Fodor's **2002**

W9-DIR-797

New England

Fodor's Travel Publications • New York, Toronto, London, Sydney, Auckland
www.fodors.com

CONTENTS

MAPS

Circled letters in text correspond to letters on the photographs. For more information on the sights pictured, turn to the indicated page number Ⓐ on each photograph.

DESTINATION
NEW ENGLAND

If New England didn't exist, Currier & Ives might have had to invent it. Its immaculate village greens, brilliant white clapboard churches, covered bridges, and lighthouses are national emblems, along with the seasons themselves: the Green Mountains in autumn oranges, the White Mountains mounded with snow, Cape Cod polka-dotted with beach-plum blossoms. But New England is much more than a colossal picture postcard: the historic sites witnessed events chronicled in classrooms across the country, the antiques shops and discount malls are legendary, and urban pleasures flourish, from lively restaurants to the performing arts. New England is a pleasure trove—if you know where to look.

Maine's rugged splendor sets it apart from its more pastoral neighbors. The state is vast—New England's Big Sky Country. Lush pine and spruce forests extend from a few miles inland all the way to the

MAINE

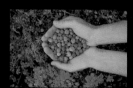

Canadian border, a ragged carpet of dark green punctuated by sparkling ponds and lakes where vacationers get cozy in rustic summer homes and generations of children have gobbled s'mores at camp. The streams that connect some of these clear blue waters, among them the celebrated Allagash River, attract canoeists from far and wide. But for most travelers Maine's coast is its big draw. You can pick wild blueberries (they are a major commercial crop on the northern end of the coast) or just enjoy the pristine quality of light at places like Ⓐ**Acadia National Park** and Ⓑ**Pemaquid Point Light.**

B▷67

Photographers and painters have long been drawn by the light, beginning with the great 19th-century landscapist Winslow Homer, who first made a name for himself as a combat artist in the Civil War.

C▷81

(As in lovely ©**Castine**, you'll see many a monument to this conflict throughout the state: in the Battle of Gettysburg the 20th Maine Infantry Regiment held a strategic knoll called Little Round Top and helped determine the course of American history.) Lobster pots and buoys, monuments to another key coastal pleasure, stand at the ready up and down the shore at Ⓓ**Boothbay Harbor** and beyond. They're a constant re-minder of what's cooking for dinner: sweet, sea-tangy lobster at sardine prices.

D▷65

MAINE

Many states front the ocean, but none has a bond to the sea as powerful as Maine's. Long before Europeans came, Native Americans harvested the sea off the rocky shores. Vikings probably made landfall here, long enough for some murderous brawls with the natives. In 1607 colonists at Popham built the *Virginia,* the first European ship launched in the Americas. The sturdy sailing vessel took them back to England when things didn't work out. Today commercial fishing is in steep decline, but the maritime museums in Bath and several other towns as well as elaborate sea captains' homes up and down the coast recall Maine's seafaring glory days. As you travel along the sawtooth coast, skirting myriad inlets and venturing onto adjacent promontories, the sea remains a presence.

Sea views greet you at every turn, and you are never far from bracing salt breezes. Even the signage—on tackle shops, boatyards, seafood restaurants—is perpetually nautical. In summer, sailors turn out by the score to compete in regattas and schooner races, windjammers give romantic travelers a feel for the ships of Maine's past, and lighthouses, most of them unromantically run by computer, have their Kodak moments.

(One of the prettiest is Ⓔ**Portland Head Light**, dating from 1791; it's also the state's oldest.) Offshore, ferries and excursion boats— Maine's everyday transport— will take you to any number of rock-bound landfalls. On much-loved Ⓕ**Monhegan Island**, wildflowers carpet the meadows and an artist's colony has taken root, with accompanying restaurants and stores. You may not find the pirate gold that legend says is buried there, but you'll discover another slice of quintessential Maine, and that's good enough.

NEW HAMPSHIRE

Ⓐ▷ 137

Just as the French refer to Burgundy as "profound France"—quintessentially French—New Hampshire might fairly call itself "profound New England." If that raises Vermonters' hackles, the folks in New Hampshire might offer simple consolation: "Get over it." (New Hampshirites don't pull punches.) There's truth to the contention. The state has a little of everything that defines New England: a seacoast around the historic city of Ⓐ**Portsmouth**, many covered bridges (including four in Ⓒ**Cornish**), and seasonal pleasures, from sailing on the central lakes to skiing and ice-skating at Ⓑ**The Balsams Wilderness,** up north, among other places. As for fall foliage, it's the region's fieriest. Ask any New Hampshirite—or see for yourself along scenic hiking trails like those in Rhododendron State Park, near Fitzwilliam (noted for its wild rhododen-

Ⓑ▷ 181

C 198

D 178

drons), and in the 770,000-acre White Mountain National Forest, way up north. It's positively soul-stirring to walk the section of the Maine-to-Georgia Appalachian Trail that passes through the forest and over the rocky, wind-pummeled summit of Mt. Washington, the Northeast's highest peak. But if you're not up to the exertion, not to worry: driving up the Ⓓ**Mt. Washington Auto Road** yields equally stunning views. With most of New Hampshire's population in the industrial south, most of the state is gloriously rustic.

NEW
HAMPSHIRE

Artist Maxfield Parrish came to the west-central wilderness early in the 20th century to paint the Technicolor sunsets over the Connecticut River. Country life here, among other factors, charmed Robert Frost away from England, where he had spent a few years becoming a famous poet, to "live cheap and get Yankier and Yankier" on a farm near tiny Franconia. Succeeding, he attained a fierce streak of independence summed up by the state motto: Live Free or Die. The same spirit makes itself felt in many ways, not the least in the absence of a state sales tax, which is instrumental in parting shoppers from their money in the outlet stores of North Conway and antiques stores far and wide. You may also detect a certain brasher-than-usual gonzo attitude among the snowboarders flipping and flying at modern winter sports venues such as Ⓔ **Attitash Bear Peak**. Maybe it's the architecture

Ⓔ 175

Ⓕ 163

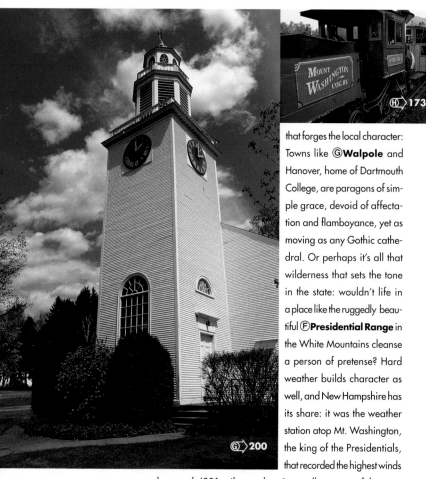

Ⓖ▷200

Ⓗ▷173

Ⓘ▷173

that forges the local character: Towns like Ⓖ**Walpole** and Hanover, home of Dartmouth College, are paragons of simple grace, devoid of affectation and flamboyance, yet as moving as any Gothic cathedral. Or perhaps it's all that wilderness that sets the tone in the state: wouldn't life in a place like the ruggedly beautiful Ⓕ**Presidential Range** in the White Mountains cleanse a person of pretense? Hard weather builds character as well, and New Hampshire has its share: it was the weather station atop Mt. Washington, the king of the Presidentials, that recorded the highest winds ever measured on earth (231 miles per hour) as well as some of the most precipitous temperature drops. Ride the venerable Ⓗ**Mt. Washington Cog Railway** to the summit in summer, or tramp up Tuckerman Ravine. Afterward repair to one of the charming inns around Jackson or to the bright, graceful veranda of the Ⓘ**Mount Washington Hotel**, sit back, and let New Hampshire nourish your soul.

VERMONT

Having spent many years of his life in New Hampshire, Robert Frost is spending eternity in Vermont, buried in a lovely old churchyard in Bennington, in the southern part of the state. Even while alive he might not have noticed when he had crossed the border. "Anything I can say about New Hampshire," he wrote, "will serve almost as well about Vermont." Today, both contemporary residents and visiting New England observers might differ, however. Over the past few decades, many parts of Vermont have absorbed waves of middle-class urban refugees bent on taking up residence year-round. Along with these well-dressed masses, yearning to be stress-free, has come a touch of semiprecious gentrification. Vermont chic exists in the form of Range Rovers and top-of-the-line cold-weather gear. Whether this is good or bad is up to the beholder, and for millions of beholders, including closet Vermontophiles from New Hampshire, it is just fine. Some of the happy visitors come to ski at world-famous resorts such as Stowe, Sugarbush, Killington, Mount Snow, and the defiantly retro Ⓐ**Mad River Glen**, where expert skiers hone their skills on natural snow and steep, narrow trails that make few concessions to the intermediates to whom almost every other U.S. ski area kowtows. Other visitors drink in the charm of picture-book villages like Ⓑ**Newfane**. Still others stop along superscenic country roads like Ⓒ**Route 100**, to learn about maple syrup in local sugar shacks, or wet their lines in trout streams like the Battenkill. If that's your fancy, make a pilgrimage to one of angling's shrines—the American Museum of Fly Fishing in Manchester, home to Bing Crosby's rod and reel.

Ⓑ>236

ⒸⅠ>220

VERMONT

Some Vermontophiles maintain, only half jokingly, that all of Vermont should be made into a national park. Chuckle at the notion if you like, but you have to commend what's behind it: the desire to preserve a national treasure, all 9,609 square miles of it, for future generations. Since the national park designation is not even remotely in the cards, Vermont tries hard to preserve itself. Billboards are banned, and laws attempt to ensure that new buildings blend harmoniously into their surroundings. Artisans open their studios to show just how long and hard they labor to craft items such as hand-woven rugs and mouth-blown glass. (Ⓓ**Simon Pearce** in Quechee is famous for his beautiful work, made in a renovated mill.) New businesses, ranging from inns and innovative restaurants to bagel shops and travel agencies, are shoehorned into vintage barns, mills, and clapboard houses. And you will never see a highrise go up near a gazebo like the one on the green of Ⓔ**Craftsbury Common**, in the heart of the Northeast Kingdom, Vermont's most rural corner. Here and around Ⓕ**South Woodstock**, the farms are picture-perfect, and the mixed coniferous forests traversed by the celebrated

Ⓓ▷242

Ⓔ▷269

Long Trail through the Green Mountains seem more like sacred groves than ordinary woods. The bits of industry that do exist trade on Vermont's distinctive character: you will find cheese and Ben & Jerry's ice cream among them. Every carton of Chunky Monkey and Bovinity Divinity shipped into stores around the country and every round of cheese that goes out from the Ⓖ**Cabot Creamery** in Cabot spreads the Vermont message a little farther. If not "America's Dairyland," like Wisconsin, it's at least New England's. There is even a cow on the official state seal, although cows no longer outnumber people.

Ⓖ 286

Massachusetts, and arguably America, began on Cape Cod: the Pilgrims landed at what is now Provincetown before moving on to nearby Ply-

MASSACHUSETTS

ANTIQUES

OPEN 11

mouth a few decades shy of 400 years ago. So it's fitting that Cape Cod is now one of America's favorite travel destinations. Sun, sand, and sparkling sea are the lures, of course, not any deep homing instinct that leads us back to ancestral ground. But it's an interesting notion, isn't it? To think that thousands of us keep returning, year after year, to the place where the first seeds of the United States were sown. There may be no other pocket of New England, not even coastal Maine, that relies more heavily on visitors than does Cape Cod. If people stopped coming, the Cape would revert to the marshlands

BUILT
AS A CHURCH
IN
1852

AUTO
SCALE

Ⓒ▷396

that still protect its inland acres from hurricanes and fear-some nor'easters. Owners of antiques shops and galleries like those packed into vintage clapboard houses in Brewster and Provincetown would soon fold up. The bunting would no longer flutter on the porches of landmarks like the Ⓐ**Brewster Store**. Boats would stand empty at the P'town docks, and 6 miles off-shore, on the Ⓑ**Stellwagen Bank**, giant whales would spend their summer feeding and frolicking in tourist-free solitude. That will never be. Full of salty, windswept beauty, the Cape— and the neighboring islands of Nantucket and Martha's Vine-yard—are irresistible, and those who love them return every year like swallows to Capistrano, to trek out to lovingly maintained lighthouses like the one at Nantucket's Ⓒ**Brant Point Light** and to body-surf, rock-hunt, look for eagles, and walk, endlessly, at beaches like Provincetown's Ⓓ**Herring Cove Beach**—some of the most glorious expanses of sand on earth.

Ⓓ▷377

MASSACHUSETTS

Throw three darts at a map of Vermont or New Hampshire and visit the points that they hit. Chances are, these places will be beautiful and eat up rolls of film. Chances are, also, that they will resemble each other in topography, architecture, and speech patterns. Try the same exercise with a map of Massachusetts—the most cosmopolitan and diverse corner of New England—and you may think you've ended up in three different states (or three centuries). In museum villages like Ⓔ**Plimoth Plantation** in Plymouth, costumed interpreters demonstrate the Pilgrim fathers' sturdy determination to make a go of it

against all odds in the New World; Ⓖ**Old Sturbridge Village** in Sturbridge, in the center of the state, documents the changes of early America confronting the Industrial Revolution. In the gently rolling Berkshire Hills to the west, at a lovely Lenox estate known as Ⓕ**Tanglewood**, magnificent hedges and spreading trees date from the late 19th century, as does some of the music that's the big draw in summer, supplied by Seiji Ozawa and the Boston Symphony Orchestra. Boston takes

303

you time traveling as well, into America's prosperous formative years along Ⓗ**Acorn Street** on Beacon Hill, into the Neverland of famous children's books in the Ⓙ**Public Garden** Swan Boats, and into the 21st century at Ⓘ**Harvard Square**, almost always mobbed with students (all born well after their parents' generation bought Bob Dylan LPs at the Harvard Coop during the activist '60s and '70s). So, although lobsters and Holsteins can serve nicely as emblems for Maine and Vermont, no single icon will do for Massachusetts, unless you agree with those who nominate a Red Sox baseball cap.

Ⓙ 313

Ⓘ 320

RHODE ISLAND

Years ago former Texas governor Pat Neff proclaimed, "Texas could wear Rhode Island as a watch fob." (One wonders whether the governor had designs on Massachusetts as a tie clip.) Yet in the smallest state in the Union, a short jaunt can transport you to sandy beaches and leafy forests, urban ethnic enclaves and farmland, and historical treasures from Colonial days and the Gilded Age.

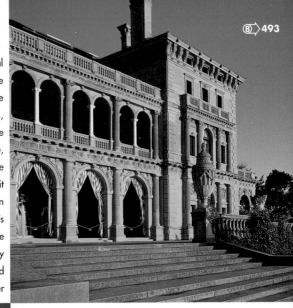

Ⓑ▷493

Ⓒ▷493

About a fifth of the National Historic Landmarks in the United States sit within Rhode Island's compact borders, some near the handsome Riverwalk in Ⓐ**Providence**, the state capital and the home of Brown University. If you visit the 1786 mansion of John Brown, one of the school's founding fathers, contemplate the source of the family wealth: the China trade and the slave trade. Many other landmarks are in Newport, including a number of marble-and-gilt "cottages" like Ⓑ Ⓒ **the Breakers**, where a Texas oilman with a jumbo ego might wish to spend his summer. Cornelius Vanderbilt II, who created the mansion, spent his Augusts clinking champagne flutes with his buddies in their own ballrooms, rallying on the grass tennis courts of the Newport Casino, and letting sea breezes put pretense behind him on the waters of Narragansett Bay, much like the Wall Street titans who summer in Rhode Island today.

Ⓐ〉571

CONNECTICUT

New England's most distinctive border with the rest of America is in Connecticut. While you don't notice much change as you move from Massachusetts or Vermont into upstate New York, the regional feeling is very striking when you come into the area from New York's Westchester County, immediately north of the Bronx. The stone walls of nearby towns and those farther afield like Ⓐ**Stonington** take on a special poignancy here, as if they are barriers to the encroachment of the glitz and bustle from points south. With the state's many highways, it's all too easy

Ⓑ〉516

Ⓒ➤ 570

Ⓓ➤ 570

to shoot past such bits of New England charm. Those who pause are rewarded along the coast by reminders of the area's seafaring past, whether at the Ⓑ**Maritime Aquarium** in Norwalk, or in ⒸⒹ**Mystic Seaport**, aboard the *Joseph Conrad* ship and in its Wendell Building, where 17 figureheads are on display. Inland and northward on up to the border with Massachusetts, all across the state, picturesque small towns such as Ridgefield, Litchfield, and Salisbury, each a study in white clapboards and green shutters, can hold their own with any on the New England scene; Woodstock's Ⓔ**Roseland Cottage,** a rosy example of the Gothic Revival style, epitomizes New England grace. Home to many a bedroom community of commuters who earn their big bucks in Manhattan, much of Connecticut is wealthy as well. (Local wags call the annual Greenwich–Darien high school football game the "BMW Bowl.") As you leave Connecticut through the lovely towns of Fairfield County, treat yourself to a gawking tour of the local streets. It's a nice place to visit, and you may want to live there, if you don't already. Come to think of it, the same could be said of New England as a whole.

Ⓔ➤ 577

GREAT ITINERARIES

Highlights of New England

14 to 19 days

In a nation where distances can often be daunting, New England packs its highlights into a remarkably compact area. Understanding Yankeedom might take a lifetime—but it's possible to get a good appreciation for the six-state region in a 2- to 2½-week drive.

HARTFORD

1 day. The Mark Twain House resembles a Mississippi steamboat beached in a Victorian neighborhood. Downtown, visit Connecticut's ornate State Capitol and the Wadsworth Atheneum, which houses fine Impressionist and Hudson River School paintings.
☞ *Hartford and the Connecticut River Valley in Chapter 6.*

LOWER CONNECTICUT RIVER VALLEY, BLOCK ISLAND SOUND

1 or 2 days. Here centuries-old towns such as Essex and Chester coexist with a well-preserved natural environment. In Rhode Island, sandy beaches dot the coast in Watch Hill, Charlestown, and Narragansett.
☞ *Hartford and the Connecticut River Valley in Chapter 6, South County in Chapter 5.*

NEWPORT

1 day. Despite its Colonial downtown and seaside parks, to most people New-

port means mansions—the most opulent, cost-be-damned enclave of private homes ever built in the United States. Turn-of-the-century "cottages" such as the Breakers and Marble House are beyond duplication today.
☞*Newport County in Chapter 5.*

PROVIDENCE
1 day. Rhode Island's capital holds treasures in places such as Benefit Street, with its Federal-era homes, and the Museum of Art at the Rhode Island School of Design. Savor a knockout Italian meal on Federal Hill and visit Waterplace Park.
☞*Providence in Chapter 5.*

CAPE COD
2 or 3 days. Meander along Massachusetts' arm-shape peninsula and explore Cape Cod National Seashore. Provincetown, at the Cape's tip, is Bohemian, gay, and touristy, a Portuguese fishing village on a Colonial foundation. In season, you can whale-watch here.
☞*Cape Cod in Chapter 4.*

PLYMOUTH
1 day. "America's home-town" is where 102 weary settlers landed in 1620. You can climb aboard the replica *Mayflower II*, then spend time at Plimoth Plantation, staffed by costumed "Pilgrims."
☞*Boston in Chapter 4.*

BOSTON
2 or 3 days. In Boston, famous buildings such as Ⓑ Faneuil Hall are not merely civic landmarks but national icons. From the Boston Common, the Freedom Trail extends to encompass foundation stones of American liberty such as Old North Church. Walk the gaslit streets of Beacon Hill, too. On your second day, explore the Museum of Fine Arts and the grand boulevards and shops of Back Bay. Another day, visit the Cambridge campus of Harvard University and its museums.
☞*Boston in Chapter 4.*

Ⓑ⟩307

SALEM AND NEWBURYPORT
1 or 2 days. In Salem, many sites, including the Peabody and Essex Museum, recall the dark days of the 1690s witch hysteria and the fortunes amassed in the China trade. Newburyport's Colonial and Federal homes testify to Yankee enterprise on the seas.
☞*The North Shore in Chapter 4.*

MANCHESTER AND CONCORD
1 day. Manchester, New Hampshire's largest city, holds the Amoskeag Textile Mills, a reminder of New England's industrial past. Smaller Concord is the state capital. Near the State House is the fine Museum of New Hampshire History, housing one of the locally built stagecoaches that carried Concord's name throughout the West.
☞*Western and Central New Hampshire in Chapter 2.*

GREEN MOUNTAINS AND MONTPELIER
1 or 2 days. Route 100 travels through the heart of the Green Mountains, whose rounded peaks assert a modest grandeur. Vermont's vest-pocket capital, Montpelier, has the gold-dome Vermont State House and the quirky Vermont Museum.
☞*Central Vermont and Northern Vermont in Chapter 3.*

WHITE MOUNTAINS
1 day. U.S. 302 threads through New Hampshire's White Mountains, passing beneath brooding Mt. Washington and through Crawford Notch. In Bretton Woods the Mt. Washington Cog Railway still chugs to the summit, and the Ⓐ Mount Washington Hotel recalls the glory days of White Mountain resorts.
☞*The White Mountains in Chapter 2.*

PORTLAND
1 day. Maine's maritime capital shows off its restored waterfront at the Old Port. Nearby, two lighthouses on Cape Elizabeth, Two Lights and Portland Head, stand vigil.
☞*Portland to Waldoboro in Chapter 1.*

Ⓐ⟩173

Fall Foliage Tour
7 to 12 days

In fall, New England's dense forests explode into reds, oranges, yellows, and purples. Like autumn itself, this itinerary works its way south from northern Vermont into Connecticut. Nature's schedule varies from year to year; as a rule, this trip is best begun around the third week of September. Book accommodations well in advance.

NORTHWESTERN VERMONT
1 or 2 days. In Burlington the elms will be turning color on the University of Vermont campus. A ferry ride across Lake Champlain affords great views of Vermont's Green Mountains and New York's Adirondacks. After visiting the resort town of Stowe, continue beneath the cliffs of Smugglers' Notch. The north country's palette unfolds in Newport, where the blue waters of Lake Memphremagog reflect the foliage.
☞*Northern Vermont in Chapter 3.*

NORTHEAST KINGDOM
1 day. After a side trip along Lake Willoughby, explore St. Johnsbury, where the St. Johnsbury Athenaeum and Fairbanks Museum reveal Victorian tastes in art and natural-history collecting. In Peacham, stock up for a picnic at the Peacham Store.
☞*Northern Vermont in Chapter 3.*

WHITE MOUNTAINS AND LAKES REGION
1 or 2 days. In New Hampshire, I-93 narrows as it winds through craggy Franconia Notch. Watch for the Old Man of the Mountain, a natural rock profile. The sinuous Kancamagus Highway passes through the mountains to Conway. In

Center Harbor in the Lakes Region, you can ride the M/S *Mount Washington* for views of the Lake Winnipesaukee shoreline, or ascend to Moultonborough's Castle in the Clouds for a falcon's-eye look at the colors.
☞*The White Mountains and Lakes Region in Chapter 2.*

MT. MONADNOCK REGION

1 or 2 days. In Concord stop at the Museum of New Hampshire History and the State House. Several trails climb Mt. Monadnock, near Jaffrey Center, and colorful vistas extend as far as Boston.
☞*Western and Central New Hampshire in Chapter 2.*

THE BERKSHIRES

1 or 2 days. The scenery around Lenox, Stockbridge, and Great Barrington has long attracted the talented and the wealthy. You can visit the homes of novelist Edith Wharton (the Mount, in Lenox), sculptor Daniel Chester French (Chesterwood, in Stockbridge), and diplomat Joseph Choate (Naumkeag, in Stockbridge).
☞*The Berkshires in Chapter 4.*

THE LITCHFIELD HILLS

1 or 2 days. This area of Connecticut combines the feel of up-country New England with exclusive exurban polish. The wooded shores of Lake Waramaug harbor country inns and wineries in New Preston and other pretty towns. Litchfield has a village green that could be the template for anyone's idealized New England town center.
☞*The Litchfield Hills in Chapter 6.*

THE MOHAWK TRAIL

1 day. In Shelburne Falls, Massachusetts, the Bridge of Flowers displays the last of autumn's blossoms. Follow the Mohawk Trail as it ascends into the Berkshire Hills—and stop to take in the view at the hairpin turn just east of North Adams. In Williamstown the Sterling and Francine Clark Art Institute houses a collection of Impressionist works.
☞*The Pioneer Valley and the Berkshires in Chapter 4.*

Newport
Lake Memphremagog
Lake Willoughby
100
5
Lake Champlain
100C
15
65 mi
46 mi
5
Smugglers' Notch
Burlington
108
St. Johnsbury
89
100
Stowe
36 mi
Peacham
93
75 mi
Montpelier
Franconia Notch
KANCAMAGUS HWY
Conway
Brunswick Bath
Freeport
White Mountains
112
16
1
39 mi
25
Portland
Center Harbor
Moultonborough
104
Lake Winnipesaukee
MAINE
1
Cape Elizabeth
93
Kennebunkport
85 mi
NEW HAMPSHIRE
40 mi
9
Concord
202
202
Portsmouth
1
Manchester
Odiorne Point State Park
Hampton Beach
1A
VERMONT
Mt. Monadnock
47 mi
Newburyport
Parker River NWR
1A
Williamstown
72 mi
MOHAWK TRAIL
Jaffrey Center
Rockport
2
North Adams
2
202
72 mi
MASSACHUSETTS
133
127 Gloucester
Shelburne Falls
Salem
65 mi
7
1A
Berkshires
ATLANTIC OCEAN
Lenox
Boston
Stockbridge
93
3
Great Barrington
Provincetown
78 mi
6
Plymouth
Litchfield Hills
3
125 mi
7
RHODE ISLAND
Cape Cod
45
Litchfield
202
Providence
6
New Preston
Narragansett Bay
Hartford
24
195
6
Lake Waramaug
114
New Bedford
CONNECTICUT
138
1
Newport
New London
Groton
66 mi
1
Mystic
Watch Hill
Long Island Sound

The Seacoast
8 to 14 days

Every New England state except Vermont borders on salt water. For history buffs this means there are plenty of vivid links to the days when the sea was the region's lifeblood; for water-sports enthusiasts, it's a guarantee of fun on beaches from the sandy shores of Long Island Sound to the bracing waters of Down East Maine. A journey along the coast also brings the promise of fresh seafood, incomparable sunrises, and a quality of light that has entranced artists from Winslow Homer to Edward Hopper.

re-created Pilgrim village.
☞ *Boston and Cape Cod in Chapter 4.*

BOSTON, THE NORTH SHORE
2 days. To savor Boston's centuries-old ties to the sea, take a half-day stroll by Faneuil Hall and Quincy Market or a boat tour of the harbor. In Salem, America's early shipping fortunes are chronicled in the Peabody and Essex Museum and the Salem Maritime National Historic Site. Spend a day exploring more of the North Shore, including the old fishing port of Gloucester and Rockport, one possible place to buy that seascape painted in oils. Newburyport, with its Federal-era shipowners'

Cape Elizabeth, with its Portland Head and Two Lights lighthouses.
☞ *The Coast in Chapter 2 and York County Coast and Portland to Waldoboro in Chapter 1.*

Campobello Island

Castine

220 mi

Camden

Rockland

Bar Harbor

Acadia National Park

SOUTHEASTERN CONNECTICUT, NEWPORT
1 to 3 days. Begin in New London, home of the U.S. Coast Guard Academy, and stop at Groton to tour the *Nautilus* at the Submarine Force Museum. In Mystic the days of wooden ships and whaling adventures live on at Mystic Seaport museum. In Rhode Island, savor the Victorian resort of Watch Hill and the Block Island Sound beaches. See the extravagant summer mansions in Newport.
☞ *New Haven and the Southeastern Coast in Chapter 6, South County and Newport County in Chapter 5.*

MASSACHUSETTS' SOUTH SHORE AND CAPE COD
2 to 4 days. New Bedford was once a major whaling center; exhibits at the New Bedford Whaling Museum capture this vanished world. Cape Cod can be nearly all things to all visitors, with quiet Colonial villages and lively resorts, gentle bay-side wavelets and crashing surf. In Plymouth visit the *Mayflower II* and Plimoth Plantation, the

homes, is home to the Parker River National Wildlife Refuge, beloved by birders and beach-walkers.
☞ *Boston and the North Shore in Chapter 4.*

NEW HAMPSHIRE AND SOUTHERN MAINE
1 or 2 days. New Hampshire fronts the Atlantic for a scant 18 miles, but its coastal landmarks range from honky-tonk Hampton Beach to quiet Odiorne Point State Park in Rye and pretty Portsmouth, whose Georgian and Federal mansions once sheltered the cream of pre-Revolutionary society. Visit a few at Strawbery Banke Museum and elsewhere. Between here and Portland, Maine's largest city and the site of a waterfront revival, you will find oceanside resorts such as Kennebunkport. Near Portland is

DOWN EAST
2 or 3 days. Beyond Portland ranges the ragged, island-strewn coast that Mainers call Down East. On your first day, travel to Camden or Castine. Some highlights are the retail mecca Freeport, home of L. L. Bean; Brunswick, with the museums of Bowdoin College; and Bath, with the Maine Maritime Museum and Shipyard. Perhaps you'll think about cruising on one of the schooners that sail out of Rockland. In Camden and Castine, exquisite inns occupy homes built from inland Maine's gold, timber. On your second day, visit the spectacular rocky coast of © Acadia National Park, near the resort town of Bar Harbor. If you have another day, drive the desolately beautiful stretch of Maine's granite coast to the New Brunswick border, where President Franklin Roosevelt's "beloved island," Campobello, and Roosevelt Campobello International Park lie across an international bridge.
☞ *Portland to Waldoboro, Penobscot Bay, Mount Desert Island, and Way Down East in Chapter 1.*

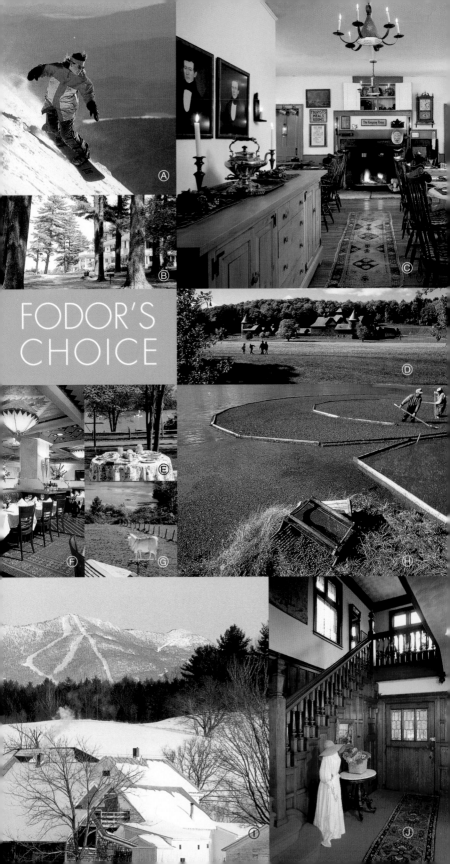

FODOR'S
CHOICE

Even with so many special places in New England, Fodor's writers and editors have their favorites. Here are a few that stand out.

DINING

ⓖ **Golden Lamb Buttery, Brooklyn, CT.** This is Connecticut's most unusual—and magical—dining experience. $$$$ ☞ p. 574

Go Fish, Mystic, CT. This big, bright, colorful restaurant serves up the bounty of the sea. $–$$ ☞ p. 570

White Barn Inn, Kennebunkport, ME. One of Maine's best restaurants, it combines fine dining with unblemished service in a rustic setting. $$$$ ☞ p. 48

Round Pond Lobstermen's Co-op, Round Pond, ME. For lobster-in-the-rough, you can't beat this dockside takeout. $ ☞ p. 68

Blantyre, Lenox, MA. If you choose to dine on the imaginative contemporary cuisine here, set aside several hours and dress up. $$$$ ☞ p. 438

Chillingsworth, Brewster, MA. The chefs at this formal spot prepare luscious French fare. $$$$ ☞ p. 365

ⓕ **Biba, Boston, MA.** The city's favorite place to see and be seen serves gutsy fare from five continents. $$$$ ☞ p. 322

The Balsams Wilderness, Dixville Notch, NH. The summer buffet lunch is heaped upon a 100-ft-long table; dinners might include salmon with caviar. $$$$ ☞ p. 181

Al Forno, Providence, RI. The Italian dishes here make the most of the region's fresh produce. $$$ ☞ p. 459

Hemingway's, Killington, VT. The chic seasonal menu celebrates native game and fresh seafood in such offerings as Vermont venison with pumpkin pudding. $$$$ ☞ p. 247

Villa Tragara, Waterbury, VT. You can sample superb northern Italian fare in tapas-style portions at this creative restaurant near Stowe. $$–$$$ ☞ p. 264

LODGING

Boulders Inn, New Preston, CT. This idyllic inn on Lake Waramaug has panoramic views. $$$$ ☞ p. 541

ⓙ **Manor House, Norfolk, CT.** Twenty stained-glass windows by Louis Comfort Tiffany are a unique feature. $$–$$$$ ☞ p. 547

Lodge at Moosehead Lake, Greenville, ME. This lumber baron's mansion is as luxurious as it gets in the North Woods. $$$–$$$$ ☞ p. 120

ⓔ **Ullikana, Bar Harbor, ME.** Within this Tudor mansion is a riot of color and art. Water views and gourmet breakfasts make it a real treat. $$$–$$$$ ☞ p. 89

Charlotte Inn, Edgartown, MA. Rooms in one of the region's finest inns are smartly furnished. $$$$ ☞ p. 386

Ritz-Carlton, Boston, MA. A perennial favorite stands for understatement combined with luxury. $$$$ ☞ p. 332

ⓒ **Historic Merrell Inn, South Lee, MA.** Built as a stagecoach stopover around 1794, this inn has an unfussy style. $$$ ☞ p. 440

ⓑ **Manor on Golden Pond, Holderness, NH.** The rooms in this English-style manor are filled with luxurious touches. $$$$ ☞ p. 156

Snowvillage Inn, Snowville, NH. Rooms in this book-filled inn near North Conway are named after authors; the nicest, with 12 windows, is a tribute to Robert Frost. $$$–$$$$ ☞ p. 182

Vanderbilt Hall, Newport, RI. There's plenty of elegance at the city's most sophisticated small hotel, a former Vanderbilt family home. $$$$ ☞ p. 496

West Mountain Inn, Arlington, VT. A former 1840s farmhouse anchors a llama ranch with 150 acres of glorious views. $$$$ ☞ p. 225

ⓓ **Inn at Shelburne Farms, Shelburne, VT.** This Tudor-style inn sits on the edge of Lake Champlain. $$$–$$$$ ☞ p. 278

SKI RESORTS

ⓐ **Sugarloaf/USA, ME.** At 2,820 ft, Sugarloaf/USA's vertical drop is greater than that of any other New England ski peak except Killington. ☞ p. 115

Sunday River, ME. Good snowmaking and reliable grooming ensure great snow from November to May. ☞ p. 111

Attitash Bear Peak, NH. There's always something innovative happening here— from demo days to race camps. ☞ p. 175

Jay Peak, VT. It gets the most natural snow of any Vermont ski area. ☞ p. 282

Mad River Glen, VT. The apt motto at this area owned by a skiers cooperative is "Ski It If You Can." ☞ p. 258

ⓘ **Smugglers' Notch, VT.** Morse Mountain at Smugglers' is tops for beginners. ☞ p. 272

Sugarbush, VT. Sugarbush is an overall great place to ski; nearly everyone will feel comfortable. ☞ p. 259

MEMORABLE SIGHTS

Long Island Sound from Stonington, CT. Wander past the historic buildings and climb up into the Old Lighthouse Museum for a spectacular view. ☞ p. 571

Sunrise from Cadillac Mountain, Mt. Desert Island, ME. From the summit you have a 360° view of the ocean, islands, woods, and lakes. ☞ p. 91

ⓗ **Cranberry harvest time, Cape Cod and Nantucket, MA.** Cape Cod's Rail Trail passes salt marshes, cranberry bogs, and ponds. On Nantucket, visit lovely Milestone Bog. ☞ p. 399

Cobblestone streets and antique houses, Nantucket, MA. Settled in the mid-17th century, Nantucket has a pristine town center. ☞ p. 394

Early October views, Kancamagus Highway, NH. The White Mountain vistas on this 34-mi drive burst into color each fall. ☞ p. 185

Bellevue Avenue, Newport, RI. Mansions with pillars and marble preside over gardens and lawns that roll to the ocean. ☞ p. 488

The Appalachian Gap, Route 17, VT. Views from this mountain pass near Bristol are a just reward for the challenging drive. ☞ p. 256

1   MAINE

At its extremes Maine measures 300 miles by
200 miles; all the other states in New
England could fit within its ample perimeters.
The Kennebunks hold classic townscapes,
rocky shorelines, sandy beaches, and quaint
downtown districts. Portland has the state's
best selection of restaurants, shops, and
cultural offerings, and Freeport is a mecca for
outlet shoppers. North of Portland, sandy
beaches give way to rocky coast and
treasures such as Acadia National Park.
Outdoors enthusiasts head to inland Maine's
lakes, mountains, and the vast North Woods.

By Hilary M.
Nangle

O N THE MAINE–NEW HAMPSHIRE BORDER is a sign that plainly announces the philosophy of the region: WELCOME TO MAINE: THE WAY LIFE SHOULD BE. Local folk say too many cars are on the road when you can't make it through the traffic signal on the first try. Romantics luxuriate in the feeling of a down comforter on an old, yellowed pine bed or in the sensation of the wind and salt spray on their faces while cruising in a historic windjammer. Families love the unspoiled beaches and safe inlets dotting the shoreline and the clear inland lakes. Hikers and campers are revived by the exalting and exhausting climb to the top of Katahdin, and adventure seekers get their thrills rafting the Kennebec or Penobscot River.

There is an expansiveness to Maine, a sense of distance between places that hardly exists elsewhere in New England, and along with the sheer size and spread of the place there is a tremendous variety of terrain. People speak of "coastal" Maine and "inland" Maine, as though the state could be summed up under the twin emblems of lobsters and pine trees. Yet the topography and character in this state are a good deal more complicated.

Even the coast is several places in one. Portland may be Maine's largest city, but its attitude is decidedly more big town than small city. South of this rapidly gentrifying city, Ogunquit, Kennebunkport, Old Orchard Beach, and other resort towns predominate along a reasonably smooth shoreline. North of Portland and Casco Bay, secondary roads turn south off U.S. 1 onto so many oddly chiseled peninsulas that it's possible to drive for days without retracing your route. Slow down to explore the museums, galleries, and shops in the larger towns and the antiques and curio shops and harborside lobster shacks in the smaller fishing villages on the peninsulas. Freeport is an entity unto itself, a place where numerous name-brand outlets and specialty stores have sprung up around the retail outpost of famous outfitter L. L. Bean. And no description of the coast would be complete without mention of popular Acadia National Park, with its majestic mountains, and the rugged scenery of the less-visited towns that lie way Down East.

Inland Maine likewise defies easy characterization. For one thing, a lot of it is virtually uninhabited. This is the land Henry David Thoreau wrote about in *The Maine Woods* more than 150 years ago; aside from having been logged over several times, much of it hasn't changed since Thoreau and his Native American guides passed through. Ownership of vast portions of northern Maine by forest-products corporations has kept out subdivision and development; many of the roads here are private, open to travel only by permit.

Wealthy summer visitors, or "sports," came to Maine beginning in the late 1800s to hunt, fish, and play in the clean air and clean water. The state's more than 6,000 lakes and more than 3,000 mi of rivers and streams still attract such people, and more and more families, for the same reasons. Sporting camps still thrive around Greenville, Rangeley, and in the Great North Woods.

Logging in the north created the culture of the mill towns, the Rumfords, Skowhegans, Millinockets, and Bangors that lie at the end of the old river drives. The logs arrive by truck today, but Maine's harvested wilderness still feeds the mills and the nation's hunger for paper.

The hunger for potatoes has given rise to an entirely different Maine culture, in one of the most isolated agricultural regions of the country. Northeastern Aroostook County is where the Maine potatoes come from. This place is also changing. In what was once called the Potato Empire, farmers are as pressed between high costs and low prices as any of their counterparts in the Midwest, and a growing national preference for Idaho baking potatoes to small, round Maine boiling potatoes has only compounded Aroostook's troubles.

If you come to Maine seeking an untouched fishing village with locals gathered around a potbellied stove in the general store, you'll likely come away disappointed; that innocent age has passed in all but the most remote villages. Tourism has supplanted fishing, logging, and potato farming as Maine's number one industry, and most areas are well equipped to receive the annual onslaught of visitors. But whether you are stepping outside a motel room for a walk or watching a boat rock at its anchor, you can sense the infinity of the natural world. Wilderness is always nearby, growing to the edges of the most urbanized spots.

Pleasures and Pastimes

Dining

Lobster and Maine are synonymous. As a general rule, the closer you are to a working harbor, the fresher your lobster will be. Aficionados eschew ordering lobster in restaurants, preferring to eat them "in the rough" at classic lobster pounds, where you select your dinner out of a pool and enjoy it at a waterside picnic table. Shrimp, scallops, clams, mussels, and crabs are also caught in the cold waters off Maine. Restaurants in Portland and in resort towns prepare shellfish in creative combinations with lobster, haddock, salmon, and swordfish. Wild blueberries are grown commercially in Maine, and local cooks use them generously in pancakes, muffins, jams, pies, and cobblers. In 1999, Maine passed a law prohibiting smoking in restaurants.

For price-category information, *see* Dining *in* Smart Travel Tips.

Lodging

The beach communities in the south beckon visitors with their weathered look. Stately digs can be found in the classic inns of Kennebunkport. Bed-and-breakfasts and Victorian inns furnished with lace, chintz, and mahogany have joined the family-oriented motels of Ogunquit, Boothbay Harbor, Bar Harbor, and the Camden–Rockport region. Although accommodations tend to be less luxurious away from the coast, Bethel, Carrabassett Valley, and Rangeley have sophisticated hotels and inns. Greenville and Rockwood have the largest selection of restaurants and accommodations in the North Woods region. Lakeside sporting camps, which range from the primitive to the upscale, are popular around Rangeley and the North Woods. Many have cozy cabins heated with woodstoves and serve three hearty meals a day. At some of Maine's larger hotels and inns with restaurants, rates may include breakfast and dinner during the peak summer season.

For price-category information, *see* Lodging *in* Smart Travel Tips.

Outdoor Activities and Sports
BOATING

Maine's long coastline is justifiably famous: all visitors should get on the water, whether on an excursion headed for Monhegan Island for the day or on a windjammer for a relaxing vacation. Windjammer trips last from just a few hours to a full week. Longer trips include hearty, homestyle meals and a traditional lobster bake often held on a remote island. Windjammers may sail past long, craggy fingers of land that jut into a sea dotted with more than 2,000 islands. Sail among these islands and you'll see hidden coves, lighthouses, boat-filled harbors, and quiet fishing villages. Some windjammers, traditional two- or

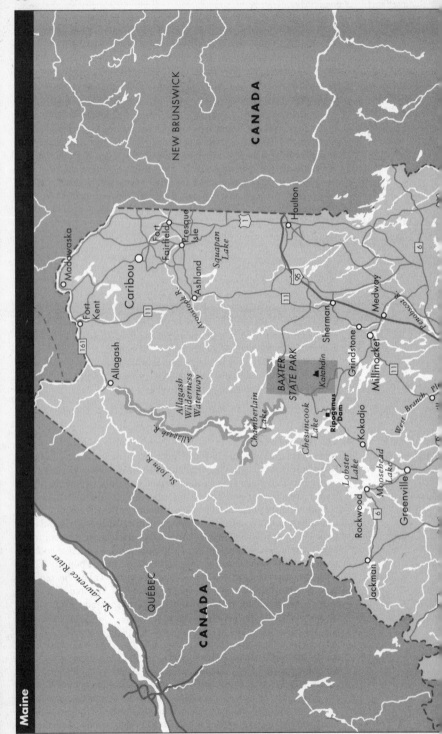

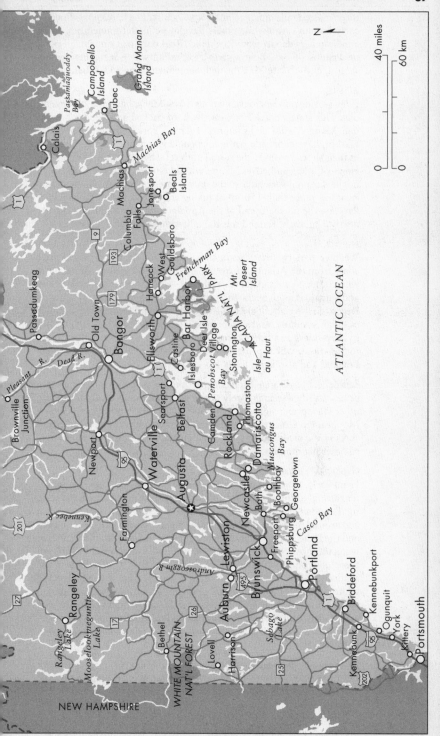

three-masted tall ships, are historic vessels that have been modified to carry human cargo while others have more modern amenities. Most windjammers depart from Rockland, Rockport, or Camden, all ports on Penobscot Bay. Boating trips, including whale-watching, run in season, mid- to late May through September or mid-October.

HIKING

From seaside rambles to backwoods hikes, Maine has a walk for everyone. This state's beaches are mostly hard packed and good for walking. Many coastal communities, such as York, Ogunquit, and Bar Harbor, have shoreside paths for people who want to keep sand out of their shoes yet enjoy the sound of the crashing surf and the cliff-top views of inlets and coves. Those who like to walk in the woods will not be disappointed: 90% of the state is forested land. Acadia National Park has more than 150 mi of hiking trails, and within Baxter State Park are the northern end of the Appalachian Trail and Katahdin. At nearly 1 mi high, Katahdin is the tallest mountain in the state.

SKIING

Weather patterns that create snow cover for Maine ski areas may come from the Atlantic or from Canada, and Maine may have snow when other New England states do not—and vice versa. Sunday River and Sugarloaf, both operated by the American Skiing Co., are the state's largest ski areas. Both are full-service destination resorts with a choice of lodging, dining, and shopping as well as more than enough terrain to keep skiers and riders content for days. It's worth the effort to get to Sugarloaf, which provides the only above-tree-line skiing in New England and also has a lively base village.

Saddleback, in Rangeley, has big-mountain skiing at little-mountain prices. Its lift system is sorely out of date, but many would have it no other way, preferring its down-home, wilderness atmosphere. Squaw Mountain in Greenville is similar in character. Its remote location ensures few crowds, and its low prices make it an attractive alternative to other big mountains.

WHITEWATER RAFTING

From early May through September, Maine has consistent whitewater rafting on three dam-controlled, Class III–V rivers: the Kennebec, the Penobscot, and the Dead. About a dozen outfitters are based in and around the Forks, Maine's whitewater capital, where the Kennebec and the Dead Rivers meet. Both are good day trips, with the Kennebec being the most popular—like a whitewater rollercoaster; big thrills but few chills. The Penobscot, which flows near Baxter State Park in the shadow of Mt. Katahdin, provides a remote trip with challenging whitewater and beautiful views of the mountain. It's not uncommon to see moose or deer while on the river. Most outfitters have facilities in this area, and most offer both day and overnight trips.

Exploring Maine

Maine is a large state that offers many different experiences. The York County Coast, in the southern portion of the state, is easily accessible and has long sand beaches, historic homes, and good restaurants. The coastal geography changes in Portland, the economic and cultural center of southern Maine. North of the city, long fingers of land jut into the sea, sheltering fishing villages. Penobscot Bay is famed for its rock-bound coast, sailing, and numerous islands. Mount Desert Island lures crowds of people to Acadia National Park, which is filled with stunning natural beauty. Way down east, beyond Acadia, the tempo changes; fast-food joints and trinket shops all but disappear, replaced by family-style restaurants and artisans' shops. Inland, the western lakes and mountains provide an entirely different experience. Summer camps, ski areas, and small villages populate this region. People head to Maine's North Woods to escape the crowds and to enjoy the great outdoors by hiking, rafting, camping, or canoeing.

Numbers in the text and in the margin correspond to numbers on the maps: Southern Maine Coast, Portland, Penobscot Bay, Mount Desert Island, Way Down East, Western Maine, and the North Woods.

Great Itineraries

You can spend days exploring just the coast of Maine, as these itineraries indicate, so plan ahead and decide whether you want to ski and dogsled in the western mountains, raft or canoe in the North Woods, or simply meander up the coast, stopping at museums and historic sites, shopping for local arts and crafts, and exploring coastal villages and lobster shacks. Trying to see everything in one visit is complicated by the lack of east–west roads in the state and heavy traffic on popular routes, such as U.S. 1 and U.S. 302. Build extra time into your schedule and relax. You'll get there eventually, and in the meantime, enjoy the view.

IF YOU HAVE 2 DAYS

A two-day exploration of the southern coast provides a good introduction to different aspects of the Maine coast. Begin in **Ogunquit** ③ with a morning walk along the Marginal Way. Then head north to **Kennebunkport** ⑥, allowing at least two hours to wander through the shops and historic homes around Dock Square. Relax on the beach for an hour or so before heading to ☖ **Portland** ⑧–⑬. If you thrive on arts and entertainment, spend the night here. Otherwise, continue north to ☖ **Freeport** ⑯, where you can shop all night at L. L. Bean. On day two, head north, stopping in **Bath** ⑱ to tour the Maine Maritime Museum, and finish up with a lobster dinner on **Pemaquid Peninsula** ㉑.

IF YOU HAVE 4 DAYS

A four-day tour of midcoast Maine up to Acadia National Park is one of New England's classic trips. From New Harbor on **Pemaquid Peninsula** ㉑, take the boat to ☖ **Monhegan Island** ㉕ for a day of walking the trails and exploring the artists' studios and galleries. The next day, continue northeast to **Rockland** ㉖ and ☖ **Camden** ㉗. On day four, visit the Farnsworth Museum in Rockland, hike or drive to the top of Mt. Battie in Camden, and meander around Camden's boat-filled harbor. Or bypass midcoast Maine in favor of ☖ **Mount Desert Island** ㉟–㊷ and Acadia National Park. To avoid sluggish traffic on U.S. 1, from Freeport, stay on I–95 to Augusta and the Maine Turnpike; then take Route 3 to Belfast and pick up U.S. 1 north there.

IF YOU HAVE 8 DAYS

An eight-day trip allows time to see a good portion of the coast. Spend two days wandering through gentrified towns and weather-beaten fishing villages from ☖ **Kittery** ① to ☖ **Portland** ⑧–⑬. On your third day explore Portland and environs, including a boat ride to **Eagle Island** ⑮ or one of the other Casco Bay islands and a visit to Portland Head Light and Two Lights in Cape Elizabeth. Continue working your way up the coast, letting your interests dictate your stops: outlet stores in **Freeport** ⑯, Maine Maritime Museum in ☖ **Bath** ⑱, antiques shops in **Wiscasset** ⑲, fishing villages and a much-photographed lighthouse on **Pemaquid Peninsula** ㉑. Allow at least one day in the **Rockland** ㉖ and ☖ **Camden** ㉗ region before taking the leisurely route to **Bar Harbor** ㉞ via the **Blue Hill** ㉛ peninsula and ☖ **Deer Isle Village** ㉜. Finish up with two days on ☖ **Mount Desert Island** ㉟–㊷.

When to Tour Maine

From July to September is the choice time for a vacation in Maine. The weather is warmest in July and August, though September is less crowded. In warm weather, the arteries along the coast and lakeside communities inland are clogged with out-of-state license plates, campgrounds are filled to capacity, and hotel rates are high. Midweek is less busy, and lodging rates are often lower then than on weekends.

Fall foliage can be brilliant in Maine and is made even more so by its reflection in inland lakes or streams or off the ocean. Late September is peak season in the north country, while in southern Maine the prime viewing dates are usually around October 5 to 10. In September and October the days are sunny and the nights crisp.

In winter, the coastal towns almost completely close down. If the sidewalks could be rolled up, they probably would be. Maine's largest ski areas usually open in mid-November and, thanks to excellent snowmaking facilities, provide good skiing often into April.

Springtime is mud season here, as in most other rural areas of New England. Mud season is followed by spring flowers and the start of wildflowers in meadows along the roadsides. Mid-May to mid-June is the main season for black flies, especially inland. It's best to schedule a trip after mid-June if possible, though this is prime canoeing time.

YORK COUNTY COAST

Maine's southernmost coastal towns, most of them in York County, won't give you the rugged, wind-bitten "Down East" experience, but they are easily reached from the south, and most have the sand beaches that all but vanish beyond Portland. These towns are highly popular in summer, an all-too-brief period. Crowds converge and gobble up rooms and dinner reservations at prime restaurants. You'll have to work a little harder to find solitude and vestiges of the "real" Maine here. Still, even day-trippers who come for a few fleeting hours will appreciate the magical warmth of the sand along this coast.

North of Kittery, the Maine coast has long stretches of hard-packed white-sand beach, closely crowded by nearly unbroken ranks of beach cottages, motels, and oceanfront restaurants. The summer colonies of York Beach and Wells Beach have the crowds and ticky-tacky shorefront overdevelopment, but quiet wildlife refuges and land reserves promise an easy escape. York's historic district is on the National Register of Historic Places. Ogunquit is more upscale and offers much to do, from shopping to taking a cliff-side walk.

More than any other region south of Portland, the Kennebunks—and especially Kennebunkport—provide the complete Maine-coast experience: classic townscapes where white clapboard houses rise from manicured lawns and gardens; rocky shorelines punctuated by sandy beaches; quaint downtown districts packed with gift shops, ice cream stands, and visitors; harbors where lobster boats bob alongside yachts; lobster pounds and well-appointed dining rooms. Continuing north, the scents of French fries, pizza, and cotton candy hover in the air above Coney Island-like Old Orchard Beach, known for its amusement pier and 7-mi-long shoreline. These towns are best explored on a leisurely holiday of two days—more if you require a fix of solid beach time. U.S. 1 travels along the coast. Inland, the Maine Turnpike (I–95) is the fastest route if you want to skip some towns.

Kittery

❶ *55 mi north of Boston, MA, 5 mi north of Portsmouth, NH.*

Kittery, which lacks a large sand beach of its own, hosts a complex of factory outlets that make it a popular destination. As an alternative to shopping, drive north past the outlets and go east on Route 103 for a peek at the hidden Kittery most people miss. There are hiking and biking trails and, best of all, great views of the water. Along this winding stretch are two forts, both open in summer.

Built in 1872, **Ft. Foster** (⊠ Pocahontas Rd., Kittery Point, ☎ 207/439–3800) was an active military installation until 1949. **Ft. McClary** (⊠ Rte. 103, Kittery Point, ☎ 207/384–5160), which dates from 1715, was staffed during five wars.

Dining and Lodging

$–$$$ ✕ **Warren's Lobster House.** A local institution, this waterfront restaurant specializes in seafood and has a huge salad bar. In season, you can dine outdoors overlooking the water. ⊠ *U.S. 1 and Water St.,* ☎ *207/439–1630. AE, MC, V.*

$$$ 🏨 **The Inn at Portsmouth Harbor.** This brick Victorian built in 1889 on the old Kittery town green overlooks the Piscataqua River and Portsmouth Harbor. An easy walk over the bridge takes you to nearby Portsmouth, NH. English antiques and Victorian watercolors decorate the no-smoking inn, and all rooms have cable TV as well as phones with voice mail. ⊠ *6 Water St., 03904,* ☎ *207/439–4040,* FAX *207/438–9286,* WEB *www.innatportsmouth.com. 5 rooms. Air-conditioning, in-room data ports. AE, MC, V. BP.*

Nightlife and the Arts

Hamilton House (⊠ 40 Vaughan's La., South Berwick, 20 mi northwest of Kittery, ☎ 603/436–3205), the Georgian home featured in Sarah Orne Jewett's historical novel *The Tory Lover,* presents "Sundays in the Garden" in July, a series of concerts ranging from classical to folk music. Concerts ($5) begin at 4. You can also visit **Jewett's home** (⊠ 5 Portland St. South Berwick, ☎ 207/436–3205) in South Berwick during summer.

Shopping

Kittery has more than 120 outlet stores. Along a several-mi stretch of U.S. 1 you can find just about anything, from hardware to underwear. Among the stores are Crate & Barrel, Eddie Bauer, Jones New York, Esprit, Waterford/Wedgwood, Lenox, Ralph Lauren, Tommy Hilfiger, DKNY, and J. Crew.

The Yorks

❷ *4 mi north of Kittery.*

The Yorks—York Village, York Harbor, York Beach, and Cape Neddick—are typical of small-town coastal communities in New England and are smaller than most. Many of their nooks and crannies can be explored in a few hours. The beaches are the big attraction here.

Most of the 18th- and 19th-century buildings within the **York Village Historic District** are clustered along York Street and Lindsay Road in York Village; seven are owned by the Old York Historical Society and charge admission. You can buy tickets for all the buildings at the **Jefferds Tavern** (⊠ U.S. 1A at Lindsay Rd.), a restored late-18th-century inn. The **Old York Gaol** (1720) was once the King's Prison for the Province of Maine; inside are dungeons, cells, and the jailer's quarters. The 1731 **Elizabeth Perkins House** reflects the Victorian style of its last

Southern Maine Coast

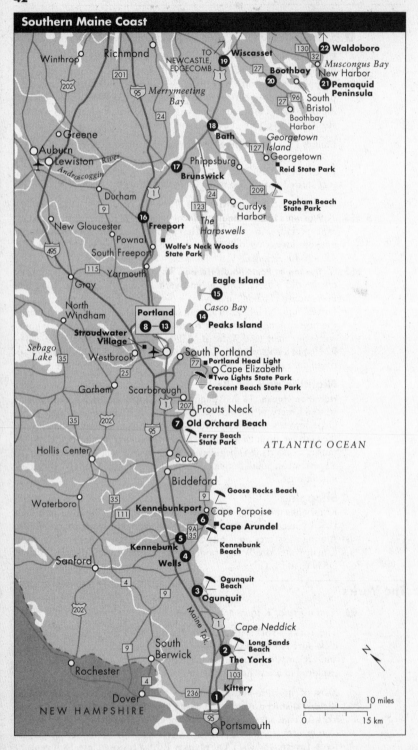

Winthrop
Richmond
TO NEWCASTLE, EDGECOMB
19 **Wiscasset**
130 32
22 **Waldoboro**
Muscongus Bay
New Harbor
201
27
Boothbay
95
Merrymeeting Bay
20
21 **Pemaquid Peninsula**
202
96
South Bristol
24
27
Boothbay Harbor
Georgetown Island
18 **Bath**
127
Greene
Phippsburg
Georgetown
■ Reid State Park
Auburn
Lewiston
Androscoggin River
17 **Brunswick**
24
209
Popham Beach State Park
Durham
1
123
Curdys Harbor
9
The Harpswells
16 **Freeport**
New Gloucester
Powna
South Freeport
495
■ Wolfe's Neck Woods State Park
115
Yarmouth
Eagle Island
Gray
15
North Windham
Casco Bay
14 **Peaks Island**
Portland
8 — **13**
Stroudwater Village
Sebago Lake
35
Westbrook
25
South Portland
77 ■ Portland Head Light
○ Cape Elizabeth
■ Two Lights State Park
Gorham
Scarborough
■ Crescent Beach State Park
1
207
Prouts Neck
35
202
95
7 **Old Orchard Beach**
Ferry Beach State Park
ATLANTIC OCEAN
Hollis Center
Saco
Biddeford
Waterboro
Goose Rocks Beach
9
35
Kennebunkport ○ Cape Porpoise
111
6 ■ **Cape Arundel**
9A 35
5
Kennebunk Kennebunk Beach
Sanford
4
Wells
4
Ogunquit Beach
9
3 **Ogunquit**
Cape Neddick
202
Long Sands Beach
2
South Berwick
The Yorks
Maine Tpk.
1
Rochester
103
4
Kittery
236
1
Dover
95
NEW HAMPSHIRE
Portsmouth

0   10 miles
0   15 km

occupants, the prominent Perkins family. Members of the Old York Historical Society lead tours. ☎ *207/363–4974.* ☞ *$7 for all buildings.* ◑ *Mid-June–mid-Oct., Tues.–Sat. 10–5, Sun. 1–5.*

The waterfront **Sayward-Wheeler House** (1718) mirrors the fortunes of a coastal village in the transition from trade to tourism. Jonathan Sayward prospered in the West Indies trade in the 18th century; by 1860 his descendants had opened the house to the public to share the story of their Colonial ancestors. The house, accessible only by guided tour, reflects both these eras. ⊠ *79 Barrell La., York Harbor,* ☎ *603/436– 3205.* ☞ *$4.* ◑ *June–mid-Oct., weekends 11–5; tours on the hr 11–4.*

If you drive down Nubble Road from U.S. 1A and go to the end of Cape Neddick, you can park and gaze out at the **Nubble Light** (1879), which sits on a tiny island just offshore. The keeper's house is a tidy Victorian cottage with gingerbread woodwork and a red roof.

Dining and Lodging

$$$$ ✕ **Cape Neddick Inn.** The American bistro-style menu at this restaurant and art gallery changes with the seasons. Past offerings have included entrées such as sage-roasted quail and poached Atlantic salmon on lobster succotash. ⊠ *U.S. 1, Cape Neddick,* ☎ *207/363–2899. D, MC, V. Closed Mon. and mid-Oct.–May. No lunch.*

$–$$$ ✕ **Cape Neddick Lobster Pound.** There's something for everyone at this casual harborside restaurant. Lobster, all kinds of seafood, and steaks appear on the menu. A children's menu and outdoor dining are available. ⊠ *Shore Rd., Cape Neddick,* ☎ *207/363–5471. MC, V. Closed Jan.–Mar..*

$$$–$$$$ ✕🏨 **York Harbor Inn.** A mid-17th-century fishing cabin with dark tim-
★ bers and a fieldstone fireplace forms the heart of this inn, to which wings and outbuildings have been added over the years. The rooms are furnished with antiques and country pieces; many have decks overlooking the water, and a few have whirlpool tubs or fireplaces. Rooms in the Harbor Cliffs next door have the intimate appeal of a classic Maine cottage. In the Harbor Hill building, all the rooms have fireplaces, whirlpool tubs, and ocean views. The dining room (no lunch off-season) has great ocean views. For dinner, start with Maine crab cakes and then try the lobster-stuffed chicken breast or the angel-hair pasta with shrimp and scallops. ⊠ *Box 573, U.S. 1A, York Harbor 03911,* ☎ *207/ 363–5119 or 800/343–3869,* 𝔽𝔸𝕏 *207/363–7151,* 𝕎𝔼𝔹 *www.yorkhar-borinn.com. 45 rooms, 2 suites. Restaurant, pub. AE, DC, MC, V. CP.*

$$–$$$ 🏨 **Edward's Harborside.** This turn-of-the-century B&B sits on the harbor's edge and is just a two-minute walk from the beach. Rooms share baths, are spacious, and have big windows to take in the water views. One room has a whirlpool tub. ⊠ *Box 866, Stage Neck Rd., York Harbor 03911,* ☎ *207/363–3037,* 𝔽𝔸𝕏 *207/363–1544,* 𝕎𝔼𝔹 *www.edward-sharborsideinn.com. 4 rooms without bath, 3 suites. Dock. MC, V. CP.*

$$–$$$ 🏨 **Union Bluff.** This fortress-like modern white structure, with balconies across the front and turrets on the ends, sits right across from Short Sands Beach with views to forever. The best rooms are in the front of the inn, but many on the north side, which cost less, also have ocean views. The front rooms in the adjacent motel have ocean views, but the motel has fewer services. ⊠ *Box 1860, 8 Beach St., York Beach 03910,* ☎ *207/363–1333 or 800/833–0721,* 𝔽𝔸𝕏 *207/363–1381,* 𝕎𝔼𝔹 *www.unionbluff.com. 36 rooms, 6 suites in inn, 21 rooms in motel. Restaurant, pub. AE, D, MC, V.*

$$ 🏨 **The Riverbed.** An oasis of calm, this clapboard home dating from before the American Revolution provides a nice counterpoint to busy York Beach, a short walk away. Each room is carefully furnished with antiques and family pieces and has a private deck; there's also a private sitting room for guests. The shared back deck, with hot tub, slopes gently down to the Cape Neddick River. ⊠ *154 Rte. 1A, 03910,* ☎ *207/363–3630. 3 rooms. Outdoor hot tub, boating. MC, V. Closed Columbus Day–Memorial Day weekend. BP.*

Nightlife and the Arts

Inn on the Blues (⊠ 7 Ocean Ave., York Beach, ☎ 207/351–3221) is a hopping blues club that attracts national bands.

Outdoor Activities and Sports

U.S. 1A runs right behind **Long Sands Beach,** a 1½-mi stretch of sand in York Beach that has roadside parking and a bathhouse. **Short Sands Beach** in York Beach has a bathhouse and is convenient to restaurants and shops. **Capt. Tom Farnon** (⊠ Rte. 103, Town Dock No. 2, York Harbor, ☎ 207/363–3234) takes passengers on lobstering trips, weekdays 10–2.

Ogunquit

❸ *10 mi north of the Yorks, 39 mi southwest of Portland.*

Probably more than any other south-coast community, Ogunquit combines coastal ambience, style, and good eating. The village became a resort in the 1880s and gained fame as an artists' colony. A mini Provincetown, Ogunquit has a gay population that swells in summer; many inns and small clubs cater to a primarily gay and lesbian clientele. Families love the protected beach area and friendly environment. Shore Road, which takes you into downtown, passes the 100-ft **Bald Head Cliff,** with views up and down the coast. On a stormy day the surf can be quite wild here.

Perkins Cove, a neck of land connected to the mainland by Oarweed Road and a pedestrian drawbridge, has a jumble of sea-beaten fish houses. These have largely been transformed by the tide of tourism to shops and restaurants. When you've had your fill of browsing and jostling the crowds at
★ Perkins Cove, stroll out along the **Marginal Way,** a mile-long footpath that hugs the shore of a rocky promontory known as Israel's Head. Benches along the route give walkers an opportunity to stop and appreciate the open sea vistas, flowering bushes, and million-dollar homes.

The small but worthwhile **Ogunquit Museum of American Art,** dedicated to 20th-century American art, overlooks the ocean and is set amid a 3-acre sculpture garden. Inside are works by Henry Strater, Marsden Hartley, Winslow Homer, Edward Hopper, Gaston Lachaise, Marguerite Zorach, and Louise Nevelson. The huge windows of the sculpture court command a superb view of cliffs and ocean. ⊠ *183 Shore Rd.,* ☎ *207/646–4909.* ⊠ *$4.* ☉ *July 1–Oct. 15, Mon.–Sat. 10:30–5, Sun. 2–5.*

Dining and Lodging

$$$$ ✕ **Arrows.** Elegant simplicity is the hallmark of this restaurant in an 18th-century farmhouse, 2 mi up a back road. Grilled salmon and radicchio with marinated fennel and baked polenta, and Chinese-style duck glazed with molasses are typical entrées on the daily-changing menu. The Maine crabmeat mousse and lobster risotto appetizers and desserts such as strawberry shortcake with Chantilly cream are also beautifully executed. ⊠ *Berwick Rd.,* ☎ *207/361–1100. Reservations essential. MC, V. Closed Mon. and mid-Dec.–mid-Apr. No lunch.*

$$–$$$$ ✕ **Gypsy Sweethearts.** The multi-ethnic fare at this popular bistro ranges from creole shrimp to chile-crusted rack of lamb to Jamaican jerk-rubbed chicken. In the dining area, cobalt blue glassware accents the white-draped tables. ⊠ *10 Shore Rd.,* ☎ *207/646–7021. MC, V. Closed Mon. and Jan.–Apr. No lunch..*

$$$-$$$$ ✕ **Hurricane.** Don't let the weather-beaten exterior or the frenzied atmosphere deter you—this small seafood bar and grill with spectacular views of the crashing surf turns out first-rate dishes. Start with lobster chowder or a chilled fresh-shrimp spring roll. Entrées may include lobster cioppino, rack of lamb, and fire-roasted veal chop. ⊠ *Oarweed La., Perkins Cove,* ☎ *207/646–6348 or 800/649–6348. AE, D, DC, MC, V. Closed early Jan.*

$$$-$$$$ ✕ **98 Provence.** Country French ambiance provides a fitting backdrop
  ★ for Chef Pierre Gignac's French fare. Begin with the duck foie gras or country-style rabbit päté, and follow it up with gigot of lotte roasted with a fresh herb crust or medallion of veal tenderloin with a wild mushroom cream sauce. ⊠ *104 Shore Rd.,* ☎ *207/646–9898. Reservations essential. MC, V.*

$$$$ ▥ **Cliff House.** Elsie Jane Weare opened the Cliff House in 1872, and her granddaughter Kathryn now presides over this sprawling oceanfront resort atop Bald Head Cliff. The complex is undergoing a renovation and expansion slated for completion in 2002: a new resort center will house a spa dining area, full health spa, 32 guest rooms, and new pools. This place has a loyal following, so reserve well in advance; be sure to call for updates on the construction. ⊠ *Box 2274, 2 East Shore Rd., 03907,* ☎ *207/361–1000,* FAX *207/361–2122,* WEB *www.cliffhousemaine.com. 178 rooms, 14 suites. 2 restaurants, 1 indoor and 1 outdoor pool, hot tub, sauna, spa, 2 tennis courts, health club. AE, D, MC, V. Closed mid-Dec.–late Mar..*

$$-$$$ ▥ **The Rockmere.** Midway along Ogunquit's Marginal Way, this shingle-style Victorian cottage is an ideal retreat from the hustle and bustle of Perkins Cove. All the rooms have corner locations and are large and airy, and all but one have ocean views. You'll find it easy to laze the day away on the wraparound porch or in the gardens. ⊠ *Box 278, 40 Stearns Rd., 03907,* ☎ *207/646–2985,* FAX *207/646–6947,* WEB *www.rockmere.com. 8 rooms. AE, D, V. CP.*

Nightlife and the Arts

Much of the nightlife in Ogunquit revolves around the precincts of Ogunquit Square and Perkins Cove, where people stroll, often enjoying an after-dinner ice cream cone or espresso. Ogunquit is popular with gay and lesbian visitors, and its club scene reflects this. **Jonathan's Restaurant** (⊠ 2 Bourne La., ☎ 207/646–4777) has live entertainment, usually blues, in season.

The **Ogunquit Playhouse** (⊠ U.S. 1, ☎ 207/646–5511), one of America's oldest summer theaters, mounts plays and musicals with name entertainment from late June to Labor Day.

Outdoor Activities and Sports

Ogunquit Beach, a 3-mi-wide stretch of sand at the mouth of the Ogunquit River, has snack bars, a boardwalk, rest rooms, and, at the Beach Street entrance, changing areas. Families gravitate to the ends; gay visitors camp at the beach's middle. The less-crowded section to the north is accessible by footbridge and has portable rest rooms, all-day paid parking, and trolley service.

Finestkind (⊠ Perkins Cove, ☎ 207/646–5227) operates cocktail cruises, lobstering trips, and cruises to Nubble Light.

Wells

❹ *5 mi north of Ogunquit, 34 mi southwest of Portland.*

This family-oriented beach community has seven mi of densely populated shoreline, along with nature preserves where you can explore salt marshes and tidal pools and see birds and waterfowl.

Extensive trails in the **Wells Reserve** lace the 1,600 acres of meadows, orchards, fields, and salt marshes, as well as two estuaries and 9 mi of seashore. Laudholm Farm, an 18th-century saltwater farm, houses the visitor center, where an introductory slide show is screened. Five rooms have exhibits. In winter, cross-country skiing is permitted. ⊠ *342 Laudholm Farm Rd.,* ☎ *207/646–1555.* ⊠ *$2 July–Aug. and week-ends Sept.–mid-Oct.* ☉ *Grounds daily 8–5. Visitor center May–Dec., Mon.–Sat. 10–4, Sun. noon–4; Jan.–Apr., Sat. 10–4, Sun. noon–4.*

Rachel Carson National Wildlife Refuge (⊠ Rte. 9, ☎ 207/646–9226) has a mi-long loop nature trail through a salt marsh. The trail borders the Little River and a white-pine forest where migrating birds and wa-terfowl of many varieties are regularly spotted.

Ⓒ A must for motor fanatics and youngsters, the **Wells Auto Museum** has 70 vintage cars, antique coin games, and a restored Model T you can ride in. ⊠ *U.S. 1,* ☎ *207/646–9064.* ⊠ *$5.* ☉ *Memorial Day–Colum-bus Day, 10–5.*

Dining and Lodging

$$–$$$$ ✕ **Billy's Chowder House.** Visitors and locals head to this simple restau-rant in a salt marsh for the generous lobster rolls, haddock sand-wiches, and chowders. ⊠ *216 Mile Rd.,* ☎ *207/646–7558. AE, D, MC, V. Closed mid-Dec.–mid-Jan.*

$–$$ ✕🏠 **Grey Gull Inn.** This century-old Victorian inn has views of the open sea and rocks on which seals like to sun themselves. The unpretentious rooms, most with ocean views, have shared or private baths. The restaurant ($$–$$$) serves excellent seafood dishes such as soft-shell crabs almandine and regional fare like Yankee pot roast or chicken breast rolled in walnuts. ⊠ *475 Webhannet Dr., at Moody Point,* ☎ *207/646–7501,* FAX *207/646–0938,* WEB *www.thegreygullinn.com. 5 rooms, 4 with bath. Restaurant. AE, D, MC, V. CP, MAP.*

$$ 🏠 **Haven by the Sea.** One block from the beach, this 1920s church was renovated in 1998 and now comforts guests with spacious rooms, some with marsh views, and four common areas, one with a fireplace. ⊠ *59 Church St., 04090,* ☎ *207/646–4194,* FAX *207/646–6883,* WEB *www.havenbythesea.com. 6 rooms, 2 suites, 1 apt.. AE, MC, V. BP.*

Outdoor Activities and Sports

Kayaking is popular along the coast, and **World Within Sea Kayaking** (☎ 207/646–0455) offers guided tours with lessons.

Shopping

Douglas N. Harding Rare Books (⊠ 2152 Post Rd. [U.S. 1], ☎ 207/646–8785) has more than 100,000 old books, maps, and prints. The **Lighthouse Depot** (⊠ U.S. 1, ☎ 207/646–0608) calls itself the world's largest lighthouse gift store. **R. Jorgensen** (⊠ 502 Post Rd. [U.S. 1], ☎ 207/646–9444) stocks 18th- and 19th-century formal and country antiques from the British Isles, Europe, and the United States.

Kennebunk

❺ *5 mi north of Wells, 29 mi southwest of Portland.*

Handsome white clapboard homes with shutters give Kennebunk, a shipbuilding center in the first half of the 19th century, a quintessen-tial New England look. The historic town is a fine place for a stroll.

The cornerstone of the **Brick Store Museum,** a block-long preservation of early 19th-century commercial buildings, is **William Lord's Brick Store.** Built as a dry-goods store in 1825 in the Federal style, the build-ing has an open-work balustrade across the roof line, granite lintels over the windows, and paired chimneys. Walking tours of Kennebunk's

National Historic Register District depart from the museum on Friday at 1 and Wednesday at 10 from June to October. ⊠ *117 Main St.,* ☎ *207/985–4802.* 🖭 *$5.* ⊙ *Tues.–Sat. 10–4:30, Wed. 10–8.*

The **Taylor-Barry House** house, owned by the (☞) Brick Store Museum, is an early 19th-century sea captain's home that's open for tours. ⊠ *24 Summer St.,* ☎ *207/985–4802.* 🖭 *$4.* ⊙ *July–Oct., Tues.–Fri. 1–4:30.*

The **Wedding Cake House** (⊠ 104 Summer St./Rte. 35) has long been a local landmark. The legend behind this confection in fancy wood fretwork is that its builder, a sea captain, was forced to set sail in the middle of his wedding; the house was his bride's consolation for the lack of wedding cake. The home, built in 1826, is not open to the public.

Lodging

$ 🖭 **St. Anthony's Franciscan Monastery Guest House.** Individuals and families in search of a quiet, contemplative retreat may want to choose one of the unadorned, motel-style rooms in a former dormitory on the grounds of a riverside monastery. The guest house is private yet within walking distance of Dock Square and the beach. The landscaped grounds, open to the public, have trails and shrines. The monks live in a Tudor mansion on the property, where Mass is said daily. This place is not recommended for those uncomfortable with Christian symbolism, although no religious participation is required. ⊠ *28 Beach Ave., 04043,* ☎ *207/967–2011. 60 rooms. Saltwater pool. No credit cards. Closed Sept. 10–June 10.*

Outdoor Activities and Sports

Kennebunk Beach has three parts: Gooch's Beach, Mother's Beach, and Kennebunk Beach. Beach Road, with its cottages and old Victorian boardinghouses, runs right behind them. Gooch's and Kennebunk attract teenagers; Mother's Beach, which has a small playground and tidal puddles for splashing, is popular with families. For parking permits (a fee is charged in summer), go to the **Kennebunk Town Office** (⊠ 1 Summer St., ☎ 207/985–2102).

Shopping

Tom's of Maine Natural Living Store (⊠ U.S. 1, ☎ 207/985–3874) sells all-natural personal-care products. **Marlow's Artisans Gallery** (⊠ 39 Main St., ☎ 207/985–2931) carries a large and eclectic collection of crafts.

Kennebunkport

❻ *5 mi east of Kennebunk, 10 mi northeast of Ogunquit.*

When George Bush was president, Kennebunkport was his summer White House. But long before Bush came into the public eye, visitors were coming to Kennebunkport to soak up the salt air, seafood, and sunshine. This is a picture-perfect town with manicured lawns, elaborate flower beds, freshly painted homes, and a small-town wholesomeness. People flock to Kennebunkport mostly in summer; some come in early December when the **Christmas Prelude** is celebrated on two weekends. Santa arrives by fishing boat and the Christmas trees are lighted as carolers stroll the sidewalks.

Route 35 merges with Route 9 in Kennebunk and takes you right into Kennebunkport's **Dock Square,** the busy town center. Boutiques, T-shirt shops, art galleries, crafts stores, and restaurants encircle the square and spread out along side streets and alleys. Although many businesses close in winter, the best bargains often are had in December. Walk onto the drawbridge to admire the tidal Kennebunk River.

The **Nott House,** known also as White Columns, is an imposing Greek Revival mansion with Doric columns that rise the height of the house. The 1853 house is furnished with the belongings of four generations of the Perkins-Nott family. It is a gathering place for village walking tours; call for schedule. ⊠ *8 Maine St.,* ☎ *207/967–2751.* ☎ *$5.* ☉ *Mid-June–mid-Oct., Tues.–Fri. 1–4, Sat. 10–1.*

Ocean Avenue follows the Kennebunk River from Dock Square to the sea and winds around the peninsula of **Cape Arundel.** Parson's Way, a small and tranquil stretch of rocky shoreline, is open to all. As you round Cape Arundel, look to the right for the entrance to George Bush's summer home at Walker's Point.

★ ℭ The **Seashore Trolley Museum** displays streetcars built from 1872 to 1972 and includes trolleys from major metropolitan areas and world capitals—Boston to Budapest, New York to Nagasaki, and San Francisco to Sydney—all beautifully restored. Best of all, you can take a trolley ride for nearly 4 mi over the tracks of the former Atlantic Shoreline trolley line, with a stop along the way at the museum restoration shop, where trolleys are transformed from junk into gems. Both guided and self-guided tours are available. ⊠ *195 Log Cabin Rd.,* ☎ *207/967–2800,* WEB *www.trolleymuseum.org.* ☎ *$7.* ☉ *Late May–mid-Oct., daily 10–4:30; reduced hrs in spring and fall.*

Intown Trolley (☎ 207/967–3686) offers 45-minute sightseeing tours.

Dining and Lodging

$$$$ ✕ **Seascapes.** The emphasis is on seafood at this pretty harborfront restaurant where the view takes center stage. You can begin with lobster spring rolls, then move on to roasted lobster or try the rack of lamb. Accompany it all with a selection from the excellent wine list. ⊠ *77 Pier Rd., Cape Porpoise Harbor, Cape Porpoise,* ☎ *207/967–8500. AE, D, DC, MC, V. Closed late Oct.–Apr.*

$$$$ ✕ **Windows on the Water.** Big windows frame Dock Square and the working harbor of Kennebunkport, and almost every window in the airy dining room shares the view. Lobster ravioli and rack of lamb are two noteworthy entrées. ⊠ *12 Chase Hill Rd.,* ☎ *207/967–3313. Reservations essential. AE, D, DC, MC, V.*

$$–$$$$ ✕ **Cape Pier Chowder House.** You can watch the surf crash over distant ledges near the Goat Island lighthouse and see lobster boats returning with their day's catch at this oceanfront lobster shack. Seating is on the deck or inside. The fare includes lobster, clams, and fried foods. ⊠ *15 Pier Rd., Cape Porpoise,* ☎ *207/967–0123 or 800/967–4268. MC, V. Closed early Nov.–mid-Apr.*

$$$$ ✕▦ **Cape Arundel Inn.** This shingle-style inn commands a magnificent ocean view that takes in the Bush estate at Walker's Point. The spacious rooms are furnished with country-style furniture and antiques, and most have sitting areas with ocean views. You can relax on the front porch or in front of the living-room fireplace. In the candlelit dining room ($$$$), open to the public for dinner, every table has a view of the surf. The menu changes seasonally. ⊠ *208 Ocean Ave., 04046,* ☎ *207/967–2125,* FAX *207/967–1199,* WEB *www.capearundelinn.com. 14 rooms. Restaurant, kitchenettes. AE, D, MC, V. Closed Jan. 15–Mar. 15.*

$$$$ ✕▦ **White Barn Inn.** For a romantic overnight stay or a superb meal,
★ you need look no further than the exclusive White Barn Inn, known for its attentive, pampering service. The meticulously appointed rooms have luxurious baths and are decorated with a blend of hand-painted pieces and period furniture; some rooms have fireplaces and whirlpool baths. Regional New England fare is served at the rustic but elegant dining room ($$$$; jacket required), one of the region's best. The fixed-

price menu, which changes weekly, might list steamed Maine lobster nestled on fresh fettuccine with carrots, ginger, and snow peas. ⊠ *Box 560C, 37 Beach Ave., 04046,* ☎ *207/967–2321,* FAX *207/967–1100,* WEB *www.whitebarninn.com. 16 rooms, 9 suites. Restaurant, pool, bicycles. AE, MC, V. CP.*

$$$$ ⚄ **The Seaside.** This handsome seaside property has been in the hands of the Severance family since 1667. The modern motel units, all with cable TVs and sliding-glass doors that open onto private decks or patios (half with ocean views), are appropriate for families; so are the cottages with one to four bedrooms. ⊠ *80 Beach Ave., 04046,* ☎ *207/ 967–4461,* FAX *207/967–1135,* WEB *www.kennebunkbeach.com. 22 rooms, 10 cottages. No-smoking rooms, beach, playground, laundry service. AE, MC, V. Cottages closed Nov.–Apr. CP.*

$$$–$$$$ ⚄ **Captain Lord Mansion.** Of all the mansions in Kennebunkport's historic district that have been converted to inns, the 1812 Captain Lord Mansion is the most stately and sumptuously appointed. The three-story Federal-style inn is topped with a widow's walk that has views of the town and harbor, just three blocks away. Distinctive architecture, including a suspended elliptical staircase and gas fireplaces in 15 rooms, and near–museum quality accoutrements make for a formal but not stuffy atmosphere. Five rooms have whirlpool tubs. The extravagant suite has two fireplaces, a double whirlpool, a hydro-massage body spa, a TV/VCR and stereo system, and a king-size canopy bed. ⊠ *Box 800, Pleasant and Green Sts., 04046,* ☎ *207/967–3141,* FAX *207/967– 3172,* WEB *www.captainlord.com. 15 rooms, 1 suite. D, MC, V. BP.*

$$$ ⚄ **Bufflehead Cove.** On the Kennebunk River at the end of a winding dirt road, this gray-shingle B&B amid quiet country fields and apple trees is only five minutes from Dock Square. Rooms in the main house have white wicker and flowers hand-painted on the walls. The Hideaway Suite, with a two-sided gas fireplace, king-size bed, and large whirlpool tub, overlooks the river. The Garden Studio has a fireplace and offers the most privacy. ⊠ *Box 499, 18 Bufflehead Cove Rd., 04046,* ☎ FAX *207/967–3879,* WEB *www.buffleheadcove.com. 2 rooms, 3 suites, 1 cottage. Dock, boating. D, MC, V. BP.*

Outdoor Activities and Sports

BEACHES

Three-mi-long **Goose Rocks,** a few minutes' drive north of town off Route 9, is a favorite of families with small children. You can pick up a **parking permit** ($5 a day, $15 a week) at the Chamber of Commerce (⊠ 17 Western Ave., Lower Village, ☎ 207/967–0857).

BIKING

Cape-Able Bike Shop (⊠ Townhouse Corners, ☎ 207/967–4382) rents bicycles.

BOATING AND FISHING

Deep Water II (⊠ Kennebunkport Marina, ☎ 207/967–5595) offers scenic cruises. **First Chance** (⊠ Arundel Wharf, Lower Village, ☎ 207/ 967–5507 or 800/967–2628) gives whale-watching cruises and guarantees sightings in season. **Maritime Productions** (⊠ Kennebunkport Marina, ☎ 207/641–2313) takes passengers on sunset theater cruises that feature tales of intrigue and horror performed by a costumed actor.

Old Orchard Beach

❼ *15 mi north of Kennebunkport, 18 mi south of Portland.*

Old Orchard Beach, a few mi north of Biddeford on Route 9, is a 7-mi strip of sand beach with an amusement park that resembles a small Coney Island. Despite the summertime crowds and fried-food odors, the atmosphere can be captivating. During the 1940s and '50s, in the heyday of the Big Band era, the pier had a dance hall where stars of the era performed. Fire claimed the end of the pier, but booths with games and candy concessions still line both sides. Plans are underway to extend the pier and offer dinner/gaming cruises. In summer the town sponsors fireworks (usually on Thursday night). The many places to stay run the gamut from cheap motels to cottage colonies to full-service seasonal hotels. You won't find free parking anywhere in town, but there are ample lots. Amtrak has a seasonal stop here.

A world away in atmosphere from the beach scene is **Ocean Park** (☎ 207/934–9068), on the southwestern edge of town. This vacation community was founded in 1881 as a summer assembly, following the example of Chautauqua, New York. Today the community still has a wide range of cultural happenings, including movies, concerts, workshops, and religious services. Most are presented in the Temple, which is on the National Register of Historic Places.

☺ **Palace Playland** (⊠ 1 Old Orchard St., ☎ 207/934–2001), open from Memorial Day to Labor Day, has rides, booths, and a roller coaster that drops almost 50 ft.

☺ **Funtown/Splashtown** (⊠ U.S. 1, Saco, ☎ 207/284–5139 or 800/878–2900) has more than 30 rides and amusements, including miniature golf, water slides, a wave pool, and Excalibur, a wooden roller coaster.

Dining and Lodging

$$$–$$$$ ✕ **Joseph's by the Sea.** Big windows frame the ocean beyond the dunes at this fine restaurant, which offers outdoor dining in season. Appetizers may include goat cheese terrine and lobster potato pancake; try the Grilled Tuscan swordfish or crabmeat Napolean for your main course. ⊠ 55 W. Grand Ave., ☎ 207/934–5044. MC, V.

$$ ⌸ **Old Orchard Beach Inn.** Dating from 1730, this is Old Orchard Beach's oldest inn. It was saved from demolition in 1997 and was completely renovated. The spacious guest rooms are furnished with antiques, area rugs cover the pine floors, quilts brighten the beds, and lace curtains frame the windows. Many have views over the town to the shimmering Atlantic. ⊠ 6 Portland Ave., 04064, ☎ 207/934–5834 or 877/700–6624, FAX 207/934–0782, WEB www.oldorchardbeachinn.com. 17 rooms, 1 suite. Air-conditioning, in-room data ports. AE, D, MC, V. CP.

Nightlife and the Arts

In season, weekly concerts are held in Town Square every Monday and Tuesday night at 7. Fireworks light the sky Thursdays at 9:30 from late June through Labor Day. Concerts are held most Sunday evenings in Ocean Park.

Outdoor Activities and Sports

Ferry Beach State Park (⊠ Rte. 9, Saco, ☎ 207/283–0067) comprises 117 acres of beach, bike paths, and nature trails. The **Maine Audubon Society** (⊠ Rte. 9, Scarborough, ☎ 207/781–2330; 207/883–5100 from mid-June to Labor Day) operates guided canoe trips and rents canoes in Scarborough Marsh, the largest salt marsh in Maine. Programs at Maine Audubon's Falmouth headquarters (north of Portland) include nature walks and a discovery room for children.

York County Coast A to Z

To research prices, get advice from other travelers, and book travel arrangements, visit www.fodors.com.

AIR TRAVEL

Portland International Jetport is 35 mi northeast of Kennebunk.

CAR TRAVEL

U.S. 1 from Kittery is the shopper's route north; other roads hug the coastline. Interstate 95 is usually faster for travelers headed to towns north of Ogunquit, but be forewarned that the Maine Turnpike/I–95 is in the midst of a widening project that will result in slowdowns and stops until completion in 2004. For information, call 877/682–9433.

The exit numbers can be confusing: as you go north from Portsmouth, Exits 1–3 lead to Kittery and Exit 4 leads to the Yorks. After the toll-booth in York, the Maine Turnpike begins, and the numbers start over again, with Exit 2 for Wells and Ogunquit and Exit 3 (and Route 35) for Kennebunk and Kennebunkport. Route 9 goes from Kenneb-unkport to Cape Porpoise and Goose Rocks. Parking is tight in Ken-nebunkport in peak season. Possibilities include the municipal lot next to the Congregational Church ($2 an hour from May to October) and 30 North St. (free year-round).

EMERGENCIES

➤ HOSPITALS AND EMERGENCY SERVICES: **Maine State Police** (⊠ Gray, ☎ 207/793–4500 or 800/482–0730). **Kennebunk Walk-in Clinic** (⊠ U.S. 1 N, ☎ 207/985–6027). **Southern Maine Medical Center** (⊠ Rte. 111, Biddeford, ☎ 207/283–7000; 207/283–7100 emergency room). **York Hospital** (⊠ 15 Hospital Dr., ☎ 207/351–2157, 800/283–7234; same phone numbers for Tel-A-Nurse).

TOURS

Gone with the Wind schedules guided kayak and windsurfing trips. Van tours of southern Maine are offered by Seacoast Tours. Routes include Portland, Ogunquit, Kittery and York, and Kennebunkport; tours are 1¼–4 hours.
➤ TOUR OPERATORS: **Gone with the Wind** (⊠ Biddeford, ☎ 207/283–8446). **Seacoast Tours** (⊠ Perkins Cove, Ogunquit, ☎ 207/646–6326 or 800/328–8687).

TRAIN TRAVEL

Amtrak offers rail service from Boston to Portland, with seasonal stops in Wells and Old Orchard Beach.
➤ TRAIN INFORMATION: **AMTRAK** (☎ 800/872–7245, WEB *www. amtrak.com*).

TRANSPORTATION AROUND YORK COUNTY COAST

Trolleys ($1–$3) serve several areas. A trolley circulates among the Yorks from June to Labor Day. Eight trolleys serve the major tourist areas and beaches of Ogunquit, including four that connect with Wells from mid-May to mid-October. The trolley from Dock Square in Kenneb-unkport to Kennebunk Beach runs from Memorial Day to Columbus Day.

VISITOR INFORMATION

➤ CONTACTS: **Maine Tourism Association & Visitor Information Cen**-ter (⊠ U.S. 1 and I–95, Kittery 03904, ☎ 207/439–1319). **Kenneb-unk-Kennebunkport Chamber of Commerce** (⊠ 17 Western Ave., Kennebunk 04043, ☎ 207/967–0857). **Kittery-Eliot Chamber of Com**-merce (⊠ 191 State Rd., Kittery 03904, ☎ 207/439–7574 or 800/639–9645). **Ogunquit Chamber of Commerce** (⊠ Box 2289, U.S. 1, Ogun-quit 03907, ☎ 207/646–2939). **Old Orchard Beach Chamber of Com**-merce (⊠ Box 600, 1st St., Old Orchard Beach 04064, ☎ 207/934–2500 or 800/365–9386). **Wells Chamber of Commerce** (⊠ Box 356, Wells 04090, ☎ 207/646–2451). The **Yorks Chamber of Commerce** (⊠ 571 U.S. 1, York 03903, ☎ 207/363–4422).

PORTLAND TO WALDOBORO

This south–mid-coast area provides an overview of Maine: a little bit of urban life, a little more coastline, and a nice dollop of history and architecture. Maine's largest city, Portland, holds some pleasant surprises, including the Old Port, among the finest urban renovation projects on the East Coast. Freeport, north of Portland, was made famous by its L. L. Bean store, whose success led to the opening of scores of other clothing stores and outlets. Brunswick is best known for Bowdoin College. Bath has been a shipbuilding center since 1607; the Maine Maritime Museum preserves its history. Wiscasset contains many antiques shops and galleries.

The Boothbays—the coastal areas of Boothbay Harbor, East Boothbay, Linekin Neck, Southport Island, and the inland town of Boothbay—attract hordes of vacationing families and flotillas of pleasure craft. The Pemaquid peninsula juts into the Atlantic south of Damariscotta and just east of the Boothbays. Near Pemaquid Beach you can view the objects unearthed at the Colonial Pemaquid Restoration.

Portland

105 mi northeast of Boston, MA, 320 mi northeast of New York City, 215 mi southwest of St. Stephen, New Brunswick.

Portland's role as a cultural and economic center for the region has given the gentrifying city of 65,000 a variety of attractions that make it well worth a day or two of exploration. Its restored Old Port balances modern commercial enterprise and salty waterfront character in an area bustling with restaurants, shops, and galleries. Water tours of the harbor and excursions to islands of Casco Bay depart from the piers of Commercial Street. Downtown Portland, in a funk for years, is now a burgeoning arts district connected to the Old Port by a revitalized Congress Street, where L. L. Bean operates a factory store.

Portland's first home was built on the peninsula now known as Munjoy Hill in 1632. The British burned the city in 1775, when residents refused to surrender arms, but it was rebuilt and became a major trading center. Much of Portland was destroyed on July 4 in the Great Fire of 1866, when a boy threw a celebration firecracker into a pile of wood shavings; 1,500 buildings burned to the ground. Poet Henry Wadsworth Longfellow said at the time that his city reminded him of the ruins of Pompeii. The Great Fire started not far from where people now wander the streets of the Old Port.

Congress Street runs the length of the peninsular city from alongside the Western Promenade in the southwest to the Eastern Promenade on Munjoy Hill in the northeast, passing through the small downtown area. A few blocks southeast of downtown, the bustling Old Port sprawls along the waterfront. Below Munjoy Hill is India Street, where the Great Fire of 1866 started.

8 The **Portland Observatory** on Munjoy Hill reopened in 2000 after a major restoration. Built in 1807 by Capt. Lemuel Moody, a retired sea captain, it is the last remaining signal tower in the country and is held in place by 122 tons of ballast. After visiting the small museum at the base, you can climb to the Orb deck and take in views of Portland, the islands, and inland to the White Mountains. ⊠ *138 Congress St.,* ☎ *207/774–5561.* ▨ *$3.* ☉ *Memorial Day–Columbus Day, Mon.–Sat. 10–6 and Sun. 1–5.*

★ **9** The Italianate-style Morse-Libby Mansion, known as **Victoria Mansion,** was built between 1858 and 1860 and is widely regarded as the most

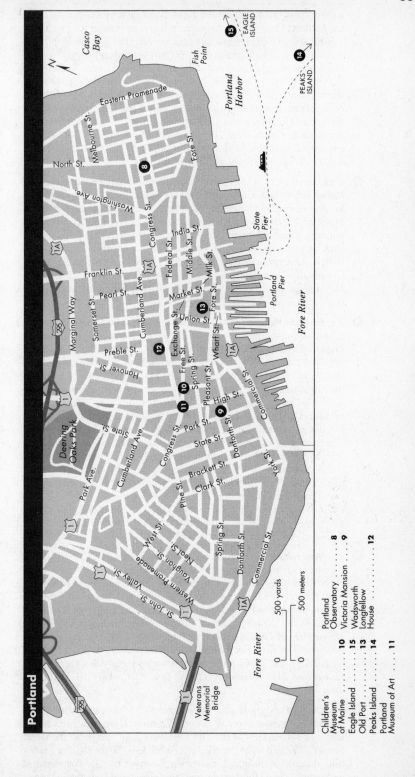

Portland

Casco Bay

N

Eastern Promenade

Fish Point

Melbourne St.

North St.

Fore St.

Washington Ave.

Congress St.

India St.

Federal St.

Middle St.

Milk St.

Franklin St.

Pearl St.

Cumberland Ave.

Market St.

Fore St.

Somerset St.

Exchange St.

Union St.

Marginal Way

Preble St.

Free St.

Spring St.

Wharf St.

Hanover St.

Pleasant St.

High St.

Deering Oaks Park

State St.

Cumberland Ave.

Congress St.

Park St.

State St.

Commercial St.

York St.

Park Ave.

Brackett St.

Clark St.

Pine St.

Danforth St.

West St.

Neal St.

Vaughan St.

Western Promenade

Spring St.

Danforth St.

St. John St.

Valley St.

Commercial St.

Fore River

Veterans Memorial Bridge

Portland Harbor

State Pier

Portland Pier

Fore River

EAGLE ISLAND

PEAKS ISLAND

⑮

⑭

⑧

⑬

⑫

⑩

⑪

⑨

500 yards

500 meters

0

0

sumptuously ornamented dwelling of its period remaining in the country. Architect Henry Austin designed the house for hotelier Ruggles Morse and his wife, Olive; the interior design—everything from the plasterwork to the furniture (much of it original)—is the only surviving commission of noted New York designer Gustave Herter. The elegant brownstone exterior of this National Historic Landmark is understated compared to the interior, which has colorful frescoed walls and ceilings, ornate marble mantelpieces, gilded gas chandeliers, stained-glass windows, and a freestanding mahogany staircase; guided tours cover all the details. ⊠ *109 Danforth St.,* ☎ *207/772–4841,* WEB *www.portlandarts.com/victoriamansion.* ⬚ *$7.* ☉ *May–Oct., Tues.–Sat. 10–4, Sun. 1–5; special Christmas hours.*

🔟 Touching is okay at the relatively small but fun **Children's Museum of Maine,** where kids can pretend they are fishing for lobster or are shopkeepers or computer experts. The majority of the museum's exhibits, many of which have a Maine theme, are best for children 10 and younger. Camera Obscura, an exhibit about optics that provides fascinating panoramic views of the city, charges a separate admission fee ($3); call for times. ⊠ *142 Free St.,* ☎ *207/828–1234.* ⬚ *$5, $6 for combination ticket with Camera Obscura.* ☉ *Memorial Day–Labor Day and school vacations, Mon.–Sat. 10–5, Sun. noon–5; early Sept.–mid-June, Wed.–Sat. 10–5, Sun. noon–5.*

★ ⑪ The **Portland Museum of Art,** Maine's largest public art institution, has a number of strong collections, including fine seascapes and landscapes by Winslow Homer, John Marin, Andrew Wyeth, Edward Hopper, Marsden Hartley, and other painters. Homer's *Pulling the Dory* and *Weatherbeaten,* two quintessential Maine-coast images, are here; the museum owns 17 paintings by Homer. The Joan Whitney Payson Collection of Impressionist and Postimpressionist art includes works by Monet, Picasso, and Renoir. Harry N. Cobb, an associate of I. M. Pei, designed the strikingly modern Charles Shipman Payson building. The renovated McLellan-Sweat House is expected to open in fall 2002 with additional galleries housing the museum's 19th-century collection and decorative art as well as interactive educational stations. ⊠ *7 Congress Sq.,* ☎ *207/775–6148; 800/639–4067 recorded information,* WEB *www.portlandmuseum.org.* ⬚ *$6; free Fri. evenings 5–9.* ☉ *Columbus Day–Memorial Day, Tues.–Wed. and weekends 10–5, Thurs.–Fri. 10–9; Memorial Day–Columbus Day, Mon.–Wed. and weekends 10–5, Thurs.–Fri. 10–9; tours daily at 2.*

⑫ The **Wadsworth Longfellow House,** the boyhood home of the poet and the first brick house in Portland, is particularly interesting because most of the furnishings are original to the house. The late-Colonial-style structure, built in 1785, sits back from the street and has a small portico over its entrance and four chimneys surmounting the hip roof. The house is part of the Center for Maine History, which includes the adjacent Maine History Gallery and a research library; the gift shop has a good selection of books about Maine. ⊠ *489 Congress St.,* ☎ *207/879–0427 or 207/774–1822,* WEB *www.mainehistory.org.* ⬚ *$6; Center $4.* ☉ *House and Maine History Gallery, June–Oct., daily 10–5; Library Tues.–Sat., 10–3..*

★ ⑬ The **Old Port** bridges the gap between the city's 19th-century commercial activities and those of today. Like the Customs House, the brick buildings and warehouses of the Old Port were built following the Great Fire of 1866 and were intended to last for ages. When the city's economy slumped in the mid-20th century, however, the Old Port declined and seemed slated for demolition. Then artists and craftspeople began opening shops in the late 1960s, and restaurants, boutiques, and bookstores followed. Allow a couple of hours to wander at leisure on Market, Exchange, Middle, and Fore streets. You can park your car at the city garage on Fore Street (between Exchange and Union streets) or opposite the U.S. Customs House at the corner of Fore and Pearl streets.

OFF THE
BEATEN PATH

CAPE ELIZABETH – This upscale Portland suburb juts out into the Atlantic. Take Route 77 south and east from Portland and follow signs to Two Lights State Park, home to Two Lights, one of the cape's three lighthouses. You can wander through old World War II bunkers and picnic on the rocky coast. Stay on Two Lights Road to the end, where you'll find another lighthouse, privately owned, and the Lobster Shack, a seafood-in-the-rough restaurant. Return to the center of Cape Elizabeth and turn right on Shore Road, which winds along the coast to Portland.

Historic **Portland Head Light,** familiar to many from photographs and Edward Hopper's painting, was commissioned by George Washington in 1791. Besides a harbor view, the park has walking paths and picnic facilities. The keeper's house is now the Museum at Portland Head Light. The lighthouse is about 2 mi from town center in Fort Williams Park. *Museum:* ⊠ *1000 Shore Rd.,* ☎ *207/799–2661.* ⌚ *$2.* ☉ *June–Oct., daily 10–4.*

Dining and Lodging

$$–$$$ ✕ **Gabriel's.** Hand-painted wall murals let you view the sea as you savor such appetizers as confit of calamari and entrées such as whole roasted rainbow trout with sweet corn and fresh herbs. The menu changes seasonally. An upstairs dining room is quieter and also has a copper-topped bar for casual dining. ⊠ *47 Middle St.,* ☎ *207/775–1510. AE, D, DC, MC, V. Closed Sun. and Mon. No lunch.*

$$–$$$ ✕ **Fore Street.** Two of Maine's best chefs, Sam Hayward and Dana Street,
★ opened this restaurant in a renovated, cavernous warehouse on the edge of the Old Port. Every table in the two-level main dining room has a view of the enormous brick oven and hearth and the open kitchen, where creative entrées such as roasted Maine lobster, applewood-grilled Atlantic swordfish loin, and wood-oven–braised cassoulet are prepared. ⊠ *288 Fore St.,* ☎ *207/775–2717. AE, MC, V. No lunch.*

$$–$$$ ✕ **Street and Co.** Fish and seafood are the specialties here, and you won't
★ find any better or fresher. You enter through the kitchen, with all its wonderful aromas, and dine, amid dried herbs and shelves of staples, at one of a dozen copper-topped tables (so your waiter can place a skillet of steaming seafood directly in front of you). There's a beer and wine bar in one of the dining rooms. Some good choices are lobster diavolo for two, scallops in Pernod and cream, and sole Française. A vegetarian dish is the only alternative to seafood. ⊠ *33 Wharf St.,* ☎ *207/775–0887. AE, MC, V. No lunch.*

$$ ✕ **Aubergine.** This casual bistro and wine bar has staked out a prime downtown location, across the street from L. L. Bean and down the street from the Portland Museum of Art. The French-inspired menu changes daily but might list appetizers such as Swiss onion soup with fresh tarragon or duck liver pâté and entrées such as spiced duck breast with fennel sauce or crispy salmon with spinach and Pernod. Wines by the glass are chosen to complement the dishes. ⊠ *555 Congress St.,* ☎ *207/874–0680. MC, V. Closed Sun.–Mon. No lunch.*

$–$$ ✕ **Portland Public Market.** Nibble your way through this handsome, airy market where 20 locally owned businesses sell fresh foods, organic produce, and imported specialty items, including fresh baked goods, soups, smoked seafood, rotisserie chicken, aged cheeses, and German meats. In 2000, celebrity chef Matthew Kenney opened **The Commissary**

(✉ ☎ 207/228–2057. MC, V.), which serves entrées such as wood-roasted free-range chicken stuffed with foie gras and pears, or poached Maine lobster with citrus and local blue potatoes. The market is open Monday–Saturday 9–7, Sunday 10–5; some vendors open at 7. ✉ *25 Preble St.,* ☎ *207/228–2000.*

$$$$ ✕⊞ **Inn by the Sea.** This all-suites inn welcomes families and dogs. All the spacious suites include kitchens and overlook the Atlantic, and it's just a short walk down a private boardwalk to sandy Crescent Beach, a popular family spot. The Audubon dining room($$), open to nonguests, serves fine seafood and regional dishes. Dogs are welcomed with a room-service pet menu, evening turn-down treats, and oversized beach towels. The cottage-style architecture throughout is typical New England. ✉ *40 Bowery Beach Rd., Cape Elizabeth 04107 (7 mi south of Portland),* ☎ *207/799–3134 or 800/888–4287,* FAX *207/799–4779,* WEB *www.innbythesea.com. 25 suites, 18 cottage condominiums. Restaurant, pool, tennis court, croquet, bicycles. AE, D, MC, V.*

$$$$ ⊞ **Black Point Inn.** Toward the tip of the peninsula that juts into the ocean at Prouts Neck stands this stylish shingled, tastefully updated old-time resort with spectacular views up and down the Maine coast. Most rooms capture an old-fashioned seaside ambiance and are nicely decorated with floral patterns and gauzy white curtains. The extensive grounds contain beaches, trails, and sports facilities; you can also use the tennis courts and golf course of the country club a few minutes' walk away. The Cliff Walk runs along the Atlantic headlands that Winslow Homer (his studio is nearby) often painted. The inn is 12 mi south of Portland and about 10 mi north of Old Orchard Beach by road. ✉ *510 Black Point Rd., Scarborough 04074,* ☎ *207/883–4126 or 800/258–2500,* FAX *207/883–9976,* WEB *www.blackpointinn.com. 68 rooms, 12 suites. Restaurant, bar, 1 indoor and 1 outdoor pool, hot tub, golf privileges, croquet, volleyball, boating, bicycles. AE, D, MC, V. BP, MAP.*

$$$$ ⊞ **Portland Regency Hotel.** The only major hotel in the center of the Old Port, the brick Regency building was Portland's armory in the late 19th century. Rooms have four-poster beds, tall standing mirrors, floral curtains, and love seats. You can walk to shops, restaurants, and museums from the hotel. ✉ *20 Milk St., 04101,* ☎ *207/774–4200 or 800/727–3436,* FAX *207/775–2150,* WEB *www.theregency.com. 87 rooms, 8 suites. Restaurant, massage, sauna, steam room, health club, nightclub, meeting room. AE, D, DC, MC, V.*

$$$–$$$$ ⊞ **Inn on Carleton.** After a day of exploring Portland's museums and shops, you'll find a quiet retreat at this elegant brick town house on the city's Western Promenade. Built in 1869, it is furnished throughout with period antiques as well as artwork by contemporary Maine artists. The entryway features a restored trompe l'oeil painting by Charles Schumacher, and more of his work has been uncovered in the back dining room. ✉ *46 Carleton St., 04102,* ☎ *207/775–1910 or 800/ 639–1779,* FAX *207/761–0956,* WEB *www.innoncarleton.com. 6 rooms. D, MC, V. BP.*

$$$–$$$$ ⊞ **Pomegranate Inn.** The classic architecture of this handsome inn in the architecturally rich Western Promenade area gives no hint of the surprises within. Vivid hand-painted walls, floors, and woodwork combine with contemporary artwork to create an ambience that is both stimulating and comforting. Rooms are individually decorated, but all have telephones and TVs, and five have fireplaces. Room 8, in the carriage house, has a private garden terrace. ✉ *49 Neal St., 04102,* ☎ *207/772–1006 or 800/ 356–0408,* FAX *207/773–4426,* WEB *www.pomegranateinn.com. 7 rooms, 1 suite. In-room data ports. MC, V. BP.*

$$–$$$ ⊞ **Inn at St. John.** This gem of a small hotel was built by railroad tycoon John Deering in 1897. Rooms are decorated with a Victorian flair, with

a mix of traditional and antique furnishings, and no two are alike. It's an uphill walk to downtown attractions from here. ✉ *939 Congress St., 04102,* ☎ *207/773–6481 or 800/636–9127,* FAX *207/756–7629,* WEB *www. innatstjohn.com. 37 rooms. In-room data ports. AE, D, DC, MC, V. CP.*

Nightlife and the Arts

NIGHTLIFE

Asylum (✉ 121 Center St., ☎ 207/772–8274) has live entertainment, dancing, and eight large screens for sports viewing. **Brian Boru** (✉ 57 Center St., ☎ 207/780–1506) is an Irish pub with occasional entertainment and an outside deck. **Gritty McDuff's—Portland's Original Brew Pub** (✉ 396 Fore St., ☎ 207/772–2739) brews fine ales and serves British pub fare and seafood dishes. **Stone Coast Brewery** (✉ 14 York St., ☎ 207/ 773–2337) is a brew pub with billiards and occasional live entertainment. For blues, head to the **Big Easy** (✉ 55 Market St., ☎ 207/871–8817).

THE ARTS

Portland Performing Arts Center (✉ 25A Forest Ave., ☎ 207/761–0591) presents music, dance, and theater performances. **Cumberland County Civic Center** (✉ 1 Civic Center Sq., ☎ 207/775–3458) hosts concerts, sporting events, and family shows. **Portland City Hall's Merrill Auditorium** (✉ 20 Myrtle St., ☎ 207/874–8200) is home to the Portland Symphony Orchestra and Portland Concert Association and the site of numerous theatrical and musical events. On most Tuesdays from mid-June to September, organ recitals ($5 donation) are given on the auditorium's huge 1912 Kotzschmar Memorial Organ. **Mad Horse Theatre Company** (✉ 92 Oak St., ☎ 207/797–3338) performs classic, contemporary, and original works. **Portland Stage Company** (✉ 25A Forest Ave., ☎ 207/774–0465) mounts productions year-round at the Portland Performing Arts Center.

Outdoor Activities and Sports

BALLOON RIDES

Balloon Rides (✉ 17 Freeman St., ☎ 207/772–4730) operates scenic flights over southern Maine.

BASEBALL

The Class AA **Portland Sea Dogs** (☎ 207/879–9500), a farm team of the Florida Marlins, play at Hadlock Field (✉ 271 Park Ave.). Tickets cost $4–$6.

BEACHES

Crescent Beach State Park (✉ Rte. 77, Cape Elizabeth, ☎ 207/767–3625), about 8 mi south of Portland, has a sand beach, picnic tables, a seasonal snack bar, and a bathhouse. Popular with families with young children, it charges a nominal fee for admittance.

BOAT TRIPS

For tours of the harbor, Casco Bay, and the scenic nearby islands, try **Bay View Cruises** (✉ Fisherman's Wharf, ☎ 207/761–0496). **Casco Bay Lines,** (✉ Maine State Pier, ☎ 207/774–7871) provides narrated cruises and transportation to Casco Bay Islands. **Eagle Island Tours** (✉ Long Wharf, ☎ 207/774–6498) offers daily cruises to Eagle Island and seal-watching cruises. **Old Port Mariner Fleet** (✉ Long Wharf, ☎ 207/ 775–0727, 207/642–3270, or 800/437–3270) has scenic cruises and whale-watching and fishing trips. **Palawan Sailing** (✉ Old Port, ☎ 207/ 774–2163) offers cruises on a catamaran.

HOCKEY

The **Portland Pirates,** the farm team of the Washington Capitals, play home games at the Cumberland County Civic Center (✉ 85 Free St., ☎ 207/828–4665). Tickets cost $10–$14.

Shopping

For a city its size, Portland has a satisfying variety of locally owned stores and art and crafts galleries, particularly those in or near the Old Port; trendy Exchange Street is great for browsing.

ART AND ANTIQUES

Abacus (⊠ 44 Exchange St., ☎ 207/772–4880), an appealing crafts gallery, has unusual gift items in glass, wood, and textiles, plus fine modern jewelry. **Greenhut Galleries** (⊠ 146 Middle St., ☎ 207/772–2693) shows contemporary art and sculpture by Maine artists. **F.O. Bailey Antiquarians** (⊠ 141 Middle St., ☎ 207/774–1479), Portland's largest retail showroom, carries antique and reproduction furniture and jewelry, paintings, rugs, and china. The **Pine Tree Shop & Bayview Gallery** (⊠ 75 Market St., ☎ 207/773–3007 or 800/244–3007) has original art and prints by prominent Maine painters. Representing 100 American artists, the spacious **Stein Gallery** (⊠ 195 Middle St., ☎ 207/772–9072) showcases decorative and sculptural contemporary glass.

BOOKS

Carlson and Turner (⊠ 241 Congress St., ☎ 207/773–4200) is an antiquarian book dealer with an estimated 70,000 titles. Besides new and used books, many of regional interest, **Emerson Books, Maps, and Prints** (⊠ 18 Exchange St., ☎ 207/874–2665) stocks antique maps, botanical and bird prints, and old posters and magazine covers.

CLOTHING

Family-owned **Casco Bay Wool Works** (⊠ 10 Moulton St., ☎ 207/879–9665) sells beautiful handcrafted wool capes and shawls, blankets and scarves.

FURNITURE

Made locally, the handsome cherry-wood pieces at **Green Design Furniture** (⊠ 267 Commercial St., ☎ 207/775–4234; 800/853–4234 orders) have a classic feel—somewhat Asian, somewhat Mission; a unique system of joinery enables easy assembly after shipping.

MALL

Maine Mall (⊠ 364 Maine Mall Rd., ☎ 207/774–0303), 5 mi south of Portland, has 145 stores, including Sears, Filene's, JCPenney, and Macy's.

Casco Bay Islands

The islands of Casco Bay are also known as the Calendar Islands because an early explorer mistakenly thought there was one for each day of the year (in reality there are only 140). The brightly painted ferries of Casco Bay Lines are the islands' lifeline. There is frequent service to the most-populated ones, including Peaks, Long, Little Diamond, and Great Diamond. A ride on the bay is a great way to experience the Maine coast.

14 **Peaks Island,** nearest to Portland, is the most developed of the Calendar Islands, but you can still commune with the wind and the sea, explore an old fort, and ramble along the alternately rocky and sandy shore. The trip to the island by boat is particularly enjoyable at or near sunset. Order a lobster sandwich or cold beer on the outdoor deck of **Jones' Landing** restaurant, steps from the dock. A circle trip without stops takes about 90 minutes. On the far side of the island you can stop on the rugged shoreline and have lunch. A small museum with Civil War artifacts, open in summer, is maintained in the **Fifth Maine Regiment** building. When the Civil War broke out in 1861, Maine was asked to raise only a single regiment to fight, but the state raised 10 and sent the 5th Maine Regiment into the war's first battle at Bull Run.

⑮ **Eagle Island,** owned by the state and open to the public for day trips in summer, was the home of Admiral Robert E. Peary, the American explorer of the North Pole. Peary built a stone-and-wood house on the 17-acre island as a summer retreat in 1904 but made it his permanent residence. Filled with Peary's stuffed Arctic birds, the quartz he brought home and set into the fieldstone fireplace, and other objects, the house remains as it was when Peary lived in it. A boat ride here offers a classic Maine experience as you pass by forested islands, and the island has a rocky beach and some trails to explore. The *Kristy K.* and *Fish Hawk* depart from Long Wharf in Portland and make four-hour narrated tours; there are also tours of Portland Head Light and seal-watching cruises. You can also visit the island from Freeport. ⊠ *Long Wharf,* ☎ *207/774–6498.* ⊒ *$8–$15, depending on tour.* ☉ *Departures late May–Labor Day, daily beginning 10* AM.

Freeport

⑯ *17 mi northeast of Portland, 10 mi southwest of Brunswick.*

Freeport, on U.S. 1, has charming back streets lined with historic buildings and old clapboard houses, and the pretty little harbor on the Harraseeket River in South Freeport is a relaxing place to linger. Most people, however, come here simply to shop—L. L. Bean is the store that put Freeport on the map, and plenty of outlets and some specialty stores have settled here. Still, if you choose, you can stay awhile and sample both parts of the Freeport experience: shopping along the town streets and easy access to nearby historic sites and outdoor activities.

☾ At the **Desert of Maine,** a 40-acre desert, a safari coach tours the sand dunes and you can walk nature trails, hunt for gemstones, and watch sand artists at work. Poor agricultural practices in the late 18th century combined with massive land clearing and overgrazing uncovered this desert, which was actually formed by a glacier during the last Ice Age. ⊠ *95 Desert Rd. (I–95, Exit 19),* ☎ *207/865–6962,* ⒲ *www.desertofmaine.com.* ⊒ *$7.50.* ☉ *Early May–Oct. 15.*

Dining and Lodging

$–$$$ ✕ **Harraseeket Lunch & Lobster Co.** Seafood baskets and lobster dinners are what this bare-bones place beside the town landing in South Freeport is all about. You can eat outside on picnic tables in good weather. ⊠ *On the pier, end of Main St.,* ☎ *207/865–4888. Reservations not accepted. No credit cards. Closed mid-Oct.–Apr.*

$$$$ ✕⌸ **Harraseeket Inn.** Despite modern appointments such as elevators and whirlpool baths in some rooms, this 1850 Greek Revival home and newer (1989 and 1997) additions provide a pleasantly old-fashioned country-inn experience just a few minutes' walk from L. L. Bean. Afternoon tea is served in the paneled drawing room, and guest rooms have print fabrics and reproductions of Federal quarter-canopy beds. The formal Maine Dining Room ($$-$$$) specializes in contemporary American regional cuisine such as lamb ragout ravioli and pan-roasted halibut with potato chowder. The more casual Broad Arrow Tavern ($-$$$), serves heartier fare. ⊠ *162 Main St., 04032,* ☎ *207/865–9377 or 800/342–6423,* ⒻⒶⓍ *207/865–1684,* ⒲ *www.stayfreeport.com. 82 rooms, 2 suites. 2 restaurants, air-conditioning, indoor pool, croquet, meeting room. AE, D, DC, MC, V. BP.*

$$–$$$ ⌸ **Isaac Randall House.** On a 5-acre lot within walking distance to downtown shops, this circa-1829 inn is a quiet retreat. Victorian antiques and country pieces fill the rooms. A red caboose in the backyard has been turned into a room that's ideal for families. Two rooms are in the town's former police station, now moved to the property. ⊠ *10 Independence Dr., 04032,* ☎ *207/865–9295 or 800/865–9295,* ⒻⒶⓍ *207/865–*

9003, WEB *www.isaacrandall.com. 12 rooms, 1 suite. Ice-skating, playground. AE, D, MC, V. BP.*

$–$$$ ⊡ **Atlantic Seal Bed & Breakfast.** The nautical decor of this 1850 waterfront Cape Cod home complements the pleasant water views from all three of its rooms. Owner Capt. Thomas Ring creates a welcoming setting, including homemade quilts, antiques, and down comforters for each room; he also offers boat trips. ⊠ *25 Main St. (Box 146), South Freeport 04078,* ☎ *207/865–6112 or 877/285–7325. 3 rooms. AE, MC, V. BP.*

$ ⊡ **Maine Idyll Motor Court.** The third and fourth generations of the Marsteller family operate this simple 1932 cottage colony. The tidy white cabins are shaded by towering pines and popular with families. Each cabin has a rustic feel, with wood floors and paneling. Baths are tiny. ⊠ *325 Rte. 1, 04032,* ☎ *207/865–4201. 20 1- to 3-bedroom cottages, 14 with fireplace, 3 with air-conditioning. In-room refrigerators, 2 playgrounds. No credit cards. Closed mid-Nov.–mid-Apr.. CP.*

Outdoor Activities and Sports

Atlantic Seal Cruises (⊠ South Freeport, ☎ 207/865–6112) operates day trips to Eagle Island and evening seal and osprey watches that are a good way to experience the coast.

L. L. Bean's year-round **Outdoor Discovery Schools** (⊠ Freeport, ☎ 888/552–3261) include half- and one-day classes, as well as longer trips, that teach canoeing, kayaking, fly-fishing, cross-country skiing, and other sports. Classes are for all skill levels; it's best to sign up several months in advance if possible.

STATE PARKS

Wolfe's Neck Woods State Park has 5 mi of good hiking trails along Casco Bay, the Harraseeket River, and a fringe salt marsh. Naturalists lead walks. The park has picnic tables and grills but no camping. ⊠ *Wolfe's Neck Rd. (follow Bow St. opposite L. L. Bean off U.S. 1),* ☎ *207/865–4465.* 🎫 *$2 Memorial Day–Labor Day, $1 off-season.*

Bradbury Mountain State Park has moderate trails to the top of Bradbury Mountain, which has views of the sea. A picnic area and shelter, a ball field, a playground, and 41 campsites are among the facilities. ⊠ *Rte. 9, Pownal (I–95, 5 mi from Freeport-Durham exit),* ☎ *207/688–4712.* 🎫 *$2 Memorial Day–Labor Day, $1 off-season.*

Shopping

The big names of designer outlets are here, from Coach, Brooks Brothers, Polo Ralph Lauren, and Cole-Haan to Hartmann and Dansk. Don't overlook the specialty stores: crafts galleries such as Abacus and Edgecombe Potters, and shops selling unique items such as the Maine Reading Pillow or Claire Murray's hand-hooked rugs. The **Freeport Visitors Guide** (☎ 207/865–1212; 800/865–1994 for a copy) lists the more than 100 shops and factory outlet stores that can be found on Main Street, Bow Street, and elsewhere.

Cuddledown of Maine (⊠ 237 U.S. 1, ☎ 207/865–1713) has a selection of down comforters, pillows, and luxurious bedding. Head upstairs for discounted merchandise. Kids get their chance to shop at the educational toy store **Play and Learn** (⊠ 140 Main St., ☎ 207/865–6434). **Thos. Moser Cabinetmakers** (⊠ 149 Main St., ☎ 207/865–4519) carries high-quality handmade furniture with clean, classic lines.

Founded in 1912 as a mail-order merchandiser of products for hunters, guides, and anglers, **L. L. Bean** (⊠ 95 Main St. [U.S. 1], ☎ 800/341–4341) attracts 3½ million shoppers a year to its giant store (open 24 hours a day) in the heart of Freeport's shopping district. You can still find the original hunting boots, along with cotton, wool, and silk sweaters; camping and ski equipment; comforters; and hundreds of other items for the home, car, boat, or campsite. The **L. L. Bean Factory Store** (⊠ Depot St., ☎ 800/341–4341) has seconds and discontinued merchandise at discount prices. **L. L. Bean Kids** (⊠ 8 Nathan Nye St., ☎ 800/341–4341) specializes in children's merchandise and has a climbing wall and other activities that appeal to kids.

Harrington House Museum Store (⊠ 45 Main St., ☎ 207/865–0477) is a restored 19th-century merchant's home owned by the Freeport Historical Society; all the period reproductions that furnish the rooms are for sale, as well as books, rugs, jewelry, crafts, Shaker items, and kitchen utensils. You can obtain a brochure with a good walking tour of Freeport here, too. **Green Design Furniture** (⊠ 45 Main St., ☎ 207/ 865–0342), in an 1830 carriage house near Harrington House, sells Maine-designed solid cherry-wood furniture that can be shipped.

Brunswick

⑰ *10 mi north of Freeport.*

Lovely brick and clapboard homes and structures are the highlights of the town's Federal Street Historic District, which includes Federal Street and Park Row and the stately campus of Bowdoin College. Pleasant Street, in the center of town, is the business district. Harriet Beecher Stowe wrote *Uncle Tom's Cabin* while living in Brunswick.

The 110-acre campus of **Bowdoin College** (⊠ Maine, Bath, and College Sts., off east end of Pleasant St.) holds an enclave of distinguished architecture, gardens, and grassy quadrangles, along with several museums. Campus tours (☎ 207/725–3000) depart daily except Sunday from the admissions office in Chamberlain Hall. Nathaniel Hawthorne and the poet Henry Wadsworth Longfellow attended Bowdoin.

Bowdoin's imposing neo-Gothic Hubbard Hall holds the **Peary–MacMillan Arctic Museum,** with photographs, navigational instruments, and artifacts from the first successful expedition to the North Pole, in 1909, by two of Bowdoin's most famous alumni, Admiral Robert E. Peary and Donald B. MacMillan. Changing exhibits document conditions in the Arctic. ☎ *207/725–3416.* ☞ *Free.* ☉ *Tues.–Sat. 10–5, Sun. 2–5.*

The **Bowdoin College Museum of Art,** in a splendid Renaissance Revival–style building designed by Charles F. McKim in 1894, has small but good collections that encompass Assyrian and classical art and works by Dutch, Italian, French, and Flemish old masters; a superb gathering of Colonial and Federal paintings, notably Gilbert Stuart portraits of Madison and Jefferson; and a Winslow Homer Gallery of engravings, etchings, and memorabilia (open in summer only). The museum's collection also includes 19th- and 20th-century American painting and sculpture, with works by Mary Cassatt, Andrew Wyeth, and Robert Rauschenberg. ⊠ *Walker Art Bldg.,* ☎ *207/725–3275.* ☞ *Free.* ☉ *Tues.–Sat. 10–5, Sun. 2–5.*

The **General Joshua L. Chamberlain Museum** displays memorabilia and documents the life of Maine's most celebrated Civil War hero. The general, who played an instrumental role in the Union army's victory at Gettysburg, was elected governor in 1867. From 1871 to 1883 he served as president of Bowdoin College. ⊠ *226 Main St.,* ☎ *207/729–6606.* ☞ *$4.* ☉ *June 1–Oct. 31, Tues.–Sat. 10–4.*

OFF THE
BEATEN PATH

THE HARPSWELLS – A side trip from Bath or Brunswick on Route 123 or Route 24 takes you to the peninsulas and islands known collectively as the Harpswells. Small coves along Harpswell Neck shelter the boats of lobstermen, and summer cottages are tucked away amid the birch and spruce trees. Along Route 123, signs with blue herons mark the studios and galleries of the Harpswell Craft Guild. For lunch, follow the signs off Route 123 to **Dolphin Marina** restaurant (⊠ End of Basin Point Rd., off Ash Point Rd.) and try the delicious fish stew and a blueberry muffin.

Dining and Lodging

\$\$ ✕ **The Great Impasta.** You can match your favorite pasta and sauce to create your own dish at this storefront restaurant, a good choice for lunch, tea, or dinner. The seafood lasagna is tasty, too. ⊠ *42 Maine St.,* ☎ *207/729–5858. Reservations not accepted. D, DC, MC, V.*

\$ ✕ **Fat Boy Drive-In.** Put your lights on for service at this old-fashioned drive-in restaurant renowned for its BLTs made with Canadian bacon, frappés (try the blueberry), and onion rings. ⊠ *Bath Rd.,* ☎ *207/729–9431. No credit cards. Closed mid-Oct.–mid-Mar.*

\$\$\$ 🏨 **Captain Daniel Stone Inn.** This Federal-style inn overlooks the Androscoggin River and Route 1. No two rooms are furnished identically, but all contain executive-style comforts and many have whirlpool baths, queen-size beds, and pullout sofas. A guest parlor, a breakfast room, and excellent service in the Narcissa Stone Restaurant (no lunch on Saturday) make this an upscale escape from college-town funkiness. ⊠ *10 Water St., 04011,* ☎ FAX *207/725–9898,* WEB *www.netquarters.net/cdsi. 34 rooms, 4 suites. Restaurant. AE, DC, MC, V. CP.*

\$\$-\$\$\$ 🏨 **Captain's Watch Bed and Breakfast and Sail Charter.** Built in 1862 and originally known as the Union Hotel, the Captain's Watch is the oldest surviving hotel on the Maine coast. Although much smaller than originally built, this National Historic Register property retains its distinctive octagonal cupola and a homey, old-fashioned feel. Two guest rooms share access to the cupola. Others have less-inspired but still-pleasant water views. Guests can arrange to go on a day sail aboard the inn's 37-ft sloop, *Symbion.* ⊠ *2476 926 Cundy's Harbor Rd., Harpswell, 04079,* ☎ *207/725–0979,* WEB *www.gwi.net/~cwatch. 4 rooms. MC, V for deposit only. BP.*

\$-\$\$\$ 🏨 **Harpswell Inn.** Spacious lawns and neatly pruned shrubs surround the stately white clapboard Harpswell Inn, built in 1761. The three-story inn was the center of a shipbuilding operation on Lookout Point, and the living room faces Middle Bay and Birch Island. Half the rooms have water views, as do the three carriage-house suites, one with a whirlpool. The inn is no-smoking. ⊠ *108 Lookout Point Rd., Harpswell 04079,* ☎ *207/833–5509 or 800/843–5509,* WEB *www.gwi.net/~harpswel. 9 rooms, 7 with bath, 1 with half bath; 3 suites. MC, V. BP.*

Nightlife and the Arts

Bowdoin Summer Music Festival (☎ 207/725–3322 information; 207/725–3895 tickets) is a six-week concert series featuring performances by students, faculty, and prestigious guest artists. **Maine State Music Theater** (⊠ Pickard Theater, Bowdoin College, ☎ 207/725–8769) stages musicals from mid-June to September. **Theater Project of Brunswick** (⊠ 14 School St., ☎ 207/729–8584) performs semiprofessional, children's, and community theater.

Outdoor Activities and Sports

H2Outfitters (⊠ Rte. 24, Orr's Island, ☎ 207/833–5257) provides sea-kayaking instruction and rentals and conducts day and overnight trips.

Shopping

ICON Contemporary Art (⊠ 19 Mason St., ☎ 207/725–8157) specializes in modern art. **O'Farrell Gallery** (⊠ 58 Maine St., ☎ 207/729–8228) represents artists such as Neil Welliver, Marguerite Robichaux, and Sheila Geoffrion. **Wyler Craft Gallery** (⊠ 150 Maine St., ☎ 207/729–1321) carries an intriguing selection of crafts, jewelry, and clothing.

Tontine Fine Candies (⊠ Tontine Mall, 149 Maine St., ☎ 207/729–4462) has chocolates and other goodies. A **farmer's market** takes place on Tuesday and Friday from May to October, on the town mall between Maine Street and Park Row.

Bath

18 *11 mi northeast of Brunswick, 38 mi northeast of Portland.*

Bath has been a shipbuilding center since 1607, so it's appropriate that a museum here explores the state's rich maritime heritage. These days the Bath Iron Works turns out guided-missile frigates for the U.S. Navy and merchant container ships. It's a good idea to avoid Bath and U.S. 1 on weekdays between 3:15 and 4:30 PM, when BIW's major shift change occurs. The massive exodus can tie up traffic for miles.

★ At the **Maine Maritime Museum,** displays in the Maritime History Building and in the buildings of the former Percy & Small shipyard examine the world of shipbuilding and the relationship between Mainers and the sea. The history building contains themed exhibits with maritime paintings, ship models, journals, photographs, artifacts, and videos. From May to November, one-hour tours (call for times) of the shipyard explain how wooden ships were built; at other times you can visit the buildings on your own. You can also watch boatbuilders wield their tools on classic Maine boats in the boatshop and learn about lobstering in a special exhibit building. In summer boat tours sail the scenic Kennebec River (extra charge); a number of boats, including the 142-ft Grand Banks fishing schooner *Sherman Zwicker,* are on display when in port. The museum has a fine gift shop and bookstore, and you can picnic on the grounds. ⊠ *243 Washington St.,* ☎ *207/443–1316.* ⊠ *$9; tickets valid for 2 consecutive days.* ☉ *Daily 9:30–5.*

The **Chocolate Church Arts Center** offers guided walking tours of private homes and historic buildings from mid-June to mid-September. Call for schedule and fees.

Reid State Park (☎ 207/371–2303), on Georgetown Island, off Route 127, has 1½ mi of sand on three beaches. Facilities include bathhouses, picnic tables, fireplaces, and a snack bar. Parking lots fill by 11 AM on summer Sundays and holidays; admission is charged.

OFF THE
BEATEN PATH

POPHAM – Follow Route 209 south from Bath to Popham, the site of the short-lived 1607 Popham Colony, where the *Virginia,* the first English ship built in the Northeast, was launched. Benedict Arnold set off from Popham in 1775 on his ill-fated march against the British in Québec. Granite-walled **Ft. Popham** (⊠ Phippsburg, ☎ 207/389–1335) was built in 1861. **Popham State Park,** at the end of Route 209, has a sand beach, a marsh area, bathhouses, and picnic tables; admission is charged.

Dining and Lodging

$$$ ✕ **Robinhood Free Meetinghouse.** Chef Michael Gagne, one of Maine's
★ best, finally has a restaurant that complements his classic and creative multiethnic cuisine. The 1855 Greek Revival–style meetinghouse has cream-color walls, pine floorboards, cherry Shaker-style chairs, and white table linens. You might begin with the artichoke strudel; veal saltimbocca and confit of duck are two entrées. Finish up with Gagne's signature "Obsession in Three Chocolates." ⊠ *Robinhood Rd.,*

Georgetown, ☎ *207/371–2188. AE, D, MC, V. Closed some weeknights mid-Oct.–mid-May. No lunch.*

$$–$$$ ✕ **Kristina's Restaurant & Bakery.** This restaurant in a frame house with a front deck prepares some of the finest pies, pastries, and cakes on the coast. The satisfying new American cuisine served for dinner usually includes fresh seafood and grilled meats. All meals can be packed to go. ⊠ *160 Centre St.,* ☎ *207/442–8577. D, MC, V. Closed Jan. No dinner Sun. Call ahead in winter.*

$$$–$$$$ ⊞ **Sebasco Harbor Resort.** This family resort sprawls over 575 ocean-front acres at the foot of the Phippsburg peninsula. The owners have retained the resort's old-fashioned feel while updating and renovating the facilities. A new all-suites building is schedule to open in 2002. Children's programs are offered in peak season. ⊠ *Route 217, Sebasco Estates 04565,* ☎ *207/389–1161 or 800/225–3819,* ℻ *207/389–2004,* WEB *www.sebasco.com. 57 rooms, cottages. 3 restaurants, lounge, in-room data ports, saltwater pool, hair salon, sauna, 9-hole golf course, 3-hole practice course, 2 tennis courts, bowling, health club, Ping-Pong, dock, boating, bicycles, shop, recreation room, children's programs, playground, airport shuttle. AE, D, MC, V. Nov.–Apr. MAP available.*

$$–$$$$ ⊞ **The Inn at Bath.** Filled with antiques, this handsome 1810 Greek Revival inn in the town's historic district makes a convenient and comfortable base for exploring Bath on foot. All rooms are air-conditioned, five have wood-burning fireplaces, and two have two-person whirlpool tubs. ⊠ *969 Washington St., 04530,* ☎ *207/443–4294,* ℻ *207/443–4295,* WEB *www.innatbath.com. 9 rooms. AE, D, MC, V. BP.*

$$–$$$ ⊞ **1774 Inn.** On the National Register of Historic Places, the 1774 Inn is a pre-Revolutionary mansion with handsome interior detailing and magnificent antiques. The inn, on a bend in the Kennebec River, has large corner guest rooms in the main house, two with fireplaces. In the attached ell is a room with a deck overlooking the river. A four-bedroom cottage on the river is available for longer stays. ⊠ *44 Parker Head Rd., Phippsburg Center 04562,* ☎ *207/389–1774,* ℻ *207/389–9076. 7 rooms, 1 cottage. No credit cards. BP.*

Nightlife and the Arts

Chocolate Church Arts Center (⊠ 804 Washington St., ☎ 207/442–8455) hosts folk, jazz, and classical concerts, theater productions, and performances for children. The gallery exhibits works in various media by Maine artists.

Shopping

On Front and Centre streets in the heart of Bath's historic downtown district, antiques shops and intriguing specialty shops invite browsing. The **Montsweag Flea Market** (⊠ U.S. 1 between Bath and Wiscasset, ☎ 207/443–2809) is a roadside attraction with trash and treasures. It's open on weekends from May to October and also on Wednesday (for antiques) and Friday during the summer. **West Island Gallery,** ⊠ 11 Centre St., ☎ 207/443–9625) carries contemporary Maine art and quality crafts.

Wiscasset

⑲ *10 mi north of Bath, 46 mi northeast of Portland.*

Settled in 1663 on the banks of the Sheepscot River, Wiscasset fittingly bills itself as Maine's Prettiest Village. Stroll through town and you'll pass by elegant sea captains' homes (many now antiques shops or galleries), old cemeteries, churches, and public buildings.

The **Nickels-Sortwell House,** maintained by the Society for the Preservation of New England Antiquities, is an outstanding example of Fed-

HOW TO USE THIS GUIDE

Great trips begin with great planning, and this guide makes planning easy. It's packed with everything you need—insider advice on hotels and restaurants, cool tools, practical tips, essential maps, and much more.

COOL TOOLS

Fodor's Choice Top picks are marked throughout with a star.

Great Itineraries These tours, planned by Fodor's experts, give you the skinny on what you can see and do in the time you have.

Smart Travel Tips A to Z This special section is packed with important contacts and advice on everything from how to get around to what to pack.

Good Walks You won't miss a thing if you follow the numbered bullets on our maps.

Need a Break? Looking for a quick bite to eat or a spot to rest? These sure bets are along the way.

Off the Beaten Path Some lesser-known sights are worth a detour. We've marked those you should make time for.

POST-IT® FLAGS

Dog-ear no more!

"Post-it" is a registered trademark of 3M.

Favorite restaurants • Essential maps • Frequently used numbers • Walking tours • Can't-miss sights • Smart Travel Tips • Web sites • Top shops • Hot nightclubs • Addresses • Smart contacts • Events • Off-the-beaten-path spots • Favorite restaurants • Essential maps • Frequently used numbers • Walking Can't-miss sights • Smart ips • Web sites • Top shops • Hot **nightclubs** • Addresses • Smart contacts • Events • Off-the-beaten-path spots • Favorite restaurants • Essential maps • Frequently used numbers • Walking tours •

ICONS AND SYMBOLS

Watch for these symbols throughout:

★	Our special recommendations
✕	Restaurant
🏠	Lodging establishment
✕🏠	Lodging establishment whose restaurant warrants a special trip
☾	Good for kids
☞	Sends you to another section of the guide for more information
✉	Address
☎	Telephone number
FAX	Fax number
WEB	Web site
🎟	Admission price
☉	Opening hours
$-$$$$	Lodging and dining price categories, keyed to strategically sited price charts. Check the index for locations.
①❶	Numbers in white and black circles on the maps, in the margins, and within tours correspond to one another.

ON THE WEB

Continue your planning with these useful tools found at **www.fodors.com**, the Web's best source for travel information.

"Rich with resources." —*New York Times*

"Navigation is a cinch." —*Forbes* "Best of the Web" list

"Put together by people bursting with know-how."
—*Sunday Times* (London)

Create a Miniguide Pinpoint hotels, restaurants, and attractions that have what you want at the price you want to pay.

Rants and Raves Find out what readers say about Fodor's picks—or write your own reviews of hotels and restaurants you've just visited.

Travel Talk Post your questions and get answers from fellow travelers, or share your own experiences.

On-Line Booking Find the best prices on airline tickets, rental cars, cruises, or vacations, and book them on the spot.

About our Books Learn about other Fodor's guides to your destination and many others.

Expert Advice and Trip Ideas From what to tip to how to take great photos, from the national parks to Nepal, Fodors.com has suggestions that'll make your trip a breeze. Log on and get informed and inspired.

Smart Resources Check the weather in your destination or convert your currency. Learn the local language or link to the latest event listings. Or consult hundreds of detailed maps—all in one place.

eral architecture. ⊠ *12 Main St.,* ☎ *207/882–6218.* 🖾 *$4.* ☉ *June–mid-Oct., Wed.–Sun. 11–5; tours on the hr 11–4.*

The 1807 **Castle Tucker,** is known for its extravagant architecture, Victorian decor, and freestanding elliptical staircase. It's run by the Society for the Preservation of New England Antiquities. ⊠ *Lee and High Sts.,* ☎ *207/882–7364.* 🖾 *$4.* ☉ *June–mid-Oct., Wed.–Sun. 11–5; tours on the hr 11–4.*

★ The 1852 **Musical Wonder House,** formerly a sea captain's home, houses a private collection of thousands of antique music boxes from around the world. ⊠ *18 High St.,* ☎ *207/882–7163 or 800/336–3725,* WEB *www.musicalwonderhouse.com.* 🖾 *$1 for grand hallway, ½-hr presentation on main floor $8; 1-hr presentation $15; 3-hr tour of entire house $30 by reservation only.* ☉ *Memorial Day–mid-Oct., daily 10–5; last tour usually at 4; call ahead for 3-hr tours.*

Dining and Lodging

$–$$$ ✕ **Le Garage.** The best tables at this automotive garage turned casual restaurant are on the glassed-in porch overlooking the Sheepscot River and Wiscasset's harbor. Entrées include homemade chicken pie, sea scallops au gratin, charbroiled lamb and vegetable kebabs, and pastas and salads. ⊠ *Water St.,* ☎ *207/882–5409. MC, V. Closed Jan.*

$$ 🏠 **Marston House.** Two carriage-house rooms provide a quiet retreat from the bustle of Main Street but are just a stone's throw from the action. Both have private entrances and fireplaces and are simply furnished with Shaker- and Colonial-style pieces. The rooms can be joined by opening a door between them. A hearty Continental breakfast is delivered to your room. ⊠ *101 Main St. (Box 517),* ☎ *207/882–6010,* FAX *207/882–6965. 2 rooms. AE, MC, V. Closed Nov.–Apr. CP.*

Shopping

The Wiscasset area rivals Searsport as a destination for antiquing. Shops line Wiscasset's main and side streets and extend over the bridge into Edgecomb. The **Butterstamp Workshop** (⊠ 55 Middle St., ☎ 207/882–7825) carries handcrafted folk-art designs from antique molds. The **Maine Art Gallery** (⊠ Warren St., ☎ 207/882–7511) presents the works of local artists. **Marston House American Antiques** (⊠ Main St. at Middle St., ☎ 207/882–6010) specializes in 18th- and 19th-century painted furniture and "smalls" (small objects), homespun textiles, and antique garden accessories and tools. The **Wiscasset Bay Gallery** (⊠ Main St., ☎ 207/882–7682) has a fine collection of the works from 19th- and 20th-century American and European artists. **Treats** (⊠ Main St., ☎ 207/882–6192) is a good place to pick up fancy foods for a picnic at Waterfront Park.

Boothbay

20 *10 mi southeast of Wiscasset, 60 mi northeast of Portland, 50 mi southwest of Camden.*

When Portlanders want a break from city life, many come north to the Boothbay region, which comprises Boothbay proper, East Boothbay, and Boothbay Harbor. This part of the shoreline is a craggy stretch of inlets where pleasure craft anchor alongside trawlers and lobster boats. Commercial Street, Wharf Street, the By-Way, and Townsend Avenue are filled with shops, galleries, and ice cream parlors. Excursion boats leave from the piers off Commercial Street. From the harbor, you can catch a boat to Monhegan Island.

☺ At the **Boothbay Railway Village,** about one mi north of Boothbay, you can ride 1½ mi on a narrow-gauge steam train through a re-creation of a century-old New England village. Among the 24 buildings is a museum with more than 50 antique automobiles and trucks. ⊠ *Rte. 27,* ☎ *207/633–4727,* ⟦WEB⟧ *www.railwayvillage.org.* ☞ *$7.* ☉ *Early June–Columbus Day, daily 9:30–5; special Halloween and Christmas schedules.*

🖐 The **Department of Marine Resources Aquarium** has a shark you can pet, touch tanks, and rare blue and multiclawed lobsters. ⊠ *194 McKown Point Rd., West Boothbay Harbor,* ☎ *207/633–9559.* ☞ *$2.50.* ☉ *Memorial Day–late-Sept., daily 10–5.*

Dining and Lodging

$$–$$$ ✗ **Christopher's Boathouse.** You can't beat the harbor view or the stylish food at this restaurant in a renovated boathouse where you can watch the chefs at work. The lobster and mango bisque with spicy lobster wontons is noteworthy. Some main-course options are lobster succotash and Asian-spiced tuna steak with Caribbean salsa; finish off with the raspberry almond flan. ⊠ *25 Union St., Boothbay Harbor,* ☎ *207/ 633–6565. DC, MC, V. Closed Mar. and Mon.–Wed. in Jan. and Feb.*

$–$$ ✗ **Lobstermen's Coop.** Crustacean lovers and landlubbers alike will find something to satisfy their cravings at this dockside working lobster pound. Lobster, steamers, hamburgers, and sandwiches are on the menu. Eat indoors or outside to watch the lobstermen at work. ⊠ *Atlantic Ave., Boothbay Harbor,* ☎ *207/633–4900. Closed mid-Oct.– mid-May.*

$$$–$$$$ ✗🛏 **Spruce Point Inn.** Escape the hubbub of Boothbay Harbor at this sprawling resort, which is a short shuttle ride from town, yet a world away. Guest rooms are in the main inn, including 39 suites added in 2000. Most are comfortable but not fancy and have ocean views. Some guests complain about inconsistent service and the nearby fog horn, which blows in inclement weather. ⊠ *Box 237, Atlantic Ave., Boothbay Harbor 04538,* ☎ *207/633–4152 or 800/553–0289,* ⟦FAX⟧ *207/633–7138,* ⟦WEB⟧ *www.sprucepointinn.com. 21 rooms, 39 suites, 7 cottages. Lounge, pool, saltwater pool, spa, 2 tennis courts, exercise room, dock. AE, D, DC, MC, V. Closed mid-Oct.–mid-May.*

$$$ 🛏 **Admiral's Quarters Inn.** This renovated 1830 sea captain's house is ideally situated for exploring Boothbay Harbor by foot. The air-conditioned rooms have private decks, many overlooking the harbor, and on rainy days you can relax by the woodstove in the solarium. ⊠ *71 Commercial St., Boothbay Harbor 04538,* ☎ *207/633–2474,* ⟦FAX⟧ *207/ 633–5904,* ⟦WEB⟧ *www.admiralsquartersinn.com. 2 rooms, 4 suites. D, MC, V. Closed Dec.–mid-Feb. BP.*

$$–$$$ 🛏 **Welch House.** This 1873 sea captain's house sits high on a hill, a few minutes walk from the center of town. Antiques, artwork, and bric-a-brac from the owner's worldwide travels adorn the rooms. From the shared third-floor deck, you can take in the 180-degree views of the harbor. ⊠ *36 McKown St., 04538,* ☎ *207/633–3431 or 800/279–7313,* ⟦WEB⟧ *www.welchhouse.com. 16 rooms. MC, V. Dec. 1–Mar. 31. BP.*

$$ 🛏 **Hodgdon Island Inn.** Every room in this 1810 inn, which is within walking distance of a lobster pound and a botanical garden, has a view of the water; two rooms open unto a shared deck. Inside, artwork from New England and the Caribbean graces the walls. ⊠ *Barters Island Road, 04571,* ☎ *207/633–7474. 6 rooms. Pool. D, MC, V. BP.*

Outdoor Activities and Sports

BOAT TRIPS

Balmy Day Cruises (⊠ Pier 8, 62 Commercial St., Boothbay Harbor, ☎ 207/633–2284 or 800/298–2284) operates day boat trips to Monhegan Island and tours of the harbor. **Cap'n Fish's Boat Trips** (⊠ Pier 1, Boothbay Harbor, ☎ 207/633–3244 or 800/636–3244) runs regional sightseeing cruises, including puffin-watching excursions, lobster-hauling and whale-watching rides, and trips to Damariscove Harbor, Pemaquid Point, and up the Kennebec River to Bath.

KAYAKING

Tidal Transit Ocean Kayak Co. (☎ 207/633–7140) offers guided tours and rentals.

Shopping

BOOTHBAY HARBOR

You can browse for hours in the trinket and T-shirt shops, crafts galleries, clothing stores, and boutiques that line the streets around the harbor. **Gleason Fine Art** (⊠ 7 Oak St., ☎ 207/633–6849) showcases fine art—regional and national, early 19th century and contemporary. **House of Logan** (⊠ 20 Townsend Ave., ☎ 207/633–2293) stocks upscale casual and fancy attire for men and women. Beautiful housewares and attractive children's clothes can be found at the **Village Store & Children's Shop** (⊠ 34 Townsend Ave., ☎ 207/633–2293).

EDGECOMB

Highly reputable **Edgecomb Potters** (⊠ Rte. 27, ☎ 207/882–6802) sells stylish glazed porcelain pottery and other crafts at rather high prices; some discontinued items or seconds are discounted. There's a store in Freeport if you miss this one. **Sheepscot River Pottery** (⊠ U.S. 1, ☎ 207/882–9410) has hand-painted pottery as well as a large collection of American-made crafts, including jewelry, kitchenware, furniture, and home accessories.

Pemaquid Peninsula

㉑ *8 mi southeast of Wiscasset.*

A detour off U.S. 1 via Routes 130 and 32 leads to the Pemaquid Peninsula and a satisfying microcosm of coastal Maine. Art galleries, country stores, antiques and crafts shops, and lobster shacks dot the country roads that meander to the tip of the point, where you'll find a much-photographed lighthouse perched on an unforgiving rock ledge, as well as a pleasant beach. Exploring here reaps many rewards, including views of salt ponds, the ocean, and boat-clogged harbors. The twin towns of Damariscotta and Newcastle anchor the region, but small fishing villages such as Pemaquid, New Harbor, and Round Pond give the peninsula its purely Maine flavor.

At what is now the **Colonial Pemaquid Restoration,** on a small peninsula jutting into the Pemaquid River, English mariners established a fishing and trading settlement in the early 17th century. The excavations at Ft. William Henry, begun in the mid-1960s, have turned up thousands of artifacts from the Colonial settlement, including the remains of an old customs house, a tavern, a jail, a forge, and homes. Some items are from even earlier Native American settlements. The state operates a museum displaying many of the artifacts. ⊠ *Off Rte. 130, New Harbor,* ☎ *207/677–2423.* ⌑ *$2.* ⊙ *Memorial Day–Labor Day, daily 9:30–5.*

★ Route 130 terminates at the **Pemaquid Point Light,** which looks as though it sprouted from the ragged, tilted chunk of granite that it commands. The former lighthouse-keeper's cottage is now the Fishermen's Museum, with photographs, models, and artifacts that explore commercial fishing in Maine. Here, too, is the Pemaquid Art Gallery, which mounts exhibitions from July to Labor Day. ⊠ *Museum: Rte. 130,* ☎ *207/677–2494.* ⌑ *$1.* ⊙ *Memorial Day–Columbus Day, Mon.–Sat. 10–5, Sun. 11–5.*

Dining and Lodging

$$ ✕ **Round Pond Lobstermen's Co-op.** Lobster doesn't get much rougher,
★   any fresher, or any cheaper than what's served at this no-frills dock-
side takeout. The best deal is the dinner special: a 1-pound lobster, steam-
ers, and corn-on-the-cob, with a bag of chips. Regulars often bring beer,
wine, bread, and salads. Settle in at a picnic table and breathe in the
fresh salt air while you drink in the view over dreamy Round Pond
Harbor. ⊠ *Round Pond Harbor, off Rte. 32, Round Pond,* ☎ *207/
529–5725. MC, V.*

$$–$$$$ ✕⌂ **Newcastle Inn.** This classic country inn with a riverside location
and an excellent dining room attracts guests year-round. All the rooms
are filled with country pieces and antiques; some rooms have fireplaces
and whirlpool baths. Breakfast is served on the back deck in fine
weather. The four-course dinners ($$$$) at the inn, open to the public by reservation, emphasize local seafood. ⊠ *60 River Rd., Newcastle
04553,* ☎ *207/563–5685 or 800/832–8669,* ℻ *207/563–6877,* ⓦⓔⓑ
*www.newcastleinn.com. 11 rooms, 3 suites. Dining room, pub. AE,
MC, V. BP.*

$$ ⌂ **Mill Pond Inn.** A quiet residential street holds this circa-1780 inn,
which is on a mill pond across the street from Damariscotta Lake. Loons,
otters, and bald eagles reside on the lake, and you can arrange a trip
with the owner, a Registered Maine Guide, on the inn's 17-ft antique
lapstrake boat. The rooms are warm and inviting and there's a pub
for guests, though you may find it hard to tear yourself away from the
hammocks-for-two overlooking the pond. ⊠ *50 Main St., off Rte. 215
N, Nobleboro 04555,* ☎ *207/563–8014,* ⓦⓔⓑ *www.millpondinn.com.
6 rooms, 1 suite. Horseshoes, boating, bicycles. No credit cards. BP.*

$–$$ ⌂ **Briar Rose.** Round Pond is a sleepy harborside village with an old-
fashioned country store, two lobster co-ops, a nice restaurant, and a
handful of antiques and crafts shops. The mansard-roof Briar Rose commands a ship captain's view over it all. Antiques and whimsies decorate the airy rooms. ⊠ *1442 Rte. 32 (Box 27), Round Pond 04564,*
☎ *207/529–5478. 2 rooms, 1 suite. No credit cards. BP.*

$–$$ ⌂ **Hotel Pemaquid.** This turn-of-the-century inn is less than 500 ft from
the lighthouse at Pemaquid Point. The main building is Victorian in style;
cottages and bungalow units have a more contemporary feel; and the
carriage house suite is ideal for honeymooners or others seeking a romantic retreat. ⊠ *3098 Bristol Rd. (Rte. 130), New Harbor 04554,* ☎
207/677–2312, ⓦⓔⓑ *www.hotelpemaquid.com. 21 rooms, 17 with bath;
4 suites, 3 cottages, 1 apt.. No credit cards. Closed mid-Oct.–mid-May.*

Nightlife and the Arts

Round Top Center for the Arts (⊠ Business Rte. 1, Damariscotta, ☎
207/563–1507) has a gallery with rotating exhibits and a performance
hall where classical, folk, operatic, and jazz concerts are held.

Outdoor Activities and Sports

Pemaquid Beach Park (⊠ Off Rte. 130, New Harbor, ☎ 207/677–2754)
has a sand beach, a snack bar, changing facilities, and picnic tables overlooking John's Bay; admission is charged.

Shopping

Of the villages on and near the Pemaquid Peninsula, downtown
Damariscotta offers boutiques, a book shop, clothing stores, and galleries. New Harbor and Round Pond have crafts and antiques shops
as well as artisans' studios. Antiques shops dot the main thoroughfares
in the region.

Bramble's (⊠ Main St., Damariscotta, ☎ 207/563–2800) is a paradise
for gardeners, with tools, sculpture, pots, artwork, and topiary. **Granite Hill Store** (⊠ Backshore Rd., Round Pond, ☎ 207/529–5864) has

penny candy, kitchen goodies, baskets, and cards on the first floor, antiques and books on the second, and an ice cream window on the side. The work of more than 50 Maine artisans is displayed in the 15 rooms of the **Pemaquid Craft Co-op** (✉ Rte. 130, New Harbor, ☎ 207/677–2077). You never know what you'll find at **Reny's** (✉ Rte. 1A, Damariscotta, ☎ 207/563–5757)—perhaps merchandise from L. L. Bean or a designer coat. This bargain chain has outlets in many Maine towns, but this is its hometown, and there are two outlets: one for clothes, the other for everything else. The **Victorian Stable Gallery** (✉ Water St., Damariscotta, ☎ 207/563–1991) is a barn with fine Maine crafts, paintings, and prints by more than 100 artisans.

Waldoboro

㉒ *10 mi. northeast of Damariscotta.*

Veer off of U.S. 1 onto Main Street or down Rtes. 220 or 32, and you'll discover a seafaring town with a proud ship-building past. The **Waldoborough Historical Society Museum** comprises the one-room Boggs Schoolhouse, built in 1857, the Town Pound, built in 1819, and a barn and museum filled with artifacts and antiques, including hooked rugs, old toys, tools, clothing, and housewares. ✉ *Route 220,* ☎ *No phone.* ⬚ *Free* ☉ *July–Labor Day, daily 1–4:30.*

One of the three oldest churches in Maine, the **Old German Church** was built in 1772 on the eastern side of the Medomak River, then moved across the ice to its present site in 1794. Inside you'll find box pews and a 9-ft-tall chalice pulpit. ✉ *Rte. 32,* ☎ *207/832–5639.* ☉ *July–Aug., daily 1–3.*

The **Fawcett's Toy Museum** delights adults and children with collectible toys, from Betty Boop and Charlie Brown to Mickey Mouse and Popeye, and original comic art. ✉ *3506 Rte. 1,* ☎ *207/832–7398.* ⬚ *$3* ☉ *Early July–Columbus Day, Thurs.–Mon., 10–3:30; fall and winter, Sat. and Sun., 12–3:30; spring most weekends and by chance.*

Dining and Lodging

$–$$$ ✕ **Pine Cone Cafe.** Paintings by local painter Eric Hopkins hang on
★ the walls of this cozy restaurant which serves up hearty soups, salads, and a mix of homestyle and creative entrées. Try the corn-fried softshell crab tower or turkey pot pie; the creme brulée is a good choice for dessert. In favorable weather ask for a table on the back deck overlooking the river. ✉ *13 Friendship St.,* ☎ *207/832–6337. MC, V.*

$–$$ ✕ **Moody's Diner.** Settle into one of the well-worn wooden booths or snag a counter stool at this old-style diner for home-cooking fare. Breakfast is served all day; don't miss the legendary walnut pie. ✉ *Rte. 1,* ☎ *207/832–5362. D, MC, V.*

$ 🛏 **La Va Tout.** An 1830 Cape Cod houses a simply decorated bed-and-breakfast and the Eliza Sweet Gallery, which shows work by contemporary Maine artists. Relax in the inn's gardens or the Swedish sauna. ✉ *218 Kalers Corner/Rte. 32 04572,* ☎ *207/832–4969,* WEB *www.midcoast.com/lavatout. 5 rooms, 3 with bath. Hot tub, sauna. MC, V. BP.*

Nightlife and the Arts

The **Waldo Theatre** (✉ 916 Main St., ☎ 207/832–6060), a Greek Revival-style cinema with an Art Deco interior, stages concerts, plays, lectures, and other performances.

Shopping

The **Waldoboro 5 & 10/Fernald's General Store** (✉ 17 Friendship St., ☎ 207/832–4624) is the oldest, continually operated 5 & 10 in the country. It has an old-fashioned soda fountain, which serves sandwiches, soups, and ice cream; there's even a penny candy counter. **Glockenspiel Imports** (✉ U.S. 1, ☎ 207/832–8000) sells traditional German lace. For a taste of authentic German sauerkraut, visit **Morse's Sauerkraut** (✉ 3856 Washington Rd./Rte. 220 north, ☎ 207/832–5569). The **Roserie at Bayfields** (✉ Rte. 32, ☎ 207/832–6330) specializes in roses. The gardens here have sweeping views over the Medomak River.

Portland to Waldoboro A to Z

To research prices, get advice from other travelers, and book travel arrangements, visit www.fodors.com.

BOAT & FERRY TRAVEL

Casco Bay Lines provides ferry service from Portland to the islands of Casco Bay.

➤ BOAT & FERRY INFORMATION: **Casco Bay Lines** (☎ 207/774–7871).

BUS TRAVEL TO & FROM PORTLAND

Greater Portland's Metro runs seven bus routes in Portland, South Portland, and Westbrook. The fare is $1; exact change ($1 bills accepted) is required. Buses run from 5:30 AM to 11:45 PM.

➤ BUS INFORMATION: **Greater Portland's Metro** (☎ 207/774–0351).

CAR TRAVEL

Congress Street leads from I–295 into the heart of Portland; the Gateway Garage on High Street, off Congress, is a convenient place to leave your car downtown. North of Portland, I–95 takes you to Exit 20 and U.S. 1, Freeport's Main Street, which continues on to Brunswick and Bath. East of Wiscasset you can take Route 27 south to the Boothbays, where Route 96 is a good choice for further exploration. To visit the Pemaquid region, take Route 129 off Business Route 1 in Damariscotta; then pick up Route 130 and follow it down to Pemaquid Point. Return to Waldoboro and U.S. 1 on Route 32 from New Harbor.

EMERGENCIES

➤ HOSPITALS: **Maine Medical Center** (✉ 22 Bramhall St., Portland, ☎ 207/871–0111). **Mid Coast Hospital** (✉ 1356 Washington St., Bath, ☎ 207/443–5524; ✉ 58 Baribeau Dr., Brunswick, ☎ 207/729–0181). **Miles Memorial Hospital** (✉ Bristol Rd., Damariscotta, ☎ 207/563–1234). **St. Andrews Hospital** (✉ 3 St. Andrews La., Boothbay Harbor, ☎ 207/633–2121).

TOURS

BUS TOURS

In Portland, the informative van tours of Mainely Tours cover the city's historical and architectural highlights (with a stop at Portland Head Light, too) from Memorial Day through October. Other tours combine a city tour with a bay cruise or take visitors to four lighthouses.

➤ TOUR OPERATOR: **Mainely Tours** (✉ 5½ Moulton St., ☎ 207/774–0808).

WALKING TOURS

Greater Portland Landmarks offers 1½-hour walking tours of the city from July through September; tours begin at the Convention and Visitors Bureau and cost $8.

➤ TOUR OPERATORS: **Greater Portland Landmarks** (✉ 165 State St., ☎ 207/774–5561). **Convention and Visitors Bureau** (✉ 305 Commercial St., ☎ 207/772–5800).

VISITOR INFORMATION

➤ CONTACTS: **Boothbay Harbor Region Chamber of Commerce** (✉ Box 356, Boothbay Harbor 04538, ☎ 207/633–2353). **Chamber of Com-**

merce of the Bath/Brunswick Region (✉ 45 Front St., Bath 04530, ☎ 207/443–9751; ✉ 59 Pleasant St., Brunswick 04011, ☎ 207/725–8797). **Convention and Visitors Bureau of Greater Portland** (✉ 305 Commercial St., Portland 04101, ☎ 207/772–5800 or 877/833–1374). **Greater Portland Chamber of Commerce** (✉ 145 Middle St., Portland 04101, ☎ 207/772–2811). **Damariscotta Region Chamber of Commerce** (✉ Box 13, Damariscotta 04543, ☎ 207/563–8340). **Freeport Merchants Association** (✉ Box 452, Freeport 04032, ☎ 207/865–1212 or 877/865–1212). **Maine Tourism Association** (✉ U.S. 1 [I–95, Exit 17], Yarmouth 04347, ☎ 207/846–0833).

PENOBSCOT BAY

Purists hold that the Maine coast begins at Penobscot Bay, where the vistas over the water are wider and bluer; the shore a jumble of broken granite boulders, cobblestones, and gravel punctuated by small sand beaches; and the water numbingly cold. Port Clyde in the southwest and Stonington in the southeast are the outer limits of Maine's largest bay, 35 mi apart across the bay waters but separated by a drive of almost 100 mi on scenic but slow two-lane highways. From Pemaquid Point at the western extremity of Muscongus Bay to Port Clyde at its eastern extent, it's less than 15 mi across the water, but it's 50 mi for the motorist, who must return north to U.S. 1 to reach the far shore. A relaxing sail on a windjammer is a great way to explore the area.

Thomaston, on the western edge of the region, has a fine collection of sea captains' homes. Rockland, the largest town on the bay, is a growing arts center, home of the Maine Lobster Festival, and the port of departure for trips to Vinalhaven, North Haven, and Matinicus islands. The Camden Hills, looming green over Camden's fashionable waterfront, turn bluer and fainter as you head toward Castine, the small town across the bay. In between Camden and Castine are Belfast and the antiques and flea-market mecca of Searsport. Deer Isle is connected to the mainland by a slender, high-arching bridge, but Isle au Haut, accessible from Deer Isle's fishing town of Stonington, can be reached by passenger ferry only: More than half of this steep, wooded island is wilderness, the most remote section of Acadia National Park.

The most promising shopping areas are Main Street in Rockland, Main and Bay View streets in Camden, and the Main Streets in Belfast, Blue Hill, Stonington. Antiques shops are clustered in Searsport and scattered around the outskirts of villages, in farmhouses and barns. Yard sales abound in summer.

Thomaston

㉓ *10 mi northeast of Waldoboro, 72 mi northeast of Portland.*

The Maine State Prison that has loomed over Thomaston for decades is slated to be replaced by a new facility in Warren in late 2001. Plans call for the dreary monstrosity to be razed and replaced with a park. Prison aside, this is a delightful town, full of beautiful sea captains' homes and dotted with antiques and specialty shops. A National Historic District encompasses parts of High, Main, and Knox streets.

Montpelier: General Henry Knox Museum was built in 1930 as a replica of the late-18th-century mansion of Major General Henry Knox, a general in the Revolutionary War and secretary of war in Washington's Cabinet. Antiques and Knox family possessions fill the interior. Architectural features of note include an oval room and a double staircase. ✉ *U.S. 1 and Rte. 131,* ☎ *207/354–8062,* **WEB** *www.gener-*

alknoxmuseum.org. ✉ *$5.* ⊙ *Memorial Day–late-Sept., Tues.–Sat. 10–4, Sun. 1–4; tours are offered on the hour and half-hour, 10–3.*

Dining

$$–$$$ ✕ **Thomaston Cafe & Bakery.** This small café is a popular spot for lunch. Entrées may include haddock cakes or grilled Black Angus. ✉ *154 Main St.,* ☎ *207/354–8589. MC, V. No dinner Sun.–Thurs.*

Shopping

Maine authors frequently sign books at the **Personal Bookstore** (✉ 144 Main St., ☎ 207/354–8058 or 800/391–8058); a small gallery is upstairs. The **Maine State Prison Showroom Outlet** (✉ Main St., ☎ 207/354–2535) carries crafts, furniture, and woodwork made by prisoners.

Tenants Harbor

② *13 mi south of Thomaston.*

Tenants Harbor is a quintessential Maine fishing town, its harbor dominated by lobster boats, its shores rocky and slippery, its center full of clapboard houses, a church, and a general store. The fictional Dunnet Landing of Sarah Orne Jewett's classic *The Country of the Pointed Firs* (1896) is based on this region. It's a favorite with artists, too, and galleries and studios invite browsing.

The keeper's house at the **Marshall Point Lighthouse** has been turned into a museum containing memorabilia from the town of St. George (a few miles north of Tenants Harbor). The setting has inspired Jamie Wyeth and other artists. You can stroll the grounds and watch the boats go in and out of Port Clyde. ✉ *Marshall Point Rd., Port Clyde,* ☎ *207/372–6450.* ✉ *Free.* ⊙ *June–Sept., weekdays 1–5 and Sat. 10–5.*

Dining and Lodging

$$–$$$ ✕🏠 **East Wind Inn & Meeting House.** Overlooking the harbor and the islands, the East Wind has unadorned but comfortable rooms, suites, and apartments in three buildings, including the main inn, the Meeting House (a converted sea captain's house), and the Wheeler Cottage; some accommodations have fireplaces. The inn is open to the public for dinner, breakfast, and Sunday brunch. Dinner options include prime rib, boiled lobster, and baked stuffed haddock. A take-out restaurant on the wharf offers lobster, clams, and lighter fare and picnic-style dining. You get a credit for breakfast at the restaurant. ✉ *Mechanic St., 04860,* ☎ *207/372–6366 or 800/241–8439,* FAX *207/372–6320,* WEB *www.eastwindinn.com. 18 rooms, 12 with bath; 3 suites; 4 apartments. 2 restaurants. AE, D, MC, V. Closed Dec.–Apr. BP.*

Shopping

Gallery-by-the-Sea (✉ Port Clyde Village, Port Clyde, ☎ 207/372–8631) carries works by a dozen local artists including Leo Brooks, Lawrence Goldsmith, and Emily Muir.

Monhegan Island

★ ② *East of Pemaquid Peninsula, 10 mi south of Port Clyde.*

Remote Monhegan Island, with its high cliffs fronting the open sea, was known to Basque, Portuguese, and Breton fishermen well before Columbus "discovered" America. About a century ago Monhegan was discovered again by some of America's finest painters, including Rockwell Kent, Robert Henri, A. J. Hammond, and Edward Hopper, who sailed out to paint its meadows, savage cliffs, wild ocean views, and fishermen's shacks. Tourists followed, and today three excursion boats dock here. The village bustles with activity in summer, when many

Penobscot Bay

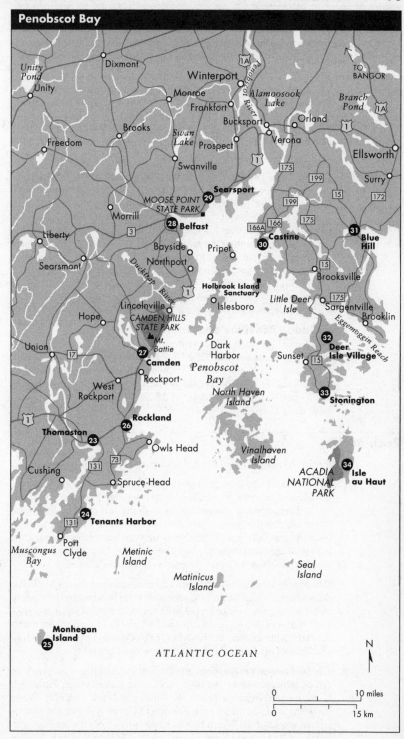

Unity Pond
Dixmont
Unity
Winterport
TO BANGOR
Monroe
Branch Pond
Frankfort
Alamoosook Lake
Bucksport
Orland
Brooks
Prospect
Verona
Ellsworth
Freedom
Swan Lake
Surry
Swanville
Searsport
29 MOOSE POINT STATE PARK
Morrill
28 Belfast
Liberty
Bayside
Pripet
31 Blue Hill
Searsmont
Northport
30 Castine
Holbrook Island Sanctuary
Brooksville
Lincolnville
Islesboro
Little Deer Isle
Sargentville
Hope
CAMDEN HILLS STATE PARK
Brooklin
Union
Mt. Battie
Dark Harbor
Sunset
Eggemoggin Reach
27 Camden
32 Deer Isle Village
Rockport
Penobscot Bay
West Rockport
North Haven Island
33 Stonington
26 Rockland
Thomaston
23 Owls Head
Vinalhaven Island
Cushing
Spruce Head
ACADIA NATIONAL PARK
34 Isle au Haut
24 Tenants Harbor
Port Clyde
Metinic Island
Muscongus Bay
Matinicus Island
Seal Island
25 Monhegan Island
ATLANTIC OCEAN
N
0   10 miles
0   15 km

artists open their studios. You can escape the crowds on the island's 17 mi of hiking trails, which lead to the lighthouse and to the cliffs. Those who overnight here have a quieter experience, since lodging is limited. Day visitors should bring lunch, as restaurants can have long waits at lunchtime.

The **Monhegan Museum,** in an 1824 lighthouse and an adjacent, newly built assistant keeper's house, has wonderful views of Manana Island and the Camden Hills in the distance. Inside, artworks and displays depict island life and local flora and birds. ⊠ *White Head Rd.,* ☎ *no phone.* 🖾 *Donations accepted.* ⊙ *July–mid-Sept., daily 11:30–3:30.*

Lodging

$$–$$$$ 🏨 **Island Inn.** This three-story inn, which dates from 1807, has a commanding presence on Monhegan's harbor. The waterside rooms, though mostly small, are the nicest, with sunset views over the harbor and stark Manana Island. Some of the meadow-view rooms have the distinct disadvantage of being over kitchen vents. New owners are gradually updating and redecorating the property, which includes the main inn, the adjacent Pierce Cottage, a small bakery-café, and a good dining room that serves breakfast, lunch, and dinner. ⊠ *Box 128, 04852,* ☎ *207/596–0371,* FAX *207/594–5517,* WEB *www.islandinnmonhegan.com. 30 rooms, 11 with bath; 4 suites in 2 buildings. Restaurant, café. MC, V. Closed Columbus Day–Memorial Day. BP.*

Outdoor Activities and Sports

Port Clyde, a fishing village at the end of Route 131, is the point of departure for the *Laura B.* (☎ 207/372–8848 schedules), the mail boat that serves Monhegan Island. The *Balmy Days* (☎ 207/633–2284 or 800/298–2284) sails from Boothbay Harbor to Monhegan on daily trips in summer. **Hardy Boat Cruises** (☎ 207/677–2026 or 800/278–3346) leave daily from Shaw's Wharf in New Harbor.

Rockland

㉖ *4 mi northeast of Thomaston, 14 mi northeast of Tenants Harbor.*

Once a place to pass through on the way to tonier ports like Camden, Rockland now attracts attention on its own, thanks to the expansion of the Farnsworth Museum. Specialty shops and galleries line Main Street and the side streets, and new restaurants and inns continue to open. A large fishing port and the commercial hub of this coastal area, with working boats moored alongside yachts and windjammers, Rockland still holds on to its working-class flavor, but it's fading.

Day trips to Vinalhaven and North Haven islands and distant Matinicus depart from the harbor, the outer portion of which is bisected by a nearly mile-long granite breakwater. At the end of the breakwater is a late-19th-century lighthouse, one of the best places in the area to watch the many windjammers sail in and out of Rockland Harbor. Owl's Head Lighthouse, off Route 73, is also a good vantage point.

★ The **Farnsworth Art Museum,** an excellent small museum of American art, contains works by Andrew, N. C., and Jamie Wyeth; Fitz Hugh Lane; George Bellows; Frank W. Benson; Edward Hopper; Louise Nevelson; and Fairfield Porter. The **Wyeth Center** is devoted to Maine-related works of the Wyeth family. Some works from the personal collection of Andrew and Betsy Wyeth include *The Patriot, Adrift, Maiden Hair, Dr. Syn, The Clearing,* and *Watch Cap.* In 2000, the **Jamien Morehouse Wing** opened, doubling the museum's gallery space. Shown here are new works by living Maine artists. The **Farnsworth Homestead,** a handsome circa-1852 Greek Revival dwelling that is part of the museum, retains its original lavish Victorian furnishings. The museum also operates the **Olson House** (⊠ Hathorn Point Rd., Cushing), which was depicted in Andrew Wyeth's famous painting *Christina's World.* ⊠ *356 Main St.,* ☎ *207/596–6457,* WEB *www.farnsworthmuseum.org.* ⊠ *$9; Olson House only, $4.* ☉ *Museum Memorial Day–Columbus Day, daily 9–5; Columbus Day–Memorial Day, Tues.–Sat. 10–5, Sun. 1–5. Home-stead Memorial Day–Columbus Day, daily 10–4. Olson House Memo-rial Day–Columbus Day, daily 11–4.*

☉ The **Shore Village Museum** displays many lighthouse and Coast Guard artifacts and has exhibits of maritime and Civil War memorabilia. ⊠ *104 Limerock St.,* ☎ *207/594–0311,* WEB *www.lighthouse.cc/shorevillage.* ⊠ *Donation suggested.* ☉ *June–mid-Oct., daily 10–4; rest of yr by chance or appointment..*

☉ **Owls Head Transportation Museum** displays antique aircraft, cars, and engines and stages air shows every other weekend May–October. ⊠ *117 Museum Lane, off Rte. 73, Owls Head (3 mi south of Rockland),* ☎ *207/594–4418, www.ohtm.org.* ⊠ *$6.* ☉ *Apr.–Oct., daily 10–5; Nov.–Mar., daily 10–4.*

OFF THE BEATEN PATH

VINALHAVEN – You can take the ferry from Rockland to this island for a pleasant day of bicycling or walking. A number of parks are within walking distance of the ferry dock, including Armbrust Hill, the site of an abandoned quarry, and Lane's Island Preserve, a 40-acre site of moors, granite shoreline, tide pools, and beach. You can learn about the is-land's quarrying history at the Historical Society Museum on High Street and even take a dip in the cool, clear waters of two quarries. Lawson's is 1 mi out on the North Haven Road; Booth Quarry is 1½ mi out East Main Street. Neither has changing facilities, so go prepared. For ferry information, call **Maine State Ferry Service** (☎ 207/596–2202).

Dining and Lodging

$$–$$$
★
✕ **Amalfi.** Delicious Mediterranean cuisine, a well-chosen and af-fordable wine list, and excellent service have made this storefront Mediterranean bistro an immediate hit. The Amalfi fish stew and lob-ster risotto are especially good; the menu changes seasonally. ⊠ *421 Main St.,* ☎ *207/596–0012. D, MC, V. Closed Sun.–Mon.*

$$–$$$
✕ **Café Miranda.** Expect to wait for a table at this cozy bistro, where the daily changing menu reflects fresh, seasonal ingredients and the chef's creative renditions of both new American and traditional home-style foods. You can make a meal from the 20 or so appetizers, many roasted in the brick oven. The two dozen entrées may include crispy panfried soft-shell crabs with red bean ragout and yellow jasmine rice. The outdoor patio is a good choice on nice days. ⊠ *15 Oak St.,* ☎ *207/594–2034. MC, V. Closed Sun.–Mon. No lunch.*

$$–$$$
★
✕ **Primo.** Chef Melissa Kelly and baker and pastry chef Price Kush-ner opened this restaurant in 2000, serving cuisine that combines fresh Maine ingredients with Mediterranean influences. The weekly chang-ing menu may include wood-roasted black sea bass, local crab-stuffed turbot or diver scallop and basil ravioli. ⊠ *2 South Main St.,* ☎ *207/ 594–0770. Reservations essential. AE, MC, V. Closed Tues.–Wed.*

$$$$
🏨 **Samoset Resort.** On the Rockland-Rockport town line next to the breakwater, this sprawling oceanside resort has excellent golf and fit-ness facilities. Plans called for all rooms and public areas to be reno-vated with new furnishings by mid-2001. Most of the spacious rooms, decorated in deep green and burgundy tones, have views of Penobscot Bay over the fairways; all have patios or decks. ⊠ *220 Warrenton St., Rockport 04856,* ☎ *207/594–2511 or 800/341–1650,* FAX *207/594– 0722,* WEB *www.samoset.com. 154 rooms, 24 suites. Restaurant, air-*

conditioning, in-room data ports, 1 indoor and 1 outdoor pool, 18-hole golf course, 4 tennis courts, exercise room, racquetball, children's programs. AE, D, DC, MC, V.

$$–$$$$ ⊡ **Berry Manor Inn.** Built in 1898 as the residence of Charles E. Berry,
★   a prominent Rockland merchant, this Victorian shingle-style inn has been carefully restored. Guest rooms are large and elegantly furnished with antiques and reproduction pieces. All have fireplaces, five have whirlpool tubs, and TVs are available upon request. A guest pantry is stocked with sweets. ⊠ 81 Talbot Ave., 04841, ☎ 207/596–7696 or 800/774–5692, FAX 207/596–9958, WEB www.berrymanorinn.com. 8 rooms. In-room data ports, library. AE, MC, V. BP.

$$–$$$ ⊡ **Limerock Inn.** You can walk to the Farnsworth and the Shore Vil-
★   lage museums from this magnificent Queen Anne–style Victorian on a quiet residential street. The meticulously decorated rooms include Island Cottage, with a whirlpool tub and doors that open onto a private deck overlooking a garden, and Grand Manan, which has a fireplace, a whirlpool tub, and a four-poster king-size bed. ⊠ 96 Limerock St., 04841, ☎ 207/594–2257 or 800/546–3762, FAX 207/594–1846, WEB www.limerockinn.com. 8 rooms. Croquet, bicycles. D, MC, V. BP.

$$ ⊡ **Beech Street Guest House.** This cozy bed-and-breakfast provides quiet, comfortable accommodations just a few minutes walk from downtown attractions. You can browse the owners' collection of rare books for sale or arrange for an in-house massage, herbal wrap, or steam treatment. Breakfasts emphasize organic and natural foods. ⊠ 41 Beech St., 04841, ☎ 207/596–7280, WEB www.midcoast.com/~beechstr. 2 rooms. Massage, spa treatments. MC, V. CP, FP.

Outdoor Activities and Sports

BOAT TRIPS

Bay Island Yacht Charters (⊠ 120 Tillison Ave., ☎ 207/596–5770 or 800/421–2492) operates bareboats and charters. The **Maine Windjammer Association** (⊠ Box 1144, Blue Hill 04614, ☎ 800/807–9463) represents the Rockland-based windjammers American Eagle, Heritage, Isaac H. Evans, J & E Riggin, Nathaniel Bowditch, Stephen Taber, and Victory Chimes, which sail on three- to eight-day cruises. The schooner **Wendameen** (⊠ Box 252, 04841, ☎ 207/594–1751) takes passengers on overnight sails.

TOURS

Downeast Air Inc. (☎ 207/594–2171 or 800/594–2171) offers scenic flights and lighthouse tours.

Shopping

Caldbeck Gallery (⊠ 12 Elm St., ☎ 207/596–5935) displays contemporary Maine works by artists such as William Thon. **Harbor Square Gallery** (⊠ 374 Main St., ☎ 207/596–8700) has roomfuls of Maine-related arts and craft. The **Islands of Maine Gallery** (⊠ 412 Main St., ☎ 207/596–0701) carries work created by residents of Maine's islands.

Camden

㉗ 8 mi north of Rockland, 19 mi south of Belfast.

"Where the mountains meet the sea," Camden's longtime publicity slogan, is an apt description, as you will discover when you look up from the harbor. The town is famous not only for geography but for its large fleet of windjammers—relics and replicas from the age of sailing. At just about any hour during warm months you're likely to see at least one windjammer tied up in the harbor. The busy downtown has some of the best shopping in the region. The district's compact size makes it perfect for exploring on foot: shops, restaurants, and galleries line

Main Street (U.S. 1) and Bayview, as well as side streets and alleys around the harbor.

Their height may not be much more than 1,000 ft, yet the hills in **Camden Hills State Park** are lovely landmarks for miles along the low, rolling reaches of the Maine coast. The 5,500-acre park contains 20 mi of trails, including the easy Nature Trail up Mt. Battie. Hike or drive to the top for a magnificent view over Camden and island-studded Penobscot Bay. The 112-site camping area, open from mid-May to mid-October, has flush toilets and hot showers. The entrance is 2 mi north of Camden. ⊠ *U.S. 1,* ☎ *207/236–3109.* ☒ *Trails and auto road up Mt. Battie $2.* ☉ *Daily dawn–dusk.*

Merryspring Horticultural Nature Park is a 66-acre retreat with herb, rose, rhododendron, hosta, and children's gardens as well as woodland trails. ⊠ *Conway Rd., off U.S. 1,* ☎ *207/236–2239.* ☒ *Free.* ☉ *Daily dawn–dusk.*

Ⓒ **Kelmscott Farm** is a rare-breed animal farm (sheep, pigs, horses, poultry, goats, and cows) with displays, a nature trail, children's activities, a picnic area, heirloom gardens, and special events. ⊠ *Rte. 52, Lincolnville,* ☎ *207/763–4088 or 800/545–9363, www.kelmscott.org.* ☒ *$5.* ☉ *May 1–Oct. 31, Tues.–Sun. 10–5; Nov. 1–Apr. 30, Tues.–Sun. 10–3.*

Dining and Lodging

$$–$$$ ✕ **Waterfront Restaurant.** A ringside seat on Camden Harbor can be had here; the best view is from the outdoor deck, open in warm weather. The fare is primarily seafood: boiled lobster, scallops, bouillabaisse, or seafood risotto. Some lunchtime highlights are lobster and crabmeat rolls. ⊠ *Bayview St.,* ☎ *207/236–3747. Reservations not accepted. MC, V.*

$$–$$$ ✕⌂ **Whitehall Inn.** One of Camden's best-known inns, just north of town, is an 1843 white clapboard sea captain's home with a wide porch and a turn-of-the-century wing. The Millay Room, off the lobby, preserves memorabilia of the poet Edna St. Vincent Millay, who grew up in the area. The sparsely furnished rooms have dark-wood bedsteads, white bedspreads, and claw-foot tubs. The dining room, which serves traditional and creative American cuisine, is open to the public for dinner. ⊠ *52 High St. (Box 558), 04843,* ☎ *207/236–3391 or 800/789–6565,* ℻ *207/236–4427,* ⓦⓔⓑ *www.whitehall.com. 44 rooms, 40 with bath. Restaurant, tennis court, shuffleboard. AE, MC, V. Closed mid-Oct.–mid-May. MAP.*

$$–$$$ ✕⌂ **Youngtown Inn.** Inside this white Federal-style farmhouse are a
  ★   French-inspired country retreat and a well-respected French restaurant ($$$). The country location guarantees quiet, and the inn is a short walk from the Fernald Neck Preserve on Lake Megunticook. Simple, airy rooms open to decks with views of the rolling countryside. Two have fireplaces. The restaurant, open to the public for dinner, serves entrées such as lobster ravioli and breast of pheasant with foie gras mousse. ⊠ *Rte. 52 at Youngtown Rd. Lincolnville 04849,* ☎ *207/763–4290 or 800/291–8438,* ℻ *207/763–4078,* ⓦⓔⓑ *www.youngtown-inn.com. 6 rooms, 1 suite. AE, MC, V. BP.*

$$$$ ⌂ **Inn at Ocean's Edge.** Perched on the ocean's edge, this shingle-style
  ★   inn looks as if it has been here for decades. In actuality, the original building dates from 1999 and the upper building from 2001. Both were built with modern-day comforts in mind. Every room has a king-size bed, an ocean view, a fireplace, and a whirlpool for two, and all have TVs, VCRs, and individually controlled heat and air-conditioning. ⊠ *U.S. 1, Lincolnville (Box 704, Camden 04843);* ☎ *207/236–0945,* ℻ *207/236–0609,* ⓦⓔⓑ *www.innatoceansedge.com. 26 rooms, 1 suite. In-room data ports, exercise room, meeting room. DC, MC, V. BP.*

$$$–$$$$ ☒ **Victorian by the Sea.** It's less than 10 minutes from downtown Camden, but with a quiet waterside location well off U.S. 1, the Victorian Inn feels a world away. Most rooms and the wraparound porch have magnificent views over island-studded Penobscot Bay. Romantic touches include canopy and brass beds, braided rugs, white wicker furniture, and floral wallpapers. Six guest rooms have fireplaces, and there are four more in common rooms, including the glass-enclosed breakfast room. ☒ *Sea View Dr., Lincolnville (Box 1385, Camden 04843),* ☎ *207/236–3785 or 800/382–9817,* 🖷 *207/236–0017,* 🕸 *www.victorianbythesea.com. 5 rooms, 2 suites. AE, MC, V. BP.*

$$–$$$ ☒ **Camden Maine Stay.** This 1802 clapboard inn on the National Register of Historic Places is within walking distance of shops and restaurants. The grounds are classic and inviting, from the flowers lining the granite walk in summer to the snow-laden bushes in winter. Fresh and colorful, the rooms contain many pieces of Eastlake furniture; six have fireplaces. ☒ *22 High St., 04842,* ☎ *207/236–9636,* 🖷 *207/236–0621,* 🕸 *www.mainestay.com. 5 rooms, 3 suites. AE, MC, V. BP.*

Nightlife and the Arts

Bay Chamber Concerts (☒ Rockport Opera House, 6 Central St., Rockport, ☎ 207/236–2823 or 888/707–2770) presents chamber music on Thursday and Friday night during July and August; concerts are given once a month from September to June. **Gilbert's Public House** (☒ 12 Bay View St., ☎ 207/236–4320) has dancing and live entertainment. **Sea Dog Tavern & Brewery** (☒ 43 Mechanic St., ☎ 207/236–6863), a popular brew pub in a converted woolen mill, has live entertainment in season. The **Whale's Tooth Pub** (☒ U.S. 1, Lincolnville Beach, ☎ 207/236–3747) has folk or acoustic entertainment on weekends.

Outdoor Activities and Sports

Brown Dog Bikes (☒ 53 Camden St., ☎ 207/236–6664) delivers rental bikes to area lodging. **Maine Sport** (☒ U.S. 1, Rockport, ☎ 207/236–8797 or 800/722–0826), the best sports outfitter north of Freeport, rents bikes, camping and fishing gear, canoes, kayaks, cross-country skis, ice skates, and snowshoes. It also conducts skiing and kayaking clinics and trips. The *Betselma* (☒ Camden Public Landing, ☎ 207/236–4446) offers one- and two-hour powerboat trips.

A voyage around the bay by windjammer, whether for an afternoon or a week, is unforgettable. The excursions are best from June through September. Eggemoggin Reach is a famous cruising ground for yachts, as are the coves and inlets around Deer Isle and the Penobscot Bay waters between Camden and Castine. The **Maine Windjammer Association** (☒ Box 1144, Blue Hill 04614, ☎ 800/807–9463) represents the Camden-based windjammers *Angelique, Grace Bailey, Lewis R. French, Mary Day,* and *Mercantile* and the Rockport-based *Timberwind.* Cruises last three to eight days.

Shopping

Shops and galleries line Camden's Bayview and Main streets and the alleys that lead to the harbor. **L. E. Leonard** (☒ 67 Pascal Ave., Rockport, ☎ 207/236–0878) sells an intriguing mix of antiques, Asian furnishings, contemporary clothing, and fun jewelry. **Maine Coast Artists** (☒ 162 Russell Ave., Rockport, ☎ 207/236–2875) specializes in contemporary Maine art. **Maine Gathering** (☒ 21 Main St., ☎ 207/236–9004) has a well-chosen selection of crafts, including Passamaquoddy and Penobscot baskets. **Maine's Massachusetts House Galleries** (☒ U.S. 1, Lincolnville, ☎ 207/789–5705) display regional art, including bronzes, carvings, sculptures, and landscapes and seascapes in pencil, oil, and watercolor. The **Owl and Turtle Bookshop** (☒ 8 Bay View St., ☎ 207/236–4769) sells books, CDs, cassettes, and cards. The two-story shop has rooms devoted to marine and children's books. The **Pine Tree Shop & Bayview Gallery** (⊠ 33 Bay View St., ☎ 207/236–4534) specializes in original art, prints, and posters, almost all with Maine themes. The **Windsor Chairmakers** (⊠ U.S. 1, Lincolnville, ☎ 207/789–5188 or 800/789–5188) sells custom-made handcrafted beds, chests, china cabinets, dining tables, highboys, and chairs.

Ski Areas

CAMDEN SNOW BOWL

The Maine coast isn't known for skiing, but this small, lively park in a Currier & Ives setting has skiing, snowboarding, tubing, and tobogganing—plus magnificent views over Penobscot Bay. ⊠ *Box 1207, Hosmer Pond Rd., 04843,* ☎ *207/236–3438.*

Downhill. The park has a 950-ft-vertical mountain, a small lodge with cafeteria, a ski school, and ski and toboggan rentals. Camden Snow Bowl has 11 trails accessed by one double chair and two T-bars. It also has night skiing.

Other Activities. Camden Snow Bowl has a small lake that is cleared for ice-skating, a snow-tubing park, and a 400-ft toboggan run that shoots sledders out onto the lake.

CROSS-COUNTRY SKIING

There are 16 km (10 mi) of cross-country skiing trails at **Camden Hills State Park** (⊠ U.S. 1, ☎ 207/236–9849). **Tanglewood 4-H Camp** (⊠ U.S. 1, ☎ 207/789–5868), about 5 mi away in Lincolnville, has 20 km (12½ mi) of trails.

Belfast

28 *19 mi north of Camden, 46 mi east of Augusta.*

Like many other Maine towns, Belfast has ridden the tides of affluence and depression since its glory days in the 1800s, when it was a shipbuilding center and home to many sea captains. Today it's hightech, namely credit-card giant MBNA, that has helped rescue the city economically. The upswing has brought the revival of the old-fashioned redbrick Victorian downtown and a lively waterfront, as well as affordable lodging and dining. The houses on Church Street are a veritable glossary of 19th-century architectural styles; pick up a map with a walking tour at the visitor center at the foot of Main Street.

A ride on the **Belfast & Moosehead Lake Railroad** (⊠ One Depot Sq., Unity, ☎ 207/948–5500 or 800/392–5500, WEB www.belfastrailroad.com), which operates from July to mid-October ($16), is especially enjoyable in the fall after the leaves begin to change colors. The railroad's timetable coordinates with a cruise boat; a discount applies if you travel on both.

Dining and Lodging

$$ ✕ **Darby's.** Tin ceilings and an old-fashioned bar create a comfortable atmosphere for the creative casual fare served here. The eclectic menu lists hearty soups and sandwiches as well as dishes with an international flavor, such as Moroccan lamb. ⊠ *155 High St.,* ☎ *207/338–2339. AE, D, DC, MC, V.*

$$–$$$ ▥ **Jeweled Turret Inn.** Turrets, columns, gables, and magnificent woodwork embellish this inn, originally built in 1898 as the home of a local attorney. The inn is named for the jewel-like stained-glass windows in the stairway turret; the gem theme continues in the den, where the ornate rock fireplace is said to include rocks from every state in the Union. Elegant Victorian pieces furnish the rooms: the Opal room has a marble bath with whirlpool tub in addition to a French armoire and a four-

poster. ⊠ *40 Pearl St., 04915,* ☎ *207/338–2304 or 800/696–2304,*
WEB *www.bbonline.com/me/jeweledturret. 7 rooms. AE, MC, V. BP.*

$$–$$$ ⊡ **The White House.** New owners have poured their hearts and purses
into renovating this fine example of Greek Revival architecture, an 1840–
1842 landmark by Maine architect Calvin Ryder. An eight-side cupola
tops the house; inside are ornate plaster ceiling medallions, Italian marble fireplaces, an elliptical flying staircase, and intricate moldings.
Crystal chandeliers, Asian rugs, and antiques and reproduction pieces
elegantly decorate the spacious rooms. Two guest rooms have whirlpool tubs. You can relax in the English garden, in the gazebo, or under
the enormous copper beech tree. ⊠ *1 Church St., 04915,* ☎ *207/338–
1901 or 888/290–1901,* FAX *207/338–5161,* WEB *www.mainebb.com. 4
rooms, 2 suites. D, MC, V. BP.*

Outdoor Activities and Sports

KAYAKING
Belfast Kayak Tours (⊠ Belfast City Pier, ☎ 207/338–6204) provides
fully outfitted trips and instruction.

PARKS
Belfast City Park (⊠ High St., 1 mi east of downtown) has a playground,
tennis courts (lighted at night), a baseball diamond, and an outdoor
swimming pool with lockers and showers. Use of the park is free.

Moose Point State Park (⊠ U.S. 1 between Belfast and Searsport, ☎
207/548–2882) is ideal for easy hikes and picnics overlooking Penobscot Bay.

TOURS
Belfast Walks (⊠ , ☎ 207/338–6306) offer 1.5–hour walking tours
that emphasize the town's history and architecture.

Shopping

Belfast's main and side streets house an eclectic selection of shops that
mirror the city's economic base. Shoppers who prefer upscale boutiques
rub elbows with those who bargain-hunt in thrift stores; fancy chocolate and pastry shops are just around the corner from the Belfast Co-
op, a popular natural foods store.

Searsport

❷⁹ *11 mi northeast of Belfast, 57 mi east of Augusta.*

Searsport, Maine's second-largest deepwater port (after Portland), has
a rich shipbuilding and seafaring history. In the 1880s, 10 percent of
all captains under deepwater sail hailed from here. Many of the former sea captains' homes are now bed-and-breakfasts. They make an
ideal base for exploring the multitude of antiques shops and flea markets lining U.S. 1 that have earned Searsport the title of Maine's Antiques Capital.

★   The fine holdings within the nine historic and five modern buildings
of the **Penobscot Marine Museum** provide fascinating documentation
of the region's seafaring way of life. These buildings, including a still-
active church and a sea captain's house, remain in their original spots
in town. The museum's outstanding collection of marine art includes
the largest collection of works by Thomas and James Buttersworth in
the country. Also of note are photos of 284 local sea captains, a collection of China trade articles, artifacts of the whaling industry (including
lots of scrimshaw), navigational instruments, treasures collected by seafarers around the globe, and models of famous ships. The museum's
newest building, a boat barn, opened in 2001 with exhibits of small

craft. ⊠ *5 U.S. 1, at Church St.,* ☎ *207/548–2529,* WEB *www.penob-scotmarinemuseum.org.* ⊠ *$6.* ☉ *Memorial Day–late-Oct., Mon.–Sat. 10–5, Sun. noon–5.*

Dining and Lodging

$$$ ✕ **The Rhumb Line.** The upscale restaurant in this 18th-century sea captain's home delivers fine dining, with formally attired waitstaff and excellent food. Pepper-glazed pork tenderloin, orange-glazed duck with potato pancakes, and horseradish-crusted salmon are typical entrées. ⊠ *U.S. 1,* ☎ *207/548–2600. MC, V. No lunch.*

$$ 🏠 **Brass Lantern** This antiques-filled Victorian bed-and-breakfast is an elegant retreat after a day of shopping nearby flea markets and antiques shops. The multi-course breakfasts are served on china and crystal by candlelight in the tin-ceiling dining room. ⊠ *81 W. Main St. (U.S. 1), 04874,* ☎ *207/548–0150 or 800/691–0150,* FAX *207/548–0304,* WEB *www.brasslanternmaine.com. 5 rooms. D, MC, V. FB.*

$–$$ 🏠 **Homeport Inn.** This 1861 inn, a former sea captain's home, provides an opulent Victorian environment that might put you in the mood to rummage through the nearby antiques and treasure shops. The back rooms downstairs have private decks and views of the bay. Families often stay in the housekeeping cottage. ⊠ *121 E. Main St. (U.S. 1),* ☎ *207/548–2259 or 800/742–5814,* WEB *www.bnbcity.com/inns/20015. 10 rooms, 7 with bath; 2 cottages. AE, D, MC, V. BP.*

Shopping

Along U.S. 1 you'll see several dozen shops and, in season, outdoor flea markets. Museum-quality model ship kits can be found at **Bluejacket Shipcrafters** (⊠ 160 E. Main St. [U.S. 1], ☎ 207/548–9970). More than 70 dealers show their wares in the two-story **Searsport Antique Mall** (⊠ 149 E. Main St. [U.S. 1], ☎ 207/548–2640); look for everything from linens and silver to turn-of-the-century oak. **Pumpkin Patch Antiques** (⊠ 15 W. Main St. [U.S. 1], ☎ 207/548–6047) displays such items as quilts, nautical memorabilia, and painted and wood furniture from about 20 dealers. It's open April through Thanksgiving or by appointment. **Penobscot Books** (⊠ 164 W. Main St. [U.S. 1], ☎ 207/ 548–6490) stocks a handsome collection of used and new books on the fine arts.

Castine

③⓪ *30 mi southeast of Searsport.*

Set on the tip of a peninsula, Castine is a quiet, peaceful place to escape most of the coastal crowds. The French, the British, the Dutch, and the Americans fought over the town from the 17th century to the War of 1812. Present-day Castine's many appealing attributes include its lively harborfront, lovely Federal and Greek Revival houses, and town common; there are two small museums and the ruins of a British fort to explore. For a nice stroll, park your car at the landing and walk up Main Street toward the white Trinitarian Federated Church, which has a tapering spire. Among the white clapboard buildings that ring the town common are the Ives House (once the summer home of the poet Robert Lowell), the Abbott School, and the Unitarian Church, capped by a whimsical belfry. Castine is also home to the Maine Maritime Academy, and its training ship often can be seen in port.

Castine's **Soldiers and Sailors Monument** (⊠ Castine Town Common) is typical of many town memorials that honor the state's participation in the Civil War. It was dedicated in May 1887 to the veterans of that conflict.

Dining and Lodging

$$–$$$ ✕🏠 **Manor Inn.** Bordering a 95-acre conservation forest with trails lead-ing to the bay, this 1895 English manor-style inn provides a quiet re-treat. Yoga classes are offered in a fully equipped studio. Rooms are individually decorated, and four have fireplaces. The dining room ($$–$$$), which specializes in regional cuisine, is on the front porch and overlooks the expansive lawn and side gardens. The pub offers a lighter menu. ✉ *15 Manor Drive, off Battle Ave. 04421,* ☎ *207/326–4861 or 877/626–6746,* FAX *207/326–0891,* WEB *www.manor-inn.com. 10 rooms, 2 suites. Restaurant, pub. AE, DC, MC, V. BP.*

$$ ✕🏠 **Castine Inn.** Upholstered easy chairs and fine prints and paintings
★ are typical of the furnishings in the no-smoking inn's airy and simply decorated rooms. The third floor has the best views: the harbor over the gardens on one side, the village on the other. The dining room ($$$), decorated with a wraparound mural of Castine and its harbor, is open to the public for breakfast and dinner; the creative menu features local ingredients and entrées such as oil-poached salmon. There's a snug, English-style pub off the lobby. ✉ *33 Main St. (Box 41), 04421,* ☎ *207/326–4365,* FAX *207/326–4570,* WEB *www.castineinn.com. 15 rooms, 4 suites. Restaurant, pub, sauna. MC, V. Closed Nov. 1–late Apr.; restau-rant closed Tues. BP.*

Outdoor Activities and Sports

Castine Kayak Adventures (✉ Dennett's Wharf, ☎ 207/326–9045) offer tours with a Registered Maine Guide. The **Steam Launch *Laurie Ellen*** (✉ Dennett's Wharf,, ☎ 207/326–9045 or 207/266–2841), the only wood-fired, steam-powered, USCG-inspected passenger steam launch in the country, offers cruises around Castine Harbor and up the Baga-duce River.

Shopping

H.O.M.E. (✉ U.S. 1, Orland, ☎ 207/469–7961) is a cooperative crafts village with a crafts and pottery shop, weaving shop, flea market, market stand, and woodworking shop. **Leila Day Antiques** (✉ Main St., ☎ 207/326–8786) specializes in antiques, quilts, folk art, and nautical accessories. **McGrath-Dunham Gallery** (✉ Main St., ☎ 207/326–9175) carries paintings, sculpture, original prints, and pottery.

Blue Hill

③ *19 mi east of Castine.*

Blue Hill has a dramatic perch over the harbor. It is renowned for its pottery and is a good spot for shopping and gallery hopping.

Jonathan Fisher was the first settled minister of Blue Hill. The **Parson Fisher House,** which he built from 1814 to 1820, provides a fascinat-ing look at his many accomplishments and talents, which included writ-ing and illustrating books and poetry, farming, painting, furniture building, and making a camera obscura. Also on view is a wooden clock he crafted while a student at Harvard; the face holds messages about time written in English, Greek, Latin, Hebrew, and French. ✉ *Rtes. 15/176,* ☎ *No phone.* 🎫 *$3.* ⏰ *July–mid-Sept., Mon.–Sat., 2-5.*

Dining and Lodging

$$–$$$ ✕ **Arborvine.** This restaurant was an immediate hit when opened in 2000 by chef/owner John Hikade. The old cape has four dining areas, all tastefully decorated. Entrées may include crispy roast duckling and medallions of lamb with wild mushrooms. A take-out lunch is avail-able at the adjacent Moveable Feasts deli. ✉ *Main St.,* ☎ *207/374–2119. MC, V. Closed Mon.; Moveable Feasts closed Sun.*

$$–$$$ ✕ **Jonathan's.** Although the ownership has changed at this in-town restaurant, chef Jonathan Chase is still in the kitchen. He's known for his use of fresh regional Maine products. Choose from Maine seacoast vegetable salad, pan-roasted mussels with potatoes, onions, and greens, or warm cranberry bread pudding, among many other delicious options. ⊠ *Main St.,* ☎ *207/374–5226. MC, V.*

$$–$$$$ 🏠 **Oakland House.** An inn, dining hall, and cottages are tucked among the towering pines at this sprawling oceanfront property. Owner Jim Littlefield is a fourth-generation innkeeper. The Shore Oaks seaside inn, built in 1907 in the Arts and Crafts style, retains an elegant turn-of-the-century ambience. Cottages, most with kitchenettes and fireplaces, are rustic but fully equipped. The inn has a ½ mi of ocean shorefront on Eggemoggin Reach as well as a lake beach. ⊠ *435 Herrick Rd., Brooksville 04617,* ☎ *207/359–8521 or 800/359–7352,* FAX *207/359–9865,* WEB *www.oaklandhouse.com. 10 rooms, 7 with bath; 15 cottages. Dining room, lake, beaches, hiking, boating, recreation room, playground. MC, V. MAP.*

$$$ 🏠 **Blue Hill Inn.** Rambling and antiques-filled, this 1830 inn is a com-
★ forting place to relax after exploring nearby shops and galleries. Original pumpkin pine and painted floors set the tone for the mix of Empire and early Victorian pieces that fill the two parlors and guest rooms; five rooms have fireplaces. ⊠ *Union St. (Box 403), 04614,* ☎ *207/ 374–2844 or 800/826–7415,* FAX *207/374–2829,* WEB *www.blue-hillinn.com. 11 rooms, 1 suite. AE, MC, V. Closed Dec.–mid-May and midweek in Nov. BP.*

Nightlife and the Arts

Kneisel Hall Chamber Music Festival (⊠ Kneisel Hall, Rte. 15, ☎ 207/ 374–2811) has concerts on Sunday and Friday in summer.

Outdoor Activities and Sports

Holbrook Island Sanctuary (⊠ off Cape Rosier Rd., Brooksville, ☎ 207/326–4012) has a gravel beach with splendid views, a picnic area, and hiking trails.

Shopping

Big Chicken Barn (⊠ U.S. 1, Ellsworth, ☎ 207/374–2715) has three floors filled with books, antiques, and collectibles. **Handworks Gallery** (⊠ Main St., ☎ 207/374–5613) carries unusual crafts, jewelry, and clothing. **Leighton Gallery** (⊠ Parker Point Rd., ☎ 207/374–5001) shows oil paintings, lithographs, watercolors, and other contemporary art in the gallery, and sculpture in its garden. **North Country Textiles** (⊠ Main St., ☎ 207/374–2715) specializes in fine woven shawls, place mats, throws, baby blankets, and pillows in subtle patterns and color schemes.

Mark Bell Pottery (⊠ Rte. 15, ☎ 207/374–5881) has received national acclaim for his porcelain bowls, bottles, and vases. **Rackliffe Pottery** (⊠ Rte. 172, ☎ 207/374–2297) is famous for its vivid blue pottery, including plates, tea and coffee sets, pitchers, casseroles, and canisters. **Rowantrees Pottery** (⊠ Union St., ☎ 207/374–5535) has an extensive selection of styles and patterns in dinnerware, tea sets, vases, and decorative items.

En Route Scenic Route 15 south from Blue Hill passes through Brooksville and takes you over the graceful suspension bridge that crosses Eggemoggin Reach to Deer Isle. The turnout and picnic area at **Caterpillar Hill,** 1 mi south of the junction of Routes 15 and 175, commands a fabulous view of Penobscot Bay, hundreds of dark-green islands, and the Camden Hills across the bay.

Deer Isle Village

32 *16 mi south of Blue Hill.*

In Deer Isle Village, thick woods give way to tidal coves. Stacks of lobster traps populate the backyards of shingled houses, and dirt roads lead to summer cottages.

Haystack Mountain School of Crafts attracts internationally renowned glassblowers, potters, sculptors, jewelers, blacksmiths, printmakers, and weavers to its summer institute. You can attend evening lectures or visit artists' studios (by appointment only). ⊠ *Rte. 15, south of Deer Isle Village (turn left at Gulf gas station and follow signs for 6 mi),* ☎ *207/ 348–2306.* ▣ *Free.* ☉ *June–Sept.*

Dining and Lodging

$$$$ ✕▦ **Goose Cove Lodge.** This wooded property has a fine stretch of ocean frontage, a sandy beach, and a long sandbar that leads to a nature preserve. Cottages and suites are in secluded woodlands and on the shore. Some are attached, some have a single large room, and still others have one or two bedrooms. All but three units have fireplaces. Dinner at the restaurant ($$$$; reservations essential) is superb, and the contemporary American fare includes at least one vegetarian entrée. On Monday night in July and August, there's a lobster feast on the beach. ⊠ *Box 40, Goose Cove Rd., Sunset 04683,* ☎ *207/348– 2508 or 800/728–1963,* ﬁⁿ *207/348–2624,* Ⓦᴱᴮ *www.goosecov- elodge.com. 2 rooms, 7 suites, 13 cottages. 2 restaurants, hiking, beach, boating. AE, D, MC, V. All but 3 units closed mid-Oct.–mid- May. BP.*

$$$ ✕▦ **Pilgrim's Inn.** A deep-red, four-story gambrel-roof house, the Pil- ★ grim's Inn dates from about 1793 and overlooks a mill pond and harbor in Deer Isle Village. Wing chairs and Oriental rugs fill the library; a downstairs taproom has a huge brick fireplace and pine furniture. Guest rooms have English fabrics and carefully selected antiques. The dining room (reservations essential; no lunch) is in the attached barn, a rustic yet elegant space with farm implements, French oil lamps, and tiny windows. The five-course menu changes nightly but might list rack of lamb or fresh seafood. ⊠ *Bridge Rd. (Rte. 15A), 04627,* ☎ *207/ 348–6615,* ﬁⁿ *207/348–7769,* Ⓦᴱᴮ *www.pilgrimsinn.com. 13 rooms, 10 with bath; 2 seaside cottages. Restaurant, bicycles. MC, V. Closed mid-Oct.–mid-May. BP, MAP.*

Shopping

Blue Heron Gallery & Studio (⊠ Rte. 15, ☎ 207/348–6051) sells the work of the Haystack Mountain School of Crafts faculty. **Harbor Farm** (⊠ Rte. 15, Little Deer Isle, ☎ 207/348–7737) carries wonderful products for the home, such as pottery, furniture, dinnerware, linens, and folk art. **Nervous Nellie's Jams and Jellies** (⊠ 474A Sunshine Rd., ☎ 800/777–6825) sells jams and jellies and operates a café. The outdoor sculpture garden is a hit with kids. **Old Deer Isle Parish House Antiques** (⊠ Rte. 15, ☎ 207/348–9964) is a place for poking around in jumbles of old kitchenware, glassware, books, and linens. **Turtle Gallery** (⊠ Rte. 15, ☎ 207/348–9977) shows contemporary painting and sculpture.

Stonington

33 *7 mi south of Deer Isle.*

Stonington's isolation at the tip of the Deer Isle peninsula has helped it retain its fishing village flavor. This is changing now, as boutiques and galleries open in summer now line its main thoroughfare. Still, Stonington remains a working port town—the principal activity is at the waterfront, where fishing boats arrive with the day's catch. At night, the town can be rowdy. The high, sloped island that rises beyond the archipelago known as Merchants Row is Isle au Haut, which contains a remote section of Acadia National Park; it's accessible by mail boat from Stonington.

The tiny **Deer Isle Granite Museum** documents Stonington's quarrying tradition. The museum's centerpiece is an 8- by 15-ft working model of quarrying operations on Crotch Island and the town of Stonington in 1900. ⊠ *Main St.,* ☎ *207/367–6331.* 🖼 *Free.* ☉ *Memorial Day–Labor Day, Mon.–Sat. 10–5 and Sun. 1–5.*

Dining and Lodging

$$–$$$ ✕ **Cafe Atlantic.** Whether you want ice cream, tasty boiled lobster, or a fancier meal, you'll find it at this harborfront eatery. Country linens and antiques decorate the restaurant, which serves fresh seafood as well as chicken and steak. For lobster in the rough, head to the deck overhanging the water. For a quick snack, visit the ice cream window. ⊠ *Main St.,* ☎ *207/367–6373. AE, D, MC, V.*

$$–$$$ ✕ **Lily's.** Local artwork embellishes the three dining rooms in this old Victorian house. The bistro-style menu emphasizes fresh, seasonal foods and may include entrées such as fresh salmon with a sesame butter sauce or curried chicken. The desserts are legendary. ⊠ *Rte. 15,* ☎ *207/367–5936. MC, V. Closed Sat.–Sun.*

$$ 🏨 **Inn on the Harbor.** From the front, this inn composed of four 100-year-old Victorian buildings is as plain and unadorned as Stonington itself. But out back it opens up, with an expansive deck over the harbor. Many guests take breakfast here in the morning. Rooms on the harbor side have views, and some have fireplaces and private decks. Those on the street side lack the views and can be noisy at night. ⊠ *Main St. (Box 69), 04681,* ☎ *207/367–2420 or 800/942–2420,* FAX *207/367–5165. 13 rooms, 1 suite. Coffee shop. AE, D, MC, V. CP.*

The Arts

Stonington Opera House (⊠ School St.) books live theater, music, and dance events.

Outdoor Activities and Sports

You can be a lobsterman for the day on the *Jacob Lewis* (☎ 207/367–5198), a 32-ft traditional Maine lobster boat. **Old Quarry** (☎ 207/367–8977) operates a charter and boat-taxi service, rents canoes, kayaks, and bicycles and offers guided kayak trips. Call for directions.

Shopping

Dockside Books & Gifts (⊠ W. Main St., ☎ 207/367–2652) on the harborfront stocks an eclectic selection of books, crafts, and gifts. The **Clown** (⊠ Main St., ☎ 207/367–6348) has fine art, antiques, a good wine selection, and specialty foods. **Eastern Bay Gallery** (⊠ Main St., ☎ 207/367–6368) carries contemporary Maine crafts; summer exhibits highlight the works of specific artists. **Firebird Gallery** (⊠ W. Main St., ☎ 207/367–0955) is a good choice for fine contemporary crafts.

Isle au Haut

❸④ *14 mi south of Stonington.*

Isle au Haut thrusts its steeply ridged back out of the sea south of Stonington. Accessible only by passenger mail boat (☎ 207/367–5193), the island is worth visiting for the ferry ride itself, a half-hour cruise amid the tiny islands of Merchants Row, where you might see terns, guillemots, and harbor seals.

More than half the island is part of **Acadia National Park**: 17½ mi of trails extend through quiet spruce and birch woods, along beaches and seaside cliffs, and over the spine of the central mountain ridge. (For more information on the park, *see* Bar Harbor *and* Acadia National Park.) From mid-June to mid-September, the mail boat docks at **Duck Harbor** within the park. The small campground here, with five lean-tos, is open from mid-May to mid-October and fills up quickly. Reservations, which are essential, can be made after April 1 by writing to Acadia National Park (✉ Box 177, Bar Harbor 04609).

Lodging

$$$$ 🏨 **The Keeper's House.** Thick spruce forest surrounds this converted lighthouse-keeper's house on a rock ledge. There is no electricity, but everyone receives a flashlight upon registering; you dine by candlelight on seafood or chicken and read in the evening by kerosene lantern. Trails link the inn with Acadia National Park's Isle au Haut trail network, and you can walk to the village. The spacious rooms contain simple, painted-wood furniture and local crafts. A separate cottage, the Oil House, has no indoor plumbing. Access to the island is via the mail boat from Stonington. ✉ *Box 26, Lighthouse Rd., 04645,* ☎ *207/367-2261,* WEB *www.keepershouse.com. 4 rooms without bath, 1 cottage. Dock, bicycles. No credit cards. Closed Nov.–Apr. FAP.*

Penobscot Bay A to Z

To research prices, get advice from other travelers, and book travel arrangements, visit www.fodors.com.

CAR TRAVEL

U.S. 1 follows the west coast of Penobscot Bay, linking Rockland, Rockport, Camden, Belfast, and Searsport. On the east side of the bay, Route 175 (south from U.S. 1) takes you to Route 166A (for Castine) and Route 15 (for Blue Hill, Deer Isle, and Stonington). A car is essential for exploring the bay area.

EMERGENCIES

➤ HOSPITALS: **Blue Hill Memorial Hospital** (✉ Water St., Blue Hill, ☎ 207/374–2836). **Island Medical Center** (✉ Airport Rd., Stonington, ☎ 207/367–2311). **Penobscot Bay Medical Center** (✉ U.S. 1, Rockport, ☎ 207/596–8000). **Waldo County General Hospital** (✉ 56 Northport Ave., Belfast, ☎ 207/338–2500).

LODGING

Camden Accommodations provides assistance for reservations around Camden.
➤ LOCAL AGENTS: **Camden Accommodations** (☎ 207/236–6090 or 800/236–1920, FAX 207/236–6091).

VISITOR INFORMATION

➤ CONTACTS: **Belfast Area Chamber of Commerce** (✉ Box 58, 1 Main St., Belfast 04915, ☎ 207/338–5900). **Blue Hill Chamber of Commerce** (✉ Box 520, Blue Hill 04614, ☎ no phone). **Castine Town Office** (✉ Emerson Hall, Court St., Castine 04421, ☎ 207/326–4502). **Deer Isle–Stonington Chamber of Commerce** (✉ Box 459, Stonington 04681, ☎ 207/348–6124). **Rockland–Thomaston Area Chamber of Commerce** (✉ Box 508, Harbor Park, Rockland 04841, ☎ 207/596–0376 or 800/562–2529). **Rockport-Camden-Lincolnville Chamber of Commerce** (✉ Public Landing, Box 919, Camden 04843, ☎ 207/236–4404 or 800/223–5459). **Waldo County Regional Chamber of Commerce** (✉ School St., Unity 04988, ☎ 207/948–5050 or 800/870–9934).

MOUNT DESERT ISLAND

Acadia is the informal name for the area east of Penobscot Bay that includes Mount Desert Island (pronounced "dessert") as well as Blue Hill Bay and Frenchman Bay. Mount Desert, 13 mi across, is Maine's largest island, and it encompasses most of Acadia National Park, an astonishingly beautiful preserve with rocky cliffs, crashing surf, and serene mountains and ponds. Maine's number-one tourist attraction, it draws more than 4 million visitors a year. The 40,000 acres of woods and mountains, lake and shore, footpaths, carriage roads, and hiking trails that make up the park extend to other islands and some of the mainland. Outside the park, on Mount Desert's eastern shore, Bar Harbor has become a busy tourist town. Less commercial and congested are the smaller island towns, such as Southwest Harbor and Northeast Harbor, and the outlying islands.

Bar Harbor

㉟ *160 mi northeast of Portland, 22 mi southeast of Ellsworth on Rte. 3.*

An upper-class resort town in the 19th century, Bar Harbor now serves visitors to Acadia National Park with inns, motels, and restaurants. Most of its grand mansions were destroyed in a fire that devastated the island in 1947, but many surviving estates have been converted into inns and restaurants. Motels abound, yet the town retains the beauty of a commanding location on Frenchman Bay. Shops, restaurants, and hotels are clustered along Main, Mt. Desert, and Cottage streets. Take a stroll down West Street, a National Historic District, where you can see some of the grand cottages that survived the fire.

The **Bar Harbor Historical Society Museum** displays photographs of Bar Harbor from the days when it catered to the very rich. Other exhibits document the fire of 1947. ⊠ *33 Ledgelawn Ave.,* ☎ *207/288–3807 or 207/288–0000.* ⌨ *Free.* ☉ *June–Oct., Mon.–Sat. 1–4 or by appointment.*

★ The **Abbe Museum,** a treasure trove of Native American artifacts, expects to be in its new downtown quarters, across from the village green, in September 2001. The museum's collections contain 50,000 objects spanning 10,000 years of Native American history, archaeology, and culture in Maine. A glass-walled archaeological laboratory will allow visitors to observe staff and volunteers working with artifacts found during the museum's scientific excavations. The 1893 building, the former home of the YMCA, is eligible for the National Register of Historic Places. Its facade is an example of the eclectic Shingle Style often used for coastal summer homes at the turn of the 20th century. ⊠ *26 Mt. Desert St.* ☎ *207/288–3519,* WEB *www.abbemuseum.org.* ⌨ *$4.50.* ☉ *Mem. Day–June 30 and Sept. 1–mid-Oct., Mon.–Wed. 10-5 and Thurs.–Sun. 10–9; July–Aug., Mon.–Tues. 10–5, Wed.–Sun. 10–9; mid-Oct.–Mem. Day, Thurs.–Sun. 1–5.*

☙ The small **Natural History Museum** at the College of the Atlantic has wildlife exhibits, a hands-on discovery room, interpretive programs, and a self-guided nature trail. ⊠ *Rte. 3,* ☎ *207/288–5015.* ⌨ *$3.50.* ☉ *Mid-June–Labor Day, Mon.–Sat. 10–5; Labor Day–Columbus Day, Thurs.–Mon. 10–4.*

☙ The **Acadia Zoo** has pastures, streams, and woods that shelter about 45 species of wild and domestic animals, including reindeer, wolves, monkeys, and a moose. A barn has been converted into a rain-forest habitat for monkeys, birds, reptiles, and other Amazon creatures. ⊠ *Rte. 3, Trenton, north of Bar Harbor,* ☎ *207/667–3244.* ⌨ *$6.* ☉ *May–Dec., daily 9:30–dusk.*

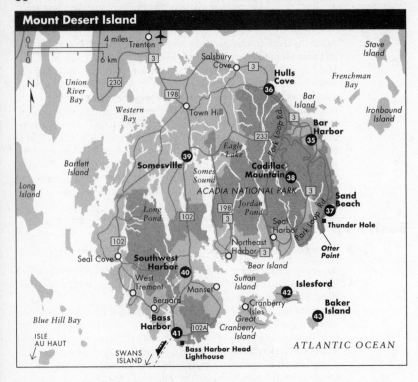

Mount Desert Island

Dining and Lodging

$$$$ ✕ **George's.** Candles, flowers, and linens grace the tables, and art fills
★ the walls of the four small dining rooms in this old house. The menu's
Mediterranean influences can be tasted in the phyllo-wrapped lobster;
the lamb and wild-game entrées are superb. The prix-fixe menu includes
an appetizer, an entrée, and dessert. Jazz musicians perform nightly in
peak season. ✉ *7 Stephen's La.,* ☎ *207/288–4505. AE, D, DC, MC,
V. Closed Nov.–mid-June. No lunch.*

$$$ ✕ **The Burning Tree.** Fresh is the key word at this casual restaurant just
outside town. The menu emphasizes seafood and organic produce and
chicken; some typical items are pan-sautéed monkfish, Cajun lobster,
crab au gratin, and chicken pot roast. There are always two or three
vegetarian choices. Local contemporary art adorns the walls in the two
dining rooms and on the porch. ✉ *Rte. 3, Otter Creek,* ☎ *207/288–
9331. D, MC, V. Closed Tues. and mid-Oct.–late May.*

$$$ ✕ **Porcupine Grill.** This restaurant, named for a cluster of islets in
Frenchman Bay, has a menu that changes regularly but might include
starters such as pan-roasted mussels or citrus barbecued quail and main
courses like grilled lobster, twin Portobello fillets, or filet mignon.
Soft-green walls, antique furnishings, and Villeroy & Boch porcelain
create an ambience that complements the sophisticated cuisine. ✉ *123
Cottage St.,* ☎ *207/288–3884. AE, MC, V. Closed Sun. and Nov.–May.*

$$–$$$ ✕ **Café This Way.** Jazz, unmatched tables and chairs, and a few couches
provide a relaxing background for the creative, internationally inspired menu at this restaurant tucked in a back street. You might begin
with crab cakes with tequila-lime sauce and then move on to cashew-
crusted chicken over sautéed greens with sesame-ginger aioli or perhaps butternut squash ravioli with roasted red peppers, broccoli, and
a rosemary maple cream sauce. Save room for the homemade desserts.
✉ *14½ Mt. Desert St.,* ☎ *207/288–4483. MC, V.*

$$-$$$ ✕ **Havana.** Pumpkin-colored walls, soft jazz, wood floors, and cloth-
★ covered tables set the tone at this storefront restaurant on the fringe
of downtown Bar Harbor. The Latin-influenced menu emphasizes
local natural and organic ingredients and changes weekly. The menu
may include crab-and-roasted-corn cakes or grilled swordfish, marinated in ginger and lime and finished with a scallion vinaigrette. ⊠
318 Main St., ☎ *207/288–2822. Reservations essential. MC, V. Closed
Sun.–Tues. late-Oct.–mid-May.*.

$$$–$$$$ ✕🏠 **Bar Harbor Inn.** The roots of this genteel inn date from the 1880s.
Rooms are spread out over three buildings on nicely landscaped wa-
terfront property, just a short walk from town. Most rooms have bal-
conies, hot tubs, fireplaces, and great views. The two-level suites are
a good choice for families. Rooms in the Oceanfront Lodge offer pri-
vate decks or patios overlooking the ocean, while those in the New-
port Lodge, behind it, are more simply furnished and smaller. The formal
waterfront Reading Room serves mostly Continental fare but has some
Maine specialties like lobster pie and a scrumptious Indian pudding.
The more casual Terrace Grill is an outdoor restaurant on the water-
front. ⊠ *Newport Dr., 04609,* ☎ *207/288–3351 or 800/248–3351,*
℻ *207/288–5296,* 🕸 *www.barharborinn.com. 138 rooms, 15 suites.
2 restaurants, no-smoking room, exercise room, pool, business services.
AE, D, DC, MC, V. CP.*

$$$$ 🏠 **Balance Rock Inn.** This grand summer cottage built in 1903 commands
a prime, secluded location on the water but is only two blocks from down-
town. The atmosphere is a bit stuffy, but service is thoughtful. Rooms
are spacious and meticulously furnished with reproduction pieces—
four-poster and canopy beds in guest rooms, crystal chandeliers and a
grand piano in common rooms. Some rooms have fireplaces, saunas, steam
rooms, whirlpool tubs, or porches, and most have views of the pool and
gardens and of the water beyond. From the bar on the veranda, you can
watch the activity in the harbor. ⊠ *21 Albert Meadow, 04609,* ☎ *207/
288–2610 or 800/753–0494,* ℻ *207/288–5534,* 🕸 *www.barharbor-
vacations.com. 13 rooms, 1 suite, 3 apartments. Bar, pool, exercise
room, concierge. AE, D, MC, V. Closed late Oct.–early May. BP.*

$$$–$$$$ 🏠 **Inn at Canoe Point.** Seclusion and privacy are the main attributes
★ of this snug, 100-year-old Tudor-style house on the water at Hulls Cove,
2 mi from Bar Harbor and ¼ mi from Acadia National Park's Hulls
Cove Visitor Center. The Master Suite, a large room with a gas fire-
place, has French doors that open onto a waterside deck. The inn's liv-
ing room has huge windows that look out on the water, a granite
fireplace, and a waterfront deck. ⊠ *Box 216, Rte. 3, 04609,* ☎ *207/
288–9511,* ℻ *207/288–2870,* 🕸 *www.innatcanoepoint.com. 3 rooms,
2 suites. D, MC, V. BP.*

$$$–$$$$ 🏠 **Ullikana.** Inside the stucco-and-timber walls of this traditional
★ Tudor cottage, the exuberant decor juxtaposes antiques with contem-
porary country pieces, vibrant color with French country wallpapers,
and abstract art with folk creations. The combination not only works—
it shines. Rooms are large, most have at least a glimpse of the water,
many have fireplaces, and some have decks. Breakfast is an elaborate
multicourse affair. The refurbished Yellow House across the drive has
six additional rooms decorated in traditional Old Bar Harbor style.
Ullikana is a short walk to downtown shops. ⊠ *16 The Field, 04609,*
☎ *207/288–9552,* ℻ *207/288–3682,* 🕸 *www.ullikana.com. 16
rooms. MC, V. Closed Nov.–May. BP.*

$$ 🏠 **Seacroft Inn.** It's an easy walk to town or the Shore Path from this
rambling multigabled inn, which is a good choice for families. One room
has a fireplace, another a kitchen, yet another a private deck, but all
have refrigerators and microwaves. A breakfast basket is delivered to
your room each morning. ⊠ *18 Albert Meadow, 04609,* ☎ *207/288–*

4669 or 800/824–9694. 3 rooms (1 with separate bath), 1 suite, 1 studio, 1 efficiency. Refrigerator. MC, V. CP.

Nightlife and the Arts

For dancing, try **Carmen Verandah** (⊠ 119 Main St., upstairs, ☎ 207/288–2766). **Geddy's Pub** (⊠ 19 Main St., ☎ 207/288–5077) has live entertainment early in the evening followed by a DJ spinning discs. At the **Lompoc Cafe & Brewpub** (⊠ 30 Rodick St., ☎ 207/288–9513) you can relax in a garden setting and play a game of bocce. Comfortable chairs, pizza, and beer make the viewing easy at **Reel Pizza Cinerama** (⊠ 33B Kennebec Pl., ☎ 207/288–3811).

Arcady Music Festival (☎ 207/288–3151) schedules concerts (primarily classical) at locations around Mount Desert Island and at some off-island sites, year-round. **Bar Harbor Music Festival** (⊠ 59 Cottage St., ☎ 207/288–5744) arranges jazz, chamber music, string-orchestra, and pop concerts by young professionals from July to early August.

Outdoor Activities and Sports

BIKING

Acadia Bike & Canoe (⊠ 48 Cottage St., ☎ 207/288–9605 or 800/526–8615) rents and sells mountain bikes. **Bar Harbor Bicycle Shop** (⊠ 141 Cottage St., ☎ 207/288–3886 or 800/824–2453) rents both recreational and high-performance bikes by the half or full day.

BOATING

Acadia Bike & Canoe has canoe and sea kayak rentals. For guided kayak tours, try **National Park Sea Kayak Tours** (⊠ 39 Cottage St., ☎ 207/288–0342 or 800/347–0940). **Coastal Kayaking Tours** (⊠ 48 Cottage St., ☎ 207/288–9605 or 800/526–8615) offers tours led by registered Maine guides. The four-mast schooner *Margaret Todd* (⊠ Bar Harbor Inn Pier, ☎ 207/288–4585) offers 1½- to 2-hour tours daily between mid-May and October.

STATE PARK

On Frenchman Bay but off Mount Desert Island, the 55-acre **Lamoine State Park** (⊠ Rte. 184, Lamoine, ☎ 207/667–4778) has a boat-launching ramp, a fishing pier, a children's playground, and a 61-site campground that's open from mid-May to mid-October.

WHALE-WATCHING

Acadian Whale Watcher (⊠ Golden Anchor Pier, 52 West St., ☎ 207/288–9794 or 800/421–3307) runs 3½-hour whale-watching cruises from June to mid-October. **Bar Harbor Whale Watch Co.** (⊠ 1 West St., ☎ 207/288–3322 or 800/508–1499) operates the catamaran *Friendship V,* for whale-watching and the *Katherine,* for lobster fishing and seal watching.

Shopping

Bar Harbor in summer is prime territory for browsing for gifts, T-shirts, and novelty items. For bargains, head for the outlets that line Route 3 in Ellsworth, which have good discounts on shoes, sportswear, cookware, and more.

Ben and Bill's Chocolate Emporium (⊠ 66 Main St., ☎ 207/288–3281) is a chocolate-lover's nirvana, and the adventurous can try lobster ice cream here. **Birdsnest Gallery** (⊠ 12 Mt. Desert St., ☎ 207/288–4054) sells fine art, paintings, and sculpture. The **Eclipse Gallery** (⊠ 12 Mt. Desert St., ☎ 207/288–9048) carries handblown glass, ceramics, art photography, and wood furniture. **Island Artisans** (⊠ 99 Main St., ☎ 207/288–4214) is a crafts cooperative. The **Lone Moose–Fine Crafts** (⊠ 78 West St., ☎ 207/288–4229) has art glass and works in clay, pottery, wood, and fiberglass. **Songs of the Sea** (⊠ 47 West St., ☎ 207/288–5653) sells handcrafted musical instruments.

Acadia National Park

★ *4 mi northwest of Bar Harbor (to Hulls Cove).*

There is no one Acadia. The park holds some of the most spectacular and varied scenery on the eastern seaboard: a rugged coastline of surf-pounded granite and an interior graced by sculpted mountains, quiet ponds, and lush deciduous forests. Cadillac Mountain, the highest point of land on the eastern coast, dominates the park. Although it's rugged, Acadia National Park also has graceful stone bridges, horse-drawn carriages, and the elegant Jordan Point Tea House. The 27-mi Park Loop Road provides an excellent introduction, yet to truly appreciate the park you must get off the main road and experience it by walking, biking, or taking a carriage ride on the carriage trails, by hiking or perhaps sea kayaking. If you get off the beaten path, you'll find places in the park that you can have practically to yourself, despite the millions of visitors who descend in summer.

36 The popular **Hulls Cove** approach to Acadia National Park, northwest of Bar Harbor on Route 3, brings you to the start of the **Park Loop Road**. Even though it is often clogged with traffic in summer, the road provides the best introduction to the park. You can drive it in an hour, but allow at least half a day or more to explore the many sites along the route. At the start of the loop, the visitor center shows a free 15-minute orientation film. Acadia Rangers lead nature walks, children's programs, mountain hikes, photography programs, and evening talks. A schedule of programs is available here. You can also pick up the *Acadia Beaver Log* (the park's free newspaper detailing guided hikes and other ranger-led programs), books, maps of hiking trails and carriage roads, the schedule for naturalist-led tours, and cassettes for drive-it-yourself tours. Traveling south on the Park Loop Road, you'll reach a small ticket booth where you pay the $10-per-vehicle entrance fee, good for seven consecutive days. ⊠ *Visitor center, Park Loop Rd. off Rte. 3,* ☎ *207/288–3338,* WEB *www.nps.gov/acad.* ☉ *Park daily. Visitor center late June–Aug., daily 8–6; mid-Apr.–mid-June and Sept.–Oct., daily 8–4:30.*

37 **Sand Beach** is a small stretch of pink sand backed by the mountains of Acadia and the odd lump of rock known as the Beehive. The **Ocean Trail,** which runs alongside the Park Loop Road from Sand Beach to the Otter Point parking area, is an easily accessible walk with some of the most awesome scenery in Maine: huge slabs of pink granite heaped at the ocean's edge, ocean views unobstructed to the horizon, and Thunder Hole, a natural seaside cave into which the ocean rushes and roars.

★ **38** **Cadillac Mountain,** at 1,532 ft, is the highest point on the eastern seaboard. From the smooth, bald summit you have an awesome 360-degree view of the ocean, islands, jagged coastline, and woods and lakes of Acadia and its surroundings. You can drive or hike to the summit.

The Sieur de Monts Spring exit off the Park Loop offers two enticing sites. The original **Abbé Museum** (a new museum is expected to open in downtown Bar Harbor in late 2001) holds a treasure trove of Maine's Native American history, including arrowheads, moccasins, tools, jewelry, and a well-documented collection of baskets. ⊠ *Sieur de Monts Spring exit from Rte. 3 or Acadia National Park Loop Rd.,* ☎ *207/288–3519.* ☒ *$2.* ☉ *July–Aug., daily 9–5; late-May–June 30 and Sept.–late Oct., daily 10–4.*

The **Wild Gardens of Acadia** present a miniature view of the plants that grow on Mount Desert Island. ⊠ *Rte. 3 at the Sieur de Monts Spring exit,* ☎ *207/288–3400.* ☒ *Free.* ☉ *Paths 24 hrs.*

Dining and Lodging

$$–$$$ ✕ **Jordan Pond House.** The restaurant's setting overlooking Jordan Pond is magnificent and serene. Come for tea and the oversize popovers with homemade strawberry jam and ice cream, a century-old tradition. If you choose to sit on the terrace or lawn, be forewarned that bees are more than a nuisance. The menu offers lunch and dinner items, including lobster stew, but these get mixed reviews. ⊠ *Park Loop Rd.,* ☎ *207/ 276–3316. AE, D, MC, V. Closed late Oct.–mid-May.*

$ ⚕ **Blackwoods and Seawall.** These two campgrounds with a total of 530 campsites fill up quickly during the summer. Space at Seawall is allocated on a first-come, first-served basis, starting at 8 AM. Between mid-June and mid-September, reserve a Blackwoods site within five months of a visit. No reservations are essential in the off-season. *Black-woods:* ⊠ *Rte. 3, Northeast Harbor,* ☎ *800/365–2267.* ☉ *Year-round. Seawall:* ⊠ *Rte. 102A, Northeast Harbor,* ☎ *207/244–3600. Closed late Sept.–late May.*

Outdoor Activities and Sports

BIKING

The carriage roads that wind through the woods and fields of Acadia National Park are ideal for biking and jogging when the ground is dry and for cross-country skiing in winter. You can pick up trail maps at the Hulls Cove Visitor Center.

HIKING

Acadia National Park maintains nearly 200 mi of foot and carriage paths, from easy strolls along flatlands to rigorous climbs that involve ladders and handholds on rock faces. Among the more rewarding hikes are the Precipice Trail to Champlain Mountain, the Great Head Loop, the Gorham Mountain Trail, and the path around Eagle Lake. The Hulls Cove visitor center has trail guides and maps and will help you match a trail with your interests and abilities.

Around Acadia

There's plenty to explore on Mount Desert Island beyond the 27-mi Park Loop Road. You can continue an auto tour of the island by heading west on Route 233 for the villages on Somes Sound, a true fjord— the only one on the East Coast—that almost bisects the island.

㊴ Somesville, the oldest settlement on the island (1621), is a carefully preserved New England village of white clapboard houses and churches, neat green lawns, and bits of blue water visible behind them.

㊵ Southwest Harbor, south from Somesville on Route 102, combines the salty character of a working port with the refinements of a summer resort community. From the town's Main Street (Route 102), turn left onto Clark Point Road to reach the harbor.

Mount Desert Oceanarium has exhibits in two locations on the fishing and sea life of the Gulf of Maine, a live-seal program, a lobster hatchery, and hands-on exhibits such as a touch tank. ⊠ *Clark Point Rd., Southwest Harbor,* ☎ *207/244–7330;* ⊠ *Rte. 3, Thomas Bay, Bar Harbor,* ☎ *207/288–5005.* 🎟 *Call for admission fees (combination tickets available).* ☉ *Mid-May–late-Oct., Mon.–Sat. 9–5.*

Wendell Gilley Museum of Bird Carving showcases bird carvings by Gilley, has carving demonstrations and workshops and natural-history programs, and exhibits wildlife art. ⊠ *4 Herrick Rd., Southwest Harbor,* ☎ *207/244–7555,* WEB *www.acadia.net/gilley.* 🎟 *$3.25.* ☉ *July–Aug., Tues.–Sun. 10–5; June and Sept.–Oct., Tues.–Sun. 10–4; May and Nov.–Dec., Fri.–Sun. 10–4..*

⁴¹ Bass Harbor, 4 mi south of Southwest Harbor (follow Route 102A when Route 102 forks), is a tiny lobstering village with cottages for rent, inns, a restaurant, and a gift shop. You can visit the **Bass Harbor Head lighthouse,** which clings to a cliff at the eastern entrance to Blue Hill Bay. It was built in 1858. Also here is the **Maine State Ferry Service's** car-and-passenger ferry (☎ 207/244–3254) to Swans Island. The ferry has six daily runs June to mid-October, fewer the rest of the year.

Dining and Lodging

$–$$ ✕ Beal's Lobster Pier. You can watch lobstermen bringing in their catch at this working lobster pound. Order lobster at one take-out window and fried foods, burgers, and dessert at another. ⊠ *End of Clark Point Rd., Southwest Harbor,* ☎ *207/244–3202, 207/244–7178, or 800/244–7178. Closed mid-Oct.–mid-May.*

$–$$ ✕ Seaweed Café. This unpretentious restaurant serves natural and organic seafood with an Asian touch. Entrées may include Thai jumbo shrimp scampi and vegetables or tuna au poivre. ⊠ *Rt. 102, Southwest Harbor,* ☎ *207/244–0572. Reservations essential. No credit cards. Closed Sun.–Tues. No lunch.*

$$–$$$$ 🏠 Claremont Hotel. Built in 1884 and operated continuously as an inn, the Claremont calls up memories of the long, leisurely vacations of days gone by. The yellow clapboard structure commands a view of Somes Sound. Croquet is played on the lawn, and cocktails and lunch are served at the Boat House in summer. Rooms are simply, some would say sparsely, decorated, and the cottages have a rustic feel. The dining room, open to the public for breakfast and dinner, has picture windows overlooking the sound. The menu changes weekly and includes fresh fish and a vegetarian entrée; reservations are essential, and a jacket is required for dinner. ⊠ *Off Clark Point Rd., Box 137, Southwest Harbor 04679,* ☎ *207/244–5036 or 800/244–5036,* 📠 *207/244–3512,* 🌐 *www.acadia.net/claremont. 31 rooms, 2 suites, 13 cottages. Restaurant, tennis court, croquet, dock, boating, bicycles. No credit cards. Hotel and restaurant closed mid-Oct.–mid-June; cottages closed Nov.–mid-May. BP, MAP.*

$$ 🏠 Island House. This sweet B&B on the quiet side of the island has four simple and bright rooms in the main house. The carriage-house suite comes complete with a sleeping loft and a kitchenette. ⊠ *Box 1006, 121 Clark Point Rd., Southwest Harbor 04679,* ☎ *207/244–5180,* 🌐 *www.acadia.net/islandhouse. 4 rooms, 1 suite. MC, V. BP.*

$$ 🏠 Moorings Inn & Cottages. Nothing is fancy here except the jaw-dropping view of Somes Sound. The Maine House dates to the late 18th century; the cottages and a small motel are more recent. Rooms in the Maine House are decorated with antiques and country touches; the motel rooms lack the atmosphere but have sliding glass doors onto decks. The homey cottage rooms offer the most privacy and have cooking facilities. Lookout Front has a fireplace, screened porch, and king-size bed. ⊠ *135 Shore Rd., Manset (Box 744, Southwest Harbor 04679),* ☎ *207/244–5523, 207/244–3210, or 800/596–5523,* 🌐 *www.mooringsinn.com. 13 rooms, 5 cottages, 1 apartment. Dock. No credit cards. Closed late Oct.–late Apr. CP.*

Outdoor Activities and Sports

BIKING

Southwest Cycle (⊠ Main St., Southwest Harbor, ☎ 207/244–5856) rents bicycles.

BOATING

Manset Yacht Service (⊠ Shore Rd., Manset, ☎ 207/244–4040) rents power boats and sailboats. **National Park Canoe Rentals** (⊠ Pretty Marsh Rd., Somesville, at the head of Long Pond, ☎ 207/244–5854) rents canoes and kayaks.

Island Cruises (⊠ Shore Rd., Bass Harbor, ☎ 207/244–5785) takes passengers on a 40-ft lobster boat through the islands of Blue Hill Bay.

Shopping
E. L. Higgins (⊠ Bernard Rd., off Rte. 102, Bernard, ☎ 207/244–3983) carries antique wicker, furniture, and glassware. **Marianne Clark Fine Antiques** (⊠ Main St., Southwest Harbor, ☎ 207/244–9247) has formal and country furniture, American paintings, and accessories from the 18th and 19th centuries. **Port in a Storm Bookstore** (⊠ Main St., Somesville, ☎ 207/244–4114) is a book-lover's nirvana.

Excursions to the Cranberry Isles

Off the southeast shore of Mount Desert Island at the entrance to Somes Sound, the five Cranberry Isles—Great Cranberry, Islesford (or Little Cranberry), Baker Island, Sutton Island, and Bear Island—escape the hubbub that engulfs Acadia National Park in summer. Sutton and Bear islands are privately owned. The **Beal & Bunker passenger ferry** (☎ 207/244–3575) serves Great Cranberry and Islesford from Northeast Harbor. **Cranberry Cove Boating Company** (☎ 207/244–5882) serves Great Cranberry and Islesford from Southwest Harbor. Baker Island is reached by the summer cruise boats of the **Islesford Ferry Company** (☎ 207/276–3717) from Northeast Harbor.

🐬 **Islesford** comes closest to having a village: a collection of houses, a church, a fishermen's co-op, a market, and a post office near the ferry dock.

The **Islesford Historical Museum,** run by Acadia National Park, has displays of tools, documents relating to the island's history, and books and manuscripts of the poet Rachel Field (1894–1942), who summered on Sutton Island. ⊠ *Isleford,* ☎ *207/244–9224.* ⬜ *Free.* ☾ *Mid-June–late Sept., daily 10–noon and 12:30–4:30.*

🐬 The 123-acre **Baker Island,** the most remote of the Cranberry Isles, looks almost black from a distance because of its thick spruce forest. The Islesford Ferry cruise boat from Northeast Harbor conducts a 4½-hour narrated tour, during which you are likely to see ospreys, harbor seals, and cormorants. Because Baker Island has no natural harbor, you take a fishing dory to get to shore.

Mount Desert Island A to Z

To research prices, get advice from other travelers, and book travel arrangements, visit www.fodors.com.

BUS TRAVEL
The free Island Explorer shuttle services the entire island from mid-June through Labor Day.
➤ Bus Information: **Island Explorer** (☎ 207/667–5796).

CAR RENTAL
➤ Local Agencies: **Avis** (⊠ Bangor International Airport, 299 Godfrey Blvd., ☎ 207/947–8383 or 800/331–1212). **Budget** (⊠ Hancock County Airport, Rte. 3, Trenton, ☎ 207/667–1200 or 800/527–0700). **Hertz** (⊠ Bangor International Airport, 299 Godfrey Blvd., ☎ 207/942–5519 or 800/654–3131). **Thrifty** (⊠ Bangor International Airport, 357 Odlin Rd., ☎ 207/942–6400 or 800/367–2277).

CAR TRAVEL
North of Bar Harbor, the scenic 27-mi Park Loop Road leaves Route 3 to circle the eastern quarter of Mount Desert Island, with one-way traffic from Sieur de Monts Spring to Seal Harbor and two-way traffic between Seal Harbor and Hulls Cove. Route 102, which serves the

western half of Mount Desert, is reached from Route 3 just after it enters the island or from Route 233 west from Bar Harbor. All these island roads pass through the precincts of Acadia National Park.

EMERGENCIES

➤ CONTACTS: **Maine Coast Memorial Hospital** (✉ 50 Union St., Ellsworth, ☎ 207/667–5311). **Mount Desert Island Hospital** (✉ 10 Wayman La., Bar Harbor, ☎ 207/288–5081). **Southwest Harbor Medical Center** (✉ Herrick Rd., Southwest Harbor, ☎ 207/244–5513).

TOURS

Acadia National Park Tours operates a 2½-hour bus tour of Acadia National Park, narrated by a naturalist, from May to October. Also offered are 2½-hour, narrated trolley tours. Bar Harbor Taxi and Tours conducts half-day historic and scenic tours of the area. Downeast Nature Tours offers personalized and small group tours highlighting the island's flora and fauna.

Acadia Air, on Route 3 in Trenton, between Ellsworth and Bar Harbor at Hancock County Airport, rents aircraft and flies seven aerial sightseeing routes, from spring to fall. A Step Back in Time uses Victorian-costumed guides to lead walking tours that highlight the 1890s in Bar Harbor. Tours leave from 48 Cottage St.
➤ CONTACTS: **Acadia National Park Tours** (☎ 207/288–3327). **Bar Harbor Taxi and Tours** (☎ 207/288–4020). **Downeast Nature Tours** (☎ 207/288–8128). **Acadia Air** (☎ 207/667–5534). **A Step Back in Time** (☎ 207/288–9605).

VISITOR INFORMATION

➤ CONTACTS: **Acadia National Park** (✉ Box 177, Bar Harbor 04609, ☎ 207/288–3338). **Bar Harbor Chamber of Commerce** (✉ Box 158, 93 Cottage St., Bar Harbor 04609, ☎ 207/288–3393, 207/288–5103, or 800/288–5103). **Southwest Harbor/Tremont Chamber of Commerce** (✉ Box 1143, Main St., Southwest Harbor 04679, ☎ 207/244–9264 or 800/423–9264).

WAY DOWN EAST

East of Ellsworth on U.S. 1 is a different Maine, a place pretty much off the beaten path that seduces with a rugged, simple beauty. Red-hued blueberry barrens dot the landscape, and scraggly jack pines hug the highly accessible shoreline. The quiet pleasures include hiking, birding, and going on whale-watching and puffin cruises. Many artists live in the region; you can often purchase works directly from them.

Hancock

44 *9 mi east of Ellsworth.*

As you approach the small town of Hancock and the summer colony of cottages at Hancock Point, stunning views await, especially at sunset, over Frenchman Bay toward Mt. Desert.

Dining and Lodging

$$$$ ✕🏨 **Le Domaine.** Owner-chef Nicole L. Purslow whips up classic French haute cuisine, the perfect accompaniments to which can be found amid the more than 5,000 bottles of French wine in the restaurant's cellar. Le Domaine is known primarily for its food, but its Provence-inspired guest rooms are also inviting; the two suites have fireplaces. Although the building fronts on U.S. 1, the well-equipped rooms open to private decks on porches overlooking the perennial gardens, private

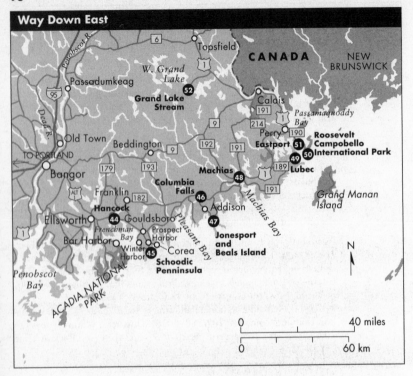

pond, and trails that meander the property's 100 acres, and the building is well insulated to block out road noise. ⊠ *U.S. 1 (HC 77, Box 496), 04640,* ☎ *207/422–3395 or 800/554–8498,* FAX *207/422–2316,* WEB *www.ledomaine.com. 5 rooms, 2 suites. Restaurant, in-room data ports, hiking. AE, D, MC, V. Closed late Oct.–mid-June; restaurant closed Sun.–Mon.. BP, MAP.*

$$$ ✕🖭 **Crocker House Inn.** Set amid tall fir trees, this century-old shingle-style cottage is a mere 200 yards from the water and holds comfortable rooms decorated with antiques and country furnishings. The accommodations in the Carriage House, which also has a TV room and a hot tub, are best for families. The inn's dining room draws Maine residents from as far away as Bar Harbor. ⊠ *Hancock Point Rd. (HC 77, Box 171), 04640,* ☎ *207/422–6806,* FAX *207/422–3105,* WEB *www.acadia.net/crocker. 11 rooms. Restaurant, hot tub, bicycles. AE, D, MC, V. BP.*

$$ 🖭 **Sullivan Harbor Farm.** Antiques and country pieces decorate this simple bed-and-breakfast in an 1829 farmhouse built by Captain James Urann, a shipbuilder who launched his boats across the road. The house, set well back from the road, has nice views of Frenchman Bay and Mount Desert Island. Cottages can be rented by the week. You can relax on the pretty grounds or take a canoe or kayak to the cove across the way. Even if you don't stay here, stop by to purchase some of the award-winning salmon cold-smoked here in the traditional Scottish manner. ⊠ *U.S. 1 (Box 96), 04664,* ☎ *207/422–3735 or 800/422–4014,* FAX *207/422–8229,* WEB *www.sullivanharborfarm.com. 2 rooms; 3 cottages. Boating. D, MC, V. Closed late Oct.–May. BP.*

Nightlife and the Arts

Pierre Monteux School for Conductors (⊠ off U.S. 1, ☎ 207/422–3931) presents orchestral and chamber concerts from mid-June through July.

Shopping

Hog Bay Pottery (⊠ 245 Hog Bay Rd., Franklin, ☎ 207/565–2282) sells pottery by Charles Grosjean and handwoven rugs by Susanne Grosjean. **Spring Woods Gallery** (⊠ 40A Willobrook Ln., Sullivan, ☎ 207/422–3006) carries contemporary art by Paul and Ann Breeden and other artists, as well as Native American pottery, jewelry, and instruments. **Sullivan Harbor Gallery** (⊠ Town Office Building, U.S. 1, ☎ no phone) shows the work of local artisans.

Schoodic Peninsula

45 *23 mi southeast of Hancock; 32 mi east of Ellsworth.*

The landscape of the Schoodic Peninsula makes it easy to understand why the overflow from Bar Harbor's wealthy summer population settled in Winter Harbor: the views over Frenchman's Bay to Mount Desert, the craggy coastline, and the towering evergreens. A drive through the community of Grindstone Neck shows what Bar Harbor might have been like before the Great Fire of 1947. Artists and craftspeople have opened galleries in and around Winter Harbor. No visit to Winter Harbor is complete without a stop at **Gerrish's Store** (⊠ Main St., ☎ 207/963–5575), an old-fashioned ice cream counter.

★ The Schoodic section of **Acadia National Park** (⊠ off Rte. 186, ☎ 207/288–3338), 2 mi east of Winter Harbor, has a scenic 6½-mi one-way loop that edges around the tip of the peninsula and yields views of Winter Harbor, Grindstone Neck, and Winter Harbor Lighthouse. At the tip of the point, huge slabs of pink granite lie jumbled along the shore, thrashed unmercifully by the crashing surf, and jack pines cling to life amid the rocks. The Fraser Point Day-Use Area at the beginning of the loop is an ideal place for a picnic. Work off your lunch with a hike up Schoodic Head for the panoramic views up and down the coast. Admission is free, but there is no visitor center here.

Prospect Harbor, on Route 186 northeast of Winter Harbor, is a small fishing village nearly untouched by tourism. There's little to do in **Corea,** at the tip of Route 195, other than watch the fishermen at work, pick your way over stone beaches, or gaze out to sea—and that's what makes it so special. **Petit Manan National Wildlife Refuge** (⊠ Pigeon Hill Rd. off Rte. 1, ☎ 207/546–2124) is a 2,166-acre refuge of fields, forest, and rocky shorefront on the peninsula east of Schoodic. You can explore the property on two walking trails; the wildlife viewing and bird-watching is renowned. Admission is free, parking is limited.

Dining and Lodging

$$$$ ✕ **Kitchen Garden.** This restaurant just off U.S. 1 in an old Cape-style house is a wonderful surprise. The five-course, fixed-price menu emphasizes organic foods, home-grown produce, and Jamaican specialties. Bring your own wine or beer, and be sure to allow time to stroll through the gardens before dinner. ⊠ *335 Village Rd., Steuben,* ☎ *207/546–2708. Reservations essential. No credit cards. Closed Mon.–Tues. and mid-Oct.–June.*

$$–$$$$ ✕ **Fisherman's Inn.** New owners have greatly improved the food, service, and ambience at this ever-popular establishment. The house specialty is lobster pie, but beef, chicken, seafood, and Italian dishes also appear on the menu. ⊠ *7 Newman St., Winter Harbor,* ☎ *207/963–5585. AE, D, MC, V. Closed mid-Oct.–Memorial Day.*

$–$$ ✕ **West Bay Lobsters in the Rough.** Lobsters, steamers, corn-on-the-cob, coleslaw, baked beans, and homemade blueberry pie are among the offerings. Eat at the outdoor tables or set up a picnic on nearby Schoodic Point. ⊠ *Rte. 186, Prospect Harbor,* ☎ *207/963–7021. AE, D, DC, MC, V. Closed Nov.–May.*

$$–$$$ ★ 🏨 **Oceanside Meadows.** Inspired by the ocean out the front door; fields, woods, and a salt marsh out back; and moose, eagles, and other wildlife, the owners created the Institute for the Arts and Sciences, an environmental center with lectures, musical performances, art shows, and other events held weekly in the barn. Rooms, furnished with antiques, country pieces, and family treasures, are spread out among two white clapboard buildings; many have ocean views. Breakfast is an extravagant multicourse affair. In the off-season, the inn is open only by special arrangement. ✉ *Corea Rd. (Rte. 195), Prospect Harbor 04669,* ☎ *207/963–5557,* FAX *207/963–5928,* WEB *www.oceaninn.com. 12 rooms, 3 suites. No-smoking rooms, croquet, horseshoes, hiking, beach. D, MC, V. Closed Nov. 1–May 1. BP.*

$$ 🏨 **Black Duck.** This small bed-and-breakfast has comfortable public areas and guest rooms, tastefully decorated with antiques and art. Two tiny cottages perch on the harbor. ✉ *Crowley Island Rd., Corea 04624,* ☎ *207/963–2689 or 877/963–2689,* FAX *207/963–7495,* WEB *www.blackduck.com. 2 rooms, 1 suite; 2 cottages. MC, V. BP.*

$ 🏨 **The Pines.** This motel's location, right at the beginning of the Schoodic Point Loop, makes it a good value. New owners have remodeled, adding cottages and log cabins and updating the decor with hand-stitched quilts. Six units have kitchenettes. ✉ *17 Rte. 186, Winter Harbor 04693,* ☎ *207/963–2296,* WEB *www.ayuh.net. 3 rooms, 4 cottages, 2 cabins. Snack bar. MC, V.*

Outdoor Activities and Sports
Moose Look Guide Service (✉ Rte. 186, Gouldsboro, ☎ 207/963–7720) provides kayak tours and rentals, rowboat and canoe rentals, and bike rentals; it also conducts guided fishing trips and all-terrain-vehicle tours.

Shopping
The wines sold at the **Bartlett Maine Estate Winery** (✉ off Rte. 1, Gouldsboro, ☎ 207/546–2408) are produced from locally grown apples, pears, blueberries, and other fruit. The **Harbor Shop** (✉ Newman St., Winter Harbor, ☎ 207/963–4117) shows the work of 80 local artisans. **Lee Art Glass Studio** (✉ Main St., Winter Harbor, ☎ 207/963–7004) carries fused-glass tableware and other items. **Pyramid Glass** (✉ Rte. 186, South Gouldsboro, ☎ 207/963–2027) sells stained-glass artwork and mosaics. **U.S. Bells** (✉ Rte. 186, Prospect Harbor, ☎ 207/963–7184) produces hand-cast bronze wind and door bells.

Columbia Falls

46 *41 mi east of Ellsworth, 78 mi west of Calais.*

Columbia Falls, founded in the late 18th century, is a small, pretty village on the Pleasant River. Once a prosperous shipbuilding center, it still has a number of stately homes dating from that era.

★ Judge Thomas Ruggles, a wealthy lumber dealer, store owner, postmaster, and Justice of the Court of Sessions, built **Ruggles House** in 1818. The house's distinctive Federal architecture, flying staircase, Palladian window, and woodwork were crafted over a period of three years by Massachusetts woodcarver Alvah Peterson with a penknife. ✉ *Main St.,* ☎ *207/483–4637.* 🎫 *$3 donation requested.* ☉ *June 1–Oct. 15 weekdays 9:30–4:30, Sun. 11–4:30.*

Lodging
$ 🏨 **Pleasant Bay Inn and Llama Keep.** This Cape-style inn takes advantage of its riverfront location. You can stroll the nature paths on the property, which winds around a peninsula and out to Pleasant Bay; you can even take a llama with you for company. The rooms, all with water

views, are decorated with antiques and have country touches. ⊠ *West Side Rd. (Box 222), Addison 04606,* ☎ *207/483–4490,* FAX *207/483–4653,* WEB *www.nemaine.com/pleasantbay. 3 rooms, 1 with bath. MC, V. BP.*

Shopping
Columbia Falls Pottery (⊠ Main St., ☎ 207/483–4075) stocks stoneware and a sampling of Maine foods.

Jonesport and Beals Island

❹ *12 mi south of Columbia Falls, 20 mi southwest of Machias.*

Jonesport and Beals Island, two fishing communities joined by a bridge over the harbor, are less polished than the towns on the Schoodic Peninsula. The birding here is superb. **Norton of Jonesport** (☎ 207/497–5933) takes passengers on day trips to Machias Seal Island, where there's a large puffin colony.

Great Wass Island Preserve (☎ 207/729–5181) a 1,540-acre nature conservancy at the tip of Beals Island, protects rare plants, stunted pines, and raised peat bogs. Trails lead through the woods and emerge onto the undeveloped, raw coast, where you can make your way along the rocks and boulders before retreating into the forest. To get to the preserve from Jonesport, cross the bridge over Moosabec Reach to Beals Island. Go through Beals to Great Wass Island. Follow the road, which eventually becomes unpaved, to Black Duck Cove, about 3 mi from Beals, where there is a parking area on the left. Admission is free.

Dining and Lodging
$$–$$$$ ✕ **Seafarer's Wife and Old Salt Room.** These two restaurants share a central kitchen. Allow at least a couple of hours to dine at the Seafarer's Wife, where a five-course meal with main dishes such as a seafood platter and baked stuffed chicken is presented at a leisurely pace in a candlelit dining room. The casual Old Salt Room, open for lunch and dinner, specializes in fresh fish and seafood. Bring your own wine—neither restaurant has a liquor license. ⊠ *Rte. 187, Jonesport,* ☎ *207/497–2365. MC, V. No lunch at the Seafarer's Wife.*

$$ ▦ **Harbor House.** The two spacious rooms on the third floor of this
★   harborfront building have big windows to take in the water view. Both are tastefully furnished with Victorian touches such as cabbage rose wallpaper and Asian-style rugs, and both have separate sleeping and sitting areas. An alcove is stocked with books, coffee, tea, snacks, a small refrigerator, and a telephone. Breakfast is served on the porch, and the owners will prepare a lobster dinner if asked in advance. ⊠ *Box 468, Sawyer Sq., Jonesport 04649,* ☎ *207/497–5417,* FAX *207/497–3211,* WEB *www.harborhs.com. 2 rooms. MC, V. BP.*

$ ▦ **Raspberry Shores.** This comfortably furnished Victorian sits on Main Street, but its backyard slopes down to a small beach on Jonesport Harbor. Rooms in the back of the house share the view, but the nicest room is in the turret and right on the road, which can be noisy. Owner Nan Ellis will prepare a Continental breakfast for guests taking early morning boat trips. ⊠ *Box 409, Rte. 187, Jonesport 04649,* ☎ *207/497–2463 or 877/710–3268,* WEB *www.jonesportmaine.com. 3 rooms without bath. Beach, bicycles, boating. MC, V. Closed Nov.–Apr. BP.*

Machias

❹ *20 mi northeast of Jonesport.*

Machias boasts of being the site of the first naval battle of the Revolutionary War. On June 12, 1775, despite being outnumbered and out-armed, a small group of Machias men under the leadership of Jeremiah O'Brien captured the armed British schooner *Margaretta* in a battle now known as the "Lexington of the Sea." The town's other claim to fame is wild blueberries. The Machias Wild Blueberry Festival, held annually during the third weekend in August, is a true community celebration complete with parade, crafts fair, concerts, and plenty of blueberry dishes. Machias is the county seat of Washington County and is home to a campus of the University of Maine.

★ The **Burnham Tavern Museum,** in a building dating to 1770, details the colorful history of Job Burnham, Mary O'Brien (his wife), and other early residents of the area. It was here that the men of Machias laid the plans that culminated in the capture of the *Margaretta*. ⊠ *Rte. 192,* ☎ *207/255–4432.* ⌨ *$2.* ☉ *Mid-June–late Sept., weekdays 9–5; late Sept.–mid-June, by appointment.*

Although small, the **Art Galleries at the University of Maine at Machias** have a strong selection of paintings by John Marin and other Maine artists. Two galleries showcase rotating exhibitions of works from the permanent collection, the Marin Foundation collection, and visiting shows. Don't miss the William Zorach sculpture just outside the front door. ⊠ *Powers Hall, University of Maine at Machias, 9 O'Brien Ave.,* ☎ *207/255–1200.* ⌨ *Free.* ☉ *Weekdays 10–noon and 2–4.*

Built by Nathan Gates in 1810, the **Gates House** houses the Machiasport Historical Society. It contains an extensive collection of photographs, tools, period furniture, housewares, memorabilia, and a genealogical library. ⊠ *Rte. 92, Machiasport,* ☎ *207/255–8461.* ⌨ *$1 donation.* ☉ *Mid-June–early-Sept., Tues.–Sat. 12:30–4:30.*

The **O'Brien Cemetery** dates from the late 18th century; many of Machias' earliest settlers and heroes are buried here. ⊠ *Bad Little Falls Park off Rte. 92, Machias (Walk through the park toward the water and look for a stairway on your right, which leads to the path. Follow it along the river until you see a white fence on a hill to your right. A small, side path leads to the cemetery.)*

OFF THE
BEATEN PATH   There's no sand in sight at **Jasper Beach,** just smooth, heather-color jasper and rhyolite stones polished by the sea. ℰ *Rte. 92, Buck's Harbor (9.5 miles south of Machias).*

Dining and Lodging

$$–$$$ ✕ **Artist's Cafe.** The white-walled dining rooms in this old house provide a simple backdrop for artwork and creative food. The menu usually has a choice of four entrées such as a catch of the day, a rib-eye steak, and "The Mex," the house vegetarian dish. You might start with Horses Standing Still, handmade Thai dumplings filled with chicken and shrimp and served with a dipping sauce. ⊠ *3 Hill St.,* ☎ *207/255–8900. MC, V. Closed Sun.–Mon.*

$$ ✕🛏 **Riverside Inn & Restaurant.** The Victorian era is captured in the furnishings and linens of this restored sea captain's home overlooking the East Machias River. Suites in the guest house have balconies, and one has a full kitchen. The restaurant ($$), open to the public for dinner Thursday–Saturday, is the best in the area, serving four-course feasts of contemporary American fare by candlelight. ⊠ *U.S. 1 (Box 373), 04630,* ☎ *207/255–4134,* ℻ *207/255–3580,* WEB *www.riversideinn-maine.com. 2 rooms, 2 suites. Restaurant. AE, MC, V. BP.*

Outdoor Activities and Sports

Machias Bay Boat Tours and Sea Kayaking (⊠ Buck's Harbor, Machiasport, ☎ 207/259–3338) operates day trips aboard the *Martha Ann* to see seals, islands and lighthouses, salmon aquaculture, and historical sites. Also offered are guided fishing and sea-kayaking trips.

Lubec

49 *28 mi east of Machias.*

Lubec is the first town in the United States to see the sunrise. Once a thriving shipbuilding and sardine packing site, it now attracts residents and visitors with its rural beauty. Lubec is best appreciated by those who enjoy outdoor pleasures; there are few shops and little entertainment. It also makes a good base for day trips to Campobello Island.

★ **Quoddy Head State Park,** the easternmost point of land in the United States, is marked by candy-striped West Quoddy Head Light. The mystical 2-mi path along the cliffs here yields magnificent views of Canada's Grand Manan island. Whales can often be sighted offshore. The 483-acre park has a picnic area. ✉ *S. Lubec Rd. off Rte. 189,* ☎ *no phone.* 🎫 *$1.* ☼ *Memorial Day–mid-Oct., daily 8–sunset; Apr.–Memorial Day and mid-Oct.–Dec., weekends 9–sunset.*

50 **Roosevelt Campobello International Park,** a joint project of the American and Canadian governments, has hiking trails and historical displays. Neatly manicured Campobello Island has always had a special appeal for the wealthy and famous. It was here that the Roosevelt family spent its summers. The 34-room **Roosevelt Cottage** was presented to Eleanor and Franklin as a wedding gift. The island can be reached by land only by crossing the International Bridge from Lubec. Stop at the information booth for an update on tides—specifically, when you will be able to walk out to East Quoddy Head Lighthouse—and details on walking and hiking trails. Once you've crossed the bridge, you're in the Atlantic time zone. ✉ *Rte. 774, Welshpool, Campobello Island, New Brunswick, Canada,* ☎ *506/752–2922.* 🎫 *Free.* ☼ *House mid-May–mid-Oct., daily 10–6; grounds daily.*

Dining and Lodging

$–$$ ✕🏠 **Home Port Inn.** Lubec's grandest accommodations are in this 1880 Colonial-style house atop a hill. The spacious rooms, some with water views, are furnished with antiques and family pieces. There are two sitting areas, and the living room has a fireplace and a television. The dining room ($$), the best in town, is open to the public for dinner. The weekly changing menu changes emphasizes seafood. ✉ *45 Main St., 04652,* ☎ *207/733–2077 or 800/457–2077,* 🌐 *www.quoddy-loop.com/hpi. 7 rooms. Restaurant. AE, D, MC, V. Closed mid-Oct.–mid-June. CP.*

$ 🏠 **Peacock House.** Four generations of the Peacock family lived in this 1860 Victorian before it was converted into an inn. A few of the simply furnished rooms have water views through lace-curtained windows; rooms on the first floor have air-conditioning. ✉ *27 Summer St., 04652,* ☎ 🖷 *207/733–2403 or 888/305–0036,* 🌐 *www.peacockhouse.com. 2 rooms, 4 suites.. MC, V. Closed Oct. 15–May 15. BP.*

En Route The road to Eastport leads through the Pleasant Point Indian Reservation, where the **Waponahki Museum and Resource Center** explains the culture of the Passamaquoddy, or "People of the Dawn." Tools, baskets, beaded artifacts, historic photos, and arts and crafts are displayed. ✉ *Rte. 190, Perry,* ☎ *207/853–4001.* 🎫 *Free.* ☼ *Weekdays 8:30–11 and noon–4.*

Eastport

⑤ *39 mi north of Lubec, 102 mi east of Ellsworth.*

Eastport is a small island connected to the mainland by a granite causeway. In the late 19th century, 14 sardine canneries operated in Eastport. The decline of that industry in the 20th century has left the city economically depressed, though a new port facility, growing aquaculture, and an increase in tourism bode well for the future. From the waterfront, you can take a ferry to Deer Island and Campobello.

The **National Historic Waterfront District** extends from the Customs House, down Water Street to Bank Square and the Peavey Library. Pick up a walking map at the **Chamber of Commerce** (⌧ 78 Water St., ☎ 207/853–4644) and wander through streets lined with historic homes and buildings. You can also take the waterfront walkway to watch the fishing boats and freighters. The tides fluctuate as much as 28 ft, which explains the ladders and steep gangways necessary to access boats.

Raye's Mustard Mill is the only remaining mill in the U.S. producing stone-ground mustard. Historically, this mill served the sardine-packing industry. You can purchase mustards made on the premises at the mill's Pantry Store; Maine-made crafts and other foods are also for sale. ⌧ *85 Washington St.,* ☎ *207/853–4451 or 800/853–1903.* 🖼 *Free.* ☾ *Jan.–Mar., weekdays 8–5; Apr.–Dec., daily 10–5. Tours on the hr Memorial Day–Labor Day; rest of year subject to guide availability.*

The short hike to **Shakford Head** (⌧ behind Washington County Technical College on Deep Cove Rd.) affords views over Passamaquoddy Bay to Campobello. From here you can see the pens for Eastport's salmon-farming industry as well as the new port facility.

Dining and Lodging

$$–$$$ ✕ **The Cannery.** Fish and seafood don't come much fresher than they do at this restaurant, where the lobsters weigh as much as 3¼ pounds. Unfortunately, neither the service nor the food is reliable. You can eat in the dining room, the downstairs pub, or out on the dock. ⌧ *167 Water St.,* ☎ *207/853–9669. MC, V. Call ahead Oct.–mid-May for hrs.*

$–$$ ✕ **WaCo Diner.** The food here is homestyle Down East, with an emphasis on seafood. You can eat at the counter with the locals, in the new dining room, or on the deck overlooking the water. The service can be slow and the food quality is uneven. ⌧ *Water St. at Bank Square,* ☎ *207/853–4046. MC, V.*

$–$$ 🏨 **Brewer House.** In 1827, Captain John Nehemiah Marks Brewer built an ornate Greek Revival house across from one of his shipyards. Now a B&B, the house is distinguished by such details as carved Grecian moldings, Ionic pilasters, marble fireplaces, silver doorknobs, and an elliptical staircase. ⌧ *U.S. 1 (Box 94), Robbinston 04671,* ☎ *207/454–2385 or 800/821–2028,* ℻ *207/454–8770,* 🌐 *www.brewerhouse.com. 4 rooms, 2 with bath; 1 apartment. MC, V. BP.*

$–$$ 🏨 **Weston House.** A Federal-style home built in 1810, the antiques-★ filled Weston House overlooks Eastport and Passamaquoddy Bay from a prime in-town location. The family room, with a fireplace and a TV, is a casual place to plan the day's activities. An elegant multicourse breakfast is served in the formal dining room, and dinner is available by advance reservation. ⌧ *26 Boynton St., 04631,* ☎ *207/853–2907 or 800/853–2907,* ℻ *207/853–0981,* 🌐 *www.virtualcities.com/me/westonhouse.htm. 4 rooms without bath. No credit cards. BP.*

Outdoor Activities and Sports

East Coast Ferries, Ltd. (☎ 506/747–2159) provides ferry service between Eastport and Deer Island and Deer Island and Campobello from late June to mid-September. **Harris Whale Watching** (⊠ Harris Point Rd., ☎ 207/853–2940 or 207/853–4303) operates three-hour tours. **Tidal Trails** (⊠ Water St., ☎ 207/853–7373) offers boat charters, natural-history tours, and guided bird-watching, canoeing, sea-kayaking, and saltwater-fishing trips.

Shopping

Dog Island Pottery (⊠ 224 Water St., ☎ 207/853–4775) stocks stoneware pottery and local crafts. The **Eastport Gallery** (⊠ 69 Water St., ☎ 207/853–4166) displays works by area artists. **45th Parallel** (⊠ U.S. 1, Perry, ☎ 207/853–9600) stocks an intriguing mix of antiques, crafts, and home furnishing. **Joe's Basket Shop** (⊠ Rte. 190, Pleasant Point, ☎ 207/853–2840) has fancy and coarse (work) baskets and jewelry made by the Passamaquoddy.

Grand Lake Stream

❺❷ *50 mi northwest of Eastport, 108 mi east of Bangor.*

This tiny community, on Grand Lake Stream between West Grand Lake and Big Lake, was once one of the largest tannery centers in the world. Today it's renowned for fishing, especially for land-locked salmon and smallmouth bass, and for the Grand Laker, a stable, square-ended, wooden canoe built specifically for use on the big and often windy lakes in this region. Outdoors-lovers will find lakes and rivers for swimming, boating, and fishing; trails for hiking; and plenty of places to spot wildlife. On the last full weekend of July, the town holds a juried folk arts festival which attracts thousands of visitors.

The tiny **Grand Lake Stream Historical Society & Museum** is jam-packed with artifacts from the town's early days. Here you can learn more about the Grand Laker canoes, the town's tannery years, and its fishing heritage. ☎ 207/796–5562. ▣ *Donation accepted.* ☉ *By chance or appt.*

Lodging

$$$$ 🏨 **Leen's Lodge.** Ten rustic cabins varying in size from one to four bedrooms are nestled on 23 wooded acres on West Grand Lake. Three have kitchens, and all have woodstoves or fireplaces and big windows to take in the views. A country-style breakfast and a hearty, homestyle dinner are served in a central lodge, where you'll also find a TV/VCR, card tables, books, and games. The lodge can arrange guided fishing trips, wildlife or photographic safaris, and other excursions. Boat rentals are available. ⊠ *Box 40, 04637,* ☎ *207/796–5575 or 800/995–3367,* WEB *www.leenslodge.com. 10 cabins. Kitchenettes (some), hiking, beach, boating, recreation room. MC, V. Closed Nov.–Apr. MAP.*

$$$$ 🏨 **Weatherby's.** Nicknamed "the fishermen's resort," Weatherby's is ideal for those who want to be in the center of the action in Grand Lake Stream. Fifteen cottages, each with an open brick or Franklin fireplace, surround the main lodge, where guests take breakfast and dinner daily. Lunch is available upon request. The main lodge also has a library, television, and piano. ⊠ *Grand Lake Stream 04637,* ☎ *207/796–5558,* WEB *www.weatherbys.com, 15 cottages. MC, V. Closed mid-Oct–Apr. MAP.*

Outdoor Activities and Sports

The **Grand Lake Stream Guides Association** (☎ 506/796–5207) maintains more than 25 lunch sites on area lakes. Guides offer fishing, family, boating, hiking, photographic, and wildlife trips.

Shopping

Shamel Boat & Canoe Works (⊠ Tough End Road, ☎ 207/796–8199) specializes in building canoes.

Way Down East A to Z

To research prices, get advice from other travelers, and book travel arrangements, visit www.fodors.com.

BOAT & FERRY TRAVEL

East Coast Ferries, Ltd. provides ferry service between Eastport and Deer Island and Deer Island and Campobello from late June to mid-September.

➤ BOAT & FERRY INFORMATION: **East Coast Ferries, Ltd.** (☎ 506/747–2159).

CAR TRAVEL

U.S. 1 is the primary coastal route, with smaller roads leading to the towns on the long fingers of land in this region. Route 182 is a pleasant inland route; Route 186 loops through the Schoodic Peninsula. The most direct route to Lubec is Route 189, but Route 191, between East Machias and West Lubec, is a scenic coastal drive.

TOURS

Quoddy Air has scenic flights. Scenic Island Tours offers tours of Eastport in a 1947 Dodge Woody bus. Picnic lunches with smoked salmon are available.

➤ TOUR OPERATORS: **Quoddy Air** (⊠ Eastport Municipal Airport, County Rd., Eastport, ☎ 207/853–0997). **Scenic Island Tours** (⊠ 37 Washington St., Eastport, ☎ 207/853–2840).

VISITOR INFORMATION

➤ CONTACTS: **Eastport Area Chamber of Commerce** (⊠ Box 254, 78 Water St., 04631, ☎ 207/853–4644). **Lubec Area Chamber of Commerce** (⊠ Box 123, 04652, ☎ 207/733–4522). **Machias Bay Area Chamber of Commerce** (⊠ Box 606, 378 Main St., 04654, ☎ 207/255–4402). **Quoddy Coastal Tourism Association of New Brunswick and Maine** (⊠ Box 1171, St. Andrews, New Brunswick, Canada E0G 2X0, ☎ 800/377–9748). **Schoodic Peninsula Chamber of Commerce** (⊠ Box 381, Winter Harbor 04693, ☎ no phone).

WESTERN LAKES AND MOUNTAINS

Less than 20 mi northwest of Portland and the coast, the sparsely populated lake and mountain areas of western Maine stretch north along the New Hampshire border to Québec. In winter this is ski country; in summer the woods and waters draw vacationers.

The Sebago–Long Lake region bustles with activity in the summer. Harrison and the Waterfords are quieter. Bridgton attracts lake visitors in summer and skiers in winter, while Lovell is a dreamy escape. Kezar Lake, tucked away in a fold of the White Mountains, has long been a hideaway of the wealthy. Children's summer camps dot the region. Bethel, in the Androscoggin River valley, is a classic New England town, its town common lined with historic homes. The more rural Rangeley Lake area brings long stretches of pine, beech, spruce, and sky—and stylish inns and bed-and-breakfasts with access to golf, boating, fishing, and hiking. Snow sports, especially snowmobiling, are popular winter pastimes. Carrabassett Valley, just north of Kingfield, is home to Sugarloaf/USA, a major ski resort with a challenging golf course.

Sebago Lake

53 *17 mi northwest of Portland.*

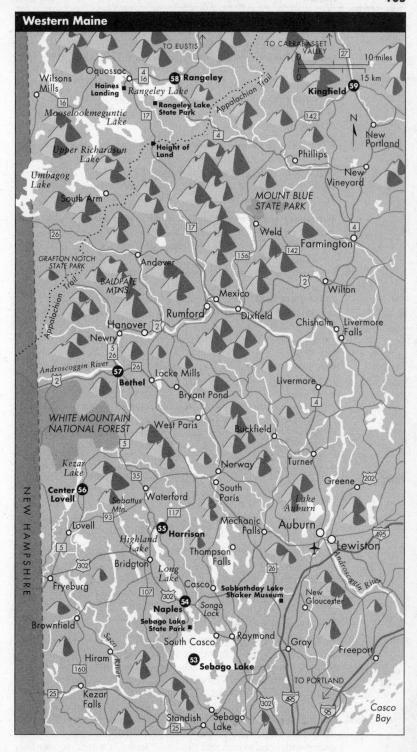

TO EUSTIS

TO CARRABASSET VALLEY

27

10 miles

0

0

15 km

Wilsons Mills

Oquossoc

4
16

58 **Rangeley**

Kingfield **59**

Haines Landing

Rangeley Lake

142

New Portland

16

Mooselookmeguntic Lake

17

Rangeley Lake State Park

Appalachian Trail

N

Upper Richardson Lake

4

Height of Land

Phillips

New Vineyard

Umbagog Lake

South Arm

MOUNT BLUE STATE PARK

26

17

156

Weld

4

Farmington

GRAFTON NOTCH STATE PARK

Andover

142

Wilton

Appalachian Trail

BALDPATE MTNS

Mexico

2

Rumford

Dixfield

Chisholm

Livermore Falls

Hanover

2

Newry

5
26

Livermore

Androscoggin River

57

26

Locke Mills

4

Bethel

Bryant Pond

WHITE MOUNTAIN NATIONAL FOREST

West Paris

Buckfield

5

Kezar Lake

35

Norway

Turner

Greene

202

Center Lovell **56**

Waterford

Sabattus Mtn.

South Paris

Lake Auburn

93

117

Lovell

Mechanic Falls

Auburn

5

55 **Harrison**

Highland Lake

Thompson Falls

Lewiston

495

NEW HAMPSHIRE

Bridgton

302

26

Long Lake

Casco

Fryeburg

107

302

Sabbathday Lake Shaker Museum

New Gloucester

Androscoggin River

Brownfield

Naples **54**

Songo Lock

Sebago Lake State Park

Raymond

Gray

Freeport

Hiram

Saco River

South Casco

160

53 **Sebago Lake**

TO PORTLAND

25

Kezar Falls

Standish

Sebago Lake

25

302

495

95

Casco Bay

Sebago Lake, which provides all the drinking water for Greater Portland, is Maine's best-known lake after Moosehead (☞ The North Woods). Many camps and year-round homes surround Sebago, which is popular with water-sports enthusiasts. At the north end of the lake, the **Songo Lock** (☎ 207/693–6231), which permits the passage of watercraft from Sebago Lake to Long Lake, is the lone surviving lock of the Cumberland and Oxford Canal. Built of wood and masonry, the original lock dates to 1830 and was expanded in 1911; today it sees heavy traffic in summer.

The 1,300-acre **Sebago Lake State Park** on the north shore of the lake provides opportunities for swimming, picnicking, camping (250 sites), boating, and fishing (salmon and togue). ⊠ *11 Park Access Rd., Casco,* ☎ *207/693–6613 May–mid-Oct.; 207/693–6231 mid-Oct.–Apr.* 🖾 *$2.50.* ☉ *Daily 9–8.*

The **Jones Museum of Glass & Ceramics** houses more than 7,000 glass, pottery, stoneware, and porcelain objects from around the world. Also on the premises are a research library and gift shop. ⊠ *35 Douglas Mountain Rd., off Rte. 107. Sebago,* ☎ *207/787–3370.* 🖾 *$5.* ☉ *Mid-May–mid-Nov., Mon.–Sat. 10–5, Sun. 1–5; tours by appointment.*

OFF THE
BEATEN PATH   **SABBATHDAY LAKE SHAKER MUSEUM** – Established in the late 18th century, this is the last active Shaker community in the United States. Members continue to farm crops and herbs, and you can see the meetinghouse of 1794—a paradigm of Shaker design—and the ministry shop with 14 rooms of Shaker furniture, folk art, tools, farm implements, and crafts from the 18th to the early 20th century. There is also a small gift shop, but don't expect to find furniture or other large Shaker items. On the busy road out front, a farmer usually has summer and fall vegetables for sale. In autumn, he sells cider, apples, and pumpkins. ⊠ *707 Shaker Rd. (Rte. 26), New Gloucester (20 mi north of Portland, 12 mi east of Naples),* ☎ *207/926–4597.* 🖾 *Tour $6, extended tour $7.50.* ☉ *Memorial Day–Columbus Day, Mon.–Sat. 10–4:30.*

Naples

54 *32 mi northwest of Portland.*

Naples swells with seasonal residents and visitors in summer. The town occupies an enviable location between Long and Sebago lakes.

🌀 **Songo River Queen II,** a 92-ft stern-wheeler, takes passengers on hour-long cruises on Long Lake and longer voyages down the Songo River and through Songo Lock. ⊠ *U.S. 302, Naples Causeway,* ☎ *207/693–6861.* 🖾 *Long Lake cruise $8, Songo River ride $11.* ☉ *July–Labor Day, daily at 9:45, 1, 2:30, 3:45, 7; call for spring and fall hrs.*

Dining and Lodging

$$–$$$ ✕ **Bistro du Lac.** The country French fare and reasonable fixed-price menu have made this restaurant in a big red farmhouse a popular choice. A four-course dinner for two, including a bottle of wine, is $49. Among the entrées are salmon with caramelized leeks, chicken with tarragon sauce, and filet mignon. ⊠ *U.S. 302 and Rte. 85, Raymond,* ☎ *207/655–4100. AE, D, MC, V. Closed Mon.–Wed. No lunch.*

$$$$ 🏨 **Migis Lodge.** The lodge's pine-panel cottages, scattered among 100 shorefront acres, have fieldstone fireplaces and are handsomely furnished with braided rugs and handmade quilts. A warm, woodsy feeling pervades the main inn. The deck has views (marvelous at sunset) of Sebago Lake. All kinds of outdoor and indoor activities are included in the room rate, and canoes, kayaks, and sailboats are available.

Guests gather in the main dining room for three fancy meals daily. ⊠ *Box 40, Migis Lodge Rd., off U.S. 302, South Casco 04077,* ☎ *207/ 655–4524,* FAX *207/655–2054,* WEB *www.migis.com. 29 cottages, 6 rooms. Dining room, 2 tennis courts, exercise room, beach, boating, waterskiing, fishing, playground. No credit cards. FAP.*

$$–$$$ 🏠 **Augustus Bove House.** Built as the Hotel Naples in the 1820s, this rambling brick B&B sits across from the Naples Causeway and has views down Long Lake. Rooms are furnished with antiques and a television. ⊠ *Box 501, R.R. 1, U.S. 302, 04055,* ☎ *207/693–6365,* WEB *www.maineguide.com/naples/augustus. 10 rooms, 7 with bath; 1 suite. Air-conditioning, hot tub. AE, D, MC, V. BP.*

Outdoor Activities and Sports

U.S. 302 cuts through Naples, and in the center at the Naples Causeway are rental craft for fishing or cruising. Sebago, Long, and Rangeley lakes are popular areas for sailing and motorboating. For boat rentals, try **Mardon Marine** (⊠ U.S. 302, ☎ 207/693–6264). **Naples Marina** (⊠ U.S. 302 and Rte. 114, ☎ 207/693–6254) rents motorboats. **Long Lake Marina** (⊠ U.S. 302, ☎ 207/693–3159) rents fishing boats and canoes.

Shopping

The **Cry of the Loon** (⊠ U.S. 302, South Casco, ☎ 207/655–5060) complex includes a gift shop, The Nest country home-furnishings shop, and the Barn, which carries specialty foods, nautical gifts, and other items.

Harrison

⑤⑤ *10 mi north of Naples, 25 mi south of Bethel.*

Harrison anchors the northern end of Long Lake but is less commercial than Naples. The combination of woods, lakes, and views makes it a good choice for leaf-peepers. The nearby towns of North Waterford, South Waterford, and tiny Waterford, a National Historic District, are ideal for outdoors-lovers who prefer to get away from the crowds.

Lodging

$$ 🏠 **Bear Mountain Inn.** After swimming at the private beach on Bear ★ Lake or hiking up Bear Mountain (across the street), it's nice to return to this rambling farmhouse inn, which the owner has meticulously decorated in a woodsy theme. The luxurious Great Grizzly Suite has a fireplace, whirlpool bath for two, and mesmerizing views, while the cozy Sugar Bear Cottage is a romantic retreat. A gourmet breakfast with an emphasis on organic ingredients is served in the dining room, which has a fieldstone fireplace and views over the lake. ⊠ *Rte. 35, South Waterford 04081,* ☎ FAX *207/583–4404,* WEB *www.bearmtninn.com. 6 rooms, 2 with bath; 3 suites; 1 cottage. Badminton, croquet, horseshoes, volleyball, beach, boating, fishing, ice-skating, cross-country skiing, snowmobiling. MC, V. BP.*

$$ 🏠 **Harrison House.** When it was built in 1867, this house at the head of Long Lake was one of the most costly and elegant residences in town. Today it charms guests with feather beds, quilts, and a porch swing. The living room, dining room, and three guest rooms have lake views. All rooms have private baths, but four of the baths are adjacent to or across the hall from the rooms. ⊠ *16 Waterford Rd., 04040,* ☎ *207/ 583–6564,* WEB *www.megalink.net/~hrsnbnb. 5 rooms. AE, MC, V. BP.*

$$ 🏠 **Waterford Inne.** This gold-painted house on a hilltop provides a good home base for trips to lakes, ski trails, and antiques shops. The bedrooms have lots of nooks and crannies. The Nantucket, with a whale motif, and the Chesapeake, with a private porch and a fireplace, are the nicest. A converted woodshed holds five additional rooms, and though they have less character than the rooms in the inn, four have sunny decks. ✉ *Box 149, 258 Chadbourne Rd., Waterford 04088,* ☎ FAX *207/583–4037. 8 rooms, 6 with bath; 1 suite. Ice-skating, cross-country skiing. AE. Closed Apr. BP.*

Nightlife and the Arts
From late June through Labor Day, **Deertrees Theater and Cultural Center** (✉ Deertrees Rd. off Rte. 117, ☎ 207/583–6747) stages musicals, dramas, dance performances, shows for children, concerts, and other events in a theater listed on the National Register of Historic Places.

Outdoor Activities and Sports
Mutiny Brook Stables (✉ Sweden Rd., South Waterford, ☎ 207/583–6650) outfits horseback tours in the Maine woods.

Center Lovell

⑤⑥ *17 mi northwest of Harrison, 28 mi south of Bethel.*

At Center Lovell you can barely glimpse the secluded Kezar Lake to the west, the retreat of wealthy and very private people. Sabattus Mountain, which rises behind Center Lovell, has a public hiking trail and stupendous views of the Presidential Range from the summit.

Dining and Lodging
$$$$ ✕▥ **Quisisana.** Music-lovers may think they've found heaven on earth at this delightful resort on Kezar Lake. After dinner, the staff—students and graduates of some of the country's finest music schools—perform everything from Broadway tunes to concert piano pieces at the music hall. White cottages have pine interiors and cheerful decor. One night dinner might be lobster and blueberry pie; the next night the choice might be saddle of lamb with a black-olive tapenade or salmon-and-leek roulade. For most of the resort's season, a one-week stay beginning Saturday is required. ✉ *Pleasant Point Rd., 04016,* ☎ *207/925–3500,* FAX *207/925–1004 in season,* WEB *www.quisisanaresort.com. 11 rooms in 2 lodges, 32 cottages. Restaurant, 3 tennis courts, windsurfing, boating, waterskiing. Closed Sept.–mid-June. FAP.*

$–$$ ✕▥ **Center Lovell Inn.** The current owners won this rambling, old-fashioned country inn in an essay contest in 1993. The eclectic decor blends furnishings from the mid-19th to mid-20th centuries in a pleasing, homey style. The best tables for dining are on the wraparound porch, which has sunset views over Kezar Lake and the White Mountains. Entrées may include veal scaloppini, chateaubriand, or chicken breast toscano. Rooms are upstairs and in the adjacent Harmon House. ✉ *Rte. 5 (Box 261) 04016,* ☎ *207/925–1575 or 800/777–2698,* WEB *www.centerlovellinn.com. 9 rooms, 4 with shared bath. Restaurant. D, MC, V. Nov.–late-Dec. and Apr.–mid-May. EP, MAP.*

Outdoor Activities and Sports
BOATING AND FISHING
For guided fishing trips, call **Carl Bois** (☎ 207/925–6262) in Lovell. **Kezar Lake Marina** (✉ West Lovell Rd. at The Narrows, Lovell, ☎ 207/925–3000) rents boats.

CANOEING
Two scenic canoeing routes on the Saco River (near Fryeburg) are the gentle stretch from Swan's Falls to East Brownfield (19 mi) and from East Brownfield to Hiram (14 mi). For rentals, try **Saco River Canoe and Kayak** (✉ Rte. 5, Fryeburg, ☎ 207/935–2369).

DOGSLEDDING
Winter Journeys (☎ 207/928–2026) in Lovell operates half- and full-day dog-sledding trips.

Bethel

57 *28 mi north of Lovell, 66 mi north of Portland.*

Bethel is pure New England, a town with white clapboard houses and white-steeple churches and a mountain vista at the end of every street. The architecture here is something to behold. In winter this is ski country: Bethel is a few miles south of Sunday River in Newry. Sunday River has plenty of action in summer, too.

A stroll in Bethel should begin at the **Moses Mason House and Museum,** a Federal home of 1813. The museum, on the town common across from the Bethel Inn and Country Club, has nine period rooms and a front hall and stairway wall decorated with murals by Rufus Porter. It is part of the Bethel Regional Historical Center, which has local history exhibits. You can pick up materials here for a walking tour of Bethel Hill Village, most of which is on the National Register of Historic Places. ⊠ *14 Broad St.,* ☎ *207/824–2908 or 800/824–2910.* ⌚ *$3.* ☉ *July–Labor Day, Tues.–Sun. 1–4; Labor Day–June, Tues.–Fri., 1–4.*

The **Major Gideon Hastings House** on Broad Street has a columned-front portico typical of the Greek Revival style. The severe white **West Parish Congregational Church** (1847), with an unadorned triangular pediment and a steeple supported on open columns, is on Church Street, around the common from the Major Gideon Hastings House. The campus of **Gould Academy** (⊠ Church St., ☎ 207/824–7777), a preparatory school, opened its doors in 1835; the dominant style of the school buildings is Georgian.

Dining and Lodging

$$$$ ✕🖼 **Victoria Inn.** It's hard to miss this turreted inn, with its beige-,
★ mauve-, and teal-painted exterior and attached carriage house topped with a cupola. Inside, Victorian details include ceiling rosettes, stained-glass windows, elaborate fireplace mantels, and gleaming oak trim. Guest rooms vary in size and decor; most are furnished with reproductions of antiques. One-bedroom-with-loft units in the carriage house are perfect for families. The restaurant, open to the public for dinner ($$–$$$; closed Monday), has three rooms, one with a wraparound mural of Italian scenes. The menu lists entrées such as beef tenderloin au poivre and rack of lamb. A children's menu is available. Rates for inn guests include a full breakfast and four-course dinner. ⊠ *32 Main St. (Box 249) 04217,* ☎ *207/824–8060 or 888/774–1235,* ℻ *207/824–3926,* 🌐 *www.victoria-inn.com. 15 rooms. Restaurant. MC, V. MAP.*

$–$$ ✕🖼 **Briar Lea.** Both children and pets are welcome at this Georgian-style inn. You can snuggle under a down comforter at night in rooms decorated in a warm and inviting country style. The dining room is open to the public for breakfast and dinner. Entrées ($–$$) may include pork chops, rainbow trout, and crispy roast duck. A children's menu is available. ⊠ *150 Mayville Rd./Rte. 2 04217,* ☎ *207/824–4717 or 877/311–1299,* ℻ *207/824–7121. 6 rooms. Restaurant, air-conditioning, no-smoking rooms. AE, D, MC, V. Restaurant closed Tues. Nov.–late Dec. and mid-Apr.–mid-June. BP.*

$$$$ 🖼 **Bethel Inn and Country Club.** Bethel's grandest accommodation, a full-service resort that includes 40 km (25 mi) of cross-country ski trails, delivers an uneven experience. Rooms in the new wing of the main inn are spacious, many with fireplaces and whirlpool tubs in the baths. Some rooms in the main section of the inn have been completely renovated; others have been spruced up with new drapes and bedding but have tiny, old-fashioned baths and peeling paint. Housekeeping, too, could be more meticulous. Winter guests will find the clanky steam heating difficult to control. Lobster specialties and updated Continental dishes are highlights of the restaurant menu. ✉ *Box 49, Village Common, 04217,* ☎ *207/824–2175 or 800/654–0125,* FAX *207/824–2233,* WEB *www.bethelinn.com. 49 rooms, 9 suites, 40 condo units. Restaurant, bar, pool, 18-hole golf course, tennis court, health club, cross-country skiing, meeting room. AE, D, DC, MC, V. MAP.*

$$$ 🏨 **Jordan Grand Resort Hotel.** A hit with Sunday River skiers, this condominium hotel provides ski-in, ski-out access to the Jordan Bowl trails. Most units have kitchenettes, and there's a heated outdoor pool to relax in after a day on the slopes. ✉ *Box 450, 1 Grand Circle, off Skiway Rd. and U.S. 2, Newry 04217,* ☎ *207/824–5000 or 800/543–2754,* FAX *207/824–5399. 195 condominiums. 2 restaurants, café, pool, health club, baby-sitting, meeting room. AE, D, MC, V.*

$$$ 🏨 **Sunday River Inn.** This homey chalet on the Sunday River ski-area access road has private rooms for families and dorm rooms (bring your sleeping bag) for groups and students, all within easy access of the slopes. A hearty breakfast and dinner are served buffet-style, and a stone hearth dominates the comfortable living room. The inn operates an excellent ski-touring center. ✉ *19 Skiway Rd., Newry 04261,* ☎ *207/824–2410,* FAX *207/824–3181,* WEB *www.sundayriverinn.com. 19 rooms; 3 with private bath; 5 dorms with shared bath. Restaurant, pool, hot tub, sauna, exercise room, cross-country skiing, downhill skiing. AE, MC, V. Closed Apr.–late-Nov. MAP.*

Nightlife and the Arts

Sunday River nightlife is spread out between the mountain and downtown Bethel. For a quiet evening, head to the piano bar at the **Bethel Inn and Country Club** (✉ Village Common, ☎ 207/824–2175). At Sunday River, the **Bumps Pub** (✉ Whitecap Lodge, ☎ 207/824–5269) has après-ski and evening entertainment. Tuesday night is comedy night, ski movies are shown on Wednesday, and bands play on weekends and holidays. **Sunday River Brewing Company** (✉ U.S. 2, ☎ 207/824–4253) has pub fare and live entertainment—usually progressive rock bands—on weekends. The **Sudbury Inn** (✉ 151 Main St., ☎ 207/824–2174) is popular for après-ski and has music that tends toward the blues.

Outdoor Activities and Sports

CANOEING

Bethel Outdoor Adventures (✉ 121 Mayville Rd., ☎ 207/824–4224) rents canoes, kayaks, bikes, and snowmobiles.

DOGSLEDDING

Mahoosuc Guide Service (✉ Bear River Rd., Newry, ☎ 207/824–2073) leads day and multiday dogsledding expeditions on the Maine–New Hampshire border.

HIKING

Telemark Inn & Llama Treks (✉ King's Hwy., Mason Township, ☎ 207/836–2703) operates one- to six-day llama-supported hiking trips in the White Mountain National Forest.

NATIONAL FORESTS AND PARKS

White Mountain National Forest straddles New Hampshire and Maine. Although the highest peaks are on the New Hampshire side, the Maine section has magnificent rugged terrain, camping and picnic areas, and hiking opportunities from hour-long nature loops to a 5½-hour scramble up Speckled Mountain. ✉ *Evans Notch Visitor Center, 18 Mayville Rd., 04217,* ☎ *207/824–2134.* 🅿 *Parking pass (good 1–7 days) $5.* 🕐 *Center early May–mid-Oct., daily 8–5; mid-Oct.–early May, daily 8:30–4:30.*

At **Grafton Notch State Park** (✉ Rte. 26, 14 mi north of Bethel, ☎ 207/824–2912) you can take an easy nature walk to Mother Walker Falls or Moose Cave and see the spectacular Screw Auger Falls, or you can hike to the summit of Old Speck Mountain, the state's third-highest peak. If you have the stamina and the equipment, you can pick up the Appalachian Trail here, hike over Saddleback Mountain, and continue on to Katahdin. The **Maine Appalachian Trail Club** (⊠ Box 283, Augusta 04330) publishes a map and trail guide.

Shopping

Bonnema Potters (⊠ 146 Lower Main St., ☎ 207/824–2821) sells plates, lamps, tiles, and vases in colorful modern designs. The **Lyons' Den** (⊠ U.S. 2, Hanover, ☎ 207/364–8634), a great barn of a place near Bethel, stocks antique glass, china, tools, prints, rugs, hand-wrought iron, and some furniture. **Mt. Mann Jewelers** (⊠ 57 Maine Street Pl., ☎ 207/824–3030) carries contemporary jewelry with unusual gems.

Ski Areas

SUNDAY RIVER

In the 1980s, Sunday River was a sleepy little ski area with minimal facilities. Today it's a sprawling resort that attracts skiers from as far away as Europe. Spread throughout the valley are three base areas, two condominium hotels, trailside condominiums, town houses, and a ski dorm. Sunday River is home to the Maine Handicapped Skiing program, which provides lessons and services for skiers with disabilities. There's plenty of summer action here, too. ⊠ *Sunday River Rd. off U.S. 2, Newry (Box 450, Bethel 04217), ☎ 207/824–3000; 207/824– 5200 snow conditions; 800/543–2754 reservations.*

Downhill. White Heat has gained fame as the steepest, longest, widest lift-served trail in the East; but skiers of all abilities will find plenty of suitable terrain, from a 5-km (3-mi) beginner run to steep glades, in-your-face bumps, and terrain parks. The area has 127 trails, the majority of them in the intermediate range. Expert and advanced runs are grouped from the peaks, and most beginner slopes are near the base. Trails spreading down from eight peaks have a total vertical descent of 2,340 ft and are served by nine quads, four triples, and two double chairlifts and three surface lifts.

Other activities. The Entertainment Center at White Cap has a lighted halfpipe, a lighted ice-skating rink, a tubing area, a teen center, and a nightclub with live music.

Child care. There are three licensed day-care centers for children from ages 6 weeks to 6 years. Coaching for children from ages 3 to 18 is available in the Children's Center at the South Ridge base area.

Summer and year-round activities. Within the housing complexes are indoor pools, outdoor heated pools, saunas, hot tubs, and 4 tennis courts. In summer, the Mountain Adventure Center attracts families with its water slides, climbing wall, BMX park, and in-line skating park, as well as hiking and mountain biking.

CROSS-COUNTRY SKIING

Bethel Inn Touring Center (⊠ Village Common, ☎ 207/824–6276) has 40 km (25 mi) of trails and offers ski and snowshoe rentals and lessons. **Carter's Cross-Country Ski Center** (⊠ 786 Intervale Rd., ☎ 207/539– 4848) offers 50 km (31 mi) for all levels of skiers; a center in Oxford has 35 km (22 mi) of trails for novice and intermediate skiing. Both centers provide lessons and snowshoe, ski, and sled rentals. **Sunday River Cross-Country Ski Center** (⊠ 23 Skiway Rd., Newry, ☎ 207/824– 2410), based at the Sunday River Inn, has 40 km (25 mi) of trails; all are tracked and most have skating lanes. A special trail is designated for skiing with dogs. Lessons and rentals are available.

En Route The routes north from Bethel to the Rangeley district are all scenic, particularly in the autumn when the maples are aflame with color. In the town of Newry, make a short detour to the **Artist's Bridge** (turn off Route 26 onto Sunday River Road and drive about 3 mi), the most painted and photographed of Maine's eight covered bridges. Route 26 continues north to the gorges and waterfalls of **Grafton Notch State Park.** Past the park, Route 26 continues to Errol, New Hampshire, where Route 16 will return you east around the north shore of Mooselookmeguntic Lake, through Oquossoc, and into Rangeley. A more direct route (if marginally less scenic) from Bethel to Rangeley still allows a stop in Newry. Follow U.S. 2 north and east from Bethel to the twin towns of Rumford and Mexico, where Route 17 continues north to Oquossoc, about an hour's drive. When you've driven for about 20 minutes beyond Rumford, the signs of civilization all but vanish and you pass through what seems like untouched territory—though the lumber companies have long since tackled the virgin forests, and sporting camps and cottages are tucked away here and there. The high point of this route is **Height of Land,** about 30 mi north of Rumford, with its unforgettable views of range after range of mountains and the island-studded blue mass of Mooselookmeguntic Lake directly below. Turnouts on both sides of the highway allow you to pull over for a long look. **Haines Landing** on Mooselookmeguntic Lake lies 7 mi west of Rangeley. Here you can stand at 1,400 ft above sea level and face the same magnificent scenery you admired at 2,400 ft from Height of Land on Route 17. Boat and canoe rentals are available at Mooselookmeguntic House.

Rangeley

⑤ *67 mi north of Bethel.*

Rangeley, north of Rangeley Lake on Route 4/16, has long lured anglers, hunters, and winter-sports enthusiasts to its more than 40 lakes and ponds and 450 square mi of woodlands. Equally popular in summer or winter, Rangeley has a rough, wilderness feel to it. Lodgings are in the woods, around the lake, and along the golf course.

The **Wilhelm Reich Museum** interprets the life and work of controversial physician-scientist Wilhelm Reich (1897–1957), who believed that a force called orgone energy was the source of neurosis. The Orgone Energy Observatory, designed for Reich in 1948, exhibits biographical materials, inventions, and the equipment used in his experiments. Also on view are Reich's library, personal memorabilia, and artwork. Trails lace the 175-acre grounds, and the observatory deck has magnificent views of the countryside. ✉ *Dodge Pond Rd.,* ☎ *207/864–3443,* WEB *www.somtel.com/~wreic.* ✇ *$4.* ⊙ *July–Aug., Wed.–Sun. 1–5; Sept., Sun. 1–5.*

OFF THE   **SANDY RIVER & RANGELEY LAKES RAILROAD** – You can ride a mile
BEATEN PATH through the woods along a narrow-gauge railroad on a century-old train drawn by a replica of the *Sandy River No. 4* locomotive. ✉ *Bridge Hill Rd., Phillips (20 mi southeast of Rangeley),* ☎ *207/778–3621,* WEB *www.srrl-rr.org.* ✇ *$3.* ⊙ *June–Oct., 1st and 3rd Sun. each month; rides hourly 11–3.*

Dining and Lodging

$$–$$$ ✕ **Gingerbread House.** A big fieldstone fireplace, well-spaced tables, and an antique marble soda fountain, all with views to the woods beyond, make for a comfortable atmosphere at this gingerbread-trim house, which is open for breakfast, lunch, and dinner. Soups, salads, and sandwiches at lunch give way to entrées such as shrimp scampi, roasted cran-

berry-maple chicken and Maine crab cakes. ✉ *Rtes. 17 and 4, Oquossoc,* ☎ *207/864–3602. AE, D, MC, V. Closed Mon. No dinner Sun.*

$$–$$$ ✗ **Porter House Restaurant.** This popular restaurant, seemingly in the middle of nowhere, draws diners from Rangeley, Kingfield, and Canada with its good service, excellent food, and casual atmosphere. Of the 1908 farmhouse's four dining rooms, the front one downstairs, which has a fireplace, is the most intimate and elegant. The broad Continental-style menu includes entrées for diners with light appetites. On the heavier side are porterhouse steak and roast duckling. Try the boneless lamb loin and lobster Brittany casserole if they're on the menu. ✉ *Rte. 27, Eustis (20 mi north of Rangeley)* ☎ *207/246–7932. Reservations essential. AE, D, MC, V. Closed Mon.–Tues.*

$$ ✗🏨 **Country Club Inn.** Built in the 1920s on the Mingo Springs Golf Course, this retreat is favored with a secluded hilltop location and sweeping lake and mountain views. The inn's baronial living room has a cathedral ceiling, a fieldstone fireplace at each end, and game trophies. Rooms downstairs in the main building and in the motel-style wing added in the 1950s are cheerfully if minimally decorated. The glassed-in dining room ($$)—open to nonguests by reservation only—has linen-draped tables set well apart. On the menu are mostly contemporary dishes using duck, veal, fresh fish, and filet mignon. ✉ *Box 680, Mingo Loop Rd., 04970,* ☎ *207/864–3831,* 🌐 *www.rangeley-maine.com/ccinn. 19 rooms. Restaurant, pub, pool, 18-hole golf course. AE, MC, V. Closed Apr.–mid-May and mid-Oct.–late-Dec. BP, MAP.*

$$ ✗🏨 **Rangeley Inn and Motor Lodge.** From Main Street you see only the three-story blue inn building (circa 1907), but behind it is a newer motel wing with views of Haley Pond, a lawn, and a garden. Some of the inn's sizable rooms have iron-and-brass beds and subdued wallpaper, some have claw-foot tubs, and others have whirlpool tubs. The dining room ($$$), open for dinner, has Continental-style choices including bouillabaisse, fresh fish, and New Zealand rack of lamb. The tavern serves casual fare such as soups, sandwiches, steaks, and ribs. You can choose to include breakfast and dinner in the rate. ✉ *Box 160, 51 Main St., 04970,* ☎ *207/864–3341 or 800/666–3687,* 📠 *207/864–3634,* 🌐 *www.rangeleyinn.com. 36 inn rooms, 15 motel rooms, 2 cabins. Restaurant, bar, meeting room. AE, D, MC, V.*

$$$$ 🏨 **Grant's Kennebago Camps.** People have been roughing it in comfort at this traditional sporting camp on Kennebago Lake for more than 85 years, lured by the mountain views, excellent fly-fishing, and hearty home-cooked meals. The wilderness setting is nothing less than spectacular. The cabins, whose screened porches overlook the lake, have woodstoves and are finished in knotty pine. Meals are served in the cheerful waterfront dining room. Motorboats, canoes, sailboats, Windsurfers, and mountain bikes are available; floatplane rides and fly-fishing instruction can be arranged. ✉ *Box 786, off Rte. 16, 04970,* ☎ *207/864–3608 in summer; 207/282–5264 in winter; 800/633–4815,* 🌐 *www.grantscamps.com. 18 cabins. Dining room, lake, hiking, boating, fishing, mountain bikes, baby-sitting, playground. MC, V. Closed Oct.–late May. FAP.*

$$–$$$ 🏨 **Hunter Cove on Rangeley Lake.** These lakeside cabins, which sleep from two to six people, provide all the comforts of home in a rustic setting. The interiors are unfinished knotty pine and include kitchens, full baths, and comfortable if plain living rooms. Cabin No. 1 has a fieldstone fireplace, and others have wood-burning stoves. Cabins No. 5 and No. 8 have hot tubs. Summer guests can take advantage of a sand swimming beach, boat rentals, and a nearby golf course. In winter, snowmobile right to your door or ski nearby (cross-country and downhill). ✉ *Mingo Loop Rd.,* ☎ *207/864–3383,* 🌐 *www.rangeleymaine.com/hunter. 8 cabins. Beach, boating. AE.*

Nightlife and the Arts

Rangeley Friends of the Arts (✉ Box 333, 04970, ☎ no phone) sponsors musical theater, fiddlers' contests, rock and jazz, classical, and other summer fare, mostly at Lakeside Park.

Outdoor Activities and Sports

BOATING

Rangeley and Mooselookmeguntic lakes are good for canoeing, sailing, and motorboating. For fishing and paddleboat rentals, call **Oquossoc Cove Marina** (✉ Oquossoc, ☎ 207/864–3463). **Dockside Sports Center** (✉ Town Cove, ☎ 207/864–2424) rents a variety of boats, canoes, and other crafts. **River's Edge Sports** (✉ Rte. 4/16, Oquossoc, ☎ 207/864–5582) rents canoes.

FISHING

Fishing for brook trout and salmon is at its best in May, June, and September; the Rangeley area is especially popular with fly-fishers. If you'd like a fishing guide, try **Westwind Charters and Guide Service** (☎ 207/864–5437).

SNOWMOBILING

More than 100 mi of maintained trails link lakes and towns to wilderness camps in the Rangeley area. The **Maine Snowmobile Association** has information about Maine's nearly 8,000-mi trail system.

STATE PARK

On the south shore of Rangeley Lake, **Rangeley Lake State Park** (✉ off Rte. 17, ☎ 207/864–3858) has superb lakeside scenery, swimming, picnic tables, a boat ramp, showers, and 50 campsites.

Ski Areas

SADDLEBACK SKI AND SUMMER LAKE PRESERVE

A down-home atmosphere prevails at Saddleback, where the quiet and the absence of crowds, even on holiday weekends, draw return visitors—many of them families. A dispute over the Appalachian Trail, which crosses Saddleback's summit ridge, prevented development here for nearly a quarter of a century, but a settlement in 2000 opens the door for expansion and modernization. ✉ *Box 490, Saddleback Rd. off Rte. 4, 04970,* ☎ *207/864–5671; 207/864–3380 snow conditions; 207/864–5364 reservations,* WEB *www.saddlebackskiarea.com.*

Downhill. The terrain is short and concentrated at the top of the mountain, accessible only by a T-bar. The middle of the mountain is mainly intermediate, with a few meandering easy trails; the beginner or novice slopes are toward the bottom. Two double chairlifts and three T-bars carry skiers to the 41 trails on the 1,830 ft mount.

Cross-country. 40 km (25 mi) of groomed cross-country trails spread out from the base area and circle Saddleback Lake and several ponds and rivers.

Child care. The nursery takes children from ages 6 weeks to 8 years. There are ski classes and programs for kids of different levels and ages.

Summer activities. Hiking is the big sport in warm weather.

Kingfield

❺❾ *33 mi east of Rangeley, 15 mi west of Phillips.*

In the shadows of Mt. Abraham and Sugarloaf Mountain, Kingfield has everything a "real" New England town should have: a general store, historic inns, and a white clapboard church. Sugarloaf/USA has golf and tennis in summer.

The **Stanley Museum** houses a collection of original Stanley Steamer cars built by the Stanley twins, Kingfield's most famous natives. ⊠ *40 School St.,* ☎ *207/265–2729.* 🎟 *$2.* 🕙 *May–Oct., Tues.–Sun. 10–4; Nov.–Apr., Mon.-Fri, 1-4.*

Nowetah's American Indian Museum displays an extensive collection of baskets as well as artifacts from native peoples of North and South America. This small museum is part of a store. ⊠ *Rte. 27, New Portland,* ☎ *207/628–4981.* 🎟 *Free.* 🕙 *Daily 10–5.*

Dining and Lodging

$–$$$ ✕ **Gepetto's.** An institution at the 'Loaf, Gepetto's combines efficient service with a wide-ranging menu: homemade soups, hearty salads, burgers, pizza, vegetarian pasta, and fresh seafood are all options. ⊠ *Sugarloaf Base Village, Carrabassett Valley,* ☎ *207/237–2953. MC, V.*

$$–$$$ ✕🖭 **Sugarloaf Inn Resort.** Guest rooms at this older inn could use a face lift, but you can't beat the ski-on access to Sugarloaf/USA. Rooms range from king-size on the fourth floor to dorm-style (bunk beds) on the ground floor. A greenhouse section of the Seasons Restaurant ($$–$$$) affords views of the slopes. At breakfast the sunlight pours into the dining room, and at dinner you can watch the snow-grooming machines prepare your favorite run. The in-house brew pub is a comfortable après-ski spot. ⊠ *Box 5000, R.R. 1, Sugarloaf Access Rd., Carrabassett Valley 04947,* ☎ *207/237–6814 or 800/843–5623,* ℻ *207/237–3773,* WEB *www.sugarloaf.com. 38 rooms, 4 dorm-style rooms. Restaurant, pub, health club, downhill skiing, meeting room. AE, D, MC, V.*

$ ✕🖭 **One and Three Stanley Avenue.** These sister properties, a fine-dining restaurant and a simple B&B, are in adjacent Victorian houses. The quiet neighborhood is a few minutes' walk from downtown Kingfield and about a 20-minute drive from Sugarloaf/USA. Both are decorated with period furnishings. The restaurant ($$-$$$$) specializes in creative Continental fare and emphasizes fresh Maine ingredients. ⊠ *Box 169, 3 Stanley Ave., 04947,* ☎ *207/265–5541. 6 rooms, 3 with bath. MC, V. Restaurant closed May–Nov. BP.*

$$–$$$ 🖭 **Grand Summit.** New England ambience and European-style service are combined at this six-story brick hotel at the base of the lifts at Sugarloaf/USA. Oak and redwood paneling in the main rooms is enhanced by contemporary furnishings. Valet parking, ski tuning, lockers, and mountain guides are available through the concierge. The Double Diamond Pub has a lively après-ski scene. ⊠ *R.R. 1, Box 2299, Carrabassett Valley 04947,* ☎ *207/237–2222 or 800/527–9879,* ℻ *207/237–2874,* WEB *www.sugarloaf.com. 100 rooms, 19 suites. Restaurant, pub, hot tub, massage, sauna, spa, concierge. AE, D, DC, MC, V.*

Nightlife and the Arts

At Sugarloaf/USA, nightlife is concentrated at the mountain's base village. Monday is blues night at the **Bag & Kettle** (☎ 207/237–2451), which is the best choice for pizza and burgers. A microbrewery on the access road called the **Sugarloaf Brewing Company** (☎ 207/237–2211) pulls in revelers who come for après-ski brewskies. **Widowmaker Lounge** (☎ 207/237–6845) frequently presents live entertainment in the base lodge.

Outdoor Activities and Sports

T.A.D. Dog Sled Services (⊠ Rte. 27, Carrabassett Valley, ☎ 207/246–4461) conducts short 1½-mi rides near Sugarloaf/USA. Sleds accommodate up to two adults and two children.

Ski Areas

SUGARLOAF/USA

Abundant natural snow, a huge mountain, and the only above-tree-line skiing in the East have made Sugarloaf one of Maine's best-known ski areas. Sugarloaf skiers like the nontrendy Maine atmosphere and the base village, which has restaurants and shops. Two slopeside hotels and hundreds of slopeside condominiums provide ski-in/ski-out access. Once you are here, a car is unnecessary—a shuttle connects all mountain operations. Summer is much quieter than winter, but you can bike, hike, golf, and fish. ⊠ *R.R. 1, Box 5000, Sugarloaf Access Rd., Carrabassett Valley 04947,* ☎ *207/237–2000; 207/237–6808 snow conditions; 800/843–5623.*

Downhill. With a vertical of 2,820 ft, Sugarloaf is taller than any other New England ski peak except Killington in Vermont. The advanced terrain begins with the steep snowfields on top, wide open and treeless. Coming down the face of the mountain, there are black-diamond runs everywhere, often blending into easier terrain. Many intermediate trails can be found down the front face, and a couple more come off the summit. Easier runs are predominantly toward the bottom, with a few long, winding runs that twist and turn from higher elevations. The mountain has three terrain parks and a halfpipe. Serving the resort's 126 trails are two high-speed quad, two quad, one triple, and eight double chairlifts and one T-bar.

Cross-country. The Sugarloaf Ski Outdoor Center has 105 km (62 mi) of cross-country trails that loop and wind through the valley. Trails connect to the resort.

Other activities. Snowshoeing and ice skating are available at the Outdoor Center. On Wednesday and Saturday nights, a snowcat takes guests to Bullwinkles, a mid-mountain restaurant, for a multi-course dining adventure ($80 per person). Reservations are essential. (☎ 207/237–2000).

Child care. A nursery takes children from ages 6 weeks to 6 years. Children's ski programs begin at age 3. A night nursery is open on Thursday and Saturday from 6 to 10 PM by reservation. Instruction is provided on a half-day or full-day basis for children from ages 4 to 14. Nightly children's activities are free. The teen club, Avalanche, is in the base lodge.

Summer and year-round activities. The resort has a superb 18-hole, Robert Trent Jones Jr.–designed golf course and six tennis courts for public use in warmer months. The Original Golf School operates from late June to late October. You can get advice on planning mountain biking and hiking trips, and the resort has canoe and bike rentals and can arrange fly-fishing instruction. The **Sugarloaf Sports and Fitness Club** (☎ 207/237–6946) has an indoor pool, six indoor and outdoor hot tubs, racquetball courts, full fitness and spa facilities, and a beauty salon. Use of club facilities is included in all lodging packages.

Western Lakes and Mountains A to Z

To research prices, get advice from other travelers, and book travel arrangements, visit www.fodors.com.

AIR TRAVEL

Mountain Air Service provides air access to remote areas, scenic flights, and charter fishing trips. Naples Flying Service operates sightseeing flights over the lakes in summer.

➤ AIRLINES & CONTACTS: **Mountain Air Service** (⊠ Rangeley, ☎ 207/864–5307). **Naples Flying Service** (⊠ Naples Causeway, Naples, ☎ 207/693–6591).

CAR TRAVEL

A car is essential to tour the western lakes and mountains. To travel from town to town in the order described in this section, drive U.S. 302 to Naples, then Route 35 to Harrison and the Waterfords. Take the Sweden Road, an ideal pick for autumn due to its vistas of the White Mountains, across to Lovell and pick up Route 5 to Bethel. From there, take Rte. 26 to U.S. 2 to Route 17 to Oquossoc, then head east on Route 16 through Rangeley to Kingfield.

EMERGENCIES

➤ HOSPITALS: **Bethel Area Health Center** (⊠ Railroad St., Bethel, ☎ 207/824–2193). **Mt. Abram Regional Health Center** (⊠ Depot St., Kingfield, ☎ 207/265–4555). **Northern Cumberland Memorial Hospital** (⊠ S. High St., Bridgton, ☎ 207/647–8841). **Rangeley Regional Health Center** (⊠ Main St., Rangeley, ☎ 207/864–3303).

VISITOR INFORMATION

Bethel's Chamber of Commerce has a reservations service. For reservations at Sugarloaf/USA, contact Sugarloaf Area Reservations Service. ➤ CONTACTS: **Bethel Area Chamber of Commerce** (⊠ Box 439, 30 Cross St., Bethel 04217, ☎ 207/824–2282 or 800/442–5526). **Bethel's Chamber of Commerce Reservation Service** (☎ 207/824–3585 or 800/442–5826). **Bridgton–Lakes Region Chamber of Commerce** (⊠ Box 236, U.S. 302, Bridgton 04009, ☎ 207/647–3472). **Greater Windham Chamber of Commerce** (⊠ Box 1015, U.S. 302, Windham 04062, ☎ 207/892–8265). **Maine Tourism Association Welcome Center** (⊠ Box 1084, U.S. 2, Bethel 04217, ☎ 207/824–4582). **Naples Business Association** (⊠ Box 412, Naples 04055, ☎ 888/627–5379). **Rangeley Lakes Region Chamber of Commerce** (⊠ Box 317, Main St., Rangeley 04970, ☎ 207/864–5571 or 800/685–2537). **Sugarloaf Area Chamber of Commerce** (⊠ R.R. 1, Box 2151, Kingfield 04947, ☎ 207/235–2100). **Sugarloaf Area Reservations Service** (☎ 800/843–2732).

THE NORTH WOODS

Maine's North Woods, the vast area in the north-central section of the state, is best experienced by canoe or raft, hiking trail, or on a fishing trip. Some great theaters for these activities are Moosehead Lake, Baxter State Park, and the Allagash Wilderness Waterway—as well as the summer resort town of Greenville, dramatically situated Rockwood, and the no-frills outposts that connect them.

Rockwood

 180 mi north of Portland, 91 mi northwest of Bangor.

Rockwood, on Moosehead Lake's western shore, is a good starting point for a wilderness trip or a family vacation on the lake. Maine's largest lake, Moosehead supplies more in the way of rustic camps, restaurants, guides, and outfitters than any other northern locale. Its 420 mi of shorefront, three-quarters of which is owned by paper manufacturers, is virtually uninhabited. Though it doesn't possess many amenities, Rockwood has the most striking location of any town on Moosehead: the dark mass of **Mt. Kineo,** a sheer cliff that rises 789 ft above the lake and 1,789 ft above sea level, looms just across the narrows (you get an excellent view just north of town on Route 6/15).

OFF THE
BEATEN PATH

KINEO – Once a thriving summer resort, the original Mount Kineo Hotel (built in 1830 and torn down in the 1940s) was accessed primarily by steamship. Today Kineo makes a pleasant day trip. You can take the

The North Woods

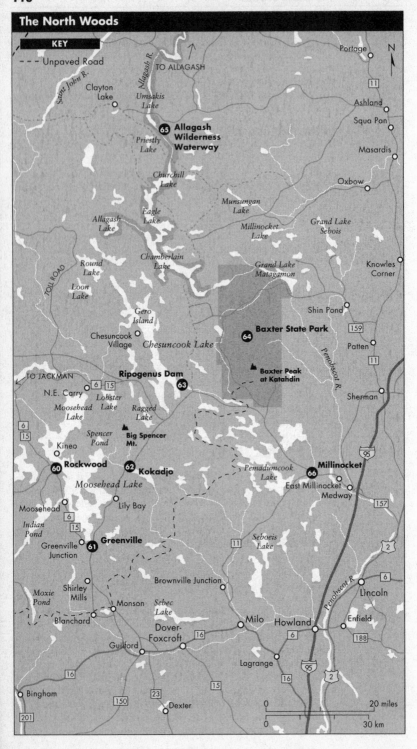

KEY

– – – Unpaved Road

N

TO ALLAGASH

Saint John R.

Allagash R.

Clayton
Lake

Umsakis
Lake

Portage

11

Ashland

Squa Pan

Masardis

65 **Allagash
Wilderness
Waterway**

Priestly
Lake

Churchill
Lake

Munsungan
Lake

Oxbow

Eagle
Lake

Allagash
Lake

Millinocket
Lake

Grand Lake
Sebois

Knowles
Corner

Round
Lake

Chamberlain
Lake

Grand Lake
Matagamon

TOLL ROAD

Loon
Lake

Gero
Island

Shin Pond

159

Chesuncook
Village

Chesuncook Lake

64 **Baxter State Park**

Patten

11

Penobscot R.

TO JACKMAN

Ripogenus Dam

63

▲ **Baxter Peak
at Katahdin**

Sherman

N.E. Carry

6   15

Lobster
Lake

Ragged
Lake

Moosehead
Lake

Spencer
Pond

▲ **Big Spencer
Mt.**

6
15

Kineo

60 **Rockwood**

62 **Kokadjo**

Pemadumcook
Lake

I-95

66 **Millinocket**

East Millinocket

Medway

157

Moosehead Lake

Moosehead

Lily Bay

6

Indian
Pond

15

61 **Greenville**

Greenville
Junction

Seboeis
Lake

11

2

6

Lincoln

Moxie
Pond

Shirley
Mills

Brownville Junction

Penobscot R.

Monson

Sebec
Lake

Enfield

Blanchard

Dover-
Foxcroft

16

Milo

Howland

188

Guilford

Lagrange

95

Bingham

16

23

15

16

2

201

150

Dexter

0 _____ 20 miles

0 _____ 30 km

Kineo Shuttle, which departs from the State Dock in Rockwood (☎ 207/ 534–8812), or rent a motorboat in Rockwood and make the journey across the lake in about 15 minutes. There's a small marina on the shore, in the shadow of Mt. Kineo, and a half dozen buildings dot the land. Some are for sale and others are being restored, but there is no real town here. A tavern sells cold libations to drink there or take with you. A walkway laces the perimeter of the mountain, and trails lead to the summit.

Lodging

$$$$ ⌂ **Attean Lake Lodge.** The Holden family has owned and operated this island lodge about an hour west of Rockwood since 1900. Log cabins, which sleep from two to six people, provide a secluded environment. The tastefully decorated central lodge has a library and games. Look for lobster, beef, and veal at the substantial meals; cookouts and picnic lunches add variety. ✉ *Box 457, off Rte. 201, Birch Island, Jackman 04945,* ☎ *207/668–3792,* FAX *207/668–4016,* WEB *www.atteanlodge.com. 18 cabins. Beach, boating, recreation room, library. AE, MC, V. Closed Oct.–May. FAP.*

$–$$ ⌂ **The Birches.** This family-oriented resort supplies the full north-country experience: Moosehead Lake, birch woods, log cabins, and boats. The century-old main lodge has guest rooms, a lobby with a trout pond, and a living room dominated by a fieldstone fireplace. Cottages have wood-burning stoves or fireplaces and sleep from 2 to 15 people. The dining room (closed in December and April) overlooking the lake is open to the public for breakfast and dinner; the fare at dinner is pasta, seafood, and steak. ✉ *Box 41, off Rte. 6/15, on Moosehead Lake, 04478,* ☎ *207/534–7305 or 800/825–9453,* FAX *207/534–8835,* WEB *www.birches.com. 4 lodge rooms without bath, 15 cottages. Dining room, hot tub, sauna, boating. AE, D, MC, V. BP.*

$ ⌂ **Rockwood Cottages.** These eight white cottages on Moosehead Lake, off Route 15 and convenient to the center of Rockwood, have screened porches and fully-equipped kitchens and sleep from two to seven people. There is a one-week minimum stay in July and August. ✉ *Box 176, Rte. 15, 04478,* ☎ FAX *207/534–7725,* WEB *www.connectmaine.com/rockwood. 8 cottages. Sauna, dock, boating. MC, V. Closed Dec. 1–Apr. 30.*

Outdoor Activities and Sports

The **Birches** (☎ 207/534–7305) operates a moose cruise. **Mt. Kineo Cabins** (✉ Rte. 6/15, ☎ 207/534–7744) rents canoes and larger boats on Moosehead Lake for the trip to Kineo. You can rent a boat or take a shuttle operated by **Rockwood Cottages** (☎ 207/534–7725) to Kineo. **Old Mill Campground** (☎ 207/534–7333) provides shuttle service to Kineo.

East Outlet of the Kennebec River, a popular Class II and III white-water run for canoeists and white-water rafters, is about 10 mi from Rockwood on Route 6/15 south. You'll come to a bridge with a dam to the left. The outlet ends at the Harris Station Dam at Indian Pond, headwaters of the Kennebec.

Greenville

61 *20 mi southeast of Rockwood, 160 mi northeast of Portland.*

Greenville, the largest town on Moosehead Lake, is an outdoors-lover's paradise. Boating, fishing, and hiking are popular in summer; snowmobiling and skiing attract visitors in winter. The town has a smattering of shops, restaurants, and inns.

Moosehead Marine Museum has exhibits on the local logging industry and the steamship era on Moosehead Lake, plus photographs of the Mount Kineo Hotel. ⊠ *Main St.,* ☎ *207/695–2716.* 🎫 *$3.* ☼ *Late May–early Oct., daily 10–4.*

★   The Moosehead Marine Museum offers three- and five-hour trips on Moosehead Lake aboard the *Katahdin,* a 1914 steamship (now diesel). The 115-ft ship, called *The Kate,* carried passengers to Kineo until 1942 and then was used in the logging industry until 1975. ⊠ *Main St. (boarding is on the shoreline by the museum),* ☎ *207/695–2716,* WEB *www.katahdincruises.com.* 🎫 *$20–$26.* ☼ *July–Columbus Day.*

Dining and Lodging

$$–$$$ ✕ **Blue Moose Cafe.** A big moose marks this special restaurant, where fresh seafood, tenderloin, and lamb are prepared with a French accent. The small menu may include entrées such as pepper-crusted tenderloin of beef, full rack of lamb, or stuffed crèpes. ⊠ *Rte. 6/15,* ☎ *207/695–0786. MC, V. Closed Sunday; no lunch.*

$–$$ ✕ **The Black Frog.** For a fun and frivolous atmosphere and the best location on the lake, head to this downtown restaurant. The wide-ranging menu runs from burgers to filet mignon, and everything is served with a sense of humor. Specialties include barbecued baby-back pork ribs and grilled salmon steak. Grab a seat on the lakefront deck or in the dining room, where the decor runs from treasures to trash. ⊠ *Pritham Ave.,* ☎ *207/695–1100. D, DC, MC, V.*

$$$ ✕🏨 **Greenville Inn.** Built more than a century ago, this rambling structure is a block from town on a rise over Moosehead Lake. The ornate cherry and mahogany paneling, Oriental rugs, and leaded glass create an aura of masculine ease. Cottages have mountain and lake views, and some have decks. The restaurant ($$$; open May–Oct.; reservations essential; no lunch) has water views. Revised daily, the menu reflects the owners' Austrian background with choices such as spicy maple-glazed salmon fillets with potato pancakes and pork tenderloin with paprika sauce and spaetzle. ⊠ *Box 1194, Norris St., 04441,* ☎ *207/695–2206 or 888/695–6000,* FAX *207/695–0335,* WEB *www.greenvilleinn.com. 4 rooms and 1 suite in main inn; 1 suite in carriage house; 6 cottages. Restaurant. D, MC, V. CP.*

$$$–$$$$ 🏨 **Blair Hill Inn.** Beautiful gardens and a hilltop location distinguish this 1891 estate. Guest rooms are spacious, and four have fireplaces; those in the front of the house have marvelous views over the lake. A restaurant, open to the public by reservation, serves dinner ($15–$24) from late-May to mid-October on Friday and Saturday nights. ⊠ *Box 1288; Lily Bay Road, 04441,* ☎ *207/ 695–0224,* FAX *207/695–4324,* WEB *www.blairhill.com, 8 rooms, 2 suites. Exercise room, outdoor hot tub, lawn games. D, MC, V. FB.*

$$$–$$$$ 🏨 **Lodge at Moosehead Lake.** This grand manor overlooking Moose-
★   head Lake is about as close as things get to luxury in the North Woods. No detail is overlooked; the service is exacting, yet the ambiance is casual. All rooms have whirlpool baths, fireplaces, and hand-carved four-poster beds; most have lake views. The carriage house suites are romantic retreats that open on to private patios. The dining room, where breakfast is served, has a spectacular view of the water. Dinners are occasionally available to guests, and dinner entrées such as pan-seared salmon with citrus and herbs have sophisticated touches. ⊠ *Box 1167, Lily Bay Rd., 04441,* ☎ *207/695–4400,* FAX *207/695–2281,* WEB *www.lodgeatmooseheadlake.com. 5 rooms, 3 suites. D, MC, V. Closed late Oct.–late Dec. and mid-Mar.–mid-May. AP.*

$$ 🏨 **Lakeview House.** You get nearly the same sweeping views over Moosehead Lake at this small, minimally decorated B&B as you do from the more exclusive and expensive Lodge at Moosehead Lake. ⊠

*Box 1102, Lily Bay Rd., 04441, ☎ 207/695–2229, FAX 207/695–2512.
2 rooms, 1 suite. Open year-round; call ahead in winter. BP.*

$ 🖼 **Chalet Moosehead.** Fifty yards off Route 6/15 and right on Moose-
head Lake, this property has efficiencies (with two double beds, a living room, and a kitchenette), motel rooms, and cabins, all with picture
windows to capture the view. The attractive grounds include a private
beach and dock. Rooms in the new building have whirlpool tubs and
private balconies overlooking the lake. ⊠ *Box 327, Rte. 6/15, Greenville
Junction 04442, ☎ 207/695–2950 or 800/290–3645,* WEB *www.moose-
headlodging.com. 19 rooms, 8 efficiencies, cabins. Horseshoes, beach,
dock, boating. AE, D, MC, V.*

Outdoor Activities and Sports

Beaver Cove Marina (☎ 207/695–3526) rents boats and snowmobiles.
Kineo Kayak Guide Service (☎ 207/474–3945 or 207/695–2896)
schedules guided kayak tours and moose safaris in the Moosehead Lake
and Kennebec Valley area. **Moose Country Safaris and Dogsled Trips**
(☎ 207/876–4907) leads moose safaris, dogsled trips, and canoe and
kayak trips. **Northwoods Outfitters** (☎ 207/695–3288) outfits a variety of sports and offers tours, moose safaris, and trail advice.

FISHING

Togue, landlocked salmon, and brook and lake trout lure thousands
of anglers to the region from ice-out in mid-May until September; the
hardiest return in winter to ice-fish. Call for current **information** (☎
207/695–3756 or 800/322–9844) on water levels.

RAFTING

The Kennebec and Dead rivers and the West Branch of the Penobscot
River offer thrilling white-water rafting (guides are strongly recommended). These rivers are dam-controlled, so trips run rain or shine
daily from May to October (day and multiday trips are conducted).
Most guided raft trips on the Kennebec and Dead rivers leave from
the Forks, southwest of Moosehead Lake, on Route 201; Penobscot
River trips leave from either Greenville or Millinocket. Many rafting
outfitters operate resort facilities in their base towns. **Raft Maine** (☎
800/723–8633) has lodging and rafting packages and information
about outfitters.

STATE PARK

Lily Bay State Park (⊠ Lily Bay Rd., ☎ 207/695–2700, 🎟 $2), 8 mi
northeast of Greenville, has a good swimming beach, two boat-launching ramps, and two campgrounds with 91 sites.

Shopping

Indian Hill Trading Post (⊠ Rte. 6/15, ☎ 207/695–2104) stocks just
about anything you might need for a North Woods vacation, including sporting and camping equipment, canoes, and fishing licenses;
there's even an adjacent grocery store. You enter **Moosehead Traders**
(⊠ Moosehead Center Mall, Rte. 6/15, ☎ 207/695–3806) through an
antler archway; inside are books, clothing, and antiques and artifacts.

Ski Areas

BIG SQUAW MOUNTAIN RESORT

The management is modernizing this remote but pretty resort overlooking
Moosehead Lake. The emphasis is on affordable family skiing—prices
are downright cheap compared with those at other in-state areas. New
snowmaking, new grooming equipment, and a new attitude make this
a wonderful place for skiers longing to escape crowds. ⊠ *Box D, Rte.
6/15, 04441, ☎ 207/695–1000.*

Downhill. Trails are laid out according to difficulty, with the easy slopes toward the bottom, intermediate trails weaving from midpoint, and steeper runs high up off the 1,750-vertical-ft peak. The 22 trails are served by one triple and one double chairlift and two surface lifts.

Child care. The nursery takes children from infants through age 6. The ski school has daily lessons and racing classes for children of all ages.

Summer activities. The resort has a recreation program for children and two tennis courts, hiking, and lawn games.

Kokadjo

❷ *22 mi northeast of Greenville.*

Kokadjo, population "not many," has a sign that reads "Keep Maine green. This is God's country. Why set it on fire and make it look like hell?" This is the last outpost before you enter the North Woods. As you leave Kokadjo, bear left at the fork and follow signs to Baxter State Park. A drive of 5 mi along this road (now dirt) brings you to the Sias Hill checkpoint, where from June to November a fee may be charged to travel the next 40 mi. Access is through a forest where you're likely to encounter logging trucks (which have the right of way), logging equipment, and work in progress. At the bottom of the hill after you pass the checkpoint, look to your right—there's a good chance you'll spot a moose.

Ripogenus Dam

❸ *20 mi northeast of Kokadjo, 25 mins southeast of Chesuncook Village by floatplane.*

Ripogenus Dam and the granite-walled Ripogenus Gorge are on Ripogenus Lake, east of Chesuncook Lake. The gorge is the jumping-off point for the famous 12-mi West Branch of the Penobscot River whitewater rafting trip and the most popular put-in point for Allagash canoe trips. The Penobscot River drops more than 70 ft-per-mi through the gorge, giving rafters a hold-on-for-your-life ride. The best spot to watch the Penobscot rafters is from Pray's Big Eddy Wilderness Campground, overlooking the rock-choked Crib Works Rapid (a Class V rapid). To get here, follow the main road northeast and turn left on Telos Road; the campground is about 10 yards after the bridge.

En Route From the Pray's Big Eddy Wilderness Campground, take the main road (here called the Golden Road for the amount of money it took the Great Northern Paper Company to build it) southeast toward Millinocket. The road soon becomes paved. After you drive over the one-lane Abol Bridge and pass through the Bowater/Great Northern Paper Company's Debsconeag checkpoint, bear left to reach Togue Pond Gatehouse, the southern entrance to Baxter State Park.

Baxter State Park

★ **❹** *24 mi northwest of Millinocket.*

Few places in Maine are as remote or as beautiful as Baxter State Park and the ☞ Allagash Wilderness Waterway. Baxter, a gift from Governor Percival Baxter, is the jewel in the crown of northern Maine, a 204,733-acre wilderness area that surrounds Katahdin, Maine's highest mountain (5,267 ft at Baxter Peak) and the terminus of the Appalachian Trail. There are 46 mountain peaks and ridges, 18 of which exceed an elevation of 3,000 ft. Day-use parking areas fill quickly in season; it's best to arrive early, before 8 AM. The park is intersected by more than 180 mi of trails. No pets, domestic animals, oversize vehicles, all-terrain vehicles, motorboats, or motorcycles are allowed in the park, and there are no pay phones, gas stations, stores, or running water or electricity. The one visitor center is at Togue Pond, for which Millinocket is the nearest gateway. ✉ *Mailing address: 64 Balsam Dr., Millinocket 04462,* ☎ *207/723–5140,* WEB *www.state.me.us.* ☞ *$8 per vehicle; free to Maine residents.*

OFF THE
BEATEN PATH
LUMBERMAN'S MUSEUM – This museum comprises 10 buildings filled with exhibits depicting the history of logging, including models, dioramas, and equipment. ✉ *Shin Pond Rd. (Rte. 159), Patten (22 mi east of Baxter State Park),* ☎ *207/528–2650,* WEB *www.lumbermensmuseum. org.* ☞ *$3.50.* ☉ *July–Aug., Tues.–Sun., 10–4; May 15–June 30 and Sept. 1–Columbus Day, Fri., Sat., and holiday Mon., 10–4.*

Lodging

$ ⚱ **Baxter State Park Authority.** Camping spaces at the 10 campgrounds here can be reserved only by mail or in person. Reservations can be made beginning the first working day in January—some sites are fully booked for midsummer weekends soon after that. The state also maintains primitive backcountry sites. ✉ *64 Balsam Dr., Millinocket 04462,* ☎ *207/723–5140.*

Outdoor Activities and Sports

Katahdin, in Baxter State Park, draws thousands of hikers every year for the daylong climb to the summit and the stunning views of woods, mountains, and lakes from the hair-raising Knife Edge Trail along its ridge. The crowds can be formidable on clear summer days, so if you crave solitude, tackle one of the 45 other mountains in the park, all of which are accessible from a 150-mi network of trails. South Turner can be climbed in a morning (if you're fit)—it has a great view of Katahdin across the valley. On the way you'll pass Sandy Stream Pond, where moose are often seen at dusk. The Owl, the Brothers, and Doubletop Mountain are good day hikes.

Allagash Wilderness Waterway

⑥⑤ *22 mi north of Ripogenus Dam.*

The Allagash is a spectacular 92-mi corridor of lakes and rivers that cuts across 170,000 acres of wilderness, beginning at the northwest corner of Baxter State Park and running north to the town of Allagash, 10 mi from the Canadian border. For information, contact the **Allagash Wilderness Waterway** (✉ 106 Hogan Rd., Bangor 04401, ☎ 207/ 941–4014).

Outdoor Activities and Sports

The Allagash rapids are ranked Class I and Class II (very easy and easy), but that doesn't mean the river is a piece of cake; river conditions vary greatly with the depth and volume of water, and even a Class I rapid can hang your canoe up on a rock, capsize you, or spin you around. On the lakes, strong winds can halt your progress for days. The Allagash should not be undertaken lightly or without planning; the complete 92-mi course requires 7 to 10 days. The canoeing season along the Allagash is from mid-May to October, although it's wise to remember that the black-fly season ends about July 1. The best bet for a novice is to go with a guide; a good outfitter will help plan your route and provide your craft and transportation.

Millinocket

66 *19 mi southeast of Baxter State Park, 70 mi north of Bangor, 90 mi northwest of Greenville.*

Millinocket, a papermill town with a population of 7,000, is a gateway to Baxter State Park. There are a number of outfitters here.

OFF THE
BEATEN PATH

KATAHDIN IRON WORKS – For a worthwhile day trip from Millinocket, take Route 11 and head southwest to a trailhead 5 mi north of Brownville Junction. Drive the gravel road 6 mi to Katahdin Iron Works, the site of a mining operation that employed nearly 200 workers in the mid-1800s; a deteriorated kiln, a stone furnace, and a charcoal-storage building are all that remain. From here, a hiking trail leads over fairly rugged terrain to **Gulf Hagas**, with natural chasms, cliffs, a 3.5-mi gorge, waterfalls, pools, exotic flora, and rock formations.

Lodging

$$$$ 🏠 **Bradford Camps.** It's tempting to laze the day away on the front porch of these lakefront log cabins or in front of the massive fieldstone fireplace in the main lodge. But alas, there are miles of trails and woods roads to explore, rivers and lakes to fish and canoe, and even the Allagash is close enough for a day trip. Rates include three hearty, home-style meals. Float plane transportation is available from Millinocket and other locations. ✉ *Box 729, Ashland, 04732,* ☎ *May 1–Nov. 30, 207/746–7777; Dec. 1–Apr. 30, 207/469–6364,* 𝗪𝗘𝗕 *www.bradford-camps.com. 8 cabins. Dining room, lake, hiking, boating. Late Nov.–May. AP.*

$$$$ 🏠 **Libby Camps.** Matt Libby, along with his wife, Ellen, represent the fifth generation of Libbys to run this sporting camp on Millinocket Lake, the headwaters of the Allagash and Aroostook rivers. Skylights brighten the well-kept cabins, where handmade quilts cover the beds and woodstoves keep the chill at bay. The main lodge is open and airy with a magnificent central stone fireplace. Rates include all meals as well as use of sea kayaks, canoes, sail and motor boats. ✉ *Box 810, Ashland, 04732,* ☎ *207/435–8274 or 207/435–6233,* 𝗙𝗔𝗫 *207/435–3230,* 𝗪𝗘𝗕 *www.libbycamps.com. 8 cabins; 10 rustic outpost cabins. Beach, boating, fishing, hiking. MC, V. Late-Nov.–May 1. MAP.*

$ 🏠 **Big Moose Inn.** There's nothing fancy about this old-fashioned inn and the cabins and campsites nestled between Ambejesus and Millinocket lakes, just 8 mi from the entrance to Baxter State Park. The inn has a big stone and brick fireplace decorated with a moose trophy and snowshoes; inn rooms are comfortably furnished with country pieces. The popular dining room, open for dinner Wednesday through Saturday, emphasizes seafood. Canoes and a store are other amenities. ✉ *Box 98, Baxter State Park Rd., 04462,* ☎ *207/723–8391,* 𝗙𝗔𝗫 *207/723–8199,* 𝗪𝗘𝗕 *www.bigmoosecabins.com. 11 rooms without bath, 11 cabins, 44 campsites. Restaurant, boating. MC, V. Closed late-Nov.–May. CP.*

$ 🏠 **Gateway Inn.** This new motel is just off I-95. Book a room with a deck facing Katahdin for the best views. ✉ *Box 637, Rte. 157, Medway 04460,* ☎ *207/746–3193,* 𝗙𝗔𝗫 *207/746–3430,* 𝗪𝗘𝗕 *www.med-waygateway.com. 30 rooms, 8 efficiencies. Air-conditioning, no-smoking rooms, indoor pool, hot tub, sauna, exercise room. AE, D, MC, V. CP.*

Outdoor Activities and Sports

Katahdin Area Guide Service (✉ 74 Water St., ☎ 207/723–9522 or 800/548–4355) outfits fishing, snowmobiling, canoeing, and camping expeditions. **Penobscot River Outfitters** (☎ 800/794–5267) rents canoes and offers a shuttle service. **New England Outdoor Center** (☎ 207/723–5438 or 800/766–7238) rents snowmobiles and offers guided trips.

The North Woods A to Z

To research prices, get advice from other travelers, and book travel arrangements, visit www.fodors.com.

AIR TRAVEL

Charter flights, usually by seaplane, from Bangor, Greenville, or Millinocket to smaller towns and remote lake and forest areas can be arranged with a number of flying services, which will transport you and your gear and help you find a guide.

➤ AIRLINES & CONTACTS: **Currier's Flying Service** (⊠ Greenville Junction, ☎ 207/695–2778). **Folsom's Air Service** (⊠ Greenville, ☎ 207/695–2821). **Katahdin Air Service** (⊠ Millinocket, ☎ 207/723–8378). **Scotty's Flying Service** (⊠ Shin Pond, ☎ 207/528–2626).

AIRPORTS

Bangor International Airport is the closest airport (☞ Maine A to Z).

CAR TRAVEL

A car is essential to negotiate this vast region but may not be useful to someone spending a vacation entirely at a wilderness camp. Public roads are scarce in the north country, but lumber companies maintain private roads that are often open to the public (sometimes by permit only). When driving on a logging road, always give lumber company trucks the right of way. Be aware that loggers often take the middle of the road and will neither move over nor slow down for you.

I–95 offers the quickest access to the North Woods. U.S. 201 (I–95, Exit 36) is the major route to Jackman and to Québec. Route 15 connects Jackman to Greenville and Bangor. The Golden Road is a private, paper company–operated road that links Greenville to Millinocket.

EMERGENCIES

➤ HOSPITALS: **Charles A. Dean Memorial Hospital** (⊠ Pritham Ave., Greenville, ☎ 207/695–2223 or 800/260–4000). **Mayo Regional Hospital** (⊠ 75 W. Main St., Dover-Foxcroft, ☎ 207/564–8401). **Millinocket Regional Hospital** (⊠ 200 Somerset St., Millinocket, ☎ 207/723–5161).

LODGING

CAMPING

Reservations for state park campsites (excluding Baxter State Park) can be made through the Bureau of Parks and Lands, which can also tell you if you need a camping permit and where to obtain one. Maine Sporting Camp Association publishes a list of its members, with details on the facilities available at each camp.

The Maine Campground Owners Association publishes a helpful annual directory of its members. The Maine Forest Service, Department of Conservation will direct you to the nearest place to get a fire permit. Maine Tourism Association publishes a listing of private campsites and cottage rentals. North Maine Woods maintains 500 primitive campsites on commercial forest land.

➤ CONTACTS: **Bureau of Parks and Lands** (⊠ State House Station 22, Augusta 04333, ☎ 207/287–3821; 800/332–1501 in ME). **Maine Sporting Camp Association** (⊠ Box 89, Jay 04239). **Maine Campground Owners Association** (⊠ 655 Main St., Lewiston 04240, ☎ 207/782–5874). The **Maine Forest Service, Department of Conservation** (⊠ State House Station 22, Augusta 04333, ☎ 207/287–2791). **Maine Tourism Association** (⊠ Box 2300, 325B Water St., Hallowell 04347, ☎ 207/623–0363; 800/533–9595 outside ME). **North Maine Woods** (⊠ Box 425, Ashland 04732, ☎ 207/435–6213).

OUTDOORS & SPORTS

CANOEING

Most canoe rental operations will arrange transportation, help plan your route, and provide a guide. Transport to wilderness lakes can be arranged through the flying services listed under Air Travel.

The Bureau of Parks and Lands provides information on independent Allagash canoeing and camping. Allagash Canoe Trips operates guided trips on the Allagash Waterway, plus the Moose, Penobscot, and St. John rivers. Allagash Wilderness Outfitters/Frost Pond Camps provides equipment, transportation, and information for canoe trips on the Allagash and the Penobscot rivers. Mahoosuc Guide Service conducts guided trips on the Penobscot, Allagash, and Moose rivers. North Country Outfitters operates a white-water canoeing and kayaking school, rents equipment, and leads guided canoe trips on the Allagash Waterway and the Moose, Penobscot, and St. John rivers. Sunrise County Canoe & Kayak outfits trips on eastern and northern Maine waterways. Willard Jalbert Camps has been leading guided Allagash trips since the late 1800s.

➤ CONTACTS: **Allagash Canoe Trips** (✉ Box 713, Greenville 04441, ☎ 207/695–3668). **Allagash Wilderness Outfitters/Frost Pond Camps** (✉ Box 620, Greenville 04441, ☎ 207/695–2821). **Mahoosuc Guide Service** (✉ Bear River Rd., Newry 04261, ☎ 207/824–2073). **North Country Outfitters** (✉ Box 41, Rockwood 04478, ☎ 207/534–2242 or 207/534–7305). **Sunrise County Canoe & Kayak** (✉ Cathance Lake, Grove Post 04657, ☎ 207/454–7708 or 800/980–2300). **Willard Jalbert Camps** (✉ 6 Winchester St., Presque Isle 04769, ☎ 207/764–0494).

GUIDES

Fishing guides are available through most wilderness camps, sporting goods stores, and canoe outfitters. For assistance in finding a guide, contact North Maine Woods (☞ Rafting).

➤ CONTACTS: **Gilpatrick's Guide Service** (✉ Box 461, Skowhegan 04976, ☎ 207/453–6959). **Maine Guide Fly Shop and Guide Service** (✉ Box 1202, Main St., Greenville 04441, ☎ 207/695–2266). **Professional Guide Service** (✉ Box 346, Sheridan 04775, ☎ 207/435–8044).

HORSEBACK RIDING

North Woods Riding Adventures, owned by registered Maine guides Judy Cross-Strehlke and Bob Strehlke, conducts one-day, two-day, and week-long pack trips (10 people maximum) through parts of Piscataquis County. A popular two-day trip explores the Whitecap–Barren Mountain Range, near Katahdin Iron Works.

➤ CONTACTS: **North Woods Riding Adventures** (✉ 64 Garland Line Rd., Dover-Foxcroft 04426, ☎ 207/564–3451).

RAFTING

Raft Maine is an association of white-water outfitters licensed to lead trips down the Kennebec and Dead rivers and the West Branch of the Penobscot River. Rafting season begins May 1 and continues through mid-October. North Maine Woods has maps; a canoeing guide for the St. John River; and lists of outfitters, camps, and campsites.

➤ CONTACTS: **Raft Maine** (☎ 800/723–8633). **North Maine Woods** (✉ Box 425, Ashland 04732, ☎ 207/435–6213).

VISITOR INFORMATION

➤ CONTACTS: **Baxter State Park Authority** (✉ 64 Balsam Dr., Millinocket 04462, ☎ 207/723–5140). **Katahdin Area Chamber of Commerce** (✉ 1029 Central St., Millinocket 04462, ☎ 207/723–4443). **Moosehead Lake Region Chamber of Commerce** (✉ Box 581, Rte. 6/15, Greenville 04441, ☎ 207/695–2702).

MAINE A TO Z

To research prices, get advice from other travelers, and book travel arrangements, visit www.fodors.com.

AIR TRAVEL

Regional flying services, operating from regional and municipal airports, provide access to remote lakes and wilderness areas as well as to Penobscot Bay islands.

AIRPORTS

Portland International Jetport is served by Air Nova, American, Business Express, Continental, Delta, Northwest, TWA, United, and US Airways. Bangor International Airport is served by Business Express, Continental, Delta/Comair, U.S. Air, and Finnair. Hancock County Airport, 8 mi northwest of Bar Harbor, is served by US Airways Express. Knox County Regional Airport, in Owls Head, 3 mi south of Rockland, has flights to Boston and Bar Harbor on US Airways Express.

➤ AIRPORT INFORMATION: **Portland International Jetport** (⊠ Westbrook St. off Rte. 9, ☎ 207/774–7301). **Bangor International Airport** (⊠ Godfrey Blvd., ☎ 207/947–0384). **Hancock County Airport** (⊠ Rte. 3, Trenton, ☎ 207/667–7329). **Knox County Regional Airport** (⊠ off Rte. 73, ☎ 207/594–4131).

BIKE [& MOPED] TRAVEL

For information on bicycling in Maine and a list of companies offering tours, contact the Bicycle Coalition of Maine.

➤ CONTACTS: **Bicycle Coalition of Maine** (☎ 207/288–3028).

BOAT & FERRY TRAVEL

Northumberland/Bay Ferries operates the Cat, a high-speed car-ferry service on a catamaran, between Yarmouth, Nova Scotia, and Bar Harbor from mid-May to mid-October. The crossing takes three hours, and the Cat has everything from a casino to sightseeing decks. Prince of Fundy Cruises operates a car ferry from May to October between Portland and Yarmouth, Nova Scotia. Maine State Ferry Service provides service from Rockland, Lincolnville, and Bass Harbor to islands in Penobscot and Blue Hill bays.

➤ BOAT & FERRY INFORMATION: **Northumberland/Bay Ferries** (☎ 888/249–7245). **Prince of Fundy Cruises** (☎ 800/341–7540; 800/482–0955 in Maine). **Maine State Ferry Service** (☎ 207/596–2202 or 800/491–4883).

BUS TRAVEL

Concord Trailways provides service between Boston and Bangor (via Portland); a coastal route connects towns between Brunswick and Searsport. Vermont Transit provides service to Augusta, Bangor, Brunswick, Lewiston, Portland, and Waterville. Vermont Transit is a subsidiary of Greyhound Lines.

➤ BUS INFORMATION: **Concord Trailways** (☎ 800/639–3317). **Vermont Transit** (☎ 207/772–6587). **Greyhound Lines** (☎ 800/231–2222).

CAR RENTAL

➤ MAJOR AGENCIES: **Alamo** (⊠ 1000 Westbrook St., ☎ 207/775–0855; 800/327–9633 in Portland). **Avis** (⊠ Portland International Jetport, ☎ 207/874–7500 or 800/831–2847). **Budget** (⊠ 1128 Westbrook St., ☎ 800/848–8005). **Hertz** (⊠ 1049 Westbrook St., Portland International Jetport, ☎ 207/774–4544 or 800/654–3131). **National** (⊠ Portland International Jetport, ☎ 207/773–0036 or 800/227–7368).

CAR TRAVEL

Interstate 95 is the fastest route to and through the state from coastal New Hampshire and points south, turning inland at Brunswick and going on to Bangor and the Canadian border. U.S. 1, more leisurely and scenic, is the principal coastal highway from New Hampshire to Canada. U.S. 302 is the primary access to the Sebago Lake region, while Route 26 leads to the western mountains and Route 27 leads to the Rangeley and Sugarloaf regions. U.S. 201 is the fastest route to Québec, and Route 9 is the inland route from Bangor to Calais.

The maximum speed limit is 65 mph, unless otherwise posted, on I–95 and the Maine Turnpike. Local municipalities post speed limits on roads within their jurisdictions. State law requires drivers to stop for pedestrians. Drivers can make right turns on red if no sign prohibits such turns. Note that Maine law requires drivers to turn on their lights when windshield wipers are operating.

In many areas a car is the only practical means of travel. The *Maine Map and Travel Guide,* available for a small fee from the Maine Tourism Association, is useful for driving throughout the state; it has directories, mileage charts, and enlarged maps of city areas. DeLorme's *Maine Atlas & Gazetteer,* sold at local bookstores, includes enlarged, detailed maps of every part of the state.

LODGING

CAMPING

Reservations for state park campsites (excluding Baxter State Park) can be made from January until August 23 through the Bureau of Parks and Lands. Make reservations as far ahead as possible (at least seven days in advance), because sites go quickly. The Maine Campground Owners Association has a statewide listing of private campgrounds.
➤ CONTACTS: **Bureau of Parks and Lands** (☎ 207/287–3824; 800/332–1501 in ME). **Maine Campground Owners Association** (⊠ 655 Main St., Lewiston 04240, ☎ 207/782–5874, FAX 207/782–4497, WEB www.campmaine.com).

OUTDOORS & SPORTS

BIRDING

The Maine Audubon Society provides information on birding in Maine and hosts field trips for novice to expert birders.
➤ CONTACTS: **Maine Audubon Society** (⊠ 20 Gilsland Farm Rd., Falmouth 04105, ☎ 207/781–6180, WEB www.maineaudubon.org).

FISHING

For information about fishing and licenses, contact the Maine Department of Inland Fisheries and Wildlife.
➤ CONTACTS: **Maine Department of Inland Fisheries and Wildlife** (⊠ 41 State House Station Augusta 04333, ☎ 207/287–8000. WEB www.state.me.us/ifw).

KAYAKING

A number of outfitters provide sea-kayaking instruction as well as tours along the Maine coast.
➤ CONTACTS: **Coastal Kayaking Tours** (⊠ 48 Cottage St., Bar Harbor, ☎ 800/526–8615 or 207/288–9605). **Maine Island Kayak Co.** (⊠ 70 Luther St., Peaks Island, ☎ 207/766–2373 or 800/796–2376). **Maine Sport Outfitters** (⊠ U.S. 1, Rockport, ☎ 207/236–8797 or 800/722–0826). **Sunrise County Canoe & Kayak** (⊠ Cathance Lake, Grove Post 04657, ☎ 207/454–7708 or 800/980–2300).

PARKS AND PUBLIC LANDS

The Bureau of Parks and Public Lands publishes the brochure "Outdoors in Maine," a listing of state parks, public reserved lands, state historic trails, boat access sites, snowmobile trails, and all-terrain-vehicle trails.

➤ CONTACTS: **Bureau of Parks and Public Lands** (✉ 22 State House Station, Augusta 04333, ☎ 207/287–3821, WEB www.state.me.us/doc/parks).

RAFTING

Raft Maine provides information on whitewater rafting on the Kennebec, Penobscot, and Dead rivers.

➤ CONTACTS: **Raft Maine** (✉ Box 3, Bethel 04217, ☎ 800/723–8633).

SKIING

For information on alpine skiing, contact Ski Maine. For information on cross-country ski centers, shops, and lodging packages, contact the Maine Nordic Ski Council.

➤ CONTACTS: **Ski Maine** (✉ Box 7566, Portland 04112, ☎ 207/622–6983; 207/761–3774; 888/624–6345 snow conditions, WEB www.skimaine.com). **Maine Nordic Ski Council** (✉ Box 645, Bethel 04217, ☎ 207/824–3694 or 800/754–9263, WEB www.mnsc.com).

SNOWMOBILING

The Maine Snowmobile Association offers an excellent state-wide trail map of about 8,000 mi of trails.

➤ CONTACTS: **Maine Snowmobile Association** (✉ Box 77, Augusta 04332, ☎ 207/622–6983; 207/626–5717 trail conditions, WEB www.mesnow.com).

SPORTING CAMPS

Maine Sporting Camp Association publishes a directory of sporting camps throughout the state.

➤ CONTACTS: **Maine Sporting Camp Association** (✉ Box 89, Jay 04249, WEB www.mainesportingcamps.com).

WINDJAMMING

The Maine Windjammer Association represents 13 schooners offering multiday cruises along the Maine coast.

➤ CONTACTS: **Maine Windjammer Association** (✉ Box 1144, Blue Hill 04614, ☎ 800/807–9463, WEB www.sailmainecoast.com).

TOURS

The Maine Professional Guides Association maintains and mails out listings of its members and their specialties.

➤ TOUR OPERATORS: **Maine Professional Guides Association** (Box 847, Augusta 04332, ☎ 207/549–5631, WEB www.maineguides.org).

TRAIN TRAVEL

Amtrak is planning to begin service from Boston to Portland in summer 2001, with stops in Saco and Wells year-round and in Old Orchard Beach in the summer.

➤ TRAIN INFORMATION: **Amtrak** (☎ 800/872–7245, WEB www.amtrak.com).

VISITOR INFORMATION

The Maine Tourism Association operates a welcome center on U.S. 2 in Bethel. State of Maine Visitor Information Centers are located on Union St. in Calais, Rte. 203 in Fryeburg, I–95 and U.S. 1 in Kittery, and on U.S. 1 in Yarmouth, I–95, Exit 17.

For a directory of members of the Maine Antique Dealer Association, send a self-addressed, stamped envelope and $3 to MADA. The Maine

Antiquarian Booksellers Association publishes a directory of members throughout Maine.

For a brochure describing eight art museums along the Maine coast, write the Maine Art Museum Trail. The Maine Crafts Association publishes a "Guide to Crafts and Culture." "The Maine Archives and Museums Directory" lists museums, historical societies, archives, and historic sites statewide. Call the Maine Garden and Landscape Trail for a map and guide. *The Maine Outdoor Sculpture Guide* is available from the Maine Arts Commission. The Web site, www.mainemusic.org, lists music-related events around the state.

➤ CONTACTS: **Maine Innkeepers Association** (✉ 305 Commercial St., Portland 04101, ☎ 207/773–7670, WEB www.maineinns.com). **Maine Tourism Association** (✉ Box 2300, 325B Water St., Hallowell 04347, ☎ 207/623–0363 or 888/624–6345, WEB www.mainetourism.com). **Maine Office of Tourism** (✉ 33 Stone St., Augusta 04333, ☎ 888/624–6345, WEB www.visitmaine.com). **Maine Antique Dealer Association,** (✉ Box 352, Scarborough 04074. WEB www.maineada.com). **Maine Antique Dealer Directory** (✉ R.R. 3, Box 1290, Winslow 04901).The **Maine Antiquarian Booksellers Association** (✉ ☎ 207/645–4122, WEB www.wworx.net/maba). **Maine Art Museum Trail** (✉ 75 Russell St., Lewiston 04240 ☎ 800/782–6497. WEB www.maineartmuseums.org). **Maine Crafts Association** (✉ 15 Walton St., Portland 04103, WEB www.mainecrafts.maine.com). "**The Maine Archives and Museums Directory**" (✉ 60 Community Dr., Augusta 04330. ☎ 800/452–8786, WEB www.mainemuseums.org). **Maine Garden and Landscape Trail** (✉ ☎ 800/782–6497). **Maine Arts Commission** (✉ 25 State House Station, Augusta 04333, ☎ 207/287–2724.

2 NEW HAMPSHIRE

The seacoast, majestic mountains, and peaceful villages are all part of New Hampshire. Along the coast is a short stretch of towns with sandy beaches, as well as the engaging city of Portsmouth. The Lakes Region is a summer and fall haven for fishing, swimming, and boating. Up north, the majestic White Mountains attract people who come to gaze on Mt. Washington, the tallest peak in the East, to ski and snowboard, to hike, and to shop at North Conway's outlet stores. Western and central New Hampshire have a string of cities along I–93 and a large unspoiled area of small towns, each with its own historic district and town green.

By Andrew
Collins

CRUSTY, INDEPENDENT-MINDED NEW HAMPSHIRE is often defined more by what it is not than by what it is. It lacks the folksy charm of neighboring Vermont, nor does it have the miles of awe-inspiring rocky coast of Maine, its neighbor to the east. And New Hampshire's politics tend toward conservative (with a distinctly libertarian slant), unlike the decidedly more liberal Massachusetts.

Whether in spite of or because of its differences, New Hampshire has been welcoming visitors for centuries. The first hiker to reach the top of Mt. Washington was Darby Field, in 1642. The first summer home appeared on one of the state's many lakes in 1763. Ralph Waldo Emerson, Henry David Thoreau, Nathaniel Hawthorne, and Louisa May Alcott all visited and wrote about the state, sparking a strong literary tradition that continues today. Filmmaker Ken Burns, writer J. D. Salinger, and poet Donald Hall all make their homes here.

New Hampshire's independent spirit nourishes other branches of the arts as well. Portsmouth has several theater groups, both cutting-edge and mainstream. New Hampshire's oldest professional theater, Tamworth's Barnstormers, claims the son of a president (Francis Cleveland) as founder. Throughout the state, a large number of stores display the work of local artisans. On back roads and in small towns, you can find makers of fine furniture and museum-quality pewter, glassblowers and potters, weavers and woodworkers. The League of New Hampshire Craftsmen operates eight stores around the state and runs the nation's oldest crafts fair each year in early August.

But it was the mountain peaks, clear air, and sparkling lakes that attracted most of New Hampshire's early visitors, the same things that draw people today. You can ski, snowboard, hike, and fish, or explore on snowmobiles, sailboats, and mountain bikes. Rock climbing and snowshoeing are popular, too. The diversity of the state's natural resources make it a popular spot with everyone from avid adventurers to young families looking for easy access to nature.

New Hampshire natives have no objection to others enjoying the natural beauty of the state as long as they leave some of their money behind. The state has long resisted both sales and income taxes, so tourism adds much-needed revenue to the state coffers.

Taxes are only one hotly debated topic in the politically minded Granite State. New Hampshire was the first colony to declare itself independent from Great Britain, the first to adopt a state constitution, and the first to require that constitution to be referred to the people for approval. From the start, New Hampshire residents took their hard-won freedoms seriously. Twenty years after the Revolutionary War's Battle of Bennington, New Hampshire native General John Stark, who led the troops to that crucial victory, wrote a letter to be read at the reunion he was too ill to attend. In it, he reminded his men, "Live free or die; death is not the worst of evils." The first half of that sentiment is now the state's motto, appearing even on its license plates. Nothing symbolizes those freedoms more than voting, and residents relish their role as host of the nation's earliest presidential primary.

With a few of its cities consistently rated among the most livable in the nation, New Hampshire has seen considerable growth over the past decade or two. Even as growth has leveled in the rest of New England, New Hampshire's population continues upward, fueled mainly by transplants seeking a higher quality of life and lower costs of living.

New Hampshire

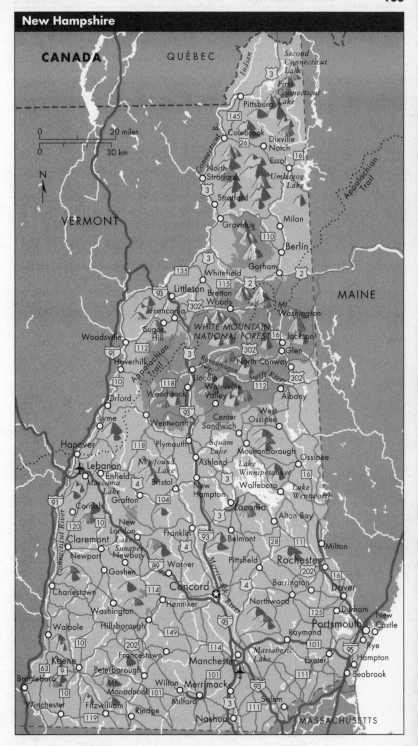

CANADA

QUÉBEC

Indian R.

Second
Connecticut
Lake

First
Connecticut
Lake

3

Pittsburg

145

Colebrook

26

Dixville
Notch

Connecticut R.

Errol

16

North
Stratford

Umbagog
Lake

3

Stratford

Appalachian Trail

Groveton

Milan

110

Berlin

3

Gorham

2

Whitefield

135

115

Littleton

93

Bretton
Woods

2

MAINE

302

Mt.
Washington

Franconia

WHITE MOUNTAIN
NATIONAL FOREST

Sugar
Hill

16

Jackson

Woodsville

112

302

Glen

91

Haverhill

Kancamagus Hwy.

3

North Conway

10

118

Lincoln

Swift River

302

Orford

Woodstock

93

Waterville
Valley

112

Albany

Lyme

Wentworth

Center
Sandwich

West
Ossipee

Hanover

118

Plymouth

Squam
Lake

Moultonborough

Ossipee

Lebanon

Newfound
Lake

Ashland

Lake
Winnipesaukee

16

Enfield

4

New
Hampton

3

Wolfeboro

Lake
Wentworth

91

Mascoma
Lake

Bristol

Cornish

Grafton

104

Laconia

120

10

New
London

Franklin

3

Alton Bay

Claremont

Lake
Sunapee

4

93

Belmont

28

11

Milton

Newport

Newbury

89

Warner

Pittsfield

Rochester

202

16

Goshen

114

Barrington

Dover

Charlestown

Concord

4

Northwood

125

Durham

Washington

Henniker

Portsmouth

New
Castle

Walpole

Hillsborough

149

Raymond

101

Rye

10

202

Francestown

114

Massabesic
Lake

95

Hampton

Keene

63

9

Peterborough

Manchester

Exeter

111

Seabrook

Brattleboro

Mt.
Monadnock

Wilton

101

Merrimack

93

Winchester

10

Fitzwilliam

Milford

3

Salem

111

119

Rindge

Nashua

MASSACHUSETTS

0   20 miles
0   30 km

N

VERMONT

Much of this population boom is in the southern section of the state, and longtime residents worry that New Hampshire will soon take on two distinct personalities: one driven by the upwardly cities of the southeast, such as Nashua, Derry, and Londonderry, and the other by the small towns and villages that make up the western and northern tiers of the state. Only time will tell how New Hampshire will cope. But while the influx of newcomers has brought inevitable change, the independent nature of the people and the state's natural beauty continue to please newcomers and locals alike.

Pleasures and Pastimes

Dining
New Hampshire prides itself on seafood, not just lobster but also salmon pie, steamed mussels, fried clams, and seared tuna steaks. Across the state you'll find country inns with upscale Continental and American menus, many of them embracing regional ingredients and cutting-edge preparations of the day. In the past two or three years, several hip contemporary eateries have opened up, especially in the southern half of the state, alongside such state traditions as greasy-spoon diners, excellent pizza restaurants, and pubs and taverns serving hearty comfort fare (especially in the ski and boating areas).

For price-category information, *see* Dining *in* Smart Travel Tips.

Lodging
In the mid-19th century, wealthy Bostonians would pack up and move to their grand summer homes in the countryside for two- or three-month stretches. Many of these homes have been restored and converted into the handsome country inns that are so strongly identified with the region. The smallest have only a couple of rooms; typically, they're done in period style. The largest contain 30 or more rooms, with in-room fireplaces and even hot tubs. Pampering amenities seem to increase each year at some properties, but others remain stuck in an earlier time, appealing for their retro value but perhaps in need of updating.

Bed-and-breakfasts and inns dominate New Hampshire's lodging scene, but you'll also find a great many well-kept, often family-owned motor lodges—particularly in the White Mountains and Lakes regions. A few of the grand old resorts still stand, with their world-class cooking staffs and tradition of top-notch service. In the Merrimack River valley, as well as along major highways, chain hotels and motels dominate the lodging scene.

For price-category information, *see* Lodging *in* Smart Travel Tips.

National and State Parks and Forests
The awesome White Mountain National Forest, the jewel of the state's park areas, covers 770,000 acres in northern New Hampshire. Major recreation parks are at Franconia Notch, Crawford Notch, and Mt. Sunapee. Rhododendron State Park, in Fitzwilliam in the Monadnock region, has a singular collection of wild rhododendrons. Mt. Washington Park crowns the highest mountain in the Northeast. Numerous state recreation areas offer camping, picnicking, hiking, boating, fishing, swimming, biking, and winter sports.

Outdoor Activities and Sports
BEACHES AND LAKES
New Hampshire makes the most of its 18-mi coastline with several good beaches, among them Hampton Beach and Wallis Sands in Rye. For warmer, fresh waters, head to pristine Lake Winnipesaukee, Lake Sunapee, Squam Lake, and Newfound Lake.

BIKING

A safe, scenic route along New Hampshire's seacoast is the bike path along Route 1A, for which you can park at Odiorne Point and follow the road 14 mi south to Seabrook. Some bikers begin at Prescott Park and take Route 1B into New Castle, but beware of the traffic. Another pretty route is from Newington Town Hall to the Great Bay Estuary. Excellent routes in the White Mountains are detailed in the mountain-bike guide map "The White Mountain Ride Guide," sold at area sports and book shops. There's also a bike path in Franconia Notch State Park at the Lafayette Campground and a mountain-biking center, Great Glen Trails, at the base of Mt. Washington. Many ski areas offer lift-serviced mountain biking in summer.

FISHING

Lake trout and salmon swim in Lake Winnipesaukee, trout and bass in smaller lakes, and trout in streams all around the Lakes Region. Alton Bay has an "Ice Out" salmon derby in spring. In winter, ice fishing takes place on all the lakes from huts known as "ice bobs." In the Sunapee region, you can fish for brook, rainbow, and lake trout; smallmouth bass; pickerel; and horned pout. The Monadnocks have more than 200 lakes and ponds stocked with a similar range of species.

SKIING AND SNOW SPORTS

Scandinavian settlers who came to New Hampshire's high, handsome, rugged peaks in the late 1800s brought their skis with them. Skiing got its modern start in the Granite State in the 1920s with the cutting of trails on Cannon Mountain; you can now ski or snowboard at nearly 20 areas, from the old, established slopes (Cannon, Cranmore, Wildcat) to more contemporary ones (Attitash, Loon, Waterville Valley). Promotional packages assembled by the ski areas allow you to sample different resorts. There's Ski 93 (referring to resorts along I–93), Ski the Mt. Washington Valley, and more.

Shopping

The absence of sales tax makes New Hampshire a hugely popular destination for shopping. Outside the outlet meccas of North Conway and Tilton, this pastime revolves around antiques and local crafts, which are plentiful and high in quality. Depression glass, silverware, and china abound, with furniture becoming scarcer and more expensive. Look for pottery, jewelry, furniture, and wooden boxes as well.

In the southern Lakes Region and in Hampton Beach, tacky souvenir shops are the norm. Summertime fairs, such as the one operated by the League of New Hampshire Craftsmen at Mt. Sunapee State Park, are a good way to see some of the state's best arts and crafts. The densest clusters of antiques shops are along U.S. 4, between Route 125 and Concord; along Route 119, from Fitzwilliam to Hinsdale; along Route 101, from Marlborough to Wilton; and in the towns of North Conway, North Hampton, Hopkinton, Hollis, and Amherst. In the Lakes Region, most shops are along the eastern side of Winnipesaukee, near Wolfeboro. Particularly in the Monadnock region, stores in barns and homes along back roads are "open by chance or by appointment."

Exploring New Hampshire

New Hampshire can be divided into four regions. The main attraction of the coast is bustling, historic Portsmouth; several somewhat quieter communities such as Durham and Exeter lie a bit further inland. The Lakes Region, in east-central New Hampshire, has good hiking trails, antiques shops, and, of course, water sports. People go to the White Mountains in the north to hike, ski, and photograph vistas and vibrant foliage. Southwestern New Hampshire is the unspoiled quiet corner of the state, hemmed in to the east by the central Merrimack Valley, which has a string of fast-growing communities along I–93 and U.S. 3.

Numbers in the text and in the margin correspond to numbers on the maps: New Hampshire Coast, New Hampshire Lakes, The White Mountains, Dartmouth–Lake Sunapee, and Monadnock Region and Central New Hampshire.

Great Itineraries

Some people come to New Hampshire to hike or ski the mountains, fish and sail the lakes, or cycle along the back roads. Others prefer to drive through scenic towns, visiting museums and shops. Although New Hampshire is a small state, roads curve around lakes and mountains, making distances longer than they appear. You can get a taste of the coast, lake, and mountain areas of the state in three to five days; eight days gives you time to make a comprehensive loop.

IF YOU HAVE 3 DAYS

Drive along Route 1A to see the coast or take a boat tour of the Isles of Shoals before exploring ⊞ **Portsmouth** ①. The next day visit ⊞ **Wolfeboro** ㉒, on the eastern edge of Lake Winnipesaukee, good for an overnight stop. The following morning drive across the scenic **Kancamagus Highway** ㊲ from Conway to **Lincoln** ㉕ to see the granite ledges and mountain streams of the White Mountains.

IF YOU HAVE 5 DAYS

After visiting ⊞ **Portsmouth** ① and ⊞ **Wolfeboro** ㉒, explore Squam and Ossipee lakes and the charming towns near them: **Moultonborough** ⑱, **Center Harbor** ⑮, and **Tamworth** ⑲. Spend your third night in the White Mountains town of ⊞ **Jackson** ㉝, which is equally beautiful in the winter, when cross-country skiing is popular, and in the summer, when hiking is the main activity. After crossing the **Kancamagus Highway** ㊲ to **Lincoln** ㉕, tour the western part of the White Mountain National Forest via Route 112 to Route 118. Take Route 25A and then Route 10 south through the upper Connecticut River valley to reach ⊞ **Hanover** ㊺, home of Dartmouth College, for an overnight. Follow I–89 back by way of **Newbury** ㊸ and the Lake Sunapee region.

When to Tour New Hampshire

In summer, people flock to seaside beaches, mountain hiking trails, and lake boat ramps. In the cities, festivals bring music and theater to the forefront. Fall brings leaf-peepers, especially to the White Mountains and along the Kancamagus Highway. Skiers take to the slopes in winter, when Christmas lights and carnivals brighten the long, dark nights. April's mud season, the black fly season in late May, and unpredictable weather keep visitor numbers low in spring, but the season has its joys, not the least of which is the appearance of New Hampshire's state flower, the purple lilac, from mid-May to early June.

THE COAST

New Hampshire's brief, shining 18-mi stretch of coastline packs in a wealth of scenery and diversions, from beaches to the historic and cultural pleasures of Portsmouth. The honky-tonk of Hampton Beach gets plenty of attention, good and bad, but first-timers are often surprised by the significant chunk of shoreline that remains pristine and unspoiled—especially through the town of Rye. This tour begins in the regional hub, Portsmouth; cuts down the coast to the beaches; branches inland to the quintessential prep school town Exeter; and then runs back up north through charming Dover, Durham (home to the University of New Hampshire), and Rochester. From here it's a short drive to the Lakes Region.

Portsmouth

★ ❶ *47 mi southeast of Concord; 50 mi southwest of Portland, ME; 56 mi north of Boston, MA.*

Originally settled in 1623 as Strawbery Banke, Portsmouth became a prosperous port before the Revolutionary War. Abundant with grand residential architecture spanning the 18th through early-20th centuries, Portsmouth has numerous historic house-museums, including the collection of buildings that make up the Strawberry Banke Museum. The energetic downtown brims with trendy eateries and both quirky and upscale shops, plus theaters and music venues. You can walk to most of these attractions from Market Square.

The **Portsmouth Harbour Trail** passes more than 70 18th- and 19th-century homes and buildings downtown, through the South End, and along State and Congress streets. You can purchase a tour map ($2.50) at the information kiosk on Market Square, the Chamber of Commerce, and at several house-museums. A guided walk can be enjoyed year–round. ☎ 603/436–3988, WEB *www.seacoastnh.com/harbourtrail* ✉ *$7,* ☉ *Thurs.–Mon.*

The **Portsmouth Black Heritage Trail** (☎ 603/431–2768, WEB www.sea-coastnh.com/blackhistory)—established in 1999—is a self-guided walk that visits sites important to black history in Portsmouth. Included are the **New Hampshire Gazette Printing Office**, where skilled slave Primus Fowle operated the paper's printing press for some 50 years beginning in 1756, and the city's 1866 **Election Hall**, outside of which the city's black citizens held annual celebrations of the Emancipation Proclamation. The yellow, hip-roof **John Paul Jones House** was a boarding house when the Revolutionary War hero lived here during his tenure in Portsmouth supervising shipbuilding for the Continental Navy. The 1758 structure, now the headquarters of the **Portsmouth Historical Society,** contains furniture, costumes, glass, guns, portraits, and documents from the late 18th century. ✉ *43 Middle St.,* ☎ *603/436–8420,* WEB *www.seacoastnh.com/touring/jpjhouse.html.* ✉ *$4.* ☉ *June–mid-Oct., Mon.–Sat. 10–4, Sun. noon–4.*

The period interior of the **Moffatt-Ladd House,** built in 1763, tells the story of Portsmouth's merchant class through portraits, letters, and fine furnishings. The Colonial Revival garden includes a horse chestnut tree, believed to be one of New Hampshire's oldest trees, planted by General William Whipple when he returned home after signing the Declaration of Independence in 1776. ✉ *154 Market St.,* ☎ *603/436–8221.* ✉ *$5.* ☉ *Mid-June–mid-Oct., Mon.–Sat. 11–5, Sun. 1–5.*

NEED A BREAK?

For some midday noshing, drop by **Annabelle's Natural Ice Cream** (✉ 49 Ceres St., ☎ 603/436–3400) for a dish of Ghirardelli chocolate chip or Almond Joy ice cream. **Cafe Brioche** (✉ 14 Market Sq., ☎ 603/430–9225), right on Market Square, serves coffees, thick deli sandwiches, and fresh-baked pastries.

★ The first English settlers named the area around today's Portsmouth for the wild strawberries abundant along the shore of the Piscataqua River. **Strawbery Banke Museum,** the city's largest and most-impressive museum, now uses the name. This attractive 10-acre outdoor museum with period gardens, exhibits, and craftspeople holds 46 buildings that date from 1695 to 1820. Ten furnished homes represent 300 years of history in one continuously occupied neighborhood. Half the interior of the **Drisco House,** built in 1795, depicts its history as a colonial dry-goods store, while the living room and kitchen are decorated as they were in the 1950s, showing how buildings are adapted. The **Shapiro House** has been restored to reflect the life of the Russian Jewish immigrant family who lived in the home in the early 1900s. Perhaps the most opulent house, decorated in decadent Victorian style, is the 1860 **Goodwin Mansion,** former home of Governor Ichabod Goodwin. ⊠ *Marcy St.,* ☎ *603/433–1100,* WEB *www.strawberybanke.org.* 🎫 *$6.* ☉ *May–Oct., daily 10–5; Nov.–Apr., Wed.–Sat. 10–4.*

Picnicking is popular in **Prescott Park,** on the waterfront between Strawbery Banke Museum and the Piscataqua River. A large formal garden with fountains is perfect for whiling away an afternoon. The park also contains **Point of Graves,** Portsmouth's oldest burial ground, and two 17th-century warehouses.

𝒞 Nineteen hands-on exhibits at the **Children's Museum of Portsmouth** explore lobstering, sound and music, computers, space travel, and other subjects. The museum is best for kids under 11. Some programs require reservations. ⊠ *280 Marcy St.,* ☎ *603/436–3853,* WEB *www.childrens-museum.org.* 🎫 *$4.* ☉ *Tues.–Sat. 10–5, Sun. 1–5; also Mon. 10– 5 in summer and during school vacations.*

The **Wentworth-Coolidge State Historic Mansion,** a National Historic Landmark that's now part of **Little Harbor State Park,** was originally the residence of Benning Wentworth, New Hampshire's first Royal Governor (1753–1770). Notable among the period furnishings in the house is the carved pine mantelpiece in the council chamber. Wentworth's imported lilac trees, believed to be the oldest in North America, bloom each May. The visitor center stages lectures and exhibits. ⊠ *Little Harbor Rd., near South Street Cemetery,* ☎ *603/436–6607.* 🎫 *$2.50.* ☉ *Grounds, daily year-round; mansion, June–Sept., Tues., Thurs.–Sat. 10– 3, Sun. noon–5.*

Docked at the **Port of Portsmouth Maritime Museum** in Albacore Park is the USS *Albacore,* built here in 1953. You can board this prototype submarine, which was a floating laboratory assigned to test a new hull design, dive brakes, and sonar systems for the navy. The nearby **Memorial Garden** and its reflecting pool are dedicated to those who lost their lives in submarine service. ⊠ *600 Market St.,* ☎ *603/436–3680.* 🎫 *$4.* ☉ *Daily 9:30–5:30.*

The **Redhook Ale Brewery,** visible from the Spaulding Turnpike, conducts tours that end with a beer tasting of three to four samples. If you don't have time to tour, you can stop in the Cataqua Public House to sample the fresh ales and have a bite to eat (open daily, lunch and dinner). ⊠ *Pease International Tradeport, 35 Corporate Dr.,* ☎ *603/ 430–8600,* WEB *www.redhook.com.* 🎫 *$1.* ☉ *Tours weekdays 11 AM, weekends 1, 3, and 5.*

Dining and Lodging

$$$–$$$$ ✗ **Dunfey's Aboard the *John Wanamaker.*** Portsmouth's floating restaurant, on a restored tugboat, prepares creative delicacies such as roasted rack of New Zealand lamb with thyme and asparagus and roasted-garlic mashed red bliss potatoes. You can watch the river from the bar, enjoy the bistro-like atmosphere of the main dining room, or relax in the romantic Captain's Room. The upper-level deck is a favorite on starry summer nights for light meals, a glass of wine, or dessert and cappuccino. ⊠ *1 Harbour Pl.,* ☎ *603/433–3111. Reservations essential on weekends. AE, MC, V.*

$$–$$$ ✕ **Blue Mermaid World Grill.** The chefs at Blue Mermaid prepare innovative, globally influenced fare on a wood-burning grill. Specialties include lobster-and-shrimp pad Thai, pan-seared cod with a coconut cream sauce and plantain chips, and grilled spiced pork chops with a rhubarb-ginger-cranberry chutney. In summer you can eat on a deck that overlooks the historic Hill neighborhood. Entertainers perform (outdoors in summer) on Friday and Saturday. ✉ *409 Hanover St.,* ☎ *603/427–2583. AE, D, DC, MC, V.*

$$–$$$ ✕ **Ciento: A Tapas Bar.** Whether nibbling on tapas or digging into substantial platters of pan-Mediterranean fare, lively yupsters and beautiful people fill Ciento nightly. The grilled flat bread sandwich with sautéed rock shrimp, applewood-smoked bacon, and citrus aioli are hard to resist. You can also try three kinds of paella. ✉ *409 Hanover St.,* ☎ *603/427–2583. AE, D, DC, MC, V.*

$$–$$$ ✕ **Library at the Rockingham House.** Most of this Portsmouth landmark, a former luxury hotel, has been converted to condominiums, but the restaurant retains the hand-carved mahogany paneling, a marble-top bar, and bookcases on every wall. Although the kitchen churns out some lighter fare such as risotto primavera, the mainstays are traditional dishes such as veal marsala and baked stuffed shrimp. The check arrives between the pages of a vintage best-seller. ✉ *401 State St.,* ☎ *603/431–5202. Reservations essential. AE, DC, MC, V.*

$$–$$$ ✕ **Porto Bello Ristorante Italiano.** This family-run restaurant brings the
★ tastes of Naples to downtown Portsmouth. In the second-story dining room overlooking the harbor, you can savor daily antipasto specials ranging from grilled calamari to stuffed baby eggplant. Pastas include spinach gnocchi and homemade ravioli. A house specialty is veal *carciofi*—a 6-ounce cutlet served with artichokes. ✉ *67 Bow St.,* ☎ *603/ 431–2989. Reservations essential. AE, D, MC, V. Closed Mon.–Tues.*

$–$$ ✕ **Muddy River Smokehouse.** Red-check tablecloths and murals of trees and meadows create the look of an outdoor summer barbecue joint— even when the weather turns cold. Roll up your sleeves and dig into platters of ribs, homemade corn bread, and molasses baked beans. Chicken, blackened catfish, exceptional burgers, and other dishes are on the menu, but devotees swear by the "pig city" platter of St. Louis– grilled ribs, with smoked sweet sausage and pulled pork. ✉ *21 Congress St.,* ☎ *603/430–9582. AE, MC, V.*

$$$ 🏨 **Sheraton Harborside Portsmouth Hotel.** Portsmouth's only luxury hotel, this five-story redbrick building is within easy walking distance of shops and attractions. Suites have full kitchens and living rooms. ✉ *250 Market St., 03801,* ☎ *603/431–2300 or 800/325–3535,* 🅵🅰🆇 *603/ 431–7805,* 🆆🅴🅱 *www.sheraton.com. 179 rooms, 24 suites. 2 restaurants, bar, room service, indoor pool, sauna, health club, nightclub, business services, meeting room. AE, D, DC, MC, V.*

$$$ 🏨 **Sise Inn.** Each room at this Queen Anne town house in Portsmouth's historic district is decorated in Victorian style, with special fabrics, antiques, and reproductions of antiques. Some rooms have hot tubs and about half are in a 1980s addition that blends well with the older section. It's close to the Market Square area. ✉ *40 Court St., 03801,* ☎ 🅵🅰🆇 *603/433–1200 or* ☎ *877/747–3466. 26 rooms, 8 suites. In-room VCRs, meeting room. AE, DC, MC, V. CP.*

$$ 🏨 **Martin Hill Inn.** Two buildings downtown—one dating from 1815, and another from 1850—hold a charming inn that's within walking distance of the historic district and the waterfront. Extensive perennial gardens enhance the B&B. The quiet rooms, furnished with antiques, are decorated in formal Colonial or country-Victorian style. The Greenhouse suite has a private solarium facing the water garden. The inn is no-smoking. ✉ *404 Islington St.,* ☎ *603/436–2287,* 🆆🅴🅱 *www.portsmouthnh.com/martinhillinn. 4 rooms, 3 suites. MC, V. BP.*

Nightlife and the Arts

The **Portsmouth Gas Light Co.** (⊠ 64 Market St., ☎ 603/430–9122) is a popular brick-oven pizzeria and restaurant that hosts local rock bands in its courtyard in summer and in the lounge at other times. People come from as far away as Boston and Portland to hang out at the **Press Room** (⊠ 77 Daniel St., ☎ 603/431–5186), which showcases folk, jazz, blues, and bluegrass performers.

The **Prescott Park Arts Festival** (⊠ 105 Marcy St., ☎ 603/436–2848) presents theater, dance, and musical events outdoors during June, July, and August. Beloved for its acoustics, the 1878 **Music Hall** (⊠ 28 Chestnut St., ☎ 603/436–2400; 603/436–9900 film line) brings the best touring events to the seacoast—from classical and pop concerts to dance and theater. The hall also hosts an ongoing art-house film series. The **Players' Ring** (⊠ 105 Marcy St., ☎ 603/436–8123) highlights more than 15 original and well-known plays and performances by local theater groups from September through June. The **Pontine Movement Theatre** (⊠ 135 McDonough St., ☎ 603/436–6660) presents dance performances in a renovated warehouse—the company also tours throughout the year around New Hampshire and northern New England. The **Seacoast Repertory Theatre** (⊠ 125 Bow St., ☎ 603/433–4472 or 800/ 639–7650) offers a year-round schedule of musicals, classic dramas, and works by up-and-coming playwrights, as well as a youth theater.

Outdoor Activities and Sports

Portsmouth doesn't have any beaches, but the **Seacoast Trolley** (☎ 603/ 431–6975) departs from Market Square on the hour (daily 10–5), servicing a continuous loop between Portsmouth sights and area beaches. You can get a schedule for the trolley, which operates from mid-June to Labor Day, at the information kiosk in Market Square or by visiting WEB www.locallink.com/seacoasttrolley. The **Urban Forestry Center** (⊠ 45 Elwyn Rd., ☎ 603/431–6774) has gardens and marked trails appropriate for short hikes on its 180 acres.

Just inland from Portsmouth, the **Great Bay Estuarine Research Reserve** preserves one of southeastern New Hampshire's most precious assets: its shoreline on the Great Bay estuary. Blue herons, ospreys, and snowy egrets, all of which are especially conspicuous during spring and fall migrations, can be found among the 4,471 acres of tidal waters, mud flats, and about 48 mi of inland shoreline that compose the reserve. New Hampshire's largest concentration of winter eagles also lives here. The best public access is via **Sandy Point Discovery Center** (⊠ 89 Depot Rd., off Rte. 101, Stratham, ☎ 603/778–0015, WEB www.greatbay.org). This excellent facility contains both outdoor and indoor exhibits, a 1,700-ft boardwalk and other trails through both mudflats and upland forest, and a library and bookshop; interpretive programs are offered year-round. The center, about 15 mi southeast of Durham and 6 mi west of exit 3 from I–95 in Portsmouth, distributes maps and information and has trails for walking. ⊠ *Information: New Hampshire Fish & Game Dept., 37 Concord Rd., Durham, 03824,* ☎ *603/ 868–1095.* ☎ *Free.* ☉ *Daily dawn–dusk.*

Shopping

Market Square, in the center of town, has gift and clothing boutiques, book and card shops, and exquisite crafts stores.

Byrne & Carlson (⊠ 121 State St., ☎ 888/559–9778) produces handmade chocolates in the finest European tradition. **Kumminz Gallery** (⊠ 65 Daniel St., ☎ 603/433–6488) carries pottery, jewelry, and fiber art

by New Hampshire artisans. **N. W. Barrett** (✉ 53 Market St., ☎ 603/
431–4262) specializes in leather, jewelry, pottery, and fiber and other arts
and crafts. It also sells furniture, including affordable steam-bent oak pieces
and one-of-a-kind lamps and rocking chairs. **Pierce Gallery** (✉ 105
Market St., ☎ 603/436–1988) has prints and paintings of the Maine and
New Hampshire coasts. The **Portsmouth Bookshop** (✉ 1–7 Islington St.,
☎ 603/433–4406) carries old and rare books and maps. At **Salamandra Glass Studios** (✉ 7 Commercial Alley, ☎ 603/743–6553), you'll find
hand-blown glass vases, bowls, and other items; you can also peruse their
wares at the **Salamandra Gallery** (✉ 67 Bow St., ☎ 603/436–1038).

Isles of Shoals

❷ *10 mi southeast of Portsmouth, by ferry.*

Many of these nine small, rocky islands (eight at high tide)—like Hog
Island, Smuttynose, and Star Island—retain the earthy names given them
by the transient 17th-century fishermen. A colorful history of piracy,
murder, and ghosts surrounds the archipelago, long populated by an
independent lot who, according to one writer, hadn't the sense to winter on the mainland. Not all the islands lie within the New Hampshire
border: after an ownership dispute between Maine and New Hampshire, they were divvied up between the two states (five went to Maine,
four to New Hampshire).

Celia Thaxter, a native islander, romanticized these islands with her
poetry in *Among the Isles of Shoals* (1873) and celebrated her garden
in *An Island Garden* (1894; now reissued with the original color illustrations by Childe Hassam). In the late 19th century, **Appledore Island** became an offshore retreat for Thaxter's coterie of writers,
musicians, and artists. The island is now used by the Marine Laboratory of Cornell University. **Star Island** contains a nondenominational
conference center and is open to those on guided tours.

New Castle

❸ *3 mi south of Portsmouth.*

Though it consists of a single square mi of land, the small island of
New Castle was once known as Great Island. The narrow roads lined
with pre-Revolutionary houses and upscale condos and homes make
the island, which is accessible from the mainland by car, perfect for a
stroll.

Wentworth by the Sea, the last of the state's great seaside resorts, is
impossible to miss as you approach New Castle on Route 1B. Empty
these days, it was the site of the signing of the Russo-Japanese Treaty
in 1905, a fact that attracts many Japanese tourists. The current owners and the town have reached a tentative agreement to bring this grand
hotel back to life; renovations begin late in 2001.

Fort Constitution was originally built in 1631 and then rebuilt in 1666
as Fort William and Mary, a British stronghold overlooking Portsmouth
Harbor. Various additions and improvements were made over the
decades, but the site earned notoriety when Rebel patriots raided the
fort in 1774 in one of revolutionary America's first overt acts of defiance against King George III. The rebels later used the captured mu-
nitions against the British at the Battle of Bunker Hill. Panels throughout
the fort explain its history. ✉ *Rte. 1B at the Coast Guard Station,* ☎
603/436–1552, WEB *www.geocities.com/Pentagon/Barracks/6402/Fort
Constitution.* ☒ *Free.* ☉ *Mid-June–Labor Day, daily 9–5; Labor Day–
mid-June, weekends 9–5.*

Rye

4 *8 mi south of Portsmouth.*

In 1623 the first European settlers landed at Odiorne Point in what is now the largely undeveloped and picturesque town of Rye, making it the birthplace of New Hampshire. Today the area's main draws are a lovely state park, oceanfront beaches, and the view from Route 1A.

★ ☺ **Odiorne Point State Park** encompasses more than 330 acres of protected land, on the site where David Thomson established the first permanent European site in what is now New Hampshire. Stroll several nature trails with interpretive panels describing the park's military history or simply enjoy the vistas of the nearby Isles of Shoals. The rocky shore's tide pools—considered the best in New England—shelter crabs, periwinkles, and sea anemones. Throughout the year, the Seacoast Science Center conducts guided nature walks and interpretive programs, has exhibits on the area's natural history, and traces the social history of Odiorne Point back to the Ice Age. The facility's tide-pool touch tank and the 1,000-gallon Gulf of Maine deepwater aquarium is popular with kids. Day camp is offered for grades K–8 throughout the summer and during school vacations. ✉ *570 Rte. 1A, north of Wallis Sands, Rye State Beach,* ☎ *603/436–8043 science center, 603/436–1552 park.* 💲 *Science center $1 ($4 for guided walks and some interpretive programs); park Memorial Day–Columbus Day and on weekends $2.50.* ☻ *Science center daily 10–5, park daily 8 AM–dusk. www.seacentr.org.*

Dining and Lodging

$$–$$$ ✕ **Saunders at Rye Harbor.** Locals and visitors have been lazing about on the waterfront deck at sunset or over lunch since this festive spot opened in the 1920s. Fresh-caught lobster, Asian-seared salmon, and baked-stuffed shrimp are among the house specialties, which also include several chicken and steak dishes. ✉ *175 Harbor Rd.,* ☎ *603/964–6466. Closed Tues. AE, D, MC, V.*

$$–$$$$ 🏠 **Rock Ledge Manor.** Built out on a point, this mid-19th-century, gambrel-roof summer house with a wraparound porch anchored a resort colony. The rooms have water views; the family suite has a private balcony. Owners Stan and Stella Smith serve breakfast in the sunny dining room overlooking the Atlantic. This no-smoking B&B has a two-night minimum on weekends and holidays, and children must be over age 11. ✉ *1413 Ocean Blvd., 03870,* ☎ *603/431–1413,* WEB *www.rockledgemanor.com. 2 rooms, 1 suite. No credit cards. BP.*

Outdoor Activities and Sports

BEACHES

Good for swimming and sunning, **Jenness State Beach,** on Route 1A, is a favorite with locals. The facilities include a bathhouse, lifeguards, and metered parking. **Wallis Sands, Rye State Beach,** on Route 1A, is a swimmers' beach with bright white sand and a bathhouse. Parking is ample and costs $8 on weekends, $5 weekdays.

FISHING

Between April and October, deep-sea anglers head out for cod, mackerel, and bluefish. For a full- or half-day charter, try **Atlantic Fishing Fleet** (✉ Rye Harbor, ☎ 603/964–5220 or 800/942–5364).

Shopping

Although Rye is not known for its shopping, **Antiques at Rye Center** (✉ 655 Wallis Rd., ☎ 603/964–8999) is worth searching out for well-presented antiques from hand-painted porcelain to early toys.

En Route On Route 1A as it winds south through Rye to North Hampton, you'll pass a group of late-19th- and early-20th-century mansions known as

Millionaires' Row. Because of the way the road curves, the drive south along this route is especially breathtaking.

Hampton Beach

5 *8 mi south of Rye.*

Hampton Beach, from Route 27 to where Route 1A crosses the causeway, is an authentic seaside amusement center—the domain of fried dough stands, loud music, arcade games, palm readers, parasailing, and bronzed bodies. An estimated 150,000 people visit the town and its free public beach on the Fourth of July, and it draws plenty of people until late September, when things close up. The 3-mi boardwalk, where kids can play games and see how saltwater taffy is made, looks as if it were snatched out of the 1940s; in fact, the whole community remains remarkably free of modern franchise eateries and chain shops. Free outdoor concerts are held on many evenings in summer, and once a week there's a fireworks display. Talent shows and karaoke performances take place in the Seashell Stage, right on the beach.

Each summer locals hold a children's festival in August and celebrate the end of the season with a huge seafood feast on the weekend after Labor Day. For a quieter time, stop by for a sunrise stroll, when only seagulls and the occasional jogger interrupt the serenity.

Away from the beach crowds, you'll find **Fuller Gardens,** a late-1920s estate garden (the original mansion was razed in 1961) designed in the Colonial Revival style by Arthur Shurtleff, with a 1938 addition by the Olmsted brothers. With 2,000 rosebushes, a hosta garden, an annual display garden, a tropical conservatory, and a Japanese garden, it blooms all summer long. The Fuller Foundation is currently restoring the gardens to original blueprints, which were recently discovered—note that certain sections may be closed off during this process. ⊠ *10 Willow Ave., North Hampton,* ☎ *603/964–5414,* WEB *www.fullergardens.org.* ☞ *$5.* ☉ *Early May–mid-Oct., daily 10–6.*

Dining and Lodging

$$–$$$$ ✗ **Ron's Landing at Rocky Bend.** Nestled in among the motels lining Ocean Boulevard is this casually elegant restaurant, which prepares fresh seafood, pasta, beef, and veal dishes. Specialties include smoked Virginia oysters and filet mignon topped with fresh horseradish sauce. In summer, you can dine on the second-floor screened porch, which has a sweeping view of the Atlantic. ⊠ *379 Ocean Blvd.,* ☎ *603/929–2122. AE, D, DC, MC, V.*

$$–$$$$ ✗🖫 **Ashworth by the Sea.** This family-owned hotel was built across the street from Hampton Beach in 1912; most rooms have private decks, and the furnishings vary from period to contemporary. Beachside rooms have breathtaking ocean views, and the others look out onto the pool or the quiet street. The Ashworth Dining Room ($$–$$$) serves steaks, poultry, and fresh seafood—including seven lobster variations. ⊠ *295 Ocean Blvd., 03842,* ☎ *603/926–6762 or 800/345–6736,* FAX *603/926–2002. 105 rooms. 3 restaurants, pool. AE, D, DC, MC, V.*

$$$ 🖫 **D. W.'s Oceanside Inn.** The square front and simple awnings of this oceanfront inn look much the same as those on all the other buildings lining Ocean Boulevard. Inside, though, carefully selected antiques and collectibles, individually decorated rooms, a cozy living room and library with a fireplace, and a second-floor veranda for watching the waves give the Oceanside the feel of a late-19th-century home. Should the resort's crush of people and noise begin to overwhelm, you'll appreciate the soundproofing that makes this inn seem like a calm port in a storm. A separate three-bedroom cottage sleeps up to six guests

and has a kitchen. ⊠ *365 Ocean Blvd., 03842,* ☎ *603/926–3542,* 𝐅𝐀𝐗
603/926–3542, 𝐖𝐄𝐁 *www.oceansideinn.com. 9 rooms, 1 cottage. In-room
safes. AE, D, MC, V. Closed mid-Oct.–mid-May. BP.*

Nightlife and the Arts

The **Hampton Beach Casino Ballroom** (⊠ 169 Ocean Blvd., ☎ 603/
929–4100), despite the name, is not a gambling casino but a late 19th-
century, 2,000-seat performance venue that has hosted everyone from
Janis Joplin to Jerry Seinfeld to Everclear. Performances are scheduled
weekly April through October.

Outdoor Activities and Sports

BEACHES

Hampton Beach State Park (⊠ Rte. 1A, ☎ 603/926–3784) is a quieter stretch of the same beach that shares its name with the town. The
park, on the southwestern edge of town at the mouth of the Hampton River, has picnic tables, a store (seasonal), parking ($8 on summer
weekends, $5 weekdays), and a bathhouse.

FISHING

Between April and October, deep-sea anglers head out for cod, mackerel, and bluefish. There are rentals and charters offering half- and full-
day cruises, as well as some night fishing. Most leave from the Hampton
State Pier on Route 1A. **Al Gauron Deep Sea Fishing** (☎ 603/926–2469)
maintains a fleet of four boats for whale watching cruises and fishing
charters. **Eastman Fishing Fleet** (⊠ Seabrook, ☎ 603/474–3461) offers whale watching and fishing cruises, with evening and morning charg-
ers. **Smith & Gilmore** (☎ 603/926–3503)hosts deep-sea fishing
expeditions, cruises, and whale watches.

Hampton

❻ *3 mi west of Hampton Beach; 11 mi south of Portsmouth; 45 mi north
of Boston, MA.* One of New Hampshire's first towns, Hampton was
settled in 1638. Its name in the 17th century was Winnacunnet, which
means "beautiful place of pines." Today busy U.S. 1 defines the center of town and makes it a crossroads for anyone traveling along the
seacoast. The center of the early town was **Meeting House Green,**
where 42 stones represent the founding families. It is still a tranquil
place surrounded by pine trees.

Tuck Museum, across from Meeting House Green, contains displays on
the town's early history. The grounds also include a 19th-century
schoolhouse, a farm museum, and a fire-fighting museum. ⊠ *40 Park
Ave.,* ☎ *603/929–0781; 603/926–3840 for appointments.* 🎟 *Free.* ☉
June–Sept., Tues.–Fri. and Sun. 1–4 PM; *and by appointment.*

At 400-acre **Applecrest Farm Orchards**—the oldest and largest apple
orchard in the region—you can pick your own apples and berries or
buy fresh fruit pies and cookies from the bakery. Fall brings cider pressing, hay rides, pumpkins, and music on weekends. In winter a cross-
country ski trail traverses the orchard. ⊠ *133 Rte. 88, Hampton Falls,*
☎ *603/926–3721,* 𝐖𝐄𝐁 *www.applecrest.com.* ☉ *Daily 9–5.*

☾ At the **Seabrook Science & Nature Center,** adjacent to the Seabrook
Station nuclear power plant 4 mi south of Hampton, you can tour exhibits on the science of power, see control-room operators in training,
walk through a replica of a cooling tunnel, and pedal a bike to create
electricity. The center maintains the ¾-mi Owascoag Nature Trail, a
touch pool for kids, and several large aquariums of local sea life. ⊠
Lafayette Rd., Seabrook, ☎ *603/474–9521 or 800/338–7482.* 🎟 *Free.*
☉ *Weekdays 10–4.*

Lodging

$$–$$$ 🏨 **Hampton Falls Inn.** Intricate Burmese wall hangings and leather furniture decorate the lobby of this modern motel only 3½ mi from Hampton Beach. The bright, airy rooms and mini-suites (with mini-refrigerators and wet bars) are large, and many have a view of the neighboring farm; all have microwave ovens. An enclosed porch by the indoor pool looks out over the woods and fields. ⊠ *11 Lafayette Rd., 03844,* ☎ *603/ 926–9545 or 800/356–1729,* FAX *603/926–4155,* WEB *www.hampton-fallsinn.com. 33 rooms, 15 suites. Restaurant, pool, hot tub, meeting room. AE, D, DC, MC, V.*

$$ 🏨 **Victoria Inn.** Easy-going innkeepers Ron and Marina Mansfield run this romantic B&B a half-mile from Hampton Beach. Built as a carriage house in 1875, this upscale inn is decorated with plush Victorian antiques and fabrics, augmented with such modern amenities as central air-conditioning and heat, cable TV, and in-room phones. A large wraparound porch and a gazebo are perfect spots for relaxing with a book on a warm summer afternoon. Savor breakfast in the inn's dining room, which overlooks the former summer home of President Franklin Pierce. ⊠ *430 High St., 03842,* ☎ *603/929–1437 or 800/291–2672,* FAX *603/929–0747,* WEB *www.thevictoriainn.com. 3 rooms, 2 suites. Dining room, bicycles. MC, V. BP.*

$ ⚠ **Tidewater Campground.** This camping area has 170 sites, a large playground, a pool, a game room, and a basketball court. ⊠ *160 Lafayette Rd., 03842,* ☎ *603/926–5474. MC, V. Closed mid-Oct.–mid-May.*

Nightlife and the Arts

From July to September, the **Hampton Playhouse** (⊠ 357 Winnacunnet Rd., ☎ 603/926–3073) brings familiar Hollywood movie and New York theater actors to the coast for five musicals, plus Saturday children's shows.

Shopping

Antiques shops line U.S. 1 (Lafayette Rd.) in Hampton and neighboring Hampton Falls. The more than 50 dealers at **Antiques at Hampton Falls** (☎ 603/926–1971) have all types of antiques and collectibles. **Antiques New Hampshire** (☎ 603/926–9603) is a group shop with 35 dealers and a range of items. **Antiques One** (☎ 603/926–5332) carries everything but furniture, including books and maps. The prodigious **Barn at Hampton Falls** (☎ 603/926–9003) is known for American and European furniture.

Exeter

❼ *9 mi northwest of Hampton, 52 mi north of Boston, MA, 47 mi southeast of Concord.*

In Exeter's center, contemporary shops mix well with the buildings of the esteemed Phillips Exeter Academy, which opened in 1783, and other equally historic buildings. During the Revolutionary War, Exeter was the state capital, and it was here that the first state constitution and the first Declaration of Independence from Great Britain were put to paper.

The **American Independence Museum,** adjacent to Phillips Exeter Academy in the Ladd-Gilman House, celebrates the birth of our nation. The story of the Revolution unfolds during each guided tour, on which you'll see drafts of the U.S. Constitution and the first Purple Heart. Other items include letters and documents written by George Washington and the household furnishings of John Taylor Gilman, one of New Hampshire's early governors. The museum also hosts a Revolutionary War Festival in June. ⊠ *1 Governor's La.,* ☎ *603/772–2622,* WEB *www.independencemuseum.org.* ⌨ *$5.* ☉ *May–Oct., Wed.–Sun. noon–5 (last tour at 4).*

Dining and Lodging

$–$$ ✕ **Loaf and Ladle.** Hearty chowders, soups, and stews and huge sandwiches on homemade bread are served cafeteria-style at this understated eatery overlooking the river. Check the blackboard for the ever-changing rotation of chef's specials, breads, and desserts, and don't miss the fresh salad bar. The café is near the shops, galleries, and historic houses along Water Street. ⊠ *9 Water St.,* ☎ *603/778–8955. Reservations not accepted. AE, D, DC, MC, V.*

$$–$$$ ✕⊡ **Exeter Inn.** This brick Georgian-style inn on the campus of Phillips Exeter Academy has been the choice of visiting parents for the past half century. It is furnished with antique and reproduction pieces and possesses plenty of modern amenities. Among the Terrace Restaurant's specialties are a fillet of salmon wrapped in a pastry crust and stuffed with wild mushrooms and onions, and a napoleon of grilled vegetables with layers of Boursin cheese. On Sunday, the line forms early for a brunch with more than 40 options. ⊠ *90 Front St., 03833,* ☎ *603/ 772–5901 or 800/782–8444,* FAX *603/778–8757. 47 rooms. Restaurant, meeting room. AE, D, DC, MC, V.*

$$–$$$$ ⊡ **Inn by the Bandstand.** Common rooms in this 1809 Federal mansion, including a 1909 large addition, are decorated in period style. Seven guest rooms have working fireplaces; some have hot tubs, marble baths, and curtained four-poster beds. After a day of sightseeing, you can relax with a glass of complimentary sherry either in the privacy of your guest room or in one of the inviting common areas. ⊠ *4 Front St., 03833,* ☎ *603/772–6352,* FAX *603/778–0212,* WEB *www.innbythebandstand.com. 5 rooms, 4 suites. AE, D, MC, V. CP.*

$ ⚠ **Exeter Elms Family Campground.** This 50-acre campground has 202 sites (some riverfront), a swimming pool, a playground, canoe rentals, and a recreation program. ⊠ *188 Court St., 03833,* ☎ FAX *603/778–7631,* WEB *www.ucampnh.com/exeterelms. MC, V. Closed mid-Sept.–mid-May.*

Shopping

The **Exeter League of New Hampshire Craftsmen** shop (⊠ 61 Water St., ☎ 603/778–8282) sells original jewelry, woodworking, and pottery. **A Picture's Worth a Thousand Words** (⊠ 65 Water St., ☎ 603/778– 1991) stocks antique and contemporary prints, old maps, town histories, and rare books. **Water Street Artisans** (⊠ 20 Water St., ☎ 603/ 778–6178) carries fine crafts including jewelry, fiber arts, and pottery.

The **Travel and Nature Bookshop** (⊠ 59 Water St., ☎ 603/772–5573) has a wide selection of travel books including guides to New Hampshire hiking spots and other specialized titles. **Water Street Books** (⊠ 125 Water St., ☎ 603/778–9731) carries new fiction and nonfiction with an emphasis on New Hampshire authors.

Durham

❽ *12 mi north of Exeter, 11 mi northwest of Portsmouth.*

Settled in 1635 and home of General John Sullivan, a Revolutionary War hero and three-time New Hampshire governor, Durham was where Sullivan and his band of rebel patriots stored the gunpowder they captured from Fort William and Mary (☞ New Castle). Easy access to Great Bay via the Oyster River made Durham a center of maritime activity in the 19th century. Among the lures today are the water, farms that welcome visitors, and the University of New Hampshire, which occupies much of the town's center.

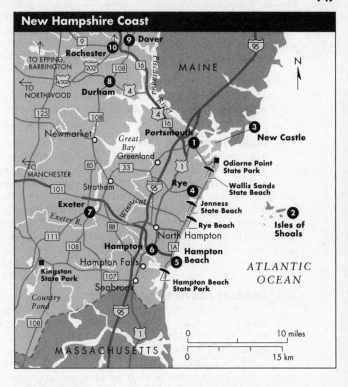

New Hampshire Coast

The **Art Gallery** at the University of New Hampshire occasionally exhibits items from a permanent collection of about 1,100 pieces but generally uses its space to host traveling exhibits of contemporary and historic art. Noted items in the collection include 19th-century Japanese woodblock prints and American landscape paintings. ⊠ *Paul Creative Arts Center, 30 College Rd.,* ☎ *603/862–3712,* WEB *www.unh.edu/arts/gallery.html.* ☒ *Free.* ☉ *Sept.–May, Mon.–Wed. 10–4, Thurs. 10–8, weekends 1–5.*

Emery Farm, which has been in the same family for 11 generations, sells fruits and vegetables in summer (including pick-your-own raspberries, strawberries, and blueberries), pumpkins in fall, and Christmas trees in December. The farm shop carries breads and pies, as well as local crafts. Children can pet the resident goats and sheep and attend storytelling events on several Tuesday mornings in July and August. ⊠ *U.S. 4, 1½ mi east of Rte. 108,* ☎ *603/742–8495.* ☉ *Late Apr.–Dec., daily 9–6.*

Dining and Lodging

$$$$ ✕🏨 **Three Chimneys Inn.** This stately yellow house on more than 3 acres has graced a hill overlooking the Oyster River since 1649. Rooms in the house and the 1795 barn, mostly named after plants from the extensive gardens, are decorated with Georgian- and Federal-period antiques and reproductions, canopy or four-poster beds with Edwardian bed drapes, and Oriental rugs—most have fireplaces. Specialties in the Maples dining room ($$-$$$$) include New England mussel salad and roast leg of farm-raised duckling. The ffrost-Sawyer Tavern ($$) serves simpler fare in a cozy setting, as does the outdoor Conservatory, which is open spring through fall. The inn is no-smoking. ⊠ *17 Newmarket Rd., 03824,* ☎ *603/868–7800 or 888/399–9777,* FAX *603/868–2964,* WEB *www.threechimneysinn.com. 23 rooms. 3 restaurants, in-room data ports, meeting room. AE, D, MC, V. BP.*

$$–$$$ ✕⊡ **New England Conference Center and Hotel.** In a lush wooded area
on the campus of the University of New Hampshire, this contemporary hotel is large enough to be a full-service conference center but quiet
enough to feel like a retreat. Acorns Restaurant specializes in American regional cuisine and is a favorite place for Sunday brunch. A signature dish is blackened red snapper with pineapple chutney. ⊠ *15
Strafford Ave., 03824,* ☎ *603/862–2801 or 800/909–6931,* 𝐅𝐀𝐗 *603/
862–4897,* 𝗪𝗘𝗕 *www.necc.unh.edu. 115 rooms. 2 restaurants, bar, in-
room data ports, health club, meeting rooms. AE, DC, MC, V.*

Nightlife and the Arts

The **Celebrity Series** (⊠ Memorial Union Building, 83 Main St., ☎ 603/
862–2290) at the University of New Hampshire brings music, theater,
and dance to Durham. The **UNH Department of Theater and Dance** (⊠
Paul Creative Arts Center, 30 College Rd., ☎ 603/862–2919) produces
a variety of shows. The University of New Hampshire's **Whittemore
Center Arena** (⊠ 128 Main St., ☎ 603/862–4000) hosts everything
from Boston Pops concerts to home shows, plus UNH sports. In nearby
Newmarket, UNH students and local yupsters head to **The Stone
Church** (⊠ 5 Granite St., ☎ 603/659–6321)—in an authentic 1835 former Methodist church—to listen to live rock, jazz, blues, and folk.

Outdoor Activities and Sports

You can take a picnic to or hike several trails at 130-acre **Wagon Hill
Farm** (⊠ U.S. 4 across from Emery Farm, ☎ no phone), overlooking
the Oyster River. The old farm wagon, sitting on the top of a hill, is
one of the most-photographed spots in New England. Park next to the
farmhouse and follow walking trails to the wagon and through the woods
to the picnic area by the water. Sledding and cross-country skiing are
winter activities.

Dover

❾ *6 mi northeast of Durham.*

Considered New Hampshire's oldest permanent settlement, Dover
Point was settled in 1623 by fishermen who worked Great Bay. By the
end of the century, the town center had moved inland to its present location. The falls on the Cocheco River made Dover a natural mill town.
Many of the brick mill buildings still stand and have been converted
to restaurants and shops that make the town worth a stop.

The **Woodman Institute** consists of three buildings: the 1675 William
Damm Garrison House, the 1813 J. P. Hale House, and the 1818
Woodman House. Exhibits focus on early American cooking utensils,
clothing, furniture, New Hampshire's involvement in the Civil War, and
natural history. Abolitionist Senator John P. Hale lived in the Hale House
from 1840 to 1873. ⊠ *182–190 Central Ave.,* ☎ *603/742–1038,* 𝗪𝗘𝗕
www.seacoastnh.com/woodman. 🎫 *$3.* ☉ *Apr.–Nov., Wed.–Sun.
12:30–4:30; Jan.–Feb., weekends 12:30–4:30.*

Dining

$–$$$ ✕ **Newick's Seafood Restaurant.** Newick's, which also has locations
in Hampton and Merrimack, might serve the best lobster roll on the
New England coast, but regulars cherish the onion rings, too. This oversize shack serves seafood and atmosphere in heaping portions. Picture
windows allow terrific views over Great Bay. ⊠ *431 Dover Point Rd.,*
☎ *603/742–3205. AE, D, MC, V.*

Shopping

Downtown Dover has a selection of crafts and specialty stores. **Downtown Dover Crafts** (⊠ 464 Central Ave., ☎ 603/749–4952) showcases country-style crafts by local artisans who are part of a collective. **Just the Thing!** (✉ 451 Central Ave., ☎ 603/742–9040) carries an engaging mix of vintage collectibles and contemporary handicrafts. **Salmon Falls Pottery & Stoneware** (✉ Oak St. Engine House, ☎ 603/749–1467 or 800/621–2030) produces handmade, salt-glaze stoneware using a method that was favored by early American potters. Potters are on hand should you want to place a special order or watch them work. **Tuttle's Red Barn** (✉ 151 Dover Point Rd., ☎ 603/742–4313) carries jams, pickles, and other farm products.

Rochester

⑩ *22 mi northwest of Portsmouth, 10 mi north of Dover, 21 mi south of Wakefield.*

This old mill factory city may lack the quaint factor of either the coastal communities or the lake hamlets, but it's an excellent base for exploring its fine Victorian architecture, both commercial and residential. Stroll around downtown's centralmost intersection at Main, Wakefield, and Congress streets to get a feel for the town's heritage, or drive up along the mighty Salmon Falls River, which once powered the towns many mills.

Dining and Lodging

$$–$$$ ✕🏨 **Governor's Inn.** Just north of downtown, this pair of neighboring early 20th-century Georgian Colonial mansions are the former homes of state governors (and brothers) Huntley and Roland Spaulding. Guests now make their way about the homes' stately marble fireplaces, elliptical staircases, sweeping garden patios, and lavishly furnished guest rooms. The restaurant (No lunch Jan.–Apr.) presents an often-changing menu of creative regional American dishes such as breast of duck with a port sauce, green figs, and local blue cheese. ✉ *78 Wakefield St., 03867,* ☎ *603/332–0107,* FAX *603/335–1984,* WEB *www.governorsinn.com. 16 rooms. Restaurant, bar. D, MC, V.*

The Coast A to Z

To research prices, get advice from other travelers, and book travel arrangements, visit www.fodors.com

AIRPORTS
Manchester Airport is a one-hour drive from the coastal region (☞ New Hampshire A to Z).

BUS TRAVEL
C&J Trailways, Concord Trailways, and Vermont Transit provide bus service to New Hampshire's coast from other regions. Coast and UNH Wildcat Transit provides limited access to towns in New Hampshire's coastal section.

➤ Bus Information: **C&J Trailways** (☎ 603/430–1100 or 800/258–7111). **Vermont Transit** (☎ 603/436–0163 or 800/451–3292). **Coast** (☎ 603/862–2328). **UNH Wildcat Transit** (☎ 603/862–2328).

CAR TRAVEL
The main route to New Hampshire's coast from other states is I–95, which runs from the Massachusetts to Maine borders. Coastal Route 1A has views of water, beaches, and summer estates. The more convenient U.S. 1 travels inland. The Spaulding Turnpike (Route 16) and U.S. 4 connect Portsmouth with Dover, Durham, and Rochester. Route 108 links Durham and Exeter. The quick route along the coast is I–95. The main route to New Hampshire's coast from other states is I–95, which travels from the border with Maine to the border with Massachusetts.

EMERGENCIES

➤ EMERGENCY SERVICES: **New Hampshire State Police** (☎ 603/271–3636 or 800/852–3411). **Portsmouth Regional Hospital** (✉ 333 Borthwick Ave., Portsmouth, ☎ 603/436–5110). **Exeter Hospital** (✉ 10 Buzell Ave., Exeter, ☎ 603/778–7311).

➤ PHARMACY: **Rite Aid** (800 Islington St., Portsmouth, ☎ 603/436–2454).

OUTDOORS & SPORTS

FISHING

Companies on the coast offer rentals and charters for deep-sea fishing and cruises. For information about fishing and licenses, call the New Hampshire Fish and Game Office.

➤ CONTACTS: **New Hampshire Fish and Game Office** (☎ 603/868–1095).

HIKING

An excellent 1-mi trail reaches the summit of Blue Job Mountain, where a fire tower has a good view. The New Hampshire Division of Parks and Recreation maintains the Rockingham Recreation Trail, which wends 27 mi from Newfields, just north of Exeter, to Manchester and is open to hikers, bikers, snowmobilers, and cross-country skiers.

➤ CONTACTS: **Blue Job Mountain** (✉ Crown Point Rd. off Rte. 202A, Rochester, 13 mi northwest of Dover). **New Hampshire Division of Parks and Recreation** (☎ 603/271–3254).

TOURS

Portsmouth Livery Company gives narrated horse-and-carriage tours through Colonial Portsmouth and Strawbery Banke. The Isles of Shoals Steamship Company runs island cruises, river trips, foliage excursions, and whale-watching expeditions from April to January. Captain Jeremy Bell hosts these voyages aboard the M/V *Thomas Laighton,* a replica of a Victorian steamship and the smaller and more modern M/V *Oceanic.* Lunch and light snacks are available on board, or you can bring your own. Some trips include a stopover and historic walking tour on Star Island.

New Hampshire Seacoast Cruises conducts naturalist-led whale-watching tours and narrated Isles of Shoals cruises aboard the 150-passenger M/V *Granite State* from May to October out of Rye Harbor State Marina. From May to October, Portsmouth Harbor Cruises operates tours of Portsmouth Harbor, trips to the Isles of Shoals, foliage trips on the Cocheco River, and sunset cruises aboard the M/V *Heritage.*

➤ TOUR-OPERATOR RECOMMENDATIONS: **Portsmouth Livery Company** (✉ Market Sq., ☎ 603/427–0044). **Isles of Shoals Steamship Company** (✉ Barker Wharf, 315 Market St., Portsmouth, ☎ 603/431–5500 or 800/441–4620). **New Hampshire Seacoast Cruises** (✉ Rye Harbor, Rte. 1A, Rye, ☎ 603/964–5545 or 800/964–5545). **Portsmouth Harbor Cruises** (✉ Ceres Street Dock, Portsmouth, ☎ 603/436–8084 or 800/776–0915).

VISITOR INFORMATION

➤ TOURIST INFORMATION: **Exeter Area Chamber of Commerce** (✉ 120 Water St., Exeter 03833, ☎ 603/772–2411, WEB www.exeterarea.org). **Greater Dover Chamber of Commerce** (✉ 299 Central Ave., Dover 03820, ☎ 603/742–2218, WEB www.dovernh.org). **Greater Portsmouth Chamber of Commerce** (✉ 500 Market St. Extension, Portsmouth 03801, ☎ 603/436–1118, WEB www.portcity.org). **Hampton Beach Area Chamber of Commerce** (✉ 836 Lafayette Rd., Hampton 03842, ☎ 603/926–8718, WEB www.hamptonbeaches.com).

For further information on the region and links to numerous attractions, visit WEB www.seacoastnh.com.

LAKES REGION

Lake Winnipesaukee, a Native American name for "smile of the great spirit," is the largest of the dozens of lakes scattered across the eastern half of central New Hampshire. With about 240 mi of shoreline full of inlets and coves, it's the largest in the state. Some claim Winnipesaukee has an island for each day of the year, but the total actually falls well short: 274.

In contrast to Winnipesaukee's summer-long bustle, the more secluded Squam Lake has a dearth of public-access points. Its tranquillity no doubt attracted the producers of *On Golden Pond*; several scenes of the Oscar-winning film were shot here. Nearby Lake Wentworth is named for the first Royal Governor of the state, who, in building his country manor here, established North America's first summer resort.

Well-preserved Colonial and 19th-century villages are among the region's many landmarks, and you'll find hiking trails, good antiques shops, and myriad water-oriented activities. This tour begins at Laconia, just off I–93, and more-or-less circles Lake Winnipesaukee clockwise, with several side trips.

Laconia

🔟 *27 mi north of Concord; 94 mi north of Boston, MA.*

When the railroad reached Laconia—then called Meredith Bridge—in 1848, the formerly sleepy community became a manufacturing center. Laconia borders both Winnisquam and Winnipesaukee lakes and is easily accessible from I–93, making it the commercial hub of the Lakes Region. If you need a McDonald's or Rite-Aid, you'll find it here.

Belknap Mill (⊠ Mill Plaza, ☎ 603/524–8813), the oldest unaltered, brick-built textile mill in the United States (1823), contains a knitting museum devoted to the textile industry and a year-round cultural center that sponsors concerts, exhibits, a lecture series, and workshops.

Dining and Lodging

$$–$$$ ✕ **Hickory Stick Farm.** This restaurant, inside a 200-year-old Cape-style inn, is renowned for its roast duckling with herb stuffing and orange-sherry sauce. Other favorites from the mostly traditional Continental and American menu include prime rib and vegetarian lasagna. ⊠ *66 Bean Hill Rd., Belmont (4 mi south of Laconia),* ☎ *603/524–3333. Closed Mon. No lunch; call for winter hours. AE, D, MC, V.*

$$–$$$ ✕ **Le Chalet Rouge.** This yellow house with two small dining rooms recalls a country-French bistro. To start, try the house pâté, escargots, or steamed mussels. The steak au poivre is tender and well spiced, and the duckling is prepared with seasonal sauces: rhubarb in spring, raspberry in summer, orange in fall, creamy mustard in winter. ⊠ *385 W. Main St., Tilton (10 mi west of Laconia),* ☎ *603/286–4035. Reservations essential. MC, V.*

$$ 🏨 **Ferry Point House.** Built in the 1800s as a summer retreat for the Pillsbury family of baking fame, this red Victorian farmhouse has superb views of Lake Winnisquam. White wicker furniture and hanging baskets of flowers decorate the 60-ft veranda, and the gazebo by the water's edge is a pleasant place to lounge and listen for loons. A paddleboat and a rowboat await those eager to get in the water. The pretty rooms have Oriental rugs and Victorian furniture. ⊠ *100 Lower Bay Rd., Sanbornton 03269,* ☎ *603/524–0087,* FAX *603/524–0959,* WEB *www.new-hampshire-inn.com. 6 rooms. Beach, boating, fishing. No credit cards. Closed Nov.–Apr. BP.*

Outdoor Activities and Sports

Bartlett Beach (⊠ Winnisquam Ave.) has a playground and picnic area. **Opechee Park** (⊠ N. Main St.) has dressing rooms, a baseball field, tennis courts, and picnic areas.

Shopping

The **Belknap Mall** (⊠ U.S. 3, ☎ 603/524–5651) has boutiques, crafts stores, and a New Hampshire state liquor store. The **Bending Birch** (⊠ 569 Main St., ☎ 603/524–7589) sells local crafts, including Laconia pottery, birdhouses made in Meredith, and lap robes in New Hampshire's official tartan. The 53 stores at the **Lakes Region Factory Stores** (⊠ Exit 20 from I–93, Tilton, ☎ 888/SHOP–333) center include Brooks Brothers, Eddie Bauer, and Black & Decker.

OFF THE
BEATEN PATH

CANTERBURY SHAKER VILLAGE – Shaker furniture and inventions are well regarded, and this outdoor museum and National Historic Landmark helps illuminate the world of the people who created them. Established as a religious community in 1792, the village flourished in the 1800s and practiced equality of the sexes and races, common ownership, celibacy, and pacifism. The last member of the community passed away in 1992. Shakers invented household items such as the clothespin and the flat broom and were known for the simplicity and integrity of their designs, especially furniture. Ninety-minute tours pass through some of the 694-acre property's 24 restored buildings, and crafts demonstrations take place daily. The Creamery Restaurant serves lunch daily and candlelight dinners Friday–Saturday (reservations essential). A large shop sells fine Shaker reproductions. ⊠ *288 Shaker Rd., 15 mi south of Laconia via Route 106, Canterbury,* ☎ *603/783–9511 or 800/982–9511,* WEB *www.shakers.org.* ☞ *$10 for 2 consecutive days.* ☉ *May–Oct., daily 10–5; Apr. and Nov.–Dec., weekends 10–5.*

Gilford

⑫ *4 mi northeast of Laconia.*

One of the larger public beaches on Lake Winnipesaukee is in Gilford, a resort community. When the town was incorporated in 1812, the inhabitants asked the oldest resident to name it. A veteran of the Battle of the Guilford Courthouse, in North Carolina, he borrowed that town's name—though apparently he didn't know how to spell it. Quiet and peaceful, Gilford remains decidedly uncommercial but offers a variety of recreational opportunities.

Lodging

$$–$$$ 🏨 **B. Mae's Resort Inn.** All the rooms in this modern resort and conference center are large and have a deck or patio; some are suites with kitchens. Close to Gunstock ski area and within walking distance of Lake Winnipesaukee, B. Mae's is popular with skiers in winter and boaters in summer. ⊠ *Rtes. 11 and 11B, 03246,* ☎ *603/293–7526 or 800/458–3877,* FAX *603/293–4340,* WEB *www.bmaesresort.com. 60 rooms, 24 suites. 2 restaurants, bar, indoor and outdoor pools, hot tub, gym, recreation room. AE, D, DC, MC, V.*

$$ 🏨 **Gunstock Inn & Fitness Center.** The original building of this Colonial-style inn, just up the road from (☞)Gunstock ski area, was built in the 1930s by Civilian Conservation Corps workers who cut the area's first ski trails. The inn has individually decorated rooms, with some large ones suitable for families. Many have views of the mountains and

Lake Winnipesaukee. The tavern serves everything from fresh seafood to burgers in a cozy setting. In the fitness center, guests can take water aerobics and body-toning classes free of charge. ⊠ *580 Cherry Valley Rd., 03246,* ☏ *603/293–2021 or 800/654–0180,* FAX *603/293–2050,* WEB *www.gunstockinn.com. 23 rooms, 2 suites. Restaurant, indoor pool, sauna, steam room, health club. AE, MC, V. BP.*

$ ⚠ **Gunstock Campground.** The campground at the Gunstock ski and recreation area has a pool and 300 tent and trailer sites. ⊠ *Box 1307, Rte. 11A, Laconia 03247,* ☏ *603/293–4341 or 800/486–7862. AE, D, MC, V.*

Nightlife and the Arts

The **New Hampshire Music Festival** (⊠ 88 Belknap Mountain Rd., ☏ 603/524–1000) presents award-winning orchestras from early July to mid-August. The outdoor stage (with 2,500 covered seats) at **Meadowbrook Farm** (⊠ Meadowbrook La., off Rte. 11B, ☏ 603/528–5550 or 888/563–2369) hosts top music acts, from Bonnie Raitt to 98°.

Outdoor Activities and Sports

Ellacoya State Beach (⊠ Rte. 11, ☏ 603/293–7821) covers just 600 ft along the southwestern shore of Lake Winnipesaukee. In season, there's a bathhouse, picnic tables, and a fee for parking.

Ski Areas

GUNSTOCK USA

High above Lake Winnipesaukee, this all-purpose area dates from the 1930s. It once had the longest rope tow lift in the country—an advantage that helped local downhill skier and Olympic silver medalist Penny Pitou perfect her craft. Gunstock allows patrons to return lift tickets for a cash refund for absolutely any reason within 75 minutes of purchase. Thrill Hill, a snowtubing park, has 10 runs, multipassenger tubes, and lift service. ⊠ *Rte. 11A (Box 1307, Laconia, 03247),* ☏ *603/293–4341 or 800/486–7862,* WEB *www.gunstock.com.*

Downhill. Clever trail cutting along with grooming and surface sculpting three times daily have made this otherwise pedestrian mountain good for intermediates. That's how most of the 44 trails are rated, with a few more challenging runs and designated sections for slow skiers and learners. Lower Ramrod trail is set up for snowboarding. Gunstock, which has one quad, two triple, and two double chairlifts and two surface tows, has the largest night-skiing facility in New Hampshire, with 15 lighted trails and five lifts in operation.

Cross-country. Gunstock has 50 km (30 mi) of trails for skiing and snowshoeing. Some 15 km (9 mi) are for advanced skiers, and there are backcountry trails as well.

Child care. The nursery takes children ages 6 months and up; the ski school teaches children ages 3–14.

Summer activities. In summer, Gunstock has a swimming pool, a children's playground, hiking trails, mountain-bike rentals and trails, a skateboarding/blading park, guided horseback trail rides, paddleboats, and a campground.

Weirs Beach

❸ *10 mi northwest of Gilford, 8 mi north of Laconia.*

Weirs Beach is Lake Winnipesaukee's center for arcade activity. Anyone who loves souvenir shops, fireworks, water slides, and hordes of children will feel right at home. Several cruise boats depart from the town dock.

The period cars of the **Winnipesaukee Scenic Railroad** carry passengers along the lake's shore on one- or two-hour rides; boarding is at Weirs Beach or Meredith. Special trips that include certain meals are also offered. ⊠ *U.S. 3, Meredith,* ☎ *603/279–5253 or 603/745–2135.* ≊ *$8.50–$22.50.* ☉ *July–mid-Sept., daily; weekends only Memorial Day–late June and late Sept.–mid-Oct. Call for hrs and for special Santa trains in Dec.*

☙ A giant **Water Slide** (⊠ U.S. 3, ☎ 603/366–5161) overlooks the lake. For an aquatic experience, visit **Surf Coaster** (⊠ U.S. 3, ☎ 603/366–4991), which has seven slides, a wave pool, and a large area for young children. Day or night you can work your way through the miniature golf course, 20 lanes of bowling, and more than 500 games at **Funspot** (⊠ Rte. 11B, at U.S. 3, ☎ 603/366–4377).

Outdoor Activities and Sports

Thurston's Marina (⊠ U.S. 3 at the bridge, ☎ 603/366–4811 or 800/834–4812) rents pontoon boats, power boats, and personal watercraft.

Meredith

❶❹ *5 mi northwest of Weirs Beach, 41 mi north of Concord.*

Meredith, on U.S. 3 at the western end of Lake Winnipesaukee, has a fine collection of crafts shops and art galleries. An information center is across from the Town Docks.

At **Annalee's Doll Museum,** you can view a collection of the famous posable felt dolls and learn about the woman who created them. Annalee Davis Thorndike began making the dolls after her graduation from high school in 1933. Her dolls caught on with collectors, and the company has grown into an empire. ⊠ *Hemlock Dr. off Rte. 104,* ☎ *603/279–3333.* ≊ *Free.* ☉ *Memorial Day–mid-Oct.; call for hrs. www.annalee.com*

Dining and Lodging

$$–$$$ ✕ **Mame's.** This 1820s tavern, once the home of the village doctor, now contains a warren of convivial dining rooms accented by exposed-brick walls, wooden beams, and wide-plank floors. Expect mostly traditional American standbys of the seafood, steak, veal, and chicken variety; the mud pie is highly recommended. ⊠ *8 Plymouth St.,* ☎ *603/279–4631. AE, D, MC, V.*

$$–$$$$ ✕▥ **The Inns at Mill Falls.** Overlooking Lake Winnipesaukee and incorporating the historic sections of the 19th-century Meredith Linen Mills, the Inns at Mill Falls offer the amenities and dining of a full resort but on a manageable scale and with a wonderful sense of warmth and personality. Choose from three different properties: the centralmost Inn at Mills Falls, which adjoins an 18-shop specialty market, has the resort's indoor pool and 54 spacious rooms; Inn at Bay Point, which faces a long and dramatic stretch of lakefront, has 24 rooms—most with balconies, some with fireplaces and whirlpool baths; and Chase House at Mill Falls, which has lake views and 23 rooms—all with fireplaces, some with balconies and whirlpool baths. Dining is a major activity here, among both inn guests and visitors from all around the lake. The upscale Boathouse Grill ($$–$$$) sits directly on the lake and serves such contemporary fare as Caesar salad with sea scallops and pan-seared almond-and-cornmeal-crusted trout with apple butter. Camp ($$–$$$) delights diners with cedar-plank salmon amid a rustic cabin-inspired motif. Other options include the breakfast/lunch-oriented Waterfall Cafe ($), which overlooks the old mill stream and 40-ft cascades, and **Giuseppe's** ($–$$), a contemporary Italian eatery with live cabaret many nights. ⊠ *U.S. 3 at Rte. 25, 03253,* ☎ *603/279–*

7006 or 800/622–6455, FAX 603/279–6797, WEB *www.millsfalls.com.*
*101 rooms. 4 restaurants, bars, indoor pool, sauna, shops, meeting
rooms. AE, D, DC, MC, V.*

$ △ **Clearwater Campground.** This wooded tent and RV campground
on Lake Pemigewasset has 153 shady sites, a large sandy beach, a recreation building, a playground, basketball and volleyball courts, and boat
rentals and slips. ⊠ *26 Campground Rd., off Rte. 104, 03253,* ☎ *603/
279–7761. Closed mid-Oct.–mid-May.*

Outdoor Activities and Sports

BEACHES

Wellington State Beach (⊠ Off Rte. 3A, Bristol, 12 mi west of Meredith), on the western shore of Newfound Lake, is one of the most beautiful area beaches. You can swim or picnic or hike along the ½-mi
shoreline, or use the boat launch.

BOATING

Meredith Marina and Boating Center (⊠ Bay Shore Dr., ☎ 603/279–
7921) rents power boats. **Wild Meadow Canoes & Kayaks** (⊠ Rte. 25
between Center Harbor and Meredith, ☎ 603/253–7536 or 800/427–
7536) has canoes and kayaks for rent.

GOLF

Waukewan Golf Course (⊠ Off U.S. 3 and Rte. 25, ☎ 603/279–6661)
is an 18-hole, par-71 course. Greens fees are $22–$28.

Shopping

About 170 dealers operate out of the three-floor **Burlwood Antique Center** (⊠ U.S. 3, ☎ 603/279–6387), open May–October. The **Meredith
League of New Hampshire Craftsmen** (⊠ U.S. 3, ½ mi north of Rte.
104, ☎ 603/279–7920) sells works of area artisans. **Mill Falls Marketplace,** part of the Inns at Mills Falls, contains shops with clothing,
gifts, and books. The **Old Print Barn** (⊠ 1008 Winona Rd., ☎ 603/
279–6479), the largest such gallery in northern New England, carries
rare prints—Currier & Ives, antique botanicals, and more—from
around the world.

Center Harbor

🔟 *5 mi northeast of Meredith.*

In the middle of three bays at the northern end of Winnipesaukee, the
town of Center Harbor also borders Lakes Squam, Waukewan, and
Winona. This prime location makes it popular in summer, especially
with boaters who spend summer weekends on the water.

Dining and Lodging

$$–$$$$ ✕🔝 **Red Hill Inn.** The large bay window in the common room of this
rambling late-19th-century inn overlooks the Sandwich Mountains.
Guest rooms are furnished with Victorian pieces and country furniture—
some of them in a neighboring 1850s farmhouse, just down the hill.
Twenty rooms have fireplaces, some have claw-foot tubs, and 10 have
two-person hot tubs. For dinner, try the Vermont goat cheese bruschetta, followed by the rack of lamb encrusted in rosemary and garlic. ⊠ *Rte. 25B and College Rd. (Box 99M, 03226),* ☎ *603/279–7001
or 800/573–3445,* FAX *603/279–7003,* WEB *www.redhillinn.com. 16
rooms, 9 suites. Restaurant, pub, pool, outdoor hot tub, cross-country skiing. AE, D, DC, MC, V. BP.*

Outdoor Activities and Sports

Red Hill, a hiking trail on Bean Road off Route 25, northeast of Center Harbor, really does turn red in autumn. The reward at the end of
the trail in any season is a view of Squam Lake and the mountains.

Shopping

Keepsake Quilting & Country Pleasures (⊠ Senter's Marketplace, Rte. 25B, ☎ 603/253–4026), reputedly America's largest quilt shop, contains 5,000 bolts of fabric, hundreds of quilting books, and countless supplies.

Holderness

🔟 *8 mi northwest of Center Harbor, 8 mi north of Meredith.*

Routes 25B and 25 lead to the small and simple town of Holderness, perched between Squam and Little Squam lakes. *On Golden Pond,* starring Katharine Hepburn and Henry Fonda, was filmed on Squam, whose quiet beauty attracts nature lovers.

★ ☾ The several trails at the 200-acre **Science Center of New Hampshire** include a ¾-mi path that passes by black bears, bobcats, otters, and other native wildlife in trailside enclosures. Educational events at the center include the "Up Close to Animals" series in July and August, at which you can study a species in an intimate setting. The Gordon Children's Activity Center has interactive exhibits. You can also tour the lake on 28-ft pontoon boats, especially useful for observing loons. ⊠ *Rtes. 113 and 25,* ☎ *603/968–7194.* 🎟 *$9.* ☉ *May–Oct., daily 9:30–4:30 (last admission 3:30). www.sciencectrofnh.org.*

Dining and Lodging

$$$$ ✕🔟 **Manor on Golden Pond.** Built in 1903, this dignified inn with a
★ British-manor ambience has well-groomed grounds and a private dock with canoes, paddle boats, and a boathouse. You can stay in the main inn, the cottages, or, during summer and fall, the carriage house. Sixteen rooms have wood-burning fireplaces; eight have two-person whirlpool baths. Three-, four-, or five-course prix-fixe dinners (reservations required) may include cumin-molasses-charred beef tenderloin with lobster mashed potatoes. ⊠ *U.S. 3 and Shepard Hill Rd., 03245,* ☎ *603/ 968–3348 or 800/545–2141,* 𝔽𝔸𝕏 *603/968–2116,* 𝕎𝔼𝔹 *www.manoron-goldenpond.com. 20 rooms, 3 cottages, 1 carriage house. Restaurant, pub, pool, tennis court, beach, boating. AE, MC, V. BP.*

$$–$$$ 🔟 **Glynn House Inn.** Innkeepers Karol and Betsy Paterman run this swanky three-story 1890s Queen Anne home with a turret and wraparound porch. Many rooms have fireplaces and hot tubs; the bi-level honeymoon suite has a whirlpool tub and fireplace downstairs and a four-poster bed and skylights above. Breakfast usually includes fresh-baked strudel. Squam Lake is minutes away. ⊠ *43 Highland St., Ashland 03217,* ☎ *603/968–3775 or 800/637–9599,* 𝔽𝔸𝕏 *603/968–3129,* 𝕎𝔼𝔹 *www.new-hampshire-lodging.com. 10 rooms, 6 suites. In-room VCRs. MC, V. BP.*

$$ 🔟 **Inn on Golden Pond.** This informal country home, built in 1879 and set on 50 wooded acres, is just up the road from Squam Lake. Rooms have a traditional country decor of hardwood floors, braided rugs, easy chairs, and calico-print bedspreads and curtains; the quietest rooms are in the rear on the third floor. The homemade jam at breakfast is made from rhubarb grown on the property. ⊠ *Box 680, U.S. 3, 03245,* ☎ *603/968–7269,* 𝔽𝔸𝕏 *603/968–9226,* 𝕎𝔼𝔹 *www.innongoldenpond.com. 7 rooms, 2 suites. Hiking. AE, MC, V. BP.*

$–$$ ⛺ **Yogi Bear's Jellystone Park.** This family-oriented camping resort has wooded, open, or riverfront sites; basic and deluxe cabins; and trailers. There's also a pool, a water playground, a hot tub, mini-golf, a basketball court, canoe and kayak rentals, and daily supervised activities. ⊠ *R.R. 1, Box 396, Rte. 132, Ashland 03217,* ☎ *603/968–9000,* 𝕎𝔼𝔹 *www.jellystonenh.com. 275 sites, 43 cabins, 7 trailers.*

Outdoor Activities and Sports

White Mountain Country Club (⊠ N. Ashland Rd., Ashland, ☎ 603/
536–2227) has an 18-hole, par-71 golf course. Greens fees are $26 to
$32.

Center Sandwich

★ **⑰** *12 mi northeast of Holderness.*

With Squam Lake to the west and the Sandwich Mountains to the north,
Center Sandwich claims one of the prettiest settings of any town in the
Lakes Region. So appealing are the town and its views that John
Greenleaf Whittier used the Bearcamp River as the inspiration for his
poem "Sunset on the Bearcamp." The town attracts artisans—crafts
shops abound among its clutch of charming 18th- and 19th-century
buildings.

The **Historical Society Museum** traces the history of Center Sandwich
through the faces of its inhabitants. Works by mid-19th-century portraitist and town son Albert Gallatin Hoit hang alongside a local pho-
tographer's exhibit portraying the town's mothers and daughters. The
museum houses a replica country store and local furniture and items.
⊠ *4 Maple St.,* ☎ *603/284–6269.* ☜ *Free.* ☉ *June–Sept., Tues.–Sat.*
11–5.

Dining

$$–$$$ ✕ **Corner House Inn.** The restaurant, in a converted barn decorated
with local arts and crafts, serves classic American fare. Before you get
to the white-chocolate cheesecake with key-lime filling, try the chef's
lobster-and-mushroom bisque or tasty garlic-and-horseradish-crusted
rack of lamb. There's story-telling Thursday evenings. ⊠ *Rtes. 109 and*
113, ☎ *603/284–6219. AE, D, MC, V. Closed Mon. Nov.–May. No*
lunch.

Moultonborough

⑱ *5 mi south of Center Sandwich.*

Moultonborough claims 6½ mi of shoreline on Lake Kanasatka, a
large chunk of Lake Winnipesaukee, and even a small piece of Squam.

The highly browsable store that is part of the **Old Country Store and**
Museum (⊠ Moultonborough Corner, ☎ 603/476–5750) has been selling maple products, cheeses aged on site, penny candy, and other items
since 1781. Much of the equipment still used in the store is antique,
and the museum (free) displays antique farming and forging tools.

The town's best-known attraction, the **Castle in the Clouds** is an odd,
elaborate stone mansion built without nails; it has 16 rooms, eight bathrooms, and doors made of lead. Construction began in 1911 and con-
tinued for three years. Owner Thomas Gustave Plant spent $7 million,
the bulk of his fortune, on this project and died penniless in 1946. A
tour includes the mansion, and the Castle Springs Microbrewery and
spring-water facility on this 5,200-acre property; there's also hiking,
pony rides, and horseback-riding. ⊠ *Rte. 171,* ☎ *603/476–2352 or*
800/729–2468, 🌐 *www.castlesprings.com.* ☜ *$12 with tour, $6 with-*
out tour. ☉ *Early June–late-Oct., daily 9–5; mid-May–early-June,*
weekends 10–4.

The **Loon Center** at the Frederick and Paula Anna Markus Wildlife Sanc-
tuary is the headquarters of the Loon Preservation Committee, an
Audubon Society project. The loon, recognizable for its eerie, haunt-
ing calls and striking black-and-white coloring, resides on many New

Hampshire lakes but is threatened by boat traffic, poor water quality, and habitat loss. The center presents changing exhibits about the birds. Two nature trails wind through the 200-acre property; vantage points on the Loon Nest Trail overlook the spot resident loons sometimes occupy in late spring and summer. ⊠ *Lees Mills Rd.,* ☎ *603/476–5666,* WEB *www.loon.org.* 🎟 *Free.* ☉ *July–Columbus Day, daily 9–5; Columbus Day–June, Mon.–Sat. 9–5.*

Dining

$$–$$$ ✕ **The Woodshed.** Farm implements and antiques hang on the walls of this enchanting, romantic converted 1860 barn. The menu offers few surprises—mostly traditional New England fare such as sea scallops baked in butter and lamb chops with mint sauce—but exceptionally fresh ingredients and delightful ambience are sure to please. ⊠ *Lee's Mill Rd.,* ☎ *603/476–2311. AE, D, DC, MC, V. Closed Mon. No lunch.*

Tamworth

🔞 *12 mi northeast of Moultonborough, 20 mi southwest of North Conway.*

President Grover Cleveland summered in what remains a village of almost unreal quaintness—it's equally photogenic in verdant summer, during fall foliage, or under a blanket of winter snow. Cleveland's son, Francis, returned to stay and founded the acclaimed Barnstormers Theater in 1931. Tamworth has a clutch of villages within its borders. At one of them—Chocorua—the view through the birches of Chocorua Lake has been so often photographed that you may feel as if you've been here before.

☙ For 99 years, Dr. Edwin Remick and his father provided medical services to the Tamworth area and operated a family farm. At the **Remick Country Doctor Museum and Farm,** endowed by Dr. Remick, exhibits focus on the life of a country doctor and on the activities of the still-working farm. There are always hands-on activities, but try to visit when ice harvesting, stone wall building, or the like is scheduled. ⊠ *58 Cleveland Hill Rd.,* ☎ *800/686–6117,* WEB *www.remickmuseum.org.* 🎟 *Free.* ☉ *Nov.–June, weekdays 10–4; July–Oct., Mon.–Sat. 10–4.*

Dining and Lodging

$$$–$$$$ ✕🏨 **Tamworth Inn.** Owners Bob and Virginia Schrader spent two
★   years completely renovating this 1833 Victorian inn anchoring the village, which is a great base both for exploring the lakes and also winter skiing in the eastern White Mountains. Common rooms range from the cozy beamed-ceiling pub to the formal dining room where tables are laid with white linen and crystal. Guest rooms have brass or antique beds, down comforters, and Caswell-Massey toiletries. The beautifully landscaped grounds border the Swift River. In the dining room (closed Sun.–Mon. in summer and Sun.–Wed. in winter), chef Jim Berry offers seasonal cuisine with specialties such as grilled salmon brushed with olive oil and cracked black pepper, with a balsamic reduction, sauteed baby spinach, and Yukon potato hash. ⊠ *Main St., 03886,* ☎ *603/323–7721 or 800/642–7352,* FAX *603/323–2026,* WEB *www.tamworth.com. 16 rooms. Restaurant, pub, pool. MC, V. BP, MAP.*

$–$$ 🏨 **Mt. Chocorua View House.** This 1845 house began as a carriage stop and has been an inn almost continuously since then. Ideally located between the Lakes Region and the White Mountains, it draws many hikers and skiers. Guest rooms can be small, but all are welcoming with flowered wallpapers, quilts, ceiling fans, and other personal touches. Common areas include a guest kitchen and a screened porch that might make hiking nearby Mt. Chocorua seem like just too much work. ✉ *Box 348, Rte. 16, Chocorua 03817,* ☎ *603/323–8350 or 888/ 323–8350,* FAX *603/323–3319,* WEB *www.mtchocorua.com. 6 rooms, 3 with bath; 1 suite. Gym. AE, D, MC, V. BP.*

Nightlife and the Arts

The **Arts Council of Tamworth** (☎ 603/323–8104) produces concerts— soloists, string quartets, revues, children's programs—September–June and an arts show in late July. **Barnstormers** (✉ Main St., ☎ 603/323– 8500) has performances in July and August. The box office opens in June.

Outdoor Activities and Sports

The 72-acre stand of native pitch pine at **White Lake State Park** (✉ Rte. 16, ☎ 603/323–7350) is a National Natural Landmark. The park has hiking trails, a sandy beach, trout fishing, canoe rentals, two sep- arate camping areas, a picnic area, and swimming.

Shopping

The many theme rooms—a Christmas room, a bride's room, a chil- dren's room, among them—at the **Country Handcrafters & Chocorua Dam Ice Cream Shop** (✉ Rte. 16, Chocorua, ☎ 603/323–8745) con- tain handcrafted items. When you're done shopping, try the ice cream, coffee, or tea and scones.

The Ossipees

⓴ *6 mi southeast of Tamworth, 21 mi south of North Conway.*

Route 16 between West Ossipee and Center Ossipee passes Ossipee Lake, known for fine fishing and swimming. Around these hamlets you'll find several antiques shops and galleries.

Dining

$$ ✕ **Jake's Seafood.** Oars and nautical trappings adorn the wood-pan- eled walls at this seafood stop between West and Center Ossipee. The kitchen serves some of the freshest and tastiest seafood in eastern New Hampshire, notably lobster pie, fried clams, and seafood casserole; steak, ribs, and chicken dishes are also offered. ✉ *2055 Rte. 16,* ☎ *603/539– 2805. Closed Mon.–Wed.. MC, V.*

$–$$ ✕ **Yankee Smokehouse.** This down-home barbecue joint's logo depicting ★ two happy pigs ironically foreshadows the gleeful enthusiasm with which patrons dive into the hefty sandwiches of sliced pork and smoked chicken and immense platters of baby back ribs and smoked sliced beef. Ample sides of slaw, beans, fries, and garlic toast complement the hearty fare. Born-and-bred Southerners have been known to come away from this place impressed. ✉ *Rtes. 16 and 25,* ☎ *603/539–RIBS. Closed Tues.–Wed. No credit cards.*

Shopping

Local craftspeople create much of the jewelry, turned wooden bowls, pewter goblets, and glassware sold at **Tramway Artisans** (✉ Rte. 16, West Ossipee, ☎ 603/539–5700).

Wakefield

㉑ *21 mi south of West Ossipee, 43 mi north of Portsmouth, 64 mi north- east of Concord.*

East of Lake Winnipesaukee, seven laid-back villages combine to form Wakefield, a town with 10 lakes. Wakefield's 26-building historic dis- trict, just off Route 16 near the Maine border, is comprised of a church, houses, and an inn that dates from the 18th century. A few mi down Route 153 in Sanbornville you'll find Wakefield's present-day commercial district.

☾ The **Museum of Childhood** displays a one-room schoolhouse, a child's room and a kitchen from 1890, model trains, antique sleds, teddy bears, 3,500 dolls, and 44 furnished dollhouses. Special events are scheduled most Fridays. ⊠ *2784 Wakefield Rd.,* ☎ *603/522–8073.* ⊡ *$3.* ☾ *Memorial Day–Labor Day, Mon. and Wed.–Sat. 11–4, Sun. 1–4.*

Lodging

$–$$ ⚕ **Wakefield Inn.** The restoration of this 1804 stagecoach inn, a high-
★   light of Wakefield's historic district, has been handled with an eye for detail. The dining-room windows retain the original panes and shutters, but the centerpiece of the building is the freestanding spiral staircase, which rises three stories. The large rooms, named for famous guests or past owners, have wide-board pine floors, big sofas, and handmade quilts. The 2-mi Wakefield Heritage Trail (for walkers) runs from the inn to the center of town. In late fall and early spring, you can learn how to quilt as part of the weekend Quilting Package. ⊠ *2723 Wake-field Rd., 03872,* ☎ *603/522–8272 or 800/245–0841,* WEB *www.wake-fieldinn.com. 7 rooms. MC, V. BP.*

Wolfeboro

❷❷ *21 mi south of West Ossipee, 28 mi northwest of Rochester, 49 mi north-west of Portsmouth.*

Quietly upscale and decidedly preppy Wolfeboro has been a resort since Royal Governor John Wentworth built his summer home on the shores of Lake Wentworth in 1763. The town center, bursting with tony boutiques and shops, fringes Lake Winnipesaukee and sees about a ten-fold population increase each summer. Expect none of the exuberant commercialism of Weirs Beach—Wolfeboro marches to a steady, relaxed beat, comfortable for all ages. It maintains a small-town feel while still offering plenty of shopping and entertainment options.

Uniforms, vehicles, and other artifacts at the **Wright Museum** illustrate the contributions of those on the home front to America's World War II effort. ⊠ *77 Center St.,* ☎ *603/569–1212,* WEB *www.wrightmu-seum.org.* ⊡ *$5.* ☾ *May–Oct., daily 10–4; Nov.–Apr., weekends 10–4.*

The artisans at the **Hampshire Pewter Company** (⊠ 43 Mill St., ☎ 603/ 569–4944 or 800/639–7704) use 17th-century techniques to make pewter tableware and accessories. Free tours are conducted at 10, 11, 1, 2, and 3 most days, Memorial Day–Columbus Day; the gift shop is open year-round.

Dining and Lodging

$$–$$$ ✕ **The Bittersweet.** This converted barn 2 mi north of downtown delights diners with its eclectic display of old quilts, pottery, sheet music, and china. Locals also love the nightly specials that range from a popular lobster pie to steak Diane. The upper level has antique tables and chairs and dining by candlelight. The lower-level lounge, decorated with Victorian wicker furniture, serves lighter fare. ⊠ *Rte. 28,* ☎ *603/ 569–3636. AE, D, MC, V.*

$–$$ ✕ **Wolfetrap Grill and Raw Bar.** The seafood at this festive shanty on Lake Winnipesaukee is guaranteed fresh—it comes from the Wolfetrap's adjacent fish market. You'll find all your favorites here, including a renowned clam boil for one that includes steamers, corn on the cob, onions, potatoes, sweet potatoes, and a hot dog. The raw bar has oysters and clams on the half shell. ⊠ *17 Bay St.,* ☎ *603/569–1503. MC, V. Closed mid-Oct.–mid-May.*

$$–$$$ ✕⚕ **Wolfeboro Inn.** Built in the early 1800s, this white clapboard house has later additions with views of the lakefront. The rooms have

polished cherry and pine furnishings, armoires, stenciled borders, and country quilts but could stand a little updating, especially the bathrooms and toiletries. Pub fare and more than 70 brands of beer are available at Wolfe's Tavern ($–$$), where fireplaces make cool evenings cozy. The 1812 Steakhouse ($$–$$$) serves fresh seafood and a popular slow-roasted prime rib. ⊠ *Box 1270, 90 N. Main St., 03894,* ☎ *603/569–3016 or 800/451–2389,* FAX *603/569–5375,* WEB *www.wolfeboroinn.com. 41 rooms, 3 suites, 1 apartment. 2 restaurants, bar, beach, boating, meeting room. AE, MC, V. CP.*

Outdoor Activities and Sports

BEACHES
Wentworth State Beach (⊠ Rte. 109, ☎ 603/569–3699) has good swimming, picnicking areas, and a bathhouse.

BOATING
Winnipesaukee Kayak Company (⊠ 17 Bay St., ☎ 603/569–9926) gives kayak lessons and leads group excursions on the lake. **Wetwolfe Boat Rentals** (⊠ 17 Bay St., ☎ 603/569–1503) rents motorboats and personal watercraft.

GOLF
Kingswood Golf Course (⊠ Rte. 28, ☎ 603/569–3569) has an 18-hole, par-72 course. Greens fees are $35–$48.

HIKING
A short (¼-mi) hike to the 100-ft post-and-beam **Abenaki Tower,** followed by a more rigorous climb to the top, rewards you with a vast view of Lake Winnipesaukee and the Ossipee mountain range. The trailhead is a few miles north of town on Route 109.

WATER SPORTS
Scuba divers can explore a 130-ft-long cruise ship that sank in 30 ft of water off Glendale in 1895. **Dive Winnipesaukee Corp.** (⊠ 4 N. Main St., ☎ 603/569–2120) runs charters out to wrecks and offers rentals, repairs, scuba sales, and lessons in waterskiing and windsurfing.

Alton Bay

❷❸ *10 mi south of Wolfeboro, 20 mi southeast of Laconia*

Neither quiet nor secluded, Lake Winnipesaukee's southern shore is alive with visitors from the moment the first flower blooms until the last maple has shed its leaves. Two mountain ridges hold 7 mi of the lake in Alton Bay, which is the name of both the inlet and the town at its tip. The lake's cruise boats dock here, and small planes land here year-round, on both the water and the ice. There's a dance pavilion, along with miniature golf, a public beach, and a Victorian-style bandstand.

Mt. Major, 5 mi north of Alton Bay on Route 11, has a 2½-mi trail with views of Lake Winnipesaukee. At the top is a four-sided stone shelter built in 1925.

Dining

$$$$ ✕ **Crystal Quail.** This tiny (12-seat) restaurant, inside an 18th-century farmhouse, is worth the drive. The prix-fixe contemporary menu changes daily but might include saffron-garlic soup, a house pâté, quenelle-stuffed sole, or duck in crisp potato shreds. ⊠ *202 Pitman Rd., Center Barnstead (12 mi south of Alton Bay),* ☎ *603/269–4151. Reservations essential. No credit cards. BYOB. Closed Mon.–Tues. No lunch.*

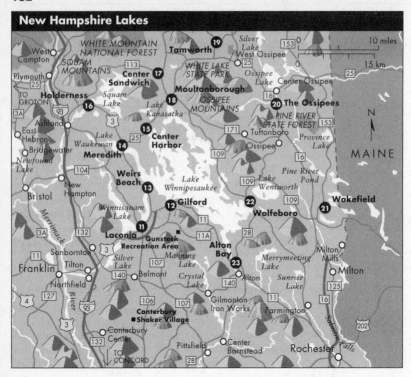

New Hampshire Lakes

Lakes Region A to Z

To research prices, get advice from other travelers, and book travel arrangements, visit www.fodors.com

AIRPORTS & TRANSFERS

Manchester Airport is about an hour to 90 minutes away by car (☞ New Hampshire A to Z).

AIRPORT TRANSFERS

Greater Laconia Transit Agency has door-to-door service from Manchester Airport to anywhere within a 10-mi radius of Laconia.
➤ SHUTTLES: **Greater Laconia Transit Agency** (☎ 603/528–2496 or 800/294–2496).

BUS TRAVEL

Concord Trailways connects Boston's South Station and Logan Airport with Center Harbor, Chocorua, Laconia, Meredith, Moultonborough, Plymouth, Tilton, and West Ossipee.
➤ BUS INFORMATION: **Concord Trailways** (☎ 800/639–3317).

CAR TRAVEL

On the western side of the Lakes Region, I–93 is the principal north–south artery. Exit 20 leads to U.S. 3 and Route 11 and the southwestern side of Lake Winnipesaukee. Take Exit 23 to Route 104 to Route 25 and the northwestern corner of the region. From the coast, the Spaulding Turnpike (Route 16) heads to the White Mountains, with roads leading to the lakeside towns.

EMERGENCIES

➤ HOSPITAL: **Lakes Region General Hospital** (✉ 80 Highland St., Laconia, ☎ 603/524–3211).

LODGING

For longer stays in the Lakes Region consider renting a lakeside house or condominium. Among the rental agencies are Preferred Vacation Rental, Inc. and Strictly Rentals, Inc.

APARTMENT & VILLA RENTALS

➤ LOCAL AGENTS: **Preferred Vacation Rentals, Inc.** (✉ Box 161, Center Harbor 03226, ☎ 603/253–7811 or 800/639–4022). **Strictly Rentals, Inc.** (✉ Box 695, Center Harbor 03226, ☎ 603/253–9800).

OUTDOORS & SPORTS

The Lakes Region Association provides boating advice. The New Hampshire Fish and Game office has information about fishing and licenses. The Alexandria headquarters of the Appalachian Mountain Club has trail information. The Laconia Office of the U.S. Forest Service can provide trail advice and information.

➤ CONTACTS: The **Lakes Region Association** (☎ 603/744–8664 or 800/925–2537). **New Hampshire Fish and Game** office (☎ 603/744–5470). **Appalachian Mountain Club** (☎ 603/744–8011). **Laconia Office of the U.S. Forest Service** (☎ 603/528–8721).

TOURS

The 230-ft M/S *Mount Washington* makes 2½-hour scenic cruises of Lake Winnipesaukee from Weirs Beach, mid-May–late October, with stops in Wolfeboro, Alton Bay, Center Harbor, and Meredith. Evening cruises include live music and a buffet dinner.

The M/V *Sophie C.* has been the area's floating post office for more than a century. The boat departs Weirs Beach with mail and passengers Monday–Saturday, mid-June–Labor Day; call for stops. Sky Bright operates airplane and helicopter tours and provides instruction on aerial photography. From May to late October, Squam Lake Tours takes up to 48 passengers on a two-hour pontoon tour of "Golden Pond." The company also operates guided fishing trips and private charters. Moultonborough Airport operates chartered flights and tours.

➤ TOUR OPERATORS: **M/S *Mount Washington*** (☎ 603/366–5531 or 888/843–6686, WEB www.msmountwashington.com). The **M/V *Sophie C.*** (☎ 603/366–5531 or 888/843–6686). **Sky Bright** (✉ Laconia Airport, Rte. 11, ☎ 800/639–6012). **Squam Lake Tours** (☎ 603/968–7577). **Moultonborough Airport** (✉ Rte. 25, Moultonborough, ☎ 603/476–8801).

VISITOR INFORMATION

➤ TOURIST INFORMATION: **Lakes Region Association** (✉ Box 430, Rte. 104, just off exit 23 of I–93, New Hampton 03256, ☎ 603/253–8555 or 800/925–2537, WEB www.lakesregion.org). **Squam Lakes Area Chamber of Commerce** (✉ Box 65, Ashland 03217, ☎ 603/968–4494. **Wolfeboro Chamber of Commerce** (✉ Box 547-WT7, Railroad Ave., Wolfeboro 03894, ☎ 603/569–2200 or 800/516–5324).

THE WHITE MOUNTAINS

Sailors approaching East Coast harbors frequently mistake the pale peaks of the White Mountains—the highest range in the northeastern United States—for clouds. It was 1642 when explorer Darby Field could no longer contain his curiosity about one mountain in particular. He set off from his Exeter homestead and became the first man to climb what would eventually be called Mt. Washington, the king of the Presidential Range. More than a mile high, Mt. Washington must have presented Field with formidable obstacles—its peak claims the highest wind velocity ever recorded and it can see snow every month of the year.

More than 350 years after Field's climb, curiosity about the mountains has not abated. People come by the tens of thousands to hike and climb in spring and summer, to photograph the vistas and the vibrant foliage in autumn, and to ski in winter. In this four-season vacation hub, many resorts (some of which have been in business since the mid-1800s) are destinations in themselves, with golf, tennis, swimming, hiking, cross-country skiing, and renowned restaurants.

Roughly 770,000 acres of forested mountains, valleys, and notches (deep mountain passes) make up the White Mountain National Forest. Long popular with hikers, campers, and skiers, and easily accessible to Bostonians and New Yorkers, it is one of the most heavily used for recreation of the nation's protected forests. The forest includes the Presidential Range of the White Mountains: these peaks, like Mt. Washington, are all named after early presidents. Notorious for its foul weather, Mt. Washington is, nonetheless, a favorite with hikers. An auto road and a railway also lead to the top. The mountain scenery of Franconia Notch, Crawford Notch, and Pinkham Notch also fall within the forest's boundaries. Crawford and Franconia notches are doubly protected, since they are state parks, too.

This section begins in Waterville Valley, off I–93, then continues to North Woodstock, where it follows the **White Mountains Trail** (☎ 888/944–8368, WEB www.whitemountainstrail.com), a magnificent 100-mi loop designated as a National Scenic & Cultural Byway in 1998. For a detailed map that notes specific photo-ops and provides additional historic background, contact or visit the **White Mountains Visitors Bureau**. The tour breaks off from the the White Mountains Trail in a few places, but you can easily follow this chapter in conjunction with the trail map.

Waterville Valley

㉔ *60 mi north of Concord.*

In 1835, visitors began arriving in Waterville Valley, a 10-mi-long cul-de-sac cut by one of New England's several Mad Rivers and circled by mountains. First a summer resort, then more of a ski area, and now a year-round getaway, Waterville Valley retains a small-town feel. There are inns and condos, restaurants, shops, conference facilities, a grocery store, and a post office. Hiking and mountain biking are popular summer sports, while ice-skating and snowshoeing supplement skiing and snowboarding in winter.

Dining and Lodging

$–$$ ✕ **Chile Peppers.** Southwest-inspired Chile Peppers caters to skiers with fajitas, tacos, enchiladas, and other Tex-Mex staples. The food here may not be authentic Mexican, but it's well priced and filling. If you're solely into Tex, the lineup includes ribs, steak, seafood, and chicken. ⊠ *Town Square,* ☎ *603/236–4646. AE, DC, MC, V.*

$$–$$$ 🏨 **Black Bear Lodge.** This family-oriented property has one-bedroom suites that sleep up to six and have full kitchens. Each unit is individually owned and decorated. Children's movies are shown at night in season, and there's bus service to the slopes. Guests can use the White Mountain Athletic Club. ⊠ *Box 357, Village Rd., 03215,* ☎ *603/236–4501 or 800/349–2327,* FAX *603/236–4114,* WEB *www.black-bear-lodge.com. 107 suites. Indoor–outdoor pool, hot tub, sauna, steam room, gym, recreation room. AE, D, DC, MC, V.*

$$–$$$ 🏨 **Golden Eagle Lodge.** Waterville's premier condominium property recalls the grand hotels of an earlier era. The full-service complex, which opened in 1989, has a two-story lobby and a capable front-desk staff. Guests have access to the White Mountain Athletic Club. ⊠ *6 Snow's*

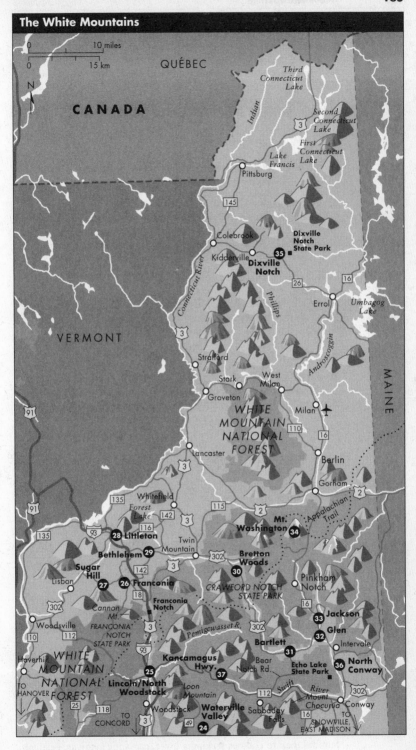

The White Mountains

0   10 miles

0   15 km

N

QUÉBEC

CANADA

Third
Connecticut
Lake

Second
Connecticut
Lake

First
Connecticut
Lake

Indian

Lake
Francis

3

Pittsburg

145

VERMONT

Connecticut River

Colebrook

Kidderville

35

Dixville
Notch
State Park

**Dixville
Notch**

26   16

Errol

Umbagog
Lake

Phillips

Strafford

Androscoggin

MAINE

Stark

West
Milan

Groveton

Milan

*WHITE
MOUNTAIN
NATIONAL
FOREST*

110   16

91

Lancaster

Berlin

3

Gorham   2

Whitefield

*Forest
Lake*

135   142   3

115   2

**Mt.
Washington** **34**

Appalachian Trail

91

135   93

28 Littleton

116

Twin
Mountain

302

**Bretton
Woods**

Bethlehem 29

30

Pinkham
Notch

**Sugar
Hill**

142   3

*CRAWFORD NOTCH
STATE PARK*

Lisbon

27 26 Franconia

18

Jackson

302   112

Cannon
Mt.

*Franconia
Notch*

33 Glen

Woodsville

10   302   112

*FRANCONIA
NOTCH
STATE PARK*

3

16

Pemigewasset R.

32

Intervale

93

302

Bartlett

31

**36 North
Conway**

Haverhill

*WHITE
MOUNTAIN
NATIONAL
FOREST*

25

TO
HANOVER

**Kancamagus
Hwy.**

25

Bear
Notch Rd.

Echo Lake
State Park

37

**Lincoln/North
Woodstock**

Loon
Mountain

Swift

River

Mount
Chocorua

Conway

302

118

TO
CONCORD

3

Woodstock

**Waterville
Valley**

49   **24**

Sabbaday
Falls

112

16

TO
SNOWVILLE,
EAST MADISON

Brook Rd., 03215, ☎ 603/236–4600 or 888/703–2453, FAX 603/236–
4947, WEB *www.goldeneaglelodge.com. 139 condominiums. Kitchenettes, indoor pool, sauna, recreation room. AE, D, DC, MC, V.*

$$–$$$ ☜ **Snowy Owl Inn.** The fourth-floor bunk-bed lofts at this inn are ideal
for families; first-floor rooms, some with whirlpool tubs, are suitable
for couples seeking a quiet getaway. The atrium lobby, where guests
are treated to afternoon wine and cheese, contains a three-story fieldstone fireplace and many prints and watercolors of snowy owls. Four
restaurants are within walking distance. Guests have access to the
White Mountain Athletic Club. ☒ *Box 407, Village Rd., 03215,* ☎
603/236–8383 or 800/766–9969, FAX *603/236–4890,* WEB
*www.snowyowlinn.com. 85 rooms. Indoor and outdoor pools, hot tubs.
AE, D, DC, MC, V. BP.*

Outdoor Activities and Sports

The **White Mountain Athletic Club** (☒ Rte. 49, ☎ 603/236–8303) has
tennis, racquetball, and squash as well as a 25-meter indoor pool, a
jogging track, exercise equipment, whirlpools, saunas, steam rooms,
and a games room. The club is free to guests of many area lodgings.

Ski Areas

WATERVILLE VALLEY

Former U.S. ski-team star Tom Corcoran designed this family-oriented resort. The lodgings and various amenities are about one mi from
the slopes, but a shuttle renders a car unnecessary. ☒ *Box 540, Rte.
49, 03215,* ☎ *603/236–8311; 603/236–4144 snow conditions; 800/
468–2553 lodging,* WEB *www.waterville.com.*

Downhill. Mt. Tecumseh has been laid out with great care. This ski area
has hosted more World Cup races than any other in the East, so most
advanced skiers will be adequately challenged. Snowboarders have a
terrain park that includes a timed boardercross course, and lift-serviced
snow tubing has been added. Most of the 52 trails are intermediate:
straight down the fall line, wide, and agreeably long. A 7-acre tree-
skiing area adds variety. Snowmaking coverage of 100% ensures good
skiing even when nature doesn't cooperate. The lifts serving the 2,020
ft of vertical rise include two high-speed detachable quads, two triple,
three double, and four surface lifts.

Cross-country. The Waterville Valley cross-country network, with the
ski center in the Town Square, has 105 km (65 mi) of trails. About two-
thirds of the trails are groomed; the rest are backcountry.

Child care. The nursery takes children 6 months to 4 years. SKIwee instruction accepts children ages 3 to 12. The Kinderpark, a children's
slope, has a slow-running lift.

Summer activities. Hiking, mountain biking, tennis, and golf are popular activities. Mountain bikes are available for rent in the Town
Square.

Lincoln/North Woodstock

㉕ *14 mi northwest of Waterville Valley, 63 mi north of Concord.*

Lincoln and North Woodstock, at the western end of the Kancamagus Highway or at Exit 32 off I–93, combine to make one of the
state's liveliest resort areas—the area appeals more to the social set and
families than to couples seeking a quiet, romantic getaway. Festivals,
such as the New Hampshire Scottish Highland Games in mid-September, keep Lincoln swarming with people year-round, while North
Woodstock maintains more of a village feel.

A ride on the **Hobo Railroad** yields scenic views of the Pemigewasset River and the White Mountain National Forest. The narrated excursions take 1 hour and 20 minutes. ⊠ *Rte. 112, Lincoln,* ☎ *603/745–2135,* WEB *www.hoborr.com.* ⊒ *$8.* ⊙ *June–Labor Day, daily, May and Sept.–Oct., weekends; call for schedule.*

⟳ At the **Whale's Tale Water Park,** you can float on an inner tube along a gentle river, careen down five water slides, take a trip down the multipassenger family tube ride, or body-surf in the large wave pool. Whale Harbor and Orca Park Play Island contain water activities for small children and toddlers. ⊠ *U.S. 3, North Lincoln,* ☎ *603/745–8810,* WEB *www.whalestale-waterpark.com.* ⊒ *$20.* ⊙ *Mid-June–Labor Day, daily 10–6.*

Dining and Lodging

$$–$$$ ✕🔟 **Woodstock Inn.** This social but laid-back inn, run by the Rice family since 1982, has rooms in three buildings, ranging from fairly simple to quite romantic (with canopy bed, whirlpool tub, and complimentary champagne). Many of them accommodate groups and families. The restaurants include the elegant Clement Room Grill ($$–$$$), where the Mediterranean seafood sauté or bison pot roast are favorite dishes; Woodstock Station ($), where the extensive menu lists everything from meat loaf to fajitas; and the Woodstock Inn Brewery. The complimentary country breakfasts (for overnight guests—are justly famous. ⊠ *Box 118, U.S. 3, North Woodstock 03262,* ☎ *603/745–3951 or 800/321–3985,* FAX *603/745–3701,* WEB *www.wood-stockinnnh.com. 21 rooms, 19 with bath. 2 restaurants, bar, refrigerator, outdoor hot tub. AE, D, MC, V. BP.*

$$–$$$$ 🔟 **Mountain Club on Loon.** This first-rate slopeside resort hotel has an assortment of accommodations: suites that sleep as many as eight, studios with Murphy beds, and 117 units with kitchens. Many can be combined to form larger units. All rooms are within walking distance of the lifts, and condominiums are on-slope and nearby. Entertainers perform in the lounge on most winter weekends. ⊠ *Rte. 112, Kancamagus Hwy., Lincoln 03251,* ☎ *603/745–2244 or 800/229–7829,* FAX *603/745–2317. 234 units. Restaurant, bar, lounge, indoor and outdoor pools, massage, sauna, tennis courts, aerobics, health club, racquetball, squash. AE, D, MC, V.*

$$–$$$ 🔟 **Indian Head Resort.** Views across the 180 acres of this resort motel near the Loon and Cannon Mountain ski areas are of Indian Head Rock Profile and the Franconia Mountains. Cross-country ski trails and a mountain-bike trail from the resort connect to the Franconia Notch trail system. The Profile Room restaurant ($$–$$$) serves a nice selection of standard American dishes. ⊠ *U.S. 3, North Lincoln 03251,* ☎ *603/745–8000 or 800/343–8000,* FAX *603/745–8414,* WEB *www.indian-headresort.com. 98 rooms, 40 cottages. Restaurant, bar, indoor and outdoor pools, lake, outdoor hot tub, sauna, tennis court, fishing, bicycles, ice-skating, cross-country skiing, recreation room. AE, D, DC, MC, V.*

Nightlife and the Arts

NIGHTLIFE

Skiers head to the **Granite Bar** at the Mountain Club at the Loon Mountain resort (⊠ Kancamagus Hwy., ☎ 603/745–8111). **Thunderbird Lounge** (⊠ Indian Head Resort, U.S. 3, North Lincoln, ☎ 603/745–8000) has nightly entertainment year-round and a large dance floor. The **Olde Timbermill Pub** (⊠ Mill at Loon Mountain, Kancamagus Hwy., ☎ 603/745–3603) brings in live dance music weekends.

THE ARTS

The **North Country Center for the Arts** (⊠ Mill at Loon Mountain, Kancamagus Hwy., Lincoln, ☎ 603/745–6032) presents theater for children and adults and art exhibitions from July to September.

Outdoor Activities and Sports

At **Lost River in Kinsman Notch** (⊠ Rte. 112, 6 mi west of North Woodstock, ☎ 603/745–8031, WEB www.findlostriver.com), open from mid-May to mid-October, you can hike along the sheer granite river gorge and view geological wonders like the Guillotine Rock and the Lemon Squeezer, or pan for gemstones. A cafeteria, extensive nature garden, and gift shop round out the amenities. Admission varies according to the activity. **Pemi Valley Excursions** (⊠ Main St., Lincoln, ☎ 603/745–2744, WEB www.i93.com/pvsr) offers moose and wildlife bus tours June–October, and guided snowmobile tours through the White Mountains in winter.

Shopping

CRAFTS

The **Curious Cow** (⊠ Main St., North Woodstock, ☎ 603/745–9230) is a multidealer shop selling country crafts. **Sunburst Fashions** (⊠ 108 Main St., North Woodstock, ☎ 603/745–8745) stocks handcrafted gemstone jewelry and imported gifts.

MALL

Millfront Marketplace, Mill at Loon Mountain (⊠ Kancamagus Hwy., Lincoln, ☎ 603/745–6261), a former paper factory, contains restaurants, boutiques, a bookstore, and a post office.

Ski Areas

LOON MOUNTAIN

A modern resort on the Kancamagus Highway and the Pemigewasset River, Loon Mountain opened in the 1960s and underwent serious development in the 1980s. In the base lodge and around the mountain are many food-service and lounge facilities. There's day and nighttime lift-serviced snow tubing on the lower slopes. Loon's Equestrian Center runs horseback-riding trips along the east branch of the Pemigewasset River. ⊠ *Kancamagus Hwy., Lincoln 03251,* ☎ *603/745–8111; 603/745–8100 snow conditions; 800/227–4191 lodging,* WEB *www.loonmtn.com.*

Downhill. Wide, straight, and consistent intermediate trails prevail at Loon. Beginner trails and slopes are set apart. Most advanced runs are grouped on the North Peak section farther from the main mountain. Snowboarders have a halfpipe and their own snowboard park, and an alpine garden with bumps and jumps provides thrills for skiers. The vertical is 2,100 ft; a four-passenger gondola, one high-speed detachable quad, two triple and three double chairlifts, and one surface lift serve the 43 trails and slopes.

Cross-country. The touring center at Loon Mountain has 35 km (22 mi) of cross-country trails.

Child care. The day-care center takes children from 6 weeks to 8 years old. The ski school runs several programs for children of different age groups. Children 5 and under ski free.

Summer activities. In summer and fall you can ride New Hampshire's longest gondola to the summit for panoramic mountain views. Among the daily activities at the summit are lumberjack shows, storytelling by a mountain man, and nature tours. You can also take self-guided walks to glacial caves. Other recreational opportunities include horseback riding, mountain biking, and in-line skating and skateboarding in a state park.

Franconia

 16 mi north of Lincoln/North Woodstock.

Travelers have long passed north-south through the White Mountains via Franconia Notch, and in the late 18th century a town evolved just to the north. It and the region's jagged rock formations and heavy coat of evergreens have stirred the imaginations of such literary icons as Washington Irving, Henry Wadsworth Longfellow, and Nathaniel Hawthorne, who penned a short story about the Old Man on the Mountain. The town remains enchanting, if sleepy (especially compared with nearby bustling Lincoln/Woodstock), touched though it is by I–93—aka Franconia Notch Parkway—and modern ski resorts.

At **Frost Place,** Robert Frost's home from 1915 to 1920, the poet wrote one of his most-remembered works, "Stopping by Woods on a Snowy Evening." Two rooms host occasional readings and contain memorabilia and signed editions of his books. Outside, you can follow short trails marked with lines from Frost's poetry. ⊠ *Ridge Rd. , off Rte. 116,* ☎ *603/823–5510.* ✏ *$3.* ⊘ *Memorial Day–June, weekends 1–5; July–Columbus Day, Wed.–Mon. 1–5.*

The **Old Man of the Mountain,** a granite profile high above the notch, defines New Hampshire; you can't easily—and shouldn't—miss glimpsing this icon. Nathaniel Hawthorne wrote about it, New Hampshire resident Daniel Webster bragged about it, and P. T. Barnum tried to buy it. Stop at the posted turn-outs from I–93 north- or southbound or along the shore of Profile Lake for the best views. There's also a small, free **Old Man of the Mountain Museum** administered by Franconia Notch State Park and located at the southbound viewing area (by the Cannon Mountain tram parking area); it's open daily 9–5.

The **Flume** is an 800-ft-long natural chasm with narrow walls that give the gorge's running water an eerie echo. The route through the flume has been built up with a series of boardwalks and stairways. The visitor center has exhibits on the region's history. ⊠ *Franconia Notch Pkwy., Exit 2,* ☎ *603/745–8391,* WEB *www.nhparks.state.nh.us/parkops/ parks/franconia.html.* ✏ *$7.* ⊘ *May–Oct., daily 9–5.*

Dining and Lodging

$$–$$$ ✕▣ **Franconia Inn.** At this 107-acre, family-friendly year-round resort, you can golf next door at Sunset Hill's nine-hole course, play tennis, swim in the pool, hike—even try soaring from the inn's airstrip. The cross-country ski barn doubles as a stable and horseback center in the warmer months. Rooms have designer chintzes, canopy beds, and country furnishings; some have whirlpool baths or fireplaces. The restaurant presents traditional American fare with some upscale twists, such as medallions of veal with apple-mustard sauce and filet mignon with green-chili butter and Madeira sauce. Meal plans are available. ⊠ *1300 Easton Rd., 03580,* ☎ *603/823–5542 or 800/473–5299,* FAX *603/823–8078,* WEB *www.franconiainn.com. 34 rooms, 1 3-bedroom cottage. Restaurant, bar, pool, hot tub, 4 tennis courts, croquet, hiking, horseback riding, bicycles, ice-skating, cross-country skiing, sleigh rides. AE, MC, V. Closed Apr.–mid-May.*

$$–$$$ ▣ **Horse and Hound Inn.** Off the beaten path yet convenient to the Cannon Mountain tram, this inn is on 8 acres surrounded by the White Mountain National Forest. Antiques and assorted collectibles provide a cheery atmosphere, and on the grounds are 65 km (39 mi) of cross-country ski trails. Pets are welcome (for a small fee). ⊠ *205 Wells Rd., 03580,* ☎ *603/823–5501 or 800/450–5501. 10 rooms, 8 with bath. Restaurant, bar, cross-country skiing. AE, D, DC, MC, V. Closed Apr.–mid-May and mid-Oct.–Thanksgiving. BP, MAP.*

$ ⚠ **Lafayette Campground.** This campground has hiking and biking trails, 97 tent sites, showers, a camp store, a bike trail, and easy access to the Appalachian Trail. ⊠ *U.S. 3 and I–93, Franconia Notch*

State Park, 03580, ☎ 603/823–9513 information; 603/271–3628 reservations. No pets. MC, V.

Shopping

Stores in the **Franconia Marketplace** (✉ Main St., ☎ 603/823–5368) include the Grateful Bread Quality Bakery and Magoons Natural Foods.

Ski Areas

CANNON MOUNTAIN

This state-run facility in Franconia Notch State Park gives strong attention to skier services, family programs, snowmaking, and grooming—all at a very sound value. It was one of the first ski areas in the country. (☞ The New England Ski Museum sits at the base of the tramway. ✉ Franconia Notch State Park, I–93, Exit 3, 03580, ☎ 603/823–8800; 603/823–7771 snow conditions; 800/237–9007 lodging, WEB www.cannonmt.com.

Downhill. The narrow, steep pitches off the peak of the 2,146 ft of vertical rise reveal the high level of skiing here. Intermediates will find newly recontoured cruising trails, and the Brookside learning slope serves beginners. Under a new fall of snow, Cannon's 42 trails present challenges rarely found elsewhere in New Hampshire. For additional fun, try the two glade-skiing trails, Turnpike and Banshee or take to the lift-serviced tubing park. A 70-passenger tramway, two quads, three triples, and one surface lift move skiers upward.

Cross-country. Nordic skiing is on a 13-km (8-mi) multiuse recreational path.

Child care. Cannon's Peabody Base Lodge takes children one and up. All-day and half-day SKIwee programs cater to kids 4–12, and season-long instruction can be arranged.

Summer activities. A multiuse recreational path runs parallel to the Franconia Notch Parkway (I–93). For $9 round-trip, the Cannon Mountain Aerial Tramway (☉ daily Memorial Day–late Oct.) can lift you 2,022 ft for a sweeping mountain vista. It's a six-minute ride to the top, where marked trails lead to the observation platform.

Sugar Hill

㉗ 6 mi west of Franconia.

Sugar Hill, a town of 500 people, is deservedly famous for its spectacular sunsets and views of the Franconia Mountains, best seen from Sunset Hill, where a row of grand hotels and summer "cottages" once stood. Quiet country charm and good-quality bed-and-breakfasts and small inns make Sugar Hill an ideal spot for a romantic getaway.

Sugar Hill may be small, but the surprisingly well-done **Sugar Hill Historical Museum** proves the town has a big history. Topics of the permanent and changing exhibits range from settlement through the resort era to the present day. ✉ Rte. 117, ☎ 603/823–5336. ☑ $2. ☉ July–mid-Oct., Thurs. and weekends 1–4.

Dining and Lodging

$ ✕ **Polly's Pancake Parlor.** This local institution, originally a carriage shed built in 1830, was converted to a tearoom during the Depression, when the Dexters began serving "all you can eat" pancakes, waffles, and French toast for 50¢. The prices have gone up some, but the descendants of the Dexters continue to serve pancakes and waffles made from grains ground on the property, their own country sausage, and pure maple syrup. ✉ Rte. 117, ☎ 603/823–5575. D, MC, V. No dinner.

$$–$$$$ ✕⊞ **Sugar Hill Inn.** The old carriage on the lawn and wicker chairs on the wraparound porch set a nostalgic mood before you even enter this converted 1789 farmhouse. Many rooms have hand-stenciled walls, views of the Franconia Mountains, and rippled antique windowpanes; all contain antiques. There are 10 rooms in the inn and six (some with fireplaces) in three country cottages. Bette Davis visited friends in this house—the room with the best view is named after her. The restaurant ($$$; reservations essential) serves such haute American fare as salmon baked with Dijon mustard and wine; the homemade desserts are always delicious. ⊠ *Rte. 117, 03585,* ☎ *603/823–5621 or 800/ 548–4748,* FAX *603/823–5639,* WEB *www.sugarhillinn.com. 16 rooms. Restaurant, pub, cross-country skiing. AE, MC, V. BP, MAP required during fall foliage season.*

$$–$$$$ ⊞ **Sunset Hill House.** Since it opened in 1882, this sprawling compound
★ has been famous for having perhaps the best sunset views of any resort in New England—it lies along a 1,700-ft ridge with panoramic views not just west toward the sun but also east out toward the Presidential Range. The meticulously kept rooms have superb views, and some have antiques dating back to the inn's first years—gas fireplaces, double whirlpool tubs, and decks grace the top units. The restaurant ($$–$$$), even apart from its fabulous views, is among the most acclaimed in the White Mountains; you might start with pan-seared ostrich with a raspberry beurre-blanc, and then move on to roasted seasoned game hen with a lemon-spinach cream. A tavern ($–$$) serves lighter but still-excellent fare (blackened tuna, chicken sandwich with blue cheese–chipotle dressing). ⊠ *Sunset Hill Rd., 03585,* ☎ *603/ 823–5522 or 800/786–4455,* WEB *www.sunsethillhouse.com. 28 rooms. 2 restaurants, bar, pool, hiking, mountain bikes, ice-skating, cross-country skiing. AE, D, MC, V. BP.*

$$–$$$ ⊞ **Foxglove.** Extensive gardens with hammocks for relaxing are just one of the sybaritic delights at this rambling turn-of-the-century home next to Lover's Lane. Common areas are decorated in country-French style with antiques, and guest rooms are thoughtfully furnished, each in a different motif. The Serengeti Room has animal-print linens, a chandelier with carnival glass shades, and black and brass fixtures in the bath. The inn is no-smoking. ⊠ *Rte. 117, 03585,* ☎ *603/823–8840 or 888/343– 2220,* FAX *603/823–5755,* WEB *www.foxgloveinn.com. 6 rooms. BP.*

$$–$$$ ⊞ **Hilltop.** Staying with innkeepers Mike and Meri Hern is just like dropping by Grandma's—they even welcome pets. The rooms in their 1895 country farmhouse are done in a quirky mix of antiques with handmade quilts, Victorian ceiling fans, piles of pillows, and big, fluffy towels. The TV room has hundreds of movies on tape. Rockers on the porch are perfect for watching the sun set behind the mountains. The large country breakfast includes homemade jams, pancakes made with homegrown berries, soufflés, and smoked ham, bacon, or salmon. The no-smoking inn has a two-night minimum during foliage season, summer weekends, and on holidays. ⊠ *Rte. 117, 03585,* ☎ *603/823– 5695 or 800/770–5695,* FAX *603/823–5518,* WEB *www.hilltopinn.com. 3 rooms, 3 suites. Bar, library. D, MC, V. BP.*

Littleton

28 *9 mi northeast of Sugar Hill, 7 mi north of Franconia, 86 miles north of Concord.*

One of the largest towns in northern New Hampshire, Littleton sits along a granite shelf along the Ammonoosuc River, whose swift current and drop of 235 ft aided in the town's early flourish as a mill center. Later, the railroad came through and Littleton grew into the trade and commerce hub of the region. In the minds of many visitors to the

White Mountains, Littleton is still more a place to stock up on supplies and basics than a bona fide tourist destination, but few New Hampshire communities have worked harder to revitalize themselves than Littleton. Today, a great wealth of engaging shops and several eateries line the town's Main Street, whose neatly kept rows of mostly 19th- and early-20th-century shopfronts suggest a scene from an old Jimmy Stewart movie.

Just off Main Street, stop by the **Littleton Grist Mill** (⊠ 22 Mill St., ☎ 603/444–7478), a recently restored 1798 mill that contains a shop selling New England–made pottery, kitchenware, and home accessories, plus stone-ground flour products; you'll also find original mill equipment on display.

Dining and Lodging

$–$$$ ✕ **Italian Oasis.** This homey spot on the second floor of Parker's Marketplace has red-checkered tablecloths, trellis wall dividers, and a separate brew pub up front, which produces a nice range of stouts and ales. You'll find an enormous menu of sandwiches, munchies, and pizzas, along with more substantial fare such as calamari platters, veal parmigiana, and spinach-and-roasted-garlic ravioli. ⊠ *106 Main St.,* ☎ *603/444–6995. AE, D, MC, V.*

$ ⊞ **Thayer's Inn.** Although this stately Greek Revival hotel, opened in
★ 1843, hasn't been converted into a cushy luxurious property the way many old White Mountains inns have, it nevertheless offers among the most charming budget accommodations in the region. The clean, well-kept rooms (some share a bath) are quaintly old-fashioned, with creaky floorboards, exposed pipes, high ceilings, comfy wing chairs, and vintage steam radiators. The friendly staff welcomes passersby to drop in for a look at a small third-floor room set up as it would have appeared in the 1840s (you view it through a display window across the door), and to take in the 360-degree views from the cupola on the sixth floor. There's no elevator, something to keep in mind if booking an upper floor. ⊠ *111 Main St., 03561,* ☎ *603/444–6469 or 800/634–8179,* WEB *www.thayersinn.com. 38 rooms. MC, V.*

Shopping

The **Village Book Store** (⊠ 81 Main St., ☎ 603/444–5263) has a vast selection of both nonfiction and fiction titles—it's one of the most comprehensive bookshops in the state.

Bethlehem

㉙ *5 mi southeast of Littleton.*

In the days before antihistamines, hay-fever sufferers came by the bus load to the town of Bethlehem, elevation 1,462 ft, whose crisp air has a blissfully low pollen count. Today this quaint hamlet is notable for its distinctive arts and crafts, Victorian and Colonial homes, art deco movie theater, and shops and eateries on its main street.

Dining and Lodging

$$–$$$ ✕ **Tim-bir Alley.** This restaurant leases space from Adair and, for eight months of the year, serves dinner in Adair's elegant dining rooms. The menu, which changes weekly, utilizes regional American ingredients in creative ways. Main dishes have included southwestern spiced tournedos of beef with corn, smoked bacon, and black-bean relish; and cinnamon-scented pork tenderloin with cranberry vinaigrette and pear-pecan chutney. Desserts, like a chocolate-glazed espresso cheesecake, are well worth saving room for. ⊠ *80 Guider La.,* ☎ *603/444–6142. No credit cards. Closed Nov.–mid-Dec. and Apr.–May; Mon.–Tues. June–Oct.; Sun.–Tues. mid-Dec.–Mar. No lunch.*

$$$$ 🏠 **Adair.** In 1927 attorney Frank Hogan built this three-story Geor-
★ gian Revival home as a wedding present for his daughter, Dorothy Adair.
Walking paths on the luxurious country inn's 200 acres wind through
gardens. The rooms, which have garden or mountain views, are decorated with period antiques and reproductions. Many have fireplaces.
One suite has a large two-person hot tub, a fireplace, a balcony, and
a king-size sleigh bed. Tim-bir Alley, which leases space here, serves
contemporary food part of the year. ✉ *80 Guider La., 03574, ☎ 603/
444–2600 or 888/444–2600,* FAX *603/444–4823,* WEB *www.adairinn.com.
7 rooms, 2 suites, 1 cottage. Restaurant, tennis court, billiards. AE,
MC, V. BP.*

Outdoor Activities and Sports

The Society for the Protection of New Hampshire Forests owns two
properties in Bethlehem open to visitors. **Bretzfelder Park** (✉ Prospect
St., ☎ 603/444–6228), a 77-acre nature and wildlife park, has a picnic shelter, hiking, and cross-country ski trails. The **Rocks Estate** (✉
113 Glessner Rd., ☎ 603/444–6228) is a working Christmas-tree farm
(you can purchase a tree here for the holiday) with walking trails, historic buildings, and educational programs.

Bretton Woods

③⓪ *14 mi southeast of Bethlehem, 28 mi northeast of Lincoln/Woodstock.*

In the early 1900s private rail cars brought the rich and famous from
New York and Philadelphia to the Mount Washington Hotel, the jewel
of Bretton Woods. The hotel was the site of a famous World Mone-
tary Fund conference in 1944, which greatly affected the post–World
War II economy. The area is also known for the cog railway and
eponymous ski resort.

In 1858 Sylvester Marsh petitioned state legislature for permission to
build a steam railway up Mt. Washington. A politico retorted that he'd
have better luck building a railroad to the moon. Just 11 years later,
★ the **Mt. Washington Cog Railway** chugged up to the summit, and so it
remains one of the state's most beloved attractions—a thrill in either
direction. Allow three hours round-trip. ✉ *U.S. 302, 6 mi northeast
of Bretton Woods,* ☎ *603/278–5404; 800/922–8825 outside NH,* WEB
www.thecog.com. 🎟 *$44 round-trip.* ☉ *Late May–mid-Oct., daily;
late-Apr.–late-May and mid-Oct.–early Nov.; call for hours.*

En Route Scenic U.S. 302 winds through the steep, wooded mountains on either
side of spectacular Crawford Notch, southeast of Bretton Woods, and
passes through **Crawford Notch State Park** (✉ U.S. 302, Harts Location, ☎ 603/374–2272), where you can stop for a picnic and a short
hike to Arethusa Falls or the Silver and Flume cascades. The visitor
center has a gift shop and a cafeteria.

Dining and Lodging

$$–$$$$ ✕🏠 **Bretton Woods Mountain Resort.** Comprising three distinct prop-
★ erties with rooms in a wide range of prices, Bretton Woods is most fa-
mous for the leviathan 1902 Mount Washington Hotel, one of the most
ambitious projects of its day. It quickly became a top grand resort, most
notable for its 900-ft-long veranda, which affords a full view of the
Presidential Range. With its stately public rooms and large, Victorian-
style bedrooms and suites, the hotel retains a turn-of-the-century for-
mality. Jacket and tie are required in the dining room ($$$$). The regional
cuisine highlights seasonal dishes such as lemon lobster ravioli with
shrimp and scallops and roast pork with onions and mushrooms. Built
in 1896, the restored Bretton Arms Country Inn predates the Mount
Washington Hotel across the way and offers mid-priced rooms in a less

dressy, country style. Reservations are essential in the contemporary dining room ($$–$$$) and should be made on arrival. Rooms at the newer Bretton Woods Motor Inn have contemporary furnishings, a balcony or patio, and mountain views. The Continental cuisine at the motor inn's Darby's Restaurant ($$) is served around a circular fireplace, and the bar is a hangout for skiers. ✉ *U.S. 302, 03575,* ☎ *603/278–1000 or 800/258–0330,* ꜰꜲꓫ *603/278–8838,* ꪡꫀꫝ *www.mtwashington.com. 281 rooms, 3 suites. 4 restaurants, 2 bars, 2 pools, sauna, driving range, 18-hole golf course, 12 tennis courts, hiking, horseback riding, bicycles, downhill skiing, sleigh rides, recreation room, children's programs (ages 5–12). AE, D, MC, V.*

$ 🏕 **Dry River Campground.** This rustic campground in Crawford Notch State Park has 30 tent sites and is a popular base for hiking the White Mountain National Forest. ✉ *U.S. 302, Harts Location (Box 177, Twin Mountain 03595),* ☎ *603/271–3628,* ꪡꫀꫝ *www.nhparks.state.nh.us/ parkops/parks/crawford.html. Closed mid-Dec.–mid-May.*

Ski Areas

BRETTON WOODS

This expansive and much-improved ski area has a three-level, open-space base lodge; a convenient drop-off area; easy parking; and an uncrowded setting. The views of Mt. Washington alone are worth the visit; the scenery is especially beautiful from the Top o' Quad restaurant and from the former Cog Railway car perched on the top of West Mountain. ✉ *U.S. 302, 03575,* ☎ *603/278–3322; 800/232–2972 information; 800/258–0330 lodging,* ꪡꫀꫝ *www.brettonwoods.com.*

Downhill. The skiing on the 64 trails is novice and intermediate, with steeper pitches near the top of the 1,500-ft vertical and glade skiing to satisfy expert skiers. Skiers and snowboarders can try a terrain park with jumps and a halfpipe. The Accelerator halfpipe is for snowboarders only. One detachable quad, one fixed-grip quad, one triple, and three double chairlifts service the trails. The area has night skiing and snowboarding on Friday, Saturday, and holidays. A limited lift-ticket policy helps keep lines short.

Cross-country. The large, full-service cross-country ski center here has 100 km (62 mi) of groomed and double-track trails, many of them lift-serviced. You can also rent snowshoes.

Child care. The nursery takes children from ages 2 months to 5 years. The ski school has an all-day program for children ages 4 to 12, using progressive instructional techniques. There's also a snowboarding program for children 8 to 12. Rates include lifts, lessons, equipment, lunch, and supervised play.

Bartlett

❸❶ *18 mi southeast of Bretton Woods.*

Bear Mountain to the south, Mt. Parker to the north, Mt. Cardigan to the west, and the Saco River to the east combine to create an unforgettable setting for the village of Bartlett, incorporated in 1790. Lovely Bear Notch Road (closed in winter) has the only midpoint access to the Kancamagus Highway.

Dining and Lodging

$$–$$$$ ✕🏨 **Grand Summit Hotel & Conference Center.** The gables and curves of this resort hotel at the base of Attitash Bear Peak mimic the mountain's peaks and slopes. The luxurious contemporary-style rooms have kitchenettes, VCRs, and stereo systems. Entrées in the Alpine Garden restaurant ($$–$$$) include grilled salmon with lobster sauce and

baked stuffed pork with chestnut herb stuffing. ⊠ *Box 429, U.S. 302, 03812,* ☎ *603/374–1900 or 888/554–1900,* ⨳ *603/374–3040,* ⊠ *www.attitash.com. 143 rooms. 2 restaurants, bar, pool, hot tub, steam room, health club, downhill skiing, recreation room. AE, D, MC, V.*

$$–$$$$ ⛺ **Attitash Mountain Village.** The style at this condo-motel complex— across the street from the mountain via a tunnel—is alpine contemporary, and the staff is young and enthusiastic. Units, some with fireplaces, kitchens, and whirlpool tubs, accommodate from 2 to 14 people. The restaurant, with a varied and family-friendly menu, has unobstructed views of the mountain. ⊠ *U.S. 302, 03812,* ☎ *603/374– 6501 or 800/862–1600,* ⨳ *603/374–6509,* ⊠ *www.attitashmtvillage.com. 300 units. Restaurant, pub, indoor and outdoor pools, sauna, tennis court, gym, hiking, fishing, mountain bikes, downhill and cross-country skiing, recreation room, playground, laundry service, meeting rooms. AE, D, MC, V.*

Ski Areas

ATTITASH BEAR PEAK

This high-profile resort, which hosts many special events and ski races, continues to expand and improve its infrastructure. Lodging at the base of the mountain is in condos and motel-style units, away from the hustle of North Conway. Attitash has a computerized lift–ticket system that allows skiers to pay as they run. Skiers can share the ticket, which is good for two years. ⊠ *Box 302, U.S. 302, 03812,* ☎ *603/374–2368 or 800/ 223–7669 snow conditions; 800/223–7669 lodging,* ⊠ *www.attitash.com.*

Downhill. Enhanced with massive snowmaking (98%), the trails now number 70 on two peaks, both with full-service base lodges. The bulk of the skiing and boarding is geared to intermediates and experts, with some steep pitches, glades, and good use of terrain. Beginners enjoy good terrain on the lower mountain and some runs from the top. The Attitash Adventure Center has a rental shop, lessons desk, and children's programs. Serving the 36 km (22 mi) of trails and the 1,750-ft vertical drop are two high-speed quads, one fixed-grip quad, three triples, three double chairlifts, and three surface tows.

Cross-country. Bear Notch Ski Touring Center (☎ 603/374–2277) has more than 70 km (43 mi) of cross-country trails, more than 60 km (37 mi) skate groomed and tracked. Backcountry skiing is unlimited. Guests staying at the Grand Summit Hotel can rent equipment, get trail passes, and connect to the trails from the hotel door.

Child care. The Attitash Adventure Center nursery takes children ages 6 months to 5 years. Other programs accommodate children up to 16.

Summer activities. Attitash Bear Park has two dry alpine slides, four water slides, Buddy Bear's Playpool for children, horseback riding, lift-serviced mountain biking, and a driving range. A chairlift whisks passengers to the White Mountain Observation Tower, which delivers 270-degree views of the Whites.

Glen

③② *6 mi northeast of Bartlett, 89 mi northeast of Concord, 71 mi northwest of Portland, ME.*

Glen is hardly more than a crossroads between North Conway and Jackson, but its central location has made it the home of a few noteworthy attractions and dining and lodging options.

⟳ That cluster of fluorescent buildings on Route 16 is **Story Land,** a children's theme park with life-size storybook and nursery-rhyme characters. The 16 rides and four shows include a flume ride, a

Victorian-theme river-raft ride, and a farm-family variety show. ⊠ *Rte. 16,* ☎ *603/383–4186,* WEB *www.storylandnh.com.* ⊡ *$18.* ☉ *Mid-June–Labor Day, daily 9–6; Memorial Day–mid-June and Labor Day–Columbus Day, weekends 10–5.*

☺ **Heritage New Hampshire,** uses theatrical sets, sound effects, and animation to render the state's history. Visitors "sail" on the *Reliance* from a village in 1634 England over tossing seas to the New World and then saunter along Portsmouth's streets in the late 1700s. Exhibits continue through the present day. ⊠ *Rte. 16,* ☎ *603/383–4186,* WEB *www.heritagenh.com.* ⊡ *$10.* ☉ *Mid-June–mid-Oct., daily 9–5.*

Dining and Lodging

$$–$$$ ✕ **Red Parka Pub.** Practically an institution, the Red Parka Pub has been in downtown Glen for more than two decades. The menu has everything a family could want, from an all-you-can-eat salad bar to scallop pie. The barbecued ribs are local favorites, and you'll find hand-carved steaks of every type, from aged New York sirloin to prime rib. ⊠ *U.S. 302,* ☎ *603/383–4344. Reservations not accepted. AE, D, MC, V.*

$–$$ ✕ **Margarita Grill.** Après-ski and hiking types congregate here, in the cozy dining rooms in cold weather and on the covered patio when it's warm, for tasty southwestern fare. The menu includes a variety of homemade salsas, wood-fired steaks, ribs, burgers, and a smattering of Tex-Mex and Cajun specialties. Unwind at the tequila bar after a day on the mountains. ⊠ *U.S. 302,* ☎ *603/383–6556. AE, D, MC, V.*

$$ ✕🏨 **Bernerhof Inn.** This Old World–style hotel is right at home in its alpine setting. The rooms have hardwood floors with hooked rugs, antiques, and reproductions. The fanciest six rooms have brass beds and spa-size bathtubs; one suite has a Finnish sauna. The menu at the Prince Palace restaurant ($–$$$) includes Swiss specialties such as fondue and Wiener schnitzel, along with new American and classic French dishes. The Black Bear pub ($–$$) pours many microbrewery beers and serves sandwiches and pastas. ⊠ *Box 240, U.S. 302, 03838,* ☎ *603/383–9132 or 800/548–8007,* FAX *603/383–0809,* WEB *www.bernerhofinn.com. 9 rooms. Restaurant, pub. AE, D, MC, V. BP.*

$$–$$$ 🏨 **Best Western Storybook Resort Inn.** On a hillside near Attitash Bear Peak, this motor inn with large rooms is well suited to families. Copperfield's Restaurant has gingerbread, sticky buns, omelets, and a children's menu. ⊠ *Box 129, intersection of U.S 302 and Rte. 16, Glen Junction 03838,* ☎ *603/383–6800,* FAX *603/383–4678. 78 rooms. Restaurant, bar, refrigerators, pool, sauna, tennis court, playground. AE, DC, MC, V.*

Jackson

★ ③③ *5 mi north of Glen.*

The village of Jackson just off Route 16 via a red covered bridge has retained its storybook New England character. Art and antiques shopping, tennis, golf, fishing, and hiking to waterfalls are among the draws. When the snow falls, Jackson becomes the state's cross-country skiing capital. The village's proximity to four downhill areas makes it popular with alpine skiers, too.

Dining and Lodging

$–$$ ✕ **Red Fox Pub & Restaurant.** Some say this restaurant overlooking the Wentworth Golf Club gets its name from a wily fox with a penchant for stealing golf balls right off the fairway. The wide-ranging menu has barbecue ribs, salads, burgers, and more sophisticated dishes such as chicken Florentine and seafood lasagna. The Sunday jazz breakfast buffet is popular with locals and visitors alike. ✉ *Rte. 16A,* ☎ *603/ 383–6659. AE, D, MC, V.*

$$$$ ✕⊡ **Inn at Thorn Hill.** Architect Stanford White designed this 1895 Vic-
★ torian house, which is a few steps from cross-country trails and Jackson village. Practical vinyl siding now covers the house, but plenty of
luxury lies within. Romantic touches in the main inn include rose-motif
papers and antiques such as a blue-velvet fainting couch, and many
rooms have spa tubs and gas fireplaces. Rooms in the carriage house
have a woodsy North Country feel, while the cottages provide extra
privacy. The restaurant ($$$; reservations essential; closed mid-week
in April) serves fine contemporary fare such grilled beef sirloin with a
cabernet–roasted tomato–sweet garlic sauce, spiced bacon, and green-
onion-mashed potatoes, garnished with a basil-gorgonzola cream. ✉
Box A, Thorn Hill Rd., 03846, ☎ *603/383–4242 or 800/289–8990,*
FAX *603/383–8062,* WEB *www.innatthornhill.com. 12 rooms, 4 suites,
3 cottages. Restaurant, pub, pool, hot tub, croquet, cross-country ski-
ing. AE, D, MC, V. BP, MAP.*

$$$–$$$$ ✕⊡ **Christmas Farm Inn.** Despite its winter-inspired name, this 1778
village inn is an all-season retreat. Rooms in the main inn and the salt-
box next door, five with whirlpool baths, are decorated in Laura Ash-
ley and Ralph Lauren prints. The suites have beamed ceilings and
fireplaces. Some standbys in the restaurant ($$–$$$) are grilled seafood
bouillabaisse and vegetable *fra diavalo* with gnocchi. ✉ *Box CC, Rte.
16B, 03846,* ☎ *603/383–4313 or 800/443–5837,* FAX *603/383–6495,*
WEB *www.christmasfarminn.com. 41 units. Restaurant, pub, pool,
sauna, hot tub, volleyball, cross-country skiing, recreation room. AE,
MC, V. MAP.*

$$$–$$$$ ✕⊡ **Wentworth.** This pale-yellow 1869 Victorian charms guests with
individually decorated rooms accented with antiques. All rooms have
TVs and telephones; some have working fireplaces and two-person whirl-
pool tubs. The dining room ($$$) serves a five-course, candlelight din-
ner with a menu that changes seasonally. Good choices are the lobster
bread pudding and the cider-poached salmon. ✉ *Rte. 16A, 03846,* ☎
603/383–9700 or 800/637–0013, FAX *603/383–4265,* WEB *www.thewent-
worth.com. 60 rooms in summer, 52 in winter. Restaurant, bar, pool,
tennis court, ice-skating, cross-country skiing, sleigh rides, billiards.
AE, D, DC, MC, V. MAP.*

$$–$$$$ ⊡ **Inn at Jackson.** The builders of this 1902 Victorian, perched impe-
riously on a hill overlooking the village, followed a design by Stanford
White. The inn has spacious rooms—six with fireplaces—with over-
size windows and an airy feel. Other than an imposing grand staircase
in the front foyer, the house is unpretentious, with hardwood floors,
braided rugs, a smattering of antiques, and mountain views. ✉ *Box
807, Thorn Hill Rd., 03846,* ☎ *603/383–4321 or 800/289–8600,* FAX
603/383–4085, WEB *www.innatjackson.com. 14 rooms. Hot tub, cross-
country skiing. AE, D, DC, MC, V. CP.*

$$–$$$$ ⊡ **Nordic Village Resort.** The light wood and white walls of these deluxe
condos near several ski areas are as Scandinavian as the snowy views.
The Club House has pools and a spa, and there is a nightly bonfire at
Nordic Falls. Larger units have fireplaces, full kitchens, and whirlpool
baths. The property is part of Luxury Mountain Getaways, which operates several additional upscale condos and hotels in the area. ✉ *Rte.
16, 03846,* ☎ *603/383–9101 or 800/472–5207,* FAX *603/383–9823,* WEB
*www.luxurymountaingetaways.com. 140 condominiums. 1 indoor
and 2 outdoor pools, hot tub, steam room, hiking, ice-skating, cross-
country skiing, sleigh rides. D, MC, V.*

$$–$$$ ⊡ **Eagle Mountain House.** This country estate, which dates from 1879,
is close to downhill ski slopes and even closer to cross-country trails,
which begin on the property. The public rooms of this showplace have

a tycoon-roughing-it feel, and the bedrooms are large and furnished with period pieces. On a warm day, you can nurse a drink in a rocking chair on the wraparound deck. ⊠ *Carter Notch Rd., 03846,* ☎ *603/383–9111 or 800/966–5779,* FAX *603/383–0854,* WEB *www.eaglemt.com. 93 rooms. Restaurant, pool, hot tub, sauna, 9-hole golf course, 2 tennis courts, health club, playground. AE, D, DC, MC, V.*

$$–$$$ ⊡ **Wildcat Inn & Tavern.** After a day of skiing, you can collapse on a comfy sofa by the fire in this small 19th-century tavern in the center of Jackson village. The fragrance of home baking permeates into suite-style guest rooms, which are full of knickknacks and furniture of various periods. The tavern, where bands often perform, attracts many skiers. In summer, dining is available in the landscaped garden. ⊠ *Rte. 16A, 03846,* ☎ *603/383–4245 or 800/228–4245,* FAX *603/383–6456,* WEB *www.wildcatinnandtavern.com. 6 rooms, 4 with bath; 7 suites; 1 cottage. Restaurant, bar. AE, MC, V. BP, MAP.*

Outdoor Activities and Sports

Nestlenook Farm (⊠ Dinsmore Rd., ☎ 603/383–9443) maintains an outdoor ice-skating rink with rentals, music, and a bonfire. Going snow-shoeing or taking a sleigh ride are other winter options; in summer you can fly-fish or ride in a horse-drawn carriage.

Ski Areas

BLACK MOUNTAIN

Black Mountain draws families and singles with its fun, friendly, and informal atmosphere. The Family Passport, which allows two adults and two juniors to ski at discounted rates, is a good value. Midweek rates here are usually the lowest in Mt. Washington valley. ⊠ *Rte. 16B, 03846,* ☎ *603/383–4490; 800/475–4669 snow conditions; 800/698–4490 lodging,* WEB *www.blackmt.com.*

Downhill. The 40 trails and two glades on the 1,100-vertical-ft mountain are evenly divided among beginner, intermediate, and expert. There are triple and double chairlifts and two surface tows. Most of the skiing is user-friendly, particularly for beginners—although recent expansion has added trails geared toward experts—and the southern exposure keeps skiers warm. In addition to trails, snowboarders can use two terrain parks and the halfpipe.

Child care. The nursery takes children 6 months to 5 years. Kids 3–12 can take classes at the ski school.

JACKSON SKI TOURING FOUNDATION

One of the top four cross-country skiing areas in the country and by far the largest in New Hampshire, Jackson offers 157 km (98 mi) of trails. About 96 km (60 mi) are track groomed, 85 km (53 mi) are skate groomed, and there are 63 km (39 mi) of marked backcountry trails. You can arrange lessons and rentals at the lodge, in the center of Jackson village. ⊠ *Main St., 03846,* ☎ *800/927–6697,* WEB *www.jacksonxc.org.*

Mt. Washington

★ ❸❹ *20 mi north of Jackson.*

In summer, you can drive to the top of spectacular Mt. Washington, the highest mountain (6,288 ft) in the northeastern United States and home of the **Mt. Washington Observatory**, a weather station that has recorded the world's highest winds. The **Mt. Washington Auto Road**, opened in 1861 and said to be the nation's first manufactured tourist attraction, begins at the **Glen House**, a gift shop and rest stop 15 mi north of Glen on Route 16. Allow two hours round-trip and check your brakes first. Cars with automatic transmissions that can't shift down into first gear aren't allowed on the road.

If you prefer not to drive on a curving, narrow mountain road, you can choose a guided tour in one of the vans (aka "stages") that leave from Great Glen Trails Outdoors Center. In winter, the vans are refitted with snowmobile-like treads and become "SnowCoaches," which travel up the mountain to just above the tree line—you have the option of cross-country skiing or snowshoeing down. (In summer, you can also take the Mt. Washington Cog Railway to the summit; ☞ Bretton Woods.)

Up top, visit the **Sherman Adams Summit Building,** which contains a museum of memorabilia from each of the three hotels that have stood on this spot and a display of native plant life and alpine flowers. Stand in the glassed-in viewing area to hear the roar of that record-breaking wind. ☎ *603/466–3988,* WEB *www.mt-washington.com.* ✉ *Auto road $16 per car and driver plus $6 for each adult passenger; van fare $22.* ☉ *Private cars, mid-May–late Oct.; van tours, year-round, daily. All tours/access are subject to weather conditions.*

Although not a town per se, scenic **Pinkham Notch** covers the eastern side of Mt. Washington and includes several ravines, including Tuckerman Ravine, famous for spring skiing. The **Appalachian Mountain Club** maintains a large visitor center here on Route 16 that provides information to hikers and travelers and has guided hikes, outdoor skills workshops, a cafeteria, lodging, regional topography displays, and a terrific outdoors shop.

Lodging

$ ⊡ **Joe Dodge Lodge at Pinkham Notch.** The Appalachian Mountain Club operates this rustic lodge at the base of Mt. Washington. Rooms are a combination of single-sex bunkrooms—rented by the bunk—for up to five people, and private rooms, all with gleaming wood, cheerful quilts, and reading lights. All share baths. The restaurant serves a buffet breakfast and lunch and a family-style dinner. Packages include breakfast and dinner, plus skiing at Great Glen Trails and/or Wildcat Ski Area. ✉ *Box 298, Rte. 16, Gorham 03581,* ☎ *603/466–2727,* FAX *603/466–3871,* WEB *www.outdoors.org. 102 beds without bath. Restaurant. MC, V. MAP.*

Ski Areas

GREAT GLEN TRAILS OUTDOOR CENTER
This center has a large, sunny base lodge that works as well for cross-country skiers in the winter as it does for hikers, mountain bikers, and backpackers in the summer. This facility, and the equipment rental shop inside, has helped turn Great Glen Trails into a year-round destination. ✉ *Box 300, Rte. 16, Gorham 03581,* ☎ *603/466–2333,* WEB *www.mt-washington.com/ggt.*

Cross-country. There are 40 km (24 mi) of cross-country trails, some with snowmaking, and access to more than 1,100 acres of backcountry. You can even ski or snowshoe the lower half of the Mt. Washington Auto Road. Trees shelter most of the trails, so Mt. Washington's famous weather shouldn't be a concern. The Great Glen Outfitters shop in the base lodge is the largest retailer of Nordic equipment in the state.

Summer activities. Great Glen Trails puts its extensive trail network to use for hiking, trail running, and mountain biking. The center also has programs in canoeing, kayaking, and fly fishing. The base lodge has equipment for rent or sale.

WILDCAT

Glade skiers favor Wildcat, with 28 acres of official tree skiing. Wildcat's runs include some stunning double-black-diamond trails. Skiers who can hold a wedge should check out the 4-km (2½ mi) long Polecat. Experts can zip down the Lynx. Views of Mt. Washington and Tuckerman Ravine are superb. The trails are classic New England—narrow and winding. ✉ *Rte. 16, Pinkham Notch, Jackson 03846,* ☎ *603/466–3326; 888/SKI–WILD snow conditions; 800/255–6439 lodging,* 𝗪𝗘𝗕 *www.skiwildcat.com.*

Downhill. Wildcat's expert runs deserve their designations and then some. Intermediates have mid-mountain-to-base trails, and beginners will find gentle terrain and a broad teaching slope. Snowboarders have several terrain parks and the run of the mountain. The 44 runs, with a 2,100-ft vertical drop, are served by a four-passenger gondola, one high-speed detachable quad, and three triple chairlifts.

Child care. The child-care center takes children ages 6 months and up. All-day SKIwee instruction, on designated slopes, is offered to kids ages 5–12.

Dixville Notch

㉟ *63 mi north of Mt. Washington, 66 mi northeast of Littleton, 149 mi north of Concord.*

If you really want to get away from it all, Dixville Notch is the place to go. Just 12 mi from the Canadian border, this tiny community is known for two things. It's the home of The Balsams Wilderness, one of the oldest and most celebrated resorts in New Hampshire. And Dixville Notch and Harts Location are the first election districts in the nation to vote in the presidential primaries and general elections. At midnight on election day, the 30 or so Dixville Notch voters gather in the little meeting room beside a hotel service bar to cast their ballots and make national news.

One of the favorite pastimes for visitors in this area is watching for moose, those large, ungainly, yet elusive members of the deer family. Although you may catch sight of one or more yourself, **Northern Forest Moose Tours** (☎ 603/752–6060) offers bus tours of the region that have a 97% success rate for spotting moose.

OFF THE
BEATEN PATH

PITTSBURG – Just north of the White Mountains, in the Great North Woods region, Pittsburg contains the four Connecticut Lakes and the springs that form the Connecticut River. The entire northern tip of the state—a chunk of about 250 square mi—lies within the town's borders, the result of a dispute between the United States and Canada. The two countries could not decide on a border, so the inhabitants of this region declared themselves independent of both countries in 1832. They named their nation the Indian Stream Republic, after the river that passes through the territory—the capital of which was Pittsburg. In 1835 the feisty, 40-man Indian Stream militia invaded Canada, with only limited success. The Indian Stream war ended more by common consent than surrender; in 1842 the Webster-Ashburton Treaty fixed the international boundary. Indian Stream was incorporated as Pittsburg, making it the largest township in New Hampshire. Canoeing, fishing, and taking photos are favorite pastimes up here; the pristine wilderness teems with moose. Contact the **North Country Chamber of Commerce** for information about the region.

Dining and Lodging

$$$$ ✕⊡ **The Balsams Wilderness.** This lavish grande dame of the North
★ Woods has been rolling out the red carpet since 1866, drawing families, golf-enthusiasts, skiiers, and others for a varied slate of activities—
from dancing to cooking demonstrations. The individually decorated
rooms vary in size but are generally spacious and comfortably furnished;
all have views of the 15,000-acre estate and the mountains beyond. In
the dining room ($$–$$$; jacket and tie), the summer buffet lunch is
heaped upon a 100-ft-long table. At dinner, a starter might be chilled
strawberry soup spiked with Grand Marnier, followed by poached
salmon with golden caviar sauce and chocolate hazelnut cake. If rates
seem high, remember they include breakfast and dinner and unlimited
use of resort facilities, including skiing and snowboarding. ⊠ *Rte. 26,
03576,* ☎ *603/255–3400; 800/255–0600; 800/255–0800 in NH,* FAX
603/255–4221, WEB *www.thebalsams.com. 204 rooms. 3 restaurants,
bar, pool, driving range, 18-hole golf course, 6 tennis courts, hiking,
boating, fishing, mountain bikes, ice-skating, cross-country skiing,
children's programs (ages 1–12). AE, D, MC, V. Closed late Mar.–mid-
May and mid-Oct.–mid-Dec. MAP.*

$$$ ⊡ **The Glen.** This rustic lodge with stick furniture, fieldstone, and
cedar is on First Connecticut Lake, surrounded by log cabins, seven
of which are right on the water. The cabins come equipped with effi-
ciency kitchens and mini-refrigerators—not that you'll need either, be-
cause rates include meals in the lodge restaurant. ⊠ *77 Glen Rd., 1
mi off U.S. 3, Pittsburg 03592,* ☎ *603/538–6500 or 800/445–4536,*
WEB *www.nhconnlakes.com/glen.htm. 8 rooms, 10 cabins. Restaurant,
kitchenettes, lake. No credit cards. Closed mid-Oct.–mid-May. FAP.*

Outdoor Activities and Sports

Dixville Notch State Park (⊠ Rte. 26, ☎ 603/823–9959), in the north-
ernmost notch in the White Mountains, has picnic areas, a waterfall,
and many hiking trails.

Ski Areas

THE BALSAMS WILDERNESS

Skiing was originally provided as an amenity for hotel guests at the
Balsams, but the area has become popular with day-trippers as well.
⊠ *Rte. 26, 03576,* ☎ *603/255–3400; 800/255–0600; 800/255–0800
in NH; 603/255–3951 snow conditions,* FAX *603/255–4221.*

Downhill. Slopes with such names as Sanguinary, Umbagog, and Ma-
galloway may sound tough, but they're only moderately difficult, lean-
ing toward intermediate. There are 14 trails and four glades from the
top of the 1,000-ft vertical for every skill level. One double chairlift
and two T-bars carry skiers up the mountain. There is a halfpipe for
snowboarders.

Cross-country. The Balsams has 95 km (59 mi) of cross-country ski-
ing, tracked and groomed for skating (a cross-country technique).
Natural-history markers annotate some trails; you can also try tele-
mark and backcountry skiing, and 29 km (18 mi) of snowshoeing trails.

Child care. The ski lodge nursery takes children ages 6 months to 5
years at no charge to hotel guests. Lessons are for kids 3 and up.

North Conway

36 *76 mi south of Dixville Notch, 7 mi south of Glen, 41 mi east of Lin-
coln/North Woodstock.*

Outlet shopping is as big a sport as skiing in this bustling, attractive
town—businesses line Route 16 for several miles. Before the arrival of

the outlets, the town drew visitors for its inspiring scenery, ski resorts, and access to White Mountain National Forest.

🕐 The **Conway Scenic Railroad** operates scenic trips of varying durations in vintage coaches pulled by steam or diesel engines. The dome observation coach on the 5½-hour trip through Crawford Notch offers views of some of the finest scenery in the Northeast. Lunch is served aboard the dining car on the Valley Train to Conway or Bartlett. The 1874 Victorian train station has displays of railroad artifacts, lanterns, and old tickets and timetables. Reserve early during foliage season for Crawford Notch or Valley dining car. ⊠ *Rte. 16/U.S. 302 (38 Norcross Circle),* ☎ *603/356–5251 or 800/232–5251,* WEB *www.conwayscenic.com.* ⊠ *$9.50–$46, depending on trip.* ☉ *Mid-Apr.–late Dec; call for times.*

At **Echo Lake State Park,** you needn't be a rock climber to glimpse views from the 700-ft **White Horse** and **Cathedral** ledges. From the top you'll see the entire valley, in which Echo Lake shines like a diamond. An unmarked trailhead another ⁷⁄₁₀ mi on West Side Road leads to **Diana's Baths,** a spectacular series of waterfalls. ⊠ *Off U.S 302,* ☎ *603/356–2672.* ⊠ *$2.50.* ☉ *Mid-June–mid-Oct., daily dawn–dusk.*

The **Hartmann Model Railroad Museum** houses 14 operating layouts (from G to Z scales), about 2,000 engines, and more than 5,000 cars and coaches. A café, a crafts store, a hobby shop, and an outdoor ride-on train are on site. ⊠ *Rte. 16/U.S. 302 and Town Hall Rd., Intervale,* ☎ *603/356–9922 or 603/356–9933,* WEB *www.hartmannrr.com.* ⊠ *$5.* ☉ *Mid-June–mid-Oct., daily 9–5; mid-Oct.–mid-June, daily 10–5.*

Weather junkies and anybody fascinating by the White Mountains' famously extreme climate conditions should check out the **Weather Discovery Center.** Its hands-on exhibits challenge visitors to understand how weather is monitored and how it in turn affects us. The facility is a collaboration between the National and Atmospheric Administration Forecast Systems lab and the nearby Mt. Washington Observatory—at the summit of Mt. Washington, the world's highest surface wind speed was clocked in at 231 mph. ⊠ *Rte. 16/U.S. 302, ⅓ mi north of rail tracks,* ☎ *603/356–2137,* WEB *www.mountwashington.org/discovery.* ⊠ *$2.* ☉ *Daily 10–5.*

Dining and Lodging

$–$$ ✕ **Delaney's Hole in the Wall.** This casual restaurant has an eclectic decor of sports and other memorabilia that includes autographed baseballs. An early photo of skiing at Tuckerman Ravine hangs over the fireplace. The menu is varied, with entrées ranging from fish-and-chips to fajitas to mussels and scallops sautéed with spiced sausage and Louisiana flavors. ⊠ *Rte. 16, ¼ mi north of North Conway,* ☎ *603/356–7776. D, MC, V.*

$–$$ ✕ **Muddy Moose.** A fun and inviting place—especially popular with younger singles and families—the Muddy Moose has a rustic lodge ambience created with fieldstone walls, exposed wood, and dark lighting. Dig into a Greek salad, grilled chicken Caesar wrap, char-grilled boneless pork chops with a maple-cider glaze, or muddy moose pie. ⊠ *Rte. 16, just south of North Conway,* ☎ *603/356–7696. AE, D, MC, V.*

$$$–$$$$ ✕▥ **Snowvillage Inn.** Journalist Frank Simonds built the main gam-
★ brel-roof house in 1916. To complement the inn's tome-jammed bookshelves, guest rooms are named for famous authors. The nicest of the rooms, with 12 windows that look out over the Presidential Range, is a tribute to native son Robert Frost. Two additional buildings—the carriage house and the chimney house—also have libraries. Snowshoe rentals are among the amenities. Menu highlights in the candlelit dining room

($$$; reservations essential) include fillet of salmon glazed with honey and mustard and roasted on a cedar board. The vegetarian selections include roasted eggplant and red peppers topped with goat cheese and served in puff pastry. ✉ *Box 68, Stuart Rd., Snowville (5 mi southeast of Conway) 03849,* ☎ *603/447–2818 or 800/447–4345,* FAX *603/ 447–5268,* WEB *www.snowvilleinn.com. 18 rooms. Restaurant, sauna, cross-country skiing. AE, D, DC, MC, V. BP, MAP.*

$$$–$$$$ ✕🏨 **White Mountain Hotel and Resort.** The rooms at this hotel at the base of Whitehorse Ledge have mountain views. Proximity to the White Mountain National Forest and Echo Lake State Park makes you feel farther away from civilization (and the nearby outlet malls) than you actually are. Dinner at the Ledges restaurant ($$$) might include White Mountain venison in a cranberry currant sauce or beef Wellington. ✉ *Box 1828, West Side Rd., 03860,* ☎ FAX *603/356–7100 or* ☎ *800/533– 6301,* WEB *www.whitemountainhotel.com. 69 rooms, 11 suites. Restaurant, bar, pool, hot tub, sauna, 9-hole golf course, tennis court, health club, hiking, cross-country skiing. AE, D, MC, V. BP, MAP.*

$$–$$$$ ✕🏨 **Darby Field Inn.** After a day of activity in the White Mountains, warm up by the fieldstone fireplace in the inn's living room or by the woodstove in the bar. Most rooms in this unpretentious 1826 converted farmhouse have mountain views, and three have fireplaces or double-whirlpool baths. The restaurant ($$$), renowned for its views, presents such haute regional American recipes as roast duckling with a raspberry Chambord sauce and rack of lamb with a burgundy sauce. The dark-chocolate pâté with white-chocolate sauce is a knock-out dessert. ✉ *Box D, 185 Chase Hill, Albany 03818,* ☎ *603/447–2181 or 800/ 426–4147,* FAX *603/447–5726,* WEB *www.darbyfield.com. 15 rooms. Restaurant, bar, pool, outdoor hot tub, cross-country skiing. AE, MC, V. Closed Apr. BP, MAP.*

$$–$$$$ 🏨 **Buttonwood Inn.** A tranquil 17-acre oasis in this busy resort area, the Buttonwood is on Mt. Surprise, 2 mi northeast of North Conway village. Rooms in the 1820s farmhouse are furnished in simple Shaker style. Wide pine floors, quilts, and period stenciling add warmth. Two rooms have gas fireplaces; one has a whirlpool bath. Innkeepers Peter and Claudia Needham supply many thoughtful extras, such as backpacks and picnic baskets. ✉ *Box 1817, Mt. Surprise Rd., 03860,* ☎ *603/356–2625 or 800/258–2625,* FAX *603/356–3140,* WEB *www.buttonwoodinn.com. 9 rooms. Pool, hiking, cross-country skiing. AE, D, MC, V. BP.*

$$ 🏨 **Cranmore Inn.** This authentic gambrel-roof country inn opened in 1863, and many of its furnishings are antiques dating from the mid-1800s. The former stables were rebuilt to house condo-style rooms with kitchens. A mere ⅓ mi from the base of Mt. Cranmore, the inn is within easy walking distance of North Conway village. Guests have privileges at a nearby health club. ✉ *Box 1349, Kearsarge St., 03860,* ☎ *603/356–5502 or 800/526–5502,* WEB *www.cranmoreinn.com. 18 rooms. Restaurant, kitchenettes, pool. AE, MC, V. BP.*

Nightlife and the Arts

Horsefeather's (✉ Main St., ☎ 603/356–6862), a restaurant and bar, often has music on weekends.

Mt. Washington Valley Theater Company (✉ Eastern Slope Playhouse, Main St., ☎ 603/356–5776) presents musicals and summer theater from mid-June to Labor Day. The Resort Players, a local group, gives pre- and postseason performances.

Outdoor Activities and Sports

Snowvillage Inn conducts a llama trek up Foss Mountain. Your picnic will include champagne and fine food. Reservations are essential.

Shopping

ANTIQUES

The **Antiques & Collectibles Barn** (⊠ 3425 Main St., ☎ 603/356–7118), 1½ mi north of the village, is a 35-dealer colony with everything from furniture and jewelry to coins and other collectibles. **Richard Plusch Fine Antiques** (⊠ Rte. 16/U.S. 302, ☎ 603/356–3333) deals in period furniture and accessories, including glass, sterling silver, Oriental porcelains, rugs, and paintings. **Sleigh Mill Antiques** (⊠ off Rte. 153, Snowville, ☎ 603/447–6791), an old sleigh and carriage mill 6 mi south of Conway, specializes in 19th-century oil lighting and early gas and electric lamps.

CRAFTS

The **Basket & Handcrafters Outlet** (⊠ Kearsarge St., ☎ 603/356–5332) sells gift baskets, dried-flower arrangements, and country furniture. **Handcrafters Barn** (⊠ Main St., ☎ 603/356–8996) stocks the work of 350 area artists and artisans. The **League of New Hampshire Craftsmen** store (⊠ 2526 Main St., ☎ 603/356–2441) carries the creations of the area's best artisans. **Zeb's General Store** (⊠ Main St., ☎ 603/356–9294 or 800/676–9294) looks like an old-fashioned country store but sells food items, crafts, and other products, all made in New England.

FACTORY OUTLETS

More than 150 factory outlets—including L. L. Bean, Timberland, Pfaltzgraff, London Fog, Anne Klein, and Reebok—line Route 16.

SPORTSWEAR

A top pick for skiwear is **Joe Jones** (⊠ 2709 Main St., ☎ 603/356–9411).

Ski Areas

KING PINE SKI AREA AT PURITY SPRING RESORT

King Pine, some 9 mi south of Conway, has been a family-run ski area for more than 100 years. Some ski-and-stay packages include free skiing for midweek resort guests. Among the facilities and activities are an indoor pool and fitness complex, ice-skating, and tubing. ⊠ *Rte. 153, East Madison 03849,* ☎ *603/367–8896; 800/367–8897; 800/373–3754 snow conditions.*

Downhill. King Pine's gentle slopes are ideal for beginner and intermediate skiers; experts won't be challenged except for a brief pitch on the Pitch Pine trail. The 16 trails are serviced by two triple chairs, a double chair, and two surface lifts. There's tubing on Saturday and Sunday afternoons and night skiing and tubing on Friday and Saturday.

Cross-country. King Pine has 15 km (9 mi) of cross-country skiing.

Child care. Children from infants up to 6 years are welcome (8:30–4) at the nursery at base lodge. Children ages 4 and up can take lessons.

CRANMORE MOUNTAIN RESORT

This ski area on the outskirts of North Conway has been a favorite of families since it opened in 1938. Five glades have opened more skiable terrain. ⊠ *Box 1640, Skimobile Rd., 03860,* ☎ *603/356–5543; 603/356–8516 snow conditions; 800/786–6754 lodging,* WEB *www.cranmore.com.*

Downhill. The mountain's 39 trails are well laid out and fun to ski. Most runs are naturally formed intermediates that weave in and out of glades. Beginners have several slopes and routes from the summit, but experts must be content with a few short but steep pitches. In addition to the trails, snowboarders have a terrain park and a halfpipe.

One high-speed quad, one triple, and three double chairlifts carry skiers to the top. There are also two surface lifts. Night skiing is an option from Thursday to Saturday and during holidays.

Other activities. Other winter activities are outdoor skating, snowshoeing, and tubing.

Child care. The nursery takes children ages 6 months–5 years. There's instruction for children ages 3–12.

Summer and year-round activities. You can take a chairlift to the top for a panoramic view of the White Mountains or mountain bike on selected trails. The fitness center has an indoor climbing wall, tennis courts, exercise equipment, and a pool.

CROSS-COUNTRY

Sixty-four kilometers (40 mi) of groomed cross-country trails weave through North Conway and the countryside along the **Mt. Washington Valley Ski Touring Association Network** (⊠ Rte. 16, Intervale, ☎ 603/356–9920 or 800/282–5220).

Kancamagus Highway

★ ㉞ *36 mi between Conway and Lincoln/North Woodstock.*

Interstate 93 is the fastest way to the White Mountains, but it's hardly the most appealing. The section of Route 112 known as the Kancamagus Highway passes through classic mountain vistas with some of the state's most unspoiled scenery. This stretch, punctuated by scenic overlooks and picnic areas, erupts into fiery color each fall, when photo-snapping drivers can really slow things down. Prepare yourself for a leisurely pace. There are also campgrounds off the highway. In bad weather, check with the **White Mountains Visitors Bureau** (☎ 800/346–3687) for road conditions.

Outdoor Activities and Sports

A couple of short hiking trails off the highway yield great rewards for relatively little effort. The **Lincoln Woods Trail** starts from the large parking lot of the Lincoln Woods Visitor Center, 4 mi east of Lincoln. You can purchase the recreation pass ($5 per vehicle, good for seven consecutive days) needed to park in any of the White Mountain National Forest lots or overlooks here; stopping to take photos or to use the rest rooms at the visitor center is permitted without a pass. The trail crosses a suspension bridge over the Pemigewasset River and follows an old railroad bed for 3 mi along the river. The parking and picnic area for **Sabbaday Falls,** about 15 mi west of Conway, is the trailhead for an easy ½-mi trail to the falls, a multilevel cascade that plunges through two potholes and a flume.

The White Mountains A to Z

To research prices, get advice from other travelers, and book travel arrangements, visit www.fodors.com

AIRPORTS

Manchester Airport is about a 60- to 90-minute drive from the region (☞ New Hampshire A to Z). Charters and private planes land at Franconia Airport & Soaring Center and Mt. Washington Regional Airport. ➤ AIRPORT INFORMATION: **Franconia Airport & Soaring Center** (⊠ Easton Rd., Franconia, ☎ 603/823–8881). **Mt. Washington Regional Airport** (⊠ Airport Rd., Whitefield, ☎ 603/837–9532).

BUS TRAVEL

Concord Trailways connects Boston's South Station and Logan Airport with Berlin, Conway, Franconia, Gorham, Jackson, Lincoln/North Woodstock, Littleton, and Pinkham Notch.

➤ BUS INFORMATION: **Concord Trailways** (☎ 800/639–3317).

CAR TRAVEL

I–93 and U.S. 3 bisect the White Mountain National Forest, running north from Massachusetts to Québec. The Kancamagus Highway (Route 112), the east–west thoroughfare through the White Mountain National Forest, is a scenic drive. U.S. 302, a longer, more leisurely east–west path, connects I–93 to North Conway. From the seacoast, Route 16 is the popular choice.

EMERGENCIES

➤ HOSPITAL: **Memorial Hospital** (✉ 3073 Main St., North Conway, ☎ 603/356–5461).

LODGING

Country Inns in the White Mountains handles reservations for a wide variety of B&Bs and inns throughout the region.

APARTMENT & VILLA RENTALS

➤ LOCAL AGENTS: **Country Inns in the White Mountains** (☎ 603/356–9460).

CAMPING

White Mountain National Forest campground reservations has 20 campgrounds with more than 900 campsites spread across the region; only some take reservations. All sites have a 14-day limit.

➤ CONTACTS: **White Mountain National Forest** (✉ U.S. Forest Service, 719 N. Main St., Laconia 03246, ☎ 603/528–8721 or 877/444–6777).

OUTDOORS & SPORTS

CANOEING AND KAYAKING

River outfitter Saco Bound Canoe & Kayak leads gentle canoeing expeditions, guided kayak trips, and white-water rafting on seven rivers and provides lessons, equipment, and transportation.

➤ CONTACTS: **Saco Bound Canoe & Kayak** (✉ Box 119, Conway 03813, ☎ 603/447–2177).

FISHING

For trout and salmon fishing, try the Connecticut Lakes, though any clear stream in the White Mountains will do. Many are stocked, and there are 650 mi of streams in the national forest alone. Conway Lake is the largest of the area's 45 lakes and ponds; it's noted for smallmouth bass and—early and late in the season—good salmon fishing. The New Hampshire Fish and Game Office has up-to-date information on fishing conditions. The North Country Angler schedules intensive guided fly-fishing weekends.

➤ CONTACTS: **New Hampshire Fish and Game Office** (☎ 603/788–3164). **North Country Angler** (✉ 3643 White Mountain Hwy., Intervale, ☎ 603/356–6000).

HIKING

With 86 major mountains in the area, the hiking possibilities are endless. Innkeepers can usually point you toward the better nearby trails; some inns schedule guided day-trips for guests. The White Mountain National Forest (☞ Visitor Information) has information on hiking and parking passes ($5) required in the national forest. These are available at visitor centers; if you can't buy one in advance, you can park and you can buy a $3 day pass (exact change only) at the parking area.

The Appalachian Mountain Club headquarters at Pinkham Notch offers lectures, workshops, slide shows, and outdoor skills instruction year-round. Accommodations include a 100-bunk main lodge, a 24-bed hostel in Crawford Notch, and two rustic cabins. The club's eight trail-side huts provide meals and dorm-style lodging, June–October, on several trails in the Whites. The rest of the year the huts are open, self-serve.

New England Hiking Holidays conducts scheduled guided hiking tours with lodging in country inns for two to eight nights. Hikes, each with two guides, allow for different levels of hiking and cover between 5 and 10 mi per day.

➤ CONTACTS: **White Mountain National Forest** (☞ Visitor Information, *below*). **Appalachian Mountain Club** (✉ Box 298, Rte. 16, Gorham 03581, ☎ 603/466–2721; 603/466–2725 trail information; 603/466–2727 reservations, 🕸 www.mountwashington.com/amc/home.html). **New England Hiking Holidays** (✉ Box 1648, North Conway 03860, ☎ 603/356–9696 or 800/869–0949, 🕸 www.nehikingholidays.com).

VISITOR INFORMATION

➤ TOURIST INFORMATION: **Mt. Washington Valley Chamber of Commerce** (✉ Box 2300, North Conway 03860, ☎ 603/356–5701, 🕸 www.4seasonresort.com). **North Country Chamber of Commerce** (✉ Box 1, Colebrook 03576, ☎ 603/237–8939 or 800/698–8939, 🕸 www.northcountrychamber.org). **White Mountains Visitors Bureau** (✉ Box 10, Kancamagus Hwy. at I–93, North Woodstock 03262, ☎ 603/745–8720 or 800/346–3687, 🕸 www.whitemtn.org). **White Mountain National Forest** (✉ U.S. Forest Service, 719 Main St., Laconia 03246, ☎ 603/528–8721 or 877/444–6777 campground reservations, 🕸 www.fs.fed.us/r9/white).

WESTERN AND CENTRAL NEW HAMPSHIRE

Western and Central New Hampshire mixes small-town charm with city hustle across three distinct regions. The Merrimack River valley includes the state's largest and fastest-growing cities of Nashua, Manchester, and Concord. Northwest of Concord, Dartmouth–Lake Sunapee—accessible from I–89—is home to the famous college in Hanover, year-round sporting activities at Lake Sunapee and its nearby mountains, and several well-preserved colonial villages. The least developed of the three areas, the Monadnocks region occupies the sleepy southwestern corner of the state. Here you'll find peaceful hilltop hamlets that appear barely changed in the past two centuries, plus many opportunities for hiking. Famous Mt. Monadnock, the largest peak in southern New Hampshire, stands guard over the area.

When you're done climbing and swimming and visiting the past, look for the wares and small studios of area artists. The region has long been an informal artists' colony where people come to write, paint, and weave in solitude. The towns in this region, beginning with Nashua, are described in counterclockwise order.

Nashua

➌⃝ *98 mi south of Lincoln/North Woodstock, 48 mi northwest of Boston, MA; 36 mi south of Concord; 50 mi southeast of Keene.*

Monadnock Region and Central New Hampshire

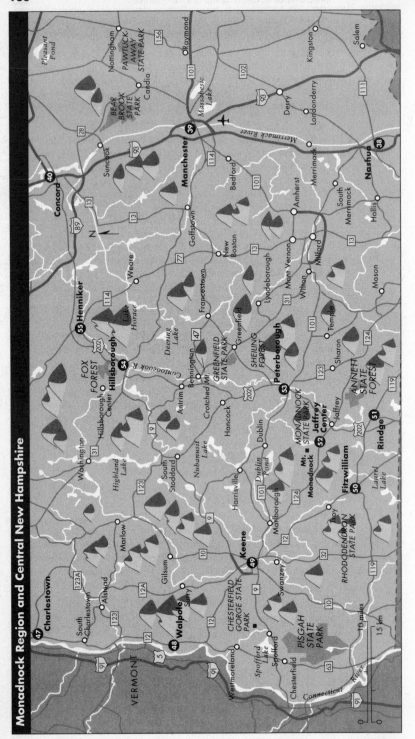

Once a prosperous manufacturing town that drew thousands of immigrant workers in the late 1800s and early 1900s, Nashua declined like its Massachusetts neighbors Lowell and Lawrence following World War II, as many factories shut down or moved to where labor was cheaper. Since the 1970s, however, the metro area has jumped in population, developing into a charming, old-fashioned community. The low-key feel is most evident in its downtown, with classic redbrick buildings that line the Nashua River, a tributary of the Merrimack River, which skirts the east side of town. Though not visited by tourists as much as other communities in the region, Nashua has some good restaurants and an engaging house-museum.

Nashua's impressive industrial history is kept alive in the Federal-style **Abbot-Spalding House** (⊠ 5 Abbot St., ☎ 603/883–0015, 🖼 donation suggested, ☉ weekdays 10–4), which is run by the Nashua Historical Society and contains both permanent and changing exhibits on the region's past.

Dining

$$–$$$ ✕ **Michael Timothy's Wine and Jazz Bar.** Part hip bistro, part jazzy wine
  ★ bar (with live music many nights), Michael Timothy's is so popular that even foodies from Massachusetts drive here. The regularly changing menu might offer Atlantic salmon and Littleneck clams braised in a lemongrass-ginger broth with baby bok choy or semi-boneless game hen pan-seared with dried cranberries, shiitake mushrooms, port wine, and shallots over crisp-fried spinach. The menu also includes wood-fired pizzas, and a stellar wine list. ⊠ *212 Main St., ☎ 603/595–9334. AE, D, MC, V. No lunch weekends.*

$–$$ ✕ **Martha's Exchange.** A casual spot with copper brewing vats, original marble floors, and booth seating, Martha's appeals both to the after-work set and office workers on lunch breaks. Burgers and sandwiches, maple-stout-barbecued chicken and ribs, Mexican fare, seafood and steak grills, and salads—all in large portions—are your options here; there's also a sweets shop attached. You can buy half-gallon jugs of house-brewed beers to go. ⊠ *185 Main St., ☎ 603/883–8781. D, MC, V.*

Nightlife and the Arts

American Stage Festival (⊠ 14 Court St., ☎ 603/886–7000), the state's largest professional theater, presents Broadway-style and newer works, music concerts, and a children's-theater series from March through October.

Manchester

㊴ *18 mi north of Nashua, 53 mi north of the Boston, MA.*

Manchester, with just over 100,000 residents, is New Hampshire's largest city. The town grew around the power of the Amoskeag Falls on the Merrimack River, which fueled small textile mills through the 1700s. By 1828, a group of investors from Boston had bought the rights to the Merrimack's water power and built on its eastern bank the Amoskeag Textile Mills, which became a testament to New England's manufacturing power. In 1906, the mills employed 17,000 people and churned out more than 4 million yards of cloth per week. This vast enterprise formed the entire economic base of Manchester; when it closed in 1936, the town was devastated.

Today Manchester is mainly a banking and business center. As part of an economic recovery plan, the old mill buildings have been converted into warehouses, classrooms, restaurants, museums, and office space. The city is also home to the state's major airport, and a new civic and convention center is under construction with a projected opening of late 2001—it will host concerts and minor-league hockey and basketball games.

The **Amoskeag Mills** houses both restaurants and museums. In 1998, the mills became home to the **SEE Science Center,** a hands-on science lab and museum that for now, unfortunately, is open only to groups. The **Millyard Museum,** which opened in spring 2001, contains state-of-the-art exhibits depicting the region's history, from when Native Americans lived alongside and fished the Merrimack River to the heyday of Amoskeag Mills. Additional features include an interactive Discovery Gallery geared toward kids, a lecture-concert hall, and one of the larger museum shops in the state. ⊠ *Mill No. 3, 200 Bedford St. (entrance at 255 Commercial St.),* ☎ *603/625–2821,* WEB *www.mv.com/org/mha.* ☜ *Free.* ⊙ *Weekdays 8–5:30.*

At the neoclassical redbrick (1931) headquarters of the **Manchester Historic Association,** you'll find a few exhibits on this city's long history and information on Amoskeag Mills. ⊠ *129 Amherst St.,* ☎ *603/622–7531,* WEB *www.mv.com/org/mha.* ☜ *Free.* ⊙ *Tues.–Fri. 9–4, Sat. 10–4.* The **Currier Gallery of Art,** in a 1929 Beaux Arts Italianate building, has a permanent collection of European and American paintings, sculpture, and decorative arts from the 13th to the 20th century, including works by Monet, Picasso, Edward Hopper, and Georgia O'Keeffe. Also part of the museum is the Frank Lloyd Wright-designed **Zimmerman House,** built in 1950. Wright called this sparse, utterly functional living space "Usonian." The house is New England's only Wright-designed residence open to the public. ⊠ *201 Myrtle Way,* ☎ *603/669–6144; 603/626–4158 Zimmerman House tours.* ☜ *$5; free Sat. 10–1; Zimmerman House $9 (reservations essentail).* ⊙ *Sun.–Mon. and Wed.–Thurs. 11–5, Fri. 11–8, Sat. 10–5; call for tour times.*

☙ Salmon, shad, and river herring "climb" the **Amoskeag Fishways** fish ladder near the Amoskeag Dam during the migration period, from May to mid-June. The visitor center has an underwater viewing window, year-round interactive exhibits and programs about the Merrimack River, and a hydroelectric-station viewing area. ⊠ *Fletcher St.,* ☎ *603/626–3474.* ☜ *Free.* ⊙ *Mon.–Sat. 9:30–5.*

Dining and Lodging

$$$–$$$$ ✕ **Richard's Bistro.** Whether you want to celebrate a special occasion or you just crave first-rate regional American cuisine, head to this romantic and hip bistro by the downtown intersection of Lowell and Elm streets. The fare bridges traditional New England ingredients with worldly preparations: try the char-broiled filet mignon with gorgonzola, baked-stuffed potato, and strawberries, or broiled fresh haddock topped with shrimp and scallops on an herb-risotto cake with a honey-peach sauce. ⊠ *36 Lowell St.,* ☎ *603/644–1180. AE, D, MC, V. No lunch Sat.*

$$–$$$ ✕ **Cotton.** This swanky eatery—with mod lighting and furnishings, and
★ an arbored patio—occupies a dapper space inside one of the old Amoskeag Mill buildings. The kitchen churns out updated comfort food with a global spin. Start off with mussels in a red curry of coconut milk, lemongrass, and kafir-lime leaves. Stellar entrée picks include a tuna-noodle casserole updated with fresh yellowfin tuna, julienne vegetables, and pappardelle pasta tossed with wild-mushroom cream and toasted lemony crumbs. ⊠ *75 Arms Park,* ☎ *603/622–5488. AE, D, DC, MC, V.*

$ ✕ **Red Arrow Diner.** A mix of hipsters and oldsters, including comedian and Manchester native Adam Sandler, favor this neon-streaked, 24-hour greasy spoon that's been going strong since 1922. Filling diner fare—

such as the platter of kielbasa, French toast, and the diner's famous pan-fries—keep patrons happy. ⊠ *61 Lowell St.,* ☎ *603/626–1118. MC, V..*

$$$$ ✕⌂ **Bedford Village Inn.** This luxurious 1810 Federal inn, just a few
★ miles southwest of downtown Manchester, was once a former farmstead that still shows horse-nuzzle marks on its old beams. Its old hayloft and the milking rooms now contain lavish suites with king-size four-poster beds, whirlpool baths, and three telephones. The restaurant, with a warren of elegant but rustic dining rooms with fireplaces and wide-pine floors—plus a casual tavern—presents an oft-changing contemporary menu that might include a starter of braised escargot in Chartreuse with chives and hazelnuts, followed by roast duckling with sage spaetzle, roast root vegetables, and vanilla-rum glaze. ⊠ *2 Village Inn La., Bedford 03110,* ☎ *603/472–2001 or 800/852–1166,* FAX *603/472–2379,* WEB *www.bedfordvillageinn.com. 12 suites, 2 apartments. Restaurant, bar, meeting room. AE, DC, MC, V.*

Nightlife and the Arts

The **Palace Theater** (⊠ 80 Hanover St., ☎ 603/668–5588) presents musicals and plays throughout the year. It's also host to the New Hampshire Philharmonic Orchestra (☎ 603/647–6476), the New Hampshire Symphony Orchestra (☎ 603/669–3559), and the Opera League of New Hampshire (☎ 603/429–9887).

Shopping

Bell Hill Antiques (⊠ Rte. 101 at Bell Hill Rd., Bedford, ☎ 603/472–5580) sells country furniture, glass, and china. The enormous **Mall of New Hampshire** (⊠ 1500 S. Willow St., ☎ 603/669–0433) has every conceivable store and is anchored by Sears and Filene's.

Concord

 20 mi north of Manchester; 67 mi northwest of Boston, MA; 46 mi northwest of Portsmouth.

New Hampshire's capital (population 38,000) is a quiet, conservative town that tends to the state's business but little else. The residents joke that the sidewalks roll up promptly at 6. The **Concord on Foot** walking trail winds through the historic district. Maps are available from the **Chamber of Commerce** (⊠ 244 N. Main St., ☎ 603/224–2508) or stores along the trail.

The **Pierce Manse** is the Greek Revival home in which Franklin Pierce lived before moving to Washington to become the 14th U.S. president. ⊠ *14 Penacook St.,* ☎ *603/225–2068 or 603/224–5954.* ⌖ *$3.* ☉ *Mid-June–Labor Day, weekdays 11–3.*

At the gilt-domed neoclassical **State House,** New Hampshire's legislature still meets in its original chambers. The building dates to 1819 and is the oldest in the United States in continuous use as a state capitol. ⊠ *107 N. Main St.,* ☎ *603/271–2154.* ☉ *Weekdays 8–4:30; guided tours by reservation.*

Among the artifacts at the **Museum of New Hampshire History** is an original Concord Coach. During the 19th century, when more than 3,000 coaches were built in Concord, this was about as technologically perfect a vehicle as you could find—many say it's the coach that won the West. Other exhibits provide an overview of New Hampshire's history, from the Abenaki to the settlers of Portsmouth up to current residents. ⊠ *6 Eagle Sq.,* ☎ *603/226–3189,* WEB *www.nhhistory.org/museum.html.* ⌖ *$5.* ☉ *Jan.–June and mid-Oct.–Nov., Tues.–Wed. and Sat. 9:30–5, Thurs.–Fri. 9:30–8:30, Sun. noon–5; Dec. and July–mid-Oct., Mon.–Wed. and Sat. 9:30–5, Thurs.–Fri. 9:30–8:30, Sun. noon–5.*

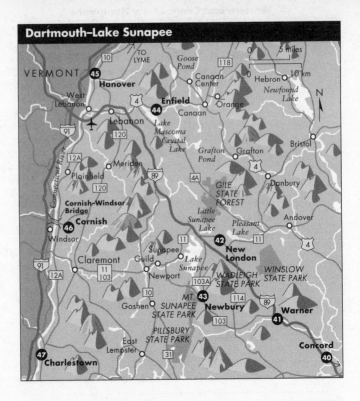

Dartmouth–Lake Sunapee

The high-tech **Christa McAuliffe Planetarium** presents shows on the solar system, constellations, and space exploration that incorporate computer graphics, sound, and special effects in the 40-ft dome theater. Children love seeing the tornado tubes, magnetic marbles, and other hands-on exhibits. Outside, explore the scale-model planet walk and the human sundial. The planetarium was named for the Concord teacher and first civilian in space, who was killed in the Space Shuttle *Challenger* explosion in 1986. ⊠ *New Hampshire Technical Institute campus, 3 Institute Dr.,* ☎ *603/271–7827.* ⚏ *Exhibit area free, shows $6.* ☉ *Tues.–Thurs. 9–5, Fri. 9–7, weekends 10–5. Call for show times and reservations.*

Dining and Lodging

$-$$ ★ ✕ **Moxy Grill.** Concord lacked for much in the way of innovative eateries before this funky little bistro opened a couple years ago, just off Main Street. Although the dining room is small—with closely spaced tables, pumpkin- and raspberry-shaded walls, and several seats crowded around a cozy central bar—the exceptional contemporary fare, such as sage-and-wild mushroom gnocchi, burgers, and other light offerings, is worth enduring the tight quarters. ⊠ *6 Pleasant St. Ext.,* ☎ *603/229–0072. MC, V.*

$ ★ ✕ **Foodee's Pizzas.** A local chain with additional parlors in Keene, Dover, Lincoln, Milford, and Wolfeboro, Foodee's serves high-caliber, creative pizzas with especially delicious crusts (such as sourdough, six-grain, and deep-dish). The capital branch is in the heart of downtown and offers such pies as the Polish (with kielbasa, sauerkraut, and three cheeses) and the El Greco (with sweet onions, sliced tomatoes, olive oil, and feta). You can also order from a selection of pastas, salads, and calzones. ⊠ *2 S. Main St.,* ☎ *603/225–3834. MC, V.*

$$-$$$ ☐ **Centennial Inn.** Built in 1896 for widows of Civil War veterans, this brick-and-stone building is set back from busy Pleasant Street. Much

of the original woodwork has been preserved. Each room is decorated with antiques and reproduction pieces, and all have ceiling fans and VCRs. In the Franklin Pierce dining room, the menu leans toward contemporary cuisine. ⊠ *96 Pleasant St., 03301,* ☎ *603/225–7102 or 800/ 360–4839,* FAX *603/225–5031. 27 rooms, 5 suites. Restaurant, bar, in-room data ports, in-room VCRs. AE, D, DC, MC, V.*

Nightlife and the Arts

The **Capitol Center for the Arts** (⊠ 46 S. Main St., ☎ 603/225–1111) has been restored to reflect its Roaring '20s origins. It hosts touring Broadway shows, dance companies, and musical acts. The lounge at **Hermanos Cocina Mexicana** (⊠ 11 Hills Ave., ☎ 603/224–5669) has live jazz Sunday through Thursday nights.

Outdoor Activities and Sports

Hannah's Paddles, Inc. (⊠ 15 Hannah Dustin Dr., ☎ 603/753–6695) rents canoes for use on the Merrimack River, which runs through Concord.

Shopping

CRAFTS

Capitol Craftsman and Romance Jewelers (⊠ 16 N. Main St., ☎ 603/ 224–6166 or 603/228–5683), which share adjoining shops, sell fine jewelry and handicrafts. The **Den of Antiquity** (⊠ 2 Capital Plaza, ☎ 603/225–4505) carries handcrafted country gifts and accessories. The **League of New Hampshire Craftsmen** (⊠ 36 N. Main St., ☎ 603/228– 8171) store exhibits crafts in many media. **Mark Knipe Goldsmiths** (⊠ 2 Capitol Plaza, Main St., ☎ 603/224–2920) sets antique stones in rings, earrings, and pendants.

MALLS

Steeplegate Mall (⊠ 270 Loudon Rd., ☎ 603/224–1523) has more than 70 stores, including chain department stores and some smaller crafts shops.

Warner

④ *22 mi northwest of Concord.*

Three New Hampshire governors were born in this quiet agricultural town just off I–89. Buildings dating from the late 1700s and early 1800s, and a charming library give the town's main street a welcoming feel.

★ **Mt. Kearsarge Indian Museum, Education and Cultural Center** gives guided tours of an extensive collection of Native American artistry, including moose-hair embroidery, quiltwork, and basketry. Signs on the Medicine Woods trail identify plants and explain how Native Americans use them as foods, medicines, and dyes. ⊠ *Kearsarge Mountain Rd., 03278,* ☎ *603/456–2600,* WEB *www.indianmuseum.org.* ☞ *$6.* ☺ *May–Oct., Mon.–Sat. 10–5, Sun. noon–5; Nov.–Dec., Sat. 10–5, Sun. noon–5.*

A 3½-mi scenic auto road at **Rollins State Park** (⊠ off Rte. 103) snakes up the southern slope of Mt. Kearsarge, where you can then tackle on foot the ½-mi trail to the summit. The road is closed November through mid-May.

New London

④ *16 mi northwest of Warner, 25 mi west of Tilton.*

New London, the home of Colby-Sawyer College (1837), is a good base for exploring the Lake Sunapee region. At the 10,000-year-old **Cricenti's Bog,** off Business Route 11 (Business Route 11 goes right through town;

Route 11 goes around town), a short trail shows off the shaggy mosses
and fragile ecosystem of this ancient pond.

Dining and Lodging

$$–$$$ ✕ **Peter Christian's Tavern.** Exposed beams, wooden tables, a smat-
tering of antiques, and half shutters on the windows make Peter Christian's a cool oasis in summer and a cozy haven in winter. Tavern fare
such as beef stew and shepherd's pie has been updated for modern tastes.
⊠ *186 Main St.,* ☎ *603/526–4042. AE, D, MC, V.*

$$–$$$ ✕🖭 **Inn at Pleasant Lake.** This rambling 1790s inn lies just across Pleas-
 ★   ant Lake from majestic Mt. Kearsage. The country antiques-filled
rooms are spacious with modern bathrooms (some with whirlpool tubs).
The restaurant ($$$$, reservations essentail) presents a nightly changing prix-fixe menu that has drawn raves for such expertly executed dishes
as pan-seared mahimahi with tropical-fruit chutney and Thai eggplant
relish, and such desserts as white-chocolate mousse with a trio of
sauces. ⊠ *Box 1030, 125 Pleasant St., 03257,* ☎ *603/526–6271 or
800/626–4907,* FAX *603/526–4111,* WEB *www.innatpleasantlake.com. 12
rooms. Restaurant, beach, boating, gym. MC, V.*

$$–$$$ ✕🖭 **New London Inn.** The two porches of this rambling 1792 coun-
try inn overlook Main Street. Rooms have Victorian decor; those in
the front of the house overlook the pretty campus of Colby-Sawyer College. The nouvelle-inspired menu in the restaurant starts with items such
as butternut squash with a sun-dried cranberry pesto and includes entrées such as grilled cilantro shrimp with a saffron risotto. The inn is
no-smoking. ⊠ *Box 8, 140 Main St., 03257,* ☎ *603/526–2791 or 800/
526–2791,* FAX *603/526–2749,* WEB *www.newlondoninn.com. 28 rooms.
Restaurant. AE, MC, V. BP.*

$$ 🖭 **Follansbee Inn.** Built in 1840, this quintessential country inn on the
shore of Kezar Lake is a perfect fit in the 19th-century village of North
Sutton, about 4 mi south of New London. The common rooms and
bedrooms are loaded with collectibles and antiques such as traveling
trunks and a wooden school desk. You can ice-fish on the lake and ski
across it in winter and swim or boat from the inn's pier in summer. A
3-mi walking trail circles the lake. The inn is no-smoking. ⊠ *Rte. 114,
North Sutton, 03260,* ☎ *603/927–4221 or 800/626–4221,* WEB *www.fol-
lansbeeinn.com. 23 rooms, 11 with bath; 1 cottage. Lake, hiking,
boating, fishing, ice-skating, cross-country skiing. MC, V. BP.*

$ 🛆 **Otter Lake Camping Area.** The 28 sites on Otter Lake have plenty
of shade, and boating and fishing are available. Facilities include a beach,
a playground, and canoe and paddleboat rentals. ⊠ *55 Otterville Rd.,
03257,* ☎ *603/763–5600. No credit cards.*

Nightlife and the Arts

The **New London Barn Playhouse** (⊠ 209 Main St., ☎ 603/526–
6710) presents Broadway-style and children's plays every summer in
New Hampshire's oldest continuously operating theater.

Shopping

Artisan's Workshop (⊠ Peter Christian's Tavern, 186 Main St., ☎ 603/
526–4227) carries jewelry, glass, and other local handicrafts.

Ski Areas

NORSK CROSS COUNTRY AND SNOWSHOE CENTER
The 70 km (43 mi) of scenic cross-country ski trails here include 45
km (28 mi) that are tracked and 24 km (15 mi) skate-groomed. Snow-
shoers have 19 km (12 mi) of groomed and backcountry trails. ⊠ *Rte.
11,* ☎ *603/526–4685 or 800/426–6775,* WEB *www.skinorsk.com.*

Newbury

43 *8 mi south of New London.*

Newbury is on the edge of Mt. Sunapee State Park. The mountain, which rises to an elevation of nearly 3,000 ft, and sparkling Lake Sunapee are the region's outdoor recreation centers. The popular League of New Hampshire Craftsmen's Fair is held at the base of Mt. Sunapee each August.

Narrated cruises aboard the **M/V Mt. Sunapee II** (⊠ Main St., Sunapee, ☎ 603/763–4030) provide a closer look at Lake Sunapee's history and mountain scenery. Dinner cruises are held on the **M/V Kearsarge** (☎ 603/763–4030). Both boats leave from the dock at Sunapee Harbor.

John M. Hay, who served as private secretary to Abraham Lincoln and secretary of state for Presidents McKinley and Theodore Roosevelt, built **The Fells** on Lake Sunapee as a summer home in 1890. House tours focus on his life in Newbury and Washington. Hay's son is responsible for the extensive gardens, a mix of formal and informal styles that includes a 75-ft perennial border and a naturalized heather garden on the hillside. More than 800 acres of the former estate are open for hiking and picnicking. ⊠ *Rte. 103A,* ☎ *603/763–4789,* WEB *www.the-fells.org.* ⚐ *$4.* ⊙ *House Memorial Day–mid-Oct., weekends 10–5; grounds daily dawn–dusk.*

Lodging

$ ⚐ **Crow's Nest Campground.** This campground has 100 sites, some directly on the Sugar River. The facilities include a recreation hall, a swimming pool, a children's wading pool, miniature golf in summer, and a warm-up room with fireplace for winter use. River swimming and fishing are summer pastimes; you can skate or sled in the winter, and area snowmobile trails connect to the campground. ⊠ *529 S. Main St., Newport 03773,* ☎ *603/863–6170. D, MC, V. Closed mid-Oct.–Nov. and Apr.–mid-May.*

Outdoor Activities and Sports

BEACHES

Sunapee State Beach has picnic areas, a beach, and a bathhouse. You can rent canoes here, too. ⊠ *Rte. 103,* ☎ *603/763–5561.* ⚐ *$2.50.* ⊙ *Daily dawn–dusk.*

FISHING

Lake Sunapee has brook and lake trout, salmon, smallmouth bass, and pickerel.

Ski Areas

MOUNT SUNAPEE

Although the resort is state-owned, the operation of Mt. Sunapee is now leased to Vermont's Okemo Mountain resort, known for its family-friendly atmosphere. The agreement brought a necessary influx of capital, and since 1998, lifts, equipment rentals, snowmaking (now at 97% coverage), parking, and trail grooming have all been vastly improved. ⊠ *Box 2021, Rte. 103, 03772,* ☎ *603/763–2356; 603/763–4020 snow conditions; 877/687–8627 lodging,* WEB *www.mt-sunapee.com.*

Downhill. This mountain is 1,510 vertical ft, tops in southern New Hampshire, and has 57 trails, mostly intermediate. Experts take to a dozen black-diamond slopes, including three nice double-black diamonds. The beginner's section is well away from other trails and has a new quad chairlift. Boarders have a 420-ft-long halfpipe and a terrain park with music. Two base lodges and a summit lodge supply the essentials. One high-speed detachable quad, one fixed-grip quad, two triple, and two double chairlifts, and three surface lifts transport skiers.

Child care. The Mother Goose Day Care takes children ages 1–5. Children's programs in skiing or snowboarding are available for kids 4 and up.

Summer activities. The Sunapee Express Quad zooms you to the summit. From here, it's just under a mile hike to Lake Solitude at the back of the mountain. Mountain bikers can use the lift to many trails, and an in-line skate park has beginner and advanced sections (plus equipment rentals).

Enfield

44 *33 mi northwest of Newbury.*

In 1782, two Shaker brothers from Mount Lebanon, New York, arrived at a community on the northeastern side of Mascoma Lake. Eventually, they formed Enfield, the ninth of 18 Shaker communities in this country, and moved it to the lake's southern shore, where they erected more than 200 buildings.

The **Enfield Shaker Museum** preserves the legacy of the Enfield Shakers, who numbered 330 members at the village's peak. By 1923, interest in the society was dwindling, and the last ten members joined the Canterbury community. A self-guided walking tour takes you through 13 of the buildings that remain, among them the Great Stone Dwelling (now the Shaker Inn) and an 1849 stone mill. Demonstrations by craftspeople of Shaker techniques and numerous special events take place year-round. ⊠ *24 Caleb Dyer La.,* ☎ *603/632–4346,* WEB *www. shakermuseum.org.* 🖃 *$7.* ☉ *Memorial Day–mid-Oct., Mon.–Sat. 10–5, Sun. noon–5; mid-Oct.–Memorial Day, Sat. 10–4, Sun. noon–4.*

Dining and Lodging

$$–$$$ ✕🏨 **The Shaker Inn.** Built between 1837 and 1841, the Great Stone Dwelling is the largest main dwelling ever built by a Shaker community. Adjacent to the Enfield Shaker Museum, it is now an inn, and the guest rooms in the original Shaker sleeping chambers have reproduction Shaker furniture and are decorated with the simplicity and style for which the religious community was known. The dining room serves Shaker-inspired cuisine such as pumpkin ravioli and maple-glazed baked ham. ⊠ *447 Rte. 4A, 03748,* ☎ *603/632–7810 or 888/707–4257,* WEB *www.theshakerinn.com. 24 rooms. Restaurant. AE, D, MC, V.*

Outdoor Activities and Sports

Anglers can try for rainbow trout, pickerel, and horned pout in **Lake Mascoma.**

Hanover

45 *12 mi northwest of Enfield, 62 mi northwest of Concord.*

Eleazer Wheelock founded Hanover's Dartmouth College in 1769 to educate the Abenaki "and other youth." When he arrived, the town consisted of about 20 families. The college and the town grew symbiotically, with Dartmouth becoming the northernmost Ivy League school. Today Hanover is still synonymous with Dartmouth, but the attractive town is also a respected medical center and the cultural center for the upper Connecticut River valley.

Robert Frost spent part of a brooding freshman semester at Ivy League **Dartmouth College** before giving up college altogether. The buildings that cluster around the green include the **Baker Memorial Library,** which houses literary treasures including 17th-century editions of Shakespeare's works. The library is also well known for the 3,000-square-ft murals by Mexican artist José Clemente Orozco that depict the story of civilization on the American continents. If the towering arcade at the entrance to the **Hopkins Center** (☎ 603/646–2422) appears familiar, it's probably because it resembles the project that architect Wallace K. Harrison completed just after designing it: New York City's Metropolitan Opera House at Lincoln Center. The complex includes a 900-seat theater for film and music, a 400-seat theater for plays, and a black-box theater for new plays. The Dartmouth Symphony Orchestra performs here, as does the Big Apple Circus (in summer). In addition to African, Peruvian, Oceanic, Asian, European, and American art, the **Hood Museum of Art** owns the Picasso painting *Guitar on a Table,* silver by Paul Revere, and a set of Assyrian reliefs from the 9th century BC. Rivaling the collection is the museum's architecture: a series of austere redbrick buildings with copper roofs arranged around a courtyard. Free guided tours of the museum are available on request. ⊠ *Museum: Wheelock St.,* ☎ *603/646–2808.* ☎ *Free.* ☉ *Tues. and Thurs.–Sat. 10–5, Wed. 10–9, Sun. noon–5.*

OFF THE
BEATEN PATH

THE UPPER VALLEY – From Hanover, you can make a 60-mi drive up Route 10 all the way to Littleton for a highly scenic tour of the upper Connecticut River Valley. You'll have views of the river from many points, as well as the mountains in Vermont. The road passes through groves of evergreens, over leafy ridges, and through some delightful hamlets. Stop at the bluff-top village green in historic **Haverhill** (28 mi north of Hanover) for a picnic amid the panorama of classic Georgian and Federal mansions and faraway farmsteads. Consider this as a scenic route to the White Mountains area, or loop back south through the mountains from Haverhill down Route 25 to Route 118 to U.S. 4 west, leading you back to Enfield—a drive of about 45 miles (and 75 minutes).

Dining and Lodging

$$ ✕ **Murphy's.** Students, visiting alums, and locals regularly descend upon this dark and pubby storefront eatery whose walls are lined with shelves of old books. The varied menu ranges from orange-chipotle–seared pork chops to buffalo chicken po' boys to Cajun salmon Caesar salads. For libations, try the extensive beer list. ⊠ *11 S. Main St.,* ☎ *603/643–4075. AE, D, DC, MC, V.*

$–$$ ✕ **Panda House/Bamboo Garden.** In a region with few decent Asian restaurants, these two-restaurants-in-one offer a welcome taste of Chinese and Japanese fare. They occupy a sedate basement space of the Hanover Park shopping arcade. Try the sashimi/sushi platters from the Bamboo Garden kitchen; Panda House favorites include tangerine beef, and whole crispy fish with a spicy Hunan sauce. ⊠ *3 Lebanon St.,* ☎ *603/643–1290. AE, D, DC, MC, V.*

$$$$ ✕🏨 **Hanover Inn.** Owned and operated by Dartmouth College, this
★ sprawling, Georgian-style brick building rises four white-trimmed stories. The original building was converted to a tavern in 1780, and this expertly run inn, now greatly enlarged, has been operating ever since. Rooms have Colonial reproductions, Audubon prints, and large sitting areas. The formal Daniel Webster Room ($$–$$$$) serves regional American dishes such as braised rabbit leg and seared loin with watercress celery salad, spiced walnuts, and cumin vinaigrette. The swank Zins wine bar ($–$$) prepares lighter but still highly innovative fare and has a fine list of vintages by the bottle, glass, and half-glass. ⊠ *Box 151, The Green, 03755,* ☎ *603/643–4300 or 800/443–7024,* ℻ *603/646–3744,* 🌐 *www.hanoverinn.com. 92 rooms. 2 restaurants. AE, D, DC, MC, V.*

$$–$$$$ ☒ **Trumbull House.** This white Colonial-style house sits on 16 acres on the outskirts of Hanover. The sunny guest rooms are furnished with king- or queen-size beds, window seats, writing desks, and other comfortable touches. Breakfast, with a choice of entrées, is served in the formal dining room or in front of the fireplace in the living room. The inn is no-smoking. ✉ *40 Etna Rd., 03755,* ☎ *603/643–2370 or 800/ 651–5141,* WEB *www.trumbullhouse.com. 5 rooms. Dining room, pond, basketball, hiking. AE, D, DC, MC, V. BP.*

Outdoor Activities and Sports

Ledyard Canoe Club of Dartmouth (☎ 603/643–6709) provides canoe and kayak rentals and classes on the swift-flowing Connecticut River, which is not suited to beginners and is safest after mid-June.

Shopping

Shops, mostly of the independent variety but with a few upscale chains sprinkled in, line Hanover's relentlessly cute and dapper Main Street—the commercial district blends almost imperceptibly with Dartmouth's campus. Goldsmith Paul Gross of **Designer Gold** (✉ 3 Lebanon St., ☎ 603/643–3864) designs settings for gemstones—all one-of-a-kind or limited-edition.

West Lebanon, south of Hanover on the Vermont border, has many more shops. The **Mouse Menagerie of Fine Crafts** (✉ Rte. 12A, ☎ 603/298–7090) sells its signature collector's series of toy mice, plus furniture, wind chimes, and other gifts. The **Powerhouse Mall** (✉ Rte. 12A, 1 mi north of Exit 20 off I–89, ☎ 603/298–5236), a former power station, comprises three buildings of specialty stores, boutiques, and restaurants.

Cornish

④⑥ *22 mi south of Hanover.*

Today Cornish is best known for its four covered bridges, but at the turn of the century the village was known primarily as the home of the country's then most popular novelist, Winston Churchill (no relation to the British prime minister). His novel *Richard Carvell* sold more than a million copies. Churchill was such a celebrity that he hosted Teddy Roosevelt during the president's 1902 visit. At that time Cornish was an enclave of artistic talent. Painter Maxfield Parrish lived and worked here, and sculptor Augustus Saint-Gaudens set up his studio and created the heroic bronzes for which he is known.

The 460-ft **Cornish-Windsor Bridge,** built in 1866, is the longest covered bridge in the United States. It spans the Connecticut River, connecting New Hampshire with Vermont.

★ The **Saint-Gaudens National Historic Site,** 1½ mi north of the Cornish-Windsor covered bridge, contains sculptor Augustus Saint-Gaudens's (1848–1907) house, studio, gallery, and 150 acres of grounds and gardens. Scattered throughout are full-size casts of his works. The property has two hiking trails, the longer of which is the Blow-Me-Down Trail. Concerts are held every Sunday afternoon in July and August. ✉ *Off Rte. 12A,* ☎ *603/675–2175,* WEB *www.sgnhs.org.* 🎫 *$4.* ☉ *Buildings mid-May–Oct., daily 9–4:30; grounds daily dawn–dusk.*

Dining and Lodging

$$$–$$$$ ✕☒ **Home Hill Inn.** This restored 1800 mansion set back from the river on 25 acres of meadow and woods is a tranquil place best suited to adults. The owners have given the inn a French influence with 19th-century antiques and collectibles. Rooms in the main house have canopy or four-poster beds, and four have fireplaces; a suite in the guest house can be a romantic hideaway. The dining room ($$$$; closed Mon.–Tues.)

serves classic and Mediterranean French cuisine such as Vermont rabbit in a pastry crust. ⊠ *River Rd., Plainfield 03781,* ☎ *603/675–6165,* WEB *www.homehillinn.com. 6 rooms, 2 suites, 1 seasonal cottage. Restaurant, pool, tennis court, cross-country skiing. AE, D, MC, V. CP.*

$$–$$$ ⚬ **Chase House Bed & Breakfast Inn.** Innkeepers Barbara Lewis and
★ Ted Doyle love sharing the history of this 1795 Federal-style house. It was the birthplace of Salmon P. Chase, who was Abraham Lincoln's secretary of the treasury, chief justice of the Supreme Court, and a founder of the Republican Party. Careful restoration with Colonial-style furnishings and Waverly wall coverings has recaptured early 19th-century elegance. Ask for a room with a canopy bed or one with a view of the Connecticut River valley and Mt. Ascutney. The inn is no-smoking. ⊠ *R.R. 2, Box 909, Rte. 12A, 03745 (1½ mi south of Cornish-Windsor covered bridge),* ☎ *603/675–5391 or 800/401–9455,* FAX *603/675–5010,* WEB *www.chasehouse.com. 5 rooms, 4 suites. Gym, boating. MC, V. Closed Nov. BP.*

Nightlife and the Arts

The beautifully restored 19th-century **Claremont Opera House** (⊠ Tremont Sq., Claremont, ☎ 603/542–4433) hosts plays and musicals from September to May.

Outdoor Activities and Sports

Northstar Canoe Livery (⊠ Rte. 12A, Balloch's Crossing, ☎ 603/542–5802) rents canoes for half- or full-day trips on the Connecticut River.

Charlestown

47 *20 mi south of Cornish, 63 mi west of Keene.*

Charlestown has the state's largest historic district: 63 homes, handsome examples of Federal, Greek Revival, and Gothic Revival architecture, are clustered about the center of town; 10 of them were built before 1800. Several merchants on Main Street distribute brochures that contain an interesting walking tour of the district.

The **Fort at No. 4,** 1½ mi north of Charlestown, was in 1747 an outpost on the lonely periphery of Colonial civilization. That year fewer than 50 militia men at the fort withstood an attack by 400 French soldiers that changed the course of New England history by ensuring that northern New England remained under British rule. Costumed interpreters at the only living-history museum from the era of the French and Indian War cook dinner over an open hearth and demonstrate weaving, gardening, and candlemaking. Each year the museum holds full reenactments of militia musters and battles of the French and Indian War. ⊠ *Rte. 11,* ☎ *603/826–5700,* WEB *www.fortat4.com.* ⊡ *$8.* ☉ *Late May–mid-Oct., Wed.–Mon. 10–4 (weekends only 1st 2 wks of Sept.).*

On a bright, breezy day you might want to detour to the **Morningside Flight Park** (⊠ Rte. 12/11, ☎ 603/542–4416), not necessarily to take hang-gliding lessons, although you could. You can watch the bright colors of the gliders as they swoop over the school's 450-ft peak.

Lodging

$$ ⚬ **MapleHedge.** The innkeepers live in the oldest section of this home, which dates from about 1755. Guest rooms, in the 1820 Federal-style part, are decorated with carefully chosen antiques. The Cobalt Room showcases an extensive collection of cobalt glass, stencil-pattern wallpaper in cobalt and burgundy, and mahogany furnishings. In Lt. R.A.D.'s Quarters, Marine Corps memorabilia and dark pine wainscoting give the room a masculine air. Freshly ironed linens and a three-course breakfast served in the formal dining room are among the

amenities. ⊠ *Box 638, 355 Main St., 03603,* ☎ *603/826–5237 or 800/
962–7539,* FAX *603/826–5237,* WEB *www.maplehedge.com. 5 rooms. MC,
V. Closed Jan.–Mar. BP.*

Walpole

48 *13 mi south of Charlestown.*

Walpole possesses one of the state's perfect town greens. This one, bordered by Elm and Washington streets, is surrounded by homes built about 1790, when the townsfolk constructed a canal around the Great Falls of the Connecticut River and brought commerce and wealth to the area. The town now has 3,200 inhabitants, more than a dozen of whom are millionaires.

OFF THE
BEATEN PATH

SUGARHOUSES – Maple-sugar season—a harbinger of spring—occurs about the first week in March when days become warmer but nights are still frigid. A drive along maple-lined back roads reveals thousands of taps and buckets catching the fresh but labored flow of unrefined sap. Plumes of smoke rise from nearby sugarhouses where sugaring off, the process of boiling down this precious liquid, takes place. Many sugarhouses are open to the public; after a tour and demonstration, you can sample the syrup with traditional unsweetened doughnuts and maybe a pickle—or taste hot syrup over fresh snow, a favorite confection. Open to the public in this area of the state are **Bacon's Sugar House** (⊠ 243 Dublin Rd., Jaffrey, ☎ 603/532–8836); **Bascom Maple Farm** (⊠ Mt. Kingsbury, off Rte. 123A, Alstead, ☎ 603/835–6361), which serves maple pecan pie and maple milk shakes; and **Stuart & John's Sugar House & Pancake Restaurant** (⊠ Rtes. 12 and 63, Westmoreland, ☎ 603/399–4486), which offers a tour and pancake breakfast.

Shopping

Walpole has a few shops that are well worth visiting. **Boggy Meadow Farm** (⊠ River Rd. S, ☎ 603/756–3300) sells the farm's Fanny Mason Farmstead Swiss cheese in its store. A window overlooks the cheese-making area. **Burdick Chocolates** (⊠ Main St., ☎ 603/756–3701) is renowned for its chocolates, especially the chocolate mice, which are shipped to trendy restaurants in New York and other cities.

Keene

49 *17 mi southeast of Walpole; 20 mi northeast of Brattleboro, VT; 56 mi west of Manchester.*

Keene is the largest city in the southwest corner of the state and the proud locus of the widest main street in America. Each year, on the Saturday before Halloween, locals use that street to hold a Pumpkin Festival, where they seek to retain their place in the record books for the most carved, lighted jack-o-lanterns—13,500 in 1997.

Keene State College, hub of the local arts community, is on the tree-lined main street. The **Thorne-Sagendorph Art Gallery** (☎ 603/358–2720) houses George Ridci's *Landscape* and presents traveling exhibitions. The **Putnam Art Lecture Hall** (☎ 603/358–2160) shows art films and international films.

Dining and Lodging

$–$$$ ✕ **176 Main.** This grand old brick house near the campus of Keene College in the heart of downtown has a varied menu that runs the gamut from pad Thai noodles to blackened catfish. The bar stocks an extensive selection of beers on draught. Weekend brunch is a big event here. ⊠ *176 Main St.,* ☎ *603/357–3100. AE, D, MC, V.*

$$$–$$$$ ✕🖭 **Chesterfield Inn.** Surrounded by gardens, the Chesterfield sits
★ above Route 9, the main road between Keene and Brattleboro, Vermont. The spacious rooms, decorated with armoires, fine antiques, and period-style fabrics, have telephones in the bathroom and refrigerators; many have fireplaces. The views from the dining room are of the gardens and the Vermont hills. Ragout of chicken with chorizo sausage and braised lamb shank with lemon and green olives are among the menu highlights. ✉ *Box 155, Rte. 9, Chesterfield 03443,* ☎ *603/256–3211 or 800/365–5515,* FAX *603/256–6131,* WEB *www.chesterfieldinn.com. 13 rooms, 2 suites. Restaurant. AE, D, DC, MC, V. BP.*

$$ 🖭 **Carriage Barn.** Antiques and wide pine floors lend this inn across from Keene State College a cozy charm. An expansive buffet is served each morning in the breakfast room, but many guests savor a second cup of coffee in the summerhouse. ✉ *358 Main St., 03431,* ☎ *603/357–3812,* WEB *www.carriagebarn.com. 4 rooms. MC, V. CP.*

$ 🛆 **Swanzey Lake Camping Area.** This 82-site campground for tents and RVs has a sandy beach, a dock, a ball field, a recreation area, and boat rentals. ✉ *88 E. Shore Rd. (Box 115, W. Swanzey 03469),* ☎ *603/352–9880,* WEB *www.swanzeylake.com.*

Nightlife and the Arts

The **Colonial Theatre** (✉ 95 Main St., ☎ 603/352–2033) opened in 1924 as a vaudeville stage. It now hosts folk and jazz concerts and has the largest movie screen in town. The **Redfern Arts Center at Brickyard Pond** (✉ 229 Main St., ☎ 603/358–2171) has year-round music, theater, and dance performances. **Elm City Brew Co.** (✉ 222 West St., ☎ 603/355–3335), at the Colony Mall, serves light food and draws a mix of college students and young professionals.

Outdoor Activities and Sports

The Monadnock region has more than 200 lakes and ponds, most of which offer good fishing. Rainbow trout, smallmouth and largemouth bass, and some northern pike swim in **Spofford Lake** in Chesterfield. **Goose Pond** in West Canaan, just north of Keene, holds smallmouth bass and white perch.

Shopping

ANTIQUES
The more than 240 dealers at **Antiques at Colony Mill** (✉ 222 West St., ☎ 603/358–6343) sell everything from furniture to dolls.

BOOKS
The extraordinary collection of used books at the **Homestead Bookshop** (✉ Rtes. 101 and 124, Marlborough, ☎ 603/876–4213) includes biographies, cookbooks, and town histories.

SHOPPING CENTER
Colony Mill Marketplace (✉ 222 West St., ☎ 603/357–1240), an old mill building, holds 30-plus stores and boutiques such as **Country Artisans** (☎ 603/352–6980), which showcases the stoneware, textiles, prints, and glassware of regional artists; the **Toadstool Bookshop** (☎ 603/352–8815), which carries many children's and regional travel and history books; and **Ye Goodie Shoppe** (☎ 603/352–0326), whose specialty is handmade chocolates and confections. There's also a food court, with excellent desserts, homemade soups, sandwiches, fish-and-chips, teas, and coffees.

Fitzwilliam

🏵 *14 mi southeast of Keene.*

A well-preserved historic district of Colonial and Federal-style houses has made the town of Fitzwilliam, on Route 119, the subject of thousands of postcards. Many show views of its landscape in winter, when a fine white snow settles on the oval common. Town business is still conducted in the 1817 meeting house.

The **Amos J. Blake House,** maintained by the Fitzwilliam Historical Society, contains a museum with period antiques and artifacts and the law office of its namesake. A town walking-tour pamphlet is available here, too. ⊠ *Village Green,* ☎ *603/585–7742.* 🎟 *Free.* ☉ *Late May–mid-Oct., Sat. 1–4 or by appointment.*

More than 16 acres of wild rhododendrons burst into bloom in mid-July at **Rhododendron State Park,** which has the largest concentration of *Rhododendron maximum* north of the Allegheny Mountains. Bring a picnic lunch and sit in a nearby pine grove, or follow the marked footpaths through the flowers. ⊠ *Off Rte. 12, 2½ mi northwest of the town common,* ☎ *603/532–8862.* 🎟 *$2.50 weekends and holidays; free at other times.* ☉ *Daily 8–sunset.*

Lodging

$$–$$$ 🏨 **Inn at East Hill Farm.** At this 1830 farmhouse resort at the base of Mt. Monadnock, children are not only allowed but expected. If you don't have kids, you might be happier elsewhere. Children collect the eggs for the next-day's breakfast, milk the cows, feed the animals, and can try arts and crafts, story-telling, hiking, and games. The innkeepers schedule weekly sleigh, hay, and pony rides. Rates include most activities and three meals in a camplike dining hall. Twice weekly in July and August trips are scheduled to a nearby lake for boating, water-skiing, and fishing. ⊠ *460 Monadnock St., Troy, 03465,* ☎ *603/242–6495 or 800/242–6495,* 𝔽𝔸𝕏 *603/242–7709,* 🌐 *www.east-hill-farm.com. 65 rooms. Restaurant, 2 outdoor pools, indoor pool, wading pool, sauna, tennis court, hiking, horseback riding, sleigh rides, recreation room, baby-sitting. D, MC, V. FAP.*

$$ 🏨 **Amos Parker House.** The garden of this Georgian B&B is the town's
★ most stunning, complete with lily ponds, Asian stone benches, and Dutch waterstones that create a gently burbling waterfall effect. Two rooms have garden views; three have wood-burning fireplaces. One of the suites is decorated with hand-painted wall murals. In winter, breakfast is served in an elegant setting in front of a roaring fire. ⊠ *Box 202, Rte. 119, 03447,* ☎ *603/585–6540. 2 rooms, 2 suites. No credit cards. BP.*

$–$$ 🏨 **Hannah Davis House.** This 1820 Federal-style house just off the vil-
★ lage green has retained its elegance. The original beehive oven still sits in the kitchen, and one suite has two Count Rumford fireplaces. Pumpkin pine floors, antique quilts, and braided rugs give the rooms a cozy glow. Your host has the scoop on area antiquing. ⊠ *106 Rte. 119, 03447,* ☎ *603/585–3344. 3 rooms, 3 suites. D, MC, V. BP.*

Shopping
ANTIQUES

You'll find about 35 dealers at **Bloomin' Antiques** (⊠ Rte. 12, 3 mi south of Rte. 119, ☎ 603/585–6688). The wares of some 40 dealers comprise **Fitzwilliam Antiques** (⊠ Rtes. 12 and 119, ☎ 603/585–9092).

Rindge

🔟 *8 mi southeast of Fitzwilliam.*

The small town of Rindge sits on a hill overlooking the Monadnock region. Most diversions center on outdoor activities in this scenic setting.

Cathedral of the Pines is an outdoor memorial to American men and women, both civilian and military, who have sacrificed their lives in service to their country. There's an inspiring view of Mt. Monadnock and Mt. Kearsarge from the **Altar of the Nation,** which is composed of rock from every U.S. state and territory. All faiths are welcome to hold services here; organ meditations take place at midday from Tuesday to Thursday in July and August. The **Memorial Bell Tower,** with a carillon of bells from around the world, is built of native stone. Norman Rockwell designed the bronze tablets over the four arches. Flower gardens, an indoor chapel, and a museum of military memorabilia share the hilltop. ⊠ *75 Cathedral Entrance Rd., off Rte. 119,* ☎ *603/899–3300.* 🎫 *Free; donations suggested.* ⊘ *May–Oct., daily 9–5.*

Dining and Lodging

$$–$$$ 🍽 **Woodbound Inn.** This rustic inn was built as a farmhouse in 1819 and became an inn in 1892. A favorite with families and outdoors and fishing enthusiasts, it occupies 200 acres on the shores of Contoocook Lake. Accommodations are functional but clean and cheerfully decorated; they range from quirky rooms in the main inn to modern hotel-style rooms in the Edgewood building to cabins by the water. ⊠ *62 Woodbound Rd., 03461,* ☎ *603/532–8341 or 800/688–7770,* 𝔽𝔸𝕏 *603/532–8341 ext. 213,* WEB *www.woodboundinn.com. 46 rooms, 42 with bath; 11 cottages. Restaurant, bar, lake, 9-hole golf course, tennis court, croquet, hiking, horseshoes, shuffleboard, volleyball, fishing, ice-skating, cross-country skiing, tobogganing, recreation room. AE, MC, V. BP, MAP.*

$–$$ 🍽 **Cathedral House Bed and Breakfast.** This 1850s farmhouse on the edge of the Cathedral of the Pines was the home of the memorial's founders. Rooms have high ceilings, flowered wallpapers, quilts, and well-stocked cookie jars, all of which help create the feeling that you've just arrived at Grandmother's house. Innkeepers Don and Shirley Mahoney are well versed in area history. ⊠ *63 Cathedral Entrance Rd., 03461,* ☎ *603/899–6790. 5 rooms, 1 with bath. MC, V. BP.*

Jaffrey Center

🔵 *8 mi north of Rindge, 7 mi northeast of Fitzwilliam.*

Novelist Willa Cather came to the historic village of Jaffrey Center in 1919 and stayed in the Shattuck Inn, which now stands empty on Old Meeting House Road. She pitched a tent not far from here in which she wrote several chapters of *My Antonia*. She returned nearly every summer thereafter until her death and was buried in the Old Burying Ground. **Amos Fortune Forum,** near the Old Burying Ground, brings nationally known speakers to the 1773 meeting house on summer evenings.

The oft-quoted statistic about **Mt. Monadnock** in **Monadnock State Park** is that it's the most-climbed mountain in America—second in the world to Japan's Mt. Fuji. Whether this is true or not, locals agree that it's never lonely at the top. Some days more than 400 people crowd its bald peak. Monadnock rises to 3,165 ft, and on a clear day the hazy Boston skyline is visible from its summit. The park maintains picnic grounds and a small campground (RVs welcome, but no hookups). Five trailheads branch into more than two dozen trails of varying difficulty that wend their way to the top. Some are shorter than others, but you should allow between three and four hours for any round-trip hike. A visitor center has exhibits documenting the mountain's history. Trail maps are available free of charge. ⊠ *Off Rte. 124, 2½ mi north of Jaffrey Center, 03452,* ☎ *603/532–8862.* 🎫 *$2.50.* ⊘ *Daily dawn–dusk.*

Dining and Lodging

$$ ✕🍽 **Inn at Jaffrey Center.** This delightful gambrel-roof inn was completely overhauled and reopened by new owners in June 2000. Rooms are done in lavenders, yellows, and peaches, with fluffy bedding and towels, fine toiletries, and period furnishings but with a hip sensibility (no phones

or TVs, however). The restaurant ($$–$$$; no lunch Sat.) offers a mix of American (pot roast, lamb shanks), Asian (chicken with mild curry, ginger-and-chipotle-steak), and Italian (sole piccata, veal marsala) dishes. ✉ *379 Main St., 03452,* ☎ *603/532–7800,* ⅁⅁ *603/532–7900,* ⎏⎀ *www.innatjaffreycenter.com. 9 rooms. Restaurant, bar. MC, V. CP.*

$–$$$ 🛏 **Benjamin Prescott Inn.** The working dairy farm surrounding this 1853 Colonial farmhouse makes guests feel as though they are miles out in the country rather than just minutes from Jaffrey Center. Stenciling and wide pine floors add to the country feel. A full breakfast of Welsh miner's cakes, baked French toast with fruit, and Jaffrey maple syrup prepares you for a day of antiquing or climbing Mt. Monadnock. ✉ *Rte. 124, 03452,* ☎ *603/532–6637 or 888/950–6637,* ⎏⎀ *www.benjamin-prescottinn.com. 10 rooms, 3 suites. AE, MC, V. BP.*

Peterborough

🟢 *9 mi northeast of Jaffrey Center, 30 mi northwest of Nashua.*

The nation's first free public library opened in Peterborough in 1833. The town, which was the first in the region to be incorporated (1760), is still a commercial and cultural hub.

The **MacDowell Colony** (✉ 100 High St., ☎ 603/924–3886) was founded by the composer Edward MacDowell in 1907 as an artists' retreat. Willa Cather wrote part of *Death Comes for the Archbishop* here. Thornton Wilder was in residence when he wrote *Our Town*; Peterborough's resemblance to the play's Grover's Corners is no coincidence. Only a small portion of the still-active colony is open to visitors.

In **Miller State Park** (✉ Rte. 101, ☎ 603/924–3672), 3 mi east of town, an auto road takes you almost 2,300 ft up Pack Monadnock Mountain. The road is closed mid-November through mid-April.

Dining and Lodging

$$–$$$ ✕ **Acqua Bistro.** At this smartly decorated, stylish downtown bistro, ★ many patrons congregate at the long bar up front. You might begin a meal with cornmeal-crusted oysters, with white-wine-braised spinach and Emmanthal fondue, before moving onto seared wild Arctic char with roasted vegetable-dill toasted couscous and basil-walnut pesto. Seven thin-crust pizzas are also offered, including a delicious chicken sausage pie with garlic cream, caramelized onions, cured Moroccan olives, and fontina. Save room for the excellent bittersweet chocolate soufflé. ✉ *9 School St.,* ☎ *603/924–9905. MC, V. No lunch.*

$$–$$$$ ✕🛏 **Hancock Inn.** This Federal-style 1789 inn is the pride of the idyllic, well-preserved town it anchors. Common areas possess the warmth of a tavern, with fireplaces, big wing chairs; couches, dark-wood paneling, and Rufus Porter murals. Rooms, done in traditional Colonial style, have antique four-poster beds. One suite has the original domed ceiling from the inn's 1800s ballroom. Updated Yankee fare is served by candlelight in the dining room ($$$); a specialty is pecan-crusted pork tenderloin with apples, maple-mustard glaze, and sweet-potato hash. ✉ *Box 96, 33 Main St., Hancock 03449,* ☎ *603/525–3318,* ⅁⅁ *603/525–9301,* ⎏⎀ *www.hancockinn.com. 11 rooms, 4 suites. Restaurant, bar. AE, D, DC, MC, V. BP.*

$$ ✕🛏 **Inn at Crotched Mountain.** This 1822 inn has nine fireplaces, four of which are in private rooms. The other five spread cheer in several common areas. The inn, whose rooms are furnished with early Colonial reproductions, is a particularly romantic place to stay when snow is falling on Crotched Mountain. The restaurant's multicultural menu lists Eastern specialties such as Indonesian charbroiled swordfish with a sauce of ginger, green pepper, onion, and lemon; cranberry-port pot roast is one of the regional entrées. Breakfast and dinner must be included in the rate

on weekends. ⊠ *Mountain Rd., Francestown 03043 (12 mi northeast of Peterborough)*, ☎ *603/588–6840. 13 rooms. Restaurant, bar, pool, tennis court, cross-country skiing. No credit cards. BP, MAP.*

$ ╳⌂ **Birchwood Inn.** Thoreau slept here, probably on his way to climb Monadnock or to visit Jaffrey or Peterborough. Country furniture and handmade quilts outfit the bedrooms of this no-smoking inn, as they did in 1775 when the house was new and no one dreamed it would someday be listed on the National Register of Historic Places. Allow time to linger in the dining room ($$$; reservations essential; BYOB; no lunch; closed Sunday and Monday), where Rufus Porter murals cover the walls and she-crab soup, roast duckling, and fresh-fruit cobblers are among the specialties. ⊠ *Box 197, Rte. 45, Temple 03084,* ☎ *603/ 878–3285,* FAX *603/878–2159,* WEB *www.birchwood.mv.com. 7 rooms, 5 with bath. Restaurant. No credit cards. BP.*

$–$$ ⌂ **Apple Gate Bed and Breakfast.** With 90 acres of apple orchards across the street, this B&B is appropriately named. The four rooms and even the yellow labrador, Macintosh, are named for types of apples. Some rooms are small, but Laura Ashley prints and stenciling make them cheery and cozy. The house dates from 1832, and the original beams and fire-place still grace the dining room. A music and reading room has a piano and a television with VCR tucked in the corner. From June to Octo-ber, there's a two-night minimum on weekends. ⊠ *199 Upland Farm Rd., 03458,* ☎ FAX *603/924–6543. 4 rooms. MC, V. BP.*

Nightlife and the Arts

Monadnock Music (☎ 603/924–7610 or 800/868–9613) produces a summer series of concerts from mid-July to late August, with solo recitals, chamber music, and orchestra and opera performances by renowned musicians. The concerts, at locations throughout the region, usually take place in the evening at 8 and on Sunday at 4; many are free.

In winter, the **Peterborough Folk Society** (☎ 603/827–2905) presents folk music concerts. The **Peterborough Players** (⊠ Stearns Farm, off Middle Hancock Rd., ☎ 603/924–7585) have performed for more than 60 seasons. Plays are staged in a converted barn. The **Temple Town Band** (☎ 603/924–3478) was founded in 1799. Members range from teenagers to septuagenarians. The band plays a selection of patriotic songs, traditional marches, and show tunes at the Jaffrey Bandstand, the Sharon Arts Center, and local festivals and events.

Outdoor Activities and Sports

Several types of trout swim in **Dublin Pond,** near Dublin.

Shopping

The corporate headquarters and retail outlet of **Eastern Mountain Sports** (⊠ 1 Vose Farm Rd., ☎ 603/924–7231) sells everything from tents to skis to hiking boots, gives hiking and camping classes, and con-ducts kayaking and canoeing demonstrations. **Harrisville Designs** (⊠ Mill Alley, Harrisville, ☎ 603/827–3333) sells hand-spun and hand-dyed yarn sheared from local sheep, as well as looms for the serious weaver. The shop also hosts classes in knitting and weaving. **North Gallery at Tewksbury's** (⊠ Rte. 101, ☎ 603/924–3224) stocks thrown pots, sconces, candlestick holders, and woodworkings. **Sharon Arts Down-town** (⊠ Depot Sq., ☎ 603/924–7256) has a gallery that exhibits lo-cally made pottery, fabric, and woodwork and other crafts.

Hillsborough

❺❹ *20 mi north of Peterborough, 23 mi west of Concord.*

Hillsborough comprises four villages, the most prominent of which lies along the roiling Contoocook River and grew up around a thriving woolen and hosiery industry in the mid-1800s. This section, which is really considered Hillsborough proper, is what you'll see as you roll through town along Route 9/U.S. 202.

Turn north from downtown up School Street, however, and continue 3 mi past Fox State Forest to reach one of the state's best-preserved historic districts, **Hillsborough Center,** where 18th-century houses surround the town green. For a wonderfully scenic drive, continue north 6 mi through the similarly quaint village of **East Washington,** and another 6 mi to reach the colonial town center of **Washington.** One of the highest-elevation villages in New Hampshire, this picturesque arrangement of white clapboard buildings made the cover of *National Geographic* several years back. You can loop back to Hillsborough proper via Route 31 south.

The nation's 14th president and arguably the least-liked of all of them, Franklin Pierce was born in Hillsborough and lived here until he married. The **Pierce Homestead,** operated by the Hillsborough Historical Society, welcomes visitors for guided tours. The house is decorated much as it was during Pierce's life. ⊠ *Rte. 31 at Rte. 9,* ☎ *603/478–3165,* WEB *www.conknet.com/~hillsboro/pierce.* ⊡ *$2.50.* ☉ *June and Sept., Sat. 10–4, Sun. 1–4; July–Aug., Mon.–Sat. 10–4, Sun. 1–4.*

NEED A
BREAK?

Families have been coming to **Diamond Acres Dairy Bar** (⊠ Rte. 9, ¼ mi west of Rte. 31, ☎ 603/478-3121), an ordinary-looking short-order seafood shanty and ice-cream stand attached to a gas station, for years to devour super-fresh clam platters, lobster rolls, and frozen sweets.

Dining and Lodging

$$–$$$ ✕ **Red Maples.** In tiny Bennington, about 10 mi south of Hillsborough, you'll find this tiny eatery in a Colonial Cape house in the center of town. Oil lamps, lace curtains, and white napery impart a romantic mood. The kitchen presents a short but ambitious menu of simply and elegantly prepared meals, such as filet mignon with wild mushroom sauce and a starter of clams in a mild Thai curry. ⊠ *12 School St., Bennington,* ☎ *603/588–3588. AE, D, MC, V. Closed Mon. and Jan.–Apr. No lunch.*

$$ ✕ **Rynborn Restaurant and Blues Club.** You may be surprised to find a blues club in such a quiet town as Antrim (8 mi south of Hillsborough), but this place serves up some vibrant sounds. The menu consists of mostly regional American fare such as blackened Cajun shrimp and pecan-crusted chicken in a honey mustard sauce. ⊠ *76 Main St., Antrim,* ☎ *603/588–6162. AE, D, MC, V. No lunch.*

Outdoor Activities and Sports

Fox State Forest (⊠ Center Rd., ☎ 603/464–3453) has 20 mi of hiking trails and an observation tower.

Shopping

At **Gibson Pewter** (⊠ 18 E. Washington Rd., ☎ 603/464–3410), Raymond Gibson and his son Jonathan create and sell museum-quality pewter in contemporary and traditional designs.

Henniker

⑤⑤ *7 mi northeast of Hillsborough, 16 mi west of Concord.*

Governor Wentworth, the first Royal Governor of New Hampshire, named this town in honor of his friend John Henniker, a London merchant and member of the British Parliament (residents delight in their town's status as "the only Henniker in the world"). Once a mill town producing bicycle rims and other light-industrial items, Henniker reinvented itself after the factories were damaged, first by spring floods in 1936 and then by the hurricane and flood of 1938. New England College was established in the following decade. One of the area's covered bridges can be found on campus.

Dining and Lodging

$$–$$$$ ✕🏠 **Colby Hill Inn.** The cookie jar is always full at this Colonial farmhouse, where guests are greeted by Delilah, the inn dog. There is no shortage of relaxing activities: you can curl up with a book by the parlor fireplace, stroll through the gardens and 5 acres of meadow, or play badminton out back. Rooms in the main house contain antiques, Colonial reproductions, and frills like lace curtains. In the carriage-house rooms, plain country furnishings, stenciled walls, and exposed beams are the norm. The frequently changing dining menu ($$$$) is excellent and focuses heavily on fish: one fine choice is spicy Malaysian pan-seared tuna with a chili relish, wasabi, and julienne gingered-vegetables. ⌧ *Box 779, 3 The Oaks, 03242,* ☎ *603/428–3281,* ℻ *603/428–9218,* WEB *www.colbyhillinn.com. 16 rooms. Restaurant, in-room data ports, pool, recreation room. AE, D, DC, MC, V. BP.*

$–$$ ✕🏠 **Meeting House Inn & Restaurant.** The owners of this 200-year-old farmhouse at the base of Pats Peak, who tout the complex as a lovers' getaway, start guests' days off with breakfast in bed. The old barn has become a restaurant ($$$) that specializes in leisurely, romantic dining. Items such as lobster pepito are served in a heart-shape puff pastry, and the chocolate-raspberry frozen mousse also comes in the shape of a heart. ⌧ *Rte. 114/Flanders Rd., 03242,* ☎ *603/428–3228,* ℻ *603/ 428–6334,* WEB *www.conknet.com/~meetinghouse. 6 rooms. Restaurant, hot tub, sauna. AE, D, MC, V. BP.*

Shopping

The **Fiber Studio** (⌧ 9 Foster Hill Rd., ☎ 603/428–7830) sells beads, hand-spun natural-fiber yarns, spinning equipment, and looms.

Ski Areas

PATS PEAK

A quick trip up I–93 from the Mass border, Pats Peak is geared to families. Base facilities are rustic, and friendly personal attention is the rule. ⌧ *Rte. 114, 03242,* ☎ *603/428–3245; 888/PATS–PEAK snow conditions,* WEB *www.patspeak.com.*

Downhill. Despite Pats Peak's short 710 vertical ft rise, the 20 trails and slopes have something for everyone. New skiers and snowboarders can take advantage of a wide slope and several short trails; intermediates have wider trails from the top; and advanced skiers have a couple of real thrillers. Night skiing and snowboarding take place in January and February. One triple and three double chairlifts and three surface lifts serve the runs. Pats Peak also has afternoon snowtubing on weekends and holidays.

Child care. The nursery takes children ages 6 months–5 years. Special nursery ski programs operate on weekends and during vacations for kids 4–12; all-day lessons for self-sufficient skiers in this age range are scheduled daily.

Western and Central New Hampshire A to Z

To research prices, get advice from other travelers, and book travel arrangements, visit www.fodors.com

AIRPORTS

Manchester Airport is the main airport in western and central New Hampshire (☞ New Hampshire A to Z). Colgan Air offers flights to Rutland,

Vermont, and Newark, New Jersey, from Keene Airport. Lebanon Municipal Airport, near Dartmouth College, is served by US Airways.
➤ AIRPORT INFORMATION: **Keene Airport** (⊠ Rte. 32 off Rte. 12, North Swanzey, ☎ 603/357–9835). **Lebanon Municipal Airport** (⊠ 5 Airpark Rd., West Lebanon, ☎ 603/298–8878).

BIKE [& MOPED] TRAVEL

Eastern Mountain Sports (☞ Visitor Information) and the Keene Chamber of Commerce have information about local bike routes.
➤ BIKE MAPS: **Keene Chamber of Commerce** (⊠ 8 Central Sq., Keene, 03431, ☎ 603/352–1303).

BUS TRAVEL

Concord Trailways runs from Concord to Boston. Dartmouth Coach connects Boston's South Station and Logan Airport with Concord and Manchester. Vermont Transit links the cities of western New Hampshire with major cities in the eastern United States. Advance Transit stops in Enfield and Hanover. Keene City Express buses run from 9 AM to 4 PM. Manchester Transit Authority has hourly local bus service around town and to Bedford from 6 AM to 6 PM.
➤ BUS INFORMATION: **Concord Trailways** (☎ 800/639–3317). **Dartmouth Coach** (☎ 603/448–2800 or 800/637–0123 out of state). **Vermont Transit** (☎ 603/351–1331 or 800/552–8737). **Advance Transit** (☎ 802/295–1824). **Keene City Express** (☎ 603/352–8494). **Manchester Transit Authority** (☎ 603/623–8801).

CAR TRAVEL

Most people who travel up from Massachusetts do so on I–93, which passes through Manchester and Concord before cutting a path through the White Mountains. I–89 connects Concord, in the Merrimack Valley, with Vermont. Route 12 runs north–south along the Connecticut River. Farther south, Route 101 connects Keene and Manchester, then continues to the seacoast. On the western border of the state, Routes 12 and 12A are picturesque but slow-moving. U.S. 4 crosses the region, winding between Lebanon and the seacoast. Other pretty drives include Routes 101, 202, and 10.

EMERGENCIES

➤ HOSPITALS: **Cheshire Medical Center** (⊠ 580 Court St., Keene, ☎ 603/352–4111). **Concord Hospital** (⊠ 250 Pleasant St., Concord, ☎ 603/225–2711). **Dartmouth Hitchcock Medical Center** (⊠ 1 Medical Center Dr., Lebanon, ☎ 603/650–5000). **Elliot Hospital** (⊠ 1 Elliot Way, Manchester, ☎ 603/669–5300). **Monadnock Community Hospital** (⊠ 452 Old Street Rd., Peterborough, ☎ 603/924–7191). **Southern New Hampshire Medical Center** (⊠ 8 Prospect St., Nashua, ☎ 603/577–2000).
➤ 24–HOUR PHARMACIES: **Brooks Pharmacy** (⊠ 53 Hookset Rd., Manchester, ☎ 603/623–1135). **CVS Pharmacy** (⊠ 271 Mammouth Rd., Manchester, ☎ 603/623–0347; ⊠ 240–242 Main St., Nashua, ☎ 603/886–1798).

LODGING

The Sunapee Area Lodging and Information Service can help with reservations.

APARTMENT & VILLA RENTALS
➤ LOCAL AGENTS: **Sunapee Area Lodging and Information Service** (☎ 603/763–2495 or 800/258–3530).

OUTDOORS & SPORTS

FISHING

For word on what's biting where, contact the New Hampshire Fish and Game Office in Keene.

➤ CONTACTS: **New Hampshire Fish and Game Office** (☎ 603/352–9669).

VISITOR INFORMATION

➤ TOURIST INFORMATION: **Concord Chamber of Commerce** (✉ 244 N. Main St., Concord 03301, ☎ 603/224–2508, WEB www.concordnhchamber.com). **Lake Sunapee Business Association** (✉ Box 400, Sunapee 03782, ☎ 603/763–2495 or 800/258–3530, WEB http://sunapee-vacations.com). **Manchester Chamber of Commerce** (✉ 889 Elm St., Manchester 03101, ☎ 603/666–6600, WEB www.manchester-chamber.org). **Monadnock Travel Council** (✉ Box 358, 8 Central Sq., Keene 03431, ☎ 800/432–7864, WEB www.monadnocktravel.com).

NEW HAMPSHIRE A TO Z

To research prices, get advice from other travelers, and book travel arrangements, visit www.fodors.com

AIRPORTS

Manchester Airport, the state's largest airport, is rapidly becoming a cost-effective and hassle-free alternative to Boston's busier Logan International Airport. It has scheduled flights by Air Canada, American Eagle, Continental, Delta, Northwest, Southwest, United, and US Airways. Lebanon Municipal Airport has commuter flights by US Airways Small local airports that handle charters and private planes are Berlin Airport, Concord Airport, Laconia Airport, Nashua Municipal Airport, and, in Rochester, Skyhaven Airport.

➤ AIRPORT INFORMATION: **Manchester Airport** (✉ 1 Airport Rd., Manchester 03103, ☎ 603/624–6539). **Lebanon Municipal Airport** (✉ 5 Airpark Rd., West Lebanon, ☎ 603/298–8878). **Berlin Airport** (✉ Rte. 16, Milan, ☎ 603/449–7383). **Concord Airport** (✉ 71 Airport Rd., Concord, ☎ 603/229–1760). **Laconia Airport** (✉ Rte. 11, Laconia, ☎ 603/524–5003). **Nashua Municipal Airport** (✉ Borie Field, Nashua, ☎ 603/882–0661). **Skyhaven Airport** (✉ 238 Rochester Hill Rd., Rochester, ☎ 603/332–0005).

BIKE [& MOPED] TRAVEL

Bike the Whites, Monadnock Bicycle Touring, and New England Hiking Holidays organize bike tours.

➤ CONTACTS: **Bike the Whites** (☎ 800/448–3534), **Monadnock Bicycle Touring** (☎ 603/827–3925), **New England Hiking Holidays** (☎ 603/356–9696 or 800/869–0949).

BUS TRAVEL

C&J serves the seacoast area of New Hampshire. Concord Trailways links Boston's South Station and Logan Airport with points all along I–93 and, around Lake Winnipesaukee and the eastern White Mountains, along Route 16. Vermont Transit links the cities of western New Hampshire with major cities in the eastern United States.

➤ BUS INFORMATION: **C&J** (☎ 603/431–2424). **Concord Trailways** (☎ 603/228–3300 or 800/639–3317). **Vermont Transit** (☎ 603/228–3300 or 800/451–3292).

CAR TRAVEL

Interstate 93 is the principal north–south route through Manchester, Concord, and central New Hampshire. To the west, I–91 traces the Vermont–New Hampshire border. To the east, I–95, which is a toll road, passes through the coastal area of southern New Hampshire on its way from Massachusetts to Maine. Interstate 89 travels from Concord to Montpelier and Burlington, Vermont.

The official state map, available free from the New Hampshire Office of Travel and Tourism Development (☞ Visitor Information), also has useful telephone numbers and information about bike, snowmobile, and scenic routes.

Speed limits on interstate and limited-access highways are generally 65 mph, except in heavily settled areas, where 55 mph is the norm. On state and U.S. routes, speed limits vary considerably. On any given stretch, the limit may be anywhere from 25 mph to 55 mph, so watch the signs carefully. Right turns are permitted on red lights unless indicated.

EMERGENCIES
➤ CONTACTS: **Ambulance, fire, police** (☎ 911).

LODGING
CAMPING
New Hampshire Campground Owners Association publishes a guide to private, state, and national-forest campgrounds.
➤ CONTACTS: **New Hampshire Campground Owners Association** (✉ Box 320, Twin Mountain, 03595, ☎ 603/846–5511 or 800/822–6764, FAX 603/846–2151).

OUTDOORS & SPORTS
BIRD-WATCHING
Audubon Society of New Hampshire schedules monthly field trips throughout the state and a fall bird-watching tour to Star Isle and other parts of the Isles of Shoals.
➤ CONTACTS: **Audubon Society of New Hampshire** (✉ 3 Silk Farm Rd., Concord 03301, ☎ 603/224–9909).

FISHING
For information about fishing and licenses, call the New Hampshire Fish and Game Office.
➤ CONTACTS: **New Hampshire Fish and Game Office** (☎ 603/271–3211).

FOLIAGE AND SNOW HOT LINES
A fall foliage hot line is updated twice weekly from mid-September through October. Two snow hot lines provide updates on snow conditions at ski centers.
➤ CONTACTS: **Foliage hot line** (☎ 800/258–3608). **Snow hot lines** (☎ 800/258–3608 New Hampshire alpine ski conditions; 800/262–6660 cross-country ski conditions).

SKIING
Ski New Hampshire has information on downhill and cross-country snow sports in the state.
➤ CONTACTS: **Ski New Hampshire** (✉ Box 10, North Woodstock 03262, ☎ 603/745–9396 or 800/887–5464).

VISITOR INFORMATION
➤ TOURIST INFORMATION: **New Hampshire Office of Travel and Tourism Development** (✉ Box 1856, Concord 03302, ☎ 603/271–2343; 800/386–4664 for free vacation packet, WEB www.visitnh.gov). **Events** (☎ 800/258–3608 or 800/262–6660). **New Hampshire Parks Department** (☎ 603/271–3556). **New Hampshire State Council on the Arts** (✉ 40 N. Main St., Concord 03301, ☎ 603/271–2789).

3 VERMONT

Southern Vermont has manicured landscapes, immaculate villages, and summer theaters, as well as a surprisingly large chunk of wilderness in the Green Mountain National Forest. Central Vermont is home to the state's largest ski resort, Killington, along with the rolling farmland vistas of the lower Lake Champlain valley. Up north, Vermont attractions include the state's largest city, cosmopolitan and collegiate Burlington; the nation's smallest state capital, Montpelier; the legendary slopes of Stowe; and the leafy back roads of the Northeast Kingdom.

Revised and
updated by
Kay and Bill
Scheller

E VERYWHERE YOU LOOK IN VERMONT, the evidence is clear: this
is not the state it was 30 years ago. That may be true for the rest
of New England as well, but the contrasts between the present
and recent past seem all the more sharply drawn in the Green Mountain State, if only because an aura of timelessness has always been at
the heart of the Vermont image. Vermont was where all the quirks and
virtues outsiders associate with up-country New England were supposed
to reside. It was where the Yankees were Yankee-est and where there
were more cows than people.

Not that you should be alarmed if you haven't been here in a while;
Vermont hasn't become southern California, or even, for that matter,
southern New Hampshire. The state's population, which increased from
335,000 to only 390,000 from 1860 to 1960, began to climb sharply
as interstate highways and resort development made their impact. By
1990 the state had 563,000 residents; today, a population of approximately 600,000 indicates some leveling off of the rate of growth. This
is still the most rural state in the Union (meaning that it has the smallest percentage of citizens living in statistically defined metropolitan areas),
and it still turns out most of New England's milk, even though there
are, finally, more people than cows. Vermont remains a place where
cars occasionally have to stop while a dairy farmer walks his herd across
a secondary road; and up in Essex County, in what George Aiken dubbed
the Northeast Kingdom, there are townships with zero population. And
the kind of scrupulous, straightforward, plainspoken politics practiced by Governor (later Senator) Aiken for 50 years shas not become
outmoded in a state that still turns out on town-meeting day.

How has Vermont changed? In strictly physical terms, the most obvi-
ous transformations have taken place in and around the two major cities,
Burlington and Rutland, and near the larger ski resorts, such as Stowe,
Killington, Stratton, and Mt. Snow. Burlington's Church Street, once
a paradigm of all the sleepy redbrick shopping thoroughfares in northern New England, is now a pedestrian mall with chic bistros; outside
the city, suburban development has supplanted farms in towns where
someone's trip to Burlington might once have been an item in a weekly
newspaper. As for the ski areas, it's no longer enough simply to boast
the latest in chairlift technology. Slopeside hotels and condos have
boomed, especially in the southern part of the state, turning ski areas
into big-time resort destinations. And once-sleepy Manchester has become one of New England's factory-outlet meccas.

The real metamorphosis in the Green Mountains, however, has to do
more with style, with the personality of the place, than with development. The past couple of decades have seen a tremendous influx of outsiders—not only skiers and "leaf peepers" but people who have come
to stay year-round—and many of them are determined either to freshen
the local scene with their own idiosyncrasies or to make Vermont even
more like Vermont than they found it. On the one hand, this trans-
lates into the fact that Vermont is the only state represented in Washington by an independent socialist congressman; on the other, it means
that sheep farming has been reintroduced to the state, largely to provide a high-quality product for the hand-weaving industry.

This ties in with another local phenomenon, one best described as Made
in Vermont. Once upon a time, maple syrup and sharp cheddar cheese
were the products that carried Vermont's name to the world. The market niche that they created has since been widened by Vermonters—a
great many of them refugees from more hectic arenas of commerce—

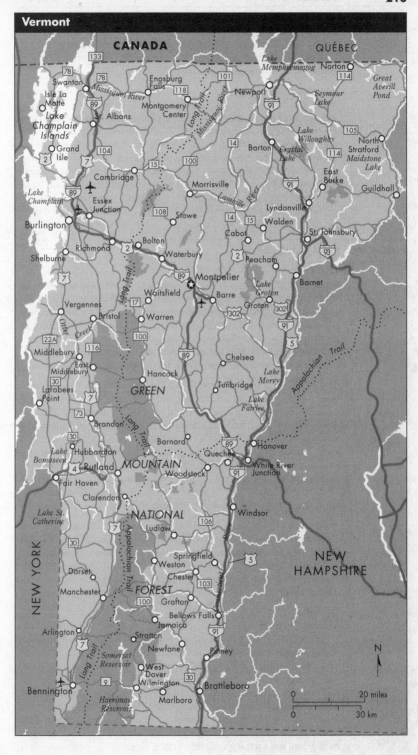

CANADA

QUÉBEC

Lake Memphremagog

Norton

133

78

78

Enosburg Falls

118

101

Newport

114

Great Averill Pond

Swanton

Isle La Motte

Missisquoi River

Montgomery Center

Seymour Lake

89

St. Albans

91

Lake Champlain Islands

Lake Willoughby

105

104

Grand Isle

15

100

Barton

Crystal Lake

North Stratford

Maidstone Lake

2

7

Cambridge

Morrisville

91

114

East Burke

Guildhall

Lamoille River

Lake Champlain

108

Stowe

Lyndonville

Essex Junction

14

15

Walden

St. Johnsbury

Burlington

Bolton

Cabot

93

Richmond

2

Waterbury

2

Peacham

Shelburne

89

Montpelier

Barnet

7

Waitsfield

Barre

Lake Groton

17

Warren

302

Groton

302

91

100

302

5

Vergennes

Chelsea

Appalachian Trail

Otter Creek

Bristol

22A

116

Middlebury

Hancock

Lake Morey

GREEN

East Middlebury

Tunbridge

30

Larabees Point

Lake Fairlee

7

73

Brandon

Long Trail

Barnard

89

Hanover

Lake Bomoseen

Hubbardton

Quechee

White River Junction

4

Rutland

MOUNTAIN

91

Woodstock

Fair Haven

Clarendon

NATIONAL

106

Windsor

Lake St. Catherine

7

Ludlow

Connecticut River

30

Springfield

5

Dorset

Weston

NEW HAMPSHIRE

Manchester

Chester

103

FOREST

100

Grafton

Appalachian Trail

Arlington

Bellows Falls

Jamaica

91

7

Stratton

Newfane

Putney

NEW YORK

Somerset Reservoir

West Dover

9

Bennington

Wilmington

30

Brattleboro

Long Trail

Marlboro

Harriman Reservoir

N

0   20 miles

0   30 km

who now offer a dizzying variety of goods with the ineffable cachet of Vermont manufacture. There are Vermont wood toys, Vermont apple wines, Vermont chocolates, even Vermont gin. The most successful Made in Vermont product is Ben & Jerry's ice cream; the company has become the largest single purchaser of Vermont milk.

The character and appearance of the landscape are what most readily ignite preservationists' passions in Vermont. Farming may be changing—in addition to sheep, there are goats, llamas, emus, and even elk grazing the Green Mountain foothills—but farms are farms, valued for their open-space counterpoint to Vermont forests and villages. The Vermont Land Trust has saved thousands of acres of farmland through the purchase of development rights; meanwhile, vast tracts of northern woodlands have been preserved for wildlife habitat, recreation, and low-impact forestry. The challenge is to bring Vermont into the 21st century while making sure it still looks like Vermont. The model might be an old farmhouse, with fiber-optic cables hidden in its walls.

Pleasures and Pastimes

Dining
Over the past few years, Vermont chefs have been working hard to fulfill two distinct responsibilities. One is the need to honor the traditions of Yankee cooking, the realm of pot roast and Indian pudding, sticky buns and homemade corn relish. As travelers and residents have become more sophisticated, there has also been a demand for the ethnic cuisines, lighter adaptations of classics, and new American treatments of seasonal ingredients that now characterize urban menus.

The more ambitious restaurants and inn kitchens have not only managed to balance these two gastronomic imperatives but also have succeeded in combining them. The trick is to take an innovative approach with Vermont game and local produce, introduce fresh herbs and other seasonings, and change menus to suit the season. Look for imaginative approaches to native New England foods such as fiddlehead ferns (available only for a short time in the spring), maple syrup (Vermont is the largest U.S. producer), dairy products (especially cheese), native fruits and berries, "new Vermont" products such as salsa and salad dressings, and venison, quail, pheasant, and other game.

Your chances of finding a table for dinner vary with the season: Many restaurants have lengthy waits during peak seasons (when it's always a good idea to make a reservation) and then shut down during the slow months of April and November. Some of the best dining is found at country inns. For price-category information, *see* Dining *in* Smart Travel Tips.

Lodging
Vermont's largest hotels are in Burlington and near the major ski resorts. There's a dearth of inns and bed-and-breakfasts in Burlington, though chain hotels provide dependable accommodations. Elsewhere you'll find a range of inns, B&Bs, and small motels. The many lovely and sometimes quite luxurious inns and B&Bs provide what many people consider the quintessential Vermont lodging experience. Rates are highest during foliage season, from late September to mid-October, and lowest in late spring and November, when many properties close. Many of the larger hotels offer package rates. For price-category information, *see* Lodging *in* Smart Travel Tips.

National Forests
The two sections of the 355,000-acre Green Mountain National Forest (GMNF) are central and southern Vermont's primary stronghold

of woodland and high mountain terrain. Like all national forests, it contains sections on which timber leases are sometimes granted, but it's possible to travel through much of this preserve without seeing significant evidence of human intrusion. In addition to the paved public highways that traverse the GMNF, many of the occasional logging roads are maintained for public use, and although unpaved, these are kept in good condition during snow-free times of the year.

The Forest Service maintains a number of picnic areas and primitive campgrounds; complete information is available from the Forest Supervisor. Fishing, subject to state laws and seasonal closings and limits, is allowed throughout the GMNF. Canoeing, cross-country skiing, and hiking are also popular; the Appalachian and Long trails run the length of the forest. Snowmobiles and other forms of motorized transportation, such as all-terrain vehicles, are permitted on marked trails, except within roadless areas designated as wilderness.

Outdoor Activities and Sports

BIKING

Vermont, especially the often deserted roads of the Northeast Kingdom, is great bicycle-touring country. Many companies lead weekend tours and weeklong trips throughout the state. If you'd like to go it on your own, most chambers of commerce have brochures highlighting good cycling routes in their area, including *Vermont Life* magazine's "Bicycle Vermont" map and guide, and many bookstores sell *25 Bicycle Tours in Vermont* by John Freidin.

FISHING

Central Vermont is the heart of the state's warm-water lake and pond fishing. Harriman and Somerset reservoirs have both warm- and cold-water species; Harriman has a greater variety. Lake Dunmore produced the state-record rainbow trout; Lakes Bomoseen and St. Catherine are good for rainbows and largemouth bass. In the east, Lakes Fairlee and Morey hold bass, perch, and chain pickerel, while the lower part of the Connecticut River contains smallmouth bass, walleye, and perch; shad are returning via the fish ladders at Vernon and Bellows Falls.

In northern Vermont, rainbow and brown trout inhabit the Missisquoi, Lamoille, Winooski, and Willoughby rivers, and there's warm-water fishing at many smaller lakes and ponds. Lakes Seymour, Willoughby, and Memphremagog and Great Averill Pond in the Northeast Kingdom are good for salmon and lake trout. The Dog River near Montpelier has one of the best wild populations of brown trout in the state. Good news is that landlocked Atlantic salmon are returning to the Clyde River following removal of a controversial dam.

Lake Champlain, stocked annually with salmon and lake trout, has become the state's ice-fishing capital; walleye, bass, pike, and channel catfish are also taken. Ice fishing is also popular on Lake Memphremagog.

SKIING

The Green Mountains run through the middle of Vermont like a bumpy spine, visible from almost every point in the state; generous accumulations of snow make the mountains an ideal site for skiing. Increased snow-making capacity and improved, high-tech computerized equipment at many areas virtually assure a good day on the slopes. Vermont has 26 alpine ski resorts with nearly 1,000 trails and some 5,000 acres of skiable terrain. Combined, the resorts operate nearly 200 lifts and have the capacity to carry some 215,000 skiers per hour. Though grooming is sophisticated at all Vermont areas, conditions usually run to a typically Eastern hard pack, with powder a rare luxury and ice a bugbear after January thaw. The best advice for skiing in Vermont is to keep your skis well tuned.

Route 100 is also known as "Skier's Highway," passing by 13 of the state's ski areas. Vermont's major resorts are Stowe, Jay Peak, Sugarbush, Killington, Okemo, Mt. Snow, and Stratton. Midsize, less hectic areas to consider include Ascutney, Bromley, Smugglers' Notch, Pico, Mad River Glen, and Burke Mountain. In 1999, Bolton Valley Holiday Resort—long a favorite because of its proximity to Burlington and ample intermediate terrain—reopened under a new owner.

Exploring Vermont

Vermont can be divided into three regions. The southern part of the state, flanked by Bennington on the west and Brattleboro on the east, played an important role in Vermont's Revolutionary War–era drive to independence (yes, there was once a Republic of Vermont) and its eventual statehood. The central part is characterized by rugged mountains and the gently rolling dairy lands near Lake Champlain. Northern Vermont is the site of the state's capital, Montpelier, and its largest city, Burlington, yet it is also home to Vermont's most rural area, the Northeast Kingdom.

Numbers in the text correspond to numbers in the margin and on the Southern Vermont, Central Vermont, and Northern Vermont maps.

Great Itineraries

There are many ways to take advantage of Vermont's beauty—skiing or hiking its mountains, biking or driving its back roads, fishing or sailing its waters, shopping for local products, visiting its museums and sights, or simply finding the perfect inn and never leaving the front porch. Distances in Vermont are relatively short, yet the mountains and many back roads will slow a traveler's pace. You can see a representative north–south section of Vermont in a few days; if you have up to a week you can hit the highlights around the state.

IF YOU HAVE 3 DAYS

Spend a few hours in historic **Bennington** ⑤ in the southern part of Vermont; then travel north to see Hildene and stay in ⊞ **Manchester** ⑦. On your second day take Route 100 through Weston and travel north through the Green Mountains to Route 125, where you turn west to explore ⊞ **Middlebury** ㉕. On day three, enter the Champlain Valley, which has views of the Adirondack Mountains to the west. Stop at Shelburne Farms and carry on to **Burlington** ㊱; catch the sunset from the waterfront and take a walk on Church Street.

IF YOU HAVE 5 TO 7 DAYS

You can make several side trips off Route 100 and also visit the Northeast Kingdom on a trip of this length. Visit **Bennington** ⑤ and ⊞ **Manchester** ⑦ on day one. Spend your second day walking around the small towns of **Chester** ⑪ and ⊞ **Grafton** ⑫. On day three head north to explore **Woodstock** ⑳ and ⊞ **Quechee** ⑲, stopping at either the Billings Farm Museum and Marsh-Billings-Rockefeller National Historical Park or the Vermont Institute of Natural Science. Head leisurely on your fourth day toward ⊞ **Middlebury** ㉕, along one of Vermont's most inspiring mountain drives, Route 125 west of Route 100. Between Hancock and Middlebury, you'll pass nature trails and the picnic spot at Texas Falls Recreation Area, then traverse a moderately steep mountain pass. Spend day five in ⊞ **Burlington** ㊱. On day six head east to **Waterbury** ㉚ and then north to ⊞ **Stowe** ㉜ and Mt. Mansfield for a full day. Begin your last day with a few hours in **Montpelier** ㉙ on your way to **Peacham** ㊸, **St. Johnsbury** ㊶, ⊞ **Lake Willoughby** ㊷, and the serenity and back roads of the Northeast Kingdom. Especially noteworthy are U.S. 5, Route 5A, and Route 14.

When to Tour Vermont

The number of visitors and the rates for lodging reach their peaks along with the color of the leaves during foliage season, from late September to mid-October. But if you have never seen a kaleidoscope of autumn colors, it is worth braving the slow-moving traffic and paying the extra money. In summer the state is lush and green. Winter, of course, is high season at Vermont's ski resorts. Rates are lowest in late spring and November, although many properties close during these times.

SOUTHERN VERMONT

The Vermont tradition of independence and rebellion began in southern Vermont. Many towns founded in the early 18th century as frontier outposts or fortifications were later important as trading centers. In the western region the Green Mountain Boys fought off both the British and the claims of land-hungry New Yorkers—some say their descendants are still fighting. In the 19th century, as many towns turned to manufacturing, the farmers here retreated to hillier regions and, as the modern ski and summer-home booms got under way, retreated even farther.

The first thing you'll notice upon entering the state is the conspicuous lack of billboards along the highways and roads. The foresight back in the 1960s to prohibit them has made for a refreshing absence of aggressive visual clutter that allows unencumbered views of working farmland, fresh-as-paint villages, and quiet back roads—but does not hide the reality of abandoned dairy barns, bustling ski resorts, and strip-mall sprawl. Visitors who reach Vermont via the well-settled districts around Brattleboro and Bennington, though, are often surprised at the beautifully desolate woodlands that lie between these gateways. Much of the Green Mountain National Forest's southern section occupies rugged uplands where homesteads and farms thrived 450 years ago.

The towns are listed in counterclockwise order, beginning in the east, south of the junction of I–91 and Route 9 in Brattleboro, and following the southern boundary of the state toward Bennington, then north up to Manchester and Weston and south back to Newfane.

Brattleboro

❶ *60 mi south of White River Junction.*

Its downtown bustling with activity, Brattleboro, with about 13,000 inhabitants, is the center of commerce for southeastern Vermont. This town at the confluence of the West and Connecticut rivers originated as a frontier scouting post and became a thriving industrial center and resort town in the 1800s. More recently, the area has become a home to political activists and a raft of earnest counterculturists.

A former railroad station, the **Brattleboro Museum and Art Center** has replaced locomotives with works created by internationally and locally renowned artists and with exhibits that chronicle the region's rich history. The organs here were made in Brattleboro between 1853 and 1961, when the city was home to the Estey Organ Company, one of the world's largest organ manufacturers. The museum hosts a lecture and concert series. ⊠ *Vernon and Main Sts.,* ☎ *802/257–0124,* Ⱳⴱ *www.brattleboromuseum.org.* ⴰ *$3.* ⊙ *Mid-May–Oct., Tues.–Sun. noon–6.*

Dining and Lodging

$$$ ✕ **Peter Havens.** In a town better known for tofu than toniness, this chic little bistro knows just what to do with a filet mignon—serve it with Roquefort walnut butter, of course. Look for the house-cured

Southern Vermont

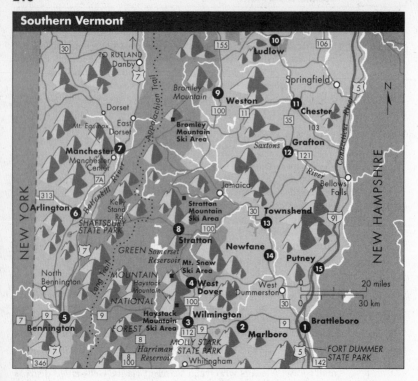

gravlax made with lemon vodka and fresh seasonal seafood, which even includes a spring fling with soft-shell crabs. The wine list is superb. ⊠ *32 Elliot St.,* ☎ *802/257–3333. MC, V. Closed Sun. and Mon. No lunch.*

$ ✕ **Common Ground.** The political posters and concert fliers that line the staircase here attest to Vermont's progressive element. The stairs lead to loft-like, rough-hewn dining rooms. Owned cooperatively by the staff, this mostly organic vegetarian restaurant serves cashew burgers, veggie stir-fries, curries, hot soup and stew, and the humble bowl of brown rice. All the desserts, including a chocolate cake with peanut butter frosting, are made without white sugar. ⊠ *25 Elliot St.,* ☎ *802/257–0855. No credit cards. Closed Mon.–Wed. No lunch Thurs.*

$ ✕ **Sarkis Market.** Gail Sarkis's Lebanese grandmother gave her many of the recipes she uses to create Middle Eastern delicacies such as falafel, stuffed grape leaves, hummus, and *kibbe*—a layered meatloaf stuffed with ground lamb, pine nuts, and onions. Undecided about what to order? Go for the combination plate and finish with a wedge of homemade baklava. ⊠ *50 Elliot St.,* ☎ *802/258–4906. AE, MC, V. Closed Sun. in winter.*

$$$ 🛏 **40 Putney Road.** Expect a warm welcome at Gwen and Dan Pasco's antiques-filled French château–style estate. Rooms are furnished with antiques and have phones, TV/VCRs, robes, and air conditioning; the suite has a gas fireplace. In warm weather, breakfast is served on the patio of the formally landscaped grounds, which lead to the shores of the West River. ⊠ *40 Putney Rd., 05301,* ☎ *802/254–6268 or 800/941–2413,* FAX *802/258–2673,* WEB *www.putney.net/40putneyrd. 3 rooms, 1 suite. Pub, in-room VCRs. AE, D, MC, V. BP.*

$–$$ 🛏 **Latchis Hotel.** Front rooms at this 1938 downtown Art Deco landmark overlook busy—and often noisy—Main Street. All the rooms have coffeemakers and are furnished comfortably, many with their original restored 1930s furniture; the suites are a bargain. Muffins arrive outside your door each morning at 8, and you can catch a movie under

the zodiac ceiling of the adjoining Latchis Theater. The Latchis Grille
(☎ 802/254–4747; closed Mon. and Tues., no lunch Mon.–Thurs.) is
home to the Windham Brewery. ⊠ *50 Main St., 05301,* ☎ *802/254–
6300,* FAX *802/254–6304,* WEB *www.brattleboro.com/latchis. 30 rooms;
3 suites. Restaurant, pub. AE, MC, V. CP.*

Nightlife and the Arts

Common Ground (⊠ 25 Elliot St., ☎ 802/257–0855) often presents
live acoustic music, especially during Sunday brunch. **Mole's Eye Cafe**
(⊠ 4 High St., ☎ 802/257–0771) hosts an open mike night every Thursday, and live bands Friday and Saturday (cover charge).

Outdoor Activities and Sports

BIKING

Brattleboro Bicycle Shop (⊠ 165 Main St., ☎ 802/254–8644 or 800/
272–8245) rents and repairs bikes. **Burrows Specialized Sports** (⊠ 105
Main St., ☎ 802/254–9430) services bikes, skis, and snowboards.

CANOEING

Vermont Canoe Touring Center (⊠ U.S. 5, ☎ 802/257–5008) has
guided and self-guided tours as well as canoe and kayak rentals and a
shuttle service.

SKATING

Nelson Withington Skating Rink (⊠ Memorial Park, 4 Guilford St., ☎
802/257–2311) rents skates.

STATE PARK

The hiking trails at **Fort Dummer State Park** (⊠ S. Main St., 2 mi south
of Brattleboro, ☎ 802/254–2610) afford views of the Connecticut River
valley; campsites are available.

Shopping

The **Book Cellar** (⊠ 120 Main St., ☎ 802/254–6026), with two floors
of volumes, carries many travel books. **Vermont Artisan Designs** (⊠
106 Main St., ☎ 802/257–7044), one of the state's best crafts shops,
displays ceramics, glass, wood, clothing, jewelry, and furniture. You
can watch **Tom and Sally's Homemade Chocolates** being made just
around the corner from their shop (⊠ 55 Elliott St., ☎ 802/258–
3065), which also sells the famous Vermont Meadow Muffins.

Marlboro

❷ *10 mi west of Brattleboro.*

Tiny Marlboro draws musicians and audiences from around the world
each summer to the Marlboro Music Festival, founded by Rudolf
Serkin and joined for many years by Pablo Casals. **Marlboro College,**
high on a hill off Route 9, is the center of musical activity. The college's white-frame buildings have outstanding views of the valley
below, and the campus is studded with apple trees.

The **Southern Vermont Natural History Museum** houses one of New
England's largest collections of mounted birds, specimens of three ex-
tinct birds, and a complete collection of mammals native to the Northeast. The museum also has weather displays and live hawk and owl
exhibits. ⊠ *Rte. 9,* ☎ *802/464–0048.* ☞ *$3.* ☉ *Memorial Day–late
Oct., daily 10–5; call for hrs rest of yr.*

Nightlife and the Arts

The **Marlboro Music Festival** (⊠ Marlboro Music Center, Marlboro College, ☎ 802/254–2394; 215/569–4690 Sept.–June) presents chamber

music at weekend concerts in July and August. The **New England Bach Festival** (☏ 802/257–4523) is held at Marlboro College in October.

Wilmington

❸ *8 mi west of Marlboro.*

Wilmington is the shopping and dining center for the Mt. Snow ski area (☞ West Dover) to the north. Main Street has a cohesive assemblage of 18th- and 19th-century buildings, many of them listed on the National Register of Historic Places. For a great stroll, pick up a self-guided tour map from the **Chamber of Commerce** (✉ Rte. 9, W. Main St., ☏ 802/464–8092 or 877-887–6884, WEB www.visitvermont.com).

North River Winery, which occupies a converted farmhouse and barn, produces fruit wines such as Green Mountain Apple and Vermont Pear. ✉ *Rte. 112, 6 mi south of Wilmington, Jacksonville,* ☏ *802/368–7557.* 🎫 *Free.* ☉ *Daily 10–5; tours late May–Dec.*

OFF THE
BEATEN PATH

SCENIC TOUR – To begin a scenic (though well-traveled) 35-mi circular tour with panoramic views of the region's mountains, farmland, and abundant cow population, drive west on Route 9 to the intersection with Route 8. Turn south and continue to the junction with Route 100; follow Route 100 through Whitingham (the birthplace of the Mormon prophet Brigham Young), and stay with the road as it turns north again and takes you back to Route 9.

Lodging

$$$–$$$$ 🏨 **White House of Wilmington.** The grand staircase in this Federal-style mansion leads to rooms with antique bathrooms and brass wall sconces. The newer section has more contemporary plumbing; some rooms have fireplaces, whirlpool tubs, and lofts. The leather wing chairs of the public rooms suggest formality, but the atmosphere is casual and comfortable. Children under 8 are welcome in the more casual Guest Cottage. The White House has a cross-country ski touring and snowshoeing center, a tubing hill, and 12 km (7 mi) of groomed trails. Guests can dine at the restaurant for a fixed price of $35. ✉ *178 Rte. 9 E, 05363,* ☏ *802/ 464–2135 or 800/541–2135,* FAX *802/464–5222,* WEB *www.whitehouseinn.com. 23 rooms. Restaurant, bar, 1 indoor and 1 outdoor pool, sauna, cross-country skiing. AE, D, DC, MC, V. BP.*

$$–$$$ 🏨 **Trail's End, A Country Inn.** This cozy four-season lodge is set on 10 acres 4 mi from Mt. Snow. The inn's centerpiece is its cathedral-ceiling living room with catwalk loft seating and a 21-ft fieldstone fireplace. Guest rooms are comfortable, if simple, though two suites have fireplaces, whirlpool tubs, cable TV, refrigerators, and microwaves; four other rooms also have fireplaces. Dinner is served during the holiday season only. There's a stocked trout pond on site, and cross-country ski trails nearby. ✉ *5 Trail's End La., 05363,* ☏ *802/464–2727 or 800/ 859–2585,* FAX *802/464–5532,* WEB *www.trailsendvt.com. 13 rooms, 2 suites. Pool, pond, game room, tennis court. AE, D, MC, V. BP.*

Nightlife and the Arts

In addition to steak and Mexican specialties, the standard fare on weekends at **Poncho's Wreck** (✉ S. Main St., ☏ 802/464–9320) is acoustic jazz or mellow rock. **Sitzmark** (✉ Rte. 100, ☏ 802/464–3384) hosts rock bands on weekends.

Outdoor Activities and Sports

SLEIGH RIDES

Adams Farm (⊠ 15 Higley Hill Rd., ☎ 802/464–3762) has three double-traverse sleighs drawn by Belgian draft horses. Rides include a narrated tour and hot chocolate. An indoor petting farm is open Wed.–Sun. from Nov.–Apr., and an outdoor version is open daily the rest of the year.

STATE PARK

Molly Stark State Park (⊠ Rte. 9, east of Wilmington, ☎ 802/464–5460) has campsites and a hiking trail that leads to a vista from a fire tower on Mt. Olga.

WATER SPORTS

Lake Whitingham (Harriman Reservoir), just west of Wilmington, is the largest lake in the state, with good fishing. Boat launch areas are at Wards Cove, Whitingham, Mountain Mills, and the Ox Bow. **Green Mountain Flagship Company** (⊠ Rte. 9, 2 mi west of Wilmington, ☎ 802/464–2975) runs a cruise boat on Lake Whitingham and rents canoes, kayaks, surfbikes, and sailboats from May to late October.

Shopping

Quaigh Design Centre (⊠ Rte. 9, W. Main St., ☎ 802/464–2780) sells New England crafts, artwork from Britain and New England—including works by Vermont woodcut artists Sabra Field and Mary Azarian—and Scottish woolens and tartans. **Wilmington Flea Market** (⊠ Rtes. 9 and 100 S, ☎ 802/464–3345) sells antiques on weekends from Memorial Day to mid-October.

West Dover

❹ *6 mi north of Wilmington.*

The Congregational church in small West Dover, a classic New England town, dates from the 1700s. The year-round population of about 1,000 swells on winter weekends as skiers flock to Mt. Snow/Haystack Ski Resort. The many condos, lodges, and inns at the base of the mountain accommodate them.

Dining and Lodging

$$$$ ✕▥ **Inn at Saw Mill Farm.** This elegant retreat close to Mt. Snow is
★ one of Vermont's two Relais & Châteaux inns (the other is the Pitcher Inn) and has all the upscale amenities expected at these properties. English chintzes, antiques, and dark wood set a comfortable tone in the common room. Each of the guest rooms is individually decorated, and many have sitting areas and fireplaces. The 19 landscaped acres are perfect for hiking; there's also a stocked trout pond. The inn's well-regarded restaurant ($$$$) has a seasonal menu that might include potato-crusted black sea bass with wild mushrooms and orzo or a grilled veal chop with wild mushroom risotto and rosemary sauce. The wine selection, with more than 30,000 bottles, is superb. ⊠ *Rte. 100 and Crosstown Rd., 05356,* ☎ *800/493–1133 or 802/464–8131,* FAX *802/464–1130,* WEB *www.vermontdirect.com/sawmill. 20 rooms. Restaurant, pool, tennis court, fishing. AE, DC, MC, V. Closed Easter–late May. MAP.*

$$$–$$$$ ✕▥ **Deerhill Inn and Restaurant.** The west-facing windows at this En-
★ glish-style country inn have views of the valley below and the ski slopes across the way. A huge fireplace dominates the living room, and English hand-painted yellow wallpaper, a garden-scene mural, and collections of antique plates accent the dining rooms. One guest room has an Asian bedroom set, several have hand-painted murals, and many have fireplaces. The three balcony rooms are the largest; they

have great views. Some rooms have whirlpool baths. In the restaurant ($$$–$$$$; closed Wednesday in summer; Tues. and Wed. in winter), the upscale comfort food might include fresh fish, a veal medallion with wild mushrooms in a lemon cream sauce, or a black-pepper sirloin steak. ⊠ *Box 136, Valley View Rd., 05356,* ☎ *802/464–3100 or 800/993–3379,* FAX *802/464–5474,* WEB *www.deerhill.com. 13 rooms, 2 suites. Restaurant, pool. AE, MC, V. BP; MAP.*

$$ ✕🗖 **Doveberry Inn.** After a day's skiing, this handsome country inn just a few minutes from the slopes offers a welcome haven. The living room has a fireplace and wine bar. Guest rooms are cheerful and bright, with TVs and VCRs; one room has a fireplace. The restaurant ($$$; closed Tuesday) serves up northern Italian specialties such as wood-grilled veal chop with wild mushrooms and pan-seared salmon with herbed risotto in intimate, candlelit dining rooms. ⊠ *Rte. 100, 05356,* ☎ *802/464–5652 or 800/722–3204,* FAX *802/464–6229,* WEB *www.doveberryinn.com. 8 rooms. Restaurant, bar. AE, MC, V. BP.*

Nightlife and the Arts

Deacon's Den Tavern (⊠ Rte. 100, ☎ 802/464–9361) hosts bands on weekends from Thanksgiving through Easter. The **Snow Barn** (⊠ near the base of Mt. Snow, ☎ 802/464–1100 ext. 4693) has live music several nights a week.

Ski Areas

MT. SNOW/HAYSTACK SKI RESORT

Mt. Snow, established in the 1950s, was purchased in 1996 by the American Skiing Company, which also owns Sugarbush, Killington, and Pico. Recent developments have included the 1998 opening of the year-round Grand Summit Hotel and Conference Center; the inauguration of the Learn to Ski and Ride Center at the Perfect Turn Discovery Center, complete with its own expanded terrain, triple chairlift, and building; and increased snowmaking capability. Two new terrain parks are the Carnival minipark for kids and the Inferno for advanced snowboarders. One lift ticket lets you ski at Mt. Snow and Haystack.

Haystack—the southernmost ski area in Vermont—is much smaller than Mt. Snow but has a more personal atmosphere. A modern base lodge is close to the lifts. A free shuttle connects the two ski areas. ⊠ *400 Mountain Rd., Mt. Snow, 05356,* ☎ *802/464–3333; 800/245–7669 for lodging; 802/464–2151 for snow conditions.*

Downhill. Mt. Snow has five separate mountain faces, each with its own personality. Most of the 1,130 trails down its 1,700-ft vertical summit are intermediate, wide, and sunny. Most of the beginner slopes are toward the bottom; most of the expert terrain is on the North Face, where there's excellent fall-line skiing. The trails are served by 23 lifts, including three high-speed quads, one regular quad, 10 triple chairs, four double chairs, and three Magic Carpets (similar to an escalator). The ski school's Perfect Turn instruction program is designed to help advanced and expert skiers.

Child care. The well-organized child care center (reservations essential) takes children from ages 6 weeks to 6 years. The center has age-appropriate toys and balances indoor play—including arts and crafts—with trips outdoors. The Pre-ski program is for 3-year-olds, and a Perfect Kids program for ages 4–12 teaches skiing and snowboarding.

Summer activities. Mt. Snow offers two- to seven-day Grand Summer Vacation packages with a variety of activities, including golf at the 18-hole Mt. Snow Golf Course, mountain biking on ski trails and forest roads, and use of the health club, with a pool, hot tubs, and spa. The Summit Local triple chairlift transports riders to the 3,600-ft peak. Swimming, boating, and a children's water play pool are available at the resort's Snow Lake. A hiking center, in-line skating park, climbing wall, and BMX track provide other summer fun.

CROSS-COUNTRY SKIING/SNOWSHOEING

Four cross-country-trail areas within 4 mi of Mt. Snow/Haystack provide more than 150 km (90 mi) of varied terrain. The **Hermitage** (⊠ Coldbrook Rd., Wilmington, ☎ 802/464–3511) has 50 km (30 mi) of groomed trails. The groomed trails at the **White House of Wilmington** (⊠ Rtes. 9 and 100, ☎ 802/464–2135) cover 50 km (30 mi). **Timber Creek** (⊠ Rte. 100, north of the Mt. Snow entrance, ☎ 802/464–0999) is appealingly small with 16 km (10 mi) of thoughtfully groomed trails.

Snowmobile Tours

At **Sitzmark** (⊠ East Dover Rd., Wilmington, ☎ 802/464-3384) guides lead snowmobile tours across a golf course and through 50 acres of woods and fields.

Bennington

⑤ *21 mi west of Wilmington.*

Bennington, college town and commercial focus of Vermont's southwest corner, lies at the edge of the Green Mountain National Forest. It has retained much of the industrial character it developed in the 19th century, when paper mills, grist mills, and potteries formed the city's economic base. It was in Bennington, at the Catamount Tavern, that Ethan Allen organized the Green Mountain Boys, who helped capture Ft. Ticonderoga in 1775. Here also, in 1777, American general John Stark urged his militia to attack the British-paid Hessian troops across the New York border: "There are the redcoats; they will be ours or tonight Molly Stark sleeps a widow!"

A brochure available at the Chamber of Commerce describes an interesting self-guided walking tour of **Old Bennington,** a National Register Historic District west of downtown. Impressive white-column Greek Revival and sturdy brick Federal homes stand around the village green. In the graveyard of the **Old First Church,** at Church Street and Monument Avenue, the tombstone of the poet Robert Frost proclaims, "I had a lover's quarrel with the world."

The **Bennington Battle Monument,** a 306-ft stone obelisk with an elevator to the top, commemorates General Stark's victory over the British, who attempted to capture Bennington's stockpile of supplies. The battle, which took place near Walloomsac Heights in New York State on August 16, 1777, helped bring about the surrender two months later of the British commander "Gentleman Johnny" Burgoyne at Saratoga in New York. ⊠ *15 Monument Ave.,* ☎ *802/447–0550.* ⊠ *$1.50.* ☉ *Mid-Apr.–Oct., daily 9–5.*

The **Bennington Museum**'s rich collections include vestiges of rural life, a percentage of which are packed into towering glass cases. The decorative arts are well represented; one room is devoted to early Bennington pottery. Two rooms cover the history of American glass and contain fine Tiffany specimens. The museum displays the largest public collection of the work of Grandma Moses (1860–1961), the popular, self-taught folk artist who lived and painted in the area. Among the 30 paintings and assorted memorabilia are her only self-portrait and the famous painted caboose window. Also here are the only surviving automobile of Bennington's Martin company, a 1925 Wasp, and the Bennington Flag, one of the oldest versions of the Stars and Stripes in existence. ⊠ *W. Main St./Rte. 9,* ☎ *802/447–1571,* WEB *www.benningtonmuseum. com.* ⊠ *$6.* ☉ *Nov.–May, daily 9–5; June–Oct., daily 9–6.*

Built in 1865 and home to two Vermont governors, the **Park-McCullough House** is a 35-room classic French Empire–style mansion furnished with period pieces. Several restored flower gardens grace the landscaped grounds, and a stable houses a collection of antique carriages. Call for details on the summer concert series, Victorian Christmas, and other special events. ⊠ *Corner of Park and West Sts., North Bennington,* ☎ *802/442–5441,* WEB *www.park/mccullough.org.* 🎫 *$6.* ⊙ *Mid-May–mid-Oct., Thurs.–Mon. 10–4; last tour at 3.*

Contemporary stone sculpture and white-frame neo-Colonial dorms surrounded by acres of cornfields punctuate the green meadows of **Bennington College**'s placid campus. The small liberal arts college, one of the most expensive to attend in the country, is noted for its progressive program in the arts. ⊠ *Rte. 67A, off U.S. 7 (look for stone entrance gate),* ☎ *800/833–6845 tour information.*

Dining and Lodging

$ ✕ **Blue Benn Diner.** Breakfast is served all day in this authentic diner, where the eats include turkey hash and breakfast burritos, with scrambled eggs, sausage, and chilies, plus pancakes of all imaginable varieties. The menu lists many vegetarian selections. Lines may be long, especially on weekends. ⊠ *U.S. 7 N,* ☎ *802/442–5140. No credit cards. Reservations not accepted. No dinner Sat.–Tues.*

$$$–$$$$ 🏠 **South Shire Inn.** Canopy beds in lushly carpeted rooms, ornate plaster moldings, and a dark mahogany fireplace in the South Shire's library re-create the grandeur of the Victorian past; fireplaces and hot tubs in some rooms add warmth. Four freshly renovated rooms in the Carriage House have whirlpool baths. The furnishings are antique except for the reproduction beds. The South Shire is in a quiet residential neighborhood within walking distance of the bus depot and downtown stores. Breakfast is served in the burgundy-and-white dining room. ⊠ *124 Elm St., 05201,* ☎ *802/447–3839,* FAX *802/442–3547,* WEB *www.southshire.com. 9 rooms. AE, MC, V. BP.*

$$ 🏠 **Molly Stark Inn.** Tidy blue-plaid wallpaper, gleaming hardwood floors, antique furnishings, and a wood-burning stove in a brick alcove of the sitting room add country charm to this 1860 Queen Anne Victorian. Molly's Room, at the back of the building, gets less noise from Route 9 and has a whirlpool bath; the attic suite is the most spacious. Three cottages have fireplaces and jacuzzis and offer more secluded accommodations. ⊠ *1067 E. Main St./Rte. 9, 05201,* ☎ *802/ 442–9631 or 800/356–3076,* FAX *802/442–5224,* WEB *www.mollystarkinn. com. 9 rooms. AE, D, MC, V. BP.*

Nightlife and the Arts

The **Bennington Center for the Arts** (⊠ Rte. 9 at Gypsy La., ☎ 802/ 442–7158), hosts a variety of cultural events, including exhibitions by local and nationally recognized artists, and of wildlife and Native American art. The **Oldcastle Theatre Co.** (☎ 802/447–0564) at the Bennington Center for the Arts, whose season runs from May through December, is one of the Northeast's finest regional theaters.

Outdoor Activities and Sports

Cutting Edge (⊠ 160 Benmont Ave., ☎ 802/442–8664) rents and repairs bicycles and also sells and rents snowboards and cross-country skis. It has one of Vermont's few skateboarding parks, open Monday through Saturday 10–6, and noon–6 on Sunday.

HIKING

Four mi east of Bennington, the **Long Trail** crosses Route 9 and runs south to the top of Harmon Hill. Allot two or three hours for this hike.

STATE PARKS

Lake Shaftsbury State Park (⌧ Rte. 7A, 10½ mi north of Bennington, ☎ 802/375–9978) is one of a few parks in Vermont with group camping. It has a swimming beach, nature trails, boat and canoe rentals, and a snack bar. **Woodford State Park** (⌧ Rte. 9, 10 mi east of Bennington, ☎ 802/447–7169) has an activities center on Adams Reservoir, campsites, a playground, boat and canoe rentals, and nature trails.

Shopping

The **Apple Barn and Country Bake Shop** (⌧ U.S. 7 S, ☎ 802/447–7780) sells home-baked goodies, fresh cider, Vermont cheeses, and maple syrup. The showroom at the **Bennington Potters Yard** (⌧ 324 County St., ☎ 802/447–7531 or 800/205–8033) stocks first-quality pottery and antiques in addition to seconds from the famed Bennington Potters. On the free tour you can follow the clay through production and hear about the Potters Yard, in business for five decades. Tours begin at 10 and 2 in spring, summer, and fall. **Hawkins House Craftsmarket** (⌧ U.S. 7/ 262 North St., ☎ 802/447–0488) showcases jewelry, woodenware, glass, pottery, rugs, and clothing from more than 450 craftspeople.

Arlington

6   *15 mi north of Bennington.*

Don't be surprised to see familiar-looking (if considerably aged) faces among the roughly 2,200 people of Arlington. The illustrator Norman Rockwell lived here from 1939 to 1953, and many of the models for his portraits of small-town life were his neighbors. First settled in 1763, Arlington was called Tory Hollow for its Loyalist sympathies— even though a number of the Green Mountain Boys lived here, too. Smaller than Bennington and more down-to-earth than upper-crust Manchester to the north, Arlington exudes a certain Rockwellian folksiness. Dorothy Canfield Fisher, a novelist popular in the 1930s and 1940s, also lived here.

There are no original paintings at the **Norman Rockwell Exhibition,** but the exhibition rooms are crammed with reproductions of the illustrator's works, arranged in every way conceivable: chronologically, by subject matter, and juxtaposed with photos of the models—several of whom work here. ⌧ *Rte. 7A/Main St.,* ☎ *802/375–6423,* WEB *www. normanrockwellexhibit.com.* ⊡ *$2.* ☉ *May–Oct., daily 9–5; Nov.–Dec. and Feb.–Apr., daily 10–4.*

Dining and Lodging

$$$$ ✕🖭 **West Mountain Inn.** A former farmhouse built in the 1840s, this
★   romantic inn has a front lawn with a spectacular view of the countryside. Its 150 acres include a llama farm. Rooms 2, 3, and 4 overlook the lawn; the three small nooks of Room 11 resemble railroad sleeper berths and are perfect for kids. The children's room, brightly painted with life-size Disney characters, is stocked with games, stuffed animals, and a TV with VCR. A low-beamed candlelit dining room ($$$) is the setting for six-course prix-fixe dinners featuring updated Continental cuisine. Aunt Min's Swedish rye and other toothsome breads, as well as desserts, are all made on the premises. Try to get a table by the window. ⌧ *River Rd., off Rte. 313, 05250,* ☎ *802/375–6516,* FAX *802/375– 6553,* WEB *www.westmountaininn.com. 18 rooms, 6 suites. Restaurant, bar, hiking, cross-country skiing, meeting room. AE, D, MC, V. MAP.*

$$–$$$$ ✕🖭 **Arlington Inn.** Greek Revival columns at the entrance to this home
★   built by a railroad magnate in 1848 lend it an imposing presence, but the atmosphere is hardly forbidding. The inn's charm is created by linens that coordinate with the Victorian-style wallpaper, claw-foot tubs in some

bathrooms, and the house's original moldings and wainscoting. The carriage house, built a century ago, contains country-French and Queen Anne furnishings. Some rooms have TVs and phones; king-size rooms have fireplaces and two-person hot tubs. The restaurant serves regional American dishes ($$$-$$$$), and polished wood floors, rose walls, and soft candlelight complement the food. The grounds have a garden, gazebo, pond, and waterfall. ⊠ *Rte. 7A, 05250, ☎ 802/375–6532 or 800/443–9442, FAX 802/375–6534,* WEB *www.arlingtoninn.com. 17 rooms, 5 suites. Restaurant, taproom. AE, D, DC, MC, V. BP.*

$$–$$$ 🔟 **Hill Farm Inn.** This homey inn on the Battenkill River has the feel of the country farmhouse it used to be. The fireplace in the informal living room, the sturdy antiques, and the spinning wheel in the upstairs hallway all convey a relaxed, friendly atmosphere. The Battenkill Suite has a beamed cathedral ceiling, and from its porch you can see Mt. Equinox. The rooms in the 1790 guest house are very private; the one- and two-bedroom cabins, open spring through fall, are charming. ⊠ *458 Hill Farm Rd., off Rte. 7A, 05250, ☎ 802/375–2269 or 800/882–2545, FAX 802/375–9918,* WEB *www.hillfarminn.com. 5 rooms (2 with kitchenettes), 6 suites, 4 cabins. D, MC, V. BP.*

Outdoor Activities and Sports

Battenkill Canoe, Ltd. (⊠ Rte. 7A, ☎ 802/362–2800 or 800/421–5268) rents canoes and offers inn-to-inn tours and day trips on the Battenkill.

Shopping

The shops at **Candle Mill Village** (⊠ Old Mill Rd., between U.S. 7 and Rte. 7A, East Arlington, ☎ 802/375–6068 or 800/772–3759) specialize in community cookbooks from around the country, music boxes, and candles. Listed on the National Register of Historic Places, the mill was built in the 1760s by Remember Baker, a cohort of Ethan Allen and one of the Green Mountain Boys. The nearby waterfall is a pleasant backdrop for a picnic.

Equinox Valley Nursery (⊠ Rte. 7A between Arlington and Manchester, ☎ 802/362–2610) is known for its perennials (more than 1,000 varieties) and materials for water gardens. The nursery has 17 greenhouses and a conservatory, sells 150 varieties of herbs, and carries many Vermont-made products in the large gift shop.

Manchester

★ ❼   *9 mi northeast of Arlington.*

Manchester, where Ira Allen proposed financing Vermont's participation in the American Revolution by confiscating Tory estates, has been a popular summer retreat since the mid-19th century. Manchester Village's tree-shaded marble sidewalks and stately old homes reflect the luxurious resort lifestyle of a century ago. Manchester Center's upscale factory outlets appeal to the affluent 20th-century ski crowd drawn by nearby Bromley and Stratton mountains. Warning: Shoppers come in droves at times, giving the place the feel of a crowded mall on the weekend before Christmas. If you're coming here from Arlington, take pretty Route 7A, which passes directly by a number of sights.

★   **Hildene,** the summer home of Abraham Lincoln's son and onetime Pullman company chairman Robert Todd Lincoln, is a beautifully preserved 412-acre estate. The 24-room mansion, with its Georgian Revival symmetry, welcoming central hallway, and grand curved staircase, is unusual in that its rooms are not roped off. When the 1,000-pipe Aeolian organ is played, the music reverberates as though from the mansion's very bones. Tours include a short film on the owner's life and a walk through the elaborate formal gardens. When snow conditions permit, you can cross-country ski on the property, which has views of nearby mountains. ⊠ *Rte. 7A,* ☎ *802/362–1788,* WEB *www.hildene.org.* 🎫 *$8.* 🕐 *Mid-May–Oct., daily 9:30–5:30, visitor center daily 9–5:30. Tours on the ½ hour (first tour at 9:30, last tour at 4. Candlelight tours Dec. 27–29, 5 PM.*

The **American Museum of Fly Fishing,** which houses the largest collection of fly-fishing equipment in the world, displays more than 1,500 rods, 800 reels, 30,000 flies, and the tackle of famous people such as Winslow Homer, Bing Crosby, and Jimmy Carter. Its library of 2,500 books is open by appointment. ⊠ *Rte. 7A at Seminary Ave.,* ☎ *802/362–3300,* WEB *www.amff.com.* 🎫 *$3.* 🕐 *Daily 10–4.*

The **Southern Vermont Arts Center** showcases rotating exhibits and its permanent collection of more than 700 pieces of 19th- and 20th-century American art in a 12,500-square-ft museum opened in July 2000. The Arts Center's original building, a graceful Georgian mansion set on 375 acres, is the frequent site of concerts, performances, and film screenings. In summer and fall, a pleasant restaurant with magnificent views opens for business. ⊠ *West Rd.,* ☎ *802/362–1405.* 🎫 *$6.* 🕐 *May–Oct., Tues.–Sat, 10–5, Sun. noon–5; Nov.–Apr., Mon.–Sat. 10–5.* WEB *www.svac.org.*

You may want to keep your eye on the temperature gauge of your car as you drive the 5-mi toll road to the top of 3,825-ft **Mt. Equinox.** Along the way you'll see the Battenkill trout stream and the surrounding Vermont countryside. Picnic tables line the drive, and there's an outstanding view down both sides of the mountain from a notch known as the Saddle. The seasonal **Inn on Mt. Equinox** (☎ 802/362–1113 or 800/868–6843) is perched on top of the mountain. ⊠ *Off Rte. 7A, south of Manchester,* ☎ *802/362–1114.* 🎫 *$6 for car and driver, $2 each additional adult.* 🕐 *May–Oct., daily 8 AM–10 PM.*

Dining and Lodging

$$$$ ✕ **Chantecleer.** Intimate dining rooms have been created in a former dairy barn that has a large fieldstone fireplace. The menu reflects the chef's Swiss background: The appetizers include *Bündnerfleisch* (air-dried Swiss beef) and frogs' legs in garlic butter; among the entrées are rack of lamb, whole Dover sole filleted table-side, and veal chops. The restaurant is 5 mi north of Manchester. ⊠ *Rte. 7A, East Dorset,* ☎ *802/362–1616. Reservations essential. AE, DC, MC, V. Closed Tues. in summer, Mon. and Tues. in winter, and mid–Oct. to mid–Nov. and mid–Apr. to mid–May; No lunch.*

$$–$$$ ✕ **Bistro Henry's.** This airy restaurant on the outskirts of town attracts a devoted clientele for authentic Mediterranean fare. The menu changes often; recent highlights include merlot-braised lamb shank with balsamic-glazed onions and garlic mashed potatoes; eggplant, mushroom, and fontina terrine Provençal; and crispy sweetbreads in Armagnac cream. The wine list is extensive. ⊠ *Rte. 11/30,* ☎ *802/362–4982. AE, DC, MC, V. Closed Mon. No lunch.*

$$$$ ✕🏠 **Barrows House.** This 200-year-old Federal-style inn and mini-re-
★ sort is a favorite with those who wish to escape the bustle of Manchester (Bromley is about 8 mi away). The rooms afford great privacy; some have gas or woodburning fireplaces, and the newly refurbished Bird's Nest Suite has a fireplace and hot tub. Dinner—served in the spacious main dining room, the greenhouse room, and the tavern—includes perennial favorites such as rack of lamb and filet mignon as well as nightly specials, which might include Maine crab cakes and native grilled trout. ⊠ *Box 98, Rte. 30, Dorset, 05251,* ☎ *802/867–4455 or 800/639–1620,* FAX *802/867–0132,* WEB *www.barrowshouse.com. 18 rooms, 10 suites. Restaurant, pool, sauna, 2 tennis courts, bicycles, cross-country skiing. AE, D, DC, MC, V. BP, MAP.*

$$$$ ✕🏨 **The Equinox.** Even before Abe Lincoln's family began summering here, this grand white-column resort was a local fixture. The spacious, sunny rooms are furnished with reproductions of antiques. In the Marsh Tavern, richly upholstered settees, stuffed armchairs, and several fireplaces create a plush traditional ambience. There are 136 rooms (including five Presidential Suites) in the main hotel; nine one- and two-bedroom suites in the Orvis Inn next door; and 27 rooms in the Town House. The three restaurants include the elegant Colonnade, where men are requested to wear jackets, and a seasonal grill at the golf course. The woodland supper of roast duck, venison sausage, and wild mushrooms is popular, and the Sunday brunch is spectacular. ⊠ *3567 Main St., Rte. 7A, Manchester Village 05254,* ☎ *802/362–4700 or 800/362–4747,* 🖷 *802/362–1595,* 🅆🄴🄱 *www.equinoxresort.com. 3 restaurants, bar, 1 indoor and 1 outdoor pool, sauna, steam room, 18-hole golf course, 3 tennis courts, croquet, health club, horseback riding, fishing, mountain bikes, ice-skating, cross-country skiing, snowmobiling. AE, D, DC, MC, V. MAP, AP.*

$$$$ 🏨 **Inn at Ormsby Hill.** During the Revolutionary War, this 1774 Federal-
★   style building provided refuge from the British for Ethan Allen, and it later served the same purpose for slaves heading north on the Underground Railroad. When renovating, the owners created interesting public spaces and romantic bedrooms. Furnished with antiques and canopied or four-poster beds, the rooms have fireplaces that can be viewed from the bed or the two-person whirlpool tub. Some have mountain views. Breakfasts in the conservatory—entrées may include baked, stuffed French toast with an apricot brandy sauce—are sumptuous. ⊠ *1842 Main St./Rte. 7A, 05255,* ☎ *802/362–1163 or 800/670–2841,* 🖷 *802/362–5176,* 🅆🄴🄱 *www.ormsbyhill.com. 10 rooms. D, MC, V. BP.*

$$$$ 🏨 **Wilburton Inn.** The Great Gatsby would have felt right at home at this turn-of-the-century Tudor mansion perched on a hill off the main road overlooking the Battenkill Valley. The common rooms, paneled in dark hardwoods, are elegant yet informal, and are decorated with part of the owners' vast art collection. Outdoor sculptures dot the spacious grounds. There are bedrooms and suites in the main house, and 25 rooms in outlying cottages. A buffet breakfast is served in the windowed Terrace Room, and dinner is served in the handsome Billiard Room. One note: Weddings take place here most summer weekends. ⊠ *River Rd., 05254,* ☎ *802/362–2500 or 800/648–4944,* 🖷 *802/362–1107,* 🅆🄴🄱 *www.wilburton.com. 31 rooms, 4 suites. Restaurant, pool, 3 tennis courts. AE, MC, V. BP.*

$$–$$$$ 🏨 **1811 House.** At this mansion once owned by President Lincoln's grand-
★   daughter, the atmosphere of an English country home can be experienced without crossing the Atlantic. The pub-style bar is decorated with horse brasses, Waterford crystal is used in the dining room, and three acres of lawn are landscaped in the English floral style. Rooms contain period antiques; six have fireplaces, and many have four-poster beds. Bathrooms are old-fashioned but serviceable. ⊠ *Box 39, Rte. 7A, 05254,* ☎ *802/ 362–1811 or 800/432–1811,* 🖷 *802/362–2443,* 🅆🄴🄱 *www.1811house. com. 14 rooms. Dining Room, bar. AE, D, MC, V. BP.*

$–$$ 🏨 **Aspen Motel.** A rare find in this area, the immaculate, family-owned Aspen is set well back from the highway and is moderately priced. The spacious, tastefully decorated rooms have Colonial-style furnishings, and all have cable TV, phones, and in-room coffeemakers; some have refrigerators. The social room has a fireplace. ⊠ *Rte. 7A N, 05255,* ☎ *802/362–2450,* 🖷 *802/362–1348,* 🅆🄴🄱 *www.thisisvermont.com/ aspen. 24 rooms, 1 cottage. Pool, playground. AE, D, MC, V.*

Nightlife and the Arts

The two pre-Revolutionary War barns of the **Dorset Playhouse** (⊠ off town green, Dorset, ☎ 802/867–5777) host a community group in winter and a resident professional troupe in summer. The **Marsh Tavern** (☎ 802/362–4700) at the Equinox has cabaret music and jazz from Wednesday to Sunday in summer and on weekends in winter. **Mulligan's** (✉ Rte. 7A, ☎ 802/362–3663) is a popular hangout in Manchester Village, especially for the après-ski set.

Outdoor Activities and Sports

BIKING

The 20-mi Dorset-Manchester trail runs from Manchester Village north on West Street to Route 30, turns west at the Dorset village green onto West Road, and heads back south to Manchester. **Battenkill Sports** (✉ Exit 4 off U.S. 7, at Rte. 11/30, ☎ 802/362–2734 or 800/340–2734) rents and repairs bikes and provides maps and route suggestions.

FISHING

Battenkill Anglers (☎ 802/362–3184) teaches the art and science of fly fishing in both private and group lessons. The **Orvis Co.** (✉ Rte. 7A, Manchester Center, ☎ 800/235–9763) hosts a nationally known fly-fishing school on the Battenkill, the state's most famous trout stream, with 2½-day courses given weekly between April and October.

HIKING

One of the most popular segments of Vermont's **Long Trail** starts at Route 11/30 west of Peru Notch and goes to the top of Bromley Mountain. The round-trip trek takes about four hours.

The **Mountain Goat** (✉ Rte. 7A south of Rte. 11/30, ☎ 802/362–5159) sells hiking, backpacking, and climbing equipment and rents snowshoes and cross-country and telemark skis. The shop also conducts rock- and ice-climbing clinics.

STATE PARK

Emerald Lake State Park (✉ U.S. 7, North Dorset, ☎ 802/362–1655), 9 mi north of Manchester, has campsites, a marked nature trail, an on-site naturalist, boat and canoe rentals, and a snack bar.

Shopping

ART AND ANTIQUES

Carriage Trade (✉ Rte. 7A north of Manchester Center, ☎ 802/362–1125) contains room after room of Early American antiques and has a fine collection of ceramics. **Danby Antiques Center** (✉ ⅛ mi off U.S. 7, Danby, ☎ 802/293–5990), 13 mi north of Manchester, has 11 rooms and a barn filled with furniture and accessories, folk art, textiles, and stoneware. Vermont-based artists have shown their oils, watercolors, and sculptures at **Gallery North Star** (✉ Rte. 7A, ☎ 802/362–4541) for more than 25 years. The **Peel Gallery of Fine Art** (✉ Peel Gallery Rd., Danby, ☎ 802/293–5230), which has celebrated its third decade in business, represents 40 professional American artists. **Tilting at Windmills Gallery** (✉ Rte. 11/30, ☎ 802/362–3022) exhibits the works of well-known artists such as Douglas Flackman of the Hudson River School.

BOOKS

Northshire Bookstore (✉ Main St., ☎ 802/362–2200 or 800/437–3700), a community bookstore for more than 20 years, carries many travel and children's books and sponsors readings year-round.

CLOTHING AND SPECIALTY ITEMS

Alfred Baier (✉ Butternut La., ☎ 802/362–3371) makes and sells pipes in his studio-workshop.

Orvis Sporting Gifts (✉ Union St., ☎ 802/362–6455), a discount outlet that carries discontinued items from the popular outdoor clothing and home furnishings mail-order company, is housed in what was Orvis's shop in the 1800s.

Anne Klein, Liz Claiborne, Donna Karan, Levi Strauss, Giorgio Armani, and Jones New York are among the shops on Route 11/30 and U.S. 7 South—a center for **designer outlet stores.**

FISHING GEAR

Orvis Retail Store (⊠ Rte. 7A, ☎ 802/362–3750), an outdoor specialty store that is one of the largest suppliers of fishing gear in the Northeast, also carries clothing, gifts, and hunting supplies.

MALLS AND MARKETPLACES

Manchester Designer Outlets (⊠ U.S. 7 and Rte. 11/30, ☎ 802/362–3736 or 800/955–7467) has such big-city names as Joan & David, Baccarat, Coach, Ralph Lauren, and Cole-Haan. At **Manchester Square** (⊠ Rte. 11/30 and Richville Rd.) you'll find outlet stores for Giorgio Armani, Yves Delorme/Palais Royal, Vermont Toy Chest, Brooks Brothers, Levi Strauss, Escada, and more.

Ski Areas

BROMLEY MOUNTAIN

The first trails at Bromley were cut in 1936. The area has a comfortable red-clapboard base lodge, built when the ski area first opened; it was later expanded. Many families appreciate the resort's convivial atmosphere. There's a large ski shop and a condominium village adjacent to the slopes. A reduced-price, two-day lift pass is available, as is a snowboard park-only lift ticket. Kids 6 and under ski free when accompanied by an adult. Eighty-four percent of the area is covered by snowmaking. ⊠ *Box 1130, Rte. 11, Manchester Center 05255,* ☎ *802/824–5522 information and snow conditions; 800/865–4786 lodging,* WEB *www.bromley.com.*

Downhill. Most ski areas are laid out to face the north or east, but Bromley faces south, making it one of the warmer spots to ski in New England. Its 43 trails are equally divided into beginner, intermediate, and advanced terrain; the last is serviced by the Blue Ribbon quad chairlift on the east side. The vertical drop is 1,334 ft. Four double chairlifts, two quad lifts, a J-bar, and two surface lifts for beginners provide transportation. The high-speed quad lift takes skiers from the base to the summit in just six minutes.

Child care. Bromley is one of the region's best places to bring children. Besides a nursery for children from ages 6 weeks to 4 years, ski instruction is provided for children ages 3 to 12.

Summer activities. The area becomes a veritable playground in summer. At the DevalKart and the Alpine Slide, passengers ride up on a chairlift and come down on wheeled sleds (or ride back down on the chair). There's also Parabounce, a helium-filled, parachute-harnessed tethered balloon, a climbing wall, kiddie bumper cars, and a huge trampoline.

CROSS-COUNTRY

With 21 km (16 mi) of marked trails, the **Meadowbrook Inn** (⊠ Rte. 11, Landgrove, ☎ 802/824–6444 or 800/498–6445) offers an idyllic setting for cross-country skiing and snowshoeing. The inn, which has eight guest rooms and a restaurant, has rental gear and provides lessons.

Stratton

❽ *18 mi southeast of Manchester.*

Stratton, home to the famous Stratton Mountain Resort, has a self-contained town center with shops, restaurants, and lodgings clustered at the base of the slopes. There's plenty of activity year-round between skiing and summer sports.

Lodging

$$–$$$$ 🏨 **Stratton Mountain Inn and Village Lodge.** The complex includes a 120-room inn—the largest on the mountain—and a 91-room lodge of studio units equipped with microwaves, refrigerators, and small wet bars. The lodge is the only slopeside ski-in, ski-out hotel at Stratton. The inn is within walking distance of the lifts. Ski packages that include lift tickets bring down room rates. ✉ *Middle Ridge Rd., 05155,* 🕿 *802/297–2500; 800/777–1700 lodgings,* FAX *802/297–1778,* WEB *www.strattonmountain.com. 120 rooms, 91 studios. Restaurant, lounge, pool, hot tub, sauna, golf course, 4 tennis courts, cross-country and downhill skiing. AE, D, DC, MC, V.*

Nightlife and the Arts

Popular **Mulligan's** (✉ Mountain Rd., 🕿 802/297–9293) serves American cuisine. Bands or DJs provide entertainment in the late afternoon and on weekends. The **Red Fox Inn** (✉ Winhall Hollow Rd., Bondville, 🕿 802/297–2488) hosts musicians in the tavern on weekends.

Ski Areas

STRATTON MOUNTAIN

Since its creation in 1961, Stratton has undergone physical transformations and upgrades, yet the area's sophisticated character has been retained. It has been the special province of well-to-do families and, more recently, young professionals from the New York–southern Connecticut corridor. Since the mid-'80s, an entire village, with a covered parking structure for 700 cars, has arisen at the base of the mountain. Adjacent to the base lodge are a condo-hotel, restaurants, and about 25 shops lining a pedestrian mall. Stratton is 4 mi up its own access road off Route 30 in Bondville, about 30 minutes from Manchester's popular shopping zone. ✉ *Box 145, R.R. 1, Stratton Mountain 05155,* 🕿 *802/297–2200; 800/843–6867; 802/297–4211 snow conditions; 800/787–2886 lodging,* WEB *www.stratton.com.*

Downhill. Stratton's skiing is in three sectors. The first is the lower mountain directly in front of the base lodge-village-condo complex; several lifts reach mid-mountain from this entry point, and practically all skiing is beginner or low-intermediate. Above that, the upper mountain, with a vertical drop of 2,000 ft, has a high-speed, 12-passenger gondola, Starship XII. Down the face are the expert trails, and on either side are intermediate cruising runs with a smattering of wide beginner slopes. The third sector, the Sun Bowl, is off to one side with two quad chairlifts and two expert trails, a full base lodge, and plenty of intermediate terrain. Stratton hosts the U.S. Open Snowboarding championships; its snowboard park has a 380-ft halfpipe. A Ski Learning Park has its own Park Packages for novice skiers. In all, Stratton has 11 lifts that service 90 trails and 90 acres of glades.

Cross-country. The resort has more than 30 km (18 mi) of cross-country skiing and two Nordic centers: Sun Bowl and Country Club.

Child care. The day-care center takes children from ages 6 weeks to 5 years for indoor activities and outdoor excursions. There is a ski school for children ages 4 to 12. A junior racing program and special instruction groups are geared toward more experienced young skiers.

Summer and year-round activities. Stratton has 15 outdoor tennis courts, 27 holes of golf, horseback riding, mountain biking and hiking accessed by a gondola to the summit, and instructional programs in tennis and golf. The sports center, open year-round, contains two

indoor tennis courts, three racquetball courts, a 25-meter indoor swimming pool, a hot tub, a steam room, a fitness facility with Nautilus
equipment, and a restaurant. Stratton also hosts summer entertainment
and family activities, including a skating park and climbing wall.

Weston

9 *20 mi northeast of Manchester.*

Although perhaps best known for the Vermont Country Store, Weston
is famed as one of the first Vermont towns to have discovered its own
intrinsic loveliness—and marketability. With its summer theater, pretty
town green, and Victorian bandstand, as well as an assortment of
shops offering variety without modern sprawl, the little village really
lives up to its vaunted image.

The **Mill Museum,** down the road from the Vermont Country Store,
has numerous hands-on displays depicting the engineering and mechanics
of one of the town's mills. The many old tools on view kept towns like
Weston running smoothly in their early days. ⊠ *Rte. 100,* ☎ *802/824–
3119.* ✍ *Donations accepted.* ☼ *July–Aug., Wed.–Sun. 1–4; Sept.–mid-
Oct., Sat. and Sun. 1-4.*

Dining and Lodging

$$$$ ✕⊞ **Inn at Weston.** Country elegance best describes this 1848 village
inn. Plush linens, Ralph Lauren comforters, fresh flowers, and chocolate truffles await in its luxurious rooms and suites. All rooms have
phones and private baths; many have whirlpool tubs, TVs, fireplaces,
and CD players. The restaurant serves contemporary regional cuisine
including herb-crusted lambchops and smoked trout in a candlelit setting. Vermont cheddar cheese and Granny Smith apple omelettes are
popular at breakfast. ⊠ *Rte. 100, Box 179, 05161,* ☎ *802/824–6789,*
FAX *802/824–3073,* WEB *www.innweston.com. 13 rooms. Restaurant, pub.
AE, MC, V. BP.*

$–$$ ⊞ **Colonial House Inn & Motel.** You'll find warmth and charm at this
family-friendly complex just two miles south of the village. Relax on
comfortable furniture in the large living room or enjoy the sun in the
solarium. Homey, country furnishings adorn both the inn rooms and
the motel units. The complimentary breakfast features fresh goodies
from the on-site bakery; there's a family-style dinner on Friday and Saturday nights. ⊠ *287 Rte. 100, 05161,* ☎ *802/824–6286 or 800/639-
5033,* FAX *802/824-3934,* WEB *www.cohoinn.com. 9 motel units; 6 inn
rooms, shared bath. Game room. D, MC, V. BP.*

Nightlife and the Arts

The members of the **Weston Playhouse** (⊠ Village Green, off Rte. 100,
☎ 802/824–5288), the oldest professional theater in Vermont, have
produced Broadway plays, musicals, and other works since 1937.
Their season runs from late June to early September.

The **Kinhaven Music School** (⊠ Lawrence Hill Rd., ☎ 802/824–3365)
stages free student concerts on Fridays at 4 PM and Sundays at 2:30 in
July and August.

Shopping

The **Vermont Country Store** (⊠ Rte. 100, ☎ 802/824–3184, WEB www.
vtcountrystore.com; closed Sun.) sets aside one room of its old-fashioned emporium for Vermont Common Crackers and bins of fudge and
other candy. For years the retail store and its mail-order catalog have
carried nearly forgotten items such as Lilac Vegetal aftershave, Monkey Brand black tooth powder, Flexible Flyer sleds, and tiny wax bottles of colored syrup, but have also sold plenty of practical items such

as sturdy outdoor clothing and even a manual typewriter. Nostalgia-evoking implements dangle from the store's walls and ceiling. (There's another store on Route 103 in Rockingham.)

Drury House Antiques (⊠ On the Village Green, ☎ 802/824–4395) specializes in antique clocks, fly rods, and fishing-related objects. The **Todd Gallery** (⊠ 614 Main St., ☎ 802/824–5606) exhibits paintings, prints, and sculptures by Vermont artists and craftspeople.

Ludlow

⑩ *9 mi northeast of Weston.*

Up until just a few years ago, Ludlow was a nondescript factory town that just happened to have a major ski area—Okemo—on its outskirts. Today the old General Electric plant is gone, its premises recycled into a rambling, block-long complex of shops and restaurants, and the town seems much more integrated into the ski scene. A beautiful, often-photographed historic church overlooks the town green.

Dining and Lodging

$–$$$ ✕ **Pot Belly Pub.** Après-ski fun seekers pile into this popular restaurant/nightspot for house specialties such as Belly burgers, smoked ribs, steaks, applejack pork, and fresh seafood. Live entertainment—from jazz and rhythm-and-blues to swing—keeps patrons warm on winter weekends. ⊠ *130 Main St.,* ☎ *802/228–8989.*

$$$–$$$$ ✕🏠 **Governor's Inn.** This 19th-century Victorian country home on the village green is a welcome retreat for those looking for gracious accommodations and creative, contemporary fare. The second- and third-floor guest rooms are decorated with antique furnishings; the third-floor rooms, including the suite, have gas-lit fire stoves. Chef/co-owner Kathy Kubec prepares prix-fixe ($45), six-course dinners Thursday through Sunday (reservations essential). An elegant breakfast is served at individual tables for two. ⊠ *86 Main St., 05149,* ☎ *802/228–8830 or 800/468–3766, ℻ 802/228–2961, WEB www.thegovernorsinn.com. 9 rooms. AE, D, MC, V. BP.*

$$$–$$$$ 🏠 **Andrie Rose Inn.** Many of the handsomely furnished, antiques-filled rooms at this lovely 1829 inn on a quiet in-town street have whirlpool tubs and views of the mountains. The inn has five buildings in all; two-person luxury suites have whirlpool tubs, fireplaces, and steam showers for two. Full-floor condo suites in the 1883 Victorian Town House sleep up to 12, and two family suites have fireplaces and kitchens. The living room, complete with fireplace, is a grand spot to enjoy a cocktail after hiking or skiing. Candlelight breakfast is served to guests staying in standard rooms; a breakfast basket is delivered to the luxury suites. A 4-course dinner with a seasonal menu is prepared Friday and Saturday evenings by award-winning chef Irene B. Maston. ⊠ *13 Pleasant St., 05149,* ☎ *802/223–4846 or 800/223-4846, ℻ 802/228–7910, WEB www.andrieroseinn.com. 9 rooms, 14 suites. Restaurant, bar, bicycles. AE, MC, V. BP.*

$$$–$$$$ 🏠 **Okemo Mountain Lodge.** The one-bedroom condominiums clustered around the base of Okemo's ski lifts come with kitchens, fireplaces, and decks. The restaurant is open for breakfast and lunch only. The Okemo Mountain Lodging Service also rents units in the Kettle Brook, Winterplace, and Solitude slopeside condominiums. Ski-and-stay packages are available for three or more non-holiday nights. ⊠ *77 Okemo Ridge Rd., off Rte. 103, 05149,* ☎ *802/228–5571, 802/228–4041, or 800/786–5366, ℻ 802/228–2079. 55 unit. Restaurant, bar, in-room VCRs, cross-country and downhill skiing. AE, MC, V. WEB www.okemo.com.*

Outdoor Activities and Sports

Cavendish Trail Horse Rides (⊠ 20 Mile Stream Rd., Proctorsville, ☎ 802/226–7821) operates horse-drawn sleigh rides in snowy weather, wagon rides at other times, and guided trail rides from mid-May to mid-October.

Ski Areas

OKEMO MOUNTAIN RESORT

An ideal ski area for families with children, family-owned Okemo has evolved into a major resort. The main attraction is a long, broad, gentle slope with two beginner lifts just above the base lodge. All the facilities at the bottom of the mountain are close together, so family members can regroup easily during the ski day. The Solitude Village Area has a triple chairlift, two new trails, and lodging. The resort offers numerous ski and snowboarding packages. ⊠ *77 Okemo Ridge Rd. (Rte. 100),* ☎ *802/228–4041; 800/786–5366 lodging; 802/228–5222 snow conditions,* WEB *www.okemo.com.*

Downhill. Above the broad beginner's slope at the base, the upper part of Okemo has a varied network of trails: long, winding, easy trails for beginners; straight fall-line runs for experts; and curving, cruising slopes for intermediates. The 98 trails are served by an efficient lift system of 14 lifts, including seven quads, three triple chairlifts, and four surface lifts; 95% are covered by snowmaking. From the summit to the base lodge, the vertical drop is 2,150 ft, the highest in southern Vermont. Okemo has a self-contained snowboarding area serviced by a surface lift; the mile-long park is home to the Pipe, a massive 420-ft by 40-ft halfpipe, and a new superpipe. There's also a snowboard park for beginners.

Cross-country/Snowshoeing. The Okemo Valley Nordic Center (⊠ Fox La., ☎ 802/228–1396) has 26 km (16 mi) of groomed trails and rents equipment.

Child care. The area's nursery, for children from ages 6 weeks to 8 years, has many indoor activities and supervised outings. Children ages 3 to 4 can get a one-hour introduction to skiing; the SnowStar program is for kids ages 4–7. Nursery reservations are essential. Okemo also offers a Kids' Night Out evening child-care program on Saturdays during the regular season and certain holiday weeks.

Summer activities. The Okemo Valley Golf Club has a new 18-hole, par-71, 6,000-yard course. Seven target greens, a putting green, a golf academy, and an indoor putting green, swing stations, and a simulator provide plenty of ways to improve your game.

Chester

⑪ *11 mi east of Weston.*

Gingerbread Victorians frame Chester's town green. The local pharmacy on Main Street has been in continuous operation since the 1860s. The **stone village** on North Street on the outskirts of town, two rows of buildings constructed from quarried stone, was built by two brothers and is said to have been used during the Civil War as a station on the Underground Railroad.

In Chester's restored 1852 train station you can board the ***Green Mountain Flyer*** for a 26-mi, two-hour round-trip journey to Bellows Falls, on the Connecticut River at the eastern edge of the state. The cars that date from the golden age of railroading travel past covered bridges and along the Brockway Mills gorge. The fall foliage trips are spectacular. ⊠ *Rte. 103,* ☎ *802/463–3069 or 800/707–3530,* WEB *www.rails-vt.com.* ⊠ *$11 in summer; $12 in fall.* ☉ *Late June–early Sept., Tues.–Sun.; mid-Sept.–late-Oct., daily. Train departs several times daily, call for schedule.*

Dining and Lodging

$ ✕ **Raspberries and Thyme.** Breakfast specials, homemade soups, a large selection of salads, homemade desserts, and a menu listing more than 40 sandwiches make this one of the area's most popular spots for casual dining. ⊠ *On the Green,* ☎ *802/875–4486. AE, D, MC, V. No dinner Tues.*

$$ ⊟ **Fullerton Inn.** Guest rooms with country quilts and lace curtains vary in size and amenities at this three-story, wooden 19th-century building with a big porch. Some favorites are the bright corner rooms and numbers 8 and 10, which share a private porch. The restaurant serves breakfast daily and dinner every night except Wednesday, offering morning delicacies such as lobster omelets and nightly entrées like roast duck and trout Provençal. There's live entertainment in the lounge Saturday night. A shuttle bus to local attractions and ski areas stops in front of the inn. ⊠ *40 Common St., on the Green, 05143,* ☎ *802/875–2444,* FAX *802/875–6414,* WEB *www.fullertoninn.com. 21 rooms, 3 suites. Restaurant, lounge. AE, D, MC, V. CP.*

Outdoor Activities and Sports

A 26-mi **driving or biking loop** out of Chester follows the Williams River along Route 103 to Pleasant Valley Road north of Bellows Falls. At Saxtons River, turn west onto Route 121 and follow along the river to connect with Route 35. When the two routes separate, follow Route 35 north back to Chester.

Shopping

The **National Survey Charthouse** (⊠ Main St., ☎ 802/875–2121) is a map-lover's paradise. The store is good for a rainy-day browse even if maps aren't your passion.

Grafton

★ ⓬ *8 mi south of Chester.*

Like many Vermont villages its size, Grafton enjoyed its heyday as an agricultural community well before the Civil War, when its citizens grazed some 10,000 sheep and spun their wool into sturdy yarn for locally woven fabric. Unlike most other out-of-the-way country towns, though, Grafton was born again, following a long decline, by preservationists determined to revitalize not only its centerpiece, the Old Tavern, but many other commercial and residential structures in the village center. Beginning in 1963, the Windham Foundation—Vermont's second-largest private foundation—commenced the rehabilitation of Grafton. The **Historical Society** documents the town's renewal. ⊠ *Townshend Rd.,* ☎ *802/843–2584 visitor center information.* ⊠ *$1.* ☉ *June–late Sept., weekends 1:30–4; late Sept.–Oct., daily 1:30–4.*

Dining and Lodging

$$$$ ✕⊟ **Old Tavern at Grafton.** White-column porches on both stories wrap around the main building of this commanding inn, which dates from 1801. The main building has 12 rooms; the rest are dispersed among other buildings in town. Two dining rooms ($$$), one with formal Georgian furniture and oil portraits, the other with rustic paneling and low beams, serve inspired New England fare such as grilled choice sirloin steeped in McNeil's stout and a blend of spices. Cross-country skiing is at the Grafton Ponds Cross-Country Ski Center, run by the inn. ⊠ *Rte. 121, 05146,* ☎ *802/843–2231 or 800/843–1801,* FAX *802/843–2245,* WEB *www.old-tavern.com. 58 rooms, 7 suites. Restaurant, bar,*

pond, tennis court, paddle tennis, mountain bikes, ice-skating, cross-country skiing, recreation room. AE, MC, V. Closed Apr. BP.

Shopping
Gallery North Star (⊠ Townshend Rd., ☎ 802/843–2465) exhibits the oils, watercolors, lithographs, and sculptures of Vermont-based artists.

Townshend

🔞 *9 miles south of Grafton.*

One of a string of pretty villages along the banks of the West River, Townshend embodies the Vermont ideal of a lovely town green presided over by a gracefully proportioned church spire. The spire belongs to the 1790 Congregational Meeting House, one of the state's oldest houses of worship. Just north on Route 30 is the Scott Bridge (closed to traffic), the state's longest single-span covered bridge.

At **Townshend State Park,** you'll find a sandy beach and a trailhead for the rigorous, 2.7-mi hike to the top of Bald Mountain. Campsites are available. ⊠ *Rte. 30 N,* ☎ *802/365-7500.*

Dining and Lodging
$–$$ ✕ **Townshend Dam Diner.** Folks come from miles around to enjoy traditional fare such as Mom's meatloaf, chili, and roast beef croquettes, as well as Townshend-raised bison burgers, and creative daily specials. Breakfast, served all day everyday, includes such tasty treats as raspberry chocolate-chip walnut pancakes and homemade French toast. ⊠ *Rte. 30,* ☎ *802/874–4107. No credit cards.*

$$$$ ✕🏨 **Windham Hill Inn.** The 1825 brick farmhouse and white barn annex house the elegant accommodations that comprise this country inn. Period antiques, Oriental carpets, and locally made furniture adorn the interior. Some rooms have fireplaces, private porches and jacuzzis; all have magnificent views of the West River valley. The Music Room has an 1888 restored Steinway piano and more than 800 CDs. A four-course candlelight dinner is served in the Frog Pond Dining Room. The seasonal menu might include marinated shiitake mushrooms and ham *en croustade* with Dijon sherry sauce. ⊠ *311 Lawrence Drive, West Townshend 05359,* ☎ *800/944–4080,*[FAX] *802/874–4702,* [WEB] *www.windhamhill.com. 21 rooms. Restaurant, pool, tennis court, hiking, cross-country skiing. MAP.*

$–$$ 🏨 **Boardman House.** This handsome Greek Revival home on the town green combines modern comfort with the relaxed charm of a 19th-century farmhouse. The uncluttered guest rooms are furnished with Shaker-style furniture, colorful duvets, and paintings. Both the breakfast room and front hall have *trompe l'oeil* floors. ⊠ *On the Green, 05353,* ☎ *802/ 365–4086,* [WEB] *www.southvermont.com/townshend/boardmanhouse, 5 rooms, 1 suite. Breakfast room, sauna. No credit cards. BP.*

Outdoor Activities and Sports
You can rent canoes, kayaks, tubes, cross-country skis, and snowshoes at **Townshend Outdoors** (⊠ Rte. 30, ☎ 802/365–7309).

Shopping
Mary Meyer Stuffed Toys Factory Store, the state's oldest stuffed toy company, offers discounts of up to 70%. (⊠ Rte. 30, ☎ 802/365–7993).

Newfane

🔞 *15 mi south of Grafton.*

With a village green surrounded by pristine white buildings, Newfane is sometimes described as the quintessential New England small town. The 1839 First Congregational Church and the Windham County

Court House, with 17 green-shuttered windows and a rounded cupola, are often open. The building with the four-pointed spire is Union Hall, built in 1832.

Dining and Lodging

$$$–$$$$ ✕⊞ **Four Columns.** The majestic white columns of this Greek Revival mansion, built in 1834 for a homesick southern bride, are more intimidating than the Colonial-style rooms inside. Rooms are decorated with a mix of antiques and turn-of-the-century reproductions. Most of the suites have cathedral ceilings; all have double whirlpool baths and gas fireplaces. The two newly remodeled suites on the third floor in the old section afford the most privacy. In the elegant restaurant ($$$; closed Tuesdays and part of April), chef Greg Parks prepares New American dishes; a favorite is roasted young chicken with herbs served in a chardonnay and mushroom sauce. The expanded Continental breakfast overflows with yogurts, cheeses, homemade breads, and the house special oatmeal. ✉ *Box 278, West St., 05345,* ☎ *802/365–7713 or 800/787–6633,* FAX *802/365–0022,* WEB *www.fourcolumnsinn.com. 9 rooms, 6 suites. Restaurant, pool, hiking. AE, D, DC, MC, V. CP.*

Shopping

The **Newfane Country Store** (✉ Rte. 30, ☎ 802/365–7916) carries many quilts (which can also be custom ordered), homemade fudge, and other Vermont foods, gifts, and crafts. Collectibles dealers from across the state sell their wares at the **Newfane Flea Market** (✉ Rte. 30, ☎ 802/365–7771), held every weekend during summer and fall. Corn-cob-smoked ham and bacon and Vermont cheeses are just a few of the delectable goodies at **Lawrence's Smoke House** (✉ Rte. 30, ☎ 802/ 365–7751).

Putney

⑮ *7 mi east of Newfane, 9 mi north of Brattleboro.*

Putney, a Connecticut River valley town just upriver from Brattleboro, was a prime destination for many of the converts to alternative rural lifestyles who swarmed into Vermont during the late 1960s and early '70s. Those who remain maintain a tradition of progressive schools, artisanship, and organic farming.

♻ **Harlow's Sugar House** (✉ U.S. 5, ☎ 802/387–5852), 2 mi north of Putney, has a working cider mill and sugar house, as well as berry picking in summer and apple picking in autumn. You can buy cider, maple syrup, and other items in the gift shop.

Tours are given of the **Green Mountain Spinnery,** a factory-shop that sells yarn, knitting accessories, and patterns. ✉ *Depot Rd. at Exit 4 off I-91,* ☎ *802/387–4528 or 800/321–9665.* 🎟 *Tours $2.* ☉ *Tours at 1:30 on the 1st and 3rd Tues. of each month.*

Dining and Lodging

$$–$$$ ✕⊞ **Putney Inn.** The inn's main building dates from the 1790s and was later part of a seminary—the present-day pub was the chapel. Two fireplaces dominate the lobby. The spacious, modern rooms in an adjacent building have Queen Anne mahogany reproductions and are 100 yards from the banks of the Connecticut River. Regionally inspired cuisine—seafood, New England potpies, a wild-game mixed grill, and burgers with Vermont cheddar—is marked by innovative flourishes. Locally raised meat is butchered on the premises. ✉ *Depot Rd., 05346,* ☎ *802/ 387–5517 or 800/653–5517,* FAX *802/387–5211,* WEB *www.putneyinn. com. 25 rooms. Restaurant, lounge. AE, D, MC, V. BP.*

$$$ ☷ **Hickory Ridge House Bed and Breakfast.** This gracious 1808 Federal mansion, listed on the National Register of Historic Places, has Palladian windows, a parlor with a Rumford fireplace, and large, comfortable guest rooms filled with antiques and country furnishings. Four rooms have wood-burning fireplaces, and one has a gas fireplace stove. A two-bedroom cottage, with a full kitchen and fireplace, can be rented as a unit, or the rooms can be rented separately. ⊠ *53 Hickory Ridge Rd., 05346,* ☎ *802/387–5709 or 800/380–9218,* FAX *802/387–4328,* WEB *www.hickoryridgehouse.com. 6 rooms, 1 cottage. Hiking, cross-country skiing. AE, MC, V. BP.*

Shopping

Allen Bros. (⊠ U.S. 5 north of Putney, ☎ 802/722–3395) bakes apple pies, makes cider doughnuts, and sells Vermont foods and products.

Southern Vermont A to Z

To research prices, get advice from other travelers, and book travel arrangements, visit ww.fodors.com.

BUS TRAVEL

Vermont Transit links Bennington, Manchester, and Brattleboro.
➤ BUS INFORMATION: **Vermont Transit** (☎ 800/552–8737).

CAR TRAVEL

In the south the principal east–west highway is Route 9, the Molly Stark Trail, from Brattleboro to Bennington. The most important north–south roads are U.S. 7; the more scenic Route 7A; Route 100, which runs through the state's center; I–91; and U.S. 5, which runs along the state's eastern border. Route 30 from Brattleboro to Manchester is a scenic drive.

EMERGENCIES

➤ HOSPITALS: **Brattleboro Memorial Hospital** (⊠ 9 Belmont Ave., Brattleboro, ☎ 802/257–0341). **Southwestern Vermont Medical Center** (⊠ 100 Hospital Dr., Bennington, ☎ 802/442–6361).

VISITOR INFORMATION

➤ CONTACTS: **Bennington Area Chamber of Commerce** (⊠ Veterans Memorial Dr., Bennington 05201, ☎ 802/447–3311, WEB www.bennington.com). **Brattleboro Area Chamber of Commerce** (⊠ 180 Main St., Brattleboro 05301, ☎ 802/254–4565, WEB www.brattleboro.com). **Chamber of Commerce, Manchester and the Mountains** (⊠ 5046 Main St., Manchester 05255, ☎ 802/362–2100, WEB www.manchesterandmtns.com). **Mt. Snow Valley Chamber of Commerce** (⊠ Box 3, W. Main St., Wilmington 05363, ☎ 802/464–8092 or 877/887-6884, WEB www.visitvermont.com).

CENTRAL VERMONT

Central Vermont's economy once centered on the mills and railroad yards of Rutland and the marble quarries that honeycomb nearby towns. Vermont's "second city" is still a busy commercial hub, but today, as in much of the rest of the state, it's tourism that drives the economic engine. The center of the dynamo is the massive ski-and-stay infrastructure around Killington, the East's largest downhill resort.

There's a lot more to central Vermont than high-speed chairlifts and slopeside condos, however. The protected (except for occasional logging) lands of the Green Mountain National Forest surround the spine of Vermont's central range; off to the west, the rolling dairyland of the

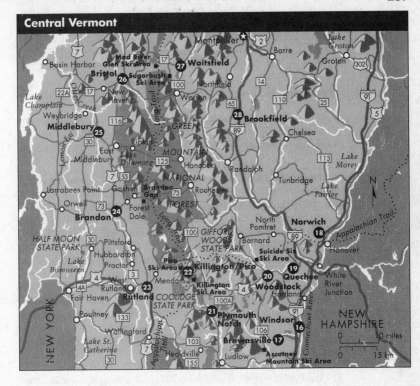

Central Vermont

southern Lake Champlain valley is one of the truly undiscovered corners of the state. To the east, in the Connecticut River valley, are towns as diverse as Calvin Coolidge's Plymouth, a Yankee Brigadoon, and busy, polished-to-perfection Woodstock, where upscale shops are just a short walk from America's newest national park.

The coverage of towns begins with Windsor, on U.S. 5 near I–91 at the state's eastern edge; winds westward toward U.S. 7; then continues north before heading over the spine of the Green Mountains.

Windsor

16 *50 mi north of Brattleboro, 42 mi east of Rutland.*

Windsor justly bills itself as the birthplace of Vermont. An interpretive exhibit on Vermont's constitution, the first in the United States to prohibit slavery and establish a system of public schools, is housed in the **Old Constitution House.** The site, where in 1777 grant holders declared Vermont an independent republic, contains 18th- and 19th-century furnishings, American paintings and prints, and Vermont-made tools, toys, and kitchenware. ⊠ *N. Main St.,* ☎ *802/828–3211.* ⬚ *$1.* ☯ *Late-May–mid-Oct., Wed.–Sun., 11–5.*

The firm of Robbins & Lawrence became famous for applying the "American system" (the use of interchangeable parts) to the manufacture of rifles. Although the company no longer exists, the **American Precision Museum** extols the Yankee ingenuity that created a major machine-tool industry here in the 19th century. The museum contains the largest collection of historically significant machine tools in the country and presents changing exhibits. ⊠ *196 Main St.,* ☎ *802/674–6628.* ⬚ *$5.* ☯ *Memorial Day–Nov. l, daily 10–5.*

The mission of the **Vermont State Craft Gallery,** in the restored 1846 Windsor House, is to advance the appreciation of Vermont crafts through education and exhibition. The center presents crafts exhibitions and operates a small museum. ⊠ *54 Main St.,* ☎ *802/674–6729.* ⊙ *Mon.–Sat. 10–5, Sun. 1–5.*

Glass blowers demonstrate their art at **Simon Pearce** (⊠ U.S. 5, ☎ 802/674–6280 or 800/774-5277), where there's also a retail shop.

At 460 ft, the **Cornish-Windsor Covered Bridge** off U.S. 5, which spans the Connecticut River between Windsor and Cornish, New Hampshire, is the longest in the state.

Dining and Lodging

$$ ✕ **Windsor Station.** This converted main-line railroad station serves such entrées as chicken Kiev, filet mignon, and prime rib. The booths, with their curtained brass railings, were created from the high-back railroad benches of the depot. ⊠ *Depot Ave.,* ☎ *802/674–2052. AE, MC, V. Closed Mon. in fall and winter; dinner only*

$$–$$$ ✕🏨 **Juniper Hill Inn.** An expanse of green lawn with Adirondack chairs and a garden of perennials sweeps up to the portico of this Greek Revival mansion, built at the turn of the century and now on the National Register of Historic Places. The central living room, with its hardwood floors, oak paneling, Oriental carpets, and thickly upholstered furniture, has a stately feel. Bedrooms are furnished with antiques; 11 have fireplaces. Four-course dinners ($34; reservations essential) served in the candlelit dining room at 7:00 p.m. Monday through Saturday may include herb-crusted rack of lamb or sautéed scallops with glazed garlic and champagne sauce. ⊠ *Box 79, Juniper Hill Rd., 05089,* ☎ *802/674–5273 or 800/359–2541,* 䕕 *802/674–2041,* ᴡᴇʙ *www.juniperhillinn.com. 16 rooms. Restaurant, pool, hiking. D, MC, V. BP.*

Nightlife and the Arts

Destiny (⊠ U.S. 5, Windsor, ☎ 802/674–6671) hosts rock bands most days and has a DJ on Sunday.

Brownsville

🛈 *5 mi southwest of Windsor.*

Brownsville, a small village at the foot of Ascutney Mountain, has everything a village needs: a country store, post office, town hall, and historic grange building. The Ascutney Mountain ski area is a self-contained four-season resort.

Lodging

$$–$$$$ 🏨 **Ascutney Mountain Resort Hotel.** One of the big attractions of this five-building resort hotel-condo complex is the ski lift outside the main door. The comfortable, well-maintained suites come in different configurations and sizes—some with kitchens, fireplaces, and decks. Slopeside multilevel condos have three bedrooms, three baths, and private entrances. The Ascutney Harvest Inn, which serves Continental cuisine, is within the complex. ⊠ *Box 699, Hotel Rd., off Rte. 44, 05037,* ☎ *802/484–7711 or 800/243–0011,* 䕕 *802/484–3117,* ᴡᴇʙ *www. ascutney.com. 212 units. 3 restaurants, 2 bars, 1 indoor and 1 outdoor pool, hot tub, health club, racquetball, ice-skating. AE, MC, V.*

$$ 🏨 **Mill Brook.** This Victorian farmhouse, built in 1880, is directly across from the Ascutney ski slopes. Making après-ski idleness easy are the four sitting rooms, decorated with antiques and contemporary furnishings. The honeymoon suite has a separate dressing room with a claw-foot bathtub; the other suites are perfect for families. Rates include afternoon tea.

⊠ *Box 410, Rte. 44, 05037,* ☎ *802/484–7283,* WEB *www.millbrookbb. com. 2 rooms, 3 suites. Hot tub. AE, MC, V. BP.*

Nightlife and the Arts

Crow's Nest Club (⊠ Ascutney Mountain Resort Hotel, Hotel Rd., off Rte. 44, ☎ 802/484–7711) has entertainment on weekends.

Ski Areas

ASCUTNEY MOUNTAIN RESORT

The Plausteiner family, whose patriarch, John, was instrumental in operations at Mt. Snow and White Face Mountain, in Lake Placid, New York, purchased this resort in the mid-1990s, and since then has been continually making improvements. In 2001, a mi-long high-speed quad on the North Peak was opened and snowmaking coverage was increased to 95%. The five buildings of the resort village have hotel suites and condominium units. ⊠ *Rte. 44, off I–91 (Box 699, Brownsville 05037),* ☎ *802/484–7711; 800/243–0011 lodging.*

Downhill. 56 trails with varying terrain are serviced by six lifts, including the quad, three triple chairs, one double chair, and a surface lift. Beginner and novice skiers stay toward the base, while intermediates enjoy the band that wraps the midsection. For experts, tougher black-diamond runs top the mountain. One disadvantage to Ascutney is that there is no easy way down from the summit, so novice skiers should not make the trip. Ascutney is popular with families because it offers some of the least-expensive junior lift tickets in the region.

Cross-country. The resort has 32 km (19 mi) of groomed cross-country trails and offers rentals.

Child care. Day care is available for children from ages 6 weeks to 10 years, with learn-to-ski options and rental equipment for toddlers and up. There are half- and full-day instruction programs for children ages 3 to 12; a Mini-Olympians program for ages 4 to 6; and a Young Olympians program for ages 7 to 12.

Summer and year-round activities. Ascutney Mountain Resort Hotel has a sports-and-fitness center with full-size indoor and outdoor pools, a hot tub, racquetball, aerobics facilities and classes, weight training, and massage. Summer activities include mountain biking, hiking, and tennis.

Norwich

⓲ *6 mi north of White River Junction, 22 mi north of Brownsville.*

Norwich is home to an excellent science museum. The town is across the river from Hanover, New Hampshire, home of Dartmouth College.

★ ☺ Numerous hands-on exhibits at the **Montshire Museum of Science** explore space, nature, and technology; there are also living habitats, aquariums, and many children's programs. A maze of trails winds through 100 acres of pristine woodland. An ideal destination for a rainy day, this is one of the finest museums in New England. ⊠ *Montshire Rd., Box 770,* ☎ *802/649–2200,* WEB *www.montshire.net.* ☒ *$5.50.* ☉ *Daily 10–5.*

Shopping

The shelves at **King Arthur Flour Baker's Store** (⊠ 135 Rte. 5 S, ☎ 802/ 649–3881) are stocked with all the tools and ingredients in the company's Baker's Catalogue, including mixes and flours, and local products. A bakery with a viewing area enables visitors to watch products being made.

Quechee

⑲   *11 mi south of Norwich, 6 mi west of White River Junction.*

Quechee is perched astride the Ottauquechee River. Quechee Gorge, 165 ft deep, is impressive, though sometimes overrun by tourists. You can see the mi-long gorge, carved by a glacier, from U.S. 4, but many people picnic nearby or scramble down one of several descents for a closer look.

More than a decade ago Simon Pearce set up **Simon Pearce,** an epony-mous glassblowing factory in an old mill by a waterfall here, using the water power to drive his furnace. Today the glassblowing factory is at the heart of a handsome, upscale shopping complex that also houses a weaver (demonstrations Tuesday through Sunday) and a pottery studio. You can watch the glassblowers at work daily, and then pur-chase their wares in the gift shop. A restaurant overlooks the water-fall. ⊠ *The Mill, Main St.,* ☎ *802/295–2711,* ⟨WEB⟩ *www.simonpearce. com.* ⊗ *Store daily 9–9.*

Dining and Lodging

$$$ ✕ **Simon Pearce.** Candlelight, sparkling glassware from the studio downstairs, contemporary dinnerware, exposed brick, and large win-dows that overlook the roaring Ottauquechee River create an ideal set-ting for contemporary American cuisine. Sesame-crusted tuna with noodle cakes and wasabi and roast duck with mango chutney sauce are house specialties; the wine cellar holds several hundred vintages. ⊠ *Main St.,* ☎ *802/295–1470. AE, D, DC, MC, V.*

$$$–$$$$ ✕▦ **Quechee Inn at Marshland Farm.** The 1793 country home of Joseph Marsh, Vermont's first lieutenant governor, has been handsomely restored; newer additions have modern amenities yet retain a traditional feeling. Each room, decorated with Queen Anne-style furnishings and period antiques, has air-conditioning and cable TV. There are groomed cross-country ski trails, bike and canoe rentals, and a fly-fishing school, but if you run short on activities, you also have privileges at the Quechee Country Club, with two 18-hole golf courses, tennis courts, and indoor and outdoor pools. Among the dining room's ($$$$) cre-ative offerings are entrées such as duck confit and seared sesame tuna. ⊠ *Clubhouse Rd., 05059,* ☎ *802/295–3133 or 800/235–3133,* ⟨FAX⟩ *802/ 295–6587,* ⟨WEB⟩ *www.pinnacle-inns.com. 22 rooms, 2 suites. Restau-rant, golf privileges, fishing, bicycles, cross-country skiing, meeting room. AE, D, DC, MC, V. BP.*

$$–$$$ ✕▦ **Parker House.** The peach-and-blue rooms of this 1857 Victorian mansion are named for former residents: Emily has a marble fireplace, Walter is the smallest room, and Joseph has a view of the Ottauquechee River. Third-floor rooms are air-conditioned. The elegant dining room ($$$) prepares sophisticated American comfort cuisine such as loin of venison with a port and balsamic vinegar sauce. Guests have access to the Quechee Country Club's first-rate golf courses, tennis courts, in-door and outdoor pool, and cross-country and downhill skiing. ⊠ *Box 0780, 1792 Quechee Main St., 05059,* ☎ *802/295–6077,* ⟨FAX⟩ *802/296–6696,* ⟨WEB⟩ *www.theparkerhouseinn.com. 7 rooms. Restaurant, golf privileges. AE, MC, V. BP.*

Outdoor Activities and Sports

FISHING

The **Vermont Fly Fishing School/Wilderness Trails** (⊠ Quechee Inn, Club-house Rd., ☎ 802/295–7620) leads workshops, rents fishing gear and mountain bikes, and arranges canoe and kayak trips. In winter, the com-pany conducts cross-country and snowshoe treks.

POLO

Quechee Polo Club (⊠ Dewey's Mill Rd., ½ mi north of U.S. 4, ☎ 802/ 295–7152) draws hundreds of spectators on summer Saturdays to its matches near the Quechee Gorge. Admission is $3 per person or $6 per carload.

Shopping

The 40 dealers at the **Hartland Antiques Center** (⊠ U.S. 4, ☎ 802/457– 4745) stock furniture, paper items, china, glass, and collectibles. More than 350 dealers sell their wares at the **Quechee Gorge Village** (⊠ U.S. 4, ☎ 802/295–1550 or 800/438–5565), an antiques and crafts mall in an immense reconstructed barn that also houses a country store and a classic diner. A merry-go-round and a small-scale working railroad operate when weather permits.

Ottauquechee Valley Winery (⊠ 5967 Woodstock Rd./U.S. 4, ☎ 802/ 295–9463) has a tasting room and sells fruit wines, such as apple and blueberry.

Scotland by the Yard (U.S. 4, ☎ 802/295–5351 or 800/295–5351) is the place to shop for all things Scottish, from kilts to Harris tweed jackets and tartan ties.

Woodstock

★ ⓴   *4 mi west of Quechee.*

Perfectly preserved Federal houses surround Woodstock's tree-lined village green, and streams flow around the town center, which is anchored by a covered bridge. The town owes much of its pristine appearance to the Rockefeller family's interest in historic preservation and land conservation.

Woodstock's history of conservationism dates from the 19th century: town native George Perkins Marsh, a congressman and diplomat, wrote the pioneering book *Man and Nature* in 1864 and was closely involved in the creation of the Smithsonian Institution in Washington, D.C.

The **Billings Farm and Museum,** on the grounds of George Perkins Marsh's boyhood home, was founded by Frederick Billings in 1870 as a model of conservation, and is one of the oldest dairy farms in the country. Billings, a lawyer and businessman, put into practice Marsh's ideas about the long-term effects of farming and grazing. Exhibits in the reconstructed Queen Anne farmhouse, school, general store, workshop, and former Marsh homestead demonstrate the lives and skills of early Vermont settlers. ⊠ *Rte. 12, ½ mi north of Woodstock,* ☎ *802/ 457-2355,* WEB *www.billingsfarm.org.* ☞ *$8.* ☉ *May–late Oct., daily 10–5; call for Thanksgiving and Dec. weekend schedules.*

The 500-acre **Marsh-Billings-Rockefeller National Historical Park,** which opened in 1998, is Vermont's only national park and the nation's first to focus on conservation and stewardship of natural resources. The park encompasses the forest lands planned by Frederick Billings according to the principles of George Perkins Marsh, as well as Billings's mansion, gardens, and carriage roads. The entire property was the gift of Laurance S. Rockefeller, who lived here with his late wife, Mary, Frederick Billings's granddaughter. It is adjacent to the ☞ Billings Farm and Museum. The residential complex is accessible by guided tour only, but you can explore the extensive network of carriage roads and trails on your own. ⊠ *Rte. 12,* ☎ *802/457–3368,* WEB *www.nps.marsh-billings.com.* ☞ *Tour $6.* ☉ *Memorial Day–Oct., daily for guided tours only (call for schedules), grounds daily dawn–dusk.*

Period furnishings of the Woodstock Historical Society fill the white clapboard **Dana House,** built circa 1807. Exhibits include the town charter, furniture, maps, and locally minted silver. The converted barn houses the Woodstock Works exhibit, an economic portrait of the town. ⊠ *26 Elm St.,* ☎ *802/457–1822.* 🖙 *$2.* ☉ *Late-May–late-Oct., Mon.–Sat. 10–4, Sun. noon–4; Mid-Oct.–mid-May, by appointment only.*

The Raptor Center of the **Vermont Institute of Natural Science** (VINS) houses 23 species of birds of prey, among them bald eagles, peregrine falcons, and 3-ounce saw-whet owls. There are also ravens, turkey vultures, and snowy owls. All the caged birds have been found injured and unable to survive in the wild. This nonprofit, environmental research and education center is on a 77-acre nature preserve with walking trails. ⊠ *Church Hill Rd.,* ☎ *802/457–2779,* WEB *www.vinsweb.org.* 🖙 *$6.* ☉ *Mon.–Sat., 10–4.*

Dining and Lodging

$$$–$$$$ ✕ **Prince and the Pauper.** Modern French and American fare with a
★ Vermont accent is the focus of this romantic restaurant in a candlelit Colonial setting. The grilled duck breast might have an Asian five-spice sauce; lamb and pork sausage in puff pastry comes with a honey-mustard sauce. A less-expensive bistro menu is available in the lounge. ⊠ *24 Elm St.,* ☎ *802/457–1818. AE, D, MC, V. No lunch.*

$–$$ ✕ **Pane & Salute.** Authentic regional Italian breads are a specialty, but this restaurant has a whole lot more to offer. You can try homemade Tuscan pizzas and soups, sandwich specials, and pasta entrées such as penne with spinach, pine nuts, raisins, and garlic. Add a glass of Chianti and *mangia bene.* Desserts include meringues with whipped cream and raspberry sauce and fruit tarts. There's outdoor seating when weather permits. The restaurant serves breakfast and lunch daily in summer, brunch all year from 10 to 2, and dinner Thursday, Friday, and Saturday; call for winter hours. ⊠ *61 Central St.,* ☎ *802/457–4882. Reservations not accepted. D, MC, V. Closed Wed..*

$$$$ ✕🖬 **Kedron Valley Inn.** Two 19th-century buildings, including the 13-
★ room Main House, and a 1968 log structure make up this inn set on 15 acres. Many rooms have a fireplace or a Franklin stove, two have decks, one has a veranda, and another has a terrace overlooking a stream. Exposed-log walls make the motel units in back more rustic than the rooms in the main inn, but they're decorated similarly, with country antiques and reproductions. The chef creates French masterpieces such as fillet of Norwegian salmon stuffed with herb seafood mousse in puff pastry, and shrimp, scallops, and lobster with wild mushrooms served with a Fra Angelico cream sauce. A terrace with views of the grounds is open in summer. ⊠ *Rte. 106, 05071,* ☎ *802/457–1473 or 800/836–1193,* FAX *802/457–4469. 21 rooms, 7 suites. Restaurant, bar, pond, beach. AE, D, MC, V. Closed Apr. and 10 days before Thanksgiving. MAP, BP.*

$$$–$$$$ ✕🖬 **Jackson House Inn.** This fine property consistently wins high ac-
★ colades for both accommodations and dining. European antiques, Oriental rugs, and French-cut crystal fill the formal parlor and cozy library. There are two wings: one for suites with gas fireplaces, Anichini linens, down duvets, and thermal massage tubs; the other, overlooking the inn's 5 acres of manicured grounds, for the cathedral-ceiling restaurant, whose focal point is a granite, open-hearth fireplace. Herb-crusted cod with an artichoke ragout and lamb shanks braised in red wine and port typify the lighter contemporary cuisine. You can choose from a prix-fixe, three-course menu ($49) or the five-course chef's tasting menu ($58). ⊠ *114-3 Senior La., 05091,* ☎ *802/457–2065 or 800/448–1890,* FAX *802/457–9290,* WEB *www.jacksonhouse.com. 9 rooms, 6 suites. Restaurant, sauna, exercise room. AE, MC, V. BP.*

$$$–$$$$ ✕🏨 **Woodstock Inn and Resort.** Country formality might sound like an oxymoron, but it best describes the relaxed yet polished atmosphere here. Resort entrepreneur Laurance Rockefeller, long a Woodstock resident, made this a flagship property of his Rockresorts chain. The lobbies and lounges hold a grand piano, decorative quilts, a monumental fieldstone fireplace, and bowls of shiny Vermont apples. Guest rooms are spacious, serene, and set well back from Woodstock's often noisy main drag. The dinner fare is nouvelle New England; the menu might list entrées such as salmon steak with avocado beurre blanc, beef Wellington, and prime rib. Guests can ski free midweek at the inn-owned Suicide Six. ✉ *14 The Green, U.S. 4, 05091,* ☎ *802/457–1100 or 800/ 448–7900,* FAX *802/457–6699,* WEB *www.woodstockinn.com. 144 rooms, 7 suites. 2 restaurants, bar, indoor lap pool, outdoor pool, sauna, 2 18-hole golf courses, 12 tennis courts, croquet, health club, racquetball, squash, cross-country skiing, meeting room. AE, MC, V. MAP.*

$$$$ 🏨 **Twin Farms.** At the center of this exclusive 300-acre resort stands the 1795 farmhouse where writers Sinclair Lewis and Dorothy Thompson lived. Not that Lewis and Thompson would recognize the place: it's been transformed into Vermont's most sumptuous—and most expensive— resort. Twin Farms' rooms and cottages are fantasy environments, drawing their inspiration from Moorish, Scandinavian, Japanese, and Adirondack design. There are fireplaces throughout, along with museum-quality artworks. The rich contemporary cuisine emphasizes local ingredients. You can help yourself at the open bar. ✉ *Stage Rd., off Rte. 12, 8 mi north of Woodstock (Box 115, Barnard 05031);* ☎ *802/234– 9999 or 800/894–6327,* FAX *802/234–9990,* WEB *www.twinfarms.com. 6 rooms, 8 cottages. 2 bars, dining room, Japanese baths, spa, exercise room, boating, bicycles, ice-skating, cross-country skiing, recreation room, meeting room. AE, MC, V. FAP.*

$$$ 🏨 **Shire Motel.** Some rooms in this immaculate, in-town motel have decks overlooking the Ottauquechee River and the Billings Farm. All have four-poster beds, wing chairs, color TVs, and telephones, and the suites have jacuzzi baths and fireplaces. Complimentary coffee is served each morning. ✉ *46 Pleasant St., 05091,* ☎ *802/457–2211,* FAX *802/ 457–5836,* WEB *www.shiremotel.com. 33 rooms, 3 suites. Refrigerators. AE, D, MC, V.*

$$–$$$ 🏨 **Winslow House.** New owners Jeff and Kathy Bendis take great pride
★ in their beautifully restored 1872 farmhouse on U.S. 4, which has hardwood and wide pine flooring, fine architectural details, and lovely but simple antique furnishings. The two guest rooms on the first floor include a suite with a private sitting room and a day bed; the three second-floor accommodations include two suites with private sitting rooms and a spacious room with a cathedral ceiling and private balcony. Breakfast is served by candlelight. ✉ *492 Woodstock Rd. (U.S. 4), 05091,* ☎ *802/457–1820,* FAX *802/457–1820,* WEB *www.scenesofvermont. com/winslowhouse. 2 rooms, 3 suites. Refrigerators. MC, V. BP.*

$$ 🏨 **Deer Brook Inn B&B.** Each spacious, immaculate guest room at this 1820 Colonial-style farmhouse has comfortable, unpretentious furnishings. The quilts are handmade by the inn's owner, Rosemary McGinty, who brings her two golden retrievers out to meet guests on request. The Deer Brook is 5 mi from downtown Woodstock and 10 mi from Killington. ✉ *5354 U.S. 4, 05091,* ☎ *802/672–3713,* WEB *www. bbhost.com/deerbrookinn. 4 rooms, 1 suite. AE, MC, V. BP.*

Outdoor Activities and Sports

BIKING

Cyclery Plus (✉ 36 U.S. 4 W, West Woodstock, ☎ 802/457–3377) rents, sells, and services bikes, and also offers a free touring map of local rides.

GOLF

Robert Trent Jones Sr. designed the 18-hole, par-69 course at **Woodstock Country Club** (⊠ South St., ☎ 802/457–6674), which is run by the Woodstock Inn. Greens fees are $32–$75; cart rentals are $38.

HORSEBACK RIDING

Kedron Valley Stables (⊠ Rte. 106, South Woodstock, ☎ 802/457–2734 or 800/225–6301) gives lessons and conducts guided trail rides and excursions in a sleigh and a wagon.

STATE PARK

Coolidge State Park (⊠ Rte. 100A, 2 mi north of Rte. 100, ☎ 802/672–3612) abuts Coolidge State Forest and has campsites (log lean-tos from the 1930s).

Shopping

The **Marketplace at Bridgewater Mills** (⊠ U.S. 4, west of Woodstock, ☎ 802/672–3332) houses shops and attractions in a three-story converted woolen mill. There's an antiques and crafts center, a bookstore, Miranda Thomas pottery, and handsome Charles Shackleton furniture. Sample Vermont stocks gourmet foods and gifts.

Stephen Huneck Studio (⊠ 49 Central St., ☎ 802/457–3206) invites canines and humans to visit the artist's gallery, filled with whimsical animal carvings, prints, and furniture. **Taftsville Country Store** (⊠ U.S. 4, Taftsville, ☎ 802/457–1135 or 800/854–0013) sells an excellent selection of Vermont cheeses, moderately priced wines, and fresh-baked breads and pastries. The **Village Butcher** (⊠ Elm St., ☎ 802/457–2756) is an emporium of Vermont comestibles. **Who Is Sylvia?** (⊠ 26 Central St., ☎ 802/457–1110), in the old firehouse, sells vintage clothing and antique linens, lace, and jewelry.

Sugarbush Farm Inc. (⊠ 591 Sugarbush Farm Rd., ☎ 802/457–1757 or 800/281–1757) taps 5,000 maple trees to make syrup each spring. You can purchase syrup here and take a self-guided tour at any time of the year. The farm also makes excellent cheeses. The road here can be messy, so call for conditions and directions.

Ski Areas

SUICIDE SIX

The site of the first ski tow in the United States (1934), this resort is owned and operated by the Woodstock Inn and Resort. The inn's package plans are remarkably inexpensive, considering the high quality of the accommodations. ⊠ *Pomfret Rd., 05091, ☎ 802/457–6661; 800/448–7900 lodging; 802/457–6666 snow conditions.*

Downhill. Despite Suicide Six's short vertical of only 650 ft, the skiing is challenging. There are steep runs down the mountain's face, intermediate trails that wind around the hill, and glade skiing. Beginner terrain is mostly toward the bottom. Two double chairlifts and one surface lift service the 23 trails and slopes. The resort also has a snowboard area with a halfpipe. Snowmaking covers 61% of the area's terrain.

Child care. The ski area has no nursery, but baby-sitting can be arranged through the Woodstock Inn if you're a guest. Lessons for children are given by the ski-school staff, and there's a children's ski-and-play park for kids ages 3 to 7.

Summer and year-round activities. Outdoor tennis courts, lighted paddle courts, croquet, and an 18-hole golf course are open in summer. The **Woodstock Health and Fitness Center** (☎ 802/457–6656), open year-round, has an indoor lap pool; indoor tennis, squash, and racquetball courts; whirlpool, steam, sauna, and massage rooms; and exercise and aerobics rooms.

The **Woodstock Ski Touring Center** (☎ 802/457–6674), headquartered at the Woodstock Country Club (✉ Rte. 106), has 60 km (37 mi) of trails. Equipment and lessons are available.

Plymouth Notch

㉑ *14 mi southwest of Woodstock.*

U.S. president Calvin Coolidge was born and buried in Plymouth Notch, a town that shares his character: low-key and quiet. The perfectly preserved 19th-century buildings of the **Plymouth Notch Historic District** look more like a large farm than a town; in addition to the homestead there's the general store once run by Coolidge's father, a visitor center, a cheese factory (with tasty cheeses for sale), and a one-room schoolhouse. Coolidge's grave is in the cemetery across Route 100A. The Aldrich House, which mounts changing historical exhibits, is open on some weekdays during the off-season. ✉ *Rte. 100A, 6 mi south of U.S. 4, east of Rte. 100,* ☎ *802/672–3773.* ✇ *$5.* ☉ *Late-May–mid-Oct., daily 9:30–5:30.*

Killington/Pico

㉒ *11 mi (Pico) and 15 mi (Killington) east of Rutland.*

The intersection of U.S. 4 and Route 100 is the heart of central Vermont's ski country, with the Killington, Pico, and Okemo resorts nearby. Unfortunate strip development characterizes the Killington access road, but the views from the top of the mountain are worth the drive.

Dining and Lodging

$$$$ × **Hemingway's.** With a national reputation reinforced by major
★ awards and a loyal clientele, Hemingway's is as good as dining gets in central Vermont. You can tuck into the celebrated cream of garlic soup and a seasonal kaleidoscope of dishes based on native game, fresh seafood, and prime meats. Recent offerings on the prix-fixe, four- to five-course menu have included autumn vegetable strudel with hazelnuts, Arctic char with flageolet beans, and Vermont venison with pumpkin sage pudding and parsnip crisps. Desserts are spectacular, as is the five-course wine tasting menu ($75–$85), which matches each dish with an appropriate glass of wine. Request seating in either the formal, vaulted dining room or the intimate wine cellar. ✉ *U.S. 4,* ☎ *802/422–3886. AE, D, DC, MC, V. Closed most Mon. and Tues., and early Nov. and mid-Apr.–mid-May. No lunch.*

$$$$ ×🏨 **Red Clover Inn.** Plushly elegant accommodations and fine dining
★ are the attractions at this romantic 1840s hideaway on 13 mountain acres 5 mi from Killington. Among the antiques-filled rooms in the inn and carriage house are three with fireplaces and whirlpool tubs for two. Many rooms have mountain views. A four-course candlelight dinner, with choice of menu, is served Monday–Saturday evenings. Appetizers might be crispy eggplant, spinach, and Parmesan fritters, or duck ravioli in a wild mushroom broth; some entrée choices have been rosemary-coated rack of lamb or fire-grilled Panama shrimp. *Wine Spectator* magazine cited the inn's wine list as one of the world's most outstanding. You can also choose to include only breakfast in the rate. Pets are allowed in the carriage house. ✉ *7 Woodward Rd., Mendon 05701,* ☎ *802/775–2290 or 800/752–0571,* 🖷 *802/773–0594,* 🕸 *www.redcloverinn.com. 14 rooms. Dining room, pool, hiking. D, MC, V. Closed Apr.–Memorial Day. MAP.*

$$$–$$$$ ×🏨 **Birch Ridge Inn.** A slate-covered carriage way leads to one of Killington's newest inns, a former executive retreat that new owners

have converted into an upscale getaway, adding a new wing to the older building. Rooms are decorated in styles that range from Colonial and Shaker to Mission, and all have a sitting area and television. Six rooms have gas fireplaces, and four of these also have whirlpool baths. The intimate dining room offers a four-course meal with two glasses of wine or an à la carte menu. Typical dishes include an appetizer of wild mushroom strudel and entrée such as potato-crusted salmon or pan-seared duckling breast. ⊠ *Butler Rd., at Killington Rd., 05751,* ☎ *802/422–4293 or 800/435–8566,* FAX *802/422–3406,* WEB *www.birchridge.com. 10 rooms. Restaurant, lounge. AE, MC, V. BP, MAP.*

$$$ 🏨 **Cortina Inn.** This large lodge and miniresort is comfortable and its location prime. About two-thirds of the contemporary country rooms have private balconies, though the views from them aren't spectacular. Two-room family suites have bunk beds. Horseback riding, sleigh rides, ice-skating, and guided snowmobile, fly-fishing, and mountain-biking tours are among the off-the-slopes activities. ⊠ *U.S. 4, Mendon 05751,* ☎ *802/773–3333 or 800/451–6108,* FAX *802/775–6948,* WEB *www.cortinainn.com. 89 rooms, 7 suites. 2 restaurants, bar, indoor pool, hot tub, sauna, 8 tennis courts, health club, ice-skating, sleigh rides. AE, D, DC, MC, V. BP.*

$$–$$$ 🏨 **Mountain Meadows Lodge.** The accommodations at this miniresort simple and a bit worn but comfortable, and the lodge offers activities for kids and adults that should exhaust even the most stalwart. There's fishing, boating (rowboats, sailboats, and canoes), and swimming in the lake, hiking on the Appalachian Trial, yard games, and pony rides. Kids are invited to the barn to help feed the animals. In winter, the lodge has sleds and dog sleds, toboggans, Norwegian kick sleds, snowshoes, and ice skates for use; a cross-country ski center next door rents skis. Mountain Meadow Munchkins provides child care. Dinner is served Friday and Saturday nights, and a light menu is available Sunday–Thursday from noon until 7. ⊠ *285 Thundering Brook Rd., 05751,* ☎ *802/ 775–1010 or 800/370–4567,* FAX *802/773–4459,* WEB *www.mtmeadowslodge.com. 20 rooms, 1 suite with fireplace. Restaurant, lake, pool, sauna, hiking, boating, fishing, recreation room, children's programs. AE, D, MC, V. Closed mid-Oct.–mid-Nov. BP, MAP.*

$–$$ ✕🏨 **Summit Lodge.** Three miles from Killington Peak, this rustic two-story country lodge caters to a varied crowd of ski enthusiasts, who are warmly met by the lodge's mascots—a pair of Saint Bernards. Country decor and antiques blend with modern conveniences to create a relaxed atmosphere. The restaurant ($$) serves continental specialties such as rack of lamb and chicken Birmingham—a boneless breast of chicken with spinach, garlic, feta cheese, and sun-dried tomatoes. ⊠ *Killington Rd. 05751,* ☎ *802/422–3535 or 800/635–6343,* FAX *802/ 422–3536,* WEB *www.summitlodgevermont.com. 43 rooms, 2 suites. Restaurant, bar, pool, pond, hot tub, massage, sauna, ice-skating, nightclub, recreation room. AE, DC, MC, V. BP.*

Nightlife and the Arts

The pub at the **Inn at Long Trail** (⊠ U.S. 4, ☎ 802/775–7181) hosts Irish music on weekends. The **Pickle Barrel** (⊠ Killington Rd., ☎ 802/422–3035), a favorite with the après-ski crowd, presents up-and-coming acts and can get pretty rowdy. The **Wobbly Barn** (⊠ Killington Rd., ☎ 802/ 422–3392), with dancing to blues and rock, is open during ski season.

Outdoor Activities and Sports

FISHING

Gifford Woods State Park's Kent Pond (⊠ Rte. 100, ½ mi north of U.S. 4, ☎ 802/775–5354) is a terrific fishing hole. Campsites are available.

The 18-hole, par 71 **Green Mountain National Golf Course** (⊠ Rte. 100 N, Sherburne, ☎ 802/422–4653) has earned accolades as one of the state's best. Greens fees are $52 mid week and $57 weekends in May and June; $57 midweek and $62 weekends from late June through fall. Cart rental is $18 per person.

Cortina Inn has an ice-skating rink and offers sleigh rides; you can also skate on Summit Pond.

Ski Areas

"Megamountain," "Beast of the East," and plain "huge" are apt descriptions of Killington. The American Skiing Company operates Killington and its neighbor Pico and over the past several years has improved lifts, snowmaking capabilities, and lodging options. A project is under way to join Pico and Killington by interconnecting trails and lifts, Green Mountain College at Killington is scheduled to open in winter 2002, and future plans call for the creation of a giant alpine village at the complex. The resort has the longest ski season in the East and some of the best package plans, as well as several new terrain parks. Killington's après-ski activities are plentiful and have been rated best in Vermont by the national ski magazines. With a single call to Killington's hot-line or a visit to their Web site, skiers can plan an entire vacation: choose accommodations; book air or railroad transportation; and arrange for rental equipment and ski lessons. Killington ticket holders can also ski at Pico. ⊠ *400 Killington Rd., 05751,* ☎ *802/422–8763; 800/621–6867 lodging; 802/422–3261 snow conditions.* WEB *www.killington.com.*

Downhill. It would probably take several weeks to test all 200 trails on the seven mountains of the Killington complex, even though all except Pico interconnect. About 70% of the 1,123 acres of skiing terrain can be covered with machine-made snow. Transporting skiers to the peaks of this complex are 32 lifts, including two gondolas, 12 quads (including six high-speed express quads), six triples, and a Magic Carpet. The K-1 Gondola goes to the area's highest elevation, at 4,241 ft off Killington Peak, and a vertical drop of 3,091 ft to the base of the Skyeship, the world's fastest and first heated eight-passenger lift, complete with piped-in music. The Skyeship base station has a rotisserie, food court, and a coffee bar. The skiing includes everything from Outer Limits, one of the steepest and most challenging trails anywhere in the country, to the 6 ½-mi Great Eastern Trail. In the Fusion Zones, underbrush and low branches have been cleared away to provide tree skiing. The Terrain Park has the longest run in the east.

Child care. Nursery care is available for children from 6 weeks to 6 years old. There's a one-hour instruction program for youngsters from ages 3 to 8; those from 6 to 12 can join an all-day program.

Summer activities. The Killington/Pico complex has a host of activities, including rides up the mountain on the Killington Skyeship or K1 Express Gondola (☎ 802/422–6200), an alpine slide, a "Bungee Thing" ride, and a swimming pool. The resort rents mountain bikes and advises hikers.

Although it's only 5 mi down the road from Killington, Pico—one of the state's first ski areas—has long been a favorite among people looking for old New England-style skiing, with lots of glades and winding and narrow trails. When modern lifts were installed and a village square was constructed at the base, some feared a change in atmosphere might occur, but the condo-hotel, restaurants, and shops have not altered the essential nature of the area. ⊠ *2 Sherburne Pass, Rutland 05701,* ☎ *802/422–3333; 800/621–6867 lodging; 802/422–3261 snow conditions.*

Downhill. Many of the 42 trails are advanced to expert, with two intermediate bail-out trails for the timid. The rest of the mountain's 2,000 ft of vertical terrain is mostly intermediate or easier. The mountain has nine lifts including two high-speed quads, two triples, and three double chairs and has 85% snowmaking coverage. Snowboarding is permitted everywhere on Pico, and there is a Terrain Park. For instruction of any kind, head to the Alpine Learning Center.

Child care. Pico's nursery takes children from ages 6 months to 6 years and provides indoor activities and outdoor play. The ski school has full- and half-day instruction programs for children ages 3 to 12.

Summer and year-round activities. A sports center (☎ 802/773–1786) at the base of the mountain has fitness facilities, a 75-ft pool, whirlpool tub, saunas, and a massage room. You can also take advantage of activities at Killington.

CROSS-COUNTRY SKIING

Mountain Meadows (⊠ Thundering Brook Rd., ☎ 802/775–7077 or 800/221–0598) has 57 km (34½ mi) of groomed trails and 10 km (6 mi) of marked outlying trails. You can also access 500 acres of backcountry skiing. **Mountain Top Inn and Resort** ☎ 802/483–6089 or 800–445-2100) is mammoth, with 120 km (72 mi) of trails, 80 km (49 mi) of which are groomed.

Rutland

㉓ *15 mi southwest of Killington, 32 mi south of Middlebury, 31 mi west of Woodstock, 47 mi west of White River Junction.*

On and around U.S. 7 in Rutland are strips of shopping centers and a seemingly endless row of traffic lights, although the mansions of the marble magnates who made the town famous still command whatever attention can be safely diverted from the traffic. Rutland's compact downtown, one of only a handful of urban centers in Vermont, has experienced a modest revival and is worth an hour's stroll. The area's traditional economic ties to railroading and marble, the latter an industry that became part of such illustrious structures as the central research building of the New York Public Library in New York City, have been rapidly eclipsed by the growth of the Pico and Killington ski areas to the east. If you're planning to visit more than one of the area's attractions, ask about the "One Great Day" admission at the Vermont Marble Exhibit, New England Maple Museum, or Wilson Castle.

The **Chaffee Center for the Visual Arts** (⊠ 16 S. Main St., ☎ 802/775–0356; closed Tues.) exhibits and sells the output of more than 250 Vermont artists who work in various media.

The highlight of the Rutland area, the **Vermont Marble Exhibit** includes a sculptor-in-residence who transforms stone into finished works of art or commerce (you can choose first-hand the marble for a custom-built kitchen counter). The gallery illustrates the many industrial and artistic applications of marble—there's a hall of presidents and a replica of Leonardo da Vinci's *Last Supper* in marble—and depicts the industry's history via exhibits and a video. Factory seconds and foreign and domestic marble items are for sale. ⊠ *62 Main St., Proctor*

(4 mi north of Rutland, off Rte. 3), ☎ *802/459–2300 or 800/427–1396.* ⊡ *$6.* ☉ *Mid-May–Oct., daily 9–5:30.*

A 32-room mansion built in 1888 by a doctor, **Wilson Castle** comes complete with turrets, towers, stained glass, and 13 fireplaces. It's magnificently furnished with European and Asian objets d'art. Head west out of Rutland on Route 4A and follow signs. ⊠ *West Proctor Rd., Proctor,* ☎ *802/773–3284,* WEB *www.wilsoncastle.com.* ⊡ *$7.* ☉ *Late-May–mid-Oct., daily 9–5:30.*

Dining and Lodging

$$ ✕ **The Palms.** This Rutland landmark, which opened its doors on Palm Sunday in 1933, was the first restaurant in the state to serve pizza. It's still owned by the same family. The menu is primarily southern Italian, with specialties such as fried mozzarella; antipasto Neapolitan (with provolone, pepperoni, mild peppers, anchovies, and house dressing); and the chef's personal creation, veal à la Palms—veal scallops topped with mushrooms, two kinds of cheese, and a special tomato sauce. Dessert choices are fairly pedestrian. ⊠ *36 Strongs St.,* ☎ *802/773–2367. AE, DC, MC, V. Closed Sun. No lunch.*

$$$$ ✕⊡ **Mountain Top Inn and Resort.** One of the state's most spectacular family resorts occupies 500 lofty acres overlooking secluded Chittenden Reservoir and the Green Mountain National Forest. It's essentially an outdoorsperson's inn, with an equestrian center, swimming and canoeing, fishing, trap and skeet shooting, and a golf school with a five-hole pitch-and-putt course and driving range. Winter brings cross-country skiing on more than 70 mi of trails, sleigh rides, and skating. The dinner menu ($$$) runs to uncomplicated American fare such as rack of lamb and roast pork tenderloin and unadventurous French fare such as sole meunière. A tip: Opt for the more-expensive deluxe rooms, which are larger and have spectacular views. If you wish, breakfast and dinner can be included in the rate. ⊠ *195 Mountaintop Rd., Chittenden 05737,* ☎ *802/483–2311 or 800/445–2100,* FAX *802/483–6373,* WEB *www.mountaintopinn.com. 35 rooms, 6 cottages, 6 chalets. Restaurant, pool, driving range, horseback riding, beach, boating, fishing, ice-skating, cross-country skiing, sleigh rides. AE, MC, V. Closed late-Oct.–late-Dec. and mid-Mar.–mid-May.*

$$–$$$ ⊡ **Inn at Rutland.** One alternative to Rutland's chain motel and hotel accommodations is this renovated Victorian mansion. The ornate oak staircase lined with heavy embossed gold and leather wainscoting leads to rooms that blend modern bathrooms with late-19th-century touches such as elaborate ceiling moldings and frosted glass. The two large common rooms, one with a fireplace, have views of surrounding mountains and valleys. The meal plan varies. ⊠ *70 N. Main St., 05701,* ☎ *802/773–0575 or 800/808–0575,* FAX *802/775–3506,* WEB *www.innatrutland.com. 11 rooms. AE, D, MC, V. BP, CP.*

Nightlife and the Arts

Crossroads Arts Council (⊠ 39 E. Center St., ☎ 802/775–5413) presents music, opera, dance, jazz, and theater year-round at venues throughout the region.

Outdoor Activities and Sports

Half Moon State Park's principal attraction is Half Moon Pond (⊠ Town Rd., 3½ mi off Rte. 30, west of Hubbardton, ☎ 802/273–2848). The park has nature trails, campsites, and boat and canoe rentals.

Shopping

Tuttle Antiquarian Books (⊠ 28 S. Main St., ☎ 802/773–8229) has a large collection of books on Asia. The store stocks rare and out-of-print books, genealogies, local histories, and miniature books.

Brandon

㉔ *15 mi northwest of Rutland.*

Straddling busy U.S. 7, Brandon nevertheless has broad side streets lined with gracious Victorian houses, lodging at the landmark Brandon Inn or at smaller B&Bs, and ready access to the mountain scenery and recreation of nearby Brandon Gap.

The **Stephen A. Douglas Birthplace** commemorates the "Little Giant" (he stood only 5 ft, 2 in tall), best known for his debates with Abraham Lincoln in 1858. Douglas, who became a U.S. representative and senator from Illinois, was born here on April 23, 1813. His boyhood home and a monument to his memory are just north of the village, next to the Baptist church. ⊠ *U.S. 7.* ☎ *802/247–6569 or 802/247–6332.* ☞ *Free.* ⊙ *June–Labor Day, Thurs. 2–5, or by appointment.*

Maple syrup is Vermont's signature product, and the **New England Maple Museum and Gift Shop** explains the history and process of turning maple sap into syrup with murals, exhibits, and a slide show. ⊠ *U.S. 7, Pittsford (9 mi south of Brandon),* ☎ *802/483–9414.* ☞ *$1.75 museum.* ⊙ *Late May–Oct., daily 8:30–5:30; Nov.–Dec. and mid-Mar.–late May, daily 10–4.*

Dining and Lodging

$$$$ ✕🖭 **Blueberry Hill Inn.** If you're looking for total peace and quiet, this is the place. In the Green Mountain National Forest and 5½ mi off a mountain pass on a dirt road, Blueberry Hill is an idyllic spot with lush gardens, a stream, and a pond with a wood-fired sauna on its bank. Many rooms have views of the mountains; all are furnished with antiques, quilts, and hot-water bottles to warm winter beds. Three rooms have lofts (good for families), and the Moosalamoo Room is in a private cottage. The restaurant menu has dishes such as garlic fish soup with mussels and venison fillet with cherry sauce. A ski-touring center with 80 km (50 mi) of marked trails focuses on hiking in the summer. Rates include breakfast and dinner, but you can choose breakfast only on weekdays. ⊠ *Forest Rd. 32, Goshen 05733,* ☎ *802/247–6735 or 800/448–0707,* ℻ *802/247–3983,* WEB *www.blueberryhillinn.com.* *12 rooms. Restaurant, sauna, hiking, volleyball, cross-country skiing, mountain bikes. MC, V. MAP.*

$$$ 🖭 **Lilac Inn.** The bridal suite at this Greek Revival mansion, which bills itself as a romantic retreat, is one of the most-elegant inn rooms in Vermont, with a pewter canopy bed, whirlpool bath for two, and fireplace. The other rooms, all uniquely furnished and with claw-foot tubs and hand-held European shower heads, are also charming. Breakfast is served on the patio or in the bright, gleaming dining room, both of which overlook the lovely gardens with 15 varieties of lilacs. The inn is a popular spot for weddings on summer weekends, and is home to two cats. ⊠ *53 Park St./Rte. 73, 05733,* ☎ *802/247–5463 or 800/221–0720,* ℻ *802/247–5499,* WEB *www.lilacinn.com. 9 rooms. Restaurant. AE, D, MC, V. Restaurant closed Nov.–Apr. BP.*

Outdoor Activities and Sports

Moosalamoo (☎ 800/448–0707) is the name given by a partnership of public and private entities to a 20,000-acre chunk of Green Mountain National Forest land (along with several private holdings) just northeast of Brandon. More than 60 mi of trails take hikers, mountain bikers, and cross-country skiers through some of Vermont's most gorgeous mountain terrain. Attractions include Branbury State Park, on the shores of Lake Dunmore; secluded Silver Lake, a trout-fishing mecca; and sections of both the Long Trail and Catamount Trail (the latter is a Massachusetts-to-Québec ski trail). Both the Blueberry Hill

Inn and Churchill House Inn (☎ 802/247–3078) have direct public access to trails.

GOLF

Neshobe Golf Club (✉ Rte. 73, east of Brandon, ☎ 802/247–3611) has 18 holes of par-72 golf on a bent-grass course totaling nearly 6,500 yards. The Green Mountain views are terrific. Several local inns offer golf packages.

HIKING

About 8 mi east of Brandon on Route 73, a trail that takes an hour to hike starts at Brandon Gap and climbs steeply up **Mt. Horrid.** South of Lake Dunmore on Route 53, a large turnout marks a trail (a hike of about two hours) to the **Falls of Lana.** Four trails—two short ones of less than a mile each and two longer ones—lead to the old abandoned Revolutionary War fortifications at **Mt. Independence**; to reach them, take the first left turn off Route 73 west of Orwell and go right at the fork. The road will turn to gravel and once again will fork; take a sharp left-hand turn toward a small marina. The parking lot is on the left at the top of the hill.

Shopping

The **Warren Kimble Gallery & Studio** (✉ Off Rte. 73 E, ☎ 802/247–3026 or 800/954–6253) is the workplace, gallery, and gift shop of the nationally renowned folk artist.

Middlebury

★ ㉕ *17 mi north of Brandon, 34 mi south of Burlington.*

In the late 1800s Middlebury was the largest Vermont community west of the Green Mountains: an industrial center of river-powered wool, grain, and marble mills. This is Robert Frost country; Vermont's late poet laureate spent 23 summers at a farm east of Middlebury. Otter Creek, the state's longest river, traverses the town center. Still a cultural and economic hub amid the Champlain Valley's serene pastoral patchwork, the town and countryside invite a day of exploration.

Smack in the middle of town, **Middlebury College** (☎ 802/443–5000), founded in 1800, was conceived as a more godly alternative to the worldly University of Vermont. The college has no religious affiliation today, however. The early-19th-century stone buildings contrast provocatively with the postmodern architecture of the Center for the Arts and the sports center. Music, theater, and dance performances take place throughout the year at the **Wright Memorial Theatre** and **Center for the Arts.**

The **Middlebury College Museum of Art** has a permanent collection of paintings, photography, works on paper, and sculpture. ✉ *Center for the Arts, Rte. 30,* ☎ *802/443–5007.* ☜ *Free.* ☼ *Tues.–Fri. 10–5, weekends noon–5. Closed major holidays and last 2 wks of Aug.*

The **Vermont Folklife Center** exhibits photography, antiques, folk paintings, manuscripts, and other artifacts and contemporary works that examine facets of Vermont life. The center is in the basement of the restored 1801 home of Gamaliel Painter, the founder of Middlebury College. ✉ *3 Court St.,* ☎ *802/388–4964.* ☜ *Donations accepted.* ☼ *Gallery May–Dec., Tues.–Sat. 11–4. Oral history archive weekdays 10–4.*

The **Sheldon Museum,** an 1829 marble merchant's house, is the oldest community museum in the country. The period rooms contain Vermont-made textiles, furniture, toys, clothes, kitchen tools, and paintings. ✉ *1 Park St.,* ☎ *802/388–2117.* ☜ *$4.* ☼ *Mon.–Sat. 10–5; open occasional Sundays.*

More than a crafts store, the **Vermont State Craft Center at Frog Hollow** mounts changing exhibitions and displays exquisite work in wood, glass, metal, clay, and fiber by more than 250 Vermont artisans. The center, which overlooks Otter Creek, sponsors classes taught by some of those artists. There are other centers in Burlington and Manchester. ⊠ *1 Mill St.,* ☎ *802/388–3177,* WEB *www.froghollow.com.* ☼ *Call for hrs.*

☾ The Morgan horse—the official state animal—has an even temper, good stamina, and slightly truncated legs in proportion to its body. The University of Vermont's **UVM Morgan Horse Farm,** about 2½ mi west of Middlebury, is a breeding and training center where in summer you can tour the stables and paddocks. ⊠ *74 Battell Dr., off Horse Farm Rd. (follow signs off Rte. 23), Weybridge,* ☎ *802/388–2011.* ☑ *$4.* ☼ *May–Oct., daily 9–5 (last tour at 4).*

About 10 mi east of town on Route 125 (1 mi west of Middlebury College's Bread Loaf campus), the easy ¾-mi **Robert Frost Interpretive Trail** winds through quiet woodland. Plaques along the way bear quotations from Frost's poems. A picnic area is across the road from the trailhead.

OFF THE
BEATEN PATH

LAKE CHAMPLAIN MARITIME MUSEUM – A replica of Benedict Arnold's Revolutionary War gunboat is part of this museum, which documents centuries of activity on the historically significant lake. The museum commemorates the days when steamships sailed along the coast of northern Vermont carrying logs, livestock, and merchandise bound for New York City. Among the 13 exhibit areas is a blacksmith's shop. A one-room stone schoolhouse built in the late 1810s houses historic maps, nautical prints, and maritime objects. Also on site are a nautical archaeology center, a conservation laboratory, and a restaurant. ⊠ *Basin Harbor Rd., Basin Harbor (14 mi west of Bristol, 7 mi west of Vergennes),* ☎ *802/475–2022.* ☑ *$7.* ☼ *Late May–Oct., daily 10–5.*

Dining and Lodging

$$–$$$ ✕ **Fire & Ice.** A 55-item salad bar (with peel-and-eat shrimp), prime rib, steak, fish, and a house specialty—homemade mashed potatoes—are all choices at this family-friendly spot. Although large, the space is divided into several rooms (each with a different theme) and has numerous intimate nooks and crannies for diners who seek privacy. Families may want to request a table next to the "children's corner," which is outfitted with cushions and a VCR. Sunday dinner begins at 1. ⊠ *26 Seymour St.,* ☎ *802/388–7166 or 800/367–7166. AE, D, DC, MC, V. No lunch Mon.*

$$–$$$ ✕ **Roland's Place.** Chef Roland Gaujac prepares classic French and
★   American dishes, elegantly served in a house built in 1796. He opened his restaurant overlooking the Adirondacks after working as a chef in various parts of the world, including the French dining room in Los Angeles's Four Seasons Hotel. Some dishes use locally raised lamb, turkey, and venison; shrimp with chipotle and roasted garlic vinaigrette on fried ravioli is one entrée. A prix-fixe menu is available, and a special menu served daily from 5 to 6 lists numerous à la carte dishes for just $9. The restaurant has three moderately priced guest rooms upstairs; the rate includes a full breakfast. ⊠ *U.S. 7, New Haven,* ☎ *802/453–6309. AE, DC, MC, V. Closed Mon. No dinner Sun. Nov.–Apr.*

$$–$$$ ✕ **Woody's.** In addition to cool jazz, diner-deco light fixtures, and abstract paintings, Woody's has a view of Otter Creek below. Seafood and Vermont lamb are the specialties—some folks say the Caesar salad is the best in the state. Sunday brunch is a popular event. ⊠ *5 Bakery La.,* ☎ *802/388–4182. AE, MC, V.*

$$-$$$$ 🏠 **Middlebury Inn.** Gracious New England–style hospitality is served up along with traditional Yankee fare in this three-story, brick Georgian building, which has been an inn since 1827. The property now encompasses a contemporary motel (decorated, like the rooms in the inn, with Early American-style furnishings) and the Victorian-era Porter House Mansion. Rooms have phones, TVs, and hair dryers; those facing the lovely town green are subject to the noise of passing traffic. Plan to arrive between 3 and 4 for the inn's complimentary afternoon tea, served daily except holidays. In nice weather, you can have lunch on the wicker-furnished porch. Dinner can be included in the price. ⊠ *14 Courthouse Sq., 05753,* ☎ *802/388–4961 or 800/842–4666,* FAX *802/388–4563,* WEB *www.middleburyinn.com. 75 rooms. Restaurant. AE, D, MC, V. CP.*

$$-$$$ 🏠 **Swift House Inn.** The main building at Swift House, the Georgian
★ home of a 19th-century governor and his philanthropist daughter, contains white-panel wainscoting, mahogany and marble fireplaces, and cherry paneling in the dining room. The rooms—most with Oriental rugs and nine with fireplaces—have period reproductions such as canopy beds, curtains with swags, and claw-foot tubs. Some bathrooms have double whirlpool tubs. Rooms in the gatehouse suffer from street noise but are charming; a carriage house holds six luxury accommodations. ⊠ *25 Stewart La., 05753,* ☎ *802/388–9925,* FAX *802/388–9927,* WEB *www.swifthouseinn.com. 21 rooms. Pub, sauna, steam room. AE, D, DC, MC, V. CP.*

$$ 🏠 **Lemon Fair.** This tidy, unfussy bed-and-breakfast occupies a building dating from 1796; it was tiny Bridport's first church before it was moved to its present location overlooking the town green in 1819. Furnishings are Early American in style, the grounds are spacious, and the entire establishment is kid-friendly. The common room is a cozy spot in which to curl up by the fireplace. Lemon Fair is just 8 mi from downtown Middlebury and 4 mi from Lake Champlain. The owners live next door and will rent out the entire house. ⊠ *Crown Point Rd., Bridport 05734,* ☎ *802/758–9238,* FAX *802/758–2135,* WEB *www.limewalk.com/lemonfair. 3 rooms; 1 suite. Pool. No credit cards. BP.*

Outdoor Activities and Sports

The **Bike and Ski Touring Center** (⊠ 74 Main St., ☎ 802/388–6666) has rentals and repairs.

HIKING

On Route 116, about 5½ mi north of East Middlebury, a U.S. Forest Service sign marks a dirt road that forks to the right and leads to the start of the two- to three-hour hike to **Abbey Pond,** which has a beaver lodge and dam as well as a view of Robert Frost Mountain.

Shopping

Historic Marble Works (⊠ Maple St., ☎ 802/388–3701), a renovated marble manufacturing facility, is a collection of unique shops set amid quarrying equipment and factory buildings. De Pasquale's (☎ 802/388–3385) prepares subs and fresh fried fish platters for take-out and sells imported Italian groceries and wines. **Danforth Pewterers** (☎ 802/388–0098) sells handcrafted pewter vases, lamps, and tableware. **Holy Cow** (⊠ 44 Main St., ☎ 802/388–6737) is where Woody Jackson sells his Holstein cattle–inspired T-shirts, memorabilia, and paintings.

Bristol

26 *13 mi northeast of Middlebury.*

At the northeastern threshold of the Green Mountain National Forest, where the rolling farmlands of the Champlain Valley meet the foothills of Vermont's main mountain chain, Bristol has a redbrick 19th-century Main Street that reflects the town's prosperous heyday as the center of a number of wood-products industries. Almost overshadowing the still-busy little downtown are the brooding heights of the Bristol Cliffs Wilderness Area, a section of national forest that has been assured permanent status as a primitive, roadless tract.

Dining

$$–$$$ ✕ **Mary's at Baldwin Creek.** This restaurant and B&B in a 1790 farmhouse provides a truly inspired culinary experience. The "summer kitchen" has a fireplace and rough-hewn barn-board walls, and the main dining room is done in pastels. The innovative fare includes a superb garlic soup, Vermont rack of lamb with a rosemary-mustard sauce, and duck cassis smoked over applewood. Farmhouse dinners on Wednesdays in summer highlight Vermont products. Four guests rooms ($$–$$$) above the restaurant have simple, comfortable furnishings. ⊠ *Rte. 116,* ☎ *802/453–2432. AE, MC, V, DC. Closed Mon. and Tues. in winter. No lunch.*

Outdoor Activities and Sports

A challenging 32-mi bicycle ride starts in Bristol. Take North Street from the traffic light in town and continue north to Monkton Ridge and on to Hinesburg. To return, follow Route 116 south through Starksboro and back to Bristol.

Shopping

Folkheart (⊠ 18 Main St., ☎ 802/453–4101) carries unusual jewelry, toys, and crafts from around the world.

En Route From Bristol, Route 17 winds eastward up and over the **Appalachian Gap,** one of Vermont's most panoramic mountain passes. The views from the top and on the way down the other side toward the ski town of Waitsfield are a just reward for the challenging drive.

Waitsfield

㉗ *20 mi east of Bristol, 55 mi north of Rutland, 32 mi northeast of Middlebury, 19 mi southwest of Montpelier.*

Although in close proximity to Sugarbush and Mad River Glen ski areas, the Mad River valley towns of Waitsfield and Warren have maintained a decidedly low-key atmosphere. The gently carved ridges cradling the valley and the swell of pastures and fields lining the river seem to keep further notions of ski-resort sprawl at bay. With a map from the Sugarbush Chamber of Commerce you can investigate back roads off Route 100 that have exhilarating valley views.

Dining and Lodging

$$$ ✕ **Spotted Cow.** Jay and Renate Young, who were previously involved in running the Sugarbush Inn, are attracting a steady clientele to their intimate dining room decorated with contemporary furnishings and warm woods. Lunch features items such as a fresh spinach salad with fried oysters and Bermuda codfish cakes (Mr. Young's family owns the Lantana Colony Club in Bermuda). For dinner, try a ragout of seafood in puff pastry or grilled breast of duckling with foie gras. Sunday brunch is served from 10:30–3. ⊠ *Bridge St.,* ☎ *802/496–5151. MC, V. Closed Mon.*

$$ ✕ **Common Man.** Although the chef is Parisian, he occasionally sneaks in dishes such as *pescespada de merida* (grilled New England swordfish steak) and ravioli *alla calabrese.* Otherwise, expect to find classics such as *entrecôte maison* (sirloin steak with an herb and garlic butter sauce), rack of lamb, and roast duck. The restaurant, a local institution since 1972, is housed in a mid-1800s barn with hand-hewn rafters

and crystal chandeliers. Dinner is served by candlelight. ⊠ *German Flats Rd., Warren,* ☎ *802/583–2800. AE, D, MC, V. No lunch. Closed Mon. Easter–Christmas.*

$ ✕ **American Flatbread.** For ideologically and gastronomically sound pizza, you won't find a better place in the Green Mountains than this modest haven between Waitsfield and Warren. Organic flour and produce fuel mind and body, and Vermont hardwood fuels the earth-and-stone oven. The "punctuated equilibrium flatbread," made with olive-pepper goat cheese and rosemary, is a dream, as are more traditional pizzas. It's open Monday–Thursday 7:30 AM–8 PM for takeout, and Friday and Saturday 5:30–9 for dinner as well. ⊠ *Rte. 100,* ☎ *802/496–8856. Reservations not accepted. MC, V. Closed Sun.*

$$$$ ✕ 🛏 **Pitcher Inn.** In 1997, four years after burning to the ground, this
★ local institution was reborn in an incarnation of *haute luxe.* Designed by architect David E. Sellers, each guest room has its own motif. In the Mallard, a curved ceiling gives the illusion of a duck blind, and the windows are etched and frosted in the likeness of the banks of a marsh. The Mountain Suite has a mountain mural, and a unique slate and mirror combination renders the effect of a waterfall. All rooms have original Vermont-inspired artwork, stereos, and a TV/VCR; most have fireplaces and steam showers. The formal dining room focuses on locally grown produce and wild game; you can also dine in the private wine cellar, one of the state's finest. Arrangements for activities such as skiing and hiking can be made here. ⊠ *Box 347, 275 Main St., Warren 05674,* ☎ *802/496–6350 or 888/867–4824,* 🅵🅰🅇 *802/496–6354,* 🆆🅴🅱 *www.pitcherinn.com. 9 rooms, 2 suites. Restaurant, billiard room, in-room data ports. AE, MC, V. BP.*

$$–$$$$ 🛏 **Inn at the Round Barn Farm.** Art exhibits have replaced cows in the big round barn here (one of only eight in the state), but the Shaker-style building still dominates the farm's 215 acres. The inn's guest rooms are in the 1806 farmhouse, where books line the walls of the cream-colored library. The rooms are sumptuous, with eyelet-trimmed sheets, elaborate four-poster beds, rich-colored wallpapers, and brass wall lamps for easy bedtime reading. Seven have fireplaces, four have whirlpool tubs, and five have steam showers. The inn offers snowshoe packages and tours. ⊠ *1661 E. Warrren Rd., 05673,* ☎ *802/496–2276,* 🅵🅰🅇 *802/ 496–8832,* 🆆🅴🅱 *www.innatroundbarn.com. 12 rooms. Indoor pool, cross-country skiing, recreation room, library. AE, D, MC, V. BP.*

$$–$$$$ 🛏 **Tucker Hill Lodge.** The 1940s lodge has a new owner and a new look. Local innkeeper David Jackson purchased the property in 1999 and modernized the rooms; all have country-casual furnishings, antiques, phones, and TV/VCRs. There are fireplaces in the living room, dining room, and pub. The menu at the Steak Place includes a 24-ounce steak and barbecue ribs, as well as fish and vegetarian choices. Lighter fare is served in the pub area for late-night patrons. Dinner can be included in the room rate if desired. ⊠ *Rte. 17, 05673,* ☎ *802/496–3983 or 800/543–7841,* 🅵🅰🅇 *802/496–3203,* 🆆🅴🅱 *www.tuckerhill.com. 18 rooms, 1 suite. Restaurant, bar, in-room data ports, pool, tennis court, hiking. AE, MC, V. CP.*

$$ 🛏 **Beaver Pond Farm Inn.** This small 1840 farmhouse less than a mile from Sugarbush overlooks rolling meadows and is next door to Sugarbush Golf Course. Guest rooms are decorated simply, and bathrooms are ample; the inn's focal point is the huge deck. The hearty breakfast might include orange-yogurt pancakes; other meals may be provided at guest's requests. The inn has a limited practice driving range, and the innkeeper is a fly-fishing guide. ⊠ *1225 Golf Course Rd., Warren 05674,* ☎ *802/583–2861,* 🅵🅰🅇 *802/583–2860,* 🆆🅴🅱 *www.beaverpondfarminn.com. 5 rooms. Dining room, driving range. MC, V. Closed Jan.–mid-May. BP.*

Nightlife and the Arts

The Back Room at **Chez Henri** (⊠ Sugarbush Village, ☎ 802/583–2600) has a pool table and is popular with the après-ski and late-night dance crowds. Local bands play music at **Gallagher's** (⊠ Rtes. 100 and 17, ☎ 802/496–8800).

The **Green Mountain Cultural Center** (⊠ Inn at the Round Barn Farm, E. Warren Rd., ☎ 802/496–7722), a nonprofit organization, brings concerts and art exhibits, as well as educational workshops, to the Mad River valley. The **Valley Players** (⊠ Rte. 100, ☎ 802/496–9612) present musicals, dramas, follies, and holiday shows.

Outdoor Activities and Sports

BIKING

The popular 14-mi Waitsfield–Warren loop begins when you cross the covered bridge in Waitsfield. Keep right on East Warren Road to the four-way intersection in East Warren; continue straight, then bear right, riding down Brook Road to the village of Warren. Return by turning right (north) on Route 100 back toward Waitsfield.

Clearwater Sports (⊠ Rte. 100, ☎ 802/496–2708) rents canoes, kayaks and camping equipment, and offers guided river trips and white water instruction in the warm months; in the winter, the store leads snowshoe tours and rents telemark equipment, snowshoes, and one-person Mad River Rocket sleds.

GOLF

Great views and challenging play are the trademarks of the Robert Trent Jones–designed 18-hole, par-72 course at **Sugarbush Resort** (⊠ Golf Course Rd., ☎ 802/583–6727). The greens fee runs from $32 to $52; a cart (sometimes mandatory) costs $17.

SLEIGH RIDES

The 100-year-old sleigh of the **Lareau Farm Country Inn** (⊠ Rte. 100, ☎ 802/496–4949) cruises along the banks of the Mad River.

Shopping

ART AND ANTIQUES

Luminosity Stained Glass Studios (☎ 802/496–2231), inside the converted Old Church on Rte. 100, specializes in stained glass, custom lighting, and art glass. **Cabin Fever Quilts** (⊠ Rte. 100, ☎ 802/496–2287), which shares a building with Luminosity Stained Glass Studios, sells fine new handmade quilts.

CRAFTS

All Things Bright and Beautiful (⊠ Bridge St., ☎ 802/496–3997) is a 12-room Victorian house jammed to the rafters with stuffed animals of all shapes, sizes, and colors as well as folk art, prints, and collectibles. **Warren Village Pottery** (⊠ Main St., Warren, ☎ 802/496–4162) sells handcrafted wares from its retail shop and specializes in functional stoneware pottery.

Ski Areas

MAD RIVER GLEN

In 1995, Mad River Glen became the first ski area to be owned by a cooperative formed by the skiing community. The hundreds of shareholders are dedicated, knowledgeable skiers devoted to keeping skiing what it used to be—a pristine alpine experience. Mad River's unkempt aura attracts rugged individualists looking for less-polished terrain: the area was developed in the late 1940s and has changed relatively little since then. It remains one of only four resorts in the country that bans snowboarding. ⊠ *Rte. 17, 05673,* ☎ *802/496–3551; 800/*

850–6742 cooperative office; 802/496–2001 snow conditions, WEB *www.madriverglen.com.*

Downhill. Mad River is steep, with natural slopes that follow the contours of the mountain. The terrain changes constantly on the 45 interconnected trails, of which 30% are beginner, 35% are intermediate, and 35% are expert. Intermediate and novice terrain is regularly groomed. Five lifts, including a single 1940s chairlift that may be the only lift of its vintage still carrying skiers, service the mountain's 2,037-ft vertical drop. Most of Mad River's trails (85%) are covered only by natural snow.

Telemark. The "Mecca of Free-Heel Skiing" sponsors telemark programs through the season and each March hosts the North America Telemark Organization, which attracts up to 1,200 skiers.

Child care. The nursery is for children ages 3 weeks to 6 years. The ski school runs classes for little ones ages 4 to 12. Junior racing is available weekends and during holidays.

SUGARBUSH

In the Warren-Waitsfield ski world, Sugarbush is Mad River Glen's alter ego. Sugarbush's current owner, the American Skiing Company, has spent millions to keep the resort on the cutting edge. The Slide Brook Express quad connects the two mountains, Sugarbush South and Sugarbush North. A computer-controlled system for snowmaking has increased coverage to nearly 70%. At the base of the mountain is a village with condominiums, restaurants, shops, bars, and a sports center. ⊠ *Box 350, Sugarbush Access Rd., accessible from Rte. 100 or Rte. 17, Warren 05674,* ☎ *802/583–6300; 800/537–8427 lodging; 802/583–7669 snow conditions,* WEB *www.sugarbush.com.*

Downhill. Sugarbush is two distinct, connected mountain complexes. The Sugarbush South area is what old-timers recall as Sugarbush Mountain: with a vertical of 2,400 ft, it is known for formidable steeps toward the top and in front of the main base lodge. Sugarbush North offers what South has in short supply—beginner runs. North also has steep fall-line pitches and intermediate cruisers off its 2,600 vertical ft. There are 115 trails in all: 23% beginner, 48% intermediate, 29% expert. The resort has 18 lifts: seven quads (including four high-speed versions), three triples, four doubles, and four surface lifts.

Child care. The Sugarbush Day School accepts children from ages 6 weeks to 6 years; older children have indoor play areas and can go on outdoor excursions. There's half- and full-day instruction available for children from ages 4 to 11. Kids have their own Magic Carpet lift. Sugarbear Forest, a terrain garden, has fun bumps and jumps.

Summer and year-round activities. The Sugarbush Mountain Biking & Technical Hiking Center (☎ 802/583–6572) has bike rentals and miles of terrain; it provides guided tours and instruction. Open year-round, the Sugarbush Health and Racquet Club (☎ 802/583–6700), near the ski lifts, has Nautilus and Universal equipment; tennis, squash, and racquetball courts; a whirlpool, a sauna, and steam rooms; one indoor pool; and a 30-ft-high climbing wall.

CROSS-COUNTRY SKIING

Blueberry Lake Cross-Country Ski Area (⊠ Plunkton Rd., Warren, ☎ 802/496–6687) has 30 km (18 mi) of groomed trails through thickly wooded glades. **Ole's** (⊠ Airport Rd., Warren, ☎ 802/496–3430) runs a cross-country center and small restaurant out of the tiny Warren airport; it has 60 km (37 mi) of groomed European-style trails that span out into the surrounding woods from the landing strips.

Brookfield

28 *26 mi southeast of Waitsfield, 15 mi south of Montpelier.*

The residents of secluded Brookfield have voted several times to keep the town's roads unpaved and even turned down an offered I–89 exit when the interstate highway was being built in the '60s. Route 14 east of town is a scenic road. Crossing the nation's only **floating bridge** (⊠ Rte. 65 between Rtes. 12 and 14) feels like driving on water. The bridge, supported by nearly 400 barrels, sits at water level. It's the scene of the annual ice-harvest festival in January, though it's closed to traffic in winter.

Lodging

$$–$$$ ★ ⊡ **Green Trails Inn.** The enormous fieldstone fireplace that dominates the living and dining area at Green Trails is symbolic of the stalwart hospitality of the innkeepers. Antique clocks fill the common areas, and the comfortably elegant rooms in two historic buildings have antiques and Oriental rugs. One room has a fireplace, and two rooms have whirlpool tubs. Vegetarians are happily accommodated. The inn overlooks Sunset Lake and is a tranquil place for a walk down a tree-shaded country road. In winter, dinner can be included in the room rate. ⊠ *Main St., 05036,* ☎ *802/276–3412 or 800/243–3412,* WEB *www. greentrailsinn.com. 13 rooms, 9 with bath. Dining room, lake, boating, cross-country skiing, ski shop, sleigh rides. D, MC, V. BP.*

Central Vermont A to Z

To research prices, get advice from other travelers, and book travel arrangements, visit ww.fodors.com.

BUS TRAVEL

Vermont Transit links Rutland, White River Junction, Burlington, and many smaller towns.
➤ BUS INFORMATION: **Vermont Transit** (☎ 800/552-8737).

CAR TRAVEL

The major east-west road is U.S. 4, which stretches from White River Junction in the east to Fair Haven in the west. Route 125 connects Middlebury on U.S. 7 with Hancock on Route 100; Route 100 splits the region in half along the eastern edge of the Green Mountains. Route 17 travels east-west from Waitsfield over the Appalachian Gap through Bristol and down to the shores of Lake Champlain. I–91 and the parallel U.S. 5 follow the state's eastern border; U.S. 7 and Route 30 are the north-south highways in the west. I–89 links White River Junction with Montpelier to the north.

EMERGENCIES

➤ HOSPITALS: **Porter Hospital** (⊠ South St., Middlebury, ☎ 802/388-7901). **Rutland Medical Center** (⊠ 160 Allen St., Rutland, ☎ 802/775-7111; 800/649-2187 in Vermont).

LODGING

Sugarbush Reservations and the Woodstock Area Chamber of Commerce provide lodging referral services.
➤ RESERVATION SERVICES: **Sugarbush Reservations** (☎ 800/537-8427). **Woodstock Area Chamber of Commerce** (☎ 802/457-3555 or 888/496-6378).

TOURS

Country Inns Along the Trail offers self-guided and guided hiking and skiing trips, and self-guided biking trips from inn to inn in Vermont.

The Vermont Icelandic Horse Farm conducts year-round guided riding expeditions on easy-to-ride Icelandic horses. Full-day, half-day, and hourly rides, weekend tours, and inn-to-inn treks are available.

➤ TOUR OPERATORS: **Country Inns Along the Trail** (✉ 834 Van Cortland Rd., Brandon 05733, ☎ 802/247–3300 or 800/838–3301). **Vermont Icelandic Horse Farm** (✉ N. Fayston Rd., Waitsfield 05673, ☎ 802/496–7141).

VISITOR INFORMATION

➤ TOURIST INFORMATION: **Addison County Chamber of Commerce** (✉ 2 Court St., Middlebury 05753, ☎ 802/388–7951 or 800/733–8376, WEB www.midvermont.com). **Quechee Chamber of Commerce** (✉ P.O. Box 106, 1789 Quechee St., Quechee 05059, ☎ 802/295–7900 or 800/295–5451, WEB www.quechee.com). **Rutland Region Chamber of Commerce** (✉ 256 N. Main St., Rutland 05701, ☎ 802/773–2747 or 800/756–8880, WEB www.rutlandvermont.com). **Sugarbush Chamber of Commerce** (✉ Box 173, Rte. 100, Waitsfield 05673, ☎ 802/496–3409 or 800/828–4748, WEB www.madrivervalley.com). **Woodstock Area Chamber of Commerce** (✉ Box 486, 18 Central St., Woodstock 05091, ☎ 802/457–3555 or 888/496–6378, WEB www.woodstockvt.com).

NORTHERN VERMONT

Vermont's northernmost region reveals the state's greatest array of contrasts. To the west, along Lake Champlain, Burlington and its Chittenden County suburbs have grown so rapidly that rural wags now say that Burlington's greatest advantage is that it's "close to Vermont." The north country also harbors Vermont's tiny capital, Montpelier, and its highest mountain, Mt. Mansfield, site of the famous Stowe ski slopes. To the northeast of Burlington and Montpelier spreads a sparsely populated and heavily wooded territory, the domain of loggers as much as farmers, where French spills out of the radio and the last snows melt toward the first of June.

You'll find plenty to do in the region's cities (Burlington, Montpelier, St. Johnsbury, and Barre), in the bustling resort area of Stowe, in the Lake Champlain Islands, and—if you like the outdoors—in the wilds of the Northeast Kingdom.

The coverage of towns in this area begins in the state capital, Montpelier; moves west toward Waterbury, Stowe, and Burlington; then goes north through the Lake Champlain Islands, east along the boundary with Canada toward Jay Peak and Newport, and south into the heart of the Northeast Kingdom before completing the circle in Barre.

Montpelier

➁ *38 mi southeast of Burlington, 115 mi north of Brattleboro.*

With only about 8,000 residents, Montpelier is the country's least populous state capital. The intersection of State and Main streets is the city hub, bustling with the activity of state and city workers during the day. It's a pleasant place to spend an afternoon shopping and browsing; in true small-town Vermont fashion, though, the streets become deserted at night.

The **Vermont State House**—with a gleaming gold dome and columns of Barre granite 6 ft in diameter—is impressive for a city this size. The goddess of agriculture tops the dome. The Greek Revival building dates from 1836, although it was rebuilt after a fire in 1859; the latter year's Victorian style was adhered to in a lavish 1994 restoration.

Northern Vermont

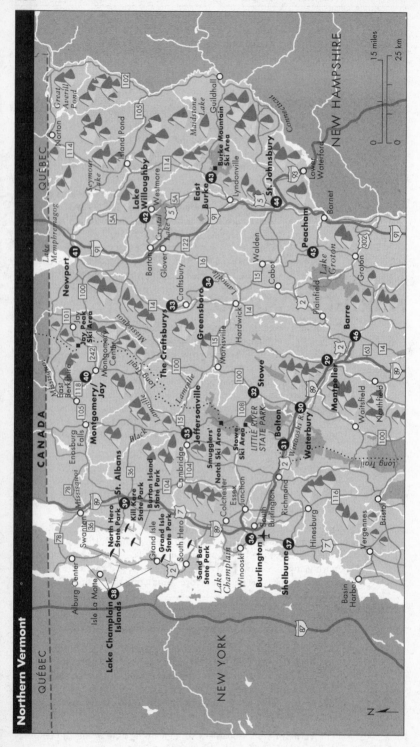

QUÉBEC

CANADA

QUÉBEC

NEW YORK

NEW HAMPSHIRE

15 miles

25 km

Great
Averill Pond

Norton

Island Pond

Maidstone
Lake

Guildhall

Burke Mountain
Ski Area

Lower
Waterford

Lake
Memphremagog

Seymour
Lake

Westmore

Lake
Willoughby

East
Burke

Lyndonville

St. Johnsbury

Barnet

Crystal
Lake

Newport

Barton

Glover

Peacham

Groton

Lake
Groton

Craftsbury

Greensboro

Walden

Cabot

Plainfield

Barre

Jay Peak
Ski Area

Jay

Montgomery
Center

The Craftsburys

Hardwick

Morrisville

Montpelier

Waitsfield

Northfield

East
Berkshire

Montgomery/
Jay

Enosburg
Falls

Jeffersonville

Stowe

Bolton

Waterbury

Cambridge

Smugglers'
Notch Ski Area

Stowe
Ski Area

LITTLE RIVER
STATE PARK

Swanton

St. Albans

Colchester

Essex
Junction

Richmond

Long Trail

Alburg
Center

Isle La Motte

Lake Champlain
Islands

North Hero
State Park

Kill Kare
State Park

Burton Island
State Park

Grand Isle

Grand Isle
State Park

South Hero

Sand Bar
State Park

Winooski

South
Burlington

Burlington

Shelburne

Hinesburg

Lake
Champlain

Vergennes

Bristol

Basin
Harbor

N

Interior paintings and exhibits make much of Vermont's sterling Civil War record. ⊠ *115 State St.,* ☎ *802/828–2228.* ⊒ *Free.* ☉ *Weekdays 8–4; tours July–mid-Oct. weekdays every ½ hr 10–3:30 (last tour begins at 3:30), also Sat. 11–3 (last tour begins at 2:30). Self-guided tours available when building is open.*

Perhaps you're wondering what the last panther shot in Vermont looked like? Why New England bridges are covered? What a niddy-noddy is? Or what Christmas was like for a Bethel boy in 1879? ("I skated on my new skates. In the morning Papa and I set up a stove for Gramper.") The **Vermont Museum,** on the ground floor of the Vermont Historical Society offices in Montpelier, satisfies the curious with intriguing and informative exhibits. ⊠ *109 State St.,* ☎ *802/828–2291,* WEB *www.state.vt. us/vhs.* ⊒ *$3.* ☉ *Tues.–Fri. 9–4:30, Sat. 9–4, Sun. noon–4.*

Dining and Lodging

$$–$$$ ✕ **Chef's Table.** Nearly everyone working here is a student at the New
★ England Culinary Institute. Although this is a training ground, the quality and inventiveness are anything but beginner's luck. The menu changes daily. The atmosphere is more formal than that of the sister operation downstairs, the Main Street Bar and Grill (open daily for lunch and dinner). A 15% gratuity is added to the bill. ⊠ *118 Main St.,* ☎ *802/229–9202; 802/223–3188 grill. AE, D, DC, MC, V. Closed Sun. No lunch Sat..*

$$–$$$ ✕ **Sarducci's.** Legislative lunches have been a lot more leisurely ever since Sarducci's came along to fill the trattoria void in Vermont's capital. These bright, cheerful rooms alongside the Winooksi River are a great spot for pizza fresh from wood-fired ovens, wonderfully textured homemade Italian breads, and imaginative pasta dishes such as pasta pugliese, which marries penne with basil, black olives, roasted eggplant, Portobello mushrooms, and sun-dried tomatoes. ⊠ *3 Main St.,* ☎ *802/223– 0229. Reservations not accepted. AE, MC, V. No lunch Sun.*

$$–$$$ ☷ **Inn at Montpelier.** This inn built in the early 1800s was renovated with the business traveler in mind, but the architectural detailing, antique four-poster beds, Windsor chairs, and the classical guitar on the stereo attract the leisure trade as well. The formal sitting room has a Federal feel to it, and the wide wraparound Colonial Revival porch is perfect for reading a good book or watching the townsfolk stroll by. The rooms in the annex, also a 19th-century building, are equally spiffy. ⊠ *147 Main St., 05602,* ☎ *802/223–2727,* FAX *802/223–0722,* WEB *www.innatmontpelier.com. 19 rooms. Meeting room. AE, D, DC, MC, V. CP.*

Waterbury

③⓪ *12 mi northwest of Montpelier.*

The face of Waterbury's compact downtown is changing as coffee shops, restaurants, and galleries begin to move into the brick buildings that once housed tired-looking furniture and hardware stores. But the anchor here remains the huge state office complex that formerly served as a hospital. The little red train station comes to life only when Amtrak's *Vermonter* stops in town, once a day in each direction. The principal draws for visitors, however, are north of I–89, along Route 100.

Ben & Jerry's Ice Cream Factory is the mecca, nirvana, and Valhalla for ice cream lovers. Ben and Jerry began selling ice cream from a renovated gas station in Burlington in the 1970s. Famous for their social and environmental consciousness, the boys do good works while living off the butterfat of the land. The tour only skims the surface of the behind-the-scenes goings-on at the plant—a flaw forgiven when the free samples are offered. ⊠ *Rte. 100, 1 mi north of I–89,* ☎ *802/244–8687,* WEB *www.benjerry.com.* ⊒ *Tour $2.* ☉ *June, daily 9-5; July–Aug.,* *daily 9–8; Sept.–Oct., daily 9–6; Nov.–May, daily 10–5. Tours every ½ hr in winter, more frequent in summer.*

Dining and Lodging

$$$-$$$$ ✕ **Mist Grill Cafe, Bakery, Roastery.** The fare is best described as country bistro, and the atmosphere casual contemporary, at this handsome restaurant in a renovated grist mill overlooking Thatcher Brook Falls just a minute from downtown. The café serves premium roasted coffee and handmade breakfast treats every day; some lunch choices are a ploughman's lunch and *panini* (Italian rolls) with Gorgonzola and greens. Traditional dinner offerings such as grilled rib steak and pork spare ribs are on the menu Friday and Saturday evenings, and on Sunday "supper" is served—a selection of comfort foods, plus delicious desserts. ⊠ *92 Stowe St.,* ☎ *802/244–2233. MC, V.*

$$-$$$ ✕ **Villa Tragara.** Intimate and creative, this northern Italian restaurant
★ with Vermont farmhouse decor consistently wins recognition as one of the state's best dining spots. Besides entrées such as the mixed grill (lamb chop, veal cutlet, and quail) and *risotto con quaglie* (roast quail stuffed with toasted bread, prosciutto, sun-dried tomatoes, sage, and Asiago cheese), the owner-chef prepares a five-course tasting menu for $40. The Italian tapas—smaller portions of some popular offerings—are moderately priced to allow patrons to pick and share dishes. (There's a $12 minimum charge per person for the tapas.) The restaurant has live entertainment Friday evenings and a popular seasonal dinner theater. ⊠ *Rte. 100, Waterbury, south of Stowe,* ☎ *802/244–5288. AE, MC, V. Closed Tues. No lunch.*

$$$ ✕🏠 **Thatcher Brook Inn.** Twin gazebos poised on both ends of the front porch of this sprawling 1899 inn define its space on busy Route 100. Three buildings hold comfortable guest rooms in a variety of sizes, with modern bathroom fixtures and Laura Ashley–style floral wallpaper. Some rooms have fireplaces and whirlpool tubs. The pine-paneled tavern is a popular socializing spot, and classic French cuisine is served in the dining room. ⊠ *Rte. 100, 05676,* ☎ *802/244–5911 or 800/292–5911,* FAX *802/244–1294,* WEB *www.thatcherbrook.com. 22 rooms. Restaurant, pub. AE, D, DC, MC, V. BP.*

Outdoor Activities and Sports

Mt. Mansfield State Forest and Little River State Park (⊠ U.S. 2, 1½ mi west of Waterbury, ☎ 802/244–7103) have extensive trail systems for hiking, including one that reaches the headquarters of the Civilian Conservation Corps unit that was stationed here in the 1930s. At Little River State Park, there are campsites, boat rentals, and trails leading to Mt. Mansfield and Camel's Hump.

Shopping

The **Cold Hollow Cider Mill** (⊠ Rte. 100, 3 mi north of I–89, ☎ 802/244–8771 or 800/327–7537) sells cider, baked goods, Vermont produce, and specialty foods. Tastes of fresh-pressed cider are offered while you watch how it is made. **Green Mountain Chocolate Complex** (⊠ Rte. 100, 2½ mi north of I–89, ☎ 802/244–1139) houses gourmet and specialty shops including the Cabot Cheese Annex Store (☎ 802/244–6334) and Shimmering Glass Studio and Gallery (☎ 802/244–8134). The **Vermont Clay Studio & Gallery** (⊠ Rte. 100, ☎ 802/244–1126) displays works by artists from around the country.

Bolton

③ *8 mi northwest of Waterbury, 20 mi northwest of Montpelier, 20 mi southeast of Burlington.*

There isn't much to the town of Bolton itself, but Bolton Valley Holiday Resort bustles with activity.

Lodging

$$$ ⚏ **Black Bear Inn.** Teddy bears in all shapes and sizes decorate this mountaintop inn near the Bolton resort and overlooking the Green Mountains. Twelve rooms have glass-door firestoves and balconies, and six have private hot tubs. Grilled Atlantic salmon with a maple-Dijon mustard glaze is a typical dish at the restaurant. ✉ *Bolton Access Rd., 05477,* ☎ *802/434–2126; 800/395–6335 outside VT,* FAX *802/434–5161,* WEB *www.blkbearinn.com. 24 rooms. Restaurant, pool, outdoor hot tub. MC, V. BP, MAP.*

$$$ ⚏ **Bolton Resort Hotel and Condominiums.** This slopeside complex includes completely renovated rooms with unexciting but functional contemporary decor, all with mountain views and most with balconies. Studios and suites with kitchens and fireplaces are available, as are condominiums. The newer rooms tend to be more spacious. Guests can use the resort's sports center, including a pool, sauna, and indoor tennis courts. Ski packages are available. ✉ *Mountain Rd., 05477,* ☎ *802/434–3444 or 877/926–5866,* FAX *802/434–2131,* WEB *www.boltonvalleyvt.com. 60 rooms, 50 suites, 100 condominiums. AE, MC, V.*

Ski Areas

BOLTON VALLEY HOLIDAY RESORT

With new owners and a multimillion-dollar face-lift, Bolton is well on the way to its goal of becoming a four-season destination. The minivillage at the base of the mountain encompasses a completely renovated hotel as well as several restaurants, a wine and cheese shop, and a sports shop. The major attraction, however, is the downhill ski facility. ✉ *Bolton Access Rd., 05477,* ☎ *802/434–3444 or 877/926–5866.*

Downhill. Bolton's six lifts include a quad chair, four double chairs, and a surface lift, which service 51 trails covering 157 acres of skiable terrain. The majority of the trails are rated for intermediates; the longest is the 2½-mi Cobrass Run. The vertical drop is 1,625 ft. The resort has 60% snowmaking coverage and offers top to bottom night skiing Monday–Saturday until 10 PM. There's a 1,500-ft terrain park for snowboarders.

Cross-country. A Nordic center offers cross-country ski, telemark, and snowshoe rentals and lessons. The resort has 35 km (22 mi) of groomed trails and 65 km (40 mi) of natural trails, including some where dogs are permitted.

Child care. The licensed Honey Bear Child Care Center provides care for children from six weeks to six years of age. There are ski programs for ages 3–15.

Summer and year-round activities. The resort has a mountain bike center that offers rentals; indoor and outdoor tennis courts; and hiking trails. A chairlift transports hikers to the top of the mountain, but not down. The sports center, open year-round, houses the indoor tennis courts and a pool, sauna, whirlpool, and weight room.

Stowe

★ ㉜ *16 mi northeast of Bolton, 22 mi northwest of Montpelier, 36 mi east of Burlington.*

Ever since the Civilian Conservation Corps cut the first downhill trails on Mt. Mansfield, ever since Austrian instructors first told weekenders to "bend mit der knees," Stowe has been the spiritual home of Vermont skiing. The village itself is tiny, just a few blocks of shops and restaurants clustered around a snow-white church spire—but it serves as the anchor for the Mountain Road, which leads north past more places to dine, stay, and shop on its way to those fabled slopes.

To many, Stowe rings a bell as the place where the von Trapp family, of *Sound of Music* fame, chose to settle after fleeing Austria. Set amid acres of pastures that fall away and allow for wide-angle panoramas of the mountains beyond, the **Trapp Family Lodge** (⌨ Luce Hill Rd., ☎ 802/253–8511 or 800/826–7000) is the site of a popular outdoor music series in summer and an extensive cross-country ski-trail network in winter.

For more than a century the history of Stowe has been determined by the town's proximity to **Mt. Mansfield**, at 4,393 ft the highest elevation in the state. As early as 1858, visitors were trooping to the area to view the mountain, which has a shape that suggests the profile of the face of a man lying on his back. If hiking to the top isn't your idea of a good time, in summer you can take the 4½-mi toll road to the top for a short scenic walk and a magnificent view. ⌨ *Mountain Rd., 7 mi from Rte. 100,* ☎ *802/253–3000.* ☞ *Toll road $14.* ☉ *Mid-May–mid-Oct., daily 10–5.*

Mt. Mansfield's upper reaches are accessible by the eight-seat gondola that shuttles continuously up to the area of "the Chin" and the Cliff House Restaurant (☎ 802/253–3000 ext. 237), where lunch is served daily from 11–2:30. ⌨ *Mountain Rd., 8 mi off Rte. 100,* ☎ *802/253–3000.* ☞ *Gondola $14.* ☉ *Mid-June–mid-Oct., daily 10–5; early Dec.–late Apr., daily 8–4 for skiers.*

Dining and Lodging

$$$ ✕ **Chelsea Grill.** Stowe's newest "in" spot successfully blends the accoutrements of a traditional Vermont country restaurant with the glitz and ambition of a big city dining room. The chef describes his cuisine as "refined country comfort food," with such appetizers as a deviled fried-oyster salad with smoked bacon and lemon parsley vinaigrette, and entrées such as grilled rack of lamb with roasted peppers and pan-roasted sea bass with citrus couscous. The homemade desserts are every bit as creative. ⌨ *Mountain Road,* ☎ *802/253–3075. MC, V. No lunch Mon.–Thurs.*

$$$ ✕ **Mes Amis.** Carole Fisher, who built her reputation as chef at the Isle
★   de France up the road, opened her own place a few years ago and has the locals queueing up for house specialties such as fresh oysters, lobster bisque, braised lamb shanks, roast duck (secret recipe), and bananas Foster. Opt for the patio on a warm summer's night. ⌨ *311 Mountain Rd.,* ☎ *802/ 253–8669. Reservations not accepted. D, MC, V. Closed Mon.*

$$–$$$ ✕ **Miguel's Stowe Away.** Miguel's serves up all the Tex-Mex standards along with tasty surprises such as coconut-fried shrimp, Cajun lamb fajitas, and a Yankee-flavored maple flan. Steaks and burgers round out the gringo menu. The cozy front room has a pool table (no quarters required) and a bar stocked with frosty Corona beer. Miguel's has an outpost on the Sugarbush Access Road in Warren (☎ 802/583–3858). ⌨ *3148 Mountain Rd.,* ☎ *802/253–7574 or 800/245–1240. AE, D, MC, V. No lunch Apr., Nov.*

$$$$ ✕▩ **Edson Hill Manor.** This French-Canadian–style manor built in 1940
★   sits atop 225 acres of rolling hills. Oriental rugs accent the dark wideboard floors, and a tapestry complements the burgundy-patterned sofas that face the huge stone fireplace in the living room. The guest rooms are pine-paneled and have fireplaces, canopy beds, and down comforters. The dining room ($$$$; no lunch; closed Sun.–Thurs. Apr.–May), the heart of the place, has walls of windows allowing contemplation of the inspiring view, wildflower paintings, and vines climbing to the ceiling. The highly designed contemporary cuisine might include rack of lamb or pan-seared salmon. ⌨ *1500 Edson Hill Rd., 05672,* ☎ *802/253–7371 or 800/621–0284,* ☏ *802/253–4036,* ▦ *www.stowevt.com.*

25 rooms. Restaurant, pool, hiking, horseback riding, cross-country ski-ing, sleigh rides. AE, D, MC, V. BP, MAP.

$$$$ ✕🏨 **Topnotch at Stowe Resort and Spa.** One of the state's poshest re-sorts occupies 120 acres overlooking Mt. Mansfield. Floor-to-ceiling windows, a freestanding circular stone fireplace, and cathedral ceilings distinguish the lobby. Country-decorated rooms have thick carpeting and accents such as painted barn-board walls or Italian prints. The large European spa offers 22 massage-treatment rooms and a fitness pro-gram. Maxwell's restaurant serves contemporary Continental cuisine. ✉ *Mountain Rd., 05672,* ☎ *802/253–8585 or 800/451–8686,* FAX *802/253–9263,* WEB *www.topnotch-resort.com. 77 rooms, 13 suites, 20 town houses. 2 restaurants, bar, 1 indoor and 1 outdoor pool, 10 ten-nis courts (4 indoor), massage, sauna, spa, horseback riding, cross-coun-try skiing, sleigh rides. AE, D, DC, MC, V. MAP.*

$$$$ 🏨 **Stone Hill Inn.** Innkeepers Hap and Amy Jordan have combined the amenities of a fine hotel with the intimacy of a B&B. Each elegantly dec-orated (and soundproof) guest room has a king-size bed, sitting area, and two-person whirlpool bath in front of a fireplace. Common areas include a sitting room and a game room, and the 10 acres of grounds are beautifully landscaped with gardens and waterfalls. For skiers there's overnight boot and glove drying service, and you can use the inn's to-boggan and snowshoes. Rates include evening hors d'oeuvres. ✉ *89 Hous-ton Farm Rd., 05672,* ☎ *802/253–6282,* FAX *802/253–7415,* WEB *www. stonehillinn.com. 9 rooms. Breakfast room, outdoor hot tub, golf priv-ileges, hiking, recreation room. AE, DC, MC, V. BP.*

$$$ 🏨 **Stoweflake Mountain Resort and Spa** You'll find scenic mountain views and a range of accommodations here, from comfortable, coun-try-inn rooms to luxurious suites with fireplaces, wet bars, refrigera-tors, and balconies. This full service resort also has one- to three-bedroom, fully equipped town houses and hosts Stowe's annual Hot Air Balloon Festival. ✉ *1746 Mountain Rd. (Box 69), 05672,* ☎ *802/253–7355,* FAX *802/253–6858,* WEB *www.stoweflake.com. 94 rooms; 30 town houses. 2 restaurants, kitchenettes (some), indoor-outdoor pools, hair salon, spa, sauna, driving range, putting green, 2 tennis courts, bicycles, sleigh rides, recreation room, business services, meeting rooms. AE, D, DC, MC, V. BP, MAP.*

$$ 🏨 **Inn at Turner Mill.** Families will feel particularly welcome at this sim-ple inn tucked well off the main road. Accommodations range from a one-bedroom unit to a two-bedroom apartment with two private baths, full kitchen, and fireplace; most units have kitchens. The inn is close to the ski area, a short walk from a swimming hole, and just across the road from miles of hiking trails. You can rent snowshoes here or purchase a pass to a nearby health club. ✉ *56 Turner Mill La., 05672,* ☎ *802/253–2062 or 800/992–0016,* WEB *www.turnermill.com. 5 units. AE, MC, V. BP.*

$–$$$ 🏨 **Sunset Motor Inn.** Strategically located among northern Vermont's big-three ski areas, this family owned, family friendly motel has clean and comfortable accommodations. Rooms numbered 70–87 in the newer section are larger and have whirlpool baths and refrigerators; the best are the ones facing the back of the motel. There's a restaurant next door. ✉ *Junction of Rtes. 15 and 100, Morrisville 05661,* ☎ *802/ 888–4956 or 800/544–2347,* FAX *802/888–3698,* WEB *www.gostowe.com/ members/sunset. 55 rooms. Pool. AE, D, MC, V. CP.*

Nightlife and the Arts

NIGHTLIFE

The **Matterhorn Night Club** (✉ Mountain Rd., ☎ 802/253–8198) has live music and dancing on weekends, DJs during the week. Live week-end entertainment takes place at **Stoweflake Mountain Resort and Spa.** Entertainers perform at the **Topnotch at Stowe** lounge on weekends.

Stowe Performing Arts (☎ 802/253–7792) sponsors a series of classical and jazz concerts during July in the Trapp Family Lodge meadow. **Stowe Theater Guild** (⊠ Town Hall Theater, Main St., ☎ 802/253–3961, summer only) performs musicals in July and August.

Outdoor Activities and Sports

A **recreational path** begins behind the Community Church in the center of town and meanders for 5⅓ mi along the river valley. There are many entry points along the way; whether you're on foot, skis, bike, or in-line skates, it's a tranquil spot to enjoy the outdoors.

BIKING

The junction of Routes 100 and 108 is the start of a 21-mi tour with scenic views of Mt. Mansfield; the course takes you along Route 100 to Stagecoach Road, to Morristown, over to Morrisville, and south on Randolph Road. The **Mountain Sports and Bike Shop** (⊠ Mountain Rd., ☎ 802/253–7919 or 800/682–4534 outside Stowe area) supplies equipment and rents bicycles.

CANOEING AND KAYAKING

Umiak Outdoor Outfitters (⊠ 849 S. Main St./Rte. 100, just south of Stowe Village, ☎ 802/253–2317) specializes in canoes and kayaks, rents them for day trips, and leads overnight excursions. The store also operates a rental outpost at Lake Elmore State Park in Elmore, and on the Winooski River off Route 2 in Waterbury.

FISHING

The **Fly Rod Shop** (⊠ Rte. 100, 3 mi south of Stowe, ☎ 802/253–7346 or 800/535–9763) provides a guiding service; gives fly-tying, casting, and rod-building classes in winter; rents fly tackle; and sells equipment, including classic and collectible firearms.

GOLF

Stowe Country Club (⊠ Mountain Rd., ☎ 802/253–4893) has a scenic 18-hole, par-72 course, a driving range, and a putting green. Greens fee is $35–$65; cart rental is $16.

HIKING

An ascent of **Mt. Mansfield** makes for a scenic day hike. Trails lead from Route 108 (the Mountain Road) to the summit ridge, where they meet the north-to-south Long Trail. An option is to take the gondola at Stowe to the top and walk down along a ski trail. Views from the summit take in New Hampshire's White Mountains, New York's Adirondacks across Lake Champlain, and southern Québec. The Green Mountain Club has a trail guide.

For the two-hour climb to **Stowe Pinnacle,** go 1½ mi south of Stowe on Route 100 and turn east on Gold Brook Road opposite the Nichols Farm Lodge; turn left at the first intersection, continue straight at an intersection by a covered bridge, turn right after 1.8 mi, and travel 2.3 mi to a parking lot on the left. The trail crosses an abandoned pasture and takes a short, steep climb to views of the Green Mountains and Stowe Valley.

ICE-SKATING

Jackson Arena (⊠ Park St., ☎ 802/253–6148 or 802/253–4402) is a public ice-skating rink. Skate rental is available.

SLEIGH RIDES

Charlie Horse Sleigh and Carriage Rides (⊠ Mountain Rd., ☎ 802/253–2215) operates rides daily from 11 to 7; reservations are suggested for evening rides.

TENNIS

Topnotch at Stowe Resort and Spa has 10 outdoor and 4 indoor courts. Public courts are located at Stowe's elementary school.

Shopping

Mountain Road is lined with shops from town up toward the ski area.

Ski Areas

STOWE MOUNTAIN RESORT

To be precise, the name of the village is Stowe and the name of the mountain is Mt. Mansfield, but to generations of skiers, the area, the complex, and the region are just plain Stowe. The resort is a classic that dates from the 1930s. Even today the area's mystique attracts as many serious skiers as social skiers. In recent years, on-mountain lodging, improved snowmaking, new lifts, and free shuttle buses that gather skiers from lodges, inns, and motels along Mountain Road have added convenience to the Stowe experience. Yet the traditions remain: the Winter Carnival in January, the Sugar Slalom in April, ski weeks all winter. Three base lodges provide the essentials, including two on-mountain restaurants. Expansion plans over the next few years include the construction of a new slopeside village with shops and accommodations. ✉ *5781 Mountain Rd., 05672,* ☎ *802/253–3000; 800/253–4754 lodging; 802/253–3600 snow conditions.*

Downhill. Mt. Mansfield, with a vertical drop of 2,360 ft, is one of the giants among Eastern ski mountains and the highest in Vermont. The mountain's symmetrical shape allows skiers of all abilities long, satisfying runs from the summit. The famous Front Four (National, Liftline, Starr, and Goat) are the intimidating centerpieces for tough, expert runs, yet there is plenty of mellow intermediate skiing, with 59% of the runs rated at that level. One long beginner trail, the Toll Road Trail, is 3.7 miles. Mansfield's satellite sector is a network of intermediate trails and one expert trail off a basin served by a gondola. Spruce Peak, separate from the main mountain, is a teaching hill and a pleasant experience for intermediates and beginners; it also has a mountaintop trail that connects with slopes at neighboring resort Smugglers' Notch. In addition to the high-speed, eight-passenger gondola, Stowe has 10 lifts, including a quad, one triple, and six double chairlifts, plus one handle tow, to service its 47 trails. Night-skiing trails are accessed by the gondola. The resort has 73% snowmaking coverage. Snowboard facilities include a halfpipe, quarterpipe, and two terrain parks—one for beginners, at the base of Spruce Peak, and one for experts on the Mt. Mansfield side.

Cross-country. The resort has 35 km (22 mi) of groomed cross-country trails and 40 km (24 mi) of backcountry trails. There are four interconnecting cross-country ski areas with more than 150 km (90 mi) of groomed trails within the town of Stowe.

Child care. The child-care center takes children from ages 6 weeks to 6 years, with kids' ski-school programs for ages 6 to 12. A center on Spruce Peak is headquarters for programs for children from ages 3 to 12, and there's another program for teenagers 13 to 17.

Summer activities. The resort offers mountain biking, hiking, in-line skating, an alpine slide, gondola rides, and an 18-hole golf course.

The Craftsburys

❸❸ *27 mi northeast of Stowe.*

The three villages of the Craftsburys—Craftsbury Common, Craftsbury, and East Craftsbury—are among Vermont's finest and oldest towns. Handsome white houses and barns, the requisite common, and terrific views make them well worth the drive. **Craftsbury General Store** in Craftsbury Village is a great place to stock up on picnic supplies and local information. The rolling farmland hints at the way Vermont used to be: the area's sheer distance from civilization and its rugged weather have kept most of the state's development farther south.

Lodging

$$$$ ✕⊞ **Inn on the Common.** All the rooms at this inn—actually a complex made of three Federal-style buildings—contain antique reproductions and contemporary furnishings; deluxe rooms have generous seating areas and fireplaces. Cocktails and hors d'oeuvres are offered in one house's cozy library. Five-course dinners (reservations essential) are served in the dining room, which overlooks the inn's gardens. The inn has an excellent wine cellar, and a dining deck open in summer. Guests have access to the facilities at the Craftsbury Sports Center and Albany's Wellness Barn, which has a lap pool, aerobics machines, a sauna, and a whirlpool. Cross-country ski trails connect with those at the Craftsbury Nordic Center. ⊠ *On the common, 05827,* ☎ *802/586–9619 or 800/521–2233,* FAX *802/586–2249,* WEB *www.innonthecommon. com. 15 rooms, 1 suite. Dining room, lounge, pool, tennis court, library, cross-country skiing. AE, MC, V. MAP.*

$$–$$$ ⊞ **Craftsbury Outdoor Center.** This outdoors-enthusiasts' haven has standard accommodations and sporting packages. Because of a long season of snowcover—it's white here when the rest of Vermont is green—the cross-country skiing is terrific on the 135 km (80 mi) of trails (85 km/50 mi groomed) on the property and through local farmland. During the rest of the year, sculling and running camps are held. Guests and nonguests alike can ski, mountain bike, and canoe at day-use rates; equipment rental is available. The buffet-style meals include soups, stews, and homemade breads and desserts. In winter, rates include use of trails. ⊠ *Box 31, Lost Nation Rd., 05827,* ☎ *802/586–7767 or 800/729–7751,* FAX *802/586–7768,* WEB *www.craftsbury.com. 49 rooms, 10 with bath; 3 cottages; 2 efficiencies. Dining room, boating, mountain bikes, cross-country skiing. MC, V. AP.*

$ ⊞ **Craftsbury Bed & Breakfast.** Craftsbury's longest operating traditional B&B is a lovely place to unwind. Owner Margaret Ramsdell creates an air of peaceful informality at her farmhouse, right down to the absence of a TV. Common rooms include a spacious country kitchen with a woodstove and a living room. In summer, relax on lawn chairs in the big yard; in winter, ski on the property's cross-country ski trails, which are part of a 105 km (65 mi) network. ⊠ *Wylie Hill, 05827,* ☎ *802/586–2206, 6 rooms without bath. MC, V. BP.*

Greensboro

㉞ *10 mi southeast of Craftsbury Common.*

Greensboro is an idyllic small town with a long history as a vacation destination.

Lodging

$$$$ ⊞ **Highland Lodge.** Tranquillity reigns at this 1860 house, which overlooks a pristine lake. The lodge's 120 acres of rambling woods and pastures are laced with hiking and skiing trails (ski rentals available). Widely known for its great front porch, this quiet family resort is part refined elegance and part casual country of the summer-camp sort. The comfortable guest rooms have Early American–style furnishings. Most rooms have views of the lake; the one- to three-bedroom cottages are more private (four with gas stoves stay open in winter). The traditional dinner menu, which incorporates Vermont foods, might include entrées

such as roasted leg of lamb and grilled Black Angus sirloin. ⊠ *E. Craftsbury Rd., 05841,* ☎ *802/533–2647,* FAX *802/533–7494. 11 rooms, 11 cottages. Restaurant, lake, tennis court, hiking, boating, cross-country skiing, recreation room. D, MC, V. Closed mid-Mar.–late May and mid-Oct.–mid-Dec. MAP.*

Shopping

The **Miller's Thumb** (⊠ Main St., ☎ 802/533–2960 or 800/680–7886) sells Italian pottery, Vermont furniture, crafts and antiques, and April Cornell clothing and linens. **Willey's Store** (⊠ Main St., ☎ 802/533–2621), with wooden floors and tin ceilings, warrants exploration. Foodstuffs, baskets, candy, kitchen paraphernalia, and more are packed to the rafters.

Jeffersonville

㉟ *36 mi west of Greensboro, 18 mi north of Stowe, 28 mi northeast of Burlington.*

Mt. Mansfield and Madonna Peak tower over Jeffersonville, whose activities are closely linked with those of Smugglers' Notch Ski Resort.

Boyden Valley Winery (⊠ Junction of Rtes. 15 and 104, Cambridge, ☎ 802/644–8151) conducts tours of its microwinery and also showcases an excellent selection of Vermont specialty products and local handicrafts, including fine furniture. The winery is closed Monday.

Lodging

$$$$ 🏨 **Smugglers' Notch Resort.** Most of the condos at this large year-round resort have fireplaces and decks. The resort is known for its many family programs. Rates include lift tickets and ski lessons in season, and kids 6 weeks to 2 years of age get free care if parents stay three or more nights. ⊠ *Rte. 108, 05464,* ☎ *802/644–8851 or 800/451–8752,* FAX *802/644–1230,* WEB *www.smugs.com. 502 condominiums. 3 restaurants, bar, indoor-outdoor pools, hot tub, sauna, 6 tennis courts, exercise room, ice-skating, down-hill skiing, recreation room, baby-sitting, children's programs (ages 3–17), nursery, playground. AE, DC, MC, V.*

$ 🏨 **Deer Run Motor Inn.** This well-kept, comfortable motel may be the north country's best bargain. Although it's right on busy Route 15, the units are set fairly well back (second-floor rooms with queen-size beds face the rear), and each has a coffeemaker, deck, sliding glass doors, and cable TV. A swing set and grills are other amenities. ⊠ *80 Deer Run Loop, 05464,* ☎ *802/644–8866 or 800/354–2728. 25 units. Picnic area, refrigerator, pool. AE, D, MC, V.*

Outdoor Activities and Sports

Applecheek Farm (⊠ 567 McFarlane Rd., Hyde Park, ☎ 802/888–4482) offers daytime and evening (by lantern) hay and sleigh rides, llama treks, and farm tours. **Smugglers' Notch State Park** (⊠ Rte. 108, 10 mi north of Mt. Mansfield, ☎ 802/253–4014) is good for picnicking and hiking on wild terrain among large boulders. **Northern Vermont Llamas** (⊠ 766 Lapland Rd., Waterville, ☎ 802/644–2257) offers half- and full-day treks from May through October along the cross-country ski trails of Smugglers' Notch. The llamas carry everything, including snacks and lunches. Advance reservations essential. **Vermont Horse Park** (⊠ Rte. 108 ☎ 802/644–5347) conducts rides on authentic horse-drawn sleighs as well as trail rides when weather permits.

Shopping

ANTIQUES

The **Buggy Man** (⊠ Rte. 15, 7 mi east of Jeffersonville, ☎ 802/635–2110) sells American furniture and collectibles including horse-drawn vehicles. **Mel Siegel** (⊠ Rte. 15, 7 mi east of Jeffersonville, ☎ 802/635–7838) specializes in 19th-century American furniture and glassware.

CLOTHING

Johnson Woolen Mills (⊠ Main St., Johnson, 9 mi east of Jeffersonville, ☎ 802/635–2271) is an authentic factory store with deals on woolen blankets, yard goods, and the famous Johnson outerwear.

CRAFTS

Vermont Rug Makers (⊠ Rte. 100C, East Johnson, 10 mi east of Jeffersonville, ☎ 802/635–2434) weaves imaginative rugs and tapestries from fabrics, wools, and exotic materials. Its International Gallery displays rugs and tapestries from countries throughout the world. The shop has a branch on Main Street in Stowe.

Ski Areas

SMUGGLERS' NOTCH RESORT

This sprawling resort complex consistently wins accolades for its family programs. Its children's ski school is one of the best in the country—and possibly *the* best. But skiers of all levels come here (in 1996, Smugglers' became the first ski area in the East to designate a triple-black-diamond run—the Black Hole). All the essentials are available at the base of the lifts. A three-phase plan, which will allow snowmaking top to bottom on all three mountains is scheduled to be completed by 2002. ⊠ *Rte. 108, 05464,* ☎ *802/644–8851 or 800/451–8752,* WEB *www.smuggs.com.*

Downhill. Smugglers' has three mountains. The highest, Madonna, with a vertical drop of 2,610 ft, is in the center and connects with a trail network to Sterling (1,500-ft vertical). The third mountain, Morse (1,150-ft vertical), is adjacent to Smugglers' "village" of shops, restaurants, and lodgings; it's connected to the other peaks by trails and a shuttle bus. The wild, craggy landscape lends a pristine, wilderness feel to the skiing experience on the two higher mountains. The tops of each of the mountains have expert terrain—a couple of double-black diamonds make Madonna memorable. Intermediate trails fill the lower sections. Morse has many beginner trails, including the new Morse Bowl, with a double chair that services five new trails for beginners and advanced beginners. Smugglers' 67 trails are served by nine lifts, including five chairs and four surface lifts. Top-to-bottom snowmaking on all three mountains allows for 62% coverage. A trail at the top of Sterling Mountain connects to Spruce Peak at the Stowe Mountain Resort. There are several terrain parks for snowboarders, including Prohibition Park, at 3,500 ft one of the longest in Vermont.

Cross-country. The area has 37 km (23 mi) of groomed and tracked cross-country trails.

Other activities. The self-contained village has ice-skating and sleigh rides. The numerous snowshoeing programs include family walks and backcountry trips. The FunZone at SmuggsCentral has an indoor pool, playground, slides, miniature golf, a hot tub, ice skating rink, and Nordic Center. A Teen Center is open from 5 PM until midnight.

Child care. The state-of-the-art Alice's Wonderland Child Care Center accepts children from ages 6 weeks to 6 years. Ski camps for kids ages 3–17 offer excellent instruction, plus movies, games, and other activities.

Summer and year-round activities. Smugglers' has a full roster of summertime programs, including a pool, complete with waterfalls and water slides, the Giant Rapid River Ride (the longest water ride in the state), lawn games, and mountain biking and hiking programs. It also has an indoor sports center, the FunZone. Horseback riding is available in summer and fall.

Burlington

★ ③⑥ *31 mi southwest of Jeffersonville, 76 mi south of Montréal, 349 mi north of New York City, 223 mi northwest of Boston, MA.*

Cited in survey after survey as one of America's most livable small cities, Burlington has the vibrant character of a college town in which a lot of the graduates have stayed behind to put down roots. The largest population center in Vermont, the city was founded in 1763 and is now the center of a rapidly growing suburban area. It has held its own against highway malls by cleverly positioning itself in the "festival marketplace" retail style, as well as by trading on its incomparable location on Lake Champlain. The Burlington area's eclectic population includes many transplants from larger urban areas as well as roughly 20,000 students from the area's five colleges. For years it was the only city in America with a socialist mayor—now the nation's sole socialist congressional representative.

The **Church Street Marketplace**—a pedestrian mall of boutiques, restaurants, sidewalk cafés, crafts vendors, and street performers—is an animated downtown focal point.

Crouched on the shores of Lake Champlain, which shimmers in the shadows of the Adirondacks to the west, Burlington's revitalized waterfront teems with outdoor enthusiasts who stroll along its recreation path and ply the waters in sailboats and motorcraft in summer. A 500-passenger, three-level cruise vessels, *The Spirit of Ethan Allen II*, takes people on narrated cruises on the lake and, in the evening, dinner and sunset sailings that drift by the Adirondacks and the Green Mountains. ⊠ *Burlington Boat House, College St. at Battery St.,* ☎ *802/862–8300.* 🎫 *$8.* ⊙ *Cruises late May–mid-Oct., daily 10–9.*

☙ Part of the waterfront's revitalization and still a work in progress, the **Lake Champlain Basin Science Center** aims to educate the public about the ecology, history, and culture of the lake region. From looking at plankton through a "kidscope" to dragging a net off the University of Vermont research boat docked on the property, there are activities for the whole family. ⊠ *1 College St.,* ☎ *802/864–1848,* WEB *www. lakechamplaincenter.org.* 🎫 *$3.* ⊙ *Mid-June–Labor Day, daily 11–5; Labor Day–mid-June, weekends and school vacations 12:30–4:30.*

Crowning the hilltop above Burlington is the campus of the **University of Vermont** (☎ 802/656–3480), known simply as UVM for the abbreviation of its Latin name, Universitas Viridis Montis—the University of the Green Mountains. With more than 10,000 students, UVM is the state's principal institution of higher learning. The most architecturally interesting buildings face the Green, which contains some of the grandest surviving specimens of the elm trees that once shaded virtually every street in Burlington, as well as a statue of UVM founder Ira Allen, Ethan's brother. The Robert Hull Fleming Art Museum (⊠ Colchester Ave., ☎ 802/656–0750), just behind the Ira Allen Chapel, houses American portraits and landscapes, including works by Sargent, Homer, and Bierstadt; two Corots and a Fragonard; and an Egyptian mummy. Contemporary Vermont works are also exhibited.

Burlington's **Intervale,** once home to Abenaki and early colonial pioneers, encompasses 700 acres of open land along the Winooski River. You can rent canoes, bicycle the 2-mi trail (which connects with Burlington's 10-mi Cycle the City loop), take a river tour, or hike the trails.

The project is under the auspices of Gardener's Supply Company (✉ 128 Intervale Rd., ☎ 802/660-3505 WEB www.gardeners.com), a major direct mail gardening company, with greenhouses and outdoor display gardens. The company provides maps, information, and a schedule of the many seasonal events held there. One of the earliest residents of the Intervale was Ethan Allen, Vermont's Revolutionary-era guerrilla fighter, who remains a captivating figure. Exhibits at the visitor center at the **Ethan Allen Homestead** answer questions about his flamboyant life. The house contains frontier hallmarks like rough saw-cut boards and an open hearth for cooking. A re-created Colonial kitchen garden resembles the one the Allens would have had. After the tour, you can stretch your legs on scenic trails along the Winooski River. ✉ *North Ave. off Rte. 127, north of Burlington,* ☎ *802/865-4556,* WEB *www.ethanallentogether.com.* ☞ *$5.* ☉ *Call for schedule.*

OFF THE
BEATEN PATH

GREEN MOUNTAIN AUDUBON NATURE CENTER – This is a wonderful place to discover Vermont's outdoor wonders. The center's 300 acres of diverse habitats are a sanctuary for all things wild, and the 5 mi of trails provide an opportunity to explore the workings of differing natural communities. Events include dusk walks, wildflower and birding rambles, nature workshops, and educational activities for kids and adults. The center is 18 mi southeast of Burlington. ✉ *Huntington-Richmond Rd., Richmond,* ☎ *802/434-3068.* ☞ *Donations accepted.* ☉ *Grounds dawn–dusk, center weekdays (and some Sat.) 8–4.*

Dining and Lodging

$$–$$$ ✕ **Isabel's.** An old lumber mill on Lake Champlain houses this restaurant with high ceilings, exposed-brick walls, and knockout views. The menu is seasonal; past dishes, all presented with an artistic flair, have included Thai seafood pasta and vegetable Wellington. Lunch and Sunday brunch are popular; be sure to dine on the outdoor patio on warm days. ✉ *112 Lake St.,* ☎ *802/865-2522. AE, D, DC, MC, V. Mon.; Nov.–Apr., lunch only and closed Mon. and Sat.*

$$–$$$ ✕ **NECI Commons.** The initials stand for New England Culinary Institute, the respected Montpelier academy whose students and teachers run this all-under-one-roof café, bakery, market, restaurant, and bar. The deli counter can get a little pricey, but everything is fresh and tasty. It's open daily for lunch and dinner and on Sundays for brunch. Mornings, homemade pastries and muffins are served in the market area. ✉ *25 Church St.,* ☎ *802/862-6324. AE, D, MC, V.*

$$–$$$ ✕ **Parima Thai Restaurant.** Chef's specials such as crispy roasted duck in tamarind sauce and seafood *phuket* (shrimp, mussels, cod, and squid sautéed in basil sauce) join a menu of traditional Thai including curries and *pad thai* (stir-fried noodles with shrimp or chicken). This handsomely appointed restaurant has one of the most elegant bars in town. ✉ *185 Pearl St.,* ☎ *802/864-7917. AE, D, DC, MC, V. No lunch Nov.–Apr.*

$$–$$$ ✕ **Trattoria Delia.** Didn't manage to rent that villa in Umbria this year? ★ The next best thing, if your travels bring you to Burlington, is this superb Italian country eatery just around the corner from City Hall Park. Local game and produce are the stars, as in roast rabbit marinated in herbs, wine, and olive oil. The chef's passion for the truly homemade extends to wild boar sausage, salami, and fresh mozzarella. Wood-grilled items are a specialty. ✉ *152 St. Paul St.,* ☎ *802/864-5253. AE, D, DC, MC, V. No lunch.*

$$ ✕ **Old Heidelberg German Restaurant.** This chef-owned restaurant, graciously appointed with linens and fresh flowers, serves such tasty Teutonic standards as *sauerbraten,* pork and veal *schnitzels,* and homemade bratwurst; hearty homemade *goulash* and potato soups round out the

luncheon and appetizer menus. German cuisine is the original "comfort food"—perfect for a cold northern Vermont winter night. German beers and wines are available. ⊠ *1016 Shelburne Rd. (Rt. 7),* ☎ *802/865–4423. AE, D, DC, MC, V. Closed Mon..*

$$$–$$$$ ✕🏨 **Basin Harbor Club.** Owned by the Beach family since 1886, this
★ outstanding resort sprawls over 700 acres of prime real estate overlooking Lake Champlain. Luxurious accommodations, a full roster of amenities including an 18-hole Geoffrey Cornish golf course, boating (with a 40-ft tour boat), and day-long children's programs make Basin Harbor a popular spot for families. Some rooms have fireplaces, decks, or porches. The restaurant menu is classic American, the wine list excellent. Coats and ties are required in common areas after 6 PM from mid-June through Labor Day. ⊠ *Basin Harbor Rd., Vergennes 05491,* ☎ *802/475–2311 or 800/622–4000,* 𝐅𝐀𝐗 *802/475–6545,* 𝐖𝐄𝐁 *www.basinharbor.com. 36 rooms, 2 suites in 3 guest houses; 77 cottages. 2 restaurants, pool, 18-hole golf course, 5 tennis courts, health club, bicycles, boating, children's programs (ages 3–15). MC, V. Closed mid-Oct.– mid-May. MAP, AP, BP available spring and fall.*

$$$–$$$$ ✕🏨 **Inn at Essex.** About 10 mi from downtown Burlington, near Essex Outlet Fair, is a state-of-the-art inn and conference center dressed in country clothing. Rooms with flowered wallpaper and reproduction period desks lend the place some character, and many of the rooms have fireplaces. The two restaurants are run by the New England Culinary Institute. Butlers serves dishes such as sweet dumpling squash with ginger-garlic basmati rice, and lobster in yellow-corn sauce with spinach pasta. Five-onion soup, burgers, and daily flatbread pizza specials are among the highlights at the Tavern. ⊠ *70 Essex Way, off Rte. 15, Essex Junction 05452,* ☎ *802/878–1100 or 800/288–7613,* 𝐅𝐀𝐗 *802/878–0063 or 800/727–4295,* 𝐖𝐄𝐁 *www.innatessex.com. 97 rooms. 2 restaurants, bar, pool, billiards, library, business services, meeting rooms. AE, D, DC, MC, V. CP.*

$$–$$$$ 🏨 **Willard Street Inn.** High in the historic hill section of Burlington, this
★ grand house with an exterior marble staircase and English gardens incorporates elements of Queen Anne and Colonial–Georgian Revival styles. The stately foyer, paneled in cherry, leads to a more formal sitting room with velvet drapes. The solarium is bright and sunny with marble floors, many plants, and big velvet couches for contemplating views of Lake Champlain. All the rooms have down comforters and phones; some have lake views and canopied beds. Orange French toast is among the breakfast favorites. ⊠ *349 S. Willard St., 05401,* ☎ *802/651–8710 or 800/ 577–8712,* 𝐅𝐀𝐗 *802/651–8714,* 𝐖𝐄𝐁 *www.willardstreetinn.com. 14 rooms. AE, D, MC, V. BP.*

Nightlife and the Arts

NIGHTLIFE

Name and local musicians come to **Higher Ground** (⊠ 1 Main St., Winooski, ☎ 802/654–8888). The music at the **Metronome** (⊠ 188 Main St., ☎ 802/865–4563) ranges from cutting-edge sounds to funk, blues, and reggae. The band Phish got its start at **Nectar's** (⊠ 188 Main St., ☎ 802/658–4771). This place is always jumping to the sounds of local bands and never charges a cover. **Ri Ra** (123 Church St., ☎ 802/860– 9401) hosts live entertainment with an Irish flair and dishes up Irish and American fare. **Vermont Pub and Brewery** (⊠ 144 College St., ☎ 802/865–0500) makes its own beer and fruit seltzers and is arguably the most popular spot in town. Folk musicians play here regularly.

THE ARTS

Burlington City Arts (☎ 802/865–7166; 802/865–9163 24-hr Artsline) has up-to-date arts-related information. **Flynn Theatre for the Performing Arts** (⊠ 153 Main St., ☎ 802/652–4500 information; 802/863–

5966 tickets), a grandiose old structure, is the cultural heart of Burlington; it schedules the Vermont Symphony Orchestra, theater, dance, big-name musicians, and lectures. The **Lyric Theater** (☎ 802/658–1484) puts on musical productions in the fall and spring at the Flynn Theatre. **St. Michael's Playhouse** (✉ St. Michael's College, Rte. 15, Colchester, ☎ 802/654–2281 box office; 802/654–2617 administrative office) performs in the McCarthy Arts Center Theater. The **UVM Lane Series** (☎ 802/656–4455 programs and times; 802/656–3085 box office) sponsors classical as well as folk music concerts in the Flynn Theatre, Ira Allen Chapel, and the UVM Recital Hall. The **Vermont Symphony Orchestra** (☎ 802/874–5741 or 800/876–9203) performs throughout the state year-round, and at the Flynn from October through May.

Outdoor Activities and Sports

BEACHES

The **North Beaches** are on the northern edge of Burlington: North Beach Park (✉ off North Ave., ☎ 802/864–0123), Bayside Beach (✉ Rte. 127 near Malletts Bay), and Leddy Beach (✉ Leddy Park Rd., off North Ave.), which is popular for sailboarding.

BIKING

Burlington's 10-mi Cycle the City loop runs along the waterfront, connecting several city parks and beaches. It also passes the Lake Champlain Basin Science Center and the Community Boathouse, and runs within several blocks of downtown restaurants and shops. **North Star Cyclery** (✉ 100 Main St., ☎ 802/863–3832) rents bicycles and provides maps of bicycle routes. **Ski Rack** (✉ 81 Main St., ☎ 802/658–3313 or 800/882–4530) rents and services bikes, and provides maps.

WATER SPORTS

Marina services are available north and south of Burlington. **Malletts Bay Marina** (✉ 228 Lakeshore Dr., Colchester, ☎ 802/862–4072) has facilities for mooring, sells gasoline, and repairs boats. **Point Bay Marina** (✉ 1401 Thompson's Point Rd., Charlotte, ☎ 802/425–2431) provides full service and repairs. **Burlington Community Boathouse** (✉ Foot of College St., Burlington Harbor, ☎ 802/865–3377) rents Jet Skis, sailboards, sailboats from 13 ft to 40 ft, and motorboats (some captained); the boathouse also gives lessons. **Marble Island Resort** (✉ Colchester, ☎ 802/864–6800) has a marina and a nine-hole golf course.

Shopping

ANTIQUES

Architectural Salvage Warehouse (✉ 53 Main St., ☎ 802/658–5011) is a great place to hunt for claw-foot tubs, stained-glass windows, mantels, andirons, and other similar items. The large rhinoceros head bursting out of the **Conant Custom Brass** (✉ 270 Pine St., ☎ 802/658–4482) storefront may tempt you in to see the custom work; the store specializes in decorative lighting and bathroom fixtures.

CRAFTS

In addition to its popular pottery, **Bennington Potters North** (✉ 127 College St., ☎ 802/863–2221 or 800/205–8033) stocks interesting gifts, glassware, furniture, and other housewares. **Vermont State Craft Center** (✉ 85 Church St., ☎ 802/863–6458) displays contemporary and traditional crafts by more than 200 Vermont artisans. **Yankee Pride** (✉ Champlain Mill, E. Canal St., Winooski, ☎ 802/655–0500) has a large inventory of quilting fabrics and supplies as well as Vermont-made quilts.

MALLS AND MARKETPLACES

Burlington Square Mall (✉ Church St., ☎ 802/658–2545) has a large Filene's department store and a few dozen other shops. The **Champlain**

Mill (⊠ U.S. 2/7, northeast of Burlington, ☎ 802/655–9477), a former woolen mill on the banks of the Winooski River, holds three floors of stores, including a bookstore and clothing shops, and several restaurants. **Church Street Marketplace** (⊠ Main St.–Pearl Sts., ☎ 802/863–1648), a pedestrian thoroughfare, is lined with boutiques, cafés, and street vendors. **University Mall** (⊠ Dorset St., ☎ 802/863–1066), home to Sears, Bon Ton, and JCPenney, continues to expand. Look for bargains at the rapidly growing **Essex Outlet Fair** (⊠ Rte 15, at Rte. 289, Essex, ☎ 802/657–2777); you'll find outlets for Brooks Brothers, Polo Ralph Lauren, and Levi's, among others.

Shelburne

③⑦ *5 mi south of Burlington.*

Once a village surrounded by small farms and lakeshore estates, Shelburne is now largely a bedroom community for Burlington. It's distinguished by one of the nation's premier repositories of Americana and by a tycoon's gilded-age fiefdom that has become a model farm and agricultural education center.

★ A few miles south of Burlington, the Champlain Valley gives way to fertile farmland, affording stunning views of the rugged Adirondacks across the lake. You can trace much of New England's history simply by wandering the 45 acres and 37 buildings of the **Shelburne Museum.** The outstanding 80,000-object collection of Americana consists of 18th- and 19th-century period homes and furniture, fine and folk art, farm tools, more than 200 carriages and sleighs, Audubon prints, an old-fashioned jail, and even a private railroad car from the days of steam. The museum also has an assortment of duck decoys, an old stone cottage, and a display of early toys—as well as the *Ticonderoga,* an old side-wheel steamship, grounded amid lawn and trees. The newest exhibit is an interactive period house from the 1950s. ⊠ *U.S. 7,* ☎ *802/ 985–3346 or 802/985–3344,* WEB *www.shelburnemuseum.org.* 🏛 *$17.50 for 2 consecutive days.* ☉ *June–mid-Oct., daily 10–5; mid.-Oct.– Dec. and Apr.–late-May, daily 1–4.*

★ ☾ **Shelburne Farms** has a history of improving the farmer's lot by developing new agricultural methods. Founded in the 1880s as a private estate, the 1,400-acre property is an educational and cultural resource center with, among other things, a working dairy farm, a Children's Farmyard, and a spot for watching the farm's famous cheddar cheese being made. Frederick Law Olmsted, co-creator of New York's Central Park, designed the magnificent grounds overlooking Lake Champlain. For an additional charge of $5, you can tour the 1891 breeding barn. ⊠ *West of U.S. 7 at Harbor and Bay Rds.,* ☎ *802/985–8686,* WEB *www. shelburnefarms.org.* 🏛 *Day pass $5, tour an additional $5.* ☉ *Visitor center and shop daily 10–5; tours mid-May–mid-Oct. (last tour at 3:30); mid-Oct.–mid-May, walking trails open, weather permitting.*

☾ On the tour of the **Vermont Teddy Bear Company,** you'll hear more puns than you ever thought possible and learn how a few homemade bears, sold from a cart on Church Street, have turned into a multimillion-dollar business. A children's play tent is set up outdoors in summer, and you can wander the beautiful 57-acre property. ⊠ *2236 Shelburne Rd.,* ☎ *802/985–3001.* 🏛 *Tour $1.* ☉ *Tours Mon.–Sat. 9:30–4, Sun. 10:30–4; store Mon.–Sat. 9–6, Sun. 10–5.*

At the 6-acre **Vermont Wildflower Farm,** the display along the flowering pathways changes constantly: violets in the spring, daisies and black-eyed Susans for summer, and for fall, flowers with colors that rival those of the trees' foliage. You can buy wildflower seeds, crafts, and books here. ⊠ *U.S. 7, Charlotte, 5 mi south of the Shelburne Museum,* ☎ *802/425–3641,* WEB *www.americanmeadows.com.* 🖃 *$3.* ☉ *Early May–late-Oct., daily 10–5.*

Dining and Lodging

$$$ ✕ **Café Shelburne.** One of the area's most popular restaurants has been
★   serving creative French bistro cuisine for more than 30 years. Some specialties are sweetbreads in a port wine and mushroom sauce in puff pastry and homemade fettuccine with prunes. Desserts such as the sweet chocolate layered terrine and maple syrup mousse with orange terrine are fabulous. ⊠ *U.S. 7,* ☎ *802/985–3939. AE, MC, V. Closed Sun.–Mon. No lunch.*

$$$–$$$$ ✕🖼 **Inn at Shelburne Farms.** This is storybook land. Built at the turn
★   of the century as the home of William Seward and Lila Vanderbilt Webb, the Tudor-style inn perches on Saxton's Point overlooking Lake Champlain, the distant Adirondacks, and the sea of pastures that make up this 1,400-acre working farm. Each room is different, from the wallpaper to the period antiques. The dining room ($$$–$$$$) defines elegance, and the seasonal contemporary menu makes clever use of local ingredients. Sunday brunch (not served in May) is one of the area's best. The inn's profits help support the farm's environmental education programs for local schools. ⊠ *Harbor Rd., 05482,* ☎ *802/985–8498,* FAX *802/985–8123,* WEB *www.shelburnefarms.org. 24 rooms, 17 with bath. Restaurant, lake, tennis court, hiking, boating, fishing, billiards. AE, D, DC, MC, V. Closed mid-Oct.–mid-May.*

Outdoor Activities and Sports

A moderately easy 18½-mi bike trail begins at the blinker on U.S. 7 in Shelburne and follows Mt. Philo Road, Hinesburg Road, Route 116, and Irish Hill Road.

Shopping

When you enter **Shelburne Country Store** (⊠ Village Green, off U.S. 7, ☎ 802/985–3657) you'll step back in time. Walk past the potbellied stove and take in the aroma emanating from the fudge neatly piled behind huge antique glass cases. The store specializes in candles, weather vanes, glassware, and local foods.

Lake Champlain Islands

❸❾   *20 mi northwest of Shelburne, 15 mi northwest of Burlington.*

South Hero, North Hero, Isle La Motte, and the Alburg peninsula compose the elongated archipelago that stretches southward from the Canadian border. Because of their temperate climate, the islands are home to several apple orchards and numerous state parks and are a center of water recreation in summer and ice fishing in winter. A scenic drive through the islands on U.S. 2 begins at I–89 and travels north to Alburg Center; Route 78 takes you back to the mainland.

Snow Farm Vineyard and Winery offers self-guided tours, a tasting room, and free concerts on the lawn for 10 Thursday evenings, beginning in mid-June. ⊠ *190 W. Shore Rd., South Hero,* ☎ *802/372–9463.* 🖃 *Free.* ☉ *May–Dec., daily 10–5, tours at 11 and 2.*

Hyde Log Cabin, built in 1783 on South Hero, is often cited as the country's oldest surviving log cabin. ⊠ *U.S. 2, Grand Isle,* ☎ *802/828–3051.* 🖃 *$3.* ☉ *July 4–Labor Day, Thurs.–Mon. 11–5*

The **Royal Lippizaner Stallions,** descendants of the noble white horses bred in Austria since the 16th century, perform intricate dressage maneuvers at their summer home on the islands. ⊠ *U.S. 2, North Hero,* ☎ *802/372–5683.* 🖃 *Barn visits free between performances; shows*

$15–$18; Fridays, children free. ☼ July–Aug.; Thurs. and Fri. at 6 pm,; Sat. and Sun. at 2:30 pm.

St. Anne's Shrine marks the site where French soldiers and Jesuits put ashore in 1665 and built a fort, creating Vermont's first European settlement. The state's first Roman Catholic Mass was celebrated here on July 26, 1666. ⊠ *W. Shore Rd., Isle La Motte,* ☎ *802/928–3362.* ▨ *Free. ☼ Mid-May–mid-Oct., daily 9–7.*

On the mainland east of the Alburg Peninsula, the **Missisquoi National Wildlife Refuge** (⊠ Off Rte. 78, Swanton, 36 mi north of Burlington, ☎ 802/868–4781) consists of 6,300 acres of federally protected wetlands, meadows, and woods. It's a beautiful setting for bird-watching, canoeing, or walking nature trails.

Dining and Lodging

$$$ ✕ **Ruthcliffe Lodge & Restaurant.** Good food and a fabulous setting make this off-the-beaten-path motel and restaurant overlooking Lake Champlain worth the drive. Owner-chef Mark Infante specializes in Italian pasta, fish, and meat dishes; save room for the homemade desserts. Fixed-price dinners include soup, salad, bread, starch, and coffee or tea. All rooms at the seven-unit motel have waterfront views. ⊠ *Old Quarry Rd., Isle La Motte,* ☎ *802/928–3200. MC, V. Closed Columbus Day–mid-May. No lunch mid-May–June and Sept.–Columbus Day.*

$$–$$$$ ⌂ **North Hero House Inn and Restaurant.** A classic country inn, North Hero House overlooks Lake Champlain and has four buildings, including the 1891 Colonial Revival main house with nine guest rooms, the restaurant, a pub room, library, and sitting room. Many rooms have water views, and each is decorated with country furnishings and antiques. Dinner is served in the informal glass greenhouse or Colonial-style dining room, or on the glassed-in veranda. Friday evenings in summer there's a lobster bake on the beach. ⊠ *U.S. 2, North Hero 05474,* ☎ *802/372–4732 or 888/525–3644,* ℻ *802/372–3218,* ⓦⓔⓑ *www.northherohouse.com. 26 rooms. Restaurant, pub, lake, hot tub, library. MC, V. CP.*

$$–$$$ ⌂ **Shore Acres Inn and Restaurant.** This lakefront motel well off the main road offers clean, comfortable rooms overlooking the water and ½ mi of private lakeshore. Breakfast and dinner are served in the restaurant overlooking the lake. The 9-hole, par-3 golf course is free to guests. ⊠ *U.S. 2, North Hero 05474,* ☎ *802/372–8722,* ⓦⓔⓑ *www.shoreacres.com. 23 rooms. Restaurant, 2 tennis courts, 9-hole golf course, beach, lawn games. AE, MC, V. Most rooms closed Nov.–Apr.; 4 rooms in annex open year-round..*

Outdoor Activities and Sports

BIKING
Hero's Welcome (⊠ U.S. 2, North Hero, ☎ 802/372–4161 or 800/372–4376) rents bicycles. **Bike Shed Rentals** (⊠ W. Shore Rd., Isle La Motte, ☎ 802/928–3440) rents bicycles.

BOATING
Apple Island Resort (⊠ U.S. 2, South Hero, ☎ 802/372–3922) rents sailboats, rowboats, canoes, and motorboats. **Henry's Sportsman's Cottages** (⊠ 218 Poor Farm Rd., Alburg, ☎ 802/796–3616) rents motorboats. **Hero's Welcome** (⊠ U.S. 2, North Hero, ☎ 802/372–4161 or 800/372–4376) has canoes and kayaks for rent.

Sea Trek Charters (⊠ Tudhope Sailing Center, U.S. 2, Grand Isle, ☎ 802/372–5391) on South Hero Island offers full-day fishing and sightseeing trips aboard a 25-ft cruiser.

Alburg Dunes State Park, one of the state's newest parks, has a sandy beach and some fine examples of rare flora and fauna along the hiking trails. ⊠ *Off U.S. 2, Alburg,* ☎ *802/893–2825.* ☞ *$2.* ☉ *Late May–Labor Day, dawn–dusk.*

Grand Isle State Park has a fitness trail, hiking trails, and boat rentals. ⊠ *U.S. 2, Grand Isle,* ☎ *802/372–4300.* ☞ *$2.* ☉ *Late May–Labor Day, dawn–dusk.*

North Hero State Park's 400 acres hold a swimming beach, nature trail, and campsites. You can rent rowboats and canoes. ⊠ *North Hero, North Hero,* ☎ *802/372–8727.* ☞ *$2.* ☉ *Late May–Labor Day, dawn–dusk.*

Sand Bar State Park, with one of Vermont's best swimming beaches, has a snack bar, changing room, and boat rental concession. ⊠ *U.S. 2, South Hero,* ☎ *802/372–8240.* ☞ *$2.* ☉ *Late May–Labor Day, dawn–dusk.*

Shopping
Open July–December, **Allenholm Farm** (⊠ 111 South St., South Hero, ☎ 802/372–5566) has a farm store that stocks local produce.

St. Albans

39 *18 miles south of Alburg Center.*

Don't let the suburban sprawl on the outskirts of St. Albans fool you. The city's compact Victorian downtown, built during its heyday as a bustling railroad center, is very much alive with shops, restaurants, and cafés. St. Albans' centerpiece is Taylor Park, a broad green space graced with an ornate bronze fountain and lined with churches and municipal buildings in an array of imposing 19th-century styles. St. Albans was the scene of the northernmost action of the Civil War, an 1864 robbery of the city's banks by a band of Confederate soldiers disguised as civilians. The **St. Albans Historical Museum** is inside an 1861 three-story brick house (Church Street ☎ 802/527–7933).

Dining and Lodging

$$$ ✕ **Jeff's Maine Seafood.** Jeff's Fish Market and Deli has long been one of the area's best spots for seafood. The market is still here, but now there's an attractive adjoining dining room, a welcoming spot to enjoy a glass of wine and sample the creatively prepared cuisine. Appetizers include crispy salmon potato cakes topped with sour cream and caviar; for entrees, try the sautéed sea scallops, plum tomatoes and scallions in an artichoke Parmesan sauce over linguine or pan-seared tuna steak glazed with pesto and topped with fresh plum tomatoes. Meat eaters can always find a steak here, too. A Light Fare menu is available Tuesday, Wednesday, and Thursday evenings. ⊠ *65 North Main St.,* ☎ *802/ 524–6135. AE, DC, MC, V.*

$–$$$ ✕ **Chow! Bella.** This narrow, handsomely decorated Victorian parlor of the former St. Albans Opera House complements chef/owner Connie Jacobs Warden's culinary creations. Pastas, individual flatbreads such as Bella Greek Shrimp with tomatoes, calamata olives and spinach, and black angus N.Y. strip steak with Gorgonzola Berkshire shiitake sauce are all worth sampling. For dessert, try the baklava cheesecake or Italian walnut tort. ⊠ *28 N. Main St.,* ☎ *802/524–1405. AE, D, MC, V.*

$ ✕ **Kept Writer Book Shop & Café.** Pairing soft classical music and the aroma of freshly brewed coffee with a fine selection of used tomes, this bookstore and café warms with ambience. The menu includes light fare like sandwich croissants and spanikopita (spinach pie), locally baked goodies, and moderately priced wine and beer. It's a cozy retreat perfect for curling up with a good book or the newspaper. ✉ *5 Lake St.,* ☎ *802/527–6242. Closed Mon.*.

$ 🏠 **Old Mill River Place.** The first owner of this 1799 five-bay Federal home was a niece of Vermont patriot Ethan Allen. When Anna Neville's family bought the home in 1926, her mother hung out a "Rooms to Rent" sign (Anna still has the sign), becoming one of the first lodging establishments in the area to take in tourists. Antiques and objets d'art her family has collected in their world travels adorn the house. The three second-floor bedrooms with shared bath are spacious and neat. There's a TV/VCR on the second floor with children's movies, and Ridley, the family dog, is apt to curl up and enjoy the show. ✉ *Georgia Shore Rd., 05478,* ☎ *802/524–7211. 3 rooms, with shared baths. Closed Nov.–Apr. No credit cards. BP.*

Shopping

Rail City Market (✉ 8 South Main St.) has an excellent selection of natural foods, teas, spices and coffees, and body creams and soaps.

Montgomery/Jay

④⓪ *51 mi northeast of Burlington.*

Montgomery is a small village near the Canadian border and Jay Peak ski resort. Amid the surrounding countryside are seven historic covered bridges. **Kilgore's Store** (✉ Main St., Montgomery Center, ☎ 802/326–3058), an old-time country store with an antique soda fountain, is a great place to stock up on picnic supplies, eat a hearty bowl of soup and an overstuffed sandwich, and check out local crafts.

Lodging

$$$ 🏠 **Hotel Jay & Jay Peak Condominiums.** Unlike a lot of other lodging places, this ski-in, ski-out hotel manages to combine cheerful simplicity, convenience, and attractive prices. Rooms on the southwest side have a view of Jay Peak, and those on the north overlook the valley; upper floors have balconies. The condominiums (most slopeside) have fireplaces, one to three bedrooms, modern kitchens, and washers and dryers; some are quite luxurious. In winter, a minimum two-night stay is required, and lift tickets and some meals are included in the rates. The summer rates are low. The meal plan varies during the year; breakfast and dinner are included in ski season. ✉ *Rte. 242, 05859,* ☎ *802/988–2611 or 800/451–4449 outside Vermont,* FAX *802/988–4049,* WEB *www.jaypeakresort.com. 48 rooms, 120 condominiums. Restaurant, bar, pool, hot tub, sauna, 2 tennis courts, downhill skiing, recreation room. AE, D, DC, MC, V. CP, MAP.*

$$ 🏠 **Black Lantern.** Built in 1803 as a hotel for mill workers, the inn has been providing bed and board ever since. Though the feeling is country, touches of sophistication abound: Provençal-print wallpaper in the dining room, a subtle rag-roll finish in the rooms in the renovated building next door. All the suites have whirlpools, and most have fireplaces. An outdoor hot tub, sheltered by a gazebo, overlooks the mountains. The restaurant menu ($$-$$$) includes pan-seared salmon with a red pepper sauce and rack of lamb. ✉ *Rte. 118, Montgomery Village 05470,* ☎ *802/326–4507 or 800/255–8661,* FAX *802/326–4077,* WEB *www.blacklantern.com. 10 rooms, 6 suites. Restaurant, outdoor hot tub. AE, D, MC, V. BP, MAP.*

$$ 🏠 **Inn on Trout River.** The large stove is often the center of attention in the two-tier living and dining area of this 100-year-old inn, though the piano, the library, and the pub with a U-shape bar are also eye-catching. Guest rooms are decorated in either English country cottage style or country Victorian, and all have down quilts and flannel sheets in winter. The back lawn rambles down to the river, and llama treks

are available for groups. The restaurant specializes in American and Continental fare with a heart-healthy emphasis. ⊠ *Main St., Montgomery Center 05471,* ☎ *802/326–4391 or 800/338–7049,* FAX *802/ 326–3194,* WEB *www.troutinn.com. 9 rooms, 1 suite. Restaurant, pub, library. AE, D, MC, V. BP, MAP.*

Ski Areas

JAY PEAK

Sticking up out of the flat farmland, Jay averages 332 in of snowfall a year—more than any other Vermont ski area. Its proximity to Québec attracts Montréalers and discourages eastern seaboarders; hence, the prices are moderate and the lift lines shorter than at other resorts. The big news is the upgrading of the aerial tram: new cars offer good visibility and a superior sound system. ⊠ *Rte. 242, Jay 05859,* ☎ *802/ 988–2611; 800/451–4449 outside VT,* WEB *www.jaypeakresort.com.*

Downhill. Jay Peak is in fact two mountains with 74 trails, the highest reaching nearly 4,000 ft with a vertical drop of 2,153 ft. The area is served by seven lifts, including Vermont's only tramway, which transports skiers to the top of the mountain in just seven minutes, and the longest detachable quad in the East. The area also has a quad, a triple, and a double chairlift, and two T-bars. The smaller mountain has more straight-fall-line, expert terrain, and the tram-side peak has many curving and meandering trails perfectly suited for intermediate and beginning skiers. Jay, highly rated for gladed skiing by major skiing publications, has 19 gladed trails. The longest trail, Ullr's Dream, is 3 mi. Every morning at 9 AM the ski school offers a free tour, from the tram down one trail. Jay has 75% snowmaking coverage. The area has a halfpipe and snowboard terrain for snowboarders.

Cross-country. A touring center at the base of the mountain has 20 km (12 mi) of groomed cross-country trails. There is a $5 trail fee. A network of 200 km (124 mi) of trails is in the vicinity.

Other activities. Snowshoes can be rented, and guided walks are led by a naturalist. Telemark rentals and instruction are available.

Child care. The child care center for youngsters ages 2 to 7 is open from 9 AM to 9 PM. Guests of the Hotel Jay and the Jay Peak Condominiums receive this nursery care free, as well as free skiing for children ages 6 and under, evening care, and supervised dining at the hotel. Infant care is available on a fee basis with advanced reservations. Children ages 5 to 10 can participate in a day-long Mountain Explorers program, which includes lunch; a Minirider program for snowboarders aged 5–10 is also available.

Summer activities. Jay Peak offers tram rides to the summit from mid-June through September ($10) and rents mountain bikes.

CROSS-COUNTRY SKIING

Hazen's Notch Cross Country Ski Center and B & B (⊠ Rte. 58, ☎ 802/ 326–4708), delightfully remote at any time of the year, has 50 km (31 mi) of marked and groomed trails and rents equipment and snow shoes.

En Route   The descent from Jay Peak on Route 101 leads to Route 100, which can be the beginning of a scenic loop tour of Routes 14, 5, 58, and back to 100, or it can take you east to the city of Newport on Lake Memphremagog. You will encounter some of the most unspoiled areas in all Vermont on the drive south from Newport on either U.S. 5 or I–91 (I–91 is faster, but U.S. 5 is prettier). This region, the Northeast Kingdom, is named for the remoteness and stalwart independence that have helped preserve its rural nature.

Newport

❹ *20 miles east of Jay Peak.*

From its rough-and-tumble days as a logging town, Newport passed through a long stretch of doldrums and decline before discovering that revitalization lay in taking advantage of its splendid location on the southern shores of Lake Memphremagog, Vermont's second-largest lake (only the southern three miles of the lake lie within the state; the northern 30 miles are in Canada). Only a block from the waterfront, downtown's main street has evolved into a busy shopping district. The waterfront has a handsome new public boat house where tours of the lake begin. One of the best ways to explore the lake on both sides of the border is aboard the 49-passenger **Stardust Princess,** which sails from the City Dock from Memorial Day through Labor Day. ⊠ *Newport City Dock,* ☎ *802/334–6617.*

Dining and Lodging

$$ ✕ **The East Side.** With an outdoor deck that overlooks the lake, this popular spot serves American fare such as beef stew and prime rib and specialties such as Crab Chicken—a boneless breast of chicken stuffed with crabmeat and napped with lobster sauce. Homeade soups and desserts also share the menu, and daily specials include a variety of over-stuffed sandwiches. ⊠ *Lake St.,* ☎ *802/334–2340. D, MC, V. No breakfast Mon.–Fri..*

$$ 🏨 **Derby Village Inn.** North of Newport on the Canadian border, the 1902 neo-classical home built by a retired Civil War general has five spacious guest rooms with private baths, original fixtures, and hardwood floors. The Passageway room has a gas fireplace; the Green Mountain Suite has its own sitting room and a clawfoot tub; it overlooks Jay Peak. ⊠ *440 Main St., Derby Line 05830,* ☎ *802/873–3604,* 𝖥𝖠𝖷 *802/873–347,* 𝖶𝖤𝖡 *www.derbyvillageinn.com. 5 rooms. BP.*

$ 🏨 **Newport City Motel.** Rooms at this reasonably priced, two-story motel, a short distance from the center of town, are clean, modern, and nicely furnished, and have cable TV and air conditioning. ⊠ *444 E. Main St., 05855,* ☎ *800/338–6558,* 𝖥𝖠𝖷 *802/334–6557. 64, 1 suite. Indoor pool, fitness center, hot tub.*

Outdoor Activities and Sports

The Great Outdoors of Newport (⊠ 177 Main St., ☎ 802/334–2831) rents boats, kayaks, and canoes, as well as cross-country skis and snowshoes. The store sells fishing supplies and bicycles.

Shopping

Bogner Haus Factory Outlet (⊠ 150 Main St., ☎ 802/334–0135) sells first-quality men's and women's skiwear and golf apparel as well as snowboarding and activewear.

Lake Willoughby

❷ *30 mi southeast of Montgomery (summer route; 50 mi by winter route), 28 mi north of St. Johnsbury.*

Flanking the eastern and western shores of Lake Willoughby, the cliffs of surrounding Mts. Pisgah and Hor drop to water's edge, giving this glacially carved, 500-ft-deep lake a striking resemblance to a Norwegian fjord. The beautiful lake is popular for summer and winter recreation, and the trails to the top of Mt. Pisgah reward hikers with glorious views.

The **Bread and Puppet Museum** is a ramshackle barn that houses a surrealistic collection of props used in past performances by the world-renowned Bread and Puppet Theater. The troupe, whose members live communally on the surrounding farm, have been performing social and political commentary with the towering (they're supported by people on stilts), eerily expressive puppets for about 30 years. ⊠ *Rte. 122, Glover, 1 mi east of Rte. 16,* ☎ *802/525–3031.* ⊇ *Donations accepted.* ⊙ *June–Oct., daily 9–5; other times by appointment.*

Lodging

$$–$$$ ⊞ **WilloughVale Inn.** Few Vermont inns can claim a more spectacular location than this waterfront property at the northern end of Lake Willoughby. The main building, with a wraparound veranda, has six spacious and nicely furnished rooms overlooking the lake. The lakefront dining room is open for dinner to guests on Friday and Saturday in winter, and Thurs.–Mon. in summer. An even better bet are the cottages on Willoughby's shore. They come with fully equipped kitchens, fireplaces, screened porches, and private docks and sleep up to four persons. Pets weighing 50 lbs or less are welcome in the cottages. Canoes and kayaks are available. ⊠ *Rte. 5A, Westmore 05860,* ☎ *802/525–4123 or 800/594–9102,* ⅋⅀ *802/525–4514,* ⅋⅀⅂ *www.willoughvale. com. 6 rooms, 4 cottages. Dining room, boating. AE, MC, V. CP.*

East Burke

43 *17 mi south of Lake Willoughby.*

A jam-packed general store, a post office, and a couple of great places to eat are in the center of East Burke, near the Burke Mountain ski area. A major attraction are the 100 miles of old logging, fire, and country roads, which are good for self-guided hiking, mountain biking, cross-country skiing, and snowshoeing. The **Kingdom Trails Association** (⊠ Box 204, East Burke 05832, ☎ 802/626–0737 ⅋⅀⅂ www.kingdom-trails.org) manages the trails and provides information.

Dining and Lodging

$$–$$$ ✕ **River Garden Café.** You can eat outdoors on the enclosed porch or the patio and view the perennial gardens that rim the grounds; the café is bright and cheerful on the inside as well. The fare includes lamb tenderloin, warm artichoke dip, bruschetta, pastas, and fresh fish. A lighter menu is offered nightly. ⊠ *Rte. 114, East Burke,* ☎ *802/626–3514. AE, D, MC, V. Closed Mon., 1 wk Apr., and month of Nov.*

$$$ ✕⊞ **Inn at Mountain View Creamery.** The 1890 redbrick Georgian-style creamery at this former gentleman's farm has been modernized as an elegant hostelry. Set high on a hilltop amid 440 acres of rolling hills and meadows, the inn has second-floor guest rooms handsomely furnished with country antiques and handmade quilts. Miles of cross-country ski, snowshoe, hiking, and mountain biking trails are right at the doorstep, and hay and sleigh rides provide a grand way to enjoy the scenery. The menu at Darling's Country Bistro ($$–$$$; dinner Thursday through Sunday) lists hearty dishes such as beef carbonnade with caramelized onions as well as fish and vegetarian fare. ⊠ *Darling Hill Rd., 05832,* ☎ *802/626–9924 or 800/572–4509,* ⅋⅀⅂ *www.innmtnview. com. 10 rooms. Restaurant, hiking, cross-country skiing. Closed Apr., Nov. AE, MC, V. BP.*

$$ ✕⊞ **Wildflower Inn.** The hilltop views are breathtaking at this ram-
★   bling complex of old farm buildings on 500 acres. Guest rooms in the restored Federal-style main house and four other buildings are decorated with reproductions and contemporary furnishings. Rooms in the carriage house are somewhat dark and cramped; they have kitchenettes and bunk beds. In warm weather, the inn is family-oriented: there's a petting barn, planned children's activities, and a kids' swimming pool. The inn quiets down in winter when it caters more to cross-country skiers. The restaurant serves gourmet fare, with dishes

such as a seasonal tricolor peppercorn cognac breast of duck, and a blackened prime rib from their own herd of Belted Galloways. ✉ *Darling Hill Rd., west of East Burke, Lyndonville 05851,* ☎ *802/626–8310 or 800/627–8310,* FAX *802/626–3039,* WEB *www.wildflowerinn.com. 10 rooms, 11 suites. Restaurant, pool, hot tub, sauna, tennis court, soccer, fishing, ice-skating, skiing, sleigh rides, tobogganing, recreation room. MC, V. Closed Apr., Nov. BP.*

$ ✕🏠 **Old Cutter Inn.** A small converted farmhouse only ½ mi from the Burke Mountain base lodge offers quaint inn rooms in the main building, as well as comfortable if less charming accommodations in an annex. The restaurant ($$–$$$) serves fare that reflects the Swiss chef-owner's heritage, as well as superb, good-value Continental cuisine including osso buco, chateaubriand, and veal piccata. You can choose to include breakfast and dinner in the price. ✉ *143 Pinkham Rd., 05832,* ☎ *802/ 626–5152 or 800/295–1943,* WEB *www.pbpub.com/cutter.htm. 9 rooms, 5 with bath; 1 suite. Restaurant, bar, pool, hiking, bicycles, cross-country skiing. D, MC, V. Closed Wed., Apr., Nov.*

Outdoor Activities and Sports

Village Sport Shop (✉ 4 Broad St., Lyndonville, ☎ 802/626–8448) rents canoes, kayaks, bikes, rollerblades, paddleboats, snowshoes, and cross-country and downhill skis.

Shopping

Bailey's & Burke, Inc. (✉ Rte. 114, ☎ 802/626–9250), an institution, sells baked goods, pizza and sandwiches, wine, clothing, and sundries. **Trout River Brewing Co.** brews all-natural premium ales and lagers and has six styles on tap daily. The tasting room is open Wed.–Sun. from 11 AM to 6 PM. (✉ Main St., Route 114, ☎ 802/626–3984 or 888/ 296–2739).

Ski Areas

BURKE MOUNTAIN

This low-key, moderately priced resort has plenty of terrain for beginners, but intermediate skiers, experts, racers, telemarkers, and snowboarders will find time-honored narrow New England trails. Many packages at Burke are significantly less expensive than those at other Vermont areas. ✉ *Mountain Rd., East Burke 05832,* ☎ *802/626–3302; 802/626–4069 snow conditions,* WEB *www.skiburke.com.*

Downhill. With a 2,000-ft vertical drop and 43 trails and glades, Burke is something of a sleeper among the larger Eastern ski areas. It has greatly increased its snowmaking capability (75%), which is enhanced by the mountain's northern location and exposure, assuring plenty of natural snow. There is a 5-acre snowboard park (with a halfpipe and snowmaking capabilities) for all levels. Burke has one quad, one double chairlift, and two surface lifts. Lift lines, even on weekends and holidays, are light to nonexistent.

Cross-country. Burke Ski Touring Center has more than 80 km (50 mi) of trails (65 km/39 mi groomed); some lead to high points with scenic views. There's a snack bar at the center.

Child care. In the Children's Center, the nursery takes children from ages 6 months to 6 years on weekends and holidays. SKIwee and MINIriders lessons through the ski school are available to children from ages 4 to 16.

Summer activities. Hiking, biking (rentals are available), and a children's swing are summer options.

St. Johnsbury

44 *16 mi south of East Burke, 39 mi northeast of Montpelier.*

St. Johnsbury is the southern gateway to the Northeast Kingdom. Though the town was chartered in 1786, its identity was not firmly established until 1830, when Thaddeus Fairbanks invented the platform scale, a device that revolutionized weighing methods that had been in use since the beginning of recorded history. Because of the Fairbanks family's philanthropic bent, this city with a distinctly 19th-century industrial feel has a strong cultural and architectural imprint.

Opened in 1891, the **Fairbanks Museum and Planetarium** attests to the Fairbanks family's inquisitiveness about all things scientific. The red-brick building in the squat Romanesque Revival architectural style of H. H. Richardson houses Vermont plants and animals, as well as ethnographic and natural history collections from around the globe. There's also a 50-seat planetarium and a hands-on exhibit room for kids. On the third Saturday in September, the museum sponsors the Festival of Traditional Crafts, with demonstrations of early American household and farm skills such as candle and soap making. ⊠ *Main and Prospect Sts.,* ☎ *802/748–2372,* WEB *www.fairbanksmuseum.org.* 🖼 *$5; planetarium $2.* ☉ *July–Aug., Mon.–Sat. 10–6, Sun. 1–5; Sept.– June, Mon.–Sat. 10–4, Sun. 1–5. Planetarium shows July–Aug., daily at 11 and 1:30; Sept.–June, weekends at 1:30.*

★ The **St. Johnsbury Athenaeum,** with its dark rich paneling, polished Victorian woodwork, and ornate circular staircases that rise to the gallery around the perimeter, is one of the oldest art galleries in the country. The gallery at the back of the building specializes in Hudson River School paintings and has the overwhelming *Domes of Yosemite* by Albert Bierstadt. ⊠ *1171 Main St.,* ☎ *802/748–8291,* WEB *www.stjathenaeum.org.* 🖼 *Free.* ☉ *Mon. and Wed. 10–8, Tues. and Thurs.–Fri. 10–5:30, Sat. 9:30–4.*

Dog Mountain is artist–dog lover Stephen Huneck's newly constructed art gallery (works are for sale) and sculpture garden, complete with a chapel where humans and their canine companions can meditate. ⊠ *Off Spaulding Rd.,* ☎ *802/748–2700 or 800/449–2580,* WEB *www.huneck.com.* 🖼 *Free.* ☉ *June–Oct., Mon.–Sat. 10–5 and Sun. 11–4, and by appointment.*

OFF THE BEATEN PATH

CABOT CREAMERY – The biggest cheese producer in the state, a dairy cooperative, has a visitor center with an audiovisual presentation about the dairy and cheese industry. You can taste samples, purchase cheese, and tour the plant. The center is midway between Barre and St. Johnsbury. ⊠ *2870 Main St./Rte. 215, 3 mi north of U.S. 2, Cabot,* ☎ *802/ 563–3393; 800/639–4031 orders only.* 🖼 *$1.* ☉ *June–Oct., daily 9–5; Nov.–Dec. and Feb.–May, Mon.–Sat. 9–4; call ahead to check cheese-making days.*

Dining and Lodging

$$$$ ✕🏨 **Rabbit Hill Inn.** Each of the guest rooms at this classic, white-
★   columned rural inn is different: the Loft, with an 8-ft Palladian window, a king canopy bed, a double whirlpool bath, and a corner fireplace, is one of the most requested. Rooms facing front have views of the Connecticut River and New Hampshire's White Mountains. Common areas, from porches to sitting rooms, make it easy to unwind. The intimate, candle-lit dining room serves a five-course fixed price dinner ($40) featuring regional dishes such as grilled sausage of Vermont pheasant with pistachios or smoked chicken and red-lentil dumplings.

Meat and fish are smoked on the premises, and the herbs and vegetables often come from gardens out back. ⊠ *Rte. 18, Lower Waterford, 11 mi south of St. Johnsbury, 05848,* ☎ *802/748–5168 or 800/762–8669,* FAX *802/748–8342,* WEB *www.rabbithillinn.com. 16 rooms, 5 suites. Restaurant, pub, hiking, cross-country skiing. AE, MC, V. Closed 1st 3 wks of Apr., 1st 2 wks of Nov. MAP.*

$$ 🏠 **Emergo Farm.** Bebo and Lori Webster rent out three guest rooms in their 1890, 15-room farmhouse on a 240-acre dairy farm that has been in the Webster family for five generations. Lori collects antiques, which are liberally sprinkled throughout the house and in the second-floor guest rooms. One room has its own bath. The other two, which share a bath, have a kitchen and can be rented out as a suite to sleep up to six. The view from the hilltop picnic grove is spectacular. ⊠ *261 Webster Hill Rd., Danville 05828,* ☎ *802/684–2215. 3 rooms, 1 with bath. BP.*

Peacham

45 *10 mi southwest of St. Johnsbury.*

Tiny Peacham's stunning scenery and 18th-century charm have made it a favorite with urban refugees, artists seeking solitude and inspiration, and movie directors looking for the quintessential New England village. *Ethan Frome,* starring Liam Neeson, was filmed here.

Gourmet soups and hearty lamb and barley stew are among the seasonally changing take-out specialties at the **Peacham Store** (⊠ Main St., ☎ 802/592–3310). You can browse through the locally made crafts while waiting for your order.

Barre

46 *7 mi southeast of Montpelier, 35 mi southwest of St. Johnsbury.*

Barre has been famous as the source of Vermont granite ever since two men began working the quarries in the early 1800s; the number of immigrant laborers attracted to the industry made the city prominent in the early years of the American labor movement. Downtown, at the corner of Maple and North Main, look for the statue of a representative Italian stonecutter of a century ago. On Route 14, just north of Barre, stop at **Hope Cemetery** to see spectacular examples of carving.

The attractions of the **Rock of Ages granite quarry** range from the awe-inspiring (the quarry resembles the Grand Canyon in miniature) to the mildly ghoulish (you can consult a directory of tombstone dealers throughout the country). You might recognize the sheer walls of the quarry from *Batman and Robin,* the film starring George Clooney and Arnold Schwarzenegger. At the crafts center, skilled artisans sculpt monuments; at the quarries themselves, 25-ton blocks of stone are cut from sheer 475-ft walls by workers who clearly earn their pay. ⊠ *Exit 6 off I–89, follow Rte. 63,* ☎ *802/476–3119.* 🎫 *Tour of active quarry $4, craftsman center and self-guided tour free.* ☉ *Visitor center May–Oct., Mon.–Sat. 8:30–5, Sun. noon–5; narrated tours every 45 mins 9:15–3 weekdays June–mid-Oct.*

Dining and Lodging

$–$$ ✕ **A Single Pebble.** Devotees of Chinese food have been making pilgrimages to this restaurant since it opened in 1997. Chef and co-owner Steve Bogart has been cooking creative, authentic Asian dishes for more than 30 years. He prepares traditional clay-pot dishes as well as wok specialties such as sesame catfish and kung po chicken. The dry fried green beans (sautéed with flecks of pork, black beans, preserved vegetables, and garlic) and mock eel (thinly sliced shiitake mushrooms) are house specialties. All dishes can be made without meat. ✉ *135 Barre-Montpelier Rd.,* ☎ *802/476–9700. D, MC, V. Reservations essential. Closed Sun.–Mon. No lunch.*

$–$$ 🏨 **Autumn Harvest Inn.** You'll be tempted to spend the whole day on the porch that graces the front of this casual inn, built in 1790. It sits atop a knoll overlooking a 46-acre workhorse farm and the surrounding valley. Rooms in the older part of the house have more character; all have phones and TVs with VCRs. Prime rib and veal dishes are among the highlights of the seasonal country menu at the restaurant (no lunch), where dinner is served by candlelight Wednesday through Saturday. ✉ *118 Clark Rd., Williamstown 05679,* ☎ *802/433–1355,* FAX *802/433–5501,* WEB *www.central-vt.com/web/autumn. 18 rooms. Restaurant, bar, pond, horseback riding, cross-country skiing. AE, MC, V. BP, MAP.*

Northern Vermont A to Z

To research prices, get advice from other travelers, and book travel arrangements, visit ww.fodors.com.

BOAT & FERRY TRAVEL
Lake Champlain Ferries, in operation since 1826, operates three ferry crossings during the summer months and one—between Grand Isle and Plattsburgh, New York—in winter through thick lake ice. Ferries leave from the King Street Dock in Burlington, Charlotte, and Grand Isle. This is a convenient means of getting to and from New York State, as well as a pleasant way to spend an afternoon.
➤ BOAT & FERRY INFORMATION: **Lake Champlain Ferries** (☎ 802/864–9804).

BUS TRAVEL
Vermont Transit links Burlington, Waterbury, Montpelier, St. Johnsbury, and Newport.
➤ BUS INFORMATION: **Vermont Transit** (☎ 800/552–8737).

CAR TRAVEL
In north-central Vermont, I–89 heads west from Montpelier to Burlington and continues north to Canada. Interstate 91 is the principal north–south route in the east, and Route 100 runs north–south through the center of the state. North of I–89, Routes 104 and 15 provide a major east–west transverse. From Barton, near Lake Willoughby, U.S. 5 and Route 122 south are beautiful drives. Strip-mall drudge bogs down the section of U.S. 5 around Lyndonville.

EMERGENCIES
➤ HOSPITALS AND EMERGENCY SERVICES: **Fletcher Allen Health Care** (✉ 111 Colchester Ave., Burlington, ☎ 802/847–2434, 24-hour emergency health care information). **Copley Hospital** (✉ Washington Hwy., Morrisville, ☎ 802/999–4231). **Northeastern Vermont Regional Hospital** (✉ Hospital Dr., St. Johnsbury, ☎ 802/748–8141).

OUTDOORS & SPORTS
HIKING
The Green Mountain Club maintains the Long Trail—the north–south border-to-border footpath that runs the length of the spine of the Green Mountains—as well as other trails nearby. The club headquarters sells maps and guides, and experts dispense advice.
➤ CONTACTS: The **Green Mountain Club** (✉ Rte. 100, Waterbury, ☎ 802/244–7037).

TOURS

P.O.M.G. Bike Tours of Vermont leads weekend and five-day adult camping-bike tours. True North Kayak Tours operates a guided tour of Lake Champlain and a natural-history tour and will arrange a custom multiday trip. The company also coordinates special trips for kids.

➤ TOUR OPERATORS: **P.O.M.G. Bike Tours of Vermont** (✉ Richmond, ☎ 802/434–2270). **True North Kayak Tours** (✉ 53 Nash Pl., Burlington, ☎ 802/860–1910).

TRAIN TRAVEL

The Champlain Valley Weekender runs between Middlebury and Burlington, with stops in Vergennes and Shelburne. The views from the coach cars, which date from the 1930s, are of Lake Champlain, the valley farmlands, and surrounding mountains. (*$12 round-trip. July–early Sept., weekends, 2 trips per day; call for foliage season schedule.*) The new Champlain Flyer, developed to ease traffic into and out of Burlington, transports passengers on weekdays between Burlington and Charlotte—with a stop in Shelburne—in just 25 minutes.

➤ TRAIN INFORMATION: **Champlain Valley Weekender** (☎ 802/463–3069 or 800/707–3530). **Champlain Flyer** (☎ 802/951–4010).

VISITOR INFORMATION

➤ TOURIST INFORMATION: **Lake Champlain Regional Chamber of Commerce** (✉ 60 Main St., Suite 100, Burlington 05401, ☎ 802/863–3489 or 877/686–5253, WEB www.champlainislands.com). **Northeast Kingdom Chamber of Commerce** (✉ 357 Western Ave., St. Johnsbury 05819, ☎ 802/748–3678 or 800/639–6379, WEB www.vermontnekchamber.org). **Northeast Kingdom Travel and Tourism Association** (✉ Box 465, Barton 05822, ☎ 802/525–4386 or 888/884–8001, WEB www.travelthekingdom.com). **Smugglers' Notch Area Chamber of Commerce** (✉ Box 364, Jeffersonville 05464, ☎ 802/644–2239, WEB www.smugnotch.com). The **Stowe Area Association** (✉ Main St., Box 1320, Stowe 05672, ☎ 802/253–7321 or 800/247–8693, WEB www.stoweinfo.com). **Vermont North Country Chamber of Commerce** (✉ The Causeway, Newport 05855, ☎ 802/334–7782 or 800/635–4643, WEB www.vtnorthcountry.com).

VERMONT A TO Z

To research prices, get advice from other travelers, and book travel arrangements, visit ww.fodors.com.

AIRPORTS & TRANSFERS

Continental, Delta, United, and US Airways fly into Burlington International Airport. Rutland State Airport has daily service to and from Boston on US Airways Express. West of Bennington and convenient to southern Vermont, Albany International Airport in New York State is served by 10 major U.S. carriers.

➤ AIRPORT INFORMATION: Continental, Delta, United, and US Airways fly into **Burlington International Airport** (✉ Airport Dr., 4 mi east of Burlington off U.S. 2, ☎ 802/863–2874). **Rutland State Airport** (✉ 1002 Airport Rd., North Clarendon, ☎ 802/786–8881). **Albany International Airport** (✉ 737 Albany Shaker Rd., Albany, ☎ 518/869–3021).

AIRPORT TRANSFERS

Aircraft charters are available at Burlington International Airport from Valet Air Services. Mansfield Heliflight provides helicopter transportation throughout New England.

➤ SHUTTLES: **Valet Air Services** (☎ 802/863–3626 or 800/782–0773). **Mansfield Heliflight** (✉ Milton, ☎ 802/893–1003 or 800/872–0884).

BUS TRAVEL

Bonanza Bus Lines connects New York City and Providence with Bennington. Vermont Transit connects Bennington, Brattleboro, Burlington, Rutland, and other Vermont cities and towns with Boston, Springfield, Albany, New York, Montréal, and cities in New Hampshire.

➤ BUS INFORMATION: **Bonanza Bus Lines** (☎ 800/556–3815). **Vermont Transit** (☎ 800/552–8737).

CAR TRAVEL

Interstate 91, which stretches from Connecticut and Massachusetts in the south to Québec in the north, reaches most points along Vermont's eastern border. I–89, from New Hampshire to the east and Québec to the north, crosses central Vermont from White River Junction to Burlington. Southwestern Vermont can be reached by U.S. 7 from Massachusetts and U.S. 4 from New York.

The official speed limit in Vermont is 50 mph, unless otherwise posted; on the interstates it's 65 mph. Right turns are permitted on a red light unless otherwise indicated. You can get a state map, which has mileage charts and enlarged maps of major downtown areas, free from the Vermont Department of Tourism and Marketing. The *Vermont Atlas and Gazetteer,* sold in many bookstores, shows nearly every road in the state and is great for driving on the back roads.

EMERGENCIES

➤ EMERGENCY SERVICES: **Ambulance, fire, police** (☎ 911). **Vermont State Police** (☎ 800/525–5555).

LODGING

The Vermont Chamber of Commerce (☞ Visitor Information) publishes the *Vermont Travelers' Guidebook,* which is an extensive list of lodgings, and additional guides to country inns and vacation rentals. The Vermont Department of Tourism and Marketing (☞ Visitor Information) has a brochure that lists lodgings at working farms.

CAMPING

Call Vermont's Department of Forests, Parks, and Recreation for a copy of the "Vermont Campground Guide," which lists state parks and other public and private camping facilities. Call the following numbers from the second Tuesday in January through May 1; after that, call the individual parks. Between Labor Day and January, reservations not accepted.

➤ CONTACTS: Department of Forests, Parks, and Recreation (☎ 802/241–3655). ☎ 802/885–8891 or 800/299–3071 in southeastern Vermont; ☎ 802/483–2001 or 800/658–1622 in southwestern Vermont; ☎ 802/879–5674 or 800/252–2363 in northwestern Vermont; ☎ 802/479–4280 or 800/658–6934 in northeastern Vermont.

NATIONAL PARKS

Vermont state parks open during the last week in May and close after the Labor Day or Columbus Day weekend, depending on location. Day-use charges are $2 per person for ages 14 and up, $1.50 for ages 4 to 13; children under 4 are free. Call individual parks or the Department of Forests, Parks, and Recreation for information.

➤ CONTACTS: **Department of Forests, Parks, and Recreation** (☎ 802/241–3655).

OUTDOORS & SPORTS

A hot line has tips on peak viewing locations and times and up-to-date snow conditions.

➤ CONTACTS: **Foliage and Snow Hot Line** (☎ 802/828–3239).

CANOEING

Umiak Outdoor Outfitters has shuttles to nearby rivers for day excursions and customized overnight trips. Vermont Canoe Trippers/Battenkill Canoe, Ltd. organizes canoe tours (some are inn-to-inn) and fishing trips.

➤ CONTACTS: **Umiak Outdoor Outfitters** (✉ 849 S. Main St., Stowe, ☎ 802/253–2317. **Vermont Canoe Trippers/Battenkill Canoe, Ltd.** (✉ River Rd., off Rte. 7A, Arlington, ☎ 802/362–2800).

FISHING

For information about fishing, including licenses, call the Vermont Fish and Wildlife Department. Strictly Trout will arrange a fly-fishing trip on any Vermont stream or river, including the Battenkill.

➤ CONTACTS: **Vermont Fish and Wildlife Department** (☎ 802/241–3700). **Strictly Trout** (☎ 802/869–3116).

HIKING

The Green Mountain Club publishes hiking maps and guides. The club also manages the Long Trail, the north–south trail that traverses the entire state.

➤ CONTACTS: **Green Mountain Club** (✉ Rte. 100, Waterbury, ☎ 802/244–7037).

HORSEBACK RIDING

Kedron Valley Stables has one- to six-day riding tours with lodging in country inns.

➤ CONTACTS: **Kedron Valley Stables** (✉ South Woodstock, ☎ 802/457–1480 or 800/225–6301).

SKIING

For information, contact Ski Vermont/Vermont Ski Area Association.

➤ CONTACTS: **Ski Vermont/Vermont Ski Area Association** (✉ Box 368, 26 State St., Montpelier 05601, ☎ 802/223–2439, WEB www.skivermont.com).

TOURS

Bicycle Holidays helps you plan your own inn-to-inn tour by providing route directions and booking your accommodations. Vermont Bicycle Touring leads numerous tours in the state and the region. New England Hiking Holidays leads guided walks with lodging in country inns. North Wind Hiking and Walking Tours conducts guided walking tours through Vermont's countryside.

➤ TOUR OPERATORS: **Bicycle Holidays** (✉ Munger St., Middlebury, ☎ 802/388–2453 or 800/292–5388). **Vermont Bicycle Touring** (✉ Monkton Rd., Bristol, ☎ 802/453–4811 or 800/245–3868). **New England Hiking Holidays** (✉ North Conway, NH, ☎ 603/356–9696 or 800/869–0949). **North Wind Hiking and Walking Tours** (✉ Waitsfield, ☎ 802/496–5771 or 800/496–5771).

TRAIN TRAVEL

Amtrak's *Vermonter* is a daytime service linking Washington, D.C., with Brattleboro, Bellows Falls, White River Junction, Montpelier, Waterbury, Essex Junction, and St. Albans. The *Adirondack,* which runs from Washington, D.C., to Montréal, serves Albany, Ft. Edward (near Glens Falls), Ft. Ticonderoga, and Plattsburgh, allowing relatively convenient access to western Vermont. The *Ethan Allen Express* connects New York City with Fair Haven and Rutland.

➤ TRAIN INFORMATION: **Amtrak** (☎ 800/872–7245, WEB www.amtrak.com).

VISITOR INFORMATION

➤ TOURIST INFORMATION: **Forest Supervisor, Green Mountain National Forest** (✉ 231 N. Main St., Rutland 05701, ☎ 802/747–6700). **Vermont Chamber of Commerce** (✉ Box 37, Montpelier 05601, ☎ 802/223–3443). **Vermont Department of Tourism and Marketing** (✉ 134 State St., Montpelier 05602, ☎ 802/828–3237 or 800/837–6668). There are **state information centers** on the Massachusetts border at I–91, the New Hampshire border at I–89, the New York border at Route 4A, and the Canadian border at I–89.

4 MASSACHUSETTS

Only a half-dozen states are smaller than Massachusetts, but few have influenced American life more profoundly. Generations of Bay State merchants, industrialists, and computer executives have charted the course of the country's economy; Massachusetts writers, artists, and academics have enriched American culture; and from the meetinghouse to the White House, the state's politicians, philosophers, and pundits have fueled national debates.

ASSACHUSETTS SEABOARD TOWNS—from Newburyport to Provincetown—were built before the Revolution, during the heyday of American shipping. These coastal villages evoke a bygone world of clipper ships, robust fishermen, and sturdy sailors bound for distant Cathay. Lowell, on the Merrimack River, was the first American city to be planned around manufacturing. This textile town introduced the rest of the nation to the routines of the Industrial Revolution. In our own time, the high-tech firms of the greater Boston area helped launch the information age, and the Massachusetts Institute of Technology (MIT) and Harvard supplied intellectual heft to deliver it to the wider world.

The Massachusetts town meeting set the tone for politics in the 13 original colonies. A century later, Boston was a hotbed of rebellion—Samuel Adams and James Otis, the "Sons of Liberty," started a war with words, inciting action against British colonial policies with patriotic pamphlets and fiery speeches at Faneuil Hall. Twentieth-century heirs to Adams include Boston's flashy mid-century mayor James Michael Curley; Thomas "Tip" O'Neill, the late Speaker of the House; and, of course, the Kennedys. In 1961, the young senator from the Boston suburb of Brookline, John Fitzgerald Kennedy, became president of the United States. JFK's service to Massachusetts was family tradition: in the years before World War I, Kennedy's grandfather John "Honey Fitz" Fitzgerald served in Congress and as mayor of Boston. But political families are nothing new here—Massachusetts has sent both a father and a son (John Adams and John Quincy Adams) to the White House.

Massachusetts has an extensive system of parks, protected forests, beaches, and nature preserves. Like medieval pilgrims, readers of *Walden* come to Concord to visit the place where Henry David Thoreau wrote his prophetic essay. Thoreau's disciples can be found hiking to the top of the state's highest peak, Mt. Greylock; shopping for organic produce in an unpretentious college burg like Williamstown; or strolling the beaches of Cape Cod. For those who prefer the hills to the ocean, the rolling Berkshire terrain defines the landscape from North Adams to Great Barrington in the western part of the state. A favorite vacation spot since the 19th century, when eastern aristocrats built grand summer residences, the Berkshire Hills have been described as an inland Newport. This area attracts vacationers seeking superb scenery and food and an active cultural scene.

The list of Bay State writers, artists, and musicians who have shaped American culture is long indeed. The state has produced great poets in every generation: Anne Bradstreet, Phillis Wheatley, Emily Dickinson, Henry Wadsworth Longfellow, William Cullen Bryant, e.e. cummings, Robert Lowell, Elizabeth Bishop, Sylvia Plath, and Anne Sexton. Massachusetts writers include Louisa May Alcott, author of the enduring classic *Little Women*; Nathaniel Hawthorne, who re-created the Salem of his Puritan ancestors in *The Scarlet Letter*; Herman Melville, who wrote *Moby-Dick* in a house at the foot of Mt. Greylock; Eugene O'Neill, whose early plays were produced at a makeshift theater in Provincetown on Cape Cod; Lowell native Jack Kerouac, author of *On the Road*; and John Cheever, chronicler of suburban angst. Painters Winslow Homer and James McNeill Whistler both hailed from the Commonwealth. Norman Rockwell, the quintessential American illustrator, lived and worked in Stockbridge. Celebrated composer and Boston native Leonard Bernstein was the first American to conduct the New York Philharmonic. Joan Baez got her start singing in Harvard Square, and contemporary Boston singer-songwriter Tracy Chapman picked up the beat with folk songs for the new age.

Pleasures and Pastimes

Dining

Massachusetts invented the fried clam, which appears on many North Shore and Cape Cod menus. Creamy clam chowder is another specialty. Eating seafood "in the rough"—from paper plates in shacklike buildings—is a revered local custom.

Boston restaurants serve New England standards and cutting-edge cuisine. At country inns in the Berkshires and the Pioneer Valley you'll find creative contemporary fare that makes the most of local ingredients, as well as traditional New England "dinners" strongly reminiscent of old England: double-cut pork chops, rack of lamb, game, Boston baked beans, Indian pudding, and the dubiously glorified "New England boiled dinner." On the Cape, ethnic specialties such as Portuguese kale soup and linguiça sausage appear on menus along with plenty of seafood. The Cape's sophisticated first-rate restaurants (with prices to match) include several in Brewster; on Nantucket and Martha's Vineyard, top-of-the-line establishments prepare traditional and innovative fare.

On the North Shore, Rockport is a "dry" town, though you can almost always take your own alcohol into restaurants; most places charge a nominal corkage fee. This law leads to early closing hours—many Rockport dining establishments close by 9 PM.

For price-category information, *see* Dining *in* Smart Travel Tips.

Lodging

Boston has everything from luxury hotels to charming B&Bs. The signature accommodation outside Boston is the country inn; in the Berkshires, where magnificent mansions have been converted into lodgings, the inns reach a very grand scale indeed. Less extravagant and less expensive are bed-and-breakfast establishments, many of them in private homes. On Cape Cod, inns are plentiful, and rental homes and condominiums are available for long-term stays. Be sure to make reservations for inns well in advance during peak periods: summer on the Cape and islands and summer through winter in the Berkshires. For price-category information, *see* Lodging *in* Smart Travel Tips.

Outdoor Activities and Sports

BEACHES

Massachusetts has many excellent beaches, especially on Cape Cod, where the waves are gentle and the water cool. Southside beaches, on Nantucket Sound, have rolling surf and are warmer. Open-ocean beaches on the Cape Cod National Seashore are cold and have serious surf. Parking lots can fill up by 10 AM in summer. Beaches not restricted to residents charge parking fees; for weekly or seasonal passes, contact the local town hall.

Bostonians head for wide sweeps of sand along the North Shore (beware of biting blackflies in late May and early June), among them Singing Beach in Manchester, Plum Island in Newburyport, and Crane Beach in Ipswich. Boston city beaches are not particularly attractive and definitely not for swimming, though the ongoing rehabilitation of Boston Harbor has made them somewhat cleaner.

BOATING

Cape Cod and the North Shore are centers for ocean-going pleasure craft, with public mooring available in many towns—phone numbers for public marinas are listed in the regional A to Z sections, or you can contact local chambers of commerce. Sea kayaking is popular along the marshy coastline of the North Shore, where freshwater canoeing is also an option. Inland, the Connecticut River in the Pioneer

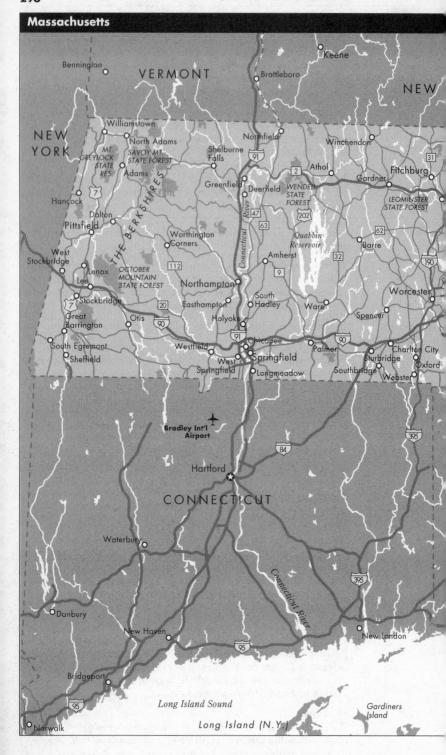

Keene

Bennington

VERMONT

Brattleboro

NEW

Williamstown

North Adams
SAVOY MT.
STATE FOREST

Northfield

Winchendon

Fitchburg

NEW
YORK

MT.
GREYLOCK
STATE
RES.

Adams

Shelburne
Falls

Athol

Gardner

31

Hancock

Dalton

Greenfield

Deerfield

WENDELL
STATE
FOREST

202

LEOMINSTER
STATE FOREST

Pittsfield

THE BERKSHIRES

Worthington
Corners

47

63

Quabbin
Reservoir

62

190

West
Stockbridge

Lenox
OCTOBER
MOUNTAIN
STATE FOREST

112

Amherst

32

Barre

Worcester

Lee
Stockbridge

20

Northampton

9

South
Hadley

Ware

Spencer

Great
Barrington

Otis

90

Easthampton

Holyoke

91

Westfield

Chicopee

Palmer

90

Sturbridge

Charlton City

South Egremont
Sheffield

West
Springfield

Springfield

Longmeadow

Southbridge

Oxford

Webster

Bradley Int'l
Airport

84

395

Hartford

CONNECTICUT

Waterbury

395

Connecticut River

Danbury

New Haven

New London

95

Bridgeport

95

Norwalk

Long Island Sound

*Gardiners
Island*

Long Island (N.Y.)

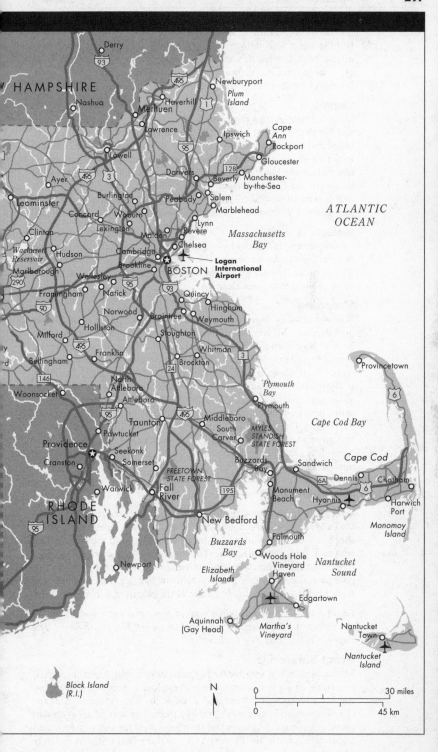

NEW HAMPSHIRE

Derry

Nashua

Methuen
Haverhill
Lawrence
Newburyport
Plum
Island

Lowell
Ipswich
Cape
Ann
Rockport

Ayer
Danvers
Gloucester
Beverly
Manchester-
by-the-Sea

Leominster
Burlington
Peabody
Salem

Concord
Woburn
Marblehead

Clinton
Lexington
Lynn
Revere

Wachusett
Reservoir
Hudson
Cambridge
Malden
Chelsea

Marlborough
Brookline
BOSTON
Logan
International
Airport

Framingham
Wellesley
Massachusetts
Bay

Natick
Quincy

Norwood
Braintree
Hingham

Holliston
Weymouth

Milford
Stoughton

Bellingham
Franklin
Whitman

Brockton

North
Attleboro
Plymouth
Bay

Woonsocket
Attleboro
Middleboro
Plymouth

Providence
Taunton
South
Carver
MYLES
STANDISH
STATE FOREST
Cape Cod Bay

Pawtucket
Provincetown

Cranston
Seekonk
Somerset
FREETOWN
STATE FOREST
Buzzards
Bay
Sandwich
Cape Cod

Warwick
Fall
River
Monument
Beach
Dennis
Chatham

RHODE
ISLAND
New Bedford
Hyannis
Harwich
Port

Newport
Buzzards
Bay
Falmouth
Monomoy
Island

Woods Hole
Vineyard
Haven
Nantucket
Sound

Elizabeth
Islands

Aquinnah
(Gay Head)
Martha's
Vineyard
Edgartown

Nantucket
Town

Nantucket
Island

ATLANTIC
OCEAN

Block Island
(R.I.)

N

0   30 miles
0   45 km

Valley is navigable by all types of craft between the Turners Falls Dam, just north of Greenfield, and the Holyoke Dam. The large dams control the water level daily, so you will notice a tidal effect; if you have a large boat, beware of sandbanks. Canoes can travel north of Turners Falls beyond the Vermont border; canoeing is also popular in the lakes and small rivers of the Berkshires.

FISHING

Deep-sea fishing trips depart from Boston, Cape Cod, and the South and North shores; surf casting is popular on the North Shore. The rivers, lakes, and streams of the Pioneer Valley and Berkshire County abound with fish—bass, pike, and perch, to name but a few. Stocked trout waters include the Hoosic River (south branch) near Cheshire; the Green River around Great Barrington; Notch Brook and the Hoosic River (north branch) near North Adams; Goose Pond and Hop Brook around Lee; and the Williams River around West Stockbridge.

WHALE-WATCHING

In summer and fall, boats leave Boston, Cape Cod, and Cape Ann two or more times a day to observe the whales feeding a few miles offshore. It's rare not to have the extraordinary experience of seeing several whales, most of them extremely close up.

Shopping

Boston has many high-quality shops, especially in the Newbury Street and Beacon Hill neighborhoods, and most suburban communities have at least a couple of main-street stores selling old furniture and collectibles. Antiques can be found on the South Shore in Plymouth; on the North Shore in Essex, Newburyport, Marblehead, and elsewhere; in the northern towns of the Pioneer Valley (especially in Amherst or along the Mohawk Trail); and just about everywhere in the Berkshires, with particularly rich hunting grounds around Sheffield and Great Barrington. On Cape Cod, Provincetown and Wellfleet are centers for fine arts and crafts. Bookstores, gift shops, jewelers, and clothing boutiques line Main Street in Hyannis. Chatham's Main Street is a pretty, upscale shopping area.

Exploring Massachusetts

Boston has the museums, the history, the shopping, and the traffic; Cape Cod and the North and South shores have beaches, more history, more shopping, and plenty of traffic. In the Berkshires and the Pioneer Valley you'll find centuries-old towns, antiques shops, green hills, and a little less traffic. There's beauty to be discovered after the tourists have gone, wandering through snowy fields or braving the elements on a winter beach, and sipping hot cider at the hearth of a local inn.

Numbers in the text and in the margin correspond to numbers on the maps: Cape Cod, Martha's Vineyard, Nantucket, The North Shore, The Pioneer Valley, and The Berkshires.

Great Itineraries

Massachusetts is a small state but one packed with appealing sights; you could easily spend several weeks exploring it. In a few days you can get a feeling for Boston and some of the historic towns near the city. Those who have a week and like to explore several areas should spend a few days in Boston and then head west for some historic and scenic highlights in the Pioneer Valley and the Berkshires. A leisurely one-week trip to Cape Cod and Martha's Vineyard is a classic summer vacation.

IF YOU HAVE 3 DAYS

Spend two days touring ⛢ **Boston.** You can hit highlights such as the Public Garden, Beacon Hill, and the Freedom Trail on the first day; check out the Museum of Fine Arts or the Isabella Stewart Gardner Museum the morning of the next day; and either explore Harvard and Cambridge or do some shopping on Newbury Street in the afternoon. On the third day either swing west on Route 2 and tour **Lexington** and **Concord** or north on Route 1A and east on Route 129 to **Marblehead** ㉘. Explore Marblehead and have lunch there before heading west on Route 114 and north on Route 1A to **Salem** ㉙.

IF YOU HAVE 7 DAYS

Follow the three-day itinerary above, and spend your third night in **Salem** ㉙. On day four take the Massachusetts Turnpike (I–90) out of Boston and make a half-day stop at Old Sturbridge Village in **Sturbridge** ㊺. Afterward, continue west on I–90 and north on I–91, stopping briefly in **Northampton** ㊶ before heading to ⛢ **Deerfield** ㊴, where you'll spend the night and day five. On day six head to the Berkshires—from Deerfield head north on I–91 to Greenfield, where you'll take Route 2 west to ⛢ **Williamstown** ㊼. On the morning of day seven tour the Sterling and Francine Clark Art Institute in Williamstown. U.S. 7 south takes you through **Pittsfield** ㊾; detour west on U.S. 20 to Hancock Shaker Village before heading on to ⛢ **Lenox** ㊿.

IF YOU HAVE 7 DAYS TO SPEND ON THE CAPE

Head south from Boston (take I–93 to Route 3 to U.S. 6). Stop in **Plymouth** and visit Plimoth Plantation. Have lunch in **Sandwich** ① and tour the town before continuing on U.S. 6 to ⛢ **Chatham** ⑪, where you'll stay the night (have dinner and stroll Main Street in the evening). The next day, drive to **Orleans** ⑫ and spend the day at Nauset Beach. On day three continue on U.S. 6 to ⛢ **Provincetown** ⑯, stopping briefly in **Wellfleet** ⑭ to tour the galleries and detouring east off U.S. 6 to Cahoon Hollow Beach. After dinner take a walk down Commercial Street. On morning four head to Race Point Beach, go on a whale-watching cruise, or take a dune-buggy tour. On day five take U.S. 6 to **Hyannis** ⑤, where you can catch the ferry to ⛢ **Martha's Vineyard** ⑰–㉔.

When to Tour Massachusetts

Fall is the best time to visit western Massachusetts, and it's the perfect season to see Boston as well. Everyone else knows this, so make reservations well ahead. Summer is ideal for visits to the Cape and the beaches. Bostonians often find their city to be too hot and humid in July and August, but if you're visiting from points south, the cool evening coastal breezes might strike you as downright refreshing. Many towns save their best for Christmas—lobster boats parade around Gloucester harbor adorned with lights, inns open their doors for goodies and caroling, shops serve eggnog, and tree-lighting ceremonies are often magical moments. The off-season is the perfect time to try cross-country skiing, take a walk on a stormy beach, or spend a night by the fire, tucked under a quilt catching up on Hawthorne or Thoreau.

BOSTON

Updated by Elizabeth Gehrman, Carolyn Heller, Rene Hertzog, Alexandra Hall, and Adam Smith

New England's largest and most important city and the cradle of American independence, Boston is more than 370 years old, far older than the republic its residents helped create. The city's most famous buildings are not merely civic landmarks but national icons, and its local heroes are known to the nation: John and Samuel Adams, Paul Revere, John Hancock, and many more who live at the crossroads of history and myth.

300

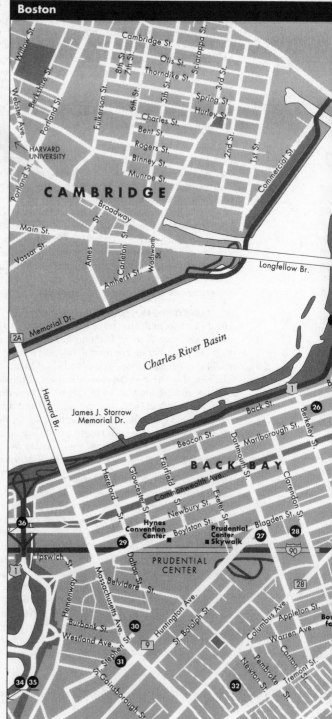

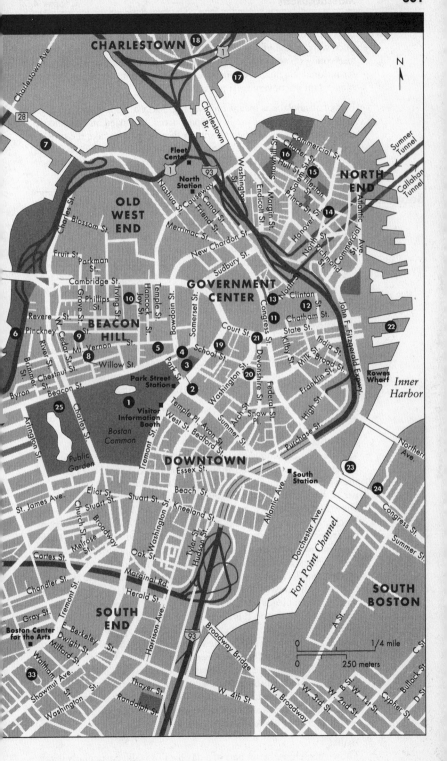

CHARLESTOWN ⓲

⓱

N

Sumner Tunnel

㉘

⑦

Charlestown Ave.

Charlestown Br.

Fleet Center

Charlestown Ave.

Charter St.

Commercial St.

Snow Hill St.

Hull St.

Salem St.

⑯

Hull St.

⑮

Prince St.

Callahan Tunnel

NORTH END

North Station

1

93

North Washington St.

Washington St.

Margin St.

Canal St.

Friend St.

Endicott St.

Hanover St.

North St.

Atlantic Ave.

Commercial Ave.

Nashua St.

Causeway

⑭

Richmond St.

Charles St.

Blossom St.

Merrimac St.

OLD WEST END

New Chardon St.

Sudbury St.

John F. Fitzgerald Expwy.

Fruit St.

Parkman St.

GOVERNMENT CENTER

Clinton

⑫

Chatham St.

Cambridge St.

Temple St.

Hancock St.

⑩

Bowdoin St.

Somerset St.

⑬

⑪

State St.

Grove St.

Phillips St.

Irving St.

Joy St.

Congress St.

Kilby St.

Mill St.

India St.

Broad St.

Revere St.

⑨

BEACON HILL

Court St.

㉑

Rowes Wharf

N. Cedar St.

Mt. Vernon St.

⑤

⑲

School St.

Devonshire St.

Franklin St.

High St.

Inner Harbor

⑥

Pinckney

River St.

⑧

Willow St.

④

③

Washington St.

⑳

Snow Pl.

Brimmer St.

Chestnut St.

Park St.

Temple Pl.

Avon St.

Summer St.

Arch St.

Federal St.

Byron

Beacon St.

②

Bedford St.

Purchase St.

Park Street Station

West St.

Northern Ave.

㉕

Charles St.

①

Visitor Information Booth

Tremont St.

DOWNTOWN

Atlantic Ave.

㉓

Arlington St.

Boston Common

Essex St.

South Station

㉔

Public Garden

Beach St.

Congress St.

St. James Ave.

Eliot St.

Kneeland St.

Dorchester Ave.

Summer St.

Stuart St.

Stuart St.

Washington St.

Tyler St.

Hudson St.

Fort Point Channel

Church St.

Broadway

Melrose St.

Oak St.

A St.

SOUTH BOSTON

Cortes St.

Marginal Rd.

Chandler St.

Tremont St.

Herald St.

Broadway Bridge

0   1/4 mile

Gray St.

E. Berkeley St.

Harrison Ave.

93

0   250 meters

Boston Center for the Arts

Dwight St.

Milford St.

B St.

W. 1st St.

C St.

Cypher St.

Bullock St.

D St.

㉝

Waltham St.

Shawmut Ave.

Washington St.

Thayer St.

Randolph St.

W. 4th St.

W. Broadway

W. 3rd St.

W. 2nd St.

A St.

SOUTH END

At the same time, Boston is a contemporary center of high finance and high technology, a place of granite and glass towers rising along what once were rutted village lanes. Its many students, artists, academics, and young professionals have made the town a haven for the arts, international cinema, late-night bookstores, ethnic food, alternative music, and unconventional politics.

Best of all, Boston is meant for walking. Most of its historical and architectural attractions are in compact areas. Its varied and distinctive neighborhoods reveal their character to visitors who take the time to stroll through them. Should you need to make short or long hops between neighborhoods, the "T"—the safe, easy-to-ride trains of the Massachusetts Bay Transportation Authority—covers the city.

Beacon Hill and Boston Common

Contender for the "Most Beautiful" award among the city's neighborhoods and the hallowed address of many literary lights, Beacon Hill is Boston at its most Bostonian. The redbrick elegance of its narrow, cobbled streets transports you back to the 19th century. From the gold-topped splendor of the State House to the neoclassical panache of its mansions, Beacon Hill exudes power, prestige, and a calm yet palpable undercurrent of history.

Beacon Hill is bounded by Cambridge Street to the north, Beacon Street to the south, the Charles River Esplanade to the west, and Bowdoin Street to the east. In contrast to "the Hill," nearby Boston Common, the country's oldest public park, has a more egalitarian feel. Beginning with its use as public land for cattle grazing, the Common has always accommodated the needs and desires of Bostonians.

Numbers in the text and in the margin correspond to numbers on the Boston map.

A Good Walk

Stock up on brochures at the **Visitor Information Center** on Tremont Street before heading into the **Boston Common** ① to see Frog Pond and the Central Burying Ground. Head back to **Beacon Street** near the corner of Park Street to reach Augustus Saint-Gaudens's Robert Gould Shaw Memorial, a commemoration of Boston's Civil War unit of free blacks. Facing the memorial, head left toward Park Street, then right on Tremont to pass the **Park Street Church** ② and the **Granary Burying Ground** ③, the final resting place of some of Boston's most illustrious figures. Return to Beacon, turn left, and you'll arrive at the **Boston Athenaeum** ④. Retrace your steps to the neoclassical **State House** ⑤. Continue ahead two blocks to Arlington Street and, to your right, the footbridge that leads to the **Esplanade** ⑥. (The **Museum of Science** ⑦, best reached by car or T, is north of the Esplanade across the Charles River.) A pedestrian overpass at the Charles/Massachusetts General Hospital T stop connects the Esplanade with **Charles Street.** Head south on Charles, east on **Chestnut Street,** and north on Willow. This will land you at photogenic **Acorn Street** ⑧ Continue on Willow across **Mt. Vernon Street** to **Louisburg Square** ⑨. Turn east (to the right) on Pinckney Street and follow it to Joy Street: Two blocks north on Smith Court is the **Museum of Afro-American History** ⑩, where you can pick up a brochure for the **Black Heritage Trail.**

TIMING

Allow yourself the better part of a day for this walk, particularly if you want to linger in the Common or browse the antiques shops on Charles Street.

Sights to See

❽ Acorn Street. Surely the most-photographed street in the city, Acorn is Ye Olde Colonial Boston at its best. Almost toylike row houses once owned by 19th-century artisans line one side; on the other are the doors to Mt. Vernon Street's hidden gardens. The cobblestone street is rough going for some.

Beacon Street. One of the city's most famous thoroughfares, Beacon Street epitomizes Boston. From the magnificent ☞ **State House** to the stately patrician mansions, the street is lined with architectural treasures. The ☞ **Boston Athenaeum** is on this street, as are the **Appleton Mansions**, at Nos. 39 and 40. Only a few buildings have panes like those of the mansions: sunlight on the imperfections in a shipment of glass sent to Boston around 1820 resulted in an amethystine mauve shade. The mansions are not open to the public.

Black Heritage Trail®. The mention of Beacon Hill conjures up images of wealthy Boston Brahmins; yet until the end of the 19th century, its north side was also home to many free blacks. The 1½-mi Black Heritage Trail celebrates that community, stitching together 14 Beacon Hill sites. Tours guided by National Park Service rangers meet at the Shaw Memorial on the Beacon Street side of the Boston Common.

★ ❹ Boston Athenaeum. Only 1,049 proprietary shares exist for membership in this cathedral of scholarship, and most have been passed down for generations—though the Athenaeum is open for use by qualified scholars who may choose to become members on a yearly basis. Once an extensive renovation project is complete in early 2002, the public will be permitted to walk through the first floor, in addition to seeing the fifth-floor Reading Room, said by poet David McCord to combine "the best elements of the Bodleian, Monticello, the frigate *Constitution,* a greenhouse, and an old New England sitting room." At press time, the Athenaeum was closed for renovation; call ahead for the latest information. ✉ *10½ Beacon St.,* ☎ *617/227–0270,* WEB *www.bostonathenaeum.org.* ☞ *Free.* ☽ *Call ahead for hours and tour availability. T stop: Park St..*

❶ Boston Common. The oldest public park in the United States is the largest and undoubtedly the most famous of the town commons around which New England settlements were traditionally arranged. As old as the city around it (it dates from 1634) and originally set aside as the spot where the freemen of Boston could graze their cattle, the Common contains intriguing sights. On the Beacon Street side of the Common—actually, just outside the park's gates—is the **Robert Gould Shaw Memorial,** executed in deep-relief bronze by Augustus Saint-Gaudens in 1897. It honors the 54th Massachusetts Regiment, the first Civil War unit made up of free blacks, led by the young Robert Gould Shaw; the regiment's stirring saga inspired the 1989 movie *Glory.* Just below the monument is the **Frog Pond**—a tame and frogless concrete depression, used as a children's wading pool during steamy summer days and for ice skating in winter—which is perhaps the Common's most recognizable feature. The **Central Burying Ground**, along the Boylston Street side, is the final resting place of Tories and Patriots, as well as many British casualties of the Battle of Bunker Hill.

Charles Street. With few exceptions, Beacon Hill lacks commercial development, but the section of Charles Street north of Boston Common more than makes up for it. Antiques shops, bookstores, small restaurants, and flower shops vie for attention, but tastefully: even the 7-Eleven storefront conforms to the Colonial aesthetic. The contemporary activity would present a curious sight to the elder Oliver Wendell Holmes, the publisher James T. Fields (of the famed Boston firm Ticknor & Fields), and many others who lived here when the neighborhood belonged to establishment literati. Charles Street sparkles at dusk from gas-fueled lamps, making it a romantic place for an evening stroll.

Chestnut Street. Delicacy and grace characterize virtually every structure along this street, from the fanlights above the entryways to the wrought-iron boot scrapers on the steps. The **Swan Houses**, at Nos. 13, 15, and 17, have elegant entrances, marble columns, and recessed arches commissioned from Charles Bulfinch by Hepzibah Swan as dowry gifts for her three daughters.

6 Esplanade. At the northern end of Charles Street is one of several footbridges crossing Storrow Drive to the Esplanade, which stretches along the Charles River. The scenic patch of green is a great place to jog, picnic, and watch the sailboats along the river. For the almost nightly entertainment in the summer, hordes of Bostonians haul chairs and blankets to the lawn in front of the **Hatch Memorial Shell.**

★ **Freedom Trail.** A 2½-mi tour of the sites of the American Revolution, the Freedom Trail is a crash course in history. There are 16 sites beginning at the Boston Common and ending at the Bunker Hill Monument in Charlestown; depending on how many are visited in depth, the walk can take an aerobic 90 minutes or a leisurely full day. Trail walks led by National Park Service rangers take place from mid-April to November and begin at the Boston National Historical Park Visitor Center; call for times. Self-guided tour maps are available here and at the Visitor Information Center on Boston Common.

3 Granary Burying Ground. "It is a fine thing to die in Boston," essayist A. C. Lyons once remarked—alluding to Boston's cemeteries, among the most picturesque and historic in America. If you found a resting place here at the Old Granary (as it's affectionately called), just to the right of Park Street Church, chances are your headstone would have been eloquently ornamented and your neighbors would have been mighty eloquent, too: Samuel Adams, John Hancock, Benjamin Franklin's parents, and Paul Revere. ⊠ *Tremont St.* ☉ *Dec.–Apr., daily 9–3; May–Nov., daily 9–5. T stop: Park St.*

Greater Boston Convention and Visitors' Bureau. You can pick up pamphlets, flyers, maps, and coupons at this kiosk at the center of the Common's Tremont Street side. ⊠ *Boston Common, Tremont St. near West St.,* ☎ *617/536–4100 or 888/733–2678,* WEB *www.bostonusa.com.* ☉ *Daily 9–5 T stop: Park St.*

★ **9 Louisburg Square.** One of the most appealing corners in a neighborhood that epitomizes charm, Louisburg (pronounce the "s" as the locals do) Square is the very heart of Beacon Hill. Its houses—many built in the 1840s—have seen their share of famous tenants, including the Alcotts at No. 10 (Louisa May died here in 1888, on the day of her father's funeral). In 1852 the popular Swedish singer Jenny Lind was married in the parlor of No. 20, the residence of Samuel Ward, brother of Julia Ward Howe.

★ **10 The Museum of Afro-American History** is an umbrella historical site that encompasses the Abiel Smith School, the African Meeting House next door, and the African Meeting House on Nantucket Island. Throughout the 19th century, abolition was the cause célèbre for Boston's intellectual elite, and during that time the black community thrived on Beacon Hill. The museum was founded in 1964 to promote this history. The first public school for black children in the United States, the **Abiel Smith School**, was open from 1835 to 1855, and educated about

200 students. The school's exhibits highlight the hardships encountered by the schoolchildren, who endured grossly inadequate learning conditions, and their will to learn. **The African Meeting House**, built in 1806, was the black community's center of social, educational, and political activity and a hotbed of abolitionist fervor. In 1832 the New England Anti-Slavery Society was formed here under the leadership of William Lloyd Garrison. The five residences on nearby **Smith Court** are typical of the homes of black Bostonians during the 1800s, including No. 3, the 1799 clapboard house where William C. Nell, America's first published black historian and a crusader for school integration, boarded from 1851 to 1865. ⌂ *8 Smith Ct. (off Joy St., between Cambridge and Myrtle Sts.),* ☎ *617/725–0022,* WEB *www.afroammuseum.org.* ✑ *Free.* ☉ *Memorial Day–Labor Day, daily 10–4; Mid–Sept.–May, Mon.–Sat. 10–4. T stop: Park St., Charles/MGH, Bowdoin, State St..*

🖐 ❼ **Museum of Science.** With 15-ft lightning bolts in the Theater of Electricity and a 20-ft-high T-rex model, this is just the place to ignite any child's Jurassic spark. In 1999 the Museum of Science joined forces with the Computer Museum, debuting its first permanent Computer Museum exhibit, the **Virtual Fish Tank**, shortly thereafter. The distinction will soon disappear as the Computer Museum is gradually subsumed. The museum, astride the Charles River Dam, has a restaurant, a gift shop, a planetarium, and a theater you can visit separately. The **Charles Hayden Planetarium**, with its sophisticated multi-image system, produces exciting programs on astronomical discoveries. The **Mugar Omni Theater** has a five-story domed screen and 27,000 watts of power driving its 84 loudspeakers. ⌂ *Science Park at the Charles River Dam,* ☎ *617/723–2500,* WEB *www.mos.org.* ✑ *$10. Reduced-price combination tickets available for museum, planetarium, and Omni Theater.* ☉ *July 5–early Sept., Sat.–Thurs. 9–7, Fri. 9–9; mid-Sept.–July 4, Sat.–Thurs. 9–5, Fri. 9–9. T stop: Science Park.*

Nichols House. The only Mt. Vernon Street home open to the public, the Nichols House—built in 1804 and attributed to Charles Bulfinch—belonged to Beacon Hill eccentric, philanthropist, peace advocate, and one of the first female landscape designers, Rose Standish Nichols. Although the Victorian furnishings passed to Miss Nichols by descent, she added a number of Colonial-style pieces, resulting in a delightful mélange of styles. ⌂ *55 Mt. Vernon St.,* ☎ *617/227–6993.* ✑ *$5 for tours only.* ☉ *May–Oct., Tues.–Sat. noon–4:15; Nov.–Dec. and Feb.–Apr., Thurs.–Sat. noon–4:15. Tours on the ¼ hr. T stop: Park St.*

❷ **Park Street Church.** If the Congregationalist Park Street Church could talk, what a joyful noise it would make. Samuel Smith's hymn "America" debuted here on July 4, 1831; two years earlier, William Lloyd Garrison began his long public campaign for the abolition of slavery. The 1810 church—designed by Peter Banner and called "the most impressive mass of brick and mortar in America" by Henry James—is easily recognized by its 217-ft steeple, considered by many to be the most beautiful in New England. ⌂ *Zero Park St., at Tremont,* ☎ *617/523–3383.* ☉ *Tours mid-June–Aug., Tues.–Sat. 9:30–3:30. Sun. services at 8:30, 11, 4:30, and 7. T stop: Park St.*

❺ **State House.** Charles Bulfinch's magnificent State House, one of the greatest works of classical architecture in America, is so striking that it hardly suffers for having been expanded in three directions by bureaucrats and lesser architects. The neoclassical design is poised between Georgian and Federal; its finest features are the delicate Corinthian columns of the portico, the graceful pediment and window arches, and the vast yet visually weightless dome, sheathed in copper from the foundry of Paul Revere. Unfortunately, much of the beauty of the

State House is to be hidden for the next couple of years; the facade is being cleaned. The restoration is due to be finished in 2003; until then, it's still worth the trip to tour the interior. ⊠ *Beacon St. between Hancock and Bowdoin Sts.,* ☎ *617/727–3676.* ⊡ *Free.* ☉ *Tours weekdays and Sat. 10–4 (last tour at 3:30); call in advance; no minimum number of people required. T stop: Park St.*

Government Center and the North End

Government Center is the section of town Bostonians love to hate. Not only does it house that which they cannot fight—City Hall—but it also holds some of the bleakest architecture since the advent of poured concrete. The sweeping brick plaza beside City Hall and the twin towers of the John F. Kennedy Federal Office Building begins at the junction where Cambridge Street becomes Tremont Street.

Separating the Government Center area from the North End is the Fitzgerald Expressway, which will eventually be replaced with an underground highway in a massive construction project dubbed "the Big Dig" by locals. In the meantime, calling the area a mess is putting it mildly. Driver alert: the rerouting of traffic and constant reconfiguration of one-way streets have changed what was once a conquerable puzzle into a nearly impenetrable maze. Trust no maps.

Opposite the pedestrian tunnel beneath the Fitzgerald Expressway is the North End, the oldest neighborhood in Boston and one of the oldest in the New World. People walked these narrow byways when Shakespeare was not yet 20 years buried and Louis XIV was new to the throne of France. In the 17th century the North End *was* Boston—much of the rest of the peninsula was still underwater or had yet to be cleared.

Today's North End is almost entirely a creation of the late 19th century, when brick tenements began to fill up with European immigrants—first the Irish, then the Eastern European Jews, then the Portuguese, and finally the Italians. Despite a recent influx of yuppies of all ethnicities, you'll still find dozens of authentic Italian restaurants, along with Old World–style groceries, bakeries, churches, social clubs, and cafés.

Numbers in the text and in the margin correspond to numbers on the Boston map.

A Good Walk

The stark expanse of Boston's City Hall Plaza introduces visitors to the urban renewal age, but across Congress Street is **Faneuil Hall** ⑪, a site of political speechmaking since Revolutionary times. Just beyond that is **Quincy Market** ⑫, where shop-till-you-droppers can sample a profusion of international taste treats. For more Bostonian fare, walk back toward Congress Street to the **Blackstone Block** ⑬ and the city's oldest restaurant, the Union Oyster House, for some oysters and ale. Around the corner to the north on Blackstone Street are the open-air produce stalls of **Haymarket,** always aflutter with activity on Friday and Saturday. To sample Italian goodies, make your way through a pedestrian tunnel underneath the Fitzgerald Highway and enter the North End at Salem Street. Follow to Parmenter Street, turn right, and continue past Hanover Street, one of the North End's main thoroughfares; here Parmenter becomes Richmond Street. At North Street, turn left, following the Freedom Trail, to the **Paul Revere House** ⑭. Take Prince Street to Hanover Street, and then continue on Hanover to St. Stephen's, the only remaining church designed by Charles Bulfinch. Directly across the street is the Prado, or Paul Revere Mall, dominated by a statue of the patriot and hero. At the end of the mall is the **Old North Church** ⑮, of "One if by land, two if by sea" fame. Continue following the Freedom Trail to Hull Street and **Copp's Hill Burying Ground** ⑯, the resting place of many Revolutionary War heroes.

TIMING

You can explore Faneuil Hall and Quincy Market in about an hour, more if you linger in the food stalls or shop. Give yourself another two to three hours to stroll through the North End. Finish the day with an Italian meal or at least a cappuccino.

Sights to See

⑬ **Blackstone Block.** For decades the butcher trade dominated the city's oldest commercial block. Today, the block is Boston at its time-machine best, with more than three centuries of architecture on view. The centerpiece of the block is the **Union Oyster House**, whose patrons have included Daniel Webster and John F. Kennedy. ⊠ *Blackstone St., between North and Hanover Sts.*

⑯ **Copp's Hill Burying Ground.** An ancient and melancholy air hovers over this Colonial-era burial ground like a fine mist. Many headstones were chipped by practice shots fired by British soldiers during the occupation of Boston, and a number of musketball pockmarks can still be seen. ⊠ *Between Hull and Snowhill Sts.* ☉ *Apr.–Nov., daily 9–5; Dec.–Mar., daily 9–3. T stop: Haymarket, State Street, Government Center.*

★ ⑪ **Faneuil Hall.** Faneuil Hall was erected in 1742 to serve as a place for town meetings and a public market. Inside are the great mural *Webster's Reply to Hayne,* Gilbert Stuart's portrait of Washington at Dorchester Heights, several worthwhile shops in the basement, and, on the top floors, the headquarters and museum of the Ancient and Honorable Artillery Company of Massachusetts, the oldest militia in the Western Hemisphere (1638). ⊠ *Faneuil Hall Sq.,* WEB *www.faneuilhallmarketplace.com* 🎫 *Free.* ☉ *Daily 9–5. T stop: Government Center, State.*

Holocaust Memorial. At night, its six 50-ft-high glass-and-steel towers glow like ghosts who vow never to forget; though during the day, the monument seems at odds with the 18th-century streetscape of Blackstone Square behind it. Recollections by Holocaust survivors are set into the glass-and-granite walls; the upper levels of the towers are etched with 6 million numbers in random sequence symbolizing the Jewish victims of the Nazi horror.

★ ⑮ **Old North Church.** Also known as Christ Church, Old North is famous not only for its status as the oldest in Boston (1723) but for the two lanterns that glimmered from its steeple on the night of April 18, 1775, signaling the departure by water of the British regulars to Lexington and Concord. Longfellow's poem aside, the lanterns—hung by a young sexton named Robert Newman—were not a signal *to* Paul Revere but *from* him to the citizens of Charlestown across the harbor. The church was designed by William Price from a study of Christopher Wren's London churches. ⊠ *193 Salem St.,* ☎ *617/523–6676,* WEB *www.oldnorth.com.* ☉ *June–Oct., daily 9–6; Nov.–May, daily 9–5. Sun. services at 9, 11, and 5; Wed. service at 9. T stop: Haymarket, North Station.*

🐣 ⑭ **Paul Revere House.** It is an interesting coincidence that the oldest house standing in one of the oldest sections of Boston should also have been the home of Paul Revere, patriot activist and silversmith. And it *is* a coincidence, since many homes of famous Bostonians have burned or been demolished over the years. It was saved from oblivion in 1902 and restored to an approximation of its original 17th-century appearance. The house was built nearly a hundred years before Revere's 1775 midnight ride through Middlesex County, on a site once occupied by the parsonage of the Reverend Increase Mather's Second Church of Boston. A few Revere furnishings are on display. Special events are scheduled throughout the year, many designed with children in mind. The immediate neighborhood surrounding the house also has Revere associations. The little park in North Square is named after Rachel Revere, his second wife, and the adjacent brick **Pierce-Hichborn House** once belonged to relatives of Revere. The garden connecting the Revere House and the Pierce-Hichborn House is planted with flowers and medicinal herbs favored in Revere's day. ✉ *19 North Sq.*, ☎ *617/523–2338,* WEB *www.paulreverehouse.org.* ✍ *$2.50; combined admission for Paul Revere and Pierce-Hichborn houses $4.* ⊘ *Jan.–Mar., Tues.–Sun. 9:30–4:15; Nov.–Dec. and first 2 wks of Apr., daily 9:30–4:15; mid-Apr.–Oct., daily 9:30–5:15. T stop: Haymarket, State.*

⑫ **Quincy Market.** Also known as Faneuil Hall Marketplace, this pioneer effort at urban recycling set the tone for many similar projects throughout America. The market consists of three block-long annexes: Quincy, North, and South markets, each 535 ft long and built to the 1826 design of Alexander Parris. Abundance and variety have been the watchwords of Quincy Market since its reopening in 1976. Some people consider it hopelessly commercial, though in the peak summer season 50,000 or so visitors a day rather enjoy the extravaganza. At the east end of Quincy Market, **Marketplace Center** has tempting boutiques and food shops. ✉ *Between Clinton and Chatham Sts.*, ☎ *617/338–2323.* ⊘ *Mon.–Sat. 10–9, Sun. noon–6. Restaurants and bars generally open daily 11 AM–2 AM; food stalls open earlier. T stop: Haymarket, Government Center, State St..*

Charlestown

Charlestown was a thriving settlement a year before Colonials headed across the Charles River to found Boston proper. The district holds two of the most visible—and vertical—monuments in Boston's history: the Bunker Hill Monument and the USS *Constitution.*

Numbers in the text and in the margin correspond to numbers on the Boston map.

A Good Walk

Charlestown can be reached by foot via the Charlestown Bridge; by taking Bus 93 from Haymarket Square, Boston; or on the MBTA water shuttle, which runs every 15 or 30 minutes year-round, from Long Wharf in downtown Boston. If you're walking, start at Copp's Hill Burial Ground; follow Hull Street to Commercial Street, and turn left to reach the bridge. The Charlestown Navy Yard will be on your right; ahead is the **USS *Constitution*** ⑰ museum and visitor center. From here, you can follow the red line of the Freedom Trail to the **Bunker Hill Monument** ⑱.

TIMING

Give yourself two or three hours for a Charlestown walk; the lengthy stroll across the bridge calls for endurance in cold weather. Many save Charlestown's stretch of the Freedom Trail for a second-day outing. You can avoid backtracking by taking the water shuttle back to Long Wharf.

Sights to See

⑱ **Bunker Hill Monument.** British troops sustained heavy losses on June 17, 1775, at the Battle of Bunker Hill—one of the earliest major confrontations of the Revolutionary War. Most of the battle took place on Breed's Hill, which is where the monument, dedicated in 1843, actually stands. The famous war cry "Don't fire until you see the whites of their eyes" may not have been uttered by American colonel William Prescott or General Israel Putnam, but if either did shout it, he was quoting an old Prussian command that was necessary due to the inaccuracy of the musket. No matter. The Americans employed a deadly delayed-action strategy and proved themselves worthy fighters. Though they lost the battle, the engagement made clear that the British could be challenged. The monument's top is reached by a flight of 294 steps. There is no elevator, but the views from the observatory are worth the arduous climb—for those in good condition. In the lodge at the base, dioramas tell the story of the battle; and ranger programs are conducted regularly. ⊠ *Main St. to Monument St., then straight uphill,* ☎ *617/ 242–5641.* ☞ *Free.* ☉ *Lodge daily 9–5, monument daily 9–4:30. T stop: Community College.*

⏱ ❶⑦ **USS** *Constitution.* Better known as "Old Ironsides," the more than two-centuries-old USS *Constitution* is docked at the Charlestown Navy Yard. Launched in 1797, the oldest commissioned ship in the U.S. fleet is from the days of "wooden ships and iron men"—when she and her crew of 200 helped to assert the sovereignty of an improbable new nation. The ship's principal service was in the War of 1812. After her 42 engagements, her record was 42–0. The adjacent **Constitution Museum** (☎ 617/426–1812) has artifacts and hands-on exhibits. It's open May–October, daily 9–6; November–April, daily 10–5. ⊠ *Charlestown Navy Yard, off Water St.,* ☎ *617/242–5670,* ᴡᴇʙ *www.ussconstitution.navy.mil, www.ussconstitutionmuseum.org.* ☞ *Free.* ☉ *Daily 9:30–sunset; 20-min tours (last tour at 3:30 PM). T stop: Haymarket; then MBTA Bus 92 or 93 to Charlestown City Sq. Or take the MBTA water shuttle from Long Wharf to Pier 4.*

Downtown Boston

The Financial District—what Bostonians usually refer to as "downtown"—may seem off the beaten track for people who are concentrating on following the Freedom Trail, yet there is much to see in a walk of an hour or two. There is little logic to the streets here; they were, after all, village lanes that only now happen to be lined with 40-story office towers.

Downtown is home to some of Boston's most idiosyncratic neighborhoods. The old Leather District directly abuts Chinatown, which is also bordered by the Theater District (and the buildings of the New England Medical Center) farther west; to the south, the red light of the once brazen and now decaying Combat Zone flickers weakly.

Numbers in the text and in the margin correspond to numbers on the Boston map.

A Good Walk

After viewing the dramatic interior of **King's Chapel** ⑲ at the corner of Tremont (that's *Treh*-mont, not *Tree*-mont) Street, visit the burying ground next door. Walk southeast on School Street, past the Globe Corner Bookstore, to Washington Street; turn right to see the **Old South Meeting House** ⑳, which seethed with Revolutionary fervor in the 1770s. Retrace your steps on Washington and continue toward Court Street to get to the **Old State House** ㉑. In a traffic island in front is a circle of stones that marks the site of the Boston Massacre, a 1770 riot in which five townspeople were killed by British troops. Follow State Street east to the harbor and the **New England Aquarium** ㉒, on Central Wharf. From here you can walk south to **Rowes Wharf,** Boston's most glamorous waterfront development. Continue on Atlantic Avenue—most likely a wall of traffic due to the construction of an underground central-artery highway nearby—to Congress Street, and then turn left onto the bridge to reach the **Boston Tea Party Ship and Museum** ㉓ aboard the *Beaver II*, a re-creation of the hapless British ship that was carrying tea in 1773. Continue over the Congress Street Bridge to the **Children's Museum** ㉔. If you're starting to crave refreshment, cross back to Atlantic Avenue and continue south past South Station toward the distinctive gate marking **Chinatown.**

TIMING

If you are traveling with small children, you may wish to limit this walk to the area around the New England Aquarium and the Children's Museum. (In fact, you'll probably want to spend two or three hours just in the museums.) Otherwise budget about three hours for the walk, and be prepared for the often cool wind coming off the harbor.

Sights to See

Boston Harbor Islands National Park Area. In 1996, the Boston Harbor Islands—the 31 islands in the inner and outer harbors—were designated a national park area, administered by a 13-member partnership. The focal point of the park is 28-acre George's Island, on which the pre–Civil War Fort Warren stands, partially restored. From May to October, you can reach George's Island on the Boston Harbor Cruises ferry; from June to September, free water shuttles run from George's to several other islands. Bumpkin and Gallops are small and easily explored within an hour; Lovell's and Grape each cover about 60 acres. You can fish, hike, and picnic—there are plenty of ruins to explore, and beautiful views. Lovell's has a rocky swimming beach with a lifeguard on duty; you can swim unsupervised on Gallops and Grape islands. No dogs are allowed on the islands. ☎ *617/223–8666. ⊠ Boston Harbor Cruises, ☎ 617/227–4321, WEB www.bostonislands.com. ☜ Trip to George's Island $8. ☉ Early June–Oct. T stop: State St..*

Boston National Historical Park Visitor Center. National Park Service ranger-led tours of the Freedom Trail leave from the center, which stocks brochures about many attractions and walking tours and has rest rooms. ⊠ *15 State St., near the Old State House, ☎ 617/242–5642, WEB www.nps.gov/bost. ☜ Free. ☉ Daily 9–5. Tours mid-Apr.–Nov., call for hours, which change seasonally.*

㉓ **Boston Tea Party Ship and Museum.** The *Beaver II*, a faithful replica of one of the ships forcibly boarded and unloaded the night Boston Harbor became a teapot, bobs in the Fort Point Channel at the Congress Street Bridge. Visitors receive a complimentary cup of tea and may be pressed into donning feathers and war paint to reenact the tea drop. The site of the actual Boston Tea Party—a revolt over a tax on tea that the British had levied—is marked by a plaque on the corner of Atlantic Avenue and the Northern Avenue bridge. ⊠ *Congress St. Bridge, ☎ 617/338–1773, WEB www.bostonteapartyship.com. ☜ $8. ☉ Late May–early Sept., daily 9–6; early Sept.–Dec. 12 and Mar.–late May, daily 9–4; reenactments on the hour and half-hour. T stop: South Station.*

☺ ㉔ **Children's Museum.** Hands-on exhibits at this popular museum include computers, video cameras, and displays designed to help children understand cultural diversity, their own bodies, the nature of disabilities, and more. Don't miss the Japanese House, "Arthur's World," or Boats Afloat, where children can build a wooden boat and float it down a 15-ft replica of the Fort Point Channel. The museum also has a full schedule of special exhibits, festivals, and performances. ✉ *Museum Wharf, 300 Congress St.,* ☎ *617/426–6500; 617/426–8855 recorded information,* WEB *www.bostonkids.org.* 🖼 *$7, $6 for kids 2-15, free for kids under 1; $1 Fri. 5–9.* ◷ *Sat.–Thurs. 10–5, Fri. 10–9. T stop: South Station.*

Chinatown. Boston's Chinatown may be geographically small, but it is home to the third-largest concentration of Chinese-Americans in the United States, after San Francisco's and New York City's Chinatowns. Beginning in the 1870s, Chinese immigrants began to trickle in, many setting up tents in a strip they called Ping On Alley. The trickle increased to a wave when immigration restrictions were lifted in 1968. In recent years, Vietnamese, Korean, Japanese, Thai, and Malaysian eateries have popped up alongside the Chinese restaurants—most along Beach and Tyler streets and Harrison Avenue. A three-story pagoda-style arch at the end of Beach Street welcomes visitors to the district. *T stop: Chinatown.*

⓳ King's Chapel. Somber yet dramatic, King's Chapel looms over the corner of Tremont and School streets. The distinctive shape of the 1754 structure was not achieved entirely by design; for lack of funds it was never topped with the steeple that architect Peter Harrison had planned. The interior is a masterpiece of elegant proportion and Georgian calm. The chapel's bell is Paul Revere's largest and, in his judgment, his sweetest-sounding. Take the path to the right from the entrance of the **King's Chapel Burying Ground,** the oldest cemetery in the city. On the left is the gravestone (1704) of Elizabeth Pain, the model for Hester Prynne in Hawthorne's *The Scarlet Letter.* Elsewhere, you'll find the graves of the first Massachusetts governor, John Winthrop, and several generations of his descendants. ✉ *58 Tremont St., at School St.,* ☎ *617/ 227–2155.* ◷ *Mid-Apr.–Nov., Mon. and Fri.–Sat. 10–4; Dec.–mid-Apr., Sat. 10–4. Year-round music program Tues. 12:15–1. Services Sun. at 11, Wed. at 12:15. T stop: Park St., Government Center.*

★ ☾ ⓴ New England Aquarium. This perennially popular attraction has added a 17,400-square-ft West Wing—with barking seals outside—to its already stunning main facility, and a new East Wing is on the planning boards, with construction to begin in 2002. Inside the main building are examples of more than 2,000 species of marine life from sharks to jellyfish, many of which make their homes in a four-story ocean reef tank. Don't miss the five-times-a-day feeding time, a fascinating procedure that lasts nearly an hour. Educational programs, like the "Science at Sea" cruise, take place year-round. Sea lion shows are held aboard *Discovery,* a floating marine mammal pavilion; and whale-watch cruises ($24) leave from the aquarium's dock from April to October. ✉ *Central Wharf (between Central and Milk Sts.),* ☎ *617/973–5200; 617/973–5277 whale-watching information,* WEB *www.neaq.org.* 🖼 *$12.50.* ◷ *July–early Sept., Mon.–Tues. and Fri. 9–6, Wed.–Thurs. 9–8, weekends 9–7; early Sept.–June, weekdays 9–5, weekends 9–6. T stop: State St.*

⓴ Old South Meeting House. Some of the most fiery pre-Revolutionary town meetings were held at Old South, culminating in the tumultuous gathering of December 16, 1773, convened by Samuel Adams to address the question of dutiable tea that activists wanted returned to England. This was also the congregation of Phillis Wheatley, the first published African-American poet. A permanent exhibition, "Voices of Protest," celebrates Old South as a forum for free speech from Revolutionary days to the present. ✉ *310 Washington St.,* ☎ *617/482–6439,* WEB *www.oldsouthmeetinghouse.org.* 🖼 *$3.* ◷ *Apr.–Oct., daily 9:30–5; Nov.–Mar., daily 10–4. T stop: State St., Downtown Crossing.*

㉑ **Old State House.** The brightly gilded lion and unicorn, symbols of British imperial power, that adorn the State Street gable of this landmark structure were pulled down in 1776 but restored in 1880. This was the seat of the Colonial government from 1713 until the Revolution, and after the evacuation of the British from Boston it served the independent Commonwealth until its replacement on Beacon Hill was completed in 1798. The permanent collection traces Boston's Revolutionary War history. ⊠ *206 Washington St.,* ☎ *617/720–3290,* WEB *www.bostonhistory.org.* ⊠ *$1–$3.* ☉ *Daily 9–5. T stop: State St..*

The Back Bay

In the folklore of American neighborhoods, the Back Bay stands with New York's Park Avenue and San Francisco's Nob Hill as a symbol of propriety and high social standing. The main east–west streets—Beacon, Marlborough, Commonwealth, Newbury, and Boylston—are bisected by eight streets named in alphabetical order from Arlington to Hereford. Note that Huntington Avenue is also known as the Avenue of the Arts, but you'll hear locals use Huntington.

Numbers in the text and in the margin correspond to numbers on the Boston map.

A Good Walk

A walk through the Back Bay properly begins with the **Public Garden** ㉕, the oldest botanical garden in the United States. Wander its paths to the corner of Commonwealth Avenue and Arlington Street. Walk up Arlington to Beacon Street and turn left to visit the **Gibson House** ㉖ museum. Follow Beacon to Berkeley and turn left to return to Commonwealth Avenue. Stroll the avenue to Clarendon, turn left, and head into **Copley Square** ㉗, where you will find **Trinity Church,** the Boston Public Library, and the **John Hancock Tower** ㉘. From Copley Square, you can walk north on Dartmouth to **Newbury Street** and its posh boutiques. For a dose of the avant-garde turn left on Hereford Street and right on Boylston and drop into the **Institute of Contemporary Art** ㉙. From there, proceed one block farther on Boylston Street to Massachusetts Avenue. Turn left to reach the **First Church of Christ, Scientist** ㉚ and **Symphony Hall** ㉛.

TIMING

The Public Garden is such a delight in the spring and summer that you should give yourself at least a hour to explore it if this is when you're visiting. Distances between sights are a bit longer here than in other parts of the city, so allow one or two hours for a walk down Newbury Street. The Museum of Contemporary Art and the First Church of Christ, Scientist can each be explored in an hour.

Sights to See

Back Bay mansions. If you like nothing better than to imagine how the other half lives, you'll suffer no shortage of old homes to sigh over in Boston's Back Bay. Most, unfortunately, are off-limits to visitors, but there's no law against gawking from the outside.

Among the grander Back Bay houses is the **Baylies Mansion** (⊠ 5 Commonwealth Ave.), of 1904, now the home of the Boston Center for Adult Education; you can enter to view its first-floor common room. Another gem is the **Burrage Mansion** (⊠ 314 Commonwealth Ave.), built in 1899 in an extravagant French château style, complete with turrets and gargoyles, that reflects a cost-be-damned attitude uncommon even among the wealthiest Back Bay families. It now houses an assisted living residence for seniors, and walk-in visitors are not encouraged.

Other mansions of note include the **Cushing-Endicott House** (✉ 163 Marlborough St.), built in 1871 and later home to William C. Endicott, secretary of war under President Grover Cleveland; the opulent **Oliver Ames Mansion** (✉ 55 Commonwealth Ave., corner of Massachusetts Ave.), built in 1882 for a railroad baron and Massachusetts governor; and the **Ames-Webster House** (✉ 306 Dartmouth St.), built in 1872 and remodeled in 1882 and 1969.

★ ✪ **㉕ Boston Public Garden.** The oldest botanical garden in the United States is beloved by Bostonians and visitors alike. The park's pond has been famous since 1877 for its foot pedal-powered **Swan Boats,** which make leisurely cruises during warm months. Its dominant statuary is Thomas Ball's equestrian **George Washington** (1869); the granite and red marble **Ether Monument,** which commemorates the advent of anesthesia at nearby Massachusetts General Hospital; and its charming fountains—though the hands-down favorite sculpture of kids (and many adults) is the *Make Way for Ducklings* **bronze statue group,** a tribute to the 1941 classic children's story by Robert McCloskey. The garden gates are always open, but it's not a good idea to visit after dark. ☎ 617/635–4505. 🎫 *Swan boats $1.75.* ☉ *Swan boats mid-Apr.–late Sept., daily 10–4. T stop: Arlington.*

★ **Boston Public Library.** When this venerable institution opened in 1895, it confirmed the status of architects McKim, Mead & White as apostles of the Renaissance Revival style, while reinforcing Boston's commitment to an enlightened citizenry. You don't need a library card to enjoy the building's magnificent art. The murals at the head of the staircase, depicting the nine muses, are the work of the French artist Puvis de Chavannes; those in the book-request processing room to the right are Edwin Abbey's interpretations of the Holy Grail legend. Upstairs, in the public areas leading to the fine arts, music, and rare books collections, is John Singer Sargent's mural series on the subject of Judaism and Christianity. Among the library's architectural perks is a Renaissance-style courtyard, where a covered arcade furnished with chairs rings a garden and fountain; the main entrance hall, with its immense stone lions by Louis Saint-Gaudens, vaulted ceiling, and marble staircase; and **Bates Hall,** one of Boston's most sumptuous interior spaces, 218 ft long and with a barrel-arch ceiling 50 ft high. ✉ *700 Boylston St. (at Copley Sq.),* ☎ *617/ 536–5400,* 🌐 *www.bpl.org.* ☉ *Mon.–Thurs. 9–9, Fri.–Sat. 9–5; Oct.– May, also Sun. 1–5. Free guided art and architecture tours Mon. at 2:30, Tues. and Thurs. at 6, Fri. and Sat. at 11, Sun. at 2. T stop: Copley.*

㉗ Copley Square. For thousands of folks in April, a glimpse of this square is a welcome sight; this is where Boston Marathon runners end their 26-mi race. The Boston Public Library, the Copley Plaza Hotel, and ☞ **Trinity Church** border the square. Copley Place, an upscale glass-and-brass urban mall, comprises two major hotels, shops, and restaurants. The ☞ **John Hancock Tower** looms over all. *T stop: Copley.*

㉚ First Church of Christ, Scientist. The world headquarters of the Christian Science faith mixes an Old World basilica with a sleek office complex designed by I. M. Pei. This church was established here by Mary Baker Eddy in 1879. Mrs. Eddy's original granite First Church of Christ, Scientist (1894) has since been enveloped by the domed Renaissance basilica, added to the site in 1906. The 670-ft reflecting pool is a splendid sight on a hot summer day. In the publishing arm's lobby is the fascinating **Mapparium,** a huge stained-glass globe whose 30-ft diameter can be traversed on a glass bridge. The Mapparium's building was closed for renovations at press time, and is due to reopen in 2002. Call ahead for the latest information. ✉ *175 Huntington Ave.,* ☎ *617/450–3790,* 🌐 *www.tfccs.com.* ☉ *Tours Mon.–Sat. 10–3 and*

Sun. 11:15–2. Sun. services 10 and 7, Wed. services noon and 7:30. T stop: Prudential.

㉖ **Gibson House.** One of the first Back Bay residences (1859), the Gibson House has been preserved as a museum with all its Victorian fixtures and furniture intact. A Gibson scion lived here until the 1950s and left things as they had always been. ⊠ *137 Beacon St.,* ☎ *617/ 267–6338.* ☜ *$5.* ⊙ *Tours May–Oct., Wed.–Sun. at 1, 2, and 3; Nov.– Apr., weekends at 1, 2, and 3. T stop: Arlington.*

㉙ **Institute of Contemporary Art.** Multimedia art, installations, film and video series, and a variety of events are showcased in this cutting-edge institution inside a 19th-century police station and firehouse. Over the years the institute has backed many groundbreaking artists, including Edvard Munch, Egon Schiele, Andy Warhol, Robert Rauschenberg, and Roy Lichtenstein. ⊠ *955 Boylston St.,* ☎ *617/266–5152,* WEB *www.ica- boston.org.* ☜ *$4–$6; free Thurs. 5–9.* ⊙ *Wed. and Fri. noon–5, Thurs. noon–9, and weekends 11–5. Tours on selected Sundays at 2:30 and every first Thurs. at 6:30. T stop: Hynes Convention Center.*

㉘ **John Hancock Tower.** The tallest building in New England is a stark and graceful reflective blue rhomboid tower designed by I. M. Pei. The 60th-floor observatory is one of the best vantage points in the city, and the "Road to Independence" light-and-sound diorama takes you through Colonial Boston until the time of the Revolution. ⊠ *Observatory ticket office, Trinity Pl. and St. James Ave.,* ☎ *617/247–1977 or 617/572–6429,* WEB *www.cityviewboston.com.* ☜ *$6.* ⊙ *Apr.–Oct., daily 9 AM–10 PM; Nov.–Mar., Mon.–Sat. 9 AM–10 PM, Sun. 9–5. T stop: Copley.*

㉛ **Symphony Hall.** The home of the Boston Symphony Orchestra since 1900, the hall was designed by the architectural firm McKim, Mead & White, but it's the acoustics, not the design, that makes this a special place for performers and concertgoers. ⊠ *301 Massachusetts Ave.,* ☎ *617/266–1492; 888/266–1200 box office,* WEB *www.bso.org.* ⊙ *Tours by appointment with volunteer office (call 1 wk ahead). T stop: Symphony.*

Trinity Church. In his 1877 masterpiece, architect Henry Hobson Richardson brought his Romanesque Revival style to maturity; all the aesthetic elements for which he was famous—bold masonry, careful arrangement of masses, sumptuously carved interior woodwork— come together magnificently. The Episcopal church remains the centerpiece of Copley Square. ⊠ *Copley Sq.,* ☎ *617/536–0944,* WEB *www.trinitychurchboston.org.* ⊙ *Daily 8–6; Sun. services at 8, 9, 11, and 6, weekday services at 7:30, 12:30, and 5:30. T stop: Copley.*

The South End

History has come full circle in the South End. Once a fashionable neighborhood, it was deserted by the well-to-do for the Back Bay toward the end of the century. Solidly back in fashion, it is today a polyglot of upscale eateries and ethnic enclaves, with redbrick row houses in various states of refurbished splendor or genteel decay. The Back Bay is French-inspired, but the South End's architectural roots are English, the houses continuing the pattern established on Beacon Hill (in a uniformly bowfront style), though aspiring to a more florid standard of decoration.

There is a substantial Latino and African-American presence in the South End, particularly along Columbus and Massachusetts Avenues, which marks the beginning of the predominantly black neighborhood of

Roxbury. Harrison Avenue and Washington Street at the north side of the South End lead to Chinatown, and consequently there is a significant Asian influence. But today the South End is known primarily for its large and well-connected gay community, which started the area's gentrification more than two decades ago and has brought with it a friendly, neighborly feel.

Numbers in the text and in the margin correspond to numbers on the Boston map.

A Good Walk

From the Back Bay, walk down Massachusetts Avenue to Columbus Avenue; turn left and follow it to **Rutland Square** ㉜ on your right. Cross to Tremont, walk northeast on Tremont, and turn right at **Union Park** ㉝. Walk south through the park to Shawmut Street, which holds a mixture of ethnic outlets and retail spaces. Walk northeast along Shawmut to East Berkeley Street, and then turn left and head back to Tremont. On Tremont Street near Clarendon is the **Boston Center for the Arts.** After a break at one of the many trendy restaurants and shops along Tremont, retrace your steps to Arlington and traverse the walkway over the Massachusetts Turnpike to reach **Bay Village,** on your right.

TIMING

You can walk through the South End in two to three hours. It's a good option on a pleasant day; go elsewhere in inclement weather, as most of what you'll see here is outdoors.

Sights to See

Bay Village. This neighborhood is a pocket of early 19th-century brick row houses that appears to be an almost toylike replication of Beacon Hill. It seems improbable that so fine and serene a neighborhood can exist in the shadow of busy Park Square; a developer might easily have leveled these blocks in an afternoon, yet they remain frozen in time, another Boston surprise. To get to Bay Village—where Edgar Allen Poe once lived—follow Columbus Avenue almost into Park Square, turn right on Arlington Street, then left onto one of the narrow streets of this neighborhood.

Boston Center for the Arts. Of Boston's many arts organizations, the city-sponsored arts and culture complex is the one that is closest "to the people." Here you can see the work of budding playwrights, view exhibits on Haitian folk art, or walk through an installation commemorating World AIDS Day. The BCA houses three small theaters, the Mills Art Gallery, and studio space for some 60 artists. ⊠ *539 Tremont St.,* ☎ *617/426–5000; 617/426–7700; 617/426–8835 Mills Gallery.* ☞ *Free.* ☉ *Weekdays 9–5; Mills Gallery Wed. and Sun. 1–4, Thurs.–Sat. 1–4 and 7–10. T stop: Back Bay.*

㉜ **Rutland Square.** Reflecting a time in which the South End was Boston's most prestigious address, this slice of park is framed by lovely Italianate bowfront houses. ⊠ *Between Columbus Ave. and Tremont St.*

㉝ **Union Park.** Cast-iron fences, Victorian town houses, and a grassy knoll add up to one of Boston's most charming mini-escapes, dating to the 1850s. ⊠ *Between Tremont St. and Shawmut Ave.*

The Fens

The marshland known as the Back Bay Fens gave this section of Boston its name, but two quirky institutions give it its character: Fenway Park, where hope for another World Series pennant springs eternal, and the Isabella Stewart Gardner Museum, the legacy of a 19th-century bon vivant Brahmin. Kenmore Square, a favorite haunt of college students, adds a bit of funky flavor to the mix.

The Fens mark the beginning of Boston's Emerald Necklace, a loosely connected chain of parks designed by Frederick Law Olmsted that extends along the Fenway, Riverway, and Jamaicaway to Jamaica Pond, the Arnold Arboretum, and Franklin Park.

Numbers in the text and in the margin correspond to numbers on the Boston map.

A Good Tour

The attractions in the Fens are best visited separately. The **Museum of Fine Arts** ㉞, between Huntington Avenue and the Fenway, and the **Isabella Stewart Gardner Museum** ㉟ are just around the corner from each other. **Kenmore Square** is at the west end of Commonwealth Avenue, a five-minute walk from **Fenway Park** ㊱.

TIMING

The MBTA Green Line stops near the attractions on this tour. The Gardner is much smaller than the Museum of Fine Arts, but each can take up an afternoon if you take a break at their cafés.

Sights to See

㊱ **Fenway Park.** Fenway may be one of the smallest parks in the major leagues (capacity 34,000), but it is one of the most loved. Since its construction in 1912, there has been no shortage of heroics: Babe Ruth pitched here when the place was new; Ted Williams and Carl Yastrzemski had epic careers here. ⊠ *4 Yawkey Way, between Van Ness and Lansdowne Sts.,* ☎ *617/267–8661 recorded information; 617/267–1700 tickets,* WEB *www.redsox.com/fenway.* 🎫 *Tours $5.* ☉ *Tours May–Sept. weekdays at 10, 11, and noon on day game days; additional tour at 2 on non-game or night-game days. T stop: Fenway.*

★ ㉟ **Isabella Stewart Gardner Museum.** A spirited young society woman named Isabella Stewart came from New York in 1860 to marry John Lowell Gardner. When it came time to create a permanent home for the old master paintings and Medici treasures she and her husband had acquired in Europe, she decided to build the Venetian palazzo of her dreams along Commonwealth Avenue. The building, whose top floor she occupied until her death in 1924, stands as a monument to one woman's extraordinary taste.

Despite the loss of several masterpieces in a film-worthy 1990 robbery, there is much to see: a trove of spectacular paintings—including masterpieces like Titian's *Rape of Europa,* Giorgione's *Christ Bearing the Cross,* Piero della Francesca's *Hercules,* and John Singer Sargent's *El Jaleo*—as well as rooms bought outright from great European houses, Spanish leather panels, Renaissance hooded fireplaces, and Gothic tapestries. An intimate restaurant overlooks the courtyard, and in the spring and summer tables and chairs spill outside. To fully conjure up the spirit of days past, attend one of the concerts held from September to May in the elegant Tapestry Room. ⊠ *280 The Fenway,* ☎ *617/566–1401; 617/566–1088 café,* WEB *www.boston.com/gardner.* 🎫 *$12; concert and galleries $17; café and gift shop free.* ☉ *Museum Tues.–Sun. 11–5; Sept.–May, weekend concerts at 1:30. T stop: Museum.*

Kenmore Square. The Kenmore Square area is home to fast-food parlors, rock-and-roll clubs, an abundance of university students, and an enormous sign advertising Citgo gasoline. The red, white, and blue neon sign put up in 1965 is so thoroughly identified with the area that historic preservationists have successfully fought to save it—proof that Bostonians are an open-minded lot who do not insist that all their landmarks be identified with the American Revolution. ⊠ *Intersection of Commonwealth Ave., Brookline Ave., and Beacon St. T stop: Kenmore Sq.*

★ ㉞ **Museum of Fine Arts.** The MFA's holdings of American art surpass those of all but two or three other U.S. museums. There are more than 50 works by John Singleton Copley, Colonial Boston's most celebrated portraitist, plus major paintings by Winslow Homer, John Singer Sargent, and Edward Hopper. Other artists represented include Mary Cassatt, Georgia O'Keeffe, and Berthe Morisot. The museum also has a sublime collection of French Impressionists—including the largest collection of Monet's work outside France—and renowned collections of Asian, Egyptian, and Nubian art. Three excellent galleries showcase the art of Africa, Oceania, and the Ancient Americas, expanding the MFA's emphasis on civilizations outside the Western tradition. In the West Wing are changing exhibits of contemporary arts, prints, and photographs. The museum has a gift shop, two restaurants, a cafeteria, and a gallery café. On the Fenway Park side of the museum, the **Tenshin-En** or "Garden in the Heart of Heaven," allows visitors to experience landscape as a work of art (daily 10–4, except Monday from April to October). ⊠ *465 Huntington Ave.,* ☎ *617/267–9300,* WEB *www.mfa.org.* ☞ *$12; voluntary admission Wed. 4–9:45.* ☉ *Mon.–Tues. and weekends 10–5:45, Wed.–Fri. 10–9:45. West Wing only Thurs.–Fri. 5–10 with admission reduced by $2. 1-hr tours weekdays. T stop: Museum.*

Cambridge

Pronounced with either prideful satisfaction or a smirk, the nickname "the People's Republic of Cambridge" sums up this independent city of nearly 100,000 west of Boston. Cambridge not only houses two of the country's greatest educational institutions—Harvard University and the Massachusetts Institute of Technology—it has a long history as a haven for freethinkers, writers, and activists of every stamp. Once a center for publishing, Cambridge has become a high-tech and biotechnology mecca.

Cambridge is easily reached on the Red Line train. The Harvard Square area is notorious for limited parking. If you insist on driving into Cambridge, you may want to avoid the local circling ritual by pulling into a garage.

Numbers in the text and in the margin correspond to numbers on the Cambridge map.

A Good Walk

Begin your tour in **Harvard Square** ① near the T station entrance. Enter Harvard Yard for a look at one of the country's premier educational institutions: **Harvard University** ②. Just past Memorial Hall (ask any student for directions) is Kirkland Street; turn right and then take a quick left onto Divinity Avenue. At 11 Divinity, you'll find an entrance to the complex of the **Peabody Museum of Archaeology and Ethnology** ③ and the **Harvard Museum of Natural History** ④. From Harvard Square, it's about a 10-min walk to Harvard's **Fogg Art Museum** ⑤, on Quincy Street, and **Arthur M. Sackler Museum** ⑥, on Broadway. The **Longfellow National Historic Site** ⑦, closed for remodeling into 2002, is a 15-min walk west of Harvard Square on Brattle Street.

In good weather, you can walk along Massachusetts Avenue through the bustle and ethnic diversity of urban Central Square and into the warehouse-like openness of the Kendall Square area, where the campus of the **Massachusetts Institute of Technology** ⑧ dominates the neighborhood. If the weather is poor, take the T Red Line heading inbound from Harvard Square two stops to Kendall Square.

Cambridge

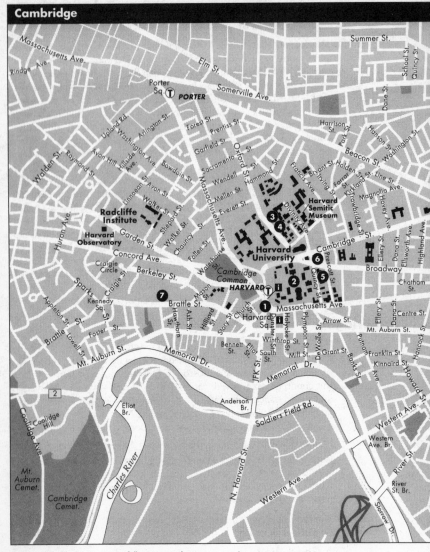

Summer St.

Massachusetts Ave.

Rindge Ave.

Elm St.

Porter Sq. T **PORTER**

Somerville Ave.

Upland Rd.

Walden St.

Raymond St.

Avon Hill St.

Washington Ave.

Arlington St.

Forest St.

Prentiss St.

Oxford St.

Francis Ave.

Harrison St.

Hamlin St.

Beacon St.

School St.

Quincy St.

Dane St.

Huron Ave.

Garden St.

Linnaean St.

Avon St.

Walker St.

Bowdoin St.

Garfield St.

Wendell St.

Sacramento St.

Hammond St.

Bryant St.

Holden St.

Kirkland St.

Irving St.

Park St.

Farrar St.

Scott St.

Frisbie St.

Divinity Ave.

Sumner Rd.

Cambridge St.

Radcliffe Institute

Harvard Observatory

Shepard St.

Walker St.

Chauncy St.

Follen St.

Waterhouse St.

Mellen St.

Everett St.

Massachusetts Ave.

3

4

Harvard University

Harvard Semitic Museum

Trowbridge St.

Oxford St.

Magnolia Ave.

Hancock St.

Ware St.

Ellery St.

Dana St.

Ellsworth Ave.

Highland St.

Concord Ave.

Berkeley St.

Craigie Circle

Sparks St.

Craigie St.

Kennedy Sq.

Cambridge Common

HARVARD

2

6

5

Prescott St.

Broadway

Chatham St.

7

Brattle St.

Hawthorn St.

Ash St.

Hilliard St.

Mason St.

1

Church St.

Story St.

Harvard Sq.

Dunster St.

Holyoke St.

Massachusetts Ave.

Quincy St.

Ellery St.

Dana St.

Centre St.

Appleton St.

Lowell St.

Brattle St.

Foster St.

Bennett St.

Eliot St.

South St.

Winthrop St.

Mill St.

DeWolfe St.

Plympton St.

Arrow St.

Mt. Auburn St.

Grant St.

Putnam Ave.

Franklin St.

Kinnaird St.

Hancock St.

Howard St.

Mt. Auburn St.

Memorial Dr.

JFK St.

Memorial Dr.

Eliot Br.

Anderson Br.

Soldiers Field Rd.

Western Ave.

2

Coolidge Ave.

Coolidge Hill

Mt. Auburn Cemet.

Cambridge Cemet.

Charles River

N. Harvard St.

Western Ave.

Western Ave. Br.

River St.

River St. Br.

Storrow Dr.

TIMING

Budget at least two hours to explore Harvard Square, plus at least three more if you plan to go to Harvard's museums. The walk down Massachusetts Avenue to MIT will take an additional 30 to 45 minutes, and you could easily spend an hour or two on the MIT campus admiring its architecture and visiting its museum or the List Visual Arts Center.

Sights to See

❻ Arthur M. Sackler Museum. The richness of the East and artistic treasures of the ancient Greeks, Egyptians, and Romans fill three of the four floors of this modern structure. The changing exhibits are first-rate, but if time is limited, make a beeline for the Ancient and Asian art galleries on the fourth floor, where you can gaze at bronze relics from a Chinese dynasty, Buddhist sculptures, Greek friezes, or Roman marbles. The fee for the Sackler gains you entrance to the ☞ **Fogg Art Museum.** ⊠ *485 Broadway,* ☎ *617/495–9400,* WEB *www.artmuseums.harvard.edu.* 🎟 *$5; free all day Wed., Sat. 10–noon.* ☉ *Mon.–Sat. 10–5, Sun. 1–5. T stop: Harvard.*

★ ❺ Fogg Art Museum. Harvard's most-famous art museum owns 80,000 works of art from every major period and from every corner of the world. The Fogg, behind Harvard Yard on Quincy Street, was founded in 1895; its collection focuses primarily on European, American, and East Asian works, with notable 19th-century French Impressionist and medieval Italian paintings. A ticket here is good for admission to the **Busch-Reisinger Museum** (☎ 617/495–9400), in the Werner Otto Hall, entered through the Fogg. From the serenity of the Fogg's old masters, you step into the jarring, mesmerizing world of German Expressionists and other 20th-century artists. Also included with Fogg admission is the **Sert Gallery**, in the adjacent Carpenter Center for the Visual Arts. Opened in 2000, the Sert hosts changing exhibits of contemporary works and also houses a café. ⊠ *32 Quincy St.,* ☎ *617/495–9400,* WEB *www.artmuseums.harvard.edu.* 🎟 *$5; free all day Wed., Sat. 10–noon.* ☉ *Mon.–Sat. 10–5, Sun. 1–5. T stop: Harvard.*

❹ Harvard Museum of Natural History. Many museums promise something for every member of the family; the Harvard museum complex actually delivers. One fee admits you to all three museums. In the **Botanical Museum**, the glass flowers, including 3,000 models of 847 plant species, were meticulously created from 1887 to 1936; everything is, indeed, made of glass. The **Museum of Comparative Zoology** traces the evolution of animals (including dinosaurs) and humans. Oversize garnets and crystals are among the holdings of the **Mineralogical and Geological Museum**, which also has an extensive collection of meteorites. ⊠ *26 Oxford St.,* ☎ *617/495–3045,* WEB *www.hmnh.harvard.edu* 🎟 *$6.50; free Sun. 9–noon, also free Wed. 3–5 (Sept.–May only).* ☉ *Daily 9–5. T stop: Harvard.*

❶ Harvard Square. Gaggles of students, street musicians, people hawking the paper *Spare Change* (as well as asking for some), end-of-the-world preachers, and political-cause proponents make for a nonstop pedestrian flow at this most celebrated of Cambridge crossroads. Harvard Square is where Massachusetts Avenue (locally, Mass Ave.), coming from Boston, turns and widens into a triangle broad enough to accommodate a brick peninsula (beneath which the MBTA station is located). Sharing the peninsula is the Out-of-Town newsstand, a local institution that occupies the restored 1928 kiosk that used to be the entrance to the MBTA station. Harvard Square is walled on two sides by banks, restaurants, and shops and on the third by Harvard University. The **Cambridge Visitor Information Booth** (☎ 617/497–1630, WEB www.cambridge-usa.org), just outside the T station entrance, is a volunteer-staffed kiosk with maps and brochures. The booth, which is open weekdays 9–5, Saturday 10–3, and Sunday 1–5, has maps for historic and literary walking tours of the city, and an excellent guide to the bookstores in the Square and beyond.

② **Harvard University.** In 1636 the Great and General Court of the Massachusetts Bay Colony established the country's first college here. Named in 1639 for John Harvard, a young Charlestown clergyman who died in 1638, leaving the college his entire library and half his estate, Harvard remained the only college in the New World until 1693, by which time it was firmly established as a respected center of learning. Students run the **Harvard University Events and Information Center,** which has maps of the university area. You can take a free hour-long walking tour of Harvard Yard. ⊠ *Holyoke Center, 1350 Massachusetts Ave.,* ☎ *617/495–1573,* WEB *www.harvard.edu.* ☉ *Tours during the academic year weekdays at 10 and 2, Sat. at 2; mid-June–Aug., Mon.–Sat. at 10, 11:15, 2, and 3:15, Sun. at 1:30 and 3. Call to confirm tour schedule, especially during holiday periods.. T stop: Harvard.*

List Visual Arts Center. Founded by Albert and Vera List, pioneer collectors of modern art, this MIT center has three galleries showcasing exhibitions of cutting-edge art and mixed media. Artworks such as Thomas Hart Benton's painting *Fluid Catalytic Crackers* are in keeping with the center's mission to explore the cultural as well as scientific contexts that surround us. ⊠ *Weisner Bldg., 20 Ames St., off Main St.,* ☎ *617/253–4680,* WEB *web.mit.edu/lvac/www.* ☒ *Free.* ☉ *Oct.–June, Tues.–Thurs. noon–6, Fri. noon–8, weekends noon–6. T stop: Kendall.*

❼ **Longfellow National Historic Site.** Once home to Henry Wadsworth Longfellow—the poet whose stirring "Miles Standish," "The Village Blacksmith," "Evangeline," "Hiawatha," and "Paul Revere's Midnight Ride" thrilled 19th-century America—this elegant mansion was a wedding gift for the poet in 1843. The National Park Service closed the house in 1998 for renovations that are expected to last until at least spring 2002. For updates on the renovation, call the park service (☎ 617/876–4491). ⊠ *105 Brattle St., ¼ mi from the Cambridge Information Booth,* WEB *www.nps.gov/long. T stop: Harvard.*

❽ **Massachusetts Institute of Technology.** MIT, at Kendall Square, occupies 135 acres 1½ mi southeast of Harvard, bordering the Charles River. The West Campus has some extraordinary buildings: the Kresge Auditorium, designed by Eero Saarinen with a curving roof and unusual thrust, rests on three, instead of four, points; the nondenominational MIT Chapel is a circular Saarinen design. Free campus tours leave from the **MIT Information Center** on weekdays at 10 and 2. ⊠ *Information center, 77 Massachusetts Ave., Bldg. 7,* ☎ *617/253–4795,* WEB *web.mit.edu.* ☉ *Weekdays 9–5. T stop: Kendall.*

MIT Museum. A place where art and science meet, the museum showcases photos, paintings, and scientific instruments and memorabilia. A popular ongoing exhibit is "The Hall of Hacks," a look at the pranks MIT students have played over the years. Most notable is a rare photo of Oliver Reed Smoot Jr., a 1958 MIT Lambda Chi Alpha pledge. Smoot's future fraternity brothers used the diminutive freshman to measure the distance of the nearby Harvard Bridge, which spans the Charles. Every 5 ft or so became "One Smoot." To this day, the markings remain painted on the bridge. ⊠ *265 Massachusetts Ave.,* ☎ *617/253–4444,* WEB *web.mit.edu/museum/.* ☒ *$5.* ☉ *Tues.–Fri. 10–5, weekends noon–5. T stop: Central.*

❸ **Peabody Museum of Archaeology and Ethnology.** The Peabody holds one of the world's most outstanding anthropological collections; exhibits focus on Native American and Central and South American cultures. The admission fee includes entrance to the ☞ **Harvard Museum of Natural History** as well. ✉ *11 Divinity Ave.,* ☎ *617/496–1027,* WEB *www.peabody.harvard.edu.* 🔄 *$6.50, free Sun. 9–noon, also free Wed. 3–5 (Sept.–May only).* ☉ *Daily 9–5. T stop: Harvard.*

Radcliffe Institute for Advanced Study. The famed women's college, with its lovely, serene yard, was founded in 1879 and wedded to Harvard University in 1977. It was subsumed under Harvard in 1999, and continues to specialize in gender issues. The **Schlesinger Library** (☎ 617/495–8647), in Radcliffe Yard, houses more than 50,000 volumes on the history of women in America, including the papers of Harriet Beecher Stowe, Julia Child, Betty Friedan, and other notable females. The library is also known for its extensive culinary collections. ✉ *10 Garden St.,* ☎ *617/495–8601,* WEB *www.radcliffe.edu. T stop: Harvard.*

Dining

Back Bay/Beacon Hill

CONTEMPORARY

$$$$ ✗ **Ambrosia on Huntington.** Chef Tony Ambrose likes his flavors vivid and his presentations dramatic. The cuisine is a thoughtful blend of New England ingredients and international fusion preparations. Don't miss the lamb and pork offerings. The decor is designer chic: burnished woods, floor-to-ceiling glass windows, and an ever-changing arrangement of modern art on the walls. ✉ *116 Huntington Ave.,* ☎ *617/247–2400. Reservations essential. AE, MC, V. No lunch weekends.*

$$$$ ✗ **Biba.** Chef and owner Lydia Shire's head-turning cuisine remains
★ the cream of Boston's culinary crop. And for good reason: the adventurous menu encourages inventive combinations, unusual cuts of meat and produce, haute comfort food, and big postmodern desserts. Indulge in "classic lobster pizza" or challenge your palate with the vanilla chicken with chestnut puree. Try to finagle a seat near the windows on the second floor for a terrific view of the Public Garden. ✉ *272 Boylston St.,* ☎ *617/426–7878. Reservations essential. AE, D, DC, MC, V.*

$$$$ ✗ **The Federalist.** Boston waited almost two years for this sophisticated
★ restaurant to open in the swanky Fifteen Beacon Hotel—and now that the initial buzz had calmed slightly, you can actually get a Saturday night reservation less than a month in advance. Chef Eric Brannan's menu is a melding of modern and traditional, driven by local ingredients; look for seared diver scallops with butternut squash and mushrooms or non-oceanic choices, such as the rack of lamb or beef Wellington. The wine list, with more than 1,000 entries, is an impressive but expensive proposition. ✉ *15 Beacon St.,* ☎ *617/670–2515. Reservations essential. AE, DC, MC, V.*

$$–$$$$ ✗ **Sonsie.** Café society blossoms along Newbury Street, particularly at Sonsie, where much of the well-heeled clientele either sips coffee up front or angles for places at the bar. The restaurant is a terrific place for breakfast, when the light pours through the long windows beautifully. Lunch and dinner are also satisfying, and during warm-weather months, the entire front of Sonsie becomes an open-air café looking out on upper Newbury Street. The dishes are basic bistro with an American twist, such as sweet pumpkin tamales with spiced pumpkin flan. ✉ *327 Newbury St.,* ☎ *617/351–2500. AE, MC, V.*

FRENCH

$$$$ ✗ **L'Espalier.** Chef-owner Frank McClelland's intoxicating master-
★ pieces are every bit as impeccable and elegant as the Victorian Back Bay town house they are served in. Grilled Hudson Valley foie gras is

accompanied by quince anise cranberry compote; Périgord black truffles intensify the poached sole. You can simplify the opulent menu by choosing a prix-fixe tasting menu, such as the innovative vegetarian *dégustation*. With two fireplaces and subtle decor in truffle colors, L'Espalier is among Boston's most romantic places. ⊠ *30 Gloucester St.,* ☎ *617/262–3023. Reservations essential. Jacket and tie. AE, D, DC, MC, V. Closed Sun. No lunch.*

$$$$ ✕ **Torch.** A little slice of the Marais hit Charles Street when Evan Deluty and wife Candice opened this bistro. Deluty is a keen culinary editor, tweaking dishes with only enough ingredients to enhance, not obscure the main flavors. Witness the sweetly simple seared sea scallops with corn bacon and mache. The Long Island duck breast comes punctuated by delicate roasted potatoes. Follow it with the thoughtfully chosen cheese plate or a deep-chocolate mousse. ⊠ *26 Charles St.,* ☎ *617/723–5939. Reservations essential. AE, D, DC, MC, V. Closed Sun. No lunch.*

PERSIAN

$$–$$$ ✕ **Lala Rokh.** ★ This beautifully detailed and delicious fantasia upon Persian food and art focuses on the Azerbaijanian corner that is now Northwest Iran. Persian miniatures and medieval maps cover the walls. The food includes exotically flavored specialties, and dishes as familiar (but superb here) as eggplant puree, pilaf, kebabs, *fesanjoon* (the classic pomegranate-walnut sauce), and lamb stews. The staff obviously enjoys explaining the menu, and the wine list is well selected for foods that often defy wine matches. ⊠ *97 Mount Vernon St.,* ☎ *617/720–5511. AE, DC, MC, V.*

SEAFOOD

$$$–$$$$ ✕ **Legal Sea Foods.** ★ What began as a tiny restaurant upstairs over a Cambridge fish market has grown to important regional status. The hallmark, as always, is extra-fresh seafood. Once puritanically simple preparations have loosened up to include Asian, European, and Caribbean sauces, and wood grilling is now the preparation of choice. Dishes come to the table in whatever order they come out of the kitchen, as freshness the priority. ⊠ *26 Park Sq.,* ☎ *617/426–4444.* ⊠ *255 State St.,* ☎ *617/227–3115. Cambridge:* ⊠ *5 Cambridge Center, Kendall Sq.,* ☎ *617/864–3400. Reservations not accepted, but a preferred seating list still allows calls ahead. AE, D, DC, MC, V.*

STEAK

$$$–$$$$ ✕ **Grill 23 & Bar.** ★ Pinstriped suits predominate at this steak house, and dark paneling, comically oversized flatware, and waiters in white jackets give it a men's-club ambience. The rotisserie tenderloin with Roquefort mashed potatoes is a winner, as is the meat loaf with mashed potatoes and truffle oil. Seafood such as the grilled Maine salmon gives beef sales a run for their money. Break out your jacket and tie. ⊠ *161 Berkeley St.,* ☎ *617/542–2255. Reservations essential. AE, D, DC, MC, V. No lunch.*

Cambridge

AMERICAN

$–$$ ✕ **Mr. and Mrs. Bartley's Burger Cottage.** It may be perfect cuisine for the student metabolism: a huge variety of variously garnished thick burgers, french fries, and onion rings. (There's also a competent veggie burger.) The nonalcoholic "raspberry lime rickey," made with fresh limes, raspberry juice, sweetener, and soda water, is the must-try classic drink. Tiny tables in a crowded space make it a convenient place for Phi Beta eavesdropping. ⊠ *1246 Massachusetts Ave., Cambridge,* ☎ *617/354–6559. Reservations not accepted. No credit cards. Closed Sun.*

Boston Dining and Lodging

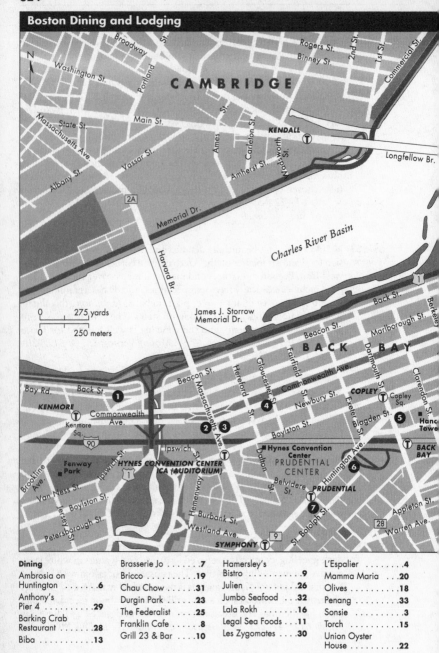

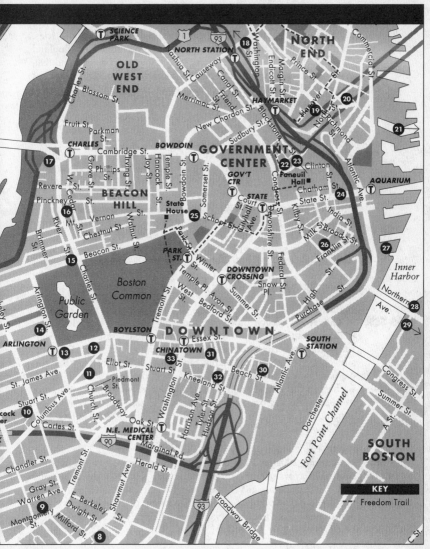

Lodging

Boston Harbor
Hotel at
Rowes Wharf **27**

Eliot Hotel **2**

Fairmont Copley
Plaza **5**

Fifteen Beacon **25**

Four Seasons **12**

Gryphon House **1**

Harborside Inn **24**

Hilton Boston
Logan Airport **21**

John Jeffries
House **17**

Le Meridien
Boston **26**

Ritz-Carlton **14**

CONTEMPORARY

$$$–$$$$ ✕ **The Harvest.** This lavish menu of up-to-date dishes is hedged with a little comfort food—mashed potatoes, baked beans, house fries. Start with raw seafood or the elaborately presented New England clam chowder with finnan haddie; then move on to roast monkfish, osso bucco, or roast lamb. Pore over the selection of Very Important Desserts, all masterminded by confectionary cult figure Lee Napoli and her up-and-coming protegé, Alice Wiebusch. The open kitchen makes some noise, but customers at the ever-popular bar don't seem to mind at all. ✉ *44 Brattle St./1 Mifflin Pl., Cambridge,* ☎ *617/868–2255. Reservations essential. AE, D, DC, MC, V.*

$$$ ✕ **Blue Room.** Totally hip, funky, and Cambridge, the Blue Room, led by Steve Johnson, the convivial owner-chef, blends a host of international cuisines with fresh, local ingredients. Brightly colored furnishings, counters where you can meet others while you eat, and a friendly staff add up to a good-time place that's serious about the food it serves. Try the seared scallops with hoisin sauce and sesame or perhaps the barrel-aged-bourbon crème brûlée with hazelnut biscotti. An extraordinary brunch with a buffet of grilled meats and vegetables as well as regular breakfast fare plus a gorgeous array of desserts is served on Sunday. ✉ *1 Kendall Sq. Cambridge,* ☎ *617/494–9034. AE, D, DC, MC, V. No lunch Mon.–Sat.*

ECLECTIC

$$$–$$$$ ✕ **Chez Henri.** French and Cuban food may make odd bedfellows, but the combination works for this sexy, comfortable restaurant. The dinner menu gets serious with duck tamale and ancho chili, garlicky salsify–oyster bisque, and a creamy, tangy lime tart. At the cozy bar you can sample turnovers, fritters, and grilled three-pork Cuban sandwiches. (It fills quickly with Cantabrigian locals—an interesting mix of students, professors, and sundry intelligentsia.) Brunch is served on Sunday. ✉ *1 Shepard St., Cambridge,* ☎ *617/354–8980. AE, DC, MC, V. No lunch.*

FRENCH

$$$–$$$$ ✕ **Sandrine's Bistro.** Chef Owner Raymond Ost goes to his Alsatian
★ roots for flavors easy and intense, but this is a bistro only in the same way that little palace at Versailles was a country house. One of the big hits is the *flammenkuche,* the Alsatian onion pizza, but much else is haute cuisine, like the trout Napoleon. ✉ *8 Holyoke St., Cambridge,* ☎ *617/497–5300. AE, MC, V.*

MEDITERRANEAN

$$$–$$$$ ✕ **Rialto.** The ultraposh Charles Hotel dining room continues a pleasant drift from its Mediterranean beginnings toward more French techniques and more New England ingredients, such as Maine crab cakes and Macomber turnips (a local, sweet, white turnip). But the savory tarts and the Tuscan-style sirloin steak with sliced Portobello mushrooms and arugula salad are lifetime commitments. ✉ *Charles Hotel, 1 Bennett St., Harvard Sq. Cambridge,* ☎ *617/661–5050. AE, DC, MC, V. No lunch.*

PORTUGUESE

$$–$$$ ✕ **Sunset Café.** Specialties at this lively cafe include kale soup thickened
★ with potatoes, *mariscada a chefe* (a great seafood combination in a casserole with fine spices), and shrimp Ana María (panfried shrimp in seafood stock). The bargain-priced wines on the list include some of the best Dão reds available anywhere outside Portugal. ✉ *851 Cambridge St. Cambridge,* ☎ *617/547–2938. AE, D, DC, MC, V.*

Charlestown

MEDITERRANEAN

$$$–$$$$ ✕ **Olives.** This bistro set the local standard for grilled pizza and smart
★ signature offerings as the appetizer "Olives tart" with marinated olives,
goat cheese, caramelized onions, and anchovies. The crowded seating,
noise, long lines, and abrupt service only add to the legend. Come early
or late or be prepared for an extended wait: reservations are taken only
for groups of six or more at 5:30 or 8:30 PM. ⊠ *10 City Sq., Cam-
bridge,* ☎ *617/242–1999. AE, DC, MC, V. Closed Sun. No lunch.*

Chinatown

CHINESE

$$–$$$ ✕ **Chau Chow.** *Chiu Chow* (or *Chaozhou* in China) is the word for
★ people from Shantou (formerly Swatow), and they are know for their
wonderful seafood. Try the clams in black bean sauce, steamed sea bass,
or any dish with their famous ginger sauce. Chau Chow has expanded
to a larger storefront called **Grand Chau Chow**, right across the street.
(⊠ ☎ 617/426–6266, AE, D, MC, V), which has live-fish tanks and
looks a little nicer on the outside. ⊠ *50–52 Beach St.,* ☎ *617/292–
5166. No credit cards.*

$$–$$$ ✕ **Jumbo Seafood.** Although this Cantonese–Hong Kong–style restau-
rant has much to be proud of, it's happily unpretentious—have a
whole sea bass with ginger and scallion and you'll understand the fuss.
The crispy fried calamari with salted pepper is a standout. The wait-
ers are understanding, though some don't speak English fluently. ⊠
5-7-9 Hudson St., ☎ *617/542–2823. AE, MC, V.*

MALAYSIAN

$–$$$ ✕ **Penang.** Penang is a resort island with a history like that of nearby
Singapore and an extraordinary cuisine of many influences—Malaysian,
Chinese, Indian, Thai, and a bit of British Trader Vic. It all comes together in favorites such as the mashed-taro "yam pot" stir-fries, the
house special squid with a dark and spicy sauce, an Indonesian beef
curry called *rendang,* and enormous fried coconut shrimp, all paired
with umbrella drinks. The open kitchen makes things loud but the drama
of watching the chefs stretch 4-ft sheets of see-through dough for *roti
canai* (an Indian bread served with curry dipping sauce) is worth it.
Reservations are accepted only for 6 or more. ⊠ *685–691 Washington St.,* ☎ *617/451–6372. MC, V.*

Downtown

FRENCH

$$$$ ✕ **Julien.** Start with the most attractive dining room in the city—a soar-
★ ing space that used to be the boardroom of the Federal Reserve Bank,
with Renaissance Revival gilded cornices and limestone walls. Then
serve some of the best French food in Boston. A ravioli appetizer is
stuffed with frogs' legs and parsley puree, garnished with garlic cream;
sautéed Maine lobster comes *en casserole* with white beans, candied
tomato, and rosemary. Little wonder Julien has become a favorite
with French business travelers and Boston Francophiles. ⊠ *Hotel
Meridien, 250 Franklin St.,* ☎ *617/451–1900. Reservations essential.
Jacket and tie. AE, D, DC, MC, V. Closed Sun. No lunch Sat.*

$$–$$$$ ✕ **Les Zygomates.** *Les zygomates,* in French, are the muscles on the
★ human face that allow you to smile—and this combination wine bar-
bistro inarguably lives up to its namesake. Les Zygomates serves clas-
sic French bistro fare that dares to be simple and simply delicious. The
restaurant offers prix fixe menus at both lunch and dinner; these could
include oysters by the half dozen or pancetta-wrapped venison with
roasted pears. ⊠ *129 South St.,* ☎ *617/542–5108. Reservations es-
sential. AE, D, DC, MC, V. No lunch weekends.*

Cambridge Dining and Lodging

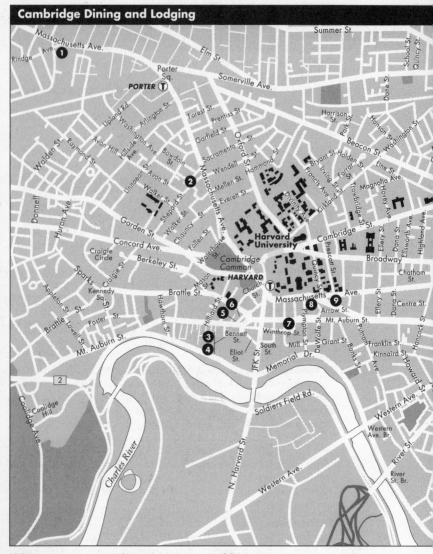

Dining

Blue Room **10**

Casablanca **6**

Chez Henri **2**

The Harvest **5**

Mr. and Mrs.
Bartley's
Burger Cottage **8**

Rialto **4**

Sandrine's Bistro . . . **7**

Sunset Café **11**

Lodging

A Cambridge
House Bed and
Breakfast **1**

The Charles Hotel . . . **3**

Inn at Harvard **9**

Walnut St.
Bow St.
Somerville Ave.
Sloane Ave.
Newton Ave.
Medford St.
Washington St.
Mansfield St.
Rossmore St.
Meridan St.
Linden St.
Allen St.
Linwood St.
Poplar
Joy St.

LECHMERE

Winter St.
Gore St.
South St.
Porter St.
Willow St.
Warren St.
Cambridge St.
3rd St.
Otis St.
7th St.
8th St.
Thorndike St.
Spring St.
Fulkerson St.
Hurley St.
6th St.
5th St.
Bent St.
Charles St.
Roger St.
Binney St.
Munroe St.
Athenaeum St.
2nd St.
1st St.
Commercial Ave.
Charlestown Ave.

Marion St.
Dimick St.
Clifton St.
Dickinson St.
Concord Ave.
Oak St.
Houghton St.
Tremont St.
Webster Ave.
Cambridge St.
Hampshire St.
Prospect St.
Windsor St.
Lincoln St.
Berkshire St.
York St.
Portland St.
Bristol St.
Binney St.

11

10

Maple Ave.
Fayette St.
Antrim St.
Inman St.
Amory St.
Norfolk St.
Elm St.
Market St.
Broadway
Harvard St.

KENDALL

West St.
Lee St.
Clifton St.
Bigelow St.
Prospect St.
Essex St.
Pine St.
Washington St.
Cross St.

Massachusetts
Institute of
Technology

Ames St.
Carleton St.
Hayward St.
Amherst St.

CENTRAL
Massachusetts Ave.
Green St.
Franklin St.
Auburn St.
Western Ave.
River St.
Joy St.
Pleasant St.
Magazine St.
Pearl St.
Brookline St.
Allston St.
Putnam St.
Henry St.
Sidney St.
Landsdowne St.
Pacific St.
Purrington St.
Albany St.
Vassar St.
Waverly St.
Amherst Alley
Main St.

Bishop Richard Allen Dr.

Memorial Dr.

Harvard
Bridge

Storrow
Drive

Beacon St.

Massachusetts Ave.

Boylston St.

Charles River

HYNES CONVENTION CENTER/
ICA (AUDITORIUM)

N

0   550 yards
0   500 meters

Faneuil Hall

AMERICAN

$$$–$$$$ ✕ **Union Oyster House.** At Boston's oldest continuing restaurant (it was established in 1826), it's best to have what Daniel Webster had—oysters on the half-shell at the ground-floor raw bar, which is the oldest part of the restaurant and still the best. The rooms at the top of the narrow staircase are dark and have low ceilings—very Ye Olde New England—and plenty of non-restaurant history. Uncomfortably small tables and chairs tend to undermine the simple, decent, but expensive food. There is valet parking after 5:30 PM. ⊠ *41 Union St., ☎ 617/ 227–2750. AE, D, DC, MC, V.*

$–$$$ ✕ **Durgin Park.** You should be hungry enough to cope with enormous portions, yet not so hungry you can't tolerate a long wait. Durgin Park was serving its same hearty New England fare (Indian pudding, baked beans, corned beef and cabbage, and a prime rib hanging over the edge of the plate) back when Faneuil Hall was a working market instead of a tourist attraction. The service is famously brusque bordering on rude or on good-natured. ⊠ *340 Faneuil Hall Marketplace, North Market Bldg., ☎ 617/227–2038. AE, D, DC, MC, V.*

North End

ITALIAN

$$$–$$$$ ✕ **Mamma Maria.** Don't let the clichéd name fool you, Mamma Maria is one of the most elegant and romantic restaurants in the North End, offering wonderfully delicious food, from the smoked-seafood ravioli appetizer to the innovative sauces and entrées to some of the North End's best desserts. You can't go wrong with the daily tiramisu or such specials as chocolate hazelnut cake with a cold champagne sabayon and raspberry compote. ⊠ *3 North Sq., ☎ 617/523–0077. AE, D, DC, MC, V.*

$$$ ✕ **Bricco.** A sophisticated but unpretentious enclave of nouveau Ital-
★   ian, Bricco has carved out quite a following. And no wonder: the velvety butternut squash soup alone is redolent of pears, sage, and the saltiness of prosciutto. Simple but well-balanced main courses, such as roasted rabbit loin wrapped in pancetta, have a sweet smokiness that lingers. You'll want to linger, too, and gaze through the floor-to-ceiling windows over a glass of Sangiovese. ⊠ *241 Hanover St., ☎ 617/ 248–6800. AE, DC, MC, V.*

South End

CONTEMPORARY

$$$–$$$$ ✕ **Hamersley's Bistro.** Gordon Hamersley has earned renown for such
★   signature dishes as grilled mushroom-and-garlic sandwich, duck confit, or souffléed lemon custard. His place has a full bar, a café area with 10 tables for walk-ins, and a larger dining room that's a little more formal and decorative than the bar and café, though nowhere near as stuffy. ⊠ *553 Tremont St., ☎ 617/423–2700. AE, D, DC, MC, V.*

$$ ✕ **Franklin Cafe.** Franklin Cafe has jumped to the head of the class by keeping things simple yet effective. (Its litmus: local chefs gather here to wind down after work.) Try anything with the great chive mashed potatoes. The vibe is generally more bar than restaurant, so be forewarned: it can get loud and smoky at times. ⊠ *278 Shawmut Ave., ☎ 617/350–0010. Reservations not accepted. AE, MC, V.*

FRENCH

$$$–$$$$ ✕ **Brasserie Jo.** This chain by Alsatian chef Jean Joho, toast of Chicago,
★   hums busily from its classy breakfast through post-Symphony snacks (it's open 'til 1 AM) in a setting evoking '40s Paris. "Brasserie" originally meant brewery—this one is bigger, louder, and more versatile than a bistro. Still, it perfectly carries off such classic bistro food as hanger

steak and onion soup gratinée as well as beer-friendly Alsatian food such as *choucroûte à l'Alsacienne* (sausages, a cured pork chop, and a pork quenelle, all on a bed of sauerkraut). ⊠ *120 Huntington Ave.,* ☎ *617/425–3240. AE, D, DC, MC, V.*

Waterfront
SEAFOOD

$$–$$$$ ✕ **Anthony's Pier 4.** This massive theme park of a restaurant rolls along, somewhat uncertainly, hosting celebration dinners for Bostonians and visitors alike. The main drawback: the famous long wait for a table. Once seated, you can dine very well on the top-quality seafood if you remember that simple preparations tend to be the best here. The wine list is remarkable, and there are scads of older wines at low prices. ⊠ *140 Northern Ave.,* ☎ *617/423–6363. Reservations essential. Jacket required. AE, D, DC, MC, V.*

$–$$$ ✕ **The Barking Crab Restaurant.** It is, believe it or not, a seaside clam shack plunk in the middle of Boston with a stunning view of the downtown skyscrapers. An outdoor lobster tent in summer, it retreats indoors to a warm-hearted version of a waterfront dive, with chestnuts roasting on a cozy wood stove, in winter. Look for the classic New England clambake—chowder, lobster, steamed clams, corn on the cob—or the spicier crab boil. The fried food lags. ⊠ *88 Sleeper St. (Northern Ave. Bridge),* ☎ *617/426–2722. AE, DC, MC, V.*

Lodging

If your biggest dilemma is deciding whether to spend $300 per night on old-fashioned elegance or extravagant modernity, you've come to the right city. The bulk of Boston's accommodations are not cheap; however, visitors with limited cash will find choices among the smaller, older establishments, the modern motels, or—perhaps the best option (if you can take early morning small talk)—the bed-and-breakfast inn.

Back Bay

$$$$ ✕🏠 **Eliot Hotel.** The luxurious suites at the Eliot have Italian marble bathrooms, two cable-equipped televisions, and tasteful pastel-hued decor. The airy restaurant, Clio, has been garnering rave reviews for its serene ambience and contemporary French-American cuisine. The Eliot is steps from Newbury Street and a short walk to Kenmore Square. ⊠ *370 Commonwealth Ave., 02215,* ☎ *617/267–1607 or 800/ 443–5468,* FAX *617/247–1997,* WEB *www.eliothotel.com. 16 rooms, 79 suites. Restaurant, bar, in-room data ports, minibars, no-smoking room, room service, meeting room, baby-sitting, laundry service, concierge, business services, parking (fee). AE, D, DC, MC, V.*

$$$$ 🏠 **Fairmont Copley Plaza.** The public spaces of this 1912 landmark ★ are decidedly grand, with high gilded and painted ceilings, mosaic floors, marble pillars, and crystal chandeliers. Guest rooms have antique and repro-antique furniture, elegant marble bathrooms, and fax machines. One of the restaurants, called the Oak Room to match its mahogany-paneled twin in New York's Plaza Hotel, has a dance floor and a raw bar. Despite the imposing Victorian surroundings, the atmosphere is gracious and welcoming, thanks to the multilingual staff. ⊠ *138 St. James Ave., 02116,* ☎ *617/267–5300 or 800/527–4727,* FAX *617/375–9648,* WEB *www.fairmont.com. 318 rooms, 61 suites. 2 restaurants, 2 bars, in-room data ports, minibars, no-smoking floor, room service, beauty salon, exercise room, baby-sitting, laundry service, concierge, business services, parking (fee). AE, D, DC, MC, V.*

$$$$ 🏠 **Four Seasons.** This stellar hotel, which overlooks the Public Gar- ★ den, is famed for luxurious personal service of the sort demanded by celebrities and heads of state. It has huge rooms with king-size beds

and new carpeting, bedspreads, and artwork. The pristine conditions continue with the marble of the foyers on each floor and a fully equipped health club with a heated 51-ft swimming pool. You can relax in the Bristol Lounge over afternoon tea, or come back at night when a pianist livens up the bar. ⊠ *200 Boylston St., 02116,* ☎ *617/338–4400 or 800/332–3442,* FAX *617/423–0154,* WEB *www.fourseasons.com. 216 rooms, 72 suites. 2 restaurants, in-room data ports, in-room safes, minibars, no-smoking floor, room service, pool, health club, baby-sitting, laundry service, concierge, business services, parking (fee). AE, D, DC, MC, V.*

$$$$ ⊞ **Ritz-Carlton.** Despite the attractions of the upstart Four Seasons, many
★ visitors to Boston would never dream of staying anywhere but the Ritz, thanks to its unmatched location, dignified elegance, and fierce devotion to its guests' comfort and privacy. Suites in the older section have parlors with working fireplaces and wonderful views of the Public Garden. If you stay in the newer section, you'll trade the garden view for larger bathrooms. ⊠ *15 Arlington St., 02117,* ☎ *617/536–5700 or 800/ 241–3333,* FAX *617/536–1335,* WEB *www.ritzcarlton.com. 233 rooms, 42 suites. 3 restaurants, bar, lounge, in-room data ports, in-room safes, minibars, no-smoking room, refrigerator, room service, beauty salon, exercise room, baby-sitting, laundry service, concierge, meeting room, parking (fee). AE, D, DC, MC, V.*

Beacon Hill

$$$$ ⊞ **Fifteen Beacon.** An intimate jewel has arrived on Beacon Hill in the form of this stylish and unrelentingly luxurious boutique hotel in a 1903 Beaux Arts building. The lobby juxtaposes the old world with the ultramodern—on one side the original cage elevators and newel post speak of a time gone by, while the sitting area is dominated by a large abstract painting. Upstairs, each floor has seven neutral-hue rooms, either a two-room suite or convertible adjoining rooms, each with a queen-size four-poster bed and a keypad-controlled gas fireplace and surround-sound stereo. ⊠ *15 Beacon St., 02108,* ☎ *617/670–1500 or 877/982–3226,* FAX *617/670–2525,* WEB *www.xvbeacon.com. 61 rooms. Restaurant, bar, in-room data ports, in-room fax, in-room safes, minibars, room service, exercise room, concierge, parking (fee). AE, D, DC, MC, V.*

$–$$$ ⊞ **John Jeffries House.** Once a housing facility for nurses, this turn-
★ of-the-century building across from Massachusetts General Hospital is now an elegant four-story inn. The Federal-style double parlor has a cluster of floral-patterned chairs and sofas. Guest rooms are furnished with handsome upholstered pieces, and nearly all have pale green kitchenettes. Triple-glazed windows block virtually all noise from busy Charles Circle; many rooms have views of the Charles River. The inn is an easy walk from most of downtown and just steps from public transportation. ⊠ *14 David G. Mugar Way, 02114,* ☎ *617/367–1866,* FAX *617/742–0313. 23 rooms, 23 suites. Kitchenettes, no-smoking floor, parking (fee). AE, D, DC, MC, V. CP.*

Cambridge

$$$$ ⊞ **The Charles Hotel.** You can't stay much closer to the center of Har-
★ vard Square than at this first-class hotel adjacent to the Kennedy School of Government. Guest rooms are equipped with terry-cloth robes, blue-and-white quilted down comforters, and Bose radios. Both restaurants are excellent, and the Regattabar attracts world-class musicians. ⊠ *1 Bennett St., 02138,* ☎ *617/864–1200 or 800/882–1818,* FAX *617/ 864–5715,* WEB *www.charleshotel.com. 293 rooms, 44 suites. 2 restaurants, 3 bars, outdoor café, in-room data ports, in-room safes, minibars, no-smoking room, pool, spa, health club, nightclub, library, baby-sitting, laundry service, concierge, business services, meeting room, parking (fee). AE, DC, MC, V.*

$$$–$$$$
★ **Inn at Harvard.** This hotel borders Harvard Yard, and its Georgian-style brick exterior mirrors the design of the university's buildings. Original 17th- and 18th-century sketches, on loan from the nearby Fogg Art Museum, and contemporary watercolors decorate the rooms, many of which have tiny balconies; most rooms have oversize windows with views of Harvard Square or Harvard Yard. Guests are granted access to the Cambridge YMCA in Central Square. ⊠ *1201 Massachusetts Ave., 02138,* ☎ *617/491–2222 or 800/458–5886,* ℻ *617/491–6520,* ᵂᴱᴮ *www.theinnatharvard.com. 111 rooms, 1 suite. Restaurant, in-room data ports, no-smoking floor, room service, dry cleaning, concierge, business services, parking (fee). AE, D, DC, MC, V.*

$$–$$$$ **A Cambridge House Bed and Breakfast.** A haven of peace and otherworldliness, this no-smoking B&B has richly carved cherry paneling, a grand cherry fireplace, elegant Victorian antiques, and polished wood floors overlaid with Oriental rugs. The Greek Revival house is on busy Massachusetts Avenue but set well back from the road. Although Harvard Square is a considerable walk away, public transportation is nearby. ⊠ *2218 Massachusetts Ave., 02140,* ☎ *617/491–6300 or 800/232–9989,* ℻ *617/868–2848,* ᵂᴱᴮ *www.acambridgehouse.com. 15 rooms. Free parking. AE, D, DC, MC, V. BP.*

Downtown

$$$$
★ **Boston Harbor Hotel at Rowes Wharf.** Everything here is done on a grand scale, starting with the dramatic entrance through an 80-ft archway. Guest rooms—at press time being renovated in one of three color schemes, and all including marble bathrooms and a custom-made desk—have either city or water views, and some have balconies. The Rowes Wharf Restaurant specializes in seafood and American cuisine. The hotel is within walking distance of Faneuil Hall, the North End, the New England Aquarium, and the Financial District. ⊠ *70 Rowes Wharf, 02110,* ☎ *617/439–7000 or 800/752–7077* ℻ *617/330–9450,* ᵂᴱᴮ *www.bhh.com. 204 rooms, 26 suites. 2 restaurants, bar, outdoor café, in-room data ports, minibars, no-smoking room, room service, indoor lap pool, massage, sauna, spa, health club, concierge, business services, meeting room, airport shuttle, parking (fee). AE, D, DC, MC, V.*

$$$$
★ **Le Meridien Boston.** Once the Federal Reserve Building, this 1922 Renaissance Revival landmark in the center of the Financial District still exudes an almost intimidating aura of money and power. Most rooms, including some bilevel, skylighted suites, have queen-size or king-size beds; all have a small sitting area. ⊠ *250 Franklin St., 02110,* ☎ *617/451–1900 or 800/543–4300,* ℻ *617/423–2844,* ᵂᴱᴮ *www.lemeridienboston.com. 326 rooms, 12 suites. 2 restaurants, bar, in-room data ports, minibars, no-smoking room, room service, pool, health club, laundry service, concierge, parking (fee). AE, D, DC, MC, V.*

$$–$$$
★ **Harborside Inn.** This 19th-century mercantile warehouse less than a block from Faneuil Hall has been transformed into a plush, sedate inn with exposed brick and granite walls, hardwood floors, Turkish rugs, and Victorian-style furnishings. An eight-story atrium is surrounded by snug, eclectically shaped rooms with queen-size sleigh beds or cherry four-posters. The inn is closed for one week over Christmas. ⊠ *185 State St., 02109,* ☎ *617/723–7500,* ℻ *617/670–2010,* ᵂᴱᴮ *www.hagopianhotels.com. 52 rooms, 2 suites. Restaurant, bar, café, in-room data ports, no-smoking floor, room service, exercise room, concierge. AE, D, DC, MC, V. CP.*

Kenmore Square

$$$–$$$$
★ **Gryphon House.** Each suite in this four-story brownstone is thematically decorated; for instance, one evokes a Victorian parlor, another a medieval castle. Each is rich with amenities—gas fireplace, wet

bar, refrigerator, TV/VCR, CD player—but nicest of all are the enormous bathrooms with oversize tubs and separate showers. Even the staircase is extraordinary: a 19th-century wallpaper mural, "El Dorado," wraps along the wall. (There is no elevator.) See if you can spot the recently commissioned faux marble work and trompe l'oeil paintings and murals by local artist Michael Ernest Kirk. ⊠ *9 Bay State Rd., 02215,* ☎ *617/375–9003,* FAX *617/425–0716,* WEB *www.gryphonhouse-boston.com. 8 suites. In-room data ports, no-smoking room, free parking. AE, D, DC, MC, V. CP.*

Logan Airport

$$–$$$$ 🖪 **Hilton Boston Logan Airport.** It's easy to get anywhere from the Hyatt, which operates its own shuttle to all Logan Airport terminals and the Airport T stop 24 hours a day; guests get a discount on the water shuttle that runs between the airport and downtown. All floors but one are nonsmoking, and all rooms are soundproofed. ⊠ *101 Harborside Dr., 02128,* ☎ *617/568–1234 or 800/233–1234,* FAX *617/567–8856. 270 rooms, 11 suites. Restaurant, bar, in-room data ports, room service, pool, sauna, exercise room, laundry service, concierge, business services, parking (fee). AE, D, DC, MC, V.*

Nightlife and the Arts

Nightlife

Good sources of nighttime happenings are the *Boston Globe* Thursday "Calendar" section, the *Boston Herald* Friday "Scene" listings. Also check out the listings in the *Boston Phoenix* (a free publication published weekly on Thursday). The Friday Music and Sunday Arts sections in the *Boston Globe* and the Saturday and Sunday Arts sections in the *Boston Herald* also contain recommendations for the week's top events. *Boston* magazine's "On the Town" feature gives a somewhat less detailed but useful monthly overview. Call clubs to check cover charges, hours, and theme nights.

BARS AND LOUNGES

Black Rose (⊠ 160 State St., Faneuil Hall, ☎ 617/742–2286), an authentic Irish pub, draws as many tourists as locals, but music by contemporary and traditional Irish musicians makes it worth the crowds. **Boston Beer Works** (⊠ 61 Brookline Ave., Kenmore Square, ☎ 617/ 536–2337) serves up its own brews to students, young professionals, and baseball fans from nearby Fenway Park. **Bull & Finch Pub** (⊠ 84 Beacon St., Beacon Hill, ☎ 617/227–9605), best known for inspiring the TV series *Cheers,* still often attracts long lines of tourists and students. **John Harvard's Brew House** (⊠ 33 Dunster St., Harvard Sq., Cambridge, ☎ 617/868–3585), an English-style pub, dispenses a range of ales, lagers, pilsners, and stouts brewed on the premises. **Sonsie** (⊠ 327 Newbury St., Back Bay, ☎ 617/351–2500) is a European-style see-and-be-seen bistro. The bar crowd is full of trendy, cosmopolitan types and professionals; in warm weather, the crowd spills out to sidewalk tables. **Top of the Hub** (⊠ Prudential Center, 800 Boylston St., Back Bay, ☎ 617/536–1775) has live jazz and fabulous views, making the steep drink prices worthwhile.

BLUES, R&B, FOLK CLUBS

Club Passim (⊠ 47 Palmer St., Harvard Sq., Cambridge, ☎ 617/492–7679) is one of the country's most famous venues for live folk music. The spare, light basement room has closely spaced tables and a separate coffee bar–restaurant counter. **House of Blues** (⊠ 96 Winthrop St., Harvard Sq., Cambridge, ☎ 617/491–2583) hosts live blues nightly at 10; on Sunday there's a gospel brunch. **Johnny D's Uptown** (⊠ 17 Holland St., Davis Sq., Somerville, ☎ 617/776–9667 or 617/776–2004) books an eclectic mix of performers and musical styles: Cajun, country, Latin, blues, jazz, swing, acoustic, and more.

CAFÉS AND COFFEEHOUSES

Caffè Vittoria (✉ 296 Hanover St., North End, ☎ 617/227–7606) is the biggest and the best of the Italian neighborhood's cafés. Stop in after dinner for coffee and tiramisu or cannoli. **Loulou's Tealuxe** (✉ Zero Brattle St., Harvard Sq., Cambridge, ☎ 617/441–0077) is a tiny "tea bar" with more than 100 different herbal and traditional blends. **1369 Coffee House** (✉ 757 Massachusetts Ave., Central Sq., Cambridge, ☎ 617/576–4600) serves coffee and tea in individual pots, as well as soups, salads, sandwiches, and pastries. The coffeehouse even provides outlets for portable computers.

COMEDY

Comedy Connection (✉ Faneuil Hall Marketplace, ☎ 617/248–9700) books local and nationally known acts nightly. **Dick Doherty's Comedy Vault** (✉ Remington's, 124 Boylston St., Theater District, ☎ 617/482–0110 or 781/729–2565), tucked away in a former bank vault, offers sketch, stand-up, improv, and open-mike comedy Thursday–Sunday nights, with a cover charge. **ImprovBoston** (✉ Back Alley Theater, 1253 Cambridge St., Cambridge, ☎ 617/576–1253) presents improv competitions and its own TV-style sitcom show—compiled on the spot from suggestions—Thursday through Saturday nights. Reservations essential. **Nick's Comedy Stop** (✉ 100 Warrenton St., Theater District, ☎ 617/482–0930) presents local comics Thursday–Saturday nights. Reservations essential.

DANCE CLUBS

Axis (✉ 13 Lansdowne St., Kenmore Sq., ☎ 617/262–2437) has high-energy dancing for more than 1,000 people. Friday is "X Night," starring DJs from alternative radio station WFNX. Dress creatively or in black rather than in khakis or jeans. Cover charge varies. **Man Ray** (✉ 21 Brookline St., Central Sq., Cambridge, ☎ 617/864–0400) is home to Boston's alternative and goth scene, with industrial, house, techno, disco, and trance music. Friday night is "Fetish Night." Wear black; dress code is enforced. The club is closed Sunday–Tuesday. The **Roxy** (✉ 279 Tremont St., Theater District, ☎ 617/338–7699), one of Boston's biggest nightclubs, is renowned for theme events such as its reggae, salsa, swing, and Top-40 nights. **Trattoria Il Panino & Club** (✉ 295 Franklin St., Financial District, ☎ 617/338–1000) attracts mostly well-heeled professionals. The multifloor complex offers informal and formal dining, a jazz bar, and dancing. Go dressy.

GAY AND LESBIAN CLUBS

For more on gay and lesbian nightlife, see the *Boston Phoenix* or *Bay Windows* newspapers.

Buzz Boston (☎ 617/267–8969), a trendy spot which stands where the Theater District meets the South End, has drinking and dancing for a 21-plus crowd. **Club Café & Lounge** (617/536–0966) is among the smartest spots in town for gay men and lesbians. It features a stylish restaurant, a piano bar, and a video bar.

JAZZ

Regattabar (✉ Charles Hotel, Bennett and Eliot Sts., Harvard Sq., Cambridge, ☎ 617/864–1200; 617/876–7777 tickets) headlines top names in jazz. Reservations essential. **Ryles Jazz Club** (✉ 212 Hampshire St., Inman Sq., Cambridge, ☎ 617/876–9330) is one of the best places for both new and established performers, with a different group playing on each floor. Sunday jazz brunches are a local institution. **Wally's Café** (✉ 427 Massachusetts Ave., South End,

☎ 617/424–1408) has a loyal clientele hooked on jazz and blues. The performers are mostly locals. Wally's is open every night of the year.

Avalon (⊠ 15 Lansdowne St., Kenmore Sq., ☎ 617/262–2424) hosts concerts by alternative, rock, and dance acts, then turns into a dance club. Themes include "Euro-night," Top-40, and techno. Ticketmaster (☎ 617/931–2000) sells advance tickets. **Lizard Lounge** (⊠ 1667 Massachusetts Ave., between Harvard Sq. and Porter Sq., Cambridge, ☎ 617/547–0759), one of the area's hottest nightspots, presents national and lesser-known folk, rock, acid jazz, and pop bands Wednesday–Saturday, and a "poetry jam" on Sundays. **Middle East Café** (⊠ 472 Massachusetts Ave., Central Sq., ☎ 617/497–0576) showcases live local and national acts as well as belly dancing, folk, jazz, and even the occasional country-tinged rock band. There's a restaurant upstairs.

The Arts

BosTix is Boston's official entertainment information center and the city's largest ticket agency. It is a full-price Ticketmaster outlet, and beginning at 11 AM, it sells half-price tickets for same-day performances; the "menu board" in front of the booth announces the available events. Only cash and traveler's checks are accepted. ⊠ *Faneuil Hall Marketplace,* ☎ *617/723–5181 recorded message.* ⊙ *Tues.–Sat. 10–6, Sun. 11–4.* ⊠ *Copley Sq., near corner of Boylston and Dartmouth Sts.* ⊙ *Mon.–Sat. 10–6, Sun. 11–4.* **NEXT Ticketing** (☎ 617/423–6398), a Boston-based outlet, handles tickets for many area theaters and nightclubs. The service, which uses a completely automated 24-hour ticket reservation system, also sells tickets online. **Ticketmaster** (☎ 617/931–2000 or 617/931–2787) allows phone charges to major credit cards, weekdays 9 AM–10 PM, weekends 9–8. There are no refunds or exchanges, and you pay a service charge. It also has outlets in local stores; call for the nearest address.

Boston Ballet (⊠ 19 Clarendon St., ☎ 617/695–6950), the city's premier dance company, performs classical and modern works, primarily at the Wang Center. Its annual *Nutcracker* is a Boston holiday tradition. **José Mateo's Ballet Theatre** (⊠ 400 Harvard St., Cambridge, ☎ 617/354–7467) offers a contemporary repertory, primarily at the Emerson Majestic Theatre. **Dance Umbrella** (⊠ 515 Washington St., ☎ 617/482–7570) performs contemporary and multicultural dance also at the Emerson Majestic Theatre.

The **Brattle Theatre** (⊠ 40 Brattle St., Harvard Sq., Cambridge, ☎ 617/876–6837) is a small downstairs cinema catering to classic-movie buffs and fans of new foreign and independent films. **Harvard Film Archive** (⊠ Carpenter Center for the Visual Arts, 24 Quincy St., Cambridge, ☎ 617/495–4700) screens the works of directors not usually shown at commercial cinemas.

Berklee Performance Center (⊠ 136 Massachusetts Ave., ☎ 617/266–1400; 617/266–7455 recorded information) is best known for its jazz programs. **Hatch Memorial Shell** (⊠ off Storrow Dr. at Embankment, ☎ 617/727–9548) is a jewel of an acoustic shell where the Boston Pops perform free summer concerts. **Jordan Hall at the New England Conservatory** (⊠ 30 Gainsborough St., ☎ 617/536–2412), ideal for everything from chamber music to a full orchestra, is home to the Boston Philharmonic. **Kresge Auditorium** (⊠ 77 Massachusetts Ave., Cambridge, ☎ 617/253–2826 or 617/253–4003) is MIT's hall for pop and classical concerts. **Orpheum Theatre** (✉ 1 Hamilton Pl., off Tremont St., ☎ 617/679–0810) is a popular forum for national and local rock acts. **Pickman Recital Hall** (✉ 27 Garden St., Cambridge, ☎ 617/876–0956) is Longy School of Music's excellent acoustical setting for smaller ensembles and recitals. **Symphony Hall** (✉ 301 Massachusetts Ave., ☎ 617/266–1492 or 800/274–8499), one of the world's most perfect acoustical settings, is home to the Boston Symphony Orchestra, conducted by Seiji Ozawa, and the Boston Pops, conducted by Keith Lockhart.

OPERA

The **Boston Lyric Opera Company** (✉ 114 State St., ☎ 617/542–6772) presents three productions each season.

PERFORMANCE VENUES

The **Colonial Theatre** (✉ 106 Boylston St., ☎ 617/426–9366) has welcomed visiting stars from Fanny Brice and Katharine Hepburn. More recently, Rosemary Harris and Lauren Bacall trodded its boards in a revival of Noel Coward's *Waiting in the Wings*. **Shubert Theatre** (✉ 265 Tremont St., ☎ 617/482–9393) has become the home for the Boston Lyric Opera Company. **Wang Center for the Performing Arts** (✉ 270 Tremont St., ☎ 617/482–9393) stages large-scale productions, such as the Boston Ballet season, and concerts by performers like Harry Connick Jr. **Wilbur Theatre** (✉ 246 Tremont St., ☎ 617/423–4008), the smallest of the traditional theater houses in the Theater District, has staged such off-Broadway hits as *Stomp*.

THEATER

The **Boston Center for the Arts** (✉ 539 Tremont St., ☎ 617/426–7700) houses more than a dozen quirky low-budget troupes in four spaces. **Charles Playhouse** (✉ 74 Warrenton St., ☎ 617/426–6912), presents two long-running shows: the avant-garde *Blue Man Group* (☎ 617/426–6912), and *Shear Madness* (☎ 617/426–5225), an audience-participation whodunit. **Emerson Majestic Theatre** (✉ 219 Tremont St., ☎ 617/824–8000) hosts everything from dance to drama to classical concerts. The **Huntington Theatre Company** (✉ 264 Huntington Ave., ☎ 617/266–0800), affiliated with Boston University, performs a mix of established 20th-century plays and classics. The **Loeb Drama Center** (✉ 64 Brattle St., Harvard Sq., Cambridge, ☎ 617/547–8300) is home to the acclaimed American Repertory Theater, which produces classic and experimental works.

Outdoor Activities and Sports

Participant Sports

Most public recreational facilities, including the many skating rinks and tennis courts, are operated by the **Metropolitan District Commission** (✉ 20 Somerset St., ☎ 617/727–5114 ext. 555; events hot line).

BIKING

The **Dr. Paul Dudley White Bikeway,** approximately 18 mi long, follows both banks of the Charles River as it winds from Watertown Square to the Museum of Science. In Boston's South End, **Community Bicycle Supply** (✉ 496 Tremont St., at E. Berkeley St., ☎ 617/542–8623) rents cycles from April through October.

BILLIARDS

Flat Top Johnny's (✉ 1 Kendall Square, Cambridge, ☎ 617/494–9565) is the hippest billiards hall around. Members of Boston's better local bands often hang out here on their nights off. At **Jillian's Billiard Club** (✉ 145 Ipswich St., ☎ 617/437–0300) businesspeople bump elbows with students and locals around 56 high-quality pool tables. Professional lessons are available, and the three bars, café, darts, shuffleboard, table tennis, and high-tech games keep everyone entertained.

IN-LINE SKATING

From April through October, **Memorial Drive** on the Cambridge side of the Charles River is closed to auto traffic on Sunday from 11 AM to 7 PM. Downstream, on the Boston side of the river, the **Esplanade** area swarms with skaters (and joggers) on weekends. **Beacon Hill Skate Shop** (⊠ 135 South Charles St., off Tremont St., ☎ 617/482–7400) rents blades and safety equipment for $8 per hour or $20 for 24 hours. You need a credit card for a deposit.

JOGGING

Both sides of the Charles River are popular with joggers. Many hotels have printed maps of nearby routes.

PHYSICAL FITNESS

The extensive facilities of the **Greater Boston YMCA** (⊠ 316 Huntington Ave., ☎ 617/536–7800) are open for $5 per day (for up to two weeks) to members of other YMCAs in the Boston area. If you have out-of-state YMCA membership, you can use the Boston Y free for up to two weeks. Nonmembers pay $10 per day or $72 for one month. The site has pools, squash, racquetball courts, cardiovascular equipment, free weights, aerobics, track, and sauna.

Spectator Sports

The **Boston Bruins** (☎ 617/624–1000; 617/931–2000 Ticketmaster) of the National Hockey League hit the ice at the FleetCenter (⊠ Causeway St. at Haverhill St.) from October until April. The **Boston Celtics** (☎ 617/624–1000; 617/931–2000 Ticketmaster) of the National Basketball Association shoot their hoops at the FleetCenter from October to May. The **Boston Red Sox** (☎ 617/267–1700 tickets) play American League baseball at Fenway Park (⊠ 4 Yawkey Way) from April to early October. The **New England Patriots** (☎ 800/543–1776) of the National Football League play their games at Foxboro Stadium in Foxborough, 45 minutes south of the city, from August (exhibition games) to January.

Every Patriot's Day (the Monday closest to April 19), fans gather along the Hopkinton-to-Boston route of the **Boston Marathon** to cheer the more than 12,000 runners from all over the world. The race ends near Copley Square in the Back Bay. For information, call the Boston Athletic Association (☎ 617/236–1652).

Shopping

Boston's shops and stores are generally open from Monday to Saturday between 9:30 and 7. Some stores, particularly those in malls and tourist areas, are open on Sunday from noon until 5. The state sales tax of 5% does not apply to clothing or to food, except in restaurants. However, there is a 5% luxury tax on clothes priced over $175 per item; the tax is levied on the amount over $175. The daily newspapers, the *Globe* and the *Herald,* are the best places to learn about sales.

Shopping Districts

The best shopping is in the area bounded by Quincy Market, the Back Bay, downtown, and Copley Square. Though locals complain that there are too many chain stores, Boston's strength remains its idiosyncratic boutiques, handcrafts shops, and galleries. Although there are few outlet stores in the city, you'll nevertheless find bargains, particularly in the Downtown Crossing area.

Pretty **Charles Street,** one of the oldest streets in the city, is crammed with antiques stores and boutiques, though they're generally a bit pricey, due to their high Beacon Hill rents. **Copley Place** (✉ 100 Huntington Ave., ☎ 617/369–5000) and the Prudential Center are Back Bay malls connected by a glass skywalk over Huntington Avenue. Copley packs more wallet-wallop, while "the Pru" contains moderately priced chain stores. **Downtown Crossing** is a jumble: entrenched independents coexist with prosaic chains, outlets snuggle against downmarket competitors, and pushcarts thrive alongside the city's two largest department stores, Macy's and Filene's (with the famous Filene's Basement beneath it). Historic **Faneuil Hall Marketplace**(☎ 617/338–2323) is an enormous complex that's hugely popular with visitors, perhaps because it successfully combines the familiar with the unique, as such chains as the Disney Store and Crate & Barrel provide the backdrop for street performers and one of the area's truly great casual dining experiences. In just eight blocks, **Newbury Street** in the Back Bay goes from Madison Avenue stylish to SoHo funky. The newly gentrified **South End** has recently become a retailing force, specializing in off-beat home furnishings and gift shops.

CambridgeSide Galleria (✉ 100 CambridgeSide Pl., ☎ 617/621–8666), accessible from the Green Line Lechmere T stop and by shuttle from the Kendall T stop, is a basic three-story mall with a food court. Traveling west along Massachusetts Avenue toward Harvard Square, you will pass through gritty **Central Square,** which holds a mix of furniture stores, used-record shops, ethnic restaurants, and small, hip performance venues. **Harvard Square** comprises just a few blocks but contains more than 150 stores selling clothes, books and records, furnishings, and a range of specialty items. **Porter Square,** on Massachusetts Ave., has several distinctive clothing and home furnishings stores, crafts shops, natural food markets, and restaurants.

Department Stores

Filene's (✉ 426 Washington St., ☎ 617/357–2100; ✉ CambridgeSide Galleria, 100 CambridgeSide Pl., Cambridge, ☎ 617/621–3800, WEB www.filenes.com), a full-service department store, carries American name-brand and designer-label men's and women's clothing. Jewelry, shoes, cosmetics, bedding, towels, and luggage are found at the Downtown Crossing store. A standout is **Filene's Basement** (✉ 426 Washington St., ☎ 617/542–2011, WEB www.filenesbasement.com), a Boston institution where items are automatically reduced in price according to the number of days they've been on the rack. **Lord & Taylor** (✉ 760 Boylston St., ☎ 617/262–6000, WEB www.mayco.com) is a reliable, if somewhat overstuffed, stop for classic clothing. **Macy's** (✉ 450 Washington St., ☎ 617/357–3000, WEB www.macys.com) carries men's and women's clothing, including top designers, as well as housewares, furniture, and cosmetics. It has direct access to the Downtown Crossing T station. **Neiman Marcus** (✉ 5 Copley Pl., ☎ 617/536–3660, WEB www.neimanmarcus.com), the flashy Texas retailer, has three levels of high fashion, cosmetics, and housewares. **Saks Fifth Avenue** (✉ 1 Ring Rd., Prudential Center, ☎ 617/262–8500, WEB www.saksfifthavenue.com) stocks top-of-the-line clothing, from more traditional styles to avant-garde apparel, plus accessories and cosmetics.

Specialty Stores

Though Newbury Street and the South End have several worthwhile shops, Charles Street has a clutch of stores where you can find everything from 18th-century paintings and early etchings of Boston land-marks to Chinese vases and complete sets of dinnerware. Don't miss the **Boston Antique Co-op** (⊠ 119 Charles St., ☎ 617/227–9810 or 617/227–9811), a two-story, flea market–style collection of dealers that carries everything from vintage photos and paintings to porcelain, silver, bronzes, and furniture. **Cambridge Antique Market** (⊠ 201 Msgr. O'Brien Hwy., Cambridge, ☎ 617/868–9655) is a bit off the beaten track but has a selection bordering on overwhelming, with four floors of dealers.

BOOKS

If Boston and Cambridge have bragging rights to anything, it is their independent bookstores, many of which stay open late and sponsor author readings and literary programs. Besides the unique places listed below, there are plenty of major chains. The **Barnes & Noble** in Kenmore Square may offer more Boston University memorabilia than books, though it has a pretty fair selection of those, too (⊠ 395 Washington St., ☎ 617/426–5184; ⊠ 660 Beacon St., Kenmore Sq., ☎ 617/267–8484). **B. Dalton** (⊠ CambridgeSide Galleria,, Cambridge, ☎ 617/923-4401) is small, but has the advantage of being conveniently located in the Cambridgeside Galleria. The **Borders** in Downtown Crossing (⊠ 10–24 School St., ☎ 617/557–7188) has 2 ½ floors of books, as well as a music section and a café that offers a respite from the hubbub; it also hosts periodic readings by such authors as John Irving, Robert Parker, and Amy Tan. **Brentano** (⊠ Copley Place, 100 Huntington Ave., ☎ 617/859–9511) offers a largish selection trade fiction, biography, history, social science, travel, and children's books. **Avenue Victor Hugo** (⊠ 339 Newbury St., ☎ 617/266–7746, WEB www.avenuevictorhugobooks.com) can divulge some startling secondhand finds (a first edition of Michelangelo's poems), plus fiction, art books, and magazines dating back to the 1800s. If the book you want is out of print, **Brattle Bookstore** (⊠ 9 West St., ☎ 617/542–0210, WEB brattlebookshop.com) has it or can probably find it. Hands down, the **Globe Corner Bookstore** (⊠ 500 Boylston St., ☎ 617/859–8008; ⊠ 28 Church St., Cambridge, ☎ 617/497–6277) is the best source in town for domestic and international travel books and maps; it also has a good selection of books about New England. The literary and academic community is well served at the **Harvard Bookstore** (⊠ 1256 Massachusetts Ave., Cambridge, ☎ 617/661–1515, WEB www.harvard.com). **Trident Bookseller and Café** (⊠ 338 Newbury St., ☎ 617/267–8688) carries books, tapes, and magazines and stays open until midnight daily. **We Think the World of You** (540 Tremont St., ☎ 617/574–5000), in the heart of the South End, stocks gay- and lesbian-oriented publications, and is a great source of posted information for the neighborhood's active gay community.

CLOTHING

The Euro-dominated **Alan Bilzerian** (⊠ 34 Newbury St., ☎ 617/536–1001) offers avant-garde men's and women's fashions. The **April Cornell** outlet (⊠ Faneuil Hall Marketplace, ☎ 617/248–0280, WEB www.aprilcornell.com) carries frilly bohemian women's clothing, furniture, linens, and toiletries at 50% off original prices. **Betsy Jenney** ⊠ 114 Newbury St., ☎ 617/536–2610) sells well-made, comfortable women's lines at moderate prices. Young trendsetters will be happiest at **Calypso** (⊠ 115 Newbury St., ☎ 617/421–1887). **Louis Boston** (⊠ 234 Berkeley St., ☎ 617/262–6100, WEB www.louisboston.com) is *the* place for the well-dressed and well-heeled to shop. **Wish** (49 Charles St., ☎ 617/227–4441) carries everything a hip young woman could wish for, from such designers as Katayone Adeli and Nanette Lepore.

GIFTS AND HOUSEHOLD ITEMS

You can travel back in time or to another country at many Boston gift shops. **Buckaroo's Mercantile** (⊠ 1297 Cambridge St., Cambridge, ☎ 617/492–4792, WEB www.buckmerc.com) rocks with retro kitsch, from pink poodle skirts to Barbie lampshades—along with everything Elvis. **Flat of the Hill** (⊠ 60 Charles St., ☎ 617/619–9977, WEB www.flatofthe-hill.com) has something for everyone on your list—including Fido—with seasonal items, gourmet foods, hard-to-find toiletries, dolls, toys, pillows, and pet products. **Kybele** (⊠ 583 Tremont St., ☎ 617/262–5522) is like a well designed Bedouin tent, with hand-woven Turkish rugs, camel covers, hookahs, and delicate cut-glass hanging lamps. Check out **Loulou's Lost & Found** (⊠ 121 Newbury St., ☎ 617/859–8593) for reproduction jazz-era tableware and wall decorations. **Mohr & McPherson** (⊠ 75 Moulton St., Cambridge, ☎ 617/520–2000; ⊠ 281–290 Concord Ave., Cambridge, ☎ 617/354–6662, WEB www.mohr-mcpherson.com) is a visual Asian feast of art and furnishings. **Tibet Emporium** (103 Charles St., ☎ 617/723–8035) goes beyond the usual masks and quilted wall hangings with delicate beaded silk pillowcases, pashmina wraps in every color imaginable, and finely wrought but affordable silver jewelry.

Side Trip: Lexington and Concord

Lexington

To reach Lexington by car from Boston, take Memorial Drive in Cambridge to the Fresh Pond Parkway, then to Route 2 west. Exit Route 2 at Routes 4/225 and continue to Massachusetts Avenue if your first stop is the Museum of Our National Heritage. For Lexington center, take the Waltham St./Lexington exit from Route 2. Follow Waltham Street just under 2 mi to Massachusetts Avenue; you'll be just east of the Battle Green.

The **MBTA** (☎ 617/222–3200, WEB www.mbta.com) operates buses to Lexington from Alewife station in Cambridge. Buses 62 and 76 make the trip in 25–30 minutes.

Lexington is a quintessential though thoroughly modern New England town where some of the first military encounters of the American Revolution took place. The events of the Revolution are very much a part of present-day Lexington, now a suburb that sprawls out from the historic sights near the town center. Each Patriot's Day (the Monday nearest April 19), groups of costume-clad "Minutemen" recreate battle maneuvers and "Paul Revere" reenacts his midnight ride.

On April 19, 1775, Minuteman captain John Parker assembled his men out on **Battle Green,** a 2-acre, triangular piece of land, to await the arrival of the British, who were marching from Boston toward Concord to "teach rebels a lesson." Parker's role is commemorated in Henry Hudson Kitson's renowned sculpture **The Minuteman,** which stands at the tip of the green, facing downtown Lexington. (Because it's on a traffic island, it's a bit hard to pose for photos.) A shot rang out from an unknown source—what Lexingtonians call "the shot heard 'round the world," although those in Concord claim the shot for their own.

The **visitor center** has a diorama of the 1775 clash on the green, plus a gift shop. ⊠ 1875 Massachusetts Ave., ☎ 781/862–1450, WEB www.lexingtonchamber.org. ☉ Mid-Apr.–Nov., daily 9–5; Dec.–mid-Apr., daily 10–4.

On the east side of Battle Green is **Buckman Tavern,** built in 1690, where the Minutemen gathered on the morning of April 19, 1775. A half-hour tour takes in the tavern's seven rooms. ⊠ 1 Bedford St., ☎ 781/

862–5598, WEB *www.lexingtonhistory.org.* ☞ *$4; combination ticket for the Buckman Tavern, Hancock-Clarke House, and Munroe Tavern $10.* ☉ *Mar.–Oct., Mon.–Sat. 10–5, Sun. 1–5.*

On the night of April 18, 1775, Paul Revere roused patriots John Hancock and Sam Adams from their sleep at the eight-room **Hancock-Clarke House,** a parsonage built in 1698. Revere rode out from Boston to "spread the alarm" that the British were approaching "through every Middlesex village and farm." Both Hancock and Adams fled to avoid capture. The house, a 10-minute walk from Lexington Common, displays the pistols of British major John Pitcairn as well as period furnishings and portraits. A 30-min tour is offered. ✉ *36 Hancock St.,* ☎ *781/861–0928,* WEB *www.lexingtonhistory.org.* ☞ *$4; combination ticket for the Buckman Tavern, Hancock-Clarke House, and Munroe Tavern $10.* ☉ *Mid-Apr.–Oct., Mon.–Sat. 10–5, Sun. 1–5.*

As April 19 dragged on, British forces met far fiercer resistance in Concord. Dazed and demoralized after the battle at Old North Bridge, the British backtracked and regrouped at the **Munroe Tavern** (built in 1695) while the Munroe family hid in nearby woods; then the troops retreated to Boston. The tavern is 1 mi east of Lexington Common; tours last about 30 minutes. ✉ *1332 Massachusetts Ave.,* ☎ *781/674–9238,* WEB *www.lexingtonhistory.org.* ☞ *$4; combination ticket for the Buckman Tavern, Hancock-Clarke House, and Munroe Tavern $10.* ☉ *Mid-Apr.–Oct., Mon.–Sat. 10–5, Sun. 1–5.*

★ The **Museum of Our National Heritage** displays items and artifacts from all facets of American life, putting them in social and political context. The "Lexington Alarm'd" exhibit highlights events leading up to April 1775 and illustrates Revolutionary-era life through everyday household objects. ✉ *33 Marrett Rd. (Rte. 2A at Massachusetts Ave.),* ☎ *781/861–6559,* WEB *www.mnh.org.* ☞ *Donation suggested.* ☉ *Mon.–Sat. 10–5, Sun. noon–5.*

DINING

$–$$ ✕ **Bertucci's.** Part of a popular chain, this Italian restaurant has good food, reasonable prices, a large menu, and a family-friendly atmosphere. Specialties include ravioli, calzones, and a wide assortment of brick oven-baked pizzas. ✉ *1777 Massachusetts Ave.,* ☎ *781/860–9000. AE, D, MC, V.*

Concord

To reach Concord from Boston, follow Route 2 west, or take I–90 (the Massachusetts Turnpike) to I–95 north, and exit at Route 2, heading west. To reach Concord from Lexington, take Routes 4 and 225 through Bedford and Route 62 west to Concord; or from Massachusetts Avenue, pick up Route 2A west at the Museum of Our National Heritage or by taking Waltham Street south from Lexington Center.

Route 2A, a longer but charming drive, takes you through parts of **Minute Man National Historical Park,** which contains many of the sites important to Concord's role in the Revolution, including the Old North Bridge, as well as two visitor centers. The free multimedia presentation, "The Road to Revolution," at the visitor center on Route 2A, makes a captivating introduction to the events of April 1775. Then stop off at the point where Revere's midnight ride ended with his capture by the British; it's marked with a boulder and plaque. You can also visit the 1732 Hartwell Tavern, a restored drover's tavern; costumed park employees frequently demonstrate musket firing or open-hearth cooking, and kids will enjoy the reproduction Colonial toys. *Minute Man Visitor Center,* ✉ *Rte. 2A, ½ mi west of Rte. 128, Lexington,* ☎ *978/369–6993 or 781/862–7753.* ☞ *Free.* ☉ *Apr.–Oct., daily 9–5; Nov.–Mar.,* *daily 9–4. North Bridge Visitor Center,* ⊠ *174 Liberty St.,* ☎ *978/369–6993,* WEB *www.nps.gov/mima.* ⊒ *Free.* ⊘ *Apr.–Oct., daily 9–5; Nov.–Mar., daily 9–4.*

While the initial Revolutionary War sorties were in Lexington, word of the American losses spread rapidly to surrounding towns: When the British marched into Concord, more than 400 Minutemen were waiting. A marker set in the stone wall along Liberty Street, behind the North Bridge Visitors Center, announces: "On this field the Minutemen and militia formed before marching down to the fight at the bridge."

At the **Old North Bridge** (⊠ Off Monument St., ½ mi from Concord center), the Concord Minutemen turned the tables on the British in the morning hours of April 19, 1775. The Americans did not fire first, but when two of their own fell dead from a redcoat volley, Major John Buttrick of Concord roared, "Fire, fellow soldiers, for God's sake, fire." The Minutemen released volley after volley, and the redcoats fled. Daniel Chester French's statue *The Minuteman* (1875) honors the country's first freedom fighters.

Of the confrontation, the essayist and poet Ralph Waldo Emerson wrote in 1837: "By the rude bridge that arched the flood/Their flag to April's breeze unfurled/Here once the embattled farmers stood/And fired the shot heard round the world." (The lines are inscribed at the foot of *The Minuteman.*) Hence, Concord claims the right to the "shot," believing that native son Emerson was, of course, referring to the North Bridge standoff. Park Service officials skirt the issue, saying the shot could refer to the battle on Lexington Green, when the very first shot rang out from an unknown source, or to Concord when Minutemen held back the redcoats in the Revolution's first major battle, or even to the Boston Massacre. What's important is Emerson's vision that here began the modern world's first experiment in democracy.

The Reverend William Emerson, the grandfather of Ralph Waldo Emerson, watched rebels and redcoats battle from behind his home, the **Old Manse,** on Monument Street, within sight of the Old North Bridge. The house, built in 1770, was occupied by the family except for a period of 3½ years, when renter Nathaniel Hawthorne lived and wrote short stories here. The furnishings date from the late 18th century. ⊠ *269 Monument St.,* ☎ *978/369–3909,* WEB *www.thetrustees.org.* ⊒ *$6 for 40-min guided tour.* ⊘ *Mid-Apr.–late Oct., Mon.–Sat. 10–5, Sun. noon–5 (last tour at 4:30).*

The **Jonathan Ball House,** built in 1753, was a station on the Underground Railroad for runaway slaves during the Civil War. Ask to see the secret room. The house, now home to the Concord Art Association, hosts rotating art exhibits, and its garden and waterfall are refreshing sights. ⊠ *37 Lexington Rd.,* ☎ *978/369–2578.* ⊒ *Free.* ⊘ *Tues.–Sat. 10–4:30, Sun. noon–4.*

Ralph Waldo Emerson lived in the (☞)Old Manse between 1834 and 1835 before moving to what is known as the **Ralph Waldo Emerson House,** where he resided until his death in 1882. Here he wrote the *Essays* ("To be great is to be misunderstood"; "A foolish consistency is the hobgoblin of little minds"). Except for items from Emerson's study, now at the nearby Concord Museum, the Emerson House furnishings have been preserved as the writer left them, down to his hat resting on the newel post. ⊠ *28 Cambridge Tpke. at Lexington Rd.,* ☎ *978/369–2236.* ⊒ *$5.* ⊘ *Mid-Apr.–mid-Oct., Thurs.–Sat. 10–4:30, Sun. 2–4:30.*

The **Concord Museum,** just east of the town center, has the original contents of Emerson's private study and a "Why Concord?" exhibit that provides a good overview of the town's history, from its Native American settlement to the 20th century. The museum, in a 1930 Colonial Revival structure, also houses several period rooms, ranging in decor from Colonial to Empire. It has the world's largest collection of Thoreau artifacts, including furnishings from the Walden Pond cabin, as well as a diorama of the Old North Bridge battle, Native American artifacts, and one of two lanterns hung at Boston's Old North Church on the night of April 18, 1775. ⊠ *200 Lexington Rd. (entrance on Cambridge Tpke.),* ☏ *978/369–9763,* WEB *www.concordmuseum.org.* ✉ *$7.* ☉ *Apr.–Dec., Mon.–Sat. 9–5, Sun. noon–5; Jan.–Mar., Mon.–Sat. 11–4, Sun. 1–4.*

The dark brown exterior of Louisa May Alcott's family home, **Orchard House,** poses a sharp contrast to the light, wit, and energy so much in evidence inside. Named for the apple orchard that once surrounded it, Orchard House was home to the Alcott family from 1857 to 1877. Here Louisa wrote *Little Women,* based on her life with her three sisters. Many of the original furnishings remain in the house. Portraits and watercolors by May Alcott (the model for Amy) abound; in her room you can see where she sketched figures on the walls—the Alcotts encouraged such creativity. ⊠ *399 Lexington Rd.,* ☏ *978/369–4118,* WEB *www.louisamayalcott.org.* ✉ *$7.* ☉ *Apr.–Oct., Mon.–Sat. 10–4:30, Sun. 1–4:30; Nov.–Dec. and mid-Jan.–Mar., weekdays 11–3, Sat. 10–4:30, Sun. 1–4:30. 30-min tours every ½ hr Apr.–Oct.; call for off-season tour schedule.*

Nathaniel Hawthorne lived at Concord's (☞)Old Manse from 1842 to 1845, working on stories and sketches; he then moved to Salem (where he wrote *The Scarlet Letter*) and later to Lenox (*The House of the Seven Gables*). In 1852 he returned to Concord, bought a rambling structure called the **Wayside,** and lived here until his death in 1864. The subsequent owner, Margaret Sidney (author of *Five Little Peppers and How They Grew*), kept Hawthorne's tower-study intact—to the fascination of visitors today. Prior to Hawthorne's ownership, the Alcotts lived here, from 1845 to 1848. ⊠ *455 Lexington Rd.,* ☏ *978/369–6975,* WEB *www.nps.gov/mima/wayside.* ✉ *$4 for 35-min guided tour; exhibit center free.* ☉ *Early May–Oct., Thurs.–Tues. 10–5. Guided tours until 4:30.*

Each Memorial Day, Louisa May Alcott's grave in **Sleepy Hollow Cemetery** is decorated in commemoration of her death. Like Emerson, Thoreau, and Hawthorne, Alcott is buried in a section of the cemetery known as **Author's Ridge.** ⊠ *Bedford St. (Rte. 62),* ☏ *978/318–3233.* ☉ *Daily 7 AM–dusk.*

A trip to Concord can include a pilgrimage to **Walden Pond,** Henry David Thoreau's most famous residence. Here, in 1845, at age 28, Thoreau moved into a one-room cabin—built for $28.12½ cents—on the shore of this 100-ft-deep kettle hole, formed 12,000 years ago by the retreat of the New England glacier. Living alone over the next two years, Thoreau discovered the benefits of solitude and the beauties of nature. Thoreau later published *Walden* (1854), a collection of essays on observations he made while living here. The site of that first cabin is staked out in stone. A full-size, authentically furnished replica of the cabin stands about ½ mi from the original site, near the Walden Pond State Reservation parking lot. Even when the cabin is closed, you can peek through its windows. Now, as in Thoreau's time, the pond is a delightful summertime spot for swimming, fishing, and rowing, and there's hiking in the nearby woods. ⊠ *Rte. 126; from Concord take Main St. west from Monument Sq., turn left on Walden St., cross over Rte. 2 onto Rte. 126, and head south ½ mi to entrance (on left),* ☏

978/369–3254, WEB *www.magnet.state.ma.us/dem/parks/wldn.htm.* ☎
*Free; parking across road from pond $2 per vehicle Memorial Day–
Labor Day, free parking rest of yr.* ☉ *Daily until approximately ½ hr
before sunset. Replica of Thoreau's cabin, daily 8* AM*–park closing.*

DINING

$$–$$$ ✕ **Walden Grille.** Contemporary fare is served in an old brick firehouse
turned upscale dining room. Lighter options include salads (such as
rare lamb over arugula) or sandwiches (hummus and cucumber wrap).
Heartier entrées may range from wild mushroom ravioli to grilled
shrimp with risotto-polenta cakes. It is near the town center. ✉ *24
Walden St.,* ☎ *978/371–2233. AE, D, DC, MC, V.*

Side Trip: Lowell

Everyone knows that the American Revolution began in Massachusetts. But the Commonwealth, and in particular the Merrimack Valley, also nurtured the Industrial Revolution. The first mill in Lowell,
30 mi northwest of Boston, opened in 1823; by the 1850s, 40 factories employed thousands of workers and produced 2 million yards of
cloth every week. By the mid-20th century, much of the textile industry had moved south, but the remnants of redbrick factories and murky
canals remain.

Lowell lies near the intersection of I–495 and U.S. 3. From Boston, take
I–93 north to I–495. Go south on I–495 to Exit 35C, the Lowell Connector. Follow the Lowell Connector to Exit 5B, Thorndike Street. Travel
time is 45 minutes to an hour. The **MBTA**'s commuter rail (☎ 617/222–
3200) runs from North Station to Lowell in about 45 minutes. Shuttle buses travel between Lowell station and downtown (about ½ mi)
every half hour weekdays 6–6, Saturday 10–4.

The **Lowell National Historical Park** tracks the history of a gritty era
when the power loom was the symbol of economic power and progress.
It encompasses several blocks in the downtown area, including former
mills turned museums, a network of canals, and a helpful visitor center in the 1902 Market Mills Complex that offers a thorough orientation to the city. Pick up a self-guiding brochure for a walking tour
that highlights aspects of local history. Park rangers also lead guided
tours on foot year-round and on turn-of-the-20th-century trolleys and
canal barges in summer and fall. ✉ *246 Market St.,* ☎ *978/970–
5000,* WEB *www.nps.gov/lowe.* ☎ *Free; barge tours generally $4–$6.*
☉ *July–Labor Day daily 9–6, early Sept.–June daily 9–5..*

The **Boott Cotton Mills Museum,** about a 10-minute walk northeast from
the visitor center, is devoted to the history of industrialization. You're
handed ear plugs for walking through an authentic re-creation of a 1920s
weave room, complete with the deafening roar of 88 working power
looms. Other exhibits at the Boott Mills complex, which dates from
the mid-19th century, show the textile worker's grueling life with all
its grit, noise, and dust. ✉ *400 Foot of John St.,* ☎ *978/970–5000.*
☎ *$4.* ☉ *Early Mar.–late-Nov., daily 9:30–5; late-Nov.–early Mar.,
Mon.–Sat. 9:30–4:30, Sun. 11–4:30.*

The **American Textile History Museum,** a short walk southwest along
Dutton Street from the national park visitor center, is housed in a former Civil War–era mill. The museum's collection of working machines
ranges from an 18th-century water wheel to an 1860s power loom to
a 1950s "weave room" where fabrics are still made. ✉ *491 Dutton
St.,* ☎ *978/441–0400,* WEB *www.athm.org.* ☎ *$6; additional fees for
some special exhibitions.* ☉ *Tues.–Fri. 9–4, weekends 10–5.*

The late Beat poet and novelist Jack Kerouac was born in Lowell in 1922. Kerouac's memory is honored in the **Eastern Canal Park** on Bridge Street (near the ☞ Boott Cotton Mills Museum), where plaques bear quotes from his Lowell novels and from *On the Road*. Kerouac's grave is in **Edson Cemetery**, 2 mi south of the Lowell Connector, the highway linking Lowell with I–495.

Dining

$$$ ✕ **The Olympia.** Lowell's diverse population includes a large Greek-American community. Among the specialties at this family-run Greek restaurant are lamb, moussaka, and fish dishes. It's about five blocks from the National Park Visitor Center. ✉ *457 Market St.,* ☎ *978/452–8092. AE, MC, V.*

Side Trip: Plymouth

If you have time to visit just one South Shore destination, make it Plymouth, a historic seaside town of narrow streets and clapboard mansions. Plymouth, 41 mi south of Boston, is known across the nation as "America's hometown" because of the 102 weary settlers (a third of whom were Separatists, or Pilgrims) who disembarked here in December 1620.

MBTA (☎ 617/222–3200, WEB www.mbta.com) commuter rail service is available to Plymouth. **Plymouth & Brockton Street Railway** (☎ 508/746–0378, WEB www.p-b.com) links Plymouth and the South Shore to Boston's South Station with frequent bus service. From the Plymouth train station or bus depot, take the **Plymouth Area Link** buses (☎ 508/746–0378, WEB www.gatra.org/pal.htm) to the town center or to Plimoth Plantation. To get to Plymouth by car, take the Southeast Expressway I–93 south to Route 3 toward Cape Cod; Exits 6 and 4 lead to downtown Plymouth and Plimoth Plantation, respectively.

★ ♿ Over the entrance of **Plimoth Plantation** is the caution: "You are now entering 1627." Believe it. Against the backdrop of the Atlantic Ocean, a Pilgrim village has been painstakingly re-created, from the thatched roofs, cramped quarters, and open fireplaces to the long-horned livestock. Throw away your preconception of white collars and funny hats; through ongoing research, the Plimoth staff has developed a portrait of the Pilgrims richer and more complex than that of the dour folk in school textbooks. Listen to the quaint accents of the "residents," who never break out of character. Feel free to engage them in conversation about their life, but expect only curious looks if you ask about anything that happened later than 1627.

Elsewhere on the plantation is **Hobbamock's Homestead**, where descendants of the Wampanoags re-create the life of a Native American who chose to live near the newcomers. In the **Carriage House Craft Center** you'll see items created using the techniques of 17th-century English craftsmanship—that is, what the Pilgrims might have imported. (You can also buy samples.) At the **Nye Barn**, youngsters can see goats, cows, pigs, and chickens bred from 17th-century gene pools or bred to represent animals raised in the original plantation. The visitor center has gift shops, a cafeteria, and multimedia presentations. Dress for the weather, since most exhibits are outdoors. ✉ *Warren Ave./Rte. 3A,* ☎ *508/746–1622,* WEB *www.plimoth.org.* ✑ *$19 (includes entry to Mayflower II); plantation only, $16.* ☉ *Apr.–Nov., daily 9–5.*

The *Mayflower II*, a replica of the 1620 *Mayflower*, is staffed by Pilgrims and hearty mates in period dress. It is 2 mi down the road from Plimoth Plantation. ✉ *State Pier,* ☎ *508/746–1622,* WEB *www.plimoth.org.* ✑ *$7 or as part of $19 Plimoth Plantation fee.* ☉ *Apr.–Nov., daily 9–5.*

Plymouth Rock, a few dozen yards from the *Mayflower II,* is popularly believed to have been the Pilgrims' stepping stone when they left the ship. Given the stone's unimpressive appearance—many people are dismayed that it's little more than a boulder—and dubious authenticity (as explained on a nearby plaque), the grand canopy overhead seems a trifle ostentatious.

A variety of historical houses are open for visits, including the 1640 **Sparrow House,** Plymouth's oldest structure. It's furnished in the spartan style of the Pilgrims' era, with periodic art and other exhibits. ⊠ *42 Summer St.,* ☎ *508/747–1240,* WEB *www.sparrowhouse.com.* ⌨ *$2.* ☉ *Apr.–Dec., Thurs.–Tues. 10–5 (Sat. till 8, or until dark).*

One of the country's oldest public museums, the **Pilgrim Hall Museum,** established in 1824, transports you back to the time before the Pilgrims' landing, with items carried by those weary travelers to the New World. Included are a carved chest, a remarkably well preserved wicker cradle, Miles Standish's sword, John Alden's Bible, Native American artifacts, and the remains of the *Sparrow-Hawk,* a 17th-century sailing ship that was wrecked in 1626. ⊠ *75 Court St. (Rte. 3A),* ☎ *508/746–1620,* WEB *www.pilgrimhall.org.* ⌨ *$5.* ☉ *Feb.–Dec., daily 9:30–4:30.*

It may be hard to imagine an entire museum devoted to a Thanksgiving side dish, but **Cranberry World,** operated by the Ocean Spray juice company, is amazingly popular. After learning how the state's local crop is grown, harvested, and processed, you can sip juices and sample other cranberry products. ⊠ *158 Water St.,* ☎ *508/747–2350.* ⌨ *Free.* ☉ *May–Nov., daily 9:30–5.*

Dining

$$–$$$ ✕ **Bert's Cove.** This local landmark just off the entrance to Plymouth Beach has great ocean views. The entrées include veal medallions, sirloin steak, risotto, and fresh seafood. ⊠ *140 Warren Ave. (Rte. 3A),* ☎ *508/746–3330. AE, D, MC, V. Nov.–Apr., closed Mon.*

Side Trip: New Bedford

New Bedford, 50 mi south of Boston, is home to the largest fishing fleet on the East Coast. Although much of the town is industrial, the restored historic district near the water is a delight. To reach New Bedford from Boston by car, follow I–93 to Route 24 south to Route 140 south, and continue to I–195 east; travel time is about one hour. **American Eagle Motorcoach Inc.** (☎ 800/453–5040) offers bus service from Boston to New Bedford.

New Bedford is the setting for the beginning of Herman Melville's masterpiece, *Moby-Dick,* a novel ostensibly about whaling. New Bedford was the world's greatest whaling port until the industry began to decline around 1850, and its whaling tradition is commemorated in the **New Bedford Whaling National Historical Park,** encompassing 13 blocks of the waterfront historic district. The park visitor center, in an 1853 Greek Revival former bank, provides maps and information about whaling-related sites. ⊠ *33 William St.,* ☎ *508/996–4095,* WEB *www.nps.gov/nebe.* ☉ *Daily 9–4.*

★ The **New Bedford Whaling Museum,** established in 1903, is the world's largest museum devoted to the history of whaling. One highlight is the skeleton of a 66-ft blue whale, one of only three on view anywhere in the world. An interactive exhibit lets you listen to the underwater sounds of whales and other sea life—plus the sounds of a thunderstorm and a whale-watching boat—as a whale might hear them. You can also peruse the collection of scrimshaw, visit exhibits on regional history, and climb aboard an 89-ft, half-scale model of the 1826 whaling ship *Lagoda*—the world's largest ship model. ☒ *18 Johnny Cake Hill,* ☎ *508/997–0046,* WEB *www.whalingmuseum.org.* ☒ *$6.* ⊙ *Memorial Day–Labor Day, Fri.–Wed. 9–5, Thurs. 9–8; Labor Day–Memorial Day, daily 9–5.*

The **Rotch-Jones-Duff House and Garden Museum,** an 1834 Greek Revival mansion a ½-mi south of downtown, was home to three prominent families in the 1800s. Set amidst a full city block of gardens, the house is filled with elegant furnishings from the era, including a mahogany piano, a massive marble-topped sideboard, and portraits of the house's occupants. A self-guided audio tour is available. ☒ *396 County St.,* ☎ *508/997–1401,* WEB *www.rjdmuseum.org.* ☒ *$4.* ⊙ *June–Dec., Mon.–Sat. 10–4, Sun. 12:30–4; Jan.–May, Tues.–Sat. 10–4, Sun 12:30–4.*

Dining

$–$$$ ✕ **Antonio's.** If you'd like to sample the traditional fare of New Bedford's large Portuguese population, friendly, unadorned Antonio's serves up hearty portions of pork and shellfish stew, *bacalau* (salt cod), and grilled sardines, often on plates piled high with crispy fried potatoes and rice. ☒ *267 Coggeshall St. (near the intersection of I–195 and Rte. 18),* ☎ *508/990–3636. No credit cards.*

Boston A to Z

To research prices, get advice from other travelers, and book travel arrangements, visit www.fodors.com.

AIRPORTS & TRANSFERS

Logan International Airport, across the harbor from downtown Boston, receives flights from most major domestic airlines and some carriers from outside the United States. If you are driving from Logan to downtown, take the Sumner Tunnel—and expect a traffic jam during morning and evening hours.

Cabs can be hired outside each terminal. Fares to and from downtown average about $15–$18 including tip via the most-direct route, the Sumner Tunnel, assuming no major traffic jams. The Ted Williams Tunnel connects the airport to points south, but is limited to taxis and commercial vehicles most of the time, until access roads are finished with the completion of the Big Dig; billboard signs will tell you when it is open to all vehicles. The toll for both tunnels is $2.

The Airport Water Shuttle crosses Boston Harbor in about seven minutes, running between Logan Airport and Rowes Wharf (a free shuttle bus operates between the ferry dock and airline terminals). Adult fare is $10 one-way. The MBTA subway, or "T," from Airport Station is one of the fastest ways to reach downtown from the airport. Shuttle bus 22 runs between Terminals A and B and the subway. Shuttle bus 33 goes to the subway from Terminals C, D, and E. US Shuttle provides door-to-door van service 24 hours a day between the airport and Boston, Cambridge, and many suburban destinations. Call and request a pickup when your flight arrives. To go to the airport, call for reservations 24 to 48 hours in advance. Sample one-way fares are $8 to downtown or the Back Bay, $16 to Cambridge.

➤ AIRPORT INFORMATION: **Logan International Airport** (☒ I–93 N, Exit 24, ☎ 617/561–1800 or 800/235–6426 24-hr information about parking and the ground transportation options). **Massport** (☎ 617/561–1751). **Airport Water Shuttle** (☎ 800/235–6426). **MBTA** (☎ 617/222–3200 or 800/392–6100). **US Shuttle** (☎ 617/889–3366 or toll-free 877/748-8853).

BUS TRAVEL TO & FROM BOSTON

South Station is the depot for most of the major bus companies that serve Boston.

➤ BUS INFORMATION: **South Station** (✉ Atlantic Ave. and Summer St., ☎ 617/345–7451).

CAR TRAVEL

Interstate 95 (also called Route 128 in some parts) skirts the western edge of Boston. Interstate 93 connects Boston to the north and to New Hampshire. The section of I–93 that runs through the city is scheduled to be turned into an underground highway as part of the massive Central Artery Project, or Big Dig,"; expect construction and delays here through at least 2004. Interstate 90 (a toll road technically known as the Massachusetts Turnpike, but called "the Mass Pike" or just "the Pike" by locals) enters the city from the west. Route 9, roughly parallel to I–90, passes through Newton and Brookline on its way into Boston from the west. Route 2 enters Cambridge from the northwest.

DISCOUNTS & DEALS

The *Arts Boston* coupon book offers discounts on admissions to 60 museums, attractions, and tour services in and around Boston. The booklets, which cost $9, can be purchased at Bostix booths in Copley Square and in Faneuil Hall.

The CityPass is a reduced-fee combination ticket to six major Boston attractions: the John F. Kennedy Library and Museum, the John Hancock Observatory, the Museum of Fine Arts, the Museum of Science, the New England Aquarium, and the Isabella Stewart Gardner Museum. The passes cost $30.25 and are available at the Greater Boston Convention and Visitors Bureau information booths (☞ Visitor Information).

EMERGENCIES

➤ DOCTORS & DENTISTS: **Physician Referral Service** (☎ 617/726–5800).

➤ EMERGENCY SERVICES: **Ambulance, fire, police** (☎ 911). **Poison control** (☎ 617/232–2120).

➤ HOSPITALS: **Massachusetts General Hospital** (☎ 617/726–2000).

➤ 24-HOUR PHARMACIES: **CVS** (✉ Porter Square Shopping Plaza, Massachusetts Ave., Cambridge, ☎ 617/876–5519; 155 Charles St., ☎ 617/227–0437 or 800/746–7287; ☎ 617/227–0437 or 800/746–7287 for other locations).

LODGING

B&BS

Bed and Breakfast Reservation Agency of Boston can book a variety of accommodations ranging from historic B&Bs to modern condominiums.

➤ RESERVATION SERVICES: **Bed and Breakfast Reservation Agency of Boston** (✉ 47 Commercial Wharf, 02110, ☎ 617/720–3540; 800/248–9262; 0800/895128 in the U.K., WEB www.boston-bnbagency.com).

TAXIS

Cabs are not easily hailed on the street; if you need to get somewhere in a hurry, use a hotel taxi stand or telephone for a cab. Taxis can also be found near South Station and in Harvard Square. Taxis charge $2–$2.10 per mile; one-way streets often make circuitous routes necessary and increase your cost. Companies offering 24-hour service include Boston Cab Association; Checker; Green Cab Association; Independent Taxi Operators Association; Town Taxi; and Cambridge Checker Cab.

➤ TAXI COMPANIES: **Boston Cab Association** (☎ 617/536–3200). **Checker** (☎ 617/536–7000). **Green Cab Association** (☎ 617/628–0600). **Independent Taxi Operators Association** (ITOA; ☎ 617/426–8700). **Town Taxi** (☎ 617/536–5000). **Cambridge Checker Cab** (☎ 617/ 497–1500).

TOURS

ORIENTATION TOURS

The red Beantown Trolleys make more than 20 stops; get on and off as many times as you like. Cost is $22. Trolleys run every half-hour from 9 AM until 4 PM. Tickets are available from hotel concierges, at many attractions, and sometimes on board. From March to November Brush Hill/Gray Line picks up passengers from hotels for a 2-hour Boston tour or a 3½-hour Cambridge–Lexington–Concord tour. Other tours are available to Plymouth, Cape Cod, Salem, Marblehead, New Hampshire, and Newport, Rhode Island. Reservations essential. Fees are $21–$45, depending on destination. The orange-and-green Old Town Trolley runs every 20 minutes from 9 AM to 3 or 4 PM; adult fares are $23. Specialty tours, such as "JFK's Boston," "Ghost and Gravestones," "The Original Chocolate Tour," and "The Holly Jolly Christmas Trolley" are available.

➤ TOUR OPERATORS: **Beantown Trolleys** (✉ Transportation Bldg., 14 Charles St. S, ☎ 617/236–2148 or 800/343–1328, WEB www.brush-hilltours.com). **Brush Hill/Gray Line** (✉ Transportation Bldg., 14 Charles St. S, ☎ 617/236–2148 or 800/343–1328, WEB www.brush-hilltours.com). **Old Town Trolley** (✉ 329 W. 2nd St., South Boston, 02127, ☎ 617/269–7010, WEB www.oldtowntrolley.com).

BOAT TOURS

Boston Harbor Cruises runs harbor tours and other cruises (including whale-watching, sunset, and evening entertainment cruises; prices vary) from mid-April to October. The Charles Riverboat Co. offers a 55-minute narrated tour of the Charles River Basin. Tours depart from the CambridgeSide Galleria mall at 10:30 AM and then on the hour from noon to 5 daily from June to August and on weekends in April, May, and September; the fare is $9. Massachusetts Bay Lines operates evening cruises with rock, blues, or reggae music and dancing, concessions, and cash bar, as well as daily harbor tours and sunset cruises. Prices vary.

Boston Duck Tours uses World War II amphibious vehicles for 80-minute tours on the city's streets and the Charles River. Tours begin and end at the Huntington Avenue entrance to the Prudential Center, at 101 Huntington Avenue. From April to November, tours leave every half hour from 9 AM till dark; the fare is about $22. Tickets are sold inside the Prudential Center 9–8 Monday–Saturday and 9–6 on Sundays; weekend tours often sell out early. Boston by Sea feature live music, drama, video, and audience participation. They meet Memorial Day through October at 1 and 3 PM, and cost $25 for adults.

➤ TOUR OPERATORS: **Boston Harbor Cruises** (✉ 1 Long Wharf, ☎ 617/ 227–4321). **Charles Riverboat Co.** (☎ 617/621–3001, WEB www.charlesriverboat.com). **Massachusetts Bay Lines** (✉ 60 Rowes Wharf, ☎ 617/542–8000). **Boston Duck Tours** (✉ 790 Boylston St., Plaza Level, ☎ 617/723–3825). **Boston by Sea** (✉ 1 Long Wharf, ☎ 617/227–4321).

WALKING TOURS

The Black Heritage Trail, a self-guided walk, explores Boston's 19th-century black community, passing 14 sites; free guided tours meet at the Shaw Memorial on Beacon Hill, Memorial Day weekend through Labor Day weekend daily at 10 AM, noon, and 2 PM. The 2½-mi Freedom Trail follows a red line past 16 of Boston's most important historic sites. The nonprofit Historic Neighborhoods Foundation covers the North End, Chinatown, Beacon Hill, the waterfront, and other urban areas on 90-minute guided walks from Wednesday to Saturday between April and November. Tours cost $5 and up. The Society for the Preservation of New England Antiquities conducts a walking tour of Beacon Hill that focuses on the neighborhood as it was in the early 1800s. Tours are given Saturdays May through October at 11 PM; tours cost $10. The Women's Heritage Trail celebrates more than 80 accomplished women on four self-guided walks. The Old State House and the Boston National Historic Park Service Visitor Center sell maps ($5) and a guidebook ($9.95), which is also available in the bookstores of most historic sites.

The volunteers of Boston by Foot conduct guided 90-minute walks of various neighborhoods daily from May to October. Most tours cost $8; no reservations are required.

➤ TOUR OPERATORS: **Black Heritage Trail** (☎ 617/742–5415, WEB www.afroammuseum.org). **Freedom Trail** (☎ 617/242–5642). **Historic Neighborhoods Foundation** (✉ 99 Bedford St., ☎ 617/426–1885, WEB www.historic-neighborhoods.org). **Society for the Preservation of New England Antiquities** (SPNEA; ✉ 141 Cambridge St., ☎ 617/227–3956). **The Old State House** (✉ 206 Washington St.) and **Boston National Historic Park Service Visitor Center** (✉ 15 State St.). **Boston by Foot** (77 N. Washington St., ☎ 617/367–2345; 617/367–3766 recorded information).

TRAIN TRAVEL

Amtrak Northeast Corridor trains from New York, Washington, D.C., and elsewhere stop at South Station, Back Bay Station, and the easy-to-access Route 128 station south of Boston. Some trains require reservations. High-speed Acela trains began running between Boston and New York in 2001. Amtrak's *Lake Shore Limited* travels daily from Boston to Chicago by way of Albany, Rochester, Buffalo, and Cleveland.

➤ TRAIN INFORMATION: **Amtrak** (☎ 617/482–3660 or 800/872–7245, WEB www.amttrak.com).

TRANSPORTATION AROUND BOSTON

Massachusetts Bay Transportation Authority dispenses 24-hour information on bus, subway, and train routes; schedules; fares; and other matters, including wheelchair access. MBTA visitor passes are available for unlimited travel on subway, local bus, and inner-harbor ferry for one-, three-, and seven-day periods (fares: $5, $9, and $18 respectively). Buy passes at the following MBTA stations: Airport, South Station, North Station, Back Bay, Government Center, and Harvard Square. Passes are also sold at the Boston Common Information Kiosk and at some hotels.

MBTA bus routes crisscross the metropolitan area and travel farther into suburbia than subway and trolley lines. Some suburban schedules are designed primarily for commuters. Current local fares are 60¢ for adults, 35¢ children from age 5 to 11, 15¢ seniors over 65 and persons with disabilities; you must pay an extra fare on an express bus, or for longer suburban trips.

The MBTA—or "T," for short—operates subways, elevated trains, and trolleys along four lines. Trains operate from about 5:30 AM to about 12:30 AM. Current T fares are 85¢ for adults, 40¢ for children from ages 5 to 11. An extra fare is required heading inbound from distant Green Line stops and in both directions for certain distant Red Line stops. The **Red Line** originates at Braintree and Mattapan to the south;

the routes join near South Boston and proceed through downtown Boston (including South Station) to the western edge of Cambridge. The **Green Line,** a combined underground and elevated surface line, uses trolleys that operate underground in the central city. It originates at Cambridge's Lechmere, heads south, and divides into four routes; these end at Boston College (Commonwealth Avenue), Cleveland Circle (Beacon Street), Riverside, and Heath Street (Huntington Avenue). Buses connect Heath Street to the old Arborway terminus. The **Blue Line** runs on weekdays from Bowdoin Square and on weeknights and weekends from Government Center to the Wonderland Racetrack in Revere, north of Boston. Logan Airport is among its stops. The **Orange Line** runs from Oak Grove in north suburban Malden to Forest Hills near the Arnold Arboretum. Park Street Station (on the Common) and State Street are the major downtown transfer points.

Boston is not an easy city to drive in—some say it's the worst in the U.S.—because of the many one-way streets, the many streets with the same name, the many streets that abruptly *change* name in the middle, and the many illogical twists and turns; not to mention the apparent disregard locals hold for rules of the road. If you must bring a car, bring a good map, keep to the main thoroughfares, and park in lots rather than on the street to avoid tickets (signage is confusing at best, and meter patrol is preternaturally quick), accidents, or theft. Some neighborhoods have strictly enforced residents-only rules, with just a handful of two-hour visitor's spaces; others have meters (25¢ for 12–15 minutes, one or two hours maximum). Major public lots are at Government Center and Quincy Market, beneath Boston Common (entrance on Charles Street), beneath Post Office Square, at the Prudential Center, at Copley Place, off Clarendon Street near the John Hancock Tower, and at several hotels. Smaller lots are scattered throughout downtown. Most are expensive (expect to pay $10 and up for an evening out, $20 and up to park all day). Some offer an hour or two of free parking with tickets stamped by local restaurants or merchants; others offer a cheaper flat rate at certain times, such as weekends. The few city-run garages are a bargain at about $10 per day—but try finding a space in them.

The Central Artery/Tunnel Project, known as "the Big Dig," is a massive highway reconstruction effort in downtown Boston that will continue through 2004 at the earliest, causing traffic delays and detours. For updates, check with the project office.

➤ CONTACTS: **Massachusetts Bay Transportation Authority** (MBTA; ☎ 617/222–3200; 800/392–6100; 617/722–5146 TTY). **MBTA** (☎ 617/222–3200, WEB www.mbta.com). **Smart Traveler** (☎ 617/374–1234). **"Big Dig" project office** (☎ 617/951–6400).

VISITOR INFORMATION
The Boston Visitor Information Pavilion is open daily 9–5. The Boston Welcome Center is open from Sunday to Thursday between 9 and 5 and on Friday and Saturday between 9 and 6 for most of the year; it's open until 7 except Sunday during the summer. Greater Boston Convention and Visitors Bureau has brochures and information.

➤ TOURIST INFORMATION: The **Boston Visitor Information Pavilion** (✉ Boston Common, Tremont St., near beginning of Freedom Trail, ☎ 617/536–4100; 888/733–2678 for recorded general information). **Boston Welcome Center** (✉ 140 Tremont St., Boston 02111, ☎ 617/451–2227). **Greater Boston Convention and Visitors Bureau** (✉ 2 Copley Pl., Suite 105, Boston 02116, ☎ 617/536–4100 or 800/888–5515).

Boston MBTA (the "T")

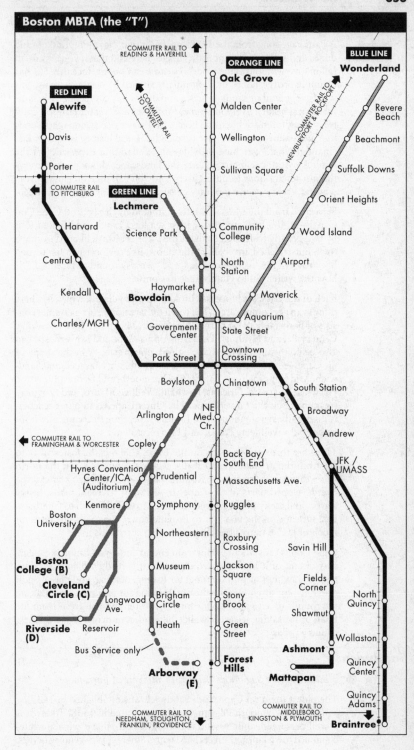

RED LINE
Alewife
Davis
Porter
Harvard
Central
Kendall
Charles/MGH

COMMUTER RAIL TO
READING & HAVERHILL

COMMUTER RAIL
TO LOWELL

COMMUTER RAIL
TO FITCHBURG

ORANGE LINE
Oak Grove
Malden Center
Wellington
Sullivan Square
Community College
North Station
Haymarket

GREEN LINE
Lechmere
Science Park

Bowdoin

Government Center
Park Street
Boylston
Arlington
Copley

COMMUTER RAIL TO
FRAMINGHAM & WORCESTER

Hynes Convention Center/ICA (Auditorium)
Kenmore
Boston University
Boston College (B)
Cleveland Circle (C)
Longwood Ave.
Riverside (D)
Reservoir

Prudential
Symphony
Northeastern
Museum
Brigham Circle
Heath

Bus Service only

Arborway (E)

NE Med. Ctr.
Downtown Crossing
Chinatown

Back Bay/South End
Massachusetts Ave.
Ruggles
Roxbury Crossing
Jackson Square
Stony Brook
Green Street
Forest Hills

COMMUTER RAIL TO
NEEDHAM, STOUGHTON,
FRANKLIN, PROVIDENCE

BLUE LINE
Wonderland
Revere Beach
Beachmont
Suffolk Downs
Orient Heights
Wood Island
Airport
Maverick
Aquarium
State Street

COMMUTER RAIL TO
NEWBURYPORT & ROCKPORT

South Station
Broadway
Andrew
JFK / UMASS
Savin Hill
Fields Corner
Shawmut
Ashmont
Mattapan

North Quincy
Wollaston
Quincy Center
Quincy Adams
Braintree

COMMUTER RAIL TO
MIDDLEBORO,
KINGSTON & PLYMOUTH

CAPE COD

Updated by
Carolyn Heller

A Patti Page song from the 1950s promises that "If you're fond of sand dunes and salty air, quaint little villages here and there, you're sure to fall in love with old Cape Cod." The tourism boom since the '50s has certainly proved her right. Continually shaped by ocean currents, this windswept land of sandy beaches and dunes has compellingly beautiful natural beauty. Everyone comes for the seaside, yet the crimson cranberry bogs, forests of birch and beech, freshwater ponds, and marshlands that grace the interior are just as splendid. Local history is equally fascinating; whale-watching provides an exhilarating experience of the natural world; cycling trails lace the landscape; shops purvey everything from antiques to pure kitsch; and you can dine on simple fresh seafood, creative contemporary cuisine, or most anything in between.

Separated from the Massachusetts mainland by the 17½-mi Cape Cod Canal—at 480 ft the world's widest sea-level canal—and linked to it by two heavily trafficked bridges, the Cape is always likened in shape to an outstretched arm bent at the elbow, its Provincetown fist turned back toward the mainland. The Cape "winds around to face itself" is how the writer Philip Hamburger has put it.

Each of the Cape's 15 towns is broken up into villages, which is where things can get complicated. The town of Barnstable, for example, consists of Barnstable, West Barnstable, Cotuit, Marstons Mills, Osterville, Centerville, and Hyannis. The terms Upper Cape and Lower Cape can also be confusing. **Upper Cape**—think upper arm, as in the shape of the Cape—refers to the towns of Bourne, Falmouth, Mashpee, and Sandwich. **Mid Cape** includes Barnstable, Yarmouth, and Dennis. Brewster, Harwich, Chatham, Orleans, Eastham, Wellfleet, Truro, and Provincetown make up the **Lower Cape.** The **Outer Cape,** as in outer reaches, is essentially synonymous with Lower Cape, though technically it includes only Wellfleet, Truro, and Provincetown.

There are three major roads on the Cape. U.S. 6 is the fastest way to get from the mainland to Orleans. Route 6A winds along the north shore through scenic towns; Route 28 dips south through some of the overdeveloped parts of the Cape. If you want to avoid malls, heavy traffic, and tacky motels, avoid Route 28 from Falmouth to Chatham. Past Orleans on the way out to Provincetown, the roadside clutter of much of U.S. 6 masks the beauty of what surrounds it.

Cape Cod is only about 70 mi from end to end—you can make a cursory circuit of it in about two days. But it is really a place for relaxing—for swimming and sunning; for fishing, boating, and playing golf or tennis; for attending the theater, hunting for antiques, and making the rounds of art galleries; for buying lobster and fish fresh from the boat; or for taking leisurely walks, bike rides, or drives along timeless country roads.

Sandwich

★ ❶ *3 mi east of the Sagamore Bridge, 11 mi west of Barnstable.*

The oldest town on Cape Cod, Sandwich was established in 1637 by some of the Plymouth Pilgrims and incorporated in 1638. Today it is a well-preserved, quintessential New England village with a white-columned town hall and streets lined with 18th- and 19th-century homes.

From 1825 until 1888, the main industry in Sandwich was the production of vividly colored glass, made in the Boston and Sandwich Glass Company's factory. The **Sandwich Glass Museum** contains relics of the town's early history, a diorama of the factory in its heyday, and displays of shimmering blown and pressed glass. Glassmaking demonstrations are held in summer, and a gift shop sells attractive glass pieces. ⊠ *129 Main St.,* ☎ *508/888–0251,* WEB *www.sandwichglassmuseum.org.* ⌦ *$3.50.* ☉ *Apr.–Dec., daily 9:30–5; Feb.–Mar., Wed.–Sun. 9:30–4.*

★ **Heritage Plantation,** a fine complex of museum buildings, gardens, and a café, sits on 76 acres overlooking Shawme Pond. The Shaker Round Barn displays historic cars, including a 1930 yellow-and-green Duesenberg built for movie star Gary Cooper. The Military Museum houses antique firearms, military uniforms, and a collection of miniature soldiers. At the Art Museum are an extensive Currier & Ives collection, antique toys, and a working 1912 Coney Island–style carousel. The grounds are planted with flowers, hostas, heather, fruit trees, and rhododendrons. Concerts are held in the gardens on summer afternoons and evenings. ⊠ *Grove and Pine Sts.,* ☎ *508/888–3300,* WEB *www.heritageplantation.org.* ⌦ *$9.* ☉ *Mid-May–late Oct., daily 10–5.*

The **Sandwich Boardwalk,** built over a salt marsh, a creek, and low dunes, leads to Town Neck Beach. Cape Cod Bay stretches out around the beach at the end of the walk, where a platform provides fine views, especially at sunset. From town cross Route 6A on Jarves Street, and at its end turn left, then right, and continue to the boardwalk parking lot.

Dining and Lodging

$$–$$$ ✕ **Aqua Grille.** The far-ranging menu and lively atmosphere at this smart-casual bistro by the marina, make it a good choice for large groups. Fried or grilled seafood, pastas, and steaks are all available. The superb lobster salad is a hearty serving of greens, avocados, baby green beans, and meaty lobster chunks. ⊠ *14 Gallo Rd.,* ☎ *508/888–8889,* WEB *www.aquagrille.com. AE, MC, V. Closed mid-Oct.–Mar..*

$$$–$$$$ ✕ **Dan'l Webster Inn.** Built in 1971 on the site of a 17th-century inn, the Dan'l Webster is a contemporary hotel with old New England friendliness and hospitality. Chef's specials at the restaurant ($$$) might include striped bass crusted with cashews and macadamia nuts and accompanied by mango sauce. You can choose to include some meals in the room price. Lodgings are in the main inn and wings or in two nearby historic houses with four suites each. All rooms have floral fabrics, reproduction mahogany and cherry furnishings, and some antiques. The eight rooms on the second floor of the Jarves Wing, which were added in 1999, are particularly spacious and have fireplaces and whirlpool tubs, as do some of the suites. ⊠ *149 Main St., 02563,* ☎ *508/888–3622 or 800/444–3566,* FAX *508/888–5156,* WEB *www.danlwebsterinn.com. 45 rooms, 9 suites. 2 restaurants, no-smoking rooms, room service, pool. AE, D, DC, MC, V. MAP available/*

$$–$$$ ✕ **Belfry Inn & Bistro.** Housed in a 1902 former church and the adjacent "painted-lady" Victorian rectory, this inn retains many of the church's original features—arches, stained-glass windows—in its six stylish rooms. In the Drew House next door, the eight rooms blend Laura Ashley prints and pastel-painted furnishings. The bistro, a dramatic space in the former sanctuary, serves contemporary fare such as grilled salmon with warm lemon vinaigrette, or duck breast with wild mushroom risotto. ⊠ *8 Jarves St., 02563,* ☎ *508/888–8550 or 800/844–4542,* FAX *508/888–3922,* WEB *www.belfryinn.com. 14 rooms. Restaurant, bar. AE, D, DC, MC, V. BP.*

$$ ⌂ **Wingscorton Farm.** This enchanting oasis is a working farm. The main house, built in 1756, has two second-floor suites, each with a fireplace, Oriental rugs, and wainscoting. Also on the property are a detached cottage and a converted stone carriage house. A private bay

Cape Cod

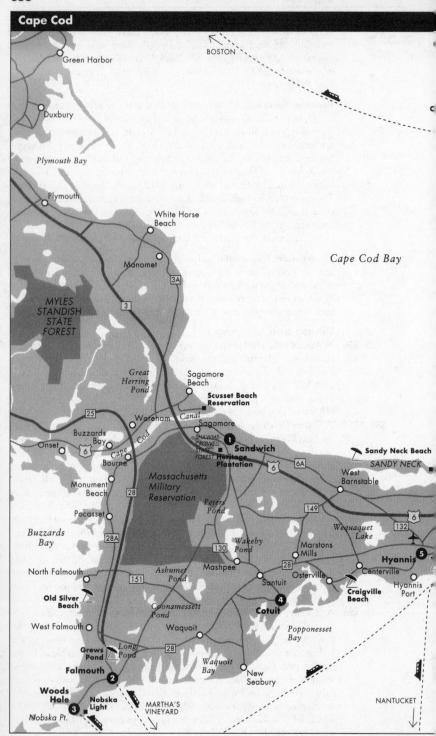

Green Harbor

Duxbury

Plymouth Bay

Plymouth

White Horse
Beach

Manomet

[3A]

[3]

*MYLES
STANDISH
STATE
FOREST*

*Great
Herring
Pond*

Sagamore
Beach

**Scusset Beach
Reservation**

Wareham

Canal

Sagamore

[25]

Buzzards
Bay

Cape Cod

*SHAWME
CROWELL
STATE
FOREST*

①

Sandwich

Onset

[6]

Bourne

Monument
Beach

[28]

*Massachusetts
Military
Reservation*

**Heritage
Plantation**

[6]

[6A]

West
Barnstable

Sandy Neck Beach

SANDY NECK

Pocasset

*Buzzards
Bay*

[28A]

*Peters
Pond*

[149]

*Wequaquet
Lake*

[132]

[6]

North Falmouth

[151]

*Ashumet
Pond*

[130]

*Wakeby
Pond*

Mashpee

[28]

Marstons
Mills

Osterville

Hyannis

⑤

**Old Silver
Beach**

*Coonamessett
Pond*

Santuit

Centerville

Hyannis
Port

**Craigville
Beach**

West Falmouth

Waquoit

④

Cotuit

*Popponesset
Bay*

**Grews
Pond**

*Long
Pond*

[28]

*Waquoit
Bay*

New
Seabury

Falmouth

②

**Woods
Hole**

**Nobska
Light**

③

Nobska Pt.

MARTHA'S
VINEYARD

NANTUCKET

BOSTON

Cape Cod Bay

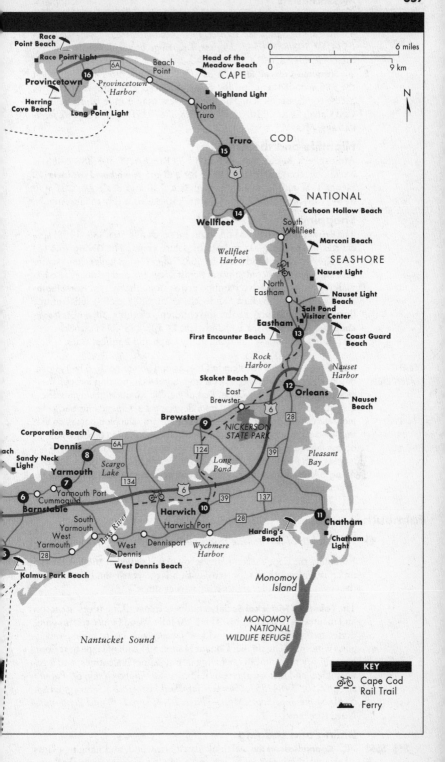

Race
Point Beach

Race Point Light

6A

Beach
Point

Head of the
Meadow Beach

CAPE

Provincetown

16

*Provincetown
Harbor*

Herring
Cove Beach

Long Point Light

Highland Light

North
Truro

COD

Truro

15

6

NATIONAL

Cahoon Hollow Beach

Wellfleet

14

South
Wellfleet

Marconi Beach

*Wellfleet
Harbor*

SEASHORE

Nauset Light

North
Eastham

Nauset Light
Beach

Salt Pond
Visitor Center

Eastham

13

Coast Guard
Beach

First Encounter Beach

*Rock
Harbor*

*Nauset
Harbor*

Skaket Beach

East
Brewster

12

Orleans

Nauset
Beach

Brewster

9

*NICKERSON
STATE PARK*

6

28

Corporation Beach

6A

124

*Pleasant
Bay*

Dennis

8

*Scargo
Lake*

Long Pond

39

ach

Sandy Neck
Light

Yarmouth

7

134

Barnstable

6

6

39

137

Cummaquid

Yarmouth Port

South
Yarmouth

West
Yarmouth

Harwich

10

Harwich Port

28

11

Chatham

Bass River

West
Dennis

Dennisport

Harding's
Beach

Chatham
Light

3

28

*Wychmere
Harbor*

West Dennis Beach

Kalmus Park Beach

*Monomoy
Island*

Nantucket Sound

*MONOMOY
NATIONAL
WILDLIFE REFUGE*

0   6 miles
0   9 km

N

KEY

Cape Cod
Rail Trail

Ferry

beach is a five-minute walk away. ⊠ *11 Wing Blvd., off Rte. 6A, about 4½ mi east of Sandwich Center, East Sandwich 02537,* ☎ *508/888–0534,* FAX *508/888–0545. 2 suites, 1 carriage house, 1 2-bedroom cottage. AE, MC, V. BP.*

$ 🔥 **Shawme-Crowell State Forest.** Open-air campfires are allowed at the 285 wooded tent and RV campsites here, and campers have free access to Scusset Beach. The forest is less than a mile from the Cape Cod Canal. ⊠ *Rte. 130, 02563,* ☎ *508/888–0351; 877/422–6762 reservations. MC, V.*

Nightlife and the Arts

Atmospheric **Bobby Byrne's Pub** (⊠ 65 Rte. 6A, ☎ 508/888–6088) is a relaxing, convivial place to stop for a drink. **Town band concerts** (⊠ Henry T. Wing Elementary School, Rte. 130 and Beale Ave., ☎ 508/888–5144) are held on Thursday at 7:30 PM from July to late August.

Shopping

The **Brown Jug** (⊠ 155 Main St., at Jarves St., ☎ 508/833–1088) specializes in antique glass and Staffordshire china. The **Giving Tree** (⊠ 550 Rte. 6A, East Sandwich, ☎ 508/888–5446), a gallery and sculpture garden, shows contemporary crafts, jewelry, and prints; it also has walking paths through a bamboo grove along the marsh. **Horsefeathers** (⊠ 454 Rte. 6A, East Sandwich, ☎ 508/888–5298) sells antique linens, lace, and vintage baby and children's clothing. **Titcomb's Bookshop** (⊠ 432 Rte. 6A, East Sandwich, ☎ 508/888–2331) stocks used, rare, and new books, including many Cape and nautical titles.

OFF THE BEATEN PATH

ROUTE 6A – If you're traveling to Orleans and you're not in a hurry, take this lovely road, which heads east from Sandwich, passing through the oldest settlements on the Cape. Part of the Old King's Highway historic district, this stretch is protected from development. Classic inns and enticing antiques shops alternate with traditional gray-shingled homes on the tree-lined route, and the woods periodically give way to broad vistas across the marshes. In autumn the foliage along the road is bright—maples with their feet wet in ponds and marshes put on a good display. Along 6A east of Sandwich center, you can stop to watch the harvesting of cranberries in flooded bogs.

Falmouth

❷ *15 mi south of the Bourne Bridge, 4 mi north of Woods Hole.*

Falmouth, the Cape's second-largest town, was settled in 1660. Although much of Falmouth is suburban, with a large year-round population, the town still includes sights from earlier times.

The **Falmouth Historical Society** conducts free walking tours in season and maintains two museums. The 1790 **Julia Wood House** retains wonderful architectural details—a widow's walk, wide-board floors, leaded-glass windows. The smaller **Conant House**, a 1724 half Cape next door, has military memorabilia, whaling items, sailors' valentines, and a genealogical and historical research library. ⊠ *Village Green, off Palmer Ave.,* ☎ *508/548–4857,* WEB *www.falmouthhistoricalsociety.org.* 🖼 *$3.* ☉ *Mid-June–mid-Sept., Mon.–Thurs. 10–4, Sun. 1–4; mid-Sept.–mid-Nov., weekends 1–4.*

Dining and Lodging

$$$–$$$$ ✕🏨 **Coonamessett Inn.** With plenty of art, wood, and hanging plants
★   all around, this is one of the best and oldest inn-restaurants on the Cape. One- or two-bedroom suites are in five buildings around a broad lawn that spills down to a wooded pond. Rooms are casually decorated, with

bleached wood or pine paneling and New England antiques or reproductions. The menu in the lovely main dining room is traditional,
maybe too much so for adventuresome palates. There are many seafood
choices, including charbroiled swordfish with grilled vegetable vinaigrette and baked scrod. ✉ *311 Gifford St., at Jones Rd., 02540,* ☎
508/548–2300, FAX *508/540–9831,* WEB *www.capecodrestaurants.org.*
28 suites, 1 cottage. AE, MC, V. CP.

$$$–$$$$ ⚑ **La Maison Cappellari at Mostly Hall.** Looking very much like a pri-
★   vate estate, this imposing 1849 house has a wraparound porch and a
dramatic widow's walk. Several bedrooms are decorated in an upscale
European style, each with a colorful mural; in the Tuscan Room, the
walls are painted to suggest an intimate Italian garden. Three rooms
are more traditionally decorated, with floral wallpaper, canopy beds,
and other antiques. Although the inn is only steps from the town cen-
ter, you can lounge in the lush gardens and feel a world away. No smok-
ing is permitted. ✉ *27 Main St., 02540,* ☎ *508/548–3786 or 800/682–*
0565, FAX *508/548–5778,* WEB *www.mostlyhall.com. 6 rooms. Bicycles,*
library. AE, D, MC, V. Closed mid-Dec.–mid-Mar. BP.

$$$ ⚑ **Wildflower Inn.** The innkeepers here call their decorating style "old
★   made new again": tables are constructed from early-1900s pedal sewing
machine bases, and the living room's sideboard was a '20s electric stove.
Guest rooms, two of which have whirlpool tubs, are also innovatively
decorated, from the romantic Moonflower Room to the bright, cheerful Geranium Room. The five-course breakfast might include sun-
flower crepes, calendula corn muffins, or other delicious concoctions
using the edible wildflowers grown out back. The inn is no-smoking.
✉ *167 Palmer Ave., 02540,* ☎ FAX *508/548–9524 or 800/294–5459,*
WEB *www.wildflower-inn.com. 5 rooms, 1 cottage. AE, MC, V. Closed*
Jan.–Feb. BP.

$–$$ ⚑ **Sjöholm Inn.** This rambling 1863 farmhouse on a country lane in West
Falmouth is comfortable and homey. The basic rooms—in the main inn
and in the adjacent cottage house—mix 1940s colonial-style furniture,
hand-me-downs, and the occasional antique. Unlike many B&Bs, the
Sjöholm (pronounced *shewr*-holm) welcomes families. No smoking is
permitted. ✉ *17 Chase Rd., off Rte. 28A, West Falmouth 02574,* ☎
508/540–5706 or 800/498–5706, WEB *www.sjoholminn.com. 15 rooms,*
7 with bath, 1 cottage. Breakfast room, croquet, bicycles. MC, V. BP.

Nightlife and the Arts

The **Nimrod Inn** (✉ 100 Dillingham Ave., ☎ 508/540–4132) presents
jazz and contemporary music at least six nights a week. **Town band
concerts** (✉ Marina Park, Scranton Ave., ☎ 508/548–8500 or 800/
526–8532) take place on summer Thursdays at 8 PM.

Outdoor Activities and Sports

BEACHES

Grews Pond, in Goodwill Park, is a pretty tree-lined freshwater pond
with a sandy beach and lifeguarded swimming area. Popular with
local families, it has picnic tables, rest rooms, and free parking. Enter
the park from Route 28 just north of Jones Road or from Gifford Street
opposite St. Joseph's Cemetery.

Old Silver Beach, a long crescent of white sand, is especially good for
small children because a sandbar keeps it shallow at one end and creates tidal pools full of crabs and minnows. There are lifeguards, rest
rooms, showers, and a snack bar. ✉ *Off Quaker Rd., North Falmouth.* 🅿 *Parking $10 in summer.*

BIKING

The **Shining Sea Trail** is an easy 3½-mi route between Locust Street in
Falmouth and the Woods Hole ferry parking lot.

FISHING

Freshwater ponds are good for perch, pickerel, and trout; the required license is available at **Eastman's Sport & Tackle** (✉ 150 Main St., ☎ 508/548–6900).

TENNIS

Falmouth Sports Center (✉ 33 Highfield Dr., ☎ 508/548–7433) has three all-weather and six indoor tennis courts, plus racquetball-hand-ball courts and a health club.

Woods Hole

❸ *4 mi southwest of Falmouth, 19 mi south of the Bourne Bridge.*

Woods Hole is home to several major scientific institutions: the Woods Hole Oceanographic Institution (WHOI), the Marine Biological Laboratory (MBL), the National Marine Fisheries Service, and the U.S. Geological Survey's Branch of Marine Geology. The town is also the departure point for ferries to Martha's Vineyard.

The WHOI is the largest independent private oceanographic laboratory in the world. Its staff led the successful U.S.–French search for the *Titanic* (found about 400 mi off Newfoundland) in 1985. Although the **Oceanographic Institution** is not open to the public, you can learn about it at the small **WHOI Exhibit Center.** ✉ *15 School St., ☎ 508/289–2663,* WEB *www.whoi.edu.* 🎟 *$2 suggested donation.* 🕙 *Memorial Day–Labor Day, Mon.–Sat. 10–4:30, Sun. noon–4:30; Apr. and Nov.–Dec., Fri.–Sat. 10–4:30, Sun. noon–4:30; May and Sept.–Oct., Tues.–Sat. 10–4:30, Sun. noon–4:30.*

The **Marine Biological Laboratory** (✉ 7 MBL St., ☎ 508/289–7623, WEB www.mbl.edu) is closed to the public, but retired scientists conduct free 1½-hour tours in summer. Make reservations one week ahead.

🔆 The exhibition tanks at the **National Marine Fisheries Service Aquarium** contain regional fish and shellfish. You can see things up close through magnifying glasses. Several hands-on pools hold banded lobsters, crabs, snails, sea stars, and other creatures. The star attractions are two harbor seals, which can be seen in the outdoor pool near the entrance. The exhibits aren't sophisticated and the facility is a bit rundown, but this popular place is definitely kid-friendly. ✉ *Albatross and Water Sts., ☎ 508/495–2267; 508/495–2001 for recorded information,* WEB *www.nefsc.nmfs.gov/nefsc/aquarium.* 🎟 *Free.* 🕙 *Mid-June–mid-Sept., daily 10–4; mid-Sept.–mid-June, weekdays 10–4.*

Dining

$$–$$$ ✕ **Fish Monger's Café.** The ambitious contemporary menu at this ★ restaurant on the sound includes a fried calamari appetizer with a hot-pepper sauce and grilled seafood dishes with tropical fruit sauces. The mango and cilantro sauce over grilled salmon is particularly delectable. ✉ *56 Water St., ☎ 508/540–5376. Reservations not accepted. AE, MC, V. Closed Dec.–mid-Feb.; also Tues. Nov. and mid-Feb.–Mar.*

Cotuit

❹ *16 mi northeast of Woods Hole.*

The center of this picturesque town is not much more than a crossroads with a coffee shop, pizza parlor, and general store, which all seem unchanged since the 1940s. Nearby Mashpee is one of two Massachusetts towns (the other is Aquinnah, formerly known as Gay Head, on Martha's Vineyard) that has municipally governed, as well as Native American–governed, areas. Mashpee also encompasses the resort community of New Seabury.

The **Cahoon Museum of American Art** is in a 1775 Georgian Colonial farmhouse that was once a tavern and an overnight way station for travelers on the Hyannis–Sandwich Stagecoach line. Its several rooms display American primitive paintings by Ralph and Martha Cahoon along with other 19th- and early 20th-century art. ⊠ *4676 Rte. 28,* ☎ *508/428–7581,* WEB *www.cahoonmuseum.org.* ☞ *Free; donations accepted.* ⊘ *Mar.–Jan., Tues.–Sat. 10–4.*

Dining and Lodging

$$$$ ✕ **Regatta of Cotuit.** The classic yet original fare here includes pâtés of rabbit, veal, and venison, and a signature seared loin of lamb with cabernet sauce, surrounded by chèvre, spinach, and pine nuts. The menu may be more haute than hot, but the restored colonial stagecoach inn is plushly filled with wood, brass, and Oriental carpets. The cozy taproom has its own bar menu. ⊠ *4613 Falmouth Rd. (Rte. 28),* ☎ *508/ 428–5715. AE, MC, V. Reservations essential. No lunch.*

$$$$ ✕⊡ **New Seabury Resort and Conference Center.** This self-contained
★   resort community on a 2,000-acre point surrounded by Nantucket Sound contains furnished apartments—available for overnight stays or longer—in some of its 13 villages. Among the amenities are fine waterfront dining ($$–$$$), a restaurant overlooking the fairways ($$–$$$), and a private beach. The resort's golf courses are open to the public from September to May. ⊠ *Box 549, Rock Landing Rd., New Seabury 02649,* ☎ *508/477–9400 or 800/999–9033,* FAX *508/477–9790,* WEB *www.newseabury.com. 140 1- or 2-bedroom units. 2 restaurants, 2 pools, 2 18-hole golf courses, 16 tennis courts, health club, jogging, beach, boating, bicycles, shops. AE, DC, MC, V.*

Hyannis

❺ *11 mi northeast of Cotuit, 23 mi east of the Bourne Bridge.*

Perhaps best known for its association with the Kennedy clan, Hyannis is the Cape's year-round commercial and transportation hub. Nearby strip malls have taken their toll on Main Street, but there are plenty of fun and fancy eateries here.

The enlarged and annotated photographs at the **John F. Kennedy Hyannis Museum** document JFK's Cape years (1934–63). ⊠ *Old Town Hall, 397 Main St.,* ☎ *508/790–3077.* ☞ *$3.* ⊘ *Mid-Apr.–mid-Oct., Mon.– Sat. 10–4, Sun. 1–4 (last admission at 3:30). Call for off-season hrs.*

Hyannis Port, 1½ mi south of Hyannis, was a mecca for Americans during the Kennedy presidency, when the **Kennedy Compound** became the summer White House. More recently, Kennedy family members waited here for news of John Kennedy Jr.'s missing plane; en route to a cousin's wedding in Hyannis in 1999, his plane crashed off Martha's Vineyard, killing himself, his wife, and her sister. The Kennedy mystique is such that tourists still seek out the compound; the best way to get a glimpse of it is from the water on one of the many harbor tours or cruises.

Dining and Lodging

$$–$$$ ✕ **The Paddock.** For more than 30 years, the Paddock has been syn-
★   onymous with excellent formal dining—in the authentically Victorian main dining room or the breezy old-style-wicker summer porch. Steak au poivre with five varieties of crushed peppercorns is but one of the many traditional yet innovative preparations. The superb Pacific Rim chicken is a grilled breast topped with oranges and mangoes, served on mixed greens and Asian noodles. Manhattans are the drink of choice in the lounge, where musicians perform in the evening. ⊠ *W. Main St. rotary, next to Melody Tent,* ☎ *508/775–7677,* WEB *www.capecod-travel.com/paddock. AE, DC, MC, V. Closed mid-Nov.–Mar..*

$$-$$$ ✗ **RooBar.** A bit of Manhattan on Main Street, RooBar has a dark, sophisticated feel, with good music and a hip bar scene at night. From the wood-fired oven come pizzas like scallop and prosciutto with asparagus and goat cheese. Also try the "Big-Ass Grilled Shrimp" in a red curry-coconut sauce, and the fire-roasted chicken rubbed with toasted fennel and cumin seeds. ⊠ *586 Main St.,* ☎ *508/778–6515,* WEB *www.roobarcitybistro.com. Reservations essential. AE, MC, V.*

$$ ✗ **Baxter's Fish N' Chips.** The delicious fried clams here are served with homemade tartar sauce. Picnic tables make it possible for you to lose no time in the sun while you dine on lobster, burgers, or delicacies from the excellent raw bar. ⊠ *Pleasant St.,* ☎ *508/775–4490. Reservations not accepted. AE, MC, V. Closed Columbus Day–Apr. and weekdays Labor Day–Columbus Day*

$$-$$$$ ▥ **Breakwaters.** If you were any closer to the water, you'd be in it—
★   that's how close these charming weathered gray-shingle cottages are to Nantucket Sound. The one-, two-, and three-bedroom condos, rented by the day or week, offer all the comforts of home. The units have one or two bathrooms; kitchens with microwaves, coffeemakers, refrigerators, toasters, and stoves; and a deck or patio with a grill. Most have water views. An added plus is daily (except Sunday) maid service. ⊠ *Box 118, 432 Sea St., 02601,* ☎ FAX *508/775–6831,* WEB *www.capecod.com/breakwaters. 18 cottages (weekly rentals only June–Aug.). Pool, beach, baby-sitting. No credit cards. Closed mid-Oct.–Apr.*

$-$$ ▥ **Sea Breeze Inn.** The rooms at this cedar-shingle seaside B&B have antique or canopied beds and are decorated with well-chosen antiques. The nicest of the three detached cottages is the three-bedroom Rose Garden, which has two baths, a TV room, a fireplace, and a washer and dryer. Innkeeper Patricia Gibney's breakfasts, served in the dining room or the gazebo, are worth rising early for. Smoking is not permitted. ⊠ *270 Ocean Ave., at Sea St., 02601,* ☎ *508/771–7213,* FAX *508/862–0663,* WEB *www.seabreezeinn.com. 14 rooms, 3 cottages. AE, D, MC, V. CP.*

Nightlife and the Arts

The **Cape Cod Melody Tent** (⊠ 21 W. Main St., ☎ 508/775–9100, WEB www.melodytent.com) presents pop concerts and comedy shows. The **Prodigal Son** (⊠ 10 Ocean St., ☎ 508/771–1337) hosts live music most nights; the lineup includes acoustic, blues, jazz, rock, and even spoken word performers. **Town band concerts** (⊠ Village Green, Main St., ☎ 508/362–5230 or 800/449–6647) take place at 7:30 PM on Wednesday in July and August.

Outdoor Activities and Sports

Kalmus Park Beach is a wide beach with a section for windsurfers and a sheltered area for children. It has a snack bar, rest rooms, showers, and lifeguards. ⊠ *South end, Ocean St.* ▤ *Memorial Day–Labor Day parking $10.*

Barnstable

❻   *4 mi north of Hyannis, 11 mi east of Sandwich.*

Barnstable is the second-oldest town on the Cape (it was founded in 1639), and you'll get a feeling for its age in Barnstable Village, a lovely area of large old homes dominated by the Barnstable County Superior Courthouse. Barnstable is also known for beautiful Sandy Neck Beach.

Dining and Lodging

$-$$ ✗ **Mill Way Fish and Lobster.** This seafood market/lunch place on Barnstable Harbor has only six outside picnic tables, but the fried clams and fish sandwiches are worth the inevitable wait. Try the fat onion rings or the almost-too-big-for-lunch clambake, which comes with chowder, lobster, steamers, and an ear of corn. Mill Way closes at 7 PM. ⊠ *275 Mill Way,* ☎ *508/362–2760. AE, D, MC, V. Closed Oct.–Mar.*

$$-$$$ ⊡ **Beechwood Inn.** This yellow and pale-green 1853 Queen Anne is
★ trimmed with gingerbread, wrapped by a wide porch with a glider swing, and shaded by beech trees. The parlor is pure mahogany-and-red-velvet Victorian; the guest rooms are decorated with antiques in lighter, earlier Victorian styles. The inn is no-smoking. ⊠ *2839 Main St. (Rte. 6A), 02630,* ☎ *508/362–6618 or 800/609–6618,* ꜰꜰ *508/362–0298,* ⱲⒺⒷ *www.beechwoodinn.com. 6 rooms. Refrigerator, bicycles. AE, D, MC, V. BP.*

$$ ⊡ **Honeysuckle Hill.** The airy, country-style guest rooms in this gray-shingle 1810 Queen Anne–style cottage have lots of white wicker, featherbeds, checked curtains, and pastel-painted floors. But it's the little touches that count here: a fridge stocked with sodas and water bottles, beach chairs with umbrellas (perfect for nearby Sandy Neck Beach), and an always-full cookie jar in the sunny dining room. Smoking is not allowed. ⊠ *591 Rte. 6A, West Barnstable 02668,* ☎ *508/362–8418 or 800/441–8418,* ⱲⒺⒷ *www.honeysucklehill.com. 3 rooms, 1 suite. AE, D, MC, V. BP.*

Outdoor Activities and Sports

Hovering above Barnstable Harbor and the 4,000-acre Great Salt Marsh, **Sandy Neck Beach** stretches 6 mi across a peninsula that ends at Sandy Neck Light. The beach is one of the Cape's most beautiful— dunes, sand, and sea spread east, west, and north. The lighthouse, a few feet from the eroding shoreline at the tip of the neck, has been out of commission since 1952. The main beach at Sandy Neck has lifeguards, a snack bar, rest rooms, and showers. ⊠ *Sandy Neck Rd. off Rte. 6A, West Barnstable.* ⊠ *Parking $10 Memorial Day–Labor Day.* ☉ *Daily 9–9, but staffed only until 5.*

Yarmouth and Yarmouth Port

❼ *4 mi east of Barnstable, 21 mi east of the Sagamore Bridge.*

Yarmouth was settled in 1639 by farmers from the Plymouth Bay Colony. By 1829, when Yarmouth Port was incorporated as a separate village, the Cape had begun a thriving maritime industry. Many impressive sea captains' houses—some now B&Bs and museums—still line the streets, and Yarmouth Port has some real old-time stores.

For a peek into the past, stop at **Hallet's,** a country drugstore preserved as it was in 1889, when the current owner's grandfather Thatcher Hallet opened it. ⊠ *139 Main St. (Rte. 6A), Yarmouth Port,* ☎ *508/362– 3362.* ⊠ *Free.* ☉ *Call for hrs.*

★ ☾ One of Yarmouth Port's most beautiful spots is Bass Hole, which stretches from Homer's Dock Road to the salt marsh. **Bass Hole Boardwalk** extends over a marshy creek. The 2½-mi **Callery-Darling nature trails** meander through salt marshes, vegetated wetlands, and upland woods. Gray's Beach is a little crescent of sand with calm waters. ⊠ *Trail entrance on Center St. near the Gray's Beach parking lot.*

Dining and Lodging

$$-$$$ ✕ **Inaho.** Yuji Watanabe's sushi and sashimi are artistically presented,
★ and his tempura is fluffy and light. The authentic Japanese ambience (there's a traditional garden out back), the attention to detail, and the remarkably high quality of the ingredients may make you forget you're still on old Cape Cod. ⊠ *157 Main St. (Rte. 6A), Yarmouth Port,* ☎ *508/362–5522. MC, V. Closed Mon. No lunch.*

$$–$$$ ✕ **Jack's Outback.** Tough to find, tough to forget, this eccentric little serve-yourself-pretty-much-anything-you-want joint goes by the motto "Good food, lousy service." Solid breakfasts give way to thick burgers and traditional favorites like Yankee pot roast. Jack's has no liquor license, and you can't BYOB. ⊠ *161 Main St. (Rte. 6A), Yarmouth Port,* ☎ *508/362–6690. Reservations not accepted. No credit cards. No dinner.*

$$–$$$ 🏠 **Blueberry Manor.** This quiet, early 19th-century Greek Revival house now serves as a wonderfully sophisticated yet homey B&B. The living room pairs Victorian furnishings and a marble fireplace with modern amenities, including a TV/VCR, a stereo, and a stash of games and books. Upstairs, the guest rooms feel crisp and clean; while the furnishings are traditional, there are no fussy lace treatments or curio shelves. The Lavender Room has a queen-size four-poster bed with a handmade quilt and an antique armoire. The inn is no-smoking. ⊠ *438 Main St. (Rte. 6A), Yarmouth Port 02675,* ☎ *508/362–7620,* ℻ *508/362–0053,* ⟨WEB⟩ *www.blueberrymanor.com. 3 rooms, 1 suite. AE, MC, V. BP.*

$$–$$$ 🏠 **Wedgewood Inn.** Black shutters and fan ornaments on the facade
★ distinguish this handsome white-painted 1812 Greek Revival building, which is on the National Register of Historic Places. Inside, the sophisticated country decor is a mix of fine Colonial antiques, handcrafted cherry pencil-post beds, antique quilts, and maritime paintings. The inn is no smoking. ⊠ *83 Main St. (Rte. 6A), Yarmouth Port 02675,* ☎ *508/362–5157 or 508/362–9178,* ℻ *508/362–5851,* ⟨WEB⟩ *www.wedgewood-inn.com. 4 rooms, 5 suites. AE, MC, V. BP.*

Shopping

Cummaquid Fine Arts (⊠ 4275 Rte. 6A, Cummaquid, ☎ 508/362–2593) has works by Cape Cod and New England artists. **Parnassus Book Service** (⊠ 220 Main St./Rte. 6A, Yarmouth Port, ☎ 508/362–6420), in an 1840 former general store, specializes in Cape Cod, maritime, and antiquarian books. **Peach Tree Designs** (⊠ 173 Main St./Rte. 6A, Yarmouth Port, ☎ 508/362–8317) carries home furnishings and accessories made by local craftspeople.

Dennis

8 *4 mi northeast of Yarmouth, 7 mi west of Brewster.*

Hundreds of sea captains lived in Dennis when fishing, salt making, and shipbuilding were the main industries. The elegant houses they constructed still line the streets. The town has conservation areas, nature trails, and numerous ponds for swimming.

The holdings of the **Cape Museum of Fine Arts** include more than 850 works by Cape-associated artists. The museum hosts film festivals, lectures, and art classes. ⊠ *60 Hope La. (on the grounds of the Cape Playhouse), off Rte. 6A,* ☎ *508/385–4477,* ⟨WEB⟩ *www.cmfa.org.* ⌑ *$5.* ☉ *Late May–mid-Oct., Mon.–Sat. 10–5, Sun. 1–5; late Oct.–mid-May, Tues.–Sat. 10–5, Sun. 1–5.*

Dining and Lodging

$$–$$$ ✕ **Gina's by the Sea.** In a funky old building tucked into a sand dune,
★ the aroma of fine northern Italian cooking blends with a fresh breeze off the bay. Look for lots of fresh pasta and seafood, and if you don't want a long wait, come early or late. ⊠ *134 Taunton Ave.,* ☎ *508/385–3213. Reservations not accepted. AE, MC, V. Closed Dec.–Mar. and Mon.–Wed. Oct.–Nov. No lunch Apr.–June and Sept.–Nov.*

$–$$ 🏠 **Four Chimneys Inn.** This three-story, four-chimney 1881 Queen
★ Anne gem is a relaxing getaway. The rooms, with hand-stenciled trim, are tastefully furnished with cherry four-poster, wicker, antique pine, or oak beds; all have views of either Scargo Lake or of the surround-

ing woods and gardens. ✉ *946 Main St. (Rte. 6A), 02638,* ☎ *508/ 385–6317 or 800/874–5502,* FAX *508/385–6285,* WEB *www.fourchim- neysinn.com. 7 rooms, 1 suite. AE, MC, V. Closed Nov.–mid-Feb. CP.*

$–$$ ☉ **Isaiah Hall B&B Inn.** Lilacs and pink roses trail the white fence out-
★ side this 1857 Greek Revival farmhouse on a residential road on the bay side. Guest rooms are decorated with country antiques, floral-print wallpapers, and homey quilts. In the carriage house, rooms have sten-ciled white walls and knotty pine, and some have small balconies over-looking gardens. Smoking is not permitted. ✉ *152 Whig St., 02638,* ☎ *508/385–9928 or 800/736–0160,* FAX *508/385–5879,* WEB *www.isa-iahhallinn.com. 9 rooms, 1 suite. Picnic area, badminton, croquet. AE, MC, V. Closed mid-Oct.–mid-Apr. CP.*

Nightlife and the Arts

The oldest professional summer theater in the country is the **Cape Play-house** (✉ 820 Main St./Rte. 6A, ☎ 508/385–3911, WEB www.cape-playhouse.com), which produces Broadway-style plays as well as children's shows. The **Reel Art Cinema** (☎ 508/385–4477) at the Cape Museum of Fine Arts shows avant garde, classic, art, and independent films on weekends; call for a schedule.

Outdoor Activities and Sports

BEACHES

Parking at these beaches is $10 per day for nonresidents from Memo-rial Day to Labor Day. Dennis's **Corporation Beach** (✉ Corporation Rd.) on Cape Cod Bay is a beautiful crescent of white sand backed by low dunes; there are lifeguards, showers, rest rooms, and a food stand. On the south shore, one of the best beaches is the long, wide **West Den-nis Beach** (✉ Davis Beach Rd., West Dennis), which has bathhouses, lifeguards, a playground, and food concessions.

Brewster

❾ *7 mi northeast of Dennis, 5 mi west of Orleans.*

Brewster is the perfect place to learn about the natural history of the Cape: the area contains conservation lands, state parks, forests, fresh-water ponds, and marshes. When the tide is low in Cape Cod Bay, you can stroll the beaches and explore tidal pools up to 2 mi from the shore on the Brewster flats.

☾ For nature enthusiasts, a visit to the **Cape Cod Museum of Natural His-tory** is a must. In the museum and on the grounds are a library, nature and marine exhibits, and trails through 80 acres of forest and marsh-land rich in birds and wildlife. The exhibit hall upstairs has a display of aerial photographs documenting the process by which the Chatham sandbar split in two. The museum also offers guided canoe and kayak trips from May through September and several cruises that explore dif-ferent Cape waterways: Nantucket Sound, Pleasant Bay, and Nauset Marsh. ✉ *869 Main St. (Rte. 6A),* ☎ *508/896–3867; 800/479–3867 in MA,* WEB *www.ccmnh.org.* ⬛ *$5.* ☾ *Mon.–Sat. 9:30–4:30, Sun. 11–4:30.*

The **Brewster Store** (✉ 1935 Main St. [Rte. 6A], at Rte. 124, ☎ 508/ 896–3744) is a local landmark. Built in 1852, this typical New England general store provides such essentials as the daily papers, penny candy, and benches out front for conversation.

Dining and Lodging

$$$$ ✕ **Chillingsworth.** This crown jewel of Cape restaurants is extremely
★ formal, terribly pricey, and completely upscale. The classic French menu and wine cellar continue to win award after award. The seven-course table d'hôte menu includes an assortment of appetizers, entrées—

like super-rich risotto, roast lobster, or grilled venison—and "amusements." At dinner, a modest bistro menu is served in the Garden Room, a patiolike area in the front of the restaurant. ⊠ *2449 Main St. (Rte. 6A),* ☎ *508/896–3640,* WEB *www.chillingsworth.com. Reservations essential. AE, DC, MC, V. Closed Mon. mid-June–Thanksgiving; some weekdays Memorial Day–mid-June and mid-Oct.–Thanksgiving; and entirely Thanksgiving–Memorial Day.*

$$$$ ✕ **High Brewster.** The restored Colonial farmhouse of this country inn
  ★   has low ceilings and exposed ceiling beams, and it overlooks a picture-perfect landscape. The five-course prix-fixe regional American menu changes frequently. Longtime dinner highlights include squash soup, grilled duck breast with a black-currant reduction, and apple-rum ice cream. ⊠ *964 Setucket Rd.,* ☎ *508/896–3636 or 800/203–2634. Reservations essential. AE, MC, V. Closed 1st 2 wks in Jan.; call for weekday hrs off-season. No lunch.*

$$–$$$$ ▣ **Captain Freeman Inn.** The opulent details at this splendid 1866 Vic-
  ★   torian include a marble fireplace, herringbone-inlay flooring, ornate Italian ceiling medallions, and 12-ft ceilings. Guest rooms in the no-smoking inn have hardwood floors, antiques, and eyelet spreads. The eight "luxury rooms" truly deserve the name. ⊠ *15 Breakwater Rd., 02631,* ☎ *508/896–7481 or 800/843–4664,* FAX *508/896–5618,* WEB *www.captainfreemaninn.com. 12 rooms. Pool, badminton, croquet, bicycles. AE, MC, V. BP.*

$–$$ ▣ **Old Sea Pines Inn.** Fronted by a white-column portico, the Old Sea Pines evokes the summer estates of an earlier time. A sweeping staircase leads to rooms decorated with framed old photographs and antique furnishings. Rooms in a newer building are sparsely but well decorated. The rooms with shared baths are *very* small but a steal in summer. No smoking is allowed. ⊠ *Box 1070, 2553 Main St. (Rte. 6A), 02631,* ☎ *508/896–6114,* FAX *508/896–7387,* WEB *www.oldseapinesinn.com. 24 rooms, 19 with bath; 3 suites and 2 family-size rooms. Restaurant. AE, D, DC, MC, V. Closed Jan.–Mar. BP.*

$ ⚠ **Nickerson State Park.** Some of the popular sites at this 2,000-acre park are right on the edges of ponds. The facilities include showers, bathrooms, barbecue areas, and a store. ⊠ *3488 Main St. (Rte. 6A), 02631,* ☎ *508/896–3491; 877/422–6762 reservations,* FAX *508/896–3103. 418 sites. No credit cards.*

Outdoor Activities and Sports

BIKING

The **Cape Cod Rail Trail** cuts through Brewster at Long Pond Road, Underpass Road, Millstone Road, and other points.

BOATING

Jack's Boat Rentals (⊠ Nickerson State Park, Flax Pond, Rte. 6A, ☎ 508/896–8556) rents canoes, kayaks, Seacycles, Sunfish, pedal boats, and sailboards.

GOLF

Captain's Golf Course (⊠ 1000 Freeman's Way, ☎ 508/896–5100) is a great 18-hole, par-72 public course with a greens fee ranging from $20 to $45; rental carts are not available. **Ocean Edge Golf Course** (⊠ Villagers Dr. (Rte. 6A), ☎ 508/896–5911), an 18-hole, par-72 course winding around five ponds, has a greens fee that ranges from $25 to $59. Carts, mandatory at certain times, cost $14.

STATE PARK

The 1,961 acres of **Nickerson State Park** (⊠ 3488 Rte. 6A, ☎ 508/896–3491) consist of oak, pitch pine, hemlock, and spruce forest dotted with freshwater kettle ponds formed by glacial action. Recreational opportunities include fishing, boating, biking along 8 mi of trails, cross-country skiing, and bird-watching. **Flax Pond** has picnic areas, a bathhouse, and water-sports rentals.

Shopping

Kemp Pottery (⊠ 258 Main St. [Rte. 6A], ☎ 508/385–5782) has functional and decorative stoneware and porcelain. **Kingsland Manor** (⊠ 440 Main St. (Rte. 6A), ☎ 508/385–9741) sells everything "from tin to Tiffany." The **Spectrum** (⊠ 369 Main St. (Rte. 6A), ☎ 508/385–3322) purveys American arts and crafts including art glass and pottery. **Sydenstricker Galleries** (⊠ 490 Main St. (Rte. 6A), ☎ 508/385–3272) is a working glass studio.

Harwich

⑩ *3 mi south of Brewster.*

Originally known as Setucket, Harwich separated from Brewster in 1694 and was renamed after the famous seaport in England. Like other townships on the Cape, Harwich is actually a cluster of seven small villages, including bustling Harwich Port. Three naturally sheltered harbors on Nantucket Sound make the town, like its English namesake, a popular spot for boaters. Each September Harwich holds a Cranberry Festival to celebrate the importance of this indigenous berry.

Once a private school, the pillared 1844 Greek Revival building of **Brooks Academy** now houses the museum of the **Harwich Historical Society.** In addition to a large photo-history collection and exhibits on artist Charles Cahoon (grandson of Alvin Cahoon, the principal cranberry grower in 1840s Harwich), the socio-technological history of the cranberry culture, and shoemaking, the museum displays antique clothing and textiles, china and glass, fans, toys, and much more. There is also an extensive genealogical collection for researchers. On the grounds is a powder house that was used to store gunpowder during the Revolutionary War, as well as a restored 1872 outhouse. ⊠ *80 Parallel St.,* ☎ *508/432–8089,* WEB *www.capecodhistory.org/harwich.* 🖾 *Donations accepted.* ☼ *June–mid-Oct., Wed.–Sun. 1–4.*

Dining and Lodging

$$–$$$ ✕ **Brax Landing.** In this local stalwart, perched alongside busy Saquatucket Harbor, you'll pass by tanks full of steamers and lobsters in the corridor leading to the dining room. The restaurant sprawls around a big bar that serves drinks like the "Moxie" (pink lemonade and vodka, "calm seas guaranteed"). The swordfish and the Chatham scrod are favorites, both served simply and well. There's a notable children's menu, and Sunday brunch, served from 10 to 2, is an institution. ⊠ *Rte. 28 at Saquatucket Harbor, Harwich Port,* ☎ *508/432–5515. Reservations not accepted. AE, DC, MC, V.*

$$$ 🏠 **Augustus Snow House.** This grand Victorian epitomizes elegance.
★ The stately dining room is the setting for the three-course breakfast, with dishes like baked pears in a raspberry-cream sauce. Guest rooms, which all have fireplaces, are decorated with Victorian-print wallpapers, luxurious carpets, and fine antiques and reproduction furnishings. ⊠ *528 Main St., Harwich Port 02646,* ☎ *508/430–0528 or 800/ 320–0528,* FAX *508/432–6638 ext. 15,* WEB *www.augustussnow.com. 5 rooms, 1 suite. AE, D, MC, V. BP.*

Outdoor Activities and Sports

Cape Water Sports (⊠ 337 Main St., Harwich Port, ☎ 508/432–7079) rents Sunfish, Hobie Cats, Lasers, powerboats, surfbikes, day sailers, and canoes. Fishing trips are operated from spring to fall on the ***Golden Eagle*** (⊠ Wychmere Harbor, Harwich Port, ☎ 508/432–5611). **Cranberry Valley Golf Course** (⊠ 183 Oak St., ☎ 508/430–7560) has a championship 18-hole, par-72 layout. The greens fee is $45; an optional cart costs $20.

Chatham

① *5 mi east of Harwich.*

At the bent elbow of the Cape, Chatham has all the charm of a quiet seaside resort, with relatively little commercialism. And it *is* charming: gray-shingle houses with tidy awnings and cheerful flower gardens, an attractive Main Street with crafts and antiques stores alongside homey coffee shops, and a five-and-ten. It's well-to-do without being ostentatious, casual and fun but refined, and never tacky.

The view from **Chatham Light** (✉ Main St., near Bridge St., ☎ 508/945–5199)—of the harbor, the sandbars, and the ocean beyond—justifies the crowds that gather to share it. The lighthouse is especially dramatic on a foggy night, as the beacon's light pierces the mist. Coin-operated telescopes allow a close look at the famous Chatham Break, the result of a fierce 1987 nor'easter that blasted a channel through a barrier beach just off the coast.

Monomoy National Wildlife Refuge is a 2,500-acre preserve including the Monomoy Islands, a fragile, 9-mi-long barrier-beach area south of Chatham. A paradise for bird-watchers, the islands are an important stop along the North Atlantic flyway for migratory waterfowl and shore birds. The Cape Cod Museum of Natural History and the Massachusetts Audubon Society in South Wellfleet conduct island tours. The **Monomoy National Wildlife Refuge headquarters,** on Morris Island, has a visitor center (✉ off Morris Island Rd., ☎ 508/945–0594), open daily from 8 to 5, where you can pick up pamphlets.

Dining and Lodging

$$$ ✕ **Christian's.** The influences at this landmark town establishment stem from two continents. Downstairs, an Old Cape–country-French motif prevails in the decor and on the menu: boneless roast duck with raspberry sauce and flaky sautéed sole with lobster and lemon-butter sauce are typical entrées. Upstairs is casual and great for families, with a seafood-based menu (with some Mexican influences), and a mahogany-paneled piano bar. ✉ 443 Main St., ☎ 508/945–3362, WEB *www.christiansrestaurant.com. AE, D, DC, MC, V. Closed weekdays Jan.–Mar.*

$$–$$$ ✕ **Vining's Bistro.** Chatham's restaurants tend to serve conservative fare,
★ but the cuisine at this bistro is among the most inventive in the area. The wood grill, where the chef employs zesty spices from all over the globe, is the center of attention. The exotic Bangkok fisherman's stew, the spit-roasted Jamaican chicken, and the Portobello mushroom sandwich are among the best dishes. ✉ 595 Main St., ☎ 508/945–5033, WEB *www.viningsbistro.com. Reservations not accepted. AE, D, MC, V. Closed mid-Jan.–Apr.*

$$$$ 🏨 **Wequassett Inn Resort & Golf Club.** This exquisite traditional resort
★ offers accommodations in 20 Cape-style cottages and an attractive hotel complex along a bay and on 22 acres of woods. Luxurious dining, attentive service, evening entertainment, and plenty of sunning and sporting opportunities are among the draws. Decor is Early American, with country pine furniture and such homey touches as handmade quilts and duck decoys. ✉ 173 Orleans Rd. (Rte. 28), Pleasant Bay 02633, ☎ 508/432–5400 or 800/225–7125, FAX 508/432–5032, WEB *www.wequassett.com. 102 rooms, 2 suites. Restaurant, grill, piano bar, room service, pool, 4 tennis courts, exercise room, windsurfing, boating. AE, D, DC, MC, V. Closed Nov.–Apr. FAP.*

$$$–$$$$ 🏨 **Queen Anne Inn.** Built in 1840 as a wedding present for the daughter of a famous clipper-ship captain, this grand structure has large rooms furnished in a casual yet elegant style. Some have working fireplaces, private balconies, and hot tubs. Lingering and lounging are encouraged—around the large pool, on the veranda, in front of the fireplace in the sitting room, and in the plush parlor. ⊠ *70 Queen Anne Rd., 02633,* ☎ *508/945-0394 or 800/545-4667,* FAX *508/945-4884,* WEB *www.queenanneinn.com. 31 rooms. Restaurant, bar, pool, 3 tennis courts. AE, D, MC, V.*

$$–$$$ 🏨 **Moses Nickerson House.** Each room in this 1839 no-smoking B&B
★ has its own look: one has dark woods, leather, Ralph Lauren fabrics, and English hunting antiques; another has a high canopy bed and a hand-hooked rug. All rooms have queen-size beds and complete modem and computer hookups. ⊠ *364 Old Harbor Rd., 02633,* ☎ *508/945-5859 or 800/628-6972,* FAX *508/945-7087,* WEB *www.capecod-travel.com/mosesnickersonhouse. 7 rooms. In-room data ports. AE, D, MC, V. BP.*

Nightlife and the Arts

Monomoy Theatre (⊠ 776 Main St., ☎ 508/945–1589) presents summer productions by the Ohio University Players. Chatham's summer **town band concerts** (⊠ Kate Gould Park, Main St., ☎ 508/945–5199) begin at 8 PM on Friday and draw up to 6,000 people.

Outdoor Activities and Sports

Harding's Beach, west of Chatham center, is open to the public and charges daily parking fees to nonresidents in season.

Shopping

Cape Cod Cooperage (⊠ 1150 Queen Anne Rd., at Rte. 137, ☎ 508/432–0788) sells traditional woodenware made by an on-site cooper. At **Chatham Glass Co.** (⊠ 758 Main St., ☎ 508/945–5547) you can watch glass being blown and buy it, too. **Fancy's Farm of Chatham** (⊠ 1291 Main St. [Rte. 28], West Chatham, ☎ 508/945–1949) sells everything you need for a beach picnic. **Yellow Umbrella Books** (⊠ 501 Main St. [Rte. 28], ☎ 508/945–0144) has an excellent selection of new and used books.

Orleans

⑫ *8 mi north of Chatham, 35 mi east of the Sagamore Bridge.*

Incorporated in 1797, Orleans is part quiet seaside village and part bustling commercial center. A walk along Rock Harbor Road, a winding street lined with gray-shingled houses, white picket fences, and neat gardens, leads to the bay-side **Rock Harbor,** the base of a small commercial fishing fleet whose catch hits the counters at the fish market here. Sunsets over the harbor are memorable.

Dining and Lodging

$$–$$$ ✕ **Kadee's Lobster & Clam Bar.** A summer landmark, Kadee's serves good clams and fish-and-chips that you can grab on the way to the beach from the take-out window. Or you can sit down in the dining room for steamers and mussels, pasta and seafood stews, or the Portuguese kale soup. There's a miniature golf course out back. Unfortunately, the prices seem to have gone through the roof. ⊠ *212 Main St.,* ☎ *508/255-6184. Reservations not accepted. MC, V. Closed day after Labor Day–week before Memorial Day and weekdays in early June.*

$$–$$$ ✕ **Nauset Beach Club.** What was once the unsung local hero has be-
★ come widely known for its fine dining. You might feel as if you're eating in someone's former living room (you are), though the sophisticated, contemporary Italian cuisine is superior to that of the finest home cooks.

Zuppa di pesce (Italian seafood stew) is one of many menu highlights. ⊠ *222 Main St., East Orleans,* ☎ *508/255–8547. AE, D, DC, MC, V. Reservations not accepted. No lunch. No dinner Sun.–Mon., mid-Oct.–Memorial Day.*

$$ ⭐ 🏠 **Kadee's Gray Elephant.** A mile from Nauset Beach, this 200-year-old house contains small vacation studio and one-bedroom apartments. They are a cheerful riot of color, from wicker painted lavender or green to beds layered in quilts and comforters mixing plaids and florals. The kitchens are equipped with microwaves, attractive glassware, irons and boards—and even lobster crackers. ⊠ *Box 86, 216 Main St., East Orleans 02643,* ☎ *508/255–7608,* 🖷 *508/240–2976. 6–8 apartments. Restaurant, miniature golf. MC, V.*

Nightlife and the Arts

The **Academy Playhouse** (⊠ 120 Main St., ☎ 508/255–1963, 🖳 www.apa1.org) hosts a dozen or so productions year-round, including original works. The **Cape & Islands Chamber Music Festival** (☎ 508/255–9509, 🖳 www.capecodchambermusic.org) presents three weeks of top-caliber performances in August.

Outdoor Activities and Sports

BEACHES

Nauset Beach (⊠ Beach Rd.)—not to be confused with Nauset Light Beach at Cape Cod National Seashore—is a 10-mi-long sweep of sandy ocean beach with low dunes and large waves good for bodysurfing or board surfing. There are lifeguards, rest rooms, showers, and a food concession. Daily parking fees are $8. **Skaket Beach** (⊠ Skaket Beach Rd., ☎ 508/240–3775) on Cape Cod Bay is a sandy stretch with calm, warm water good for children. There are rest rooms, lifeguards, and a snack bar. Daily parking fees are $8.

BOATING AND FISHING

Arey's Pond Boat Yard (⊠ 43 Arey's La., off Rte. 28, South Orleans, ☎ 508/255–0994) has a sailing school where individual and group lessons are taught. **Goose Hummock Shop** (⊠ 15 Rte. 6A, off the U.S. 6 rotary, ☎ 508/255–0455) sells licenses, which are required for fishing in Orleans's freshwater ponds. **Rock Harbor Charter Boat Fleet** (⊠ Rock Harbor, ☎ 508/255–9757; 800/287–1771 in MA) goes for bass and blues in the bay from spring to fall. Walk-ons are welcome.

Shopping

Addison Holmes Gallery (⊠ 43 Rte. 28, ☎ 508/255–6200), housed in four rooms of a brick-red Cape, represents area artists. **Hannah** (⊠ 47 Main St., ☎ 508/255–8234) has unique women's fashions. **Tree's Place** (⊠ Rte. 6A, at Rte. 28, ☎ 508/255–1330) displays the works of New England artists.

Eastham

⑬ *3 mi north of Orleans.*

Like many other Cape towns, Eastham (incorporated in 1651) started as a farming community, later turning to the sea and to salt making for its livelihood. A more atypical industry here was asparagus growing; from the late 1800s through the 1920s, Eastham was known as the "Asparagus Capital."

The park on busy U.S. 6 at Samoset Road has as its centerpiece the **Eastham Windmill,** the oldest windmill on Cape Cod. ⊠ *U.S 6.* ☞ *Free.* ☉ *Late June–Labor Day, Mon.–Sat. 10–5, Sun. 1–5.*

⭐ Along 30 mi of shoreline from Chatham to Provincetown, the 27,000-acre **Cape Cod National Seashore** encompasses superb ocean beaches, rolling dunes, wetlands, pitch pine and scrub oak forest, wildlife, and several historic structures. Self-guided nature, hiking, biking, and horse trails lace these landscapes. **Salt Pond Visitor Center** has a museum and offers guided tours, boat trips, and lectures, as well as evening beach walks and campfire talks in summer. ⊠ *Visitor center, Doane Rd., off U.S. 6,* ☎ *508/255–3421,* WEB *www.nps.gov/caco.* *Free; beach parking $7 per day mid-June–Labor Day or $20 for yearly pass good at all seashore beaches.* ⊙ *Mar.–June and Sept.–Dec., daily 9–4:30; July–Aug., daily 9–5; Jan.–Feb., weekends 9–4:30.*

Roads and bicycle trails lead to Coast Guard and Nauset Light beaches, which begin an unbroken 30-mi stretch of barrier beach extending to Provincetown—the "Cape Cod Beach" of Thoreau's 1865 classic, *Cape Cod.* You can still walk its length, as Thoreau did. Tours of the much-photographed red and white **Nauset Light** (⊠ Ocean View Dr. and Cable Rd., ☎ 508/240–2612) are given on weekends in season.

Lodging

$$$–$$$$ Whalewalk Inn. With windows galore, this 1830 whaling master's home on 3 acres of rolling lawns and gardens has an airy feeling. Wide-board pine floors, fireplaces, and 19th-century country antiques provide historical appeal. The spacious rooms at the no-smoking inn have floral fabrics and antique or reproduction furniture. ⊠ *220 Bridge Rd., 02642,* ☎ *508/255–0617,* FAX *508/240–0017,* WEB *www.whalewalkinn.com. 11 rooms, 5 suites. Bicycles. MC, V. BP.*

$$–$$$ Penny House Inn. Antiques and collectibles decorate the rooms in this rambling, no-smoking inn sheltered by a wave of privet hedge. Common areas include the Great Room, with a fireplace and lots of windows, a combination sunroom-library, and a garden patio set with umbrella tables. ⊠ *4885 County Rd. (U.S. 6), 02642,* ☎ *508/255–6632 or 800/554–1751,* FAX *508/255–4893,* WEB *www.pennyhouseinn.com. 11 rooms. AE, D, MC, V. BP.*

$ Atlantic Oaks Campground. Primarily an RV camp, this campground forest is less than one mi north of the Salt Pond Visitor Center. RV hookups, including cable TV, cost $40 for two people; tent sites are $28 for two people. Showers are free. ⊠ *3700 U.S. 6, 02642,* ☎ *508/255–1437 or 800/332–2267,* WEB *www.atlanticoaks.com. 100 RV sites, 30 tent sites. Bicycles, playground, coin laundry. D, MC, V. Closed Nov.–Apr.*

Outdoor Activities and Sports

Low grass and heathland back the long **Coast Guard Beach** (⊠ Off Ocean View Dr.). It has no parking lot, so park at the Salt Pond Visitor Center or the lot up Doane Road from the center and take the free shuttle or walk the 1¾-mi Nauset Trail to the beach. A great spot for watching sunsets over the bay, **First Encounter Beach** (⊠ Samoset Rd., off U.S. 6) is laden with history. Near the parking lot, a bronze marker commemorates the first encounter between local Indians and passengers from the *Mayflower,* who explored the area for five weeks in late 1620.

Wellfleet

⑭ *10 mi northwest of Eastham, 13 mi southeast of Provincetown.*

Tastefully developed Wellfleet attracts many artists and writers because of its fine restaurants, historic houses, and many art galleries.

★ The **Massachusetts Audubon Wellfleet Bay Sanctuary,** a 1,000-acre haven for more than 250 species of birds, is a superb place for walking, birding, and looking west over the salt marsh and bay at wondrous sunsets. The Audubon Society hosts naturalist-led wildlife tours year-round;

reservations essential. ⊠ *Off U.S. 6, Box 236, South Wellfleet,* ☎ *508/ 349–2615,* WEB *www.wellfleetbay.org.* 🖃 *$3.* ⊙ *Daily 8 AM–dusk.*

A good stroll around town would take in Commercial and Main streets and end at **Uncle Tim's Bridge** (⊠ Off E. Commercial St.). The short walk across this arcing landmark—with its much-photographed view over marshland and a tidal creek—leads to a small wooded island.

For a **scenic loop** through a classic Cape landscape near Wellfleet's Atlantic beaches—with scrub and pines on the left, heathland meeting cliffs and the ocean below on the right—take LeCount Hollow Road north of the Marconi Station turnoff. Access to the first and last of four beaches on this stretch, **LeCount Hollow** and **Newcomb Hollow,** is restricted to residents in season. Between the two hollows are the lovely public Atlantic beaches **White Crest** and **Cahoon Hollow.** Backtrack to Cahoon Hollow Road and turn west for the southernmost entrance to the town of Wellfleet proper, across U.S. 6.

Dining and Lodging

$$$–$$$$ ✕ **Aesop's Tables.** Inside this 1805 captain's house—a worthy choice
   ★   for a special dinner—are five dining rooms; aim for a table on the porch overlooking the town center. This is a great place to sample various preparations of local seafood; the signature dish is an exotic bouillabaisse with mounds of fresh-off-the-boat seafood. "Death by Chocolate" is a popular dessert. On some nights in summer, the tavern hosts jazz musicians. ⊠ *316 Main St.,* ☎ *508/349–6450. AE, DC, MC, V. Closed Columbus Day–Mother's Day. No lunch.*

$$ ✕ **Finely JP's.** The dining room is noisy, but the wonderful Italian-in-
   ★   fluenced fish and pasta dishes are worth it. The appetizers, among them the warm spinach and scallop salad and the blackened beef with charred-pepper relish, are especially good, and the Wellfleet paella draws raves. ⊠ *U.S. 6, South Wellfleet,* ☎ *508/349–7500. Reservations not accepted. D, MC, V. Closed Mon.–Wed. Thanksgiving– Memorial Day; Mon.–Tues. Memorial Day–mid-June and Oct.–Thanksgiving; Tues. Labor Day–Oct.*

$$–$$$ 🏠 **Surf Side Colony Cottages.** These one- to three-bedroom cottages
   ★   on the Atlantic shore of the Outer Cape have fireplaces, kitchens, and screened porches. The exteriors are retro-Florida, but the interiors are tastefully decorated. ⊠ *Box 937, Ocean View Dr., South Wellfleet 02663,* ☎ *508/349–3959,* FAX *508/349–3959,* WEB *www.capecod.net/surfside. 18 cottages. Picnic area, coin laundry. MC, V. 1- to 2-wk minimum in summer. Closed Nov.–Mar..*

$–$$ 🏠 **Holden Inn.** If you're watching your budget and can deal with modest basics, try this old-time place just out of the town center. The lodge has shared baths, an outdoor shower, and a screened-in porch with a view of the bay. Rooms with private baths that have old porcelain sinks are available in adjacent 1840 and 1890 buildings. All rooms are clean and simple. ⊠ *140 Commercial St., 02667,* ☎ *508/349–3450. 25 rooms, 10 with bath. No credit cards. Closed mid-Oct.–mid-Apr.*

Nightlife and the Arts

The **Beachcomber** (⊠ Ocean View Dr., Cahoon Hollow Beach, off U.S. 6, ☎ 508/349–6055) has live music and dancing in summer. The drive-in movie is alive and well at the **Wellfleet Drive-In Theater** (⊠ 51 U.S. 6, Eastham-Wellfleet line, ☎ 508/349–7176 or 508/255–9619). Art galleries host cocktail receptions during the **Wellfleet Gallery Crawl,** on Saturday evenings in July and August. The **Wellfleet Harbor Actors Theater** (⊠ Kendrick St., past E. Commercial St., ☎ 508/349–6835) stages American plays, satires, and farces mid-May–mid-October.

Outdoor Activities and Sports

BEACHES

The spectacular dune-bordered Atlantic **public beaches** White Crest and Cahoon Hollow charge daily parking fees of $10 to nonresidents in season only. Cahoon Hollow has lifeguards, rest rooms, and a restaurant and music club on the sand. **Marconi Beach,** part of Cape Cod National Seashore, charges $7 for daily parking or $20 for a yearly pass that provides access to all seven national seashore beaches. **Mayo Beach,** just west of Wellfleet Harbor, is free.

BOATING

Jack's Boat Rentals (⊠ Gull Pond, ☎ 508/349–7553) rents canoes, kayaks, sailboats, and sailboards.

Shopping

Blue Heron Gallery (⊠ 20 Bank St., ☎ 508/349–6724), one of the Cape's best galleries, carries contemporary works. **Karol Richardson** (⊠ 11 W. Main St., ☎ 508/349–6378) designs women's wear in luxurious fabrics. **Kendall Art Gallery** (⊠ 40 E. Main St., ☎ 508/349–2482) carries contemporary art and has a serene sculpture garden.

Truro

⓯ *2 mi north of Wellfleet, 7 mi southeast of Provincetown.*

☾ Truro, a town of high dunes and rivers fringed by grasses, is a popular retreat for artists, writers, and politicos. Edward Hopper, who summered here from 1930 to 1967, found the Cape light ideal for his austere realism. At **Pamet Harbor,** off Depot Road, you can walk out on the flats at low tide and discover the creatures of the salt marsh.

Lodging

$$ ☷ **Moorlands Inn.** The artful touches at this proud Victorian beauty include the creative works—both visual and musical—of innkeepers Bill and Skipper Evaul. Antiques adorn the bright, uncluttered rooms in the main house, and the spacious penthouse provides a full kitchen, two bedrooms, and plenty of living space. Guests can gather in the communal hot tub out back. ⊠ *11 Hughes Rd., North Truro 02652,* ☎ *508/487–0663. 5 rooms, 1 apartment, 3 cottages. Croquet, outdoor hot tub. MC, V. BP.*

Outdoor Activities and Sports

BEACH

Head of the Meadow Beach (⊠ Off U.S. 6, North Truro), a relatively uncrowded part of the national seashore, has only temporary rest-room facilities available in summer and no showers. The daily parking fee is $7 mid-June–Labor Day or $20 for an annual pass.

BIKING

The **Head of the Meadow Trail** is 2 mi of easy cycling between dunes and salt marshes from the Head of the Meadow Beach parking lot to High Head Road, off Route 6A in North Truro. Bird-watchers love this area.

GOLF

Highland Golf Links (⊠ Lighthouse Rd., North Truro, ☎ 508/487–9201), a nine-hole, par-36 course on a cliff overlooking the Atlantic, has a greens fee of $16; an optional cart costs $13.

Provincetown

★ ⓰ *7 mi northwest of Truro, 27 mi north of Orleans, 62 mi from the Sagamore Bridge.*

Provincetown's shores form a curled fist at the very tip of the Cape. The town was for decades a bustling seaport, with fishing and whaling as its major industries. Fishing is still an important source of income for many Provincetown natives, although the town is a major whale-watching, rather than hunting, mecca.

One of the first of many historically important visitors to anchor in this hospitable natural harbor was Bartholomew Gosnold, who arrived in 1602 and named the area Cape Cod after the abundant codfish he found in the local waters. The Pilgrims arrived on Monday, November 21, 1620, when the *Mayflower* dropped anchor in Provincetown Harbor after a difficult 63-day voyage; while in the harbor they signed the Mayflower Compact, the first document to declare a democratic form of government in America. They stayed in the area for five weeks before moving on to Plymouth. During the American Revolution, Provincetown Harbor was controlled by the British, who used it as a port from which to sail to Boston and launch attacks on Colonial and French vessels.

Provincetown is the nation's oldest continuous arts colony: painters began coming here in 1899 for the unique Cape Cod light. Eugene O'Neill's first plays were written and produced here, and the Fine Arts Work Center continues to have in its ranks some of the most important writers of our time. In the busy downtown, Portuguese-American fishermen mix with painters, poets, writers, whale-watching families, cruise-ship passengers on brief stopovers, and many lesbian and gay residents and visitors, for whom P-town, as it's almost universally known, is one of the most popular East Coast seashore spots.

In summer, Commercial Street, the main thoroughfare, is packed with sightseers and shoppers browsing through the galleries and crafts shops. At night, raucous music and people spill out of bars, drag shows, and sing-along lounges. It's a fun, crazy place, with the extra dimension of the fishing fleet unloading the day's catch at MacMillan Wharf, in the center of the action. On the wharf are a municipal parking facility and the Chamber of Commerce, so it's a sensible place to start a tour of town.

Driving from one end of 3-mi-long Commercial Street to the other could take forever in season—walking is definitely the way to go. Many architectural styles—Victorian, Second Empire, Gothic, and Greek Revival, to name a few—were used to build houses for sea captains and merchants. The Provincetown Historical Society publishes walking-tour pamphlets, available for about $1 at many shops in town. Free Provincetown gallery guides are also available.

The quiet East End of town is mostly residential, with some top galleries. The similarly quiet West End has a number of small inns with neat lawns and elaborate gardens.

The **Pilgrim Monument,** which stretches incongruously into the sky over the small town, commemorates the first landing of the Pilgrims in the New World and their signing of the Mayflower Compact, America's first rules of self-governance. Climb the 252-ft-high tower (116 steps and 60 ramps) for a panoramic view—dunes on one side, harbor on the other, and the entire bay side of Cape Cod beyond. At the base is a museum of Lower Cape and Provincetown history. ⊠ *High Pole Hill,* ☎ *508/487–1310.* ☜ *$5.* ☉ *Apr.–June and Sept.–Nov., daily 9–5; July–Aug., daily 9–7 (last admission 45 mins before closing).*

Founded in 1914 to collect and show the works of Provincetown-associated artists, the **Provincetown Art Association and Museum** (PAAM) houses a 1,650-piece permanent collection. Exhibits here combine the works of up-and-comers with established artists of the 20th century. ⊠ *460 Commercial St.,* ☎ *508/487–1750,* WEB *www.paam.org.* ☞ *$3.* ☼ *Nov.–Apr., weekends noon–4 and by appointment; Memorial Day–Labor Day, daily noon–5 and 8–10; May (until Memorial Day) and Labor Day–Oct., Fri.–Sun. noon–5.*

Near the Provincetown border, **massive dunes** meet the road in places, turning U.S. 6 into a sand-swept highway. Scattered among the dunes are primitive cottages, called dune shacks, built from flotsam and other found materials, that have provided atmospheric as well as cheap lodgings to artists and writers over the years—among them Eugene O'Neill, e. e. cummings, Jack Kerouac, and Norman Mailer.

The **Province Lands,** scattered with ponds, cranberry bogs, and scrub, begin at High Head in Truro and stretch to the tip of Provincetown. Bike and walking trails wind through forests of stunted pines, beech, and oak and across desertlike expanses of rolling dunes—these are the "wilds" of the Cape. A national seashore visitor center is in this area. ⊠ *Visitor center, Race Point Rd.,* ☎ *508/487–1256.* ☼ *Apr.–Nov., daily 9–5.*

Dining and Lodging

$$$$
★ ✕ **Café Edwige.** Delicious contemporary cuisine, friendly service, a homey setting—Café Edwige delivers night after night. Two good starters are the Maine crab cake and the warm goat cheese on crostini; for an entrée try lobster and Wellfleet scallops over pasta with a wild mushroom and tomato broth. Don't pass on the wonderful desserts. ⊠ *333 Commercial St.,* ☎ *508/487–2008. AE, MC, V. Closed Nov.–May.*

$$$$
✕ **Chester.** Elegant and understated, this golden-hued dining room in a Greek Revival sea captain's house has earned notice for its memorable, beautifully presented contemporary fare. The small menu changes regularly and emphasizes local ingredients. Try seasonal choices such as asparagus-and-fiddlehead risotto and lamb with cranberry jus, potatoes, and vegetables. ⊠ *404 Commercial St.,* ☎ *508/487–8200,* WEB *www.chesterrestaurant.com. Reservations essential. AE, MC, V. Closed part of Dec.–Mar; call for Dec. dates.*

$$$$
★ ✕ **Front Street.** Many consider this the best restaurant in town. Well versed in classic Italian cooking, chef-owners Donna Aliperti and Kathleen Cotter also venture into other Mediterranean regions. Duck smoked in Chinese black tea is served with a different lusty sauce every day—one of the best is fresh tropical fruit with mixed peppercorns. The wine list is a winner. Call well ahead for a reservation. ⊠ *230 Commercial St.,* ☎ *508/487–9715,* WEB *www.capecod.net/frontstreet. Reservations essential. AE, D, MC, V. Closed Jan.–mid-May.*

$$–$$$
✕ **Lobster Pot.** Provincetown's Lobster Pot is fit to do battle with all the Lobster Pots anywhere on the Cape. As you enter you'll pass through one of the hardest-working kitchens on the Cape, which consistently turns out fresh New England classics and some of the best chowder around. ⊠ *321 Commercial St.,* ☎ *508/487–0842,* WEB *www.ptownlobsterpot.com . Reservations not accepted. AE, D, DC, MC, V. Closed Jan.*

$$–$$$
★ ✕ **Napi's.** The zesty meals on Napi's internationally inspired menu include many vegetarian choices and Greco-Roman items like delicious shrimp feta (shrimp flambé in ouzo and Metaxa, served with a tomato, garlic, and onion sauce). Both the food and the whimsically tasteful interior share a penchant for unusual, striking juxtapositions. ⊠ *7 Freeman St.,* ☎ *508/487–1145,* WEB *www.provincetown.com/napis. Reservations essential. AE, D, DC, MC, V. No lunch June–mid-Sept.*

$$-$$$ ✕ **Bubala's by the Bay.** Personality abounds at this funky restaurant inside a building painted bright yellow and adorned with campy carved birds. The kitchen serves three meals, with lots of local seafood, and the wine list is priced practically at retail. The bar scene picks up in the evening. ✉ 183 Commercial St., ☎ 508/487–0773, WEB www.capecodaccess.com/bubala's. AE, D, MC, V. Closed Halloween–Mar.

$$-$$ ✕ **Mojo's.** At Provincetown's fast-food institution, the tiniest of kitchens
★   turns out everything from fresh-cut french fries to fried clams, tacos, and tofu burgers. How they crank it out so fast and so good is anybody's guess. ✉ 5 Ryder St. Ext., ☎ 508/487–3140. Reservations not accepted. No credit cards. Closed occasionally mid-Oct.–early May, depending on weather and crowds; call ahead.

$$$-$$$$ 🏨 **Brass Key.** Convenient to Commercial Street's restaurants, shops,
★   and nightlife, this gay-popular complex is fast becoming Provincetown's most luxurious resort. In season, complimentary cocktails are served in the courtyard; in winter, wine is served before a roaring fire in the common room. Rooms have antique furniture and decidedly modern amenities; all have Bose stereos, minirefrigerators, and TV/VCRs. Deluxe rooms have gas fireplaces and whirlpool baths. Smoking is not allowed. ✉ 67 Bradford St., 02657, ☎ 508/487–9005 or 800/842–9858, FAX 508/487–9020, WEB www.brasskey.com. 36 rooms. In-room safes, pool. AE, D, MC, V. CP.

$$-$$$$ 🏨 **Bayshore and Chandler House.** A great option for longer stays, this
★   apartment complex is on the water, ½ mi from the town center. Many of the units have fireplaces, decks, and large water-view windows; all have full kitchens, modern baths, and phones. Rentals are mostly by the week in season. Pets are welcome. ✉ 493 Commercial St., 02657-2413, ☎ 508/487–9133, FAX 508/487–0520, WEB www.provincetown.com/bayshore. 25 apartments. Beach. AE, MC, V.

$$-$$$$ 🏨 **Fairbanks Inn.** This comfortable inn a block from Commercial Street includes a 1776 main house and auxiliary buildings. Many rooms have four-poster or canopy beds, fireplaces, Oriental rugs on wide-board floors, and antique furnishings. The wicker-filled sunporch and the garden are good places to take your afternoon cocktail. ✉ 90 Bradford St., 02657, ☎ 508/487–0386 or 800/324–7265, FAX 508/487–3540, WEB www.fairbanksinn.com. 13 rooms, 1 efficiency. Free parking. AE, MC, V. CP.

$$-$$$ 🏨 **The Masthead.** Hidden away in the quiet west end of Commercial Street, this charming cluster of shingled houses overlooks a lush lawn, a 450-ft-long boardwalk, and a private beach. Spacious rooms, efficiencies, apartments, and cottages are among the lodging options. The cottages, which sleep four to seven, are ideal for families or larger groups and for longer stays. ✉ Box 577, 31–41 Commercial St., 02657, ☎ 508/487–0523 or 800/395–5095, FAX 508/487–9251, WEB www.capecodtravel.com/masthead. 9 rooms, 7 apartments, 3 cottages, 2 efficiencies. Beach, dock. AE, D, DC, MC, V.

Nightlife and the Arts

NIGHTLIFE

During the summer the **Boatslip Beach Club** (✉ 161 Commercial St., ☎ 508/487–1669) holds a mixed gay and lesbian tea dance daily from 3:30 to 6:30 on the outdoor deck. A pianist plays easy-listening tunes on weekends (nightly in season) at **Napi's.** The **Pied Piper** (✉ 193A Commercial St., ☎ 508/487–1527) draws hordes of gay men to its post-tea dance gathering. Later in the evening, the crowd is mostly, though not exclusively, women.

THE ARTS

The **Provincetown Playhouse Mews Series** (✉ Town Hall, 260 Commercial St., ☎ 508/487–0955) presents varied summer concerts. The **Provincetown Repertory Theatre** (☎ 508/487–0600) mounts productions of classic and modern drama in the summer. The **Provincetown Theatre Company** (☎ 508/487–8673) stages classics, modern drama, and new works by local authors year-round.

Outdoor Activities and Sports

BEACHES

Herring Cove Beach, a national seashore beach, is calmer (and a little warmer) than Race Point Beach, though it's not as pretty since the parking lot isn't hidden behind dunes. But the lot to the right of the bathhouse is a great place to watch the sunset, and there's a hot-dog stand. From mid-June through Labor Day, parking costs $7 per day, or $20 for a yearly pass good at all national seashore beaches. **Race Point Beach** (⊠ Race Point Rd.), at the end of U.S. 6, has a remote feeling, with a wide swath of sand stretching around the point. Because it faces north, the beach gets sun all day long.

BIKING

The **Province Lands Trail** is a fairly strenuous 5¼-mi loop off the Beech Forest parking lot on Race Point Road in Provincetown, with spurs to Herring Cove and Race Point beaches and to Bennett Pond.

FISHING

You can go for fluke, bluefish, and striped bass on a walk-on basis from spring to fall with **Cap'n Bill & Cee Jay** (⊠ MacMillan Wharf, ☎ 508/ 487–4330 or 800/675–6723).

GUIDED TOUR

Art's Dune Tours are hour-long narrated van tours through the national seashore and the dunes around Provincetown. ⊠ *Standish and Commercial Sts.,* ☎ *508/487–1950; 800/894–1951 in MA,* WEB *www.artsdunetours.com.* ≊ *$12 daytime, $15 sunset.* ☉ *Tours mid-Apr.–late Oct.; call for schedule.*

WHALE-WATCHING

One of the joys of Cape Cod is spotting whales while they're swimming in and around the feeding grounds at Stellwagen Bank, about 6 mi off the tip of Provincetown. Many people also come aboard for birding, especially during spring and fall migration. Several tour operators take whale-watchers out to sea for three- to four-hour morning, afternoon, or sunset trips.

The naturalist-narrated **Cape Cod Whale Watch** trips leave three times daily from MacMillan Wharf. ⊠ *Ticket office at MacMillan Wharf or 293 Commercial St.,* ☎ *508/487–4079 or 877/487–4079,* WEB *www.capecodwhalewatch.com.* ≊ *$18 (seasonal variations).* ☉ *Tours Apr.–Oct. Call for hours.*

Dolphin Fleet tours are accompanied by scientists from the Center for Coastal Studies in Provincetown who know many of the whales by name and tell you about their habits and histories. Reservations essential. ⊠ *Tickets: MacMillan Wharf, Chamber of Commerce building,* ☎ *508/ 349–1900 or 800/826–9300,* WEB *www.whalewatch.com.* ≊ *$18 (varies with season).* ☉ *Tours Apr.–Oct.*

Shopping

Berta Walker Gallery (⊠ 208 Bradford St., ☎ 508/487–6411) represents Provincetown-affiliated artists working in various media. **Giardelli Antonelli** (⊠ 417 Commercial St., ☎ 508/487–3016) specializes in handmade clothing by local designers. **Remembrances of Things Past** (⊠ 376 Commercial St., ☎ 508/487–9443) deals in articles from the 1920s to the 1960s. **West End Antiques** (⊠ 146 Commercial St., ☎ 508/487– 6723) specializes in variety: $4 postcards, a $3,000 model ship, handmade dolls, and glassware.

Cape Cod A to Z

To research prices, get advice from other travelers, and book travel arrangements, visit www.fodors.com.

AIRPORTS

Barnstable Municipal Airport, the Cape's main air gateway, is served by Cape Air/Nantucket Airlines, and US Airways Express. Provincetown Municipal Airport has Boston service through Cape Air.

➤ AIRPORT INFORMATION: **Barnstable Municipal Airport** (⊠ 480 Barnstable Rd., Hyannis, ☎ 508/775–2020). **Provincetown Municipal Airport** (⊠ Race Point Rd., ☎ 508/487–0241).

BIKE [& MOPED] TRAVEL

The Cape's premier bike path, the Cape Cod Rail Trail, follows the paved right-of-way of the old Penn Central Railroad. About 25 mi long, the easy-to-moderate trail passes salt marshes, cranberry bogs, ponds, and Nickerson State Park. The trail starts at the parking lot off Route 134 south of U.S. 6, near Theophilus Smith Road in South Dennis, and it ends at the post office in South Wellfleet. If you want to cover only a segment, there are parking lots in Harwich (across from Pleasant Lake Store on Pleasant Lake Avenue) and in Brewster (at Nickerson State Park). For bike and trailer rentals, try Bert & Carol's Lawnmower & Bicycle Shop; the Little Capistrano Bike Shop; the Rail Trail Bike Shop.

➤ BIKE RENTALS: **Bert & Carol's Lawnmower & Bicycle Shop** (⊠ 347 Orleans Rd., North Chatham, ☎ 508/945–0137); **Little Capistrano Bike Shop** (⊠ Salt Pond Rd. across from the Salt Pond Visitor Center, Eastham, ☎ 508/255–6515); **Rail Trail Bike Shop** (⊠ 302 Underpass Rd., Brewster, ☎ 508/896–8200).

BOAT & FERRY TRAVEL

Bay State Cruise Company makes the three-hour trip between Commonwealth Pier in Boston and MacMillan Wharf in Provincetown Friday, Saturday, and Sunday from Memorial Day to Labor Day. The company also runs a two-hour express boat from Boston to Provincetown's Fisherman's Wharf daily from Memorial Day to Columbus Day. *3-hr boat $18 one-way, $5 bicycles; same-day round-trip $30, $10 bicycles. 2-hr express boat $28 one-way, $5 bicycles; same-day round-trip $49, $10 bicycles.*

➤ BOAT & FERRY INFORMATION: **Bay State Cruise Company** ☎ (617/ 748–1428 in Boston; 508/487–9284 in Provincetown), WEB www.baystatecruisecompany.com.

BUS TRAVEL

Bonanza Bus Lines operates direct service to Bourne, Falmouth, and Woods Hole from Boston and Providence. Plymouth & Brockton Street Railway provides bus service to Provincetown from Boston and Logan Airport, with stops in several Cape towns en route.

The Cape Cod Regional Transit Authority operates its SeaLine service along Route 28 daily except Sunday between Hyannis and Woods Hole and connects in Hyannis with the Plymouth & Brockton line. The driver will stop when signaled along the route. The "b-bus" is a fleet of minivans that transport passengers daily door-to-door anywhere on the Cape. Make reservations, which are essential, no later than 11 AM on the day before you want to depart. The H2O Line operates scheduled service several times daily, year-round, between Hyannis and Orleans along Route 28.

➤ BUS INFORMATION: **Bonanza Bus Lines** (☎ 508/548–7588 or 800/ 556–3815, WEB www.bonanzabus.com). **Plymouth & Brockton Street Railway** (☎ 508/771–6191 or 508/746–0378, WEB www.p-b.com).

The **Cape Cod Regional Transit Authority** (☎ 508/385–8326 or 800/352–7155 in MA, WEB www.capecodtransit.org).

CAR RENTAL

Budget rents cars at the Barnstable and Provincetown airports.

➤ MAJOR AGENCIES: **Budget** (☎ 508/771–2744 or 800/527–0700).

CAR TRAVEL

From Boston (60 mi), take Route I–93 south to Route 3 south, across the Sagamore Bridge, which becomes U.S. 6, the Cape's main artery. From western Massachusetts, northern Connecticut, and northeastern New York State, take I–84 east to the Massachusetts Turnpike (I–90 east) and take I–495 south and east to the Bourne Bridge. From New York City, and all other points south and west, take I–95 north toward Providence, where you'll pick up I–195 east (toward Fall River/New Bedford) to Route 25 east to the Bourne Bridge.

From the Bourne Bridge, you can take Route 28 south to Falmouth and Woods Hole (about 15 mi), or go around the rotary, following the signs to U.S. 6; this will take you to the Lower Cape and central towns more quickly. On summer weekends, avoid arriving in the late afternoon. U.S. 6, Route 6A, and Route 28 are heavily congested eastbound on Friday evening, westbound on Sunday afternoon, and in both directions on summer Saturdays. When approaching one of the Cape's numerous rotaries (traffic circles), keep in mind that vehicles already in the rotary have the right of way.

EMERGENCIES

➤ HOSPITALS: **Cape Cod Hospital** (✉ 27 Park St., Hyannis, ☎ 508/771–1800). **Falmouth Hospital** (✉ 100 Ter Heun Dr., Falmouth, ☎ 508/548–5300).

➤ LATE-NIGHT PHARMACIES: **CVS** (✉ 64 Davis Straits, Falmouth, ☎ 508/540–4307, WEB www.cvs.com); 176–182 North St., Hyannis, ☎ 508/775–8346.

LODGING

APARTMENT & VILLA RENTALS

Commonwealth Associates can assist in finding rentals in the Harwiches. Donahue Real Estate lists apartments and houses in the Falmouth area. Roslyn Garfield Associates lists rentals for Wellfleet, Truro, and Provincetown.

➤ LOCAL AGENTS: **Commonwealth Associates** (✉ 551 Main St., Harwich Port 02646, ☎ 508/432–2618, WEB www.commonwealthrealestate.com). **Donahue Real Estate** (✉ 850 Main St., Falmouth 02540, ☎ 508/548–5412, WEB www.falmouthhomes.com). **Roslyn Garfield Associates** (✉ 115 Bradford St., Provincetown 02657, ☎ 508/487–1308).

B&BS

➤ RESERVATION SERVICES: **Bed and Breakfast Cape Cod** (✉ Box 1312, Orleans 02653, ☎ 508/255–3824 or 800/541–6226, FAX 508/240–0599, WEB www.bedandbreakfastcapecod.com).

CAMPING

The Cape Cod Chamber of Commerce (☞ Visitor Information) maintains a list of private campgrounds.

OUTDOORS & SPORTS

BASEBALL

The Cape Cod Baseball League, considered the country's best summer collegiate league, is scouted by all the major-league teams. Ten teams play a 44-game season from mid-June to mid-August; games held at all 10 fields are free.

➤ CONTACTS: The **Cape Cod Baseball League** (☎ 508/432–6909, WEB www.capecodbaseball.org).

FISHING

The Cape Cod Chamber of Commerce's *Sportsman's Guide* describes fishing regulations and surf-fishing access locations and contains a map of boat-launching facilities. The Division of Fisheries and Wildlife has a book of maps of Cape ponds. Freshwater fishing licenses are available for a nominal fee at bait and tackle shops. The Cape Cod Canal is a good place to fish; the Army Corps of Engineers operates a canal fishing hot line.

➤ CONTACTS: **Army Corps of Engineers canal fishing hot line** (☎ 508/759–5991).

TAXIS

➤ CONTACTS: **All Village Taxi** (Falmouth, ☎ 508/540–7200). **Cape Cab** (Provincetown, ☎ 508/487–2222). **Eldredge Taxi** (Chatham, ☎ 508/945–0068). **Hyannis Taxi** (☎ 508/775–0400 or 800/773–0600).

TOURS

The Cape Cod Central Railroad offers two-hour, 42-mi scenic rail tours from Hyannis to the Cape Cod Canal and back. ✉ *Memorial Day–Oct., Tues.–Sun.; Mar.–May, Christmas, and New Year's, off-season, call for schedule.*

➤ TOUR-OPERATOR RECOMMENDATIONS: **Cape Cod Central Railroad** ✉ Hyannis Train Depot, 252 Main St., Hyannis, ☎ 508/771–3800 or 888/797–7245, WEB www.capetrain.com.

VISITOR INFORMATION

➤ TOURIST INFORMATION: **Army Corps of Engineers 24-hour recreation hot line** (☎ 508/759–5991). **Cape Cod Chamber of Commerce** (✉ U.S. 6 and Rte. 132, Hyannis, ☎ 508/862–0700 or 888/332–2732, WEB www.capecodchamber.org). **Tide, marine, and weather forecast hot line** (☎ 508/771–5522).

MARTHA'S VINEYARD

Updated by
Carolyn Heller

Far less developed than Cape Cod yet more cosmopolitan than Nantucket, Martha's Vineyard is an island with a double life. From Memorial Day through Labor Day the quieter, some might say real, Vineyard quickens into a vibrant, star-studded frenzy. The busy main port, Vineyard Haven, welcomes day-trippers fresh off a ferry or private yacht. Oak Bluffs, where pizza and ice cream emporiums reign supreme, has the air of a boardwalk. Edgartown is flooded with seekers of chic who wander tiny streets that hold boutiques, stately whaling captains' homes, and charming inns. Summer regulars include a host of celebrities, among them William Styron, Walter Cronkite, and Sharon Stone. If you're planning to stay overnight on a summer weekend, be sure to make reservations well in advance; spring is not too early. Things begin to slow down in mid-September, though, and in many ways the Vineyard's off-season persona is even more appealing than its summer self. There's more time to linger over pastoral and ocean vistas, free from the throngs of cars, bicycles, and mopeds.

The island is roughly triangular, with maximum distances of about 20 mi east to west and 10 mi north to south. The Down-Island end comprises Vineyard Haven, Oak Bluffs, and Edgartown, the most popular and most populated towns; ferry docks, shops, and centuries-old houses and churches line the main streets. Up-Island, the west end of the Vineyard, is more rural. In Chilmark, West Tisbury, and Aquinnah (formerly called Gay Head), country roads meander through woods and tranquil farmland.

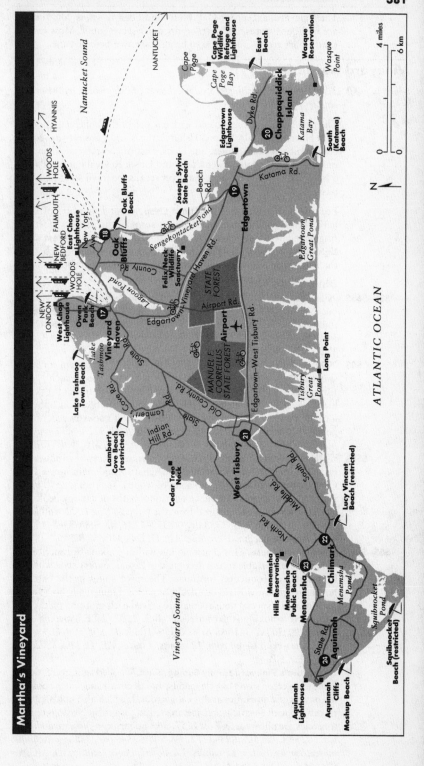

Martha's Vineyard

ATLANTIC OCEAN

Vineyard Sound

Nantucket Sound

NANTUCKET

HYANNIS

WOODS HOLE

FALMOUTH

NEW YORK

NEW BEDFORD

WOODS HOLE

NEW LONDON

4 miles

6 km

N

Cape Poge Wildlife Refuge and Lighthouse

Cape Poge

Cape Poge Bay

East Beach

Wasque Reservation

Wasque Point

Edgartown Lighthouse

Chappaquiddick Island

Katama Bay

South (Katama) Beach

20

Joseph Sylvia State Beach

Beach Rd.

Katama Rd.

19

Edgartown

Oak Bluffs Beach

Sengekontacker Pond

Felix Neck Wildlife Sanctuary

Edgartown Great Pond

East Chop Lighthouse

18

Oak Bluffs

County Rd.

STATE FOREST

Airport Rd.

Edgartown–Vineyard Haven Rd.

Edgartown–West Tisbury Rd.

West Chop Lighthouse

Owen Park Beach

17

Vineyard Haven

Lagoon Pond

Lake Tashmoo

MANUEL F. CORRELLUS STATE FOREST

Airport

Long Point

Tisbury Great Pond

Lake Tashmoo Town Beach

State Rd.

Lambert's Cove Rd.

Indian Hill Rd.

Lambert's Cove Beach (restricted)

Cedar Tree Neck

State Rd.

Old County Rd.

21

West Tisbury

North Rd.

Middle Rd.

South Rd.

Lucy Vincent Beach (restricted)

22

Chilmark

Menemsha Pond

Menemsha Hills Reservation

Menemsha Public Beach

23

Menemsha

State Rd.

24

Aquinnah

Squibnocket Pond

Squibnocket Beach (restricted)

Aquinnah Lighthouse

Aquinnah Cliffs

Moshup Beach

Dyke Rd.

The Vineyard, except for Oak Bluffs and Edgartown, is "dry": there are no liquor stores, and restaurants don't serve liquor. Most restaurants in dry towns allow you to bring your own beer or wine.

Vineyard Haven (Tisbury)

🔞 *3½ mi west of Oak Bluffs, 8 mi northwest of Edgartown by the inland route.*

The past and the present blend with a touch of the bohemian in Vineyard Haven (officially named Tisbury), the island's busiest year-round community. **William Street,** one block west of commercial Main, is a quiet stretch of white picket fences and Greek Revival houses. Part of a National Historic District, the street recalls the town's 19th-century past.

Beautiful and green, exclusive **West Chop,** about 2 mi north of Vineyard Haven along Main Street, claims some of the island's most distinguished residents. The 52-ft white-and-black brick **West Chop Lighthouse** (⊠ W. Chop Rd.) was built in 1838. On the point beyond the lighthouse is a landscaped scenic overlook with benches.

Dining and Lodging

$$$–$$$$ ✕ **Le Grenier.** Calling a restaurant French in a dry town is a stretch, but the cuisine here is authentic and expert. For frogs' legs, sweetbreads, tournedos, and calves' brains, Le Grenier is the clear choice. ⊠ *Upper Main St.,* ☎ *508/693–4906,* ⅦⅢ *www.tiac.net/users/lgrenier. AE, MC, V. BYOB. No lunch.*

$$$ ✕ **Black Dog Tavern.** This island landmark (widely known for its T-shirts and other merchandise) serves all the usual suspects, such as codfish and pasta. The food—if that still matters—is just fine at breakfast, lunch, or dinner. Waiting for a table is something of a tradition, although locals have generally adopted Yogi Berra's line: it's so crowded, no one goes there anymore. ⊠ *Beach St. Ext.,* ☎ *508/693–9223,* ⅦⅢ *www.the-blackdog.com. Reservations not accepted. AE, D, MC, V. BYOB.*

$$$$ 🏨 **Thorncroft Inn.** Fine Colonial and Renaissance Revival antiques and ★ tasteful reproductions adorn the somewhat formal main inn, a 1918 Craftsman bungalow set on 3½ acres of woods. Ten rooms have working fireplaces; some rooms have whirlpool baths or canopy beds. The no-smoking inn is about a mile from the ferry. ⊠ *Box 1022, 460 Main St., 02568,* ☎ *508/693–3333 or 800/332–1236,* ℻ *508/693–5419,* ⅦⅢ *www.thorncroft.com. 14 rooms. AE, D, DC, MC, V. BP.*

$$$–$$$$ 🏨 **Hanover House.** This charming inn within walking distance of the ferry has comfortable rooms decorated in casual country style with antiques and reproduction furniture. The three suites in the carriage house are roomy, with private decks or patios. Homemade breads and muffins and a special house cereal are served each morning on the sun porch. No smoking is permitted. ⊠ *Box 2107, 28 Edgartown Rd., 02568,* ☎ *508/693–1066 or 800/339–1066,* ℻ *508/696–6099,* ⅦⅢ *www.hanoverhouseinn.com. 12 rooms, 3 suites. AE, D, MC, V. Closed Dec.–Mar. CP.*

$ ⛺ **Martha's Vineyard Family Campground.** Wooded sites, recreational facilities, a camp store, bicycle rentals, and electrical and water hookups are among the amenities at this campground, which also holds 12 rustic cabins (with electricity, refrigerators, and gas grills). No dogs or motorcycles are allowed. ⊠ *Box 1557, 569 Edgartown–Vineyard Haven Rd., 02568,* ☎ *508/693–3772,* ℻ *508/693–5767,* ⅦⅢ *www.camp-mvfc.com. 180 sites, 12 cabins. Picnic area, coin laundry. D, MC, V. Closed mid-Oct.–mid-May.*

Nightlife and the Arts

Town band concerts (☎ 508/693–0085) take place every other Sunday in summer at 8 PM at Owen Park off Main Street. The **Vineyard Playhouse** (✉ 24 Church St., ☎ 508/693–6450 or 508/696–6300, WEB www.vineyardplayhouse.org) presents community theater and Equity productions, including summer programs at a natural amphitheater.

Outdoor Activities and Sports

Lake Tashmoo Town Beach, at the end of Herring Creek Road, has swimming in a warm, relatively shallow lake or in the cooler Vineyard Sound. There is parking, and lifeguards are on duty. **Owen Park Beach,** a small harbor beach off Main Street, has a children's play area and lifeguards. **Public tennis courts** are on Church Street; they're open in season only, and a fee is charged (reserve with the attendant the previous day). **Martha's Vineyard Strictly Bikes** (✉ 24 Union St., ☎ 508/693–0782) rents bicycles. **Wind's Up!** (✉ 199 Beach Rd., ☎ 508/693–4252 or 508/693–4340) rents catamarans, surfboards, sea kayaks, canoes, Sunfish, and windsurfers.

Shopping

Bramhall & Dunn (✉ 19 Main St., ☎ 508/693–6437) carries crafts, linens, hand-knit sweaters, and fine antique country-pine furniture. **Bunch of Grapes Bookstore** (✉ 44 Main St., ☎ 508/693–2291, WEB www.bunchofgrapes.com) sells new books and sponsors book signings. **C. B. Stark Jewelers** (✉ 53A Main St., ☎ 508/693–2284, WEB www.cbstark.com) creates one-of-a-kind pieces, including island charms. **Paper Tiger** (✉ 29 Main St., ☎ 508/693–8970) stocks handmade paper and gift items, plus works by local artists.

Oak Bluffs

⓲ *3½ mi east of Vineyard Haven, 22 mi northeast of Aquinnah.*

Circuit Avenue is the bustling center of the Oak Bluffs action, with most of the town's shops, bars, and restaurants. Colorful gingerbread-trimmed guest houses and food and souvenir joints enliven Oak Bluffs Harbor, once the setting for several grand hotels (the 1879 Wesley Hotel on Lake Avenue is the last of them). This small town is more high-spirited than haute, more fun than refined.

On the way from Vineyard Haven to Oak Bluffs, **East Chop Lighthouse** stands atop a bluff with views of Nantucket Sound. The 40-ft tower was built of cast iron in 1876. ✉ *E. Chop Dr., off Highland Dr.* ☞ *$2.* ☉ *Late June–late Sept., hr before sunset–hr after sunset.*

The **Flying Horses Carousel,** a National Historic Landmark, is the nation's oldest continuously operating carousel. The carousel was handcrafted in 1876—the horses have real horse hair and glass eyes. ✉ *Oak Bluffs Ave.,* ☎ *508/693–9481,* WEB *www.vineyard.net/org/mvpt/carousel.html.* ☞ *Rides $1; $8 for a book of 10.* ☉ *Easter–Memorial Day, weekends 10–5; Memorial Day–Labor Day, daily 10–10; Labor Day–Columbus Day, weekdays 11–4:30, weekends 10–5.*

★ The **Oak Bluffs Camp Ground,** a 34-acre warren of streets off Circuit Avenue, contains more than 300 Carpenter Gothic Victorian cottages gaily painted in pastels and with wedding-cake trim. Methodist summer camp meetings have been held here since 1835. Each year on Illumination Night, the end of the season is celebrated with lights, song, and open houses. Because of the overwhelming crowds of onlookers, the date is not announced until the week before the event.

Dining and Lodging

$$$$ ✕ **Lola's.** Open 364 days a year (closed only on Christmas), this boisterous spot draws a party crowd, with live music several nights a
week. Ribs and Louisiana standards such as jambalaya fill its menu,
and Sunday mornings offer an all-you-can-eat buffet. The bar is big
and welcoming. ⊠ *Beach Rd., just over 1 mi from Oak Bluffs, ☎ 508/
693–5007. D, MC, V.*

$$$$ ✕ **Tsunami.** In a quaint gingerbread house overlooking the harbor, this
restaurant features an Asian-influenced menu (a rarity for the island),
focusing on Thai flavors but ranging to Japan, China, Burma, and In-
donesia. All the spring-roll appetizers (vegetable, mango and crab, tuna
and avocado) are delicate and subtle, while entrees may include tender smoked lemongrass duck or grilled tuna with shiitake mushrooms
in a fig soy glaze. ⊠ *6 Circuit Ave., ☎ 508/696–8900. AE, MC, V.
Closed Columbus Day–mid-May.*

$$$–$$$$ ✕ **Sweet Life Café.** An island favorite, this café has a interior that's so
★   subdued you may feel like you've entered someone's home, but the cook-
ing is more sophisticated than home-style. Cod may be served Basque
style, with chorizo, peppers, onion, and local clams, while the halibut
may be paired with eggplant puree and curried onion rings. Desserts
remain superb. ⊠ *63 Upper Circuit Ave., ☎ 508/696–0200. Reser-
vations essential. AE, D, MC, V. Closed Jan.–Mar.*

$$$–$$$$ ✕ **Smoke 'n Bones.** This is the island's only rib joint, with a smoker
out back and hickory, apple, oak, and mesquite wood stacked around
the lot. The place has a cookie-cutter, prefab feeling, but it's fun, with
details kids can really enjoy, like a hole in each tabletop for a bucket
to hold discarded ribs. As the menu says, "Bone appetit." ⊠ *Siloam
Rd., about 7 blocks from Oak Bluffs, ☎ 508/696–7427. Reservations
not accepted. No credit cards. Closed Nov.–Apr.*

$$$ 🏠 **Oak House.** The wraparound veranda of this pastel-painted 1872
★   Victorian looks across a busy street to the beach. The well-preserved
wood of the inn's name provides a solid backdrop (in ceilings and wainscoting) for the choice antique furniture and nautical-theme accessories.
An elegant afternoon tea with cakes and cookies is served in a glassed-
in sunporch. The inn is no-smoking. ⊠ *Box 299, 75 Sea View Ave.,
02557, ☎ 508/693–4187 or 800/245–5979,* FAX *508/696–7385,* WEB
*www.vineyard.net/biz/inns/oakhouse. 8 rooms, 2 suites. AE, D, MC,
V. Closed mid-Oct.–mid-May. CP.*

$$–$$$ 🏠 **Admiral Benbow Inn.** The Benbow, on a busy road between Vine-
yard Haven and Oak Bluffs Harbor, is endearing. This small turn-of-
the-century B&B is decked out with elaborate woodwork, a comfortable
hodgepodge of antique furnishings, and a parlor with a stunning tile-
and-carved-wood fireplace. Next door to the rather drab yard is a gas
station, but the price is right, and the location a few blocks from the
harbor is convenient. The inn is no-smoking. ⊠ *Box 2488, 81 New
York Ave., 02557, ☎ 508/693–6825,* FAX *508/693–1131. 6 rooms.
AE, D, MC, V. CP.*

$$–$$$ 🏠 **Sea Spray Inn.** This porch-wrapped Victorian overlooks expansive
Waban Park, with views of the ocean beyond; public tennis and the
beach are within walking distance. The rooms are outfitted with king-
size, four-poster beds and other personal touches. One room has a cedar-
lined bath with an extra-large shower; a garden-side room opens to a
private enclosed porch. Smoking is not permitted. ⊠ *Box 2355, 2
Naumkeag Ave., 02557, ☎ 508/693–9388,* FAX *508/696–7765. 5 rooms,
3 with bath, 2 suites. MC, V. Closed Dec.–Apr. CP.*

Nightlife and the Arts

Atlantic Connection (⊠ 124 Circuit Ave., ☎ 508/693–7129) hosts reggae, R&B, funk, and blues performers and has a strobe-lit dance floor.

Offshore Ale (✉ Kennebec Ave., ☎ 508/693–2626), the island's only brewpub, has live entertainment (usually jazz) year-round. **Town band concerts** take place every other Sunday in summer at 8 PM at the gazebo in Ocean Park on Beach Road.

Outdoor Activities and Sports

BEACH

Joseph A. Sylvia State Beach (✉ Off Beach Rd.), between Oak Bluffs and Edgartown, is a 2-mi-long beach with calm water and a view of Cape Cod. Vendors sell food here, and there's parking along the roadside.

BIKING

DeBettencourt's (✉ Circuit Ave. Ext., ☎ 508/693–0011) rents bikes, mopeds, scooters, and four-wheel-drive vehicles.

BOATING AND FISHING

Dick's Bait and Tackle (✉ New York Ave., ☎ 508/693–7669) rents gear, sells bait, and has a current list of fishing regulations. The party boat **Skipper** (☎ 508/693–1238) leaves for deep-sea fishing trips out of Oak Bluffs Harbor in summer. **Vineyard Boat Rentals** (✉ Dockside Marketplace, Oak Bluffs Harbor, ☎ 508/693–8476) rents Boston Whalers, wave runners, and kayaks.

GOLF

Farm Neck Golf Club (✉ County Rd., ☎ 508/693–3057), a semiprivate club, has 18 holes in a par-72 championship layout. Reservations are required at least 48 hours in advance.

TENNIS

Niantic Park (☎ 508/693–6535) has courts that cost a small fee to use.

Shopping

Book Den East (✉ New York Ave., ☎ 508/693–3946) stocks 20,000 out-of-print, antiquarian, and paperback books. **Laughing Bear** (✉ 138 Circuit Ave., ☎ 508/693–9342) carries women's wear made of Balinese or Indian batiks plus jewelry and accessories from around the world.

Edgartown and Chappaquiddick Island

6 mi southeast of Oak Bluffs, 9 mi southeast of Vineyard Haven via Beach Rd., 8½ mi east of West Tisbury.

⑲ Once a well-to-do whaling town, **Edgartown** remains the Vineyard's toniest town and has preserved some of its elegant past. Sea captains' houses from the 18th and 19th centuries, ensconced in well-manicured gardens and lawns, line the streets, including the architecturally pristine upper section of North Water Street. The many shops here attract see-and-be-seen crowds. The **Old Whaling Church** (✉ 89 Main St., ☎ 508/627–8619 for tour), built in 1843 as a Methodist church and now a performing-arts center, has a six-column portico, unusual triple-sash windows, and a 92-ft clock tower. The stylish 1840 **Dr. Daniel Fisher House** (✉ 99 Main St.) has a wraparound roof walk, a small front portico with fluted Corinthian columns, and a side portico with thin fluted columns.

The Martha's Vineyard Historical Society administers a complex of buildings and lawn exhibits that constitute the **Vineyard Museum and Oral History Center.** The Francis Foster Museum houses the Gale Huntington Reference Library and 19th-century miniature photographs of 110 Edgartown whaling masters. The Capt. Francis Pease House, an 1850s Greek Revival structure, exhibits Native American, prehistoric, pre-Columbian, and more recent artifacts. ✉ *School St.,* ☎ *508/627–*

4441, WEB *www.vineyard.net/org/mvhs.* 🖃 *$6.* ⊙ *Mid-June–mid-Oct.,*
Tues.–Sat. 10–5; mid-Oct.–mid-June, Wed.–Fri. 1–4, Sat. 10–4.

★ ✆ The 350-acre **Felix Neck Wildlife Sanctuary,** a Massachusetts Audubon
Society preserve 3 mi out of Edgartown toward Oak Bluffs and Vineyard Haven, has 6 mi of hiking trails traversing marshland, fields, woods,
seashore, and waterfowl and reptile ponds. Naturalist-led events include sunset hikes, stargazing, snake or bird walks, and canoeing. 🖃
Off Edgartown–Vineyard Haven Rd., ☎ *508/627–4850,* WEB *www.mas-*
saudubon.org. 🖃 *$3.* ⊙ *Center June–Sept., daily 8–4; Oct.–May,*
Tues.–Sun. 9–4. Trails daily sunrise–7 PM.

⑳ **Chappaquiddick Island,** a sparsely populated area with many nature
preserves, makes for a pleasant day trip or bike ride on a sunny day.
The island is actually connected to the Vineyard by a long sand spit
that begins in South Beach in Katama. It's a spectacular 2¾-mi walk,
or you can take the On Time ferry, which departs about every five minutes from 7 AM to midnight in season.

★ The 200-acre **Wasque Reservation** (pronounced "*wayce*-kwee") connects Chappaquiddick Island with the Vineyard and forms Katama Bay.
Wasque Beach is accessed by a flat boardwalk with benches overlooking the west end of Swan Pond. Beyond that are beach, sky, and
boat-dotted sea. From the picnic grove, a long boardwalk leads down
amid the grasses to **Wasque Point.** There's plenty of wide beach here
to sun on, but swimming is dangerous because of strong currents.
East end of Wasque Rd., 5 mi from Chappaquiddick ferry landing, ☎
508/627–7260. 🖃 *$3 cars, plus $3 per adult, Memorial Day–mid-Sept.;*
free rest of yr. ⊙ *Property 24 hrs; gatehouse Memorial Day–Colum-*
bus Day, daily 9–5.

At the end of Dyke Road is the **Dyke's Bridge,** infamous as the scene
of the 1969 accident in which a young woman died in a car driven by
Senator Edward M. Kennedy. The **Cape Poge Wildlife Refuge,** across
Dyke's Bridge, is more than 6 mi of wilderness—dunes, woods, cedar
thickets, moors, salt marshes, ponds, tidal flats, and barrier beach. The
best way to get to the refuge is as part of a naturalist-led Jeep drive
(☎ 508/627–3599). Permits for four-wheel-drive vehicles (the cost
ranges from $90 to $110) are available on-site or through Coop's Bait
and Tackle. 🖃 *East end of Dyke Rd., 3 mi from the Chappaquiddick*
ferry landing.

Dining and Lodging

$$$$ ✕ **L'étoile.** Both the stunning setting—a glass-enclosed dining room in
★ the Charlotte Inn—and the classic yet creative French food have preserved L'étoile's reputation as perhaps the Vineyard's finest restaurant.
Not to be missed are a terrine of grilled vegetable appetizer, roasted
ivory king salmon with a horseradish and scallion crust, and Black Angus
sirloin with zinfandel and oyster sauce. The Californian and European
wines are well selected, if a little pricey. 🖃 *27 S. Summer St.,* ☎ *508/*
627–5187. Reservations essential. AE, MC, V. Closed Jan.–mid-Feb.
and weekdays Oct.–Dec. and late Feb.–Apr. No lunch.

$$$$ ✕ **Savoir Fare.** Drawing everyone from Walter Cronkite to Bill Clin-
★ ton, Savoir Fare has carved out a reputation as the Vineyard's celebrity
favorite. They come for the food. The fish and meat are top quality;
try "Summer on a Plate"—roasted striped bass with peach and tomato
jelly, grilled Vidalia onion and basil salad, and handmade potato chips.
🖃 *14 Church St., in courtyard opposite town hall,* ☎ *508/627–9864.*
Reservations essential. AE, MC, V. Closed Nov.–Apr. No lunch.

$$$$ ✕🛏 **Charlotte Inn.** As you approach the Scottish barrister's desk at check-
★ in, you enter a tasteful and elegant bygone era. Guests are hand-writ-

ten into the register by the attentive staff. Beautiful antique furnishings and paintings fill the property—your bed could be a hand-carved four-poster. Come to the inn for an Edwardian fantasy, an utterly tranquil winter holiday, or a sumptuous meal at L'étoile. ⊠ *27 S. Summer St., 02539,* ☎ *508/627–4751,* FAX *508/627–4652,* WEB *www.charlotteinn.com. 23 rooms and 2 suites in 5 buildings. Restaurant. AE, MC, V. CP.*

$$$$ ⊞ **Harbor View Hotel.** This historic hotel, centered in an 1891 gray-shingle main building with wraparound veranda and a gazebo, is part of a complex in a residential neighborhood a few minutes from town. Town houses have cathedral ceilings, decks, kitchens, and large living areas with sofa beds. Rooms in other buildings, however, resemble up-scale motel rooms. A good beach for walking stretches ¾ mi from the hotel's dock. ⊠ *131 N. Water St., 02539,* ☎ *508/627–7000 or 800/ 225–6005,* FAX *508/627–7845,* WEB *www.harbor-view.com. 102 rooms, 22 suites. Restaurant, room service, pool, 2 tennis courts, laundry service, concierge. AE, DC, MC, V.*

$$$–$$$$ ⊞ **Daggett House.** The flower-bordered lawn that separates the main house
★ from the harbor makes a great retreat after a day of exploring town, a minute away. All four no-smoking inn buildings—the main 1660 Colonial house, the Captain Warren house across the street, the Henry Lyman Thomas house around the corner, and a three-room cottage between the main house and the water—are decorated with fine wallpapers, antiques, and reproductions. Breakfast and dinner are served in the 1750 tavern. ⊠ *Box 1333, 59 N. Water St., 02539,* ☎ *508/627–4600 or 800/ 946–3400,* FAX *508/627–4611,* WEB *www.mvweb.com/daggett. 27 rooms, 4 suites. AE, D, MC, V.*

Outdoor Activities and Sports

East Beach on Chappaquiddick Island, one of the area's best beaches, is accessible only by boat or Jeep from the Wasque Reservation. The relatively isolated strand, a good place to bird-watch, has heavy surf. **South Beach** (⊠ Katama Rd.), also called Katama Beach, is the island's largest, a 3-mi ribbon of sand on the Atlantic with strong surf and occasional riptides. Check with the lifeguards before swimming here. Parking is limited.

Big Eye Charters (☎ 508/627–3649) operates fishing charters that leave from Edgartown Harbor. **Coop's Bait and Tackle** (⊠ 147 W. Tisbury Rd., ☎ 508/627–3909) sells accessories and bait, rents fishing gear, and has a list of fishing regulations. **Wheelhappy** (⊠ 8 S. Water St., ☎ 508/627–5928) rents bicycles and will deliver them to you.

Shopping

Bickerton & Ripley Books (⊠ Main and S. Summer Sts., ☎ 508/627–8463, WEB www.bickertonandripley.com) carries current and island-related titles. **Edgartown Scrimshaw Gallery** (⊠ 17 N. Water St., ☎ 508/627–9439) stocks some antique pieces, as well as Nantucket lightship baskets and nautical paintings. The **Old Sculpin Gallery** (⊠ 58 Dock St. (next to the Chappy Ferry), ☎ 508/627–4881) displays original works by island artists. **Optional Art** (⊠ 35 Winter St., ☎ 508/627–5373) carries handcrafted fine jewelry.

West Tisbury

❷❶ *9 mi west of Edgartown.*

Very much the small New England village, complete with a white steepled church, West Tisbury has a vibrant agricultural life, with several active horse and produce farms. The **West Tisbury Farmers' Market**—Massachusetts's largest—is held mid-June to mid-October on Saturdays from 9 to noon and Wednesdays from 2:30 to 5:30 at the

1859 **Old Agricultural Hall** (⊠ South Rd., ☎ 508/693–9549) near the town hall.

Winery at Chicama Vineyards was started in 1971 by George and Cathy Mathiesen and their six children. From 3 acres of trees and rocks, they created a winery that today produces nearly 100,000 bottles a year from chardonnay, cabernet, and other European grapes. ⊠ *Stoney Hill Rd.,* ☎ *508/693–0309.* ☛ *Free tours and tastings.* ☉ *Memorial Day–Columbus Day, Mon.–Sat. 11–5, Sun. 1–5; call for off-season hrs and tastings.*

Long Point, a 633-acre preserve, is an open area of grassland and heath bounded on the east by the freshwater Homer's Pond, on the west by the saltwater West Tisbury Great Pond, and on the south by a mile of fantastic South Beach on the Atlantic Ocean. Arrive early on summer days if you're coming by car—the lot fills quickly. ⊠ *Mid-June–mid-Sept., turn left onto the unmarked dirt road (Waldron's Bottom Rd., look for mailboxes) ³/₁₀ mi west of airport on Edgartown–West Tisbury Rd., at end, follow signs to Long Point parking lot. Mid-Sept.–mid-June, follow unpaved Deep Bottom Rd. (1 mi west of airport) 2 mi to lot.* ☎ *508/693–3678,* WEB *www.thetrustees.org.* ☛ *Mid-June–mid-Sept., $7 per vehicle, $3 per adult; free rest of yr.* ☉ *Daily 9–6.*

★ At the center of the island, the **Manuel F. Correllus State Forest** is a 2,000-acre pine and scrub-oak forest crisscrossed with hiking trails and circled by a paved but rough bike trail (mopeds are prohibited). There's a 2-mi nature trail, a 2-mi course for exercisers, and horse trails. ⊠ *Headquarters on Barnes Rd. by the airport,* ☎ *508/693–2540,* WEB *www.state.ma.us/dem/parks/corr.htm.* ☛ *Free.* ☉ *Daily dawn–dusk.*

Dining and Lodging

$$$–$$$$ ✕🏨 **Lambert's Cove Country Inn.** A narrow road winds through pine woods to this secluded inn surrounded by gardens and old stone walls. Rooms in the 1790 farmhouse have light floral wallpapers and a country feel. Those in outbuildings have screened porches or decks. The soft candlelight and excellent contemporary cuisine make the restaurant ($$$–$$$$; reservations essential; BYOB) a destination for a special occasion. The fare is classic New England with an original spin. Especially good are the grilled duck breast on caramelized onions and the buttery-smooth mint-infused rack of lamb. ⊠ *Off Lambert's Cove Rd., West Tisbury (R.R. 1, Box 422, Vineyard Haven 02568),* ☎ *508/693–2298,* FAX *508/693–7890,* WEB *www.vineyard.net/biz/lambertscoveinn. 15 rooms. Restaurant, tennis court. AE, MC, V. BP.*

$ 🏨 **Hostelling International–Martha's Vineyard.** The only budget alternative in season, this hostel is one of the country's best. You'll catch up on local events from the bulletin board, and there is a large common kitchen. Doing morning chores is required in summer. ⊠ *Box 158, Edgartown–West Tisbury Rd., 02575,* ☎ *508/693–2665 or 800/909–4776 ext. 27,* WEB *www.usahostels.org. 78 dorm-style beds. Volleyball, coin laundry. MC, V. Closed Nov.–Apr.* 11 PM *curfew June–Aug.*

Nightlife and the Arts

Hot Tin Roof (⊠ Martha's Vineyard Airport, Edgartown–West Tisbury Rd., ☎ 508/693–1137), owned by Carly Simon, is the island's hottest club, with big-name artists. **WIMP** (⊠ Grange Hall, State Rd., ☎ 508/696–8475), the island's premier comedy improvisation troupe, performs Wednesdays at 8 PM from mid-June to mid-October.

Outdoor Activities and Sports

Lambert's Cove Beach (⊠ Lambert's Cove Rd.), on the Vineyard Sound, has fine sand and very clear water. In season the beach is restricted to residents and those staying in West Tisbury.

Stop at the grammar school on Old County Road to reserve one of its hard-surface **tennis courts. Misty Meadows Horse Farm** (⊠ Old County Rd., ☎ 508/693–1870) conducts trail rides.

Shopping

Granary Gallery (⊠ Red Barn Emporium, Old County Rd., ☎ 508/693–0455 or 800/472–6279, WEB www.granarygallery.com) showcases sculptures and mostly representational paintings by island and international artists, including the photographs of the late Alfred Eisenstaedt.

Chilmark

㉒ *5½ mi southwest of West Tisbury, 12 mi southwest of Vineyard Haven.*

Chilmark is a rural village whose ocean-view roads, rustic woodlands, and lack of crowds have drawn chic summer visitors and resulted in stratospheric real estate prices. Laced with rough roads and winding stone fences that once separated fields and pastures, Chilmark reminds people of what the Vineyard was like in an earlier time, before developers took over.

Dining and Lodging

$$$$ ✕ **Feast of Chilmark.** Civilized and calming, the Feast is a welcome break from the Vineyard's busier joints. The seafood entrées, light appetizers, and fresh salads play up summer tastes and flavors, and the whole menu takes advantage of local produce. ⊠ *Beetlebung Corner,* ☎ *508/645–3553. AE, MC, V. BYOB. No lunch.*

$$$$ ✕🏠 **Inn at Blueberry Hill.** Exclusive and secluded, this unique property comprising 56 acres of former farmland puts you in the heart of the rural Vineyard. The restaurant ($$$–$$$$; open to the public by reservation only) is relaxed and elegant, and the fresh, innovative, and health-conscious food is superb. Guest rooms are simply and sparsely decorated with Shaker-inspired island-made furniture. Some less-expensive rooms are on the small side; a number of rooms can be combined to create larger units. Though the restaurant serves only dinner, the cooks will prepare box lunches for guests. ⊠ *R.R. 1, Box 309, 74 North Rd., 02535,* ☎ *508/645–3322 or 800/356–3322,* FAX *508/645–3799,* WEB *www.blueberryinn.com. 25 rooms. Restaurant, lap pool, massage, tennis court, exercise room, meeting room, airport shuttle. AE, MC, V. Closed Nov.–Apr. CP.*

Outdoor Activities and Sports

A dirt road leads off South Road to beautiful **Lucy Vincent Beach,** which in summer is open only to Chilmark residents and those staying in town.

Menemsha

★ **㉓** *1½ mi northwest of Chilmark.*

Unspoiled by the "progress" of the past few decades, Menemsha is a jumble of weathered fishing shacks, fishing and pleasure boats, drying nets, and lobster pots.

Dining and Lodging

$$ ✕ **The Bite.** Fried everything—clams, fish-and-chips, you name it—is on the menu at this roadside shack, where two outdoor picnic tables are the only seating options. The Bite closes at 3 PM on weekdays and 7 PM on weekends. ⊠ *Basin Rd.,* ☎ *no phone. No credit cards. Closed Oct.–late-Mar.*

$–$$ ✕ **Larson's.** Basically a retail fish store, with reasonable prices and superb quality, Larson's will open oysters, stuff quahogs, and cook a lob-
★ ster to order. The best deal is a dozen littlenecks or cherrystones for $7.50. They taste especially good with a bottle of your own wine, sitting at an

outdoor picnic table or on a blue bench. Larson's closes at 6 PM on weekdays and at 7 PM on weekends. ⊠ *Dutcher's Dock,* ☏ *508/645–2680. MC, V. No seating. BYOB. Closed mid-Oct.–mid-May.*

$$$ 🈁 **Menemsha Inn and Cottages.** All with screened porches, fireplaces,
★   and full kitchens, the cottages here are spaced on 10 acres; some have more privacy and better water views than others. The 1989 inn building and the pleasant Carriage House have plush blue or sea-green carpeting and Appalachian-pine reproduction furniture. All rooms and suites have private decks, most with fine sunset views. The meal plan is for the inn and Carriage House only. ⊠ *Box 38, North Rd., 02552,* ☏ *508/ 645–2521,* 🌐 *www.menemshainn.com. 9 rooms, 6 suites, 12 cottages, 1 3-bedroom house. No credit cards. Closed Dec.–mid-Apr. CP.*

Outdoor Activities and Sports

Menemsha Public Beach, adjacent to Dutcher's Dock, is a pebbly beach with gentle surf on Vineyard Sound. The views to the west make it a great place to catch the sunset. There are rest rooms, food concessions, lifeguards, and parking spaces.

Aquinnah

㉔ *4 mi west of Menemsha, 12 mi southwest of West Tisbury.*

Aquinnah, formerly called Gay Head, is an official Native American township. The Wampanoag tribe is the guardian of the 420 acres that constitute the Aquinnah Native American Reservation. In 1997, the town voted to change Gay Head back to its original Native American name, Aquinnah (pronounced "a-*kwih*-nah"), which is Wampanoag for "land under the hill." The town is best known for the red-hued Aquinnah Cliffs.

Quitsa Pond Lookout (⊠ State Rd.) has a good view of the adjoining Menemsha and Nashaquitsa ponds, the woods, and the ocean beyond. From a roadside iron pipe, **Aquinnah spring** (⊠ State Rd.) gushes water cold enough to slake a cyclist's thirst on the hottest day. Feel free to fill a canteen. Locals come from all over the island to fill
★ jugs. The spring is just over the town line.The spectacular **Aquinnah Cliffs** (⊠ State Rd.), a National Historic Landmark, are part of the Wampanoag reservation land. These dramatically striated walls of red clay are the island's major attraction, as evidenced by the tour bus– filled parking lot. Native American crafts and food shops line the short approach to the overlook, from which you can see the Elizabeth Islands to the northeast across Vineyard Sound and Noman's Land Island—part wildlife preserve, part military bombing-practice site—3 mi off the Vineyard's southern coast.Adjacent to the cliffs overlook, the redbrick **Aquinnah Lighthouse** is precariously stationed atop the rapidly eroding cliffs. The lighthouse is open to the public on summer weekends at sunset, weather permitting; private tours can also be arranged. ⊠ *Lighthouse Rd.,* ☏ *508/645–2211.* 🎫 *$2.*

Dining and Lodging

$$$$ ✕🈁 **Outermost Inn.** Standing alone on acres of moorland, the inn is
★   wrapped with windows revealing breathtaking views of sea and sky. The restaurant (reservations essential; BYOB; no lunch) seats twice for dinner, at 6 and 8 PM four to six nights a week from spring to fall. Dinners ($65) are prix-fixe; try the crab cakes or baked stuffed seafood platter. The overall decor of the inn is clean and contemporary, with white walls, local art, and polished light-wood floors. Each room has a phone, and one has a whirlpool tub. ⊠ *R.R. 1, Box 171, Lighthouse Rd., 02535,* ☏ *508/645–3511,* 📠 *508/645–3514,* 🌐 *www.outer-*

*mostinn.com. 7 rooms. Restaurant. AE, D, MC, V. Closed mid-Oct.–
May. BP.*

Martha's Vineyard A to Z

To research prices, get advice from other travelers, and book travel arrangements, visit www.fodors.com.

AIRPORTS

Martha's Vineyard Airport (☎ 508/693-7022) is in West Tisbury, about
5 mi west of Edgartown. Cape Air/Nantucket Airlines connects the Vineyard year-round with Boston (including an hourly summer shuttle), Hyannis, Nantucket, and New Bedford. It offers joint fares and ticketing and
baggage agreements with several major carriers. Continental Express
has seasonal nonstop flights to the Vineyard from Newark, New Jersey. Direct Flight is a year-round charter service based on the Vineyard.
US Airways Express has service to the Vineyard out of Boston and New
York City's LaGuardia Airport, as well as to Hyannis and Nantucket,
and seasonal service from Washington, D.C. For airline telephone numbers, *see* Air Travel *in* Smart Travel Tips A to Z.

BOAT & FERRY TRAVEL

Car-and-passenger ferries travel to Vineyard Haven from Woods Hole
on Cape Cod year-round. In season, passenger ferries from Falmouth
and Hyannis on Cape Cod, and from New Bedford, serve Vineyard
Haven and Oak Bluffs. All provide parking where you can leave your
car overnight—the fees range from $7 to $12 a night.

FROM FALMOUTH: The *Island Queen* makes the 35-min trip to Oak Bluffs
from late May to Columbus Day. Round-trip $10, $6 bicycles. One-way
$6, $3 bicycles. Patriot Boats allows passengers on its daily Falmouth
Harbor–Oak Bluffs mail runs ($6 one-way) and operates a year-round
24-hour water taxi. You can also charter a boat for about $300.

FROM HYANNIS: Hy-Line makes the 1¾-hour run to Oak Bluffs between
May and October. From June to mid-September, the "Around the
Sound" cruise makes a one-day round-trip from Hyannis with stops
at Nantucket and Martha's Vineyard ($36). Call to reserve a space in
summer, because the parking lot often fills up. ✉ . One-way $13.50,
$5 bicycles.

FROM NANTUCKET: Hy-Line makes 2¼-hour runs to and from Oak Bluffs
from early June to mid-September—the only interisland passenger service. (To get a car from Nantucket to the Vineyard, you must return
to the mainland and drive from Hyannis to Woods Hole.) One-way
$13.50, $5 additional for bicycles.

FROM NEW BEDFORD: The *Schamonchi* travels between Billy Woods
Wharf and Vineyard Haven from mid-May to mid-October. The 600-
passenger ferry makes the 1½-hour trip at least once a day, several times
in high season, allowing you to avoid Cape traffic. Note that round-trip fares apply only for same-day travel; overnight stays require the
purchase of two one-way tickets. Round-trip $18 adults, $6 bicycles.
One-way $10.00, $3 bicycles.

FROM NEW LONDON: Fox Navigation carries passengers between
State Pier in New London, Connecticut, and Vineyard Haven from June
to early September. The 257-passenger high-speed ferry makes the
two-hour trip Friday through Monday only, once per day. Passengers
sit in either Clipper Class or the more expensive Admiral Class. Round-
trip Admiral Class $89, Clipper Class $59.

FROM WOODS HOLE: The Steamship Authority runs the only car ferries, which make the 45-minute trip to Vineyard Haven year-round and to Oak Bluffs from late May through September. If you plan to take a car, you'll definitely need a reservation in summer or on weekends in the fall (passenger reservations are not necessary). Passengers one-way year-round $5; bicycles $3 additional. Car one-way mid-May–mid-Oct. $52; call for off-season rates.

The three-car On Time ferry makes the five-minute run to Chappaquiddick Island. ⊠ . Round-trip $1.50 individual, $6 car and driver, $4 bicycle and rider, $5.50 moped and rider, $5 motorcycle. Memorial Day–mid-October, about every 5 mins, daily 7 AM–midnight, less frequently off-season.

➤ BOAT & FERRY INFORMATION: The *Island Queen* ⊠ (Falmouth Harbor, ☎ 508/548–4800, WEB www.islandqueen.com). **Patriot Boats** (⊠ Scranton Ave., Falmouth Harbor, ☎ 508/548–2626 or 800/734-0088 in MA, WEB www.sunsol.com/patriot). **Hy-Line** ⊠ (Ocean St. dock, ☎ 508/778–2600; 888/778–1132; 508/778–2602 reservations; 508/693–0112 in Oak Bluffs). **Hy-Line** ☎ (508/778–2600 in Hyannis; 508/693–0112 in Oak Bluffs; 508/228–3949 in Nantucket, WEB www.hy-linecruises.com). *Schamonchi* ☎ (508/997–1688 in New Bedford; Martha's Vineyard ticket office: ⊠ Beach Rd., Vineyard Haven, ☎ 508/693–2088, WEB www.mvferry.com). **Fox Navigation** ☎ (888/724–5369, WEB www.foxnavigation.com; ⊠ Pier 44, Beach Rd., Vineyard Haven). **Steamship Authority** ☎ (508/477–8600 information and car reservations; 508/693–9130 on the Vineyard; 508/540–1394 TTY), WEB www.islandferry.com. **On Time** ⊠ (Dock St., Edgartown, ☎ 508/627–9427).

➤ TOWN HARBOR FACILITIES: **Edgartown** (☎ 508/627–4746). **Menemsha** (☎ 508/645–2846). **Oak Bluffs** (☎ 508/693–4355). **Vineyard Haven** (☎ 508/696–4249).

BUS TRAVEL
Bonanza Bus Lines travels to the Woods Hole ferry port on Cape Cod from Boston's Logan Airport, Rhode Island, Connecticut, and New York year-round.

Martha's Vineyard Transit Authority (VTA) buses run on a summer schedule (mid-May through September), with in-town services and selected routes such as Edgartown to Vineyard Haven, West Tisbury to Chilmark and Aquinnah, and Edgartown to South Beach. The fare is 50¢ per town, with the exception of trips to South Beach, which are $1.50. For the latest schedules and fare informations, call the VTA. The VTA also has three in-town minibus routes, two in Edgartown and one in Vineyard Haven. One-way fares are $1.50 or less; weekly, monthly, and seasonal passes are available.

From late June to early September, shuttles operate between Vineyard Haven, Oak Bluffs, and Edgartown. Buses from the Down-Island towns to Aquinnah—stopping at the airport, West Tisbury, Chilmark, and on demand wherever it's safe to do so—run every couple of hours in July and August. For the current bus schedule, call the shuttle hot line.
➤ BUS INFORMATION: **Bonanza Bus Lines** (☎ 508/548–7588 or 800/556–3815, WEB www.bonanzabus.com). The **Martha's Vineyard Transit Authority** (☎ 508/627–9663 or 508/627–7448, WEB www.vineyardtransit.com). **Shuttle hot line** (☎ 508/693–1589 or 508/693–0058).

CAR RENTAL
You can book rentals through the Woods Hole ferry terminal free phone. The following agencies have rental desks at the airport; be aware, though, that cars rented from the airport incur a small surcharge.

> ➤ MAJOR AGENCIES: **Budget** (☎ 508/693–1911). **Hertz** (☎ 508/693–2402). **All Island** (☎ 508/693–6868).

CAR TRAVEL

Driving on the island is fairly simple (though the few main roads can be crowded in summer). Four-wheel-drive vehicles are allowed from Katama Beach to Wasque Reservation with $50 annual permits ($75 for vehicles not registered on the island) sold on the beach in summer, or anytime at the Dukes County Courthouse. Wasque Reservation has a separate mandatory permit (also available at the courthouse) and requires that vehicles carry certain equipment, such as a shovel, tow chains, and rope; call the rangers before setting out.

EMERGENCIES

Dial **911** for the hospital, physicians, ambulance services, police, fire departments, or Coast Guard. Vineyard Medical Services provides walk-in care; call for days and hours. Leslie's Drug Store is open daily and has a pharmacist on 24-hour call for emergencies.

➤ HOSPITAL AND EMERGENCY SERVICES: **Martha's Vineyard Hospital** (⊠ Linton La., Oak Bluffs, ☎ 508/693–0410). **Vineyard Medical Services** (⊠ State Rd., Vineyard Haven, ☎ 508/693–6399).

➤ LATE-NIGHT PHARMACY: **Leslie's Drug Store** (⊠ 65 Main St., Vineyard Haven, ☎ 508/693–1010).

LODGING

B&BS

➤ RESERVATION SERVICES: **Martha's Vineyard and Nantucket Reservations** (⊠ Box 1322, Lagoon Pond Rd., Vineyard Haven 02568, ☎ 508/693–7200; 800/649–5671 in MA, WEB www.mvreservations.com).

APARTMENT & VILLA RENTALS

➤ RESERVATION SERVICES: **Martha's Vineyard Vacation Rentals** (⊠ Box 1207, 107 Beach Rd., Vineyard Haven 02568, ☎ 508/693–7711 or 800/556–4225, WEB www.mvvacationrentals.com). **Sandcastle Vacation Home Rentals** (⊠ Box 2488, 256 Vineyard Haven Rd., Edgartown 02539, ☎ 508/627–5665, WEB www.sandcastlemv.com).

TAXIS

Muzik's Limousine Service provides limousine service on- and off-island.

➤ CONTACTS: **All Island Taxi** (☎ 508/693–2929 or 800/693–8294). **Martha's Vineyard Taxi** (☎ 508/693–8660). **Muzik's Limousine Service** (☎ 508/693–2212, WEB www.mvy.com/muzik).

TOURS

The teakwood sailing yacht *Ayuthia* sails to Nantucket or the Elizabeth Islands out of Coastwise Wharf in Vineyard Haven. Liz Villard Vineyard History Tours leads walking tours of Edgartown's "history, architecture, ghosts, and gossip."

➤ TOUR OPERATORS: *Ayuthia* (☎ 508/693–7245). **Liz Villard** (☎ 508/627–8619).

VISITOR INFORMATION

Martha's Vineyard Chamber of Commerce is two blocks from the Vineyard Haven ferry. There are town information booths by the Vineyard Haven Steamship terminal, on Circuit Avenue in Oak Bluffs, and on Church Street in Edgartown; these are generally open daily in season. Weekdays 9–5. ⊠

➤ CONTACTS: **Martha's Vineyard Chamber of Commerce** ⊠ (Beach Rd., Vineyard Haven 02568, ☎ 508/693–0085, WEB www.mvy.com).

NANTUCKET

Updated by
Carolyn Heller

At the height of its prosperity in the early to mid-19th century, the little island of Nantucket was the foremost whaling port in the world. Its harbor bustled with whaling ships and merchant vessels. Ship's chandleries, cooperages, and other shops stood cheek by jowl along the wharves. Barrels of whale oil were off-loaded from ships onto wagons, then wheeled along cobblestone streets to refineries and candle factories. Strong sea breezes carried the smoke and smells of booming industry through town as its inhabitants eagerly took care of business. Shipowners and sea captains built elegant mansions that today remain remarkably unchanged, thanks to a very strict code regulating any changes to structures within the town of Nantucket, an official National Historic District.

Day-trippers usually take in the architecture and historical museums, dine at one of the many fine restaurants, and browse in the art galleries, crafts shops, and boutiques downtown. One signature item is the now-expensive ($300 and up) Nantucket lightship basket, woven of oak or cane. Those who stay longer will have time to explore more of the island. Its moors—swept with fresh salt breezes and scented with bayberry, wild roses, and cranberries—and its miles of white-sand beaches make Nantucket a respite from the rush and regimentation of life elsewhere. Most shops stay open until Christmas. If you do plan to linger, however, make reservations well in advance; for summer weekends, early spring would not be too early.

Nantucket Town

②⑤ *30 mi southeast of Hyannis, 107 mi southeast of Boston.*

Nantucket Town has one of the country's finest historical districts, with beautiful 18th- and 19th-century architecture and a museum of whaling history. The **Nantucket Historical Association** (NHA; ☎ 508/228–1894, WEB www.nha.org) operates a dozen historic properties along Nantucket Town's streets as museums. At any of them you can purchase an NHA Visitor Pass ($10), which entitles you to entry at all NHA museums, or you can pay single admission at each (prices vary). Most NHA properties are open daily from Memorial Day to Columbus Day; hours vary from year to year, so call ahead.

The **Peter Foulger Museum** hosts engaging changing exhibits from the NHA's permanent collection, including portraits, historical documents, and furniture. ⊠ *15 Broad St.,* ☎ *508/228–1655.* 🎫 *$5 or NHA pass. Research permit $10 (2 days).* ☉ *Memorial Day–mid-June and Columbus Day–Thanksgiving, weekends 11–3; mid-June–Labor Day, daily 10–5; Labor Day–Columbus Day, daily 11–3.*

An 1846 factory built for refining spermaceti and making candles houses the excellent **Whaling Museum.** The exhibits here include a fully rigged whaleboat, harpoons and other implements, portraits of sea captains, a large scrimshaw collection, and the skeleton of a 43-ft finback whale. Lectures on whaling history are given daily. ⊠ *13 Broad St.,* ☎ *508/228–1894.* 🎫 *$5 or NHA pass.* ☉ *Apr. and Columbus Day–Nov., weekends 11–3; May (until Memorial Day), daily 11–3; Memorial Day–Columbus Day, daily 10–5. www.nha.org/whalingmuseum.htm.*

Built in 1818, the **Pacific National Bank,** at the corner of Main and Fair streets, is a monument to the Nantucket whaling ships it once financed. Above the old-style teller cages, murals show the town as it was in its whaling heyday. At 93–97 Upper Main Street are the **"Three**

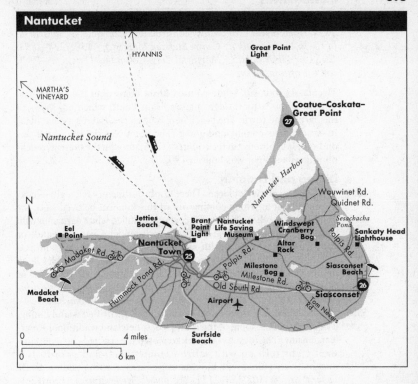

Nantucket

HYANNIS

MARTHA'S
VINEYARD

Nantucket Sound

Great Point
Light

Coatue–Coskata–
Great Point
27

Nantucket Harbor

Wauwinet Rd.
Quidnet Rd.

*Sesachacha
Pond*

N

Eel
Point

Jetties
Beach

Brant
Point
Light

Nantucket
Life Saving
Museum

Windswept
Cranberry
Bog

Sankaty Head
Lighthouse

**Nantucket
Town**
25

Altar
Rock

Polpis Rd.

Madaket Rd.

Polpis Rd.

Milestone
Bog

Siasconset
Beach

Hummock Pond Rd.

Milestone Rd.

Madaket
Beach

Old South Rd.

Siasconset
26

Tom Nevers

Airport

Surfside
Beach

0   4 miles

0   6 km

Bricks," identical redbrick mansions with columned Greek Revival porches at their front entrances. They were built between 1836 and 1838 by a whaling merchant for his three sons.

Two white porticoed Greek Revival mansions built in 1845–46 stand across the street from the "Three Bricks." One of the buildings, the **Hadwen House,** is a museum that surveys Nantucket's affluent whaling era. A guided tour points out the grand circular staircase, fine plasterwork, carved Italian marble fireplace mantels, and Victorian gas chandeliers and furnishings. ⊠ *96 Main St.,* ☎ *508/228–1894,* WEB *www.nha.org/HadwenHouse.html.* 🎟 *$3 or NHA pass.* ☉ *Memorial Day–Labor Day, daily 10–5; Labor Day–Columbus Day, daily 11–3.*

Several windmills sat on Nantucket hills in the 1700s, but only the **Old Mill,** a 1746 Dutch-style octagonal structure made of lumber from shipwrecks, remains. When the wind is strong enough, corn is ground into meal that is sold here. ⊠ *50 Prospect St., at S. Mill St.,* ☎ *508/228–1894.* 🎟 *$2 or NHA pass.* ☉ *Memorial Day–Labor Day, daily 10–5; Labor Day–Columbus Day, daily 11–3.*

★ The tower of the **First Congregational Church** provides the best view of Nantucket—for those who climb the 92 steps. Rising 120 ft, the tower is capped by a weather vane that depicts a whale catch. Peek in at the church's 1850 trompe l'oeil ceiling. ⊠ *62 Centre St.,* ☎ *508/228–0950,* WEB *www.nantucket.org/congregational.* 🎟 *Tour $2.50.* ☉ *Mid-June– mid-Oct., Mon.–Sat. 10–4; call for schedule of tower tours. Services Sun. at 8, 9, and 10:15 AM.*

The **Oldest House,** a 1686 saltbox also called the Jethro Coffin House, really is the oldest house on the island. The structure's most noteworthy element is the massive central brick chimney with a giant brick horseshoe adornment. Other highlights of the sparsely furnished interior are the enormous hearths and diamond-pane leaded-glass windows. Cutaway panels reveal 17th-century construction techniques. ⊠ *Sunset Hill (a 10- to 15-min walk up Centre St. from Main St.),* ☎ *508/228–1894.* ☞ *$3 or NHA pass.* ☉ *Memorial Day–Columbus Day, daily 10–5; call for off-season hrs.*

Twenty-six-foot tall, white-painted **Brant Point Light** (⊠ end of Easton St., across a footbridge) sits on Brant Point, which has views of the harbor and town. The beach here is not large, but it's a great place to watch boats coming and going. The point was the site of the second-oldest lighthouse in the country (1746), though the present, much-photographed light was built in 1902.

Dining and Lodging

$$$$ ✕ **Company of the Cauldron.** There's only one menu each night—luckily, just about anything coming out of this kitchen, beloved since the mid-'70s, is excellent. You might encounter chilled white gazpacho with sliced lobster meat and fresh basil, fork-tender Châteaubriand, or chocolate ganache cake with raspberries. The tiny dining room is a sconce-lit haven of handsome architectural salvage, with tables lined up in rows that are more comradely than intimate. ⊠ *7 India St.,* ☎ *508/228–4016,* WEB *www.companyofthecauldron.com. Reservations essential. MC, V. No smoking. Closed Nov.–May. No lunch.*

$$$$ ✕ **21 Federal.** The epitome of sophisticated, gentrified island dining,
★ 21 Federal serves some of the island's best new and traditional American cuisine. The food has a spark to match the spirited clientele: soft-shell crabs turn up with saffron fennel salad, and swordfish is imaginatively paired with mole sauce, salsa, and corn pudding. ⊠ *21 Federal St.,* ☎ *508/228–2121,* WEB *www.21federal.net. AE, MC, V. Closed Jan.–Mar.*

$$$–$$$$ ✕ **American Seasons.** The culinary context here is geographic: from
★ the four corners of the continental United States, chef-owner Michael Getter gathers specialties. You can mix and match, with choices ranging from tuna tempura or Hudson Valley foie gras to grilled Wyoming trout or crayfish ravioli. ⊠ *80 Centre St.,* ☎ *508/228–7111,* WEB *www.americanseasons.com. Reservations essential. AE, MC, V. Closed late Dec.–May. No lunch.*

$$$ ✕ **Atlantic Cafe.** Long popular with visitors and locals alike for fairly predictable bar food, the AC has begun adding little flourishes, such as gnocchi sauced with cream, asparagus, and oyster mushrooms, and sea scallops paired with ricotta-crab ravioli. The room's nautical flotsam is not some decorator's scheme but vestiges of the real thing. ⊠ *15 S. Water St.,* ☎ *508/228–0570,* WEB *www.atlanticcafe.com. AE, D, DC, MC, V.*

$–$$$ ✕ **Nantucket Tapas.** The first thing you see in this converted cottage is a counter beckoning with rich desserts that can round off a meal of tasty appetizer-size dishes. The 33 items on the main tapas menu are eclectic with an Asian bent, and expensive. Pick and choose; try the pork fried dumplings or crab cakes, throw in some tuna carpaccio or Szechuan beef, and you've got a meal. The place fills up fast, so expect a wait or take advantage of the takeout option. ⊠ *15 S. Beach St.,* ☎ *508/228–2033,* WEB *www.nantuckettapas.com. MC, V.*

$$$$ ▥ **Harbor House.** This family-oriented complex near the center of
★ town comprises an 1886 main inn and several "town houses" on a flower-filled quadrangle. Standard rooms are decorated English-country style, with bright floral fabrics and queen-size beds. The hotel's restaurant ($$–$$$) serves simple New England fare; it's popular with families and their hungry children. ⊠ *Box 1139, S. Beach St., 02554,* ☎ *508/228–1500; 800/475–2637 reservations,* FAX *508/228–7639,* WEB *www.harborhouseack.com. 109 rooms. Restaurant, lounge, concierge, children's programs, business services. AE, D, DC, MC, V. CP.*

$$$$ ⬚ **White Elephant.** Long a hallmark of service and style, the White Elephant is right on Nantucket Harbor, separated from the water by a wide lawn. The main hotel has a formal restaurant with a waterside outdoor café. Rooms and common areas are elegantly appointed, with a fresh, floral, white-wicker atmosphere. The garden cottages, named for flowers and connected by landscaped walkways, are ideal for families. ✉ *Box 1139, Easton St., 02554,* ☎ *508/228–2500; 800/475–2637 room reservations,* ℻ *508/325–1195,* ⬛ *www.whiteelephanthotel.com. 24 rooms, 30 suites, 12 cottages. Restaurant, lounge, room service, putting green, dock, concierge, meeting rooms. AE, D, DC, MC, V. Closed late Oct.–mid-May. BP.*

$$$–$$$$ ⬚ **Centerboard Guest House.** White walls, blond-wood floors, and natural woodwork create a dreamy atmosphere at this no-smoking inn a
★ few blocks from the center of town. Stained-glass lamps, antique quilts, and fresh flowers adorn the rooms; the first-floor suite is stunning, with 11-ft ceilings, a Victorian living room with fireplace and bar, parquet floors, and a green-marble bath with whirlpool tub. ✉ *Box 456, 8 Chester St., 02554,* ☎ *508/228–9696,* ⬛ *www.nantucket.net/lodging/centerboard. 6 rooms, 1 suite. AE, MC, V. CP.*

$$$–$$$$ ⬚ **Westmoor Inn.** The many common areas in this yellow 1917 Federal-style mansion include a wide lawn set with Adirondack chairs, a garden patio secluded behind 11-ft hedges, and a wicker-filled sunroom. The guest rooms are decorated in country French style; most have soft florals and stenciled walls. One first-floor room has a giant bath with a whirlpool tub and French doors opening onto the lawn. The inn is no-smoking. ✉ *Cliff Rd., 02554,* ☎ *508/228–0877 or 888/236–7310,* ℻ *508/228–5763,* ⬛ *www.westmoorinn.com. 14 rooms. Bicycles. AE, MC, V. Closed early Dec.–mid-Apr. CP.*

$$–$$$ ⬚ **76 Main Street.** This 1883 B&B just beyond the downtown shops blends antiques and reproductions, Oriental rugs, handmade quilts, and lots of fine woods. Room 3 has wonderful woodwork, a carved-wood armoire, and twin four-posters; Room 1 has large windows, massive redwood pocket doors, and a canopy bed. The motel-like annex rooms have low ceilings, but they are spacious enough for families. No smoking is permitted. ✉ *76 Main St., 02554,* ☎ *508/228–2533,* ⬛ *www.nantucketonline.com/lodging/76main. 18 rooms. AE, D, MC, V. Closed Jan.–Mar. CP.*

$ ⬚ **Nesbitt Inn.** This family-run guest house in the center of town has comfortable, shared-bath rooms (including inexpensive singles) done in Victorian style, with lace curtains, some marble-top and brass antiques, and a sink in each room. Some beds are not as firm as they should be, but the Nesbitt is a very good buy in this town. Ask for a room away from the popular bar-restaurant next door. ✉ *Box 1019, 21 Broad St., 02554,* ☎ *508/228–0156,* ℻ *508/228–2446. 12 rooms without bath. No-smoking rooms, refrigerator. MC, V. Closed Jan.–Mar. CP.*

Nightlife and the Arts

NIGHTLIFE

The **Box** (a.k.a. Chicken Box; ✉ 16 Dave St., off Lower Orange St., ☎ 508/228–9717) has live music, from reggae to rock, six nights a week in season, weekends off-season. The **Brotherhood of Thieves** (✉ 23 Broad St., ☎ no phone) presents folk musicians and has a well-stocked bar. **Rose and Crown** (✉ 23 S. Water St., ☎ 508/228–2595) is a friendly, noisy seasonal restaurant with a big bar, a small dance floor, live bands, DJs, and karaoke nights. Folks of all ages dance at the **Muse** (✉ 44 Surfside Rd., ☎ 508/228–6873) to a variety of sounds from rock to reggae, both live and recorded.

Actors Theatre of Nantucket (⊠ Methodist Church, 2 Centre St., at Main St., ☎ 508/228–6325, WEB www.nantuckettheatre.com) presents Broadway-style plays between Memorial Day and Columbus Day, children's post-beach matinees in July and August, comedy nights, and other events. **Band concerts** (☎ 508/228–7213) are held at 6 PM Thursdays and Sundays, July 4–Labor Day, at Children's Beach. The **Nantucket Musical Arts Society** (☎ 508/228–1287) presents Tuesday-evening concerts in July and August at the First Congregational Church (⊠ 62 Centre St.). **Theatre Workshop of Nantucket** (⊠ Bennett Hall, 62 Centre St., ☎ 508/228–4305, WEB www.theatreworkshop.com), a community theater, stages plays, musicals, and readings.

Outdoor Activities and Sports

BEACHES

Children's Beach (⊠ S. Beach St.), a calm harbor beach suited to small children, is an easy walk from town. It has a park and playground, a lifeguard, food service, and rest rooms. Six miles west of town and accessible only by foot, **Eel Point** (⊠ Eel Point Rd., off Cliff Rd. near Madaket) has one of the island's most beautiful and interesting beaches—a sandbar extends out 100 yards, keeping the water shallow, clear, and calm. There are no services, just lots of birds, wild berries and bushes, and solitude.

Jetties Beach (⊠ Hulbert Ave.), a short bike or shuttle ride from town, is the most popular beach for families because of its calm surf, lifeguards, bathhouse, snack bar, water-sports rentals, and tennis. Known for great sunsets and surf, **Madaket Beach** is reached by shuttle bus or by the Madaket bike path (5½ mi) off Cliff Road. Lifeguards are on duty, and there are rest rooms. **Surfside** (⊠ Surfside Rd.) is the premier surf beach, with lifeguards, rest rooms, a snack bar, and a wide strand. About 2 mi south of the center of town, the beach attracts college students and families and is great for kite-flying and surf-casting.

BOATING

Nantucket Harbor Sail (⊠ Swain's Wharf, ☎ 508/228–0424) rents sailboats.

FISHING

Barry Thurston's Fishing Tackle (⊠ Harbor Sq., ☎ 508/228–9595) dispenses fishing tips and rents gear. The **Herbert T.** (⊠ Slip 14, ☎ 508/228–6655) and other boats are available for seasonal charter from Straight Wharf.

WHALE-WATCHING

Nantucket Whale Watch (⊠ Hy-Line dock, Straight Wharf, ☎ 508/283–0313 or 800/322–0013, WEB www.yankeefleet.com) operates naturalist-led full-day excursions ($88; reservations essential) on Tuesday and Friday from mid-July through August.

Shopping

ANTIQUES

Forager House Collection (⊠ 20 Centre St., ☎ 508/228–5977) specializes in folk art and Americana. **Janis Aldridge** (⊠ 50 Main St., ☎ 508/228–6673) sells home furnishings and beautifully framed antique engravings. **Nina Hellman Antiques** (⊠ 48 Centre St., ☎ 508/228–4677) stocks scrimshaw, ship models, nautical instruments, and other marine antiques, plus folk art and Nantucket memorabilia. **Paul La Paglia** (⊠ 38 Centre St., ☎ 508/228–8760) has moderately priced antique prints.

BOOKS

The stock at **Mitchell's Book Corner** (⊠ 54 Main St., ☎ 508/228–1080) includes books on Nantucket and whaling and ocean-related children's titles. **Nantucket Bookworks** (⊠ 25 Broad St., ☎ 508/228–4000) sells hardcover and paperback books, with an emphasis on children's books and literary works.

CLOTHING

Cordillera Imports (⊠ 18 Broad St., ☎ 508/228–6140) sells jewelry, affordable clothing in natural fibers, and crafts from Latin America, Asia, and elsewhere. **Murray's Toggery Shop** (⊠ 62 Main St., ☎ 508/228–0437) stocks traditional footwear and clothing—including the famous Nantucket Reds (cotton pants that fade to pink with washing)—for men, women, and children. An outlet store (⊠ 7 New St., ☎ 508/228–3584) has discounts of up to 50%.

CRAFTS

Four Winds Craft Guild (⊠ 6 Ray's Ct., ☎ 508/228–9623) sells antique and new scrimshaw and lightship baskets, as well as ship models, duck decoys, and a kit for making your own lightship basket.

GALLERIES AND GIFTS

The **Museum Shop** (⊠ 11 Broad St. next to the Whaling Museum, ☎ 508/228–5785) has island-related books, antique whaling tools, reproduction furniture, and toys. **Robert Wilson Galleries** (⊠ 34 Main St., ☎ 508/228–6246 or 508/228–2096) carries contemporary American marine, impressionist, and other art. **Seven Seas Gifts** (⊠ 46 Centre St., ☎ 508/228–0958) stocks inexpensive gift and souvenir items, including shells, baskets, toys, and Nantucket jigsaw puzzles.

Siasconset

★ ㉖ *7 mi east of Nantucket Town.*

First a whaling town and then an artist's colony, Siasconset (or 'Sconset, as locals call their town) is a charming village of streets with tiny rose-covered cottages and driveways of crushed white shells. At the central square are the post office, a market, two restaurants, and a liquor store–cum–informal lending library.

★ The **Milestone Bog** (⊠ off Milestone Rd., west of Siasconset), more than 200 acres of working cranberry bogs surrounded by conservation land, is always a beautiful sight to behold, especially during the fall harvest, which begins in September and continues for six weeks. At any time of year, the bog and the moors have a remarkable, quiet beauty that's well worth experiencing.

★ An unmarked dirt track off Polpis Road between Wauwinet and Nantucket Town leads to **Altar Rock,** from which the view is spectacular. The rock sits on a high spot amid open moor and bog land—technically called lowland heath—which is very rare in the United States. The entire area, of which the Milestone Bog is a part, is laced with paths leading in every direction. Keep track of the trails you travel so you'll be able to find your way back.

Dining and Lodging

$$$$ ✕ **Chanticleer.** For more than 20 years, Anne and Jean-Charles Berruet
★ have been serving superb French food in a formal country setting. Some people feel that the food and ambience have become heavy and overbearing. Still, for many, a Nantucket visit would not be complete without getting dressed up and coming here, where dining is a commitment to a classic form of elegance. ⊠ *9 New St.,* ☎ *508/257–6231,* WEB

www.thechanticleerinn.com. Jacket required. AE, MC, V. Closed Mon. and mid-Oct.–early May.

$$$$ ✕ **'Sconset Café.** It looks like a modest lunchroom, but this tiny institution, treasured by summering locals since 1983, prepares wonderful breakfasts, great lunches, and outright astounding dinners. The nightly menus shift every two weeks to take advantage of seasonal bounty, with a focus on local seafood. If you can't get in, order out and feast on the beach. ⊠ *Post Office Sq.,* ☎ *508/257–4008. Reservations essential. No credit cards. BYOB. Closed Oct.–mid-May.*

$$$$ ✕🏠 **Summer House.** Clustered around a flower-filled lawn across from 'Sconset Beach, these one- and two-bedroom rose-covered cottages are furnished in romantic English country style: trompe l'oeil–bordered white walls, white eyelet spreads, and stripped English-pine antique furnishings. The restaurant ($$$–$$$$; reservations essential for dinner) has ocean views and live piano music. The seafood specials are often the menu highlights. ⊠ *Box 880, 17 Ocean Ave., 02564,* ☎ *508/257–4577,* FAX *508/257–4590,* WEB *www.thesummerhouse.com. 8 cottages. 2 restaurants, bar, piano bar, pool. AE, MC, V. Closed Nov.– late Apr. CP.*

$$–$$$$ 🏠 **Wade Cottages.** On a bluff overlooking the ocean, this complex of guest rooms, apartments, and cottages in 'Sconset couldn't be better located for beach lovers: the buildings are arranged around a central lawn with a great ocean view. Most inn rooms and cottages have sea views, and all have phones. Furnishings are generally in somewhat worn beach style, with some antique pieces. ⊠ *Box 211, Shell St., 02564,* ☎ *508/ 257–6308; 212/989–6423 off-season,* FAX *508/257–4602,* WEB *www.wade-cottages.com. 8 rooms (3-night minimum), 4 with bath; 6 apartments (1-wk minimum); 3 cottages (2-wk minimum). Badminton, Ping-Pong, beach, coin laundry. AE, MC, V. Closed mid-Oct.–late May. CP.*

Outdoor Activities and Sports

BEACHES

Siasconset Beach (⊠ end of Milestone Rd.) has a golden-sand beach with moderate to heavy surf and a lifeguard, showers, rest rooms, and playground. Restaurants are a short walk away.

BIKING

The 8-mi **Polpis Bike Path,** a long trail with gentle hills, winds alongside Polpis Road past the moors, the cranberry bogs, and Sesachacha Pond almost into Siasconset. The 6½-mi **'Sconset Bike Path** starts at the rotary east of Nantucket Town and parallels Milestone Road, ending in 'Sconset. It is mostly level, with some gentle hills and benches and drinking fountains at strategic locations along the way.

Coatue–Coskata–Great Point

🔟 *13 mi from Nantucket Town to Great Point, 11 mi from Siasconset.*

Wauwinet Road leads to the gateway of Coatue–Coskata–Great Point, an unpopulated spit of sand comprising three cooperatively managed wildlife refuges that can be entered only on foot or by four-wheel-drive over-sand vehicle (☎ 508/228–2884 information). The area's beaches, dunes, salt marshes, and stands of oak and cedar provide a major habitat for marsh hawks, oystercatchers, terns, herring gulls, and other birds. Because of frequent dangerous currents and riptides and the lack of lifeguards, swimming is strongly discouraged, especially around the Great Point Light.

The **Nantucket Life Saving Museum,** on the road back to Nantucket Town from Great Point, is housed in a re-creation of an 1874 Life Saving Service station. Exhibits include original rescue equipment and boats, artifacts recovered from the wreck *Andrea Doria,* and photos and accounts of daring rescues. ⊠ *158 Polpis Rd.,* ☎ *508/228–1885,* WEB *www.nantucket.net/museums/lifesaving.* ⊡ *$3.* ☉ *Mid-June–Columbus Day, Tues.–Sun. 9:30–4.*

Dining and Lodging

$$$$
★ ✕⊡ **Wauwinet.** Some people say this luxurious 19th-century hotel is the only place to stay on Nantucket. The tasteful Topper's restaurant ($$$–$$$$; reservations essential) serves alluring dishes like pan-seared sea scallops with lobster risotto and roasted rack of venison with polenta and forest-mushroom glaze. The rooms and cottages are decorated in country-beach style, with pine antiques; some have water views. A boat shuttles to Coatue beach across the harbor, and the innkeeper runs a Land Rover tour of the Great Point reserve. Jitney service to and from Nantucket Town (8 mi away), plus Steamship pickup, makes this a convenient place to stay if you don't have a car. ⊠ *Box 2580, 120 Wauwinet Rd., Nantucket 02584,* ☎ *508/228–0145 or 800/ 426–8718,* FAX *508/228–7135,* WEB *www.wauwinet.com. 25 rooms, 5 cottages. Restaurant, bar, room service, 2 tennis courts, croquet, boating, mountain bikes, library, concierge, business services. AE, DC, MC, V. Closed Nov.–Apr. BP.*

Outdoor Activities and Sports

The Trustees of Reservations sponsor naturalist-led **Great Point Natural History Tours** (☎ 508/228–6799) from June to October.

Nantucket A to Z

To research prices, get advice from other travelers, and book travel arrangements, visit www.fodors.com.

AIRPORTS

Nantucket Memorial Airport is about 3½ mi southeast of town via Old South Road; cars and four-wheel-drive vehicles can be rented at the airport. American Eagle/American Airlines flies from Boston in season and from New York (JFK) year-round. Cape Air/Nantucket Air flies from Hyannis year-round and runs charters. US Airways Express has nonstops from New York (LaGuardia) and Boston year-round.
➤ AIRPORT INFORMATION: **Nantucket Memorial Airport** (☎ 508/325–5300).

BIKE & MOPED TRAVEL

Nantucket Bike Shop, open between April and October, rents bicycles and mopeds and provides a touring map. Daily rentals typically cost from $18 to $30 for a bicycle and from $45 to $70 for a moped.
➤ BIKE RENTALS: **Nantucket Bike Shop** (⊠ Steamboat Wharf and Straight Wharf, ☎ 508/228–1999).

BOAT & FERRY TRAVEL

Year-round service is available from Hyannis only. Hy-Line has two boats, one of which runs between Nantucket and Martha's Vineyard in summer only. The only way to get a car to Nantucket is on the Steamship Authority. To get a car from the Vineyard to Nantucket, you would have to return to Woods Hole, drive to Hyannis, and take the ferry from there.

The Steamship Authority runs car-and-passenger ferries to the island from Hyannis year-round (one-way $12.50; bicycles $5; cars $160 mid-May–mid-Oct., $100 mid-Oct.–mid-May. High-speed passenger ferry $24 one-way, $5 bicycles). The trip takes 2¼ hours. A newer, faster passenger ferry takes just an hour.

Hy-Line departs from Hyannis from early May through October. The trip takes from 1¼ to 2 hours. The cost one-way is $13.50, plus $5 for bicycles. There is also service from Oak Bluffs on Martha's Vineyard from early June to mid-September; that trip takes 2¼ hours and costs the same.

Hy-Line's high-end, high-speed boat, *The Grey Lady*, ferries passengers from Hyannis and back year-round (one-way $31, bicycles $5). The trip takes just over an hour. That speed has its downside in rough seas—lots of bouncing and lurching that some find nauseating.

➤ BOAT & FERRY INFORMATION: **Steamship Authority** (☎ 508/228–3274 on Nantucket; 508/477–8600 on the Cape, WEB www.islandferry.com). **Hy-Line** (☎ 508/228–3949 on Nantucket; 508/778–2602 in Hyannis for reservations; 508/778–2600 in Hyannis for information; 508/693–0112 from Oak Bluffs on Martha's Vineyard, WEB www.hy-linecruises.com). **Hy-Line** ✉ (Ocean St. dock, ☎ 508/778–0404 or 800/492–8082).

HARBOR FACILITIES

The Boat Basin operates harbor facilities year-round, with shower and laundry facilities, electric power, cable TV, phone hookups, a fuel dock, and summer concierge service.

➤ CONTACT: **Boat Basin** (☎ 508/228–1350 or 800/626–2628, WEB www.nantucketboatbasin.com).

BUS TRAVEL

From mid-June to Labor Day, Barrett's Tours, across from the Information Bureau in Nantucket Town, runs beach shuttles to Siasconset ($5 round-trip, $3 one-way), Surfside ($3 round-trip, $2 one-way), and Jetties ($1 one-way) several times daily. Children pay half fare to 'Sconset and Surfside. The Nantucket Regional Transit Authority runs shuttle buses around the island between June and September. Most service begins at 7 AM and ends at 11 PM. Fares are 50¢ in town, $1 to 'Sconset and Madaket, $10 for a three-day pass, $15 for a seven-day pass, and $30 for a one-month pass. Seasonal passes are also available.

➤ BUS INFORMATION: **Barrett's Tours** (✉ 20 Federal St., ☎ 508/228–0174 or 800/773–0174). **Nantucket Regional Transit Authority** (☎ 508/228–7025; 508/325–0788 TTY, WEB www.nantucket.net/trans/nrta).

CAR RENTAL

➤ LOCAL AGENCIES: **Budget** (☎ 508/228–5666 or 888/228–5666). **Hertz** (☎ 508/228–9421 or 800/654–3131). **Nantucket Windmill** (☎ 508/228–1227 or 800/228–1227).

EMERGENCIES

➤ HOSPITAL AND EMERGENCY SERVICES: **Police or fire** (911). **Nantucket Cottage Hospital** (✉ 57 Prospect St., ☎ 508/228–1200).
➤ LATE-NIGHT PHARMACY: **Nantucket Pharmacy** (✉ 45 Main St., ☎ 508/228–0180).

LODGING

➤ RESERVATION AGENCIES: **Congdon & Coleman** (✉ 57 Main St., Nantucket 02554, ☎ 508/325–5000, FAX 508/325–5025, WEB www.congdonandcoleman.com). **'Sconset Real Estate** (✉ Box 122, Siasconset 02564, ☎ 508/257–6335; 508/228–1815 in winter). **Martha's Vineyard and Nantucket Reservations** (✉ Box 1322, 73 Lagoon Pond Rd., Vineyard Haven 02568, ☎ 508/693–7200; 800/649–5671 in MA, WEB www.mvreservations.com.).

TAXIS

➤ CONTACTS: **A-1 Taxi** (☎ 508/228–3330 or 508/228–4084). **All Points Taxi** (☎ 508/228–5779). **BG's Taxi** (☎ 508/228–4146).

TOURS

The third-generation Nantucketers at Barrett's Tours conduct 1½-hour bus tours of the island. Carried Away takes people on narrated carriage rides through Nantucket's historic district in season. Sixth-generation Nantucketer Gail Johnson of Gail's Tours narrates a lively 1½-hour van tour of island highlights. Nantucket Whale Watch runs excursions in season.

➤ TOUR-OPERATOR RECOMMENDATIONS: **Barrett's Tours** (✉ 20 Federal St., ☎ 508/228–0174 or 800/773–0174). **Carried Away** (☎ 508/228–0218). **Gail's Tours** (☎ 508/257–6557 WEB www.nantucket.net/tours/gails). **Nantucket Whale Watch** (✉ Straight Wharf, Hy-Line dock, ☎ 508/283–0313 or 800/322–0013).

VISITOR INFORMATION

The Nantucket Visitors Service and Information Bureau monitors room availability in season and at holidays for last-minute bookings. At night, check the board outside for available rooms.

➤ TOURIST INFORMATION: **Nantucket Visitors Service and Information Bureau** (✉ 25 Federal St., ☎ 508/228–0925). **Chamber of Commerce** (✉ 48 Main St., Nantucket 02554, ☎ 508/228–1700, WEB www.nantucketchamber.org). **Nantucket Visitor Services and Information Bureau** (✉ 25 Federal St., ☎ 508/228–0925).

THE NORTH SHORE

Updated by
Carolyn Heller

The slice of Massachusetts's Atlantic coast known as the North Shore extends past grimy docklands and through Boston's well-to-do northern suburbs to the picturesque Cape Ann region, and beyond Cape Ann to Newburyport, just south of New Hampshire. In addition to miles of fine beaches, the North Shore encompasses Marblehead, a quintessential New England sea town; Salem, which thrives on a history of witches, millionaires, and maritime trade; Gloucester, the oldest seaport in America and now a popular spot for whale-watching; quaint Rockport, crammed with crafts shops and artists' studios; and Newburyport, with its redbrick center and rows of clapboard Federal mansions. Bright and busy in the short summer season, the North Shore is calmer between November and June. Since many restaurants, inns, and attractions operate with reduced hours or close in the off-season, it's worth calling ahead.

Marblehead

❷❽ *15 mi north of Boston.*

Marblehead's narrow, winding streets and old clapboard houses retain much of the character of the village founded in 1629 by fishermen from Cornwall and the Channel Islands. The proud spirit of the ambitious merchant sailors who made Marblehead prosper in the 18th century can still be felt in many of the impressive Georgian mansions that line downtown streets. It's a sign of the times that today's fishing fleet is small compared to the armada of pleasure craft in the harbor. This is one of New England's premier sailing capitals, and Race Week (usually the last week of July) draws boats from all along the eastern seaboard. Parking in town can be difficult; try the 30-car public lot at the end of Front Street, the lot on State Street by the Landing restaurant, or the metered areas on the street. The Marblehead Chamber of Commerce has a complete visitor guide with a walking tour of the city.

Marblehead's Victorian-era municipal building, **Abbott Hall,** built in 1876, houses Archibald Willard's painting *The Spirit of '76.* One of America's treasured patriotic icons, it depicts three Revolutionary veterans with fife, drum, and flag. The deed used to buy the town from the Nana-

The North Shore

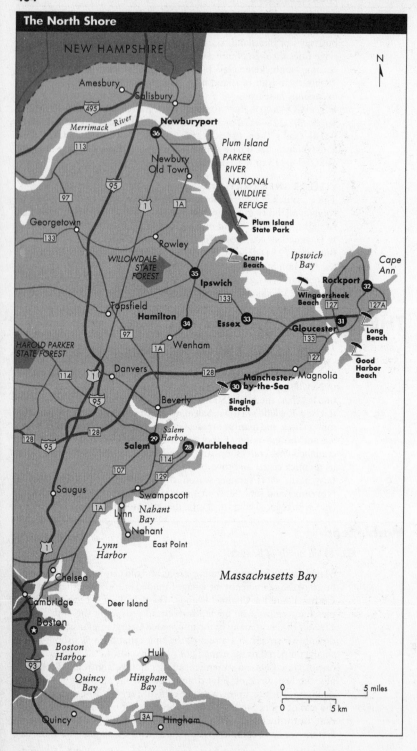

NEW HAMPSHIRE

Amesbury

Salisbury

495

Merrimack River

113

Newburyport 36

Newbury
Old Town

95

97

1

1A

Plum Island

PARKER
RIVER
NATIONAL
WILDLIFE
REFUGE

Plum Island
State Park

Georgetown

133

Rowley

WILLOWDALE
STATE
FOREST

Crane
Beach

Ipswich
Bay

Cape
Ann

Ipswich 35

133

Rockport 32

Wingaersheek
Beach

127

127A

Topsfield

Hamilton 34

Essex 33

31

Long
Beach

HAROLD PARKER
STATE FOREST

97

Wenham

1A

Gloucester

133

127

Good
Harbor
Beach

114

1

95

Danvers

128

**Manchester-
by-the-Sea** 30

Magnolia

Beverly

Singing
Beach

128

128

95

Salem
Harbor

Salem 29

28 **Marblehead**

Saugus

107

114

129

Swampscott

1A

Lynn

*Nahant
Bay*

Nahant

*Lynn
Harbor*

East Point

1

Chelsea

Massachusetts Bay

Cambridge

Deer Island

★ Boston

*Boston
Harbor*

93

Hull

*Quincy
Bay*

*Hingham
Bay*

0   5 miles

0   5 km

Quincy

3A   Hingham

pashemet and other artifacts of Marblehead's history are also on display. ⊠ *188 Washington St.,* ☎ *781/631–0528.* ☉ *May–Oct., Mon.–Tues. and Thurs. 8–5, Wed. 7:30–7:30, Fri. 8–6, Sat. 9–6, Sun. 11–6; Nov.–Apr., Mon.–Tues. and Thurs. 8–5, Wed. 7:30–7:30, Fri. 8–1.*

Dining and Lodging

$$$ ✕ **The Landing.** Right on Marblehead harbor, this pleasant restaurant has indoor and outdoor dining. The menu mixes classic New England fare (clam chowder, lobster, broiled scrod) with more contemporary dishes, such as sesame-crusted salmon, seafood cioppino, and grilled duck risotto. There's also a pub with a lighter menu. ⊠ *81 Front St.,* ☎ *781/639–1266,* WEB *www.thenewlanding.com. AE, D, DC, MC, V.*

$–$$ ✕ **King's Rook.** At this cozy café and wine bar, the crisp single-serving pizzas include one with goat cheese, roasted red peppers, and caramelized onions and another loaded with veggies. The restaurant also serves tasty sandwiches like the curried egg salad with raisins and the overstuffed turkey. ⊠ *12 State St.,* ☎ *781/631–9838. D, MC, V. Closed Mon.*

$ ✕ **Truffles.** This gourmet café–take-out shop has everything needed for a picnic or a quick coffee break. Prepared items include stuffed baby eggplant and smoked-turkey calzone, as well as intriguing sandwiches. The house-made pastries complement the strong coffee. ⊠ *114 Washington St.,* ☎ *781/639–1104. AE, MC, V. No dinner.*

$$$–$$$$ 🏨 **Marblehead Inn.** This rambling mansard-roof mansion, built as a private home in 1872, sits on the main road between Salem and Marblehead. The two-room suites with Victorian-style furnishings have living rooms, bedrooms (some with pineapple four-poster beds), and kitchenettes. Several have whirlpool tubs, and two have a private patio or terrace. There's no smoking on the premises. ⊠ *264 Pleasant St. (Rte. 114), 01945,* ☎ *781/639–9999 or 800/399–5843,* FAX *781/639–9996,* WEB *www.marbleheadinn.com. 10 suites. AE, MC, V. CP.*

$$–$$$$ 🏨 **Harbor Light Inn.** If you were to describe the ideal New England inn, ★ it might resemble the Harbor Light. Stately antiques are arranged in rooms with floral wallpaper or period-color paint. Most guest rooms have fireplaces, and several have hot tubs or skylights. Traditional touches, including four-poster and canopy beds, carved arched doorways, wide-board floors, and Oriental rugs—plus afternoon tea and wine and cheese on winter Saturday nights—make a stay here special. ⊠ *58 Washington St., 01945,* ☎ *781/631–2186,* FAX *781/631–2216,* WEB *www.harborlightinn.com. 21 rooms. Pool, meeting room. AE, MC, V. CP.*

Outdoor Activities and Sports

BEACHES

Marblehead is not known for sprawling beaches, but the ones it does have are well maintained and mostly used for family outings or quick ocean dips. **Deveraux Beach** (⊠ Ocean Ave. before the causeway to Marblehead Neck), the most spacious, has some sandy and some pebbled areas, as well as a playground. Parking is $5 for nonresidents.

BOATING

Boating is popular, but the town has long waiting lists for mooring space. The **harbormaster** (☎ 781/631–2386) can inform you of nightly fees at public docks when space is available.

Salem

★ ㉙ *4 mi west of Marblehead, 15 mi north of Boston.*

Salem unabashedly calls itself "Witch City." During the town's wildly popular October "Haunted Happenings," museums and businesses are converted into haunted houses, graveyards, or dungeons, as the town celebrates its spooky past. Year-round, witches astride broomsticks decorate the police cars; numerous witch-related attractions and shops, as well current-day resident witchcraft practitioners, recall the city's infamous connection with the witchcraft hysteria and trials of 1692. That witchcraft mania began in January 1692 when several Salem-area girls fell ill, and William Griggs, the village physician, declared that the girls were bewitched. More than 150 men and women were charged with practicing witchcraft, a crime punishable by death. After the resulting trials later that year, 19 innocent people were hanged.

Witchcraft aside, Salem's charms include compelling museums, trendy waterfront stores and restaurants, and a wide common with a children's playground. Settled in 1626, the town has a rich maritime tradition; frigates out of Salem opened the Far East trade routes and generated the wealth that created America's first millionaires. Among Salem's native sons were writer Nathaniel Hawthorne, navigator Nathaniel Bowditch, and architect Samuel McIntire.

A good place to start your Salem tour is the large **National Park Service Visitor Center,** which has a wide variety of booklets and pamphlets, including a "Maritime Trail" and "Early Settlement Trail" for Essex County, as well as a free 27-minute film. ⊠ 2 New Liberty St., ☎ 978/740–1650, WEB www.nps.gov/sama. ⊙ Daily 9–5.

One way to explore Salem is to follow the 1¾-mi **Heritage Trail** (painted in red on the sidewalk) around town. For those who prefer to ride rather than walk, the **Salem Trolley** leaves every hour (and sometimes more often) for a guided tour from near the National Park Visitor Center. You may get off and back on the trolley en route. ⊠ Trolley Depot, 191 Essex St., ☎ 978/744–5469 or 800/821–8179, WEB www.trolley-depot.com. ☑ $10. ⊙ Apr.–June and Sept.–Oct., daily 10–5; July–Aug., daily 10–7; Nov. and Mar., weekends 10–4.

★   Tour highlights at the **House of the Seven Gables,** which was immortalized in the classic 1851 novel of the same name by Nathaniel Hawthorne, include the period furnishings, a secret staircase, and a garret containing an antique scale model of the house. The complex of 17th-century buildings includes the small house where Hawthorne was born in 1804; it was moved from its original location elsewhere in Salem. ⊠ 54 Turner St. (off Derby St.), ☎ 978/744–0991, WEB www.7gables.org. ☑ Guided tours $8, combination ticket with Salem 1630 Pioneer Village $13. ⊙ Apr.–Dec., daily 10–5; mid-Jan.–Mar., Mon.–Sat. 10–5, Sun. noon–5.

The **Salem Maritime National Historic Site,** run by the National Park Service, focuses on Salem's heritage as a major seaport with a thriving overseas trade. The park site includes an orientation center with an 18-minute film; the 1762 home of Elias Derby, America's first millionaire; the 1819 Customs House, made famous in Nathaniel Hawthorne's The Scarlet Letter; several sites relating to sea trade; and a replica of **The Friendship,** a 171-ft, three-masted 1797 trader merchant vessel, scheduled to open in 2002. ⊠ 174 Derby St., ☎ 978/740–1660, WEB www.nps.gov/sama. ☑ Guided tours $3, grounds free. ⊙ Daily 9–5.

★   Salem's vast, dazzling maritime riches are the focal point of the **Peabody Essex Museum.** The galleries are filled with maritime art and history and the spoils of the Asian export trade—ranging from 16th-century Chinese blue porcelain to Indian colonial silver. In 2000, the museum embarked on a major renovation and expansion, designed by architect Moshe Safdie; construction is expected to continue through 2003, but the museum plans to remain open in the interim. ⊠ East India Sq., ☎ 978/745–9500 or 800/745–4054, WEB www.pem.org. ☑ $10; good *for 2 consecutive days.* ☉ *Apr.–Oct., Mon.–Sat. 10–5, Sun. noon–5; Nov.–Mar., Tues.–Sat. 10–5, Sun. noon–5.*

For an informative if somewhat hokey introduction to the 1692 witchcraft hysteria, visit the **Salem Witch Museum,** which stages a half-hour multisensory re-creation of the 1692 events, using 13 sets, life-size models, and a taped narration. A 10-minute walk-through exhibit, "Witches' Evolving Perceptions," describes witch history and witch hunts through the years. The museum also sells an interesting pamphlet detailing the events that led to the witch trials. ⊠ *19½ Washington Sq. N,* ☎ *978/744–1692,* 🕸 *www.salemwitchmuseum.com.* 🎟 *$6.* ☉ *Sept.–June, daily 10–5; July–Aug., daily 10–7.*

The figures at the **Salem Wax Museum of Witches and Seafarers** tell the town's story, detailing its rich maritime tradition and the witch-related hysterics of 1692. The **Salem Witch Village** (managed by the wax museum) across the street focuses on historic and modern witchcraft's spiritual and religious practices. ⊠ *282–288 Derby St.,* ☎ *978/740–2929,* 🕸 *www.salemwaxmuseum.com.* 🎟 *Each site $4.95, combination ticket $8.95.* ☉ *Nov.–Mar., Sun.–Thurs. 11–4, Fri.–Sat. 10–5; Apr.–June, daily 10–6; July–Sept. daily 10–7; extended hrs in Oct.*

The **Witch Dungeon Museum** features a guided tour of dungeons where accused witches were kept and a live reenactment of one trial, as adapted from 1692 transcripts. ⊠ *16 Lynde St.,* ☎ *978/741–3570,* 🕸 *www.witchdungeon.com.* 🎟 *$5.* ☉ *Apr.–Nov., daily 10–5; evening hrs around Halloween.*

Ⓒ Children will enjoy the small **Salem 1630 Pioneer Village,** where costumed interpreters help re-create the Salem of the early 17th century, when it was a fishing village and the Commonwealth's first capital. Replicas of thatched-roof cottages, period gardens, and wigwams have been constructed at the site. ⊠ *Forest River Park (follow Rte. 114 east, then turn left onto West Ave.),* ☎ *978/744–0991,* 🕸 *www.7gables.org/ 1630.html.* 🎟 *$7, combination ticket with House of Seven Gables $13.* ☉ *Apr.–late Nov., Mon.–Sat. 10–5, Sun. noon–5.*

Ⓒ **Salem Willows Park,** at the eastern end of Derby Street, has picnic grounds, beaches, food stands, amusements, games, boat rentals, and fishing bait.

Although Salem became famous as the witch-trials city, it is Danvers (formerly Salem Village)—several miles northwest of present-day Salem—that has the real relics of the witchcraft episode. The **Rebecca Nurse Homestead** was the home of aged, pious Rebecca, a devout churchgoer accused of being a witch. The charge caused shock waves in the community. Her trial was a mockery (she was first pronounced innocent, but the jury was urged to change its verdict), and she was hanged in 1692. Her family secretly buried her body somewhere on the grounds of this house, which has period furnishings and 17th-century vegetable and herb gardens. ⊠ *149 Pine St., Danvers,* ☎ *978/774–8799,* 🕸 *www.rebeccanurse.org.* 🎟 *$4.* ☉ *Mid-June–Labor Day, Tues.–Sun. 1–4:30; Labor Day–Oct., weekends 1–4:30 or by appointment; May– mid-June, by appointment.*

Dining and Lodging

$$–$$$ ✕ **The Grapevine.** Contemporary northern Italian fare is served up at this inviting upscale bistro opposite Pickering Wharf. The changing menu may include fish stew with Sardinian couscous, grilled lamb with black pepper vinaigrette, or capellini with arugula, garlic, and crab, as well as vegetarian selections. ⊠ *26 Congress St.,* ☎ *978/745–9335,* 🕸 *www.grapevinesalem.com. AE, MC, V. No lunch.*

$$$-$$$$ ✕⊡ **Hawthorne Hotel.** An imposing redbrick structure, this hotel stands on the green, just a short walk from the commercial center, the waterfront, and other attractions. Guest rooms are appointed with reproduction 18th-century armchairs and desks. The hotel's formal, chandelier-bedecked restaurant, Nathaniel's, is one of the more elegant eateries in Salem; the ambitious menu may include lobster, pink peppercorn-crusted salmon, and wild mushroom ravioli. ⊠ *18 Washington Sq. W, 01970,* ☎ *978/744–4080 or 800/729–7829,* 𝔽𝔸𝕏 *978/745–9842,* WEB *www.hawthornehotel.com. 83 rooms, 6 suites. Restaurant, bar, lounge, exercise room, meeting room. AE, D, DC, MC, V.*

$$-$$$$ ⊡ **Inn at Seven Winter St.** Built in 1871, this inn has been authentically restored to re-create the Victorian era. Rooms are spacious and well furnished, with heavy mahogany and walnut antiques. Some open to a deck, some have whirlpool tubs, and some have marble fireplaces; the suites also have kitchenettes. The no-smoking inn is better suited to couples than families. ⊠ *7 Winter St., 01970,* ☎ *978/745–9520 or 800/932–5547,* 𝔽𝔸𝕏 *978/745–0523,* WEB *www.inn7winter.com. 8 rooms, 2 suites. Breakfast room, free parking. AE, MC, V. CP.*

$$ ⊡ **Amelia Payson Guest House.** This elegantly restored 1845 Greek Revival house near all the historic attractions has been converted into a bright, airy bed-and-breakfast. Floral-print wallpaper, brass and canopy beds, and white wicker furnishings decorate the pretty rooms, which have nonworking marble fireplaces. The downstairs parlor has a grand piano. Smoking is not allowed. ⊠ *16 Winter St., 01970,* ☎ *978/744–8304,* WEB *www.ameliapaysonhouse.com. 4 rooms. Breakfast room, free parking. AE, D, MC, V. Mid-Dec.–Mar. CP.*

Shopping

Crow Haven Corner (⊠ 125 Essex St., ☎ 978/745–8763) is the former haunt of Laurie Cabot, once dubbed Salem's "official" witch. Her daughter, Jody, now presides over crystal balls, herbs, tarot decks, healing stones, and books about witchcraft. **Pyramid Books** (⊠ 214 Derby St., ☎ 978/745–7171) stocks New Age and metaphysical books.

Manchester-by-the-Sea

③⓪ *13 mi northeast of Salem, 28 mi northeast of Boston.*

Incorporated in 1645, Manchester became a fashionable summer community for well-to-do urbanites in the mid-19th century. Today it is a small seaside commuter suburb built around a picturesque harbor.

Outdoor Activities and Sports

Bostonians visit Manchester for its lovely, long **Singing Beach** (⊠ Off Rte. 127), so called because of the noise your feet make against the white sand. The beach has lifeguards, food stands, and rest rooms, but no parking; either take the commuter train from Boston or park in the private pay lot ($15 per day for nonresidents) by the railroad station—a ½-mi walk to the beach.

Gloucester

③① *8 mi northeast of Manchester, 36 mi northeast of Boston.*

On Gloucester's fine seaside promenade is a famous statue of a man steering a ship's wheel, his eyes searching the horizon. The statue, which honors those "who go down to the sea in ships," was commissioned by the town citizens in 1923 in celebration of Gloucester's 300th anniversary. The oldest seaport in the nation, this workaday town is still a major fishing port. One portrait of Gloucester's fishing community can be found in Sebastian Junger's best-selling 1997 book, *A Perfect Storm,* about a Gloucester fishing boat caught in "the storm of the century" in October 1991; in 2000, the book was made into a movie, filmed on location in Gloucester. Whale-watching is popular here, too.

The town's creative side is illuminated by the **Rocky Neck** neighborhood, the first-settled artists' colony in the United States. Its alumni include Winslow Homer, Maurice Prendergast, Jane Peter, and Cecilia Beaux. Today Rocky Neck remains home to many artists; its galleries are usually open daily 10 AM to 10 PM in summer. To get here, follow East Main Street from downtown toward Eastern Point.

Hammond Castle Museum, a stone "medieval" castle built in 1926 by the inventor John Hays Hammond Jr., who is credited with more than 500 patents, contains medieval-style furnishings and paintings. The Great Hall houses an organ impressive for its 8,200 pipes. From the castle you can also see "Norman's Woe Rock," made famous by Longfellow in his poem *The Wreck of the Hesperus.* ⊠ *80 Hesperus Ave. (on the south side of Gloucester off Rte. 127),* ☎ *978/283–2080 or 978/283–7673.* ☞ *$6.50.* ☉ *Memorial Day–Labor Day, daily 9–5; Labor Day–Columbus Day, Wed.–Sun. 10–4; Columbus Day–Memorial Day, weekends 10–3; closed last 2 wks in Oct. The museum often closes to host weddings or special events; call ahead to check hrs.*

Dining and Lodging

$$$ ✕ **White Rainbow.** This excellent restaurant is in the basement of a down-
★   town store, and candlelight provides a romantic atmosphere. The contemporary American specialties include Maui onion soup, grilled filet mignon, lobster, and fresh fish. ⊠ *65 Main St.,* ☎ *978/281–0017. AE, D, DC, MC, V. Closed Mon.–Tues.; no lunch*

$$–$$$ ✕ **Franklin Café.** Under the same ownership as the Franklin Café in Boston's South End, this funky nightspot brings hip comfort food to the North Shore. Think bistro-style chicken, roast cod, and upscale meat-loaf, perfect for the late-night crowd (they're open till midnight). Tuesday evenings generally feature live jazz. There's no sign, so look for the signature martini glass over the door. ⊠ *118 Main St.,* ☎ *978/283–7888. AE, DC, D, MC, V. No lunch.*

$$ ☷ **Cape Ann Motor Inn.** This wood-shingle, three-story motel is as close to the sand as they come, right on Long Beach on the Gloucester-Rockport line. Half the smallish rooms have kitchenettes, and all have balconies and superb views over beach, sea, and the twin lights of Thatcher's Island. ⊠ *33 Rockport Rd., 01930,* ☎ *978/281–2900 or 800/464–8439,* FAX *978/281–1359,* WEB *www.capeannmotorinn.com. 30 rooms, 1 suite. AE, D, MC, V. CP.*

$–$$ ☷ **Cape Ann's Marina Resort.** This year-round hostelry less than a mile from Gloucester really comes alive in summer, when a full-service restaurant (open mid-April–October), a whale-watch boat, and deep-sea fishing excursions operate on and from the premises. The rooms, with views of the water, have color TVs, balconies, and air-conditioning, should the Atlantic breezes be insufficient. ⊠ *75 Essex Ave., 01930,* ☎ *978/283–2116 or 800/626–7660,* FAX *978/283–2116,* WEB *www.capeannmarina.com. 52 rooms. Restaurant, pool. AE, D, DC, MC, V.*

Nightlife and the Arts

The **Rhumb Line** (⊠ 40 Railroad Ave., ☎ 978/283–9732) has good food and live entertainment every night but Tuesday, with rock-and-roll on Friday and Saturday and acoustic music on Sunday.

The **Gloucester Stage Company** (⊠ 267 E. Main St., ☎ 978/281–4099) is a nonprofit professional group that stages new plays and revivals May–October. The **Hammond Castle Museum** (⊠ 80 Hesperus Ave., ☎ 978/283–2080) has a summer chamber-music concert series.

Outdoor Activities

BEACHES

Gloucester has some of the best beaches on the North Shore. Parking costs about $10 on weekdays and about $15 on weekends, when the lots often fill by 10 AM. **Wingaersheek Beach** (⊠ Exit 13 off Rte. 128) is a picture-perfect, well-protected cove of white sand and dunes, with the white Annisquam lighthouse in the bay. **Good Harbor Beach** (⊠ signposted from Rte. 127A) is a huge, sandy, dune-backed beach with a rocky islet just offshore. **Long Beach** (⊠ off Rte. 127A on Gloucester-Rockport town line) is an excellent place for sunbathing; parking here is only $5.

BOATING

You can sail along the harbor and coast aboard the 65-ft schooner ***Thomas E. Lannon*** (⊠ 63R Rogers St., Seven Seas Wharf, ☎ 978/281–6634, WEB www.schooner.org), crafted in Essex in 1996 and modeled after the great boats built a century ago. From mid-May through October, there are several two-hour sails daily, including sunset sails, lobster bake sails, music cruises, and storytelling sails. Advance reservations are recommended.

FISHING

Captain Bill's Deep Sea Fishing/Whale Watch (⊠ 30 Harbor Loop, ☎ 978/283–6995 or 800/339–4253, WEB www.cape-ann.com/captbill.html) operates half-day excursions from May to October. **Coastal Fishing Charters,** under the same ownership as Cape Ann Whale Watch (⊠ Rose's Wharf, 415 Main St., ☎ 978/283–5113 or 800/877–5110, WEB www.caww.com), operates day and evening fishing trips by private charter for up to six people. The **Yankee Fishing Fleet** (⊠ 75 Essex Ave., ☎ 978/283–0313 or 800/942–5464, WEB www.yankeefleet.com) conducts deep-sea fishing trips.

WHALE-WATCHING

The most popular special-interest tours on the North Shore are whale-sighting excursions. **Cape Ann Whale Watch** (⊠ 415 Main St., ☎ 978/283–5110 or 800/877–5110, WEB www.caww.com) runs daily trips from mid-April to mid-October. **Captain Bill's Whale Watch** generally operates excursions between May and October. **Yankee Fishing Fleet** runs daily whale-watch trips from mid-June through September; call for spring and fall schedules.

Rockport

㉜   *4 mi north of Gloucester, 40 mi north of Boston.*

At the very tip of Cape Ann, Rockport derives its name from its granite formations. Many Boston-area structures are made of stone from the town's long-gone quarries. Rockport is a mecca for summer tourists attracted by its hilly rows of colorful clapboard houses, historic inns, artists' studios, and small bathing beaches. (It's also very accessible to Boston—the commuter rail stops in town.) Though it's a tourist haunt, Rockport has not gone overboard on T-shirt shacks and the like: shops sell crafts, folk and fine art, clothing, and cameras, and restaurants serve seafood or home-baked cookies rather than fast food.

You can walk out to the end of **Bearskin Neck** for an impressive view of the open Atlantic. The nearby lobster shack in view is known as "Motif No. 1" because of its popularity as a subject for artists and amateur painters. The **Rockport Art Association Gallery** (⊠ 12 Main St., ☎ 978/546–6604), open all year except January, displays the best work of local artists.

Dining and Lodging

$$$–$$$$ ✕ **My Place by the Sea.** This restaurant is perched right at the tip of Bearskin Neck, with a lower deck on rocks over the ocean. The menu lists New England seafood specialties such as lobster, plus steaks, pasta, salads, and sandwiches. ✉ *Bearskin Neck,* ☎ *978/546–9667. AE, D, DC, MC, V. BYOB. Closed Nov.–Mar.*

$$–$$$ ✕ **Brackett's Oceanview Restaurant.** The big bay window of this homey restaurant has an excellent view across the beach. On the menu are scallop casserole, fish cakes, and other seafood dishes. ✉ *27 Main St.,* ☎ *978/546–2797,* WEB *www.bracketts.com. AE, D, DC, MC, V. BYOB. Closed Nov.–Mar.*

$$$$ 🏨 **Yankee Clipper Inn.** This perfectly located inn in an imposing Geor-
★ gian mansion sits on a rocky point jutting into the sea. Guest rooms vary in size, but most are spacious. Furnished with antiques, they contain four-poster or canopy beds, and all but one have an ocean view. Smoking is not permitted. ✉ *127 Granite St., 01966,* ☎ *978/546–3407 or 800/545–3699,* FAX *978/546–9730,* WEB *www.yankeeclipperinn.com. 8 rooms. Pool. AE, MC, V. Closed Dec.–Feb. BP.*

$$–$$$ 🏨 **Addison Choate Inn.** This historic inn sits inconspicuously among pri-
★ vate homes, just a minute's walk from the center of Rockport. The spacious rooms, with large tile bathrooms, are beautifully decorated; the navy-and-white captain's room contains a canopy bed, handmade quilts, and Oriental rugs. Other rooms—all with polished pine floors—have their share of antiques and local seascape paintings. In the third-floor suite, huge windows look out over the rooftops to the sea. The two comfortably appointed duplex stable-house apartments have skylights, cathedral ceilings, and exposed wood beams. ✉ *49 Broadway, 01966,* ☎ *978/546–7543 or 800/245–7543,* FAX *978/546–7638,* WEB *www.addisonchoate.com. 5 rooms, 1 suite, 2 apartments. AE, DC, MC, V. CP.*

$$–$$$ 🏨 **Seacrest Manor.** Surrounded by large gardens, this distinctive 1911 clapboard mansion sits atop a hill overlooking the sea; the inn's motto is "Decidedly small, intentionally quiet." Two elegant sitting rooms are furnished with antiques and leather chairs; one has a huge looking glass salvaged from the old Philadelphia Opera House. The hall and staircase are hung with paintings—some depicting the inn—by local artists. Guest rooms vary in size and character and combine simple traditional and antique furnishings; some have large, private decks. ✉ *99 Marmion Way, 01966,* ☎ *978/546–2211,* WEB *www.seacrestmanor.com. 8 rooms, 6 with bath. No credit cards. Closed Dec.–Mar. BP.*

$–$$ 🏨 **Sally Webster Inn.** Sally Webster was a member of Hannah Jumper's
★ so-called hatchet gang, which smashed up the town's liquor stores in 1856 and turned Rockport into the dry town it remains today. Sally lived in this house for much of her life, and the guest rooms are named for members of her family. They contain rocking chairs; nonworking brick fireplaces; pineapple four-poster, brass, canopy, or spool beds; and wide-board pine floors covered with Oriental rugs. ✉ *34 Mt. Pleasant St., 01966,* ☎ *978/546–9251 or 877/546–9251,* WEB *www.sallywebster.com. 8 rooms. MC, V. Closed Jan. CP.*

Essex

㉝ *12 mi west of Rockport, 31 mi north of Boston.*

The small, picturesque town of Essex, once an important shipbuilding center, is surrounded by salt marshes and is filled with antiques stores and seafood restaurants.

The **Essex Shipbuilding Museum,** which is still an active shipyard, has exhibits on 19th-century shipbuilding, including displays of period tools and ship models. One-hour tours are available, taking in the museum's several buildings and boats, including the *Evelina M. Goulart*—one of only seven remaining Essex-built schooners. ⊠ *66 Main St. (Rte. 133),* ☎ *978/768–7541,* WEB *www.essexshipbuildingmuseum.com.* ⌐ *$4.* ☉ *Memorial Day–Columbus Day, Wed.–Mon. 12–4; Columbus Day–Memorial Day, weekends 12–4.*

From April through October, **Essex River Cruises** (⊠ Essex Marina, 35 Dodge St., ☎ 978/768–6981 or 800/748–3706, WEB www.essex-cruises.com) explores the area's salt marshes, rivers, and local wildlife during a 1½-hour narrated cruise on the *Essex River Queen.*

Dining

$$–$$$ ✕ **Jerry Pelonzi's Hearthside.** This 250-year-old converted farmhouse is the epitome of coziness; its small dining rooms have exposed beams and open fireplaces. Traditional entrées include baked stuffed haddock, seafood casserole, sirloin steak, lobster, and chicken. ⊠ *109 Eastern Ave. (Rte. 133),* ☎ *978/768–6002 or 978/768–6003. AE, MC, V. Closed Mon. in winter.*

$–$$ ✕ **Woodman's of Essex.** Back in 1916, Lawrence "Chubby" Woodman
★ dipped a shucked clam in batter and threw it into the french fryer as a kind of joke, apparently creating the first fried clam in town. Today this large wooden shack with unpretentious booths is *the* place for seafood in the rough. The menu includes lobster, a raw bar, clam chowder, and, of course, fried clams. ⊠ *121 Main St. (Rte. 133),* ☎ *978/768–6451 or 800/649–1773,* WEB *www.woodmans.com. No credit cards.*

Shopping

Essex is a popular antiquing destination. Most of the shops are along Main Street (Route 133). The **White Elephant** (⊠ 32 Main St., ☎ 978/768–6901), one of the region's largest consignment shops, offers furniture, china, and collectibles. **Chebacco Antiques** (⊠ 38 Main St., ☎ 978/768–7371) concentrates on American pine and country furniture.

Hamilton

㉞ *3 mi south of Ipswich, 33 mi north of Boston.*

Settled in 1638, incorporated in 1793, and named after Alexander Hamilton, the town of Hamilton is said to have the highest horse-to-person ratio in the Northeast. Most of the property in this small town is owned by a few families who are dedicated to keeping the landscape rural and undeveloped—there are miles of wooded trails.

The lovely **Sedgwick Gardens at Long Hill** surround the former summer home of Ellery Sedgwick, editor of the *Atlantic Monthly* from 1909 to 1938. The 114-acre property includes numerous gardens, a lotus pool, Chinese pagoda, and a woodland path lined with unusual plants. The gardens are on the town line with Beverly. ⊠ *572 Essex St. (Rte. 22), Exit 18 from Rte. 128, Beverly,* ☎ *978/921–1944,* WEB *www.thetrustees.org.* ⌐ *Donation suggested.* ☉ *Daily 8 AM–dusk.*

Dining and Lodging

$$$ ✕ **The Black Cow.** A young professional crowd hangs out at this comfortable tap and grill. The food is similar to what you'd find at an upscale bar in Boston: lobster ravioli; grilled tuna with mango salsa; New York strip steak; and grilled duck breast with sticky rice. ⊠ *16 Bay Rd. (Rte. 1A),* ☎ *978/468–1166,* WEB *www.blackcowtapandgrill.com. AE, MC, V.*

$$–$$$$ ⊡ **Miles River Country Inn.** Staying in this sprawling Colonial home
★ amid acres of lawns and gardens is like being a guest at a private country estate. The guest rooms, living room, and sunporch are all comfortably appointed with country-style antiques. In winter you can

cross-country ski for miles in fields and woods, right from the front door; in milder weather, you can wander the fields and gardens. Breakfast often includes eggs from the hens of the gracious innkeepers, Gretel and Peter Clark, and honey from Gretel's beehives. In the main house, an apartment (with a full kitchen) sleeps six; a separate four-room cottage on the property rents by the week. ✉ *823 Bay Rd. (Rte. 1A), 01936,* ☎ *978/468–7206,* FAX *978/468–3999,* WEB *www.milesriver.com. 8 rooms, 6 with bath; 1 apartment, 1 cottage. Skiing. AE, MC, V. BP.*

Outdoor Activities and Sports

The very grand **Myopia Hunt Club** (☎ 978/468–4433; 978/468–7656 polo schedules in season, WEB www.myopiapolo.com)—one of the most exclusive clubs in America—stages polo matches (open to the public) on weekends Memorial Day through October at its grounds along Route 1A. Admission is $10.

Ipswich

35 *5 mi north of Hamilton, 6 mi northwest of Essex, 36 mi north of Boston.*

Quiet little Ipswich, settled in 1633 and famous for its clams, is said to have more 17th-century houses standing and occupied than any other place in America; more than 40 were built before 1725. The **Visitor Information Center** has a booklet with a suggested walking tour. ✉ *20 S. Main St., next to Town Hall,* ☎ *978/356–8540.* ☉ *Summer and fall, daily 10–4.*

The **Crane Estate,** comprising more than 2,000 acres along the Essex and Ipswich rivers, includes Castle Hill, Crane Beach, and the Crane Wildlife Refuge. Also on the estate is the Great House, a 59-room Stuart-style mansion built in 1927 for Richard Crane—of the Crane plumbing company—and his family. The house has been elaborately refurnished in period style. The Great House is open for one-hour tours and hosts concerts and other special events. ✉ *290 Argilla Rd.,* ☎ *978/356–4351,* WEB *www.thetrustees.org.* 🎫 *House tours $7.* ☉ *Tours late May–mid-Oct., Wed.–Thurs. 10–4.*

Several small islands can be explored by taking a **Crane Island Tour** (☎ 978/356–4351, 🎫 $12, ☉ Memorial Day through Columbus Day) across the Castle Neck River. You can take a hay-wagon tour of Hog Island, view sets from the 1996 film *The Crucible* (filmed here and in nearby Essex), and admire the many birds and wildlife at this refuge. The tour lasts two hours; the boats to the island leave at 10 and 2. (The boat ride takes less than 10 minutes.)

☺ At **Russell Orchards,** a short drive from the Crane Estate, you can pick-your-own of whatever fruit is in season or buy apples and other produce, while the kids feed the barnyard animals. A winery produces hard cider and fruit wines. Regular cider is made with wood presses in the back of the barn. ✉ *123 Argilla Rd.,* ☎ *978/356–5366,* WEB *www.russellorchardsma.com.* ☉ *May–Nov. daily 9–6.*

Dining and Lodging

$–$$ ✕ **Clam Box.** No visit to Ipswich is complete without a sampling of the town's famous clams, and where better than at a restaurant shaped like a box of fried clams? Since 1932, people have come to this casual spot for excellent clams, fries, and onion rings. ✉ *246 High St. (Rte. 1A),* ☎ *978/356–9707. No credit cards. Closed Dec.–Feb.*

$$$–$$$$ 🏨 **The Inn at Castle Hill.** Nothing but marsh, dunes, and ocean, as far as you can see—that's the view from the spectacular wraparound porch at this secluded luxury retreat. On the grounds of the Crane Estate and owned by the Trustees of Reservations, this former farmhouse was built in the 1840s with Italianate flourishes. Furnishings range from the traditional to the more contemporary and crisp, almost spare; the vistas from the top-floor rooms are especially dramatic. You can take your afternoon tea on the verandah or by the fire in the cozy sitting room; smoking is not permitted. ⊠ *280 Argilla Rd., 01938,* ☎ *978/ 412–2555,* FAX *978/412–2556,* WEB *www.theinnatcastlehill.com. 9 rooms, 1 suite. AE, MC, V. Breakfast room, air-conditioning. CP. Closed Jan.*

Nightlife and the Arts

The **Great House at Castle Hill** (⊠ Argilla Rd., ☎ 978/356–4351) holds an annual picnic concert series of pop, folk, and classical music on Thursday evenings in July and August, plus a winter holiday concert and other special events.

Outdoor Activities and Sports

BEACHES

Crane Beach, one of the North Shore's most beautiful beaches, is a sandy, 4-mi-long stretch backed by dunes and a nature trail. There are lifeguards and changing rooms. Public parking is available. Sand Blast!, an annual sand sculpture competition, is held here in late August. ⊠ *290 Argilla Rd.,* ☎ *978/356–4354,* WEB *www.thetrustees.org.* ☞ *Mid-May–early Sept., parking $10 weekdays, $15 weekends; early Sept.– mid-May, parking $5.* ☼ *Daily 8–sunset.*

HIKING

The Massachusetts Audubon Society's **Ipswich River Wildlife Sanctuary** (⊠ 87 Perkins Row, Topsfield, ☎ 978/887–9264, WEB www.massaudubon.org) contains trails through marshland hills with remains of early Colonial settlements as well as abundant wildlife. You can pick up a self-guiding trail map from the office, but note that the office and trails are closed Mondays. The sanctuary is southwest of Ipswich, 1 mi off Route 97.

Newburyport

③⑥ *12 mi north of Ipswich, 38 mi north of Boston.*

Newburyport's High Street is lined with some of the finest examples of Federal-era (1790–1810) mansions in New England. The city was once a leading port and shipbuilding center, and the houses were built for prosperous sea captains. An energetic downtown renewal program brought new life to the town's brick-front center. Renovated buildings house restaurants, taverns, galleries, and shops that sell everything from nautical brasses to antique Oriental rugs. The civic improvements have been matched by private restorations of the town's housing stock, much of which dates from the 18th century, with a scattering of 17th-century homes in some neighborhoods.

Newburyport is a good walking city, and there is free all-day parking down by the water. A stroll through the **Waterfront Park and Promenade** yields a good view of the harbor and the fishing and pleasure boats that moor here. The **Custom House Maritime Museum,** built in 1835 in Classical Revival style, contains ship models, tools, paintings, and exhibits on maritime history, as well as a tidal tank housing lobsters, eels, and other marine life. ⊠ *25 Water St.,* ☎ *978/462–8681.* ☞ *$3.* ☼ *Apr.–Dec., Mon.–Sat. 10–4, Sun. 1–4.*

A causeway leads from Newburyport to the narrow spit of land known as **Plum Island,** which harbors a summer colony (rapidly becoming year-round) at one end. **Parker River National Wildlife Refuge,** on Plum Island, comprises 4,662 acres of salt marsh, freshwater marsh, beaches, and dunes. Bird-watching, surf fishing, plum and cranberry picking, swimming, and hiking are among the exhilarating pastimes here. The 2-mi Hellcat Swamp Trail cuts through the marshes and sand dunes, taking in the best of the sanctuary. Trail maps are available at the office. The refuge is so popular in summer, especially on weekends, that cars begin to line up at the gate before 7 AM. Only a limited number of cars are let in, though there's no restriction on the number of people using the beach. ⊠ *Sunset Dr., about ½ mi south of bridge to Plum Island,* ☎ *978/465–5753,* WEB *www.parkerriver.org.* ⊠ *$5 per car; $2 for bicycles and walk-ins.* ☉ *Daily dawn–dusk. Beach sometimes closed during endangered-species nesting season in spring and early summer. No pets.*

Dining and Lodging

$$$ ✕ **Scandia.** This restaurant is well known locally for its fine Continental
★ cuisine; among the house specialties are Caesar salad prepared tableside and a veal and lobster sauté. The narrow 15-table dining room is lighted with candles on the tables and chandeliers with candle bulbs. Sunday brunch has hot entrées, cold salads, crepes, waffles, and omelets, while at lunch, the menu offers upscale sandwiches, salads, and several seafood dishes. ⊠ *25 State St.,* ☎ *978/462–6271,* WEB *www.scandiarestaurant.com. AE, D, MC, V.*

$$–$$$ 🏨 **Clark Currier Inn.** The care, taste, and imagination with which this
★ 1803 Federal mansion has been restored make it one of the best inns on the North Shore. Guest rooms are spacious and furnished with antiques, including one with a glorious sleigh bed dating from the late 19th century. ⊠ *45 Green St., 01950,* ☎ *978/465–8363,* WEB *www.clarkcurrierinn.com. 8 rooms. AE, D, MC, V. CP.*

Nightlife and the Arts

The **Grog Shop** (⊠ 13 Middle St., ☎ 978/465–8008) hosts blues and rock bands several nights weekly.

Outdoor Activities and Sports

Surf casting is popular—bluefish, pollock, and striped bass can be taken from the ocean shores of Plum Island. Permits to remain on the beach after dark are free for anyone entering Parker River National Wildlife Refuge with fishing equipment in the daylight. You don't need a permit to fish from the public beach at Plum Island. The best spot is around the mouth of the Merrimack River.

Newburyport Whale Watch (⊠ 54 Merrimac St., ☎ 978/465–9885 or 800/848–1111) operates deep-sea fishing charters and whale-watching and dinner cruises.

The North Shore A to Z

To research prices, get advice from other travelers, and book travel arrangements, visit www.fodors.com.

BOAT & FERRY TRAVEL

A boat leaves Boston for Gloucester daily in the summer at 10 AM; from Memorial Day through June, boats run weekends only, and from July through Labor Day, there are departures every day except Monday. The return boat leaves Gloucester at 3 PM. For information, contact A. C. Cruise Lines.
➤ BOAT & FERRY INFORMATION: **A. C. Cruise Lines** (⊠ 290 Northern Ave., Boston, ☎ 617/261–6633 or 800/422–8419, WEB www.accruiseline.com).

BUS TRAVEL

The Coach Company bus line runs a commuter bus between New-buryport and Boston on weekdays. MBTA buses leave daily from Boston's Haymarket Station for Marblehead and Salem. Travel time is about 1 to 1¼ hours. The Cape Ann Transportation Authority covers the Gloucester, Rockport, and Essex region with buses and water shuttles.

➤ Bus INFORMATION: **Coach Company** (☎ 800/874–3377 WEB www. coachco.com). **MBTA** (☎ 617/222–3200 schedulesWEB www.mbta.com). **Cape Ann Transportation Authority** (CATA; ☎ 978/283–7916).

CAR TRAVEL

The primary link between Boston and the North Shore is Route 128, which breaks off from I–95 and follows the coast northeast to Glouces-ter. To pick up Route 128 from Boston, take I–93 north to I–95 north to Route 128. If you stay on I–95, you'll reach Newburyport. A less direct route, but a scenic one north of Lynn, is Route 1A, which leaves Boston via the Callahan Tunnel. Beyond Beverly, Route 1A travels in-land toward Ipswich and Essex; at this point, Route 127 follows the coast to Gloucester and Rockport.

From Boston to Salem or Marblehead, follow Route 128 to Route 114 into Salem and on to Marblehead. An alternate route to Marblehead: follow Route 1A north, and then pick up Route 129 north along the shore through Swampscott and into Marblehead.

EMERGENCIES

➤ HOSPITAL: **Beverly Hospital** (✉ 85 Herrick St., Beverly, ☎ 978/922–3000).

➤ LATE-NIGHT PHARMACY: **CVS Pharmacy** (✉ 53 Dodge St., Beverly, ☎ 978/927–3291WEB www.cvs.com). **Walgreen's** (✉ 201 Main St., Gloucester, ☎ 978/283–7361WEB www.walgreens.com).

TAXIS

➤ CONTACTS: **A-1 Taxi** (☎ 508/228–3330 or 508/228–4084). **All Points Taxi** (☎ 508/228–5779). **BG's Taxi** (☎ 508/228–4146).

TRAIN TRAVEL

MBTA trains travel from Boston's North Station to Salem (25–30 minutes), Manchester (40–50 minutes), Gloucester (55–60 minutes), Rockport (70 minutes), Ipswich (50–55 minutes), and Newburyport (60–65 minutes).

➤ TRAIN INFORMATION: **MBTA** (☎ 617/222–3200 schedules WEB www.mbta.com).

VISITOR INFORMATION

➤ TOURIST INFORMATION: **Cape Ann Chamber of Commerce** (✉ 33 Com-mercial St., Gloucester 01930, ☎ 978/283–1601 or 800/321–0133, WEB www.capeannvacations.com). **Marblehead Chamber of Commerce** (✉ Box 76, 62 Pleasant St., Marblehead 01945, ☎ 781/631–2868, WEB www.marbleheadchamber.org). **National Park Service Visitor Infor-mation** (✉ 2 New Liberty St., Salem 01970, ☎ 978/740–1650, WEB www.nps.gov/sama). **North of Boston Visitors and Convention Bureau** (✉ 17 Peabody Sq., Peabody 01960, ☎ 978/977–7760 or 800/742–5306, WEB www.northofboston.org). **Rockport Chamber of Commerce** (✉ Box 67, 3 Main St., Rockport 01966, ☎ 978/546–6575, WEB www.rockportusa.com).

THE PIONEER VALLEY

Updated by
Kay and Bill
Scheller

The Pioneer Valley, a string of historic settlements along the Connecticut River from Springfield in the south up to the Vermont border, formed the western frontier of New England from the early 1600s until the late 18th century. The river and its fertile banks first attracted farmers and traders, and the Connecticut later became a source of power and transport for the earliest industrial cities in America. The northern regions of the Pioneer Valley remain rural and tranquil; farms and small towns have typical New England architecture. Farther south, the cities of Holyoke and Springfield are more industrial. Educational pioneers came to this region as well—to form Mount Holyoke College, America's first college for women, and four other major colleges, as well as several well-known prep schools.

Northfield

37 *97 mi northwest of Boston.*

Just south of the Vermont border, this country town is known mainly as a center for hikers, campers, and other lovers of the outdoors.

The **Northfield Mountain Recreation and Environmental Center** has 29 mi of hiking trails, and you can rent canoes and kayaks at the large campground at Barton Cove. From here you can paddle to the Munn's Ferry campground, accessible only by canoe. Free one-hour bus tours head up the mountain, where you can see a large underground power station at work. The center also runs 1½-hour sightseeing tours of the Pioneer Valley, along a 12-mi stretch of the Connecticut River between Northfield and Gill, on a riverboat. In winter, the center rents cross-country skis and snowshoes and offers lessons. ⊠ *99 Miller's Falls Rd.,* ☎ *413/659–3714 or 800/859–2960.* ◻ *Riverboat tour $8.* ☉ *Riverboat tour mid-June–mid-Oct., Wed.–Sun. 11, 1:15 and 3. Reservations essential. Bus tour May–Oct., Wed.–Sun. 11 and 3.*

Lodging

$$–$$$ ⊡ **Centennial House.** Once home to presidents of the town's Mount Hermon School, this 1811 Colonial bed and breakfast has five spacious, antiques-filled guest rooms and a third-floor suite that sleeps up to four, has a kitchen, living and dining areas, a TV/VCR, and a full bath. The inn's large, glassed-in sunroom (screened in summer) is a delightful place to curl up and read a book; the pine-paneled living room has a huge fireplace, perfect for a cozy retreat on a cold winter's night. There are 2 1/2 acres of yard to play in, or to just sit and watch the sun set. The owners have a friendly English Springer Spaniel. ⊠ *Main St.,* ☎ *413/498-5921. 5 (3 with bath); 1 suite. MC, V, AE. BP.* WEB *www.thecentennialhouse.com*

Shelburne Falls

38 *20 mi southwest of Northfield.*

A near-perfect example of small-town America, Shelburne Falls straddles the Deerfield River. A sprinkling of quality antiques shops and the Copper Angel Restaurant overlooking the river make the village a good place to spend a half day. From May to October an arched, 400-ft abandoned trolley bridge is transformed by Shelburne Falls' Women's Club into the **Bridge of Flowers** (⊠ *at Water St.,* ☎ *413/625–2544*), a gardened promenade bursting with colors. In the riverbed just downstream from the town are 50 immense **glacial potholes** ground out of granite during the last ice age.

The Pioneer Valley

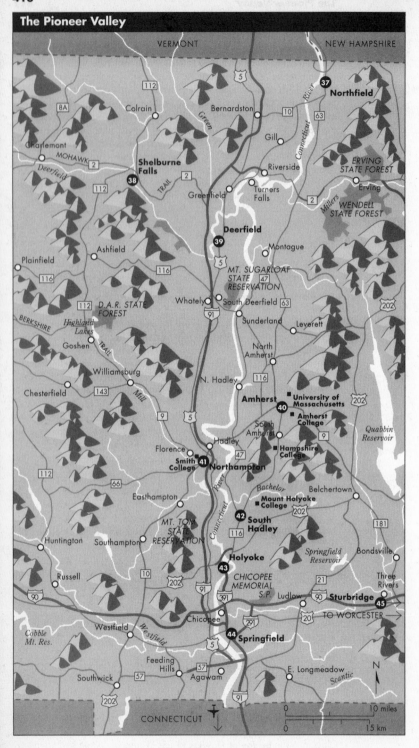

VERMONT

NEW HAMPSHIRE

Colrain

Bernardston

Northfield **37**

Gill

Green

River

Charlemont

MOHAWK

Shelburne
Falls **38**

Riverside

*ERVING
STATE FOREST*

Deerfield

TRAIL

Greenfield

Turners
Falls

Erving

*WENDELL
STATE FOREST*

Millers

Ashfield

Deerfield **39**

Montague

Plainfield

MT. SUGARLOAF
STATE
RESERVATION

Whately

South Deerfield

*D.A.R. STATE
FOREST*

Sunderland

Leverett

BERKSHIRE

*Highland
Lakes*

TRAIL

North
Amherst

Goshen

Mill

Chesterfield

Williamsburg

N. Hadley

*Quabbin
Reservoir*

Amherst **40** ■ University of
Massachusetts

■ Amherst
College

South
Amherst

Florence

Hadley

Smith
College **41** Northampton

■ Hampshire
College

Easthampton

Bachelor

Belchertown

MT. TOM
STATE
RESERVATION

■ Mount Holyoke
College

South **42**
Hadley

Huntington

Southampton

Holyoke **43**

CHICOPEE
MEMORIAL
S.P.

*Springfield
Reservoir*

Bondsville

Russell

Three
Rivers

Ludlow

Sturbridge **45**

Connecticut

River

44 Springfield

TO WORCESTER →

Cobble
Mt. Res.

Westfield

Westfield

Chicopee

Feeding
Hills

Southwick

Agawam

E. Longmeadow

Scantic

N

CONNECTICUT

0   10 miles

0   15 km

Dining and Lodging

$$–$$$ ✕ **Copper Angel Restaurant.** This restaurant between the Deerfield River and State Street specializes in vegetarian cuisine but also offers poultry and fish. The organic produce–based menu includes lentil cutlets with vegetarian gravy, a tofu stir-fry with peanut sauce, stuffed chicken breast with garlic mashed potatoes, and orange-pepper shrimp. A deck over the water is pleasant for summer dining. The restaurant serves three meals in the summer, and dinner only the rest of the year. ✉ *2 State St.,* ☎ *413/625–2727. Reservations not accepted. MC, V. Closed Mon.–Tues. May–Oct., Sun.–Wed. the rest of the year.*

$ 🛏 **Penfrydd Farm.** In the middle of a 160-acre working farm, this serene B&B occupies a rejuvenated farmhouse and has exposed beams, skylights, and a big hot tub. The ideal place to get away from it all, Penfrydd Farm has fabulous fall foliage and plenty of snow for snowshoeing and cross-country skiing in winter at nearby H.O. Cook State Park. Three of the 4 rooms share bath; the room with the private bath has a whirlpool tub. ✉ *Box 100A, R.R. 1, 105 Hillman Rd., Colrain 01340,* ☎ *413/624–5516,* 🌐 *www.penfrydd.com. 4 rooms. Hot tub, skiing. AE, MC, V. CP weekends, BP weekdays.*

Outdoor Activities and Sports

You can raft along the Deerfield River at Charlemont, on the Mohawk Trail. From April to October **Zoar Outdoor** (☎ 800/532–7483) operates one-day raft tours over 10 mi of Class II–III rapids daily as well as family float trips on the lower section of the Deerfield River. The outfit also conducts canoe and kayak tours and rock climbs.

Shopping

The **Salmon Falls Artisans Showroom** (✉ Ashfield St., ☎ 413/625–9833) carries sculpture, pottery, glass (including hand-blown pieces by Josh Simpson), and furniture by more than 185 local artisans.

Deerfield

39 *10 mi southeast of Shelburne Falls.*

In Deerfield, a horse pulling a carriage clip-clops past perfectly maintained 18th-century homes, neighbors leave their doors unlocked and tip their hats to strangers, kids play ball in fields by the river, and the bell of the impossibly beautiful brick church peals from a white steeple. This is the perfect New England village, though not without a past darkened by tragedy. Settled by Native Americans more than 8,000 years ago, Deerfield was originally a Pocumtuck village—deserted after deadly epidemics and a war with the Mohawks that all but wiped out the tribe. English pioneers eagerly settled into this frontier outpost in the 1660s and 1670s, but two bloody massacres at the hands of the natives and the French caused the village to be abandoned until 1707, when construction began on the buildings that remain today.

★ Although it has a turbulent past, **Historic Deerfield** now basks in a genteel aura. With 52 buildings on 93 acres, this village provides an impressive glimpse into 18th- and 19th-century American life. The **Street,** a tree-lined avenue of 18th- and 19th-century houses, is protected and maintained as a museum site, with 14 of the preserved buildings open to the public year-round (in winter, homes are shown according to interest). Some homes contain antique furnishings and decorative arts; other buildings exhibit textiles, silver, pewter, or ceramics. The well-trained guides converse knowledgeably about the exhibits and Deerfield's history. Start your visit at the information center in Hall Tavern and don't miss the **Wells-Thorn House,** where rooms depict life as it changed from 1725 to 1850. Purchase of an all-house admission ticket

includes access to the **Flynt Center of Early New England Life** (⊠ 37D
Old Main St.), which houses two exhibit galleries. One of the galleries
holds 2,500 decorative objects from 1600 to the present. Quilts, Native American artifacts, furniture, and other objects are on display at
Memorial Hall Museum (☎ 413/664–3768), one of the oldest museums in the country. ⊡ $6 ☉ May–Oct., daily 9:30–4:30. Plan to spend
at least one full day at Historic Deerfield. ⊠ *The Street,* ☎ *413/774–
5581,* WEB *www.historic-deerfield.org.* ⊡ *1-wk admission to all houses
and museum $12; single-house admission $6.* ☉ *Daily 9:30–4:30.*

You can take a walk back in history at **Old Greenfield Village,** where for
more than 30 years Waine Morse has built a carefully documented replica
of a New England town in 1895. Among the 15 buildings are a general
store, a church, a schoolhouse, and a print shop. ⊠ *Rte. 9, Greenfield,*
☎ *413/774–7138.* ⊡ *$5.* ☉ *Mid-May–mid-Oct., Wed.–Mon. 10–4.*

ℭ The massive store at the **Yankee Candle Company and Car Museum**
holds millions of candles, Christmas decorations, and foodstuffs. The
Bavarian Christmas Village provides an imaginative shopping experience; kids love the Dip-Your-Own Candle station. The outdoor patio
at Chandler's Tavern Restaurant is a pleasant spot for lunch. The car
museum exhibits more than 70 antique classics, and novelty dragsters.
⊠ *U.S. 5 (Rte. 10), South Deerfield,* ☎ *413/665–2929,* WEB *www.yan-
keecandle.com.* ⊡ *Store free; museum $5.* ☉ *Daily 9:30–6; call for
holiday hrs.*

Dining and Lodging

$$$$ ✕ **Sienna.** The atmosphere here is soothing and the service well man-
★   nered, but the food is what really shines. Choices from the ever-changing menu might grilled tuna on chèvre ravioli. After an irresistible dessert
such as a chocolate hazelnut tart, your evening ends with the personal
touch of a handwritten check on stationery. ⊠ *6 Elm St., South Deerfield,* ☎ *413/665–0215. Reservations essential. MC, V. Closed Mon.–
Tues. No lunch.*

$$$$ ✕▥ **Deerfield Inn.** Period wallpapers decorate the rooms in the main
★   inn, which was built in 1884; the rooms in an outbuilding have identical papers but are newer (1981) and closer to the parking lot. All rooms
have antiques and replicas, sofas, and bureaus, and some have four-
poster or canopy beds. The restaurant's menu ($$$$), which showcases
contemporary American cuisine, changes monthly, but a house specialty,
Indian pudding, is always available. The inn is no-smoking. ⊠ *81 Old
Main St., 01342,* ☎ *413/774–5587 or 800/926–3865 outside Mass,*
FAX *413/773–8712,* WEB *www.deerfieldinn.com. 23 rooms. Restaurant,
bar, coffee shop. AE, DC, MC, V. BP.*

$$ ✕▥ **Whately Inn.** Antiques and four-poster beds slope gently on old-
wood floors of the guest rooms here. The dining room ($$–$$$) has a
fireplace and exposed beams, tables on a raised stage at one end, and
some booths; it's dimly lighted, with candles on the tables. Prime Angus
steaks, baked lobster, rack of lamb, and other entrées come with salad,
appetizer, dessert, and coffee. The restaurant is busy on weekends; Sun-
day dinner begins at 1 PM. The full menu is also served in the casual
lounge. ⊠ *Chestnut Plain Rd., Whately Center 01093,* ☎ *413/665–3044
or 800/942–8359,* WEB *www.whateyinn.com 4 rooms. Restaurant.
AE, D, MC, V.*

$$–$$$ ▥ **Brandt House Country Inn.** The owner of this 16-room, turn-of-the-
★   century Colonial Revival mansion set on 3½ manicured acres is an in-
terior decorator, and her touch is evident throughout. The sunlit,
spacious common rooms are filled with plants, plump easy chairs, and
handsome contemporary furnishings; the elegantly appointed guest
rooms have feather beds. Still, the emphasis is on comfort and homi-

ness, and kids and well-behaved dogs are welcome. Room 8, with a full kitchen and sleeping loft, sleeps up to five. Continental breakfast is served on weekdays, full on weekends. ⊠ *29 Highland Ave., Greenfield 01301,* ☎ *413/774–3329 or 800/235–3329,* FAX *413/772–2908,* WEB *www.brandthouse.com. 8 rooms, 6 with bath; 1 suite. Billiards, tennis court. AE, D, MC, V. BP. CP.*

$–$$ 🏠 **Yellow Gabled House.** Edna Stahelek's home, built circa 1800 on the Street, is sunny and gracious, with an elegant dining room and a living room with a grandfather clock and other antiques. The upstairs guest rooms include a suite with a private bath and sitting room. The no-smoking B&B is just off I–91, 4 mi from Historic Deerfield and a mile from Yankee Candle. ⊠ *111 N. Main St., South Deerfield 01373,* ☎ *413/ 665–4922. 2 rooms with shared bath, 1 suite. No credit cards. BP.*

$ 🏠 **Sunnyside Farm Bed and Breakfast.** Maple antiques and family heirlooms decorate this inn's country-style rooms, all of which are hung with fine-art reproductions and have views across the fields. A full country breakfast is served family-style in the dining room. The farm is about 8 mi south of Deerfield, convenient to cross-country skiing, mountain biking, and hiking. ⊠ *21 River Rd., Whately 01093,* ☎ *413/665–3113. 5 rooms without bath. Pool. BP. No credit cards.*

Shopping

Lunt Silversmiths Outlet Store and More (⊠ 298 Federal St., Greenfield, ☎ 413/772–0767 or 800/344–5868) has daily demonstrations of silversmithing and glassblowing, a retail area, a restaurant (serving lunch Wed.–Sat., and Sun. brunch buffet), and a museum. The Outlet Store sells merchandise at a savings of 20-60%.

Amherst

➍ *14 mi south of Deerfield.*

Three of the Pioneer Valley's five major colleges—the University of Massachusetts (UMass), Amherst College, and Hampshire College—are in small but lively Amherst, which has a large village green. Its bookstores, bars, and cafés reflect the area's youthful orientation.

The poet Emily Dickinson (1830–86) was born and died in the **Emily Dickinson Homestead.** The house contains some of the poet's belongings, but most of her manuscripts are elsewhere. Guided tours are the only way to visit the house, and reservations are advisable. ⊠ *280 Main St.,* ☎ *413/542–8161.* ☜ *$4.* ☉ *Wed.–Sat.; call for hrs.*

The **Amherst History Museum at the Strong House,** built in the mid-1700s, has an extensive collection of household tools, furniture, china, and clothing that reflects changing styles of interior decoration. Most items are Amherst originals, dating from the 18th to the mid-20th century. ⊠ *67 Amity St.,* ☎ *413/256–0678,* WEB *www.amhersthistory.org* ☜ *$4.* ☉ *May–Oct., Wed.–Sat. 12:30–3:30; Nov, Dec., and Feb.–Apr., Fri. and Sat. 12:30–3:30.*

★ The effort to save Yiddish books and preserve Jewish culture has become a major movement, and the **National Yiddish Book Center** is its core. The center is housed in a thatched-roof building that resembles a cluster of structures typical of a shtetl, or traditional Eastern European Jewish village. Inside, a contemporary space contains more than 1.3 million books, a fireside reading area, a kosher dining area, and a visitor center with exhibits. The work here is performed out in the open: hundreds of books pour in daily, and workers come across everything from family keepsakes to rare manuscripts. ⊠ *Harry and Jeanette Weinberg Building, Hampshire College, Rte. 116,* ☎ *800/535–3595,* WEB *www.yiddishbookcenter.org.* ☜ *Free.* ☉ *Sun.–Fri. 10–3:30.*

Dining and Lodging

$$–$$$ ✕ **Judie's.** For more than 20 years students have crowded around small tables on the glassed-in porch, ordering burgers, salads, stuffed popovers, fancy pastas, and delicious desserts. The atmosphere is casual and artsy—a painting on canvas covers each tabletop. ✉ *51 N. Pleasant St.,* ☎ *413/253–3491. Reservations not accepted. AE, D, MC, V.*

$$ ✕ **Black Sheep.** Newspapers and books are strewn about the tables at this student-oriented counter-service café, which typifies Amherst dining. A half dozen coffee selections complement excellent desserts and creative, high-quality sandwiches that include the "C'est la brie" (a baguette smothered with brie, roasted peppers, spinach, and raspberry mustard) and the "French Kiss" (truffle pâté, Dijon mustard, and red onion on a baguette). The Black Sheep opens at 7 AM (7:30 on Sunday). ✉ *79 Main St.,* ☎ *413/253–3442. D, MC, V.*

$$–$$$ ✕🛏 **Lord Jeffery Inn.** This gabled brick inn sits on the green between the town center and Amherst College. Many bedrooms have a light floral decor; others have stencils and pastel woodwork. The formal dining room, where traditional dishes are served, is collegiate and Colonial, with old wood panels, heavy drapery, and a large fireplace. Burgers and salads are served at Boltwood's Tavern, which has a small bar and a wraparound porch. ✉ *30 Boltwood Ave., 01002,* ☎ *413/253–2576 or 800/742–0358,* FAX *413/256–6152,* WEB *www.lordjefferyinn.com. 40 rooms, 8 suites. 2 restaurants, bar. AE, DC, MC, V.*

$$–$$$ 🛏 **Allen House Victorian Inn.** A rare find, this inn built in 1886 has
★ been gloriously restored with precision to the Aesthetic period of the Victorian era. Busy, colorful wallcoverings reach to the high ceilings. Antiques include a burled walnut headboard and dresser set, wicker "steamship" chairs, screens, and carved golden-oak beds. Lace curtains grace the windows in the rooms, which have supremely comfortable beds with goose-down comforters. Allen House is a short walk from the center of Amherst. The inn's owners have recently opened the Amherst Inn, an 1850 Victorian inn similar to the Allen House, across from the Emily Dickinson House. Amenities and rates for the seven guest rooms at this "painted lady" are the same as at the Allen House. ✉ *599 Main St., 01002,* ☎ *413/253–5000,* WEB *www.allenhouse.com. 7 rooms. No credit cards. BP.*

$$ 🛏 **Campus Center Hotel.** Atop the UMass campus and convenient to all of Amherst, this modern hotel has spacious rooms with large windows that allow excellent views over campus and countryside. The walls are exposed cinderblock, and the rooms have simple furnishings. Guests can use university exercise facilities—as well as the pool and tennis courts—with prior reservation. Because the hotel is at a college, no tax is charged for accommodations. ✉ *University of Massachusetts, Murray D. Lincoln Tower, 01003,* ☎ *413/549–6000,* FAX *413/545–1210,* WEB *www.aux.umass.edu/hotel. 116 rooms, 2 suites and 4 parlors with kitchen facilities. AE, D, DC, MC, V.*

Nightlife and the Arts

Major ballet and modern dance companies appear in season at the **UMass Fine Arts Center** (✉ Haigis Hall, ☎ 413/545–2511). The **William D. Mullens Memorial Center** (✉ University Dr., University of Massachusetts, ☎ 413/545–0505) hosts concerts, theatrical productions, and other entertainment.

Outdoor Activities and Sports

BIKING

Valley Bicycles (✉ 319 Main St., ☎ 413/256–0880) rents bikes and dispenses cycling advice.

FISHING

The Connecticut River sustains shad, salmon, and several dozen other fish species. From May to October, at **Waterfield Farms Recreational Fishing** (✉ 500 Sunderland Rd., ☎ 413/549–3558), you pay $3 ($8 for a family of four) to drop your line, plus an amount that varies depending on what fish you catch and the size. Poles can be rented, and bait is sold.

Shopping

The **Leverett Crafts and Arts Center** (✉ Montague Rd., Leverett, ☎ 413/548–9070) houses 20 resident artists who create jewelry, ceramics, glass, and textiles. An institution in the Pioneer Valley, **Atkins Farms Country Market** (✉ Rte. 116, South Amherst, ☎ 413/253–9528) is surrounded by apple orchards and gorgeous views of the Holyoke Ridge. Hay rides are offered in the fall, and there are children's events year-round. The farm sells apples and has a bakery and deli.

Northampton

41 *8 mi southwest of Amherst.*

The small, bustling college town of Northampton is listed on the National Register of Historic Places. Tracy Kidder's 1999 nonfiction book *Home Town* describes how the community has successfully absorbed an influx of new residents over the past few decades. Packed with numerous ethnic restaurants and activists, the town, first settled in 1654, is most famous as the site of **Smith College,** the nation's largest liberal arts college for women. The redbrick quadrangles of this institution founded in 1871 resemble the layouts of the women's colleges at Cambridge University, England, which were built around the same period. Worth visiting are the **Lyman Plant House** (☎ 413/585–2740) and the **botanic gardens.**

Historic Northampton maintains three houses that are open for tours: Parsons House (1730), Shepherd House (1798), and Damon House (1813).Exhibits in the headquarters chronicle the history of Northampton. ✉ *Headquarters, 46 Bridge St.,* ☎ *413/584–6011.* 🖃 *Headquarters exhibits by donation; Houses $3.* ⊙ *Headquarters exhibits open Tues.–Fri., 10–4; houses open Sat. and Sun. 12–4.*

Northampton was the Massachusetts home of the 30th U.S. president, Calvin Coolidge. He practiced law here and served as mayor from 1910 to 1911. The **Coolidge Room** at the **Forbes Library** (✉ 20 West St., ☎ 413/587–1011) contains a collection of his papers and memorabilia.

🕲 Within the 150-acre **Look Memorial Park** (✉ 300 N. Main St. (Rt.9), Florence, ☎ 413/584–5457) are a small zoo, a wading pool, children's playgrounds, paddleboats, a train,and bumper boats.

At the wide place in the Connecticut River known as the Oxbow is the Massachusetts Audubon Society's 700-acre **Arcadia Nature Center and Wildlife Sanctuary,** where you can try the hiking and nature trails and scheduled canoe trips. ✉ *127 Combs Rd., Easthampton (3 mi south of Northampton),* ☎ *413/584–3009.* 🖃 *$3 (free for Massachusetts Audubon members).* ⊙ *Trails Tues.–Sun. and Mon. holidays dawn–dusk, nature center Mon.–Sat. 8–4.*

Dining and Lodging

$–$$$ ✗ **Spoleto.** Among the new and traditional Italian specialties served in a casual setting are appetizers such as phyllo ravioli and entrées such as *ravioli alla vodka* (three-cheese ravioli in a tomato and vodka cream sauce) and veal scallopini with shrimp and artichokes. The entrée price includes pasta, vegetable, and salad. Save room for the homemade desserts. ✉ *50 Main St.,* ☎ *413/586–6313. AE, MC, V. No lunch.*

$$–$$$ ✕ **Eastside Grill.** One of the dining rooms here is a glassed-in porch, and the other is wood-paneled with comfortable wood-and-leather booths. The menu lists a large selection of appetizers, great if you've just stopped by for a drink, and 35 entrées daily such as blackened fish of the day and oysters on the half shell. ⊠ *19 Strong Ave.,* ☎ *413/ 586–3347. AE, D, DC, MC, V. No lunch.*

$–$$$ ✕ **Hunan Gourmet.** In a college town that knows its Chinese food, the Gourmet has been favored by discerning locals for years. The prices are low enough to appeal to students, and there are plenty of red-star items to satisfy hot-and-spicy fans. Among the house specialties are Hunan Triple Crown (jumbo shrimp, chicken, and roast pork with fresh vegetables in a spicy sauce) and Tsing Tao Duck (shredded Beijing duck sautéed with shredded vegetables in a special sauce). ⊠ *261 King St.,* ☎ *413/585–0202. AE, MC, V.*

$$$ ▦ **Hotel Northampton.** Room furnishings at this downtown hotel include Colonial reproductions and heavy curtains. Some rooms have four-poster beds, balconies overlooking a busy street or the parking lot, whirlpool tubs, and heated towel racks. Wiggins Tavern (no lunch) serves American fare and an elaborate Sunday brunch; the café serves lighter fare. ⊠ *36 King St., 01060,* ☎ *413/584–3100 or 800/547–3529,* FAX *413/584–9455,* WEB *www/hotelnorthampton.com. 99 rooms, 6 suites, 2 efficiency units. 2 restaurants, bar, exercise room. AE, D, DC, MC, V. CP.*

$$–$$$ ▦ **Clark Tavern Inn.** Early customers at this 1742 inn included Min-
   ★   utemen on their way to fight in Concord and Lexington. Two centuries later, when the planned route for I–91 ran right through the property, two dedicated preservationists saved the house by moving it to its new site. Braided rugs, canopy beds, and stencils create a Colonial atmosphere. Fires warm two large but cozy common rooms; in summer, you can nap in the garden hammock or take a dip in the pool. Breakfast can be served fireside, on the screened-in porch, or in your room.One of the guest rooms has a fireplace. ⊠ *98 Bay Rd., Hadley 01035,* ☎ *413/586–1900,* FAX *413/587–9788,* WEB *www.clarktaverninn.com. 3 rooms. Pool. AE, D, DC, MC, V. BP.*

$ ▦ **Twin Maples Bed and Breakfast.** Fields and woods surround this 200-year-old farmhouse, which is 7 mi northwest of Northampton near the village of Williamsburg. Colonial-style antiques and reproductions furnish the small rooms, which have restored brass beds. ⊠ *106 South St., Williamsburg 01096,* ☎ *413/268–7925 or 413/268–7244,* FAX *413/ 268–7243,* WEB *www.berkbb33£javanet.com. 3 rooms without bath. AE, MC, V.*

Nightlife and the Arts

The **Center for the Arts in Northampton** (⊠ 17 New South St., ☎ 413/ 584-7327) hosts more than 250 gallery exhibitions and theater, dance, and musical events each year, as well as First Night festivities New Year's Eve.

Outdoor Activities and Sports

The **Norwottuck Rail Trail,** part of the Connecticut River Greenway State Park (☎ 413/586–8706), is a paved 10-mi path that links Northampton with Belchertown. Great for pedaling, rollerblading, jogging, and cross-country skiing, it runs along the old Boston & Maine Railroad Bed.**Sportsman's Marina Boat Rental Company** (⊠ Rte. 9, Hadley, ☎ 413/586–2426) rents canoes and kayaks during summer and early fall.

Shopping

The 8,000-square-ft **Antique Center of Northampton** (⊠ 9½ Market St., ☎ 413/584–3600) houses 60 dealers. **Pinch** (⊠ 179 Main St., ☎

413/586–4509) sells contemporary ceramics, jewelry, and glass. **Thorne's Marketplace** (⌧ 150 Main St., ☎ 413/584–5582) is a funky four-floor indoor mall in a former department store. **Williamsburg General Store** (⌧ Village Center, Rte. 9, Williamstown, ☎ 413/268–3036), a Pioneer Valley landmark for more than a century, sells breads, specialty foods, penny candy, ice cream, and lots of gift items.

South Hadley

42 *8 mi southeast of Northampton.*

Although it remained a farming community well into the 20th century, South Hadley has long been known primarily as a college town. **Mount Holyoke College,** founded in 1837, was the first women's college in the United States. Among the college's alumnae are Emily Dickinson and playwright Wendy Wasserstein. The handsome wooded campus, encompassing two lakes and lovely walking or riding trails, was landscaped by Frederick Law Olmsted. ⌧ *Rte. 116,* ☎ *413/538–2000.*

Mount Holyoke's **College Art Museum,** scheduled to reopen in February 2002 after extensive renovations, has exhibits of Asian, Egyptian, and classical art. ⌧ *Rte. 116,* ☎ *413/538–2245.* ▨ *Free.* ☉ *Tues.– Fri. 11–5, weekends 1–5.*

Shopping

The **Hadley Antique Center** (⌧ 227 Russell St./Rte. 9, ☎ 413/586–4093) contains more than 70 different booths. The **Village Commons** (⌧ College St.), across from Mount Holyoke College, is an outdoor mall with a movie theater, several restaurants, and shops with everything from handmade picture frames to lingerie. The **Odyssey Bookstore** (⌧ Village Commons, 9 College St., ☎ 413/534–7307) stocks gifts, cards, and more than 50,000 new and used titles. Drop into **Tailgate Picnic** (⌧ Village Commons, 7 College St., ☎ 413/532–7597) for specialty bagels, sandwiches, cold pastas, wine, and crackers; you can order the prepared foods to go.

Holyoke

43 *5 mi south of South Hadley.*

Working hard to overcome its days as a factory town, Holyoke has an imaginatively restored industrial city center, a children's museum, a hall of fame, and the largest indoor mall in the valley.

☾ The **Heritage State Park** tells the story of this papermaking community, the nation's first planned industrial city. The merry-go-round is a popular attraction. ⌧ *221 Appleton St.,* ☎ *413/534–1723.* ▨ *Free; merry-go-round, $1 per ride.* ☉ *Tues.–Sun. and school vacations, 10:30–4.*

☾ The **Children's Museum,** beside Heritage State Park in a converted mill by a canal, is packed with hands-on games and educational toys. Within the museum are a state-of-the-art TV station, a multitiered interactive exhibit on the body, a giant bubblemaker, and a sand pendulum. ⌧ *444 Dwight St.,* ☎ *413/536–5437.* ▨ *$4.* ☉ *Tues.–Sat. 9:30– 4:30, Sun. noon–5.*

Volleyball was invented at the Holyoke YMCA in 1895, and the **Volleyball Hall of Fame** pays homage to the sport with interactive videos and displays of memorabilia, and a hitmaster and jumpmaster to test your skills. ⌧ *444 Dwight St.,* ☎ *413/536–0926.* ▨ *$3.50.* ☉ *Tues.– Sat. 9:30–4:30, Sun. noon–4:30.*

Dining and Lodging

$$$$ ✕ **Delaney House.** Eating here always feels like an event, in part because of the elegantly set tables and tasteful Victorian decor in the several dining rooms in the hundred-plus-year-old portion of the building. It's also because of the live music that flows out of the comfortable lounge. The biggest plus is the food, tasty and beautifully presented in ample portions. Most choices are standard American: prime rib, baked sea scallops, and rack of lamb. Among the more ambitious offerings are chicken Portobello, grilled salmon pesto, and lobster regale—a 2½-pound lobster with mussels, clams, shrimp, and scallops. On Sunday, the restaurant opens at 1 for dinner. ⊠ *U.S. 5 at Smith's Ferry,* ☎ *413/ 532–1800. AE, D, DC, MC, V. No lunch.*

$$–$$$ ✕🏠 **Yankee Pedlar Inn.** Antiques and four-poster or canopy beds furnish the charming rooms at this sprawling inn at a busy crossroads near I–91. The elaborate Victorian bridal suite is heavy on lace and curtains; the beamed carriage house has rustic appointments and simple canopy beds. Walnut crusted chicken, garlic salmon and nightly game specials are among the dishes served in the Grill Room, which is painted burgundy and accented with stained glass. The more casual Oyster Bar hosts local musicians Thursday through Saturday evenings. A 6-floor, 57-room Radisson Country Inn is scheduled to open next door in the summer of 2001. ⊠ *1866 Northampton St., 01040,* ☎ *413/532–9494,* ᖴᗩᕽ *413/ 536–8877,* ᗯᗴᗷ *www.yankeepedlar.com. 28 rooms, 11 suites. Restaurant, bar, nightclub, meeting room. AE, D, DC, MC, V. CP.*

Outdoor Activities and Sports

A 3⅓-mi round-trip hike at the **Mt. Tom State Reservation** (⊠ U.S 5, ☎ 413/536–0416) leads to the summit, whose sheer basalt cliffs were formed by volcanic activity 200 million years ago. At the top are excellent views over the Pioneer Valley and the Berkshires.

Springfield

④ *8 mi south of Holyoke, 101 mi southwest of Boston.*

Springfield is the largest city in the Pioneer Valley, an industrial town where modern skyscrapers rise between grand historic buildings. The city has several rewarding museums and historic sites. The late children's book author Theodore Geisel, also known as Dr. Seuss, was born here.

★   Dr. James Naismith invented basketball in Springfield in 1891. The **Naismith Memorial Basketball Hall of Fame,** dedicated to preserving and promoting all facets of the sport, has a cinema with a 600-square-ft screen, a two-story basketball fountain, and a moving walkway from which you can shoot baskets into 20 different-size hoops. Special exhibits include the Elks FANtasy virtual reality game and the Honors Court, which pays tribute to Basketball Hall of Fame enshrinees. An expansion that will almost double the size of the Hall of Fame is scheduled for completion in summer of 2002. ⊠ *1150 W. Columbus Ave., at Union St.,* ☎ *413/781–6500 or 877-4HOOPLA,* ᗯᗴᗷ *www.hoophall.com.* 🎟 *$9.* ☉ *daily except major holidays, 9:30–5:30.*

★   Four museums near downtown make up the **Springfield Museums at the Quadrangle.** The **Connecticut Valley Historical Museum** commemorates the history of the Pioneer Valley. The **George Walter Vincent Smith Art Museum** contains a private collection of Japanese armor, ceramics, and textiles and a gallery of American paintings. The **Museum of Fine Arts** has paintings by Gauguin, Renoir, Degas, and Monet, as well as 18th-century American paintings and contemporary works. The **Springfield Science Museum** has an "Exploration Center" of touchable displays, a planetarium, a kid-focused eco-center, and dinosaur exhibits. The **Dr. Seuss National Memorial,** six bronze statues around the quadrangle, honor Springfield's famous native son. ⊠ *200 State St., State and Chestnut Sts.,* ☎ *413/263–6800,* WEB *www.quadrangle.org.* ⊠ *$6 pass valid for all museums.* ☉ *Wed.–Fri. noon–5, Sat. and Sun., 11–4; Tues. July and Aug.*

🖑 **Forest Park,** Springfield's leafy 735-acre retreat, is an ideal urban green space. There are hiking paths, paddleboats on Porter Lake, tennis courts, picnic groves, a kiddie train, and a wonderful pond filled with hungry ducks. The **Zoo in Forest Park,** one of the highlights for children, is home to nearly 200 domestic and exotic animals. ⊠ *Sumner Ave. (Rte. 83),* ☎ *413/787–6461; 413/733–2251 zoo.* ⊠ *Park $4 out-of-state cars weekdays, $2 in-state cars weekdays; $5 out-of-state cars weekends; $3 in-state cars weekends; zoo $3.50.* ☉ *Park daily. Zoo Apr. 15–Nov.15, daily 10–4; Nov.15–Dec., weekends; Feb. school vacation, and weekends to Apr. 15.*

★ 🖑 **Six Flags New England.** Riverside, New England's largest theme park and water park, got even better since it was purchased by the country's largest amusement park company. Among the more than 160 rides and shows are the new SuperHeroes Adventure Area featuring Superman-Ride of Steel, the tallest and fastest steel coaster on the east coast, and the Batman Thrill Spectacular stunt show. ⊠ *1623 Main St. (Rte. 159), south from Rte. 57 west of Springfield, Agawam,* ☎ *877-4-SIXFLAGS,* WEB *www.sixflags.com.* ⊠ *$36.99 (after 4 pm, $21.99); $8 parking.* ☉ *late Apr.–Oct., daily 10–10.*

Dining

$$–$$$ ✕ **Student Prince and Fort Restaurant.** Named after a 1930s operetta, this downtown restaurant established in 1935 is known for its rendition of classic German food—bratwurst, schnitzel, and sauerbraten—and steaks, chops, and seafood. It also holds a collection of more than 2,000 beer steins. ⊠ *8 Fort St.,* ☎ *413/734–7475. D, DC, MC, V.*

$$–$$$ ✕ **Theodore's.** "Booze, blues, and barbecue" are the specialties of this popular downtown restaurant, which stays open until 2 AM Friday–Sunday. You can dine saloon style in booths near the bar or in a small adjacent dining room. The decor is yard-sale eclectic, with framed old-time advertisements lending a whimsical air. Burgers, sandwiches, chicken, and seafood are on the menu. The blues are performed Friday and Saturday nights. ⊠ *201 Worthington St.,* ☎ *413/736–6000. AE, MC, V. No lunch Sat. and Sun.*

Nightlife and the Arts

THE ARTS

The city's newest professional, nonprofit theater, **CityStage** (⊠ 1 Columbus Center, ☎ 413/733–2500 tickets; 413/788–7033 box office) showcases musicals, dramas, and comedy. The **Springfield Symphony Orchestra** (☎ 413/733–2291) performs at Symphony Hall (⊠ 75 Market Pl.) year-round and mounts a summer program of concerts in the Springfield area.

Sturbridge

45 *31 mi northeast of Springfield, 55 mi southwest of Boston.*

Sturbridge is best known as the home of an outstanding open-air museum. **Old Sturbridge Village,** one of the country's finest period restorations and the star attraction of central Massachusetts, is just east of the Pioneer Valley. The village is a model of an early 1800s New England town, with more than 40 historic buildings (moved here from other towns) on a 200-acre site. Some of the village houses are furnished with canopy beds and elaborate decoration; in the simpler, single-story cottages, interpreters wearing period costumes demonstrate home-based crafts like spinning, weaving, shoe-making, and cooking. Also here are several mills, including a saw mill. On the informative short boat ride along the Quinebaug River, you can learn about river life in 19th-century New England and catch a glimpse of ducks, geese, turtles, and other local wildlife. The village store contains an amazing variety of goods necessary for everyday life in the 19th century. ✉ *1 Old Sturbridge Village Rd.,* ☎ *508/ 347–3362 or 800/733–1830,* WEB *www.osv.org.* ✆ *$20, valid for 2 consecutive days.* ☉ *Apr.–Oct., daily 9–5; call for off-season hrs.*

Dining and Lodging

$$–$$$ ✕ **Rom's.** A local institution, this 700-seat restaurant attracts crowds with a classic formula: good food at low prices. The six dining rooms have an Early American decor, with wood paneling and beamed ceilings. Italian and American choices range from pizza to roast beef; the veal Parmesan is very popular, as is the Thursday lunch buffet and the Wednesday dinner buffet. ✉ *Rte. 131,* ☎ *508/347–3349. AE, DC, MC, V.*

$$ ✕🖻 **Publick House Historic Inn Complex.** Each of the three inns and
★ the motel in this complex has its own character. The 17 rooms in the Publick House, which dates to 1771, are Colonial in design, with uneven wide-board floors; some have canopy beds. The neighboring Chamberlain House consists of larger suites, and the Country Motor Lodge has more modern rooms. The Crafts Inn, about a mile away, has a library, lounge, pool, and eight rooms with four-poster beds and painted wood paneling (Continental breakfast is included in the price here). The big, bustling restaurant at the Publick House is very busy on weekends. The fare is traditional Yankee—lobster pies, double-thick lamb chops, Indian pudding, and pecan bread pudding. ✉ *Rte. 131, On-the-Common, 01566,* ☎ *508/347–3313 or 800/782–5425,* FAX *508/347–5073,* WEB *www.publickhouse.com. 113 rooms, 13 suites. Restaurant, bar, pool, tennis court, jogging, shuffleboard, playground, meeting room. AE, D, DC, MC, V.*

$$$–$$$$ 🖻 **Sturbridge Host.** This hotel across the street from Old Sturbridge Village on Cedar Lake has luxuriously appointed bedrooms with Colonial decor and reproduction furnishings. Some rooms have fireplaces, balconies, or patios. Dinner is served nightly in Portobella's Italian Restaurant, and a pub menu with club sandwiches and burgers is offered at lunch and dinner in the Ox Head Tavern. ✉ *U.S. 20, 01566,* ☎ *508/347–7393 or 800/582–3232,* FAX *508/347–3944. 220 rooms, 6 suites. 2 restaurants, bar, pool, miniature golf, sauna, basketball, health club, racquetball, boating, fishing, meeting room. AE, D, DC, MC, V.*

$$–$$$ 🖻 **Sturbridge Country Inn.** The atmosphere at this onetime farmhouse on Sturbridge's busy Main Street is between that of an inn and a plush business hotel. Guest rooms—all with working gas fireplaces and whirlpool tubs—have reproduction antiques; the best is the top-floor suite. ✉ *Box 60, 530 Main St., 01566,* ☎ *508/347–5503,* FAX *508/347– 5319,* WEB *www.sturbridgecountryinn.com. 6 rooms, 3 suites. Bar, hot tub. AE, D, MC, V. CP.*

The Pioneer Valley A to Z

To research prices, get advice from other travelers, and book travel arrangements, visit www.fodors.com.

AIRPORTS

Bradley International Airport in Windsor Locks, Connecticut, is the most convenient airport for flying into the Pioneer Valley. American, Continental, Delta, Midway, Northwest, TWA, United, and US Airways serve Bradley.

➤ AIRPORT INFORMATION: **Bradley International Airport** (✉ Rte. 20 [take Exit 40 off I–91], ☎ 860/292–2000).

BUS TRAVEL

Peter Pan Bus Lines provides daily service to all the major cities in the Northeast, including Boston, New York City and Washington, D.C. It also links many of the Pioneer Valley's larger cities, including Springfield, Holyoke, Northampton, Amherst, and South Hadley, and offers transportation to Bradley and Logan Airports.

Pioneer Valley Transit Authority provides service in 24 communities throughout the Pioneer Valley. Greenfield/ Montague Transportation Area serves the Greenfield-Montague area.
➤ BUS INFORMATION: **Peter Pan Bus Lines** (☎ 413/781–3320 or 800/ 237–8747). **Pioneer Valley Transit Authority** (☎ 413/781–7882). **Greenfield Montague Transportation Area** (☎ 413/773–9478).

CAR TRAVEL

Interstate 91 runs north–south through the valley, from Deerfield to Springfield. Interstate 90 links Springfield to Boston. Route 2 connects Boston with Greenfield and, via U.S. 5, Deerfield.

Interstate 91 passes through or near Springfield, Holyoke, Northampton, Hadley, Deerfield, and Greenfield. Northfield is east (via Route 10) of I–91 on Route 63. Route 2 heads west from Greenfield to Shelburne Falls. Amherst is east of Northampton on Route 9. Sturbridge is east of Springfield, I–90 to I–84.

EMERGENCIES

➤ HOSPITALS AND EMERGENCY SERVICES: **Baystate Medical Center** (✉ 759 Chestnut St., Springfield, ☎ 413/794–0000). **Cooley Dickenson Hospital** (✉ 30 Locust St., Northampton, ☎ 413/582–2000). **Holyoke Hospital** (✉ 575 Beech St., Holyoke, ☎ 413/534–2500).

LODGING
B&BS
Berkshire Bed-and-Breakfast Service provides information and takes reservations for B&B and other Pioneer Valley accommodations.
➤ RESERVATION SERVICES: **Berkshire Bed-and-Breakfast Service** (☎ 413/ 268–7244 or 800/762–2751, FAX 413/268–7243).

TRAIN TRAVEL

Amtrak serves Springfield from New York City. The *Lake Shore Limited* between Boston and Chicago calls at Springfield once daily in each direction, and three more trains run between Boston and Springfield every day.
➤ TRAIN INFORMATION: **Amtrak** (☎ 800/872–7245, WEB www.amtrak.com).

VISITOR INFORMATION

For a list of members of the Pioneer Valley Antique Dealers Association, write to Maggie Herbert.
➤ TOURIST INFORMATION: **Amherst Area Chamber of Commerce** (✉ 409 Main St., 01002, ☎ 413/253–0700). **Greater Northampton Chamber of Commerce** (✉ 99 Pleasant St., 01060, ☎ 413/584–1900). The **Greater Springfield Convention and Visitors Bureau** (✉ 1441 Main St., Springfield 01115, ☎ 413/787–1548 or 800/723–1548). **Pioneer Valley Antique Dealers Association,** write to Maggie Herbert (✉ 201 N. Elm St., Northampton 01060).

THE BERKSHIRES

Updated by
Kay and Bill
Scheller

More than a century ago, wealthy families from New York and Boston built "summer cottages" in western Massachusetts's Berkshire Hills—great country estates that earned Berkshire County the nickname "inland Newport." Most of those grand houses have been converted into schools or hotels. Occupying the entire far western end of the state, the area is only about a 2½-hour drive directly west from Boston or north from New York City, yet it lives up to the storybook image of rural New England with wooded hills, narrow winding roads, and compact charming villages. Many cultural events take place in summer, among them the renowned Tanglewood classical music festival in Lenox. The foliage blazes brilliantly in fall, skiing is popular in winter, and spring is the time for maple sugaring. The scenic Mohawk Trail runs east to west across the northern section of the region.

North Adams

46 *130 mi northwest of Boston.*

Once a railroad boomtown and a thriving industrial city, North Adams is still industrial but no longer thriving. It's worth a stop if you're intrigued by the ghosts of the Industrial Revolution or are a railway buff.

The only natural bridge in North America caused by water erosion is the marble arch at 49-acre **Natural Bridge State Park.** The bridge crosses a narrow 500-ft chasm containing numerous faults and fractures. ⊠ *Rte. 8 N,* ☎ *413/663–6392.* 🖾 *$2 per car.* ☾ *Memorial Day–Columbus Day, weekdays 8:30–4:30, weekends 10–6.*

★ Opened in 1999 to much fanfare, the **Massachusetts Museum of Contemporary Arts,** or Mass MoCA, is the nation's largest center for contemporary performing and visual arts. The vast, 13-acre 19th-century complex of 27 buildings once housed the now defunct Sprague Electric Co. Six of the factory buildings have been transormed into more than 250,000 square feet of galleries, studios, performance venues, cafés, and shops. Its size enables the museum to display monumentally scaled works such as Robert Rauschenberg's ¼ *Mile or 2 Furlong Piece.* Exhibits and performances include everything from art exhibitions to dance and music concerts and film presentations. ⊠ *87 Marshall St.,* ☎ *413/664–4481,* WEB *www.massmoca.org.* 🖾 *$8.* ☾ *June–Oct. 10–5, Fri. and Sat. until 7; Nov.–May, Tues.–Sun. 10–4.*

Lodging

$$–$$$ 🏠 **Blackington Manor B& B.** Dan and Betsy Epstein's meticulously re-
★ stored 1849 Italianate mansion is furnished with antiques and filled with music. The Epsteins are both professional musicians, and the couple hosts concerts and chamber music workshops throughout the year. Several of the elegantly appointed guest rooms have pianos. The mansion, built by a wealthy textile manufacturer, is notable for its intricate wrought-iron balconies, floor-to-ceiling windows, a spacious bay window, and decorative corbels. A kosher kitchen is available for stays of one week or longer. ⊠ *1391 Massachusetts Ave., 01247,* ☎ *413/663–5795, 800/795–8613, or 413/663–3121,* WEB *www.blackington-manor.com. 5 rooms. Pool. MC, V. BP.*

Outdoor Activities and Sports

Picnic tables at the **Mohawk Trail State Forest** (⊠ Rte. 2, Charlemont, ☎ 413/339–5504) are set up under large evergreen trees. A few well-maintained hiking trails of a mile or so lead to a scenic lookout. A camping area and a few log cabins, which can be rented for under $10 a night, are available.

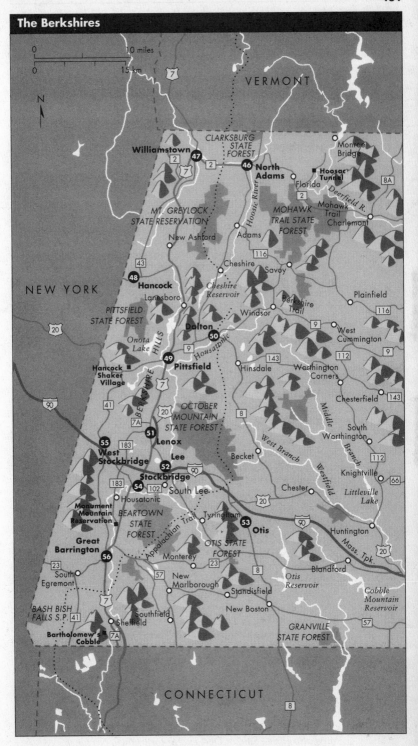

The Berkshires

0   10 miles
0   15 km

N

VERMONT

NEW YORK

CONNECTICUT

Williamstown 47
CLARKSBURG STATE FOREST
46 North Adams
Monroe Bridge
Hoosac Tunnel
Florida
8A
Deerfield R.
MT. GREYLOCK STATE RESERVATION
New Ashford
Adams
Mohawk Trail
MOHAWK TRAIL STATE FOREST
Charlemont
Cheshire
116
Savoy
43
48 Hancock
Cheshire Reservoir
Berkshire Trail
Plainfield
Lanesboro
PITTSFIELD STATE FOREST
Windsor
116
Onota Lake
Dalton 50
9
West Cummington
49 Pittsfield
Hinsdale
143
Worthington Corners
112
Chesterfield
143
Hancock Shaker Village
90
41
20
OCTOBER MOUNTAIN STATE FOREST
8
Middle Branch
South Worthington
112
7A
51 Lenox
West Branch
Becket
Knightville
66
55 West Stockbridge
183
52 Lee
90
Chester
Westfield Branch
Littleville Lake
Stockbridge 54
183
102
South Lee
20
90
Mass. Tpk.
Huntington
20
Housatonic
BEARTOWN STATE FOREST
Tyringham
53 Otis
Monument Mountain Reservation
Appalachian Trail
OTIS STATE FOREST
Blandford
Great Barrington 56
Monterey
23
Otis Reservoir
Cobble Mountain Reservoir
23
South Egremont
57
New Marlborough
8
Standisfield
New Boston
57
BASH BISH FALLS S.P.
41
Southfield
GRANVILLE STATE FOREST
Sheffield
7A
Bartholomew's Cobble
7
8

Hoosic River
Housatonic
BERKSHIRE HILLS

En Route Many people approach the Berkshires along Route 2 from Boston and the East Coast. The **Mohawk Trail,** a more than 50-mi stretch from Orange to Williamstown, follows the path blazed long ago by Native Americans that ran along the Deerfield River through the Connecticut River valley to the Berkshire Hills. It is lovely in fall. Just beyond the town of Charlemont stands *Hail to the Sunrise,* a 900-pound bronze statue of an Indian facing east, with arms uplifted, dedicated to the five Native American nations that lived along the Mohawk Trail. Some mostly tacky "Indian trading posts" on the highway carry out the Mohawk theme. Also along the road are antiques stores, flea markets, and places to pull off the road, picnic, and take photos.

Williamstown

⑰ *10 mi west of North Adams.*

When Colonel Ephraim Williams left money to found a free school in what was then known as West Hoosuck, he stipulated that the name be changed to Williamstown. Williams College opened in 1793, and even today life in this placid town revolves around it. Graceful campus buildings like the Gothic cathedral, built in 1904, line wide Main Street. The collection and exhibits at the **Williams College Museum of Art** focus on American and 20th-century art. ⊠ *Main St.,* ☎ *413/597–2429,* WEB *www.williams.edu/WCMA.* ☞ *Free.* ☉ *Tues.–Sat. 10–5, Sun. 1–5.*

★ The **Sterling and Francine Clark Art Institute** is one of the nation's notable small art museums. Its famous works include more than 30 paintings by Renoir (among them *Mademoiselle Fleury in Algerian Costume*), as well as canvases by Monet and Pisarro. *The Little Dancer,* an important sculpture by Degas, is another notable work. ⊠ *225 South St.,* ☎ *413/458–2303,* WEB *www.clark.williams.edu.* ☞ *July–Oct. $5; free rest of year and on Tues..* ☉ *Sept.–June, Tues.–Sun. 10–5; July–Aug., daily 10–5.*

The **Chapin Library of Rare Books and Manuscripts** at Williams College contains original copies of the Four Founding Documents of the United States—the Declaration of Independence, the Articles of Confederation, the Constitution, and the Bill of Rights—and 35,000 books, manuscripts, and illustrations dating from as far back as the 9th century. ⊠ *Stetson Hall, Main St.,* ☎ *413/597–2462.* ☞ *Free.* ☉ *Weekdays 10–noon and 1–5.*

Dining and Lodging

$$$ ✕ **Main Street Cafe.** Delicious northern Italian treats have earned the
★ restaurant rave reviews. The appetizer sampler includes spinach stuffed eggplant with fontina cheese, and calamari fritti with a basil emulsion. Among the entrées are a seafood combination of mussels, clams, calamari, jumbo shrimp and grilled scallops in a white wine and garlic marinara, and chicken and sausage with braised onions and mushrooms. Pizza is always on the menu. ⊠ *16 Water St.,* ☎ *413/458–3210. AE, DC, MC, V. No lunch.*

$$–$$$ ✕ **Mezze Bistro.** Live entertainment, cabarets, and seasonal parties set the tone for one of Williamstown's most popular spots. Like the entertainment, the menu changes often, featuring entrées such as veal sweetbreads with artichoke hearts and radicchio, sautéed pork with roasted shallots, prosciutto over soft polenta, and oven-roasted fennel gazpacho. ⊠ *84 Water St.,* ☎ *413/458–0123. AE, MC, V. Closed Mon. Sept.– May; also closed Sun. in Dec. except for brunch. No lunch.*

$$–$$$ ✕ **Wild Amber Grill.** The White Amber's simple decor belies the ambitiousness of its menu. The owners–chefs describe the cuisine as "creative, eclectic American," but the menu changes frequently, featuring

such dishes as osso bucco, frog's legs, a Japanese-inspired salmon cake appetizer, and an excellent apple strudel. The extensive wine list has been shrewdly selected. ☒ *101 North St.,* ☎ *413/458–4000. AE, MC, V. Closed Tues. No lunch.*

$$$ 🏨 **The Orchards Hotel.** Although it's right on Route 2 and surrounded by parking lots, this hotel compensates for these shortcomings with a beautiful central courtyard with fruit trees and a pond stocked with koi. English antiques furnish most of the spacious accommodations. The inner rooms, which have one-way windows looking onto the courtyard, are best for summer stays. The outer rooms have less-distinguished views, but their fireplaces add appeal for winter visits. Morning coffee and afternoon high tea are complimentary. ☒ *222 Adams Rd., 01267,* ☎ *413/458–9611 or 800/225–1517,* FAX *413/458–3273,* WEB *www.orchardshotel.com. 47 rooms. Restaurant, bar, pool, hot tub, sauna, exercise room, meeting room. AE, DC, MC, V.*

$$–$$$ 🏨 **Field Farm Guest House.** Built in 1948 on 296 acres, this house holds
★ a number of contemporary artworks on loan from Williams College. It was donated as part of a land trust by the former owners (art lovers who gave part of their collection to Williams) and is now run as a B&B by a nonprofit organization. The large windows in the guest rooms have expansive views of the grounds. Three rooms have private decks; two rooms have working fireplaces with tiles depicting various animals. Guests can prepare simple meals in the pantry area. The grounds, open to the public, include a pond, sculptures, a nature center, and 4 mi of trails. ☒ *554 Sloan Rd., off Rte. 43, 01267,* ☎ FAX *413/458–3135,* WEB *www.berkshireweb.comtrustees/field. 5 rooms. Pool, tennis court, fishing. D, MC, V. BP.*

$$ 🏨 **River Bend Farm.** One of the founders of Williamstown built this 1170 Georgian Colonial farmhouse, now restored with complete authenticity. The kitchen, through which guests enter, contains an open-range stove and an oven hung with dried herbs. Some bedrooms have wide-plank walls, curtains of unbleached muslin, and four-poster beds with canopies or rope beds (yes, they really are comfortable). All rooms are sprinkled with antique pieces—chamber pots, washstands, wing chairs, and spinning wheels. ☒ *643 Simonds Rd., 01267,* ☎ *413/458–3121. 4 rooms without bath. No credit cards. Closed Nov.–Mar. CP.*

$$–$$$ 🏨 **Berkshire Hills Motel.** All the rooms at this two-story brick-and-clapboard motel about 3 mi south of Williamstown are furnished in Colonial style. The lounge has a fireplace, and guests can use the barbecue on the deck. Although the motel is close to the road, the spacious grounds in back encompass a brook, woodlands, landscaped gardens, and an outdoor heated pool. ☒ *U.S. 7, 01267,* ☎ *413/458–3950 or 800/388—9677,* FAX *413/458–5878. 21 rooms. Pool. AE, D, MC, V. CP.*

Nightlife and the Arts

Friday evening is folk music night; on Saturday jazz and blues are played at the tavern in the **Williams Inn** (☒ On-the-Green, ☎ 413/458–9371). The **Williamstown Theatre Festival** (☒ Williams College, Adams Memorial Theatre, ☎ 413/597–3400 for tickets or 413/597-3399 for information), which runs from June to August, presents well-known theatrical works with famous performers on the Main Stage and contemporary works on the Other Stage.

Outdoor Activities and Sports

BIKING

The gently rolling Berkshire Hills are excellent cycling terrain. Mountain bike trails can be found at the Mt. Greylock State Reservation. You can rent a bike from **Mountain Goat Bicycle Shop** (☒ 130 Water St., ☎ 413/458-8445), which is about 7 mi west of Mt. Greylock.

Waubeeka Golf Links (⊠ U.S. 7, ☎ 413/458–8355), an 18-hole, par-72 course, is open to the public and rents golf clubs. Greens fees are $30 weekdays and $35 weekends and holidays; carts are $13 per rider or $26 per cart.

En Route   The centerpiece of the 10,327-acre **Mt. Greylock State Reservation** (⊠ Rockwell Rd., Lanesboro, ☎ 413/499–4262 or 413/499–4263) is 3,491-ft-high Mt. Greylock, the highest point in Massachusetts. The reservation, south of Williamstown, has facilities for cycling, fishing, horseback riding, camping, and snowmobiling. Many treks—including a portion of the Appalachian Trail—start from the parking lot at the summit, an 8-mi drive from the base of the mountain. **Bascom Lodge** (☎ 413/743–1591 or 413/443–0011), also at the summit, provides overnight accommodations, snacks, and souvenirs from mid–May to mid–Oct. A visitor center at the base of the mountain is open daily, year-round. The Sperry Road turn-off leads to a camping-picnic area; there's a modest charge.

Hancock

48   *15 mi south of Williamstown.*

Hancock, the closest village to the Jiminy Peak ski resort, comes into its own during ski season, though summer guests have a number of options.

Lodging

$$$–$$$$ 🏨 **Country Inn at Jiminy Peak.** Massive stone fireplaces in its lobby and lounge lend this hotel a ski-lodge atmosphere. The modern condo-style suites accommodate up to four people and have kitchenettes separated from the living area by a bar and high stools; the suites at the rear of the building overlook the slopes. Lodging-skiing packages are available. ⊠ *Corey Rd., 01237,* ☎ *413/738–5500; 800/882–8859 outside MA,* FAX *413/738–5513,* WEB *www.jiminypeak.com. 96 suites. Restaurant, bar, pool, 2 hot tubs, 2 saunas, miniature golf, 5 tennis courts, exercise room, meeting room. AE, D, DC, MC, V.*

$$ 🏨 **Hancock Inn.** This country Victorian inn, which dates from the late 1700s, provides cozy accommodations a mile from Jiminy Peak. Two small dining rooms (no lunch) have fireplaces, stained-glass windows, and candles on the tables. ⊠ *Rte. 43, 01237,* ☎ *413/738–5873,* FAX *413/738–5719,* WEB *www.inntopia.com. 6 rooms. Restaurant. AE, MC, V. BP.*

Ski Areas

BRODIE

The snow can be green, the beer is often green, and the decor is *always* green here. Yet it's more than the Irish ambience that attracts crowds for weekend and night skiing: the base lodge has a restaurant and bar with live entertainment, lodging (not fancy) is within walking distance of the lifts, and RV trailers can be accommodated. Brodie and Jiminy Peak are now under the same ownership, and a Value Card can be used at both areas. There's express bus service from New York City on weekends. ⊠ *U.S. 7, New Ashford 01237,* ☎ *413/443–4752; 413/443–4751 snow conditions.*

Downhill. Almost all the 40 trails at Brodie are beginner and intermediate despite the black diamonds, which designate steeper (but not expert) runs; the vertical is 1,250 ft. Four double chairlifts and one surface lift serve the trails. Snowmaking covers 95% of the area's skiable terrain.

Cross-country. The area's cross-country skiing covers 25 km (16 mi) of trails, half of which are groomed daily.

Tubing. The area's new tubing center is open Wed.–Fri. from 4–10:30 and all day and night on weekends.

Other activities. A sports center, **Brodie Racquet Club** (☎ 413/458–4677), 1 mi from the ski area, has five indoor courts for tennis and five for racquetball, an exercise room, and a snack bar.

Child care. The nursery takes infants through age 8 by the hour, half day, or full day. There are afternoon, weekend, and holiday ski-instruction programs for children.

JIMINY PEAK

This area, 2½ hours from New York City and three hours from Boston, has all the amenities of a major mountain resort. A high speed, six-passenger Berkshire Express chair lift wisks skiers three-quarters of a mile to the summit (and the summit lodge) in just five minutes. Condominiums and an all-suites country inn are within walking distance of the ski lifts; more condominium complexes are nearby; and two restaurants and bars are at the slopes. Rentals are available on a nightly or weekly basis. ⊠ *Corey Rd., 01237, ☎ 413/738–5500; 888/454–6469 outside MA; 413/738–7325 snow conditions.*

Downhill. With a vertical of 1,140 ft, 40 trails, and nine lifts, Jiminy has near big-time status. It is mostly a cruising mountain—trails are groomed daily, and only on some are small moguls left to build up along the side of the slope. The steepest black-diamond runs are on the upper headwalls; longer outer runs make for good intermediate terrain. There's skiing nightly in season, and snowmaking covers 93% of the skiable terrain.

Other activities. Jiminy has a snowboard park and an old-fashioned ice rink.

Child care. The nursery takes children from 6 months. Children from age 4 to 12 can take daily SKIwee lessons; those from 6 to 15 can take a series of eight weekends of instruction with the same teacher. The kids' ski area has its own lift.

Summer activities. The resort has an alpine slide, a putting course, tennis courts, swimming facilities, and trout fishing. You can ride up the mountain on a high-speed chairlift.

Pittsfield

㊾ *22 mi south of Williamstown.*

Fast-food chains and run-down storefronts dominate downtown Pittsfield, the county seat and geographic center of the Berkshires. But not every town in the region can be relentlessly quaint, and Pittsfield does have an engaging small-town atmosphere.

☻ Three floors of exhibits at the **Berkshire Museum** display an excellent collection of objects relating to history, the natural world, and art–including a fine collection of Hudson River School paintings. ⊠ *39 South St., ☎ 413/443–7171,* WEB *www.berkshiremuseum.org.* ⊡ *$7.* ☉ *10–5 daily 1–5.*

The **Herman Melville Memorial Room** at the **Berkshire Athenaeum** houses books, letters, and memorabilia of the author of *Moby-Dick.* ⊠ *Berkshire Public Library, 1 Wendell Ave., ☎ 413/499–9486.* ⊡ *Free, but request admission at the Local History Department.* ☉ *Call for hrs.*

Arrowhead, the house Herman Melville purchased in 1850, is just outside Pittsfield; the underwhelming tour includes the study in which *Moby-*

Dick was written. ⊠ *780 Holmes Rd.,* ☎ *413/442–1793,* WEB *www.mobydick.org.* ⊠ *$5.* ⊙ *Memorial Day–Oct., daily 10–5, with guided tours on the hr; Nov.–late May, weekdays by appointment.*

★ **Hancock Shaker Village** was founded in the 1790s, the third Shaker community in America. At its peak in the 1840s, the village had almost 300 inhabitants, who made their living farming, selling seeds and herbs, making medicines, and producing crafts. The religious community officially closed in 1960, its 170-year life span a small miracle considering its population's vows of celibacy (they took in orphans to maintain their constituency). Many examples of Shaker ingenuity are visible at Hancock today: the **Round Stone Barn** and the **Laundry and Machine Shop** are two of the most interesting buildings. Also on site are a farm, some period gardens, a museum shop with reproduction Shaker furniture, a picnic area, and a café. ⊠ *U.S. 20, 6 mi west of Pittsfield,* ☎ *413/443–0188 or 800/817–1137,* WEB *hancockshakervillage.org.* ⊠ *Guided tour $10; self-guided tour $13.50.* ⊙ *Memorial Day–late Oct. 9:30–5 for self-guided tours; rest of year, 10–3 for guided tours.*

Dining and Lodging

$$–$$$ ✕ **Dakota.** Moose and elk heads watch over diners, and the motto is "Steak, Seafood, and Smiles" at this large, highly acclaimed restaurant decorated like a rustic hunting lodge. Meals cooked on the mesquite grill include steaks and salmon, shrimp, and trout; the 32-item salad bar has many organic foods. A hearty brunch buffet is served on Sunday. ⊠ *U.S. 7/20,* ☎ *413/499–7900. AE, D, DC, MC, V. No lunch Mon.–Sat.*

$$ ▥ **Crowne Plaza Pittsfield.** Two tiers of rooms surround the large, glass-dome swimming pool at this freshly renovated downtown hotel. Some rooms have a view of the mountains. ⊠ *Berkshire Common, South St., 01201,* ☎ *413/499–2000,* FAX *413/442–0449,* WEB *www.crowne-plaza.com. 179 rooms. 3 restaurants, bar, pool, hot tub, sauna, exercise room, meeting room. AE, D, DC, MC, V.*

Nightlife and the Arts

The **Albany Berkshire Ballet** (⊠ Koussevitzky Arts Center, Berkshire Community College, West St., ☎ 413/445–5382) performs classical and contemporary works year-round, including *The Nutcracker* at Christmastime. **Berkshire Opera Company** (⊠ 297 North St., ☎ 413/443-7400) stages performances throughout the summer at the Koussevitzky Arts Center at Berkshire Community College. On weekends in winter a DJ at the **Tamarack Lounge** (⊠ Dan Fox Dr., ☎ 413/442–8316), in the Bousquet ski area's base lodge, spins dance tunes.

Outdoor Activities and Sports

The **Housatonic River** flows south from Pittsfield between the Berkshire Hills and the Taconic Range toward Connecticut. You can rent canoes, rowboats, paddleboats, small motorboats, and even pontoon party boats from the **Onota Boat Livery** (⊠ 463 Pecks Rd., ☎ 413/442–1724), which also provides dock space on Onota Lake and sells fishing tackle and bait.

U-Drive Boat Rentals (⊠ 1651 North St., ☎ 413/442-7020) has rentals on Pontoosuc Lake.

Ski Areas

BOUSQUET SKI AREA

Other areas have entered an era of glamour and high prices, but Bousquet remains an economical, no-nonsense place to ski. The inexpensive lift tickets are the same price every day, and there's night skiing except Sunday. You can go tubing for just $10 for the day when conditions allow. ⊠ *Dan Fox Dr., 01201,* ☎ *413/442–8316; 413/442–2436 snow conditions,* WEB *www.bousquets.com.*

Downhill. Bousquet, with a 750-ft vertical drop, has 21 trails, but only if you count every change in steepness and every merging slope. Though this is a generous figure, you will find some good beginner and intermediate runs, with a few steeper pitches. There are three double chairlifts and two surface lifts.

Child care. Bous-Care Nursery watches children age 6 months and up by the hour; reservations are suggested. Ski instruction classes are offered twice daily on weekends and holidays for children ages 5 and up.

Summer and year-round activities. The facilities at the **Berkshire West Athletic Club** (⊠ Dan Fox Dr., ☎ 413/499–4600), across the street from Bousquet, include four handball courts, indoor and outdoor tennis courts, cardiovascular and weight machines, and indoor and outdoor pools.

Dalton

50 *3 mi northeast of Pittsfield.*

The paper manufacturer Crane and Co., started by Zenas Crane in 1801, is the major employer in working-class Dalton. Exhibits at the **Crane Museum of Paper Making,** in the handsomely restored Old Stone Mill (1844), trace the history of American papermaking from 1801 to the present. ⊠ *E. Housatonic St., off Rte. 9,* ☎ *413/684–6481.* 🎟 *Free.* ☉ *June–mid-Oct., weekdays 2–5.*

Lodging

$$–$$$ 🏨 **Dalton House.** Cheerful guest rooms decorated in an eclectic mix of Shaker and period furnishings, folk art, plants, and collectibles are spread out in three interconnected buildings; the original structure was built in 1810 by a Hessian soldier. Common rooms include a living room with a stone fireplace and a sunny breakfast area. Two suites in the carriage house have sitting areas, exposed beams, and quilts. ⊠ *955 Main St., 01226,* ☎ *413/684–3854,* 📠 *413/684–0203,* WEB *www.thedalton-house.com. 9 rooms, 2 suites. Pool. AE, MC, V. CP winter, BP summer.*

Lenox

51 *8 mi southwest of Dalton, 5 mi south of Pittsfield, 146 mi west of Boston.*

In the thick of the "summer cottage" region, rich with old inns and majestic buildings, the sophisticated village of Lenox epitomizes the Berkshires. The outstanding Tanglewood music festival takes place here.

★ **The Mount,** a Classical Revival mansion built in 1902, was the former summer home of novelist Edith Wharton. The house and grounds were designed by Wharton, who is considered by many to have set the standard for 20th-century interior decoration. In designing the Mount, she followed the principles set forth in her book *The Decoration of Houses* (1897), creating a calm and well-ordered home. A "Women of Achievement" lecture series takes place here on Mondays in July and August. ⊠ *Plunkett St.,* ☎ *413/637–1899,* WEB *www.edithwharton.org.* 🎟 *$6.* ☉ *Memorial Day weekend–Oct., daily 9–3, with tours on the hr (last tour at 2).*

☺ The **Railway Museum,** in a restored 1902 railroad station in central Lenox, contains period exhibits and a large working model railway. It's the starting point for the diesel-hauled **Berkshire Scenic Railway,** which travels for 15 minutes over a portion of the historic New Haven Railway's Housatonic Valley Line. ⊠ *Willow Creek Rd.,* ☎ *413/637–2210,* WEB *www.RegionNet.com/colberk/berkshirerailway.html.* 🎟 *$2.* ☉ *May–Nov., weekends and holidays, 10–3:30.*

The **Frelinghuysen Morris House & Studio** exhibits the works of American abstract artists Suzy Frelinghuysen and George L.K. Morris as well as those of contemporaries including Picasso, Braque, and Gris. It's best to call in advance to set up a tour. ⊠ *92 Hawthorne St.,* ☎ *413/637–0166,* WEB *www.frelinghuysen.org.* ⊠ *$8.* ⊗ *July–Aug., Thurs.–Sun. 10–3; Sept.–Columbus Day, Thurs.–Sat. 10–3; guided tours on the hr.*

Dining and Lodging

$$$ ✕ **Café Lucia.** *Bistecca alla fiorentina* (porterhouse steak grilled with olive oil, garlic, and rosemary) and *ravioli basilico e pomodoro* (homemade ravioli with fresh tomatoes, garlic, and basil) are among the dishes that change seasonally at this northern Italian restaurant. The sleek decor includes track lighting and photographs of the owners' Italian ancestors. Weekend reservations are essential up to a month ahead during Tanglewood. ⊠ *90 Church St.,* ☎ *413/637–2640. AE, DC, MC, V. Closed Mon. July–Oct. and Sun.–Mon. Nov.–June. No lunch.*

$$–$$$ ✕ **Trattoria Il Vesuvio.** *Proprietaria* Anna Arace, a native of Pompeii,
★ is on hand nightly to assure that every dish meets her exacting standards. Among the house specialties are *arrosto di vitello,* roast breast of veal stuffed with sliced prosciutto and spinach, cooked in a brick oven and served with red wine sauce; *linguini con vongole,* baby clams sautéed in virgin olive oil, white wine, garlic, and parsley, served over pasta; and *lasagna di verdura,* homemade pasta layered with eggplant, sweet red onions, braised spinach, cheeses, and marinara sauce. Save room for Anna's homemade tiramisu. ⊠ *242 Pittsfield Rd.,* ☎ *413/637–4904. AE, D, MC, V. Closed Sun. Sept.–June. No lunch.*

$$$$ ✕🏠 **Blantyre.** Modeled after a castle in Scotland, this supremely ele-
★ gant manor house sits amid 100 acres of manicured lawns and woodlands. Lavishly decorated rooms in the main house have hand-carved four-poster beds, overstuffed chaise lounges, and Victorian bathrooms. The rooms in the carriage house are well-appointed but can't compete with the formal grandeur of the main house. The restaurant (reservations essential; jacket and tie) serves "refined Country House cuisine"—no cream or heavy sauces, light on the butter—and offers a $75 prix-fixe menu. After-dinner coffee and cognac are served in the music room, where a harpist plays. ⊠ *16 Blantyre Rd., off U.S. 20, 01240,* ☎ *413/637–3556,* FAX *413/637–4282,* WEB *www.blantyre.com. 13 rooms, 11 suites. Restaurant, pool, hot tub, sauna, 4 tennis courts, croquet, hiking. AE, DC, MC, V. Closed early Nov.–early May. CP.*

$$$$ ✕🏠 **Wheatleigh Hotel.** Set amid 22 wooded acres, this mellow brick estate based on a 16th-century Florentine palazzo has rooms with high ceilings, intricate plaster moldings, English antiques, and some modern furnishings. The main restaurant, a huge room with marble fireplaces and cut-glass chandeliers, serves "contemporary classical" cuisine; the $82 three-course prix-fixe menus include roast antelope, pheasant, rabbit, and lobster. The Library offers a more casual setting. ⊠ *Hawthorne Rd., 02140,* ☎ *413/637–0610,* FAX *413/637–4507,* WEB *www.wheatleigh.com. 19 rooms. 2 restaurants, bar, pool, tennis court, exercise room, meeting room. AE, DC, MC, V.*

$$$–$$$$ 🏠 **Cliffwood Inn.** Six of the seven guest rooms in this 1889 Georgian Revival inn have fireplaces, and four more fireplaces glow in the common areas. Much of the inn's furniture comes from Europe; most guest rooms have canopy beds. The patio and pool area are well designed; indoors there's a counter-current pool. ⊠ *25 Cliffwood St., 01240,* ☎ *413/637–3330 or 800/789–3331,* FAX *413/637–0221,* WEB *www.cliffwood.com. 7 rooms. 1 pool, hot tub. No credit cards.*

$$$–$$$$ 🏠 **Cranwell Resort and Hotel.** The best rooms in this 380-acre, five-building complex are in the century-old Tudor mansion; they're furnished with antiques and have marble bathrooms. Two smaller buildings have

20 rooms each, and there are several small cottages, each with a kitchen. Most of the facilities are open to the public, as are the resort's restaurants, where you can dine formally or informally. ✉ *55 Lee Rd., 02140,* ☎ *413/637–1364 or 800/272–6935,* FAX *413/637–4364,* WEB *www.cranwell.com. 107 rooms. 3 restaurants, pool, exercise room, driving range, golf, 2 tennis courts, bicycles, skiing. AE, D, DC, MC, V. CP.*

$$$–$$$$ 🏠 **Garden Gables.** This 250-year-old "summer cottage" on 5 acres of wooded grounds has been an inn since 1947. The three common parlors have fireplaces, and one long, narrow room has a unique five-legged Steinway piano. Rooms come in various shapes, sizes, and colors; some have brass beds, and others have pencil four-posters. Some rooms have sloping ceilings, fireplaces, whirlpool baths, or woodland views. Three have private decks. Breakfast is served buffet-style in the airy dining room. ✉ *Box 52, 135 Main St., 01240,* ☎ *413/637–0193,* FAX *413/637–4554,* WEB *www.lenoxinn.com. 18 rooms. Pool. AE, D, MC, V. BP.*

$$–$$$$ 🏠 **Whistler's Inn.** The antiques decorating the parlor of this intown
★ English Tudor mansion are ornate, with a touch of the exotic. The library, formal parlor, music room (with a Steinway Grand piano and Louis XVI original furniture), and grand dining room all impress. Designer drapes and bedspreads adorn the rooms, three of which have working fireplaces. The carriage house is only open May through October; one room in it has African decor, and another is done in southwestern style. The inn is nestled amidst seven acres of gardens and woods across from Kennedy Park. ✉ *5 Greenwood St., 01240,* ☎ *413/637–0975,* FAX *413/637–2190,* WEB *www.whistlersinnlenox.com. 14 rooms. Badminton, croquet, library. AE, D, MC, V. BP.*

Nightlife and the Arts

Tanglewood (✉ West St., off Rte. 183, ☎ 413/637–5165; 617/266–1492; 617/266–1200 to order tickets from Symphony Charge), the 200-acre summer home of the Boston Symphony Orchestra, attracts thousands every year to concerts by world-famous performers from mid-June to Labor Day. The 5,000-seat main shed hosts larger concerts; the Seiji Ozawa Hall (named for the BSO conductor) seats around 1,200 and is used for recitals, chamber music, and more intimate performances by summer program students and soloists. One of the most rewarding ways to experience Tanglewood is to purchase lawn tickets, arrive early with blankets or lawn chairs, and have a picnic. The season's schedule is posted on their Web site: WEB www.bso.org.

Shakespeare and Company (✉ Plunkett St., ☎ 413/637–1199 or, for tickets, 413/637-3353) performs the works of Shakespeare and Edith Wharton from late May through Oct. at the Mount and at two new theatres on the former grounds of the National Music Center at 70 Kemble St.

The **Robbins-Zust Family Marionettes** (☎ 413/698–2591) have been pleasing audiences for decades. Performances are Tuesday, Thursday and Saturday at 11 and 2 at the Lenox House Shops (✉ U.S. 7/20) the lst two weeks of July and the first two weeks in August, and year-round throughout the Berkshires.

Outdoor Activities and Sports

Undermountain Farm (✉ 400 Undermountain Rd., ☎ 413/637–3365) gives horseback-riding lessons and conducts guided trail rides year-round, weather permitting.

Shopping

Stone's Throw Antiques (✉ 51 Church St., ☎ 413/637–2733) carries fine 19th- and early-20th-century antiques. The **Ute Stubich Gallery** (✉ 69 Church St., ☎ 413/637–3566) sells folk and contemporary art. **Si-**

enna Gallery (✉ 80 Main St., ☎ 413/637-8386) displays the creations of more than 40 contemporary studio jewelers from around the world. **Perfect Picnics** (✉ 72 Church St., ☎ 413/637–3015) prepares gourmet picnic baskets and delivers them free of charge (including to Tanglewood).

Lee

❷ *6 mi south of Lenox.*

A 65-store outlet mall and the reopening of an 1817 inn on the National Register of Historic Places downtown have breathed new life into tiny Lee, just off the Massachusetts Turnpike.

Santarella Museum and Gardens, which resembles a dwelling from the fairy tales of the Brothers Grimm, was the home and last studio of Sir Henry Hudson Kitson (1863–1947), sculptor of *The Minuteman* in Lexington and other renowned works. Today the studio is open as a museum and gallery, and the 4 acres of grounds designed by the artist-naturalist are a sculpture park. ✉ *75 Main Rd., Tyringham,* ☎ *413/243–3260.* 🎟 *$4.* ☉ *Memorial Day–Columbus Day weekend, Thurs.-Mon. 10–5.*

Lodging

$$$ 🏨 **Historic Merrell Inn.** Built more than 200 years ago as a private res-
★   idence (it was later a stagecoach stopover), this inn has some good-size rooms, several with working fireplaces. Meticulously maintained, the Merrell has an unfussy yet authentic style, with polished wide-board floors, painted walls, and wood antiques. The sitting room has an open fireplace and contains the only intact "bird cage" Colonial bar—a semi-circular bar surrounded by wooden slats—in the country. Breakfast is cooked to order. ✉ *1565 Pleasant St./Rte. 102, South Lee 01260,* ☎ *413/243–1794 or 800/243–1794,* 📠 *413/243–2669,* 🌐 *www.merrell-inn.com. 9 rooms, 1 suite. MC, V. BP.*

$$–$$$ 🏨 **Morgan House.** This landmark 1817 Federal inn, once owned by Nat King Cole's wife, Maria, has been reopened by new owners after extensive restoration and renovation. Each room has a sitting area, brightly painted wood furniture, four-poster beds, stenciled walls, and well-worn antiques. Dinner, mainly American comfort foods, is served nightly. ✉ *33 Main St., 01238,* ☎ *413/243–3661.* 📠 *413/243-3103,* 🌐 *www.morganhouseinn.com 11 rooms, 6 with bath. 2 restaurants. AE, MC, V. BP.*

Otis

❸ *15 mi southeast of Lee, 21 mi southeast of Lenox.*

A more rustic alternative to the polish of Stockbridge and Lenox, Otis, with a ski area and 20 lakes and ponds, supplies plenty of what made the Berkshires desirable in the first place—the great outdoors. The dining options here are slim; your best bet is to pack a picnic of goodies from a Lenox gourmet shop. Nearby Becket hosts the outstanding Jacob's Pillow Dance Festival in summer.

Dining

$–$$ ✕ **Dream Away Lodge.** When the Dream Away reopened in 1998, folk-music fans hailed the revival of the "middle of nowhere" roadhouse once run by the late "Mama" Maria Fresca, a spirited hostess who befriended many performers (scenes from Bob Dylan's road-show movie *Renaldo and Clara* were filmed here). Wednesday is music night, with acoustic folk, blues, and other traditional sounds. Bar-menu Wednesdays features burgers, pastas, and spicy fries; four-course prix-fixe offerings other nights might include roast cilantro chicken or salmon fillet in puff pastry, and homemade desserts. ⊠ *County Rd., Becket,* ☎ *413/623–8725. No credit cards. Closed Mon.–Tues. Brunch Sat. and Sun. beginning at noon.*

Nightlife and the Arts

For nine weeks each summer, the tiny town of Becket, a few miles north of Otis, comes to life and becomes a mecca of the dance world during **Jacob's Pillow Dance Festival** (⊠ George Carter Rd. at U.S. 20, Becket, ☎ 413/637–1322; 413/243–0745 box office mid-May–Aug. WEB www.jacobspillow.org), which showcases world-renowned performers of ballet, modern, and ethnic dance. Before the main events, showings of works-in-progress and even of some of the final productions are staged outdoors, often free of charge. You can picnic on the grounds or eat at the restaurant.

Outdoor Activities and Sports

Deer Run Maples (⊠ Ed Jones Rd., ☎ 413/269–7588) is one of several sugar houses where you can spend the morning tasting freshly tapped maple syrup that's been drizzled onto a dish of snow. Sugaring season varies with the weather; it can be anytime between late February and early April.

You can hike, bike, or cross-country ski at the 3,800-acre **Otis State Forest** (⊠ Rte. 23, ☎ 413/269–6002). The 8,000-acre **Tolland State Forest** (⊠ Rte. 8, ☎ 413/269–6002) allows swimming in the Otis Reservoir and camping.

Stockbridge

54 *7 mi south of Lenox, 149 mi west of Boston.*

Stockbridge, a major tourist destination, has the look of small-town New England down pat. Its artistic and literary inhabitants have included sculptor Daniel Chester French, writers Norman Mailer and Robert Sherwood, and, fittingly enough, that champion of small-town America, painter Norman Rockwell, who lived here from 1953 until his death in 1978.

★ The **Norman Rockwell Museum** owns more than 570 of the artist's works, beginning with the first *Saturday Evening Post* cover from 1916. A summer 2001 exhibition will display 70 original paintings and 322 *Post* covers. The museum also mounts exhibits by other artists. On the 36-acre grounds is Rockwell's studio, complete with his brushes. You can picnic here or stroll along the river walk. ⊠ *Rte. 183 (2 mi from Stockbridge),* ☎ *413/298–4100,* WEB *www.nrm.org.* ☜ *$9.* ☺ *Mon.–Fri. 10-4, Sat. and Sun. until 5.*

★ **Chesterwood** was for 33 years the summer home of the sculptor Daniel Chester French (1850–1931), who created *The Minuteman* in Concord and the Lincoln Memorial in Washington, D.C. Tours are given of the house, which is maintained in the style of the 1920s, and of the studio, where you can view the casts and models French used to create the Lincoln Memorial. ⊠ *Williamsville Rd. off Rte. 183,* ☎ *413/298–3579,* WEB *www.chesterwood.net.* ☜ *$6.50.* ☺ *May–Oct., daily 10–5.*

The 15-acre **Berkshire Botanical Gardens** contain greenhouses, ponds, nature trails, and perennial, rose, and herb gardens. Picnicking is encouraged. ⊠ *Rtes. 102 and 183,* ☎ *413/298–3926.* ☜ *$5.* ☺ *May–Oct., daily 10–5.*

★ **Naumkeag,** a Berkshire cottage once owned by Joseph Choate, an ambassador during the administration of U.S. president William McKinley and a successful New York lawyer, provides a glimpse into the gracious living of the "gilded era of the Berkshires. The 26-room gabled mansion, designed by Stanford White in 1886, sits atop Prospect Hill. It is decorated with many original furnishings and art that spans three centuries; the collection of Chinese export porcelain is also noteworthy. The meticulously kept 8 acres of formal gardens designed by Fletcher Steele are themselves worth a visit. ✉ *South Prospect Hill,* ☎ *413/298–3239,* WEB *www.thetrustees.org.* 💲 *$8.* 🕐 *Memorial Day–Columbus Day, daily 10–5.*

Dining and Lodging

$$$ ✕ **Once Upon a Table.** The atmosphere is casual yet vaguely romantic at this little restaurant in an alley off Stockbridge's main street. The Continental and new American cuisine includes seasonal dishes, with appetizers such as escargots, and potpie entrées. It's best to call ahead for seasonal hours. ✉ *36 Main St.,* ☎ *413/298–3870. Reservations essential AE, MC, V. Open daily for lunch, seasonally for dinner; call for hrs.*

$$–$$$$ ✕🏠 **Red Lion Inn.** An inn since 1773, the Red Lion has a large main building and seven annexes, each of which is different (one is a converted fire station). Many rooms are small; the ones in the annex houses tend to be more appealing. All the rooms are furnished with antiques and reproductions and hung with Rockwell prints; some have Oriental rugs. The same menu—with an emphasis on New England specialties—is served in both of the dining rooms and (in season) in the garden. Jacket and tie (no jeans) is required in the formal dining room. Evenings, there's live entertainment in the Lion's Den. ✉ *30 Main St., 02162,* ☎ *413/298–5545,* FAX *413/298–5130,* WEB *www.redlion-inn.com. 110 rooms, 96 with bath; 26 suites. 2 restaurants, bar, pool, massage, exercise room, meeting room. AE, D, DC, MC, V.*

$$$$ 🏠 **Inn at Stockbridge.** Antiques and feather comforters are among the accents in the rooms of this inn run by the attentive Alice and Len Schiller. The two serve breakfast in their elegant dining room, and every evening they provide wine and cheese. Each of the junior suites in the adjacent "cottage" building has a decorative theme such as Kashmir, St. Andrews, and Provence; the junior suites in the new "carriage" building have Berkshire themes. Some rooms have fireplaces or whirlpool baths. ✉ *Box 618, U.S. 7, 02162,* ☎ *413/298–3337 or 888/466–7865,* FAX *413/298–3406,* WEB *www.stockbridgeinn.com. 16 rooms. Pool. AE, D, MC, V. BP.*

Nightlife and the Arts

The **Berkshire Theatre Festival** (☎ 413/298–5536; 413/298–5576 box office) stages nightly performances during summer in Stockbridge. Plays written by local schoolchildren are performed occasionally during the summer. The **Red Lion's Lion's Den** presents live jazz, folk, or blues nightly.

West Stockbridge

🔵 *5 mi west of Stockbridge.*

The Williams River winds through this pretty little town, whose streets are dotted with galleries, antiques and specialty shops, and restaurants.

At the **Berkshire Center for Contemporary Glass** you can watch glassblowers create magnificent pieces and, in summer, create your own paperweight. This handsome gallery displays and sells the works of some of the country's foremost artists working in this medium. ✉ *6 Harris St.,* ☎ *413/232–4666.* 💲 *Free.* 🕐 *May–Oct., daily 10–6; Nov.–Apr., daily 10–4:30.*

Dining

$$–$$$ ✕ **Truc Orient Express.** "Happy Pancake," "Shaking Beef," and "Beef on Rice Noodles" are just a few of the well-prepared Vietnamese specialties at this restaurant just across from the Berkshire Center for Contemporary Glass. Plenty of wood, windows, and artwork create a lovely setting. Portions tend to be on the small side but are beautifully presented. ⊠ *3 Harris St.,* ☎ *413/232–4204. AE, D, MC, V. No lunch.*

Shopping

Sawyer Antiques (⊠ Depot St., ☎ 413/232–7062) sells Early American furniture and accessories in a spare clapboard structure that was a Shaker mill.

Great Barrington

56 *10 mi south of West Stockbridge.*

The largest town in the southern Berkshires was the first place to free slaves under due process of law and was also the birthplace of W. E. B. Du Bois, the civil rights leader, author, and educator. The many ex–New Yorkers who live in Great Barrington expect great food and service, and the restaurants here deliver complex, tasteful fare. The town is also a favorite of antiques hunters, as are the nearby villages of South Egremont and Sheffield.

Bartholomew's Cobble, south of Great Barrington, is a natural rock garden beside the Housatonic River (the Native American name means "river beyond the mountains"). The 277-acre site is filled with trees, ferns, wildflowers, and hiking trails. The visitor center has a museum. ⊠ *Rte. 7A,* ☎ *413/229–8600.* 💰 *$3.* 🕐 *Daily dawn–dusk.*

Dining and Lodging

$$$ ✕ **Helsinki Tea Company.** The emphasis is on Finnish, Russian, and Jewish cuisines, prepared with lots of spices and served in big portions, at this restaurant, which suggests a lost world of Old European elegance. A hodgepodge of colorful cushions, fringed draperies, and objets d'art create the feeling of an intimate café. It doesn't get much cozier than sitting by a roaring fire, tucking into an order of "Midnight Train to Moscow" (chicken-apple bratwurst, hot cabbage slaw, and potato latkes), and then lingering over one of the numerous tea offerings (or something stronger—the restaurant has a full liquor license) and live music at the Club Helsinki next door. Sunday brunch is a popular affair. ⊠ *284 Main St.,* ☎ *413/528–3394. D, MC, V.*

$$–$$$ ✕🖫 **Egremont Inn.** The public rooms in this 1780 inn are enormous, and each has a fireplace. Bedrooms are on the small side but have four-poster beds (some have claw-foot baths), and, like the rest of the inn, unpretentious furnishings. Windows sweep around two sides of the stylish restaurant ($$$; reservations essential on weekends in season), where flames flicker in a huge fireplace. The menu changes frequently but always includes salmon or another fresh fish, a homemade pasta, and a hearty meat dish like rib-eye steak with caramelized onions. There's a three-night minimum in season. ⊠ *10 Old Sheffield Rd., South Egremont 01258,* ☎ *413/528–2111 or 800/859–1780,* ℻ *413/528–3284,* WEB *www.egremontinn.com. 19 rooms, 1 suite. Restaurant, bar, pool, tennis court. AE, D, MC, V. CP, EP, MAP.*

$$$–$$$$ 🖫 **The Old Inn on the Green and Gedney Farm.** Five distinctive lodgings make up this property in the historic village of New Marlborough. The 1760 Old Inn has five authentically restored, antiques-filled guest rooms. The ultradeluxe, freshly restored Thayer House includes five elegantly appointed rooms and a courtyard terrace with a pool. Just up the road is Gedney Farm, with two turn-of-the-century, Normandy-style

barns with 16 rooms and suites—all with queen beds and many with fireplaces and whirlpool baths. Other properties include the mid-nineteenth century Gedney Manor House with 12 guest rooms, and the four-bedroom Colonial Hannah Stebbins House on the Green. The restaurant in the Old Inn is lit entirely by candlelight and has fireplaces in each dining room. ⊠ *Rte. 57, New Marlborough 01230,* ☎ *413/229–3131 or 800/286–3139,* ⅢX *413/229–8236,* Ⓦ *www.oldinn.com. 42 rooms and suites. Restaurant, pool. AE, MC, V. CP.*

$$$–$$$$ 🖭 **Weathervane Inn.** Originally a farmhouse, this 1785 inn on 10 landscaped acres has period-appointed guest rooms and comfortable sitting rooms. Home-baked cookies and cakes are served at afternoon tea, and the owners will prepare gourmet boxed picnic dinners and formal dinners for groups. Golf courses and tennis courts are nearby. ⊠ *Box 388, Rte. 23, South Egremont 01258,* ☎ *413/528–9580 or 800/ 528–9580,* ⅢX *413/528–1713,* Ⓦ *www.weathervaneinn.com. 10 rooms. Bar, pool. AE, MC, V. BP.*

$$–$$$ 🖭 **Stagecoach Hill Inn.** Built in 1765, this handsome redbrick inn has been welcoming travelers since 1829. An eclectic mix of family heirlooms, antiques, and period reproductions furnishes the rooms in both the main building and the mid-nineteenth century cottage, where there are four guest rooms. Dinner is served in the dining room and the tavern, where smoking is permitted. ⊠ *854 S. Undermountain Rd., Sheffield 01257,* ☎ *413/229–8585,* ⅢX *413/229–8584. 11 rooms, 10 with bath. Bar, restaurant, pool. AE, MC, V.*

$–$$ 🖭 **Ivanhoe Country House.** The Appalachian Trail runs right across the property of this 1780 house. The antiques-furnished rooms are generally spacious; four have working fireplaces, several have private porches or balconies, and all have excellent views. The large sitting room has antique desks, a piano, a fireplace, and comfortable couches. The owners have several golden retrievers; dogs are welcome. ⊠ *254 S. Undermountain Rd. (Rte. 41), Sheffield, 01257,* ☎ *413/229–2143,* Ⓦ *www.innweb.com. 9 rooms, 2 suites. Refrigerator, pool. No credit cards. CP.*

Nightlife and the Arts

Jazz musicians perform at the **Egremont Inn** on Friday and Saturday. Club Helsinki at **Helsinki Tea Company** has live music Thurs., Sat. and some Fri. evenings, and open mike every Sun.

Outdoor Activities and Sports

North of Great Barrington is the large and untamed **Beartown State Forest,** which has miles of hiking trails and a small campground where the fee for a site is $4 a night (first come, first served). ⊠ *Blue Hill Rd., Monterey,* ☎ *413/528–0904.*

Three miles north of Great Barrington, you can leave your car in a parking lot beside U.S. 7 and climb Squaw Peak in **Monument Mountain Reservation** (☎ 413/298–3239). The 2½-mi circular hike (a trail map is displayed in the parking lot) takes you up 900 ft, past glistening white quartzite cliffs from which Native Americans are said to have leapt to their deaths to placate the gods. The view of the surrounding mountains from the peak is superb.

Shopping

The Great Barrington area, including the small towns of Sheffield and South Egremont, has the greatest concentration of antiques stores in the Berkshires. Some shops are open sporadically, and many are closed on Tuesday. For a list of storekeepers, send a self-addressed, stamped envelope to the **Berkshire County Antiques Dealers Association.** (⊠ 604 Sheffield Plain, Sheffield 01257, ☎ 413/229-2716).

The 200-plus dealers at **Coffman's Country Antiques Markets** (⊠ Jennifer House Commons, U.S. 7, ☎ 413/528–9282)fill two buildings with primitive to formal antiques. The **Splendid Peasant** (⊠ Rte. 23 and Sheffield Rd., South Egremont, ☎ 413/528-5199) houses an extensive collection of museum-quality 18th- and 19th-century American folk art.

Bradford Galleries (⊠ U.S. 7, Sheffield, ☎ 413/229–6667) holds monthly auctions of furniture, paintings and prints, china, glass, silver, and Oriental rugs. A tag sale of household items occurs daily. Some of the pottery on display at **Great Barrington Pottery** (⊠ Rte. 41, Housatonic, ☎ 413/274–6259) is crafted on-site; there are gallery-style showrooms, European and Japanese gardens, and a tea room where a full tea ceremony is performed Wed. at noon in July and Aug.

Ski Areas

BUTTERNUT BASIN

This friendly resort has good base facilities, pleasant skiing, 100% snow-making capabilities, and the longest quad lift in the Berkshires. There are two top-to-bottom terrain parks for snowboarders. Ski and snowboard lessons are available. Kids six and under ski free midweek on nonholidays if accompanied by a paying adult. ⊠ *Rte. 23, 01230,* ☎ *413/528–2000 ext. 112; 413/528–4433 ski school; 800/438–7669 snow conditions.* WEB *www.skibutternut.com*

Downhill. Only a steep chute or two interrupt the mellow terrain on 22 trails. Eight lifts keep skier traffic spread out.

Cross-country. Butternut Basin has 8 km (4 mi) of groomed cross-country trails.

Child care. The nursery takes children from 6 months to age 6. The ski school has programs for children from 4 to 12 years old.

The Berkshires A to Z

To research prices, get advice from other travelers, and book travel arrangements, visit www.fodors.com.

BUS TRAVEL

Bonanza Bus Lines connects points throughout the Berkshires with Albany, New York City, and Providence. Peter Pan Bus Lines serves Lee and Pittsfield from Boston and Albany. Berkshire Regional Transit Authority provides transportation throughout the Berkshires.

➤ BUS INFORMATION: **Bonanza Bus Lines** (☎ 800/556–3815). **Peter Pan Bus Lines** (☎ 413/442–4451 or 800/237–8747). **Berkshire Regional Transit Authority** (☎ 800/292–2782).

CAR TRAVEL

The Massachusetts Turnpike (I–90) connects Boston with Lee and Stockbridge and continues into New York, where it becomes the New York State Thruway. To reach the Berkshires from New York City take either I–87 or the Taconic State Parkway. The main north–south road within the Berkshires is U.S. 7. Route 2 runs from the northern Berkshires to Greenfield at the head of the Pioneer Valley and continues across Massachusetts into Boston. The scenic section of Route 2 known as the Mohawk Trail runs from Williamstown to Orange.

EMERGENCIES

➤ HOSPITALS: **Fairview Hospital** (⊠ 29 Lewis Ave., Great Barrington, ☎ 413/528–0790). **Berkshire Medical Hospital** (⊠ 725 North St. Pittsfield, ☎ 413/447-2000) **North Adams Regional Hospital** (⊠ Hospital Ave., North Adams, ☎ 413/663–3701).

ENGLISH-LANGUAGE MEDIA
NEWSPAPERS & MAGAZINES

The daily *Berkshire Eagle* covers the area's arts festivals; from June to Columbus Day the *Eagle* publishes *Berkshires Week,* the summer bible for events information. The *Williamstown Advocate* prints general arts listings. The Thursday edition of the *Boston Globe* publishes news of major concerts.

OUTDOORS & SPORTS
CANOEING

Pleasant canoe trips in the Berkshires include Lenox–Dalton (19 mi), Lenox–Stockbridge (12 mi), Stockbridge–Great Barrington (13 mi), and, for experts, Great Barrington–Falls Village (25 mi).

➤ CONTACTS: **Berkshire Region Headquarters** (✉ 740 South St., Pittsfield, ☎ 413/442–8928).

HIKING

Berkshire Region Headquarters of the state's Dept. of Environmental Management Division of Forests and Parks has information about trails and hiking in state parks. New England Hiking Holidays of North Conway, New Hampshire, organizes guided hiking vacations through the Berkshires, with overnight stays at country inns. Hikes cover from 5 to 9 mi per day.

➤ CONTACTS: **New England Hiking Holidays** (☎ 603/356–9696 or 800/869–0949).

TAXIS

Abbott's Limousine and Livery Service, Inc. provides transportation to and from airports throughout the region, including New York, Boston, and Hartford. It requires 24-hr notice.

➤ CONTACTS: **Abbott's Limousine and Livery Service, Inc.** (☎ 413/243–1645).

TRAIN TRAVEL

Amtrak runs the *Lake Shore Limited,* which stops at Pittsfield once daily in each direction on its route between Boston and Chicago.

➤ TRAIN INFORMATION: **Amtrak** (☎ 800/872–7245, WEB www.amtrak.com).

VISITOR INFORMATION

➤ TOURIST INFORMATION: **Berkshire Visitors Bureau** (✉ Berkshire Common, Pittsfield 01201, ☎ 413/443–9186 or 800/237–5747). **Lenox Chamber of Commerce** (✉ Lenox Academy Building, 75 Main St., 01240, ☎ 413/637–3646). **Mohawk Trail Association** (✉ P.O. Box 1044, North Adams 01247, ☎ 413/743-8127). **Northern Berkshires Chamber of Commerce** (✉ 57 Main St. North Adams, ☎ 413/663-3735)

MASSACHUSETTS A TO Z

To research prices, get advice from other travelers, and book travel arrangements, visit www.fodors.com.

AIRPORTS

Boston's Logan International Airport has scheduled flights by most major domestic and foreign carriers. Bradley International Airport in Windsor Locks, Connecticut, 18 mi south of Springfield on I–91, has scheduled flights by major U.S. airlines.

BIKE [& MOPED] TRAVEL

The Massachusetts Bicycle Coalition, an advocacy group that works to improve conditions for area cyclists, has information on organized rides and sells good bike maps of Boston and the state.

➤ CONTACTS: The **Massachusetts Bicycle Coalition** (MassBike; ✉ 44 Bromfield St., Boston 02178, ☎ 617/542–2453).

BUS TRAVEL

Bonanza Bus Lines serves Boston, as far as Woods Hole on Cape Cod, and the eastern part of the state from Providence, with connecting service to New York. Greyhound buses connect Boston with all major cities in North America. Peter Pan Bus Lines connects Boston with cities elsewhere in Massachusetts and in Connecticut, New Hampshire, and New York. Plymouth & Brockton Buses link Boston with the South Shore and Cape Cod.

➤ BUS INFORMATION: **Bonanza Bus Lines** (☎ 800/556–3815). **Greyhound** (☎ 800/231–2222). **Peter Pan Bus Lines** (☎ 617/426–7838 or 800/237–8747). **Plymouth & Brockton Buses** (☎ 508/746–0378). **South Station** (✉ Atlantic Ave. and Summer St., ☎ 617/345–7451).

CAR TRAVEL

Boston is the traffic hub of New England, with interstate highways approaching it from every direction. New England's chief coastal highway, I–95, skirts Boston; I–90 leads west to the Great Lakes and Chicago. I–91 brings visitors to the Pioneer Valley in western Massachusetts from Vermont and Canada to the north and Connecticut and New York to the south. The speed limit on interstate highways is 65 mph; 55 mph may be posted near urban areas. Other highways are 50 mph, except as indicated in settled areas. Rights turns on red are permitted unless otherwise posted.

EMERGENCIES

➤ EMERGENCY SERVICES: **Ambulance, fire, police** (☎ 911).

LODGING

CAMPING

A list of private campgrounds throughout Massachusetts can be obtained free from the Massachusetts Office of Travel and Tourism.

OUTDOORS & SPORTS

FISHING

For information about fishing and licenses, call the Massachusetts Division of Fisheries and Wildlife.

➤ CONTACTS: **Massachusetts Division of Fisheries and Wildlife** (☎ 617/727–3151).

TRAIN TRAVEL

The Northeast Corridor service of Amtrak links Boston with the principal cities between it and Washington, D.C. High-speed Acela service is now available between the two cities. The *Lake Shore Limited*, which stops at Springfield and the Berkshires, carries passengers from Chicago to Boston.

➤ TRAIN INFORMATION: **Amtrak** (☎ 800/872–7245, WEB www.amtrak.com).

VISITOR INFORMATION

➤ TOURIST INFORMATION: **Massachusetts Office of Travel and Tourism** (✉ 10 Park Plaza, Suite 4510, Boston 02116, ☎ 617/973-8500; 800/447–6277 for brochures) WEB www.massvacation.com.

5   RHODE ISLAND

Though it's just 37 mi wide and 48 mi long, Rhode Island changes from pristine coastline to wooded hills to bustling city in the space of an hour's drive. From Newport, a city of gilded-age mansions and Colonial homes, it's a short, 25-mi trip to the Ocean State's capital, Providence; 20 mi farther north is the Blackstone Valley, birthplace of the American Industrial Revolution. Easily accessible and remarkably well-preserved history, an abundance of natural beauty, and a lively culture of arts make Rhode Island an appealing New England destination.

WITH PROPER PLANNING, a traveler in Rhode Island can pick apples in the morning in the Blackstone Valley, tour a historic house in Providence by noon, spend the afternoon shopping for antiques in South County, and end the day with a sunset sail in Newport. Besides possessing such recreational offerings, the smallest state in the nation—just 1,500 square mi (500 of that being water)—is packed with American history: the state holds 20% of the country's National Historic Landmarks and has more restored Colonial and Victorian buildings than anywhere else in the United States.

Updated by
Paula M.
Bodah

In May 1776, before the Declaration of Independence was issued, Rhode Island and Providence Plantations—the state's official name— passed an act removing the king's name from all state documents. This action was typical of the independent-thinking colony. A steadfast insistence upon separation of church and state made Rhode Island attractive to Baptists, Jews, and Quakers, who in the 17th and 18th centuries fled puritanical Massachusetts for Newport and Providence. The first public school was established in forward-thinking Newport in 1664. (Rhode Island continues to be a force in education, with 70,000 students at 10 colleges and universities.) In the 19th century the state flourished, as its entrepreneurial leaders constructed some of the nation's earliest cotton mills, textile mills, and foundries for jewelry. Industry attracted workers from French Canada, Italy, Ireland, England, and Eastern Europe, descendants of whom have retained much of their heritage in numerous ethnic enclaves all across the state.

The qualities that define Rhode Island's unique personality—its small size and diversity from community to community—also contribute to some less-attractive elements: crowded state highways, especially around Providence, and sprawling commercial development that has gone almost unchecked for the past two decades. But as tourism has grown into the state's biggest money maker, a more thoughtful approach to development seems to be the norm. Neighborhoods, remote villages, and even rough-hewn cities like Pawtucket and Woonsocket are now constructing bike paths, historic walkways, and visitor centers. Leading the way is the capital city of Providence, where leaders are aggressively reshaping the city.

Rhode Island's 39 towns and cities—none more than 50 mi apart— all hold architectural gems and historic sights. You can tour a gilded-age mansion in Newport and, an hour later, be inside the 1786 John Brown House in Providence, once considered the finest home in North America. Natural attractions such as Narragansett Bay—the second-largest bay on the East Coast and a mecca for world-class sailors— and the barrier beaches of South County round out Rhode Island's list of attractions; inspired culinary artistry and fine accommodations complement the mix. With so many offerings in such a compact space, it's easy to explore the Rhode Island that fits your interests.

Pleasures and Pastimes

Beaches
Rhode Island has 400 mi of shoreline with more than 100 salt- and freshwater beaches. Almost all the ocean beaches around the resort communities of Narragansett, Watch Hill, Newport, and Block Island are open to the public. Deep sands blanket most Rhode Island beaches, and their waters are clear and clean—in some places, the water takes on the turquoise color of the Caribbean Sea. Newport's harbor glimmers from the beach at Fort Adams State Park; nearby Middletown

Rhode Island

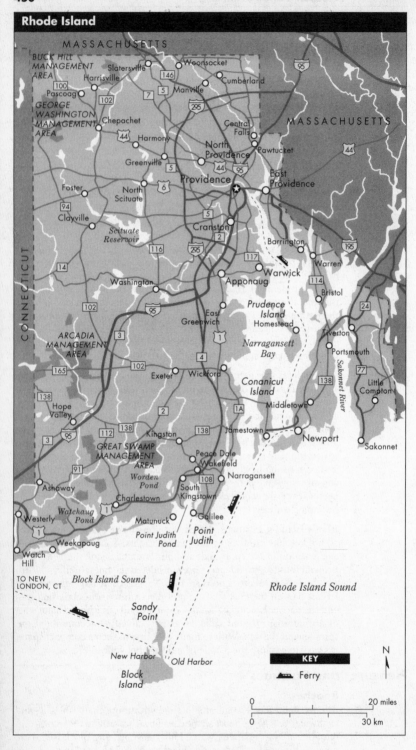

MASSACHUSETTS

BUCK HILL
MANAGEMENT
AREA

GEORGE
WASHINGTON
MANAGEMENT
AREA

Slatersville
Woonsocket
Harrisville
Cumberland
Pascoag
100
102
146
7
5
Manville
295
Chepachet
44
Harmony
MASSACHUSETTS
44
Central
Falls
North
Providence
Pawtucket
Greenville
5
44
95
Providence
East
Providence
Foster
6
North
Scituate
94
Clayville
Scituate
Reservoir
5
Cranston
2
195
Barrington
116
295
117
Washington
Warwick
Warren
Apponaug
114
Bristol
Prudence
Island
24
95
East
Greenwich
Homestead
Tiverton
ARCADIA
MANAGEMENT
AREA
102
3
1
Narragansett
Bay
Portsmouth
77
165
102
4
Conanicut
Island
138
Little
Compton
Exeter
Wickford
1A
Middletown
138
Hope
Valley
2
Sakonnet River
3
95
112
138
Kingston
138
Jamestown
Newport
GREAT SWAMP
MANAGEMENT
AREA
Peace Dale
91
Wakefield
Worden
Pond
Narragansett
Sakonnet
Ashaway
108
South
Kingstown
Charlestown
1
Westerly
Watchaug
Pond
Matunuck
Galilee
1
Point Judith
Pond
Point
Judith
Weekapaug
Watch
Hill

CONNECTICUT

TO NEW
LONDON, CT

Block Island Sound

Rhode Island Sound

*Sandy
Point*

New Harbor — Old Harbor

*Block
Island*

KEY

🚢 Ferry

N

| 0 | | 20 miles |
| 0 | | 30 km |

has a long beach adjacent to a wildlife refuge; and Jamestown's Mackerel Cove Beach is sheltered from heavy surf, making it a good choice for families. With naturally occurring white sands and a rock reef to the north that's ideal for snorkeling, Mansion Beach on Block Island is one of the most splendid coastal stretches in New England.

Boating

It should come as no surprise that a place nicknamed the Ocean State would attract boaters. Colonial Newport prospered from shipbuilding and trading, and even today boating is the city's second-largest industry after tourism. Point Judith Pond, close to deep Atlantic waters, harbors New England's second-largest commercial fishing fleet (behind New Bedford, Massachusetts) and nearly four dozen sportfishing charter boats. Block Island's Great Salt Pond is New England's busiest summertime harbor, hosting more than 1,700 boats on weekends. At the head of Narragansett Bay, Waterplace—Providence's riverfront park— is a destination for small boats, canoes, and kayaks. Many tidal rivers and salt ponds in South County are ideal for kayaking and canoeing.

Dining

Rhode Island has been winning national accolades for its restaurants, which serve cuisine from every part of the world. Visitors can still find regional fare such as johnnycakes, a corn cake–like affair cooked on a griddle, and the native clam, the quahog (pronounced "*ko*-hog"), which is served stuffed, fried, and in chowder. "Shore dinners" consist of clam chowder, steamed soft-shell clams, clam cakes, sausage, corn-on-the-cob, lobster, watermelon, and Indian pudding (a steamed pudding made with cornmeal and molasses). The Federal Hill neighborhood in Providence holds superlative Italian restaurants, and several dozen other restaurants in the city rival many of Boston's finest eateries. For price-category information, *see* Dining *in* Smart Travel Tips.

Lodging

The major chain hotels are represented in Rhode Island, but the state's many smaller bed-and-breakfasts and other inns offer a more down-home experience. Rates are very much seasonal; in Newport, for example, winter rates are often half those of summer. Many inns in coastal towns are closed in winter. For price-category information, *see* Lodging *in* Smart Travel Tips.

Shopping

Newport is a shopper's—but not a bargain-hunter's—city. You can find antiques, souvenirs, fine crafts, clothing, and marine supplies in abundance. Antiques are a specialty of South County; more than 30 stores are within an hour's drive of each other. Villages such as Wickford and Watch Hill have unique shops in postcard waterside settings. An upscale shopping mall in downtown Providence has 150 stores and several movie theaters, and the city's ethnic communities sell specialties such as Italian groceries and Hmong (Laotian) clothing. Providence's student population supports a variety of secondhand boutiques and funky shops on Wickenden and Thayer streets. The Blackstone Valley contains myriad outlet stores; unlike suburban "factory outlets," these places, often low on decor, have great deals and are usually a short walk from the factory floor.

Exploring Rhode Island

The Blackstone Valley region and the capital city of Providence compose the northern portion of Rhode Island. South County to the west and Newport County to the east make up the southern portion of the state. The museums and country roads of the Blackstone Valley make it a good family destination; Providence has history, intellectual and cultural vitality, and great food. Both southerly regions have beaches, boating, and historical sights, with Newport being more historically significant, more upscale, and more crowded.

Numbers in the text and in the margin correspond to numbers on the maps: Central Providence, The Blackstone Valley, South County and Newport County, Block Island, Downtown Newport, and Greater Newport.

Great Itineraries

By car it's less than an hour from any one place in Rhode Island to another. Though the distances are short, the state is densely populated, and getting around its cities and towns can be confusing; it's best to map out your route in advance. In five days, you can visit all four regions of the state, as well as Block Island. On a shorter visit of several days, you can still take in two regions, such as Providence and Newport. Most of the sights in Providence can be seen in one day. The Blackstone Valley will also occupy one day, but during fall foliage season, you will want to spend more time here. Newport has many facets and will require two busy days. South County, with its superb beaches, is generally a relaxing two-day destination.

In Rhode Island, however, just one day can be an unforgettable adventure. A day-long drive from Watch Hill to Newport can include a beach hike at Napatree Point or go-cart rides in Misquamicut, a fishing trip out of Galilee, a tour of a Newport mansion, and dinner at an exquisite French restaurant.

IF YOU HAVE 3 DAYS

Spend a day and a half in the historic waterfront city of **Newport** ㊴–㊹, and then make the 40-minute drive north to **Providence** ①–⑯. Though this city's attractions are less packaged than Newport's, they include sophisticated restaurants, historic districts, two large city parks, and an outdoor skating rink.

IF YOU HAVE 5 DAYS

Spend your first three days in **Newport** ㊴–㊹ and **Providence** ①–⑯; then take two days to explore South County. With pristine beaches and no shortage of restaurants and inns, South County encourages a take-it-as-it-comes attitude that's just right for summer and fall touring. Shop and soak up the turn-of-the-century elegance of **Watch Hill** ㉒, and then spend a day on the beach in **Charlestown** ㉔ or **South Kingstown** ㉕ (try **Misquamicut** ㉓ if you prefer beaches with a carnival atmosphere). **Narragansett** ㉖, which has great beaches and numerous B&Bs, is one option for a second South County night. A day trip to **Block Island** ㉘–㊲ allows enough time to see some of its treasures, but it's easy to linger longer.

When to Tour Rhode Island

The best time to visit Rhode Island is between May and October. Newport hosts several high-profile music festivals in summer; Providence is at its prettiest; and Block Island and the beach towns of South County are in full swing (though not nearly as crowded as Newport). Because of the light traffic and the often gorgeous weather, October is a great time to come to Rhode Island. The colorful fall foliage of the Blackstone Valley is as bright and varied as any in New England.

PROVIDENCE

With a new convention center, the completion of Waterplace Park, the opening of an outdoor ice rink in Kennedy Plaza that's larger than the one in New York, and the 1999 debut of a glittering shopping mall, Providence has nearly completed the renovation it began in the 1980s.

Long considered an awkward stepchild of greater Boston (50 mi to the north) by even its own residents, Providence is shrugging off its apparent inferiority complex.

The second half of the 20th century was rough on Providence. The decline of its two main industries, textiles and jewelry, precipitated a population exodus in the 1940s and '50s. In the '60s and '70s, the state's major naval installations were phased out, and the 1990s began with a statewide banking crisis. But the bad news has ended, and New England's third-largest city (with a population of 200,000, behind Boston and Worcester) is starting the 21st century as a renaissance city. In the past decade, rivers have been rerouted and railroad tracks have been put underground. Dilapidated neighborhoods are being rejuvenated and new development is taking place all over the city. Many travelers now prefer the expanding T. F. Green State Airport to Boston's Logan International Airport.

Providence's renaissance isn't all looks. Besides the glitzy new shopping center, hotels, and parks, the city has cultivated a more worldly, sophisticated spirit. As a result, it was chosen to host the 1999 NCAA Hockey finals, the 2000 annual meeting of the International Association of Culinary Professionals, and the 2001 National Governors Conference. The city also forged an annual cultural exchange program with Florence, Italy, that brings Italian artwork and artisans to Providence. Time spent courting Hollywood dealmakers has resulted in a string of movies being filmed in the city, including *There's Something About Mary* and *Outside Providence,* and the popular NBC show "Providence." With more restaurants per capita than any other major city in America, Providence—home to the Johnson and Wales University Culinary Institute—legitimately lays claim to being one of the nation's best places to get a bite to eat.

Roger Williams founded Providence in October 1635 as a refuge for freethinkers and religious dissenters escaping the dictates of the Puritans of Massachusetts Bay Colony. The city still embraces independent thinking in business, the arts, and academia. Brown University, the Rhode Island School of Design (RISD), and Trinity Square Repertory Company are major forces in New England's intellectual and cultural life. Playing to that strength, Providence is striving to have its once-abandoned downtown (now called Downcity, to erase the connotations of the old downtown) populated by artists and art studios. A state referendum has exempted such artists from income taxes. Such statewide support is not surprising, because improvements here are typically a boon to the rest of the state.

The narrow Providence River cuts through the city north to south. West of the river lies the compact business district. An Italian neighborhood, Federal Hill, pushes west from here along Atwells Ave. To the north you'll see the white-marble capitol. South Main and Benefit streets run parallel to the river, on the East Side. College Hill constitutes the western half of the East Side. At the top of College Hill, the area's primary thoroughfare, Thayer Street, runs north to south. Don't confuse East Providence, a city unto itself, with Providence's East Side.

A Good Walk and Tour

Begin at the **Rhode Island State House** ①, where the south portico looks down over the city of Providence and the farthest reach of Narragansett Bay. After touring the capitol, proceed to Smith Street, at the north end of the State House grounds. Follow the road east to **Roger Williams National Memorial** ②. **Benefit Street** ③ is one block east (up the hill).

Walk south on this historic street to the **Museum of Art, Rhode Island School of Design** ④ and the **Providence Athenaeum** ⑤, with its changing exhibits from the library's collections.

Head east (away from the Providence River) on College Street and north (to the left) on Prospect Street to visit the **John Hay Library** ⑥ and its specialized collections. The handsome **Brown University** ⑦ campus is across the street. Walk east on Waterman Street; you can enter the grounds at Brown Street. After you've toured the campus, exit from the gate at George Street (to the south) and turn right, which will take you back to Benefit Street. Walk south for one block, where you'll see the Romanesque **First Unitarian Church of Providence** ⑧. The magnificent **John Brown House** ⑨ is two blocks south of here. From the Brown house, walk one block downhill on Power Street and turn right on South Main Street. Proceed north until you reach the **Market House** ⑩, a remnant of the Colonial economy, and, one block farther north, the Georgian **First Baptist Church in America** ⑪. Turn left at Steeple Street (also called Thomas Street), and you will shortly reach **Waterplace Park and Riverwalk** ⑫, centerpiece of the city's revitalization.

The Italian neighborhood of **Federal Hill** ⑬ and the fun shops of **Wickenden Street** ⑭ are best visited via car or taxi. The stately **Governor Henry Lippit House Museum** ⑮ and the **Museum of Rhode Island History at Aldrich House** ⑯ are four blocks apart in the eastern end of Providence; you'll need a car or taxi to visit them.

TIMING

The timing of the walk from the State House to Waterplace Park will vary greatly depending on how much time you spend at each sight. If you stop for a half hour at most sights and an hour at the RISD Museum of Art, the tour will take about six hours. To see the rest of the sights, add in several hours.

Sights to See

❸ **Benefit Street.** The centerpiece of any visit to Providence is the "Mile of History," where a cobblestone sidewalk passes a row of early 18th- and 19th-century candy-color houses crammed shoulder-to-shoulder on a steep hill overlooking downtown. Romantic Benefit Street, with one of the nation's highest concentrations of historic architecture, is a reminder of the wealth brought to Colonial Rhode Island through the triangular trade of slaves, rum, and molasses. The **Providence Preservation Society** (⊠ 21 Meeting St., at Benefit St., ☎ 401/831–7440) offers maps and pamphlets with self-guided tours.

❼ **Brown University.** The nation's seventh-oldest college, founded in 1764, is an Ivy League institution with more than 40 academic departments, including a school of medicine. Gothic and Beaux Arts structures dominate the campus, which has been designated a National Historic Landmark. University tours leave Mon.–Fri. at 10, 11, 1, 3, and 4 from the admissions office, in the Corliss-Brackett House. The university is on College Hill, a neighborhood with handsome 18th- and 19th-century architecture well worth a stroll. Thayer Street is the campus's principal commercial thoroughfare. ⊠ *Corliss-Brackett House, 45 Prospect St.,* ☎ *401/863–2378; 401/863–2703 tour information.*

❸ **Federal Hill.** You're as likely to hear Italian as English in this neighborhood, which is vital to Providence's culture and sense of self. The stripe down Atwells Avenue is repainted each year in red, white, and green, and a huge *pigna* (pinecone), an Italian symbol of abundance and quality, hangs on an arch soaring over the street. Hardware shops sell bocce sets and grocers sell a range of pastas and Italian pastries.

Central Providence

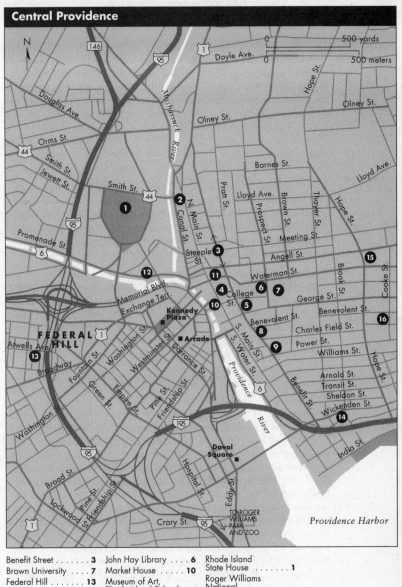

The neighborhood truly shines at the Columbus Weekend Festival (held on the Sunday of that weekend), with music, food stands, and parades.

⓫ First Baptist Church in America. This historic house of worship was built in 1775 for a congregation established in 1638 by Rhode Island founder Roger Williams and his fellow Puritan dissenters. The church, one of the finest examples of Georgian architecture in the United States, has a carved wood interior, a Waterford crystal chandelier, and graceful but austere Ionic columns. ⊠ *75 N. Main St.,* ☎ *401/751–2266.* ⊡ *Free; donations accepted.* ☉ *Mon.–Fri. 9–12, 1–3; call ahead on Sat. Guided tours Memorial Day–Columbus Day, self-guided tours Columbus Day–Memorial Day. Sept.–June, Sun. service at 11, guided tour at 12:15; July–Aug., Sun. service at 10, guided tour at 11:15.*

❽ First Unitarian Church of Providence. This Romanesque house of worship made of Rhode Island granite was built in 1816. Its steeple houses a 2,500-pound bell, the largest ever cast in Paul Revere's foundry. ⊠ *1 Benevolent St., at Benefit St.,* ☎ *401/421–7970.* ⊡ *Free.* ☉ *Guided tours by appointment; Sun. service at 9:30 and 11.*

⓯ Governor Henry Lippit House Museum. The two-term Rhode Island governor made his fortune selling textiles to both armies during the Civil War, and he spared no expense in building his home, an immaculate Renaissance Revival mansion, in 1863. The floor of the billiard room is made with nine types of inlaid wood; the ceilings are intricately hand-painted (some look convincingly like tiger maple), and the neoclassical chandeliers are cast in bronze. The home was fitted with central heating and electricity, quite an extravagance at the time. ⊠ *199 Hope St.,* ☎ *401/453–0688.* ⊡ *$5.* ☉ *Open year-round. Tours by appointment only.*

★ ❾ John Brown House. John Quincy Adams called it "the most magnificent and elegant private mansion that I have ever seen on this continent." George Washington and other notables also visited the house. Designed by Joseph Brown for his brother in 1786, the three-story Georgian mansion has elaborate woodwork and is filled with decorative art, furniture, silver, and items from the China trade, which is how John Brown made his fortune. In addition to opening trade with China, Brown is famous for his role in the burning of the British customs ship *Gaspee.* He was also a slave trader: his abolitionist brother, Moses, brought charges against him for illegally engaging in the buying and selling of human lives. John Brown donated the land for what became Brown University. Across the street and open only on Friday from 1 to 4 is Nightingale House, built by Brown's chief rival in the China trade. ⊠ *52 Power St.,* ☎ *401/331–8575,* ⓦⓔⓑ *www.rihs.org.* ⊡ *$6.* ☉ *Mar.–Dec., Tues.–Sat. 10–4:30, Sun. noon–4:30; Jan.–Feb., Mon.–Thurs. by appointment, Fri.–Sat. 10–5, Sun. noon–4.*

❻ John Hay Library. Built in 1910 and named for Abraham Lincoln's secretary, "the Hay" houses 11,000 items related to the 16th president. The noncirculating research library, part of **Brown University**, also stores American drama and poetry collections, 500,000 pieces of American sheet music, the Webster Knight Stamp Collection, the letters of horror and science-fiction writer H. P. Lovecraft, military prints, and a world-class collection of toy soldiers. ⊠ *20 Prospect St.,* ☎ *401/863–2146.* ⊡ *Free.* ☉ *Weekdays 9–5.*

❿ Market House. Designed by Joseph Brown and now owned by the Rhode Island School of Design, this brick structure was central to Colonial Providence's trading economy. Tea was burned here in March 1775, and the upper floors were used as barracks for French soldiers during the Revolutionary War. From 1832 to 1878, Market House served as the seat of city government. A plaque shows the height reached by flood-waters during the Great Hurricane of 1938. The building is not open to the public. ⊠ *Market Sq. at S. Main St.*

★ ❹ **Museum of Art, Rhode Island School of Design.** This small college museum is amazingly comprehensive. Many exhibitions, which change annually, are of textiles, a long-standing Rhode Island industry. The museum's permanent holdings include the Abby Aldrich Rockefeller collection of Japanese prints, Paul Revere silver, 18th-century porcelain, and French Impressionist paintings. Popular with children are the 10-ft statue of Buddha and the Egyptian mummy from the Ptolemaic period (circa 300 BC). Admission includes the adjoining **Pendleton House,** a replica of an early 19th-century Providence house. ⊠ *224 Benefit St.,* ☎ *401/454–6500,* WEB *www.risd.edu.* ⊡ *$5.* ☉ *Tues.–Sun. 10–5.*

⓰ **Museum of Rhode Island History at Aldrich House.** The Federal-style Aldrich House, built in 1822, was given to the Rhode Island Historical Society in 1974 by the heirs of New York financier Winthrop W. Aldrich. The first comprehensive museum about Rhode Island history, it presents rotating exhibits. ⊠ *110 Benevolent St.,* ☎ *401/331–8575,* WEB *www.rihs.org.* ⊡ *$2.* ☉ *Tues.–Fri. 9–5, Sun. 1–4; until 9 PM 3rd Thurs. of each month.*

★ ❺ **Providence Athenaeum.** Established in 1753 and housed in a granite 1838 Greek Revival structure, this is among the oldest lending libraries in the world. The Athenaeum was the center of the intellectual life of old Providence. Here Edgar Allan Poe, visiting Providence to lecture at Brown, met and courted Sarah Helen Whitman, who was said to be the inspiration for his poem "Annabel Lee." The library holds Rhode Island art and artifacts, an original set of elephant folio *Birds of America* prints by John J. Audubon, and one of the world's best collections of travel literature. Changing exhibits showcase parts of the collection. ⊠ *251 Benefit St.,* ☎ *401/421–6970,* WEB *www.providenceathenaeum.org.* ⊡ *Free.* ☉ *June–Labor Day, Mon.–Thurs. 10–8, Fri. 10–5; Labor Day–May, Mon.–Thurs. 10–8, Fri.–Sat. 10–5, Sun. 1–5.*

❶ **Rhode Island State House.** Capitols are often planned to inspire awe (or at least respect), and this one, designed by the noted firm of McKim, Mead & White and erected in 1900, achieves that effect. It has the first unsupported marble dome in the United States (and the fourth largest in the world), which was modeled on St. Peter's Basilica in Rome. The gilded statue *Independent Man* tops the ornate white Georgia marble exterior. Engraved on the south portico is a passage from the Royal Charter of 1663: "To hold forth a lively experiment that a most flourishing civil state may stand and best be maintained with full liberty in religious concernments." In the state room you'll see a full-length portrait of George Washington by Rhode Islander Gilbert Stuart, the same artist who created the likeness on the $1 bill. You'll also see the original parchment charter granted by King Charles to the colony of Rhode Island in 1663 and military accoutrements of Nathaniel Greene, Washington's second-in-command during the Revolutionary War. Booklets are available for self-guided tours, and there's a gift shop on the basement level. ⊠ *82 Smith St.,* ☎ *401/222–2357.* ☉ *Weekdays 8:30–4:30; guided tours by appointment.*

❷ **Roger Williams National Memorial.** Roger Williams contributed so significantly to the development of the concepts that underpin the Declaration of Independence and the Constitution that the National Park Service dedicated a 4½-acre park to his memory. Displays provide a quick glimpse into the life and times of Rhode Island's founder, who wrote the first-ever book on the languages of the native people of North

---

America. ✉ 282 N. Main St., ☎ 401/521–7266. 🎟 Free. ☉ Daily 9–4:30.

OFF THE BEATEN PATH **ROGER WILLIAMS PARK AND ZOO –** This beautiful 430-acre Victorian park is immensely popular. You can picnic, feed the ducks in the lakes, ride a pony, or rent a paddleboat or miniature speedboat. At Carousel Village, kids can ride the vintage carousel or a miniature train. There's also the Museum of Natural History and the Cormack Planetarium, and the Tennis Center has Rhode Island's only public clay courts. More than 900 animals of 156 different species live at the zoo. Among the attractions are the Tropical Rain Forest Pavilion, the African Plains and Australasia exhibits, and an open-air aviary. To get here from downtown, take I-95 south to U.S. 1 south (Elmwood Avenue); the park entrance will be the first left turn. ✉ Elmwood Ave., ☎ 401/785–3510 zoo; 401/785–9457 museum. 🎟 $6. ☉ Zoo daily 9–5 (until 4 in winter), museum daily 10–5.

⑫ **Waterplace Park and Riverwalk.** Romantic Venetian-style footbridges, cobblestone walkways, and an amphitheater encircling a tidal pond set the tone at this 4-acre tract, which has won national and international design awards since its completion in 1997. The Riverwalk passes the junction of three rivers—the Woonasquatucket, Providence, and Moshassuck—a nexus of the shipping trade during the city's early years. It's the site of the popular Waterfire, a multimedia installation featuring music and nearly 100 burning braziers that rise from the water and are tended from boats; the dusk-to-midnight Waterfires attract 500,000 visitors annually and are held several times each year. The amphitheater hosts free concerts and plays. Ask about upcoming events at the visitor information center, in the clock tower. ✉ Boat House Clock Tower, 2 American Express Way, ☎ 401/751–1177. ☉ Daily 10–4.

⑭ **Wickenden Street.** The main artery in the Fox Point district, a working-class Portuguese neighborhood that is undergoing gentrification, Wickenden Street is chockablock with antiques stores, galleries, and trendy cafés. Professors, artists, and students are among the newer residents here. Many of the houses along Wickenden, Transit, Gano, and nearby streets are still painted the pastel colors of Portuguese homes.

Dining

American/Casual

$$ ✗ **Union Station Brewery.** The historic brick building that houses this brew pub was once the freight house for the Providence Train Station. You can wash down a tasty chipotle-glazed pork quesadilla, an old-fashioned chicken potpie, or ale-batter fish-and-chips with a pint of Providence cream ale or one of several other fine beers brewed here. ✉ 36 Exchange Terr., ☎ 401/274–2739, WEB www.johnharvards.com. AE, D, DC, MC, V.

Contemporary

$$$–$$$$ ✗ **The Gatehouse.** A redbrick cottage houses this much-praised restaurant, where the views of the Seekonk River and the classy decor (which includes works from owner Henry Kate's art collection) complement the New Orleans–influenced New England cuisine. Chef James Maxwell might prepare something as complex as a grilled pork tenderloin with whipped yams and sauteed smoked onions accompanied by pecan chutney and blueberry-horseradish sauce, or as simple but inspired as a roasted rack of veal encrusted with porcino mushrooms. ✉ 4 Richmond Sq., ☎ 401/521–9229, WEB www.gatehouserestaurant.com. Reservations essential. AE, DC, MC, V. No lunch Sat.

$$$ ✕ **Neath's.** The large, open dining room of this converted warehouse is one reason why Neath's is a place to be seen. Views of the Providence River are nice, too, but it's the food that has made this the trendiest restaurant in town. Seafood with Asian accents is the primary focus, such as crisp Cambodian spring rolls with bean sprouts and grilled shrimp, and roasted sea bass with Chinese black bean marinade and jasmine rice. Don't pass up the chocolate-stuffed fried wontons for dessert. ⊠ *262 S. Water St.,* ☎ *401/751–3700,* WEB *www.neaths.com. AE, MC, V. Closed Mon. No lunch.*

$$$ ✕ **Rue de l'Espoir.** At this homey, longtime Providence favorite, dishes are designed to be fun. A few of the many eclectic choices include a lobster Madeira crepe, Szechuan duck quesadillas, and Caribbean-spiced grilled pork porterhouse chops. Wide-plank pine floors, an ornate tin ceiling, and wooden booths set the mood in the dining room. The spacious barroom, where many locals prefer to dine, has a mural in bright pastels and a fine selection of jazz CDs. Breakfast is served on weekdays, brunch on weekends. ⊠ *99 Hope St.,* ☎ *401/751–8890. AE, D, DC, MC, V. Closed Mon.*

French

$$$–$$$$ ✕ **Pot au Feu.** As night falls, business-driven downtown Providence
★ clears out, and this bastion of French country cuisine lights up. For more than a quarter century the chefs here have worked to perfect the basics, such as pâté du foie gras, beef bourguignon, and potatoes au gratin. Such classically rendered dishes—and a distinctive list of French wines—have inspired a devoted corps of regulars. The dining experience is more casual at the downstairs Bistro than at the upstairs Salon. ⊠ *44 Custom House St.,* ☎ *401/273–8953. AE, DC, MC, V. Salon closed Sun.–Mon.*

Indian

$$ ✕ **India.** Mango chicken curry and swordfish kabobs are two of the entrées at this downtown restaurant filled with Oriental rugs, colorful paintings, and plants. India is known for its freshly made breads, including *paratha,* wheat bread cooked on a grill and stuffed with various fillings. ⊠ *123 Dorrance St.,* ☎ *401/278–2000. AE, MC, V.*

Italian

$$$ ✕ **Al Forno.** The owners, George Germon and Johanne Killeen, wrote
★ *Cucina Simpatica,* an acclaimed book on the art of food, and their restaurant cemented the city's reputation as a culinary center in New England. Try a wood-grilled pizza as an appetizer, followed by roasted clams and spicy sausage in a tomato broth, or charcoal-seared tournedos of beef with mashed potatoes (called "dirty steak" by regulars) and onion rings. Your dessert could be crepes with apricot puree or a fresh cranberry tart. Meals are served both upstairs, in the rustic dining room, and downstairs, in a room with white marble flooring. ⊠ *577 S. Main St.,* ☎ *401/273–9760. Reservations not accepted. AE, DC, MC, V. Closed Sun.–Mon. No lunch.*

$$$ ✕ **Camille's Roman Garden.** Perhaps the most classic of the Italian eateries on Federal Hill, the second-oldest family-run restaurant in the United States serves traditional fare such as veal scallopini and shrimp scampi. Black-tie service and reproductions of early Renaissance murals in the massive dining room (which was a speakeasy in the 1920s) impart an air of sophistication. ⊠ *71 Bradford St.,* ☎ *401/751–4812. AE, DC, MC, V. Closed Sun. July–Aug.*

$$$ ✕ **L'Epicureo.** One of Providence's most refined restaurants was founded as half of a Federal Hill butcher shop called Joe's Quality. Joe's daughter Rozann and son-in-law Tom Buckner transformed the former market into an Italian bistro that has won high marks for its wood-grilled steaks, veal chops, and such pasta dishes as fettuccine tossed with arugula, garlic, and lemon. ⊠ *238 Atwells Ave.,* ☎ *401/454–8430. AE, D, DC, MC, V. Closed Sun.–Mon. No lunch.*

$$ ✕ **Angelo's Civita Farnese.** On Federal Hill in the heart of Little Italy, lively (even boisterous) Angelo's is a family-run place with Old World charm. Locals come here for its good-size portions of fresh, simply prepared pasta. ⊠ *141 Atwells Ave.,* ☎ *401/621–8171. Reservations not accepted. No credit cards.*

Japanese

$–$$ ✕ **Tokyo Restaurant.** New carpeting and a fresh coat of paint may be in order at Tokyo, but the Japanese cuisine served here is the best in the state. Choose traditional or American seating—or take a stool at the sushi bar, where local fish such as tuna, mackerel, and eel are prepared alongside red snapper and fish from points beyond. The designer rolls include beef, squid, duck, and seaweed. Bring your own wine or beer. ⊠ *123 Wickenden St.,* ☎ *401/331–5330. AE, D, MC, V.*

Steak

$$$ ✕ **Capital Grille.** Dry-aged beef is the star, but lobster and fish also highlight the menu at the cavernous Capital Grille. The mashed potatoes, cottage fries, and Caesar salads are served in portions that will sate even the heartiest appetite. Leather, brass, mahogany, oil portraits, a mounted wooden canoe, and Bloomberg News ticking away in the barroom lend this establishment the feel of an opulent men's club. ⊠ *1 Cookson Pl.,* ☎ *401/521–5600,* WEB *www.thecapitalgrille.com. AE, D, DC, MC, V. No lunch weekends.*

Lodging

$$–$$$$ ⊞ **Providence Marriott.** This chain hotel near the capitol lacks the old-fashioned grandeur of the Providence Biltmore, but it has all the modern conveniences. Tones of mauve and green grace the good-size rooms. The Bluefin Grille restaurant specializes in local seafood prepared with a French flair. ⊠ *Charles and Orms Sts. near Exit 23 off I–95, 02904,* ☎ *401/272–2400 or 800/937–7768,* FAX *401/273–2686,* WEB *www.marriott.com. 351 rooms, 6 suites. Restaurant, 1 indoor and 1 outdoor pool, sauna, health club, meeting rooms. AE, D, DC, MC, V.*

$$$ ⊞ **Providence Biltmore.** The Biltmore, completed in 1922, has a sleek Art Deco exterior, an external glass elevator with delightful views of Providence, a grand ballroom, and an Italian restaurant that rivals the best in the city. The personal attentiveness of its staff (there is a European-style concierge system), the downtown location, and modern amenities make this hotel one of the city's best. ⊠ *Kennedy Plaza, Dorrance and Washington Sts., 02903,* ☎ *401/421–0700 or 800/294–7709,* FAX *401/455–3040,* WEB *www.grandheritage.com. 84 rooms, 157 suites. Restaurant, café, health club, meeting room. AE, D, DC, MC, V.*

$$$ ⊞ **Westin Providence.** The multiturreted 25-story Westin towers over
★ Providence's compact downtown, connected by skywalks to the city's gleaming convention center and the Providence Place mall. Its rooms have reproduction period furniture, and half have king-size beds; many have views of the city. The redbrick hotel's Agora restaurant has an award-winning wine cellar. ⊠ *1 W. Exchange St., 02903,* ☎ *401/598–8000 or 800/937–8461,* FAX *401/598–8200,* WEB *www.westin.com. 364 rooms, 22 suites. 2 restaurants, 2 bars, pool, hot tub, health club, meeting room. AE, D, DC, MC, V.*

$$–$$$ ⊞ **Old Court Bed & Breakfast.** This three-story Italianate inn on historic Benefit Street was built in 1863 as a rectory. Antique furniture, richly colored wallpaper, and memorabilia throughout the house reflect the best of 19th-century style. The comfortable, spacious rooms

have high ceilings and chandeliers; most have nonworking marble fireplaces and some have views of the statehouse and downtown. ⊠ *144 Benefit St., 02903,* ☎ *401/751–2002,* FAX *401/272–4830,* WEB *www.oldcourt.com. 10 rooms, 1 suite. AE, D, MC, V. BP.*

$$ ★ ⌆ **State House Inn.** The beautifully restored rooms of this inviting, classy inn near the statehouse are furnished with Shaker- or Colonial-style pieces, and a few have working fireplaces. Some rooms in the 1880s Colonial Revival home are on the small side. The neighborhood isn't great for a late-night stroll, but there is convenient parking. The inn is no-smoking. ⊠ *43 Jewett St., 02903,* ☎ *401/351–6111,* FAX *401/351–4261,* WEB *www.providence-inn.com. 10 rooms. AE, D, MC, V. BP.*

$–$$ ⌆ **C. C. Ledbetter's.** Innkeeper C. C. Ledbetter's mansard-roof 1770 home has a vibrant, welcoming interior and a great location on College Hill, the city's historic East Side. Lively art, photographs, quilts, and a shrewd blend of contemporary furnishings and antiques fill the place. The rooms at this B&B across from the John Brown House are priced well below the competition, making it a favorite of the parents of Brown University students. ⊠ *326 Benefit St., 02903,* ☎ FAX *401/351–4699. 5 rooms, 2 with bath. D, MC, V. CP.*

Nightlife and the Arts

For events listings, consult the daily *Providence Journal* and the weekly *Providence Phoenix* (free in restaurants and bookstores). Brown University and the Rhode Island School of Design often present free lectures and performances.

Nightlife

BARS

The **Custom House Tavern** (⊠ 36 Weybosset St., ☎ 401/751–3630) is a friendly downtown gathering place. Fashionable with professionals, **Hot Club** (⊠ 575 S. Water St., ☎ 401/861–9007) is where the waterside scenes in the movie *There's Something About Mary* were shot. **Oliver's** (⊠ 83 Benevolent St., ☎ 401/272–8795), a popular hangout for Brown students that serves good pub food, has three pool tables. **Snookers** (⊠ 145 Clifford St., ☎ 401/351–7665) is a stylish billiard hall in the Jewelry District. Through a double doorway at the rear of the billiard room is a '50s-style lounge where food is served.

MUSIC CLUBS

AS220 (⊠ 111 Empire St., ☎ 401/831–9327) is a gallery and performance space; the musical styles run the gamut from techno-pop, hip-hop, and jazz to folk music. Talent shows and comedy nights are also scheduled. The **Call** (⊠ 15 Elbow St., ☎ 401/751–2255), a large blues bar, hosts such top local groups as Roomful of Blues. In the same building and under the same management as the Call is the **Century Lounge,** which hosts a variety of progressive bands. Proclaiming itself "Rhode Island's number one reason to party," the **Complex** (⊠ 180 Pine St., ☎ 401/751–4263) is home to four different clubs, the most popular being a mecca for swing dancers. **Gerardo's Alternative Dance Club** (⊠ 1 Franklin Sq., ☎ 401/274–5560) is a popular gay and lesbian disco. The **Living Room** (⊠ 23 Rathbone St., ☎ 401/521–5200) presents live entertainment nightly, often by prominent local blues musicians. **Lupo's Heartbreak Hotel** (⊠ 239 Westminster St., ☎ 401/272–5876), a roadhouse-style nightclub, books local and international talents.

The Arts

FILM

The **Cable Car Cinema** (⊠ 204 S. Main St., ☎ 401/272–3970) is on the musty side, but the theater showcases a fine slate of alternative and foreign flicks. There are couches rather than seats, and street performers entertain prior to most shows. An espresso café substitutes for the traditional soda-and-popcorn concession. The **Providence Place** mall (✉ 1 Providence Pl., ☎ 401/270–1000), near the Westin, has an IMAX theater and a multiscreen cinema.

MUSIC

Rock bands and country acts occasionally perform at the 14,500-seat **Providence Civic Center** (✉ 1 LaSalle Sq., ☎ 401/331–6700). The **Providence Performing Arts Center** (✉ 220 Weybosset St., ☎ 401/421–2787), a 3,200-seat theater and concert hall that opened in 1928, hosts touring Broadway shows, concerts, and other large-scale happenings. Its lavish interior contains painted frescoes, Art Deco chandeliers, bronze moldings, and marble floors. The **Rhode Island Philharmonic** (☎ 401/831–3123) presents 18 concerts at Veterans Memorial Auditorium between October and May. **Veterans Memorial Auditorium** (✉ 69 Brownell St., ☎ 401/222–3150) hosts concerts, plays, children's theater, and ballet.

THEATER

Sandra Feinstein-Gamm Theatre (✉ 31 Elbow St., ☎ 401/831–2919), an ambitious offshoot of Trinity Square Repertory, presents innovative versions of classic and contemporary plays in a tiny, 75-seat space. **Brown University** (✉ Leeds Theatre, 77 Waterman St., ☎ 401/863–2838) mounts productions of contemporary, sometimes avant-garde, works as well as classics. **Trinity Square Repertory Company** (✉ 201 Washington St., ☎ 401/351–4242), one of New England's best theater companies, presents plays in the renovated Majestic movie house. The varied season generally includes classics, foreign plays, and new works. The **Providence Performing Arts Center** and **Veterans Memorial Auditorium** host a variety of plays.

Outdoor Activities and Sports

Basketball

The **Providence College Friars** play Big East basketball at the Providence Civic Center (✉ 1 LaSalle Sq., ☎ 401/331–6700 events information; 401/331–2211 tickets).

Biking

The best biking in the Providence area is along the 14½-mi **East Bay Bicycle Path,** which hugs the Narragansett Bay shore from India Point Park through four towns before it ends in Independence Park in Bristol. **Esta's Too** (✉ 257 Thayer St., ☎ 401/831–2651), which rents bicycles, is near the East Bay Bicycle Path.

Boating

Prime boating areas include the Providence River, the Seekonk River, and Narragansett Bay. The **Narragansett Boat Club** (✉ River Rd., ☎ 401/272–1838) has information about local boating. **Paddle Providence** (✉ 222 S. Water St., ☎ 401/453–1633) rents canoes and kayaks from April to October and conducts guided tours of Providence's waterfront.

Football

The **Brown Bears** (☎ 401/863–2773) of Brown University play at Brown Stadium (✉ Elmgrove and Sessions Sts.).

Golf

The 18-hole, par-72 **Triggs Memorial Golf Course** (✉ 1533 Chalkstone Ave., ☎ 401/521–8460) has lengthy fairways. The greens fee ranges from $25 to $30; an optional cart costs $24.

Hockey

The **Providence Bruins** (☎ 401/331–6700), a farm team of the Boston Bruins, play at the Providence Civic Center (✉ 1 LaSalle Sq.). The **Brown Bears** (☎ 401/863–2773) play high-energy hockey at Meehan Auditorium (✉ 235 Hope St.).

Ice-skating

The outdoor ice rink downtown, **Fleet Skating Center** (✉ Kennedy Plaza, ☎ 401/331–5544), has become a popular destination. It's open October through April, daily 10–8. Skates are available for rent.

Jogging

Three-mi-long **Blackstone Boulevard** draws joggers with its wide, level, and tree-lined trail.

Shopping

Antiques

Wickenden Street contains many antiques stores and several art galleries. **CAV** (✉ 14 Imperial Pl., ☎ 401/751–9164) is a large restaurant, bar, and coffeehouse (with music Friday and Saturday nights) in a revamped factory space. It sells fine rugs, tapestries, prints, portraits, and antiques. **Tilden-Thurber** (✉ 292 Westminster St., ☎ 401/272–3200) carries high-end Colonial- and Victorian-era furniture, antiques, and estate jewelry.

Art

The **Alaimo Gallery** (✉ 301 Wickenden St., ☎ 401/421–5360) specializes in hand-colored engravings, magazine and playbill covers, political cartoons, antique prints and posters, and box labels. **JRS Fine Art** (✉ 218 Wickenden St., ☎ 401/331–4380) sells works by national, regional, and Rhode Island artists. The **Peaceable Kingdom** (✉ 116 Ives St., ☎ 401/351–3472) stocks folk art. The store's strengths include Native American crafts, Haitian paintings, Oriental rugs, and kilims. Hmong story cloths (from Laos) are another specialty.

Food

Constantino's Venda Ravioli (✉ 265 Atwells Ave., ☎ 401/421–9105) on Federal Hill sells a variety of imported and homemade gourmet Italian foods. **Roma Gourmet Foods** (✉ 310 Atwells Ave., ☎ 401/331–8620) sells homemade pasta, bread, pizza, pastries, and meats and cheeses. **Tony's Colonial** (✉ 311 Atwells Ave., ☎ 401/621–8675), a superb Italian grocery and deli, stocks freshly prepared foods.

Malls

America's first shopping mall is the **Arcade** (✉ 65 Weybosset St., ☎ 401/598–1199), built in 1828. A National Historic Landmark, this graceful Greek Revival building has three tiers of shops and restaurants. Expect the unusual at **Copacetic Rudely Elegant Jewelry** (✉ The Arcade, 65 Weybosset St., ☎ 401/273–0470), which sells the work of more than 130 diverse artists. The **Game Keeper** (✉ The Arcade, 65 Weybosset St., ☎ 401/351–0362) sells board games, puzzles, and gadgets.

Downtown's upscale **Providence Place** (✉ 1 Providence Pl., at Francis and Hayes Sts., ☎ 401/270–1000), with 150 shops, is anchored by Filene's, Lord & Taylor, and Nordstrom.

Maps

The **Map Center** (✉ 671 N. Main St., ☎ 401/421–2184) carries maps of all types and nautical charts.

Providence A to Z

To research prices, get advice from other travelers, and book travel arrangements, visit www.fodors.com.

BUS TRAVEL TO & FROM PROVIDENCE

Rhode Island Public Transit Authority buses run around town and to T. F. Green State Airport; the main terminal is in Kennedy Plaza. The fares range from $1 to $3.

➤ BUS INFORMATION: **Rhode Island Public Transit Authority** (RIPTA; ☎ 401/781–9400; 800/244–0444 in RI). Kennedy Plaza (⊠ Washington and Dorrance Sts.).

CAR TRAVEL

Overnight parking is not allowed on Providence streets, and during the day it can be difficult to find curbside parking, especially downtown and on Federal and College hills. The Westin Providence downtown has a large parking garage; parking is also available at the Providence Place Mall. To get from T. F. Green Airport to downtown Providence, take I–95 north to Exit 22.

EMERGENCIES

➤ HOSPITALS: **Rhode Island Hospital** (⊠ 593 Eddy St., ☎ 401/444–4000).

➤ 24-HOUR PHARMACIES: **Brooks Pharmacy** (⊠ 1200 N. Main St., ☎ 401/272–3048).

TAXIS

Fares are $2 at the flag drop, then $2 per mi. The ride from the airport to downtown takes about 15 minutes and costs about $22.

➤ TAXI COMPANIES: **Airport Taxi** (☎ 401/737–2868). **Checker Cab** (☎ 401/273–2222). **Economy Cab** (☎ 401/944–6700). **Yellow Cab** (☎ 401/941–1122).

TOURS

Providence Preservation Society publishes a walking-tour guidebook ($2.50) to historic Benefit Street and leads house tours on the second weekend in June.

➤ CONTACTS: **Providence Preservation Society** (⊠ 21 Meeting St., ☎ 401/831–7440, WEB www.providencepreservation.org).

VISITOR INFORMATION

➤ TOURIST INFORMATION: **Greater Providence Convention and Visitors Bureau** (⊠ 1 W. Exchange St., 02903, ☎ 401/274–1636, WEB www.providencecvb.com).

THE BLACKSTONE VALLEY

New England today calls up images of rural charm, but 200 years ago the region was being transformed by industry into the young nation's manufacturing powerhouse. Much of that industry is gone now, but its heritage remains to be explored. The 45-mi-long Blackstone River, a federally designated American Heritage River, runs from Worcester, Massachusetts, to Pawtucket, Rhode Island, where its power was first harnessed in 1790, setting off America's Industrial Revolution. Along the river and its tributaries are many old mill villages and towns separated by woods and farmland. Pawtucket and Woonsocket grew into large cities in the 1800s when a system of canals, and later railroads, became distribution channels for local industry, which attracted a steady flow of French, Irish, and Eastern European immigrants.

This area in the northern portion of the state is named for William Blackstone, who in 1628 became the first European to settle in Boston. In 1635, having grown weary of the ways of the Puritan settlers who had become his neighbors, this Anglican clergyman built a new home in what was wilderness and is now called Rhode Island. His cabin and his writings were destroyed in 1675, during the year-long King Philip's War, a devastating conflict between European settlers and Native Americans.

In 1986 the National Park Service designated the Blackstone Valley a National Heritage Corridor. A planned bike path will run from Worcester to the Narragansett Bay, and a prominent new museum in Woonsocket relates the region's history through multimedia exhibits. The valley is gradually emerging as a destination for people interested in antiques, architecture, country drives, and fall foliage, as well as history. The new visitor center in Pawtucket is a great place to begin a tour of the region.

Pawtucket

⑰ *5 mi north of Providence.*

In Algonquian, "petuket" (similar to standard Rhode Island pronunciation of the city's name, accent on the second syllable) means "water falls." A small village was established at the falls in 1670 by Joseph Jenks Jr., who considered the area a prime spot for an iron forge. When Samuel Slater arrived 120 years later, he was delighted to find a corps of skilled mechanics ready to assist him in his dream of organizing America's first factory system. Many older buildings were torn down as part of urban renewal projects in the 1970s, but significant portions of the city's history have been preserved and are worth a visit.

The **Blackstone Valley Visitor Center,** across the street from Slater Mill, has information kiosks, maps, and hospitable tourism consultants. A large screening room shows documentaries on the region. ⊠ *175 Main St.,* ☎ *401/724–2200 or 800/454–2882,* WEB *www.tourblackstone.com.* 🎦 *Free.* ☉ *Daily 9–5.*

☾ In 1793, Samuel Slater and two Providence merchants built the first factory in America to produce cotton yarn from water-powered machines. The yellow clapboard **Slater Mill Historic Site** houses classrooms, a theater, and machinery illustrating the conversion of raw cotton to finished cloth. A 16,000-pound waterwheel powers an operational 19th-century machine shop; the shop and the adjacent 1758 Sylvanus Brown House are open to the public. ⊠ *67 Roosevelt Ave.,* ☎ *401/ 725–8638,* WEB *www.slatermill.org.* 🎦 *$6.50.* ☉ *June–Nov., Mon.–Sat. 10–5, Sun. 1–5; Mar.–May, weekends 1–5; Dec.–Feb., weekends, 1 PM tour only. Guided tours daily; call for times.*

☾ **Slater Memorial Park** stretches along Ten mi River. Within this stately grounds are picnic tables, tennis courts, playgrounds, a river walk, and two historic sites. Eight generations of Daggetts lived in the **Daggett House,** Pawtucket's oldest home, which was built in 1685. Among the 17th-century antiques on display are bedspreads owned by Samuel Slater. The **Loof Carousel,** built by Charles I. D. Loof, has 42 horses, three dogs, and a lion, camel, and giraffe that are the earliest examples of the Danish immigrant's work. ⊠ *Newport Ave./Rte. 1A,* ☎ *401/728–0500 park information.* 🎦 *Park and carousel free; Daggett House $2.* ☉ *Park daily dawn–dusk; Daggett House June–Sept., weekends 2–5; carousel July–Labor Day, daily 10–5, late-Apr.–June and Labor Day– Columbus Day, weekends 10–5.*

The Blackstone Valley

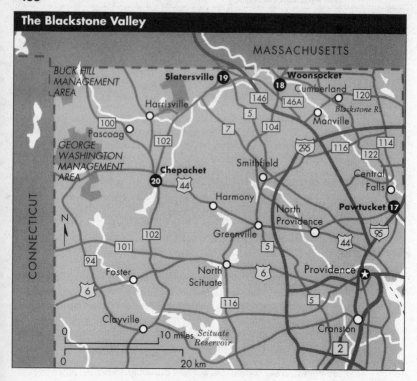

Dining

$–$$ ✕ **Modern Diner.** This 1941 Sterling Streamline eatery—a classic from the heyday of the stainless-steel diner—was the first diner to be listed on the National Register of Historic Places. The Modern serves standard diner fare and some specialty items, including lobster Benedict and French toast with custard sauce and berries. ⊠ *364 East Ave.,* ☎ *401/726–8390. No credit cards. No dinner.*

Outdoor Activities and Sports

The **Pawtucket Red Sox,** the Triple-A farm team of baseball's Boston Red Sox, play at the newly remodeled and expanded McCoy Stadium (⊠ 1 Columbus Ave., ☎ 401/724–7300).

Woonsocket

18 *10 mi north of Pawtucket, 15 mi north of Providence.*

Rhode Island's sixth-largest city (population 40,000) was settled in the late 17th century, home to a sawmill and Quaker farmers for its first 100 years. A steep hill on the northern end of the city looks down on the Blackstone River, which makes a dozen turns in its 5-mi course through Woonsocket. The river's flow spawned textile mills that made Woonsocket a thriving community in the 19th and early 20th centuries; today a museum is dedicated to this industrial heritage. Manufacturing plants remain the city's leading employers.

Multimedia and more traditional exhibits at the **Museum of Work and Culture** examine the lives of American factory workers and owners during the Industrial Revolution. The genesis of the textile-workers' union is described, as are the events that led to the National Textile Strike of 1934. A model of the triple-decker (a three-family tenement building) demonstrates the practicality behind what was once the region's preeminent style of home. Youngsters may be interested in presentations about child labor. ⊠ *42 S. Main St.,* ☎ *401/769–9675.* 🖼 *$5.* ☉ *Weekdays 9:30–4, Sat. 10–5, Sun. 1–5.*

Dining and Lodging

$–$$ ✕ **Ye Olde English Fish & Chips.** Fresh fried fish and potatoes have been served at this statewide institution for generations. The decor is simple—wood paneling and booths—so it must be the inexpensive and consistently excellent food, served in red plastic baskets, that has kept folks returning to this joint since 1922. ⊠ *Market Sq. at S. Main St.,* ☎ *401/762–3637. No credit cards. Closed Sun.–Mon.*

$–$$ 🏠 **Pillsbury House.** Stately Prospect Street stretches along the crest of the ridge north of the Blackstone River; its mansions, like the mansard-roof Pillsbury House, were built by mill owners in the late 1800s. The common room has a baby grand piano, a parquet floor, and a fireplace with a maple hearth. The two guest rooms on the second floor are furnished in Victorian style, with antiques, plants, high beds, and fringed lamp shades. The third-floor suite has a more rustic-country decor. ⊠ *341 Prospect St., 02895,* ☎ 🖷 *401/766–7983,* ☎ *800/205–4112,* 🌐 *www.pillsburyhouse.com. 2 rooms, 1 suite. AE, D, DC, MC, V. BP.*

Nightlife and the Arts

The impressive entertainment lineup at **Chan's Fine Oriental Dining** (⊠ 267 Main St., ☎ 401/765–1900) includes blues, jazz, and folk performers. Reservations are essential; ticket prices range from $10 to $24.

Shopping

Storefront renovations have made for much better shopping along Main Street. **Main Street Antiques** (⊠ 32 Main St., ☎ 401/762–0805) is a good place to browse.

Slatersville

⑲ *3 mi west of Woonsocket.*

Samuel Slater's brother, John, purchased a small sawmill and blacksmith shop along the Branch River and turned the area (now part of the town of North Smithfield) into America's first company town, Slatersville, beginning in 1807. With their factory well removed from population centers, Slater and his partners built homes, a town green, a Congregational church, and a general store for their workers. The village, west of the junction of Routes 102 and 146, has been well preserved, and though it doesn't have many amenities for visitors, it is a fine place for an afternoon stroll.

Dining

$ ✕ **Wright's Farm Restaurant.** Chicken family-style (all-you-can-eat bread, salad, roast chicken, pasta, and potatoes, a northern Rhode Island tradition, was born of a Woonsocket social club's need to feed many people efficiently. More than a dozen restaurants in the Blackstone Valley serve this food combo; Wright's Farm, the largest, dishes up 300 tons of chicken each year. ⊠ *84 Inman Rd., Burrillville, 2 mi west of Slatersville off Rte. 102,* ☎ *401/769–2856. No credit cards. Closed Mon.–Tues. No lunch.*

Chepachet

⑳ *12 mi south of Slatersville, 20 mi northwest of Providence.*

Antiques shops and other businesses line Main Street in the village of Chepachet, at the intersection of Routes 44 and 102 in the township of Glocester. The setting feels so much out of a storybook that you might find it jolting to see paved roads and automobiles upon exiting its many emporiums. **Snowhurst Farm** (✉ 421 Chopmist Hill Rd., ☎ 401/568–8900) grows 16 varieties of apples that you pick yourself for 55¢ per pound, from late August until about Columbus Day. This working farm has cattle, horses, and sheep. From Chepachet, drive 2 mi south on U.S. 44 to Route 102; the farm is 2 mi south of the intersection.

Dining

$$ ✕ **Stagecoach Tavern.** Formerly a stagecoach stop between Providence and Hartford, this establishment serves hearty meat dishes and pastas at reasonable prices. Locals hang out at the casual bar. ✉ *1157 Main St.*, ☎ *401/568–2275. AE, D, MC, V.*

Shopping

Established in 1809, **Brown & Hopkins Country Store** (✉ 79 Main St., ☎ 401/568–4830) has been in operation longer than any other country store in America. Crafts, penny candy, a deli, antiques, and a pot-bellied stove await you.

Harold's (✉ 1191 Main St., ☎ 401/568–6030) specializes in antique lamps. **The Lion and the Swan** (✉ 1187 Main St., ☎ 401/568–1800) carries antique dark-wood furniture and dolls. **Old Chepachet Village** (✉ 11 Money Hill Rd., ☎ 401/568–3511) houses 30 crafts and antiques stores in a 10,000-square-ft building.

OFF THE   **BUCK HILL MANAGEMENT AREA –** Tucked away in the remote northwest
BEATEN PATH   corner of the state, 7 mi northwest of Chepachet, this area supports waterfowl, songbirds, deer, pheasant, owls, foxes, and wild turkeys. Hiking trails traverse the preserve and cross into Connecticut and Massachusetts. ✉ *Buck Hill Rd. off Rte. 100 (Wallum Lake Rd.),* ☎ *401/222–2632.* ▣ *Free.* ☉ *Daily, from ½ hr before sunrise to ½ hr after sunset.*

Blackstone Valley A to Z

To research prices, get advice from other travelers, and book travel arrangements, visit www.fodors.com.

BUS TRAVEL

Rhode Island Public Transit Authority buses travel from Providence's Kennedy Plaza to towns in the Blackstone Valley.
➤ Bus Information: **Rhode Island Public Transit Authority** (RIPTA; ☎ 401/781–9400; 800/244–0444 in RI) Kennedy Plaza (✉ Washington and Dorrance Sts.).

CAR TRAVEL

Pawtucket is north of Providence on I–95. To reach Woonsocket, take Route 146 northwest from Providence and head north at Route 99; from Woonsocket, take Route 146A west to Route 102 to get to Slatersville. Chepachet is southwest of Slatersville on Route 102 and west of Providence on U.S. 44.

The easiest way to explore the Blackstone Valley is by car, though a good map is needed because signage satisfying visitors' needs is not yet in place. *Street Atlas Rhode Island* is available at most gas stations.

EMERGENCIES

➤ Hospital: **Landmark Medical Center** (✉ 115 Cass Ave., Woonsocket, ☎ 401/769–4100).

TOURS

Blackstone Valley Explorer is a 49-passenger, canopied riverboat offering various tours of the Blackstone River. Tours are given from April to October and depart from a number of landings along the river. ➤ CONTACT: *Blackstone Valley Explorer* (✉ 171 Main St., Pawtucket, ☎ 800/619–2628).

VISITOR INFORMATION

The Blackstone Valley Tourism Council operates the Blackstone Valley Visitor Center, a good starting point for visitors to northern Rhode Island. A complete list of factory stores is also available. ➤ TOURIST INFORMATION: **Blackstone Valley Tourism Council** (✉ 171 Main St., Pawtucket 02860, ☎ 401/724–2200 or 800/454–2882, WEB www.tourblackstone.com). **Northern Rhode Island Chamber of Commerce** (✉ 6 Blackstone Valley Pl., Suite 105, Lincoln 02865, ☎ 401/334–1000, WEB www.nrichamber.com).

SOUTH COUNTY

When the principal interstate traffic shifted from U.S. 1 to I–95 in the 1960s, coastal Rhode Island—known within the state as South County—was given a reprieve from the inevitabilities of development. In the past three decades, strong local zoning laws have been instituted and a wide-ranging park system established. In some communities, land trusts were set up to buy open space with monies generated from land-transaction fees. Always a summertime destination, South County is now growing into a region of year-round residents. The southern coast is, indeed, the fastest-growing region in the state, but the changes are being well managed by the respective communities; and the area's appeal as a summer playground has not diminished.

Westerly

㉑ *50 mi southwest of Providence, 100 mi southwest of Boston, MA, 140 mi northeast of New York City.*

The city of Westerly is a busy little railroad town that grew up in the late 19th century around a major station on what is now the New York–Boston Amtrak corridor. The 30-square-mi community of 15 villages has since sprawled out along U.S. 1. Victorian and Greek Revival mansions line many streets off the town center, which borders Connecticut and the Pawcatuck River. During the Industrial Revolution and into the 1950s, Westerly was distinguished for its flawless red granite, from which monuments throughout the country were made.

Watch Hill and Misquamicut are summer communities recognized without mention of the city to which they belong, Westerly. Casinos in Uncasville and Ledyard, Connecticut (less than an hour away), are slowly changing Westerly's economic climate. Many residents work in the Mohegan Sun and Foxwoods casinos, and visitors are discovering that Westerly's B&Bs provide alternatives to casino hotels.

Wilcox Park (✉ 71½ High St., ☎ 401/596–8590), designed in 1898 by Warren Manning, an associate of Frederick Law Olmsted and Calvert Vaux, is an 18-acre park in the heart of town with a garden designed so that people with visual and other impairments can identify—by taste, touch, and smell—such plants as chives and thyme.

Dining and Lodging

$$$$ ✕🏨 **Weekapaug Inn.** Weekapaug is a picturesque coastal village 6 mi
★ southeast of Westerly center and 3 mi from Misquamicut Beach. This

South County and Newport County

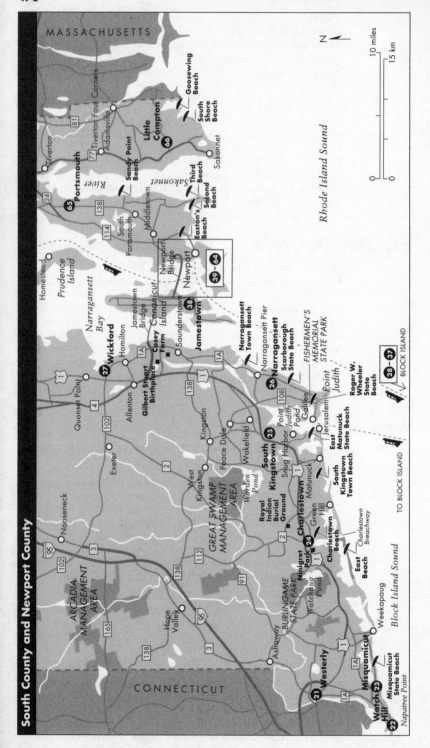

MASSACHUSETTS

CONNECTICUT

Rhode Island Sound

Narragansett Bay

Block Island Sound

Goosewing Beach

South Shore Beach

Little Compton 66

Sakonnet

Sandy Point Beach

Third Beach

Second Beach

Easton's Beach

Portsmouth 65

Middletown

South Portsmouth

Newport Bridge

Newport 39-64

Tiverton Four Corners

Tiverton

Adamsville

Sakonnet River

Homestead

Prudence Island

Jamestown Bridge

Casey Conanicut Farm Island

Jamestown 38

Saunderstown

Wickford 27

Hamilton

Gilbert Stuart Birthplace

Allenton

Quonset Point

Kingston

Peace Dale

Wakefield

Exeter

West Kingston

Nooseneck

GREAT SWAMP MANAGEMENT AREA

Worden Pond

Royal Indian Burial Ground

South Kingstown 25

Snug Harbor

Point Judith Pond

Galilee

Jerusalem

Narragansett Pier

Narragansett Town Beach

Scarborough State Beach

Narragansett 26

Point Judith

FISHERMEN'S MEMORIAL STATE PARK

Roger W. Wheeler State Beach

28-37 BLOCK ISLAND

East Matunuck State Beach

South Kingstown Town Beach

Matunuck

Green Hill

Charlestown 24

Charlestown Beach

Charlestown Breachway

East Beach

Ninigret Park

BURLINGAME STATE PARK

Watchaug Pond

ARCADIA MANAGEMENT AREA

Hope Valley

Ashaway

Weekapaug

Westerly 21

Misquamicut 23

Watch Hill 22

Misquamicut State Beach

Napatree Point

TO BLOCK ISLAND

N

10 miles

15 km

inn, with a peaked roof and huge wraparound porch, sits on a peninsula surrounded on three sides by salty Quonochontaug Pond. The rooms are cheerful, if not particularly remarkable; most are big and bright, with wide windows that have impressive views. The standards at the restaurant, which has a full-time baker, are high: each new daily menu emphasizes seafood and lists four to six entrées. You can choose to include breakfast and dinner in the price. ⊠ *25 Spring Ave., Weekapaug 02891,* ☎ *401/322–0301,* ℻ *401/322–1016. 55 rooms. Restaurant. No credit cards. Closed Oct.–May.*

$$–$$$ ✕🏠 **Shelter Harbor Inn.** This inn, about 6 mi east of downtown in a quiet, rural setting not far from the beach, started out as a summer musicians' colony. The rooms are furnished with a combination of Victorian antiques and reproduction pieces; bedspreads and curtains are in muted floral patterns. Many of the rooms have fireplaces and decks. The frequently changing menu at this excellent restaurant might include smoked scallops and cappellini or pecan-crusted duck breast. Breakfast is good every day, but Sunday brunch is legendary. ⊠ *10 Wagner Rd., off U.S. 1, 02891,* ☎ *401/322–8883 or 800/468–8883,* ℻ *401/ 322–7907. 23 rooms. Restaurant, hot tub, croquet, paddle tennis. AE, D, DC, MC, V. BP.*

$$ 🏠 **Grandview Bed and Breakfast.** Relaxed and affordable, this B&B on a rise above Route 1A has comfortable, if nondescript, rooms (the front ones have ocean views). The common room has a TV with VCR. Breakfast is served on the porch year-round. ⊠ *212 Shore Rd., Dunn's Corners (between Misquamicut and Weekapaug), 02891,* ☎ *401/596– 6384 or 800/447–6384,* ℻ *401/596–6384,* 🕸 *www.grandview-bandb.com. 9 rooms, 5 with bath. AE, MC, V. CP.*

Watch Hill

★ ㉒   *5 mi south of downtown Westerly.*

Watch Hill, a Victorian-era resort village, contains mi of beautiful beaches. Many of its well-kept summer houses are owned by wealthy families who have passed ownership down through generations. Sailing and socializing are the top activities for Watch Hill residents. This is a good place to tour the attractive streets, shop, and hit the beaches. Long before the first Europeans showed up, southern Rhode Island was inhabited by the Narragansetts, a powerful Native American tribe. The Niantics, ruled by Chief Ninigret in the 1630s, were one branch of the tribe. A statue of Ninigret stands watch over Bay Street.

🐚 **Flying Horse Carousel,** at the beach end of Bay Street, is the oldest merry-go-round in America. It was built by the Charles W. F. Dare Co. of New York in about 1867. The horses, suspended from above, swing out when in motion. Each is hand-carved from a single piece of wood. Adults are not permitted to ride the carousel. ⊠ *Bay St.* 🎫 *50¢.* ⊙ *Mid-June– Labor Day, weekdays 1–9, weekends 11–9.*

The **Watch Hill Lighthouse,** an active U.S. Coast Guard station, has great views of the ocean and of Fishers Island, New York. A tiny museum contains exhibits about the lighthouse. Parking is for the elderly only; everyone else must walk from lots at the beach. The grounds here are worth a stroll, whether the museum is open or not. ⊠ *Lighthouse Rd.,* ☎ *no phone.* 🎫 *Free.* ⊙ *May–Sept., Tues. and Thurs. 1–3.*

Dining and Lodging

$$$ ✕ **Three Fish.** Housed in a former 19th-century woolen mill, literally straddling the Pawcatuck River, this restaurant's homey atmosphere seems an unlikely place for fine seafood. But amid its dishes of chowder and crab cakes, and nautical decor—navy, gold, and green, polished wood furniture, and water visible from every window—you'll also find innovative dishes such as miniature duck and cabbage pierogi and filet mignon topped with boursin cheese ravioli. ⊠ *37 Main St.,* ☎ *401/348–9700. AE, MC, V. Closed Sun.*

$$–$$$ ✕ **Olympia Tea Room.** A step back in time, this small restaurant, which
   ★   opened in 1916, has varnished wood booths and a soda fountain behind a long marble counter. It also has a great reputation. The menu items are all memorable—some being Rhode Island classics (stuffed quahogs) and others the chef's own creations (duck egg rolls wrapped in phyllo dough). The "world-famous Avondale swan" dessert is a fantasy of ice cream, whipped cream, chocolate sauce, and puff pastry. ⊠ *30 Bay St.,* ☎ *401/348–8211. Reservations not accepted. AE, MC, V. Closed Nov.–Mar.*

$$$–$$$$ ☎ **Ocean House.** The immensity of this yellow-clapboard Victorian hotel will just about take your breath away. Built by George Nash in 1868, the Ocean House helped earn Watch Hill its fame as a 19th-century resort. Though the place is a bit down at the heels these days, it has a private beach and one of the best seaside porches in New England. Casual, relaxing, and quiet, the inn has a reassuring, if faded, elegance. The furniture can best be described as maple eclectic. Ask for a room with an ocean view. ⊠ *2 Bluff Ave., 02891,* ☎ *401/348–8161. 59 rooms. Restaurant, lounge, beach. MC, V. Closed Sept.–June. BP, MAP.*

Shopping

Bay Street is a good place to shop for jewelry, summer clothing, and antiques. The **Book and Tackle Shop** (⊠ 7 Bay St., ☎ 401/596–1770) buys, sells, and appraises old and rare books, prints, autographs, and photographs. **Puffins of Watch Hill** (⊠ 60 Bay St., ☎ 401/596–1140) carries fine American crafts, collectibles, pottery, jewelry, and gifts.

Misquamicut

㉓ *2 mi northeast of Watch Hill.*

Strip motels jostle for attention in Misquamicut, where a giant water slide, a carousel, miniature golf, a game arcade, children's rides, batting cages, and fast-food stands attract visitors by the thousands. The mi-long beach is accessible year-round, but the amusements are open only between Memorial Day and Labor Day.

Atlantic Beach Park (⊠ 337 Atlantic Ave., ☎ 401/322–9298) offers more games and rides for kids than any other Misquamicut facility.

Dining and Lodging

$$ ✕ **Paddy's Seafood Restaurant.** The food is good and the portions are generous at this no-frills, family-style beachside restaurant. Lobster, scrod, stuffed shrimp, grilled tuna, and other seafood plates rule the menu, but you can also order pastas and salads. ⊠ *159 Atlantic Ave.,* ☎ *401/ 596–2610. AE, D, MC, V. Closed Oct.–Apr.*

$$–$$$ ☎ **Breezeway Motel.** The Bellone family takes great pride in its business and offers a variety of accommodations: villas with fireplaces and hot tubs, suites, efficiencies, and standard rooms. The grounds hold a swing set, shuffleboard, and floodlighted fountains. ⊠ *70 Winnapaug Rd., (Box 1368), 02891,* ☎ *401/348–8953 or 800/462–8872,* FAX *401/ 596–3207. 52 rooms, 14 suites, 2 villas. Refrigerators, pool, recreation room. AE, D, DC, MC, V. Closed Nov.–May. CP.*

Nightlife and the Arts

The **Windjammer** (⊠ 337 Atlantic Ave., ☎ 401/322–9298), open Memorial Day to Labor Day, hosts dancing to rock bands in a room that holds 1,500.

Outdoor Activities and Sports

Two-mi-long **Misquamicut State Beach** (✉ Atlantic Ave., ☎ 401/596–9097), open to the public, has parking, shower facilities, and a snack bar at the state-run beach pavilion.

Charlestown

㉔ *10 mi northeast of Misquamicut.*

Charlestown stretches along the Old Post Road (Route 1A). The 37-square-mi town has parks, the largest saltwater marsh in the state, 4 mi of pristine beaches, and many oceanfront motels, summer chalets, and cabins.

Ninigret Park (✉ Park La. off Rte. 1A, ☎ 401/364–1222) is a 172-acre park with picnic grounds, ball fields, a bike path, tennis courts, nature trails, and a spring-fed pond; also here is the **Frosty Drew Observatory and Nature Center** (☎ 401/364–9508), which presents nature and astronomy programs on Friday evenings.

Ninigret National Wildlife Refuge consists of two stretches of beach-lands and marshes, plus the abandoned naval air station on Ninigret Pond. Nine mi of trails cross 400 acres of diverse upland and wetland habitats—including grasslands, shrublands, wooded swamps, and freshwater ponds. ✉ *Rte. 1A,* ☎ *401/364–9124.* ▣ *Free.* ☉ *Daily dawn–dusk.*

Many Narragansetts still live in the Charlestown area, but their historic sites are unmarked and easy to miss. The **Royal Indian Burial Ground,** on the left side of Narrow Lane north of U.S. 1, is the resting place of *sachems* (chiefs). You'll recognize it by the tall fences, but there's no sign. It's not open for visits except during the annual Narragansett meeting, usually the second Sunday in August, when tribal members from around the nation convene for costumed dancing and rituals.

Dining and Lodging

$$ ✕▥ **General Stanton Inn.** For helping pay the ransom of a native princess in 1655, the Narragansetts rewarded Thomas Stanton with the land where this inn stands. Stanton, a trader from England, first ran it as a schoolhouse for African-American and Native American children. Since the 18th century, it has provided dining and lodging in a Colonial atmosphere. The rooms have low ceilings, uneven floorboards, small windows, and period antiques and wallpapers. The dining rooms in the restaurant (closed November–April) have brick fireplaces, beams, and wooden floors. Traditional New England fare—steaks, lobster, scrod, rack of lamb—is prepared. ✉ *4115A Old Post Rd. (Rte. 1A), 02813,* ☎ *401/364–8888,* 📠 *401/364–3333. 16 rooms. Restaurant, bar. AE, MC, V. BP.*

Outdoor Activities and Sports

The 2,100-acre **Burlingame State Park** (✉ 75 Burlingame Park Rd., ☎ 401/322–7337 or 401/322–7994) has nature trails, picnic and swimming areas, and campgrounds, as well as boating and fishing on Watchaug Pond.

BEACHES

The two beaches in Charlestown have deep sand and stretch for mi. Both have parking, a snack bar, and rest rooms. **Charlestown Town Beach** (✉ Charlestown Beach Rd.) ends at a breachway that is part of Ninigret National Wildlife Refuge. Glorious **East Beach** (✉ East Beach Rd.), composed of 3½ mi of dunes backed by the crystal-clear waters of Ninigret Pond, is a 2-mi hike from the breachway at Charlestown Town Beach. Parking is at the end of East Beach Road.

BOATING

Ocean House Marina (⊠ 60 Town Dock Rd., ☎ 401/364–6040), at the Cross Mills exit off U.S. 1, is a full-service marina with boat rentals and fishing supplies.

Shopping

Artists Guild and Gallery (⊠ 5429 Post Rd., off U.S. 1, ☎ 401/322–0506) exhibits 19th- and 20th-century art. **Fox Run Country Antiques** (⊠ Intersection of U.S. 1 and Rte. 2, Crossland Park complex, ☎ 401/364–3160; 401/377–2581 appointments), open May through October, sells jewelry, lighting devices, Orientalia, antiques, china, and glassware.

The **Fantastic Umbrella Factory** (⊠ 4920 Old Post Rd., off U.S. 1, ☎ 401/364–6616) comprises four rustic shops and a barn built around a wild garden. For sale are hardy perennials and unusual daylilies, greeting cards, kites, crafts, tapestries, and incense. There is also an art gallery, a greenhouse, and a café that serves organic foods.

South Kingstown

㉕ *4 mi northeast of Charlestown.*

In summer months, the 55-square-mi town of South Kingstown—encompassing Wakefield, Snug Harbor, Matunuck, Green Hill, Kingston, and 10 other villages—offers a wealth of history, outdoor recreation and beaches, and entertainment.

At the old **Washington County Jail,** built in 1792 in Wakefield, the largest South Kingstown village, you can view jail cells, rooms from the Colonial period, a Colonial garden, and exhibits about South County life. ⊠ *1348 Kingstown Rd.,* ☎ *401/783–1328.* 🎟 *Free.* ☉ *May–Oct., Tues., Thurs., and Sat. 1–4.*

Dining and Lodging

$$ ✕ **Mews Tavern.** The food at this cheery tavern is consistently excellent. Rhode Islanders consider it the best place in the state to get a hamburger (buy one, get one free on Thursday night), but you can also order seafood. Beer is also popular here; 69 varieties are on tap. ⊠ *465 Main St.,* ☎ *401/783–9370. Reservations not accepted. AE, D, MC, V.*

$$ ✕🏠 **Larchwood Inn.** This 169-year-old country inn with a Scottish flavor is set in a grove of larch trees. The dining room ($–$$) is open for three meals daily; the halibut stuffed with scallops is delicious. Ask for a table near the fireplace in winter or a patio spot under the trees in summer. Rooms range from suites with grand views to smaller, back-of-the-house affairs. ⊠ *521 Main St., Wakefield 02879,* ☎ *401/783–5454,* 🖷 *401/783–1800,* 🌐 *www.xpos.com/larchwoodinn.html. 18 rooms. Restaurant. AE, D, DC, MC, V.*

$$ 🏠 **Admiral Dewey Inn.** Victorian antiques furnish the rooms of this inn, which was built in 1898 as a seaside hotel—it's across the road from Matunuck Beach—and is now on the National Register of Historic Places. Some rooms have views of the ocean; others are tucked cozily under the eaves. Smoking is permitted only on the wraparound veranda, which is filled with old-fashioned rocking chairs. ⊠ *668 Matunuck Beach Rd., 02881,* ☎ *401/783–2090,* 🌐 *www.admiraldewey.com. 10 rooms, 8 with bath. MC, V. CP.*

Nightlife and the Arts

Ocean Mist (⊠ 145 Matunuck Beach Rd., ☎ 401/782–3740) is a distinctive beachfront barroom with music nightly in summer and on weekends off-season. The hard-drinking crowd at this hangout of South County's younger generation can be as rough-hewn as the building. The barn-style **Theatre-by-the-Sea** (⊠ Cards Pond Rd., off U.S. 1, ☎

401/782–8587), built in 1933 and listed on the National Register of Historic Places, presents musicals and plays in summer.

Outdoor Activities and Sports

BEACHES

East Matunuck State Beach (⊠ Succotash Rd.) is popular with the college crowd for its white sand and picnic areas. Crabs, mussels, and starfish populate the rock reef that extends to the right of **Matunuck Beach** (⊠ Succotash Rd.). Southward, the reef gives way to a sandy bottom. When the ocean is calm, you can walk on the reef and explore its tide pools. **Roy Carpenter's Beach** (⊠ Matunuck Beach Rd.) is part of a cottage-colony of seasonal renters but is open to the public for a fee. **South Kingstown Town Beach** (⊠ Matunuck Beach Rd.) draws many families.

FISHING

Gil's Custom Tackle (⊠ 101 Main St., Wakefield, ☎ 401/783–1370) sells recreational fishing gear. **Snug Harbor Marina** (⊠ 410 Gooseberry Rd., Wakefield, ☎ 401/783–7766) sells bait, rents kayaks, and arranges fishing charters. At Snug Harbor it is not uncommon to see on the docks giant tuna and sharks weighing more than 300 pounds.

WATER SPORTS

The **Watershed** (⊠ 396 Main St., Wakefield, ☎ 401/789–3399) rents surfboards, Windsurfers, body boards, and wet suits. Owner Peter Pan gives lessons at nearby Narragansett Town Beach.

Shopping

Historic downtown Wakefield has a number of unique shops. **Dove and Distaff Antiques** (⊠ 365 Main St., Wakefield, ☎ 401/783–5714) is a good spot for early American furniture. **Hera Gallery** (⊠ 327 Main St., Wakefield, ☎ 401/789–1488), a women's art cooperative, exhibits the work of emerging local artists. It's open Wednesday–Friday 1–5, Saturday 10–4.

Narragansett

🟢 *2 mi east of South Kingstown.*

The popular beach town of Narragansett is on the peninsula east of Point Judith Pond and the Pettaquamscutt River. Its 16 villages include Galilee, Bonnett Shores, and Narragansett Pier.

Narragansett Pier, the beach community often called simply the Pier, was named for an amusement wharf that no longer exists. The Pier, now populated by summertime "cottagers," college students, and commuting professionals, was in the late 1800s a posh resort linked by rail to New York and Boston. Many summer visitors headed for the Narragansett Pier Casino, which had a bowling alley, billiard tables, tennis courts, a rifle gallery, a theater, and a ballroom. The grand edifice burned to the ground in 1900. Only the **Towers** (⊠ Rte. 1A, ☎ 401/783–7121), the grand stone entrance to the former casino, remains. Most of the mansions built during Narragansett's golden age are along Ocean Road, from Point Judith to Narragansett Pier.

The village of **Galilee** is a busy, workaday fishing port from which whale-watching excursions, fishing trips, and the **Block Island Ferry** (⊠ Galilee State Pier, ☎ 401/783–4613) depart. The occasionally pungent smell of seafood and bait will lead you to the area's fine restaurants and markets. From the port of Galilee it's a short drive to the **Point Judith Lighthouse** (⊠ 1460 Ocean Rd., ☎ 401/789–0444) and a beautiful ocean view. The lighthouse is open from dawn to dusk.

🟢 **Adventureland in Narragansett** has bumper boats, miniature golf, batting cages, and a go-cart track. ⊠ *Rte. 108,* ☎ *401/789–0030.* 🖥 *Com-*

bination tickets $1.50–$9.50. ⊙ *Mid-June–Labor Day, daily 10–10; Labor Day–Oct. and mid-Apr.–mid-June, weekends 10–10.*

Ⓒ The seven buildings of the **South County Museum** house 20,000 artifacts dating from 1800 to 1933. Exhibits include a country kitchen, a carpentry shop, a cobbler's shop, a tack shop, a working print shop, and an antique carriage collection. ✉ *Canonchet Farm, Anne Hoxie La., off Rte. 1A,* ☎ *401/783–5400.* 🖃 *$3.50.* ⊙ *May–June and Sept.– Oct., Wed.–Sun. 11–4; July–Aug., Wed.–Mon. 10–4.*

Dining and Lodging

$$$ ✕ **Basil's.** French and Continental cuisine are served in an intimate setting within walking distance of Narragansett Town Beach. Dark floral wallpaper and fresh flowers decorate the small dining room. The specialty is veal topped with a light cream-and-mushroom sauce; among the other dishes are fish and duck à l'orange. ✉ *22 Kingstown Rd.,* ☎ *401/789–3743. AE, DC, MC, V. Closed Mon., and Tues. Oct.–June. No lunch.*

$$–$$$ ✕ **Spain Restaurant.** South County's only Spanish restaurant is known
★   for its generous portions and fine service by well-trained professionals. Worthy appetizers include shrimp in garlic sauce, stuffed mushrooms, and Spanish sausages; lobster, steak, and paella are some of the main courses. Even basic dishes, such as chicken with rice, are unforgettable. Arched entryways and tall plants help create Mediterranean mood. ✉ *1144 Ocean Rd.,* ☎ *401/783–9770. AE, D, DC, MC, V.*

$$ ✕ **Aunt Carrie's.** This popular family-owned restaurant has been serving up Rhode Island shore dinners, clam cakes and chowder, and fried seafood for nearly 80 years. At the height of the season the lines can be long; one alternative is to order from the take-out window and picnic on the grounds of the nearby lighthouse. ✉ *Rte. 108 and Ocean Rd., Point Judith,* ☎ *401/783–7930. Reservations not accepted. MC, V. Closed Oct.–Mar. and Mon.–Thurs. Apr.–May and Sept.*

$$ ✕ **Coast Guard House.** This restaurant, housed in an 1888 building that served as a lifesaving station for 50 years, displays interesting photos of Narragansett Pier and the Casino. Candles light the tables, and picture windows on three sides allow views of the ocean. The fare is American—seafood, pasta, veal, steak, and lamb. The upstairs lounge hosts entertainers and has a DJ on Friday and Saturday night. ✉ *40 Ocean Rd.,* ☎ *401/789–0700. AE, D, DC, MC, V.*

$$ ✕ **George's of Galilee.** This restaurant at the mouth of the Point Judith harbor has been a must for tourists since 1948. The "stuffies" (baked stuffed quahogs) are some of the best in the state. The menu lists a variety of fried and broiled seafood, chicken, steak, and pasta, all at reasonable prices. Its proximity to the beach and its large outside bar on the second floor make George's a very busy place all summer. ✉ *Sand Hill Cove Rd., Port of Galilee,* ☎ *401/783–2306. Reservations not accepted. AE, D, MC, V. Closed Dec. and weekdays Nov. and Jan.*

$–$$ 🏠 **The Richards.** Imposing and magnificent, this mansion has a broodingly Gothic mystique that is quite different from the spirit of the typical summer house. French windows in the wood-paneled common rooms downstairs open up to views of a lush landscape, and a grand swamp oak is the centerpiece of the garden. A fire crackles in the library fireplace on chilly afternoons. Some rooms have 19th-century English antiques, floral-upholstered furniture, and fireplaces. ✉ *144 Gibson Ave., 02882,* ☎ *401/789–7746. 4 rooms, 1 2-bedroom suite. No credit cards. BP.*

Outdoor Activities and Sports

BEACHES

Popular **Narragansett Town Beach** (✉ Rte. 1A) is within walking distance of many hotels and guest houses. Its pavilion has changing rooms, showers, and concessions. **Roger W. Wheeler State Beach** (✉ Sand Hill Cove Rd., Galilee) has a pavilion; the beach, sheltered from ocean swells, has picnic areas and a playground. **Scarborough State Beach** (✉ Ocean Rd.), considered by many the jewel of the Ocean State's beaches, has a pavilion with showers and concessions. On weekends, teenagers and college students blanket the sands.

FISHING

The **Lady Frances** (✉ Frances Fleet, 2 State St., Point Judith, ☎ 401/783–4988 or 800/662–2824) operates day and overnight fishing trips. Narragansett-based charter boats include the **Persuader** (☎ 401/783–5644), **Prowler** (☎ 401/783–8487), and **Seven B's V** (☎ 401/789–9250). **Maridee Canvas–Bait & Tackle** (✉ 120 Knowlesway Ext., ☎ 401/789–5190) stocks supplies and provides helpful advice.

WHALE-WATCHING

Whale-watching excursions aboard the **Lady Frances** depart at 1 PM and return at 6 PM. The fare is $30. The trips operate Monday through Saturday from July to Labor Day.

Wickford

★ ㉗ *10 mi north of Narragansett Pier, 15 mi south of Providence.*

The Colonial village of Wickford has a little harbor, dozens of 18th- and 19th-century homes, several antique shops, and boutiques selling locally made jewelry and crafts, home accents and gifts, and clothing. This bayside spot is the kind of almost-too-perfect, salty New England period piece that is usually conjured up only in books and movies. In fact, Wickford was John Updike's model for the New England of his novel *The Witches of Eastwick.*

Old Narragansett Church, now called St. Paul's, was built in 1707. It's one of the oldest Episcopal churches in America. ✉ *55 Main St.,* ☎ *401/294–4357.* ☉ *July–Labor Day, Fri.–Sat. 11–4, Sun. services at 8 and 9:30.*

Smith's Castle, built in 1678 by Richard Smith Jr., is a beautifully preserved saltbox plantation house on the quiet shore of an arm of Narragansett Bay. It was the site of many orations by Roger Williams, from whom Smith bought the surrounding property. The grounds have one of the first military burial grounds (open during daylight hours) in the country: interred in a marked mass grave are 40 colonists killed in the Great Swamp battle of 1675. The Narragansetts were nearly annihilated, ending King Philip's War in Rhode Island. ✉ *55 Richard Smith Dr., 1 mi north of Wickford,* ☎ *401/294–3521.* ✍ *$3.* ☉ *May and Sept., Fri.–Sun. noon–4; June–Aug., Thurs.–Mon. noon–4. Castle tours by appointment Oct.–Apr.*

Historic **Silas Casey Farm,** off Route 1A south of Wickford, still functions much as it has since the 18th century. The farmhouse contains original furniture, prints, paintings, and 300 years of political and military documents. Nearly 30 mi of stone walls surround the 360-acre farmstead. ✉ *2325 Boston Neck Rd., Saunderstown,* ☎ *401/295–1030.* ✍ *$3.* ☉ *June–mid-Oct., Tues., Thurs., and Sat. 1–5.*

En Route Built in 1751, the **Gilbert Stuart Birthplace** was the home of America's foremost portraitist of George Washington. It lies on a pretty country road along little Mattatuxet River. The adjacent 18th-century snuff mill was the first in America. You can hike the trail along the river. ✉ *815 Gilbert Stuart Rd., Saunderstown,* ☎ *401/294–3001.* ✍ *$3.* ☉ *Apr.–Oct., Thurs.–Mon. 11–4:30.*

Shopping

The **Hour Glass** (⊠ 15 W. Main St., ☎ 401/295–8724) carries antique barometers, clocks, tide clocks, thermometers, and the like. **Mentor Antiques** (⊠ 7512 Post Rd., ☎ 401/294–9412) receives monthly shipments of antique English mahogany, pine, and oak furniture. **Wickford Antiques Centre** (⊠ 16 Main St., ☎ 401/295–2966) sells wooden kitchen utensils, country furniture, china, glass, linens, and jewelry.

Needlepoint pillows, Florentine leather books, lamps, and woven throws are a few of the gifts and home furnishings at **Askham & Telham Inc.** (⊠ 12 Main St., ☎ 401/295–0891).

South County A to Z

To research prices, get advice from other travelers, and book travel arrangements, visit www.fodors.com.

The closest major airport is in Warwick, south of Providence. Westerly Airport is served by New England Airlines, which flies from Westerly to Block Island and operates charter flights.

➤ AIRPORT INFORMATION: **Westerly Airport** (⊠ Airport Rd., 2 mi south of Westerly off U.S. 1, ☎ 401/596–2460). **New England Airlines** (☎ 401/596–2460 or 800/243–2460).

Rhode Island Public Transit Authority provides service from Providence and Warwick to Kingston, Wakefield, and Narragansett.

➤ BUS INFORMATION: **Rhode Island Public Transit Authority** (RIPTA; ☎ 401/781–9400; 800/244–0444 in RI).

Interstate 95 passes 10 mi north of Westerly before heading inland toward Providence. U.S. 1 and Route 1A follow the coastline along Narragansett Bay and are the primary routes through the South County resort towns.

➤ HOSPITALS: **South County Hospital** (⊠ 100 Kenyon Ave., Wakefield, ☎ 401/782–8000). **Westerly Hospital** (⊠ 25 Wells St., Westerly, ☎ 401/596–6000).

➤ 24-HOUR PHARMACY: **CVS Pharmacy** (⊠ Granite Shopping Center, 114 Granite St., Westerly, ☎ 401/596–0306).

Amtrak trains running between Washington and Boston stop in Westerly and Kingston.

➤ TRAIN INFORMATION: **Amtrak** (☎ 800/872–7245, WEB www.amtrak.com).

The state operates a visitor information center off I–95 at the Connecticut border.

➤ TOURIST INFORMATION: **Charlestown Chamber of Commerce** (⊠ 4945 Old Post Rd., Charlestown 02813, ☎ 401/364–3878). **Greater Westerly Chamber of Commerce** (⊠ 74 Post Rd., Westerly 02891, ☎ 401/596–7761 or 800/732–7636). **Narragansett Chamber of Commerce** (⊠ The Towers, Rte. 1A, Narragansett 02882, ☎ 401/783–7121). **South County Tourism Council** (⊠ 4808 Tower Hill Rd., Wakefield 02879, ☎ 401/789–4422 or 800/548–4662).

BLOCK ISLAND

Visitors have been seeking out Block Island, 12 mi off Rhode Island's southern coast, since the 19th century. Despite the many people who come here each summer, and thanks to the efforts of local conservationists, the island's beauty has been preserved; its 365 freshwater ponds support more than 150 species of migrating birds.

The original inhabitants of the island were Native Americans who called it Manisses, or "Isle of the Little God." Following a visit in 1614 by the Dutch explorer Adrian Block, the island was given the name Adrian's Eyelant, and later Block Island. In 1661 the island was settled by farmers and fishermen from Massachusetts Bay Colony. They gave Block Island what remains its second official name, the Town of New Shoreham, when it became part of Rhode Island in 1672.

Block Island is a laid-back community. Phone numbers are exchanged by the last four digits (466 is the prefix), and you can dine at any of the island's establishments in shorts and a T-shirt. The heaviest visitor activity takes place between May and Columbus Day—at other times, most restaurants, inns, stores, and visitor services close down. If you plan to stay overnight in summer, make reservations well in advance; for weekends in July and August, March is not too early.

Block Island has two harbors, Old Harbor and New Harbor. Approaching Block Island by sea from New London (Connecticut), Newport, or Point Judith, you'll see Old Harbor and its group of Victorian hotels. The Old Harbor area is the island's only village. Most of the inns, shops, and restaurants are here, and it's a short walk from the ferry landing to any hotel and to most of the interesting sights.

With the exception of a short strip called Moped Alley (actually Weldon's Way), where visitors test-drive mopeds, there's not a bad walk on all of Block Island. The West Side loop (West Side Road to Cooneymus Road) is gorgeous.

(28) Three docks, two hotels, and four restaurants huddled in the southeast corner of the Great Salt Pond make up the **New Harbor** commercial area. The harbor itself—also called Great Salt Pond—shelters as many as 1,700 boats on busy weekends, hosts sail races and fishing tournaments, and is the landing point for two ferries that run from Montauk on Long Island (New York) to Block Island.

(29) The **Island Cemetery,** ½ mi west on West Side Road from New Harbor, has held the remains of island residents since the 1700s. At this well-maintained graveyard you can spot the names of long-standing Block Island families (Ball, Rose, Champlin) and take in fine views of the Great Salt Pond, the North Light, and the Rhode Island coast; on a clear day, the Jamestown–Newport Bridge will be visible to the northeast.

To explore the island's lovely **west side,** head west from New Harbor on West Side Road; after the Island Cemetery, you will pass a horse farm and some small ponds. You get to the beach by turning right on Dories Cove Road or Cooneymus Beach Road; both dirt roads dead-end at the island's tranquil west shore. One mi past Dories Cove Road, peaceful West Side Road jogs left and turns into Cooneymus Road. On your right ½ mi farther is a deep ravine.

★ (30) **Rodman's Hollow** (⊠ off Cooneymus Rd.) is a fine example of a glacial outwash basin. This was the first piece of property purchased in the island's quarter-century-long tradition of land conservation, an effort that has succeeded in saving 25% of the island from development. At Rodman's you can descend along winding paths to the ocean, where

Block Island

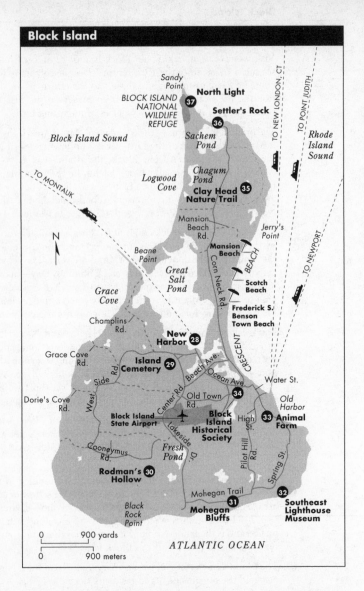

you can hike the coastline, lie on beaches at the foot of sand and clay cliffs, or swim if the waters are calm.

31 The 200-ft cliffs along Mohegan Trail, the island's southernmost road, are called **Mohegan Bluffs**—so named for an Indian battle in which the local Manisses pinned down an attacking band of Mohegans at the base of the cliffs. From **Payne Overlook**, west of the Southeast Lighthouse Museum, you can see to Montauk Point, New York, and beyond. An intimidating set of stairs leads down to the beach.

32 The small **Southeast Lighthouse Museum** occupies a "rescued" 1873 redbrick beacon with gingerbread detail that was moved back from eroded cliffs in 1993. The lighthouse is a National Historic Landmark. ⊠ *Mohegan Trail,* ☎ *401/466–5009.* 🎫 *$5.* ⊗ *Memorial Day–Labor Day, daily 10–4.*

33 The owners of the 1661 Inn and Hotel Manisses run a small **Animal Farm** with a collection of llamas, emus, sheep, goats, and ducks. The animals happily coexist in a meadow next to the hotel. ⊠ *Off Spring or High St.,* ☎ *401/466–2063.* 🎟 *Free.* ⊙ *Daily dawn–dusk.*

㉞ Exhibits at the **Block Island Historical Society** describe the island's farming and maritime pasts. Many original pieces furnish the society's headquarters, an 1850 mansard-roof home that's well worth a visit. ⊠ *Old Town Rd.,* ☎ *401/466–2481 or 401/466–5009.* 🎟 *$2.* ⊙ *July–Aug., daily 10–4; June and Sept., weekends 10–4.*

★ **㉟** The outstanding **Clay Head Nature Trail** meanders past Clay Head Swamp and along 150-ft-high oceanside cliffs. Songbirds chirp and flowers bloom along the paths that lead into the interior—an area called the Maze. The trailhead, recognizable by a simple white-post marker, is at the end of a dirt road that begins at Corn Neck Road, just past Mansion Beach Road. It's about a mi, but other trails lead off of it. Trail maps are available at the **Nature Conservancy** (⊠ Ocean Ave., ☎ *401/466–2129*).

㊱ **Settler's Rock,** on the spit of land between Sachem Pond and Cow Beach, is a monument that lists the names of the original settlers and marks the spot where they landed in 1661. Hiking 1 mi over sandy terrain will get you to the somber North Light.

★ **㊲** **North Light,** an 1867 granite lighthouse on the northernmost tip of the Block Island National Wildlife Refuge, was reopened as a maritime museum in 1993. The protected area nearby is a temporary home to American oystercatchers, piping plovers, and other rare migrating birds. From a parking lot at the end of Corn Neck Road, it's a mi-long hike over sand to the lighthouse. ⊠ *Corn Neck Rd.,* ☎ *401/466–3200.* 🎟 *$2.* ⊙ *Mid-June–Labor Day, daily 10–4 (weather permitting).*

Dining and Lodging

$$–$$$ ✕ **Eli's.** Though the noise level is high and the napkins are paper, the
★ food keeps people coming back to Block Island's preferred restaurant. Pastas are the menu's mainstays, but the kitchen makes extensive excursions into local seafood, Asian dishes, and steaks like the "Carpetbagger," a 12-ounce filet mignon filled with lobster, mozzarella, and sun-dried tomatoes, topped with a béarnaise sauce. ⊠ *Chapel St.,* ☎ *401/466–5230. Reservations not accepted. MC, V. Closed Jan.–Feb., and Mon.–Wed. Mar.–May.*

$$–$$$ ✕ **Finn's.** A Block Island institution, Finn's serves reliable fried and broiled seafood and prepares a wonderful smoked bluefish pâté. For lunch try the "Workman's Special" platter—a burger, cole slaw, and french fries. You can eat inside or out on the deck, or get food to go. Finn's raw bar is on an upstairs deck that overlooks Old Harbor. ⊠ *Ferry Landing,* ☎ *401/466–2473. Reservations not accepted. AE, MC, V. Closed mid-Oct.–May.*

$ ✕ **The BeacHead.** The food—especially the Rhode Island clam chowder—is very good, the price is right, and you won't feel like a tourist at this locals' hangout. Play pool, catch up on town gossip, or sit at the bar and stare out at the sea. The menu and service are unpretentious; burgers are served on paper plates with potato chips and pickles. ⊠ *Corn Neck Rd.,* ☎ *401/466–2249. Reservations not accepted. No credit cards.*

$$$–$$$$ ✕🛏 **Atlantic Inn.** Bravely facing the elements on a hill above the ocean,
★ this long, white, classic Victorian resort has big windows, high ceilings, and a sweeping staircase. Most of the oak and maple furnishings in the rooms are original to the building. And then there are the views: isolated from the hubbub of the Old Harbor area, you can perch on a hillside, look out over the harbor, and contemplate the shape of the

island. Each morning the inn's pastry chef prepares a buffet breakfast with fresh-baked goods. The restaurant ($$$$; reservations essential; no lunch; closed from November to April) serves creative prix-fixe meals that use local ingredients. ⊠ *Box 1788, High St., 02807,* ☎ *401/466–5883 or 800/224–7422,* FAX *401/466–5678. 20 rooms, 1 suite. Restaurant, 2 tennis courts, croquet, playground, meeting room. D, MC, V. Closed Nov.–Easter. CP.*

$$$–$$$$ ✕🛏 **Hotel Manisses.** The chef at the island's premier restaurant (closed November–April) for American cuisine uses herbs and vegetables from the hotel's garden and locally caught seafood to prepare superb dishes such as littleneck clams Dijonnaise. Period furnishings and knickknacks fill the rooms in the 1872 mansion, some of which were named after shipwrecks; because of the antiques, the hotel is not suitable for children. The extras here include picnic baskets, an animal farm, island tours, afternoon wine and hors d'oeuvres in the parlor, and many rooms with whirlpool baths. ⊠ *1 Spring St., 02807,* ☎ *401/466–2421 or 800/626–4773,* FAX *401/466–3162,* WEB *www.blockisland.com/biresorts. 17 rooms. Restaurant, fans. MC, V. BP.*

$$$–$$$$ 🛏 **Blue Dory Inn.** This Old Harbor district inn has been a guest house
★ since its construction in 1898. Thanks to Ann Loedy, the dynamic owner-manager, things in the main building and the three small shingle-and-clapboard outbuildings run efficiently. Though not large, the rooms are tastefully appointed, and each has either an ocean or a harbor view. Couples looking for a romantic hideaway often enjoy the Tea House, which has a porch overlooking Crescent Beach. ⊠ *Box 488, Dodge St., 02807,* ☎ *401/466–2254 or 800/992–7290.* WEB *www.thebluedoryinn.com. 12 rooms, 4 cottages, 3 suites. AE, D, MC, V. BP.*

$$$–$$$$ 🛏 **1661 Inn and Guest House.** If your island vacation fantasy includes
★ lounging in bed while gazing at swans in the marshes that overlook the blue Atlantic, you might consider the 1661. Even if your room doesn't face the water, you can loll on the inn's expansive deck or curl up in a chair on the lawn; from both spots you'll enjoy the panorama of the water below. The room decor reflects the innkeepers' attention to detail: floral wallpaper in one room matches the colors of the hand-painted tiles atop its antique bureau, and another room has a collection of wooden model ships. The ample breakfast buffet might consist of fresh bluefish, corned-beef hash, sausage, Belgian waffles, roast potatoes, French toast, scrambled eggs, hot and cold cereal, fruit juices, and fresh muffins. ⊠ *Spring St., 02807,* ☎ *401/466–2421 or 800/626–4773,* FAX *401/466–2858,* WEB *www.blockisland.com/biresorts. 21 rooms, 19 with bath. Playground. AE, MC, V. Closed mid-Nov.–mid-Apr. BP.*

$$–$$$ 🛏 **Barrington Inn.** When a former Welcome Wagon hostess decides to open a B&B, you can bet she'll do things right. Owners Joan and Howard Ballard run a tidy, inviting place and enjoy helping you plan your days; the breakfast table is known as "command central." The inn, meticulously clean, precisely arranged, and thoroughly soundproofed, has unusual views of Trims Pond, Great Salt Pond, and Crescent Beach. Three rooms have private decks; there's also a large common deck. Two apartments (rented by the week in season) in a separate building are good options for families. ⊠ *Box 397, Beach Ave., 02807,* ☎ *401/466–5510,* FAX *401/466–5880,* WEB *www.blockisland.com/barrington. 6 rooms, 2 apartments. D, MC, V. CP.*

$$–$$$ 🛏 **Surf Hotel.** A stone's throw from the ferry dock, in the heart of the Old Harbor area and near Crescent Beach, the Surf seems to have changed little over the years; in fact, it's not hard to imagine what the hotel must have been like when it first opened in 1876. Dimly lighted hallways take you to small rooms furnished with a jumble of antique furniture and odds and ends. The rooms have sinks but share toilets

and baths, but the many return guests don't seem to mind sharing. ✉ *Box C, Dodge St., 02807, ☎ 401/466–2241. 38 rooms, 3 with bath. Breakfast room. MC, V. Closed mid-Oct.–Apr.. CP.*

Nightlife and the Arts

Many regular visitors consider Block Island's nightlife one of its best offerings, and you'll find a good number of places to get a drink. Check the *Block Island Times* for band listings. **Captain Nick's Rock and Roll Bar** (✉ 34 Ocean Ave., ☎ 401/466–5670), a fortress of summertime debauchery, has four bars and two decks on two floors. In season, bands play nightly. A 360-degree mural that depicts Block Island in the 1940s covers the walls at atmospheric **Club Soda** (✉ 35 Connecticut Ave., ☎ 401/466–5397). **McGovern's Yellow Kittens Tavern** (✉ Corn Neck Rd., ☎ 401/466–5855) has bands on weekend nights in summer.

Outdoor Activities and Sports

Beaches

The east side of the island has a number of beaches. The 2½-mi **Crescent Beach** runs from Old Harbor to Jerry's Point. **Frederick J. Benson Town Beach,** a family beach less than 1 mi down Corn Neck Road from Old Harbor, has a beach pavilion, parking, showers, and lifeguards. Young summer workers congregate ½ mi north of Town Beach at **Scotch Beach** to play volleyball, to surf, and to sun themselves. **Mansion Beach,** off Mansion Beach Road south of Jerry's Point, has deep white sand and is easily one of New England's most beautiful beaches. In the morning, you may spot deer on the dunes.

Boating

Block Island Boat Basin (✉ West Side Rd., New Harbor, ☎ 401/466–2631) is the island's best-stocked ship's store. **New Harbor Kayak** (✉ Ocean Ave., New Harbor, ☎ 401/466–2890) rents kayaks. **Oceans & Ponds** (✉ Ocean and Connecticut Aves., ☎ 401/466–5131) rents kayaks and books charter-boat trips.

Fishing

Most of Rhode Island's record fish have been caught on Block Island. From almost any beach, skilled anglers can land tautog and bass. Bonito and fluke are often hooked in the New Harbor channel. Shellfishing licenses may be obtained at the town hall, on Old Town Road. **Oceans & Ponds** sells tackle and fishing gear, operates charter trips, and provides guide services. **Twin Maples** (✉ Beach Ave., ☎ 401/466–5547) is the island's only bait shop.

Hiking

The **Greenway,** a well-maintained trail system, meanders across the island, but some of the best hikes are along the beaches. You can hike around the entire island in about eight hours. Trail maps for the Greenway are available at the Chamber of Commerce (✉ Water St., ☎ 401/466–2982) and the Nature Conservancy (✉ Ocean Ave. near Payne's Dock, ☎ 401/466–2129). The Nature Conservancy conducts nature walks; call for times or check the *Block Island Times.*

Water Sports

Island Outfitters (✉ Ocean Ave., ☎ 401/466–5502) rents wet suits, spearguns, and scuba gear. PADI-certification diving courses are available, and beach gear and bathing suits are for sale. **Parasailing on Block Island** (✉ Old Harbor Basin, ☎ 401/466–2474) offers parasailing and also rents jet boats.

Shopping

Scarlet Begonia (⊠ Dodge St., ☎ 401/466–5024) carries unusual jewelry and crafts, including place mats and handmade quilts. **Spring Street Gallery** (⊠ Spring St., ☎ 401/466–5374) shows and sells paintings, photographs, stained glass, serigraphs, and other work by island artists and artisans. **Watercolors** (⊠ Dodge St., ☎ 401/466–2538) showcases distinctive jewelry and clothing, much of it locally made.

Block Island A to Z

To research prices, get advice from other travelers, and book travel arrangements, visit www.fodors.com.

AIRPORTS

Block Island Airport is served by a few small airlines. Action Air flies in from Groton, Connecticut, between June and October. New England Airlines flies from Westerly to Block Island and operates charter flights.
➤ AIRPORT INFORMATION: **Block Island Airport** (⊠ Center Rd., ☎ 401/466–5511). **Action Air** (☎ 203/448–1646 or 800/243–8623). **New England Airlines** (☎ 401/466–5881 or 800/243–2460).

BIKE [& MOPED] TRAVEL

The best way to explore the island is by bicycle (about $15 a day to rent) or moped (about $40). Most rental places are open spring through fall and have child seats for bikes, and all offer bicycles in a variety of styles and sizes, including mountain bikes, hybrids, tandems, and children's biles.
➤ BIKE RENTALS: **Island Bike & Moped** (⊠ Weldon's Way, ☎ 401/466–2700). **Moped Man** (⊠ Weldon's Way, ☎ 401/466–5011). **Old Harbor Bike Shop** (south of the ferry dock, Old Harbor ☎ 401/466–2029).

BOAT & FERRY TRAVEL

Interstate Navigation Co. operates ferry service from Galilee, a one-hour trip, for $16.30 round-trip; there are six or seven trips a day. Make auto reservations well ahead. Foot passengers cannot make reservations; you should arrive 45 minutes ahead in high season—the boats do fill up. Ferries run daily from Memorial Day to October from Providence's India Street Pier to Newport's Fort Adams State Park, and to Block Island, and then return along the same route in the afternoon. The company also has summer service from New London, Connecticut. A new high-speed ferry is expected to be operating in 2001; call for details.

Nelseco Navigation operates an auto ferry from New London, Connecticut, in summer. Reservations are advised for the two-hour trip. One-way fares from New London are $15 per adult and $28 per vehicle. Viking Ferry Lines operates passenger and bicycle service from Montauk, Long Island (New York), from mid-May to mid-October. The trip, which takes 1¾ hours, costs $16 each way, plus $3 per bicycle.
➤ BOAT & FERRY INFORMATION: **Interstate Navigation Co.** (⊠ Galilee State Pier, Narragansett, ☎ 401/783–4613, WEB www.blockisland-ferry.com). **Nelseco Navigation** (⊠ 2 Ferry Rd., New London, CT, ☎ 860/442–7891). **Viking Ferry Lines** (☎ 516/668–5709).

CAR RENTAL
➤ LOCAL AGENCIES: **Block Island Car Rental** (☎ 401/466–2297).

CAR TRAVEL

Corn Neck Road runs north to Settler's Rock from Old Harbor. West Side Road loops west from New Harbor; to return to the Old Harbor area, take Cooneymus Road east and Lakeside Drive, Center Road, and Ocean Avenue north.

LODGING

Inns and hotels on Block Island are booked well in advance for weekends in July and August. Many visitors rent homes for stays of a week or more. Many houses, however, are booked solid by April.

➤ LOCAL AGENTS: **Ballard Hall Real Estate** (✉ Ocean Ave., 02807, ☎ 401/466–8883). **Sullivan Real Estate** (✉ Water St., 02807, ☎ 401/466–5521).

TAXIS

Taxis are plentiful at the Old Harbor and New Harbor ferry landings.
➤ CONTACTS: **Kirb's Cab** (☎ 401/466–2928). **Ladybird Taxi** (☎ 401/466–3133). **O.J.'s Taxi** (☎ 401/741–0500).

VISITOR INFORMATION

➤ TOURIST INFORMATION: **Block Island Chamber of Commerce** (✉ Drawer D, Water St., 02807, ☎ 401/466–2982).

NEWPORT COUNTY

Perched gloriously on the southern tip of Aquidneck Island and bounded on three sides by water, Newport is one of the great sailing cities of the world and the host to world-class jazz, blues, folk, and classical music festivals. Colonial houses and gilded-age mansions grace the city. Newport County encompasses the three communities of Aquidneck Island—Newport, Middletown and Portsmouth—plus Conanicut Island, also known as Jamestown, and Tiverton and Little Compton, which abut Massachusetts to Newport's east. Little Compton is a remote, idyllic town that presents a strong contrast to Newport's quick pace.

Jamestown

38 *25 mi south of Providence, 3 mi west of Newport.*

Summer residents have come to Jamestown since the 1880s, but never to the same extent as to Watch Hill, Narragansett, or Newport. The locals' "We're not a T-shirt town" attitude has resulted in a relatively low number of visitors, even in July and August, making this a peaceful alternative to the bustle of nearby Newport and South County.

The east and west passages of Narragansett Bay encompass the 9-mi-long, 1-mi-wide landmass that goes by the names Jamestown and Conanicut Island. Valuable as a military outpost in days gone by, the island was once considered an impediment to commercial cross-bay shipping. In 1940 the Jamestown Bridge linked the island to western Rhode Island, and in 1969 the Newport Bridge completed the cross-bay route, connecting Newport to the entire South County area.

The conditions range from tranquil to harrowing at **Beavertail State Park,** which straddles the southern tip of Conanicut Island. The currents and surf here are famously deadly during rough seas and high winds; but on a clear, calm day, the park's craggy shoreline seems intended for sunning, hiking, and climbing. The **Beavertail Lighthouse Museum,** in what was the lighthouse keeper's quarters, has displays about Rhode Island's lighthouses. ✉ *Beavertail Rd.,* ☎ *401/423–3270.* 🆓 *Free.* ☉ *Museum June–Labor Day, daily 10–4. Park daily.*

Thomas Carr Watson's family had worked the **Watson Farm** for 190 years before he bequeathed it to the Society for the Preservation of New England Antiquities when he died in 1979. The 285-acre spread, dedicated to educating the public about agrarian history, has 2 mi of trails along Jamestown's southwestern shore with amazing views of Narragansett Bay and North Kingstown. ⊠ *455 North Rd.,* ☎ *401/423–0005.* ⊡ *$3.* ⊙ *June–mid-Oct., Tues., Thurs., and Sun. 1–5.*

The English-designed **Jamestown Windmill,** built in 1789, ground corn for nearly 100 years—and it still works. Mills like this one were once common in Rhode Island. ⊠ *North Rd., east of Watson Farm,* ☎ *401/ 423–1798.* ⊡ *Free.* ⊙ *Mid-June–Sept., weekends 1–4.*

⟳ A working 1859 hand tub and a horse-drawn steam pump are among the holdings of the **Jamestown Fire Department Memorial Museum,** an informal display of firefighting equipment in a garage that once housed the fire company. ⊠ *50 Narragansett Ave.,* ☎ *401/423–0062.* ⊡ *Free.* ⊙ *Daily 7–3; inquire next door at fire department if door is locked.*

Fort Wetherill State Park, an outcropping of stone cliffs at the tip of the southeastern peninsula, has been a picnic destination since the 1800s. There's great swimming at the small cove here, and it's a favorite spot for local snorkelers and scuba divers. ⊠ *Ocean St.,* ☎ *401/ 423–1771.* ⊡ *Free.* ⊙ *Daily dawn–dusk.*

The **Jamestown and Newport Ferry Co.** stops in Newport at Bowen's Landing and Long Wharf and will stop on request at Fort Adams or Goat Island. The 26-ft passenger ferry departs on its half-hour voyage from Ferry Wharf about every 1½ hours, from 9 AM to 10 PM (11:30 PM on weekends). The last run leaves from Newport at 10:30 PM (midnight on weekends). The ferry operates from Memorial Day to mid-October. ⊠ *Ferry Wharf,* ☎ *401/423–9900.* ⊡ *About $6.*

Dining and Lodging

$$$ ✕ **Trattoria Simpatico.** A jazz trio plays on sunny weekends at Jamestown's signature restaurant, while patrons dine alfresco under a 275-year-old copper beech tree. An herb garden, fieldstone walls, and white linen complete the picture. You can munch splendid salads, taste pasta dishes cooked northern-Italian style, or try meats prepared with a Continental flair. One memorable appetizer is crispy-skin duck confit with deep-fried fettuccine, savoy cabbage, and onion marmalade. Reservations are essential on summer weekends. ⊠ *13 Narragansett Ave.,* ☎ *401/423–3731. AE, D, MC, V. No lunch weekdays Labor Day– Memorial Day, no lunch weekends Memorial Day–Labor Day.*

$$ ✕ **Jamestown Oyster Bar.** Whether you're ordering clam chowder
★ and a dollar draft or grilled swordfish and a martini, you'll feel right at home here. Oysters are kept on ice behind the bar, where tenders pour fine microbrews and wines. The burgers are locally renowned, but for something more delicate, try one of the seafood specials listed on the chalkboard. ⊠ *22 Narragansett Ave.,* ☎ *401/423–3380. Reservations not accepted. AE, MC, V. No lunch weekdays.*

$$$$ ▦ **Bay Voyage.** In 1889 this Victorian inn was shipped to its current location from Newport and named in honor of its trip. The one-bedroom suites, furnished in floral prints and pastels, have been sold as time shares, which makes availability tight in summer months. The facilities are plentiful, the view memorable. The restaurant is known for its Sunday brunch. ⊠ *150 Conanicus Ave., 02835,* ☎ *401/423–2100,* 𝔽𝔸𝕏 *401/423–3209,* 𝖶𝖤𝖡 *www.easternresorts.com. 32 suites. Restaurant, bar, kitchenettes, pool, sauna, exercise room. AE, D, DC, MC, V.*

$ ▦ **East Bay B&B.** If Karen Montoya's three rooms aren't booked, you can get a great deal at her humble B&B. The circa-1896 Victorian is peaceful day and night, even though it's only a block from Jamestown's two main streets and bustling wharf. The original trim and bullnose molding are all in great shape, as is the formal living room, which has a fireplace and Oriental rugs. ⊠ *14 Union St., 02835,* ☎ *401/423–2715. 3 rooms, 1 with bath. No credit cards. CP.*

Outdoor Activities and Sports

BEACHES

Sandy **Mackerel Cove Beach** (⊠ Beavertail Rd.) is sheltered from the currents of Narragansett Bay, making it a great spot for families. Parking costs $10 for nonresidents.

DIVING AND KAYAKING

Ocean State Scuba (⊠ 79 N. Main Rd., ☎ 401/423–1662 or 800/933–3483) rents kayaks and diving equipment.

GOLF

Jamestown Country Club (⊠ 245 Conanicus Ave., ☎ 401/423–9930) has a crisp nine-hole course, where for $10 you can play all day.

Newport

30 mi from Providence, 80 mi from Boston, MA.

The island city of Newport preserves Colonial industry and gilded-age splendor like no other place in the country. Settled in 1639 by a small band of religious dissenters from Massachusetts, Newport earned a reputation for tolerance and its prime location at the mouth of Narragansett Bay ensured its success in the Colonial period. The golden age of Newport ran from roughly 1720 to the 1770s, when products such as cheese, candles, clocks, and furniture, as well as livestock and the slave trade, put the city on a par with Charleston, South Carolina; the two cities trailed only Boston as centers of New World maritime commerce. In the mid-1700s, Newport was home to the best shipbuilders in North America. Their small, swift, and reliable slave ships were the stars of the triangle trade (rum to Africa for slaves; slaves to the West Indies for molasses; molasses and slaves back to America, where the molasses was made into rum). This unsavory scheme guaranteed investors a 20% return on their money and earned Newport the dubious distinction of being the largest slave-trading port in the North. In 1774, progressive Rhode Island became the first colony to outlaw trading in slaves.

In the 19th century, Newport became a summer playground for the wealthy, the titans of the gilded age who built the fabulous "cottages" overlooking the Atlantic. Newport's mansions served as proving grounds for the country's best young architects. Richard Upjohn, Richard Morris Hunt, and firms like McKim, Mead & White have left a legacy of remarkable homes, many now open to the public.

Recreational sailing, a huge industry in Newport today, convincingly melds the attributes of two eras: the conspicuous consumption of the late 19th century and the nautical expertise of the Colonial era. Tanned young sailors often fill Newport bars and restaurants, where they talk of wind, waves, and expensive yachts. For those not arriving by water, a sailboat tour of the harbor is a great way to get your feet wet.

Newport in summer can be exasperating, its streets jammed with visitors, the traffic slowed by sightseeing buses (3½ million people visit the city each year). Yet the quality of Newport's sights and its arts festivals persuade many people to brave the crowds. In fall and spring, you can explore the city without having to stand in long lines.

Downtown Newport

More than 200 pre-Revolutionary buildings (mostly private residences) remain in Newport, more than in any other city in the country. Most of these treasures are in the neighborhood known as the Point.

A GOOD WALK

The ideal first sight in a walking tour is the Colonial-era **Hunter House** ㊴. Walk north from Hunter House on Washington Street. At Van Zandt Avenue, turn right and proceed to the **Common Burial Ground** ㊵. Cross aptly-named Farewell Street through the cemetery, then head southeast. At the Marlborough Street intersection you'll pass the country's oldest bar and restaurant, the **White Horse Tavern** ㊶. Across Farewell Street stands **Friends Meeting House** ㊷. To the east, Marlborough intersects Spring Street and Broadway; ahead on your right you'll see the **Wanton-Lyman-Hazard House** ㊸, the oldest home in Newport. Follow Spring Street three short blocks south to Washington Street, which heads west into Washington Square. Over your left shoulder is the imposing **Colony House** ㊹, site of a number of historic events. At the bottom of Washington Square is the **Museum of Newport History at the Brick Market** ㊺.

Walk two blocks east on Touro Street (on the south side of the square); **Touro Synagogue** ㊻, the country's oldest Jewish house of worship, will be on your left. Next door is the **Newport Historical Society** ㊼. Cross the road and follow High Street one block; then turn right on Church Street to see the immaculate **Trinity Church** ㊽. Proceed east on Church Street. Across Bellevue Avenue are the four pillars of the **Redwood Library** ㊾. The **Newport Art Museum and Art Association** ㊿ is one block south.

Timing. This walk covers 2½ mi. If you spend time inside each building, it should take about 4½ hours to reach Bellevue Avenue. It's best to do this walk one day and the mansions of Bellevue Avenue another. If you have only one day, you will have to limit the number of sights you visit.

SIGHTS TO SEE

㊹ **Colony House.** This redbrick structure above downtown Washington Square was where, on May 4, 1776, Rhode Island and Providence Plantations signed an act that removed King George's name from all state documents. The same year, from the balcony of this building, the Declaration of Independence was read to Newporters. In 1781, George Washington met here with French commander Count Rochambeau to plan the Battle of Yorktown, which led to the end of the Revolutionary War. ⊠ *Washington Sq.*, ☎ *401/846–2980.* ☼ *Tours by appointment.*

㊵ **Common Burial Ground.** Farewell Street is lined with historic cemeteries; the many tombstones at this 17th-century graveyard are fine examples of Colonial stone carving, much of it the work of John Stevens.

㊷ **Friends Meeting House.** Built in 1699, this is the oldest Quaker meetinghouse in the country. With its wide-plank floors, simple benches, balcony, and beam ceiling (considered lofty by Colonial standards), the two-story shingle structure reflects the quiet reserve and steadfast faith of Colonial Quakers. ⊠ *29 Farewell St.*, ☎ *401/846–0813.* ◪ *$5.* ☼ *Tours by appointment.*

★ ㊴ **Hunter House.** The French admiral Charles Louis d'Arsac de Ternay used this lovely 1748 home as his Revolutionary War headquarters. The carved pineapple over the doorway was a symbol of welcome throughout Colonial America; a fresh pineapple placed out front signaled an invitation to neighbors to visit a returned seaman or to look

---

489

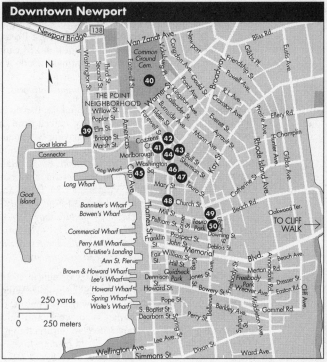

over a shop's new stock. The elliptical arch in the central hall is a typical Newport detail. Pieces made by Newport artisans Townsend and Goddard furnish much of the house, which also contains the first commissioned painting by a young Gilbert Stuart, best known for his portraits of George Washington. ⊠ *54 Washington St.,* ☎ *401/847–7516,* WEB *www.newportmansions.org.* ⊡ *$8.* ☉ *May–Sept., daily 10–5; Oct., weekends 10–5.*

45 **Museum of Newport History at the Brick Market.** This restored building once used for slave trading houses a city museum with multimedia exhibits that explore Newport's social and economic influences. Antiques such as the printing press of James Franklin (Ben's brother) inspire the imagination. Built in 1760 and designed by Peter Harrison, who was also responsible for the Touro Synagogue and the Redwood Library, the building served as a theater and a town hall. The museum and the Gateway Information Center are departure points for walking tours of Newport; call for times. ⊠ *127 Thames St.,* ☎ *401/841–0813.* ⊡ *$5.* ☉ *May–Nov., Mon. and Wed.–Sat. 10–5, Sun. 1–5; Dec.–Apr., Fri.–Sat. 10–4, Sun. 1–5.*

50 **Newport Art Museum and Art Association.** Richard Morris Hunt designed the Stick-style Victorian building that houses this community-supported center for the arts. The galleries exhibit contemporary works by New England artists. ⊠ *76 Bellevue Ave.,* ☎ *401/848–8200,* WEB *www.newportartmuseum.com.* ⊡ *$4.* ☉ *Memorial Day–Labor Day, Mon.–Sat. 10–5, Sun. noon–5; Labor Day–Memorial Day, Fri.–Sun. 10–4.*

47 **Newport Historical Society.** The headquarters of the historical society has a library and a small exhibit with Newport memorabilia, furniture, and maritime items. ⊠ *82 Touro St.,* ☎ *401/846–0813.* ⊡ *Free.* ☉ *Mid-June–Aug., Tues.–Sat. 9:30–4:30; Sept.–mid-June, Tues.–Fri. 9:30–4:30, Sat. 9:30–noon.*

49 **Redwood Library.** This magnificent building by Peter Harrison was built as a library in 1747 and has been in use for that purpose ever since, a record in America. Although it may look like a Roman temple, it is actually made of wood; the exterior paint is mixed with sand to make it resemble cut stone. The library's paintings include works by Gilbert Stuart and Rembrandt Peale. ⊠ *50 Bellevue Ave.,* ☎ *401/847–0292.* 🎟 *Free.* ☾ *Mon.–Sat. 9:30–5:30.* WEB *www.redwood1747.org.*

46 **Touro Synagogue.** Jews, like Quakers and Baptists, were attracted by Rhode Island's religious tolerance; they arrived from Amsterdam and Lisbon as early as 1658. The oldest surviving synagogue in the United States was dedicated in 1763. Although simple on the outside, the Georgian building, designed by Peter Harrison, has an elaborate interior. Its classical style influenced Thomas Jefferson in the building of Monticello and the University of Virginia. ⊠ *85 Touro St.,* ☎ *401/847–4794,* WEB *www.tourosynagogue.org.* 🎟 *Free.* ☾ *July 4–Labor Day, Sun.–Fri. 10–5; Memorial Day–July 4 and Labor Day–Columbus Day, Sun. 11–3 and weekdays 1–3; Columbus Day–Memorial Day, Sun. 1– 3 and weekdays for 2 PM tour only. Guided tours on the ½ hr. Services Fri. at 6 or 7 PM, Sat. at 8:45 AM; call to confirm.*

48 **Trinity Church.** This Colonial beauty was built in 1724 and modeled after London churches designed by Sir Christopher Wren. A special feature of the interior is the three-tier wineglass pulpit, the only one of its kind in America. The lighting, woodwork, and palpable feeling of history make attending services here an unforgettable experience. ⊠ *Queen Anne Sq.,* ☎ *401/846–0660.* 🎟 *Free.* ☾ *June–Sept., daily 10– 4; Oct.–May, daily 10–1. Services Sun. at 8 and 10; off-season (call for months) at 8 and 10:30.*

43 **Wanton-Lyman-Hazard House.** Newport's oldest residence dates from the mid-17th century and presents a window on the fascinating Colonial and Revolutionary history of Newport. The dark red building was site of the city's Stamp Act riot of 1765; after the British Parliament levied a tax on most printed material, the Sons of Liberty stormed the house, which was occupied by the English stamp master. It underwent extensive restoration in 1999. ⊠ *17 Broadway,* ☎ *401/846–0813.* 🎟 *$4.* ☾ *By appointment.*

41 **White Horse Tavern.** William Mayes, the father of a successful and notorious pirate, received a tavern license in 1687, which makes this building, built in 1673, the oldest tavern in America. Its gambrel roof, low dark-beam ceilings, cavernous fireplace, and uneven plank floors epitomize Newport's Colonial charm. ⊠ *Marlborough and Farewell Sts.,* ☎ *401/849–3600,* WEB *www.whitehorsetavern.com.*

Greater Newport

The gilded-age mansions of Bellevue Avenue are what many people associate most with Newport. These late-19th-century homes are almost obscenely grand, laden with ornate rococo detail and designed with a determined one-upmanship. Also in this area are some museums.

The **Preservation Society of Newport County** (☎ 401/847–1000) maintains 12 mansions. Guided tours are given of each; you can purchase a combination ticket at any of the properties for a substantial discount. The hours and days the houses are open during the off-season are subject to change, so it's wise to call ahead. Chateau-sur-Mer, the Elms, and, in some years, the Marble House or the Breakers are decorated for Christmas and usually open for tours daily from Thanksgiving Day to Christmas Day.

At the corner of Memorial Boulevard and Bellevue Avenue is the **International Tennis Hall of Fame Museum at the Newport Casino** ⑤, birthplace of the U.S. Open. Before you visit the mansions (or stop by when you're done), you can walk south on Bellevue Avenue, make a right on Bowery Street, and turn left at Thames Street to visit the **International Yacht Restoration School** ㊿. Back on Bellevue Avenue, catercorner from Newport Casino is **Kingscote** ㊿, a Victorian "cottage." The neoclassical **Elms** ㊿ is two blocks south. Three blocks farther is the Gothic-style **Chateau-sur-Mer** ㊿, and **Rosecliff** ㊿, modeled after the Grand Trianon, is four more blocks in the same direction. **Astors' Beechwood** ㊿ and the **Marble House** ㊿, a Vanderbilt mansion, are on the same side of this lengthy block of palaces. Farther down, on the corner of Lakeview and Bellevue, is **Belcourt Castle** ㊿. Beyond this mansion, Bellevue Avenue turns 90 degrees west and dead-ends at what most consider the end of the **Cliff Walk** ㊿, a stunning promenade. From here you can stroll along the Rhode Island Sound to Newport's most renowned mansion, the **Breakers** ㊿, which can be reached from the Cliff Walk by heading west on Ruggles Avenue and north on Ochre Point Avenue. If you're up for the hike, you can continue on the Cliff Walk all the way down to **Rough Point** ㊿ to catch a backyard glimpse of the home of Doris Duke.

You can walk the first part of this tour, although you may well prefer to save your energy for touring the houses, but you'll need a car to visit three sights. The **Museum of Yachting** ㊿ is at Fort Adams State Park. From downtown Newport, drive south on Thames Street to Wellington Avenue. Turn right and follow Wellington to the bend where Wellington becomes Halidon Avenue. Turn right on Harrison Avenue. One mi to the right is the entrance to the park; the museum is at the end of Fort Adams Road. To get back to town, follow Ocean Drive to Bellevue Avenue. To reach the **Naval War College Museum** ㊿, at the intersection with Memorial Boulevard, turn left; Memorial becomes America's Cup Avenue. At the cemetery, turn left on Farewell Street. Farewell runs into Bridge Access Road, where you will veer left to reach the Connell Highway traffic circle. Exit at the west end of the circle on Training Station Road. A small bridge will take you to Coasters Harbor Island. Park at the naval base entrance and walk two blocks along the same road to the museum, which is on a hill to your right.

Timing. If you have one day, it's best to tour two or three mansions and see the others only from the outside. To avoid long lines in summer, go early or choose the less-popular but still amazing mansions—the Elms, Kingscote, and Belcourt Castle. It's less than 2 mi from Kingscote to Belcourt—the first and last mansions on Bellevue Avenue. Plan on spending one hour at each mansion you visit. The full Cliff Walk is 3½ mi long. Seeing the Tennis Hall of Fame, three mansions, walking the length of Bellevue Avenue, and returning via the Cliff Walk takes five or six hours. The driving portion of the tour is about 11 mi long. You could easily spend an hour at each sight on the drive.

❺❼ **Astors' Beechwood.** The original mistress of this oceanfront mansion, Caroline Schermerhorn Astor, was the queen of American society in the late 19th century; her list of "The Four Hundred" was the first social register. Her husband, William Backhouse Astor, was a reserved businessman and a member of one of the wealthiest families in the nation (much of the Astors' fortune came from real estate, the China trade, and fur trading in North America). As they guide visitors through the 1857 mansion, actors in period costume play the family, their servants, and their household guests. ✉ *580 Bellevue Ave.,* ☎ *401/846–3772,*

Greater Newport

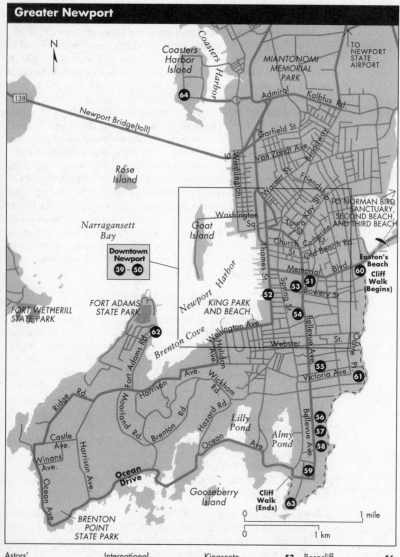

N

138

Newport Bridge (toll)

Coasters Harbor Island

64

Coasters Harbor

MIANTONOMI MEMORIAL PARK

TO NEWPORT STATE AIRPORT

Admiral

Kalbfus Rd.

Garfield St.

Van Zandt Ave.

Broadway

Warner St.

Friendship St.

Washington St.

Rose Island

Washington Sq.

Goat Island

Narragansett Bay

Downtown Newport

39 — 50

Touro St.

Kay St.

Church St.

Catherine St.

Old Beach Rd.

TO NORMAN BIRD SANCTUARY, SECOND BEACH, AND THIRD BEACH

Easton's Beach

Cliff Walk (Begins)

60

Memorial Blvd

Thames St.

Newport Harbor

KING PARK AND BEACH

53

51

52

Spring St.

Bowery St.

FORT ADAMS STATE PARK

FORT WETHERILL STATE PARK

62

Brenton Cove

54

Wellington Ave.

Webster St.

Halidon Ave.

Ave.

Wickham Rd.

55

Victoria Ave.

61

Harrison

Ave.

Brenton Rd.

Hazard Rd.

Lilly Pond

Almy Pond

Bellevue Ave.

56

57

58

Ridge Rd.

Moorland Rd.

Ocean Ave.

59

Castle Ave.

Winans Ave.

Ocean Ave.

Harrison Ave.

Ocean Drive

Gooseberry Island

Cliff Walk (Ends)

63

BRENTON POINT STATE PARK

0   1 mile

0   1 km

Astors'
Beechwood **57**

Belcourt Castle **59**

The Breakers **61**

Chateau-sur-Mer .. **55**

Cliff Walk **60**

The Elms **54**

International
Tennis Hall of Fame
Museum at the
Newport Casino ... **51**

International
Yacht Restoration
School **52**

Kingscote **53**

Marble House **58**

Museum of
Yachting **62**

Naval
War College
Museum **64**

Rosecliff **56**

Rough Point **63**

WEB *www.astors-beechwood.com.* ☎ *$9.* ☉ *Mid–May–Oct., daily 10–5; Nov.–Dec., daily 10-4; Feb.–mid-May, Fri.–Sun. 10–4; call about Christmas hrs and events.*

59 **Belcourt Castle.** Richard Morris Hunt based this 1894 Gothic Revival mansion, built for banking heir Oliver H. P. Belmont, on Louis XIII's hunting lodge. The house is so filled with European and Asian treasures that locals have dubbed it the Metropolitan Museum of Newport. Sip tea and admire the stained glass and carved wood, and don't miss the Golden Coronation Coach. ⊠ *657 Bellevue Ave.,* ☎ *401/846-0669 or 401/849–1566.* ☎ *$8.* ☉ *Apr.–Oct., daily 10–5; Nov.–Dec., daily 10–3; Feb.–Mar., daily 10–3.*

★ **61** **The Breakers.** It's easy to understand why it took 2,500 workers in the early 1890s two years to build the most magnificent Newport palace, the 70-room home of railroad heir Cornelius Vanderbilt II. A few of the marvels within the four-story Italian Renaissance–style palace are a gold-ceiling music room, a blue marble fireplace, rose alabaster pillars in the dining room, and a porch with a mosaic ceiling that took Italian artisans six months, lying on their backs, to install. To build the Breakers today would cost $400 million. ⊠ *Ochre Point Ave.,* ☎ *401/847–6544,* WEB *www.newportmansions.org.* ☎ *$12.* ☉ *Mar.–Oct., daily 10–5; Nov., weekends 10–4; open Dec. some years (call ahead).*

55 **Chateau-sur-Mer.** Bellevue Avenue's first stone mansion was built in the Victorian Gothic style in 1852 for William S. Wetmore, a tycoon involved in the China trade, and enlarged in the 1870s by Richard Morris Hunt. The Gold Room by Leon Marcotte and the Renaissance Revival-style dining room and library by the Florentine sculptor Luigi Frullini are sterling examples of the work of leading 19th-century designers. Upstairs, the bedrooms are decorated in the English Aesthetic style with wallpaper by Arts and Crafts designers William Morris and William Burges. ⊠ *Bellevue Ave. at Shepard Ave.,* ☎ *401/847–1000,* WEB *www.newportmansions.org.* ☎ *$9.* ☉ *May–Sept., daily 10–5; Oct.–Thanksgiving, weekends 10–4; Thanksgiving–Dec. 23, daily 10–4; Jan.–Mar., weekends 10–4; Apr., weekends 10–5.*

★ **60** **Cliff Walk.** Easton's Beach (also called First Beach) is the beginning of this spectacular 3½-mi path, which runs south along Newport's cliffs to Bailey's Beach. The promenade has views of sumptuous mansions on one side and the rocky coastline on the other; walking any section of it is worth the effort. The Cliff Walk can be accessed from any road running east off Bellevue Avenue. The unpaved sections can be difficult for small children or people with mobility problems.

54 **The Elms.** In designing this graceful 48-room French neoclassical mansion, architect Horace Trumbauer paid homage to the style, fountains, broad lawn, and formal gardens of the Château d'Asnières near Paris. The Elms was built for Edward Julius Berwind, a bituminous coal baron, in 1899. The energy magnate's home was one of the first in the nation to have central heat and to be piped for hot water. The trees throughout the 12-acre backyard are labeled, providing an exemplary botany lesson. ⊠ *Bellevue Ave.,* ☎ *401/842–0546,* WEB *www.newportmansions.org.* ☎ *$9.* ☉ *Daily 10–5.*

51 **International Tennis Hall of Fame Museum at the Newport Casino.** The photographs, memorabilia, and multimedia exhibits at the Hall of Fame provide a definitive chronicle of the game's greatest moments and characters. The magnificent, shingle-style Newport Casino, a social club, was designed by Stanford White and built in 1880 for publisher James Gordon Bennett Jr., who quit the nearby club, the Newport Reading Room, after a polo player—at Bennett's behest—rode a horse into the building and was subsequently banned. Bennett further retaliated by commissioning the Casino, which has 13 grass courts and one court-tennis facility (court tennis is the precursor to modern tennis). The Casino quickly became the social and recreational hot spot of the gilded age. ✉ *194 Bellevue Ave.*, ☎ *401/849–3990*, WEB *www.tennisfame.com.* ⌧ *$8; tennis courts $35 per person per hr.* ☉ *Daily 9:30–5.*

❺❷ International Yacht Restoration School. This school, off Thames Street in a former power plant, lets you watch shipwrights and students as they overhaul historically significant sailboats and power boats. Plac-ards recount each boat's past. The 1885 racing schooner *Coronet* and the original "cigarette boat" are two standouts. ✉ *449 Thames St.*, ☎ *401/848–5777*, WEB *www.iyrs.org.* ⌧ *Free.* ☉ *Apr.–Nov., daily 9–5; Dec.–Mar., Mon.–Sat. 10–5.*

Isaac Bell House. Considered one of the finest examples of American shingle-style architecture, this Bellevue Avenue home currently being restored is open to the public as a work in progress. The exterior has been completed; inside, a short film documents the effort to revitalize the McKim, Mead & White design, and you are given a tour of vari-ous rooms. Bell, who built the home in 1883, was a wealthy cotton broker. ✉ *Bellevue Ave., at Perry St.*, ☎ *401/847–1000*, WEB *www.new-portmansions.org.* ⌧ *$9.* ☉ *May–Oct., Fri.–Sat. 10–5.*

❺❸ Kingscote. This Victorian mansion completed in 1841 was designed by Richard Upjohn for George Noble Jones, a plantation owner from Savannah, Georgia. (Newport was popular with Southerners before the Civil War.) Decorated with antique furniture, glass, and Asian art, it contains a number of Tiffany windows. ✉ *Bowery St., off Bellevue Ave*, ☎ *401/847–1000*, WEB *www.newportmansions.org.* ⌧ *$9.* ☉ *May–Sept., daily 10–5; Apr. and Oct., weekends 10–4.*

★ ❺❽ Marble House. Perhaps the most opulent Newport mansion, the Mar-ble House is known for its extravagant gold ballroom. The house was the gift of William Vanderbilt to his wife, Alva, in 1892. Alva divorced William in 1895 and married Oliver Perry Belmont, becoming the lady of Belcourt Castle. When Oliver died in 1908, she returned to Mar-ble House. Mrs. Belmont was involved with the suffragist movement and spent much of her time campaigning for women's rights. The Chi-nese teahouse behind the estate was built in 1913. ✉ *Bellevue Ave., near Ruggles St.*, ☎ *401/847–1000*, WEB *www.newportmansions.org.* ⌧ *$9.* ☉ *Apr.–Oct., daily 10–5; Jan.–Mar., weekends 10–4; open Dec. some years (call ahead).*

❻❷ Museum of Yachting. The museum has four galleries: Mansions and Yachts, Small Craft, America's Cup, and the Hall of Fame for Single-handed Sailors. In summer, eight wooden yachts constitute a floating exhibition. ✉ *Ft. Adams Park, Ocean Dr.*, ☎ *401/847–1018.* ⌧ *$3.* ☉ *Mid-May–Oct., daily 10–5; Nov.–mid-May, by appointment.*

❻❹ Naval War College Museum. The Naval War College, the oldest school of its kind in the world, represents the pinnacle of education in the U.S. Navy. The museum's exhibits analyze the history of naval warfare and tactics and trace the history of the navy in Narragansett Bay. ✉ *Founders Hall, Gate 1, Naval Education and Training Center, Cush-ing Rd.*, ☎ *401/841–4052*, WEB *www.nwc.navy.mil/museum.* ⌧ *Free.* ☉ *Oct.–May, weekdays 10–4; June–Sept., weekdays 10–4, weekends noon–4.*

❺❻ Rosecliff. Newport's most romantic mansion was built for Mrs. Her-mann Oelrichs in 1902; her father had amassed a fortune from Nevada silver mines. Stanford White modeled the palace after the Grand Trianon at Versailles. Rosecliff has a heart-shape staircase, and its 40 rooms include the Court of Love and a grand ballroom. ⊠ *Bellevue Ave., at Marine Ave.,* ☎ *401/847–5793,* WEB *www.newportmansions.org.* ⛝ *$9.* ⊙ *Apr.–Oct., daily 10–5.*

➅ **Rough Point.** The late tobacco heiress and preservationist Doris Duke hosted such celebs as Elizabeth Taylor at her Newport mansion, which is open for small tours that leave from the Newport visitors center. (And only from the center: You can't drive or walk here and be admitted.) The 105-room home was built in the English-manor style for an heir to the Vanderbilt railroad fortune. The furnishings range from the grand to the peculiar (count the mother-of-pearl bedroom suite among the latter), but Duke's taste in art, especially English portraiture, was pretty sharp: Of all the Newport mansions, Duke's has the best art collection. ⊠ *Bellevue Ave., at Ocean Dr.,* ☎ *401/849–7300.* ⛝ *$25 (first-come, first-served basis).* ⊙ *Tours leave from the Newport Gateway visitors center (23 America's Cup Avenue) at 10, 12:30, and 3.*

Dining and Lodging

$$$$ ✕ **The Black Pearl.** Visitors and yachters flock to this dignified converted dock shanty, where award-winning clam chowder is sold by the quart. Dining is in the casual tavern or the formal Commodore's Room (reservations essential). The latter serves an appetizer of black-and-blue tuna with red-pepper sauce. The French and American entrées include duck breast with green peppercorn sauce and swordfish with Dutch pepper butter. ⊠ *Bannister's Wharf,* ☎ *401/846–5264. Jacket required. AE, MC, V.*

$$$$ ✕ **Clarke Cooke House.** Waiters in tuxedos and the richly patterned cushions on wood chairs and booths underscore this restaurant's luxurious Colonial atmosphere. Formal dining is on the upper level, in a room with a timber-beam ceiling, green latticework, and water views; there's open-air dining in warm weather. The refined, pricey Mediterranean menu incorporates local seafood; game dishes often appear as specials. ⊠ *Bannister's Wharf,* ☎ *401/849–2900. Reservations essential. Jacket required. AE, D, DC, MC, V.*

$$$–$$$$ ✕ **Asterix & Obelix.** Danish chef John Bach-Sorensen makes fine din-
★ ing as fun and colorful as the madcap French cartoon strip after which this eatery was named. An auto repair garage before Sorensen took it over, the restaurant has a concrete floor painted to look like it's been covered with expensive tiling. The garage doors can be opened or closed depending on the weather. Asian twists enliven the French-influenced Mediterranean fare, and there is a carefully selected menu of wines, brandies, and aperitifs. Sunday brunch is served year-round. ⊠ *599 Thames St.,* ☎ *401/841–8833. AE, D, DC, MC, V. No lunch.*

$$$ ✕ **La Petite Auberge.** The colorful owner-chef, who once worked for General Charles de Gaulle, prepares such traditional delicacies as trout with almonds, duck flambé with orange sauce, and medallions of beef with goose-liver pâté. The setting for his exquisite cooking is a series of intimate rooms inside a Colonial house. In summer, dinner is served in the courtyard. ⊠ *19 Charles St.,* ☎ *401/849–6669. AE, MC, V.*

$$$ ✕ **Restaurant Bouchard.** There are regional takes on French cuisine at this upscale yet homey restaurant. Sautéed local cod, for instance, is topped with fresh Maine crab and asparagus, then finished with a light beurre blanc. ⊠ *505 Thames St.,* ☎ *401/846–0123. AE, D, MC, V.*

$$$ ✕ **White Horse Tavern.** The nation's oldest operating tavern, once a meeting house for Colonial Rhode Island's General Assembly, offers intimate dining with black-tie service, a top-notch wine cellar, and consistently excellent food. The tavern serves suave American cuisine, including local seafood and beef Wellington, along with more exotic entrées such as cashew-encrusted venison tenderloin topped with an apple-cider demi-glace. ⊠ *Marlborough and Farewell Sts.,* ☎ *401/849–3600,* WEB *www.whitehorsetavern.com. Reservations essential. Jacket required. No lunch Mon.–Wed. AE, D, DC, MC, V.*

$$–$$$ ✕ **The Mooring.** The seafood chowder at this family-oriented restaurant won the local cook-off so many times that it was removed from further competition. Slowly braised beef short loin and any fish special are good choices. In fine weather you can dine on the enclosed patio overlooking the harbor; on chilly winter evenings, take advantage of the open fire in the sunken interior room. ⊠ *Sayer's Wharf,* ☎ *401/846–2260. AE, D, DC, MC, V.*

$$–$$$ ✕ **Scales & Shells.** Busy, sometime noisy, but always excellent, this restaurant serves as many as 15 types of superbly fresh wood-grilled fish, including grilled lobster. The cooks occasionally send your server to the table with your future dinner so you'll know exactly how fresh the fish is. Similar offerings are available in a more formal setting upstairs at Upscales. Reservations are not accepted downstairs. ⊠ *527 Thames St.,* ☎ *401/848–9378. No credit cards.*

$$ ✕ **Flo's Clam Shack.** Fried seafood, steamed clams, cold beer, and the best raw bar in town keep the lines long here in summer. The rest of the year, Flo's, established in 1936, is a favorite with locals. An upstairs bar serves baked, chilled lobster, and outside seating is available. This place is across the street from First Beach. ⊠ *4 Wave Ave.,* ☎ *401/847–8141. Reservations not accepted. MC, V. Closed Jan.*

$$ ✕ **Puerini's.** The aroma of garlic and basil greets you as soon as you enter this laid-back neighborhood Italian restaurant. Lace curtains hang in the windows, and black-and-white photographs of Italy cover the soft-pink walls. The long and intriguing menu includes green noodles with chicken in marsala sauce, tortellini with seafood, and cavatelli with four cheeses. ⊠ *24 Memorial Blvd.,* ☎ *401/847–5506. Reservations not accepted. MC, V.*

$ ✕ **Ocean Coffee Roasters.** Known to locals as Wave Café, this nonchalant diner draws fans aplenty for fresh-roasted coffee and fresh-baked muffins as well as bagels, salads, and homemade Italian soups. Breakfast is served until 2 PM; lines can be long in summer. ⊠ *22 Washington Sq.,* ☎ *401/846–6060. Reservations not accepted. MC, V.*

$$$$ ✕🖬 **Vanderbilt Hall.** Originally built with funds donated by the Vanderbilt family, this former YMCA has been converted into the city's most sophisticated inn and restaurant. A butler greets arriving guests, a musician solos nightly at the grand piano in the center of the home, and there's a classy billiard room. Room 35 has a king-size bed and three windows with views of Newport Harbor and Trinity Church; suites have office space and sitting rooms. All the rooms have bathrobes and are decorated with antiques. The butler offers canapés and cocktails in the common room while patrons peruse the options for dinner: Continental cuisine, including beef Wellington, served on Wedgwood china at tables set with silver. ⊠ *41 Mary St., 02840,* ☎ *401/846–6200,* FAX *401/846–0701,* WEB *www.vanderbilthall.com. 40 rooms, 10 suites. Restaurant, in-room data ports, indoor pool, sauna, billiards. AE, D, DC, MC, V.*

$$$$ 🖬 **Cliffside Inn.** Grandeur and comfort come in equal supply at this swank Victorian home on a tree-lined street near the Cliff Walk. The rooms are furnished with Victorian antiques and down comforters, and many have bay windows; more than 100 paintings by artist Beatrice Turner, who lived in the house for many years and painted hundreds of self portraits, are a signature touch. The Governor's Suite (named for Governor Thomas Swann, of Maryland, who built the home in 1880) has a two-sided fireplace, a whirlpool bath, a four-poster king-size bed, and a brass birdcage shower. Seven other rooms also have whirlpool baths; 10 have working fireplaces. ⊠ *2 Seaview Ave., 02840,* ☎ *401/847–1811 or 800/845–1811,* FAX *401/848–5850,* WEB *www.cliffsideinn.com. 16 rooms. AE, D, DC, MC, V. BP.*

$$$$ 🏠 **Elm Tree Cottage.** William Ralph Emerson, Ralph Waldo's cousin, designed the Elm Tree, a shingle-style house. This 1882 architectural treasure has massive guest rooms (most with fireplaces) furnished with English antiques and decorated by owner Priscilla Malone, an interior designer. Guests rave about her creative breakfasts, served on linen-bedecked tables. The inn is no-smoking; there's a two-night minimum weekends, three on holiday weekends. ⊠ *336 Gibbs Ave., 02840,* ☎ *401/849–1610 or 800/882–3356,* FAX *401/849–2084,* WEB *www.elm-tree.com. 5 rooms, 1 suite. Lounge. AE, MC, V. BP.*

$$$$ 🏠 **Francis Malbone House.** The design of this stately painted-brick house
★ is attributed to Peter Harrison, the architect responsible for the Touro Synagogue and the Redwood Library. A lavish inn with period reproduction furnishings, the 1760 structure was tastefully doubled in size in the mid-1990s. The rooms in the main house are all in corners (with two windows) and look out over the courtyard, which has a fountain, or across the street to the harbor. Fifteen rooms have working fireplaces and many have whirlpool tubs. ⊠ *392 Thames St., 02840,* ☎ *401/846–0392 or 800/846–0392,* FAX *401/848–5956,* WEB *www.malbone.com. 16 rooms, 2 suites. AE, MC, V. BP.*

$$$–$$$$ 🏠 **Castle Hill Inn and Resort.** Much of the furniture at this inn is orig-
★ inal to the structure, a summer home built in 1874 on a cliff at the mouth of the Narragansett Bay. Views over the bay are enthralling, and the public areas have tremendous charm. Renovated in 1999, Castle Hill also has luxurious rooms in the more modern Beach Houses and Harbor Houses. The inn, 3 mi from the center of Newport, is famous for its Sunday brunches. On Sunday afternoons, the lawn is crowded with people enjoying cocktails. ⊠ *590 Ocean Dr., 02840,* ☎ *401/849–3800 or 888/466–1355,* FAX *401/849–3838,* WEB *www.castlehillinn.com. 35 rooms. Restaurant, 3 beaches. AE, D, MC, V. BP.*

$$$–$$$$ 🏠 **Hotel Viking.** An inn expressly built in 1926 for the guests of mansion owners, the redbrick Viking is elegantly situated at the north end of Bellevue Avenue. The wood paneling and original chandeliers evoke the hotel's sophisticated history. The place got a major sprucing-up in 2000 but retains its old-style grandeur. The roomy suites (one is 4,000 square ft) have refrigerators and VCRs. ⊠ *1 Bellevue Ave., 02840,* ☎ *401/847–3300 or 800/556–7126,* FAX *401/848–4864,* WEB *www.hotelviking.com. 218 rooms, 9 suites. Restaurant, bar, indoor pool, hot tub, sauna, meeting room. AE, D, DC, MC, V.*

$$$–$$$$ 🏠 **Hyatt Regency Newport.** On Goat Island across from the Colonial Point District, the Hyatt has great views of the harbor and the Newport Bridge. Most rooms have water views. There's free parking, and although the hotel is a 15-minute walk to Newport's center, bike and moped rentals are nearby. All rooms have oak furnishings and multicolor jewel-tone fabrics. ⊠ *1 Goat Island, 02840,* ☎ *401/851–1234,* FAX *401/846–7210,* WEB *www.hyatt.com. 264 rooms. Restaurant, indoor pool, saltwater pool, beauty salon, sauna, spa, tennis court, health club, racquetball, boating, meeting room. AE, D, DC, MC, V.*

$$$–$$$$ 🏠 **Inntowne.** This small town-house hotel is in the center of Newport, 1½ blocks from the harbor. The neatly appointed rooms are decorated in a floral motif. Light sleepers may prefer rooms on the upper floors, which let in less traffic noise. The staff members are on hand throughout the day to give sightseeing advice. ⊠ *6 Mary St., 02840,* ☎ *401/846–9200 or 800/457–7803,* FAX *401/846–1534,* WEB *www.newportrhodeisland.com/users/inntowne. 26 rooms. AE, MC, V. CP.*

$$$ 🏠 **Ivy Lodge.** The only B&B in the mansion district, this grand (though
★ small by Newport's standards) Victorian has gables and a Gothic turret. Designed by Stanford White, the home has 11 fireplaces, large and lovely rooms, a spacious dining room, window seats, and two common rooms. The defining feature is a Gothic-style oak entryway with

a three-story turned baluster staircase and a dangling wrought-iron chandelier. Summer guests congregate on the wraparound front porch, which has wicker chairs. ⊠ *12 Clay St., 02840,* ☏ *401/849–6865,* ℻ *401/849–2919. 7 rooms, 1 suite. AE, MC, V. BP.*

$$–$$$$ 🄷 **Newport Marriott.** This luxury hotel on the harbor at Long Wharf has an atrium lobby with marble floors and a nautical theme. Rooms that don't border the atrium overlook the city or the waterfront. Fifth-floor rooms facing the harbor have sliding French windows that open onto large decks. Rates vary greatly according to season and location; harbor-view rooms cost more. ⊠ *25 America's Cup Ave., 02840,* ☏ *401/849–1000 or 800/228–9290,* ℻ *401/849–3422,* 🕸 *www.court-yard.com. 317 rooms, 7 suites. Restaurant, bar, indoor pool, hot tub, sauna, health club, racquetball, meeting room. AE, D, DC, MC, V.*

$$–$$$ 🄷 **Admiral Benbow Inn.** Listed on the National Register of Historic Places, this tidy 1855 Victorian is ideally situated on Newport's tranquil Historic Hill, between Bellevue Avenue and Thames Street. Maple and pine trees shade the front yard. Period antiques decorate the rooms, each of which has either an antique brass or hand-carved wood bed. Two rooms have fireplaces, and one has a private deck with a harbor view. Kitchen facilities are available. ⊠ *93 Pelham St., 02840,* ☏ *401/846–4256,* ℻ *401/848–8006,* 🕸 *www.admiralsinns.com. 15 rooms. AE, D, MC, V. CP.*

$–$$ 🄷 **Harbor Base Pineapple Inn.** This basic, clean motel is the least expensive lodging in Newport. All rooms contain two double beds; some also have kitchenettes. Close to the naval base and jai alai, it's a five-minute drive from downtown. ⊠ *372 Coddington Hwy., 02840,* ☏ *401/847–2600,* 🕸 *www.newportrhodeisland.com/users/pineapple. 48 rooms. AE, D, DC, MC, V.*

Nightlife and the Arts

Detailed events calendars can also be found in *Newport This Week* and the *Newport Daily News.*

NIGHTLIFE

For a sampling of Newport's lively nightlife, you need only stroll down **Thames Street** after dark. The **Candy Store** (⊠ Bannister's Wharf, ☏ 401/849–2900) in the Clarke Cooke House restaurant is a snazzy place for a drink. There's a DJ during the summer at **The Cheeky Monkey,** (14 Perry Mill Wharf, ☏ 401/845–9494) where you can dance with the chic set; the mood at the bar is lighthearted and casual year-round. **Newport Blues Café** (⊠ 286 Thames St., ☏ 401/841–5510) hosts great blues performers. **One Pelham East** (⊠ 270 Thames St., ☏ 401/847–9460) draws a young crowd for progressive rock, reggae, and R&B.

The **JVC Newport Jazz Festival** (☏ 401/847–3700) takes place in mid-August. Performers in recent years have included Bobby Short, Dave Brubeck, Cassandra Wilson, John Zorn, and Stefan Harris.

THE ARTS

Murder-mystery plays are performed on Thursday evening from June to October at 8 PM at the **Astors' Beechwood** (⊠ 580 Bellevue Ave., ☏ 401/846–3772). **Newport Children's Theatre** (⊠ Box 144, ☏ 401/848–0266) mounts several productions each year. **Newport Playhouse & Cabaret** (⊠ 102 Connell Hwy., ☏ 401/848–7529) stages comedies and musicals; dinner packages are available.

The **Newport International Film Festival** (☏ 401/848–9443; 🕸 www.newportfilmfestival.com) a small but impressive festival, takes place in June.

Outdoor Activities and Sports

BASEBALL

Sunset League Baseball (✉ America's Cup Ave. and Marlborough St., ☎ 401/847–5609), an amateur league, has played at Cardines Field since 1908. The ticket price is $1, and the talent level is impressive.

BEACHES

Easton's Beach (✉ Memorial Blvd.), also known as First Beach, is popular for its carousel. **Fort Adams State Park** (✉ Ocean Dr.), a small beach with a picnic area and lifeguards in summer, has views of Newport Harbor and is fully sheltered from ocean swells. **Sachuest Beach,** or Second Beach, east of First Beach in the Sachuest Point area of Middletown, is a beautiful sandy area adjacent to the Norman Bird Sanctuary and Sachuest Wildlife Reserve. Dunes and a campground make it popular with young travelers and families. **Third Beach,** in the Sachuest Point area of Middletown, is on the Sakonnet River. It has a boat ramp and is a favorite of windsurfers.

BIKING

The 12-mi swing down Bellevue Avenue, along Ocean Drive and back, is a great route to ride your wheels. **Ten Speed Spokes** (✉ 18 Elm St., ☎ 401/847–5609) rents bikes for $25 per day.

BOATING

Adventure Sports (✉ The Inn at Long Wharf, America's Cup Ave., ☎ 401/849–4820) rents sailboats, kayaks, and canoes. **Newport Yacht Services** (✉ 580 Thames St., ☎ 401/846–7720) charters yachts. **Oldport Marine Services** (✉ Sayer's Wharf, ☎ 401/847–9109) operates harbor tours and daily and weekly crewed yacht charters, rents moorings, and provides launch services. **Sail Newport** (✉ Ft. Adams State Park, ☎ 401/846–1983) rents sailboats by the hour.

DIVING

Newport Diving Center (✉ 550 Thames St., ☎ 401/847–9293) operates charter dive trips, refills Nitrox, conducts PADI training and certification, and has rentals, sales, and service.

FISHING

Fishin' Off (✉ American Shipyard, Goat Island Causeway, ☎ 401/849–9642) runs charter fishing trips on a 36-ft Trojan. The **Saltwater Edge** (✉ 561 Thames St., ☎ 401/842–0062) sells fly-fishing tackle, gives lessons, and conducts guided trips. **Sam's Bait & Tackle** (✉ 36 Aquidneck Ave., ☎ 401/849–5909) stocks gear and live bait.

JAI ALAI

Newport Jai Alai (✉ 150 Admiral Kalbfus Rd., ☎ 401/849–5000) hosts live jai alai from March to mid-September. Simulcast racing and video slot machines are available year-round.

Shopping

Many of Newport's art and crafts galleries and antiques shops are on Thames Street; others are on Spring Street, Franklin Street, and at Bowen's and Bannister's wharves. The Brick Market area—between Thames Street and America's Cup Avenue—has more than 40 shops. Bellevue Avenue just south of Memorial Boulevard (near the International Tennis Hall of Fame) contains a strip of pricey shops with high-quality merchandise.

ANTIQUES

Aardvark Antiques (✉ 475 Thames St., ☎ 401/849–7233) carries architectural pieces such as mantels, doors, and stained glass; the nearby yard sells unique fountains and garden statuary. The 125 dealers at the **Armory** (✉ 365 Thames St., ☎ 401/848–2398), a vast 19th-century structure, carry antiques, china, and estate jewelry. **Harbor Antiques** (⊠ 134 Spring St., ☎ 401/848–9711) has a stock of unusual furniture and prints and glassware.

ART AND CRAFTS GALLERIES

Arnold Art Store and Gallery (⊠ 210 Thames St., ☎ 401/847–2273) has a large collection of marine-inspired paintings and prints. **DeBlois Gallery** (138 Bellevue Ave., ☎ 401/847–9977) exhibits the works of Newport's emerging artists.

MacDowell Pottery (⊠ 140 Spring St., ☎ 401/846–6313) showcases the wares of New England potters. The delicate, dramatic blown-glass gifts at **Thames Glass** (⊠ 688 Thames St., ☎ 401/846–0576) are designed by Matthew Buechner and created in the adjacent studio. **William Vareika Fine Arts** (⊠ 212 Bellevue Ave., ☎ 401/849–6149) exhibits and sells American paintings and prints from the 18th to the 20th century.

BEACH GEAR

Water Brothers (⊠ 39 Memorial Blvd., ☎ 401/849–4990) is the place to go for surf supplies, including bathing suits, wet suits, sunscreen, sunglasses, and surfboards.

BOOKS

The **Armchair Sailor** (⊠ 543 Thames St., ☎ 401/847–4252) stocks marine and travel books, charts, and maps.

CLOTHING

JT's Ship Chandlery (⊠ 364 Thames St., ☎ 401/846–7256) is a major supplier of clothing, marine hardware, and equipment. **Michael Hayes** (⊠ 204 Bellevue Ave., ☎ 401/846–3090) sells upscale clothing for men, women, and children. **Tropical Gangsters** (⊠ 375 Thames St., ☎ 401/847–9113) stocks hip clothes for men and women.

JEWELRY

Angela Moore (⊠ 119 Bellevue Ave., ☎ 401/849–1900 or 800/927–5470) designs jewelry and other accessories that have been featured in *Vogue*, *InStyle*, and other publications.

Portsmouth

65 *8 mi north of Newport.*

Portsmouth is now mainly a bedroom community for professionals who work in other parts of Rhode Island and Massachusetts, but it also has a topiary garden and a beach. Its most significant resident was its founder, Anne Hutchinson. A religious dissident and one of the country's first feminists, she led a group of settlers to the area in 1638 after being banished from the Massachusetts Bay Colony.

Half the fun of a trip to Portsmouth is a ride on the **Old Colony & Newport Railway,** which follows an 8-mi route along Narragansett Bay. The vintage diesel train and two century-old coaches make three-hour round-trips, with a 1¼-hour stop at the gardens. ⊠ *19 America's Cup Ave., Newport,* ☎ *401/624–6951,* WEB *www.ocnrr.com.* ⬚ *$6.* ☉ *May–mid-Nov.*

Green Animals, a large topiary garden on a Victorian estate, contains sculpted shrubs, flower gardens, winding pathways, and a variety of trees. Most notable are the animal-shape plants: an elephant, a camel, a giraffe, and even a teddy bear. Also on the grounds are a remarkable Victorian toy collection and a plant shop. ⊠ *Cory La. off Rte. 114,* ☎ *401/847–1000,* WEB *www.newportmansions.org.* ⬚ *$9.* ☉ *May–Oct., daily 10–5.*

Outdoor Activities and Sports

Sandy Point Beach (✉ Sandy Point Ave.) is a choice spot for families and beginning windsurfers because of the calm surf along the Sakonnet River.

En Route Route 77, the main thoroughfare to Little Compton, passes through **Tiverton Four Corners**, a great place to stretch your legs and catch your first breath of East Bay air. **Provender** (✉ 3883 Main Rd., ☎ 401/624–8096), in a former general store and post office, is a gourmet foods store, coffee shop, and bakery. Also within walking distance are a half-dozen galleries and gift shops. The delicious **Gray's Ice Cream** (✉ Intersection of Rtes. 77 and 179, ☎ 401/624–4500) is produced and sold in this stout building.

Little Compton

⑥⑥ *19 mi southeast of Portsmouth.*

The rolling estates, lovely homes, farmlands, woods, and gentle western shoreline make Little Compton one of the Ocean State's prettiest areas. Little Compton and Tiverton were part of Massachusetts until 1747—to this day, residents here often have more roots in Massachusetts than in Rhode Island. "Keep Little Compton little" is a popular sentiment, but considering the town's remoteness and its steep land prices, there may not be all that much to worry about.

Little Compton Commons (✉ Meetinghouse La.) is the epitome of a New England town square. As white as the clouds above, the spire of the Georgian-style United Congregational Church rises over the tops of adjacent oak trees. Within the triangular lawn is a cemetery with Colonial headstones, among them that of Elizabeth Padobie, said to be the first white girl born in New England. Surrounding the green is a rock wall and all the elements of a small community: town hall, a community center, the police station, and the school. You will find town squares only in a few northern Rhode Island towns, ones that were once a part of the Massachusetts Bay Colony. Rhode Islanders, adamant about separating church and state, did not favor this layout.

A neatly kept relic of Rhode Island living, the 1680 **Wilbor House** was occupied by eight generations of Wilburs—the first of which included 11 children born between 1690 and 1712. Curiously, later generations used a half-dozen variations on the spelling of the same last name. The Common Room is 17th century; the bedrooms 18th and 19th; the kitchen 19th; and the living room 18th. The barn museum holds a one-horse shay, an oxcart, and a buggy and coach. ✉ 548 W. Main Rd., ☎ 401/635–4035. 🎟 $4. ☉ Mid-June–mid-Sept., Thurs.–Sun. 2–5; mid-Sept.–early Oct., weekends 2–5.

Sakonnet Point, a surreal spit of land, reaches out toward three tiny islands. The point begins where Route 77 ends. The ½-mi hike to the tip of Sakonnet Point passes tide pools, a beach composed of tiny stone, and outcroppings that recall the surface of the moon. Parking is sometimes available in the lot adjacent to Sakonnet Harbor.

Tours and tastings are free at **Sakonnet Vineyard,** New England's largest winery. A few of its brands are well known, including Eye of the Storm, which was born of compromise: a power outage caused by a hurricane forced the wine makers to blend finished wine with what was in the vats. ✉ 162 W. Main Rd., ☎ 401/635–8486, 🕸 www.sakonnetwines.com. 🎟 Free. ☉ Oct.–May, daily 11–5, tours on the hr noon–4; June–Sept., daily 10–6, tours on the hr 11–5.

Dining and Lodging

$$ ✕ **Abraham Manchester's.** Little Compton's former general store houses a restaurant with a basic menu of chicken, steak, seafood, and pasta. Antiques adorn the walls of the bar and the dimly lit, dark-paneled dining room, enhancing the feel of history. Take time to cross the street and look for the Rhode Island Red Monument (actually a plaque in the ground)—this community developed the famous Rhode Island Red breed of chicken. ⊠ *Main Rd.,* ☎ *401/635–2700. MC, V.*

$–$$ ✕ **Commons Lunch.** This unpretentious old-Yankee restaurant, across from the church on the town square, opens daily at 5 AM. The food may not be spectacular, but it's reliable and priced to move. The menu is greasy-spoon standard, with Rhode Island favorites such as cabinets (milk shakes). ⊠ *South of Commons Rd.,* ☎ *401/635–4388. No credit cards. No dinner.*

$$ ⌶ **The Roost.** A former farmhouse amid the fields of Sakonnet Vineyards is an intimate B&B that's remote yet accessible to rural pleasures such as hiking, biking, and main-street shopping. Rooms are smartly furnished. Call well ahead for stays on summer weekends. ⊠ *170 W. Main Rd., 02837,* ☎ *401/635–8486,* ᶠᴬˣ *401/635–2101,* ᵂᴱᴮ *www.sakonnetwines.com. 3 rooms. AE, MC, V. CP.*

Outdoor Activities and Sports

FISHING

The 38-ft boat *Oceaneer* (⊠ Sakonnet Point Marina, ☎ 401/635–4292) can accommodate up to six people on chartered fishing trips.

HIKING

Wilbur Woods (⊠ Swamp Rd.), a 30-acre hollow with picnic tables and a waterfall, is a good place for a casual hike. A trail winds along and over Dundery Brook.

Newport County A to Z

To research prices, get advice from other travelers, and book travel arrangements, visit www.fodors.com.

AIRPORTS

Newport State Airport is 3 mi northeast of Newport. Charters fly from here to T. F. Green State Airport in Warwick, south of Providence. Cozy Cab runs a shuttle service ($15) between the airport and Newport's visitors bureau.

➤ AIRPORT INFORMATION: **Newport State Airport** (☎ 401/846–2200). **Cozy Cab** (☎ 401/846–2500).

BOAT & FERRY TRAVEL

The Jamestown and Newport Ferry Co. runs a passenger ferry about every 1½ hours from Newport's Bowen's Landing and Long Wharf (and, on request, Fort Adams and Goat Island) to Jamestown's Ferry Wharf. The ferry operates from Memorial Day to mid-October. Old Port Marine Company operates a water-taxi service for boaters in Newport Harbor.

➤ BOAT & FERRY INFORMATION: **Jamestown and Newport Ferry Co.** (☎ 401/423–9900). **Old Port Marine Company** (☎ 401/847–9109).

BUS TRAVEL

Rhode Island Public Transit Authority buses leave from Providence for Newport and also serve the city from other Rhode Island destinations.

➤ BUS INFORMATION: **Rhode Island Public Transit Authority** (RIPTA; ☎ 401/847–0209; 800/244–0444 in RI).

CAR TRAVEL

From Providence take I–95 east into Massachusetts and head south on Route 24. From South County, take U.S. 1 north to Route 138 east. From Boston take I–93 south to Route 24 south. With the exception of Ocean Drive, Newport is a walker's city. In summer, traffic thickens, and the narrow one-way streets can constitute an unbearable maze. It's worth parking in a pay lot and leaving your car behind while you visit in-town sights; one lot is at the Gateway Information Center.

EMERGENCIES

➤ HOSPITAL: **Newport Hospital** (✉ Friendship St., ☎ 401/846–6400).
➤ 24-HOUR PHARMACY: **Brooks Pharmacy** (✉ 268 Bellevue Ave., ☎ 401/849–4600).

LODGING

➤ LOCAL AGENTS: **Newport Reservations** (☎ 800/842–0102).

TOURS

More than a dozen yacht companies operate tours of Narragansett Bay and Newport Harbor. Outings usually last just two hours and cost about $25 per person. *Flyer Sailing,* a 57-ft catamaran, departs from Long Wharf. *Madeline,* a 72-ft schooner, departs from Bannister's Wharf. *RumRunner II,* a vintage 1929 motor yacht, once carried "hooch"; it leaves from Bannister's Wharf. *The Spirit of Newport,* a 200-passenger multideck ship, departs for tours of Narragansett Bay and Newport Harbor from the Newport Harbor Hotel, on America's Cup Avenue, from May to mid-October.

Viking Bus and Boat Tours of Newport conducts Newport tours in buses from April to October. One-hour boat tours of Narragansett Bay operate from mid-May to Columbus Day weekend. The Newport Historical Society sponsors walking tours on Saturday from May to November.
➤ TOUR OPERATORS: *Flyer Sailing* (☎ 401/848–2100). *Madeleine* (☎ 401/847–0298). *RumRunner II* (☎ 401/847–0299). *The Spirit of Newport* (☎ 401/849–3575). **Viking Bus and Boat Tours of Newport** (✉ Gateway Information Center, 23 America's Cup Ave., ☎ 401/847–6921). The **Newport Historical Society** (✉ 82 Touro St., ☎ 401/846–0813).

VISITOR INFORMATION

Newport County Convention and Visitors Bureau shows an orientation film and provides maps and advice.
➤ TOURIST INFORMATION: **Newport County Convention and Visitors Bureau** (✉ Gateway Information Center, 23 America's Cup Ave., ☎ 401/849–8048 or 800/326–6030 WEB www.gonewport.com).

RHODE ISLAND A TO Z

To research prices, get advice from other travelers, and book travel arrangements, visit www.fodors.com.

AIRPORTS

T. F. Green State Airport, 10 mi south of Providence, has scheduled daily flights by several major airlines, including American, Continental/Northwest, Southwest, United, and US Airways, with additional service by regional carriers. The main regional airports in Rhode Island are in Westerly, Newport State, and Block Island.
➤ AIRPORT INFORMATION: **T. F. Green State Airport** (✉ U.S. 1, Warwick, ☎ 401/737–4000).

BUS TRAVEL

Bonanza Bus Lines, Greyhound, and Peter Pan Bus Lines serve the Providence Bus Terminal. A shuttle service connects the Providence Bus Terminal with Kennedy Plaza in downtown Providence, where you can board the local public transit buses. Bonanza runs a bus from Boston's Logan Airport to Providence. Rhode Island Public Transit Authority buses crisscross the state.

➤ BUS INFORMATION: **Bonanza Bus Lines** (☎ 800/556–3815). **Greyhound** (☎ 800/231–2222). **Peter Pan Bus Lines** (☎ 800/237–8747). **Providence Bus Terminal** (✉ Bonanza Way, off Exit 25 from I–95, ☎ 401/751–8800) Kennedy Plaza (✉ Washington and Dorrance Sts.). **Bonanza. Rhode Island Public Transit Authority** (RIPTA; ☎ 401/781–9400; 800/244–0444 in RI).

CAR TRAVEL

Interstate 95, which cuts diagonally across the state, is the fastest route to Providence from Boston, coastal Connecticut, and New York City. Interstate 195 links Providence with New Bedford and Cape Cod. Route 146 connects Providence to Worcester and I–90, passing through the northeastern portion of the Blackstone Valley. U.S. 1 follows much of the Rhode Island coast east from Connecticut before turning north to Providence. Route 138 heads east from Route 1 to Jamestown, Newport, and Tiverton in easternmost Rhode Island.

The speed limit on interstate highways varies from 55 mph to 65 mph; state routes vary, with 55 mph the top speed. Right turns are permitted on red lights after stopping, except in downtown Providence. Free state maps are available at all chambers of commerce and at visitor information centers in Providence and Newport and at T. F. Green State Airport. The detailed *Street Atlas Rhode Island,* published by Arrow Map, Inc., is available at many bookstores and gas stations.

EMERGENCIES

➤ CONTACTS: **Ambulance, fire, police** (☎ 911).

LODGING

B&BS

Bed and Breakfast of Rhode Island, Inc. represents about 100 B&Bs.
➤ RESERVATION SERVICES: **Bed and Breakfast of Rhode Island, Inc.** (✉ Box 3291, Newport 02840, ☎ 401/849–1298 or 800/828–0000 WEB www.visitnewport.com/bedandbreakfast).

OUTDOORS & SPORTS

For information on pricing and where to buy licenses for freshwater fishing, contact the Department of Environmental Management's Division of Licensing. No license is needed for saltwater fishing.

One of the best trail guides for the region is the *AMC Massachusetts and Rhode Island Trail Guide,* available at local outdoors shops or from the Appalachian Mountain Club. The Rhode Island Audubon Society leads interesting hikes and field expeditions around the state.
➤ CONTACTS: **Division of Licensing** (☎ 401/222–3576). **Appalachian Mountain Club** (✉ 5 Joy St., Boston, MA 02114, ☎ 617/523–0636). **Rhode Island Audubon Society** (✉ 12 Sanderson Rd., Smithfield 02917, ☎ 401/949–5454).

TRAIN TRAVEL

Amtrak service between New York City and Boston makes stops at Westerly, Kingston, and Providence. Providence Station is the city's main station. The MBTA commuter rail service connects Boston and Prov-

idence during weekday morning and evening rush hours for about half
the cost of an Amtrak ride.

➤ TRAIN INFORMATION: **Amtrak** (☎ 800/872–7245, WEB www.
amtrak.com). **Providence Station** (✉ 100 Gaspee St., ☎ 401/727–
7379). **MBTA commuter rail service** (☎ 617/722–3200).

VISITOR INFORMATION

➤ TOURIST INFORMATION: **Rhode Island Department of Economic Development, Tourism Division** (✉ 1 W. Exchange St., Providence 02903,
☎ 401/222–2601 [ask to be transferred to Tourism Divison]; 800/556–
2484).

6 CONNECTICUT

The southern gateway to New England
is a small state with plenty of variety.
Southwestern Connecticut is home to
commuters, celebrities, and others who
enjoy its sophisticated atmosphere and
convenience to New York City. The
Connecticut River valley has a stretch of
river villages punctuated by a few small
cities and Hartford. The northwest's Litchfield
Hills have grand inns and rolling farmlands.
Along the southeastern coast are New
Haven, home to Yale and some fine
museums, and quiet shoreline villages.
The sparsely populated towns in the
northeast's Quiet Corner are known for
their antiquing potential.

Updated by
Michelle
Bodak Acri

ONNECTICUT MAY BE the third smallest state in the nation, but it is among the hardest to define. Indeed, you can travel from any point in the Nutmeg State, as it is known, to any other in less than two hours, yet the land you travel—fewer than 60 mi top to bottom and 100 mi across—is as varied as a drive across the country. Connecticut's 253 mi of shoreline blows salty sea air over such beach communities as Old Lyme and Stonington. The state's patchwork hills and peaked mountains fill the northwestern corner, and the once-upon-a-time mill towns line its rivers such as the Housatonic. Finally, Connecticut has seemingly endless farmland in the northeast, where cows just might outnumber people (and definitely outnumber the traffic lights), as well as chic bedroom communities of New York City such as Greenwich and New Canaan, where boutique shopping bags seem to be the dominant species. Each section of the state is unique; each defines Connecticut.

Just as diverse as the landscape are the state's residents, who numbered close to 3½ million at last count. There really is no such thing as the definitive Connecticut Yankee, however. Yes, families can trace their roots back to the 1600s, when Connecticut was founded as one of the 13 original colonies, but the state motto is also "He who transplanted still sustains." And so the face of the Nutmegger is that of the family from Naples who tend the pizza ovens in New Haven and the farmer in Norfolk whose land dates back five generations, the grandmother from New Britain who makes the state's best pierogi and the ladies who lunch from Westport, not to mention the celebrity nestled in the Litchfield Hills and the Bridgeport entrepreneur working to close the gap between Connecticut's struggling cities and its affluent suburbs.

A unifying characteristic of the Connecticut Yankee, however, is his or her propensity for inventiveness. You might say that Nutmeggers have been setting trends for centuries. They are historically known for both their intellectual abilities and their desire to have a little fun. As evidence of the former, consider that the nation's first public library was opened in New Haven in 1656 and its first statehouse built in Hartford in 1776; Tapping Reeve opened the first law school in Litchfield in 1784; and West Hartford's Noah Webster published the first dictionary in 1806. As proof of the latter, note that Lake Compounce in Bristol was the country's first amusement park, Bethel's P. T. Barnum staged the first three-ring circus, and the hamburger, the lollipop, the Frisbee, and the Erector set were all invented within the state's 5,009 square mi.

Not surprisingly, Nutmeggers have a healthy respect for their history. For decades, the Mystic Seaport museum, which traces the state's rich maritime past through living history exhibits, has been the premier tourist attraction. Today, however, slot machines in casinos in the southeastern woods of Connecticut are giving the sailing ships a run for their money. Foxwoods Casino near Ledyard, opened in 1992 and run by the Mashantucket Pequots, is the world's largest casino—it draws more than 55,000 visitors per day—and the Mohegan Sun Casino in nearby Uncasville is working hard to catch up. Thanks in large part to the lure of these casinos, not to mention the state's rich cultural attractions, cutting-edge restaurants, shopping outlets, first-rate lodgings, and abundance of natural beauty (including 91 state parks and 30 state forests), tourism is now the second leading industry in the state. Anyone who has explored even part of Connecticut will discover that a small state can have big diversity—and appeal.

Pleasures and Pastimes

Antiquing

Although you'll find everything from chic boutiques to vast outlet malls in Connecticut, the state is an antiquer's paradise. The Litchfield Hills region, in the state's northwest corner, is the heart of antiques country. In the Quiet Corner, east of the Connecticut River, are several hundred dealers and complexes. Mystic, Old Saybrook, and other towns along the coast are filled with markets, galleries, and shops, many specializing in antique prints, maps, books, and collectibles.

Dining

Call it the fennel factor or the arugula influx: southern New England has witnessed a gastronomic revolution in recent years. Preparation and ingredients reflect the culinary trends of nearby Manhattan and Boston; indeed, the quality and diversity of Connecticut restaurants now rival those of such sophisticated metropolitan areas. Although traditional favorites remain—such as New England clam chowder, buttery lobster rolls, Yankee pot roast, and grilled haddock—Grand Marnier is now favored on ice cream over hot fudge sauce, sliced duck is wrapped in phyllo and served with a ginger-plum sauce (the orange glaze decidedly absent), and everything from lavender to fresh figs is used to season and complement dishes. Dining in the cities and suburbs is increasingly international: you'll find Indian, Vietnamese, Thai, Malaysian, South American, and Japanese restaurants, even Spanish tapas bars. The locals are also going a tad decadent; designer martinis are quite the rage, brew pubs have popped up all around the state—even caviar is making a comeback. The one drawback of this turn toward sophistication is that finding an under-$10 dinner entrée is difficult. For price-category information, *see* Dining *in* Smart Travel Tips.

Fishing

Connecticut teems with possibilities for anglers, from deep-sea fishing in coastal waters to fly-fishing in the state's many streams. Try the Litchfield Hills region for freshwater fish: if you're just a beginner, don't fret—you'll be catching trout or bass in the Housatonic River in no time. Southeastern Connecticut is the charter- and party-boat capital of the state. Charter fishing boats take passengers out on Long Island Sound for half-day, full-day, and overnight trips.

Lodging

Connecticut has plenty of business-oriented chain hotels and low-budget motels, but the state's unusual inns, resorts, bed-and-breakfasts, and country hotels are far more atmospheric and typical of New England. You'll pay dearly for rooms in summer on the coast and in autumn in the hills, where thousands peek at the changing foliage. Rates are lowest in winter, but so are the temperatures, making spring the best time for bargain seekers to visit. For price-category information, *see* Lodging *in* Smart Travel Tips.

State Parks

Sixty percent of Connecticut is forest land, some of it under the jurisdiction of the state parks division, which also manages several beaches on the southern shoreline. Many parks have campgrounds. Trails meander through most of the parks—the hiking is especially spectacular around the cool, clear water at Lake Waramaug State Park and the 200-ft-high waterfall at Kent Falls State Park. Popular Gillette Castle State Park in East Haddam has several trails, some on former railroad beds. Some state parks have no entrance fees year-round. At others the fee varies ($5–$12), depending on the time of year, day of the week, and whether or not your car bears a Connecticut license plate.

Exploring Connecticut

Southwestern Connecticut contains the wealthy coastal communities. Moving east along the coast (in most states you usually travel north or south along the coast, but in Connecticut you actually travel east or west), you'll come to New Haven and the southeastern coast, which is broken by many small bays and inlets. The Quiet Corner in the northeast, bordered by Rhode Island to the east and Massachusetts to the north, contains rolling hills and tranquil countryside. To the west are the fertile farmland of the Connecticut River valley and the state's capital, Hartford. In the northwestern part of the state is the Litchfield Hills area, covered with mi of forests, lakes, and rivers.

Numbers in the text and in the margin correspond to numbers on the maps: Southwestern Connecticut, Connecticut River Valley, Downtown Hartford, Litchfield Hills, Southeastern Connecticut, Downtown New Haven, and The Quiet Corner.

Great Itineraries

The Nutmeg State is a confluence of different worlds, where farm country meets country homes, and fans of the New York Yankees meet downeastern Yankees. To get the best sense of this variety, especially if you have only a few days, start in the scenic Litchfield Hills, where you can see historic town greens and trendy cafés juxtaposed in a way that's uniquely Connecticut. If you have a bit more time, head south to the wealthy southwestern corner of the state and then over to New Haven, with its cultural pleasures. If you have five days or a week (the minimum time needed to truly sample the state's myriad flavors), take in the capital city of Hartford and the surrounding towns of the Connecticut River valley and head down to the southeastern shoreline. If you have kids or an interest in the sea, Mystic alone could occupy a few days.

IF YOU HAVE 1 DAY

Begin a day in the Litchfield Hills in **New Preston** ㉝ and then head for Lake Waramaug. In West Cornwall, near **Cornwall** ㉟, have a look at the state's largest covered bridge. Working your way north, stop in **Lakeville** ㊱ and **Salisbury** ㊲ (a good place to stop for lunch). Turning south, spend a couple of hours in **Litchfield** ㊸, where you can tour historic houses before continuing south via **Bethlehem** ㊺ to **Woodbury** ㊼ to visit the town's churches and antiques shops.

IF YOU HAVE 2 DAYS

Old Saybrook ㊶, once a lively ship-building and fishing town, is a picture-perfect example of the Connecticut shoreline. Start your day here with some shopping on Main Street or a stroll along the coastline. Next, head across the Connecticut River to **Old Lyme** ㊷, home to the Florence Griswold Museum, where members of the Old Lyme Impressionist Art Colony once lived and painted *en plein air.* Continue up the coast, stopping if you like in **Waterford** ㊸, to take in the glorious water views at Harkness Memorial State Park, or in **Groton** ㊼ to see the world's first nuclear-powered submarine and the Submarine Force Museum. On your way to **Mystic** ㊽, stop in Noank for a late lunch or early dinner of lobster-in-the-rough seated at a picnic table at the edge of Noank Harbor. End your day in Mystic, where you'll find a wide assortment of hotels, inns, and restaurants to chose from. You won't have far to travel on day two: Mystic is home to the highly esteemed Mystic Seaport Museum and Mystic Aquarium, which can easily fill your day. Afterward, if you have the stamina, head inland to **Ledyard** ㊻ and try your luck at Foxwood Resort Casino's 5,500-plus slot machines—it's open 24 hours.

Connecticut

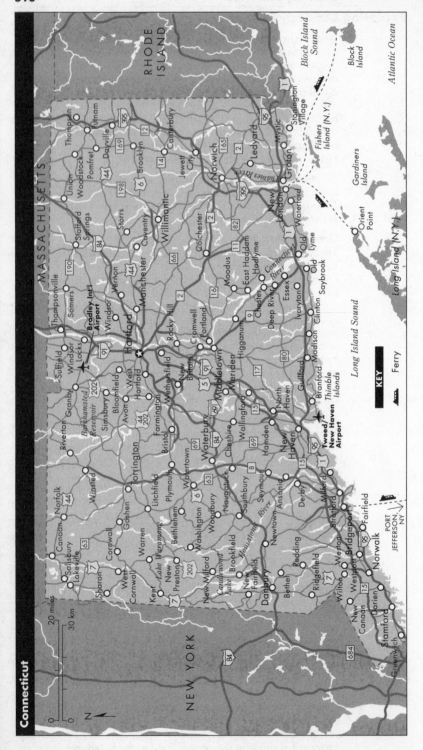

MASSACHUSETTS

RHODE ISLAND

NEW YORK

Atlantic Ocean

Block Island Sound

Block Island

Fishers Island (N.Y.)

Gardiners Island

Orient Point

Long Island (N.Y.)

Long Island Sound

PORT JEFFERSON, NY

KEY

Ferry

N

20 miles

30 km

Thompson
Putnam
Woodstock
Pomfret
Dayville
Union
Brooklyn
Canterbury
Jewett City
Norwich
Ledyard
Mystic
Stonington Village
Groton
Stafford Springs
Storrs
Coventry
Willimantic
Colchester
New London
Waterford
Somers
Thompsonville
Vernon
Manchester
Moodus
East Haddam
Hadlyme
Old Lyme
Bradley Int'l Airport
Windsor
Rocky Hill
Portland
Chester
Deep River
Essex
Old Saybrook
Suffield
Windsor Locks
Hartford
Cromwell
Higganum
Ivoryton
Clinton
Granby
West Hartford
Wethersfield
New Britain
Middletown
Madison
Guilford
Branford
Riverton
Bloomfield
Avon
Farmington
Meriden
Wallingford
North Haven
Thimble Islands
Norfolk
Canaan
Simsbury
Bristol
Cheshire
Hamden
New Haven
Tweed/ New Haven Airport
Winsted
Torrington
Watertown
Waterbury
Southbury
Seymour
Ansonia
Derby
Milford
Goshen
Litchfield
Plymouth
Naugatuck
Stratford
Fairfield
Cornwall
Warren
Washington
Woodbury
Newtown
Bridgeport
Salisbury
Lakeville
West Cornwall
Bethlehem
Brookfield
Redding
Weston
Westport
Norwalk
Sharon
Kent
New Preston
New Milford
New Fairfield
Danbury
Bethel
Ridgefield
Wilton
New Canaan
Darien
Stamford
Greenwich

Burkhamsted Reservoir
Lake Waramaug
Candlewood Lake
Housatonic River
Naugatuck River
Connecticut River
Thames River

Greenwich ①, a wealthy community with grand homes and great restaurants, is a good starting point for a several-day tour that begins near New York. From here head to **Stamford** ②, where you can visit the Whitney Museum of American Art at Champion or hit the mall across the street. East along the coast is **Norwalk** ③, whose SoNo commercial district and Maritime Aquarium are popular attractions. Have dinner in **Westport** ⑨, and end your first day in ⛯ **Ridgefield** ⑥. After touring Ridgefield the next morning, head for the Litchfield Hills, driving north via **Cornwall** ㉟ to **Norfolk** ㊳. Then it's south to **Litchfield** ㊸ and ⛯ **New Preston** ㉝, where you may want to conclude your day. If not, travel a little farther south to charming ⛯ **Washington** ㊻. Begin day three in **Woodbury** ㊼ and then head to **New Haven** ㊿–㊾. Near the Yale University campus are many great museums, shops, and restaurants.

With five days you can explore some of the state's cities as well as its historic interior towns and coastal villages. Spend the morning of your first day in **Hartford** ⑳–㉗ and the early part of the afternoon in **West Hartford** ㉘ before heading to ⛯ **Farmington** ㉙, which has two excellent house museums, and ⛯ **Simsbury** ㉚, where you can visit the Phelps Homestead. Spend the night in either town. On your second day, head west to **Woodbury** ㊼, stopping in **Litchfield** ㊸ and **Kent** ㉞. Stay the night in ⛯ **Washington** ㊻ or ⛯ **Ridgefield** ⑥. Begin your third day in southwestern Connecticut in **Greenwich** ①, followed by stops in **Stamford** ②, **Westport** ⑨, and **Bridgeport** ⑪. Spend the remainder of your day in ⛯ **New Haven** ㊿–㊾. Start your fourth day in **Essex** ⑬ and visit the Connecticut River Museum. At Gillette Castle State Park in **East Haddam** ⑯ you can tour the hilltop estate built by the actor William Gillette. From here, backtrack to the coastal town of **Old Saybrook** ㊽ and then cross the river to ⛯ **Old Lyme** ㊾, a former art colony. On the fifth day, continue touring the coast, starting in either **New London** ㊿ or **Groton** ㊿, and head east toward **Mystic** ㊿. Take time to visit Mystic Seaport before heading to the little village of **Stonington** ㊿.

When to Tour Connecticut

Connecticut is lovely year-round, but fall and spring are particularly appealing times to visit. A drive in fall along the rolling hills of the state's back roads or the Merritt Parkway (a National Scenic Byway) is a memorable experience. Leaves of yellow, orange, and red color the fall landscape, but the state blooms in springtime, too—town greens are painted with daffodils and tulips, and blooming trees punctuate the rich green countryside. Many attractions that close in winter reopen in April or May. Summer, of course, is prime time for most attractions; travelers have the most options then but also plenty of company, especially along the shore.

SOUTHWESTERN CONNECTICUT

Southwestern Connecticut is a rich swirl of old New England and new New York. This region consistently reports the highest cost of living and most expensive homes of any area in the country. Its bedroom towns are home primarily to white-collar executives; some still make the nearly two-hour dash to and from New York, but most enjoy a more civilized morning drive to Stamford, which is reputed to have more corporate headquarters per square mi than any other U.S. city. Strict zoning has preserved a certain privacy and rusticity uncommon in other such densely populated areas, and numerous celebrities—Paul Newman, David Letterman, Vince McMahon, and Mel Gibson, among them—live in Fairfield County.

Venture away from the wealthy communities, and you'll discover cities struggling in different stages of urban renewal: Stamford, Norwalk, Bridgeport, and Danbury. These four have some of the region's best cultural and shopping opportunities, but the economic disparity between Connecticut's troubled cities and its upscale towns is perhaps nowhere more visible than in Fairfield County.

Greenwich

❶ *28 mi northeast of New York City, 64 mi southwest of Hartford.*

You'll have no trouble believing that Greenwich is one of the wealthiest towns in the United States when you drive along U.S. 1 (called Route 1 by the locals, and which goes by the names West Putnam Avenue, East Putnam Avenue, and the Post Road, among others), where the streets are lined with ritzy car dealers, posh boutiques, and chic restaurants. The median price of a house sold in Greenwich is $485,000; the average is more than $1.4 million. In other words, bring your charge cards.

The **Bruce Museum** is a must-visit for both kids and adults. A section devoted to environmental history has a wigwam, a spectacular mineral collection, a marine touch tank, and a 16th-century woodland diorama. There's also a small but worthwhile collection of American Impressionist paintings. ⊠ *1 Museum Dr. (I–95, Exit 3),* ☎ *203/869–0376,* WEB *www.brucemuseum.com.* ⊠ *$4, free on Tues.* ⊙ *Tues.–Sat. 10–5, Sun. 1–5.*

The small, barn-red **Putnam Cottage,** built in 1690 and operated as Knapp's Tavern during the Revolutionary War, was a frequent meeting place of Revolutionary War hero General Israel Putnam. You can meander through an herb garden and examine the cottage's Colonial furnishings and fieldstone fireplaces. ⊠ *243 E. Putnam Ave./U.S. 1,* ☎ *203/869–9697.* ⊠ *$4.* ⊙ *Apr.–Dec., Wed., Fri., and Sun. 1–4.*

The circa-1732 **Bush–Holley Historic Site,** a handsome central-chimney saltbox, contains a wonderful collection of 19th- and 20th-century artworks by sculptor John Rogers, potter Leon Volkmar, and painters Childe Hassam, Elmer Livingstone MacRae, and John Twachtman. The visitor center, set in the historic site's circa-1805 storehouse, holds exhibition galleries and a gift shop. ⊠ *39 Strickland Rd.,* ☎ *203/869–6899.* ⊠ *$6.* ⊙ *Jan.–Mar., Sat. 11–4, Sun. 1–4; Apr.–Dec., Wed.–Fri. noon–4, Sat. 11–4, Sun. 1–4.*

More than 1,000 species of flora and fauna have been recorded at the 522-acre **Audubon Center** in northern Greenwich, where exhibits survey the local environment. 15 mi of trails traverse woods and fields. ⊠ *613 Riversville Rd.,* ☎ *203/869–5272,* WEB *www.greenwich.center.audubon.org.* ⊠ *$3.* ⊙ *Daily 9–5.*

Dining and Lodging

$$–$$$$ ✕ **Dome.** Eclectic contemporary fare with shock appeal is served in a sophisticated, arty setting with colorful murals, faux leopard carpeting, and bright blue banquettes. Standouts have been sesame-peanut glass noodles and lacquered tuna with wasabi caviar. There is also a wide assortment of veggie risottos and napoleons. ⊠ *253 Greenwich Ave.,* ☎ *203/661–3443. AE, DC, MC, V.*

$$–$$$ ✕ **Restaurant Jean-Louis.** Roses, Limoges china, and white tablecloths
★ with lace underskirts complement this restaurant's world-class cuisine. On any given night, the five-course Celebration Menu or the four-course Le Classic Menu might include diced vegetables cooked in saffron bouil-

Southwestern Connecticut

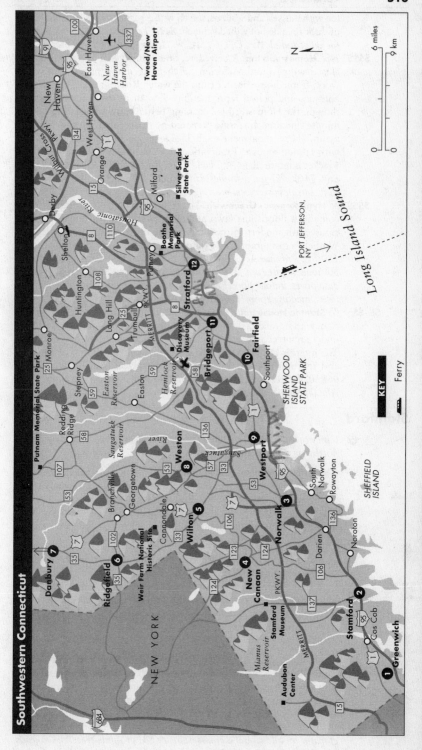

New Haven

Tweed/New
Haven Airport

New
Haven Harbor

East Haven

West Haven

Orange

Milford

Silver Sands
State Park

Derby

Shelton

Putney

Boothe
Memorial Park

Stratford **12**

Housatonic River

Huntington

Long Hill

Trumbull

Monroe

Stepney

Putnam Memorial State Park

Redding
Ridge

Easton

Easton
Reservoir

Hemlock
Reservoir

Discovery
Museum

Bridgeport **11**

Fairfield **10**

Southport

SHERWOOD
ISLAND
STATE PARK

PORT JEFFERSON,
NY

Long Island Sound

Branchville

Georgetown

Saugatuck
Reservoir

Weston **8**

Saugatuck
River

Westport **9**

Danbury **7**

Ridgefield **6**

Weir Farm National
Historic Site

Cannondale

Wilton **5**

Norwalk **3**

South
Norwalk

Rowayton

SHEFFIELD
ISLAND

N E W   Y O R K

New
Canaan **4**

Stamford
Museum

Miamus
Reservoir

MERRITT PKWY

Darien

Noroton

Audubon
Center

Stamford **2**

Cos Cob

Greenwich **1**

KEY

Ferry

6 miles

9 km

N

lon with mussels and scallops, served with a parsley coulis, or roast breast of duck on a bed of wilted spinach. ⊠ *61 Lewis St.,* ☎ *203/622–8450. Jacket required. AE, D, DC, MC, V. No lunch Sat. Closed Sun.*

$$$$
★ ✕🏨 **Homestead Inn.** A belvedere, ornate bracketed eaves, and an enclosed wraparound Victorian porch grace this enormous Italianate wood-frame house not far from the water. Rooms are decorated with antiques and period reproductions. For all its architectural appeal, though, the Homestead is becoming better known for the up-to-the-minute fine French cuisine prepared by master chef Thomas Henkelmann. The seasonal menu might list Dover sole filets poached and filled with salmon mousse. Reservations are essential for dinner, for which a jacket is required. ⊠ *420 Field Point Rd.,* ☎ *203/869–7500,* ℻ *203/869–7502,* 🌐 *www.homesteadinn.com. 17 rooms, 6 suites. Restaurant, business services, meeting room. AE, MC, V.*

$$$$
🏨 **Hyatt Regency Greenwich.** The Hyatt's vast but comfortable atrium contains a flourishing lawn and abundant flora. The rooms are spacious, with modern furnishings and many amenities. The pleasant Winfield's restaurant serves innovative renditions of classic dishes. ⊠ *1800 E. Putnam Ave., 06870,* ☎ *203/637–1234,* ℻ *203/637–2940,* 🌐 *www.hyatt.com. 374 rooms, 16 suites. Restaurant, bar, in-room data ports, indoor pool, beauty salon, sauna, health club, business services, meeting room. AE, D, DC, MC, V.*

$$–$$$
🏨 **Stanton House Inn.** The original structure of this Federal-style mansion, within walking distance of downtown, was built in 1840. In 1899, under architect Stanford White's supervision, the house was enlarged. The interior has been carefully decorated with a mixture of antiques and reproductions; two rooms have fireplaces. ⊠ *76 Maple Ave., 06830,* ☎ *203/869–2110,* ℻ *203/629–2116. 24 rooms, 2 suites. Pool. AE, D, MC, V. No smoking. CP.*

Stamford

❷ *6 mi northeast of Greenwich, 38 mi southwest of New Haven, 33 mi northeast of New York City.*

Glitzy office buildings, chain hotels, and major department stores are among the new landmarks in revitalized Stamford, the most dynamic city on the southwestern shore. Restaurants, nightclubs, and shops line Atlantic and lower Summer streets, poised to harness the region's affluence and satisfy the desire of suburbanites to spend an exciting night on the town without having to travel to New York City.

The primary focus of the **Whitney Museum of American Art Fairfield County,** a facility affiliated with the Whitney Museum in New York City, is 20th-century American painting and photography. Past exhibitions (there is no permanent collection) have included works by Edward Hopper, Alexander Calder, and Georgia O'Keeffe. Free gallery talks are held on Tuesday, Thursday, and Saturday at 12:30. ⊠ *400 Atlantic St.,* ☎ *203/358–7630.* 🎟 *Free.* ☉ *Tues.–Sat. 11–5.*

☙ Oxen, sheep, pigs, and other animals roam the **Stamford Museum and Nature Center,** a New England–style farmstead with many nature trails for visitors to explore. Exhibits survey natural history, art, and Americana. Two enjoyable times to visit are spring harvest and maple-sugaring season—call for exact dates. ⊠ *39 Scofieldtown Rd./Rte. 137,* ☎ *203/322–1646,* 🌐 *www.stamfordmuseum.org.* 🎟 *Grounds $5, planetarium an additional $2, observatory $3; grounds free.* ☉ *Grounds Mon.–Sat. 9–5, Sun. 1–5; farm daily 9–5; planetarium shows Sun. 3 PM; observatory Fri. 8–10 PM.*

The 64-acre **Bartlett Arboretum,** owned by the University of Connecticut, holds natural woodlands, cultivated gardens, marked ecology trails, a swamp walk, and a pond. The wildflower garden is stunning in the spring. ⊠ *151 Brookdale Rd., off High Ridge Rd. (Merritt Pkwy., Exit 35),* ☎ *203/322–6971.* ⌨ *Free.* ☉ *Grounds daily 8:30– dusk, visitor center weekdays 9–4.*

Dining and Lodging

\$\$–\$\$\$ ✕ **Beacon.** Wraparound harbor views and a brick exterior highlight
★ this stylish waterfront restaurant. Its open kitchen prepares shared platters—try the one with house-made sausages, lamb, chicken, and chorizo—and stand-out entrées such as Argentine ranch-grazed rib-eye steak and grilled calves' livers with apple-soaked bacon. If you want to linger before or after dinner, head to the bar upstairs for some lively chatter. ⊠ *183 Harbor Dr.,* ☎ *203/327–4600. AE, MC, V.*

\$\$–\$\$\$ ✕ **Druid Restaurant.** Upscale contemporary Continental fare is the focus at this restaurant on bustling Bedford Street. The Tudor-style dining room has elaborate woodwork, antiques, white linens, and gleaming oak floors reminiscent of an Irish manor house. It seems an appropriate setting for favorite dishes such as pan-roasted pheasant and lamb carpaccio. ⊠ *120 Bedford St.,* ☎ *203/316–8588. AE, D, DC, MC, V. Closed Sun.*

\$\$ ✕ **Macarena.** The virgin of Macarena was the patron saint of bullfighting. This restaurant, which has infused a touch of Spain into downtown, has a colorful mural of a Spanish matador as the focus of its dining room. The cuisine ranges from such tasty tapas as tortilla española and roasted peppers stuffed with shrimp and saffron-flavored rice, to hearty portions of paella. ⊠ *78 W. Park Pl.,* ☎ *203/323– 7421. AE, D, DC, MC, V. No lunch weekends.*

\$\$\$\$ 🏨 **Stamford Marriott Hotel.** The Marriott stands out for its up-to-date facilities and convenience to trains and airport buses. Furnishings are modern and comfortable. ⊠ *2 Stamford Forum, 06901,* ☎ *203/357– 9555,* ℻ *203/324–6897,* ⛛ *www.marriott.com. 499 rooms, 7 suites. Restaurant, bar, indoor-outdoor pool, barbershop, beauty salon, basketball, health club, racquetball. AE, D, DC, MC, V.*

\$\$\$\$ 🏨 **Westin Stamford.** The ultramodern entrance of this downtown luxury hotel should prepare you for the dramatic atrium lobby, which has a brass-and-glass-enclosed gazebo. The attractive rooms are understated and elegant, with subdued colors and comfortable wing chairs; bathrooms are spacious. ⊠ *1 First Stamford Pl.,* ☎ *203/967–2222,* ℻ *203/ 967–3475,* ⛛ *www.starwood.com. 470 rooms, 28 suites. Restaurant, indoor pool, 2 tennis courts, health club, meeting room. AE, D, DC, MC, V. CP.*

Nightlife and the Arts

NIGHTLIFE

For alternative dance music try the **Art Bar** (⊠ 84 W. Park Pl., ☎ 203/ 973–0300), which draws a collegiate crowd. At the **Terrace Club** (⊠ 1938 W. Main St., ☎ 203/961–9770) you can dance to everything from ballroom and country western to Top 40 and Latin. **Tigin Pub** (⊠ 175 Bedford St., ☎ 203/353–8444) has the feel of an Irish pub; there's live music Sunday nights.

THE ARTS

The **Stamford Center for the Arts** (☎ 203/325–4466) presents everything from one-act plays and comedy shows to musicals and film festivals. Performances are held at the Rich Forum (⊠ 307 Atlantic St.) and the Palace Theatre (⊠ 61 Atlantic St.). The **Stamford Symphony Orchestra** (☎ 203/325–1407) has performances from September to April, including a family concert series. The **Connecticut Grand Opera and**

Orchestra (☎ 203/327–2867) perform at the Palace Theatre. Opera season runs from September to May.

Outdoor Activities and Sports

The greens fee at the 18-hole, par-72 **Sterling Farms Golf Course** (✉ 1349 Newfield Ave., ☎ 203/461–9090) is $45; an optional cart costs $24.

Shopping

The **Stamford Town Center** (✉ 100 Greyrock Pl., ☎ 203/356–9700) houses 130 chiefly upscale shops, including Saks Fifth Avenue, Talbots, a Pottery Barn Studio Store, and Williams-Sonoma. Northern Stamford's **United House Wrecking** (✉ 535 Hope St., ☎ 203/348–5371) sells acres of architectural artifacts, decorative accessories, antiques, nautical items, and lawn and garden furnishings.

Norwalk

❸ *14 mi northeast of Stamford, 47 mi northeast of New York City.*

In the 19th century, Norwalk became a major New England port and also manufactured pottery, clocks, watches, shingle nails, and paper. It later fell into a state of neglect, in which it remained for much of the 20th century. During the past decade, however, Norwalk's coastal business district has been the focus of a major redevelopment project. Art galleries, restaurants, and trendy boutiques have blossomed on and around Washington Street; the stretch is now known as the **SoNo** (short for South Norwalk) commercial district.

Norwalk is the home of Yankee Doodle Dandies: in 1756, Colonel Thomas Fitch threw together a motley crew of Norwalk soldiers and led them off to fight at Fort Crailo, near Albany, New York. Supposedly, Norwalk's women gathered feathers for the men to wear as plumes in their caps in an effort to give them some appearance of military decorum. Upon the arrival of these foppish warriors, one of the British officers sarcastically dubbed them "macaronis"—slang for dandies. The saying caught on, and so did the song.

★ ♨ The cornerstone of the SoNo district is the **Maritime Aquarium at Norwalk,** a 5-acre waterfront center that explores the ecology and history of Long Island Sound. The 20 habitats include the vast Open Ocean Tank and separate otter and seal areas; a new Environmental Education Center recently opened. Besides the huge aquarium, there are marine-mammal cruises aboard the *Oceanic* and an IMAX theater. Although not as popular as Mystic Seaport, the aquarium is one of the state's most worthwhile attractions—especially for families. ✉ *10 N. Water St.,* ☎ *203/852–0700,* 🌐 *www.maritimeaquarium.org.* 🎟 *Aquarium $8.75, IMAX theater $6.75, combined $13.25.* ☺ *Labor Day–June, daily 10–5; July–Labor Day, daily 10–6.*

Restoration continues at the **Lockwood-Mathews Mansion Museum,** an ornate tribute to Victorian decorating that was the summer home of LeGrand Lockwood in the late 19th century. It's hard not to be impressed by the octagonal rotunda and 50 rooms of gilt, frescoes, marble, woodwork, and etched glass. ✉ *295 West Ave.,* ☎ *203/838–9799,* 🌐 *www.lockwoodmathews.org.* 🎟 *$8.* ☺ *Mid-Mar.–Dec., Wed.–Sun. 12–5, or by appointment.*

The 3-acre park at the **Sheffield Island Lighthouse** is a prime spot for a picnic. The 1868 lighthouse has four levels and 10 rooms to explore. *Ferry service from Hope Dock (corner of Washington and North Water Sts.),* ☎ *203/838–9444 ferry and lighthouse,* 🌐 *www.seaport.org.* 🎟 *Round-trip ferry service and lighthouse tour $15.* ☺ *Ferry early May–mid-June and mid-Sept.–mid-Oct., weekends 11 and 2;*

mid-June–Labor Day, weekdays 11 and 3:30, weekends 10, 1, and 4.
Lighthouse open when ferry is docked.

The colorful exhibits at the **Stepping Stones Museum for Children,** encourage hands-on exploration for kids ages 1–10, and incorporate the themes of science and technology, arts and culture, and heritage. An "I Spy Connecticut" exhibit, where kids can climb aboard a train, fly a helicopter, or submerge themselves in a research submarine, combines educational role-playing with an introduction to the state's landmarks, landscapes, and history. ☒ *Mathews Park, 303 West Ave.,* ☎ *203/899–0606,* WEB *www.steppingstonesmuseum.org.* ☒ *$6.* ☉ *Tues.–Sat. 10–5, Sun. 12–5, also Mon.10–5 from Memorial Day–Labor Day.*

Dining and Lodging

$$ ✕ **Habana.** Ceiling fans, banana trees, and a high energy level characterize Habana, which serves contemporary Cuban cuisine with some Argentinian, Peruvian, Mexican, Puerto Rican, and Brazilian dishes thrown in for spice. Some favorites are roasted sea bass with a crispy plantain crust, empanadas stuffed with minced duck or chorizo, ceviche, and baby-back ribs with guava sauce. ☒ *70 N. Main St.,* ☎ *203/852–9790. AE, D, MC, V. No lunch.*

$$ ✕ **Match.** This chic South Norwalk hot spot is renowned for its imaginative designer pizza: potato (with roasted fingerling potatoes, caramelized onions, garlic and mozzarella) and wild mushroom (with black truffles, mozzarella, goat cheese, and truffle oil) are two popular varieties. A centerpiece wood-burning stove also turns out entrées such as steak au poivre and pan-roasted salmon. ☒ *98 Washington St.,* ☎ *203/852–1088. AE, MC, V. No lunch Mon.–Tues.*

$$–$$$ ✕🏠 **Silvermine Tavern.** The simple rooms at this inn are furnished with hooked rugs and antiques along with some modern touches. The large, low-ceiling dining rooms ($$$; closed on Tuesday) are romantic, with an eclectic Colonial decor; many tables overlook a millpond. Traditional New England favorites receive modern accents—roast duckling, for instance, is often served with maple mashed sweet potatoes and a peach reduction. Sunday brunch is a local tradition. ☒ *194 Perry Ave., 06850,* ☎ *203/847–4558,* FAX *203/847–9171,* WEB *www.silverminetavern.com. 10 rooms, 1 suite. Restaurant, shop. AE, DC, MC, V. CP.*

Nightlife and the Arts

Some good bars can be found in the SoNo district of South Norwalk. **Barcelona** (☒ 63 N. Main St., ☎ 203/899–0088), a wine bar, is a hot spot for Spanish tapas. Brewing memorabilia adorns the **Brewhouse** (☒ 13 Marshall St., ☎ 203/853–9110).

Shopping

Stew Leonard's (☒ 100 Westport Ave., ☎ 203/847–7213), the self-proclaimed "Disneyland of Supermarkets," has a petting zoo, animated characters lining the aisles, scrumptious chocolate chip cookies, and great soft ice cream. Along **Washington Street** in the South Norwalk (SoNo) area are some excellent art galleries and crafts dealers.

New Canaan

❹ *5 mi northwest of Norwalk, 33 mi southwest of New Haven.*

So rich and elegant is the landscape in New Canaan that you may want to pick up a local street map and spend the afternoon driving around the estate-studded countryside, which includes everything from a Frank Lloyd Wright home and Philip Johnson's Glass House to imposing Georgians and clapboard farmhouses. Or you might prefer lingering on **Main Street,** which is loaded with upscale shops.

The **New Canaan Nature Center** comprises more than 40 acres of woods and habitats. You can try the hands-on natural science exhibits at the Discovery Center in the main building or walk along the many nature trails. Demonstrations take place in fall at the cider house and in spring at the maple sugar shed (reservations essential). ⊠ *144 Oenoke Ridge,* ☎ *203/966–9577,* WEB *www.newcanaannaturecenter.org.* ⊡ *Donation suggested for museum.* ☉ *Grounds daily dawn–dusk, museum Mon.–Sat. 9–4.*

Lodging

$$$$ 🏠 **Maples Inn.** This yellow clapboard structure a short drive from downtown has 13 gables, most of which are veiled by a canopy of maples. Bedrooms in the no-smoking inn are furnished with antiques and queen-size canopy beds. Mahogany chests, gilt frames, and brass lamps gleam from energetic polishing. The Mural Room, whose walls are painted with images of New Canaan in each of the four seasons, is an ideal setting for breakfast. ⊠ *179 Oenoke Ridge, 06840,* ☎ *203/966–2927,* FAX *203/966–5003,* WEB *www.maplesct.com. 12 rooms. AE, MC, V. CP.*

Wilton

⑤ *6 mi northeast of New Canaan, 27 mi southwest of New Haven.*

Quiet and unassuming, this lovely, tree-shaded town with graceful turn-of-the-century houses is one of Fairfield County's many bedroom communities.

★ **Weir Farm National Historic Site** is dedicated to the legacy of painter J. Alden Weir (1852–1919), one of the earliest American Impressionists. Tours of Weir's studio and sculptor Mahonri Young's studio are given, and you can take a self-guided walk past Weir's painting sites. The property's 60 wooded acres include hiking paths, picnic areas, and a restored rose and perennial garden. ⊠ *735 Nod Hill Rd.,* ☎ *203/834–1896,* WEB *www.nps.gov/wefa.* ⊡ *Free.* ☉ *Grounds daily dawn–dusk, visitor center Wed.–Sun. 8:30–5.*

The forest and wetlands of 146-acre **Woodcock Nature Center** (⊠ 56 Deer Run Rd., ☎ 203/762–7280, WEB www.wcol.net/woodcock) are the site of botany walks, birding and geology lectures, and hikes.

Shopping

Antiques sheds and boutiques can be found along and off U.S. 7. **Cannondale Village** (⊠ off U.S. 7, ☎ 203/762–2233), a pre-Civil War farm village, overflows with antiques vendors.

Ridgefield

⑥ *8 mi north of Wilton, 43 mi west of New Haven.*

In Ridgefield, you'll find a rustic Connecticut atmosphere within an hour of Manhattan. The town center, which you approach from Wilton on Route 33, is a largely residential sweep of lawns and majestic homes.

The **Aldrich Museum of Contemporary Art** presents changing exhibitions of cutting-edge work rivaling that of any small collection in New York and has an outstanding 2-acre sculpture garden. ⊠ *258 Main St.,* ☎ *203/438–4519,* WEB *www.aldrichart.org.* ⊡ *$5; Tues. free.* ☉ *Tues.–Thurs. and weekends noon–5, Fri. noon–8.*

A British cannonball is lodged in a corner of the **Keeler Tavern Museum,** a historic inn and the former home of the noted architect Cass Gilbert (1859–1934). Furniture and Revolutionary War memorabilia fill the museum, where guides dressed in Colonial costumes conduct tours. The sunken garden is lovely in the spring. ⊠ *132 Main St.,* ☎ *203/438–5485.* ☜ *$4.* ☉ *Feb.–Dec., Wed. and weekends 1–4.*

Dining and Lodging

$$$–$$$$ ✕☷ **The Elms Inn.** The best rooms here are in the frame house built by a Colonial cabinetmaker in 1760; antiques and reproductions furnish all the rooms. Chef Brendan Walsh presents fine new American cuisine in the restaurant ($$$–$$$$)—pan-roasted Maryland crab cakes with three-pepper relish, maple-thyme grilled loin of venison, and the like. ⊠ *500 Main St.,* ☎ FAX *203/438–2541,* WEB *www.theelmsinn.com. 20 rooms. Restaurant, pub. AE, DC, MC, V. CP.*

$$–$$$$ ✕☷ **Stonehenge Inn & Restaurant.** The manicured lawns and bright white-clapboard buildings of Stonehenge are visible just off U.S. 7. Its tasteful rooms are a mix of Waverly and Schumacher fabrics; the gem of a restaurant ($$) is run by Bruno Crosnier. Featured on the changing menu may be medallions of venison with dauphine potatoes (fried croquettes) laced with garlic and sweet green peppercorns or simple and elegant Dover sole. ⊠ *Stonehenge Rd. off U.S. 7, 06877,* ☎ *203/438–6511,* FAX *203/438–2478. 12 rooms, 4 suites. Restaurant. AE, MC, V. CP.*

Shopping

The **Hay Day Market** (⊠ 21 Governor St., ☎ 203/431–4400) stocks hard-to-find fresh produce, jams, cheeses, sauces, baked goods, flowers, and much more. Other locations are in Greenwich (☎ 203/637–7600) and Westport (☎ 203/254–5200).

Danbury

❼ *9 mi north of Ridgefield, 20 mi northwest of Bridgeport.*

A middle-class slice of suburbia, Danbury was the hat capital of America for nearly 200 years—until the mid-1950s. Rumors persist that the term "mad as a hatter" originated here. Hat makers suffered widely from the injurious effects of mercury poisoning, a fact that is said to explain the resultant "madness" of veteran hatters.

The **Military Museum of Southern New England** exhibits an impressive collection of U.S. and Allied forces memorabilia from World War II, plus 19 tanks dating from that war to the present. A computer program allows access to the names on the Vietnam Veterans Memorial in Washington. ⊠ *125 Park Ave.,* ☎ *203/790–9277,* WEB *www. usmilitarymuseum.org.* ☜ *$4.* ☉ *Apr.–Nov., Tues.–Sat. 10–5, Sun. noon–5; Dec.–Mar., Fri.–Sat. 10–5, Sun. noon–5.*

☾ A station built in 1903 for the New Haven Railroad houses the **Danbury Railway Museum.** In the train yard are 20 or so examples of freight and passenger railroad stock, including a restored 1944 caboose, a 1948 Alco locomotive, and an operating locomotive turntable. Museum exhibits include vintage American Flyer model trains. ⊠ *120 White St.,* ☎ *203/ 778–8337,* WEB *www.danbury.org/drm.* ☜ *$3.* ☉ *Jan.–Mar., Wed.–Sat. 10–4, Sun. noon–4; Apr.–Dec., Tues.–Sat. 10–5, Sun. noon–5.*

Dining

$$–$$$$ ✕ **Ondine.** Drifts of flowers, soft lighting, hand-written menus, and waiters in white jackets make every meal feel like a celebration. The five-course prix-fixe traditional French menu, updated once a week, might list medallions of venison with a hunter's sauce made of dried cherries or fresh salmon with a crushed peppercorn crust served with red wine-butter sauce. Grand Marnier soufflé is the signature dessert. ⊠ *69 Pembroke Rd. (Rte. 37),* ☎ *203/746–4900. AE, D, DC, MC, V. Closed Mon. No lunch.*

Outdoor Activities and Sports

The 18-hole, par-72 **Richter Park Golf Course** (⊠ 100 Aunt Hack Rd., ☎ 203/792–2550) is a superb, challenging public course. The greens fee is $48; an optional cart costs $24.

Shopping

The **Danbury Fair Mall** (⊠ I–84, Exit 3, ☎ 203/743–3247) has more than 225 shops as well as a huge working carousel in the food court. **Stew Leonard's** (⊠ 99 Federal Rd., ☎ 203/790–8030), with a petting zoo, animated characters in the aisles, and great soft ice cream, is an experience as much as a supermarket.

Weston

❽ *15 mi southeast of Danbury, 36 mi southwest of New Haven.*

Heavily wooded Weston is Fairfield County's version of a peaceful—and posh—New England town.

The 1,746 acres of woodlands, wetlands, and rock ledges at the **Nature Conservancy's Devil's Den Preserve** (⊠ 33 Pent Rd., ☎ 203/226–4991, WEB www.tnc.org/states/connecticut/preserves) include 20 mi of hiking trails. Trail maps are available in the parking lot registration area, and guided walks take place year-round. There are no rest rooms, and pets and bikes are not allowed.

OFF THE
BEATEN PATH
PUTNAM MEMORIAL STATE PARK – In the winter of 1778–79, three brigades of Continental Army soldiers under the command of General Israel Putnam made their winter encampment at this site, known as "Connecticut's Valley Forge." Superb for hiking, picnicking, and cross-country skiing, the park has a small history museum. ⊠ *Rtes. 58 and 107, West Redding(10 mi north of Weston),* ☎ *203/938–2285.* ⊠ *Donation suggested.* ⊘ *Grounds 8 am–dusk; museum May–Oct. weekends 10–5.*

Dining

$$–$$$ ✕ **Cobb's Mill Inn.** Ducks and swans frolic in the waterfall outside this former mill and inn, now a charming restaurant. The pheasant pistachio pâté is a good starter. The Continental menu is heavy on red meat dishes, but lighter fare might include grilled swordfish and roasted Chilean sea bass with a shiitake glaze. Sunday brunch is a favorite. ⊠ *12 Old Mill Rd., off Rte. 57,* ☎ *203/227–7221. AE, D, DC, MC, V. No lunch Mon. or Sat.*

Westport

❾ *7 mi south of Weston, 47 mi northeast of New York City.*

Westport, an artists' mecca since the turn of the century, continues to attract creative types. Despite commuters and corporations, the town remains more artsy and cultured than its neighbors: if the rest of Fairfield County is stylistically five years behind Manhattan, Westport lags by just five months. Paul Newman and Joanne Woodward have their main residence here.

Summer visitors to Westport congregate at **Sherwood Island State Park,** which has a 1½-mi sweep of sandy beach, two water's-edge picnic groves, a nature center, and several food concessions. The museum and concessions are open seasonally. ⊠ *I–95, Exit 18,* ☎ *203/226–6983.* ⊠ *$5–$12.* ⊘ *Daily 8 AM–dusk.*

Dining and Lodging

$$–$$$ ✕ **Da Pietro's.** This romantic storefront café serves a savory mix of Italian and French specialties. Roasted monkfish with curry-coconut sauce,

lasagna filled with snails and spinach, and sautéed veal tenderloins are possible choices. ⊠ *36 Riverside Ave.,* ☎ *203/454–1213. AE, DC, MC, V. Closed Sun. No lunch.*

$$ ✕ **Tavern on Main.** This intimate restaurant takes the tavern concept
★ to a new level—fresh flowers and soft music included. In winter the glow of fireplaces reaches every table, and in summer a terrace with an awning beckons. The sophisticated comfort food includes starters such as wild mushroom ravioli and a roasted walnut and endive salad. Among the notable entrées are potato-wrapped sea bass with cabernet sauce and certified Black Angus steak with caramelized shallots. ⊠ *146 Main St.,* ☎ *203/221–7222. AE, DC, MC, V.*

$$$$ ✕🏨 **Inn at National Hall.** Each whimsically exotic room at this tow-
★ ering Italianate redbrick inn is a study in innovative restoration, wall-stenciling, and decorative painting—including magnificent trompe l'oeil designs. The furniture collection, with antique and new pieces, is exceptional. The rooms and suites are magnificent; some have sleeping lofts and 18-ft windows overlooking the Saugatuck River. At Miramar restaurant, Todd English, a Boston superstar, turns out such dishes as grilled sirloin over Tuscan bruschetta and butternut squash tortellini with brown butter and sage. ⊠ *2 Post Rd. W, 06880,* ☎ *203/221–1351; 800/628–4255; 203/222–2267 restaurant,* FAX *203/221–0276,* WEB *www.innatnationalhall.com. 8 rooms, 7 suites. Restaurant, refrigerator, in-room VCRs, meeting room. AE, D, DC, MC, V. CP.*

$$–$$$ ✕🏨 **Westport Inn.** Bedrooms in this upscale motor lodge have attractive contemporary furniture. Rooms surrounding the large indoor pool are set back nicely and are slightly larger than the rest. The on-site restaurant, Gennaro's of Westport ($$–$$$), serves updated Italian classics such as Black Angus filet mignon with cognac, Gorgonzola cheese, Portobello mushrooms, and fresh–picked lobster meat. ⊠ *1595 Post Rd. E,,* ☎ *203/259–5236; 800/446–8997; 203/255–8889 restaurant,* FAX *203/254–8439,* WEB *www.westportinn.com. 116 rooms, 2 suites. Restaurant, bar, indoor pool, sauna, health club. AE, D, DC, MC, V.*

Nightlife and the Arts

The **Levitt Pavilion for the Performing Arts** (⊠ Jesup Rd., ☎ 203/221–4422) sponsors an excellent series of summer concerts, most of them free, that range from jazz to classical, folk-rock to blues. The venerable **Westport Country Playhouse** (⊠ 25 Powers Ct., ☎ 203/227–4177) presents six productions each summer in a converted barn.

Shopping

J. Crew, Ann Taylor, Coach, Laura Ashley, Pottery Barn, and other fashionable shops have made **Main Street** in Westport the outdoor equivalent of upscale malls such as Stamford Town Center.

Fairfield

🔟 *9 mi east of Westport, 33 mi south of Waterbury.*

Fairfield, founded in 1639, was one of the first settlements along the old Post Road (Route 1). Although it was primarily an agricultural community in its early days, Fairfield turned its attention to the shipping industry in order to recover after it was burned to the ground by the British in 1779. The Greenfield Hill section of town is home to thousands of dogwood trees—and the popular Dogwood Festival each May. Southport has grand estates and panoramic views of the Long Island Sound, while downtown Fairfield is just the place to browse through a bookstore and lick an ice cream cone.

The **Connecticut Audubon Center of Fairfield** (⊠ 2325 Burr St., ☎ 203/259–6305, WEB www.ctaudubon.org/centers/fairfield) maintains a 160-

acre wildlife sanctuary that includes 6 mi of rugged hiking trails and special walks for people with visual impairments and mobility problems.

The **Connecticut Audubon Birdcraft Museum** (⊠ 314 Unquowa Rd., ☎ 203/259–0416, WEB www.ctaudubon.org/centers/birdcraft), operated by the Connecticut Audubon Society, has a children's activity corner, 6 acres with trails, and a pond that attracts waterfowl during their spring and fall migrations.

Dining

$$ ✕ **Voilà.** A stone fireplace and and lace curtains add cozy warmth to this intimate French bistro. On any given day the menu may include escargots au Roquefort, pâté du chef, or veal chasseur. Save room for dessert: the tarte tartin is said to be a work of art. ⊠ 70 Reef Rd., ☎ 203/254–2070. AE, MC, V. Closed Sun.

$ ✕ **Rawley's Hot Dogs.** The legendary franks at this drive-in are deep-fried in vegetable oil, then grilled for a few seconds—a recipe the stand has been following since it opened in 1946. The cheesedog with the works is a favorite. ⊠ 1886 Post Rd., ☎ 203/259–9023. No credit cards. Closed Sun.

Nightlife and the Arts

The **Quick Center for the Arts** (⊠ Fairfield University, N. Benson Rd., ☎ 203/254–4010) hosts musical and theatrical performances, children's shows, and a lecture series with international speakers.

Bridgeport

❶ 5 mi northeast of Fairfield, 63 mi west of New London.

Bridgeport, a city that has endured some economic hard times, is working hard to overcome its negative image. Recent improvements by civic leaders, as well as a number of unique attractions, make it a worthwhile stop.

☺ Exhibits at the **Barnum Museum,** associated with past resident and former mayor P. T. Barnum, depict the life and times of the great showman, who presented performers such as General Tom Thumb and Jenny Lind, the Swedish Nightingale. You can tour a scaled-down model of Barnum's legendary five-ring circus. ⊠ 820 Main St., ☎ 203/331–1104, WEB www.barnum-museum.org. ⊠ $5. ⊗ Tues.–Sat. 10–4:30, Sun. noon–4:30.

☺ The indoor walk-through South American rain forest at the **Beardsley Park and Zoological Gardens** itself justifies a visit. Also in the park, which has 36 acres of exhibits north of downtown Bridgeport, are a working carousel and museum, and a New England farmyard. ⊠ 1875 Noble Ave., ☎ 203/394–6565, WEB www.beardsleyzoo.org. ⊠ $6. ⊗ Park daily 9–4, rain forest daily 10–3:30.

Captain's Cove on historic Black Rock Harbor is the home port of the Lightship #112 Nantucket. Band concerts take place on Sunday afternoon in summer. The boardwalk, a popular warm-weather hangout, holds a small assortment of shops and a casual seafood restaurant. ⊠ 1 Bostwick Ave. (I–95, Exit 26), ☎ 203/335–1433, WEB www.captainscoveseaport.com. ⊠ Cove free, lightship tour $2, frigate tour (when it's in port) $5. ⊗ Tours on the hr Memorial Day–Labor Day, weekends noon–4.

☺ The draws at the **Discovery Museum and Wonder Workshop** include a planetarium, several hands-on science exhibits, a computer-art exhibit, Hoop Smarts (a virtual basketball game), the Challenger learning center (which has a simulated space flight), and a children's museum.

The Wonder Workshop schedules storytelling, arts-and-crafts, science, and other programs. ⊠ *4450 Park Ave.,* ☎ *203/372–3521,* WEB *www.discoverymuseum.org.* ⌸ *$7.* ☉ *Sept.–June, Tues.–Sat. 10–5, Sun. noon–5; July–Aug., Mon.–Sat. 10–5, Sun. noon–5.*

Outdoor Activities and Sports

The **Bridgeport Bluefish** (⊠ Harbor Yard, 500 Main St., off I–95, ☎ 203/345–4800) play in the Atlantic League of Professional Baseball.

Stratford

⑫ *3 mi northeast of Bridgeport, 15 mi southwest of New Haven.*

Stratford, named after the English town Stratford-upon-Avon, has more than 150 historic homes, many of which are on Long Island Sound. The Academy Hill neighborhood, near the intersection of Main (Route 113) and Academy Hill streets, is a good area to stroll.

Boothe Memorial Park & Museum, a 32-acre complex with several unusual buildings, includes a blacksmith shop, carriage and tool barns, and a museum that traces the history of the trolley. Also on the grounds are a beautiful rose garden and a children's playground. ⊠ *Main St.,* ☎ *203/381–2046.* ⌸ *Free.* ☉ *Park daily dawn–dusk; museum June–Oct., Tues.–Fri. 11–1, weekends 1–4.*

Southwestern Connecticut A to Z

To research prices, get advice from other travelers, and book travel arrangements, visit www.fodors.com.

BUS TRAVEL

Bonanza Bus Lines provides service to Danbury from Hartford, New York, and Providence. Peter Pan Bus Lines stops in Bridgeport en route from Hartford, Boston, Providence, and New York.

Connecticut Transit buses stop in Greenwich, Stamford, and Norwalk. The Greater Bridgeport Transit District's People Movers provide bus transportation in Norwalk, Bridgeport, Stratford, and Fairfield. Norwalk Transit provides bus service in Norwalk and Westport.
➤ BUS INFORMATION: **Bonanza Bus Lines** (☎ 800/556–3815, WEB www.bonanzabus.com). **Peter Pan Bus Lines** (☎ 800/343–9999, WEB www.peterpan-bus.com). **Connecticut Transit** (☎ 203/327–7433, WEB www.cttransit.com). **People Movers** (☎ 203/333–3031). **Norwalk Transit** Norwalk (☎ 203/852–0000) and Westport (☎ 203/226–0422).

CAR TRAVEL

The main routes into southwestern Connecticut are Route 15 (called the Merritt Parkway in this area) and I–95 (also known as the Connecticut Turnpike). The Merritt Parkway and I–95 are the main arteries; both can have harrowing rush-hour snarls. Greenwich, Stamford, Norwalk, Westport, Fairfield, Bridgeport, and Stratford are on or just off I–95. From I–95 or the Merritt Parkway take Route 124 north to New Canaan; U.S. 7 north to Wilton or Danbury; U.S. 7 and Route 33 north to Ridgefield; and Route 53 north to Weston.

EMERGENCIES

➤ HOSPITALS: **Norwalk Hospital** (⊠ 34 Maple St., Norwalk, ☎ 203/852–2000, WEB www.norwalkhosp.org). **St. Vincent's Medical Center** (⊠ 2800 Main St., Bridgeport, ☎ 203/576–6000, WEB www.stvincents.org).
➤ 24-HOUR PHARMACY: **CVS Pharmacy** (⊠ 235 Main St., Norwalk, ☎ 203/847–6057, WEB www.cvs.com).

TRAIN TRAVEL

Amtrak stops in Stamford and Bridgeport. Metro-North Railroad trains stop in Greenwich, Stamford, Norwalk, New Canaan, Wilton, Danbury, Redding, Westport, Fairfield, Bridgeport, and Stratford.

➤ TRAIN INFORMATION: **Amtrak** (☎ 800/872–7245, WEB www.amtrak.com). **Metro-North Railroad** (☎ 800/638–7646; 212/532–4900 from New York City, WEB www.mta.nyc.ny.us).

VISITOR INFORMATION

➤ TOURIST INFORMATION: **Coastal Fairfield County Convention and Visitors Bureau** (✉ The Gate Lodge–Mathews Park, 297 West Ave., Norwalk 06850, ☎ 203/899–2799 or 800/866–7925, WEB www.coastalct.com). **Housatonic Valley Tourism District** (✉ 30 Main St., Danbury 06810, ☎ 203/743–0546 or 800/841–4488, WEB www.housatonic.org).

HARTFORD AND THE CONNECTICUT RIVER VALLEY

Westward expansion in the New World began along the meandering Connecticut River. Dutch explorer Adrian Block first explored the area in 1614, and in 1633 a trading post was set up in what is now Hartford. Within five years, throngs of restive Massachusetts Bay colonists had settled in this fertile valley. What followed was more than three centuries of shipbuilding, shad hauling, and river trading with ports as far away as the West Indies and the Mediterranean.

Less touristy than the coast and northwest hills, the Connecticut River valley is a swath of small villages and uncrowded state parks punctuated by a few small cities and a large one: the capital city of Hartford. To the south of Hartford, with the exception of industrial Middletown, genuinely quaint hamlets vie for a share of Connecticut's tourist crop with antiques shops, scenic drives, and trendy restaurants.

Essex

⑬ *29 mi east of New Haven.*

Essex, consistently named one of the best small towns in America, looks much as it did in the mid-19th century, at the height of its shipbuilding prosperity. So important to a young America was Essex's boat manufacturing that the British burned more than 40 ships here during the War of 1812. Gone are the days of steady trade with the West Indies, when the aroma of imported rum, molasses, and spices hung in the air. Whitewashed houses—many the former roosts of sea captains—line Main Street, which has shops that sell clothing, antiques, paintings and prints, and sweets.

In addition to pre-Colonial artifacts and displays, the **Connecticut River Museum** has a full-size reproduction of the world's first submarine, the *American Turtle*; the original was built by David Bushnell in 1775. Views of the river from the museum are spectacular. ✉ *Steamboat Dock, 67 Main St.,* ☎ *860/767–8269,* WEB *www.ctrivermuseum.org.* 🎟 *$4.* ☉ *Tues.–Sun. 10–5.*

The **Essex Steam Train and Riverboat** travels alongside the Connecticut River and through the lower valley; if you wish to continue, you can take a riverboat up the river. The train trip lasts an hour; the riverboat ride, 90 minutes. ✉ *Valley Railroad, 1 Railroad Ave., Rte. 9, Exit 3,* ☎ *860/767–0103,* WEB *www.essexsteamtrain.com.* 🎟 *Train fare $10.50, train-boat fare $16.50.* ☉ *May–Dec.; call for schedule.*

Dining and Lodging

$$–$$$ ✕🏠 **Griswold Inn.** Two-plus centuries of catering to changing tastes at what's billed as America's oldest continuously operating inn has resulted in a kaleidoscope of decor—some Colonial, a touch of Federal, a little Victorian, and just as many modern touches as are necessary to meet present-day expectations. The chefs at the restaurant ($$–$$$) prepare country-style and more-sophisticated dishes—try the famous 1776 sausages, which come with sauerkraut and German potato salad, or the risotto croquettes. The Tap Room, built in 1738 as a schoolhouse, is ideal for after-dinner drinks. The "English Hunt Breakfast," a feast of muffins, eggs, fresh cod, creamed chipped beef, and smoked bacon, is a Sunday event. ✉ *36 Main St., 06426,* ☎ *860/767–1776,* FAX *860/767–0481,* WEB *www.griswoldinn.com. 18 rooms, 12 suites. Restaurant, bar, no-smoking room. AE, MC, V. CP.*

$$–$$$ 🏠 **Riverwind.** All the guest rooms at this splendid inn have antique furnishings, collectibles, and touches of stenciling. One room has a country-pine bed and a painted headboard; another holds a carved oak bed; a third contains an 18th-century bird's-eye-maple four-poster with a canopy. Co-owner Barbara Barlow serves a hearty country breakfast of Smithfield ham, her own baked goods, and several casseroles. Freshly brewed tea and coffee and home-baked cookies are always on hand, and you can relax in multiple common rooms. ✉ *209 Main St., Deep River 06417,* ☎ *860/526–2014,* WEB *www.riverwindinn.com. 7 rooms, 1 suite. No-smoking room AE, MC, V. BP.*

$$ ✕ **Steve's Centerbrook Café.** Latticework and gingerbread trim are among the architectural accents of the Victorian house that holds this bright café. The culinary accents lean toward the ornate as well, especially in the few classic French dishes. Although the menu changes regularly, you can usually find rack of lamb or grilled salmon. Save room for the *marjolaine,* a hazelnut torte covered with chocolate. ✉ *78 Main St., Centerbrook,* ☎ *860/767–1277. AE, MC, V. Closed Mon. No lunch.*

Ivoryton

14 *4 mi west of Essex.*

Ivoryton was named for its steady import of elephant tusks from Kenya and Zanzibar during the 19th century—piano keys were Ivoryton's leading export during this time. At one time, the Comstock-Cheney piano manufacturers processed so much ivory that Japan regularly purchased Ivoryton's surplus, using the scraps to make souvenirs. The Depression closed the lid on Ivoryton's pianos, and what remains is a sleepy, shady hamlet.

The **Museum of Fife and Drum,** said to be the only one of its kind in the world, contains martial sheet music, instruments, and uniforms chronicling America's history of parades, from the Revolutionary War to the present. ✉ *62 N. Main St.,* ☎ *860/767–2237 or 860/399–6519,* WEB *www.fifedrum.com/thecompany.* 🎫 *$3.* ⊙ *June–Sept., first and last Sun. of the month 1–5 or by appointment.*

Dining and Lodging

$$–$$$$ ✕🏠 **Copper Beech Inn.** A magnificent copper beech tree shades the imposing main building of this Victorian inn, set on 7 wooded acres. The four rooms in the main house have an old-fashioned feel, right down to the claw-foot tubs; the nine rooms in the Carriage House are more modern and have decks. The distinctive country-French menu in the romantic dining room ($$–$$$; reservations essential; jacket and tie required; no lunch) changes seasonally. Specials might include the inn's renowned bouillabaisse or lamb with an herb crust. Dinner starts at 1

Connecticut River Valley

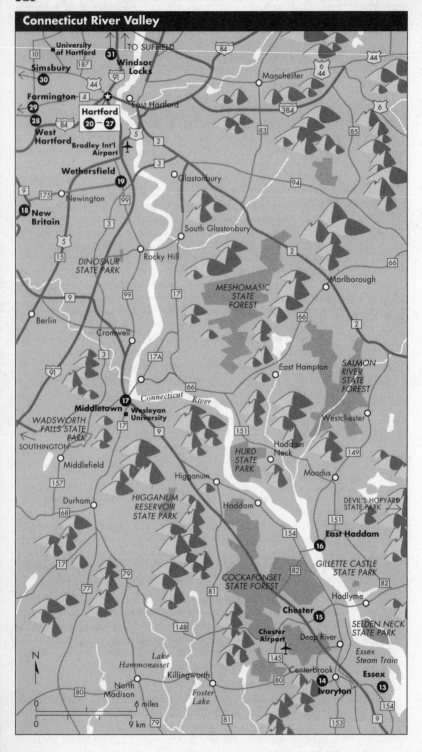

TO SUFFIELD

University of Hartford

10

187

31 Windsor Locks

Simsbury

30

44

91

Manchester

6
44

44

Farmington

4

East Hartford

384

6

29

Hartford
20 — 27

5

83

85

28

84

West Hartford

Bradley Int'l Airport

2

Wethersfield

3

Glastonbury

94

9

175

19

Newington

99

18 New Britain

3

South Glastonbury

2

66

5

Rocky Hill

15

DINOSAUR STATE PARK

99

17

MESHOMASIC STATE FOREST

Marlborough

9

Berlin

66

2

Cromwell

3

17A

SALMON RIVER STATE FOREST

91

East Hampton

Connecticut River

66

Middletown 17

Wesleyan University

Westchester

WADSWORTH FALLS STATE PARK

17

151

SOUTHINGTON

9

HURD STATE PARK

Haddam Neck

149

Middlefield

Moodus

157

Higganum

DEVIL'S HOPYARD STATE PARK

Durham

68

HIGGANUM RESERVOIR STATE PARK

Haddam

151

154

East Haddam

17

16

79

82

GILLETTE CASTLE STATE PARK

77

COCKAPONSET STATE FOREST

81

Hadlyme

82

17

148

Chester 15

SELDEN NECK STATE PARK

N

Chester Airport

Deep River

Essex Steam Train

Lake Hammonasset

145

Centerbrook

80

Killingworth

14

Essex 13

80

North Madison

Foster Lake

Ivoryton

0   6 miles

0   9 km

79

81

153

9

154

PM on Sunday. ⊠ *46 Main St., 06442,* ☎ *860/767–0330 or 888/809–2056,* WEB *www.copperbeechinn.com. 13 rooms. Restaurant, in-room data ports. AE, DC, MC, V. CP.*

Chester

🔟 *5 mi north of Ivoryton, 24 mi northwest of New London.*

Upscale boutiques and artisans' studios fill chiefly 19th-century buildings along Chester's quaint and well-preserved Main Street. Chester sits on a portion of the Connecticut River that has been named "one of the last great places on earth" by the Nature Conservancy and is the starting point of the Chester-Hadlyme Ferry, which crosses the river in a grand total of five minutes.

Chester Airport offers fantastic open-cockpit biplane rides over the lower Connecticut River valley. Bring your own bomber jacket and you're set. ⊠ *Off Rte. 9,* ☎ *860/526–4321 or 800/752–6371.* 🎫 *$85 half hr, $165 hr.* ☉ *By appointment.*

Sometimes the simple pleasures mean the most. The *Selden III* is the second-oldest continually operating ferry in the country. Although its trip across the Connecticut River to Hadlyme is swift, you'll still catch nice views of the valley and Gillette Castle. ⊠ *148 Ferry Rd.,* ☎ *860/526–2743.* 🎫 *$2.25 vehicle and 1 person, 75¢ each additional person.* ☉ *Apr.–Nov., daily upon demand.*

Dining

$$–$$$ ✕ **Restaurant du Village.** A black wrought-iron gate beckons you away from the antiques stores of Chester's Main Street, and an off-white awning draws you through the door of this classic little Colonial storefront, painted in historic Newport blue and adorned with flower boxes. Here you can sample exquisite classic French cuisine—escargots in puff pastry and filet mignon—while recapping the day's shopping coups. ⊠ *59 Main St.,* ☎ *860/526–5301. AE, MC, V. Closed Mon. No lunch.*

$$ ✕ **Fiddler's.** The specialties at this fine fish house are the rich bouillabaisse and the lobster with a sauce of peaches, peach brandy, shallots, mushrooms, and cream. Blond bentwood chairs, lacy stenciling on the walls, prints of famous schooners, and the amber glow of oil lamps lend the place a gentrified air. ⊠ *4 Water St.,* ☎ *860/526–3210. DC, MC, V. Closed Mon. No lunch Sun.*

Shopping

Ceramica (⊠ 36 Main St., ☎ 800/782–1238) carries hand-painted Italian tableware and decorative accessories. The **Connecticut River Artisans** (⊠ 4 Water St., ☎ 860/526–5575), a crafts cooperative, sells one-of-a-kind works, including pottery, jewelry, and folk art.

East Haddam

🔟 *7 mi north of Chester, 28 mi southeast of Hartford.*

Fishing, shipping, and musket-making were the chief enterprises at East Haddam, the only town in the state that occupies both banks of the Connecticut River. This lovely town retains much of its old-fashioned charm.

★ ☙ At **Allegra Farm and the Horsedrawn Carriage and Sleigh Museum of New England,** John and Kate Allegra not only offer sleigh, hay, and carriage rides using authentic vehicles right out of a Currier & Ives scene, but they also have a post-and-beam barn museum that houses more than 30 restored antique carriages and sleighs. Children love the pony rides and the opportunity to visit the livery stable and its tenants—a donkey, llama, sheep, and 30 horses. ⊠ *Junction of Rte. 82 and Petticoat La.*, ☎ *860/873–9658*, WEB *www.allegrafarm.com.* ⊠ *$2.50.* ☉ *Weekends 11–5; call for weekday hrs, which vary.*

★ **Gillette Castle State Park** holds the outrageous 24-room oak-and-fieldstone hilltop castle built by the eccentric actor and dramatist William Gillette between 1914 and 1919; he modeled it after the medieval castles of the Rhineland. You can tour the castle and hike on trails near the remains of the 3-mi private railroad that chugged about the property until the owner's death in 1937. Gillette, who was born in Hartford, wrote two famous Civil War plays and was beloved for his play *Sherlock Holmes* (he performed the title role). In his will, Gillette demanded that the castle not fall into the hands of "some blithering saphead who has no conception of where he is or with what surrounded." To that end, the castle and 200-acre grounds were designated a state park that's an excellent spot for hiking and picnicking. ⊠ *67 River Rd., off Rte. 82*, ☎ *860/526–2336.* ⊠ *Castle $4, grounds free.*

★ The upper floors of the 1876 Victorian gingerbread **Goodspeed Opera House** have served as a venue for theatrical performances for more than 100 years. In the 1960s the Goodspeed underwent a restoration that included the stage area, the Victorian bar, the sitting room, and the drinking parlor. More than 14 Goodspeed productions have gone on to Broadway, including *Annie*. The performance season runs from April to December. ⊠ *Rte. 82*, ☎ *860/873–8668*, WEB *www.goodspeed.org.* ⊠ *Tour $2.* ☉ *Tours Memorial Day–Columbus Day; call for times.*

St. Stephen's Church is listed in the *Guinness Book of Records* as having the oldest bell in the United States. Crafted in Spain in the year 815, the bell is believed to have been taken from a monastery by Napoléon and used for ballast in a ship. A Captain Andrews from East Haddam discovered it in Florida and brought it back to his hometown, where it now sits in the belfry of St. Stephen's, a small stone Episcopal church with cedar shingles. The church was built in 1794 and was moved to its present site in 1890. ⊠ *Main St. (Rte. 149)*, ☎ *860/873–9547.* ☉ *Call for hrs and service times.*

The three formal herb gardens at the **Sundial Herb Garden**—a knot garden of interlocking hedges, a typical 18th-century geometric garden with central sundial, and a topiary garden—surround an 18th-century farmhouse. An 18th-century barn serves as a formal tearoom and a shop with herbs, books, and rare and fine teas. Sunday afternoon teas and special programs take place throughout the year. ⊠ *59 Hidden Lake Rd., Higganum (6 mi from Higganum Center; head south on Rte. 81, turn right on Brault Hill Rd., and right again when road ends)*, ☎ *860/345–4290*, WEB *www.sundialgardens.com.* ⊠ *$1.* ☉ *Jan.–late-Nov., weekends 10–5 (except last 2 weekends of Oct.); late Nov.–Dec. 24, daily 10–5.*

Sixty-foot cascades flow down Chapman Falls at the 860-acre **Devil's Hopyard State Park,** an idyllic spot for picnicking, fishing, camping, and hiking. ⊠ *366 Hopyard Rd., 3 mi north of junction of Rtes. 82 and 156*, ☎ *860/873–8566.* ⊠ *Free.* ☉ *Park daily 8 AM–dusk.*

Lodging

$$–$$$ 🏠 **Bishopsgate Inn.** An 1818 Federal-style inn near the landmark Goodspeed Opera House, the Bishopsgate contains cozy and inviting rooms furnished with period reproductions, a smattering of antiques, and fluffy featherbeds. Four rooms have fireplaces, and one has a sauna. You can order elaborate candlelight dinners served in your room. ⊠ *Box 290, 7 Norwich Rd. (Rte. 82), 06423*, ☎ *860/873–1677*, FAX *860/873–3898*, WEB *www.bishopsgate.com. 6 rooms. MC, V. BP.*

Middletown

⑰ *15 mi northwest of East Haddam, 24 mi northeast of New Haven.*

Middletown, once a bustling river city, was named for its location halfway between Hartford and Long Island Sound (it's also halfway between New York City and Boston). It is home to Wesleyan University. The wealthiest town in the state from about 1750 to 1800, Middletown had been in decline for more than a century before being chosen to take part in the National Trust for Historic Preservation's "Main Street Program." The town is currently undergoing a multiyear rehabilitation project to revitalize the downtown area.

The imposing campus of **Wesleyan University,** founded here in 1831, is traversed by High Street, which Charles Dickens once called "the loveliest Main Street in America"—even though Middletown's actual Main Street runs parallel to it a few blocks east. High Street is an architecturally eclectic thoroughfare. Note the massive, fluted Corinthian columns of the Greek Revival Russell House (circa 1828) at the corner of Washington Street, across from the pink Mediterranean-style Davison Arts Center, built just 15 years later; farther on are gingerbreads, towering brownstones, Tudors, and Queen Annes. A few hundred yards up on Church Street, which intersects High Street, is the Olin Library. The 1928 structure, Wesleyan University's library, was designed by Henry Bacon, the architect of the Lincoln Memorial.

The Federal **General Mansfield House** has 18th- and 19th-century decorative arts, Civil War memorabilia and firearms, and local artifacts. ⊠ *151 Main St.,* ☎ *860/346–0746.* 🎫 *$2.* ☉ *Sun. 2–4:30, Mon. 1–4, and by appointment.*

Dinosaurs once roamed the area around **Dinosaur State Park,** north of Middletown. Tracks dating from the Jurassic period, 200 million years ago, are preserved here under a giant geodesic dome. From May to October you can make plaster casts of tracks on a special area of the property; call ahead to learn what materials you need to bring. An exhibit center with interactive displays interprets the dinosaurs, geology, and paleontology of the Connecticut River valley region. A pleasant place for hiking, the park has nature trails that run through woods, along a ridge, and through swamps on a boardwalk. ⊠ *West St., east of I–91, Exit 23 Rocky Hill,* ☎ *860/529–8423,* 🌐 *www.dinosaurstatepark.org.* 🎫 *$2.* ☉ *Exhibits Tues.–Sun. 9–4:30, trails daily 9–4:30.*

You can pick your own fruits and vegetables—berries, peaches, pears, apples, and even pumpkins—at **Lyman Orchards** (⊠ Rtes. 147 and 157, Middlefield, ☎ 860/349–3673, 🌐 www.lymanorchard.com), just south of Middletown, from June to October.

Dining

$ ✕ **O'Rourke's Diner.** For a university town, Middletown has surprisingly few eateries. The food at this stainless-steel-and-glass-brick diner, which opens at 4:30 AM, is a cut above that at any of the "real" restaurants. You'll find the expected diner fare, along with a tasty Irish stew, corned-beef hash, and regional delicacies such as steamed cheeseburgers (not served on weekends); it's all unusually good. The weekend breakfast menu is extensive. ⊠ *728 Main St.,* ☎ *860/346–6101. No credit cards. No dinner.*

Nightlife and the Arts

Wesleyan University's **Center for the Arts** (⊠ between Washington Terr. and Wyllys Ave., ☎ 860/685–3355) frequently hosts concerts, theater, films, and art exhibits. At last count, **Eli Cannon's** (⊠ 695 Main

St., ☎ 860/347–3547) had 28 beers on tap and more than 100 bottled selections.

Outdoor Activities and Sports

Called by some "a public course with a private feel," the **Lyman Orchards Golf Club** (⊠ Rte. 157, Middlefield, ☎ 860/349–8055) has two 18-hole championship courses. The greens fee at both the par-72 course designed by Robert Trent Jones and par-71 course designed by Gary Player ranges between $35 and $47. Carts ($11) are mandatory.

Shopping

Tours of the **Wesleyan Potters** (⊠ 350 S. Main St., ☎ 860/347–5925) pottery and weaving studios can be arranged in advance. Jewelry, clothing, baskets, pottery, weavings, and more are for sale.

Ski Areas

POWDER RIDGE

The trails here drop straight down from the 500-ft-high ridge for which this ski area is named. Half the 15 trails are designed for intermediate skiers, with the others split between beginner trails and expert black diamonds; all the trails are lighted for night skiing. One quad lift, two doubles, and a handle tow cover the mountain. Special features include a snowtubing area, a snowboard park, an alpine park, a full-service restaurant, and ski instruction for children ages 4 and up. ⊠ 99 Powder Hill Rd., Middlefield 06455, ☎ 860/349–3454.

New Britain

⑱ 13 mi northwest of Middletown, 10 mi southwest of Hartford.

New Britain got its start as a manufacturing center producing sleigh bells. From these modest beginnings, it soon became known as "Hardware City," distributing builders' tools, ball bearings, locks, and other such items. No longer a factory town, New Britain is home to the Central Connecticut State College University and a first-rate museum of American art.

The **New Britain Museum of American Art,** in a turn-of-the-century house, holds 19 galleries and more than 4,000 works of art that survey the entire history of American art. Though the collection includes luminaries such as Thomas Cole, Georgia O'Keeffe, and Thomas Hart Benton, the selection of Impressionist artists deserves special note— Mary Cassatt, William Merritt Chase, Childe Hassam, and John Henry Twachtman, among others. ⊠ 56 Lexington St., ☎ 860/229–0257, WEB www.nbmaa.org. ☞ $4;. ⊙ Tues., Thurs., Fri., Sun. noon–5, Wed. noon–7, Sat. 10–5.

The **Copernican Observatory & Planetarium,** on the campus of Central Connecticut State University, has one of the largest public telescopes in the nation and schedules a variety of programs geared to both children and adults. ⊠ 1615 Stanley St., ☎ 860/832–3399. ☞ $3.50. ⊙ Shows Fri.–Sat.; call for times.

Outdoor Activities and Sports

The **New Britain Rock Cats,** the Double-A affiliate of baseball's Minnesota Twins, play at New Britain Stadium (⊠ Willow Brook Park, S. Main St., ☎ 860/224–8383) from April to September.

Wethersfield

⑲ 7 mi northeast of New Britain, 32 mi northeast of New Haven.

Wethersfield, a vast Hartford suburb, dates from 1634 and has the state's largest historic district, with more than 100 buildings from before

1840. As was the case throughout early Connecticut, the Native Americans indigenous to these lands fought the arriving English with a vengeance; here their struggles culminated in the 1637 Wethersfield Massacre, when Pequot Indians killed nine settlers. Three years later, the citizens held a public election, America's first defiance of British rule, for which they were fined five British pounds.

The Joseph Webb House, Silas Deane House, and Isaac Stevens House, all built in the mid- to late 1700s, form one of the state's best historic-house museums, the **Webb-Deane-Stevens Museum.** The structures, well-preserved examples of Georgian architecture, reflect their owners' lifestyles as, respectively, a merchant, a diplomat, and a tradesman. The Webb House, a registered National Historic Landmark, was the site of the strategy conference between George Washington and the French general Jean-Baptiste Rochambeau that led to the British defeat at Yorktown. ⊠ *211 Main St. (I–91, Exit 26),* ☎ *860/529–0612.* ☑ *$8.* ☉ *May–Oct., Wed.–Mon. 10–4; Nov.–Apr., weekends 10–4.* ⊞ *www.webb-deane-stevens.org.*

Comstock Ferre & Co. (⊠ 263 Main St., ☎ 860/571–6590, ⊞ www.comstockferre.com), founded in 1820, is the country's oldest continuously operating seed company. It sells more than 800 varieties of seeds and 3,000 varieties of perennials in a chestnut post-and-beam building that dates from the late 1700s.

Hartford

4 mi north of Wethersfield, 45 mi northwest of New London, 81 mi northeast of Stamford.

Formerly one of the nation's most powerful cities, Connecticut's capital seems past its prime. Although the decline of the insurance and defense industries in the past two decades has left the once-lovely city in some disrepair, it still offers many notable sights for travelers. Some ambitious long-term programs for downtown renewal are in the works, however, including riverfront beautification. America's insurance industry was born here in the early 19th century—largely in an effort to protect the Connecticut River valley's tremendously important shipping interests. Throughout the 19th century, insurance companies expanded their coverage to include fires, accidents, life, and (in 1898) automobiles. Through the years, Hartford industries have included the inspection and packing of tobacco (once a prominent industry in the northern river valley) and the manufacture of everything from bedsprings to artificial limbs, pool tables, and coffins. Hartford's distinctive office towers make what is actually an ever-expanding suburban development seem more urban.

❷⓪ The Federal **Old State House,** a building with an elaborate cupola and roof balustrade, was designed in the early 1700s by Charles Bulfinch, architect of the U.S. Capitol. The Great Senate Room, where everyone from Abraham Lincoln to George Bush has spoken, contains a Gilbert Stuart portrait of George Washington that remains in its commissioned location. For a chance to see a two-headed calf, drop by the small but distinctive museum of oddities upstairs. And at 12:15 every Tuesday, the trial of the Africans who mutinied on the *Amistad* in 1839—an event depicted in Stephen Spielberg's 1997 film of the same name—is reenacted in the very courtroom where it was first held. ⊠ *800 Main St.,* ☎ *860/522–6766.* ☑ *Free.* ☉ *Weekdays 10–4, Sat. 11–4.*

★ **❷①** With more than 50,000 artworks and artifacts spanning 5,000 years, the **Wadsworth Atheneum Museum of Art** is the second-largest public art museum in New England and the oldest in the nation, predating the

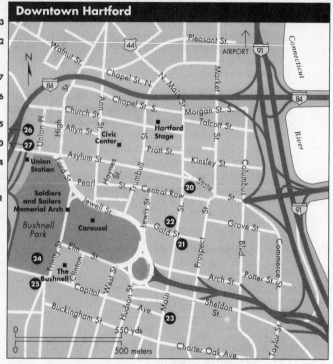

Downtown Hartford

Metropolitan Museum of Art in New York by 35 years. Among notable items to look for are five wall drawings by Connecticut's own Sol LeWitt, the well-known conceptual artist, as well as the first American acquisitions of works by Salvador Dalí and the Italian artist Caravaggio. Particularly impressive are the museum's collections of Baroque, Impressionist, and Hudson River School artists—including pieces by Frederic Church and Thomas Cole—as well as what some consider the world's finest collection of Pilgrim-era furnishings. The Museum Café, though a bit pricey, is a lovely spot for lunch. ⊠ *600 Main St.,* ☎ *860/278–2670,* WEB *www.wadsworthatheneum.org..* 💲 *$7; free Sat. 11–noon and Thurs..* ☉ *Tues.–Sun. 11–5 (1st Thurs. of most months until 8).*

❷❷ The **Center Church,** built in 1807, is a classic temple-with-spire design with a soaring, barrel-vaulted ceiling. The parish itself dates from 1632 and was started by Puritan clergyman Thomas Hooker (1586–1647), one of the chief founders of Hartford. Five of the stained-glass windows were created by Louis Tiffany. The Ancient Burying Ground, in the churchyard, is filled with granite and brownstone headstones, some dating from the 1600s. ⊠ *675 Main St.,* ☎ *860/249–5631.* 💲 *Free.* ☉ *Open by appointment.*

❷❸ The **Butler-McCook Homestead,** built in 1782 and occupied continuously by the same family until 1971, has furnishings that show the evolution of American taste over time. There's an extensive collection of Japanese armor and Asian bronzes, Victorian-era toys, and a restored Victorian garden, originally designed by Jacob Weidenmann in 1865. ⊠ *396 Main St.,* ☎ *860/522–1806 or 860/247–8996,* WEB *www.hartnet.org/als.* 💲 *$5.* ☉ *Wed.–Sat 10–4, Sun. 1–4.*

Bushnell Park, which fans out from the State Capitol building, was the first public space (1850) in the country with natural landscaping instead of a traditional village-green configuration. The park was created by the firm of Frederick Law Olmsted, the Hartford-born landscape architect who, with Calvert Vaux, designed New York City's Central Park. Amid Bushnell's 40 acres are 150 varieties of trees and such landmarks as a 1914 Stein & Goldstein carousel (open May–October) and the 100-ft-tall, 30-ft-wide medieval-style Soldiers and Sailors Memorial Arch, dedicated to Civil War soldiers.

㉔ Rising above Bushnell Park and visible citywide is the grandiose **State Capitol,** a colossal edifice composed of wholly disparate architectural elements. Built in 1879 of marble and granite—to a tune of $2.5 million—this gilt-dome wonder is replete with crockets, finials, and pointed arches. It houses the governor's office and legislative chambers and displays historic statuary, flags, and furnishings. ⊠ *210 Capitol Ave.,* ☎ *860/240–0222.* ⌨ *Free.* ⊙ *Weekdays 9–3; tours weekdays 9:15–1:15 every hr and Sat. 10:15–2:15 every hr Apr.–Oct.*

㉕ The **Museum of Connecticut History** exhibits artifacts of Connecticut military, industrial, and political history, including the state's Colonial charter. It holds a vast assemblage of Samuel Colt firearms; the so-called Arm of Law and Order was manufactured in Hartford. ⊠ *231 Capitol Ave.,* ☎ *860/757–6535,* WEB *www.cslib.org.* ⌨ *Free.* ⊙ *Mon.–Fri 9–4, Sat. 10–4, Sun. noon-4.*

Nook Farm, a late-19th-century neighborhood, was home to several prominent families. Samuel Langhorne Clemens, better known as Mark Twain, built his Stick-style Victorian mansion here in 1874. ★ ㉖ During his residency at the 19-room **Mark Twain House,** he published seven major novels, including *Tom Sawyer, Huckleberry Finn,* and *The Prince and the Pauper.* Personal memorabilia and original furnishings are on display, and one-hour guided tours of the house discuss its spectacular Victorian interior and Twain's family life. Also on tour are the rooms of the family butler, George Griffin, a prominent member of Hartford's African-American community. ⊠ *351 Farmington Ave., at Woodland St.,* ☎ *860/247–0998,* WEB *www.marktwainhouse.org.* ⌨ *$9.* ⊙ *May–Oct. and Dec., Mon.–Sat. 9:30–4, Sun. noon–4; Jan. 2–Apr. and Nov., Mon. and Wed.–Sat. 9:30–4, Sun. noon–4.*

㉗ The **Harriet Beecher Stowe House,** a Victorian Gothic cottage erected in 1871, stands as a tribute to the author of one of 19th-century America's most popular and influential works of literature, the antislavery novel *Uncle Tom's Cabin.* Stowe (1811–96) spent her final years here. Inside are her personal writing table and effects, several of her paintings, a period pinewood kitchen, and a terrarium of native ferns, mosses, and wildflowers. ⊠ *71 Forest St.,* ☎ *860/525–9258,* WEB *www.hartnet.org/stowe.* ⌨ *$6.50.* ⊙ *Memorial Day–Columbus Day and Dec., Mon.–Sat. 9:30–4:30, Sun. noon–4:30; mid-Oct.–Nov. and Jan.–Memorial Day, Tues.–Sat. 9:30–4:30, Sun. noon–4:30.*

Dining and Lodging

$$$–$$$$ ✕ **Max Downtown.** One of restaurateur Richard Rosenthal's culinary
★ creations, upscale Max Downtown serves cuisine from around the world—everything from Portobello mushroom napoleon and steamed miso-sake–glazed Chilean sea bass to aged New York strip steak and grilled veal loin chop. A separate cigar bar serves classic port and single-malt liquor. ⊠ *CityPlace, 185 Asylum St.,* ☎ *860/522–2530. Reservations essential. AE, DC, MC, V. No lunch weekends.*

$$–$$$ ✕ **Savannah.** The dining experience at this chic eatery is truly eclec-
★ tic: dishes combine French, Spanish, Asian, and southern influences. Favorites often include an appetizer of ravioli filled with a puree of sweet potato and topped with chive butter sauce and a touch of nutmeg, and an entrée of tuna crusted with sesame seeds and served with

risotto and jicama-ginger salsa. ⊠ *391 Main St.,* ☎ *860/278–2020. AE, MC, V. Closed Sun.–Mon. No lunch Sat.*

$$ ✕ **Peppercorn's Grill.** This mainstay of Hartford's restaurant scene presents contemporary Italian cuisine in a setting that is both lively (colorful murals adorn the walls) and formal (tables are topped with white linen). Some of the specials might be smoked Sicilian swordfish carpaccio, grilled and roasted veal with a truffle and porcino glaze, or Tuscan seafood stew. ⊠ *357 Main St.,* ☎ *860/547–1714. AE, DC, MC, V. Closed Sun.*

$$ ✕ **Hotep's.** This exotic restaurant—named for Imhotep, an Egyptian sage who lived in 2680 BC and was later deified—entices diners with international cuisine spiced with everything from Caribbean to Italian influences. You can muse at the decorative hieroglyphics and busts of Ramses and Nefertiti while sampling such starters as dahl soup and scallop seviche. Favored entreées include jerk-roasted chicken and fresh grouper crusted with yucca. ⊠ *283-291 Asylum St.,* ☎ *860/548–1675. AE, MC, V. Closed Sun. No lunch Sat. No dinner Mon.*

$$ ✕ **First and Last Tavern.** What looks to be a simple neighborhood joint south of downtown is actually one of the state's most hallowed pizza parlors. The long, old-fashioned wooden bar in one room is jammed most evenings with suburbia-bound daily-grinders shaking off their suits. The main dining room, which is just as noisy, has a brick outer wall covered with an array of celebrity photos. ⊠ *939 Maple Ave.,* ☎ *860/ 956–6000. Reservations not accepted. AE, D, DC, MC, V.*

$–$$ ✕ **Pastis.** Homey French cuisine such as steak frites, coq au vin, and beef bourguignon is the mainstay of this Parisian-style brasserie. Tile floors, lace curtains, and French prints set the mood. ⊠ *201 Ann St.,* ☎ *860/278–8852. AE, DC, MC, V. Closed Sun.*

$$$$ 🏨 **Goodwin Hotel.** Connecticut's only truly grand city hotel looks a
★   little odd in the downtown business district—the Civic Center dwarfs the ornate dark red structure, a registered historic landmark built in 1881. Its rooms are large and tastefully done in Colonial style and have Italian marble baths. The clubby, mahogany-panel Pierpont's Restaurant serves popular new American fare. ⊠ *1 Haynes St., 06103,* ☎ *860/246–7500 or 800/922–5006,* FAX *860/247–4576,* WEB *www.goodwinhotel.com.. 111 rooms, 13 suites. Restaurant, bar, gym, meeting room. AE, D, DC, MC, V.*

$$$ 🏨 **Hilton Hartford Hotel.** At 15 stories, this is the city's largest hotel. It's not sumptuous, but touches of elegance such as the street-level lobby abloom with fresh flowers abound. The Hilton connects to the Civic Center by an enclosed bridge and is within walking distance of the downtown area. ⊠ *315 Trumbull St. (at the Civic Center Plaza), 06103,* ☎ *860/728–5151,* FAX *860/240–7246,* WEB *www.hilton.com. 390 rooms, 6 suites. Restaurant, bar, indoor pool, hot tub, sauna, health club. AE, D, DC, MC, V.*

$ 🏨 **Ramada Inn Capitol Hill.** Adjacent to Bushnell Park, the Ramada has an unobstructed view of the State Capitol. Ask for a room in front—the ones facing the rear overlook the train station around the corner, a parking lot, and a busy highway. The restaurant serves steaks, hamburgers, and other traditional American fare. ⊠ *440 Asylum St., 06103,* ☎ *860/246–6591,* FAX *860/728–1382,* WEB *www.ramada.com. 96 rooms. Restaurant. AE, D, DC, MC, V. CP.*

Nightlife and the Arts

NIGHTLIFE

The **Arch Street Tavern** (⊠ 85 Arch St., ☎ 860/246–7610) hosts local rock bands. For barbecue and blues head to **Black-Eyed Sally's** (⊠ 350 Asylum St., ☎ 860/278–7427). **Coach's Sports Bar** (⊠ 117 Allyn St., ☎ 860/525–5141)is a always a happening spot to watch the game. **Mozzi-**

cato–De Pasquale's Bakery, Pastry Shop & Caffe (⊠ 242 Pittsfield Rd., ☎ 860/296–0426) serves up late-night Italian pastries in the bakery and espresso, cappuccino, and gelato in the café, which has a full bar.

THE ARTS

The Tony Award–winning **Hartford Stage Company** (⊠ 50 Church St., ☎ 860/527–5151) turns out future Broadway hits, innovative productions of the classics, and new plays. **The National Theatre of the Deaf** (⊠ 55 Van Dyke Ave., ☎ 860/724–5179) has moved its headquarters to Hartford. The award-winning ensemble performs in sign and spoken language. **Theatreworks** (⊠ 233 Pearl St., ☎ 860/527–7838), the Hartford equivalent of Off-Broadway, presents experimental new dramas. The **Bushnell** (⊠ 166 Capitol Ave., ☎ 860/246–6807) hosts the Hartford Symphony (☎ 860/244–2999) and tours of major musicals. The **Hartford Conservatory** (⊠ 834 Asylum Ave., ☎ 860/246–2588) presents musical performances, with an emphasis on traditional works. The mammoth **Meadows Music Theater** (⊠ 63 Savitt Way, ☎ 860/548–7370) hosts nationally known acts. **Real Art Ways** (⊠ 56 Arbor St., ☎ 860/232–1006) presents modern and experimental musical compositions in addition to avant-garde and foreign films.

Outdoor Activities and Sports

The **Hartford Wolf Pack** (☎ 860/246–7825) of the American Hockey League play at the 16,500-seat Civic Center (⊠ 1 Civic Center Plaza).

Ski Areas

MT. SOUTHINGTON

This mountain, an easy half-hour drive southwest of Hartford, has 14 trails off the 425 ft of vertical range split equally among basic beginner, intermediate, and advanced. All trails are lighted for night skiing and are serviced by one triple chairlift, one double, two T-bars, 1 J-bar, and a handle tow. Snowboarders will find a halfpipe and terrain park. The ski school (with 150 instructors) includes a popular SKIwee program for kids from 4 to 12 years old. The Mountain Room provides respite for skiers and snowboarders alike. ⊠ *396 Mount Vernon Rd., Southington 06489,* ☎ *860/628–0954; 860/628–7669 snow conditions.*

West Hartford

㉘ *5 mi west of Hartford.*

More metropolitan than many of its suburban neighbors, West Hartford is alive with a sense of community. Gourmet food and ethnic grocery stores abound, as do unusual boutiques and shops. A stroll around West Hartford Center (I–84, Exit 42) reveals well-groomed streets busy with pedestrians and lined with coffee shops.

★ ⊙ A life-size walk-through replica of a 60-ft sperm whale greets patrons of the **Science Center of Connecticut,** whose attractions include a wildlife sanctuary and planetarium. The Kids Factory teaches about magnetics, motion, optics, sound, and light through colorful hands-on exhibits. Some "Mathmagical" toys in the lower exhibit hall are a giant bubble maker, a hands-on weather station, and "Kaleidovision"—a 30-ft by 9-ft walk-in kaleidoscope. ⊠ *950 Trout Brook Dr.,* ☎ *860/231–2824,* WEB *www.sciencecenterct.org.. ⊠ Science Center $6, laser and planetarium shows $3 additional.* ⊙ *Sept.–June, Tues.–Wed. and Fri.–Sat. 10–5, Thurs. 10–8, Sun. noon–5; July–Aug., Mon.–Wed. and Fri.–Sat. 10–5, Thurs. 10–8, Sun. noon–5.*

The **Noah Webster House/Museum of Hartford History** is the birthplace of the famed author (1758–1843) of the *American Dictionary.* The 18th-century farmhouse contains Webster memorabilia and period furnishings. ⊠ *227 S. Main St.,* ☎ *860/521–5362,* WEB *www.ctstateu.edu/ noahweb.* ☞ *$5.* ⊙ *Sept.–May, Mon., Thurs.–Sun. 1–4; June–Aug., Mon. and Thurs.–Fri. 11–4, weekends 1–4.*

The **Museum of American Political Life** houses a staggering collection of rare political materials and memorabilia—buttons, posters, bumper stickers, and pamphlets—from the campaigns of U.S. presidents from George Washington to the present. A small section is devoted to memorabilia from the women's rights and temperance movements. ⊠ *University of Hartford, 200 Bloomfield Ave.,* ☎ *860/768–4090,* WEB *www.hartford.edu/polmus.* ☞ *Donation suggested.* ⊙ *Sept.–May, Tues.–Fri. 11–4, weekends noon–4; call for summer hours noon–4.*

Dining

$ ✕ **Butterfly Chinese Restaurant.** The piano entertainment suggests that this is not your ordinary order-by-number Chinese restaurant; indeed, the food is authentic, the staff outgoing. Among the 140 mostly Cantonese (some Szechuan) entrées are Peking duck and sesame chicken. ⊠ *831 Farmington Ave.,* ☎ *860/236–2816. AE, MC, V.*

Farmington

㉙ *5 mi southwest of West Hartford*

Busy Farmington, incorporated in 1645, is a classic river town with lovely estates, a perfectly preserved main street, and the prestigious **Miss Porter's School** (⊠ *60 Main St.*), the late Jacqueline Kennedy Onassis's alma mater. Antiques shops can be found near the intersection of Routes 4 and 10, along with some excellent house-museums.

★ The **Hill-Stead Museum** was converted from a private home into a museum by its talented owner, Theodate Pope, a turn-of-the-century architect. She also designed the elaborate sunken garden, now the elegant stage for poetry readings by nationally known writers every other week in summer. The Colonial Revival farmhouse contains a superb collection of French Impressionist art. Paintings of haystacks by Monet hang at each end of the drawing room, and Manet's *The Guitar Player* hangs in the middle. ⊠ *35 Mountain Rd.,* ☎ *860/677–4787,* WEB *www.hillstead.org.* ☞ *$7.* ⊙ *May–Oct., Tues.–Sun. 10–5; Nov.–Apr., Tues.–Sun. 11–4.*

A museum since the 1930s, the **Stanley-Whitman House** was built in 1720 and has a massive central chimney, an overhanging second story, and superlative 18th-century furnishings. ⊠ *37 High St.,* ☎ *860/677– 9222.* ☞ *$5.* ⊙ *Nov.–Apr., Sun. noon–4 and by appointment; May– Oct., Wed.–Sun. noon–4.*

Dining and Lodging

$$ ✕ **Ann Howard's Apricots.** A white Colonial with dozens of windows looking out over gardens and the Farmington River holds the area's best eatery. Fine new American cuisine—such as the grilled filet mignon with crispy fried Bermuda onions and a shiitake demi-glace or the duck with cashew wild rice—is presented in the quiet, cozy formal dining room; less expensive fare is available in the convivial pub. ⊠ *1593 Farmington Ave.,* ☎ *860/673–5903. AE, DC, MC, V.*

$$$–$$$$ ☗ **Farmington Inn.** Antiques and reproductions decorate guest rooms that are generous in size and appointed tastefully. Fresh flowers and paintings by local artists are nice touches. Much nicer than a chain hotel, the inn is very close to Miss Porter's and area museums. ⊠ *827 Farmington Ave., 06032,* ☎ *860/677–2821 or 800/648–9804,* FAX *860/677– 8332,* WEB *www.farmingtoninn.com. 72 rooms. Business services, meeting room. AE, D, DC, MC, V. CP.*

Shopping

The upscale 160-shop **Westfarms Mall** (⊠ New Britain Ave., or I–84, Exit 40, ☎ 860/561–3024) includes Nordstrom, April Cornell, Williams-Sonoma, and Restoration Hardware.

Simsbury

30 *12 mi north of Farmington via Rte. 10.*

Colonial-style shopping centers, a smattering of antiques shops, and a proliferation of insurance-industry executives define this chic bedroom community near Hartford.

The highlight of the Simsbury Historical Society's **Phelps Homestead** is the period-furnished 1771 Colonial home of Elijah Phelps and his family. A new permanent exhibit highlights the use of the home as a tavern from 1786–1849, when it was a stop on the Farmington Canal. You'll also learn about the 300-year, largely agrarian history of Simsbury, which was settled around 1640 and incorporated in 1670. Other buildings on the property include a Victorian carriage house (circa 1880), a 1795 cottage and herb garden, a 1740 schoolhouse, and a replica of the town's original meeting house that can be seen on special tours. You can view the houses only on a tour, but the highly strollable grounds are also accessible. ⊠ *800 Hopmeadow St.,* ☎ *860/658-2500.* ☜ *$6.* ☉ *Tues.–Sat. 10–4.*

The **Old New-Gate Prison and Copper Mine,** 7 mi north of Simsbury, was the country's first chartered copper mine (in 1707) and, later (in 1773), Connecticut's first Colonial prison. Tours of the underground mine (where temperatures rarely top 55°F) are a great way to chill out in summer. There are hiking trails and a picnic area. ⊠ *Newgate Rd., East Granby,* ☎ *860/653–3563 or 860/566–3005.* ☜ *$4.* ☉ *Mid-May–Oct., Wed.–Sun. 10–4:30.*

Lodging

$$$ ⌂ **Avon Old Farms Hotel.** This 20-acre compound of redbrick Colonial-style buildings is set into the Avon countryside at the foot of Talcott Mountain, about midway between Farmington and Simsbury. An immense place that caters largely to business travelers, it has quietly elegant rooms. ⊠ *279 Avon Mountain Rd., Avon 06001,* ☎ *860/677–1651,* FAX *860/677–0364,* WEB *www.avonoldfarmshotel.com. 160 rooms. Restaurant, pub, pool, sauna, exercise room, meeting room. AE, D, DC, MC, V. CP.*

$$$ ⌂ **Simsbury 1820 House.** The rooms at this inn perched on a hillside contain a judicious mix of antiques and modern furnishings. The main house was built in 1820 and has an 1890 addition on its west side; each room and suite here has a special feature—a decorative fireplace or balcony, a patio, a wet bar, a dormer with a cozy window seat. Across the parking lot is a former carriage house with 10 rooms; the split-level Executive Suite has a private patio, entrance, and hot tub. ⊠ *731 Hopmeadow St., 06070,* ☎ *860/658–7658 or 800/879–1820,* FAX *860/651–0724,* WEB *www.simsbury1820house.com. 30 rooms, 3 suites. Restaurant. AE, D, DC, MC, V. CP.*

Outdoor Activities and Sports

ICE-SKATING

The **International Skating Center of Connecticut** is a world-class twin-rink facility used for practice by skating luminaries such as Viktor Petrenko, Ekaterina Gordeeva, Scott Davis, and Isabelle Brasseur and Lloyd Eisler. Lessons and public skating sessions are offered, and ice shows are held periodically throughout the year. ⊠ *1375 Hopmeadow St.,* ☎ *860/651–5400.* ☜ *Call for public hrs and rates.*

A 1½-mi climb from the parking lot at the southern section of **Talcott Mountain State Park** to the 165-ft Heublein Tower, a former private home, rewards you with views of four states. ⊠ *Rte. 185,* ☎ *860/242–1158.* 🎫 *Free.* ☉ *Park daily 8 AM–sunset. Tower late Apr.–Labor Day, Thurs.–Sun. 10–5; Labor Day–late Oct., daily 10–5.*

Shopping
Arts Exclusive Gallery (⊠ 690 Hopmeadow St., ☎ 860/651–5824) represents more than 30 contemporary artists. The **Farmington Valley Arts Center** (⊠ 25 Arts Center La., Avon, ☎ 860/678–1867) shows the works of nationally known artists.

Windsor Locks

③ *13 mi northeast of Simsbury, 94 mi northeast of Greenwich, 48 mi northeast of New Haven, 56 mi northwest of New London.*

Windsor Locks was named for the locks of a canal built to bypass falls in the Connecticut River in 1833; in 1844 the canal closed to make way for a railroad line. You'll see long, low tobacco barns in the area. The town is home to Bradley International Airport, the state's central transportation hub.

★ The more than 70 aircraft at the **New England Air Museum** include flying machines that date from 1870, among them gliders and helicopters. A World War II–era P-47 Thunderbolt and B-29 Superfortress are on display, along with other vintage fighters and bombers. There's even a jet fighter simulator. *Next to Bradley International Airport, off Rte. 75,* ☎ *860/623–3305,* WEB *www.neam.org.* 🎫 *$7.* ☉ *Daily 10–5.*

The **Hatheway House,** 7 mi north of Windsor Locks, is one of the finest architectural specimens in New England. The walls of its neoclassical north wing (1794) still wear their original 18th-century French hand-blocked wallpaper. The double front doors and gambrel roof of the main house (1761) were typical accoutrements of Connecticut River valley homes. An ornate picket fence fronts the property. ⊠ *55 S. Main St. (take Rte. 75 north from Windsor Locks), Suffield,* ☎ *860/668–0055 or 860/247–8996.* 🎫 *$4.* ☉ *Mid-May–June and Sept.–mid-Oct., Wed. and weekends 1–4; July–Aug., Wed.–Sun. 1–4.*

Hartford and the Connecticut River Valley A to Z

To research prices, get advice from other travelers, and book travel arrangements, visit www.fodors.com.

AIRPORTS
Bradley International Airport, 12 mi north of Hartford, is served by American, Continental, Delta, Midway, Northwest, Southwest, United, and US Airways.
➤ AIRPORT INFORMATION: **Bradley International Airport** (⊠ Rte. 20, Windsor Locks; take I–91, Exit 40, ☎ 860/627–3000, WEB www. bradleyairport.com).

BUS TRAVEL
Hartford's renovated Union Station is the main terminus for Greyhound and Peter Pan bus lines buses. Bus service is available to most major northeastern cities. Connecticut Transit provides bus service throughout the greater Hartford area. The fare varies according to destination.
➤ BUS INFORMATION: **Union Station** (⊠ 1 Union Pl.).**Greyhound** (☎ 800/231–2222, WEB www.greyhound.com). **Peter Pan bus lines**(☎ 800/ 237–8747, WEB www.peterpan-bus.com). **Connecticut Transit** (☎ 860/ 525–9181, WEB www.cttransit.com).

CAR TRAVEL

Interstates 84 and 91, Route 2, and U.S. 44 intersect in Hartford. The junction of I–84 and I–91 in downtown Hartford is notorious for near-gridlock conditions during rush hour.

The major road through the valley is Route 9, which extends from south of Hartford at I–91 to I–95. Old Saybrook. Essex, Ivoryton, Chester, Middletown, and New Britain are all on or near Route 9; Wethersfield is east of Route 9. From just below Deep River to just above Higganum, Route 154 loops east of Route 9; head east from Route 154 on Route 151 to reach East Haddam. Farmington is west of Hartford on Route 4. To reach Simsbury head west from Hartford on U.S. 202/44 and north on U.S. 202. To reach Windsor Locks, take I–91 north from Hartford and head north on Route 159.

EMERGENCIES

➤ HOSPITALS: **Hartford Hospital** (⊠ 80 Seymour St., ☎ 860/545–5000, WEB www.hartfordhosp.org). **Middlesex Hospital** (⊠ 28 Crescent St., Middletown, ☎ 860/344–6000, WEB www.midhosp.org).
➤ LATE-NIGHT PHARMACIES: CVS (⊠ 1099 New Britain Ave., West Hartford, ☎ 860/236–6181, WEB www.cvs.com; 154 Main St., Old Saybrook, ☎ 860/388–1045).

TRAIN TRAVEL

Hartford's renovated Union Station is the main terminus for Amtrak trains. Train service is available to most major northeastern cities. The fare varies according to destination.
➤ TRAIN INFORMATION: **Union Station**(⊠ 1 Union Pl.). **Amtrak**(☎ 800/872–7245, WEB www.amtrak.com).

VISITOR INFORMATION

➤ TOURIST INFORMATION: **Central Connecticut Tourism District** (⊠ 1 Grove St., Suite 310, New Britain 06053, ☎ 860/225–3901, WEB www.centralct.org). **Connecticut's North Central Tourism Bureau** (⊠ 111 Hazard Ave., Enfield 06082, ☎ 860/763–2578 or 800/248–8283, WEB www.cnctb.org). **Connecticut River Valley and Shoreline Visitors Council** (⊠ 393 Main St., Middletown 06457, ☎ 860/347–0028 or 800/486–3346, WEB www.cttourism.org). **Greater Hartford Tourism District** (⊠ 234 Murphy Rd., Hartford 06114, ☎ 860/244–8181 or 800/793–4480, WEB www.enjoyhartford.com).

THE LITCHFIELD HILLS

Here in the foothills of the Berkshires is some of the most spectacular and unspoiled scenery in Connecticut. Two scenic highways, I–84 and Route 8, form the southern and eastern boundaries of the region. New York, to the west, and Massachusetts, to the north, complete the rectangle. Grand old inns are plentiful, as are sophisticated eateries. Rolling farmlands abut thick forests, and trails—including a section of the Appalachian Trail—traverse the state parks and forests. Two rivers, the Housatonic and the Farmington, attract anglers and canoeing enthusiasts, and the state's three largest natural lakes, Waramaug, Bantam, and Twin, are here. Sweeping town greens and stately homes anchor Litchfield and New Milford. Kent, New Preston, and Woodbury draw avid antiquers, and Washington, Salisbury, and Norfolk provide a glimpse into New England village life as it might have existed two centuries ago.

Favorite roads for admiring fall foliage are U.S. 7, from New Milford through Kent and West Cornwall to Canaan; Route 41 to Route 4 from Salisbury through Lakeville, Sharon, Cornwall Bridge, and Goshen to

Torrington; and Route 47 to U.S. 202 to Route 341 from Woodbury through Washington, New Preston, and Warren to Kent.

New Milford

❸❷ *28 mi west of Waterbury, 46 mi northeast of Greenwich.*

If you're approaching the Litchfield Hills from the south, New Milford is a practical starting point to begin a visit. It was also a starting point for a young cobbler named Roger Sherman, who, in 1743, opened his shop where Main and Church streets meet. A Declaration of Independence signatory, Sherman also helped draft the Articles of Confederation and the Constitution. You'll find old shops, galleries, and eateries all within a short stroll of New Milford green—one of the longest in New England.

OFF THE BEATEN PATH **THE SILO –** New Yorkers who miss Zabar's and Balducci's feel right at home in this silo and barn packed with objets de cookery, crafts, and an array of goodies and sauces. The founder and music director of the New York Pops, Skitch Henderson, and his wife, Ruth, own and operate this bazaar, where culinary superstars give a variety of cooking classes between March and December. ⊠ *44 Upland Rd., 4 mi north of the New Milford town green on U.S. 202,* ☎ *860/355–0300.* ☉ *Daily 10–5.* WEB www.thesilo.com.

Dining and Lodging

$$ ✕ **Adrienne.** Set in an 18th-century farmhouse with terraced gardens, Adrienne serves award-winning American cuisine from a seasonal menu. You may be lucky enough to encounter seared scallops, garlic, rosemary, and spinach in a roasted tomato cream sauce over pasta or an Indonesian stew of chicken and potatoes with curry, coconut milk, and steamed broccoli. ⊠ *218 Kent Rd.,* ☎ *860/354–6001. AE, D, DC, MC, V. Closed Mon.*

$–$$ ✕ **Bistro Café.** Copper pots and vintage black-and-white photos adorn the walls of this café in a redbrick corner building. The well-crafted regional American dishes change weekly—tender grilled swordfish with whipped potatoes, veggies, and a chive aioli one week, oven-roasted duck with pecans and cranberry coulis the next. You can sample buffalo, moose, antelope, kangaroo, alligator, or northern black bear—they're all farm-raised and low in cholesterol. Upstairs is a taproom where you can relax with a bottle of wine or feast from the same menu as downstairs. ⊠ *31 Bank St.,* ☎ *860/355–3266. AE, MC, V.*

$$ ▦ **Homestead Inn.** The Homestead, high on a hill overlooking New Milford's town green, was built in 1853 and opened as an inn in 1928. Life is casual here, and the owners, Rolf and Peggy Hammer, are always game for a leisurely chat. Breakfast is served in a cheery living room, where you can sit by the fire. The eight rooms in the main house have more personality than those in the motel-style structure next door. ⊠ *5 Elm St., 06776,* ☎ *860/354–4080,* FAX *860/354–7046,* WEB *www.homesteadct.com. 14 rooms. AE, D, DC, MC, V. CP.*

New Preston

❸❸ *4 mi north of New Milford.*

The crossroads village of New Preston, perched above a 40-ft waterfall on the Aspetuck River, has a little town center that's packed with antiques shops specializing in everything from 18th-century furnishings to out-of-print books.

Lake Waramaug, north of New Preston on Route 45, is an area that reminds many of Austria and Switzerland. The lake is named for Chief Waramaug, one of the most revered figures in Connecticut's Native

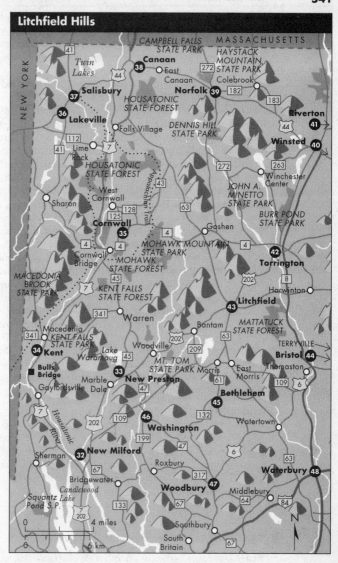

Litchfield Hills

MASSACHUSETTS

NEW YORK

Twin Lakes

CAMPBELL FALLS STATE PARK

HAYSTACK MOUNTAIN STATE PARK

Canaan 38 ○ East Canaan

Colebrook

Salisbury 37

Norfolk 39

HOUSATONIC STATE FOREST

Lakeville 36

○ Falls Village

DENNIS HILL STATE PARK

Riverton 41

Winsted 40

Lime Rock

HOUSATONIC STATE FOREST

Winchester Center

JOHN A. MINETTO STATE PARK

BURR POND STATE PARK

Sharon ○

West Cornwall

Cornwall 35

Goshen

MOHAWK MOUNTAIN STATE PARK

Cornwall Bridge

MOHAWK STATE FOREST

Torrington 42

MACEDONIA BROOK STATE PARK

KENT FALLS STATE PARK

Warren

Litchfield 43

Harwinton ○

MATTATUCK STATE FOREST

Kent 34

Macedonia KENT FALLS STATE PARK

Lake Waramaug

Woodville

Bantam

TERRYVILLE

Bristol 44

Bulls Bridge

New Preston 33

MT. TOM STATE PARK

Morris

East Morris

Thomaston

Gaylordsville

Marble Dale

Bethlehem

New Milford 32

Sherman

Washington 46

Watertown

Roxbury

Waterbury 48

Bridgewater

Candlewood Lake

Squantz Pond S.P.

Woodbury 47

Middlebury

Southbury

South Britain

0   4 miles

0   6 km

N

American history. A drive around the 8-mi perimeter of the lake takes you past beautiful inns—many of which serve delicious food—and homes. **Lake Waramaug State Park** (⊠ 30 Lake Waramaug Rd., ☎ 860/868–0220 or 860/868–2592), at the northwest tip of the lake, is an idyllic 75-acre spread, great for picnicking and lakeside camping.

The popular **Hopkins Vineyard,** overlooking Lake Waramaug, produces more than 13 varieties of wine, from sparkling to dessert. A weathered red barn houses a gift shop and a tasting room, and there's a picnic area. The wine bar serves a fine cheese-and-pâté board. ⊠ 25 Hopkins Rd., ☎ 860/868–7954, WEB *www.hopkinsvineyard.com.* 🖙 Free. ☉ Jan.–Feb., Fri.–Sat. 10–5, Sun. 11–5; Mar.–Apr., Wed.–Sat. 10–5, Sun. 11–5; May–Dec., Mon.–Sat. 10–5, Sun. 11–5.

Dining and Lodging

$$$$ ✕ ☒ **Boulders Inn.** The most idyllic and prestigious of the inns along Lake
★   Waramaug opened in 1940 but still looks like the private home it was

a century ago. Apart from the main house, a carriage house and several guest houses command panoramic views of the countryside and the lake. The rooms, four with double whirlpool baths, contain Victorian antiques and wood-burning fireplaces. The exquisite menu at the window-lined, stone-wall dining room ($$–$$$) changes seasonally but might include hickory-glazed pork mignon or pan-seared halibut with wild mushroom duxelle. ⊠ *E. Shore Rd. (Rte. 45), 06777,* ☎ *860/868–0541 or 800/552–6853,* FAX *860/868–1925,* WEB *www.bouldersinn.com. 17 rooms. Restaurant, lake, beach, boating. AE, MC, V. MAP.*

$$$–$$$$ ✕⊡ **Birches Inn.** One of the area's poshest inns, the Birches is some-
★ thing of a Lake Waramaug institution. Antiques and reproductions decorate the rooms; three on the waterfront have private decks. Executive chef Frederic Faveau presides over the lakeview dining room ($$; closed Tuesday and Wednesday; no lunch). Among his signature dishes are grilled marinated leg of lamb with herb risotto cake, sautéed mustard greens, and a roasted garlic sauce. ⊠ *233 West Shore Rd., 06777,* ☎ *860/868–1735,* FAX *860/868–1815,* WEB *www.thebirchesinn.com. 8 rooms. Restaurant, beach. AE, MC, V. CP.*

$–$$ ✕⊡ **Hopkins Inn.** A grand 1847 Victorian that sits on a hill overlooking
★ Lake Waramaug, the Hopkins is one of the best bargains in the Hills. Most rooms have plain white bedspreads, simple antiques, and pastel floral wallpaper. In winter, the inn smells of burning firewood; year-round, it is redolent with the aromas from the rambling dining rooms ($$$; closed January through late March), which serve outstanding Swiss and Austrian dishes—calves' brains in black butter and sweetbreads Viennese. When the weather is kind, you can dine on the terrace and view the lake. ⊠ *22 Hopkins Rd. (1 mi off Rte. 45), 06777,* ☎ *860/ 868–7295,* FAX *860/868–7464,* WEB *www.thehopkinsinn.com. 11 rooms. Restaurant, beach. AE, D, MC, V.*

Shopping

More than a dozen shops with art, antiques, and related items can be found within walking distance of downtown New Preston. **Ray Boas, Bookseller** (⊠ 6 Church St., ☎ 860/868–9596) stocks thousands of antiquarian and out-of-print books. **J. Seitz & Co.** (⊠ Main St., ☎ 860/ 868–0119) fills 5,000 square feet with stylish home furnishings, fashions, and gifts.

Kent

🄴 *12 mi northwest of New Preston.*

Kent has the area's greatest concentration of art galleries, some nationally renowned. Home to a prep school of the same name, Kent once held many ironworks. The Schaghticoke Indian Reservation is also here. During the Revolutionary War, one hundred Schaghticokes helped defend the Colonies by transmitting messages of army intelligence from the Litchfield Hills to Long Island Sound, along the hilltops, by way of shouts and drum beats. **Bulls Bridge** (⊠ U.S. 7, south of Kent), one of three covered bridges in Connecticut, is open to cars.

Hardware-store buffs and vintage-tool aficionados will feel at home at the **Sloane-Stanley Museum.** Artist and author Eric Sloane (1905–1985) was fascinated by Early American woodworking tools, and his collection (on display) ranges from the 17th to the 19th century. The museum, a re-creation of Sloane's last studio, also encompasses the ruins of a 19th-century iron furnace. Sloane's books and prints, which celebrate vanishing aspects of American heritage such as barns and covered bridges, are on sale here. ⊠ *U.S. 7,* ☎ *860/927–3849 or 860/566–3005.* 🖽 *$3.50.* ⊙ *Mid-May–Oct., Wed.–Sun. 10–4.*

Dining and Lodging

$$ ✕⚏ **Fife 'n Drum.** If you like to shop, eat, and have a cozy place to rest your head, you can do all three at this family owned inn, restaurant, and gift shop. The shop sells everything from cards and candles to jewelry and accessories. The eight inn rooms (most above the shop) are decorated with a pleasing assortment of antiques, reproductions, and flowery decorative accessories. The restaurant serves a mix of continental and American choices. ✉ *53 N. Main St., 06757,* ☎ *860/927–3509,* FAX *860/927–4595,* WEB *www.fifendrum.com. 8 rooms. Restaurant, shop. AE, MC, V. Closed Tues.*

Outdoor Activities and Sports

The **Appalachian Trail**'s longest riverwalk, off Route 341, is the almost 8-mi hike from Kent to Cornwall Bridge along the Housatonic River. The early season trout fishing is superb at 2,300-acre **Macedonia Brook State Park** (✉ Macedonia Brook Rd. off Rte. 341, ☎ 860/927–3238), where you can also hike and cross-country ski.

Shopping

The **Bachelier-Cardonsky Gallery** (✉ 10 Main St., ☎ 860/927–3129), one of the foremost galleries in the Northeast, exhibits works by local artists and contemporary masters such as Alexander Calder, Carol Anthony, and Jackson Pollock. The **Paris–New York–Kent Gallery** (✉ Kent Station, off U.S. 7, ☎ 860/927–4152) shows museum-quality contemporary works by local and world-famous artists. **Pauline's Place** (✉ 79 N. Main St., ☎ 860/927–4475) specializes in Victorian, Georgian, Art Deco, Edwardian, and contemporary jewelry.

En Route Heading north from Kent toward Cornwall, you'll pass the entrance to 295-acre **Kent Falls State Park** (✉ U.S. 7, ☎ 860/927–3238, ⌸ $5–$8), where you can hike a short way to one of the most impressive waterfalls in the state and picnic in the green meadows at the base of the falls.

Cornwall

③⑤ *12 mi northeast of Kent.*

Connecticut's Cornwalls can get confusing. (Try saying *that* five times fast.) There's Cornwall, Cornwall Bridge, West Cornwall, Cornwall Hollow, East Cornwall, and North Cornwall. What this quiet corner of the Litchfield Hills is known for is its fantastic vistas of woods and mountains and its covered bridge, which spans the Housatonic and is easily one of the most photographed spots in the state.

A romantic reminder of the past, the wooden, barn-red, one-lane, covered **Cornwall Bridge** is not in the town of the same name but several mi up U.S. 7 on Route 128 in West Cornwall. The bridge was built in 1841 and incorporates strut techniques that were copied by bridge builders around the country.

With many trails and nature walks, the **Sharon Audubon Center,** a 890-acre sanctuary with a wide variety of birds, is one of the best places to hike in Connecticut. On-site are an exhibit center, a gift shop, and a picnic area. ✉ *325 Cornwall Bridge Rd., Sharon,* ☎ *860/364–0520,* WEB *www.audubon.org/local/sanctuary/sharon. ⌸ $3. ☉ Mon.–Sat. 9–5, Sun. 1–5; trails daily dawn–dusk.*

Dining and Lodging

$$ ✕⚏ **The Cornwall Inn.** This 19th-century inn on scenic Route 7 combines country charm with up-to-date elegance; eight rooms in the adjacent "lodge" are slightly more rustic in tone. The restaurant ($$) serves American cuisine with French undertones on a seasonally changing menu. Entrées might include steak au poivre with cracked peppercorns and

cognac sauce or ravioli with sautéed shrimp, scallops, mushrooms, and tomatoes in a cognac-lobster sauce. ⊠ *270 Kent Rd. (Rte. 7), 06754,* ☏ *860/672–6884 or 800/786–6884,* <u>WEB</u> *www.cornwallinn.com. 14 rooms. Restaurant, bar. AE, MC, V.*

Outdoor Activities and Sports

CANOEING AND KAYAKING

Clarke Outdoors (⊠ U.S. 7, West Cornwall, ☏ 860/672–6365) rents canoes and kayaks and operates 10-mi trips from Falls Village to Housatonic Meadows State Park from April to October.

FISHING

Housatonic Anglers (⊠ U.S. 7, West Cornwall, ☏ 860/672–4457), which operates half- and full-day tours, provides fly-fishing instruction for trout and bass on the Housatonic and its tributaries. **Housatonic River Outfitters** (⊠ Rte. 128, West Cornwall, ☏ 860/672–1010) is a full-service fly shop offering guided trips of the region as well as classes in fly fishing, fly tying, and casting; it also stocks a good selection of vintage and antique gear.

STATE PARKS

Housatonic Meadows State Park (⊠ U.S. 7, Cornwall Bridge, ☏ 860/672–6772 or 860/927–3238) is marked by its tall pine trees near the Housatonic River. Fly-fishers consider this 2-mi stretch of the river among the best places in New England to test their skills against trout and bass. The riverside campsites are excellent.

Mohawk Mountain State Park (⊠ 1 mi south of Cornwall off Rte. 4, ☏ 860/927–3238) is a great spot for a picnic. The view at the top of 1,683-ft Mohawk Mountain is breathtaking, especially during foliage season; the hike up is 2½ mi.

Shopping

Cornwall Bridge Pottery Store (⊠ Rte. 128, West Cornwall, ☏ 860/672–6545) sells its own pottery and some glass by Simon Pearce. **Ian Ingersoll Cabinetmakers** (⊠ 1 Main St., by the Cornwall Bridge, West Cornwall, ☏ 860/672–6334) stocks Shaker-style furniture.

Ski Areas

MOHAWK MOUNTAIN

Mohawk's 23 trails, ranging down 640 vertical ft, include plenty of intermediate terrain, with a few trails for beginners and a few steeper sections toward the top of the mountain. A small section is devoted to snowboarders. Trails are serviced by one triple lift and four doubles and are lit for night skiing except on Sunday. The base lodge has munchies and a retail shop, and the Pine Lodge, halfway up the slope, has an outdoor patio. Mohawk's SKIwee program is for kids from age 5 to 12. There are facilities for ice-skating. ⊠ *46 Great Hollow Rd., off Rte. 4, 06753,* ☏ *860/672–6100; 860/672–6464 snow conditions.*

Lakeville

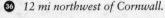 *12 mi northwest of Cornwall.*

You can usually spot an original Colonial home in handsome Lakeville by looking for the grapevine design cut into the frieze above the front door. It's the trademark of the builder of the town's first homes. Take a peak at the lake of Lakeville, **Lake Wononscopomuc,** as you drive along U.S. 44 or Route 41. A closer look is unlikely, however, as most of the shoreline lies on private property.

The holdings of the **Holley House Museum,** which chronicles 18th- and 19th-century life, include a 1768 ironmaster's home with an 1808 Classical Revival wing filled with family furnishings, Colonial portraits, and a Holley Manufacturing Co. pocketknife exhibit. "From Corsets to Freedom" is a popular hands-on exhibit, set in the 1870s, demonstrating the debate between women's rights versus "women's sphere" in the home. Tours are conducted. Admission also includes the on-site **Salisbury Cannon Museum**, which surveys the contributions of area residents and the local iron industry to the American Revolution. ⊠ *15 Millerton Rd.,* ☎ *860/435–2878,* WEB *www.salisburyassociation.org.* ⊠ *$3.* ☉ *Mid-June–mid-Oct., weekends noon–5 and by appointment.*

Nightlife and the Arts

From mid-June to mid-September, **Music Mountain** (⊠ Falls Village, ☎ 860/824–7126) presents chamber music concerts on Sunday afternoon and some Saturday evenings, and jazz concerts on Saturday nights.

Outdoor Activities and Sports

Auto racing at renowned **Lime Rock Park** (⊠ Rte. 112, ☎ 860/435–5000 or 800/722–3577) takes place on occasional Saturday and holiday Mondays from late April to mid-October; amphitheater-style lawn seating allows for great views all around.

Rustling Wind Stables (⊠ 160 Mountain Rd., Falls Village, ☎ 860/824–7634) gives riding lessons and operates pony rides for the kids by appointment.

Salisbury

㊲ *6 mi north of Lakeville.*

Were it not for the obsolescence of its ironworks, Salisbury might today be the largest city in Connecticut. Instead, it settles for having both the state's highest mountain, Bear Mountain (2,355 ft), and its highest point, the shoulder of Mt. Frissel (2,380 ft)—whose peak is in Massachusetts. There's a spot on Mt. Frissel where, if the urge strikes you (as it does many), you can stretch your limbs across the Connecticut, Massachusetts, and New York borders.

Iron was discovered here in 1732, and for the next century, the slopes of Salisbury's Mt. Riga produced the finest iron in America. Swiss and Russian immigrants, and later Hessian deserters from the British army, worked the great furnaces. The spread of rail transport opened up better sources of ore, the region's lumber supply was depleted, and the introduction of the Bessemer process of steel manufacturing—partially invented by Salisbury native Alexander Holley—reduced the demand for iron products. Most signs of cinder heaps and slag dumps are long gone, replaced by grand summer homes and gardens.

Harney & Sons Fine Teas supplies its high-quality Darjeeling, Earl Grey, Keemun, and other blends to some of the world's best hotels and restaurants. The tasting room has samples of some of the 100 varieties, and there's a gift shop. If you call ahead you might even be able to schedule a tour, led by founder John Harney himself, of the factory, where the tea is blended and packaged. ⊠ *11 Brook St.,* ☎ *860/435–5050,* WEB *www.harney.com.* ⊠ *Free.* ☉ *Mon.–Sat. 10–5, Sun. 11–4.*

Dining and Lodging

$$$$ ✕🏨 **Under Mountain Inn.** The nearest neighbors of this white-clapboard farmhouse are the horses grazing in the field across the road. Antiques, knickknacks, and objets d'art fill every space; chess and checkers games are set up by the fireplace. The hospitality has a pronounced British flavor (there's a British video lounge and "The Pub"—a replica of an English taproom); dinner, too, recalls Britain with dishes such as hearty steak-and-kidney pie. You can work off some of those calories with a hike on the nearby Appalachian Trail. ⊠ *482 Under Mountain Rd. (Rte. 41), 06068,* ☎ *860/435–0242,* FAX *860/435–2379. 7 rooms. Restaurant, pub, hiking. MC, V. MAP.*

Shopping

The **Salisbury Antiques Center** (⊠ 46 Library St., off U.S. 44, ☎ 860/435–0424) carries a varied selection of high-end American and English pieces. The **Village Store** (⊠ 19 Main St./U.S. 44, ☎ 860/435–9459) stocks quality sportswear, hiking boots, and maps, as well as bicycles, cross-country skis, and showshoes for sale or rent.

Canaan

38 *10 mi northeast of Salisbury, 84 mi northeast of Stamford, 42 mi northwest of Hartford.*

Canaan is one of the more developed towns in the Litchfield region. It was the site of some important late-18th-century industry, including a gun-barrel factory and a paper mill, and was also the home of Captain Gershom Hewitt, who is credited with securing the plans of Fort Ticonderoga for Ethan Allen.

Dining

$$ ✕ **Cannery Café.** The eggshell-color walls of this storefront American bistro are painted with a pattern of gleaming gold stars; elegant brass fixtures reflect the muted lighting. All is crisp and clean, the service chatty but refined. Pistachio-crusted salmon and grilled lamb are popular menu items. Sunday brunch is a favorite with locals. ⊠ *85 Main St. (U.S. 44 and 7),* ☎ *860/824–7333. AE, MC, V. No lunch.*

$ ✕ **Collin's Diner.** There's no denying that this 1942 O'Mahony diner,
★ inspired by the jazzy railroad dining cars of the '20s and '30s, is a classic beauty. Locals count on Collin's for classic diner fare, but the specials are the biggest draw—on Friday there's usually baked stuffed shrimp, on Saturday a meaty 2-inch cut of prime rib. The diner closes at 3 PM (at 1 PM on Wednesday); call for extended summer hours. ⊠ *U.S. 44,* ☎ *860/824–7040. No credit cards. No dinner.*

Shopping

The **Connecticut Woodcarvers Gallery** (⊠ U.S. 44, East Canaan, ☎ 860/824–0883) sells the work of woodcarver Joseph Cieslowski, whose unique relief carvings embellish clocks, mirrors, and decorative panels.

Norfolk

39 *7 mi southeast of Canaan, 59 mi north of New Haven.*

Norfolk, thanks to its severe climate and terrain, is one of the best-preserved villages in the Northeast. Notable industrialists have been summering here for two centuries, and many enormous homesteads still exist. The striking town green is at the junction of Route 272 and U.S. 44. At its southern corner is a fountain (designed by Augustus Saint-Gaudens and executed by Stanford White), a memorial to Joseph Battell, who turned Norfolk into a major trading center.

Dr. Frederick Shepard Dennis lavishly entertained guests, among them President Howard Taft and several Connecticut governors, in the stone pavilion at the summit of what is now **Dennis Hill State Park.** From its 1,627-ft height, you can see Haystack Mountain, New Hampshire and, on a clear day, New Haven harbor, all the way across the state. Picnic on the park's 240-acre grounds or hike one of its many trails. ⊠ *Rte. 272,* ☎ *860/482–1817.* ☜ *Free.* ⊙ *Daily 8 AM–dusk.*

Dining and Lodging

$–$$$ ✕ **The Pub.** Bottles of trendy beers line the shelves of this down-to-earth
★   restaurant on the ground floor of a redbrick Victorian near the town
green. Burgers and other pub fare are on the menu alongside strip steak
and lamb curry. This place is a real melting pot. ⊠ *U.S. 44,* ☎ *860/
542–5716. AE, MC, V. Closed Mon.*

$$–$$$$ ⊞ **Manor House.** Among this 1898 Bavarian Tudor's remarkable fea-
★   tures are its bibelots, mirrors, carpets, antique beds, and prints—not
to mention the 20 stained-glass windows designed by Louis Tiffany.
The vast Spofford Room has windows on three sides, a king-size
canopy bed with a cheery fireplace opposite, and a balcony. The Morgan Room has the most remarkable feature—a private wood-panel elevator (added in 1939). It also has a private deck. ⊠ *Box 447, 69 Maple
Ave., 06058,* ☎ FAX *860/542–5690,* WEB *www.manorhouse-norfolk.com.
8 rooms. AE, MC, V. BP.*

Nightlife and the Arts

The **Norfolk Chamber Music Festival** (☎ 860/542–3000), at the Music
Shed on the Ellen Battell Stoeckel Estate at the northwest corner of the
Norfolk green, presents world-renowned artists and ensembles on Fri-
day and Saturday summer evenings. Students from the Yale School of
Music perform on Thursday evening and Saturday morning. Early ar-
rivals can stroll or picnic on the 70-acre grounds or visit the art gallery.

The newly renovated **Greenwoods Theatre at Norfolk** (U.S. 44, ☎ 860/
542–0026), has its own professional resident company that performs
from June–October; a vintage film series runs the rest of the year.

Outdoor Activities and Sports

One of the most spectacular views in the state can be seen from
Haystack Mountain State Park (⊠ Rte. 272, ☎ 860/482–1817), with
a challenging trail to the top for the brave and a road halfway up for
the rest of us.

Shopping

Norfolk Artisans Guild (⊠ 24 Greenwoods Rd. E, ☎ 860/542–5487)
carries works by more than 60 local artisans—from hand-painted pillows to hand-crafted baskets.

Winsted

40   *9 mi southeast of Norfolk, 28 mi north of Waterbury, 25 mi northwest of Hartford.*

With its rows of old homes and businesses seemingly untouched since
the 1940s, Winsted still looks a bit like the set of a Frank Capra movie.
Though it's far less fashionable than nearby Norfolk, the town, which
was devastated by a major flood in 1955, is still worth a brief stop.
You can drive around the hills and alongside the reservoirs.

Nightlife and the Arts

The **Gilson Café and Cinema** (⊠ 354 Main St., ☎ 860/379–6069), a
refurbished Art Deco movie house, serves food and drinks unobtru-
sively during movies, every evening except Monday. You must be 21
or older for shows on the weekend.

Outdoor Activities and Sports

Main Stream Canoe and Kayaks (⊠ U.S. 44, New Hartford, ☎ 860/
693–6791) rents and sells canoes and kayaks, conducts day trips on
the Farmington River, and offers lessons. Moonlight trips take place
on summer evenings. **North American Canoe Tours** (⊠ Satan's Kingdom State Recreation Area, U.S. 44, New Hartford, ☎ 860/739–
0791) rents tubes and flotation devices for exhilarating self-guided tours

along the Farmington River. The company is open for business on weekends from Memorial Day to June and daily from June to Labor Day.

Ski Area
SKI SUNDOWN

This area has the state's most challenging trails plus some neat touches—a sundeck on the top of the mountain and a Senior Spree social club for skiers 55 and older—as well as excellent facilities and equipment. The vertical drop is 625 ft. Of the 15 trails, 8 are for beginners, 4 for intermediates, and 3 for advanced skiers. All are lighted at night and serviced by three triple chairs and one double. Terrain features are set up on the mountain; lessons are available for ages 4 and up. ⊠ *Ratlum Rd., New Hartford 06057, ☎ 860/379–9851; 860/379–7669 snow conditions.*

Riverton

41 *6 mi north of Winsted.*

Almost every New Englander has sat in a Hitchcock chair. Riverton, formerly Hitchcockville, is where Lambert Hitchcock built the first one, in 1826. The Farmington and Still rivers meet in this tiny hamlet. It's in one of the more unspoiled regions in the Hills, great for hiking and driving.

The **Hitchcock Museum,** showcasing beautiful examples of 18th- and 19th-century furniture, is in the gray granite Union Church. The nearby Hitchcock Factory Store, which sells first-quality merchandise at outlet prices and also has a seconds department, is open year-round and makes arrangements for tours. ⊠ *Rte. 20, ☎ 860/379–4826. ☜ Free. ☉ By appointment only.*

Dining and Lodging

$$–$$$$ ✕🏨 **Old Riverton Inn.** This historic inn, built in 1796 and overlooking the west branch of the Farmington River and the Hitchcock Chair Factory, is a peaceful weekend retreat. Rooms are small—except for the fireplace suite—and the decorating, which includes Hitchcock furnishings, is for the most part ordinary, but the inn always delivers warm hospitality. The inviting dining room serves traditional New England fare; the stuffed pork chops are local favorites. ⊠ *Rte. 20, 06065, ☎ 860/379–8678 or 800/378–1796, ℻ 860/379–1006. 11 rooms, 1 suite. Restaurant. AE, D, DC, MC, V. BP.*

Outdoor Activities and Sports

American Legion and People's State Forests (⊠ Off Rte. 181, ☎ 860/379–2469) border the west bank and the east bank, respectively, of the West Branch of the Farmington River—a designated National Wild and Scenic River. You can picnic beneath 200-year-old pines along the riverbank, and the hiking, fishing, tubing, and canoeing are superb.

Torrington

42 *14 mi southwest of Riverton.*

This old industrial town has a few hidden charms for those willing to overlook its rougher sections. Torrington's pines were for years used for shipbuilding, and its factories produced brass kettles, needles, pins, and bicycle spokes. Torrington was the birthplace of abolitionist John Brown and also of Gail Borden, who developed the first successful method for the production of evaporated milk.

The **Hotchkiss-Fyler House,** a 16-room century-old Queen Anne structure with a slate and brick exterior, is one of the better house museums in Connecticut. The design high points include hand-stenciled walls and intricate mahogany woodwork and ornamental plaster. European porcelains, American and British glass, and paintings by Winfield S. Clime are on display. If you plan to arrive around noon on a weekday, call ahead; the house sometimes closes briefly at lunchtime. ⊠ *192 Main St.,* ☎ *860/482–8260.* ☞ *$2.* ⊙ *Tours Apr.–Oct. and last 2 wks of Dec., Tues.–Fri. 10–4, weekends noon–4.*

Nightlife and the Arts

The **Warner Theatre** (⊠ 68 Main St., ☎ 860/489–7180), an Art Deco former movie palace, presents live Broadway musicals, ballet, and concerts by touring pop, classical, and country musicians.

Outdoor Activities and Sports

The lures at 436-acre **Burr Pond State Park** (⊠ Rte. 8, ☎ 860/482–1817) are a crystal-clear pond, hiking paths, and wheelchair-accessible picnic grounds.

Litchfield

㊸ *5 mi southwest of Torrington, 48 mi north of Bridgeport, 34 mi west of Hartford.*

Everything in Litchfield, the wealthiest and most noteworthy town in the Litchfield Hills, seems to exist on a larger scale than in neighboring burgs, especially the impressive **Litchfield Green** and the white Colonial and Greek Revival homes that line the broad elm-shaded streets. Harriet Beecher Stowe, author of *Uncle Tom's Cabin,* and her brother, abolitionist preacher Henry Ward Beecher, were born and raised in Litchfield, and many famous Americans earned their law degrees at the Litchfield Law School. Today lovely but exceptionally expensive boutiques and hot-spot restaurants line the downtown, attracting celebrities and the town's monied citizens.

★ In 1773, Judge Tapping Reeve enrolled his first student, Aaron Burr, in what was to become the first law school in the country. (Before Judge Reeve, students studied the law as apprentices, not in formal classes.) The **Tapping Reeve House and Law School** is dedicated to Reeve's remarkable achievement and to the notable students who passed through its halls: Oliver Wolcott Jr., John C. Calhoun, Horace Mann, three U.S. Supreme Court justices, and 15 governors, not to mention senators, congressmen, and ambassadors. Renovations in 1998 made the museum into one of the state's most worthy attractions, with interactive multimedia exhibits, an excellent introductory film, and beautifully restored facilities. ⊠ *82 South St.,* ☎ *860/567–4501,* WEB *www.litchfieldhistoricalsociety.org.* ☞ *$5 (includes Litchfield History Museum).* ⊙ *Mid Apr.–late Nov., Tues.–Sat. 11–5, Sun. 1–5.*

The well-organized galleries at the **Litchfield History Museum** display decorative arts, paintings, and antique furnishings. The extensive reference library has information about the town's historic buildings, including the Sheldon Tavern (where George Washington slept on several occasions) and the Litchfield Female Academy, where in the late 1700s Sarah Pierce taught girls not just sewing and deportment but also mathematics and history. ⊠ *7 South St., at Rtes. 63 and 118,* ☎ *860/ 567–4501,* WEB *www.litchfieldhistoricalsociety.org.* ☞ *$5 (includes Tapping Reeve House and Law School).* ⊙ *Mid-Apr.–late Nov., Tues.– Sat. 11–5, Sun. 1–5.*

A stroll through the landscaped grounds of **White Flower Farm** is nearly always a pleasure, and gardeners will find many ideas here. The farm is the home base of a mail-order operation that sells perennials and bulbs to gardeners throughout the United States. ⊠ *Rte. 63 (3 mi*

south of Litchfield), ☎ *860/567–8789,* WEB *www.whiteflowerfarm.com.*
☞ *Free.* ⊘ *Oct.–Mar., daily 10–5; Apr.–Sept., daily 9–6.*

Haight Vineyard and Winery flourishes despite the area's severe climate. You can stop in for vineyard walks, winery tours, and tastings.
⊠ *29 Chestnut Hill Rd. (Rte. 118) (1 mi east of Litchfield),* ☎ *860/
567–4045,* WEB *www.ctwine.com/haight.html.* ☞ *Free.* ⊘ *Mon.–Sat.
10:30–5, Sun. noon–5.*

The 4,000-acre **White Memorial Conservation Center,** Connecticut's
largest nature center and wildlife sanctuary, contains fishing areas, bird-
watching platforms, two self-guided nature trails, several boardwalks,
and 35 mi of hiking, cross-country skiing, and horseback-riding trails.
The main conservation center houses natural-history exhibits and a gift
shop. ⊠ *U.S. 202 (2 mi west of village green),* ☎ *860/567–0857,* WEB
www.whitememorialcc.org. ☞ *Grounds free, conservation center $4.*
⊘ *Grounds daily; conservation center Mon.–Fri. 8:30–4:30, Sat. 9–
4:30, Sun. noon–4.*

The chief attractions at **Topsmead State Forest** are a Tudor-style cottage built by architect Henry Dana Jr., and a 40-acre wildflower preserve. The forest holds picnic grounds, hiking trails, and cross-country
ski areas. ⊠ *Buell Rd. off E. Litchfield Rd.* ☎ *860/567–5694.* ☞ *Free.*
⊘ *Forest daily 8 AM–dusk; house tours June–Oct., 2nd and 4th weekends of the month.*

Dining and Lodging

$$$ ✕ **West Street Grill.** This sophisticated dining room on the town green
★   is *the* place to see and be seen, both for patrons and for the state's up-
and-coming chefs, many of whom have gotten their start here. Imag-
inative grilled fish, steak, poultry, and lamb dishes are served with fresh
vegetables and pasta or risotto. The ice cream and sorbets, made by
the restaurant, are worth every calorie. ⊠ *43 West St.,* ☎ *860/567–
3885. AE, MC, V.*

$–$$ ✕ **Village Restaurant.** The folks who run this storefront eatery in a redbrick town house serve food as tasty as any in town—inexpensive pub
grub in one room, updated New England cuisine in the other. Whether
you order burgers or homemade ravioli, you'll get plenty to eat. ⊠ *25
West St.,* ☎ *860/567–8307. AE, MC, V.*

$$–$$$ ⌂ **The Litchfield Inn.** This reproduction Colonial-style inn lies little more
than a mi west of the center of Litchfield. Period accents adorn its modern rooms, including themed "designer" rooms such as an "Irish" room
(which has a four-poster bed draped in green floral chintz) and a "Western" room (which employs a rustic picket fence as a headboard). ⊠ *Rte.
202 06759,* ☎ *860/567–4503 or 800/499–3444,* FAX *860/567–5358,* WEB
www.litchfieldinnct.com. 32 rooms. Restaurant, bar. AE, MC, V. CP.

Outdoor Activities and Sports

Lee's Riding Stables (⊠ 57 E. Litchfield Rd., ☎ 860/567–0785) conducts trail and pony rides. At **Mt. Tom State Park** (⊠ U.S. 202, ☎ 860/
567–8870), you can boat, hike, swim, and fish in summer. The view
from atop the mountain is outstanding.

Shopping

Black Swan Antiques (⊠ 17 Litchfield Commons, U.S. 202, ☎ 860/
567–4429) carries 17th- and 19th-century English and Continental furniture and accessories. **Carretta Glass Studio** (⊠ 513 Maple St., ☎ 860/
567–4851), open by appointment, makes and sells remarkable glass
sculptures and works. The **P. S. Gallery** (⊠ 41 West St., ☎ 860/567–
1059) showcases paintings, prints, and sculptures by area artists. **Susan
Wakeen Dolls** (⊠ 425 Bantam Rd., ☎ 860/567–0007) creates stunning limited-edition and play dolls.

Bristol

44 *17 mi southeast of Litchfield.*

There were some 275 clock makers in and around Bristol during the late 1800s—it is said that by the end of the 19th century just about every household in America told time to a Connecticut clock. Eli Terry (for whom nearby Terryville is named) first mass-produced clocks in the mid-19th century. Seth Thomas (for whom nearby Thomaston is named) learned under Terry and carried on the tradition.

★ ☺ **Lake Compounce,** which opened in 1846, is the oldest amusement park in the country. The rides and attractions at the 325-acre facility include an antique carousel, a classic wooden roller coaster, and a white-water raft ride. The park also has picnic areas, a beach, and a water playground with slides, spray fountains, and a wave pool. The Sky Coaster and Zoomerang offer hair-raising rides. ⊠ *Rte. 229 N, I–84, Exit 31,* ☎ *860/583–3631,* WEB *www.lakecompounce.com.* ☞ *Rides and general admission $25.95; general admission $7.95.* ☉ *Memorial Day–late Sept., call for hrs.*

★ The **Carousel Museum of New England** displays carousel art, much of it full-size pieces, in the Coney Island, Country Fair, and Philadelphia styles. Miniature carousels are also on display, and volunteers occasionally demonstrate the craft at the antique carving shop. ⊠ *95 River-side Ave.,* ☎ *860/585–5411,* WEB *www.thecarouselmuseum.com.* ☞ *$4.* ☉ *Apr.–Nov., Mon.–Sat. 10–5, Sun. noon–5; Dec.–Mar., Thurs.–Sat. 10–5, Sun. noon–5.*

You can set your watch by the **American Clock & Watch Museum**— one of the few in the country devoted entirely to clocks and watches. More than 3,000 timepieces are on display in an 1801 house. ⊠ *100 Maple St.,* ☎ *860/583–6070,* WEB *www.plads.com/acwmuseum.* ☞ *$5.* ☉ *Apr.–Nov., daily 10–5.*

Lodging

$$–$$$ 🏨 **Chimney Crest Manor.** All the rooms in this impressive circa-1930 Tudor mansion have spectacular views of the Farmington Valley. The 40-ft-long Garden Suite, in what was the mansion's ballroom, has gleaming hardwood floors, a fireplace, a queen-size canopy bed, its own kitchen, and tile walls with a dazzling sunflower motif. Breakfast, which might include yogurt pancakes, is served on fine china in the formal dining room or, more casually, on the grand fieldstone patio. Among the handsome public spaces in the no-smoking inn are a library, sunroom, and salon. ⊠ *5 Founders Dr., 06010,* ☎ *860/582–4219,* FAX *860/584–5903. 5 rooms, 1 suite. AE, MC, V. BP.*

Bethlehem

45 *16 mi west of Bristol.*

Come Christmas, Bethlehem is the most popular town in Connecticut. Cynics say that towns such as Canaan, Goshen, and Bethlehem were named primarily with the hope of attracting prospective residents and not truly out of religious deference. In any case, the local post office has its hands full postmarking the 220,000 pieces of holiday greetings mailed from Bethlehem every December.

The **Bethlehem Christmas Town Festival** (☎ 203/266–5557), which takes place in early December, draws quite a crowd. Year-round, the **Christmas Shop** (⊠ 18 East St., ☎ 203/266–7048) showcases the trimmings and trappings that help set the holiday mood.

The Benedictine nuns at the **Abbey of Regina Laudis,** who were made famous by their best-selling CD *Women in Chant,* make and sell fine handcrafts, honey, cheese, herbs, beauty products, and more. An 18th-century Neapolitan crèche with 80 hand-painted Baroque porcelain figures is on view from March to December. ⊠ *Flanders Rd.,* ☎ *203/266–7637.* ☺ *Mon.–Tues. and Thurs.–Sun. 10–noon and 1:30–4.*

Washington

46 *11 mi west of Bethlehem.*

The beautiful buildings of the Gunnery prep school mingle with stately Colonials and churches in Washington, one of the best-preserved Colonial towns in Connecticut. The Mayflower Inn, south of the Gunnery on Route 47, attracts an exclusive clientele. Washington, which was settled in 1734, became in 1779 the first town in the United States to be named for the first president.

Dining and Lodging

$$$$ ×☷ **Mayflower Inn.** Though the most-expensive suites at this inn cost
★ an unbelievable $1,300 a night, the Mayflower is always booked months in advance—and with good reason. Running streams, rambling stone walls, and rare specimen trees fill the inn's 28 impeccably groomed acres. Each of the rooms is an individual work of art with fine antiques, 18th- and 19th-century art, and four-poster canopy beds. The colossal baths have mahogany wainscoting, much marble, and handsome Belgian tapestries on the floors. At the posh restaurant ($$$–$$$$), the contemporary menu may list favorites such has potato-crusted Atlantic salmon or Asian barbecue pork chops. ⊠ *118 Woodbury Rd. (Rte. 47), 06793,* ☎ *860/868–9466,* FAX *860/868–1497,* WEB *www.mayflowerinn.com. 17 rooms, 8 suites. Restaurant, pool, tennis court, health club, meeting room. AE, MC, V.*

En Route The **Institute for American Indian Studies,** between Roxbury and Washington, is a small but excellent and thoughtfully arranged collection of exhibits and displays that details the history of Northeastern Woodland Native Americans. Highlights include a replicated longhouse and nature trails. The institute is at the end of a forested residential road (just follow the signs from Route 199). ⊠ *Curtis Rd. off Rte. 199,* ☎ *860/868–0518,* WEB *www.americanindianinstitute.org.* ⊠ *$4.* ☺ *Jan.–Mar., Wed.–Sat. 10–5, Sun. noon–5; Apr.–Dec., Mon.–Sat. 10–5, Sun. noon–5.*

Woodbury

47 *10 mi southeast of Washington.*

There may very well be more antiques shops in the quickly growing town of Woodbury than in all the towns in the rest of the Litchfield Hills combined. Five magnificent **churches** and the Greek Revival **King Solomon's Temple,** formerly a Masonic lodge, line U.S. 6; they represent some of the finest-preserved examples of Colonial religious architecture in New England.

The **Glebe House** is the large gambrel-roof Colonial in which Dr. Samuel Seabury was elected America's first Episcopal bishop in 1783. It holds an excellent collection of antiques. Renowned British horticulturist Gertrude Jekyll designed the historic garden. ⊠ *Hollow Rd.,* ☎ *203/263–2855.* ⊠ *$5.* ☺ *Apr.–Oct., Wed.–Sun. 1–4; June–Aug. also Sat. 10–4; Nov., weekends 1–4; Dec.–Mar. by appointment.*

Dining and Lodging

$$ ✕ **Good News Café.** Carole Peck is a well-known name in these parts,
★ and her decision to open a restaurant in Woodbury was met with
cheers. The emphasis is on healthful, innovative fare: venison filet
mignon with a horseradish crust, wok-seared shrimp with new pota-
toes, grilled green beans, and a garlic aioli good choices. You can drop
by for cappuccino and munchies in a separate room decorated with
fascinating vintage radios. ⊠ *694 Main St. S,* ☎ *203/266–4663. AE,
MC, V. Closed Tues.*

$$$–$$$$ 🏨 **The Heritage.** Extensive renovations completed in 1998 have given
this large resort a much-needed face-lift, including a new Colonial look
and improved facilities. Guest rooms have dark traditional furniture
and modern amenities such as two phones; some have river or golf-
course views. Drop by the pub Schadrack's for light fare or a drink
after a day on the greens. ⊠ *522 Heritage Rd., Southbury 06488,* ☎
203/264–8200 or 800/932–3466, FAX *203/264–5035,* WEB
*www.dolce.com/heritage. 158 rooms, 5 suites. Restaurant, bar, 18-hole
golf course, 3 tennis courts, health club. AE, D, DC, MC, V.*

$–$$ 🏨 **Curtis House.** Connecticut's oldest inn (1754), at the foot of Woodbury's antiques row, may also be its cheapest; some rooms are under
$70. The inn has seen dozens of alterations and renovations over the
years, but the floorboards still creak like friendly ghosts, and the TVs
in some rooms look to be from the Ed Sullivan era. A fireplace roars
downstairs, where the restaurant serves filling dishes in the steak-and-
potato genre. ⊠ *506 Main St. (Rte. 6), 06798,* ☎ *203/263–2101,* WEB
*www.thecurtishouse.com. 18 rooms, 12 with bath. Restaurant. D,
MC, V.*

Shopping

Country Loft Antiques (⊠ 557 Main St. S, ☎ 203/266–4500) sells
18th- and 19th-century French antiques. **David Dunton** (⊠ Rte. 132
off Rte. 47, ☎ 203/263–5355) is a respected dealer of formal American Federal furniture. **Mill House Antiques** (⊠ 1068 Main St. N, ☎
203/263–3446) carries formal and country English and French furniture and has the state's largest collection of Welsh dressers. The **Woodbury Pewterers** (⊠ 860 Main St. S., ☎ 203/263–2668) factory store
offers discounts on fine reproductions of Early American tankards, Revere bowls, candlesticks, and more.

Outdoor Activities and Sports

G. E. M. Morgans (⊠ 75 N. Poverty Rd., Southbury, ☎ 203/264–
6196) conducts hay and carriage rides using registered Morgan horses.

Ski Areas

WOODBURY SKI AREA

This small, laid-back ski area with a 300-ft vertical drop has 18 downhill trails of varying difficulty that are serviced by a double chairlift,
three rope tows, a handle tow, and a T-bar. About half of the 15 km
(9 mi) of cross-country trails are groomed, and 2 km (1 mi) are lighted
and covered by snowmaking when necessary. There's a snowboard and
alpine park, a skateboard and in-line skating park, and a special area
for sledding and tubing serviced by two lifts and three tows. Snow biking and snowshoeing are other options. Ski parties are held on Friday
and Saturday nights in the base lodge; lessons are given for adults and
for children ages 2 and up. ⊠ *Rte. 47, 06798,* ☎ *203/263–2203.*

Waterbury

48 *15 mi east of Woodbury, 28 mi southwest of Hartford, 28 mi north
of Bridgeport.*

Waterbury, in the Naugatuck River valley, was once known as Brass City for its role as the country's top producer of brass products in the 19th and early 20th centuries. Evidence of the prosperity of the city's brass barons can still be seen in the hillside district northwest of downtown, where grand old Queen Anne, Greek and Georgian Revival, and English Tudor homes remain, a few of which have been turned into bed-and-breakfasts. Today Waterbury and its shops and restaurants serves as the urban center for people in the nearby Litchfield Hills. The dramatic 240-ft **Clock Tower** (⊠ 389 Meadow St.) in the historic downtown was modeled after the city hall tower in Siena, Italy.

Pick up a brochure at the **Waterbury Region Convention and Visitors Bureau** (⊠ 21 Church St., ☎ 203/597–9527, WEB www.wrcvb.org) and follow their fascinating self-guided walking tour of the downtown area.

The **Mattatuck Museum** has a fine collection of 19th- and 20th-century Connecticut art and memorabilia documenting the state's industrial history, as well as a charming museum café. ⊠ 144 W. Main St., ☎ 203/753–0381, WEB www.mattatuckmuseum.org. ⊡ Free. ☉ Sept.–June, Tues.–Sat. 10–5, Sun. noon–5; July–Aug., Tues.–Sat. 10–5.

Dining and Lodging

$$–$$$ ✕ **Carmen Anthony Steak House.** A worthy re-creation of the steak
★   houses of old, Carmen Anthony has rich wood paneling, handsome oil paintings on the walls, and white linen on the tables. You can order Delmonico, filet mignon, porterhouse, and other steaks; the popular "Italian" steaks are served on a bed of rotini pasta. ⊠ 496 Chase Ave., ☎ 203/757–3040. AE, D, DC, MC, V. No lunch weekends.

$$–$$$ ✕ **Diorio Restaurant and Bar.** The dining room at Diorio, a Waterbury
★   tradition for more than a half-century, retains its original mahogany bankers' booth, marble brass bar, high tin ceilings, exposed brick, and white-tile floors. The dishes here are expertly prepared, from the juicy shrimp scampi to the dozens of pasta, chicken, veal, steak, and seafood plates. ⊠ 231 Bank St., ☎ 203/754–5111. AE, D, DC, MC, V. Closed Sun. No lunch Sat.

$$$ ⌂ **House on the Hill.** Owner-innkeeper Marianne Vandenburgh's fanciful B&B is surrounded by lush gardens in a historic hillside neighborhood. The three-story 1888 Victorian, former home of a brass baron, has a glorious exterior color scheme of teal, sage green, red, and ivory. The rich original woodwork and details remain, and guest rooms are furnished in a welcoming blend of antiques and nostalgia. ⊠ 92 Woodlawn Terr., 06710, ☎ 203/757–9901. 4 suites. Library. AE, D, DC, MC, V. Closed Dec. 15–Jan. 15. BP.

Nightlife and the Arts

Seven Angels Theatre (⊠ Hamilton Park Pavilion, Plank Rd., ☎ 203/757–4676) presents first-rate plays, musicals, children's theater, cabaret concerts, and youth programs.

Shopping

Howland-Hughes (⊠ 120 Bank St., ☎ 203/753–4121) is stocked entirely with items made in Connecticut, from Wiffle balls to Pez candies, fine pottery to glassware.

Litchfield Hills A to Z

To research prices, get advice from other travelers, and book travel arrangements, visit www.fodors.com.

AIR TRAVEL TO AND FROM LITCHFIELD HILLS

The airport nearest to the Litchfield Hills region is Hartford's Bradley International Airport.

BUS TRAVEL

Bonanza Bus Lines operates daily buses between New York City's Port Authority terminal and Southbury, in the southern part of the region. There is no local bus service in the Litchfield Hills.

➤ BUS INFORMATION: **Bonanza Bus Lines** (☎ 800/556–3815, WEB www.bonanzabus.com).

CAR TRAVEL

U.S. 44 west and U.S. 6 south are the most direct routes from Hartford to the Litchfield Hills. To get here from New York, take I–684 to I–84, from which the roads off Exits 7 to 18 head north into the hills.

U.S. 7 winds from New Milford through Kent, Cornwall Bridge, Cornwall, and West Cornwall to Canaan. Sharon is west of U.S. 7 on Route 4; continue north from Sharon on Route 41 to get to Lakeville and Salisbury. U.S. 44 heading east from Salisbury passes through Canaan, Norfolk, and Winsted. Route 63 travels southeast from South Canaan through Litchfield to Waterbury; at Watertown head west from Route 63 on U.S. 6 and north on Route 61 to get to Bethlehem. Southbury is at the junction of U.S. 6 and I–84. Route 8, the main north–south road through the eastern part of the Litchfield Hills, passes through Winsted, Torrington, and Waterbury; Bristol is east of Route 8 off U.S. 6, and Riverton is east of Route 8 on Route 20.

EMERGENCIES

➤ HOSPITALS: **New Milford Hospital** (✉ 21 Elm St., ☎ 860/355–2611, WEB www.newmilfordhospital.org). **Sharon Hospital** (✉ 50 Hospital Hill Rd., ☎ 860/364–4141, WEB www.sharonhospital.org).
➤ 24-HOUR PHARMACY: **CVS** (✉ 627 Farmington Ave., Bristol, ☎ 860/582–8167).

VISITOR INFORMATION

➤ TOURIST INFORMATION: **Litchfield Hills Visitors Council** (✉ Box 968, Litchfield 06759, ☎ 860/567–4506, WEB www.litchfieldhills.com).

NEW HAVEN AND THE SOUTHEASTERN COAST

As you drive northeast along I–95, culturally rich New Haven is the final urban obstacle between southwestern Connecticut's overdeveloped coast and southeastern Connecticut's quieter shoreline villages. The remainder of the jagged coast, which stretches all the way to the Rhode Island border, consists of small coastal villages, quiet hamlets, and undisturbed beaches. The only interruptions along this mostly undeveloped seashore are the industry and piers of New London and Groton. Mystic, Stonington, Old Saybrook, Clinton, and Guilford are havens for fans of antiques and boutiques. North of Groton, near the town of Ledyard, the Mashantucket Pequot Reservation owns and operates Foxwoods Casino and the Mashantucket Pequot Museum & Research Center. The Mohegan Indians run the Mohegan Sun casino in Uncasville.

Milford

49 *6 mi northeast of Stratford.*

Milford, established in 1639, is Connecticut's sixth-oldest municipality, and it retains the feel of a small-town coastal community despite its more than 48,000 residents and the commercial stretch of the Boston Post Road that runs through its center. The large town green is at the heart of this community, and it sparkles in winter with thousands of tiny white lights strung in its trees. The duck pond and waterfall behind city hall is a pleasant place to while away a spring afternoon, and Milford's many beaches, open to the public for the price of parking, are inviting in summer.

The **Connecticut Audubon Coastal Center,** an 840-acre reserve, where the Housatonic River meets the Long Island Sound, has an observation tower with a view of all the reserve has to offer: a boardwalk to a sandy beach for exploring (swimming is not allowed), observation platforms at the water's edge, a nature center, and an amazing assortment of birds year-round. Popular guided canoe trips through the salt marsh are scheduled from May to September. ✉ *1 Milford Point Rd.,* ☎ *203/878–7440,* WEB *www.ctaudubon.org/centers/coastal.* ☞ *Center $2; grounds free.* ⊙ *Center Tues.–Sat. 10–4, Sun. noon–4; grounds daily dawn–dusk.*

Dining

$$ ✕ **Jeffrey's.** This popular restaurant serves up-to-the-minute new American cuisine in a refined yet welcoming setting that includes an antique Dutch armoire and a grand piano. Some of the changing specials have been rainbow trout with lemon butter and filet mignon with cranberry-wild mushroom bordelaise sauce. ✉ *501 New Haven Ave.,* ☎ *203/878–1910. AE, D, DC, MC, V. No lunch weekends.*

$ ✕ **Paul's Famous Hamburgers.** "Not serving numbers, but generations" is the motto of this drive-in established in 1946. It's the place to go for extraordinarily friendly service and juicy, fresh burgers, hot dogs on toasted buns, fries, reubens, and milk shakes thick enough to stand a spoon in. ✉ *829 Boston Post Rd.,* ☎ *203/874–7586. No credit cards. Closed Sun.*

Outdoor Activities and Sports

BEACHES
The state recently completed the first phase of a renovation of **Silver Sands State Park,** with its signature beach and old-fashioned wooden boardwalk. You can walk out to Charles Island at low tide. ✉ *600 E. Broadway,* ☎ *203/783–3280.* ☞ *Free.* ⊙ *Daily, 8 AM–dusk.*

BOATING
Milford Landing (✉ 37 Helwig St., ☎ 203/874–1610), open April– November, is an attractive complex for temporary docking at the head of Milford Harbor. The 50 slips are for vessels up to 50 ft. Overnight slips are available; there are rest rooms, showers, a coin laundry, and tennis and basketball courts. Several restaurants are within walking distance.

JAI-ALAI
Milford Jai-Alai is one of the few remaining forums on the East Coast where you can watch the sport known as the world's fastest ball game. ✉ *311 Old Gate La.,* ☎ *203/877–4242.* ☞ *$2 weekends; free weekdays.* ⊙ *Mon. and Wed.–Sun.; call for game times.*

New Haven

9 mi east of Milford, 46 mi northeast of Greenwich.

New Haven's history goes back to the 17th century, when its squares, including a lovely central green for the public, were laid out. The city, a cultural center, is home to Yale University. The historic district surrounding Yale and the shops, museums, theaters, and restaurants on nearby **Chapel Street** are handsome and prosperous. Visitors should be careful about exploring areas away from the campus and city common at night.

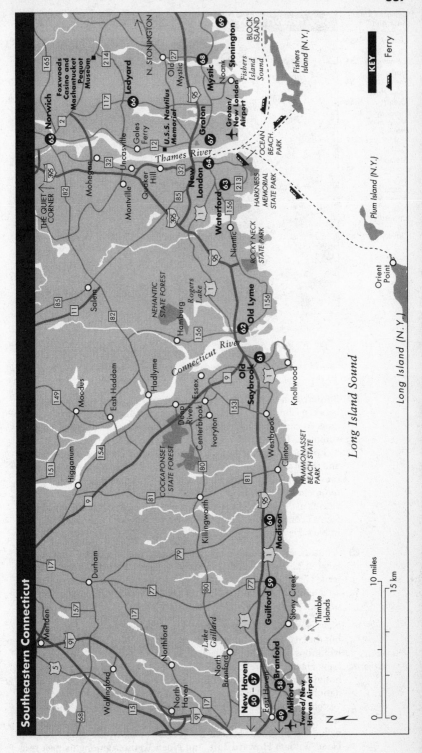

Southeastern Connecticut

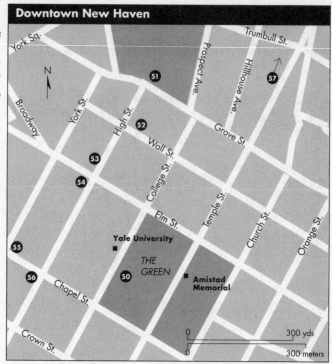

Downtown New Haven

50 Bordered on one side by the Yale campus, the **New Haven Green** (⊠ between Church and College Sts.) is a fine example of early urban planning. As early as 1638, village elders set aside the 16-acre plot as a town common. Three early-19th-century churches—the Gothic-style **Trinity Episcopal Church,** the Georgian-style **Center Congregational Church,** and the predominantly Federal-style **United Church**—contribute to its present appeal. Sculptor Ed Hamilton's three-sided, 14-ft-high *Amistad* **memorial** in front of City Hall (⊠ 165 Church St.) shows key incidents in the life of Joseph Cinque, one of the Africans kidnapped from Sierra Leone in 1839. Part of the Africans' battle for freedom took place in New Haven.

51 A historic example of New Haven's innovation is the **Grove Street Cemetery** (⊠ 227 Grove St., ☎ 203/787–1443), the first planned public cemetery (1797) in the nation. Walk under the imposing Egyptian Revival arch, circa 1845, and you can see the final resting place of such Connecticut greats as Noah Webster, Eli Whitney, and Charles Goodyear.

New Haven is a manufacturing center dating from the 19th century, but the city owes its fame to merchant Elihu Yale. In 1718, Yale's contributions enabled the Collegiate School, founded in 1701, to settle in

★ New Haven, where it changed its name to **Yale University,** for which honor he never donated another dime to the school. This is one of the nation's great universities, and its campus holds some handsome neo-Gothic buildings and a number of noteworthy museums. The university's knowledgeable guides conduct one-hour walking tours that include Connecticut Hall in the Old Campus, which counts Nathan Hale, William Howard Taft, and Noah Webster among its past residents. ⊠ *Yale Visitors Center, 149 Elm St.,* ☎ *203/432–2300,* <u>WEB</u> *www.yale.edu.* ☉ *Tours weekdays at 10:30 and 2, weekends at 1:30. Tours start from 149 Elm St. on north side of New Haven Green.*

52 The collections at Yale's **Beinecke Rare Book and Manuscript Library** (⊠ 121 Wall St., ☎ 203/432–2977, WEB www.library.yale.edu/beinecke) include a Gutenberg Bible, illuminated manuscripts, and original Audubon bird prints, but the building is almost as much of an attraction—the walls are made of marble cut so thinly that the light shines through, making the interior a breathtaking sight on sunny days.

53 James Gamble Rogers, an American architect, created many buildings for Yale, his alma mater, including the **Sterling Memorial Library** (⊠ 120 High St., ☎ 203/432–2798, WEB www.library.yale.edu), which he designed in 1930 to be "a cathedral of knowledge and a temple of learning." This is evident in the major interior area, which resembles a Gothic cathedral.

54 The most notable example of the Yale campus's neo-Gothic architecture is the **Harkness Tower** (⊠ High St.), built between 1917 and 1921, which was modeled on St. Botolph's Tower in Boston, England. The university's famous motto, inscribed on Memorial Gate near the tower, is sometimes described as the world's greatest anticlimax: "For God, for country, and for Yale."

55 Since its founding in 1832, the **Yale University Art Gallery** has amassed more than 85,000 objects from around the world, dating from ancient Egypt to the present day. Highlights include works by van Gogh, Manet, Monet, Picasso, Winslow Homer, and Thomas Eakins, as well as Etruscan and Greek vases, Chinese ceramics and bronzes, and early Italian paintings. The gallery's collection of American decorative arts is considered one of the finest in the world. Be certain not to miss the re-creation of a Mithraic shrine downstairs. ⊠ *1111 Chapel St.,* ☎ *203/432–0600,* WEB *www.yale.edu/artgallery.* ⌷ *Free.* ☉ *Tues.–Sat. 10–5, Sun. 1–6.*

★ **56** The **Yale Center for British Art** has the most comprehensive collection of British art outside Britain and surveys the development of English art, life, and thought from the Elizabethan period to the present. The center's skylighted galleries, designed by Louis I. Kahn, contain works by Constable, Hogarth, Gainsborough, Reynolds, and Turner, to name but a few. You'll also find rare books and paintings documenting English history. ⊠ *1080 Chapel St.,* ☎ *203/432–2800,* WEB *www.yale.edu/ycba.* ⌷ *Free.* ☉ *Tues.–Sat. 10–5, Sun. noon–5.*

57 Yale's **Peabody Museum of Natural History** opened in 1876; with more than 9 million specimens, it's one of the largest natural history museums in the nation. In addition to exhibits on Andean, Mesoamerican, and Pacific cultures, the venerable museum has an excellent collection of birds, including a stuffed dodo and passenger pigeon. But the main attractions for children and amateur paleontologists alike are some of the world's earliest reconstructions of dinosaur skeletons. ⊠ *170 Whitney Ave.,* ☎ *203/432–5050,* WEB *www.peabody.yale.edu.* ⌷ *$5.* ☉ *Mon.–Sat. 10–5, Sun. noon–5.*

Dining and Lodging

$$–$$$ ✗ **Hot Tomato's.** This café in the former 1912 Taft Hotel has a stately Old World elegance—cathedral-like windows, walls embellished with classic motifs in bas-relief, and a sweeping staircase that leads to a balcony dining room. Its contemporary menu includes everything from pork-and-vegetable wontons to fettuccine with lobster, mushrooms, and asparagus in a cream sauce. ⊠ *261 College St.,* ☎ *203/624–6331. AE, MC, V. No lunch weekends.*

$–$$ ✗ **Frank Pepe's.** Does this place serve the best pizza in the world, as
★ some reviewers claim? If it doesn't, it comes close. Pizza is the only thing prepared here—try the famous white-clam pie. Expect to wait an hour or more for a table—or, on weekend evenings, come after 10

PM. The Spot (☎ 203/865–7602), right behind the restaurant, is owned by Pepe's and is usually open when Pepe's is not. ⊠ *157 Wooster St.,* ☎ *203/865–5762. Reservations not accepted. No credit cards. Closed Tues. No lunch Mon. or Wed.–Thurs.*

$–$$ ✕ **Pika Tapas Café.** Chic and colorful, this cosmopolitan café serves
★ delicate Spanish hors d'oeuvres meant for sharing; each region in Spain is well represented on the menu. *Gambas al ajillo* (shrimp sautéed in a pungent, good-to-the-last-drop garlic sauce) and baked goat cheese on parsley toast are among the popular tapas. A few salads and entrées—the paella is a standout—are also prepared. ⊠ *39 High St.,* ☎ *203/865–1933. AE, MC, V. No lunch Sun.–Tues.*

$ ✕ **Louis' Lunch.** This all-American luncheonette on the National Register of Historic Places claims to be the birthplace of the hamburger in America. The first-rate burgers are cooked in an old-fashioned, upright broiler and served with either a slice of tomato or cheese on two slices of toast. (Don't even think about asking for ketchup.) ⊠ *263 Crown St.,* ☎ *203/ 562–5507. No credit cards. Closed Sun.–Mon. No dinner Tues.–Wed.*

$$$ ▦ **Three Chimneys Inn.** This 1870 Victorian mansion is one of the classi-
★ est small inns in the state. Rooms have posh Georgian furnishings: mahogany four-poster beds, oversize armoires, Chippendale desks, and Oriental rugs. The sitting room and library have working fireplaces. ⊠ *1201 Chapel St., 06511,* ☎ *203/789–1201,* ℻ *203/776–7363,* WEB *www.threechimneysinn.com. 11 rooms. Library, business services, meeting room. AE, D, DC, MC, V. BP.*

$$–$$$ ▦ **Omni New Haven Hotel at Yale.** This 19-floor Omni opened in 1998 and is the only large hotel in the city. With modern amenities and a view of the green, it's comfortable and convenient to the heart of New Haven. The rooftop restaurant ($$) is named Galileo's for its lofty height, though the menu is somewhat more down to earth, with traditional hotel fare such as salmon and filet mignon at reasonable prices. ⊠ *155 Temple St., 06511,* ☎ *203/772–6664,* ℻ *203/974–6777,* WEB *www.omnihotel.com. 306 rooms. Restaurant, lounge, health club, business services, meeting room. AE, D, MC, V.*

$$ ▦ **New Haven Hotel.** A quiet spot in the heart of the city, the New Haven has the feel of a small, exclusive hotel, but the amenities are those of a large facility. The Queen Anne-style rooms are comfortable and modern, and the restaurant, Templeton's ($–$$), serves innovative American cuisine. ⊠ *229 George St., 06510,* ☎ *203/498–3100,* ℻ *203/498– 3190,* WEB *www.newhavenhotel.com. 92 rooms. Restaurant, bar, indoor lap pool, hot tub, business services, meeting room. AE, D, DC, MC, V.*

Nightlife and the Arts

NIGHTLIFE

Anna Liffey's (⊠ 17 Whitney Ave., ☎ 203/773–1776) is the city's liveliest Irish pub. **BAR** (⊠ Crown St. at College St., ☎ 203/495–1111) is a cross between a nightclub, a brick-oven pizzeria, and a brew pub. **Richter's** (⊠ 990 Chapel St., ☎ 203/777–0400) is famous for its half-yard glasses of beer. Alternative and traditional rock bands play at **Toad's Place** (⊠ 300 York St., ☎ 203/624–8623).

THE ARTS

The century-old **New Haven Symphony Orchestra** (☎ 203/865–0831) plays at Yale University's Woolsey Hall (⊠ College and Grove Sts.). The **SNET Oakdale Theatre** (⊠ 95 S. Turnpike Rd., ☎ 203/265–1501) in Wallingford, 18 mi north of New Haven, presents nationally known theatrical and musical performances. **Yale School of Music** (☎ 203/432– 4157) presents an impressive roster of performers, from classical to jazz; most events take place in the Morse Recital Hall in Sprague Memorial Hall (⊠ College and Wall Sts.).

The well-regarded **Long Wharf Theatre** (⊠ 222 Sargent Dr., ☎ 203/787–4282) presents works by new writers and imaginative revivals of neglected classics. The **Shubert Performing Arts Center** (⊠ 247 College St., ☎ 203/562–5666 or 800/228–6622) hosts Broadway musicals and dramas, usually following their run in the Big Apple, plus dance, classical music, and cabaret acts. The **Yale Cabaret** (⊠ 217 Park St., ☎ 203/432–1566) can be counted on for unusual plays and good food at great prices during the school year. The highly professional **Yale Repertory Theatre** (⊠ Chapel and York Sts., ☎ 203/432–1234) mounts world premieres and is known for its fresh interpretations of the classics.

Outdoor Activities and Sports

A public beach, nature trails, excellent birding, and a stunning antique carousel in a century-old beach pavilion are attractions of the 88-acre **Lighthouse Point Park** (⊠ Lighthouse Rd. off Rte. 337, ☎ 203/946–8005), in southeastern New Haven.

The **New Haven Knights** (☎ 203/498–7825), members of the United Hockey League, play home games at Veterans Memorial Coliseum (⊠ George Street,) from October to March.

The **New Haven Ravens** (☎ 800/728–3671), the Class AA affiliate of baseball's St. Louis Cardinals, play home games at Yale Field (⊠ 252 Derby Ave., West Haven) from April to September.

Shopping

Chapel Street, near the town green, has a pleasing assortment of shops and eateries. **Arethusa Book Shop** (⊠ 87 Audubon St., ☎ 203/624–1848) carries a huge selection of out-of-print and used books, including first editions. **Atticus Bookstore & Café** (⊠ 1082 Chapel St., ☎ 203/776–4040), in the heart of Yale University, was one of the first stores to combine books and food; it's been a favorite among museum groupies and theatergoers for years.

En Route The oldest rapid-transit car and the world's first electric freight locomotive are among classic trolleys on display at the **Shoreline Trolley Museum.** Admission includes a 3-mi round-trip ride aboard a vintage trolley. ⊠ *17 River St., East Haven (midway between New Haven and Branford),* ☎ *203/467–6927,* WEB *www.bera.org.* ⌧ *$6.* ☉ *Memorial Day–Labor Day, daily 10–4:30; May, Sept.–Oct., and Dec., weekends 10–4:30; Apr. and Nov., Sun. 10–4:30.*

Branford

58 *8 mi east of New Haven.*

Founded in 1644, Branford was a prosperous port and the site of a saltworks that during the Revolutionary War provided salt to preserve food for the Continental Army. Today it is a charming seaside town with a close-knit community of artists and craftspeople. The summer cottages are shoulder to shoulder, with tiny, well-kept yards and colorful gardens.

The small Branford village of Stony Creek, with a few tackle shops, antiques shops, a general store, and a marina, is the departure point for cruises around the **Thimble Islands.** This group of more than 90 tiny islands was named for its abundance of thimbleberries, which are similar to gooseberries. Legend has it that Captain Kidd buried pirate gold on one island. Two sightseeing vessels vie for your patronage, the *Volsunga IV* (☎ 203/488–9978, WEB www.thimbleislands.com) and the *Sea Mist II* (☎ 203/488–8905). Both depart from Stony Creek Dock, at the end of Thimble Island Road, from May to Columbus Day.

Dining

$–$$$ ✕ **USS Chowder Pot III.** There's no doubt about the specialty of the
★   house here: seafood with a capital "S"—clams, scallops, lobster, sole,
and more. The casual, nautical atmosphere (fish nets hang from every
available surface) sets the mood for digging into the heaping fried seafood
platters. One word of caution: the restaurant does not accept reser-
vations for small parties and the lines are often out the door. It's worth
the wait, but try to arrive early or plan on drinks in the extensive
bar/lounge while you wait. ⊠ 560 E. Main St., ☎ 203/481–2356. AE,
DC, MC, V. Reservations not accepted.

Shopping

Branford Craft Village (⊠ 779 E. Main St., ☎ 203/488–4689), on the
150-year-old, 85-acre Bittersweet Farm, contains a dozen crafts shops
and studios, an herb garden, an antiques shop, and a small café. The
village is closed Monday.

Guilford

59 5 mi northeast of Branford, 37 mi west of New London.

The Guilford town green, crisscrossed by pathways, dotted with
benches, and lined with historic homes and specialty shops, is consid-
ered by many to be the prettiest green in the state and is actually the
third largest in the Northeast. The group of English settlers who
founded Guilford in 1639 was led by the Reverend Henry Whitfield.

The **Henry Whitfield State Museum,** built by the Reverend Whitfield
in 1639, is the oldest house in the state and the oldest stone house in
New England. The furnishings in the medieval-style building were
made between the 17th and 19th centuries. The visitor center has two
exhibition galleries and a gift shop. ⊠ 248 Old Whitfield St., ☎ 203/
453–2457, WEB www.hbgraphics.com/whitfieldmuseum. ⊡ $3.50. ☉
Feb.–mid-Dec., Wed.–Sun. 10–4:30; mid-Dec.–Jan. by appointment.

Dining

$$ ✕ **Esteva.** A wall of windows overlooking stately Guilford Green and
a colorful mural and open kitchen create a comfortable, yet lively
atmosphere perfect for enjoying the eclectic cuisine served here. You
might find rack of lamb with a pomegranate and molasses glaze,
monkfish and mahogany clams with green olives and prosciutto, or
duck breast glazed with ponzu coloring your plate. ⊠ 25 Whitfield St.,
☎ 203/458–1300. AE, MC, V. Closed Mon.

$–$$$ ✕ **Quattro's.** The two owner-chefs here are Ecuadoran but are trained
★   in the Italian style of cooking. Although their menu includes traditional
pasta dishes, these pros really cut loose with the daily specials. Look
for delicacies such as the smoky bacon–wrapped scallops served over
a bed of lobster sauce and the filet mignon topped with fresh spinach,
sautéed shrimp, and cognac sauce. ⊠ 1300 Boston Post Rd., ☎ 203/
453–6575. Reservations essential. AE, DC, MC, V.

Shopping

The **Guilford Handcrafts Center** (⊠ 411 Church St., ☎ 203/453–5947)
sponsors seven crafts exhibitions a year and has an excellent shop that
represents more than 300 artists.

Madison

60 5 mi east of Guilford, 62 mi northeast of Greenwich.

Coastal Madison has an understated charm. Ice cream parlors, antiques
stores, and quirky gift boutiques prosper along U.S. 1, the town's
main street.

Hammonasset Beach State Park, the largest of the state's shoreline sanctuaries, has 2 mi of white sandy beaches, a nature center, excellent birding, and a hugely popular 541-site campground. ⊠ *I–95, Exit 62,* ☎ *203/245–2785 park; 203/245–1817 campground.* ☞ *Park $5–$12 Apr.–Sept., free Oct.–Mar.* ◔ *Park daily 8 AM–dusk.*

Dining and Lodging

$$$$ ✕⊡ **Inn at Lafayette.** Skylights, painted murals, and handcrafted woodwork are among the design accents at this airy hostelry in a converted 1830s church. The rooms may be small, but they are decorated with beautiful fabrics and reproduction 17th- and 18th-century antique furniture. The modern marble baths come equipped with telephones. Fresh food and flawless service are highlights at Café Allegre ($$; closed Mon.), the inn's popular restaurant. The menu is largely southern Italian, with a dash of French. ⊠ *725 Boston Post Rd., 06443,* ☎ *203/245–7773,* FAX *203/245–6256,* WEB *www.allegrecafe.com. 5 rooms. Restaurant, bar, business services. AE, DC, MC, V.*

En Route   Among the 70 upscale discount stores at **Clinton Crossing Premium Outlets** (⊠ 20 Killingworth Turnpike, I–95, Exit 63, Clinton, ☎ 860/664–0700), you can find Off 5th–Saks Fifth Avenue, Donna Karan, Coach, Tommy Hilfiger, Barneys New York, and Lenox. Represented at **Westbrook Factory Stores** (⊠ I–95, Exit 65, Westbrook, ☎ 860/399–8656) are Carter's, Springmaid/Wamsutta, Oneida, J. Crew, and Timberland, among more than 60 others.

Old Saybrook

⊕ *9 mi east of Madison, 29 mi east of New Haven.*

Old Saybrook, once a lively shipbuilding and fishing town, bustles with summer vacationers and antiques shoppers. In July and August a trolley run by the chamber of commerce shows you the sights, from restaurants to shops to the old-fashioned soda fountain where you can share a sundae with your sweetie.

Dining and Lodging

$$ ✕ **Café Routier.** Duck-leg ragout in a rich red-wine sauce, fried oys-
★ ters with a chipotle rémoulade, and steak au poivre with potatoes Dauphinois are among the entrées at this classy café. White tablecloths and candlelight provide a fitting atmosphere in which to enjoy the snappy French and American cuisine. Some of France's finest vintages are served from the copper wine bar. ⊠ *1080 Boston Post Rd.,* ☎ *860/ 388–6270. AE, D, DC, MC, V. Closed Mon. No lunch.*

$–$$ ✕ **Aleia's.** This restaurant is as light, bright, and bountiful as the Ital-
★ ian countryside. Raffia, silk flowers, and hand-painted plates from Capri decorate the walls, and trompe l'oeil fruits, vegetables, and herbs adorn the tabletops. Chef-owner Kimberly Snow adds nouvelle touches to her mother's tried-and-true recipes, such as the grilled veal chop with Yukon Gold potatoes, garlic-scented greens, and a wild mushroom reduction and the seafood risotto with clams, shrimp, scallops, and chorizo. ⊠ *1687 Boston Post Rd.,* ☎ *860/399–5050. AE, MC, V. Closed Sun.–Mon. No lunch.*

$ ✕ **Pat's Kountry Kitchen.** Upbeat service and traditional New England fare have made this home-style restaurant a local institution and a family favorite. Best-sellers are the fresh clam hash, pork chops, and apple-cranberry-raisin pie. ⊠ *U.S. 1,* ☎ *860/388–4784. AE, MC, V.*

$$$$ ✕⊡ **Saybrook Point Inn & Spa.** Rooms at the Saybrook are furnished mainly in 18th-century style, with reproductions of British furniture and Impressionist art. The health club and pools overlook the inn's ma-

rina and the Connecticut River. The Terra Mar Grille ($$$–$$$), which sit on the river, serves stylish Continental cuisine. ✉ *2 Bridge St., 06475,* ☎ *860/395–2000,* ℻ *860/388–1504,* WEB *www.saybrook.com. 50 rooms, 12 suites. Restaurant, 1 indoor and 1 outdoor pool, spa, health club, marina, meeting room. AE, D, DC, MC, V.*

$$$$
★   🏨 **Water's Edge Inn & Resort.** With its spectacular setting on Long Island Sound, this traditional weathered gray-shingle compound in Westbrook is one of the Connecticut shore's premier resorts. The main building has warm, bright public rooms furnished with antiques and reproductions, and its upstairs bedrooms, with wall-to-wall carpeting and clean, modern bathrooms, afford priceless views of the sound. ✉ *1525 Boston Post Rd., Westbrook 06498,* ☎ *860/399–5901 or 800/ 222–5901,* ℻ *860/399–6172,* WEB *www.watersedge-resort.com. 99 rooms, 67 suites. Restaurant, bar, 1 indoor and 1 outdoor pool, spa, health club, 2 tennis courts, volleyball, beach, business services, meeting room. AE, D, DC, MC, V.*

$$–$$$ 🏨 **Deacon Timothy Pratt Bed & Breakfast.** Small but inviting, this B&B has an excellent location in the heart of the shopping and historic districts and within a mi of a train station and beaches. Each room in the 1746 center-chimney Colonial reflects the owner's attention to detail, respect for history, and eye for romance. Three rooms have working fireplaces and three have whirlpool baths. ✉ *325 Main St., 06475,* ☎ *860/395–1229,* ℻ *860/395–4748,* WEB *www.connecticut-bed-and-breakfast.com. 4 rooms. In-room data ports. AE, MC, V. BP.*

Outdoor Activities and Sports

The **African Queen** (✉ Saybrook Yacht Basin, 142 Ferry Rd., ☎ 860/ 388–2007), the original steam launch made famous by Kate (a resident of Old Saybrook) and Bogey, offers tours from July through October. **Deep River Navigation Company** (✉ Saybrook Point, ☎ 860/ 526–4954) runs narrated cruises up the Connecticut River, along the shoreline, or out into Long Island Sound.

Shopping

More than 120 dealers operate out of the **Essex-Saybrook Antiques Village** (✉ 345 Middlesex Turnpike, ☎ 860/388–0689). **North Cove Outfitters** (✉ 75 Main St., ☎ 860/388–6585) is Connecticut's version of L. L. Bean. **Saybrook Country Barn** (✉ 2 Main St., ☎ 860/388–0891) has everything country, from tiger-maple dining-room tables to hand-painted pottery. **James Gallery and Soda Fountain** (✉ 2 Pennywise La., ☎ 860/395–1229) sells both watercolors and ice cream sodas in a historic former general store–pharmacy.

Old Lyme

62 *4 mi east of Old Saybrook, 40 mi south of Hartford.*

Old Lyme, on the other side of the Connecticut River from Old Saybrook, is renowned among art-lovers for its history as America's foremost Impressionist art colony. Artists continue to be attracted to the area for its lovely countryside and shoreline. The town also has handsome old houses, many built for sea captains.

★   Central to Old Lyme's artistic reputation is the **Florence Griswold Museum,** a columned, Georgian-style former boarding house that hosted members of the Old Lyme art colony, including Willard Metcalf, Clark Voorhees, Childe Hassam, and Henry Ward Ranger, in the early 20th century. Griswold, the descendant of a well-known family, offered artistic encouragement as well as housing. The artists painted for their hostess the double row of panels in the dining room that now serve as the museum's centerpiece. Many of their other works are on display in revolving exhibits, along with 19th-century furnishings and decorative items. The landscaped 11-acre estate is a perfect setting for the 1817 late-Georgian mansion. The museum is part of the Connecticut Impressionist Art Trail, a self-guided tour of 10 sites. ✉ *96 Lyme St.,* ☎ *860/434–5542,* WEB *www.flogris.org.* 🖼 *$5.* ☉ *Jan.–Apr., Wed.–Sun. 1–5; May–Dec., Tues.–Sat. 10–5, Sun. 1–5.*

The **Lyme Academy of Fine Arts,** in a Federal-style home built in 1817, has a popular gallery with works by contemporary artists, including the academy's students and faculty. ✉ *84 Lyme St.,* ☎ *860/434–5232,* WEB *www.lymeacademy.edu.* 🖼 *$2 donation suggested.* ☉ *Tues.–Sat. 10–4, Sun. 1–4.*

Dining and Lodging

$$$–$$$$ ✕🏨 **Bee & Thistle Inn.** Behind a weathered stone wall in the Old Lyme
★ historic district is a three-story 1756 Colonial house with 5½ acres of broad lawns, blooming flowers in a formal garden, and herbaceous borders. The scale of rooms throughout is small and inviting, with fireplaces in the parlors and dining rooms and light and airy curtains in the multipaned guest-room windows. Most rooms have canopy or four-poster beds with old quilts and afghans; breakfast (not included in the price) can be brought to your room. Fireplaces and candlelight create a romantic atmosphere in the fine restaurant ($$$–$$$$; closed on Tuesday and the first three weeks in January), where American cuisine—like crab ravioli and roasted rack of lamb—is served with style. ✉ *100 Lyme St., 06371,* ☎ *860/434–1667 or 800/622–4946,* FAX *860/434–3402,* WEB *www.beeandthistleinn.com. 11 rooms, 1 cottage. Restaurant. AE, DC, MC, V.*

$$–$$$ ✕🏨 **Old Lyme Inn.** A white clapboard 1850s farmhouse with blue shutters is the centerpiece of this dining and lodging establishment in the heart of Old Lyme's historic district. Behind the ornate iron fence, tree-shaded lawn, and banister front porch are spacious guest rooms impeccably decorated with antiques and contemporary furnishings. The inn's elegant dining rooms ($$–$$$) offer creative American dishes such as pan-grilled tuna with basil butter and veal ravioli. ✉ *85 Lyme St., 06371 (just north of I–95),* ☎ *860/434–2600 or 800/434–5352,* FAX *860/434–5352,* WEB *www.oldlymeinn.com. 13 rooms. Restaurant. AE, D, DC, MC, V. CP.*

Waterford and Niantic

㊻ *13 mi east of Old Lyme (Waterford).*

Less cutesy than Mystic and less military than Groton, Waterford and Niantic are working shoreline towns, but not without their down-to-earth charms.

Harkness Memorial State Park, the former summer estate of Edward Stephen Harkness, a silent partner in Standard Oil, encompasses formal gardens, picnic areas, a beach for strolling and fishing (but not swimming), and the 42-room Italian villa-style mansion, Eolia. Classical, pop, and jazz talents perform at the **Summer Music at Harkness** (☎ *860/ 442–9199*) festival in July and August. ✉ *275 Great Neck Rd. (Rte. 213), Waterford,* ☎ *860/443–5725.* 🖼 *Memorial Day–Labor Day $4–$8, free rest of yr.* ☉ *Daily 8 AM–dusk. House tours Memorial Day–Labor Day; call for hrs.*

The **Children's Museum of Southeastern Connecticut,** about a mi from Waterford, is an excellent facility that uses a hands-on approach to engage kids in the fields of science, math, and current events. ✉ *409 Main St., Niantic,* ☎ *860/691–1255,* WEB *www.childmuseumsect.conncol-*

lege.edu. ⊡ *$4.* ⊙ *Labor Day–Memorial Day, Tues.–Sat. 9:30–4:30, Fri. 9:30–8, Sun. noon–5; also Mon. 9:30–4:30 Memorial Day–Labor Day.*

Outdoor Activities and Sports

In Waterford **Captain John's Dock** (☎ 860/443–7259) operates lighthouse cruises, as well as sightseeing tours in search of whales, seals, eagles, or lighthouses aboard the 100-ft-long *Sunbeam Express.* Naturalists from Mystic Aquarium accompany the boat.

Among the attributes of **Rocky Neck State Park** are its picnic facilities, saltwater fishing, and historic stone and wood pavilion, which was built in the 1930s. The park's mi-long crescent-shape strand is one of the finest beaches on Long Island Sound. ⊠ *Rte. 156, I–95, Exit 72, Niantic,* ☎ *860/739–5471.* ⊡ *Apr.–Sept. $5–$12; free Oct.–Mar.* ⊙ *Daily 8 AM–dusk.*

New London

🚗 *3 mi northeast of Waterford, 46 mi east of New Haven.*

New London, on the banks of the Thames River, has long had ties to the sea. In the mid-1800s it was the second-largest whaling port in the world. Today it is home to the U.S. Coast Guard Academy, which uses its campus on the Thames to educate and train its cadets. Ocean Beach Park, an old-fashioned beach resort with a wooden boardwalk, provides an up-close-and-personal view of New London's connection to the deep blue sea.

The 100-acre cluster of redbrick buildings at the **U.S. Coast Guard Academy** includes a museum and visitors pavilion with a gift shop. The three-mast training bark, the USCGC *Eagle,* may be boarded on weekends when in port. ⊠ *15 Mohegan Ave.,* ☎ *860/444–8270,* ⓦ *www.cga.edu.* ⊡ *Free.* ⊙ *Academy daily 9–5; May–Oct., daily 10–5.*

The **Lyman Allyn Museum of Art,** at the southern end of the Connecticut College campus, was named by founder Harriet U. Allyn after her father, a whaling merchant. Housed in a neoclassical building designed by Charles Platt are collections of American fine arts from the country's earliest years through today. The galleries of Connecticut's decorative arts and American Impressionist paintings are noteworthy. ⊠ *625 Williams St.,* ☎ *860/443–2545,* ⓦ *www.lymanallyn.conncollege.edu.* ⊡ *$4.* ⊙ *Tues.–Sat. 10–5, Sun. 1–5.*

⚲ It's a toss-up who will enjoy **Lyman Allyn Dolls & Toys** more, children or their parents, who can find the toys of their youth at this museum. A lovingly refurbished Victorian dollhouse, a hall of dolls, a construction site with classic toys, and a Lego playstation are just a few of the attractions. Many galleries include interactive "playzones" where children (and adults) can play. ⊠ *Harris Place, 165 State St.,* ☎ *860/437–1947.* ⊡ *$4.* ⊙ *Tues.–Fri. 1–5.*

The **Monte Cristo Cottage,** the boyhood home of Pulitzer and Nobel prize-winning playwright Eugene O'Neill, was named for the literary count, his actor-father's greatest role. The setting figures in two of O'Neill's landmark plays, *Ah, Wilderness!* and *Long Day's Journey into Night.* ⊠ *325 Pequot Ave.,* ☎ *860/443–0051.* ⊡ *$5.* ⊙ *Memorial Day–Labor Day, Tues.–Sat. 10–5, Sun. 1–5.*

Dining and Lodging

$ ✕ **Recovery Room.** It's a favorite game of Connecticut pizza parlors to declare "We're as good as Pepe's"—a reference to the famed New

Haven eatery. But this white Colonial storefront eatery, presided over by the friendly Cash family, lives up to its claim. Plenty of "boutique" toppings are available, but don't ruin a great pizza with too many flavors. Perfection is realized by the three-cheese pizza with grated Parmesan, Romano, and Gorgonzola. ⊠ *445 Ocean Ave.,* ☎ *860/443–2619. MC, V. No lunch weekends.*

$$–$$$ 🏨 **Radisson Hotel.** The rooms are quiet and spacious at this downtown property convenient to State Street, I–95, and the Amtrak station. ⊠ *35 Gov. Winthrop Blvd., 06320,* ☎ *860/443–7000,* FAX *860/443–1239,* WEB *www.radisson.com. 116 rooms, 4 suites. Restaurant, bar, indoor pool, health club. AE, D, DC, MC, V.*

Nightlife and the Arts

The **El 'n' Gee Club** (⊠ 86 Golden St., ☎ 860/437–3800) presents heavy metal, reggae, and local and national bands. The **Garde Arts Center** (⊠ 325 State St., ☎ 860/444–7373) hosts national and international Broadway, music, dance, and theater touring companies. Connecticut College's **Palmer Auditorium** (⊠ Mohegan Ave., ☎ 860/439–2787) plans a full schedule of dance and theater programs.

Outdoor Activities and Sports

The beach at **Ocean Beach Park** (⊠ 1225 Ocean Ave., ☎ 860/447–3031) is ½-mi long. Also here are an Olympic-size outdoor pool (with a triple water slide), a miniature golf course, a video arcade, a boardwalk, and a picnic area.

Norwich

65 *15 mi north of New London, 37 mi southeast of Hartford.*

Outstanding Georgian and Victorian structures surround the triangular town green in Norwich, and more can be found downtown by the Thames River. The former mill town is still hard at work at restoration and rehabilitation efforts begun in the 1990s.

The **Slater Memorial Museum & Converse Art Gallery,** on the grounds of the Norwich Free Academy, has the largest plaster-cast collection of classical statues in the country, including *Winged Victory, Venus de Milo,* and Michelangelo's *Pietà.* ⊠ *108 Crescent St.,* ☎ *860/887–2505 or 860/887–2506,* WEB *www.norwichfreeacademy.com/slater museum.* 🎟 *$3.* ☉ *Sept.–June, Tues.–Fri. 9–4, weekends 1–4; July–Aug., Tues.–Sun. 1–4.*

Lodging

$$$–$$$$ 🏨 **The Spa at Norwich Inn.** This posh Georgian-style inn is on 42 rolling acres right by the Thames River. The spa provides an entire spectrum of fitness classes, massages, and beauty treatments. You'll find four-poster beds, wood-burning fireplaces and a complete galley kitchen in the posh villas, and comfy country decor in the guest rooms. The inn's elegant restaurant serves both luxe Continental fare and lighter spa favorites. ⊠ *607 W. Thames St. (Rte. 32), 06360,* ☎ *860/886–2401 or 800/275–4772,* FAX *860/886–4492,* WEB *www.spaatnorwichinn.com. 49 rooms, 54 villas. Restaurant, indoor pool, beauty salon, spa, 18-hole golf course, 2 tennis courts. AE, DC, MC, V.*

Outdoor Activities and Sports

The **Norwich Navigators** (☎ 800/644–2867), the Class AA affiliate of baseball's New York Yankees, play at Senator Thomas J. Dodd Stadium (⊠ 14 Stott Rd.).

Ledyard

⑥⑥   *10 mi south of Norwich, 37 mi southeast of Hartford.*

There's no doubt that Ledyard, in the woods of southeastern Connecticut between Norwich and the coastline, is known first and foremost for the vast Mashantucket Pequot Tribal Nation's Foxwoods Resort Casino, which draws more than 55,000 visitors a day. With the opening of the excellent Mashantucket Pequot Museum & Research Center, however, the tribe has moved beyond gaming to educating the public about their history, as well as that of other Northeast Woodland tribes.

Foxwoods Resort Casino, on the Mashantucket Pequot Indian Reservation near Ledyard, is the world's largest gambling operation and a major draw. The skylighted compound draws more than 55,000 visitors daily to its more than 5,800 slot machines, 3,200-seat high-stakes bingo parlor, poker rooms, keno station, smoke-free gaming area, theater, and Race Book room. This massive complex includes the Grand Pequot Tower, the Great Cedar Hotel, and Two Trees Inn, which have more than 1,400 rooms combined, as well as a full–service day spa, retail concourse, food court, and 24 restaurants. A large game room and arcade and a movie theater in-the-round keep the kids entertained, along with Turbo Ride, which has specially engineered seats that simulate takeoffs and G-force pressure. ⊠ *Rte. 2, Mashantucket,* ☎ *860/ 312–3000 or 800/752–9244,* WEB *www.foxwoods.com.* ☉ *Daily.*

★   Opened in 1998, the **Mashantucket Pequot Museum & Research Center,** a large complex across from Foxwoods Resort Casino, explores the history and culture of Northeastern Woodland tribes in general and the Pequots in particular with exquisitely researched detail. Some highlights include re-creations of a glacial crevasse, a caribou hunt from 11,000 years ago, and a 17th-century fort. Perhaps most remarkable is a sprawling "immersion environment"—a 16th-century village with life-size figures and real smells and sounds—in which you use audio devices to obtain detailed information about the sights. The research center, open to scholars and schoolchildren free of charge, holds thousands of books and artifacts. Native American cuisine is available at the restaurant, and the shop sells contemporary Native American arts and crafts. ⊠ *110 Pequot Trail, Mashantucket,* ☎ *800/411–9671,* WEB *www.mashantucket.com.* ⊡ *$12.* ☉ *Memorial Day–Labor Day, daily 10–7; Labor Day–Memorial Day, Wed.–Mon. 10–6.*

The Mohegan Indians, known as the Wolf People, operate the **Mohegan Sun,** which currently has more than 3,000 slot machines, 192 gaming tables, bingo, a theater, "Kids Quest" family entertainment complex, and, among 20 food-and-beverage suppliers, three fine-dining restaurants. For betting on the ponies or even on greyhounds, you'll find Race Book, a Simulcast theater with New York Racing Association broadcasts. Free entertainment, including nationally known acts, is presented nightly in the Wolf Den. An expansion, to be completed in 2002, will include a 1,200-room luxury hotel, nine new restaurants, a day spa, a 10,000–seat arena, and an additional 115,000–square–ft of gaming space. Uncasville is west of Ledyard, across the Thames River. ⊠ *Mohegan Sun Blvd. off I–395, Uncasville,* ☎ *888/226–7711,* WEB *www.mohegansun.com.*

Dining and Lodging

$$$–$$$$ ✕☰ **Stonecroft.** This well-regarded inn has become even more popu-
★   lar after the 1999 renovation of a historic barn on the property and the addition of a restaurant and more deluxe guest rooms. The sunny 1807 Georgian Colonial is set on 6 ½ acres of green meadows, woodlands, and rambling stone walls. The rooms are decorated with unique

themes but are united in their refined but welcoming country atmosphere. Sea scallops with truffle butter, braised leeks, wild mushrooms, and a sweet corn reduction are good options at the sophisticated restaurant. ✉ *515 Pumpkin Hill Rd., 06339,* ☎ *860/572–0771,* FAX *860/572–9161,* WEB *www.stonecroft.com. 10 rooms. Restaurant, croquet, horseshoes. AE, D, MC, V. BP.*

$$$$ 🏨 **Grand Pequot Tower.** Foxwoods' showcase hotel is an imposing 17 stories. Mere steps from the gaming floors, the expansive showpiece contains deluxe rooms and suites in pleasantly neutral tones. ✉ *Box 3777, Rte. 2, Mashantucket 06339,* ☎ *800/369–9663,* FAX *860/312–5044,* WEB *www.foxwoods.com. 824 rooms. 4 restaurants, 2 bars, indoor pool, beauty salon, spa, 2 18-hole golf courses, health club, meeting room. AE, D, DC, MC, V.*

Groton

67 *10 mi south of Ledyard.*

Home to the United States naval submarine base and the Electric Boat Division of General Dynamics, designer and manufacturer of nuclear submarines, Groton is often referred to as "the submarine capital of the world." The submarine *Nautilus,* a National Historic Landmark, is a major draw, as is the Submarine Force Museum.

The world's first nuclear-powered submarine, the *Historic Ship Nautilus,* launched from Groton in 1954, is permanently berthed at the **Submarine Force Museum.** You're welcome to climb aboard and imagine yourself as a crew member during the boat's trip under the North Pole more than 40 years ago. The adjacent museum, outside the entrance to the submarine base, charts submarine history with memorabilia, artifacts, and displays, including working periscopes and controls. ✉ *Crystal Lake Rd.,* ☎ *860/694–3174 or 800/343–0079,* WEB *www.ussnautilus.org.* 🎫 *Free.* ⏱ *Mid-May–Oct., Wed.–Mon. 9–5, Tues. 1–5; Nov.–early May, Wed.–Mon. 9–4.*

Fort Griswold Battlefield State Park contains the remnants of a Revolutionary War fort. Historic displays at the museum mark the site of the massacre of American defenders by Benedict Arnold's British troops in 1781. A sweeping view of the shoreline can be had from the top of the Groton monument. ✉ *Monument St. and Park Ave.,* ☎ *860/445–1729,* WEB *www.revwar.com/ftgriswold.* 🎫 *Free.* ⏱ *Park daily 8 AM–dusk. Museum and monument Memorial Day–Labor Day, daily 10–5.*

Outdoor Activities and Sports

Striped bass and blues are the catch of the day on **Hel-Cat II,** a 144-ft party fishing boat, from June to October. Cod, pollock, mackerel, blackfish, and sea bass are the goals in winter and spring. ✉ *181 Thames St.,* ☎ *860/535–2066 or 860/445–5991.* 🎫 *$28–$48.* ⏱ *Jan.–May, weekends; June–Oct., daily; call for hrs.*

Mystic

68 *8 mi east of Groton.*

Mystic has tried with dedication (if also with excessive commercialism) to recapture the seafaring spirit of the 18th and 19th centuries. This is where some of the nation's fastest clipper ships were built in the mid-19th century; today's Mystic Seaport is the state's most-popular museum. Downtown Mystic has an interesting collection of boutiques and galleries.

★ ☾ **Mystic Seaport,** the world's largest marine museum, encompasses 17 acres of indoor and outdoor exhibits that provide a fascinating look at the area's rich maritime heritage. In the narrow streets and historic homes and buildings (some moved here from other sites), craftspeople give demonstrations of open-hearth cooking, weaving, and other skills of yesteryear. The museum's more than 480 vessels include the *Charles W. Morgan,* the last remaining wooden whaling ship afloat, and the 1882 training ship *Joseph Conrad.* You can climb aboard for a look or for sail-setting demonstrations and reenactments of whale hunts. Among the other attractions here are dozens of spectacular ship's figureheads, the world's largest collection of maritime art, 19th-century cruises on 19th-century vessels, thousands of manuscripts and maps, and a period tavern. The museum can be very crowded in summer and early fall; if possible, plan to visit between October and May. In December, tours by lantern light are led by a costumed interpreter doing his 19th-century Christmas errands; reservations are essential. ✉ 75 Greenmanville Ave., ☎ 860/572-0711, WEB *www.mysticseaport.org.* 🎫 *$16.* ☾ *May–Oct., daily 9–5; Nov.–Apr., daily 10–4.*

★ ☾ Sea lions and penguins and whales—oh, my! The **Mystic Aquarium and Institute for Exploration,** with more than 3,500 specimens and 34 exhibits of sea life, includes Seal Island, a 2½-acre outdoor exhibit that shows off seals and sea lions from around the world; the Marine Theater, where California sea lions perform; and the beloved Penguin Pavilion. You'll also find exhibits such as a re-creation of the Alaska coastline, with the world's largest (750,000-gallon) outdoor beluga whale habitat. World-renowned ocean explorer Dr. Robert Ballard uses high-tech exhibits to take a simulated dive 3,000 ft below the ocean surface. ✉ *55 Coogan Blvd.,* ☎ *860/572-5955,* WEB *www.mysticaquarium.org.* 🎫 *$15.* ☾ *Labor Day–June, daily 9–5; July–Labor Day, daily 9–6.*

Dining and Lodging

$-$$ ✕ **Abbott's Lobster in the Rough.** If you want some of the state's best
★ lobsters, mussels, crabs, or clams on the half shell, grab a bottle of wine and slip down to this unassuming seaside lobster shack in sleepy Noank, a few mi southwest of Mystic. Most seating is outdoors or on the dock, where the views are magnificent. ✉ *117 Pearl St., Noank,* ☎ *860/536-7719. AE, MC, V. BYOB. Closed Columbus Day–1st Fri. in May and weekdays Labor Day–Columbus Day.*

$-$$ ✕ **Go Fish.** In this town by the sea, it's only right to dine on seafood,
★ and this sophisticated restaurant captures all the tastes—and colors—of the ocean. The black granite sushi bar, with its myriad tiny, briny morsels, is worth the trip in itself. The glossy blue tables in the two large dining rooms are the perfect setting for the signature bouillabaisse with aioli, fennel toast, and saffron-scented broth. The menu offers options for vegetarians and carnivores as well, but the lobster ravioli in a light cream sauce is a must-try. ✉ *Olde Mistick Village, Coogan Blvd. (I–95, Exit 90),* ☎ *860/536-2662. AE, MC, V.*

$-$$ ✕ **Mystic Pizza.** It's hard to say who benefited more from the success of the 1988 sleeper film *Mystic Pizza:* then-budding actress Julia Roberts or the pizza parlor on which the film is based (though no scenes were filmed here). This joint, which is often teeming with customers in summer, serves other dishes but is best known for its pizza, garlic bread, and grinders. ✉ *56 W. Main St.,* ☎ *860/536-3700 or 860/536-3737. D, MC, V.*

$$$$ ✕🍽 **Inn at Mystic.** The highlight of this inn, which sprawls over 15
★ hilltop acres and overlooks picturesque Pequotsepos Cove, is the five-bedroom Georgian Colonial mansion. Almost as impressive are the rambling four-bedroom gatehouse (where Lauren Bacall and Humphrey

Bogart honeymooned) and the unusually attractive motor lodge. The convivial, sun-filled Flood Tide restaurant specializes in contemporary Continental fare and New England classics such as beef Wellington and pan-seared veal chops. Brunch fans flock here on Sunday. ⊠ *U.S. 1 and Rte. 27, 06355,* ☎ *860/536–9604 or 800/237–2415,* FAX *860/ 572–1635,* WEB *www.innatmystic.com. 67 rooms. Restaurant, pool, tennis court, dock, boating. AE, D, DC, MC, V.*

$$–$$$$ ✕⌂ **Whaler's Inn and Motor Court.** A perfect compromise between a chain motel and a country inn, this complex with public rooms that contain lovely antiques is one block from the Mystic River and downtown. Motel-style guest rooms are decorated in a Victorian manner with quilts and reproduction four-poster beds. The restaurant, Bravo Bravo, serves nouvelle Italian food: the fettuccine might come with grilled scallops, roasted apples, sun-dried tomatoes, and a Gorgonzola cream sauce. ⊠ *20 E. Main St., 06355,* ☎ *860/536–1506 or 800/243–2588,* FAX *860/ 572–1250,* WEB *www.whalersinnmystic.com. 41 rooms. Restaurant, outdoor café, meeting room. AE, MC, V.*

$$$$ ⌂ **Steamboat Inn.** The rooms at this inn are named after famous Mystic schooners, but it's hardly a creaky old establishment—many of the rooms look as though they've been arranged for the cover shot of *House Beautiful.* Six have wood-burning fireplaces, all have whirlpool baths, and most have dramatic river views. Despite the inn's busy downtown location (within earshot of the eerie hoot of the Bascule Drawbridge and the chatter of tourists), the rooms are the most luxurious and romantic in town. ⊠ *73 Steamboat Wharf, off W. Main St., 06355,* ☎ *860/536– 8300,* WEB *www.visitmystic.com/steamboat. 10 rooms. AE, D, MC, V. CP.*

Outdoor Activities and Sports

Private charter boats depart from **Noank Village Boatyard** (⊠ 38 Bayside Ave., Noank, ☎ 860/536–1770).

Shopping

Finer Line Gallery (⊠ 48 W. Main St., ☎ 860/536–8339) exhibits nautical and other prints. At the **Mystic Factory Outlets** (⊠ Coogan Blvd.), nearly two dozen stores discount famous-name clothing and other merchandise. **Olde Mistick Village** (⊠ Coogan Blvd., I–95, Exit 90, ☎ 860/536–1641), a re-creation of what an American village might have looked like in the early 1700s, is at once hokey and picturesque. The stores here sell crafts, clothing, souvenirs, and food. **Tradewinds Gallery** (⊠ 7 Cottrell St., ☎ 860/536–0119) represents some New England artists but specializes in antique maps and prints and marine art.

Stonington

⑥⑨ *7 mi southeast of Mystic, 57 mi east of New Haven.*

The pretty village of Stonington pokes into Fishers Island Sound. Today a quiet fishing community clustered around white-spired churches, Stonington is far less commercial than Mystic. In the 19th century, though, this was a bustling whaling, sealing, and transportation center. Historic buildings line the town green and border both sides of Water Street up to the imposing Old Lighthouse Museum.

The **Captain Nathaniel B. Palmer House** is the Victorian home of the man who discovered Antarctica in 1820. Exhibits focus on both his career and family life. ⊠ *40 Palmer St.,* ☎ *860/535–8445.* ⌦ *$4.* ☉ *May–Oct., Tues.–Sun. 10–4.*

The **Old Lighthouse Museum** has six rooms of exhibits depicting life in a coastal town circa 1649. It occupies a lighthouse built in 1823, which was moved to higher ground 17 years later. Climb to the top of the tower for a spectacular view of Long Island Sound and three states. ⊠ *7 Water St.,* ☎ *860/535–1440.* ☜ *$4.* ⊙ *July–Aug., daily 10–5; May–June and Sept.–Oct., Tues.–Sun. 10–5, or by appointment.*

The **Stonington Vineyards,** a small coastal winery, has grown premium vinifera, including chardonnay and French hybrid grape varieties, since 1987. You can browse through the works of local artists in the small gallery or take a picnic lunch on the grounds. ⊠ *523 Taugwonk Rd.,* ☎ *860/535–1222,* 🕸 *www.stoningtonvineyards.com.* ☜ *Free.* ⊙ *Daily 11–5; tours at 2.*

Dining and Lodging

$$$–$$$$ ✕▥ **Randall's Ordinary.** The waiters dress in Colonial garb at this inn known for its open-hearth cooking. The prix-fixe menu ($$$; reservations essential for dinner) changes daily; choices might include tasty Nantucket scallops or rosemary-rhubarb lamb. The 17th-century John Randall House provides very simple accommodations, but all rooms have modern baths with whirlpool tubs and showers. The barn houses irregular-shape guest rooms, all with authentic early Colonial decor. ⊠ *Box 243, Rte. 2, North Stonington, 7 mi north of Stonington, 06359,* ☎ *860/599–4540,* 🖷 *860/599–3308,* 🕸 *www.randallsordinary.com. 14 rooms, 1 suite. Restaurant. AE, MC, V.*

$$$$ ▥ **Antiques & Accommodations.** The British influence is evident in the
★ Georgian formality of this Victorian country home, built about 1861. Exquisite furniture and accessories decorate the rooms. An 1820 house has similarly furnished suites. Aromatic candles and fresh flowers create an inviting atmosphere. Breakfast is a grand four-course affair served by candlelight on fine china, sterling silver, and crystal. ⊠ *32 Main St., North Stonington, 7 mi north of Stonington, 06359,* ☎ *860/ 535–1736 or 800/554–7829,* 🕸 *www.visitmystic.com/antiques. 3 rooms, 2 suites. MC, V. BP.*

New Haven and the Southeastern Coast A to Z

To research prices, get advice from other travelers, and book travel arrangements, visit www.fodors.com.

AIR TRAVEL TO AND FROM NEW HAVEN AND THE SOUTHEASTERN COAST
Tweed/New Haven Airport, 5 mi southeast of New Haven, is served by US Airways Express.
➤ AIRPORT INFORMATION: **Tweed/New Haven Airport** (⊠ Burr St. off I–95, ☎ 203/466–8833 or 800/428–4322, 🕸 www.tweednewhavenairport.com). **US Airways Express** (☎ 203/466–8833 or 800/428–4322).

BOAT & FERRY TRAVEL
From New London, Cross Sound Ferry operates year-round passenger and car service to and from Orient Point, Long Island, New York. The high-speed ferry can make the trip in 90 minutes. Fishers Island Ferry has passenger and car service to and from Fishers Island, New York, from New London. Interstate Navigation Co. operates passenger and car service from New London to and from Block Island, Rhode Island, from June to early September.
➤ BOAT & FERRY INFORMATION: **Cross Sound Ferry** (☎ 860/443–5281, 🕸 www.longislandferry.com). **Fishers Island Ferry** (☎ 860/ 443–6851). **Interstate Navigation Co.** (☎ 401/783–4613, 🕸 www.blockislandferry.com).

BUS TRAVEL

Peter Pan Bus Lines services New Haven from Boston, Hartford, and New York. Prime Time Shuttle provides shuttle service between New Haven and LaGuardia and John F. Kennedy airports in New York City. Connecticut Transit's local bus service connects New Haven and the surrounding towns; there is also service to and from Tweed/New Haven Airport.

➤ BUS INFORMATION: **Peter Pan Bus Lines** (☎ 800/237–8747, WEB www.peterpan-bus.com). **Prime Time Shuttle** (☎ 800/733–8267, WEB www.primetimeshuttle.com). **Connecticut Transit** (☎ 203/624–0151, WEB www.cttransit.com).

CAR TRAVEL

Interstate 95 and U.S. 1, which run mostly parallel but sometimes intertwine, are the main routes to and through southeastern Connecticut; the two roads intersect with I–91 (coming south from Hartford) in New Haven.

Most of the southeastern Connecticut towns in New Haven and the Southeastern Coast are on or just off I–95 and U.S. 1, and a car is the easiest way to explore much of the area. Interstate 395 branches north from I–95 to Norwich.

EMERGENCIES

➤ HOSPITALS: **Lawrence & Memorial Hospital** (⊠ 365 Montauk Ave., New London, ☎ 860/442–0711, WEB www.lmhospital.org). **Yale–New Haven Hospital** (⊠ 20 York St., New Haven, ☎ 203/688–4242, WEB www.ynhh.org).
➤ LATE-NIGHT PHARMACY: **CVS** (⊠ 1168 Whalley Ave., New Haven, ☎ 203/389–4714, WEB www.cvs.com).

TAXIS

Metro Taxi serves New Haven and environs.
➤ CONTACTS: **Metro Taxi** (☎ 203/777–7777).

TRAIN TRAVEL

Amtrak trains make stops in New Haven, New London, and Mystic. Metro-North Railroad trains from New York stop in New Haven.

The Connecticut Department of Transportation's Shore Line East operates commuter rail service (weekdays, westbound in the morning, eastbound in the evening) connecting New Haven, Branford, Guilford, Madison, Clinton, Westbrook, Old Saybrook, and New London.

FARES & SCHEDULES
➤ TRAIN INFORMATION: **Amtrak** (☎ 800/872–7245, WEB www.amtrak.com). **Metro-North Railroad** (☎ 800/638–7646; 212/532–4900 in New York City, WEB www.mta.nyc.ny.us). **Shore Line East** (☎ 800/255–7433 in Connecticut, WEB www.rideworks.com).

VISITOR INFORMATION

➤ TOURIST INFORMATION: **Connecticut River Valley and Shoreline Visitors Council** (⊠ 393 Main St., Middletown 06457, ☎ 860/347–0028 or 800/486–3346, WEB www.cttourism.org). **Connecticut's Mystic and More** (⊠ Box 89, 470 Bank St., New London 06320, ☎ 860/444–2206 or 800/863–6569, WEB www.mysticmore.com). **Greater New Haven Convention and Bureau District** (⊠ 59 Elm St., Suite 100, New Haven 06510, ☎ 203/777–8550 or 800/332–7829, WEB www.newhavencvb.org). **Mystic Coast & Country Travel & Leisure Council** (☎ 800/692–6278, WEB www.mycoast.com).

THE QUIET CORNER

Few visitors to Connecticut experience the old-fashioned ways of the state's "Quiet Corner," a vast patch of sparsely populated towns that seem a world away from the rest of the state. The Quiet Corner has a reclusive allure: people used to leave New York City for the Litchfield Hills; now many are leaving for northeastern Connecticut, where the stretch of Route 169 from Brooklyn past Woodstock has been named a National Scenic Byway.

The cultural capital of the Quiet Corner is Putnam, a small mill city on the Quinebaug River whose formerly industrial town center has been transformed into a year-round antiques mart. Smaller jewels in and around the Putnam area are Brooklyn, Pomfret, and Woodstock—three towns where authentic Colonial homesteads still seem to outnumber the contemporary, charmless clones that are springing up all too rapidly across the state.

Brooklyn

⑦⓪ *45 mi east of Hartford.*

The village of Brooklyn bears no resemblance to the more famous borough of New York City that carries the same name. White picket fences and beautifully restored Colonial homes are the norm here.

The **New England Center for Contemporary Art,** housed in a four-story pre-Revolutionary barn, hosts exhibitions of 20th-century art and has a gift shop. ⊠ *Rte. 169,* ☎ *860/774–8899.* ⬛ *Free.* ☉ *Apr.–Nov., Wed.–Sun. 1–5.*

Ever think that a Connecticut dairy farm is the home where buffalo roam? At **Creamery Brook Bison** they do. This working farm, with a herd of more than 70, offers wagon rides to the fields where the herd grazes and has a store with various buffalo-themed items such as T-shirts, stuffed animals, figurines, and even frozen buffalo meat. ⊠ *19 Purvis Rd.,* ☎ *860/779–0837,* WEB *www.creamerybrookbison.com.* ⬛ *$6.* ☉ *Weekdays 2–6, Sat. 9–2; wagon rides July–Sept., weekends at 1:30.*

Logee's Greenhouses, a family business founded in 1892, has eight greenhouses overflowing with more than 1,500 varieties of indoor plants. Begonias—more than 400 varieties—are a specialty. ⊠ *141 North St., Danielson,* ☎ *860/774–8038,* WEB *www.logees.com.* ⬛ *Free.* ☉ *Mon.–Sat. 9–5, Sun. 11–5.*

Dining and Lodging

$$$$ ✕ **Golden Lamb Buttery.** Connecticut's most unusual and magical din-
★ ing experience has achieved almost legendary status. Eating here is far more than a chance to enjoy good Continental food: it's a social and gastronomical event. There is one seating each for lunch and dinner in this converted barn. Owners Bob and Virginia "Jimmie" Booth have a vintage Jaguar roadster and a hay wagon that guests can ride in before dinner (a musician accompanies you). Choose from one of three daily soups and four entrées, which might include medallions of lamb or pan-fried beef tenderloin. ⊠ *499 Bush Hill Rd. (off Rte. 169),* ☎ *860/774–4423. Reservations essential. No credit cards. Closed Jan.–mid-Apr. and Sun.–Mon. No dinner Tues.–Thurs.*

The Quiet Corner

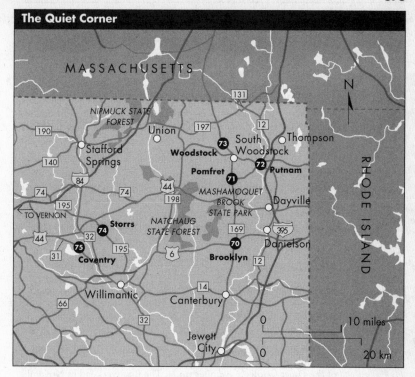

Pomfret

71 *6 mi north of Brooklyn.*

Pomfret, one of the grandest towns in the region, was once known as the inland Newport because it attracted the wealthy, who summered here in large "cottages." Today it is a quiet stopping-off point along Route 169, designated one of the 10 most scenic byways in the country. The hilltop campus of the Pomfret School offers some of Connecticut's loveliest views.

Sharpe Hill Vineyard is centered on an 18th-century-style barn in the hills of Pomfret. Tours and tastings are given, and you can nibble on smoked salmon and fruit and cheese in the European-style wine garden or the Fireside Tavern, which also serves dinner on Friday evenings. ⊠ *108 Wade Rd.,* ☎ *860/974–3549,* WEB *www.sharpehill.com.* ☞ *Free.* ☉ *Fri.–Sun. 11–5.*

Dining

$$ ✕ **The Harvest.** This romantic country restaurant is alive with fresh flowers, glimmering candles, antiques, and touches of chintz. It serves a variety of seafood, vegetable, and pasta dishes. Its large assortment of "prime entrées," include steaks, filets, and chops with your choice of such accompaniments as shiitake mushrooms with wasabi Béarnaise sauce or roasted garlic and tomatoes. ⊠ *37 Putnam St.,* ☎ *860/928–0008. AE, MC, V. No lunch weekends.*

$ ✕ **Vanilla Bean Café.** A perfect stop for lunch, this tan Colonial-style barn serves salads and hearty sandwiches in an informal dining room. Dinner entrées such as smoked mozzarella and basil ravioli and roast pork with winter vegetables are offered until 8. From May to October, fare from the outside grill is served on the patio until 9; the indoor grill is fired up for burgers year-round. The cheesecake gets rave reviews. Breakfast is available on weekends. ⊠ *450 Deerfield Rd. (U.S. 44, Rte. 97, and Rte. 169),* ☎ *860/928–1562. No credit cards. No dinner Mon.–Tues.*

Outdoor Activities and Sports

Mashamoquet Brook State Park was formed by combining Mashamoquet Brook, Wolf Den, and Saptree Run into an 860-acre park with an attractive trail system. The park also has swimming, fishing, and camping facilities. ⊠ *U.S. 44,* ☎ *860/928–6121.* ☞ *Memorial Day–Labor Day, $5–$8; Labor Day–Memorial Day, free.* ☉ *Daily 8* AM*–dusk.*

Shopping

Majilly (⊠ 56 Babbitt Hill Rd., ☎ 860/974–3714), an upscale line of hand-painted ceramic pottery crafted in Italy, is based in a 150-year-old barn. Open Tuesday through Saturday, the outlet sells still-gorgeous seconds at 50%–70% off the retail prices. **Martha's Herbary** (⊠ 589 Pomfret St., ☎ 860/928–0009), in a 1780 home, is an herb-theme gift shop and garden. Classes in the demonstration kitchen cover everything from cooking with herbs to making herbal facial masks.

Putnam

🕖 *5 mi northeast of Pomfret.*

Ambitious antiques dealers have reinvented Putnam, a mill town 30 mi west of Providence, R.I. that became neglected after the Depression. Putnam's downtown, with more than 400 antiques dealers, is the heart of the Quiet Corner's antiques trade. The first weekend in November is **Antiquing Weekend,** when nearly two dozen area shops offer discounts and give workshops.

Dining

$$–$$$ ✕ **White Horse Inn.** This historic country inn from the early 1800s has been updated with a sophisticated white-on-white color scheme. Favorite dishes among the robust country fare are New Zealand lamb tenderloin and shellfish fantasy (a mix of scallops, shrimp, crab, and lobster). ⊠ *351 Thompson Rd. (Rtes. 193 and 200),* ☎ *860/923–9571. AE, D, DC, MC, V. Closed Mon.–Tues.*

$–$$ ✕ **The Vine.** This stylish trattoria-bistro is *the* place to go for a break from antiquing. Don't miss the eggplant rollatini (thinly sliced eggplant rolled with ricotta, mozzarella, Parmesan, and sun-dried tomatoes with a marinara sauce), a starter. You can follow with the house special: Pasta D'Vine (sautéed chicken breast with artichoke hearts, tomatoes, black olives, mushrooms, and homemade angel-hair pasta). ⊠ *85 Main St.,* ☎ *860/928–1660. Reservations essential. AE, MC, V. Closed Mon.*

Shopping

The four-level **Antiques Marketplace** (⊠ 109 Main St., ☎ 860/928–0442) houses the wares of nearly 300 dealers, from fine furniture to tchotchkes and collectibles. The 30,000-square-ft **Putnam Antique Exchange** (⊠ 75–83 Main St., ☎ 860/928–1905) stocks 18th-century to Art Deco-era paintings, stained glass, architectural elements, and fine furnishings.

Woodstock

🕖 *5 mi northwest of Putnam.*

The landscape of this enchanting town is splendid in every season—the gently rolling hills seem to stretch for mi.

Roseland Cottage, probably the region's most notable historic dwelling, is a pink board-and-batten Gothic Revival house built in 1846 by New York publisher and merchant Henry Bowen. The pride of its grounds is an 1850s boxwood parterre garden that four presidents—Ulysses S. Grant, Rutherford B. Hayes, Benjamin Harrison, and William McKinley—have visited. An hour-long stroll around the grounds is one of several dozen walks held during the Quiet Corner's **Walking Weekend,** offered each Columbus Day weekend. ☒ *556 Rte. 169,* ☏ *860/ 928–4074,* WEB *www.spnea.org/visit/homes/bowen.htm.* ☒ *$4.* ☉ *June– mid-Oct., Wed.–Sun. 11–5. Tours on the hr, last one at 4.*

Dining and Lodging

$$–$$$ ✕🏠 **Inn at Woodstock Hill.** This inn on a hill overlooking the countryside has sumptuous rooms with antiques, four-poster beds, fireplaces, pitched ceilings, and timber beams. The chintz-and-prints restaurant ($$; reservations essential) next door serves excellent Continental and American variations on seafood, veal, beef, pork, and chicken dishes. ☒ *94 Plaine Hill Rd., South Woodstock 06267,* ☏ *860/928–0528,* FAX *860/928–3236,* WEB *www.woodstockhill.com. 22 rooms. Restaurant, meeting room D, MC, V. CP.*

Shopping

The **Christmas Barn** (☒ 835 Rte. 169, ☏ 860/928–7652) has 12 rooms of country and Christmas goods. **Scranton's Shops** (☒ 300 Rte. 169, ☏ 860/928–3738) sells antiques and the wares of 90 local artisans. **Whispering Hill Farm** (☒ Rte. 169, ☏ 860/928–0162) sells supplies for rug hooking and braiding, quilting, and needlework mixed with an assortment of antiques.

Storrs

74 *25 mi southwest of Woodstock.*

The majority of the rolling hillside and farmland of Storrs is occupied by the 4,400 acres and some 12,000 students of the main campus of the University of Connecticut (UConn). Many cultural programs, sporting events, and other happenings take place here. University Parking Services and the Student Union supply campus maps.

Hand puppets, rod puppets, body puppets, shadow puppets, marionettes—the **Ballard Institute and Museum of Puppetry** has more than 2,000 puppets in its extraordinary collection. Half were created by Frank Ballard, a master of puppetry who established the country's first complete undergraduate and graduate degree program in puppetry at UConn more than three decades ago. Exhibits change seasonally. If you're lucky you might even catch Oscar the Grouch from *Sesame Street* on display. ☒ *Univ. of Connecticut Depot Campus, 6 Bourn Place, U-212,* ☏ *860/486–4605.* ☒ *$2.* ☉ *Late-Apr.–early Nov., Fri.–Sun. noon–5.* WEB *www.sp.uconn.edu/~wwwsfa/bimp.html.*

The permanent collection of the **William Benton Museum of Art** includes European and American paintings, drawings, prints, and sculptures from the 16th century to the present. ☒ *Univ. of Connecticut, 245 Glenbrook Rd.,* ☏ *860/486–4520,* WEB *www.benton.uconn.edu.* ☒ *Free.* ☉ *Tues.–Fri. 10–4:30, weekends 1–4:30. Closed between exhibitions.*

Talk about diversity—the **University of Connecticut Greenhouses** are internationally acclaimed for their more than 3,000 different kinds of plants, from 900 varieties of exotic orchids to banana plants and a redwood tree. Organized tours are given weekends by advance appoint-

ment. ⊠ *Univ. of Connecticut, 75 N. Eagleville Rd.,* ☎ *860/486–4052.*
🎫 *Free.* ☉ *Weekdays 8–4.*

Nightlife and the Arts

The **Jorgenson Auditorium** (⊠ Univ. of Connecticut, 2132 Hillside Rd.,
☎ 860/486–4226) presents music, dance, and theater programs.
Downstairs in the Jorgenson Auditorium in the Harriet S. Jorgensen
Theatre (aka "Baby" Jorgensen), the **Connecticut Repertory Theatre**
(☎ 860/486–3969) produces musicals, Shakespeare, and modern dramas. **Mansfield Drive-In** (⊠ Rtes. 31 and 32, Mansfield, ☎ 860/423–
4441), with three big screens, is one of the state's few remaining
drive-in theaters.

Shopping

The **Eastern Connecticut Flea Market** (⊠ Mansfield Drive-In, Rtes. 31
and 32, Mansfield, ☎ 860/456–2578), with more than 150 vendors
selling everything from T-shirts to toys and jewelry, unfolds on Sunday from the first weekend of spring until Thanksgiving weekend.

Coventry

 *5 mi southwest of Storrs.*

Historians will recognize Coventry as the birthplace of the Revolutionary
War hero Captain Nathan Hale, who was hanged as a spy by the British
in 1776. It was Hale who spoke the immortal last words, "I only re-
gret that I have but one life to lose for my country." Gardeners and
herbalists, on the other hand, regard Coventry first and foremost as
the home of Caprilands Herb Farm, which the late Adelma Grenier
Simmons built into a center of worldwide renown.

The **Nathan Hale Homestead** was rebuilt by Deacon Richard Hale,
Nathan's father, in 1776. Ten Hale children, six of whom served in the
Revolutionary War, were raised here. Family artifacts are on exhibit
in the completely furnished house. The grounds include a corncrib and
an 18th-century barn. ⊠ *2299 South St.,* ☎ *860/742–6917.* 🎫 *$4.* ☉
Mid-May–mid-Oct., daily 1–4.

Coventry's **Caprilands Herb Farm** (⊠ 534 Silver St., ☎ 860/742–7244,
WEB www.caprilands.com) draws thousands of visitors annually to 38
gardens with more than 300 varieties of herbs, which are for sale. There's
a noon luncheon lecture program, and tea is held on the weekends (phone
for reservations).

The Quiet Corner A to Z

*To research prices, get advice from other travelers, and book travel ar-
rangements, visit www.fodors.com.*

CAR TRAVEL

You'll need a car to reach and explore the Quiet Corner. Many Nutmeggers live their entire lives without even noticing I–395, let alone
driving on it, but this is the main highway connecting Worcester,
Massachusetts, with New London—and it passes right through the Quiet
Corner. From Hartford take I–84 east to U.S. 44 east, and from Providence, Rhode Island, take either U.S. 44 or 6 west. The main towns
in the Quiet Corner are on or near historic Route 169.

EMERGENCIES

➤ Hospitals: **Rockville General Hospital** (⊠ 31 Union St., Vernon, ☎
860/872–5292, WEB www.echn.orh/rgh.htm). **Windham Community**

Memorial Hospital (✉ 112 Mansfield Ave., Willimantic, ☎ 860/456–6715, WEB www.windhamhospital.org).

➤ PHARMACY: **CVS** (✉ Mansfield Shopping Plaza, Storrs, ☎ 860/487–0223, WEB www.cvs.com, ⊙ Mon.–Fri. until 9 PM, Sat.–Sun. until 10 PM).

VISITOR INFORMATION

➤ TOURIST INFORMATION: **Northeast Connecticut Visitors District** (✉ 13 Canterbury Rd., Suite 3, Box 145, Brooklyn 06234, ☎ 860/779–6383 or 888/628–1228, WEB www.ctquietcorner.org).

CONNECTICUT A TO Z

To research prices, get advice from other travelers, and book travel arrangements, visit www.fodors.com.

AIRPORTS

Many people visiting Connecticut fly into New York City's John F. Kennedy International Airport or LaGuardia Airport, both of which are served by many major carriers. Another option is Bradley International Airport, north of Hartford.

➤ AIRPORT INFORMATION: **John F. Kennedy International Airport** (☎ 718/244–4444, WEB www.panynj.gov/aviation/jfkframe.htm). **LaGuardia Airport** (☎ 718/533–3400, WEB www.panynj.gov/aviation/jgaframe/htm). **Bradley International Airport**, north of Hartford.

AIRPORT TRANSFERS

The Airport Connection has scheduled service from Bradley to Hartford's Union Station, as well as door-to-door service. Connecticut Limo operates bus and van service between Connecticut and the New York airports and to and from Bradley International Airport. Prime Time Shuttle serves New Haven and Fairfield counties with service to and from both New York airports.

➤ TAXIS & SHUTTLES: **Airport Connection** (☎ 860/627–3400). **Connecticut Limo** (☎ 800/472–5466, WEB www.ctlimo.com). **Prime Time Shuttle** (☎ 800/733–8267, WEB www.primetimeshuttle.com).

BUS TRAVEL

Bonanza Bus Lines connects Hartford, Farmington, Southbury, Waterbury, Manchester, and Danbury with Boston and New York. Greyhound links Connecticut with most major cities in the United States. Peter Pan Bus Lines serves the eastern seaboard, including many New England cities.

➤ BUS INFORMATION: **Bonanza Bus Lines** (☎ 800/556–3815, WEB www.bonanzabus.com). **Greyhound** (☎ 800/231–2222, WEB www.greyhound.com). **Peter Pan Bus Lines** (☎ 800/237–8747, WEB www.peterpan-bus.com).

CAR TRAVEL

From New York City head north on I–95, which hugs the Connecticut shoreline into Rhode Island or, to reach the Litchfield Hills and Hartford, head north on I–684, then east on I–84. From Springfield, Massachusetts, go south on I–91, which bisects I–84 in Hartford and I–95 in New Haven. From Boston take I–95 south through Providence or take the Massachusetts Turnpike west to I–84. Interstate 395 runs north–south from southeastern Connecticut to Massachusetts.

The interstates are the quickest routes between many points in Connecticut, but they are busy and ugly. The speed limits on Connecticut's interstates change, sometimes going from 65 mph to 45 mph and back quite quickly through the cities. Be certain to check for posted speed limits. Right turns on red are legal unless posted otherwise.

If time allows, skip the interstates in favor of the historic Merritt Parkway (Route 15), which winds between Greenwich and Middletown; U.S. 7 and Route 8, extending between I–95 and the Litchfield Hills; Route 9, which heads south from Hartford through the Connecticut River valley to Old Saybrook; and scenic Route 169, which meanders through the Quiet Corner. Maps are available free from the Connecticut Office of Tourism (☞ Visitor Information).

EMERGENCIES

Ambulance, fire, police (☎ 911).

LODGING

B&BS

➤ RESERVATION SERVICES: **B&B, Ltd.** (☎ 203/469–3260). **Mystic Country Inns** (☎ 800/598–7116, WEB www.mysticcountryinns.com). Covered Bridge B&B Reservation Service (☎ 860/542–5944). **Nutmeg B&B Agency** (☎ 860/236–6698, WEB www.bnb-link.com).

OUTDOORS & SPORTS

For information about fishing licenses and regulations and a copy of the annual angler's guide to state lakes and ponds and the fish that inhabit them, call the Fisheries Division of the Department of Environmental Protection.

➤ CONTACTS: **Fisheries Division of the Department of Environmental Protection** (☎ 860/424–3474).

TOURS

The Connecticut Freedom Trail features 36 historic sights associated with the state's African-American heritage. The Connecticut Impressionist Art Trail is a self-guided tour of 10 museums important to the 19th-century American Impressionist movement. Write to the below address for a map. The Connecticut Wine Trail travels between eight member vineyards.

➤ TOUR OPERATORS: **Connecticut Impressionist Art Trail** (✉ Box 793, Old Lyme 06371). **Connecticut Wine Trail** (✉ 131 Tower Rd., Brookfield 06804, ☎ 203/775–1616).

TRAIN TRAVEL

Amtrak runs from New York to Boston, stopping in Stamford, Bridgeport, and New Haven before heading either north to Hartford or east to Mystic. Metro-North Railroad trains from New York stop locally between Greenwich and New Haven, and a few trains head inland to New Canaan, Danbury, and Waterbury.

➤ TRAIN INFORMATION: **Amtrak** (☎ 800/872–7245, WEB www.amtrak.com). **Metro-North Railroad** (☎ 800/638–7646; 212/532–4900 from New York City, WEB www.mta.nyc.ny.us).

VISITOR INFORMATION

State welcome centers, in Darien and Westbrook on I–95 northbound, North Stonington on I–95 southbound, Danbury on I–84 eastbound, and Willington on I–84 westbound, have visitor information.

➤ TOURIST INFORMATION: **Connecticut Office of Tourism** (✉ 505 Hudson St., Hartford 06106, ☎ 800/282–6863 brochures, WEB www.ctbound.org). **State Parks Division Bureau of Outdoor Recreation** (✉ 79 Elm St., Hartford 06106, ☎ 860/424–3200). **Antiquarian and Landmarks Society** (✉ 66 Forest St., Hartford 06105, ☎ 860/247–8996, WEB www.hartnet.org/als). **Connecticut Campground Owners Association** (⌑ 14 Rumford St., West Hartford 06107, ☎ 860/521–4704, 🆆🅴🅱 www.campconn.org). **Connecticut State Golf Association** (⌑ 35 Cold Spring Rd., Suite 212, Rocky Hill 06067, ☎ 860/257–4171, 🆆🅴🅱 www.csgalinks.org).

7 BACKGROUND AND ESSENTIALS

Smart Travel Tips A to Z

ESSENTIAL INFORMATION

AIR TRAVEL

Most travelers will head for a major gateway and then rent a car to enjoy the sights. The New England states form a fairly compact region, with few important destinations more than six hours apart by car, and intraregional air transportation facilities are mainly patronized by business travelers (exceptions include flights to island resort destinations such as Martha's Vineyard and Nantucket from Boston's Logan International Airport). Should you wish to fly, be advised that intraregional fares can be high and flights limited.

BOOKING

When you book **look for nonstop flights** and **remember that "direct" flights stop at least once.** Try to avoid connecting flights, which require a change of plane. For more booking tips and to check prices and make online flight reservations, log on to www.fodors.com.

CARRIERS

➤ MAJOR AIRLINES: American (☎ 800/433–7300). Continental (☎ 800/525–0280). Delta (☎ 800/221–1212). Northwest (☎ 800/225–2525). Southwest (☎ 800/435–9792). Sun Country (☎ 800/359-5786). TWA (☎ 800/221–2000). United (☎ 800/241–6522). US Airways (☎ 800/428–4322).

➤ REGIONAL AIRLINES: Cape Air/Nantucket Airlines (☎ 508/790–3122 or 800/352–0714). Midway (☎ 800/446–4392).

➤ FROM THE U.K.: American (☎ 0345/789–789). British Airways (☎ 0345/222–111). Virgin Atlantic (☎ 01293/747–747).

➤ FROM AUSTRALIA AND NEW ZEALAND: Qantas (from Australia, ☎ 13–1313, 0800/808–767, or 09/357–8900; from New Zealand, outside Auckland, ☎ 0800/808–767; from Auckland area, ☎ 09/357–8900).

CHECK-IN & BOARDING

Assuming that not everyone with a ticket will show up, airlines routinely overbook planes. When everyone does, airlines ask for volunteers to give up their seats. In return, these volunteers usually get a certificate for a free flight and are rebooked on the next flight out. If there are not enough volunteers, the airline must choose who will be denied boarding. The first to get bumped are passengers who checked in late and those flying on discounted tickets, so **get to the gate and check in as early as possible,** especially during peak periods.

Always **bring a government-issued photo I.D. to the airport;** a passport is best. You may be asked to show it before you are allowed to check in.

CUTTING COSTS

The least expensive airfares to New England must usually be purchased in advance and are non-refundable. It's smart to **call a number of airlines, and when you are quoted a good price, book it on the spot**—the same fare may not be available the next day. Always **check different routings** and look into using different airports. Travel agents, especially low-fare specialists (☞ Discounts & Deals), are helpful.

Consolidators are another good source. They buy tickets for scheduled international flights at reduced rates from the airlines, then sell them at prices that beat the best fare available directly from the airlines, usually without restrictions. Sometimes you can even get your money back if you need to return the ticket. Carefully read the fine print detailing penalties for changes and cancellations, and **confirm your consolidator reservation with the airline.**

➤ CONSOLIDATORS: **Cheap Tickets** (☎ 800/377–1000) **Discount Airline Ticket Service** (☎ 800/576–1600). **Unitravel** (☎ 800/325–2222). **Up & Away Travel** (☎ 212/889–2345). **World Travel Network** (☎ 800/409–6753).

ENJOYING THE FLIGHT

For more legroom, **request an emergency-aisle seat.** Don't sit in the row in front of the emergency aisle or in front of a bulkhead, where seats may not recline. If you have dietary concerns, **ask for special meals when booking.** These can be vegetarian, low-cholesterol, or kosher, for example. On long flights, try to maintain a normal routine, to help fight jet lag. At night, **get some sleep.** By day, **eat light meals, drink water** (not alcohol), and **move around the cabin** to stretch your legs. For additional jet-lag tips consult *Fodor's FYI: Travel Fit & Healthy* (available at bookstores everywhere).

All flights within the U.S. are strictly nonsmoking, as are international flights on American-based carriers. Smoking regulations vary among non-U.S.–based carriers, so call if this is important to you. It is uncommon for U.S. airports to allow smoking, although a few permit it in specially designated areas.

FLYING TIMES

Flying time to Boston is 1 hour from New York, 2 hours and 15 minutes from Chicago, 6 hours from Los Angeles, 4 hours from Dallas, and 8 hours from London. Flying time from Sydney, Australia, to Boston (via Los Angeles) is 20 hours; flying time from Auckland, New Zealand, to Boston (via Los Angeles) is 17 hours.

HOW TO COMPLAIN

If your baggage goes astray or your flight goes awry, complain right away. Most carriers require that you **file a claim immediately.**

➤ AIRLINE COMPLAINTS: U.S. Department of Transportation **Aviation Consumer Protection Division** (✉ C-75, Room 4107, Washington, DC 20590, ☎ 202/366–2220, WEB www.dot.gov/airconsumer). **Federal Aviation Administration Consumer Hotline** (☎ 800/322–7873).

AIRPORTS

The main gateway to New England is Boston's Logan International Airport (BOS), the region's largest. Bradley International Airport (BDL), in Windsor Locks, Connecticut, 12 mi north of Hartford, is convenient to western Massachusetts and all of Connecticut. T. F. Green State Airport (PVD), just outside Providence, Rhode Island, is another major airport. Additional New England airports served by major carriers include Manchester Airport (MHT) in Manchester, New Hampshire (a rapidly growing, lower-cost alternative to Boston); Portland International Jetport (PWM) in Maine; and Burlington International Airport (BTV) in Vermont. Other airports are in Bangor, Maine, and Hyannis and Worcester, Massachusetts.

➤ AIRPORT INFORMATION: **Bradley International Airport** (☎ 888/624-1533). **Burlington International Airport** (☎ 802/863–1889). **Logan International Airport** (☎ 800/235-6426). **Manchester Airport** (☎ 603/624-6539). **Portland International Jetport** (☎ 207/774–7301). **T. F. Green State Airport** (☎ 888/268-7222).

BIKE TRAVEL

Cyclists favor New England because overnight destinations are seldom far apart. Inns and B&Bs are plentiful, and some operators offer guided inn-to-inn tours. In general, northern (except for far northern Maine) and western New England have the best cycling opportunities, with plenty of lightly traveled secondary roads and pleasant small towns to explore en route. Make sure you're in shape if you plan to tackle the hills of Vermont and New Hampshire, and **consider a mountain bike** if you're going to be on dirt roads. Both mountain and touring bikes are available for rent in resort areas and in most larger towns and cities for as little as $20 a day.

BIKES IN FLIGHT

Most airlines accommodate bikes as luggage, provided they are dismantled and boxed. Airlines sell bike boxes, which are often free at bike shops, for about $5 (it's at least $100 for bike bags). International travelers can sometimes substitute a bike for a piece of checked luggage at no charge; otherwise, the cost is about $100. Domestic and Canadian airlines charge $25–$50.

BOAT & FERRY TRAVEL

Principal ferry routes in New England connect Cape Cod with Martha's Vineyard and Nantucket, and Connecticut with New York's Long Island; other routes provide access to many islands off the Maine coast. In addition, ferries cross Lake Champlain between Vermont and upstate New York. International service between Portland and Bar Harbor, Maine, and Yarmouth, Nova Scotia, is also available. With the exception of the Lake Champlain ferries, which are first-come, first-served, car reservations are always advisable.

BUS TRAVEL

All New England states have bus service; fares are generally moderate and buses normally run on schedule, although service can be infrequent and travel time can be long due to traffic and frequent stops. Smoking is not permitted on buses.

CUTTING COSTS

Greyhound offers Ameripass, which allows riders to travel throughout New England at discounted fares for varying lengths of time from seven to 60 days.

➤ BUS INFORMATION: **Bonanza Bus Lines** (☎ 800/556–3815). **Concord Trailways** (☎ 800/639–3317). **Greyhound** (☎ 800/231–2222; 888/454–7277 for Ameripass). **Peter Pan Bus Lines** (☎ 800/343–9999). **Vermont Transit** (☎ 800/642-3133 in Vermont; 800-552-8737 elsewhere).

BUSINESS HOURS

Banks in New England are generally open weekdays from 9 AM until 3 PM, with longer hours on Thursdays and Fridays. Post offices are open weekdays between 8 AM and 5 PM; many branches operate Saturday morning hours. Business hours tend to be weekdays from 9 to 5. Banks and post offices close on all national holidays; retail businesses generally close only on Thanksgiving, Christmas, New Year's Day, and Easter. Convenience stores, especially in urban areas, are often open 365 days a year.

GAS STATIONS

Except along major highways, gas stations frequently close at around 10 or 11 PM and reopen at 5 or 6 AM.

MUSEUMS & SIGHTS

While some major museums and attractions are open daily—at least during peak tourist season—Monday closings are common. In resort areas, museums and attractions are frequently closed or on significantly reduced schedules from mid-October to late May. Hours of sights and attractions are denoted throughout this book by the clock icon, ☉ .

PHARMACIES

In larger cities, pharmacies near around hospitals and/or medical centers generally stay open 24 hours.

SHOPS

Many stores may not open until 10 or 11, but they remain open until 6 or 7; most carry on brisk business on Saturday and Sunday as well. Suburban shopping malls are generally open seven days a week, with evening hours every day except Sunday. All across New England, so-called convenience stores sell food and sundries until about 11 PM. Along the highways and in major cities you can usually find all-night diners, supermarkets, drugstores, and convenience stores.

CAMERAS & PHOTOGRAPHY

Seascapes and fall foliage are the most commonly photographed subjects in New England. Both can make for memorable images, provided you remember that saltwater and autumn leaves photograph better when there's something else included in the picture. Include a lighthouse or fog-shrouded sailboat in your ocean shots, and look for that covered bridge or church steeple tucked among the birches and maples. The *Kodak Guide to Shooting Great Travel Pictures* (available at bookstores everywhere) is loaded with tips.

➤ PHOTO HELP: **Kodak Information Center** (☎ 800/242–2424).

EQUIPMENT PRECAUTIONS

Don't pack film and equipment in checked luggage, where it is much more susceptible to damage. X-ray machines used to view checked luggage are becoming much more powerful and therefore are much more likely to ruin your film. Always **keep film and tape out of the sun.** Carry an extra supply of batteries, and **be prepared to turn on your camera or camcorder** to prove to security personnel that the device is real. Always **ask for hand inspection of film,** which becomes clouded after repeated exposure to airport X-ray machines, and **keep videotapes away from metal detectors.**

Be careful on sailboat cruises—saltwater can corrode metal camera parts. Remember to **stock up on film at home or in big cities.** Prices are a lot higher in airports, resort areas, and small towns, and the film options are often limited.

CAR RENTAL

Rates in Boston begin at $34 a day and $220 a week for an economy car with air-conditioning, an automatic transmission, and unlimited mileage. This rate does not include taxes and surcharges that can add as much as 25% if you rent a car at the airport.

➤ MAJOR AGENCIES: **Alamo** (☎ 800/327–9633; 020/8759–6200 in the U.K.). **Avis** (☎ 800/331–1212; 800/879–2847 in Canada; 02/9353–9000 in Australia; 09/525–1982 in New Zealand; 0870/606–0100 in the U.K.). **Budget** (☎ 800/527–0700; 0144/227–6266 in the U.K., through affiliate Europcar). **Dollar** (☎ 800/800–4000; 0124/622–0111 in the U.K., where it is known as Sixt Kenning; 02/9223–1444 in Australia). **Hertz** (☎ 800/654–3131; 800/263–0600 in Canada; 020/8897–2072 in the U.K.; 02/9669–2444 in Australia; 09/256–8690 in New Zealand). **National Car Rental** (☎ 800/227–7368; 0845/722–2525 in the U.K., where it is known as National Europe).

CUTTING COSTS

To get the best deal, **book through a travel agent who will shop around.** Also **price local car-rental companies,** although the service and maintenance may not be as good as those of a major player. Remember to ask about required deposits, cancellation penalties, and drop-off charges if you're planning to pick up the car in one city and leave it in another. If you're traveling during a holiday period, also make sure that a confirmed reservation guarantees you a car.

INSURANCE

When driving a rented car you are generally responsible for any damage to or loss of the vehicle as well as for any property damage or personal injury that you may cause. Before you rent, see what coverage your personal auto-insurance policy and credit cards provide.

For about $15 to $20 per day, rental companies sell protection, known as a collision- or loss-damage waiver (CDW or LDW), that eliminates your liability for damage to the car.

In Massachusetts the car-rental company must pay for damage to third parties up to a preset legal limit, beyond which your own liability insurance kicks in. However, **make sure you have enough coverage to pay for the car.** If you do not have auto insurance or an umbrella policy that covers damage to third parties, purchasing liability insurance and a CDW or LDW is highly recommended.

REQUIREMENTS & RESTRICTIONS

In New England you must be 21 to rent a car, and rates may be higher if you're under 25. You'll pay extra for child seats (about $3 a day), which are compulsory for children under five, and for additional drivers (about $2 per day). Non-U.S. residents need a reservation voucher (for prepaid reservations that were made in the traveler's home country), a passport, a driver's license, and a travel policy that covers each driver, when picking up a car.

SURCHARGES

Before you pick up a car in one city and leave it in another, **ask about drop-off charges or one-way service fees,** which can be substantial. Note, too, that some rental agencies charge extra if you return the car before the time specified in your contract. To avoid a hefty refueling fee, **fill the tank just before you turn in the car,** but be aware that gas stations near the rental outlet may overcharge.

CAR TRAVEL

Because public transportation is spotty or completely lacking in the outer reaches of New England, a car is the most convenient means of transportation. The region is well served by the interstate highway system, on which you can expect to average 60 mph, except near major metropolitan areas (in rush hour around Hartford and Boston, you will cut that average in half). On other federal and state highways, your average will more likely be 40–50 mph. In northern New England, east–west travel is notoriously slow, due to several mountain ranges and no limited-access highways.

GASOLINE

Self-service gas stations are the norm in New England, though in some of the less-populated regions you'll find stations with one or two pumps and a friendly attendant who provides full service (pumping your gas, checking your tires and oil, washing your windows). Stations are plentiful. Most stay open late (24 hours along large highways and in big cities), except in rural areas, where Sunday hours are limited and where you may drive long stretches without a refueling opportunity. At press time, rates for unleaded regular gas at self-service stations in New England were about $1.70 per gallon (somewhat higher in Boston and Connecticut); rates at full-service stations are often slightly more.

ROAD CONDITIONS

Federal and state highways throughout New England are maintained in excellent condition and are promptly plowed and salted in winter. Secondary roads maintained by local municipalities are sometimes in poor repair, especially in spring, when frost heaves—bumps and dips in the pavement—are caused by melting ground frost. Northern New England has many miles of unpaved roads, but these are usually well graded and pleasant to travel, except in mud season in late March and early April. Far northern Maine is crisscrossed by privately owned logging roads, for which a pass is frequently required (pay at gates at entrances to logging company lands).

City traffic can be particularly trying in New England, as many streets were laid out centuries ago. Boston's traffic snarls are legendary; avoid driving here if at all possible. Rush hours in the city run roughly from 6 to 9 AM and from 4 to 7 PM.

ROAD MAPS

Each state in New England makes available a free map that has directories, mileage, and other useful information—contact the state offices of tourism (☞ Visitor Information). Jimapco produces detailed maps of Massachusetts. Hagstrom sells maps of Connecticut. Rand McNally prints a detailed map of Rhode Island. Delorme publishes topographical atlases of Connecticut/Rhode Island, Maine, New Hampshire, and Vermont that include most back roads and many outdoor recreation sites. The maps are widely available in the state.

RULES OF THE ROAD

The speed limit in much of New England is 65 mph on interstate and some limited-access highways (55 mph in densely populated areas), and 50 mph on most other roads (25–30 mph in towns and cities). Speed limits are stringently enforced throughout the region, particularly in populated areas. Fines can easily exceed $100 for driving 15–20 miles in excess of the speed limit. In New England, drivers can turn right at a red light (unless signs indicate otherwise) providing they come to a full stop and check to see that the intersection is clear first.

There is zero tolerance for drunk driving. The blood alcohol content that defines legal intoxication for adults varies between .08 and .10 percent, depending on the state, and penalties are severe.

CHILDREN IN NEW ENGLAND

In New England, there's no shortage of things to do with children. Major museums have children's sections, and you'll find children's museums in cities large and small. Many tourist areas have roadside attractions, and miniature golf courses are easy to come by. Attractions such as beaches and boat rides, parks and planetariums, lighthouses and llama treks can be fun for youngsters, as can special events such as crafts fairs and food festivals. *Fodor's Around Boston with Kids* (available in bookstores everywhere) can help you plan your days together.

Be sure to plan ahead and **involve your youngsters** as you outline your trip. When packing, include things to keep them busy en route. On sightseeing days try to schedule activities of special interest to your children. If you are renting a car, don't forget to **arrange for a car seat** when you reserve. For general advice about traveling with children, consult *Fodor's FYI: Travel with Your Baby* (available in bookstores everywhere).

FLYING

If your children are two or older, **ask about children's airfares.** As a general rule, infants under two not occupying a seat fly at greatly reduced fares or even for free.

Experts agree that it's a good idea to use safety seats aloft for children weighing less than 40 pounds. Airlines set their own policies: U.S. carriers usually require that the child be ticketed, even if he or she is young enough to ride free, since the seats must be strapped into regular seats. Do **check your airline's policy about using safety seats during takeoff and landing.** And since safety seats are not allowed everywhere in the plane, get your seat assignments early.

When reserving, **request children's meals or a freestanding bassinet** if you need them. But note that bulk-head seats, where you must sit to use the bassinet, may lack an overhead bin or storage space on the floor.

LODGING

Chain hotels and motels welcome children, and New England has many family-oriented resorts with lively children's programs. You'll also find farms that accept guests and can be lots of fun for children. Rental houses and apartments abound, particularly around ski areas; off-season, these can be economical as well as comfortable touring bases. Some country inns, especially those with a quiet, romantic atmosphere and those furnished with antiques, are less enthusiastic about little ones, so **be up front about your traveling companions** when you reserve.

Most hotels allow children under a certain age to stay in their parents' room at no extra charge; others charge them as extra adults; be sure to **find out the cutoff age for children's discounts.**

Most lodgings that welcome infants and small children will be glad to provide a crib or cot, but **be sure to give advance notice** so that one will be available for you. Most resort and hotels with extended amenities will also arrange to have a baby-sitter come to your room. Many family resorts make special accommodations for small children during meals. Be sure to ask in advance.

SIGHTS & ATTRACTIONS

Places that are especially appealing to children are indicated by a rubber-duckie icon (🐤) in the margin.

TRANSPORTATION

Each New England state has specific requirements regarding age and weight requirements for children in car seats. If you're renting a car, **be sure to ask about the state(s) you're planning to drive in.** If you will need a car seat, make sure the agency you select provides them and **reserve well in advance.**

CONSUMER PROTECTION

Whenever shopping or buying travel services in New England, **pay with a major credit card,** if possible, so you can cancel payment or get reimbursed if there's a problem. If you're doing business with a particular company for the first time, **contact your local Better Business Bureau and the attorney general's offices** in your state and (for U.S. businesses) the company's home state as well. Have any complaints been filed? Finally, if you're buying a package or tour, always **consider travel insurance** that includes default coverage (☞ Insurance).

➤ BBBs: **Council of Better Business Bureaus** (✉ 4200 Wilson Blvd., Suite 800, Arlington, VA 22203, ☎ 703/276–0100, FAX 703/525–8277, WEB www.bbb.org).

CRUISE TRAVEL

Several cruise companies have ships that set sail from Boston to cruise the coast of New England. Many head north to Canada, stopping in Montréal or Halifax. Others head south out of Boston to Newport, Rhode Island. To learn how to plan, choose, and book a cruise-ship voyage, check out Cruise How-to's on www.fodors.com and consult *Fodor's FYI: Plan & Enjoy Your Cruise* (available in bookstores everywhere).

➤ CRUISE LINES: **American Canadian Caribbean Line** (☎ 800/556–7450). **Clipper Cruise Line** (☎ 800/325–0010). **Royal Caribbean International** (☎ 800/327–6700).

CUSTOMS & DUTIES

IN AUSTRALIA

Australian residents who are 18 or older may bring home $A400 worth of souvenirs and gifts (including jewelry), 250 cigarettes or 250 grams of tobacco, and 1,125 ml of alcohol (including wine, beer, and spirits). Residents under 18 may bring back $A200 worth of goods. Prohibited items include meat products. Seeds, plants, and fruits need to be declared upon arrival.

➤ INFORMATION: **Australian Customs Service** (Regional Director, ✉ Box 8, Sydney, NSW 2001, Australia, ☎ 02/9213–2000, FAX 02/9213–4000, WEB www.customs.gov.au).

IN CANADA

Canadian residents who have been out of Canada for at least seven days may bring home C$500 worth of goods duty-free. If you've been away fewer than seven days but more than 48 hours, the duty-free allowance drops to C$200; if your trip lasts 24–48 hours, the allowance is C$50. You may not pool allowances with family members. Goods claimed under the C$500 exemption may follow you by mail; those claimed under the lesser exemptions must accompany you. Alcohol and tobacco products may be included in the seven-day and 48-hour exemptions but not in the 24-hour exemption. If you meet the age requirements of the province or territory through which you reenter Canada, you may bring in, duty-free, 1.14 liters (40 imperial ounces) of wine or liquor *or* 24 12-ounce cans or bottles of beer or ale. If you are 16 or older you may bring in, duty-free, 200 cigarettes and 50 cigars. Check ahead of time with Revenue Canada or the Department of Agriculture for policies regarding meat products, seeds, plants, and fruits.

You may send an unlimited number of gifts worth up to C$60 each duty-free to Canada. Label the package UNSOLICITED GIFT—VALUE UNDER $60. Alcohol and tobacco are excluded.

➤ INFORMATION: **Revenue Canada** (✉ 2265 St. Laurent Blvd. S, Ottawa, Ontario K1G 4K3, Canada, ☎ 613/993–0534; 800/461–9999 in Canada, FAX 613/991–4126, WEB www.ccra-adrc.gc.ca).

IN NEW ZEALAND

Homeward-bound residents 17 or older may bring back $700 worth of souvenirs and gifts. Your duty-free allowance also includes 4.5 liters of wine or beer; one 1,125-ml bottle of spirits; and either 200 cigarettes, 250 grams of tobacco, 50 cigars, or a combination of the three up to 250 grams. Prohibited items include meat products, seeds, plants, and fruits.

➤ INFORMATION: **New Zealand Customs** (Custom House, ✉ 50 Anzac Ave., Box 29, Auckland, New Zealand, ☎ 09/300–5399, FAX 09/359–6730), WEB www.customs.govt.nz.

IN THE U.K.

From countries outside the EU, including the U.S., you may bring home, duty-free, 200 cigarettes or 50 cigars; 1 liter of spirits or 2 liters of fortified or sparkling wine or liqueurs; 2 liters of still table wine; 60 ml of perfume; 250 ml of toilet water; plus £136 worth of other goods, including gifts and souvenirs. If returning from outside the EU, prohibited items include meat products, seeds, plants, and fruits.

➤ INFORMATION: **HM Customs and Excise** (✉ Dorset House, Stamford St., Bromley, Kent BR1 1XX, U.K., ☎ 020/7202–4227, WEB www.hmce. gov.uk).

DINING

Thoughts of dining in New England center on seafood, and the coast and many inland locations have restaurants specializing in lobster, clams, scallops, and fresh fish. Restaurants in New England's cities have an impressive variety of menus and price ranges. The best dining in rural areas is often to be found in country inns, the larger of which are often quite proud of their chefs and their commitment to using local meats and produce.

Restaurant prices in New England are generally on a par with those elsewhere in the country, but travelers may experience sticker shock at even more modest seafood restaurants. Catch limits on many favorite ocean species, as well as the premium charged for lobster and other shellfish, have sent prices soaring. Lobsters are sold by the pound ("market price" is the phrase that appears on many menus), and a $20 lobster dinner or a $10 lobster roll is not uncommon.

The restaurants we list are the cream of the crop in each price category. Properties indicated by an ✕☰ are lodging establishments whose restaurant warrants a special trip. Following is the price chart used in this book; note that prices do not include tax, which is 6% in Connecticut, 5% in Maine (7% on alcohol), 5% in Massachusetts, 8% in New Hampshire, 7% in Rhode Island, and 9% in Vermont (10% on alcohol).

CATEGORY	COST*
$$$$	over $25
$$$	$17–$25
$$	$9–$16
$	under $9

*per person, for a main course dinner

MEALTIMES

In general, the widest variety of mealtime options in New England is in larger cities and at resort areas.

For an early breakfast, pick places that cater to a working clientele. City, town, and roadside establishments specializing in breakfast for the busy often open their doors at 5 or 6 AM. At country inns and B&Bs, breakfast is seldom served before 8; if you need to get an earlier start, ask ahead of time if your host or hostess can accommodate you.

Unless otherwise noted, the restaurants listed in this guide are open daily for lunch and dinner. Lunch in New England generally runs from around 11 to 2:30; dinner is usually served from 6 to 9 (many restaurants have early-bird specials beginning at 5). Only in the larger cities will you find full dinners being offered much later than 9, although you can usually find a bar or bistro serving a limited menu late into the evening in all but the smallest towns.

Many restaurants in New England are closed on Mondays, although this is never true in resort areas in high season. However, resort-town eateries often shut down completely in the off-season.

Credit cards are accepted for meals throughout New England, in all but the most modest establishments.

RESERVATIONS & DRESS

Reservations are always a good idea: we mention them only when they're essential or not accepted. Book as far ahead as you can, and reconfirm as soon as you arrive. We mention dress only when men are required to wear a jacket or a jacket and tie.

SPECIALTIES

Clam favorites include chowder, made with big, meaty quahogs (and featuring milk or cream, unlike the tomato-based Manhattan version); fried clams; and steamers. Some lobster classics include plain boiled lobster—a staple at "in the rough" picnic-bench-and-paper-plate spots along the Maine coast—and lobster rolls, a lobster meat and mayo (or just melted butter) preparation served in a hot dog bun. The leading fin fish is scrod—young cod or haddock—best sampled baked or broiled.

Inland specialties run to the plain and familiar dishes of old-fashioned Sunday-dinner America—pot roast, roast turkey, baked ham, hefty stacks of pancakes (with local maple syrup, of course), and apple pie. One regional favorite is Indian pudding, a long-boiled cornmeal and molasses concoction that's delicious with vanilla ice cream. As for ethnic menus, New England has welcomed Chinese, Thai, Middle Eastern, and all the other international cuisines popular in America. The region's deeper ethnic traditions, though, take in the hearty Portuguese pork and fish dishes and spicy sausages of southern Massachusetts and Rhode Island; the festival of Italian flavors that is Boston's North End; and the pork pie (*tortière*) and pea soup of northern New England's French-Canadians.

WINE, BEER & SPIRITS

In recent years, New England has been in the forefront of the micro-brew revolution. The granddaddy of New England's independent beermakers is Boston's Samuel Adams, producing brews available throughout the region. Following the Sam Adams lead in offering hearty English-style ales and special seasonal brews are breweries such as Vermont's Long Trail and Catamount; Maine's Shipyard; and New Hampshire's Old Man Ale.

New England is beginning to earn some respect as a wine-producing region. Varieties capable of withstanding the region's harsh winters have been the basis of promising enterprises such as Rhode Island's Sakonnet Vineyards, Chicama Vineyards on Martha's Vineyard, and Connecticut's Hopkins Vineyard. Even Vermont is getting into the act with the new Snow Farm Vineyard in the Lake Champlain Islands and Boyden Valley Winery in Cambridge.

Although a patchwork of state and local regulations affect the hours and locations of places that sell alcoholic beverages, New England licensing laws are fairly liberal. State-owned or -franchised stores sell hard liquor in New Hampshire, Maine, and Vermont; many travelers have found that New Hampshire offers the region's lowest prices. Look for state-run liquor "supermarkets" on interstate highways in the southern part of the state; these also have good wine selections.

DISABILITIES & ACCESSIBILITY

➤ LOCAL RESOURCES: **Cape Cod Chamber of Commerce** (✉ U.S. 6 and Rte. 132, Hyannis 02601, ☎ 508/362–3225 or 888/332–2732) has two publications with accessibility ratings: "Visitor's Guide" and "Accommodations Directory." The **Cape Cod National Seashore** (✉ South Wellfleet 02663, ☎ 508/349–3785) publishes "Cape Cod National Seashore Accessibility." **Connecticut Office of Tourism** (☞ Visitor Information) prints accessibility codes in the *Connecticut Vacation Guide*. **MBTA** (✉ MBTA, Office for Transportation Access, 10 Boylston Pl., Boston 02116, ☎ 617/222–5123; 617/222–5415 TTY) has a brochure, "MBTA: Access." The **New Hampshire Office of Travel and Tourism Development** (☞ Visitor Information) *New Hampshire Guide Book* includes accessibility ratings for lodgings and restaurants. **Vermont Chamber of Commerce** (☞ Visitor Information) includes accessibility codes for attractions in the *Vermont Traveler's Guidebook*. **VSA** (✉ 2 Boylston St., Room 211, Boston 02116, ☎ 617/350–7713) sells "Access Expressed! Massachusetts" for $5.

RESERVATIONS

When discussing accessibility with an operator or reservations agent, **ask hard questions.** Are there any stairs, inside *or* out? Are there grab bars next to the toilet *and* in the shower/tub? How wide is the doorway to the room? To the bathroom? For the most extensive facilities meeting the latest legal specifications, **opt for newer accommodations.**

SIGHTS & ATTRACTIONS

In Boston, many sidewalks are brick or cobblestone and may be uneven or sloping; many have curbs cut at one end and not the other. To make matters worse, Boston drivers are notorious for running yellow lights and ignoring pedestrians. Back Bay has flat, well-paved streets; older Beacon Hill is steep and difficult; Quincy Market's cobblestone and brick malls are crisscrossed with smooth, tarred paths. The downtown financial district and Chinatown are accessible, while areas such as the South End and the Italian North End may prove more problematic for people who use wheelchairs.

In Cape Cod, a number of towns such as Wellfleet, Hyannis, and Chatham have wide streets with curb cuts; and the Cape Cod National Seashore has several accessible trails. The narrow streets of Provincetown, the Cape's most-popular destination, are difficult for anyone to navigate. Travelers using wheelchairs would be well advised to visit "P-town" in the off-season, when pedestrian and vehicular traffic is less chaotic.

In Kennebunkport, as in many of Maine's coastal towns south of Portland, travelers with mobility impairments will have to cope with crowds as well as with narrow, uneven steps and sporadic curb cuts. L. L. Bean's outlet in Freeport is fully accessible, and Acadia National Park has some 50 accessible mi of carriage roads that are closed to motor vehicles. In New Hampshire, many of Franconia Notch's natural attractions are accessible.

TRANSPORTATION

Many major rental agencies provide special cars for people with disabilities on request. Most ask that you provide your own handicapped sticker or plate, which will be honored throughout the region. Be sure to reserve well in advance.

➤ COMPLAINTS: **Aviation Consumer Protection Division** (☞ Air Travel) for airline-related problems. **Civil Rights Office** (✉ U.S. Department of Transportation, Departmental Office of Civil Rights, S-30, 400 7th St. SW, Room 10215, Washington, DC 20590, ☎ 202/366–4648, FAX 202/366–9371, WEB www.dot.gov/ost/docr/index.htm) for problems with surface transportation. **Disability Rights Section** (✉ U.S. Department of Justice, Civil Rights Division, Box 66738, Washington, DC 20035-6738, ☎ 202/514–0301 or 800/514–0301; 202/514–0383 TTY; 800/514–0383 TTY, FAX 202/307–1198, WEB www.usdoj.gov/crt/ada/adahom1.htm) for general complaints.

TRAVEL AGENCIES

In the United States, the Americans with Disabilities Act requires that travel firms serve the needs of all travelers. Some agencies specialize in working with people with disabilities.

➤ TRAVELERS WITH MOBILITY PROBLEMS: **Access Adventures** (✉ 206 Chestnut Ridge Rd., Scottsville, NY 14624, ☎ 716/889–9096, dltravel@prodigy.net), run by a former physical-rehabilitation counselor. **Accessible Vans of America** (✉ 9 Spielman Rd., Fairfield, NJ 07004, ☎ 877/282–8267, FAX 973/808–9713, WEB www.accessiblevans.com). **CareVacations** (✉ 5-5110 50th Ave., Leduc, Alberta T9E 6V4, Canada, ☎ 780/986–6404 or 877/478–7827, FAX 780/986–8332, WEB www.carevacations.com), for group tours and cruise vacations. **Flying Wheels Travel** (✉ 143 W. Bridge St., Box 382, Owatonna, MN 55060, ☎ 507/451–5005 or 800/535–6790, FAX 507/451–1685, WEB www.flyingwheelstravel.com).

➤ TRAVELERS WITH DEVELOPMENTAL DISABILITIES: **Sprout** (✉ 893 Amsterdam Ave., New York, NY 10025, ☎ 212/222–9575 or 888/222–9575, FAX 212/222–9768, WEB www.gosprout.org).

DISCOUNTS & DEALS

Be a smart shopper and **compare all your options** before making decisions. A plane ticket bought with a promotional coupon from travel clubs, coupon books, and direct-mail offers or on the Internet may not be cheaper than the least expensive fare from a discount ticket agency. And always keep in mind that what you get is just as important as what you save.

DISCOUNT RESERVATIONS

To save money, **look into discount reservations services** with toll-free numbers, which use their buying power to get a better price on hotels, airline tickets, even car rentals. When booking a room, always **call the hotel's local toll-free number** (if one is available) rather than the central reservations number—you'll often get a better price. Always ask about special packages or corporate rates.

➤ AIRLINE TICKETS: ☎ **800/FLY–ASAP.**

➤ HOTEL ROOMS: **Accommodations Express** (☎ 800/444–7666, WEB www.accommodationsexpress.com). **Central Reservation Service (CRS)** (☎ 800/548–3311). **Players Express Vacations** (☎ 800/458–6161, WEB www.playersexpress.com). **RMC Travel** (☎ 800/245–5738, WEB www.rmcwebtravel.com). **Steigenberger Reservation Service** (☎ 800/223–5652, WEB www.srs-worldhotels.com). **Turbotrip.com** (☎ 800/473–7829, WEB www.turbotrip.com).

PACKAGE DEALS

Don't confuse packages and guided tours. When you buy a package, you travel on your own, just as though you had planned the trip yourself. Fly/drive packages, which combine airfare and car rental, are often a good deal.

GAY & LESBIAN TRAVEL

As one of the country's most socially and politically progressive regions, New England is almost invariably accepting of gay and lesbian travelers. Some exceptions might be found in some areas less frequented by visitors, but in general, people in the tourism business here are hospitable to travelers regardless of sexual orientation.

The capitals of gay New England are Boston and Cambridge and, on Cape Cod, Provincetown. Most sizable college and university towns in New England have gay communities. Alternative publications in all of these areas carry listings of gay bars, nightclubs, and special events. For details about the gay and lesbian scene in Boston and Provincetown, Massachusetts, and in Ogunquit, Maine, consult *Fodor's Gay Guide to the USA* (available in bookstores everywhere).

➤ GAY- & LESBIAN-FRIENDLY TRAVEL AGENCIES: **Different Roads Travel** (✉ 8383 Wilshire Blvd., Suite 902, Beverly Hills, CA 90211, ☎ 323/651–5557 or 800/429–8747, FAX 323/651–3678. **Kennedy Travel** (✉ 314 Jericho Turnpike, Floral Park, NY 11001, ☎ 516/352–4888 or 800/237–7433, FAX 516/354–8849, WEB www.kennedytravel.com). **Now Voyager** (✉ 4406 18th St., San Francisco, CA 94114, ☎ 415/626–1169 or 800/255–6951, FAX 415/626–8626, WEB www.nowvoyager.com). **Skylink Travel and Tour** (✉ 1006 Mendocino Ave., Santa Rosa, CA 95401, ☎ 707/546–9888 or 800/225–5759, FAX 707/546–9891, WEB www.skylinktravel.com), serving lesbian travelers.

GUIDEBOOKS

Plan well and you won't be sorry. Guidebooks are excellent tools—and you can take them with you. You may want to check out the color-photo-illustrated *Fodor's Exploring Boston and New England* and *Compass American Guide: Boston,* thorough on culture and history, and pocket-size *Citypack Boston,* with a supersize map. *Fodor's CITYGUIDE Boston,* for residents, is loaded with colorful listings and *Flashmaps Boston* with theme maps. All are available at on-line retailers and bookstores everywhere.

HEALTH

LYME DISEASE

Lyme disease, so named for its having been first reported in the town of Lyme, Connecticut, is a potentially debilitating disease carried by deer ticks, which thrive in dry, brush-covered areas, particularly on the coast. Always **use insect repellent;** outbreaks of Lyme disease all over the East Coast make it imperative that you protect yourself from ticks from early spring through summer. To prevent bites, **wear light-colored clothing and tuck pant legs into socks.** Look for black ticks about the size of a pin head around hairlines and the warmest parts of the body. If you have been bitten, **consult a physician, especially if you see the telltale bull's-eye bite pattern.** Influenza-like symptoms often accompany a Lyme infection. Early treatment is imperative. Also **ask your physician about Lymerix**; it takes three shots and 12 months to be 80% effective but is worth considering.

PESTS & OTHER HAZARDS

New England's two greatest insect pests are black flies and mosquitoes. The former are a phenomenon of late spring and early summer and are generally a problem only in the densely wooded areas of the far north. Mosquitoes, however, can be a nuisance just about everywhere in summer—they're at their worst following snowy winters and wet springs. The best protection against both pests is repellant containing DEET; if you're camping in the woods during black fly season, you'll also want to **use fine mesh screening in eating and sleeping areas, and even wear mesh headgear.** A particular pest of coastal areas, especially salt marshes, is the greenhead fly. Their bite is nasty, and they are best repelled by a liberal application of Avon Skin So Soft.

SHELLFISHING

Coastal waters attract seafood lovers who enjoy harvesting their own clams, mussels, and even lobsters; permits are required, and casual harvesting of lobsters is strictly forbidden. Amateur clammers should be aware that New England shellfish beds are periodically visited by red tides, during which microorganisms can render shellfish poisonous. To keep abreast of the situation, inquire when you apply for a license (usually at town halls or police stations) and pay attention to red tide postings as you travel.

HOLIDAYS

Expect banks and post offices to be closed on all national holidays, but not much else—except on Thanksgiving, Christmas, New Year's Day, and Easter, when the majority of businesses close. Exceptions are restaurants and hotels, which, depending on location, may be even busier at holiday times. Christmas in Boston or in ski country, for instance, will require early advance dining and lodging reservations. Public transportation schedules will also be affected on major holidays; in general, schedules will be similar for those of normal Sundays.

Major national holidays include New Year's Day (Jan. 1); Martin Luther King, Jr. Day (3rd Mon. in Jan.); President's Day (3rd Mon. in Feb.); Memorial Day (last Mon. in May); Independence Day (July 4); Labor Day (1st Mon. in Sept.); Thanksgiving Day (4th Thurs. in Nov.); Christmas Day (Dec. 25); and New Year's Eve (Dec. 31). Patriot's Day (the Monday closest to April 19) is a state holiday in Massachusetts.

INSURANCE

The most useful travel-insurance plan is a comprehensive policy that includes coverage for trip cancellation and interruption, default, trip delay, and medical expenses (with a waiver for pre-existing conditions).

Without insurance you will lose all or most of your money if you cancel your trip, regardless of the reason. Default insurance covers you if your tour operator, airline, or cruise line goes out of business. Trip-delay covers expenses that arise because of bad weather or mechanical delays. Study the fine print when comparing policies.

Always **buy travel policies directly from the insurance company**; if you buy them from a cruise line, airline, or tour operator that goes out of business you probably will not be covered for the agency or operator's default, a major risk. Before making any purchase, **review your existing health and home-owner's policies** to find what they cover away from home.

➤ TRAVEL INSURERS: In the U.S.: **Access America** (⊠ 6600 W. Broad St., Richmond, VA 23230, ☎ 804/285–3300 or 800/284–8300, ℻ 804/673–1586, **Travel Guard International** (⊠ 1145 Clark St., Stevens Point, WI 54481, ☎ 715/345–0505 or 800/826–1300, ℻ 800/955–8785, WEB www.noelgroup.com).

FOR INTERNATIONAL TRAVELERS

For information on customs restrictions, *see* Customs & Duties, *above.*

CONSULATES & EMBASSIES

➤ AUSTRALIA: **Consulate** (✉ 150 East 42nd St., 34th Floor New York NY 10017, ☎ 212/351-6500).

➤ CANADA: **Consulate** (✉ 3 Copley Pl., Suite 400, Boston, Massachusetts 02216, ☎ 617/262–3760).

➤ UNITED KINGDOM: **Consulate** (✉ 600 Atlantic Ave., Boston, MA 02210, ☎ 617/248–9555).

CURRENCY

The dollar is the basic unit of U.S. currency. It has 100 cents. Coins include the copper penny (1¢); the silvery nickel (5¢), dime (10¢), quarter (25¢), and half-dollar (50¢); and the golden $1 coin, replacing a now-rare silver dollar. Bills are denominated $1, $5, $10, $20, $50, and $100, all green and identical in size; designs vary. The exchange rate at press time was US$1.40 per British pound, $.65 per Canadian dollar, $.57 per Australian dollar, and $.47 per New Zealand dollar. The European Union Euro was at $.85 Euro to the dollar.

CAR TRAVEL

Interstate highways—limited-access, multilane highways whose numbers are prefixed by "I–"—are the fastest routes. Interstates with three-digit numbers beginning with an even digit encircle urban areas; those beginning with an odd digit lead into central cities. The region also has other limited-access expressways, freeways, and parkways. Tolls may be levied on limited-access highways. So-called U.S. highways and state highways are not necessarily limited-access but may have several lanes.

Along larger highways, roadside stops with rest rooms, fast-food restaurants, gasoline, and sundries stores are well spaced. State police and tow trucks patrol major highways and lend assistance. If your car breaks down on an interstate, pull onto the shoulder and wait for help, or have your passengers wait while you walk to an emergency phone. If you carry a cell phone, dial *55, noting your location on the small green roadside mileage markers.

Driving in the United States is on the right. **Obey speed limits** posted along roads and highways. Watch for lower limits in small towns and on back roads.

Book stores, gas stations, convenience stores, and rest stops sell maps (about $3) and multiregion road atlases (about $10).

For more information, *see* Car Travel.

ELECTRICITY

The U.S. standard is AC, 110 volts/60 cycles. Plugs have two flat pins set parallel to each other.

EMERGENCIES

For police, fire, or ambulance, **dial 911** (0 in rural areas).

INSURANCE

Britons and Australians need extra medical coverage when traveling overseas.

➤ INSURANCE INFORMATION: In the U.K.: **Association of British Insurers** (✉ 51–55 Gresham St., London EC2V 7HQ, U.K., ☎ 020/7600–3333, FAX 020/7696–8999, WEB www.abi.org.uk). In Australia: **Insurance Council of Australia** (✉ Level 3, 56 Pitt St., Sydney NSW 2000, ☎ 03/9614–1077, FAX 03/9614–7924). In Canada: **RBC Insurance** (✉ 6880 Financial Dr., Mississauga, Ontario L5N 7Y5, Canada, ☎ 905/816–2400 or 800/668–4342 in Canada, FAX 905/816–2498, WEB www.royalbank.com). In New Zealand: **Insurance Council of New Zealand** (✉ Box 474, Wellington, New Zealand, ☎ 04/472–5230, FAX 04/473–3011, WEB www.icnz.org.nz).

MAIL & SHIPPING

You can buy stamps and aerograms and send letters and parcels in post offices. Stamp-dispensing machines can occasionally be found in airports, bus and train stations, office buildings, drugstores, and the like. You can also deposit mail in the stout, dark blue, steel bins at strategic locations everywhere and in the mail chutes of large buildings; pickup schedules are posted.

For mail sent within the United States, you need a 34¢ stamp for first-class letters weighing up to 1 ounce (21¢ for each additional ounce) and 20¢ for domestic postcards. For overseas mail, you pay 80¢ for 1-ounce airmail letters, 70¢ for airmail postcards, and 35¢ for surface-rate postcards. For Canada and Mexico you need a 60¢ stamp for a 1-ounce letter and 50¢ for a postcard. For 70¢ you can buy an aerogram—a single sheet of lightweight blue paper that folds into its own envelope, stamped for overseas airmail.

To receive mail on the road, have it sent c/o General Delivery at your destination's main post office (use the correct five-digit zip code). You must pick up mail in person within 30 days and show a driver's license or passport.

PASSPORTS & VISAS

When traveling internationally, **carry your passport** even if you don't need one (it's always the best form of I.D.) and **make two photocopies of the data page** (one for someone at home and another for you, carried separately from your passport). If you lose your passport, promptly call the nearest embassy or consulate and the local police.

Visitor visas are not necessary for Canadian citizens, or for citizens of Australia and the United Kingdom who are staying fewer than 90 days.

➤ Australian Citizens: **Australian Passport Office** (☎ 131–232). **U.S. Office of Australia Affairs** (✉ MLC Centre, 19-29 Martin Pl., 59th floor, Sydney NSW 2000, Australia).

➤ Canadian Citizens: **Passport Office** (☎ 819/994–3500; 800/567–6868 in Canada).

➤ New Zealand Citizens: **New Zealand Passport Office** (☎ 04/494–0700 for application procedures; 0800/225–050 in New Zealand for application-status updates). **U.S. Office of New Zealand Affairs** (✉ 29 Fitzherbert Terr., Thorndon, Wellington, New Zealand).

➤ U.K. Citizens: **London Passport Office** (☎ 0870/521–0410) for application procedures and emergency passports. **U.S. Embassy Visa Information Line** (☎ 01891/200–290).

U.S. Embassy Visa Branch (✉ 5 Upper Grosvenor Sq., London W1A 1AE, U.K.); send a self-addressed, stamped envelope. **U.S. Consulate General** (✉ Queen's House, Queen St., Belfast BTI 6EO, Northern Ireland).

TELEPHONES

All U.S. telephone numbers consist of a three-digit area code and a seven-digit local number. Within most local calling areas, dial only the seven-digit number. Within the same area code, dial "1" first. To call between area-code regions, dial "1" then all 10 digits; the same goes for calls to numbers prefixed by "800," "888," and "877"—all toll-free. For calls to numbers preceded by "900" you must pay—usually dearly.

For international calls, dial "011" followed by the country code and the local number. For help, dial "0" and ask for an overseas operator. The country code is 61 for Australia, 64 for New Zealand, 44 for the United Kingdom. Calling Canada is the same as calling within the United States. Most local phone books list country codes and U.S. area codes. The country code for the United States is 1.

For operator assistance, dial "0". To obtain someone's phone number, call directory assistance, 555–1212 or occasionally 411 (free at public phones). To have the person you're calling foot the bill, phone collect; dial "0" instead of "1" before the 10-digit number.

At pay phones, instructions are usually posted. Usually you insert coins in a slot (10¢–35¢ for local calls) and wait for a steady tone before dialing. When you call long-distance, the operator will tell you how much to insert; prepaid phone cards, widely available in various denominations, are easier. Call the number on the back, punch in the card's personal identification number when prompted, then dial your number.

LODGING

Hotel and motel chains provide standard rooms and amenities in major cities and at or near traditional vacation destinations. At small inns, where each room is different and amenities vary in number and quality, price isn't always a reliable indicator; fortunately, when you call to make reservations, most hosts will be happy to give all manner of details about their properties, down to the color scheme of the handmade quilts—so **ask all your questions before you book.** Also **ask if the property has a Web site;** sites can have helpful information and pictures, although it's always wise to confirm how up-to-date the information is. The rooms in the lodgings reviewed here have private baths unless otherwise indicated.

The lodgings we list are the cream of the crop in each price category. We always list the facilities that are available—but we don't specify whether they cost extra. When pricing accommodations, always ask what's included and what costs extra. Lodgings are indicated in the text by a little house icon, 🏠 ; lodging establishments whose restaurants warrant a special trip, by ✕🏠 . Following is the price chart used in this book; note that prices do not include tax, which is 12% in Connecticut, 5% in Maine, 5% state tax plus up to 7% local tax in some cities in Massachusetts, 8% in New Hampshire, 5% in Rhode Island, and 9% in Vermont.

CATEGORY	BOSTON, THE CAPE, AND THE ISLANDS*	OTHER AREAS*
$$$$	over $220	over $180
$$$	$160–$220	$130–$180
$$	$110–$160	$80–$130
$	under $110	under $80

*All prices are for a standard double room during peak season and do not include tax or gratuities. Some inns add a 15% service charge.

Assume that hotels operate on the **European Plan** (EP, with no meals) unless we specify that they use the **Continental Plan** (CP, with a Continental breakfast), **Breakfast Plan** (BP, with a full breakfast), **Modified American Plan** (MAP, with breakfast and dinner), or the **Full American Plan** (FAP, with all meals).

APARTMENT & VILLA RENTALS

If you want a home base that's roomy enough for a family and comes with cooking facilities, **consider a furnished rental.** These can save you money, especially if you're traveling with a group. Home-exchange directories sometimes list rentals as well as exchanges. In New England, you are most likely to find a house, apartment, or condo rental in areas in which ownership of second homes is common, such as beach resorts and ski country. A good strategy is to **inquire about rentals in what would be the off-season** for those resort areas—for instance, it's fairly easy to rent ski chalets during the summer. Home-exchange directories sometimes list rentals as well as exchanges. Another good bet is to **contact real estate agents in the area in which you are interested.**

➤ INTERNATIONAL AGENTS: **Hideaways International** (✉ 767 Islington St., Portsmouth, NH 03801, ☎ 603/430–4433 or 800/843–4433, 📠 603/430–4444, 🌐 www.hideaways.com; membership $129).

B&BS & INNS

The bed-and-breakfasts and small inns of New England offer some of the region's most distinctive lodging experiences. Some are homey and casual, others provide a stay in a historic property in a city or out in the country, and still others are modern and luxurious. At even the poshest country inns, rooms frequently lack telephones or televisions; many proprietors feel that their guests are actively escaping from the modern world. These properties are also not likely to feature air-conditioning, which is often superfluous in New England's mountains or seashore. Most inns offer breakfast—hence the name bed-and-breakfast—yet this formula varies; at one B&B you may be served muffins and coffee, at another a multicourse feast with fresh flowers on the table. In keeping with the preferences of their guests, most inns and B&Bs prohibit smoking, and some of the inns with antiques or other expensive furnishings do not allow children. Almost all say no to pets. Always be sure to **ask about any restrictions** when you're making a reservation. It's also necessary to **inquire about minimum stays**; many inns require a two-night stay on weekends, for example.

CAMPING

The state offices of tourism (☞ Visitor Information) supply information about privately operated campgrounds and ones in parks run by state agencies and the federal government.

HOME EXCHANGES

If you would like to exchange your home for someone else's, **join a home-exchange organization**, which will send you its updated listings of available exchanges for a year and will include your own listing in at least one of them. It's up to you to make specific arrangements.

➤ EXCHANGE CLUBS: HomeLink International (⊠ Box 47747, Tampa, FL 33647, ☎ 813/975–9825 or 800/638–3841, FAX 813/910–8144, WEB www.homelink.org; $98 per year). Intervac U.S. (⊠ Box 590504, San Francisco, CA 94159, ☎ 800/756–4663, FAX 415/435–7440, WEB www.intervacus.com; $93 yearly fee includes one catalogue and on-line access).

HOSTELS

No matter what your age, you can **save on lodging costs by staying at hostels.** In some 5,000 locations in more than 70 countries around the world, Hostelling International (HI), the umbrella group for a number of national youth-hostel associations, offers single-sex, dorm-style beds and, at many hostels, rooms for couples and family accommodations. Membership in any HI national hostel association, open to travelers of all ages, allows you to stay in HI-affiliated hostels at member rates; one-year membership is about $25 for adults (C$26.75 in Canada, £9.30 in the U.K., $30 in Australia, and $30 in New Zealand); hostels run about $10–$25 per night. Members have priority if the hostel is full; they're also eligible for discounts around the world, even on rail and bus travel in some countries.

➤ ORGANIZATIONS: Hostelling International—American Youth Hostels (⊠ 733 15th St. NW, Suite 840, Washington, DC 20005, ☎ 202/783–6161, FAX 202/783–6171, WEB www.hiayh.org). Hostelling International—Canada (⊠ 400–205 Catherine St., Ottawa, Ontario K2P 1C3, Canada, ☎ 613/237–7884, FAX 613/237–7868, WEB www.hostellingintl.ca). Youth Hostel Association of England and Wales (⊠ Trevelyan House, 8 St. Stephen's Hill, St. Albans, Hertfordshire AL1 2DY, U.K., ☎ 0870/8708808, FAX 01727/844126, WEB www.yha.org.uk). Australian Youth Hostel Association (⊠ 10 Mallett St., Camperdown, NSW 2050, Australia, ☎ 02/9565–1699, FAX 02/9565–1325, WEB www.yha.com.au). Youth Hostels Association of New Zealand (⊠ Box 436, Christchurch, New Zealand, ☎ 03/379–9970, FAX 03/365–4476, WEB www.yha.org.nz).

HOTELS

Hotel and motel chains are amply represented in New England. Some of the large chains, such as Holiday Inn, Hilton, Hyatt, Marriott, and Ramada, operate all-suites, budget, business-oriented, or luxury resorts, often variations on the parent corporation's name (Courtyard by Marriott, for example). Though some chain hotels and motels may have a standardized look to them, this "cookie-cutter" approach also means that you can rely on the same level of comfort and efficiency at all properties in a well-managed chain, and at a chain's premier properties—its so-called flagship hotels—the decor and services may be outstanding.

New England is liberally supplied with small, independent motels, which run the gamut from the tired to the tidy. Don't overlook these mom-and-pop operations; they frequently offer cheerful, convenient accommodations at lower rates than the chains.

While reservations are always a good idea, they are particularly recommended in summer and winter resort areas; in college towns during September and at graduation time in the spring; and at areas renowned for autumn foliage.

Most hotels and motels will hold your reservation until 6 PM; **call ahead if you plan to arrive late.** All will hold a late reservation for you if you guarantee your reservation with a credit-card number.

When you call to make a reservation, **ask all the necessary questions up front.** If you are arriving with a car, ask if there is a parking lot or covered garage and whether there is an extra fee for parking. If you like to eat your meals in, ask if the hotel has a restaurant or whether it has room service (most do, but not necessarily 24 hours a day—and be forewarned that it can be expensive). Most hotels and motels have in-room TVs, often with cable movies, but verify this if you like to watch TV. If you want an in-room crib for your child, there will probably be an additional charge.

All hotels listed have private bath unless otherwise noted.

➤ TOLL-FREE NUMBERS: **Best Western** (☎ 800/528–1234, WEB www.best-western.com). **Choice** (☎ 800/221–2222, WEB www.hotelchoice.com). **Clarion** (☎ 800/252–7466, WEB www.hotelchoice.com). **Colony** (☎ 800/777–1700, WEB www.colony.com). **Comfort** (☎ 800/228–5150, WEB www.comfortinn.com). **Days Inn** (☎ 800/325–2525, WEB www.daysinn.com). **Doubletree and Red Lion Hotels** (☎ 800/222–8733, WEB www.doubletree.com). **Embassy Suites** (☎ 800/362–2779, WEB www.embassysuites.com). **Fairfield Inn** (☎ 800/228–2800, WEB www.marriott.com). **Hilton** (☎ 800/445–8667, WEB www.hilton.com). **Holiday Inn** (☎ 800/465–4329, WEB www.basshotels.com). **Howard Johnson** (☎ 800/654–4656, WEB www.hojo.com). **Hyatt Hotels & Resorts** (☎ 800/233–1234, WEB www.hyatt.com). **La Quinta** (☎ 800/531–5900, WEB www.laquinta.com). **Marriott** (☎ 800/228–9290, WEB www.marriott.com). **Quality Inn** (☎ 800/228–5151, WEB www.qualityinn.com). **Radisson** (☎ 800/333–3333, WEB www.radisson.com). **Ramada** (☎ 800/228–2828, WEB www.ramada.com). **Sheraton** (☎ 800/325–3535, WEB www.starwood.com). **Sleep Inn** (☎ 800/753–3746, WEB www.sleepinn.com). **Westin Hotels & Resorts** (☎ 800/228–3000, WEB www.westin.com).

MAIL AND SHIPPING

➤ OVERNIGHT SERVICES: FedEx (☎ 800/463–3339). UPS (☎ 800/742–5877).

MEDIA

NEWSPAPERS & MAGAZINES

The New York Times and the national *USA Today* are available in all but the most remote regions of New England; of the two, the *Times* is by far the more thorough and is considered the U.S. newspaper of record. The *Boston Globe,* a respected morning daily, is also available throughout the region. Most cities with 10,000 or more inhabitants generally have their own daily newspapers, many of which carry comprehensive listings of local events at least once a week. Larger cities and college towns often have at least one alternative publication that provides extensive coverage on the local cultural and social scene. Among regional magazines, the most noteworthy are *Yankee, Vermont Life, Down East* (Maine), and *Boston.*

RADIO & TELEVISION

As in the rest of the U.S., talk shows are usually found on AM radio stations, while FM stations are devoted primarily to music. National Public Radio (NPR), which has FM affiliates in each New England state, offers a combination of both, including *Morning Edition* and *All Things Considered,* the most comprehensive radio news programs in the U.S.

Although New England's half-dozen or so major metropolitan areas each have their own local television stations and public television affiliates, cable and satellite TV bring dozens of channels to most hotels and motels. Cable News Network (CNN) offers the most comprehensive national and international news coverage. Boston's public television affiliate, WGBH, is a flagship station of the U.S. Public Television Network.

MONEY MATTERS

It costs about the same to travel in New England as it does throughout the rest of the northeastern United States. As a rule, this is slightly more expensive than touring just about anywhere else in the country, with the exception of metropolitan California and major resort areas. The regional capital, Boston, is among the more expensive U.S. cities; it's cheaper than New York City and perhaps comparable to San Francisco. Out in the countryside, or in lesser metropolitan centers, you'll find consistent good value, with the exception of places such as Cape Cod and the Massachusetts islands (in summer) and times such as fall foliage season (along the well-traveled routes of western and northern New England).

British, Australian, and New Zealand travelers will find hotel and restaurant tariffs comparable to those they're familiar with at home; Canadians, however, may be in for a bit of sticker shock due to the prevailing exchange rate between the two currencies. However, a number of hotel and resort operators, and places frequented by Canadian travelers, often offer exchange rates at or close to par as a promotional come-on.

Unless you're out slumming or deliberately going posh, figure on paying about $1 for a cup of coffee in New England, $2–$3 for a draft beer, and $4 for a ham sandwich with a few pickles and chips. A 1-mi ride in a Boston taxi will set you back $5, including tip; admission to a major museum such as Boston's Museum of Fine Arts will average about $10.

Prices throughout this guide are given for adults. Substantially reduced fees are almost always available for children, students, and senior citizens. For information on taxes, *see* Taxes.

ATMS

Automatic teller machines (ATMs) are a useful way to obtain cash. A debit card, also known as a check card, deducts funds directly from your checking account and helps you stay within your budget. When you want to rent a car, though, you may still need an old-fashioned credit card. Although you can always *pay* for your car with a debit card, some agencies will not allow you to *reserve* a car with a debit card.

ATMs are located just about everywhere in New England, from big-city banks to Vermont general stores.

CREDIT CARDS

Using a credit card on the road allows you to delay payment and gives you certain rights as a consumer (☞ Consumer Protection).

Throughout this guide, the following abbreviations are used: **AE**, American Express; **D**, Discover; **DC**, Diner's Club; **MC**, MasterCard; and **V**, Visa.

➤ REPORTING LOST CARDS: To report lost or stolen credit cards, call the following toll-free numbers: **American Express** (☎ 800/327–2177); **Discover Card** (☎ 800/347–2683); **Diner's Club** (☎ 800/234–6377); **MasterCard** (☎ 800/307–7309); and **Visa** (☎ 800/847–2911).

NATIONAL PARKS

National parks and forests offer a broad range of visitor facilities, including campgrounds, picnic grounds, hiking trails, nature walks, boating, and ranger programs. For more information on any of these, contact the state tourism offices or specific national park or forest headquarters.

Look into discount passes to save money on park entrance fees. The National Parks Pass ($50) gets you and your companions free admission to all parks for one year. (Camping and parking are extra.) A percentage of the proceeds from sales of the pass will fund National Parks projects. Both the Golden Age Passport ($10), for those 62 and older, and the Golden Access Passport (free), for travelers with disabilities, entitle holders to free entry to all national parks, plus 50% off fees for the use of many park facilities and services. You must show proof of age and of U.S. citizenship or permanent residency (such as a U.S. passport, driver's license, or birth certificate) and, if requesting Golden Access, proof of disability. The Golden Age and Golden Access passes are available at all national parks wherever entrance fees are charged. The National Parks Pass is available by mail or through the Internet.

➤ PASSES BY MAIL: **National Park Service** (⊠ National Park Service/Department of Interior, 1849 C St. NW, Washington, DC 20240, ☎ 202/208–4747, WEB www.nps.gov). **National**

Parks Pass (✉ 27540 Ave. Mentry, Valencia, CA 91355, ☎ 888/GO–PARKS, 🌐 www.nationalparks.org).

OUTDOORS & SPORTS

State information offices (☞ Visitor Information) have further information about New England's sporting opportunities. For information on skiing New England, see state chapters.

BEACHES

Long, wide beaches edge the New England coast from southern Maine to southern Connecticut; the most popular are on Cape Cod, Martha's Vineyard, Nantucket, and the shore areas north and south of Boston; on Maine's York County coast; Block Island Sound in Rhode Island; and the coastal region of New Hampshire. Many are maintained by state and local governments and have lifeguards on duty; they may have picnic facilities, rest rooms, changing facilities, and concession stands. Depending on the locale, you may need a parking sticker to use the lot. The waters are at their warmest in August, though they're cold even at the height of summer along much of the Maine coast. Inland, there are small lake beaches, most notably in New Hampshire and Vermont.

BIKING

Cape Cod, in Massachusetts, has miles of bike trails, some paralleling the national seashore, most on level terrain. On either side of the Cape Cod Canal is an easy 7-mi straight trail with views of the canal traffic. Other favorite areas for bicycling are the Massachusetts Berkshires, the New Hampshire Lakes Region, and Vermont's Green Mountains and Champlain Valley. Nantucket, Martha's Vineyard, and Block Island can be thoroughly explored by bicycle. Biking in Maine is especially scenic in and around Kennebunkport, Camden, Deer Isle, and the Schoodic Peninsula. The carriage paths in Acadia National Park are ideal. Many ski resorts allow mountain bikes during the summer months.

➤ BIKING: **Cambridge Bicycle** (259 Massachusetts Ave., Cambridge, MA 02139, ☎ 617/876–6555) rents bicycles. **Vermont Bicycle Touring** (Box 711, Bristol, VT 05443, ☎ 802/

453–4811 or 800/245–3868) operates tours throughout the region.

BOATING

Along many of New England's larger lakes, sailboats, rowboats, canoes, and outboards can be rented at local marinas. Sailboats are available for rent at a number of seacoast locations; you may be required to demonstrate competence. Lessons are also frequently available. In Rhode Island, Block Island Sound, Narragansett Bay, and Newport are revered by sailors worldwide. Maine's Penobscot Bay draws boaters, including windjammers. Lakes in New Hampshire and Vermont are splendid for all kinds of boating. In Massachusetts, the Connecticut River in the Pioneer Valley and the Housatonic River in the Berkshires are popular for canoeing, as are the salt marshes around Essex. Maine's Allagash Wilderness Waterway is one of the region's premier places to canoe.

FISHING

Anglers will find sport aplenty throughout the region—surf-casting along the shore; deep-sea fishing in the Atlantic on party and charter boats; fishing for trout in streams; and angling for bass, landlocked salmon, and other fish in freshwater lakes. Maine's Moosehead and Rangeley Lakes regions are draws for serious anglers, as are Vermont's Lakes Champlain and Memphremagog and the Connecticut Lakes of far northern New Hampshire. Coastal towns in southeastern Connecticut and Rhode Island (notably Narragansett) are home to scores of deep-sea charter boats. Sporting-goods stores and bait-and-tackle shops are reliable sources for licenses—necessary in fresh waters—and for leads to the nearest hot spots.

GOLF

Golf caught on early in New England, with Massachusetts courses such as those at the Country Club in Brookline and the Myopia Hunt Club in Hamilton (both, alas, private) among the oldest in the country. The region has an ample supply of public and semi-private courses, many of which are attached to distinctive resorts or even ski areas. One dilemma facing golfers is keeping their eyes on the ball instead of the scenery: in Manchester, Vermont, the Gleneagles Course at the Equinox Hotel is ringed by mountain splendor, as are the links at the Balsams Grand Resort in Dixville Notch, New Hampshire, and the nearby course at the splendid old Mount Washington Hotel in Bretton Woods. Even the windswept little Highland nine-hole course in Truro on Cape Cod has its adherents, if only for the sense it offers of playing golf out at sea. During prime season, make sure you reserve ahead for tee times, particularly near urban areas and at resorts.

HIKING

Probably the most famous trails are the 255-mi Long Trail, which runs north–south through the center of Vermont, and the Maine-to-Georgia Appalachian Trail, which runs through New England on both private and public land. The Appalachian Mountain Club (AMC) maintains a system of staffed huts in New Hampshire's Presidential Range, with bunk space and meals available by reservation. You'll find good hiking in many state parks throughout the region.

➤ HIKING: **Audubon Society of New Hampshire** (3 Silk Farm Rd., Concord, NH 03301, ☎ 603/224–9909). **Appalachian Mountain Club** (Box 298, Gorham, NH 03581, ☎ 603/ 466–2725). **Green Mountain Club** (Box 650, Rte. 100, Waterbury, VT 05677, ☎ 802/244–7037). **White Mountain National Forest** (719 North Main St., Laconia, NH 03246, ☎ 603/528–8721).

PACKING

The principal rule on weather in New England is that there are no rules. A cold, foggy morning in spring can and often does become a bright, 60° afternoon. A summer breeze can suddenly turn chilly, and rain often appears with little warning. Thus, the best advice on how to dress is to **layer your clothing** so that you can peel off or add garments as needed for comfort. Showers are frequent, so **pack a raincoat and umbrella.** Even in summer you should bring long pants, a sweater or two, and a waterproof

windbreaker, for evenings are often chilly and sea spray can make things cool.

Casual sportswear—walking shoes and jeans or khakis—will take you almost everywhere, but swimsuits and bare feet will not: shirts and shoes are required attire at even the most casual venues. Dress in restaurants is generally casual, except at some of the distinguished restaurants of Boston, Newport, and Maine coast towns such as Kennebunkport; a number of inns in the Berkshires; and in Litchfield and Fairfield counties in Connecticut. Upscale resorts will, at the very least, require men to wear collared shirts at dinner, and jeans are often frowned upon.

In summer, **bring a hat and sunscreen.** Remember also to **pack insect repellent**; to prevent Lyme disease you'll need to guard against ticks from early spring through the summer (☞ Health).

In your carry-on luggage, **pack an extra pair of eyeglasses or contact lenses and enough of any medication** you take to last the entire trip. You may also ask your doctor to write a spare prescription using the drug's generic name, since brand names may vary from country to country. In luggage to be checked, **never pack prescription drugs or valuables.** To avoid customs delays, carry medications in their original packaging. And don't forget to carry with you the addresses of offices that handle refunds of lost traveler's checks. Check *Fodor's How to Pack* (available in bookstores everywhere) for more tips.

CHECKING LUGGAGE

How many carry-on bags you can bring with you is up to the airline. Most allow two, but not always, so make sure that everything you carry aboard will fit under your seat or in the overhead bin, and get to the gate early. Note that if you have a seat at the back of the plane, you'll probably board first, while the overhead bins are still empty.

If you are flying internationally, note that baggage allowances may be determined not by piece but by weight—generally 88 pounds (40 kilograms) in first class, 66 pounds (30 kilograms) in business class, and 44 pounds (20 kilograms) in economy.

Airline liability for baggage is limited to $1,250 per person on flights within the United States. On international flights it amounts to $9.07 per pound or $20 per kilogram for checked baggage (roughly $640 per 70-pound bag) and $400 per passenger for unchecked baggage. You can buy additional coverage at check-in for about $10 per $1,000 of coverage, but it excludes a rather extensive list of items, shown on your airline ticket.

Before departure, **itemize your bags' contents** and their worth, and label the bags with your name, address, and phone number. (If you use your home address, cover it so potential thieves can't see it readily.) Inside each bag, **pack a copy of your itinerary.** At check-in, **make sure that each bag is correctly tagged** with the destination airport's three-letter code. If your bags arrive damaged or fail to arrive at all, file a written report with the airline before leaving the airport.

PASSPORTS & VISAS

For information on passports for non-U.S. citizens, *see* For International Travelers.

PASSPORT OFFICES

The best time to apply for a passport or to renew is in fall and winter. Before any trip, check your passport's expiration date, and, if necessary, renew it as soon as possible.

➤ U.S. CITIZENS: **National Passport Information Center** (☎ 900/225–5674 or 888/362-8668, WEB www. travel.state.gov/passport services; calls to the 900 number are 35¢ per minute for automated service, $1.05 per minute for operator service); calls to the 888 number, for Visa, MC, or AE card holders, are billed at a flat rate of $4.95.

SAFETY

Rural New England is one of the country's safest regions, so much so that residents often leave their doors unlocked. In the cities, particularly in Boston, observe the usual precautions; it's worth noting, however, that crime rates have been dropping in metropolitan areas. You should avoid out-of-the-way or poorly lit areas at night; clutch handbags close to your body and don't let them out of your sight; and be on your guard in subways, not only during the deserted wee hours but in crowded rush hours, when pickpockets are at work. Keep your valuables in hotel safes. Try to use ATMs in busy, well-lighted places such as bank lobbies.

If your vehicle breaks down in a rural area, **pull as far off the road as possible,** tie a handkerchief to your radio antenna (or use flares at night—check if your rental agency can provide them), and stay in your car with the doors locked until help arrives. Don't pick up hitchhikers. If you're planning to leave a car overnight to make use of off-road trails or camping facilities, **make arrangements for a supervised parking area** if at all possible. Cars left at trailhead parking lots are subject to theft and vandalism.

The universal telephone number for crime and other emergencies throughout New England is 911.

SENIOR-CITIZEN TRAVEL

To qualify for age-related discounts, **mention your senior-citizen status up front** when booking hotel reservations (not when checking out) and before you're seated in restaurants (not when paying the bill). When renting a car, ask about promotional car-rental discounts, which can be cheaper than senior-citizen rates.

➤ EDUCATIONAL PROGRAMS: **Elderhostel** (✉ 11 Ave. de Lafayette, Boston, MA 02111-1746, ☎ 877/426–8056, FAX 877/426–2166, WEB www. elderhostel.org). **Interhostel** (✉ University of New Hampshire, 6 Garrison Ave., Durham, NH 03824, ☎ 603/862–1147 or 800/733–9753, FAX 603/862–1113, WEB www.learn. unh.edu).

SHOPPING

Antiques, crafts, maple syrup and sugar, and fresh produce lure shoppers to New England's flea markets, bazaars, yard sales, country stores, and farmers' markets.

KEY DESTINATIONS

Best bets for antiquing in Connecticut include U.S. 7 (in Wilton and Ridgefield, and also in western Litchfield County), New Preston, Putnam and Woodstock, Woodbury and Litchfield, and the area of West Cornwall just east of the covered bridge. Antiques stores are plentiful in Newport but are a specialty of Rhode Island's South County: the best places to browse are Wickford, Charlestown, and Watch Hill. In Massachusetts, there's a large concentration of antiques stores on the North Shore around Essex, but there are also plenty in Salem and Cape Ann and along Boston's Charles Street at the base of Beacon Hill. Also try the Berkshires around Great Barrington, South Egremont, and Sheffield. One of America's biggest open-air antiques markets is held at Brimfield, Massachusetts, on several dates in summer and fall. Particularly in the Monadnock region of New Hampshire, dealers abound in barns and home stores strung along back roads—along Route 119, from Fitzwilliam to Hinsdale; Route 101, from Marlborough to Wilton; and in the towns of Hopkinton, Hollis, and Amherst. In southern New Hampshire, the stretch of U.S. 4 between Durham and Concord is another mecca. In Vermont, antiques shops and barns are scattered just about everywhere but are especially concentrated along the southern portions of U.S. 7 and along Route 30, particularly in and around Newfane. In Maine, antiques shops are clustered in Wiscasset and Searsport and along U.S. 1 between Kittery and Scarborough.

For crafts, try Washington Street in South Norwalk, Connecticut; in Massachusetts, there are some good shops in Provincetown on Cape Cod and in the Berkshires. In Vermont, galleries in Burlington, Middlebury, and Windsor sell work by some of the best of the state's craftspeople, although artisans have set up shop throughout the state. The League of New Hampshire Craftsmen operates seven fine shops, including locations in Concord, Exeter, and North Conway. On Maine's Deer Isle, Haystack Mountain School of Crafts attracts internationally renowned craftspeople to its summer institute. The Schoodic Peninsula is home to many skilled artisans. Passamaquoddy baskets can be found in Eastport.

Opportunities abound for obtaining fresh farm produce from the source; some farms allow you to pick your own strawberries, raspberries, blueberries, and apples. October in Maine is prime time for pumpkins and potatoes. There are maple-syrup producers who demonstrate the process to visitors, most notably in Vermont. Maple syrup is available in different grades; while Grade AA, "fancy," is the lightest in color and the most refined, many Vermonters prefer grade B, which has a deeper flavor and is often used in cooking. Grade A, medium amber in color, has a light caramel flavor and is often used with pancakes and hot cereals.

SMART SOUVENIRS

Distinctive New England souvenirs include Nantucket lightship baskets; authentic handbag versions are available at several Nantucket shops and will cost several hundred dollars (watch out for imported knockoffs). Less expensive options are Blue Hill pottery, sturdy, brightly colored tableware made in Blue Hill, Maine, and available at several shops in the area; Bennington Pottery, attractive, utilitarian items made in the Vermont town (Bennington Potters North in Burlington sells inexpensive seconds); moccasins of moose and deer hide made by Maine Native Americans and sold throughout the state; and whimsical animal prints by Woody Jackson (cows) and Stephen Huneck (dogs), available at several Vermont galleries.

WATCH OUT

When you're looking for pure maple syrup, a sugarhouse can be the most or the least expensive place to shop, depending on how tourist-oriented it is. Small grocery stores are often a good source of less-expensive syrup. **Look for the word "pure" and the state designation;** much artificially flavored sugarcane syrup is sold as "maple."

With any crafts item, always **be aware that some vendors substitute mass-produced imports** for the real thing; if the price seems too good to be true, it probably is.

As the U.S. is signatory to treaties involving trade and products made from endangered animal species, you won't need to worry about purchasing souvenirs that you won't be able to bring into your home country. Visitors to New Hampshire should be aware that one item for sale in this state—fireworks, found at many roadside stands—is strictly forbidden as airline baggage and cannot be imported into most countries.

STUDENTS IN NEW ENGLAND

Most major attractions throughout New England offer discount admissions to students. This is particularly true in and around Boston, which has America's highest concentration of colleges and universities.

➤ I.D.s & SERVICES: **Council Travel** (CIEE; ✉ 205 E. 42nd St., 15th floor, New York, NY 10017, ☎ 212/822–2700 or 888/268–6245, FAX 212/822–2699, WEB www.councilexchanges.org) for mail orders only, in the U.S. **Travel Cuts** (✉ 187 College St., Toronto, Ontario M5T 1P7, Canada, ☎ 416/979–2406 or 800/667–2887 in Canada, FAX 416/979–8167, WEB www.travelcuts.com).

TAXES

See Dining *and* Lodging for information about taxes on restaurant meals and accommodations.

SALES TAX

Sales taxes in New England are as follows: Connecticut 6% (with an exemption on clothing purchases up to $50); Maine 5%; Massachusetts 5%; Rhode Island 7%; Vermont 5% (with an exemption on purchase of one clothing item of up to $110). No sales tax is charged in New Hampshire. Some states and municipalities levy an additional tax (from 1% to 10%) on lodging or restaurant meals. Alcoholic beverages are sometimes taxed at a higher rate than that applied to meals.

TIME

New England is in the Eastern time zone.

TIPPING

At restaurants, a 15% tip is standard for waiters; up to 20% is expected at more expensive establishments. The same goes for taxi drivers, bartenders, and hairdressers. Coat-check operators usually expect $1; bellhops and porters should get $1 per bag; hotel maids should get about $1.50 per day of your stay. Hotel concierges should be tipped if you utilize their services; the amount varies widely depending on the nature of service. On package tours, conductors and drivers usually get $10 per day from the group as a whole; check whether this has already been figured into your cost. For local sightseeing tours, you may individually tip the driver-guide $1–$5, depending on the length of the tour and the number of people in your party, if he or she has been helpful or informative.

TOURS & PACKAGES

Because everything is prearranged on a prepackaged tour or independent vacation, you spend less time planning—and often get it all at a good price.

BOOKING WITH AN AGENT

Travel agents are excellent resources. But it's a good idea to collect brochures from several agencies as some agents' suggestions may be influenced by relationships with tour and package firms that reward them for volume sales. If you have a special interest, **find an agent with expertise in that area**; the American Society of Travel Agents (ASTA) (☞ Travel Agencies) has a database of specialists worldwide.

Make sure your travel agent knows the accommodations and other services of the place they're recommending. Ask about the hotel's location, room size, beds, and whether it has a pool, room service, or programs for children, if you care about these. Has your agent been there in person or sent others whom you can contact?

Do some homework on your own, too: local tourism boards can provide information about lesser-known and small-niche operators, some of which may sell only direct.

BUYER BEWARE

Each year consumers are stranded or lose their money when tour operators—even large ones with excellent reputations—go out of business. So **check out the operator.** Ask several travel agents about its reputation, and try to **book with a company that has a consumer-protection program.** (Look for information in the company's brochure.) In the United States, members of the National Tour Association and the United States Tour Operators Association are required to set aside funds to cover your payments and travel arrangements in the event that the company defaults. It's also a good idea to choose a company that participates in the American Society of Travel Agents' Tour Operator Program (TOP); ASTA will act as mediator in any disputes between you and your tour operator.

Remember that the more your package or tour includes the better you can predict the ultimate cost of your vacation. Make sure you know exactly what is covered, and **beware of hidden costs.** Are taxes, tips, and transfers included? Entertainment and excursions? These can add up.

➤ TOUR-OPERATOR RECOMMENDATIONS: **American Society of Travel Agents** (☞ Travel Agencies). **National Tour Association** (NTA; ✉ 546 E. Main St., Lexington, KY 40508, ☎ 859/226–4444 or 800/682–8886, WEB www.ntaonline.com). **United States Tour Operators Association** (USTOA; ✉ 342 Madison Ave., Suite 1522, New York, NY 10173, ☎ 212/599–6599 or 800/468–7862, FAX 212/599–6744, WEB www.ustoa.com).

TRAIN TRAVEL

State-run and national train service are options in New England: Massachusetts's MBTA connects Boston with outlying areas on the north and south shores of the state; Amtrak offers frequent daily service along its Northeast Corridor route from Washington and New York to Boston.

Amtrak's new high-speed *Acela* trains now link Boston and Washington, with a stop at Penn Station in New York.

Other Amtrak services include the *Vermonter* between Washington, D.C., and St. Albans, Vermont; the *Ethan Allen* between New York and Rutland, Vermont; and the *Lake Shore Limited* between Boston and Chicago, with stops at Worcester and Springfield, Massachusetts. These trains run on a daily basis. Amtrak sells passes good for travel within specific regions for a set period of time and also has a schedule of reduced children's fares. Overnight accommodations exist on only one New England train, the *Lake Shore Limited*. Reservations are required for certain trains and for all overnight accommodations.

Private rail lines have scenic train trips throughout New England, particularly during fall foliage season. Several use vintage steam equipment; the most notable is the Cog Railway to Mt. Washington in New Hampshire.

➤ TRAIN INFORMATION: **Amtrak** (☎ 800/872–7245, WEB www.amtrak.com). **MBTA** (☎ 617/722–5000).

TRANSPORTATION AROUND NEW ENGLAND

If you plan to travel around a sizable portion of New England, a car or car rental will be a *must*. Frequent rail connections between major cities exist only within Amtrak's Northeast Corridor (most notably New Haven, Providence, and Boston), and regional travel by air is expensive. Buses connect major cities and towns, but schedules are often inconvenient and routes are generally not the most scenic. Since one of New England's primary attractions is its picturesque countryside and innumerable small villages, only the automobile traveler (or bicyclist) can really appreciate all the region has to offer. If, however, you plan to concentrate your trip in and around Boston, where streets and roads are tangled and hectic, you're better off relying on public transportation.

TRAVEL AGENCIES

A good travel agent puts your needs first. Look for an agency that has been in business at least five years, emphasizes customer service, and has someone on staff who specializes in your destination. In addition, **make sure the agency belongs to a professional trade organization.** The American Society of Travel Agents (ASTA), with more than 26,000 members in some 170 countries, is the largest and most influential in the field. Operating under the motto "Without a travel agent, you're on your own," it maintains and enforces a strict code of ethics and will step in to help mediate any agent-client disputes if necessary. ASTA also maintains a Web site that includes a directory of agents. (If a travel agency is also acting as your tour operator, *see* Buyer Beware *in* Tours & Packages.)

➤ LOCAL AGENT REFERRALS: American Society of Travel Agents (ASTA; ☎ 800/965–2782 24-hr hot line, FAX 703/739–7642, WEB www.astanet.com). Association of British Travel Agents (✉ 68–71 Newman St., London W1T 3AH, U.K., ☎ 020/7637–2444, FAX 020/7637–0713, WEB www.abtanet.com). Association of Canadian Travel Agents (✉ 130 Albert St., Ste. 1705, Ottawa, Ontario K1P 5G4, Canada, ☎ 613/237–3657, FAX 613/237–7502, WEB www.acta.net). Australian Federation of Travel Agents (✉ Level 3, 309 Pitt St., Sydney NSW 2000, Australia, ☎ 02/9264–3299, FAX 02/9264–1085, WEB www.afta.com.au). Travel Agents' Association of New Zealand (✉ Box 1888, Wellington 10033, New Zealand, ☎ 04/499–0104, FAX 04/499–0827, WEB www.taanz.org.nz).

VISITOR INFORMATION

Each New England state offers a helpful free information kit, including a guidebook, map, and listings of attractions and events. All include listings and/or advertisements for lodging and dining establishments. Each state also has an official Web site with material on sights and lodgings; most of these sites have a calendar of events and other special features.

➤ TOURIST INFORMATION: Connecticut Office of Tourism (✉ 505 Hudson St., Hartford, CT 06106, ☎ 860/270–8081 or 800/282–6863, WEB www.ctbound.org). Maine Tourism Association (✉ 325B Water St., Box 2300, Hallowell, ME 04347, ☎ 207/623–0363 or 888/624–6345, WEB www.visitmaine.com). Massachusetts Office of Travel and Tourism (✉ 10 Park Plaza, Suite 4510, Boston, MA 02116, ☎ 617/727–3201; 800/227–6277; 800/447–6277 brochures, WEB www.mass-vacation.com). New Hampshire Office of Travel and Tourism Development (✉ Box 1856, Concord, NH 03302, ☎ 603/271–2343; 800/258–3608 seasonal events; 800/386–4664 brochures, WEB www.visitnh.gov). Rhode Island Department of Economic Development, Tourism Division (✉ 1 W. Exchange St., Providence, RI 02903, ☎ 401/222–2601; 800/556–2484 brochures, WEB www.visitrhodeisland.com). Vermont Department of Tourism and Marketing (✉ 134 State St., Montpelier, VT 05602, ☎ 802/828–3237; 800/837–6668 brochures). Vermont Chamber of Commerce, Department of Travel and Tourism (✉ Box 37, Montpelier, VT 05601, ☎ 802/223–3443, WEB www.1-800-vermont.com).

➤ IN THE U.K.: Discover New England (✉ Admail 4 International, Greatness La., Sevenoaks TN14 5BQ, ☎ 01732/742777).

WEB SITES

Do check out the World Wide Web when planning your trip. You'll find everything from weather forecasts to virtual tours of famous cities. Be sure to **visit Fodors.com** (www.fodors.com), a complete travel-planning site. You can research prices and book plane tickets, hotel rooms, rental cars, vacation packages, and more. In addition, you can post your pressing questions in the Travel Talk section and, in the site's Rants & Raves section, read comments about some of the restaurants and hotels in this book—and chime in yourself. Other planning tools include a currency converter and weather reports, and there are loads of links to travel resources.

CONNECTICUT

The Connecticut Impressionist Art Trail has a site at www.arttrail.org; the Connecticut Wine Trail is at ctwine.com.

MAINE

The site of Ski Maine (www.ski-maine.com) has information about alpine snow sports. Maine's Nordic Ski Council provides cross-country info at www.mnsc.com.

MASSACHUSETTS

Boston.com (www.boston.com), home of the *Boston Globe* online, has news and feature articles, ample travel information, and links to towns throughout Massachusetts. The site for Boston's arts and entertainment weekly, the *Boston Phoenix* (www.bostonphoenix.com), has nightlife, movie, restaurant, and fine and performing arts listings. The site of the Cape Cod Information Center (www.allcapecod.com) carries events information and has town directories with weather, sightseeing, lodging, and dining entries.

NEW HAMPSHIRE

For information on downhill and cross-country skiing, www.skinh.com is the site of Ski New Hampshire.

RHODE ISLAND

The official site of Providence (www.providencecvb.com) tells you what's happening in town.

VERMONT

The Vermont Ski Areas Association covers the downhill scene at www.skivermont.com. Up-to-date foliage reports are given at www.1800vermont.com.

GENERAL INTEREST

Visit New England (www.visitnewengland.com) covers the entire region. The Great Outdoor Recreation Page (www.gorp.com) is arranged into three easily navigated categories: attractions, activities, and locations; within most of the "locations" are links to the state parks office. The National Park Service site (www.nps.gov) lists all the national parks and has extensive historical, cultural, and environmental information.

WHEN TO GO

All six New England states are largely year-round destinations. But you might want to **stay away from rural areas during mud season in April and black-fly season from mid-May to mid-June.** Many smaller museums and attractions are open only from Memorial Day to mid-October, at other times by appointment only.

Memorial Day is the start of the migration to the beaches and the mountains, and summer begins in earnest on July 4. Those who are driving to Cape Cod in July or August should know that Friday and Sunday are the days weekenders clog the overburdened Route 6; a better time to visit the beach areas and the islands may be after Labor Day. The same applies to the Maine coast and its feeder roads, I–95 and U.S. 1.

Fall is the most colorful season in New England, a time when many inns and hotels are booked months in advance by foliage-viewing visitors. New England's dense hardwood forests explode in color as the diminishing hours of autumn daylight signal trees to stop producing chlorophyll. As green is stripped away from the leaves of maples, oaks, birches, beeches, and other deciduous species, a rainbow of reds, oranges, yellows, purples, and other vivid hues is revealed. The first scarlet and gold colors emerge in mid-September in northern areas; "peak" color occurs at different times from year to year. Generally, it's best to **visit the northern reaches in late September and early October** and move southward as October progresses.

All leaves are off the trees by Halloween, and hotel rates fall as the leaves do, dropping significantly until ski season begins. November and early December are hunting season in much of New England; those who venture into the woods should wear bright orange clothing.

Winter is the time for downhill and cross-country skiing. New England's major ski resorts are well equipped with snowmaking equipment if nature falls short. Along the coast, bed-and-breakfasts that remain open will often rent rooms at far lower prices than in summer.

In spring, despite mud season, maple sugaring goes on in Maine, New Hampshire, and Vermont, and the fragrant scent of lilacs is never far away.

CLIMATE

In winter, coastal New England is cold and damp; inland temperatures may be lower, but generally drier conditions make them easier to bear. Snowfall is heaviest in the interior mountains and can range up to several hundred inches per year in northern Maine, New Hampshire, and

Vermont. Spring is often windy and rainy; in many years it appears as if winter segues almost immediately into summer. Coastal areas can be quite humid in summer, making even moderate temperatures uncomfortable. One of the delights of inland northern New England, particularly at higher elevations, is the prevalence of cool summer nights. Autumn temperatures can be quite mild in more southerly areas well into October, although northern portions of the region can be quite cold by Columbus Day. In some years, a period of unseasonably mild weather occurs in late October and early November.

HARTFORD, CT

Jan.	36F	2C	May	70F	21C	Sept.	74F	23C
	20	– 7		47	8		52	11
Feb.	38F	3C	June	81F	27C	Oct.	65F	18C
	20	– 7		56	13		43	6
Mar.	45F	7C	July	85F	29C	Nov.	52F	11C
	27	– 3		63	17		32	0
Apr.	59F	15C	Aug.	83F	28C	Dec.	38F	3C
	38	3		61	16		22	– 6

BOSTON, MA

Jan.	36F	2C	May	67F	19C	Sept.	72F	22C
	20	– 7		49	9		56	13
Feb.	38F	3C	June	76F	24C	Oct.	63F	17C
	22	– 6		58	14		47	8
Mar.	43F	6C	July	81F	27C	Nov.	49F	9C
	29	– 2		63	17		36	2
Apr.	54F	12C	Aug.	79F	26C	Dec.	40F	4C
	38	3		63	17		25	– 4

BURLINGTON, VT

Jan.	29F	– 2C	May	67F	19C	Sept.	74F	23C
	11	–12		45	7		50	10
Feb.	31F	– 1C	June	77F	25C	Oct.	59F	15C
	11	–12		56	13		40	4
Mar.	40F	4C	July	83F	28C	Nov.	45F	7C
	22	6		59	15		31	– 1
Apr.	54F	12C	Aug.	79F	26C	Dec.	31F	– 1C
	34	1		58	14		16	– 9

PORTLAND, ME

Jan.	31F	– 1C	May	61F	16C	Sept.	68F	20C
	16	– 9		47	8		52	11
Feb.	32F	0C	June	72F	22C	Oct.	58F	14C
	16	– 9		54	15		43	6
Mar.	40F	4C	July	76F	24C	Nov.	45F	7C
	27	– 3		61	16		32	0
Apr.	50F	10C	Aug.	74F	23C	Dec.	34F	1C
	36	2		59	15		22	– 6

➤ FORECASTS: **Weather Channel Connection** (☎ 900/932–8437), 95¢ per minute from a Touch-Tone phone.

FESTIVALS AND SEASONAL EVENTS

➤ JANUARY: The Bethel (ME) **Winter Festival** has snowshoe and cross-country races, sleigh rides, and a snowman contest. Stowe's (VT) festive **Winter Carnival** heats up late in the month. Brookfield (VT) holds its **Ice Harvest Festival,** one of New England's largest. The weeklong **Winter Carnival** in Jackson (NH) includes ski races and ice sculptures.

➤ FEBRUARY: The Camden Snow Bowl in Camden (ME) is the site of the **U.S. National Toboggan Championships.** On tap at the **Brattleboro Winter Carnival** (VT), held during the last week of the month, are jazz concerts and an ice fishing derby. The **Mad River Valley Winter Carnival** (VT) is a week of winter festivities, including dogsled races and ski races and fireworks; Burlington's **Vermont Mozart Festival** showcases the Winter Chamber Music Series. Flower lovers flock to Hartford's Expo Center for the annual **Flower and Garden Show.**

➤ MARCH: This is the season for **maple-sugaring festivals and events:** throughout the month and into April, New England sugarhouses demonstrate procedures from maple-tree tapping to sap boiling. During **Maine Maple Sunday** Maine sugarhouses open for tours and tastings. Maine's Moosehead Lake has a renowned **Ice-Fishing Derby.** Rangeley's **New England Sled Dog Races** attract more than 100 teams. Stratton Mountain (VT) hosts the **U.S. Open Snowboarding Championships.** Boston's **St. Patrick's Day Parade** is one of the nation's largest. Five acres of landscaped gardens bloom at Boston's **New England Spring Flower Show.** At Lyman Plant House on the Smith College Campus in Northampton, more than 2,500 flowering bulbs and spring flowers are on display at the **Spring Bulb Show.**

➤ APRIL: During **Reggae Weekend** at Sugarloaf/USA (ME), Caribbean reggae bands play outdoors and inside. At Sunday River's (ME) annual **Bust 'n' Burn Mogul Competi-**

tion, professional and amateur bump skiers test their mettle. Early blooms are the draw of Nantucket's (MA) **Daffodil Festival,** which celebrates spring with a flower show and a procession of antique cars along roadsides bursting with daffodils. You can gorge on sea grub at Boothbay Harbor's (ME) **Fishermen's Festival,** held on the third weekend in April. Dedicated runners draw huge crowds to the **Boston Marathon,** run each year on Patriot's Day (the Monday nearest April 19). Colonial Minute Men battle the British at the annual **Battle of Lexington and Concord Reenactment.** At the **Maple Festival,** held early each April in St. Albans (VT), you can try Sugar on Snow, a taffylike treat.

➤ MAY: The Shelburne Museum in Shelburne (VT) is awash in purple glory in mid-May, when the **Lilac Festival** blossoms. **Lilac Sunday,** at Boston's Arnold Arboretum, celebrates the blooming of more than 250 varieties. If you want to see a moose, visit Greenville (ME) during **Moosemania,** which runs from mid-May to mid-June. Events include moose safaris and mountain bike and canoe races. **Lobsterfest** kicks off Mystic Seaport's (CT) summer of festivities with live entertainment and good food. Holyoke's (MA) **Shad Fishing Derby** is said to be the largest freshwater fishing derby in North America.

➤ JUNE: In Vermont, you can listen to jazz at Burlington's **Discover Jazz Festival. Lake Champlain International Fishing Derby** entices anglers to try their fishing skills. **Jacob's Pillow Dance Festival** at Becket (MA) in the Berkshires hosts performers of various dance traditions from June to September. The **Boothbay Harbor Windjammer Days** starts the high season for Maine's boating set. The **Blessing of the Fleet** in Provincetown (MA) culminates a weekend of festivities. Mystic Seaport in Mystic (CT) hosts its annual **Small Craft Weekend.** The **Sea Music Festival,** in Mystic, is a celebration of New England's quintessential folk music. **A Taste of Hartford** lets you eat your way through Connecticut's capital city while enjoying outdoor music, dance, comedy, and magic. Burlington, Vermont's **Green Mountain Chew Chew** offers a variety of entertainment including outdoor music and comedy. New Haven (CT) hosts the two-week **International Festival of Arts and Ideas,** showcasing music, dance, theater, film, visual arts, and literature. During the **Strawberry Festival** in Wiscasset (ME), you can get your fill of strawberry goodies. You can visit Providence's (RI) stately homes, some by candlelight, on one of the **Providence Preservation Society's** tours. At the **Great Chowder Cookoff** in Newport (RI), restaurants compete for the distinction of having the best chowder in New England.

➤ JULY: Independence day is celebrated with concerts, family entertainment, an art show, a parade, and fireworks in Bath (ME). Exeter (NH) holds a **Revolutionary War Festival** at the American Independence Museum with battle reenactments and period crafts and antiques. The **Mashpee Powwow** (MA) brings together Native Americans from North and South America for three days of dance contests, drumming, a fireball game, and a clambake. The **Marlboro Music Festival** presents classical music at Marlboro College (VT). Newport's (RI) **Music Festival** brings together celebrated musicians for two weeks of concerts in Newport mansions. Newport's **Rhythm & Blues Festival** hosts an array of top performers. The **Bar Harbor Festival** (ME) hosts classical, jazz, and popular music concerts into August. The **Tanglewood Music Festival** at Lenox (MA) shifts into high gear with performances by the Boston Symphony Orchestra and major entertainers. Glorious outdoor concert sites and sumptuous picnics are sidelines to fine music at the **Vermont Mozart Festival,** held throughout central and northern Vermont in July and August. The two-day **Stoweflake Hot Air Balloon Festival** in Stowe is one of the state's most popular events. Admire the furnishings of homes during **Open House Tours** in Litchfield (CT) and Camden (ME). Folks flock to the **Mashantucket Pequot Thames River Fireworks** in New London (CT) to view one of the country's largest fireworks events. In Mystic (CT),

vintage powerboats and sailboats are on view at the **Antique and Classic Boat Rendezvous.** The **Yarmouth Clam Festival** (ME) is more than a seafood celebration—expect continuous entertainment and a crafts show throughout the three-day event.

➤ AUGUST: **Ben & Jerry's Newport Folk Festival** is one of the region's most popular musical events. Newport (RI) hosts the **JVC's Jazz Festival.** The historic streets of Essex (CT) rock with sounds of the **Great Connecticut Traditional Jazz Festival.** Stowe (VT) hosts a popular **Antique and Classic Car Rally.** The **Southern Vermont Crafts Fair** in Manchester (VT) features popular arts, crafts, and antiques. The **Outdoor Arts Festival** in Mystic (CT) presents the works of fine local artists. Sellers and collectors throng to the **Maine Antiques Festival** in Union. There's a **Lobster Festival** in Rockland (ME). Everything's coming up blueberries at the **Wild Maine Blueberry Festival** in Machias (ME). In Rangeley Lake (ME), the blueberry is king at the annual **Blueberry Festival.** Rhode Islanders honor their favorite shellfish at the **International Quahog Festival** in Wickford. A **Bluefish Festival** takes place in Clinton (CT). Brunswick's **Maine Festival** is a four-day celebration of Maine arts. Maine's **Annual Maine Highland Games** features traditional Scottish athletic events and music entertainment. The **Martha's Vineyard Agricultural Fair** (MA) includes animal shows, a carnival, and evening entertainment. In New Bedford, Massachusetts, the **Feast of Blessed Sacrament** is the country's largest Portuguese feast.

➤ SEPTEMBER: New England's Labor Day fairs include the **Vermont State Fair** in Rutland, with agricultural exhibits and entertainment. The **Providence Waterfront Festival** (RI) is a weekend of arts, crafts, ethnic foods, music, and boat races. The **International Seaplane Fly-In Weekend,** sets Moosehead Lake (ME) buzzing. The **Champlain Valley Fair,** in Burlington (VT), has all the features of a large county fair. Foot stomping and guitar strumming are the activities of choice at several musical events: the **Rhythm and**

Roots festival of Cajun food, music, and dancing is held in Charlestown (RI). Many of the country's finest fiddlers compete at the **National Traditional Old-Time Fiddler's Contest** in Barre (VT). Folk music is the highlight at the **Rockport Folk Festival** in Rockport (ME). In Stratton (VT), artists and performers gather for the **Stratton Arts Festival.** Providence (RI) shows off its diversity during its **Heritage Day Festival.** The **Common Ground Country Fair** in Unity (ME) is an organic farmer's delight. The **Deerfield Fair** (NH) is one of New England's oldest agricultural fairs. The **Eastern States Exposition**) is New England's largest agricultural fair/carnival. The six small Vermont towns of Walden, Cabot, Plainfield, Peacham, Barnet, and Groton host the weeklong **Northeast Kingdom Fall Foliage Festival.** Crafts, entertainment, and fried scallops are served up at the **Bourne Scallopfest** in Buzzards Bay (MA). For the **Martha's Vineyard Striped Bass and Bluefish Derby,** from mid-September to mid-October, locals cast their lines in search of a prize-winning whopper. The **Eastport Salmon Festival** (ME), the first Sunday after Labor Day, hosts entertainers and crafts artists. At the **Annual Seafood Festival** in Hampton Beach (NH), you can sample seafood specialties, dance to live bands, and watch fireworks.

➤ OCTOBER: The **Fryeburg Fair** (ME) presents agricultural exhibits, harness racing, and a pig scramble. The **Nantucket Cranberry Harvest** in Massachusetts is a three-day celebration including bog and inn tours and a crafts fair. Connecticut's Quiet Corner holds a **Walking Weekend,** with 50 guided scenic walks through the towns, along rivers, and in the woods of this rural area. **Hildene Farm, Food and Crafts Fair** in Manchester (VT) has farm activities, entertainment, and lots of events for kids.

➤ NOVEMBER: The **International Film Festival** presents films dealing with environmental, human rights, and political issues for a week in Burlington (VT). The **Bradford Wild Game Supper** (VT) draws thousands to taste large and small game animals and birds. New Haven's (CT) **Annual Celebration of American Crafts** exhibits and sells works of more than 400 juried craftspeople.

➤ DECEMBER: The **reenactment of the Boston Tea Party** takes place on the *Beaver II* in Boston Harbor. In Nantucket (MA), the first weekend of the month sees an early Christmas celebration with elaborate decorations, costumed carolers, theatrical performances, art exhibits, and a tour of historic homes. In Newport (RI), several Bellevue Avenue mansions open for the holidays, and there are candlelight tours of Colonial homes. At **Mystic Seaport** (CT), costumed guides escort visitors on lantern-light tours. **Old Saybrook** (CT) has a Christmas Torchlight Parade and Muster of Ancient Fife and Drum Corps, which ends with a carol sing. The little town of **Bethlehem** (CT) is the site of a large Christmas festival each December. More than 200 spectacularly decorated trees and wreaths grace the Wadsworth Atheneum in Hartford (CT) during its annual **Festival of Trees.** Historic **Strawbery Banke** (NH) has a Christmas Stroll, with carolers, through nine historic homes. **Christmas Prelude** in Kennebunkport (ME) celebrates winter with concerts, caroling, and special events. The final day of the year is observed with festivals, entertainment, and food in many locations during **First Night Celebrations.** Some of the major cities hosting First Nights are Portland (ME); Burlington, Montpelier, and St. Johnsbury (all in VT); Providence (RI); Boston; and Danbury, Hartford, and Mystic (in CT).

INDEX

FODOR'S NEW ENGLAND 2002

EDITOR: William Travis

Editorial Contributors: Michelle Bodak Acri, Paula Bodah, Andrew Collins, Elizabeth Gehrman, Alexandra Hall, Carolyn Heller, Rene Hertzog, Hilary M. Nangle, Bill Scheller, Kay Scheller, Adam Smith.

Editorial Production: Ira-Neil Dittersdorf

Maps: David Lindroth, *cartographer*; Rebecca Baer and Bob Blake, *map editors*

Design: Fabrizio La Rocca, *creative director*; Guido Caroti, *art director*; Jolie Novak, *senior picture editor*; Melanie Marin, *photo editor*.

Cover Design: Pentagram

Production/Manufacturing: Yexenia (Jessie) Markland

ISBN 0–679–00855–1

ISSN 0192–3412

SPECIAL SALES
Fodor's Travel Publications are available at special discounts for bulk purchases for sales promotions or premiums. Special editions, including personalized covers, excerpts of existing guides, and corporate imprints, can be created in large quantities for special needs. For more information, contact your local bookseller or write to Special Markets, Fodor's Travel Publications, 280 Park Avenue, New York, NY 10017. Inquiries from Canada should be directed to your local Canadian bookseller or sent to Random House of Canada, Ltd., Marketing Department, 2775 Matheson Boulevard East, Mississauga, Ontario L4W 4P7. Inquiries from the United Kingdom should be sent to Fodor's Travel Publications, 20 Vauxhall Bridge Road, London SW1V 2SA, England.

PRINTED IN THE UNITED STATES OF AMERICA

10 9 8 7 6 5 4 3 2 1

IMPORTANT TIP
Although all prices, opening times, and other details in this book are based on information supplied to us at press time, changes occur all the time in the travel world, and Fodor's cannot accept responsibility for facts that become outdated or for inadvertent errors or omissions. So always confirm information when it matters, especially if you're making a detour to visit a specific place.

PHOTOGRAPHY
Corbis: *Craig Aurness*, cover (Manchester, Vermont).

Attitash Bear Peak: *Sharon McNeil*, p. 12E.

Balsams Grand Resort Hotel, p.10B.

Biba, p. 30E.

The Golden Lamb Buttery, p. 30G.

Blaine Harrington, p. 15B.

Historic Merrell Inn, p. 30C.

Robert Holmes, p. 10A.

The Image Bank: Alan Becker, p. 15C. Walter Bibikow, p. 7D, 21H. Bullaty/Lomeo, p. 12F. Andy Caulfield, p. 21J. Joe Devenney, p. 7C, 9F, 16D. Steve Dunwell, p. 1, 3 bottom right, 11C, 13H, 13I, 17F, 23B, 23C, 25C, 25D, 25E. Brett Froomer, p. 24 center. David W. Hamilton, p. 19B. Patti McConville, p. 9E, 17 bottom right. Paul McCormick, p. 6 top. Michael Melford, p. 2 bottom left, 4-5, 7B, 8, 9 center, 15 bottom right, 16E, 18 top, 24A, 32. Derek Redfearn, p. 3 top left. Alvis Upitis, p. 6A. Pete Turner, p. 11D. Stephen Wilkes, p. 18A.

Inn at Shelburne Farms, p. 2 top left, 30D.

William H. Johnson/Johnson's Photography, p. 13G.

James Lemass, p. 22A.

The Lodge at Moosehead Lake: *Macduff Everton*, p. 2 top right.

Mad River Glen: *T.J. Greenwood*, p. 14A.

The Manor on Golden Pond: *George W. Gardner*, p. 30B.

Manor House: *Randy O'Rourke*, p. 30J.

The Maritime Aquarium of Norwalk: *Norma Mondazzi*, p. 24B.

Massachusetts Office of Travel & Tourism: *Kindra Clineff*, p. 2 bottom center, p. 3 center, 19D, 20E, 20F, 20G, 21I, 30H, 27B.

The Mount Washington Hotel & Resort, p. 27A.

Nantucket Island Chamber of Commerce: *Thomas P. Benincas, Jr.*, p.19C.

Random House Photo Library, p. 28, 29C, 29 bottom.

Rhode Island Tourism Division: p. 3 top right. *Chuck Browning*, p. 23 bottom.

Smugglers' Notch Resort, p. 30I.

State of Vermont Department of Tourism, p. 2 bottom right.

Sugarloaf/USA: p. 30A. *Gary Pearl*, p.3 bottom left.

Ullikana Bar Harbor, p. 30F.

Vermont Travel & Tourism, p. 17G.

ABOUT OUR WRITERS

The more you know before you go, the better your trip will be. New England's most fascinating antique store or its finest seafood restaurant could be just around the corner from your hotel, but if you don't know it's there, it might as well be on the other side of the globe. That's where this book comes in. It's a great step toward making sure your next trip lives up to your expectations. As you plan, check out the Web as well. Guidebooks have been helping smart travelers find the special places for years; the Web is one more tool. Whatever reference you consult, be savvy about what you read, and always consider the source. Images and language can be massaged to make places appear better than they are. And one traveler's quaint is another's grimy. Here at Fodor's, and at our on-line arm, fodors.com, our focus is on providing you with information that's not only useful but accurate and on target. Every day Fodor's editors put enormous effort into getting things right, beginning with the search for the right contributors—people who have objective judgment, broad travel experience, and the writing ability to put their insights into words. There's no substitute for advice from a like-minded friend who has just come back from where you're going, but our writers, having seen all corners of New England, are the next best thing. They're the kind of people you'd poll for tips yourself if you knew them.

Hilary M. Nangle, formerly travel editor for a daily newspaper in Maine, is now a freelancer based in the state's scenic midcoast. Her Fodor's beat is Maine, and she writes regularly about travel, food, and skiing for publications in the United States and Canada.

Former Fodor's editor and New England native **Andrew Collins,** who updated and expanded the New Hampshire chapter, is the author of several books on travel in New England including handbooks on Connecticut and Rhode Island.

Kay and Bill Scheller, who revised and expanded the Vermont chapter as well as the Berkshires and Pioneer Valley sections of Massachusetts, have a total of more than 30 years' experience as contributors to Fodor's guides. They are the authors of several books on travel in New England and the Northeast. The Schellers live in northern Vermont.

A number of talented writers worked on the Massachusetts chapter. Food and travel writer **Alexandra Hall,** the features and lifestyle editor of *Boston Magazine,* updated the Boston dining scene. **Elizabeth Gehrman,** a freelance writer based in Boston, served as the Boston shopping maven and explorer extraordinaire. **Carolyn Heller,** a Cambridge-based travel writer, provided the latest updates on Cambridge, Boston side trips, the North Shore, Cape Cod, Martha's Vineyard, and Nantucket. She has contributed to several Fodor's New England guidebooks and other publications. Boston lodging updater **Rene Hertzog,** a writer and editor, explored the city's best digs. Boston nightlife and the arts scout **Adam Smith** writes a weekend-events column for the *Boston Herald* that appears every Saturday.

Rhode Island updater **Paula Bodah** is the editor of *Rhode Island Monthly* and a native of Rhode Island. She's written for Yankee, Yankee's Travel Guide to New England, *Walking* magazine, and Rodale Press cookbooks. She is also the author "Rhode Island: The Spirit of America" from Harry Abrams Press.

Michelle Bodak Acri, who updated the Connecticut chapter, has lived in the Nutmeg State for 31 years, the last nine of them working as an editor for *Connecticut* magazine. She enthusiastically shares her state's glories with the uninitiated.

Don't Forget to Write

Your experiences—positive and negative—matter to us. If we have missed or misstated something, we want to hear about it. We follow up on all suggestions. Contact the New England editor at editors@fodors.com or c/o Fodor's, 280 Park Avenue, New York, New York 10017. And have a fabulous trip!

Karen Cure
Editorial Director